PRAISE FOR *WAYS OF READING*

"*Ways of Reading* is full of engaging, thought-provoking selections that encourage students to develop their reading, writing, and thinking skills. The assignment sequences invite students to make a meaningful contribution to the conversation of ideas. *Ways of Reading* gives students the dignity of being treated as intelligent adults who are capable of challenging work."
— Nathanael Myers, *University of Georgia*

"*Ways of Reading* is a thoughtful, challenging text. It expects that students will be able to read, understand, model, and respond to some of the most important intellectual developments in society. It does not condescend to students and it requires them — as well as their professors — to struggle. This struggle can be immensely productive. At the end of the semester, I can see that my first-year students have grown. Their habits of mind have evolved. And they approach writing with different attitudes and ambitions."
— Laura Albritton, *Ringling School of Art and Design*

"In presenting students with difficult but ultimately understandable and relevant texts to respond to, *Ways of Reading* has helped me to become a better teacher." — Malkiel Choseed, *Onondaga Community College*

"For those teachers who believe that reading, broadly defined, plays a crucial role in writing instruction, for those of us who, following Quintilian, believe that all of the language arts — writing, reading, speaking, and listening — have a place in our composition classrooms, *Ways of Reading* remains the undisputed standard." — Frank Farmer, *University of Kansas*

"The most valuable aspect of *Ways of Reading* for me is that it consists of 'real' essays: that is, essays that are not commissioned exclusively for a student textbook but which continue to be read and engaged with by active thinkers in the academy and beyond. This quality helps students recognize writing not as a task or a static activity but as a mode of thinking, an engagement in an ongoing conversation, a way of being in the world."
— Jeffrey Norman, *University of Wisconsin–Milwaukee*

"*Ways of Reading* has taught me a lot about how to teach writing. The demands it makes on instructors are as great as those it makes on students — but the rewards are about equal, too. It works like a very stimulating and challenging colleague, and it's been a key part of my experience and on-the-job training as a teacher of writing. I couldn't be more grateful for it."
— Matthew Parfitt, *Boston University, College of General Studies*

WAYS OF READING

An Anthology for Writers

WAYS OF READING

An Anthology for Writers

Eighth Edition

David Bartholomae

UNIVERSITY OF PITTSBURGH

Anthony Petrosky

UNIVERSITY OF PITTSBURGH

BEDFORD/ST. MARTIN'S

Boston ♦ New York

For Bedford/St. Martin's

Developmental Editor: John Sullivan
Assistant Editor: Alicia Young
Production Supervisor: Andrew Ensor
Senior Marketing Manager: Karita dos Santos
Project Management: Books By Design, Inc.
Text Design: Jean Hammond
Cover Design: Donna Dennison
Cover Art: Page 9 from *A Humument*, a treated book by Tom Phillips, based
   on the Victorian novel *A Human Document*, by W. H. Mallock.
Composition: Books By Design, Inc.
Printing and Binding: RR Donnelley & Sons Company

President: Joan E. Feinberg
Editorial Director: Denise B. Wydra
Director of Marketing: Karen Melton Soeltz
Director of Editing, Design, and Production: Marcia Cohen
Manager, Publishing Services: Emily Berleth

Library of Congress Control Number: 2007929905

Manufactured in the United States of America.

2   1   0   9

f   e   d

For information, write: Bedford/St. Martin's, 75 Arlington Street, Boston,
MA 02116   (617-399-4000)

ISBN-10: 0-312-45413-9
ISBN-13: 978-0-312-45413-5

ACKNOWLEDGMENTS

Preface

WAYS OF READING is designed for a course where students are given the opportunity to work on what they read, and to work on it by writing. When we began developing such courses, we realized the problems our students had when asked to write or talk about what they read were not "reading problems," at least not as these are strictly defined. Our students knew how to move from one page to the next. They could read sentences. They had, obviously, been able to carry out many of the versions of reading required for their education — skimming textbooks, cramming for tests, strip-mining books for term papers.

Our students, however, felt powerless in the face of serious writing, in the face of long and complicated texts — the kinds of texts we thought they should find interesting and challenging. We thought (as many teachers have thought) that if we just, finally, gave them something good to read — something rich and meaty — they would change forever their ways of thinking about English. It didn't work, of course. The issue is not only *what* students read, but what they can learn to *do* with what they read. We learned that the problems our students had lay not in the reading material (it was too hard) or in the students (they were poorly prepared) but in the classroom — in the ways we and they imagined what it meant to work on an essay.

There is no better place to work on reading than in a writing course, and this book is intended to provide occasions for readers to write. You will find a number of distinctive features in *Ways of Reading*. For one thing, it contains selections you don't usually see in a college reader: long, powerful, mysterious pieces like John Berger's "Ways of Seeing," Susan Griffin's "Our Secret," Adrienne Rich's "When We Dead Awaken: Writing as Re-Vision," Clifford Geertz's "Deep Play: Notes on the Balinese Cockfight," Mary Louise Pratt's "Arts of the Contact Zone," John Edgar Wideman's "Our Time," W. G. Sebald's "The Rings of Saturn," and Michel Foucault's "Panopticism." These are the sorts of readings we talk about when we talk with our colleagues. We have learned that we can talk about them with our students as well.

When we chose the essays, we were looking for "readable" texts—that is, texts that leave some work for a reader to do. We wanted selections that invite students to be active, critical readers, that present powerful readings of common experience, that open up the familiar world and make it puzzling, rich, and problematic. We wanted to choose selections that invite students to be active readers and to take responsibility for their acts of interpretation. So we avoided the short set-pieces you find in so many anthologies. In a sense, those short selections misrepresent the act of reading. They can be read in a single sitting; they make arguments that can be easily paraphrased; they solve all the problems they raise; they wrap up Life and put it into a box; and so they turn reading into an act of appreciation, where the most that seems to be required is a nod of the head. And they suggest that a writer's job is to do just that, to write a piece that is similarly tight and neat and self-contained. We wanted to avoid pieces that were so plainly written or tightly bound that there was little for students to do but "get the point."

We learned that if our students had reading problems when faced with long and complex texts, the problems lay in the way they imagined a reader—the role a reader plays, what a reader does, why a reader reads (if not simply to satisfy the requirements of a course). When, for example, our students were puzzled by what they read, they took this as a sign of failure. ("It doesn't make any sense," they would say, as though the sense were supposed to be waiting on the page, ready for them the first time they read through.) And our students were haunted by the thought that they couldn't remember everything they had read (as though one could store all of Geertz's "Deep Play" in memory); or if they did remember bits and pieces, they felt that the fragmented text they possessed was evidence that they could not do what they were supposed to do. Our students were confronting the experience of reading, in other words, but they were taking the problems of reading—problems all readers face—and concluding that there was nothing for them to do but give up.

As expert readers, we have all learned what to do with a complex text. We know that we can go back to a text; we don't have to remember it—in fact, we've learned to mark up a text to ease that re-entry. We know that a reader is a person who puts together fragments. Those coherent readings we construct begin with confusion and puzzlement, and we construct those readings by writing and rewriting—by working on a text.

These are the lessons our students need to learn, and this is why a course in reading is also a course in writing. Our students need to learn that there is something they can do once they have first read through a complicated text; successful reading is not just a matter of "getting" an essay the first time. In a very real sense, you can't begin to feel the power a reader has until you realize the problems, until you realize that no one "gets" Geertz or Rich or Griffin or Wideman all at once. You work on what you read, and then what you have at the end is something that is yours, something you made. And this is what the teaching apparatus in *Ways of Reading* is designed to do. In a sense, it says to students, "OK, let's get to work on these essays; let's see what you can make of them."

This, then, is the second distinctive feature you will find in *Ways of Reading:* reading and writing assignments designed to give students access to the essays. After each selection, for example, you will find "Questions for a Second Reading." We wanted to acknowledge that rereading is a natural way of carrying out the work of a reader, just as rewriting is a natural way of completing the work of a writer. It is not something done out of despair or as a punishment for not getting things right the first time. The questions we have written highlight what we see as central textual or interpretive problems. Geertz, for example, divides his essay into seven sections, each written in a different style. By going back through the essay with this in mind and by asking what Geertz is doing in each case (what his method is and what it enables him to accomplish), a student is in a position to see the essay as the enactment of a method and not just as a long argument with its point hidden away at the end. These questions might serve as preparations for class discussion or ways of directing students' work in journals. Whatever the case, they both honor and direct the work of rereading.

Each selection is also followed by two sets of writing assignments, "Assignments for Writing" and "Making Connections." The first set directs students back into the work they have just read. While the assignments vary, there are some basic principles behind them. They ask students to work on the essay by focusing on difficult or problematic moments in the text; they ask students to work on the author's examples, extending and testing his or her methods of analysis; or they ask students to apply the method of the essay (its way of seeing and understanding the world) to settings or experiences of their own. Students are asked, for example, to give a "Geertzian" reading to scenes from their own immediate culture (the behavior of people at a shopping mall, characteristic styles of dress), and they are asked to imagine that they are working alongside Geertz and making his project their own. Or they are asked to consider the key examples in Rich's "When

We Dead Awaken" (poems from various points in her career) to see how as writers they might use the key terms of her argument ("structures of oppression," "renaming") in representing their own experience. The last assignments—"Making Connections"—invite students to read one essay in the context of another, to see, for example, if Pratt's account of the "literate arts of the contact zone" can be used to frame a reading of Gloria Anzaldúa's prose, Harriet Jacobs's narrative, or Paulo Freire's account of education. In a sense, then, the essays are offered as models, but not as "prose models" in the strictest sense. What they model is a way of seeing or reading the world, of both imagining problems and imagining methods to make those problems available to a writer.

At the end of the book, we have included several longer assignment sequences and a goodly number of shorter sequences. A single sequence provides structure for an entire course. (There are a number of additional sequences included in the instructor's manual.) In some cases these incorporate single assignments from earlier in the book; in most cases they involve students in projects that extend anywhere from two to three weeks for the shorter sequences to an entire semester's worth of work for the longer ones. Almost all the sequences include several of the essays in the anthology and require a series of separate drafts and revisions. Alternative essays and assignments are included with the sequences so that they can be adapted easily. In academic life, readers seldom read single essays in isolation, as though one were "finished" with Geertz after a week or two. Rather, they read with a purpose—with a project in mind or a problem to solve. The assignment sequences are designed to give students a feel for the rhythm and texture of an extended academic project. They offer, that is, one more way of reading and writing. Because these sequences lead students through intellectual projects proceeding from one week to the next, they enable them to develop authority as specialists, to feel the difference between being an expert and being a "common" reader on a single subject. And, with the luxury of time available for self-reflection, students can look back on what they have done, not only to revise what they know, but also to take stock and comment on the value and direction of their work.

Because of their diversity, it is difficult to summarize the assignment sequences. Perhaps the best way to see what we have done is to turn to the back of the book and look at them. They are meant to frame a project for students but to leave open possibilities for new directions. You should feel free to add or drop readings, to mix sequences, and to revise the assignments to fit your course and your schedule.

You will also notice that there are few "glosses" appended to the essays. We have not added many editors' notes to define difficult words or to identify names or allusions to other authors or artists. We've omitted them because their presence suggests something we feel is false about reading. They suggest that good readers know all the words or pick up all the allusions or recognize every name that is mentioned. This is not true. Good readers do what they can and try their best to fill in the blanks; they ignore seemingly unimportant references and look up the important ones. There is no reason for students to feel they lack the knowledge necessary to complete a reading of these texts. We have translated foreign phrases and glossed some technical terms, but we have kept the selections as clean and open as possible.

We have been asked on several occasions whether the readings aren't finally just too hard for students. The answer is no. Students will have to work on the selections, but that is the point of the course and the reason, as we said before, why a reading course is also a course in writing. College students want to believe that they can strike out on their own, make their mark, do something they have never done before. They want to *be* experts, not just hear from them. This is the great pleasure, as well as the great challenge, of undergraduate instruction. It is not hard to convince students they ought to be able to speak alongside of (or even speak back to) Clifford Geertz, Adrienne Rich, or Cornelius Eady. And, if a teacher is patient and forgiving—willing, that is, to let a student work out a reading of Walker Percy, willing to keep from saying, "No, that's not it," and filling the silence with the "right" reading—then students can, with care and assistance, learn to speak for themselves. It takes a certain kind of classroom, to be sure. A teacher who teaches this book will have to be comfortable turning the essays over to the students, even with the knowledge that they will not do immediately on their own what a professional could do—at least not completely, or with the same grace and authority.

In our own teaching, we have learned that we do not have to be experts on every figure or every area of inquiry represented in this book. And, frankly, that has come as a great relief. We can have intelligent, responsible conversations about Geertz's "Deep Play" without being experts on Geertz or on anthropology or ethnography. We needed to prepare ourselves to engage and direct students as readers, but we did not have to prepare ourselves to lecture on Foucault or Rich, or poststructuralism, French Impressionism, or American feminism. The classes we have been teaching, and they have been some of the most exciting we have ever taught, have been classes where students—together and with their instructors—work on what these essays might mean.

So here we are, imagining students working shoulder to shoulder with Geertz and Rich and Foucault, even talking back to them as the occasion arises. There is a wonderful Emersonian bravado in all this. But such is the case with strong and active readers. If we allow students to work on powerful texts, they will want to share the power. This is the heady fun of academic life, the real pleasure of thinking, reading, and writing. There is no reason to keep it secret from our students.

Note to the Eighth Edition. The eighth edition of *Ways of Reading* contains five new selections by Kwame Anthony Appiah, Cornelius Eady, Michael McKeon, Linda Nochlin, and W. G. Sebald.

Our principle of selection remains the same—we were looking for "readable" texts, pieces that instructors and students would find challenging and compelling, pieces that offer powerful readings of ordinary experience, pieces worth extended work.

We revised the assignment sequences, some to incorporate the new selections, others because, after teaching them again, we thought about them differently. We have continued to offer sequences focusing on autobiographical writing and the personal essay. While there have always been assignments in *Ways of Reading* that ask students to use their experience as subject matter, these assignments invite students to look critically and historically at the genre and insist that reading and thinking can *also* be represented as part of one's "personal" experience. Teaching these as examples of reading and writing projects has taught us that they have much to offer that students can study and imitate. We remain convinced that this kind of work helps students to think about sentences in useful ways. And we have continued to focus attention on prose models that challenge conventional forms and idioms, that complicate the usual ways of thinking about and representing knowledge and experience. There are several assignment sequences that ask students to write as though they too could participate in such revisionary work.

We've also updated *Resources for Teaching* WAYS OF READING, by including three new pedagogical essays, by Rashmi Bhatnagar, Thomas E. Recchio, and Richard E. Miller. We continue to offer essays by graduate students; these essays give advice on how to work with the book. They stand as examples of the kinds of papers graduate students might write when they use *Ways of Reading* in conjunction with a teaching seminar. They stand best, however, as examples of graduate students speaking frankly to other graduate students about teaching and about this book. Additional pedagogical essays are on the Web site, bedfordstmartins.com/waysofreading.

With our colleagues, we have taught most of the selections in this book, including the new ones. Several of us worked together to prepare the assignment sequences; most of these, too, have been tested in class. As we have traveled around giving talks, we've met many people who have used *Ways of Reading*. We have been delighted to hear them speak about how it has served their teaching, and we have learned much from their advice and example. It is an unusual and exciting experience to see our course turned into a text, to see our work read, critiqued, revised, and expanded. We have many people to thank. The list that follows can't begin to name all those to whom we owe a debt. And it can't begin to express our gratitude.

Acknowledgments. We owe much to the friendship and wisdom of our colleagues at the University of Pittsburgh. There are old friends and colleagues with whom we have worked for a very long time: Don Bialostosky, Ellen Bishop, Jean Ferguson Carr, Steve Carr, Nick Coles, Kathryn Flannery, Paul Kameen, Geeta Kothari, Mariolina Salvatori, Philip Smith, Susan Smith, and Jim Seitz. We also want to thank students and colleagues who gave particular help and attention to the work in preparation of the Eighth Edition; in particular Anna Redcay, who helped significantly with the research for the headnotes. Kathleen Welsch, at Clarion University, has worked as a reviewer on several editions. For this one, we asked her to provide a detailed review of the headnotes and apparatus from the selections that have stood the test of time, to reread them, and to make suggestions for cuts and revision. She had a fine eye, a good ear, and a wicked red pen.

And we owe much to colleagues at other schools who have followed our work with interest and offered their support and criticism. We are grateful for the notes, letters, and student papers.

We are fortunate to have a number of outstanding reviewers on the project: Barclay Barrios, Florida Atlantic University; Diane Burton, University of Tulsa; John Champagne, Penn State Erie, The Behrend College; G. Matthew Jenkins, University of Tulsa; Beverly Neiderman, Kent State University; Richard Parent, University of Vermont; Thomas Recchio, University of Connecticut; Patricia Suzanne Sullivan, Northeastern University; Kathleen Welsch, Clarion University; Chris Warnick, College of Charleston; Jennifer Whatley, University of Pittsburgh; Nicole Willey, Kent State University.

We would also like to thank those who responded to our questionnaire: Laura Albritton, University of Miami; Barclay Barrios, Florida Atlantic University; Larry Beason, University of South Alabama; Rashmi D. Bhatnagar, Boise State University; Barbara Biasiolli, St. Mary's University; Jacqueline Cason, University of Alaska; Becky Caouette, University of Connecticut; Malkiel Choseed, Onondaga Community College; Pamelyn Dane, Lane Community College; Michael G. Davros, Northeastern Illinois University; Lynn Dornink, Northeastern University; Robert Fanning, West Virginia University; Frank Farmer, University of Kansas; Rochelle H. Grey, Park University; Kurtis Haas, Mesa State College; Catherine Ann Laskaya, University of Oregon; Keming Liu, Medgar Evers College; Drew M. Loewe, Texas Christian University; Mary Bauer Morley, University of North Dakota; Claire Moroney, Emerson College; Michael Myers, University of Georgia; Jeffrey Norman, University of Wisconsin, Milwaukee; Matthew Parfitt, College of General Studies, Boston University; Thomas Recchio, University of Connecticut; Lori Robison, University of North Dakota; Joseph Scallorns, Virginia Tech; Virginia Stein, Community College of Allegheny County, Allegheny Campus; Patricia Suzanne Sullivan, Northeastern University; Carol A. Zieman, Northeastern University; and James Zukowski, Lake Superior State University.

Chuck Christensen and Joan Feinberg helped to shape this project from its very beginning. They remain fine and thoughtful friends as well as fine and thoughtful editors. John Sullivan joined the group for the Fifth Edition. He had taught from an earlier edition of *Ways of Reading* and had, for us, a wonderful sense of the book's approach to reading, writing, and teaching. John is organized, resourceful, generous, quick to offer suggestions and to take on extra work. He soon became as much a collaborator as an editor.

His care and dedication held everything together at times when we were falling apart. It was a real pleasure to work with him. Sandy Schechter and Linda Finigan handled permissions. Alicia Young assisted with many details. Emily Berleth and Nancy Benjamin of Books By Design expertly guided the manuscript through production. Joan Flaherty was an excellent copyeditor, sensitive to the quirks of our prose and attentive to detail.

And, finally, we are grateful to Joyce and Ellen, and to Jesse, Dan, Kate, Matthew, and Ben, for their love and support.

Contents

Preface   *vii*

Introduction: Ways of Reading   1

Making a Mark   *1*
Ways of Reading   *5*
Strong Readers, Strong Texts   *8*
Reading with and against the Grain   *10*
Working with Difficulty   *12*
Reading and Writing: The Questions and Assignments   *16*

The Readings   25

GLORIA ANZALDÚA   27
Entering into the Serpent   *29*
How to Tame a Wild Tongue   *42*
[FROM *Borderlands/La frontera*]

KWAME ANTHONY APPIAH *55*
  The Ethics of Individuality *56*
  [FROM *The Ethics of Identity*]

JOHN BERGER *95*
  Ways of Seeing *97*
  [FROM *Ways of Seeing*]

  On Rembrandt's Woman in Bed *119*
  On Caravaggio's The Calling of St. Matthew *121*
  [SELECTIONS FROM *And Our Faces, My Heart, Brief as Photos*]

SUSAN BORDO *129*
  Beauty (Re)discovers the Male Body *131*
  [FROM *The Male Body*]

CORNELIUS EADY *182*
  Brutal Imagination *184*
  [FROM *Brutal Imagination*]

MICHEL FOUCAULT *207*
  Panopticism *209*
  [FROM *Discipline and Punish*]

PAULO FREIRE *242*
  The "Banking" Concept of Education *243*
  [FROM *Pedagogy of the Oppressed*]

CLIFFORD GEERTZ *258*
  Deep Play: Notes on the Balinese Cockfight *259*
  [FROM *The Interpretation of Cultures*]

SUSAN GRIFFIN *297*
  Our Secret *299*
  [FROM *A Chorus of Stones*]

HARRIET JACOBS *351*
  Incidents in the Life of a Slave Girl *353*
  [SELECTIONS FROM *Incidents in the Life of a Slave Girl*]

MICHAEL McKEON *394*
  Subdividing Inside Spaces *396*
  [FROM *The Secret History of Domesticity*]

LINDA NOCHLIN   447
  Renoir's **Great Bathers***: Bathing as Practice,
    Bathing as Representation*   449

  [FROM *Bathers, Bodies, Beauty*]

WALKER PERCY   480
  The Loss of the Creature   481

  [FROM *The Message in the Bottle*]

MARY LOUISE PRATT   497
  Arts of the Contact Zone   499

  [FROM *Profession 91*]

ADRIENNE RICH   517
  When We Dead Awaken: Writing as Re-Vision   520

  [FROM *On Lies, Secrets, and Silence*]

  Sources   533
  [FROM *Your Native Land, Your Life*]

RICHARD RODRIGUEZ   544
  The Achievement of Desire   545

  [FROM *Hunger of Memory*]

EDWARD SAID   567
  States   570
  [FROM *After the Last Sky*]

W. G. SEBALD   611
  The Rings of Saturn   613

  [SELECTIONS FROM *The Rings of Saturn*]

JANE TOMPKINS   646
  *"Indians": Textualism, Morality, and the Problem
    of History*   647

  [FIRST APPEARED IN *Critical Inquiry*]

ALICE WALKER   667
  In Search of Our Mothers' Gardens   668
  [FROM *In Search of Our Mothers' Gardens*]

JOHN EDGAR WIDEMAN   679
  Our Time   681
  [FROM *Brothers and Keepers*]

Assignment Sequences 723

Working with Assignment Sequences 725
Working with a Sequence 726

SEQUENCE ONE *The Aims of Education* 729

FREIRE *The "Banking" Concept of Education*
RICH *When We Dead Awaken: Writing as Re-Vision*
PRATT *Arts of the Contact Zone*
GRIFFIN *Our Secret*

Alternative Selections

APPIAH *The Ethics of Individuality*
SEBALD *The Rings of Saturn*

Assignments

1. *Applying Freire to Your Own Experience as a Student* [FREIRE] **730**
2. *Studying Rich as a Case in Point* [FREIRE, RICH] **731**
3. *Tradition and the Writing of the Past* [RICH] **733**
4. *The Contact Zone* [PRATT] **734**
5. *The Pedagogical Arts of the Contact Zone* [PRATT] **735**
6. *Writing against the Grain* [GRIFFIN] **736**
7. *The Task of Attention* [GRIFFIN] **737**
8. *Putting Things Together* [FREIRE, RICH, PRATT, GRIFFIN] **738**

Alternative Assignments

Considering Common Pursuits [APPIAH] **738**
A Mental Ramble [SEBALD] **739**

SEQUENCE TWO *The Arts of the Contact Zone* 740

PRATT *Arts of the Contact Zone*
ANZALDÚA *Entering into the Serpent; How to Tame a Wild Tongue*
JACOBS *Incidents in the Life of a Slave Girl*
SAID *States*

Alternative Selection

WIDEMAN *Our Time*

Assignments

1. *The Literate Arts of the Contact Zone* [PRATT] **741**
2. *Borderlands* [PRATT, ANZALDÚA] **743**
3. *Autoethnography* [PRATT, JACOBS] **744**
4. *A Dialectic of Self and Other* [PRATT, SAID] **745**
5. *On Culture* [PRATT, ANZALDÚA, JACOBS, SAID] **746**

Alternative Assignment

Counterparts [WIDEMAN] **747**

SEQUENCE THREE *Autobiographical Explorations* **748**

RODRIGUEZ *The Achievement of Desire*
SAID *States*
SEBALD *The Rings of Saturn*

Alternative Selections

APPIAH *The Ethics of Individuality*
RICH *When We Dead Awaken: Writing as Re-Vision*
WIDEMAN *Our Time*
TOMPKINS *"Indians": Textualism, Morality, and the Problem of History*
GRIFFIN *Our Secret*
ANZALDÚA *Entering into the Serpent; How to Tame a Wild Tongue*
JACOBS *Incidents in the Life of a Slave Girl*

Assignments

1. *Desire, Reading, and the Past* [RODRIGUEZ] **750**
2. *A Photographic Essay* [SAID] **750**
3. *Personal Experience as Intellectual Experience* [SEBALD] **752**
4. *The "I" of the Personal Essay* [RODRIGUEZ, SAID, SEBALD] **752**

Alternative Assignments

Plans of Life [APPIAH] **753**
Possible Narratives [APPIAH] **754**
A Moment of Hesitation [RICH] **754**
Old Habits [WIDEMAN] **755**
Personal Experience as Intellectual Experience (II) [TOMPKINS] **756**
The Matrix [GRIFFIN] **756**
La conciencia de la mestiza/Toward a New Consciousness [ANZALDÚA] **757**
The Voice of the Unwritten Self [JACOBS] **758**

SEQUENCE FOUR *Experts and Expertise* **760**

RICH *When We Dead Awaken: Writing as Re-Vision*
GEERTZ *Deep Play: Notes on the Balinese Cockfight*
WIDEMAN *Our Time*
PERCY *The Loss of the Creature*

Alternative Selections

APPIAH *The Ethics of Individuality*
EADY *Brutal Imagination*
McKEON *Subdividing Inside Spaces*
NOCHLIN *Renoir's* Great Bathers: *Bathing as Practice,*
   Bathing as Representation
SEBALD *The Rings of Saturn*

Assignments

1. *Looking Back* [RICH] **761**
2. *Seeing Your World through Geertz's Eyes* [GEERTZ] **762**

3. *Wideman as a Case in Point* [WIDEMAN]   **763**
4. *On Experts and Expertise* [RICH, GEERTZ, WIDEMAN, PERCY]   **763**

Alternative Assignments

A Parallel Project [APPIAH]   **765**
Writing (and Re-Writing) History [EADY]   **765**
Subdividing Interior Spaces [McKEON]   **766**
Practice and Presentation [NOCHLIN]   **767**
A Mental Ramble [SEBALD]   **768**

SEQUENCE FIVE   *Reading the Lives of Others*   **769**

GEERTZ   *Deep Play: Notes on the Balinese Cockfight*
PRATT   *Arts of the Contact Zone*
EADY   *Brutal Imagination*
WIDEMAN   *Our Time*

Assignments

1. *Close Reading* [GEERTZ]   **770**
2. *Reading Others* [PRATT]   **771**
3. *Writing (and Re-Writing) History* [EADY]   **772**
4. *A Writer's Guide* [WIDEMAN, GEERTZ, PRATT, EADY]   **773**
5. *Revision* [GEERTZ]   **774**

SEQUENCE SIX   *On Difficulty*   **775**

FOUCAULT   *Panopticism*
APPIAH   *The Ethics of Individuality*
SEBALD   *The Rings of Saturn*
NOCHLIN   *Renoir's* Great Bathers: *Bathing as Practice,
Bathing as Representation*

Alternative Selections

BORDO   *Beauty (Re)discovers the Male Body*
WIDEMAN   *Our Time*

Assignments

1. *Foucault's Fabrication* [FOUCAULT]   **776**
2. *Thinking about the State* [APPIAH]   **777**
3. *Erudition* [SEBALD]   **777**
4. *Technical Terms* [NOCHLIN]   **778**
5. *A Theory of Difficulty* [FOUCAULT, WIDEMAN, BORDO]   **779**

Alternative Assignments

The Pleasures of the Text [BORDO]   **779**
A Story of Reading [WIDEMAN]   **780**

SEQUENCE SEVEN   *Reading Culture*   782

BERGER *Ways of Seeing*
BORDO *Beauty (Re)discovers the Male Body*
NOCHLIN *Renoir's* Great Bathers: Bathing as Practice,
    Bathing as Representation
FOUCAULT *Panopticism*

Alternative Selection

McKEON *Subdividing Inside Spaces*

Assignments

1. *Looking at Pictures* [BERGER]   *783*
2. *Berger and After* [BERGER, BORDO]   *784*
3. *Reading the Body* [BORDO]   *784*
4. *High and Low* [BORDO, NOCHLIN]   *785*
5. *On Agency* [BERGER, BORDO, NOCHLIN, FOUCAULT]   *786*
6. *Reading Culture* [BERGER, BORDO, NOCHLIN, FOUCAULT]   *787*

Alternative Assignment

The Mechanisms of Power [FOUCAULT, McKEON]   *788*

SEQUENCE EIGHT   *The Uses of Reading*   *790*

RODRIGUEZ *The Achievement of Desire*
HOGGART *The Scholarship Boy*
BORDO *Beauty (Re)discovers the Male Body*
BERGER *Ways of Seeing*
APPIAH *The Ethics of Individuality*
WALKER *In Search of Our Mothers' Gardens*
BARTHOLOMAE AND PETROSKY *Introduction to* Ways of Reading

Alternative Selection

EADY *Brutal Imagination*

Assignments

1. *The Scholarship Boy* [RODRIGUEZ, HOGGART]   *791*
2. *Sources* (I) [BORDO, BERGER]   *792*
3. *Sources* (II) [APPIAH]   *792*
4. *Contrary Instincts* [WALKER]   *793*
5. *Ways of Reading* [BARTHOLOMAE, PETROSKY]   *794*

Alternative Assignment

Writing (and Re-Writing) History [EADY]   *794*

Additional Assignment Sequences Included in Resources for Teaching WAYS OF READING

Writing with Style

Assignments

1. *Language, Rhythm, Tone* [WIDEMAN]
2. *The Sentence* [SEBALD]
3. *The Line* [EADY]
4. *Character, Point of View* [BERGER]
5. *The Paragraph, the Essay* [GRIFFIN]
6. *The Pleasure of the Text* [BORDO]
7. *A Classroom Lesson* [HACKER]

Alternative Assignment

Punctuating the Essay [APPIAH]

Experiments in Reading and Writing

Assignments

1. *A Mix of Personal and Academic Writing* [GRIFFIN]
2. *Unconventional, Hybrid, and Fragmentary Forms* [SAID]
3. *Turning This Way and That* [WIDEMAN]
4. *A Crazy Dance* [ANZALDÚA]
5. *Writing and Schooling* [GRIFFIN, SAID, WIDEMAN, ANZALDÚA]

Alternative Assignments

Erudition [SEBALD]
Imitating Design and Order [SEBALD]
Poems in Sequence [EADY]
Giving Voice to a Figure [EADY]

Ways of Seeing (I)

Assignments

1. *Ways of Seeing* [BERGER]
2. *A Painting in Writing* [BERGER]
3. *Berger Writing* [BERGER]
4. *Practice and Representation* [NOCHLIN]
5. *Writing Berger* [BORDO, BERGER]
6. *Revision* [BERGER]

Working with the Past

Assignments

1. *A Scholarship Boy* [RODRIGUEZ, HOGGART]
2. *A Slave Narrative* [JACOBS]

3. *Working with the Past* [WALKER]

4. *Legacies* [WALKER, JACOBS]

5. *Writing History* [SAID]

Alternative Assignment

Words and Images [SEBALD]

Writing Projects

Assignments

1. *Words and Images* [SAID]

2. *Poems in Sequence* [EADY]

3. *Subdividing Interior Spaces* [McKEON]

4. *Instruments of Thought* [APPIAH]

5. *Commentary* [SAID, EADY, McKEON, APPIAH]

Alternative Assignments

A Project [RICH]
Writing the "Real" [WIDEMAN]

Reading Walker Percy

Assignments

1. *Who's Lost What in "The Loss of the Creature"?* [PERCY]

2. *Telling a "Percian" Story of Your Own* [PERCY]

3. *Complex and Common Readings of "The Loss of the Creature"* [PERCY]

4. *Rodriguez as One of Percy's Examples* [PERCY, RODRIGUEZ]

5. *The Anthropologist as a Person with a Way of Seeing* [GEERTZ]

6. *Taking Your Turn in the Conversation* [PERCY, RODRIGUEZ, GEERTZ]

A Way of Composing

Assignments

1. *Posing a Problem for Writing* [FREIRE]

2. *Giving Advice to a Fellow Student* [BERGER]

3. *Writing a Second Draft* [FREIRE, BERGER]

4. *Writing as Re-Vision* [RICH]

5. *Preparing a Final Draft* [FREIRE, BERGER, RICH]

Ways of Seeing (II)

Assignments

1. *Berger's Example of a Way of Seeing* [BERGER]

2. *Applying Berger's Methods to a Painting* [BERGER]

3. *A Way of Seeing Your Way of Seeing* [BERGER]

4. *Reviewing the Way You See* [BERGER]

Working with Foucault

Assignments

1. *Foucault's Fabrication* [FOUCAULT]
2. *The Technology of Mastery (A Revision)* [FOUCAULT]
3. *Prisons, Schools, Hospitals, and Workplaces* [FOUCAULT]
4. *Writing, Surveillance, and Control* [FOUCAULT]
5. *The Two-Step* [FOUCAULT]

WAYS OF READING

READING

An Anthology for Writers

Introduction:
Ways of Reading

Making a Mark

READING involves a fair measure of push and shove. You make your mark on a book and it makes its mark on you. Reading is not simply a matter of hanging back and waiting for a piece, or its author, to tell you what the writing has to say. In fact, one of the difficult things about reading is that the pages before you will begin to speak only when the authors are silent and you begin to speak in their place, sometimes for them—doing their work, continuing their projects—and sometimes for yourself, following your own agenda.

This is an unusual way to talk about reading, we know. We have not mentioned finding information or locating an author's purpose or identifying main ideas, useful though these skills are, because the purpose of our book is to offer you occasions to imagine other ways of reading. We think of reading as a social interaction—sometimes peaceful and polite, sometimes not so peaceful and polite.

We'd like you to imagine that when you read the works we've collected here, somebody is saying something to you, and we'd like you to imagine that you are in a position to speak back, to say something of your own in turn. In other words, we are not presenting our book as a miniature library (a place to find information) and we do not think of you, the reader, as a term-paper writer (a person looking for information to summarize or report).

When you read, you hear an author's voice as you move along; you believe a person with something to say is talking to you. You pay attention, even when you don't completely understand what is being said, trusting that it will all make sense in the end, relating what the author says to what you already know or expect to hear or learn. Even if you don't quite grasp everything you are reading at every moment (and you won't), and even if you don't remember everything you've read (no reader does—at least not in long, complex pieces), you begin to see the outlines of the author's project, the patterns and rhythms of that particular way of seeing and interpreting the world.

When you stop to talk or write about what you've read, the author is silent; you take over—it is your turn to write, to begin to respond to what the author said. At that point this author and his or her text become something you construct out of what you remember or what you notice as you go back through the text a second time, working from passages or examples but filtering them through your own predisposition to see or read in particular ways.

In "The Achievement of Desire," one of the essays in this book, Richard Rodriguez tells the story of his education, of how he was drawn to imitate his teachers because of his desire to think and speak like them. His is not a simple story of hard work and success, however. In a sense, Rodriguez's education gave him what he wanted—status, knowledge, a way of understanding himself and his position in the world. At the same time, his education made it difficult to talk to his parents, to share their point of view; and to a degree, he felt himself becoming consumed by the powerful ways of seeing and understanding represented by his reading and his education. The essay can be seen as Rodriguez's attempt to weigh what he had gained against what he had lost.

If ten of us read his essay, each would begin with the same words on the page, but when we discuss the chapter (or write about it), each will retell and interpret Rodriguez's story differently; we will emphasize different sections—some, for instance, might want to discuss the strange way Rodriguez learned to read, others might be taken by his difficult and changing relations to his teachers, and still others might want to think about Rodriguez's remarks about his mother and father.

Each of us will come to his or her own sense of what is significant, of what the point is, and the odds are good that what each of us makes of the essay will vary from one to another. Each of us will understand Rodriguez's story in his or her own way, even though we read the same piece. At the same time, if we are working with Rodriguez's essay (and not putting it aside or ignoring its peculiar way of thinking about education), we will be working within a framework he has established, one that makes education stand, metaphorically, for a complicated interplay between permanence and change, imitation and freedom, loss and achievement.

In "The Achievement of Desire," Rodriguez tells of reading a book by Richard Hoggart, *The Uses of Literacy*. He was captivated by a section of this book in which Hoggart defines a particular kind of student, the "scholarship boy." Here is what Rodriguez says:

> Then one day, leafing through Richard Hoggart's *The Uses of Literacy*, I found, in his description of the scholarship boy, myself. For the first time I realized that there were other students like me, and so I was able to frame the meaning of my academic success, its consequent price—the loss.

For Rodriguez, this phrase, "scholarship boy," became the focus of Hoggart's book. Other people, to be sure, would read that book and take different phrases or sections as the key to what Hoggart has to say. Some might argue that Rodriguez misread the book, that it is really about something else, about British culture, for example, or about the class system in England. The power and value of Rodriguez's reading, however, are represented by what he was able to *do* with what he read, and what he was able to do was not record information or summarize main ideas but, as he says, "frame the meaning of my academic success." Hoggart provided a frame, a way for Rodriguez to think and talk about his own history as a student. As he goes on in his essay, Rodriguez not only uses this frame to talk about his experience, but he resists it, argues with it. He casts his experience in Hoggart's terms but then makes those terms work for him by seeing both what they can and what they cannot do. This combination of reading, thinking, and writing is what we mean by *strong reading,* a way of reading we like to encourage in our students.

When we have taught "The Achievement of Desire" to our students, it has been almost impossible for them not to see themselves in Rodriguez's description of the scholarship boy (and this was true of students who were not minority students and not literally on scholarships). They, too, have found a way of framing (even inventing) their own lives as students—students whose histories involve both success and loss. When we have asked our students to write about this essay, however, some students have argued, and quite convincingly, that Rodriguez had either to abandon his family and culture or to remain ignorant. Other students have argued equally convincingly that Rodriguez's anguish was destructive and self-serving, that he was trapped into seeing his situation in terms that he might have replaced with others. He did not necessarily have to turn his back on his family. Some have contended that Rodriguez's problems with his family had nothing to do with what he says about education, that he himself shows how imitation need not blindly lead a person away from his culture, and these student essays, too, have been convincing.

Reading, in other words, can be the occasion for you to put things together, to notice this idea or theme rather than that one, to follow a writer's announced or secret ends while simultaneously following your own. When this happens, when you forge a reading of a story or an essay, you make your mark on it, casting it in your terms. But the story makes its mark on you as well, teaching you not only about a subject (Rodriguez's struggles with his teachers and his parents, for example) but about a way of seeing and understanding a subject. The text provides the opportunity for you to see through someone else's powerful language, to imagine your own familiar settings through the images, metaphors, and ideas of others. Rodriguez's essay, in other words, can make its mark on readers, but they, too, if they are strong, active readers, can make theirs on it.

Readers learn to put things together by writing. It is not something you can do, at least not to any degree, while you are reading. It requires that you work on what you have read, and that work best takes shape when you sit down to write. We will have more to say about this kind of thinking in a later section of the introduction, but for now let us say that writing gives you a way of going to work on the text you have read. To write about a story or an essay, you go back to what you have read to find phrases or passages that define what for you are the key moments, that help you interpret sections that seem difficult or troublesome or mysterious. If you are writing an essay of your own, the work that you are doing gives a purpose and a structure to that rereading.

Writing also, however, gives you a way of going back to work on the text of your own reading. It allows you to be self-critical. You can revise not just to make your essay neat or tight or tidy but to see what kind of reader you have been, to examine the pattern and consequences in the choices you have made. Revision, in other words, gives you the chance to work on your essay, but it also gives you an opportunity to work on your reading—to qualify or extend or question your interpretation of, say, "The Achievement of Desire."

We can describe this process of "re-vision," or re-seeing, fairly simply. You should not expect to read "The Achievement of Desire" once and completely understand the essay or know what you want to say. You will work out what you have to say while you write. And once you have constructed a reading—once you have completed a draft of your essay, in other words—you can step back, see what you have done, and go back to work on it. Through this activity—writing and rewriting—we have seen our students become strong, active, and critical readers.

Not everything a reader reads is worth that kind of effort. The pieces we have chosen for this book all provide, we feel, powerful ways of seeing (or framing) our common experience. The selections cannot be quickly summarized. They are striking, surprising, sometimes troubling in how they challenge common ways of seeing the world. Some of them (we're thinking of pieces by Michel Foucault, Clifford Geertz, and Adrienne Rich) have captured and altered the way our culture sees and understands daily experience. The essays have changed the ways people think and write. In fact, every selection in the book is one that has given us, our students, and our colleagues that dramatic experience, almost like a discovery, when we suddenly saw things as we had never seen them before and, as a consequence, we had to work hard to understand what had happened and how our thinking had changed.

If we recall, for example, the first time we read Susan Griffin's "Our Secret" or John Edgar Wideman's "Our Time," we know that they have radically shaped our thinking. We carry these essays with us in our minds, mulling over them, working through them, hearing Griffin and Wideman in sentences we write or sentences we read. We introduce the essays in classes we teach whenever we can; we are surprised, reading them for the third or fourth time, to find things we didn't see before. It's not that we failed to "get" these essays the first time around. In fact, we're not sure we have captured them yet, at least not in any final sense, and we disagree in basic ways about what Griffin and Wideman are saying or about how these essays might best be used. Essays like these are not the sort that you can "get" like a loaf of bread at the store. We're each convinced that the essays are ours in that we know best what's going on in them, and yet we have also become theirs, creatures of these essays, because of the ways they have come to dominate our seeing, talking, reading, and writing. This captivity is something we welcome, yet it is also something we resist.

Our experience with these texts is a remarkable one and certainly hard to provide for others, but the challenges and surprises are reasons we read — we hope to be taken and changed in just these ways. Or, to be more accurate, it is why we read outside the daily requirements to keep up with the news or conduct our business. And it is why we bring reading into our writing courses.

Ways of Reading

Before explaining how we organized this book, we would like to say more about the purpose and place of the kind of strong, aggressive, labor-intensive reading we've been referring to.

Readers face many kinds of experiences, and certain texts are written with specific situations in mind and invite specific ways of reading. Some texts, for instance, serve very practical purposes — they give directions or information. Others, like the short descriptive essays often used in English textbooks and anthologies, celebrate common ways of seeing and thinking and ask primarily to be admired. These texts seem self-contained; they announce their own meanings with little effort and ask little from the reader, making it clear how they want to be read and what they have to say. They ask only for a nod of the head or for the reader to take notes and give a sigh of admiration ("yes, that was very well said"). They are clear and direct. It is as though the authors could anticipate all the questions their essays might raise and solve all the problems a reader might imagine. There is not much work for a reader to do, in other words, except, perhaps, to take notes and, in the case of textbooks, to work step-by-step, trying to remember as much as possible.

This is how assigned readings are often presented in university class-rooms. Introductory textbooks (in biology or business, for instance) are good examples of books that ask little of readers outside of note-taking and memorization. In these texts the writers are experts and your job, as novice, is to digest what they have to say. And, appropriately, the task set before you is to summarize—so you can speak again what the author said, so you can better remember what you read. Essay tests are an example of the writing tasks that often follow this kind of reading. You might, for instance, study the human nervous system through textbook readings and lectures and then be asked to write a summary of what you know from both sources. Or a teacher might ask you during a class discussion to paraphrase a paragraph from a textbook describing chemical cell communication to see if you understand what you've read.

Another typical classroom form of reading is reading for main ideas. With this kind of reading you are expected to figure out what most people (or most people within a certain specialized group of readers) would take as the main idea of a selection. There are good reasons to read for main ideas. For one, it is a way to learn how to imagine and anticipate the values and habits of a particular group—test-makers or, if you're studying business, Keynesian economists, perhaps. If you are studying business, to continue this example, you must learn to notice what Keynesian economists notice—for instance, when they analyze the problems of growing government debt—to share key terms, to know the theoretical positions they take, and to adopt for yourself their common examples and interpretations, their jargon, and their established findings.

There is certainly nothing wrong with reading for information or reading to learn what experts have to say about their fields of inquiry. These are not, however, the only ways to read, although they are the ones most often taught. Perhaps because we think of ourselves as writing teachers, we are concerned with presenting other ways of reading in the college and university curriculum.

A danger arises in assuming that reading is only a search for information or main ideas. There are ways of thinking through problems and working with written texts which are essential to academic life, but that are not represented by summary and paraphrase or by note-taking and essay exams.

Student readers, for example, can take responsibility for determining the meaning of the text. They can work as though they were doing something other than finding ideas already there on the page and they can be guided by their own impressions or questions as they read. We are not, now, talking about finding hidden meanings. If such things as hidden meanings can be said to exist, they are hidden by readers' habits and prejudices (by readers' assumptions that what they read should tell them what they already know), or by readers' timidity and passivity (by their unwillingness to take the responsibility to speak their minds and say what they notice).

Reading to locate meaning in the text places a premium on memory, yet a strong reader is not necessarily a person with a good memory. This point may seem minor, but we have seen too many students haunted because they could not remember everything they read or retain a complete essay in their minds. A reader could set herself the task of remembering as much as she could from Walker Percy's "The Loss of the Creature," an essay filled with stories about tourists at the Grand Canyon and students in a biology class, but a reader could also do other things with that essay; a reader might figure out, for example, how students and tourists might be said to have a common problem seeing what they want to see. Students who read Percy's essay as a memory test end up worrying about bits and pieces (bits and pieces they could go back and find if they had to) and turn their attention away from the more pressing problem of how to make sense of a difficult and often ambiguous essay.

A reader who needs to have access to something in the essay can use simple memory aids. A reader can go back and scan, for one thing, to find passages or examples that might be worth reconsidering. Or a reader can construct a personal index, making marks in the margin or underlining passages that seem interesting or mysterious or difficult. A mark is a way of saying, "This is something I might want to work on later." If you mark the selections in this book as you read them, you will give yourself a working record of what, at the first moment of reading, you felt might be worth a second reading.

If Percy's essay presents problems for a reader, they are problems of a different order from summary and recall. The essay is not the sort that tells you what it says. You would have difficulty finding one sentence that sums up or announces, in a loud and clear voice, what Percy is talking about. At the point you think Percy is about to summarize, he turns to one more example that complicates the picture, as though what he is discussing defies his attempts to sum things up. Percy is talking about tourists and students, about such things as individual "sovereignty" and our media culture's "symbolic packages," but if he has a point to make, it cannot be stated in a sentence or two.

In fact, Percy's essay is challenging reading in part because it does not have a single, easily identifiable main idea. A reader could infer that it has several points to make, none of which can be said easily and some of which, perhaps, are contradictory. To search for information, or to ignore the rough edges in search of a single, paraphrasable idea, is to divert attention from the task at hand, which is not to remember what Percy says but to speak about the essay and what it means to you, the reader. In this sense, the Percy essay is not the sum of its individual parts; it is, more accurately, what its readers make of it.

A reader could go to an expert on Percy to solve the problem of what to make of the essay—perhaps to a teacher, perhaps to the Internet or to a book in the library. And if the reader pays attention, he could remember what the expert said or she could put down notes on paper (or in an e-file). But in doing either, the reader only rehearses what he or she has been told, abandoning the responsibility to make the essay meaningful. There are ways of reading, in other words, in which Percy's essay "The Loss of the Creature" is not what it means to the experts but what it means to you as a reader willing to take the chance to construct a reading. You can be the authority on Percy; you don't have to turn to others. The meaning of the essay, then, is something you develop as you go along, something for which you must take final responsibility. The meaning is forged from reading the essay, to be sure, but it is determined by what you do with the essay, by the connections you can make and your explanation of why those connections are important, and by your account of what Percy might mean when he talks about "symbolic packages" or a "loss of sovereignty" (phrases Percy uses as key terms in the essay). This version of Percy's essay will finally be yours; it will not be exactly what Percy said. (Only his words in the order he wrote them would say exactly what he said.) You will choose the path to take through his essay and support it as you can with arguments, explanations, examples, and commentary.

If an essay or a story is not the sum of its parts but something you as a reader create by putting together those parts that seem to matter personally, then the way to begin, once you have read a selection in this collection, is by reviewing what you recall, by going back to those places that stick in your memory—or, perhaps, to those sections you marked with checks or notes in the margins. You begin by seeing what you can make of these memories and notes. You should realize that with essays as long and complex as those we've included in this book, you will never feel, after a single reading, as though you have command of everything you read. This is not a problem. After four or five readings (should you give any single essay that much attention), you may still feel that there are parts you missed or don't understand. This sense of incompleteness is part of the experience of reading, at least the experience of reading serious work. And it is part of the experience of a strong reader. No reader could retain one of these essays in her mind, no matter how proficient her memory or how experienced she might be. No reader, at least no reader we would trust, would admit that he understood everything that Michel Foucault or Adrienne Rich or Edward Said had to say. What strong readers know is that they have to begin, and they have to begin regardless of their doubts or hesitations. What you have after your first reading of an essay is a starting place, and you begin with your marked passages or examples or notes, with questions to answer, or with problems to solve. Strong readings, in other words, put a premium on individual acts of attention and composition.

Strong Readers, Strong Texts

We chose pieces for this book that invite strong readings. Our selections require more attention (or a different form of attention) than a written summary, a reduction to gist, or a recitation of main ideas. They are not "easy" reading. The challenges they present, however, do not make them inaccessible to college students. The essays are not specialized studies; they have interested, pleased, or piqued general and specialist audiences alike. To say that they are challenging is to say, then, that they leave some work for a reader to do. They are designed to teach a reader new ways to read (or to step outside habitual ways of reading), and they anticipate readers willing to take the time to learn. These readers need not be experts on the subject matter. Perhaps the most difficult problem for students is to believe that this is true.

You do not need experts to explain these stories and essays, although you could probably go to the library and find an expert guide to most of the selections we've included. Let's take, for example, Adrienne Rich's "When We Dead Awaken: Writing as Re-Vision." This essay looks at the history of women's writing (and at Rich's development as a poet). It argues that women have been trapped within a patriarchal culture—speaking in men's voices and telling stories prepared by men—and, as a consequence, according to Rich, "We need to know the writing of the past, and know it differently than we have ever known it; not to pass on a tradition but to break its hold over us."

You could go to the library to find out how Rich is regarded by experts, by literary critics or feminist scholars, for example; you could learn how her work fits into an established body of work on women's writing and the representation of women in modern culture. You could see what others have said about the writers she cites: Virginia Woolf, Jane Austen, and Elizabeth Bishop. You could see how others have read and made use of Rich's essay. You could see how others have interpreted the poems she includes as part of her argument. You could look for standard definitions of key terms like "patriarchy" or "formalism."

Though it is often important to seek out other texts and to know what other people are saying or have said, it is often necessary and even desirable to begin on your own. Rich can also be read outside any official system of interpretation. She is talking, after all, about our daily experience. And when she addresses the reader, she addresses a person—not a term-paper writer. When she says, "We need to know the writing of the past, and know it differently than we have ever known it," she means us and what we know and how we know what we know. (The "we" of her essay could be said to refer most accurately to women readers, leading men to feel the kind of exclusion women must feel when the reader is always "he.")

The question, then, is not what Rich's words might mean to a literary critic, or generally to those who study contemporary American culture. The question is what you, the reader, can make of those words given your own experience, your goals, and the work you do with what she has written. In this sense, "When We Dead Awaken" is not what it means to others (those who have already decided what it means) but what it means to you, and this meaning is something you compose when you write about the essay; it is your account of what Rich says and how what she says might be said to make sense.

A teacher, poet, and critic we admire, I. A. Richards, once said, "Read as though it made sense and perhaps it will." To take command of complex material like the selections in this book, you need not subordinate yourself to experts; you can assume the authority to provide such a reading on your own. This means you must allow yourself a certain tentativeness and recognize your limits. You should not assume that it is your job to solve the problems between men and women. You can speak with authority while still acknowledging that complex issues *are* complex.

There is a paradox here. On the one hand, the essays are rich, magnificent, too big for anyone to completely grasp all at once, and before them, as before inspiring spectacles, it seems appropriate to stand humbly, admiringly. And yet, on the other hand, a reader must speak with authority.

In "The American Scholar," Ralph Waldo Emerson says, "Meek young men grow up in libraries, believing it their duty to accept the views, which Cicero, which Locke, which Bacon, have given, forgetful that Cicero, Locke, and Bacon were only young men in libraries when they wrote these books." What Emerson offers here is not a fact but an attitude. There is creative reading, he says, as well as creative writing. It is up to you to treat authors as your equals, as people who will allow you to speak, too. At the same time, you must respect the difficulty and complexity of their texts and of the issues and questions they examine. Little is to be gained, in other words, by turning Rich's essay into a message that would fit on a poster in a dorm room: "Be Yourself" or "Stand on Your Own Two Feet."

Reading with and against the Grain

Reading, then, requires a difficult mix of authority and humility. On the one hand, a reader takes charge of a text; on the other, a reader gives generous attention to someone else's (a writer's) key terms and methods, commits his time to her examples, tries to think in her language, imagines that this strange work is important, compelling, at least for the moment.

Most of the questions in *Ways of Reading* will have you moving back and forth in these two modes, reading with and against the grain of a text, reproducing an author's methods, questioning his or her direction and authority. With the essay "When We Dead Awaken," for example, we have asked students to give a more complete and detailed reading of Rich's poems (the poems included in the essay) than she does, to put her terms to work, to extend her essay by extending the discussion of her examples. We have asked students to give themselves over to her essay — recognizing that this is not necessarily an easy thing to do. Or, again in Rich's name, we have asked students to tell a story of their own experience, a story similar to the one she tells, one that can be used as an example of the ways a person is positioned by a dominant culture. Here we are saying, in effect, read your world in Rich's terms. Notice what she would notice. Ask the questions she would ask. Try out her conclusions.

To read generously, to work inside someone else's system, to see your world in someone else's terms—we call this "reading with the grain." It is a way of working *with* a writer's ideas, in conjunction with someone else's text. As a way of reading, it can take different forms. In the reading and writing assignments that follow the selections in this book, you will sometimes be asked to summarize and paraphrase, to put others' ideas into your terms, to provide your account of what they are saying. This is a way of getting a tentative or provisional hold on a text, its examples and ideas; it allows you a place to begin to work. And sometimes you will be asked to extend a writer's project—to add your examples to someone else's argument, to read your experience through the frame of another's text, to try out the key terms and interpretive schemes in another writer's work. In the assignments that follow the Rich essay, for example, students are asked both to reproduce her argument and to extend her terms to examples from their own experience.

We have also asked students to read against the grain, to read critically, to turn back, for example, *against* Rich's project, to ask questions they believe might come as a surprise, to look for the limits of her vision, to provide alternate readings of her examples, to find examples that challenge her argument, to engage her, in other words, in dialogue. How might her poems be read to counter what she wants to say about them? If her essay argues for a new language for women, how is this language represented in the final poem or the final paragraphs, when the poem seems unreadable and the final paragraph sounds familiarly like the usual political rhetoric? If Rich is arguing for a collective movement, a "we" represented by the "we" of her essay, who is included and who excluded by the terms and strategies of her writing? To what degree might you say that this is a conscious or necessary strategy?

Many of the essays in this book provide examples of writers working against the grain of common sense or everyday language. This is true of John Berger, for example, who redefines the "art museum" against the way it is usually understood. It is true of John Edgar Wideman, who reads against his own text while he writes it—asking questions that disturb the story as it emerges on the page. It is true of Harriet Jacobs, Susan Griffin, and W. G. Sebald, whose writings show the signs of their efforts to work against the grain of the standard essay, habitual ways of representing what it means to know something, to be somebody, to speak before others.

This, we've found, is the most difficult work for students to do, this work against the grain. For good reasons and bad, students typically define their skill by reproducing rather than questioning or revising the work of their teachers (or the work of those their teachers ask them to read). It is important to read generously and carefully and to learn to submit to projects that others have begun. But it is also important to know what you are doing—to understand where this work comes from, whose interests it serves, how and where it is kept together by will rather than desire, and what it might have to do with you. To fail to ask the fundamental questions—Where am I in this? How can I make my mark? Whose interests are represented? What can

I learn by reading with or against the grain?—to fail to ask these questions is to mistake skill for understanding, and it is to misunderstand the goals of a liberal education. All of the essays in this book, we would argue, ask to be read, not simply reproduced; they ask to be read and to be read with a difference. Our goal is to make that difference possible.

Working with Difficulty

When we chose the selections for this textbook, we chose them with the understanding that they were difficult to read. And we chose them knowing that students were not their primary audience (that the selections were not speaking directly to you). We chose them, in other words, knowing that we would be asking you to read something you were most likely not prepared to read. But this is what it means to be a student and it was our goal to take our students seriously. Students have to do things they are not yet ready to do; this is how they learn. Students need to read materials that they are not yet ready to read. This is how they get started; this is where they begin. It is also the case that, in an academic setting, difficulty is not necessarily a problem. If something is hard to read, it is not necessarily the case that the writer is at fault. The work can be hard to read because the writer is thinking beyond the usual ways of thinking. It is hard because it is hard, in other words. The text is not saying the same old things in the same old ways.

We believe the best way to work on a difficult text is by rereading, and we provide exercises to direct this process ("Questions for a Second Reading"), but you can also work on the difficult text by writing—by taking possession of the work through sentences and paragraphs of your own, through summary, paraphrase, and quotation, by making another writer's work part of your work. The textbook is organized to provide ways for you to work on these difficult selections by writing and rereading. Each of the selections is followed by questions designed to help you get started.

To get a better sense of what we mean by "working with difficulty," it might be useful to look at an example. One of the selections in *Ways of Reading* is a chapter from a book titled *Pedagogy of the Oppressed*, by the Brazilian educator Paulo Freire. The chapter is titled "The 'Banking' Concept of Education," and the title summarizes the argument at its most simple level. The standard forms of education, Freire argues, define the teacher as the active agent and the student as the passive agent. The teacher has knowledge and makes deposits from this storehouse into the minds of students, who are expected to receive these deposits completely and without alteration—like moving money from a wallet to the bank vault. And this, he argues, is not a good thing.

One of the writing assignments attached to this selection asks students to think along with Freire and to use his argument to examine a situation from their own experience with schooling. Here is an essay (a very skillful essay) that we received from a freshman in the opening weeks of class. It is relatively short and to the point. It will be familiar. You should have no trouble following it, even if you haven't read the selection by Freire.

The "Banking" Concept of Education

As a high school senior, I took a sociology class that was a perfect example of the "banking" concept of education, as described by Freire. There were approximately thirty students enrolled in the class. Unless each of our brains was computerized for long-term memorization, I don't understand how we were expected to get anything out of the class.

Each class began with the copying of four to five pages of notes, which were already written on the blackboards when we entered the classroom. Fifteen to twenty minutes later, the teacher proceeded to pass out a worksheet, which was to be filled out using only the notes we previously copied as our reference. If a question was raised, her reply was, "It's in the notes."

With approximately ten minutes left in the period, we were instructed to pass our worksheets back one desk. Then, she read the answers to the worksheets and gave a grade according to how many questions we answered correctly.

During the semester, we didn't have any quizzes, and only one test, which consisted of matching and listing-type questions. All test information was taken directly from the daily worksheets, and on no occasion did she give an essay question. This is an example of a test question:

Name three forms of abuse that occur in the family.

1.
2.
3.

In order to pass the class, each piece of information printed on her handouts needed to be memorized. On one occasion, a fellow classmate summed up her technique of teaching perfectly by stating, "This is nothing but education by memorization!"

Anyone who cared at all about his grade in the class did quite well, according to his report card. Not much intelligence is required to memorize vocabulary terms. Needless to say, not too many of us learned much from the class, except that "education by memorization" and the "banking" concept of education, as Freire puts it, are definitely not an interesting or effective system of education.

The essay is confident and tidy and not wrong in its account of the "banking" concept of education. In five short paragraphs, the writer not only "got" Freire, he also worked his high school sociology teacher and her teaching methods into the "banking" narrative. We asked the student (as we have asked many students since then): How did you do this? What was the secret? And he was quick to answer, "I read through the Freire essay and I worked with what I understood and I ignored the rest." And it's true. He did. And it is true that this is one way to get started. It's OK. You work with what you can.

The difficult sections of Freire's argument (the hard parts, the sections, and the passages our writer ignored) are related to a Marxist analysis of a *system* of education and its interests. Freire does not write just about individuals—a bad teacher and a smart student—although it is certainly easier (and in some ways more comforting) to think that schooling is just a matter of individual moments and individual actors, good and bad. What is happening in our classrooms, Freire argues, is bigger than the intentions or actions of individuals. He says, for example, "Education as the exercise of domination stimulates the credulity of students, with the ideological intent (often not perceived by educators) of indoctrinating them to adapt to the world of oppression." He writes about how schools "regulate the way the world 'enters into' students." He calls for "problem-posing education": "Problem-posing education is revolutionary futurity." What is at stake, he says, is "humanity." What is required is "*conscientização*." He is concerned to promote education in service of "revolution": "A deepened consciousness of their situation leads people to apprehend that situation as an historical reality susceptible of transformation." There is more going on here, in other words, than can be represented simply by a teacher who is lazy or unimaginative.

The student's essay marks a skillful performance. He takes Freire's chapter and makes it consistent with what he knows how to say. You hear that in this statement: "'education by memorization' and the 'banking' concept of education, as Freire puts it, are definitely not an interesting or effective system of education." Freire's language becomes consistent with his own (the "banking" concept can be filed away under "education by memorization") and, once this is achieved, the writer's need to do any real work with Freire's text becomes unnecessary—"needless to say." Working with difficult readings often requires a willingness to step outside of what you can conveniently control, and this process often begins with revision. As important as it was for this student to use his essay to get a hold of Freire, to open a door or to get a handhold, a place of purchase, a way to begin, it is equally important for a writer to take the next step—and the next step is to revise, particularly where revision is a way of reworking rather than just "fixing" what you have begun.

This was a student of ours and, after talking with him about the first draft, we suggested that he reread "The 'Banking' Concept of Education," this time paying particular attention to the difficult passages, the passages that were hard to understand, those that he had ignored the first time around. And we suggested that his revised essay should bring some of those passages into the text. He did just this and by changing the notion of what he was doing (by working with rather than in spite of difficulty), he wrote a very different essay. This was real revision, in other words, not just a matter of smoothing out the rough edges. The revision changed the way the writer read and it changed the way the reader wrote. The revised essay was quite different (and not nearly so confident and skillful—and this was a good thing, a sign of learning). Here is a representative passage:

> We never really had to "think" in the class. In fact, we were never permitted to "think," we were merely expected to take in the information and store it like a computer. Freire calls this act a "violation of men's humanity" (p. 266). He states, "Any situation in which some men prevent others from engaging in the process of inquiry is one of violence" (p. 266). I believe what Freire is speaking of here is . . . .

We'll keep his conclusion to ourselves, since the conclusion is not nearly so important as what has happened to the writer's understanding of what it means to *work* on a reading. In this revised paragraph, he brings in phrases from the text and the phrases he brings in are not easy to handle; he has to struggle to put them to use or to make them make sense. The writer is trying to figure out the urgency in Freire's text. The story of the sociology class was one thing but how do you get from there to a statement about a "violation of men's humanity"? So the passage that is quoted is not just dumped in for color; it is there for the writer to work with, to try to deploy. And that is what comes next:

> He states, "Any situation in which some men prevent others from engaging in the process of inquiry is one of violence" (p. 266). I believe what Freire is speaking of here is . . . .

The key moment in writing like this is the moment of translation: "I believe what Freire is speaking of here is . . . ." This is where the writer must step forward to take responsibility for working inside the terms of Freire's project.

There is much to admire in this revision. It was early in the semester when writing is always risky, and it took courage and determination for a student to work with what she (or he) couldn't quite understand, couldn't sum up easily, couldn't command. We are a long way from the first draft and "needless to say." You can see, even in this brief passage, that the writing has lost some of the confidence (or arrogance) of the first draft and, as the writer works to think with Freire about education as a system, the characters of the "student" and the "teacher" become different in this narrative. And this is good writing. It may not be as finished as it might need to be later in the semester, but it is writing where something is happening, where thought is taken seriously.

So, how do you work with a difficult text? You have to get started somewhere and sometime and you will almost always find yourself writing before you have a sense that you have "mastered" the text, fully comprehended what you have read. (We would argue that these are dangerous goals, "mastery" and "comprehension." We value what students can bring themselves to *do* with what they read and we measure their success in relation to the success of the project.) You have to get started somewhere and then you can go back to work again on what you have begun by rereading and rewriting. The textbook provides guidelines for rereading.

When you are looking for help with a particular selection, you can, for example, turn to the "Questions for a Second Reading." Read through *all* of them whether they are assigned or not, since they provide several entry points, different ways in, many of them suggested to us by our students in class and in their essays. You might imagine that these questions and the writing assignments that follow (and you might read through these writing assignments, too) provide starting points. Each suggests a different path through the essay. No one can hold a long and complicated essay in mind all at once. Every reader needs a starting point, a way in. Having more than one possible starting point allows you to make choices.

Once you have an entry point, where you have entered and how you have entered will help to shape your sense of what is interesting or important in the text. In this sense, you (and not just the author) are organizing the essay or chapter. The text will present its shape in terms of sections or stages. You should look for these road signs—breaks in the text or phrases that indicate intellectual movement, like "on the other hand" or "in conclusion." You can be guided by these, to be sure, but *you* also give shape to what you read—and you do this most deliberately when you reread. This is where you find (and impose) patterns and connections that are not obvious and not already articulated but that make sense to you and give you a way to describe what you see in what you are reading. In our own teaching, we talk to our students about "scaffolds." The scaffold, we say, represents the way you are organizing the text, the way you are putting it together. A scaffold is made up of lines and passages from the text, the terms you've found that you want to work with, ideas that matter to you, your sense of the progress of the piece.

The scaffold can also include the work of others. In groups or in class discussion, take notes on what other students say. This is good advice generally (you can always learn from your colleagues), but it is particularly useful in a class that features reading and writing. Your notes can document the ideas of others, to be sure, but most important they can give you a sense of where other people are beginning, of where they have entered the text and what they are doing once they have started. You can infer the scaffold they have constructed to make sense of what they read and this can give highlight and relief, even counterpoint, to your own. And use your teacher's comments and questions, including those on your first drafts, to get a sense of the shape of your work as a reader and a writer. This is not a hunt for ideas, for the right or proper or necessary thing to say about a text. It is a hunt for a method, for a way of making sense of a text without resorting only to simple summary.

Reading and Writing:
The Questions and Assignments

Strong readers, we've said, remake what they have read to serve their own ends, putting things together, figuring out how ideas and examples relate, explaining as best they can material that is difficult or problematic, translating phrases like Richard Rodriguez's "scholarship boy" into their own terms. At these moments, it is hard to distinguish the act of reading from the act of writing. In fact, the connection between reading and writing can be seen as almost a literal one, since the best way you can show your reading of a rich and dense essay like "The Achievement of Desire" is by writing down your thoughts, placing one idea against another, commenting on what you've done, taking examples into account, looking back at where you began, perhaps changing your mind, and moving on.

Readers, however, seldom read a single essay in isolation, as though their only job were to arrive at some sense of what an essay has to say. Although we couldn't begin to provide examples of all the various uses of reading in academic life, it is often the case that readings provide information and direction for investigative projects, whether they are philosophical or scientific in nature. The reading and writing assignments that follow each selection in this book are designed to point you in certain directions, to give you ideas and projects to work with, and to challenge you to see one writer's ideas through another's.

Strong readers often read critically, weighing, for example, an author's claims and interpretations against evidence—evidence provided by the author in the text, evidence drawn from other sources, or the evidence that is assumed to be part of a reader's own knowledge and experience. Critical reading can produce results as far-reaching as a biochemist publicly challenging the findings and interpretations in an article on cancer research in the *New England Journal of Medicine* or as quiet as a student offering a personal interpretation of a story in class discussion.

You will find that the questions we have included in our reading and writing assignments often direct you to test what you think an author is saying by measuring it against your own experience. Paulo Freire, for example, in "The 'Banking' Concept of Education" talks about the experience of the student, and one way for you to develop or test your reading of his essay is to place what he says in the context of your own experience, searching for examples that are similar to his and examples that differ from his. If the writers in this book are urging you to give strong readings of your common experience, you have access to what they say because they are talking not only to you but about you. Freire has a method that he employs when he talks about the classroom—one that compares "banking" education with "problem-posing" education. You can try out his method and his terms on examples of your own, continuing his argument as though you were working with him on a common project. Or you can test his argument as though you want to see not only where and how it will work but where and how it will not.

You will also find questions that ask you to extend the argument of the essay by looking in detail at some of the essay's own examples. John Berger, for example, gives a detailed analysis of two paintings by Frans Hals in "Ways of Seeing." Other paintings in the essay he refers to only briefly. One way of working on his essay is to look at the other examples, trying to do with them what he has done for you earlier.

Readers, as we have said, seldom read an essay in isolation, as though, having once worked out a reading of Adrienne Rich's "When We Dead Awaken: Writing as Re-Vision," they could go on to something else, something unrelated. It is unusual for anyone, at least in an academic setting, to read in so random a fashion. Readers read most often because they have a project in hand—a question they are working on or a problem they are trying to solve. For example, if as a result of reading Rich's essay you become interested in the difference between women's writing and men's writing, and you begin to notice things you would not have noticed before, then you can read other essays in the book through this frame. If you have a project in mind, that project will help determine how you read these other essays. Sections of an essay that might otherwise seem unimportant suddenly become important—Gloria Anzaldúa's unusual prose style, or the moments when Harriet Jacobs addresses the "women of the North." Rich may enable you to read Jacobs's narrative differently. Jacobs may spur you to rethink Rich.

In a sense, then, you do have the chance to become an expert reader, a reader with a project in hand, one who has already done some reading, who has watched others at work, and who has begun to develop a method of analysis and a set of key terms. You might read Jacobs's narrative "Incidents in the Life of a Slave Girl," for example, in the context of Mary Louise Pratt's discussion of "autoethnography," or you might read the selections by Gloria Anzaldúa, Cornelius Eady, and John Edgar Wideman as offering differing accounts of racism in America. Imagining yourself operating alongside some of the major figures in contemporary thought can be great fun and heady work—particularly when you have the occasion to speak back to them.

In every case, then, the material we provide to direct your work on the essay, story, or poem will have you constructing a reading, but then doing something with what you have read—using the selection as a frame through which you can understand (through which you can "read") your own experience, the examples of others, or the ideas and methods of other writers.

You may find that you have to alter your sense of who a writer is and what a writer does as you work on your own writing. Writers are often told that they need to begin with a clear sense of what they want to do and what they want to say. The writing assignments we've written, we believe, give you a sense of what you want (or need) to do. We define a problem for you to work on, and the problem will frame the task for you. You will have to decide where you will go in the texts you have read to find materials to work with, the primary materials that will give you a place to begin as you work on your essay. It would be best, however, if you did not feel that you need to have a clear sense of what you want to say before you begin. You may begin to develop a sense of what you want to say while you are writing—as you begin, for example, to examine how and why Anzaldúa's prose could be said to be difficult to read, and what that difficulty might enable you to say about what Anzaldúa expects of a reader. It may also be the case, however, that the subjects you will be writing about are too big for you to assume that you need to have all the answers or that it is up to you to have the final word or to solve the problems once and for all. When you work on your essays, you should cast yourself in the role of one who is exploring a question, examining what might be said, and speculating on possible rather than certain conclusions. If you consider your responses to be provisional, examples of what might be said by a bright and serious student at this point in time, you will be in a position to learn more, as will those who read what you write. Think of yourself, then, as a writer intent on opening a subject up rather than closing one down.

Let us turn briefly now to the three categories of reading and writing assignments you will find in the book.

Questions for a Second Reading

Immediately following each selection are questions designed to guide your second reading. You may, as we've said, prefer to follow your own instincts as you search for the materials to build your understanding of the essay or story or poem. These questions are meant to assist that process or develop those instincts. Most of the selections in the book are longer and more difficult than those you may be accustomed to reading. They are difficult enough that any reader would have to reread them and work to understand them; these questions are meant to suggest ways of beginning that work.

The second-reading questions characteristically ask you to consider the relations between ideas and examples in what you have read or to test specific statements in the essays against your own experience (so that you can get a sense of the author's habit of mind, his or her way of thinking about subjects that are available to you, too). Some turn your attention to what we take to be key terms or concepts, asking you to define these terms by observing how the writer uses them throughout the essay.

These are the questions that seemed "natural" to us; they reflect our habitual way of reading and, we believe, the general habits of mind of the academic community. These questions have no simple answers; you will not find a correct answer hidden somewhere in the selection. In short, they are not the sorts of questions asked on SAT or ACT exams. They are real questions, questions that ask about the basic methods of an essay or about the issues the essay raises. They pose problems for interpretation or indicate sections where, to our minds, there is some interesting work for a reader to do. They are meant to reveal possible ways of reading the text, not to indicate that there is only one correct way, and that we have it.

You may find it useful to take notes as you read through each selection a second time, perhaps in a journal you can keep as a sourcebook for more formal written work. We will often also divide our students into groups, with each group working together with one of the second-reading questions in preparation for a report to the class. There are important advantages for you as a *writer* when you do this kind of close work with the text. Working through a second time you get a better sense of the argument and of the *shape* of the argument; you get a sense of not only what the author is *saying* but what she is *doing* and this prepares you to provide not only summary and paraphrase but a sense of the author and his or her project. And the work of rereading sends you back to the text; the second time through you can locate passages you might very well want to use in your own writing — passages that are particularly interesting to you, or illustrative, or even puzzling and obscure. These become the block quotations you can use to bring the author's words into your essay, to bring them in as the object of scrutiny and discussion.

Assignments for Writing

This book actually offers three kinds of writing assignments: assignments that ask you to write about a single essay or story, assignments that ask you to read one selection through the frame of another, and longer sequences of assignments that define a project within which three or four of the selections serve as primary sources. All of these assignments serve a dual purpose. Like the second-reading questions, they suggest a way for you to reconsider the stories or essays; they give you access from a different perspective. The assignments also encourage you to be a strong reader and actively interpret what you have read. In one way or another, they all invite you to use a story or an essay as a way of framing experience, as a source of terms and methods to enable you to interpret something else — some other text, events and objects around you, or your own memories and experience. The assignment sequences can be found at the end of the book and on the companion Web site at bedfordstmartins.com/waysofreading. The others (titled "Assignments for Writing" and "Making Connections") come immediately after each selection.

"Assignments for Writing" ask you to write about a single selection. Although some of these assignments call for you to paraphrase or reconstruct difficult passages, most ask you to interpret what you have read with a specific purpose in mind. The work you are to do is generally of two sorts. For most of the essays, one question asks you to interpret a moment from your own experience through the frame of the essay. This, you will remember, is the use that Rodriguez made of Richard Hoggart's *The Uses of Literacy*.

Other assignments, however, ask you to turn an essay back on itself or to extend the conclusions of the essay by reconsidering the examples the writer has used to make his or her case. Adrienne Rich's essay "When We Dead Awaken: Writing as Re-Vision" is built around a series of poems she wrote at various stages in her career. She says that the development represented by these poems reflects her growing understanding of the problems women in a patriarchal society have in finding a language for their own experience. She presents the poems as examples but offers little detailed discussion of them. One of the assignments, then, asks you to describe the key differences in these poems. It next asks you to comment on the development of her work and to compare your account of that development with hers.

In her essay, Rich also says that writing is "renaming." This is an interesting and, one senses, a potentially powerful term. For it to be useful, however, a reader must put it to work, to see what results when you accept the challenge of the essay and think about writing as renaming. Another assignment, then, asks you to apply this term to one of her poems and to discuss the poem as an act of renaming. The purpose of this assignment is not primarily to develop your skill as a reader of poems but to develop your sense of the method and key terms of Rich's argument.

A note on the writing assignments: When we talk with teachers and students using *Ways of Reading*, we are often asked about the wording of these assignments. The assignments are long. The wording is often unusual, unexpected. The assignments contain many questions, not simply one. The directions seem indirect, confusing. "Why?" we're asked. "How should we work with these?" When we write assignments, our goal is to point students toward a project, to provide a frame for their reading, a motive for writing, a way of asking certain kinds of questions. In that sense, the assignments should not be read as a set of directions to be followed literally. In fact, they are written to resist that reading, to forestall a writer's desire to simplify, to be efficient, to settle for the first clear line toward the finish. We want to provide a context to suggest how readers and writers might take time, be thoughtful. And we want the projects students work on to become their own. We hope to provoke varied responses, to leave the final decisions to the students. So the assignments try to be open and suggestive rather than narrow and direct. We ask lots of questions, but students don't need to answer them all (or any of them) once they begin to write. Our questions are meant to suggest ways of questioning, starting points. "What do you want?" Our own students ask this question. We want writers to make the most they can of what they read, including our questions and assignments.

So, what's the best way to work with an assignment? The writing assignments we have written will provide a context for writing, even a set of expectations, but the assignments do not provide a set of instructions. The first thing to do, then, is to ask yourself what, within this context, do you want to write about? What is on your mind? What is interesting or pressing for you? What direction can you take that will best allow you to stretch or to challenge yourself or to do something that will be new and interesting? We will often set aside class time to talk through an assignment and what possibilities it might suggest for each student's work. (We don't insist that everyone take the same track.) And we invite students to be in touch with us and with each other outside of class or via the Internet. At this stage (at least to our minds), sharing your thoughts with others is one way to do the work of the academy. Writers and scholars rely on their friends and colleagues to help them get an angle, think about where to begin, understand what is new and interesting and what is old and dull. And, then, finally, the moment comes and you just sit down to the keyboard and start writing. There is no magic here, unfortunately. You write out what you can and then you go back to what you have written to see what you are saying and to see what comes next and to think about how to shape it all into an essay to give to readers in the hope that they might say "eloquent," "persuasive," "beautiful."

Making Connections

The connections questions will have you work with two or more readings at a time. These are not so much questions that ask you to compare or contrast the essays or stories as they are directions on how you might use one text as the context for interpreting another. Mary Louise Pratt, for example, in "Arts of the Contact Zone" looks at the work of a South American native, an Inca named Guaman Poma, writing in the seventeenth century to King Philip III of Spain. His work, she argues, can be read as a moment of contact, one in which different cultures and positions of power come together in a single text—in which a conquered person responds to the ways he is represented in the mind and the language of the conqueror. Pratt's reading of Guaman Poma's letter to King Philip, and the terms she uses to describe the way she reads it, provides a powerful context for a reader looking at essays by other writers, like Harriet Jacobs or Gloria Anzaldúa, for whom the "normal" or "standard" language of American culture is difficult, troubling, unsatisfactory, or incomplete. There are, then, assignments that ask you both to extend and to test Pratt's reading through your reading of alternative texts.

The purpose of all these assignments is to demonstrate how the work of one author can be used as a frame for reading and interpreting the work of another. This can be exciting work, and it demonstrates a basic principle of liberal arts education: students should be given the opportunity to adopt different points of view, including those of scholars and writers who have helped to shape modern thought. These kinds of assignments give you the chance, even as a novice, to try your hand at the work of professionals.

Reading one essay through the lens of another becomes a focused form of rereading. To write responses to these assignments, you will need to reread both of the assigned selections. The best way to begin is by taking a quick inventory of what you recall as points of connection. You could do this on your own, with a colleague, or in groups, but it is best to do it with pen and paper (or laptop) in hand. And before you reread, you should come to at least a provisional sense of what you want to do with the assignment. Then you can reread with a project in mind. Be sure to mark passages that you can work with later, when you are writing. And look for passages that are interestingly different as well as those that complement each other.

The Assignment Sequences

The assignment sequences are more broad-ranging versions of the "Making Connections" assignments; in the sequences, several reading and writing assignments are linked and directed toward a single goal. They allow you to work on projects that require more time and incorporate more readings than would be possible in a single assignment. And they encourage you to develop your own point of view in concert with those of the professionals who wrote the essays and stories you are reading.

The assignments in a sequence build on one another, each relying on the ones before. A sequence will usually make use of four or five reading selections. The first is used to introduce an area of study or inquiry as well as to establish a frame of reference, a way of thinking about the subject. In the sequence titled "The Aims of Education," you begin with readings by Paulo Freire. The goal of the sequence is to provide a point for you to work from, one that you can open up to question. Subsequent assignments ask you to develop examples from your own schooling as you work through other accounts of education in, for example, Adrienne Rich's "When We Dead Awaken," Mary Louise Pratt's "Arts of the Contact Zone," or Susan Griffin's "Our Secret."

The sequences allow you to participate in an extended academic project, one in which you take a position, revise it, look at a new example, hear what someone else has to say, revise it again, and see what conclusions you can draw about your subject. These projects always take time — they go through stages and revisions as a writer develops a command over his or her material, pushing against habitual ways of thinking, learning to examine an issue from different angles, rejecting quick conclusions, seeing the power of understanding that comes from repeated effort, and feeling the pleasure writers take when they find their own place in the context of others whose work they admire. This is the closest approximation we can give you of the rhythm and texture of academic life, and we offer our book as an introduction to its characteristic ways of reading, thinking, and writing.

The Readings

GLORIA
ANZALDÚA

GLORIA ANZALDÚA (1942–2004) grew up in south-west Texas, the physical and cultural borderland between the United States and Mexico, an area she called "una herida abierta," *an open wound, "where the Third World grates against the first and bleeds." Defining herself as lesbian, feminist, Chicana—a representative of the new* mestiza—*she dramatically revised the usual narrative of American autobiography. "I am a border woman," she said. "I grew up between two cultures, the Mexican (with a heavy Indian influence) and the Anglo (as a member of a colonized people in our own territory). I have been straddling that* tejas-*Mexican border, and others, all my life." Cultural, physical, spiritual, sexual, linguistic—the borderlands defined by Anzaldúa extend beyond geography. "In fact," she said, "the Borderlands are present where two or more cultures edge each other, where people of different races occupy the same territory, where under, lower, middle, and upper classes touch, where the space between two individuals shrinks with intimacy." In a sense, her writing argues against the concept of an "authentic," unified, homogeneous culture, the pure "Mexican experience," a nostalgia that underlies much of the current interest in "ethnic" literature.*

In the following selections, which represent two chapters from her book Borderlands/La frontera: The New Mestiza *(1987), Anzaldúa mixes genres, moving between poetry and prose, weaving stories with sections that resemble the work of a cultural or political theorist. She tells us a story about her childhood, her culture, and her people that is at once both myth and history. Her prose, too, is mixed, shifting among Anglo-American English, Castilian Spanish, Tex-Mex, Northern Mexican dialect, and Nahuatl (Aztec), speaking to us in the particular mix that represents her linguistic heritage: "Presently this infant language, this bastard language, Chicano Spanish, is not approved by any society. But we Chicanos no longer feel that we need to beg entrance, that we need always to make the first overture—to translate to Anglos, Mexicans, and Latinos, apology blurting out of our mouths with every step. Today we ask to be met halfway. This book is our invitation to you." The book is an invitation, but not always an easy one. The chapters that follow make a variety of demands on the reader. The shifting styles, genres, and languages can be confusing or disturbing, but this is part of the effect of Anzaldúa's prose, part of the experience you are invited to share.*

In a chapter from the book that is not included here, Anzaldúa gives this account of her writing:

> *In looking at this book that I'm almost finished writing, I see a mosaic pattern (Aztec-like) emerging, a weaving pattern, thin here, thick there. I see a preoccupation with the deep structure, the underlying structure, with the gesso underpainting that is red earth, black earth. . . . This almost finished product seems an assemblage, a montage, a beaded work with several leitmotifs and with a central core, now appearing, now disappearing in a crazy dance. The whole thing has had a mind of its own, escaping me and insisting on putting together the pieces of its own puzzle with minimal direction from my will.*

Beyond her prose, she sees the competing values of more traditionally organized narratives, "art typical of Western European cultures, [which] attempts to manage the energies of its own internal system. . . . It is dedicated to the validation of itself. Its task is to move humans by means of achieving mastery in content, technique, feeling. Western art is always whole and always 'in power.'"

Anzaldúa's prose puts you, as a reader, on the borderland; in a way, it re-creates the position of the mestiza. As you read, you will need to meet this prose halfway, generously, learning to read a text that announces its difference.

In addition to Borderlands/La frontera, *Anzaldúa edited* Haciendo Caras: Making Face/Making Soul *(1990) and coedited an anthology,* This Bridge Called My Back: Writings by Radical Women of Color *(1983). She published a book for children,* Prietita and the Ghost Woman *(1996), which retells traditional Mexican folktales from a feminist perspective. A collection of interviews,* Interviews/Entrevistas, *was published in 2000, and a coedited anthology of multicultural feminist theory titled* This Bridge We Call Home: Radical Visions for Transformation *was published in 2002.*

Entering into the Serpent

Sueño con serpientes, con serpientes del mar,
Con cierto mar, ay de serpientes sueño yo.
Largas, transparentes, en sus barrigas llevan
Lo que puedan arebatarle al amor.
Oh, oh, oh, la mató y aparese una mayor.
Oh, con mucho más infierno en digestión.

I dream of serpents, serpents of the sea,
A certain sea, oh, of serpents I dream.
Long, transparent, in their bellies they carry
All that they can snatch away from love.
Oh, oh, oh, I kill one and a larger one appears.
Oh, with more hellfire burning inside!
　　　　　　　　　　　— SILVIO RODRÍGUES,
　　　　　　　　　　　"Sueño con serpientes"[1]

　　In the predawn orange haze, the sleepy crowing of roosters atop the trees. *No vayas al escusado en lo oscuro.* Don't go to the outhouse at night, Prieta, my mother would say. *No se te vaya a meter algo pour allá.* A snake will crawl into your *nalgas,*[2] make you pregnant. They seek warmth in the cold. *Dicen que las culebras* like to suck *chiches,*[3] can draw milk out of you.

　　En el escusado in the half-light spiders hang like gliders. Under my bare buttocks and the rough planks the deep yawning tugs at me. I can see my legs fly up to my face as my body falls through the round hole into the sheen of swarming maggots below. Avoiding the snakes under the porch I walk back into the kitchen, step on a big black one slithering across the floor.

Ella tiene su tono[4]

　　　　　　　　　　　　　Once we were chopping cotton in the fields of Jesus Maria Ranch. All around us the woods. *Quelite*[5] towered above me, choking the stubby cotton that had outlived the deer's teeth.

　　　　　　　　　　　　　I swung *el ázadón*[6] hard. *El quelite* barely shook, showered nettles on my arms and face. When I heard the rattle the world froze.

　　　　　　　　　　　　　I barely felt its fangs. Boot got all the *veneno.*[7] My mother came shrieking, swinging her hoe high, cutting the earth, the writhing body.

　　　　　　　　　　　　　I stood still, the sun beat down. Afterwards I smelled where fear had been: back of neck, under arms, between my legs, I felt its heat slide down my body. I swallowed the rock it had hardened into.

　　　　　　　　　　　　　When Mama had gone down the row and was out of sight, I took out my pocketknife. I made an X over each prick. My body followed the blood, fell onto the soft ground. I put my mouth over the red and sucked and spit between the rows of cotton.

I picked up the pieces, placed them end on end. *Culebra de cascabel.*[8] I counted the rattlers: twelve. It would shed no more. I buried the pieces between the rows of cotton.

That night I watched the window sill, watched the moon dry the blood on the tail, dreamed rattler fangs filled my mouth, scales covered my body. In the morning I saw through snake eyes, felt snake blood course through my body. The serpent, *mi tono,* my animal counterpart. I was immune to its venom. Forever immune.

Snakes, *víboras*: since that day I've sought and shunned them. Always when they cross my path, fear and elation flood my body. I know things older than Freud, older than gender. She—that's how I think of *la Víbora,* Snake Woman. Like the ancient Olmecs, I know Earth is a coiled Serpent. Forty years it's taken me to enter into the Serpent, to acknowledge that I have a body, that I am a body and to assimilate the animal body, the animal soul.

Coatlalopeuh, She Who Has Dominion over Serpents

Mi mamagrande Ramona toda su vida mantuvo un altar pequeño en la esquina del comedor. Siempre tenía las velas prendidas. Allí hacía promesas a la Virgen de Guadalupe. My family, like most Chicanos, did not practice Roman Catholicism but a folk Catholicism with many pagan elements. *La Virgen de Guadalupe*'s Indian name is *Coatlalopeuh.* She is the central deity connecting us to our Indian ancestry.

Coatlalopeuh is descended from, or is an aspect of, earlier Mesoamerican fertility and Earth goddesses. The earliest is *Coatlicue,* or "Serpent Skirt." She had a human skull or serpent for a head, a necklace of human hearts, a skirt of twisted serpents, and taloned feet. As creator goddess, she was mother of the celestial deities, and of *Huitzilopochtli* and his sister, *Coyolxauhqui,* She with Golden Bells, Goddess of the Moon, who was decapitated by her brother. Another aspect of *Coatlicue* is *Tonantsi.*[9] The Totonacs, tired of the Aztec human sacrifices to the male god, *Huitzilopochtli,* renewed their reverence for *Tonantsi* who preferred the sacrifice of birds and small animals.[10]

The male-dominated Azteca-Mexica culture drove the powerful female deities underground by giving them monstrous attributes and by substituting male deities in their place, thus splitting the female Self and the female deities. They divided her who had been complete, who possessed both upper (light) and underworld (dark) aspects. *Coatlicue,* the Serpent goddess, and her more sinister aspects, *Tlazolteotl* and *Cihuacoatl,* were "darkened" and disempowered much in the same manner as the Indian *Kali.*

Tonantsi—split from her dark guises, *Coatlicue, Tlazolteotl,* and *Cihuacoatl*—became the good mother. The Nahuas, through ritual and prayer, sought to oblige *Tonantsi* to ensure their health and the growth of their crops. It was she who gave *México* the cactus plant to provide her people with milk and pulque. It was she who defended her children against the wrath of the Christian God by challenging God, her son, to produce mother's milk (as she had done) to prove that his benevolence equalled his disciplinary harshness.[11]

After the Conquest, the Spaniards and their Church continued to split *Tonantsi/Guadalupe*. They desexed *Guadalupe*, taking *Coatlalopeuh*, the serpent/sexuality, out of her. They completed the split begun by the Nahuas by making *la Virgen de Guadalupe/Virgen María* into chaste virgins and *Tlazolteotl/Coatlicue/la Chingada* into *putas*; into the Beauties and the Beasts. They went even further; they made all Indian deities and religious practices the work of the devil.

Thus *Tonantsi* became *Guadalupe*, the chaste protective mother, the defender of the Mexican people.

> *El nueve de diciembre del año 1531*
> *a las cuatro de la madrugada*
> *un pobre indio que se llamaba Juan Diego*
> *iba cruzando el cerro de Tepeyác*
> *cuando oyó un cantó de pájaro.*
> *Alzó al cabeza vío que en la cima del cerro*
> *estaba cubierta con una brillante nube blanca.*
> *Parada en frente del sol*
> *sobre una luna creciente*
> *sostenida por un ángel*
> *estaba una azteca*
> *vestida en ropa de india.*
> *Nuestra Señora María de Coatlalopeuh*
> *se le apareció.*
> *"Juan Diegito, El-que-habla-como-un-águila,"*
> *la Virgen le dijo en el lenguaje azteca.*
> *"Para hacer mi altar este cerro eligo.*
> *Dile a tu gente que yo soy la madre de Dios,*
> *a los indios yo les ayudaré.*
> *Estó se lo contó a Juan Zumarraga*
> *pero el obispo no le creyo.*
> *Juan Diego volvió, lleño su tilma*[12]
> *con rosas de castilla*
> *creciendo milagrosamiente en la nieve.*
> *Se las llevó al obispo,*
> *y cuando abrío su tilma*
> *el retrato de la Virgen*
> *ahí estaba pintado.*

Guadalupe appeared on December 9, 1531, on the spot where the Aztec goddess, *Tonantsi* ("Our Lady Mother"), had been worshiped by the Nahuas and where a temple to her had stood. Speaking Nahua, she told Juan Diego, a poor Indian crossing Tepeyac Hill, whose Indian name was *Cuautlaohuac* and who belonged to the *mazehual* class, the humblest within the Chichimeca tribe, that her name was *María Coatlalopeuh*. *Coatl* is the

Nahuatl word for serpent. *Lopeuh* means "the one who has dominion over serpents." I interpret this as "the one who is at one with the beasts." Some spell her name *Coatlaxopeuh* (pronounced *"Cuatlashupe"* in Nahuatl) and say that *"xopeuh"* means "crushed or stepped on with disdain." Some say it means "she who crushed the serpent," with the serpent as the symbol of the indigenous religion, meaning that her religion was to take the place of the Aztec religion.[13] Because *Coatlalopeuh* was homophonous to the Spanish *Guadalupe*, the Spanish identified her with the dark Virgin, *Guadalupe*, patroness of West Central Spain.[14]

From that meeting, Juan Diego walked away with the image of *la Virgen* painted on his cloak. Soon after, Mexico ceased to belong to Spain, and *la Virgen de Guadalupe* began to eclipse all the other male and female religious figures in Mexico, Central America, and parts of the U.S. Southwest. *"Desde entonces para el mexicano ser Guadalupano es algo esencial*/Since then for the Mexican, to be a *Guadalupano* is something essential."[15]

Mi Virgen Morena	My brown virgin
Mi Virgen Ranchera	my country virgin
Eres nuestra Reina	you are our queen
México es tu tierra	Mexico is your land
Y tú su bandera.	and you its flag.
	– "La Virgen Ranchera"[16]

In 1660 the Roman Catholic Church named her Mother of God, considering her synonymous with *la Virgen María*; she became *la Santa Patrona de los mexicanos*. The role of defender (or patron) has traditionally been assigned to male gods. During the Mexican Revolution, Emiliano Zapata and Miguel Hidalgo used her image to move *el pueblo mexicano* toward freedom. During the 1965 grape strike in Delano, California, and in subsequent Chicano farmworkers' marches in Texas and other parts of the Southwest, her image on banners heralded and united the farmworkers. *Pachucos* (zoot suiters) tattoo her image on their bodies. Today, in Texas and Mexico she is more venerated than Jesus or God the Father. In the Lower Rio Grande Valley of south Texas it is *la Virgen de San Juan de los Lagos* (an aspect of *Guadalupe*) that is worshiped by thousands every day at her shrine in San Juan. In Texas she is considered the patron saint of Chicanos. *Cuando Carito, mi hermanito*, was missing in action and, later, wounded in Viet Nam, *mi mamá* got on her knees *y le prometío a Ella que si su hijito volvía vivo* she would crawl on her knees and light novenas in her honor.

Today, *la Virgen de Guadalupe* is the single most potent religious, political, and cultural image of the Chicano/*mexicano*. She, like my race, is a synthesis of the old world and the new, of the religion and culture of the two races in our psyche, the conquerors and the conquered. She is the symbol of the *mestizo* true to his or her Indian values. *La cultura chicana* identifies with the mother (Indian) rather than with the father (Spanish). Our faith is rooted in indigenous attributes, images, symbols, magic, and myth. Because *Guadalupe* took upon herself the psychological and physical devastation of the conquered and oppressed *indio*, she is our spiritual, political, and psychological symbol. As a symbol of hope and faith, she sustains and insures our survival. The Indian, despite extreme despair, suffering, and near genocide, has survived. To Mexicans on both sides of the border, *Guadalupe* is the symbol of our rebellion against the rich, upper and middle class; against their subjugation of the poor and the *indio*.

Guadalupe unites people of different races, religions, languages: Chicano protestants, American Indians, and whites. *"Nuestra abogada siempre serás/* Our *mediatrix* you will always be."* She mediates between the Spanish and the Indian cultures (or three cultures as in the case of *mexicanos* of African or other ancestry) and between Chicanos and the white world. She mediates between humans and the divine, between this reality and the reality of spirit entities. *La Virgen de Guadalupe* is the symbol of ethnic identity and of the tolerance for ambiguity that Chicanos-*mexicanos*, people of mixed race, people who have Indian blood, people who cross cultures, by necessity possess.

La gente Chicana tiene tres madres. All three are mediators: *Guadalupe*, the virgin mother who has not abandoned us, *la Chingada (Malinche)*, the raped mother whom we have abandoned, and *la Llorona*, the mother who seeks her lost children and is a combination of the other two.

Ambiguity surrounds the symbols of these three "Our Mothers." *Guadalupe* has been used by the Church to mete out institutionalized oppression: to placate the Indians and *mexicanos* and Chicanos. In part, the true identity of all three has been subverted—*Guadalupe* to make us docile and enduring, *la Chingada* to make us ashamed of our Indian side, and *la Llorona* to make us long-suffering people. This obscuring has encouraged the *virgen/puta* (whore) dichotomy.

Yet we have not all embraced this dichotomy. In the U.S. Southwest, Mexico, Central and South America the *indio* and the *mestizo* continue to worship the old spirit entities (including *Guadalupe*) and their supernatural power, under the guise of Christian saints.[17]

> *Las invoco diosas mías, ustedes las indias*
> *sumergidas en mi carne que son mis sombras.*
> *Ustedes que persisten mudas en sus cuevas.*
> *Ustedes Señoras que ahora, como yo,*
> *están en desgracia.*

For Waging War Is My Cosmic Duty: The Loss of the Balanced Oppositions and the Change to Male Dominance

Therefore I decided to leave
The country [Aztlán],
Therefore I have come as one charged with a special duty,
Because I have been given arrows and shields,

> For waging war is my duty,
> And on my expeditions I
> Shall see all the lands,
> I shall wait for the people and meet them
> In all four quarters and I shall give them
> Food to eat and drinks to quench their thirst,
> For here I shall unite all the different peoples!
>   — HUITZILOPOCHTLI
>   speaking to the Azteca-Mexica[18]

Before the Aztecs became a militaristic, bureaucratic state where male predatory warfare and conquest were based on patrilineal nobility, the principle of balanced opposition between the sexes existed.[19] The people worshiped the Lord and Lady of Duality, *Ometecuhtli* and *Omecihuatl*. Before the change to male dominance, *Coatlicue*, Lady of the Serpent Skirt, contained and balanced the dualities of male and female, light and dark, life and death.

The changes that led to the loss of the balanced oppositions began when the Azteca, one of the twenty Toltec tribes, made the last pilgrimage from a place called Aztlán. The migration south began about the year A.D. 820. Three hundred years later the advance guard arrived near Tula, the capital of the declining Toltec empire. By the eleventh century, they had joined with the Chichimec tribe of Mexitin (afterwards called Mexica) into one religious and administrative organization within Aztlán, the Aztec territory. The Mexitin, with their tribal god *Tetzauhteotl Huitzilopochtli* (Magnificent Humming Bird on the Left), gained control of the religious system.[20] (In some stories *Huitzilopochtli* killed his sister, the moon goddess *Malinalxoch*, who used her supernatural power over animals to control the tribe rather than wage war.)

Huitzilopochtli assigned the Azteca-Mexica the task of keeping the human race (the present cosmic age called the Fifth Sun, *El Quinto Sol*) alive. They were to guarantee the harmonious preservation of the human race by unifying all the people on earth into one social, religious, and administrative organ. The Aztec people considered themselves in charge of regulating all earthly matters.[21] Their instrument: controlled or regulated war to gain and exercise power.

After one hundred years in the central plateau, the Azteca-Mexica went to Chapultepec, where they settled in 1248 (the present site of the park on the outskirts of Mexico City). There, in 1345, the Azteca-Mexica chose the site of their capital, Tenochtitlan.[22] By 1428, they dominated the Central Mexican lake area.

The Aztec ruler, *Itzcoatl*, destroyed all the painted documents (books called codices) and rewrote a mythology that validated the wars of conquest and thus continued the shift from a tribe based on clans to one based on classes. From 1429 to 1440, the Aztecs emerged as a militaristic state that preyed on neighboring tribes for tribute and captives.[23] The "wars of flowers" were encounters between local armies with a fixed number of warriors, operating within the Aztec World, and, according to set rules, fighting ritual battles at fixed times and on predetermined battlefields. The religious purpose of these wars was to procure prisoners of war who could be sacrificed to the deities of the capturing party. For if one "fed" the gods, the human race would be saved from total extinction. The social purpose was to enable males of noble families and warriors of low descent to win honor, fame, and administrative offices, and to prevent social and cultural decadence of the elite. The Aztec people were free to have their own religious faith, provided it did not conflict too much with the three fundamental principles of state ideology: to fulfill the special duty set forth by *Huitzilopochtli* of unifying all peoples, to participate in the wars of flowers, and to bring ritual offerings and do penance for the purpose of preventing decadence.[24]

Matrilineal descent characterized the Toltecs and perhaps early Aztec society. Women possessed property, and were curers as well as priestesses. According to the codices, women in former times had the supreme power in Tula, and in the beginning of the Aztec dynasty, the royal blood ran through the female line. A council of elders of the Calpul headed by a supreme leader, or *tlactlo*, called the father and mother of the people, governed the tribe. The supreme leader's vice-emperor occupied the position of "Snake Woman" or *Cihuacoatl*, a goddess.[25] Although the high posts were occupied by men, the terms referred to females, evidence of the exalted role of women before the Aztec nation became centralized. The final break with the democratic Calpul came when the four Aztec lords of royal lineage picked the king's successor from his siblings or male descendants.[26]

La Llorona's wailing in the night for her lost children has an echoing note in the wailing or mourning rites performed by women as they bid their sons, brothers, and husbands good-bye before they left to go to the "flowery wars." Wailing is the Indian, Mexican, and Chicana woman's feeble protest when she has no other recourse. These collective wailing rites may have been a sign of resistance in a society which glorified the warrior and war and for whom the women of the conquered tribes were booty.[27]

In defiance of the Aztec rulers, the *macehuales* (the common people) continued to worship fertility, nourishment, and agricultural female deities, those of crops and rain. They venerated *Chalchiuhtlicue* (goddess of sweet or inland water), *Chicomecoatl* (goddess of food), and *Huixtocihuatl* (goddess of salt).

Nevertheless, it took less than three centuries for Aztec society to change from the balanced duality of their earlier times and from the egalitarian traditions of a wandering tribe to those of a predatory state. The nobility kept the tribute, the commoner got nothing, resulting in a class split. The conquered tribes hated the Aztecs because of the rape of their women and the heavy taxes levied on them. The *Tlaxcalans* were the Aztec's bitter enemies and it was they who helped the Spanish defeat the Aztec rulers, who were by this time so unpopular with their own common people that they could not even mobilize the populace to defend the city. Thus the Aztec nation fell not because *Malinali (la Chingada)* interpreted for and slept with Cortés, but because the ruling elite had subverted the solidarity between men and women and between noble and commoner.[28]

Sueño con serpientes

Coatl. In pre-Columbian America the most notable symbol was the serpent. The Olmecs associated womanhood with the Serpent's mouth which was guarded by rows of dangerous teeth, a sort of *vagina dentate*. They considered it the most sacred place on earth, a place of refuge, the creative womb from which all things were born and to which all things returned. Snake people had holes, entrances to the body of the Earth Serpent; they followed the Serpent's way, identified with the Serpent deity, with the mouth, both the eater and the eaten. The destiny of humankind is to be devoured by the Serpent.[29]

> Dead,
> the doctor by the operating table said.
> I passed between the two fangs,
> the flickering tongue.
> Having come through the mouth of the serpent,
> swallowed,
> I found myself suddenly in the dark,
> sliding down a smooth wet surface
> down down into an even darker darkness.
> Having crossed the portal, the raised hinged mouth,
> having entered the serpent's belly,
> now there was no looking back, no going back.
>
> Why do I cast no shadow?
> Are there lights from all sides shining on me?
> Ahead, ahead,
> curled up inside the serpent's coils,
> the damp breath of death on my face.
> I knew at that instant; something must change
> or I'd die.
> *Algo tenía que cambiar.*

After each of my four bouts with death I'd catch glimpses of an otherworld Serpent. Once, in my bedroom, I saw a cobra the size of the room, her hood expanding over me. When I blinked she was gone. I realized she was, in my psyche, the mental picture and symbol of the instinctual in its collective impersonal, prehuman. She, the symbol of the dark sexual drive, the chthonic (underworld), the feminine, the serpentine movement of sexuality, of creativity, the basis of all energy and life.

The Presences

> She appeared in white, garbed in white,
> standing white, pure white.
> — BERNARDINO DE SAHAGÚN[30]

On the gulf where I was raised, *en el Valle del Río Grande* in South Texas — that triangular piece of land wedged between the river *y el golfo* which serves as the Texas-U.S./Mexican border — is a Mexican *pueblito* called Hargill (at one time in the history of this one-grocery-store, two-service-stations town there were thirteen churches and thirteen *cantinas*). Down the road, a little ways from our house, was a deserted church. It was known among the *mexicanos* that if you walked down the road late at night you would see a woman dressed in white floating about, peering out the church window. She would follow those who had done something bad or who were afraid. *Los mexicanos* called her *la Jila*. Some thought she was *la Llorona*. She was, I think, *Cihuacoatl*, Serpent Woman, ancient Aztec goddess of the earth, of war and birth, patron of midwives, and antecedent of *la Llorona*. Covered with chalk, *Cihuacoatl* wears a white dress with a decoration half red and half black. Her hair forms two little horns (which the Aztecs depicted as knives) crossed on her forehead. The lower part of her face is a bare jawbone, signifying death. On her back she carries a cradle, the knife of sacrifice swaddled as if it were her papoose, her child.[31] Like *la Llorona*, *Cihuacoatl* howls and weeps in the night, screams as if demented. She brings mental depression and sorrow. Long before it takes place, she is the first to predict something is to happen.

Back then, I, an unbeliever, scoffed at these Mexican superstitions as I was taught in Anglo school. Now, I wonder if this story and similar ones were the culture's attempts to "protect" members of the family, especially girls, from "wandering." Stories of the devil luring young girls away and having his way with them discouraged us from going out. There's an ancient Indian tradition of burying the umbilical cord of an infant girl under the house so she will never stray from it and her domestic role.

> *A mis ancas caen los cueros de culebra,*
> *cuatro veces por año los arrastro,*
> *me tropiezo y me caigo*
> *y cada vez que miro una culebra le pregunto*
> *¿Qué traes conmigo?*

Four years ago a red snake crossed my path as I walked through the woods. The direction of its movement, its pace, its colors, the "mood" of the trees and the wind and the snake — they all "spoke" to me, told me things. I look for omens everywhere, everywhere catch glimpses of the patterns and cycles of my life. Stones "speak" to Luisah Teish, a Santera; trees whisper their secrets to Chrystos, a Native American. I remember listening to the voices of the wind as a child and understanding its messages. *Los espíritus* that ride the back of the south wind. I remember their exhalation blowing in through the slits in the door during those hot Texas afternoons. A gust of wind raising the linoleum under my feet, buffeting the house. Everything trembling.

We're not supposed to remember such otherworldly events. We're supposed to ignore, forget, kill those fleeting images of the soul's presence and of the spirit's presence. We've been taught that the spirit is outside our bodies or above our heads somewhere up in the sky with God. We're supposed to forget that every cell in our bodies, every bone and bird and worm has spirit in it.

Like many Indians and Mexicans, I did not deem my psychic experiences real. I denied their occurrences and let my inner senses atrophy. I allowed white rationality to tell me that the existence of the "other world" was mere pagan superstition. I accepted their reality, the "official" reality of the rational, reasoning mode which is connected with external reality, the upper world, and is considered the most developed consciousness — the consciousness of duality.

The other mode of consciousness facilitates images from the soul and the unconscious through dreams and the imagination. Its work is labeled "fiction," make-believe, wish-fulfillment. White anthropologists claim that Indians have "primitive" and therefore deficient minds, that we cannot think in the higher mode of consciousness — rationality. They are fascinated by what they call the "magical" mind, the "savage" mind, the *participation mystique* of the mind that says the world of the imagination — the world of the soul — and of the spirit is just as real as physical reality.[32] In trying to become "objective," Western culture made "objects" of things and people when it distanced itself from them, thereby losing "touch" with them. This dichotomy is the root of all violence.

Not only was the brain split into two functions but so was reality. Thus people who inhabit both realities are forced to live in the interface between the two, forced to become adept at switching modes. Such is the case with the *india* and the *mestiza*.

Institutionalized religion fears trafficking with the spirit world and stigmatizes it as witchcraft. It has strict taboos against this kind of inner knowledge. It fears what Jung calls the Shadow, the unsavory aspects of ourselves. But even more it fears the suprahuman, the god in ourselves.

"The purpose of any established religion . . . is to glorify, sanction, and bless with a superpersonal meaning all personal and interpersonal activities. This occurs through the 'sacraments,' and indeed through most religious rites." But it sanctions only its own sacraments and rites. Voodoo, Santeria, Shamanism, and other native religions are called cults and their beliefs are called mythologies. In my own life, the Catholic Church fails to give meaning to my daily acts, to my continuing encounters with the "other world." It and other institutionalized religions impoverish all life, beauty, pleasure.

The Catholic and Protestant religions encourage fear and distrust of life and of the body; they encourage a split between the body and the spirit and totally ignore the soul; they encourage us to kill off parts of ourselves. We are taught that the body is an ignorant animal; intelligence dwells only in the head. But the body is smart. It does not discern between external stimuli and stimuli from the imagination. It reacts equally viscerally to events from the imagination as it does to "real" events.

So I grew up in the interface trying not to give countenance to *el mal aigre*,[33] evil nonhuman, noncorporeal entities riding the wind, that could come in through the window, through my nose with my breath. I was not supposed to believe in *susto*, a sudden shock or fall that frightens the soul out of the body. And growing up between such opposing spiritualities how could I reconcile the two, the pagan and the Christian?

No matter to what use my people put the supranatural world, it is evident to me now that the spirit world, whose existence the whites are so adamant in denying, does in fact exist. This very minute I sense the presence of the spirits of my ancestors in my room. And I think *la Jila* is *Cihuacoatl*, Snake Woman; she is *la Llorona*, Daughter of Night, traveling the dark terrains of the unknown searching for the lost parts of herself. I remember *la Jila* following me once, remember her eerie lament. I'd like to think that she was crying for her lost children, *los* Chicanos/*mexicanos*.

La facultad

La facultad is the capacity to see in surface phenomena the meaning of deeper realities, to see the deep structure below the surface. It is an instant "sensing," a quick perception arrived at without conscious reasoning. It is an acute awareness mediated by the part of the psyche that does not speak, that communicates in images and symbols which are the faces of feelings, that is, behind which feelings reside/hide. The one possessing this sensitivity is excruciatingly alive to the world.

Those who are pushed out of the tribe for being different are likely to become more sensitized (when not brutalized into insensitivity). Those who do not feel psychologically or physically safe in the world are more apt to develop this sense. Those who are pounced on the most have it the strongest—the females, the homosexuals of all races, the darkskinned, the outcast, the persecuted, the marginalized, the foreign.

When we're up against the wall, when we have all sorts of oppressions coming at us, we are forced to develop this faculty so that we'll know when the next person is going to slap us or lock us away. We'll sense the rapist when he's five blocks down the street. Pain makes us acutely anxious to avoid more of it, so we hone that radar. It's a kind of survival tactic that people, caught between the worlds, unknowingly cultivate. It is latent in all of us.

I walk into a house and I know whether it is empty or occupied. I feel the lingering charge in the air of a recent fight or lovemaking or depression.

I sense the emotions someone near is emitting—whether friendly or threatening. Hate and fear—the more intense the emotion, the greater my reception of it. I feel a tingling on my skin when someone is staring at me or thinking about me. I can tell how others feel by the way they smell, where others are by the air pressure on my skin. I can spot the love or greed or generosity lodged in the tissues of another. Often I sense the direction of and my distance from people or objects—in the dark, or with my eyes closed, without looking. It must be a vestige of a proximity sense, a sixth sense that's lain dormant from long-ago times.

Fear develops the proximity sense aspect of *la facultad*. But there is a deeper sensing that is another aspect of this faculty. It is anything that breaks into one's everyday mode of perception, that causes a break in one's defenses and resistance, anything that takes one from one's habitual grounding, causes the depths to open up, causes a shift in perception. This shift in perception deepens the way we see concrete objects and people; the senses become so acute and piercing that we can see through things, view events in depth, a piercing that reaches the underworld (the realm of the soul). As we plunge vertically, the break, with its accompanying new seeing, makes us pay attention to the soul, and we are thus carried into awareness—an experiencing of soul (Self).

We lose something in this mode of initiation, something is taken from us: our innocence, our unknowing ways, our safe and easy ignorance. There is a prejudice and a fear of the dark, chthonic (underworld), material such as depression, illness, death, and the violations that can bring on this break. Confronting anything that tears the fabric of our everyday mode of consciousness and that thrusts us into a less literal and more psychic sense of reality increases awareness and *la facultad*.

NOTES

[1] From the song *"Sueño con serpientes"* by Silvio Rodrígues, from the album *Días y flores*. Translated by Barbara Dane with the collaboration of Rina Benmauor and Juan Flores.

[2] *Nalgas*: vagina, buttocks.

[3] *Dicen que las culebras* like to suck *chiches*: they say snakes like to suck women's teats.

[4] *Ella tiene su tono*: she has supernatural power from her animal soul, the *tono*.

[5] *Quelite*: weed.

[6] *Ázadón*: hoe.

[7] *Veneno*: venom, poison.

[8] *Culebra de cascabel*: rattlesnake.

[9] In some Nahuatl dialects *Tonantsi* is called *Tonatzin*, literally "Our Holy Mother." "*Tonan* was a name given in Nahuatl to several mountains, these being the congelations of the Earth Mother at spots convenient for her worship." The Mexica considered the mountain mass southwest of Chapultepec to be their mother. Burr Cartwright Brundage, *The Fifth Sun: Aztec Gods, Aztec World* (Austin, TX: University of Texas Press, 1979), 154, 242.

[10] Ena Campbell, "The Virgin of Guadalupe and the Female Self-image: A Mexican Case History," *Mother Worship: Themes and Variations*, James J. Preston, ed. (Chapel Hill, NC: University of North Carolina Press, 1982), 22.

[11] Alan R. Sandstrom, "The Tonantsi Cult of the Eastern Nahuas," *Mother Worship: Themes and Variations*, James J. Preston, ed.

[12] *Una tela tejida con asperas fibras de agave*: it is an oblong cloth that hangs over the back and ties together across the shoulders.

[13] Andres Gonzales Guerrero, Jr., *The Significance of Nuestra Señora de Guadalupe and La Raza Cósmica in the Development of a Chicano Theology of Liberation* (Ann Arbor, MI: University Microfilms International, 1984), 122.

[14] *Algunos dicen que Guadalupe es una palabra derivida del lenguaje arabe que significa "Río Oculto."* Tomie de Paola, *The Lady of Guadalupe* (New York, NY: Holiday House, 1980), 44.

[15] *"Desde el cielo una hermosa mañana,"* from *Propios de la misa de Nuestra Señora de Guadalupe*, Guerrero, 124.

[16] From *"La Virgen Ranchera,"* Guerrero, 127.

[17] *La Virgin María* is often equated with the Aztec *Teleoinam*, the Maya *Ixchel*, the Inca *Mamacocha*, and the Yoruba *Yemayá*.

[18] Geoffrey Parrinder, ed., *World Religions: From Ancient History to the Present* (New York, NY: Facts on File Publications, 1971), 72.

[19] Lévi-Strauss's paradigm which opposes nature to culture and female to male has no such validity in the early history of our Indian forebears. June Nash, "The Aztecs and the Ideology of Male Dominance," *Signs* (Winter, 1978), 349.

[20] Parrinder, 72.

[21] Parrinder, 77.

[22] Nash, 352.

[23] Nash, 350, 355.

[24] Parrinder, 355.

[25] Jacques Soustelle, *The Daily Life of the Aztecs on the Eve of the Spanish Conquest* (New York, NY: Macmillan Publishing Company, 1962). Soustelle and most other historians got their information from the Franciscan father, Bernardino de Sahagún, chief chronicler of Indian religious life.

[26] Nash, 252–253.

[27] Nash, 358.

[28] Nash, 361–362.

[29] Karl W. Luckert, *Olmec Religion: A Key to Middle America and Beyond* (Norman, OK: University of Oklahoma Press, 1976), 68, 69, 87, 109.

[30] Bernardino de Sahagún, *General History of the Things of New Spain* (Florentine Codex), Vol. I Revised, trans. Arthur Anderson and Charles Dibble (Sante Fe, NM: School of American Research, 1950), 11.

[31] The Aztecs muted Snake Woman's patronage of childbirth and vegetation by placing a sacrificial knife in the empty cradle she carried on her back (signifying a child who died in childbirth), thereby making her a devourer of sacrificial victims. Snake Woman had the ability to change herself into a serpent or into a lovely young woman to entice young men, who withered away and died after intercourse with her. She was known as a witch and a shape-shifter. Brundage, 168–171.

[32] Anthropologist Lucien Levy-Bruhl coined the word *participation mystique*. According to Jung, "It denotes a peculiar kind of psychological connection . . . [in which] the subject cannot clearly distinguish himself from the object but is bound to it by a direct relationship which amounts to partial identity." Carl Jung, "Definitions," in *Psychological Types, The Collected Works of C. G. Jung*, Vol. 6 (Princeton, NJ: Princeton University Press, 1953), par. 781.

[33] Some *mexicanos* and Chicanos distinguish between *aire*, air, and *mal aigre*, the evil spirits which reside in the air.

How to Tame a Wild Tongue

"We're going to have to control your tongue," the dentist says, pulling out all the metal from my mouth. Silver bits plop and tinkle into the basin. My mouth is a motherlode.

The dentist is cleaning out my roots. I get a whiff of the stench when I gasp. "I can't cap that tooth yet, you're still draining," he says.

"We're going to have to do something about your tongue," I hear the anger rising in his voice. My tongue keeps pushing out the wads of cotton, pushing back the drills, the long thin needles. "I've never seen anything as strong or as stubborn," he says. And I think, how do you tame a wild tongue, train it to be quiet, how do you bridle and saddle it? How do you make it lie down?

> Who is to say that robbing a people of
> its language is less violent than war?
> —RAY GWYN SMITH[1]

I remember being caught speaking Spanish at recess—that was good for three licks on the knuckles with a sharp ruler. I remember being sent to the corner of the classroom for "talking back" to the Anglo teacher when all I was trying to do was tell her how to pronounce my name. "If you want to be American, speak 'American.' If you don't like it, go back to Mexico where you belong."

"I want you to speak English. *Pa' hallar buen trabajo tienes que saber hablar el inglés bien. Qué vale toda tu educación si todavía hablas inglés con un 'accent,'*" my mother would say, mortified that I spoke English like a Mexican. At Pan American University, I and all Chicano students were required to take two speech classes. Their purpose: to get rid of our accents.

Attacks on one's form of expression with the intent to censor are a violation of the First Amendment. *El Anglo con cara de inocente nos arrancó la lengua.* Wild tongues can't be tamed, they can only be cut out.

Overcoming the Tradition of Silence

> *Ahogadas, escupimos el oscuro.*
> *Peleando con nuestra propia sombra*
> *el silencio nos sepulta.*

En boca cerrada no entran moscas. "Flies don't enter a closed mouth" is a saying I kept hearing when I was a child. *Ser habladora* was to be a gossip and a liar, to talk too much. *Muchachitas bien criadas*, well-bred girls don't answer back. *Es una falta de respeto* to talk back to one's mother or father. I remember one of the sins I'd recite to the priest in the confession box the few times I went to confession: talking back to my mother, *hablar pa' 'tras, repelar. Hociocona, repelona, chismosa*, having a big mouth, questioning, carrying tales are all signs of being *mal criada*. In my culture they are all words that are derogatory if applied to women—I've never heard them applied to men.

The first time I heard two women, a Puerto Rican and a Cuban, say the word *"nosotras,"* I was shocked. I had not known the word existed. Chicanas use *nosotros* whether we're male or female. We are robbed of our female being by the masculine plural. Language is a male discourse.

> And our tongues have become
> dry   the wilderness has
> dried out our tongues   and
> we have forgotten speech.
> —IRENA KLEPFISZ[2]

Even our own people, other Spanish speakers *nos quieren poner candados en la boca*. They would hold us back with their bag of *reglas de academia*.

Oyé como ladra: el lenguaje de la frontera

Quien tiene boca se equivoca.
—Mexican saying

"Pocho, cultural traitor, you're speaking the oppressor's language by speaking English, you're ruining the Spanish language," I have been accused by various Latinos and Latinas. Chicano Spanish is considered by the purist and by most Latinos deficient, a mutilation of Spanish.

But Chicano Spanish is a border tongue which developed naturally. Change, *evolución, enriquecimiento de palabras nuevas por invención o adopción* have created variants of Chicano Spanish, *un nuevo lenguaje. Un lenguaje que corresponde a un modo de vivir.* Chicano Spanish is not incorrect, it is a living language.

For a people who are neither Spanish nor live in a country in which Spanish is the first language; for a people who live in a country in which English is the reigning tongue but who are not Anglo; for a people who cannot entirely identify with either standard (formal, Castilian) Spanish nor standard English, what recourse is left to them but to create their own language? A language which they can connect their identity to, one capable of communicating the realities and values true to themselves—a language with terms that are neither *español ni inglés*, but both. We speak a patois, a forked tongue, a variation of two languages.

Chicano Spanish sprang out of the Chicanos' need to identify ourselves as a distinct people. We needed a language with which we could communicate with ourselves, a secret language. For some of us, language is a homeland closer than the Southwest—for many Chicanos today live in the Midwest and the East. And because we are a complex, heterogeneous people, we speak many languages. Some of the languages we speak are

1. Standard English
2. Working-class and slang English
3. Standard Spanish
4. Standard Mexican Spanish
5. North Mexican Spanish dialect
6. Chicano Spanish (Texas, New Mexico, Arizona, and California have regional variations)
7. Tex-Mex
8. *Pachuco* (called *caló*)

My "home" tongues are the languages I speak with my sister and brothers, with my friends. They are the last five listed, with 6 and 7 being closest to my heart. From school, the media, and job situations, I've picked up standard and working-class English. From Mamagrande Locha and from reading Spanish and Mexican literature, I've picked up Standard Spanish and Standard Mexican Spanish. From *los recién llegados*, Mexican immigrants, and *braceros*, I learned the North Mexican dialect. With Mexicans I'll try to speak either Standard Mexican Spanish or the North Mexican dialect. From my parents and Chicanos living in the Valley, I picked up Chicano Texas Spanish, and I speak it with my mom, younger brother (who married a Mexican and who rarely mixes Spanish with English), aunts, and older relatives.

With Chicanas from *Nuevo México* or *Arizona* I will speak Chicano Spanish a little, but often they don't understand what I'm saying. With most California Chicanas I speak entirely in English (unless I forget). When I first moved to San Francisco, I'd rattle off something in Spanish, unintentionally embarrassing them. Often it is only with another Chicana *tejano* that I can talk freely.

Words distorted by English are known as anglicisms or *pochismos*. The *pocho* is an anglicized Mexican or American of Mexican origin who speaks Spanish with an accent characteristic of North Americans and who distorts and reconstructs the language according to the influence of English.[3] Tex-Mex, or Spanglish, comes most naturally to me. I may switch back and forth from English to Spanish in the same sentence or in the same word. With my sister and my brother Nune and with Chicano *tejano* contemporaries I speak in Tex-Mex.

From kids and people my own age I picked up *Pachuco*. *Pachuco* (the language of the zoot suiters) is a language of rebellion, both against Standard Spanish and Standard English. It is a secret language. Adults of the culture and outsiders cannot understand it. It is made up of slang words from both English and Spanish. *Ruca* means girl or woman, *vato* means guy or dude, *chale* means no, *simón* means yes, *churro* is sure, talk is *periquiar*, *pigionear* means petting, *que gacho* means how nerdy, *ponte águila* means watch out, death is called *la pelona*. Through lack of practice and not having others who can speak it, I've lost most of the *Pachuco* tongue.

Chicano Spanish

Chicanos, after 250 years of Spanish/Anglo colonization, have developed significant differences in the Spanish we speak. We collapse two adjacent vowels into a single syllable and sometimes shift the stress in certain words such as *maíz/maiz, cohete/cuete*. We leave out certain consonants when they appear between vowels: *lado/lao, mojado/mojao*. Chicanos from South Texas pronounce *f* as *j* as in *jue (fue)*. Chicanos use "archaisms," words that are no longer in the Spanish language, words that have been evolved out. We say *semos, truje, haiga, ansina,* and *naiden*. We retain the "archaic" *j*, as in *jalar*, that derives from an earlier *h* (the French *halar* or the Germanic *halon* which was lost to standard Spanish in the sixteenth century), but which is still found in several regional dialects such as the one spoken in South Texas. (Due to geography, Chicanos from the Valley of South Texas were cut off linguistically from other Spanish speakers. We tend to use words that the Spaniards brought over from Medieval Spain. The majority of the Spanish colonizers in Mexico and the Southwest came from Extremadura—Hernán Cortés was one of them—and Andalucía. Andalucians pronounce *ll* like a *y*, and their *d*'s tend to be absorbed by adjacent vowels: *tirado* becomes *tirao*. They brought *el lenguaje popular, dialectos, y regionalismos*.)[4]

Chicanos and other Spanish speakers also shift *ll* to *y* and *z* to *s*.[5] We leave out initial syllables, saying *tar* for *estar*, *toy* for *estoy*, *hora* for *ahora* (*cubanos* and *puertorriqueños* also leave out initial letters of some words). We also leave out the final syllable such as *pa* for *para*. The intervocalic *y*, the *ll* as in *tortilla, ella, botella*, gets replaced by *tortia* or *toriya, ea, botea*. We add an additional syllable at the beginning of certain words: *atocar* for *tocar*, *agastar* for *gastar*. Sometimes we'll say *lavaste las vacijas*, other times *lavates* (substituting the *ates* verb endings for the *aste*).

We use anglicisms, words borrowed from English: *bola* from ball, *carpeta* from carpet, *máchina de lavar* (instead of *lavadora*) from washing machine. Tex-Mex argot, created by adding a Spanish sound at the beginning or end of an English word such as *cookiar* for cook, *watchar* for watch, *parkiar* for park, and *rapiar* for rape, is the result of the pressures on Spanish speakers to adapt to English.

We don't use the word *vosotros/as* or its accompanying verb form. We don't say *claro* (to mean yes), *imagínate*, or *me emociona*, unless we picked up Spanish from Latinas, out of a book, or in a classroom. Other Spanish-speaking groups are going through the same, or similar, development in their Spanish.

Linguistic Terrorism

Deslenguadas. Somos los del español deficiente. We are your linguistic nightmare, your linguistic aberration, your linguistic *mestisaje*, the subject of your *burla*. Because we speak with tongues of fire we are culturally crucified. Racially, culturally, and linguistically *somos huérfanos* — we speak an orphan tongue.

Chicanas who grew up speaking Chicano Spanish have internalized the belief that we speak poor Spanish. It is illegitimate, a bastard language. And because we internalize how our language has been used against us by the dominant culture, we use our language differences against each other.

Chicana feminists often skirt around each other with suspicion and hesitation. For the longest time I couldn't figure it out. Then it dawned on me. To be close to another Chicana is like looking into the mirror. We are afraid of what we'll see there. *Pena.* Shame. Low estimation of self. In childhood we are told that our language is wrong. Repeated attacks on our native tongue diminish our sense of self. The attacks continue throughout our lives.

Chicanas feel uncomfortable talking in Spanish to Latinas, afraid of their censure. Their language was not outlawed in their countries. They had a whole lifetime of being immersed in their native tongue; generations, centuries in which Spanish was a first language, taught in school, heard on radio and TV, and read in the newspaper.

If a person, Chicana or Latina, has a low estimation of my native tongue, she also has a low estimation of me. Often with *mexicanas y latinas* we'll speak English as a neutral language. Even among Chicanas we tend to speak English at parties or conferences. Yet, at the same time, we're afraid the other will think we're *agringadas* because we don't speak Chicano Spanish. We oppress each other trying to out-Chicano each other, vying to be the "real" Chicanas, to speak like Chicanos. There is no one Chicano language just as there is no one Chicano experience. A monolingual Chicana whose first language is English or Spanish is just as much a Chicana as one who speaks several variants of Spanish. A Chicana from Michigan or Chicago or Detroit is just as much a Chicana as one from the Southwest. Chicano Spanish is as diverse linguistically as it is regionally.

By the end of this [the twentieth] century, Spanish speakers will comprise the biggest minority group in the United States, a country where students in high schools and colleges are encouraged to take French classes because French is considered more "cultured." But for a language to remain alive it must be used.[6] By the end of this century English, and not Spanish, will be the mother tongue of most Chicanos and Latinos.

So, if you want to really hurt me, talk badly about my language. Ethnic identity is twin skin to linguistic identity—I am my language. Until I can take pride in my language, I cannot take pride in myself. Until I can accept as legitimate Chicano Texas Spanish, Tex-Mex, and all the other languages I speak, I cannot accept the legitimacy of myself. Until I am free to write bilingually and to switch codes without having always to translate, while I still have to speak English or Spanish when I would rather speak Spanglish, and as long as I have to accommodate the English speaker rather than having them accommodate me, my tongue will be illegitimate.

I will no longer be made to feel ashamed of existing. I will have my voice: Indian, Spanish, white. I will have my serpent's tongue—my woman's voice, my sexual voice, my poet's voice. I will overcome the tradition of silence.

> My fingers
> move sly against your palm
> Like women everywhere, we speak in code. . . .
> —MELANIE KAYE/KANTROWITZ[7]

"Vistas," corridos, y comida: My Native Tongue

In the 1960s, I read my first Chicano novel. It was *City of Night* by John Rechy, a gay Texan, son of a Scottish father and a Mexican mother. For days I walked around in stunned amazement that a Chicano could write and could get published. When I read *I Am Joaquín*[8] I was surprised to see a bilingual book by a Chicano in print. When I saw poetry written in Tex-Mex for the first time, a feeling of pure joy flashed through me. I felt like we really existed as a people. In 1971, when I started teaching High School English to Chicano students, I tried to supplement the required texts with works by Chicanos, only to be reprimanded and forbidden to do so by the principal. He claimed that I was supposed to teach "American" and English literature. At the risk of being fired, I swore my students to secrecy and slipped in Chicano short stories, poems, a play. In graduate school, while working toward a Ph.D., I had to "argue" with one adviser after the other, semester after semester, before I was allowed to make Chicano literature an area of focus.

Even before I read books by Chicanos or Mexicans, it was the Mexican movies I saw at the drive-in—the Thursday night special of $1.00 a carload—that gave me a sense of belonging. *"Vámonos a las vistas,"* my mother would call out and we'd all—grandmother, brothers, sister, and cousins—squeeze into the car. We'd wolf down cheese and bologna white bread sandwiches while watching Pedro Infante in melodramatic tearjerkers like *Nosotros los pobres,* the first "real" Mexican movie (that was not an imitation of European movies). I remember seeing *Cuando los hijos se van* and surmising that all Mexican movies played up the love a mother has for her children and what ungrateful sons and daughters suffer when they are not devoted to their mothers. I remember the singing-type "westerns" of Jorge Negrete and Miguel Aceves Mejía. When watching Mexican movies, I felt a sense of

homecoming as well as alienation. People who were to amount to something didn't go to Mexican movies, or *bailes*, or tune their radios to *bolero*,
rancherita, and *corrido* music.

The whole time I was growing up, there was *norteño* music sometimes
called North Mexican border music, or Tex-Mex music, or Chicano music,
or *cantina* (bar) music. I grew up listening to *conjuntos*, three- or four-piece
bands made up of folk musicians playing guitar, *bajo sexto*, drums, and button accordion, which Chicanos had borrowed from the German immi-
grants who had come to Central Texas and Mexico to farm and build brew-
eries. In the Rio Grande Valley, Steven Jordan and Little Joe Hernández
were popular, and Flaco Jiménez was the accordion king. The rhythms of
Tex-Mex music are those of the polka, also adapted from the Germans, who
in turn had borrowed the polka from the Czechs and Bohemians.

I remember the hot, sultry evenings when *corridos*—songs of love and
death on the Texas-Mexican borderlands—reverberated out of cheap am-
plifiers from the local *cantinas* and wafted in through my bedroom window.

Corridos first became widely used along the South Texas/Mexican border during the early conflict between Chicanos and Anglos. The *corridos* are
usually about Mexican heroes who do valiant deeds against the Anglo oppressors. Pancho Villa's song, "*La cucaracha*," is the most famous one. *Corridos* of John F. Kennedy and his death are still very popular in the Valley.
Older Chicanos remember Lydia Mendoza, one of the great border *corrido*
singers who was called *la Gloria de Tejas*. Her "*El tango negro*," sung during
the Great Depression, made her a singer of the people. The ever-present
corridos narrated one hundred years of border history, bringing news of
events as well as entertaining. These folk musicians and folk songs are our
chief cultural mythmakers, and they made our hard lives seem bearable.

I grew up feeling ambivalent about our music. Country-western and
rock-and-roll had more status. In the fifties and sixties, for the slightly educated and *agringado* Chicanos, there existed a sense of shame at being caught
listening to our music. Yet I couldn't stop my feet from thumping to the
music, could not stop humming the words, nor hide from myself the exhilaration I felt when I heard it.

There are more subtle ways that we internalize identification, especially
in the forms of images and emotions. For me food and certain smells are
tied to my identity, to my homeland. Woodsmoke curling up to an immense blue sky; woodsmoke perfuming my grandmother's clothes, her
skin. The stench of cow manure and the yellow patches on the ground; the
crack of a .22 rifle and the reek of cordite. Homemade white cheese sizzling
in a pan, melting inside a folded *tortilla*. My sister Hilda's hot, spicy *menudo*,
chile colorado making it deep red, pieces of *panza* and hominy floating on
top. My brother Carito barbequing *fajitas* in the backyard. Even now and
3,000 miles away, I can see my mother spicing the ground beef, pork, and
venison with *chile*. My mouth salivates at the thought of the hot steaming
tamales I would be eating if I were home.

Si le preguntas a mi mamá, "¿Qué eres?"

Identity is the essential core of who
we are as individuals, the conscious
experience of the self inside.
−GERSHEN KAUFMAN[9]

Nosotros los Chicanos straddle the borderlands. On one side of us, we are constantly exposed to the Spanish of the Mexicans, on the other side we hear the Anglos' incessant clamoring so that we forget our language. Among ourselves we don't say *nosotros los americanos, o nosotros los españoles, o nosotros los hispanos.* We say *nosotros los mexicanos* (by *mexicanos* we do not mean citizens of Mexico; we do not mean a national identity, but a racial one). We distinguish between *mexicanos del otro lado* and *mexicanos de este lado.* Deep in our hearts we believe that being Mexican has nothing to do with which country one lives in. Being Mexican is a state of soul — not one of mind, not one of citizenship. Neither eagle nor serpent, but both. And like the ocean, neither animal respects borders.

Dime con quien andas y te diré quien eres.
(Tell me who your friends are and I'll tell you who you are.)
−Mexican saying

Si le preguntas a mi mamá, "¿Qué eres?" te dirá, "Soy mexicana." My brothers and sister say the same. I sometimes will answer *"soy mexicana"* and at others will say *"soy Chicana" o "soy tejana."* But I identified as *"Raza"* before I ever identified as *"mexicana"* or "Chicana."

As a culture, we call ourselves Spanish when referring to ourselves as a linguistic group and when copping out. It is then that we forget our predominant Indian genes. We are 70–80 percent Indian.[10] We call ourselves Hispanic[11] or Spanish-American or Latin American or Latin when linking ourselves to other Spanish-speaking peoples of the Western hemisphere and when copping out. We call ourselves Mexican-American[12] to signify we are neither Mexican nor American, but more the noun "American" than the adjective "Mexican" (and when copping out).

Chicanos and other people of color suffer economically for not acculturating. This voluntary (yet forced) alienation makes for psychological conflict, a kind of dual identity — we don't identify with the Anglo-American cultural values and we don't totally identify with the Mexican cultural values. We are a synergy of two cultures with various degrees of Mexicanness or Angloness. I have so internalized the borderland conflict that sometimes I feel like one cancels out the other and we are zero, nothing, no one. *A veces no soy nada ni nadie. Pero hasta cuando no lo soy, lo soy.*

When not copping out, when we know we are more than nothing, we call ourselves Mexican, referring to race and ancestry; *mestizo* when affirming both our Indian and Spanish (but we hardly ever own our Black) ancestry; Chicano when referring to a politically aware people born and/or raised in the United States; *Raza* when referring to Chicanos; *tejanos* when we are Chicanos from Texas.

Chicanos did not know we were a people until 1965 when Cesar Chavez and the farmworkers united and *I Am Joaquín* was published and *la Raza Unida* party was formed in Texas. With that recognition, we became a distinct people. Something momentous happened to the Chicano soul—we became aware of our reality and acquired a name and a language (Chicano Spanish) that reflected that reality. Now that we had a name, some of the fragmented pieces began to fall together—who we were, what we were, how we had evolved. We began to get glimpses of what we might eventually become.

Yet the struggle of identities continues, the struggle of borders is our reality still. One day the inner struggle will cease and a true integration take place. In the meantime, *tenémos que hacer la lucha. ¿Quién está protegiendo los ranchos de mi gente? ¿Quién está tratando de cerrar la fisura entre la india y el blanco en nuestra sangre? El Chicano, si, el Chicano que anda como un ladrón en su propia casa.*

Los Chicanos, how patient we seem, how very patient. There is the quiet of the Indian about us.[13] We know how to survive. When other races have given up their tongue we've kept ours. We know what it is to live under the hammer blow of the dominant *norteamericano* culture. But more than we count the blows, we count the days the weeks the years the centuries the aeons until the white laws and commerce and customs will rot in the deserts they've created, lie bleached. *Humildes* yet proud, *quietos* yet wild, *nosotros los mexicanos-Chicanos* will walk by the crumbling ashes as we go about our business. Stubborn, persevering, impenetrable as stone, yet possessing a malleability that renders us unbreakable, we, the *mestizas* and *mestizos*, will remain.

NOTES

[1] Ray Gwyn Smith, *Moorland Is Cold Country*, unpublished book.

[2] Irena Klepfisz, "*Di rayze aheym*/The Journey Home," in *The Tribe of Dina: A Jewish Women's Anthology*, Melanie Kaye/Kantrowitz and Irena Klepfisz, eds. (Montpelier, VT: Sinister Wisdom Books, 1986), 49.

[3] R. C. Ortega, *Dialectología Del Barrio*, trans. Hortencia S. Alwan (Los Angeles, CA: R. C. Ortega Publisher & Bookseller, 1977), 132.

[4] Eduardo Hernandéz-Chávez, Andrew D. Cohen, and Anthony F. Beltramo, *El Lenguaje de los Chicanos: Regional and Social Characteristics of Language Used by Mexican Americans* (Arlington, VA: Center for Applied Linguistics, 1975), 39.

[5] Hernandéz-Chávez, xvii.

[6] Irena Klepfisz, "Secular Jewish Identity: Yidishkayt in America," in *The Tribe of Dina*, Kaye/Kantrowitz and Klepfisz, eds., 43.

[7] Melanie Kaye/Kantrowitz, "Sign," in *We Speak in Code: Poems and Other Writings* (Pittsburgh, PA: Motheroot Publications, Inc., 1980), 85.

[8] Rodolfo Gonzales, *I Am Joaquín/Yo Soy Joaquín* (New York, NY: Bantam Books, 1972). It was first published in 1967.

[9] Gershen Kaufman, *Shame: The Power of Caring* (Cambridge, MA: Schenkman Books, Inc., 1980), 68.

[10] John R. Chávez, *The Lost Land: The Chicano Images of the Southwest* (Albuquerque, NM: University of New Mexico Press, 1984), 88–90.

[11] "Hispanic" is derived from *Hispanis* (*España,* a name given to the Iberian Peninsula in ancient times when it was a part of the Roman Empire) and is a term designated by the U.S. government to make it easier to handle us on paper.

[12] The Treaty of Guadalupe Hidalgo created the Mexican-American in 1848.

[13] Anglos, in order to alleviate their guilt for dispossessing the Chicano, stressed the Spanish part of us and perpetrated the myth of the Spanish Southwest. We have accepted the fiction that we are Hispanic, that is Spanish, in order to accommodate ourselves to the dominant culture and its abhorrence of Indians. Chávez, 88–91.

. . . .

QUESTIONS FOR A SECOND READING

1. The most immediate challenge to many readers of these chapters will be the sections that are written in Spanish. Part of the point of a text that mixes languages is to give non-Spanish-speaking readers the feeling of being lost, excluded, left out. What is a reader to do with this prose? One could learn Spanish and come back to reread, but this is not a quick solution and, according to Anzaldúa, not even a completely satisfactory one, since some of her Spanish is drawn from communities of speakers not represented in textbooks and classes.

   So how do you read this text if you don't read Spanish? Do you ignore the words? sound them out? improvise? Anzaldúa gives translations of some words or phrases, but not all. Which ones does she translate? Why? Reread these chapters with the goal of explaining how you handled Anzaldúa's polyglot style.

2. These chapters are made up of shorter sections written in a variety of styles (some as prose poems, some with endnotes, some as stories). And, while the sections are obviously ordered, the order is not a conventional argumentative one. The text is, as Anzaldúa says elsewhere in her book, "an assemblage, a montage, a beaded work, . . . a crazy dance":

   > In looking at this book that I'm almost finished writing, I see a mosaic pattern (Aztec-like) emerging, a weaving pattern, thin here, thick there. . . . This almost finished product seems an assemblage, a montage, a beaded work with several leitmotifs and with a central core, now appearing, now disappearing in a crazy dance. The whole thing has had a mind of its own, escaping me and insisting on putting together the pieces of its own puzzle with minimal direction from my will. It is a rebellious, willful entity, a precocious girl-child forced to grow up too quickly, rough, unyielding, with pieces of feather sticking out here and there, fur, twigs, clay. My child, but not for much longer. This female being is angry, sad, joyful, is Coatlicue, dove, horse, serpent, cactus. Though it is a flawed thing—clumsy, complex, groping, blind thing, for me it is alive, infused with spirit. I talk to it; it talks to me.

   This is not, in other words, a conventional text; it makes unexpected demands on a reader. As you reread, mark sections you could use to talk about how, through the text, Anzaldúa invents a reader and/or a way of reading. Who is Anzaldúa's ideal reader? What does he or she need to be able to do?

3. Although Anzaldúa's text is not a conventional one, it makes an argument and proposes terms and examples for its readers to negotiate. How might you summarize Anzaldúa's argument in these two chapters? How do the individual chapters mark stages or parts of her argument? How might you explain the connections between the chapters? As you reread this selection, mark those passages where Anzaldúa seems to you to be creating a case or an argument. What are its key terms? its key examples? its conclusions?

ASSIGNMENTS FOR WRITING

1. Anzaldúa has described her text as a kind of crazy dance (see the second "Question for a Second Reading"); it is, she says, a text with a mind of its own, "putting together the pieces of its own puzzle with minimal direction from my will." Hers is a prose full of variety and seeming contradictions; it is a writing that could be said to represent the cultural "crossroads" which is her experience/sensibility.

   As an experiment whose goal is the development of an alternate (in Anzaldúa's terms, a mixed or *mestiza*) understanding, write an autobiographical text whose shape and motives could be described in her terms: a mosaic, woven, with numerous overlays; a montage, a beaded work, a crazy dance, drawing on the various ways of thinking, speaking, understanding that might be said to be part of your own mixed cultural position, your own mixed sensibility.

   To prepare for this essay, think about the different positions you could be said to occupy, the different voices that are part of your background or present, the competing ways of thinking that make up your points of view. Imagine that your goal is to present your world and your experience to those who are not necessarily prepared to be sympathetic or to understand. And, following Anzaldúa, you should work to construct a mixed text, not a single unified one. This will be hard, since you will be writing what might be called a "forbidden" text, one you have not been prepared to write.

2. In *"La conciencia de la mestiza*/Towards a New Consciousness," the last essaylike chapter in her book (the remaining chapters are made up of poems), Anzaldúa steps forward to define her role as writer and yours as reader. She says, among other things,

   > Many women and men of color do not want to have any dealings with white people. . . . Many feel that whites should help their own people rid themselves of race hatred and fear first. I, for one, choose to use some of my energy to serve as mediator. I think we need to allow whites to be our allies. Through our literature, art, *corridos*, and folktales we must share our history with them so when they set up committees to help Big Mountain Navajos or the Chicano farmworkers or los *Nicaragüenses* they won't turn people away because of their racial fears and ignorances. They will come to see that they are not helping us but following our lead.
   >
   > Individually, but also as a racial entity, we need to voice our needs. We need to say to white society: We need you to accept the fact that Chicanos are different, to acknowledge your rejection and negation of us.

> We need you to own the fact that you looked upon us as less than human, that you stole our lands, our personhood, our self-respect. We need you to make public restitution: to say that, to compensate for your own sense of defectiveness, you strive for power over us, you erase our history and our experience because it makes you feel guilty—you'd rather forget your brutish acts. To say you've split yourself from minority groups, that you disown us, that your dual consciousness splits off parts of yourself, transferring the "negative" parts onto us. . . . To say that you are afraid of us, that to put distance between us, you wear the mask of contempt. Admit that Mexico is your double, that she exists in the shadow of this country, that we are irrevocably tied to her. Gringo, accept the doppelganger in your psyche. By taking back your collective shadow the intracultural split will heal. And finally, tell us what you need from us.

This is only a part of the text—one of the ways it defines the roles of reader and writer—but it is one that asks to be taken account of, with its insistent list of what a white reader must do and say. (Of course not every reader is white, and not all white readers are the same. What Anzaldúa is defining here is a "white" way of reading.)

Write an essay in which you tell a story of reading, the story of your work with the two chapters of *Borderlands/La frontera* reprinted here. Think about where you felt at home with the text and where you felt lost, where you knew what you were doing and where you needed help; think about the position (or positions) you have taken as a reader and how it measures up against the ways Anzaldúa has figured you in the text, the ways she has anticipated a response, imagined who you are and how you habitually think and read.

3. In "How to Tame a Wild Tongue" (p. 42), Anzaldúa says, "I will no longer be made to feel ashamed of existing. I will have my voice: Indian, Spanish, white. I will have my serpent's tongue—my woman's voice, my sexual voice, my poet's voice." Anzaldúa speaks almost casually about "having her voice," not a single, "authentic" voice, but one she names in these terms: Indian, Spanish, white; woman, lesbian, poet. What is "voice" as defined by these chapters? Where does it come from? What does it have to do with the act of writing or the writer?

As you reread these chapters, mark those passages that you think best represent Anzaldúa's voices. Using these passages as examples, write an essay in which you discuss how these voices are different—both different from one another and different from a "standard" voice (as a "standard" voice is imagined by Anzaldúa). What do these voices represent? How do they figure in your reading? in her writing?

4. Anzaldúa's writing is difficult to categorize as an essay or a story or a poem; it has all of these within it. The writing may appear to have been just put together, but it is more likely that it was carefully crafted to represent the various voices Anzaldúa understands to be a part of her. She speaks directly about her voices—her woman's voice, her sexual voice, her poet's voice; her Indian, Spanish, and white voices on page 47 of "How to Tame a Wild Tongue."

Following Anzaldúa, write an argument of your own, one that requires you to use a variety of voices, in which you carefully present the various voices that you feel are a part of you or a part of the argument.

When you have completed this assignment, write a two-page essay in which you explain why the argument you made might be worth a reader's attention.

MAKING CONNECTIONS

1. In "Arts of the Contact Zone" (p. 499), Mary Louise Pratt talks about the "autoethnographic" text, "a text in which people undertake to describe themselves in ways that engage with representations others have made of them," and about "transculturation," the "processes whereby members of subordinated or marginal groups select and invent from materials transmitted by a dominant or metropolitan culture."

   Write an essay in which you present a reading of these two chapters as an example of an autoethnographic and/or transcultural text. You should imagine that you are writing to someone who is not familiar with either Pratt's argument or Anzaldúa's book. Part of your work, then, is to present Anzaldúa's text to readers who don't have it in front of them. You have the example of Pratt's reading of Guaman Poma's *New Chronicle and Good Government*. And you have her discussion of the "literate arts of the contact zone." Think about how Anzaldúa's text might be similarly read, and about how her text does and doesn't fit Pratt's description. Your goal should be to add an example to Pratt's discussion and to qualify it, to give her discussion a new twist or spin now that you have had a chance to look at an additional example.

2. Both Adrienne Rich in "When We Dead Awaken: Writing as Re-Vision" (p. 520) and Gloria Anzaldúa in these two chapters could be said to be writing about the same issues—writing, identity, gender, history. Both texts contain an argument; both, in their peculiar styles, enact an argument—they demonstrate how and why one might need to revise the usual ways of writing. Identify what you understand to be the key points, the key terms, and the key examples in each selection.

   Beginning with the passages you have identified, write an essay in which you examine the similarities and differences in these two texts. Look particularly for the differences, since they are harder to find and harder to explain. Consider the selections as marking different positions on writing, identity, politics, history. How might you account for these differences (if they represent more than the fact that different people are likely to differ)? How are these differences significant?

KWAME ANTHONY
APPIAH

KWAME ANTHONY APPIAH (pronounced **Ap**-eea, with the accent on the first syllable) was born in London; he grew up in Ghana, in the town of Asante; he took his MA and PhD degrees from Cambridge University in England; he is now a citizen of the United States. He has taught at Yale, Cornell, Duke, and Harvard and, most recently, at Princeton, where he is the Laurence S. Rockefeller University Professor of Philosophy and a member of the University Center for Human Values. Appiah's father was Ghanaian and a leader in the struggle for Pan-Africanism and Ghanaian independence from Britain; his mother, originally Peggy Cripps, was British and the daughter of a leading figure in the Labour government. Appiah's recent book, The Ethics of Identity, which questions the labels we glibly use to name racial, cultural, and national identity, is quite beautifully and appropriately dedicated to his partner, Henry Finder. He says, "the name on the title page is mine, and I take responsibility for the book and its claims, but it is ours, I think, as substantially as [John Stuart] Mill claimed On Liberty to be a joint production with [his partner] Harriet Taylor."

Appiah's life illustrates the virtues of a "rooted cosmopolitanism," a term he offers to describe a desired way of living in the world, and it illustrates the difficulties

55

we face in naming someone as black or white or African or American. In the preface to The Ethics of Identity, *he says,*

> What has proved especially vexatious, though, is the effort to take account of those social forms we now call identities: genders and sexual orientations, ethnicities and nationalities, professions and vocations. Identities make ethical claims because—and this is just a fact about the world we human beings have created—we make our lives as men and as women, as gay and as straight people, as Ghanaians and as Americans, as blacks and as whites. Immediately, conundrums start to assemble. Do identities represent a curb on autonomy, or do they provide its contours: What claims, if any, can identity groups as such justly make upon the state? These are concerns that have gained a certain measure of salience in recent political philosophy, but, as I hope to show, they are anything but newfangled. What's modern is that we conceptualize identity in particular ways. What's age-old is that when we are asked—and ask ourselves—who we are, we are being asked what we are as well. (xiv)

    Appiah is a prolific writer; he is both a political philosopher and a cultural theorist. His books include Assertion and Conditionals *(1985);* For Truth in Semantics *(1986);* In My Father's House: Africa in the Philosophy of Culture *(1992);* Color Conscious: The Political Morality of Race *(with Amy Gutmann, 1996);* The Ethics of Identity, *from which the following selection is chosen (2004); and* Cosmopolitanism: Ethics in a World of Strangers *(2007). He is also the author of three mystery novels,* Avenging Angel *(1991),* Nobody Likes Letitia *(1994), and* Another Death in Venice *(1995); a textbook,* Thinking It Through: An Introduction to Contemporary Philosophy *(2003); and, with Henry Louis Gates Jr., the* Encarta Africana *CD-ROM encyclopedia.*

The Ethics of Individuality

THE GREAT EXPERIMENT — LIBERTY AND INDIVIDUALITY — PLANS OF LIFE — THE SOUL OF THE SERVITOR — SOCIAL CHOICES — INVENTION AND AUTHENTICITY — THE SOCIAL SCRIPTORIUM — ETHICS IN IDENTITY — INDIVIDUALITY AND THE STATE — THE COMMON PURSUIT

The Great Experiment

    Depending upon how you look at it, John Stuart Mill's celebrated education was either a case study in individuality or a vigorous attempt to erase it. He himself seems to have been unable to decide which. He called his education "the experiment," and the account he provided in his *Autobiography* ensured that it would become the stuff of legend. He was learning Greek at three, and by the time he was twelve, he had read the whole of Herodotus, a fair amount of Xenophon, Virgil's *Eclogues* and the first six books of the *Aeneid*, most of Horace, and major works by Sophocles, Euripides, Polybius, Plato, and Aristotle, among others. After studying Pope's Homer, he set about composing a "continuation of the *Iliad*," at first on whim and then on command. He had also made serious forays into geometry, algebra, and differential calculus.

The young Mill was kept away as much as possible from the corrupting influence of other boys ("the contagion," as he put it, "of vulgar modes of thought and feeling"); and so, in his fourteenth year, when John Stuart was about to meet some new people beyond the range of his father's supervision, James Mill took his son for a walk in Hyde Park to prepare him for what he might expect to encounter. If he found that he was ahead of other children, he must attribute it not to his own superiority, but to the particular rigors of his intellectual upbringing: "it was no matter of praise to me, if I knew more than those who had not had a similar advantage, but the deepest disgrace to me if I did not." This was the first inkling he had that he was precocious, and Mill had every reason to be astonished. "If I thought anything about myself, it was that I was rather backward in my studies," he recounts, "since I always found myself so, in comparison with what my father expected from me."[1]

But James Mill was a man with a mission, and it was his eldest son's appointed role to carry forward that mission. James, as Jeremy Bentham's foremost disciple, was molding yet another disciple—someone who, trained in accordance with Benthamite principles, would extend and promulgate the grand *raisonneur*'s creed for a new era. He was, so to speak, the samurai's son. In the event, self-development was to be a central theme of Mill's thought and, indeed, a main element of his complaint against his intellectual patrimony. When he was twenty-four, he wrote to his friend John Sterling about the loneliness that had come to overwhelm him: "There is now no human being (with whom I can associate on terms of equality) who acknowledges a common object with me, or with whom I can cooperate even in any practical undertaking, without feeling that I am only using a man, whose purposes are different, as an instrument for the furtherance of my own."[2] And his sensitivity about using another in this way surely flows from his sense that he himself had been thus used—that he had been conscripted into a master plan that was not his own.

Mill memorably wrote about the great crisis in his life—a sort of midlife crisis, which, as befitted his precocity, visited when he was twenty—and the spiral of anomie into which he descended, during the winter of 1826.

> In this frame of mind it occurred to me to put the question directly to myself: "Suppose that all your objects in life were realized; that all the changes in institution and opinions which you

are looking forward to, could be completely effected at this very
instant: would this be a great joy and happiness to you?" And
an irrepressible self-consciousness distinctly answered, "No!"
At this my heart sank within me: the whole foundation on
which my life was constructed fell down.[3]

He pulled out of it, stepped blinking into the light; but for a long while
thereafter found himself dazed and adrift. Intent on deprogramming himself from the cult of Bentham, he plunged into an uncritical eclecticism, unwilling to exercise his perhaps overdeveloped faculties of discrimination.
He was determinedly, even perversely, receptive to the arguments of those
he would once have considered the embodiment of Error, whether the
breathless utopianism of the Saint-Simonians or the murky Teutonic mysti-
cisms of Coleridge and Carlyle. When intellectual direction returned to his
life, it was through the agency of his new friend and soul mate, Mrs. Harriet Hardy Taylor. "My great readiness and eagerness to learn from everybody, and to make room in my opinions for every new acquisition by adjusting the old and the new to one another, might, but for her steadying
influence, have seduced me into modifying my early opinions too much,"
he would write.[4]

It was a relationship that was greeted with considerable censure, not
least by James Mill. So there is some irony that it was she, more than anyone, who seems to have returned the rudderless craft he had become to the
tenets of the patrimonial cause. His love for her was at once rebellion and
restoration—and the beginning of an intellectual partnership that spanned
almost three decades. Only when Mrs. Taylor was widowed, in 1851, could
she and Mill live together as man and wife, and in the mid-1850s their collaboration bore its greatest fruit: *On Liberty*, surely the most widely read
work of political philosophy in the English language.

I retell this familiar story because so many of the themes that preoccupied Mill's social and political thought wend their way through his life. It is
a rare convenience. Buridan's ass did not itself tap out any contributions to
decision theory before succumbing to starvation. Paul Gauguin, the emblem
and avatar of Bernard Williams's famous analysis of "moral luck," was not
himself a moral philosopher. Yet Mill's concern with self-development and
experimentation was a matter of both philosophical inquiry and personal
experience. *On Liberty* is an impasto of influences—ranging from German
romanticism, by way of Wilhelm von Humboldt and Coleridge, to the
sturdy, each-person-counts-for-one equality and tolerance that were Mill's
intellectual birthright. But my interest in Mill's work is essentially and ten-
dentiously presentist, for it adumbrates the main themes of this book, as it
does so many topics in liberal theory.

Consider his emphasis on the importance of diversity; his recognition
of the irreducibly plural nature of human values; his insistence that the
state has a role in promoting human flourishing, broadly construed; his effort to elaborate a notion of well-being that was at once individualist and
(in ways that are sometimes overlooked) profoundly social. Finally, his ro-

bust ideal of individuality mobilizes, as we'll see, the critical notions of autonomy and identity. My focus on Mill isn't by way of *argumentum ad verecundiam*; I don't suppose (nor did he) that his opinions represented the last word. But none before him—and, I am inclined to add, none since— charted out the terrain as clearly and as carefully as he did. We may cultivate a different garden, but we do so on soil that he fenced in and terraced.

Liberty and Individuality

"If it were felt that the free development of individuality is one of the leading essentials of well-being; that it is not only a coordinate element with all that is designated by the terms civilization, instruction, education, culture, but is itself a necessary part and condition of all those things; there would be no danger that liberty should be undervalued, and the adjustment of the boundaries between it and social control would present no extraordinary difficulty."[5] So Mill wrote in the book's celebrated third chapter, "On Individuality, as One of the Elements of Wellbeing," and it is a powerful proposal. For it seems to suggest that individuality could be taken as prior even to the book's titular subject, liberty itself. Our capacity to use all our faculties in our individual ways was, at least in part, what made liberty valuable to us. In Mill's accounting, individuality doesn't merely conduce to, it is constitutive of, the social good. And he returns to the point, lest anyone miss it: "Having said that Individuality is the same thing with development, and that it is only the cultivation of individuality which produces, or can produce, well-developed human beings, I might here close the argument: for what more or better can be said of any condition of human affairs, than that it brings human beings themselves nearer to the best thing they can be? or what worse can be said of any obstruction to good, than that it prevents this?[6]

To be sure, Mill does offer conventionally consequentialist arguments for liberty—arguments that liberty is likely to have good effects. His most famous arguments for freedom of expression assume that we will find the truth more often and more easily if we allow our opinions to be tested in public debate, in what we all now call the marketplace of ideas. But he argued with especial fervor that the cultivation of one's individuality is itself a part of well-being, something good *in se*, and here liberty is not a means to an end but part of the end. For individuality means, among other things, choosing for myself instead of merely being shaped by the constraint of political or social sanction. It was part of Mill's view, in other words, that freedom mattered not just because it enabled other things—such as the discovery of truth—but also because without it people could not develop the individuality that is an essential element of human good.[7] As he writes,

> He who lets the world, or his own portion of it, choose his plan of
> life for him, has no need for any other faculty than the ape-like
> one of imitation. He who chooses his plan for himself, employs

all his faculties. He must use observation to see, reasoning and judgment to foresee, activity to gather materials for decision, discrimination to decide, and when he has decided, firmness and self-control to hold to his deliberate decision. And these qualities he requires and exercises exactly in proportion as the part of his conduct which he determines according to his own judgment and feelings is a large one. It is possible that he might be guided in some good path, and kept out of harm's way, without any of these things. But what will be his comparative worth as a human being? It really is of importance, not only what men do, but also what manner of men they are that do it.[8]

Individuality is not so much a state to be achieved as a mode of life to be pursued. Mill says that it is important that one choose one's own plan of life, and liberty consists, at least in part, in providing the conditions under which a choice among acceptable options is possible. But one must choose one's own plan of life not because one will necessarily make the wisest choices; indeed, one might make poor choices. What matters most about a plan of life (Mill's insistence on the point is especially plangent coming from the subject of James and Jeremy's great experiment) is simply that it be chosen by the person whose life it is: "If a person possesses any tolerable amount of common sense and experience, his own mode of laying out his existence is best, not because it is the best in itself, but because it is his own mode." Not only is exercising one's autonomy valuable in itself, but such exercise leads to self-development, to the cultivation of one's faculties of observation, reason, and judgment.[9] Developing the *capacity* for autonomy is necessary for human well-being, which is why it matters not just what people choose but "what manner of men they are that do it." So Mill invokes "individuality" to refer both to the precondition and to the result of such deliberative choice making.[10]

The account of individuality that Mill offers in chapter 3 of *On Liberty* does not distinguish consistently between the idea that it is good to be different from other people and the idea that it is good to be, in some measure, self-created, to be someone who "chooses his plan for himself."[11] Still, I think it is best to read Mill as finding inherent value not in diversity—being different—but in the enterprise of self-creation. For I might choose a plan of life that was, as it happened, very like other people's and still not be merely aping them, following them blindly as a model. I wouldn't, then, be contributing to diversity (so, in one sense, I wouldn't be very individual), but I would still be constructing my own—in another sense, individual— plan of life. *On Liberty* defends freedom because only free people can take full command of their own lives.

Plans of Life

Why does Mill insist that individuality is something that develops in coordination with a "plan of life"? His training as a utilitarian means that he wouldn't have separated well-being from the satisfaction of wants; but he was well aware that to make sense of such wants, we had to see them as structured in particular ways. Our immediate desires and preferences so often run contrary to other, longer-term ones. We wish to have written a book, but we don't wish to write one. We wish to ace our gross anatomy exam, but don't wish to study for it on this sunny afternoon. It's for this reason that we devise all manner of mechanisms to bind ourselves . . . , so that, as we often say, we "force ourselves" to do what our interest requires. Moreover, many of our goals are clearly intermediate in nature, subordinate to more comprehensive goals. You want to ace your gross anatomy exam because you want to be a surgeon; you want to be a surgeon because you want to mend cleft palates in Burkina Faso or, as the case may be, carve retroussé noses in Beverly Hills; and these ambitions may be in the service of still other ambitions. . . . It's worth bearing in mind that for Mill the activity of choosing freely had a *rational* dimension, was bound up in observation, reason, judgment, and deliberation. In *A System of Logic*, Mill even suggests that the consolidation of fleeting preferences into steadier purposes is what constitutes maturity:

> A habit of willing is commonly called a purpose; and among the causes of our volitions, and of the actions which flow from them, must be reckoned not only likings and aversions, but also purposes. It is only when our purposes have become independent of the feelings of pain or pleasure from which they originally took their rise, that we are said to have a confirmed character. "A character," says Novalis, "is a completely fashioned will," and the will, once so fashioned, may be steady and constant, when the passive susceptibilities of pleasure and pain are greatly weakened, or materially changed.[12]

Precisely this notion became central to a subsequent theorist of "life plans," Josiah Royce, who essentially defined a person as someone in possession of one. Rawls, too, was working within this Millian discourse when he stipulated that "a person's plan of life is rational if, and only if, (1) it is one of the plans that is consistent with the principles of rational choice when these are applied to all the relevant features of his situation, and (2) it is that plan among those meeting this condition which would be chosen by him with full deliberative rationality, that is, with full awareness of the relevant facts and after a careful consideration of the consequences."[13]

The currency such talk of "plans" has acquired in contemporary liberal theory has invited some gimlet-eyed scrutiny. "In general, people do not and cannot make an overall choice of a total plan of life," J. L. Mackie observes. "They choose successively to pursue various activities from time to time, not once and for all." Daniel A. Bell, in a critique of the sort of liberal individualism associated with Rawls, maintains that "people do not necessarily have a 'highest-order interest' in rationally choosing their career and marriage partner, as opposed to following their instincts, striving for ends and goals set for them by others (family, friends, community groups, the government, God), and letting fate do the rest of the work. . . .

This, combined with an awareness of the unchosen nature of most of our social attachments, undermines those justifications for a liberal form of social organization founded on the value of reflective choice." And Michael Slote has raised concerns about the ways in which such "plans of life" mobilize preferences across time. Sometimes, given certain future uncertainties, we will be better served if we cultivate a measure of passivity, of watchful waiting. It's also the case that, as he puts it, "rational life-planfulness is a virtue with a temporal aspect"—it's not advisable for children to arrive at hard-and-fast decisions about their careers, because the activity requires the sort of prudence they're unlikely to possess. What's more, there are important human goods, like love or friendship, that we don't exactly "plan" for.[14]

The critics have a point. No doubt such talk of plans can be misleading if we imagine that people stride around with a neatly folded blueprint of their lives tucked into their back pocket—if we imagine life plans to be singular and fixed, rather than multiple and constantly shifting.[15] Dickens hardly needed to underscore the irony when he had Mr. Dombey announce, of his doomed young heir, "There is nothing of chance or doubt in the course before my son. His way in life was clear and prepared, and marked out before he existed."[16] Plans can evolve, reverse course, be derailed by contingencies large and small; and to speak of them should not commit us to the notion that there's one optimal plan for an individual. (It's noteworthy that even the great embodiments of ambition in European fiction—Stendhal's Julien Sorel, say, or Trollope's Phineas Finn—stumble into their careers through a succession of fortuities. Sorel's choice of the black over the red reflects not inner conviction, but the particular positions of the army and the church during the French restoration.) Mill himself did not labor under any such illusions. Nobody would have planned to fall in love with another man's wife and spend the next two decades in a nerve-racking ménage à trois.[17] Precisely because of his temperamental constancy, he was acutely aware of the ways in which his thought and goals shifted over time. That's one reason he came to think that the exploration of the ends of life would yield to "experiments in living," although he had reason to know that conducting an experiment and having one conducted upon you were two different things.

The Soul of the Servitor

Though talk of plans can sound overly determinate, Mill's rhetorical excesses were frequently in the opposite direction—suggesting not too much structure but too little. The way he wrote about individuality, the product (and condition) of the freely chosen life plan, occasionally makes it sound like a weirdly exalted affair—an existence of ceaseless nonconformity, de novo judgments, poeticizing flights. It may conjure the whirling, willowy performance artist the cartoonist Jules Pfeiffer likes to draw, a character who perpetually expresses her every velleity in dance. This is not Mill's view,[18] any more than the engineering-schematic view is, but because Mill speaks abstractly, it may help to imagine a more concrete example. Consider, then, Mr. Stevens, the butler in Kazuo Ishiguro's celebrated novel *The Remains of the Day*. Mr. Stevens has spent a whole life in service in a "great house," and his aim has been to perform his task to the very best of his ability. He sees himself as part of the machinery that made the life of his master, Lord Darlington, possible. Since his master has acted on the stage of public history, he sees Lord Darlington's public acts as part of what gives meaning to his own life. As he puts it: "Let us establish this quite clearly: a butler's duty is to provide good service. It is not to meddle in the great affairs of the nation. The fact is, such great affairs will always be beyond the understanding of those such as you and I, and those of us who wish to make our mark must realize that we best do so by concentrating on what *is* within our realm."[19]

Mr. Stevens takes what is "within our realm" extremely seriously; for example, he feels, as he says, "uplifted" by a "sense of triumph" when he manages to pursue his duties unflustered on the evening that the woman he barely realizes he loves has announced to him that she is going to marry somebody else.[20] By the time he tells us about this fateful day, we know him well enough to understand how such a sentiment is possible.

At the end of the book, Mr. Stevens is returning to Darlington Hall from the holiday during which he has reviewed his life with us, and he tells us he is going back to work on what he calls his "bantering skills" in order to satisfy his new American master.

> I have of course already devoted much time to developing my bantering skills, but it is possible I have never previously approached the task with the commitment I might have done. Perhaps, then, when I return to Darlington Hall tomorrow . . . I will begin practicing with renewed effort. I should hope, then, by the time of my employer's return, I shall be in a position to pleasantly surprise him.[21]

Few readers of Ishiguro's novel will aspire to be a butler, least of all the sort of butler that Mr. Stevens aimed to be. And there is, indeed, something mildly ridiculous in the thought of an elderly man working on his skills at light conversation in order to entertain his young "master." Ishiguro specializes in starchy, self-deceived narrators, and readers are likely to feel when they come to these last words a tremendous sadness at what is missing from Mr. Stevens's life.

Nevertheless, Mr. Stevens is continuing to live out the life he has chosen. And it does seem to me that we can understand part of what Mill is suggesting by saying that bantering is something of value to Mr. Stevens because he has chosen to be the best butler he can be. This is not a life *we* would have chosen; but for someone who *has* chosen it, it is intelligible that improving one's bantering skills is a good. Mill isn't very clear in *On Liberty* about how "individuality" might relate to other kinds of goods. But he recognized that sometimes a thing matters because a person has chosen to make a life in which it matters, and that it would not matter if he or she had not chosen to make such a life. To say that bantering is of value to Mr. Stevens is not just to say that he wants to be able to do it well, as he might want to be good at bridge or bowling. It is to say that, given his aims, his "plan of life," bantering matters to him; we, for whom bantering does not matter in this way, can still see that it is a value for him within the life he has chosen.

You may think that this is not a life that anyone who had other reasonable options should have chosen, and that even someone who was forced into it should not have taken to it with the enthusiasm and commitment that Mr. Stevens manifests. You might even explain this by saying that the life of the perfect servant is not one of great dignity. But the fact is that Mr. Stevens did choose this mode of life, in the full awareness of alternatives, and pursued it with focused ambition: among other things, he clearly sought to surpass his father's own considerable achievement in the profession. It is because of his commitment that he has engaged in such vigorous self-development, cultivating and improving his various skills. And the seriousness with which he takes the imperative of self-development is one that Mill could only have applauded. As Mill wrote in an emphatic letter to his friend David Barclay, "there is only one plain rule of life eternally binding, and independent of all variations in creeds, and in the interpretation of creeds, embracing equally the greatest moralities and the smallest; it is this: try thyself unweariedly till thou findest the highest thing thou art capable of doing, faculties and outward circumstances being both duly considered, and then DO IT."[22] Mill also says that "a sense of dignity" is something that "all human beings possess in one form or another,"[23] and dignity is something that Mr. Stevens himself knows a good deal about. He even offers a definition of it in response to the questioning of a doctor he meets on his travels.

> "What do *you* think dignity's all about?"
>   The directness of the inquiry did, I admit, take me rather by surprise. "It's rather a hard thing to explain in a few words, sir," I said. "But I suspect it comes down to not removing one's clothing in public."[24]

This is more than a joke. Mr. Stevens *believes* in decorum, good manners, formality. These compose the world that he has chosen to inhabit and make it the world that it is. Once again, these may not be values for us, but they *are* values for him, given his plan of life. When he is serious, when he is explaining to a room full of villagers what makes the difference between a gentleman and someone who is not, he says: "one would suspect that the quality . . . might be most usefully termed 'dignity.'" This is a quality that he, like many conservatives, believes to be far from equally distributed. "Dignity's not just something for gentlemen," says a character called Harry Smith. And Mr. Stevens observes in his narrative voice, "I perceived, of course, that Mr. Harry Smith and I were rather at cross purposes on this matter."[25]

If Mr. Stevens is a helpful illustration of individuality—of the values of self-development and autonomy—it is in part because he must seem an unlikely representative of such things; to cite him as such is to read Ishiguro's novel against the grain. Ishiguro is like you and me, a modern person, and his novel is sad (and comic) because Mr. Stevens's life seems, in ways he does not recognize, a failure. Mr. Stevens is also a contentious example because . . . some philosophers would want to deny that he was fully autonomous, and so to ascribe autonomy to him is to challenge a certain conception of what autonomy requires. At first blush, Mr. Stevens represents precisely the dead hand of convention and custom that Mill railed against in *On Liberty*. Yet Mill's view of convention and custom was rather more complicated than such denunciations suggest. In a somewhat wistful passage in *A System of Logic*, he writes:

> The longer our species lasts, and the more civilized it becomes, the more, as Comte remarks, does the influence of past generations over the present, and of mankind en masse over every individual in it, predominate over other forces; and though the course of affairs never ceases to be susceptible of alteration both by accidents and by personal qualities, the increasing preponderance of the collective agency of the species over all minor causes, is constantly bringing the general evolution of the race into something which deviates less from a certain and preappointed track.[26]

At the same time, Stevens's rather circumscribed conception of what belongs in his "realm" of interest and expertise does make him especially vulnerable to the vagaries of moral luck. For Lord Darlington turns out to be a weak man, an easy mark for the National Socialist Joachim von Ribbentrop, Germany's prewar ambassador to London. The result is that (at least in the novel's apparent accounting) Mr. Stevens's life is a failure because his master's life has proved one, not because service is, in fact, bound to lead to failure. After all, if Mr. Stevens had been working for Winston Churchill, he, at least, could deny that he had failed; he could claim to have been the faithful servant of a great man, just as he set out to be.[27] Instead, Mr. Stevens's pursuit of his vocation robs him both of his dignity and of a love life, since the only woman he might have married works in the same household and he believes a relationship with her would most likely have compromised their professional relations. Though Mr. Stevens makes a mess of this, there is, as I say, no reason to think that these losses are the fault of his vocation.[28]

Then again, perhaps the reason his life seems a failure is that he is servile. Servility, as Thomas E. Hill has suggested we understand the term, isn't just happily earning your living by working for another; it's acting as an unfree person, a person whose will is somehow subjected to another's—a person who, in Hill's formulation, disavows his own moral rights.[29] And yet Mr. Stevens might be defended even from this charge. Has he, in fact, disavowed his own moral rights? His sense of duty to his employer seems derivative from his sense of duty to himself and his own amour propre, for we have no doubt that he could let standards slip without his employer's being any the wiser. Mr. Stevens, who holds to his sense of what is proper despite the caviling of his peers and the inattentiveness of his employer, is conscious that he represents a way of life that is endangered; his conservatism is decidedly not that of conformity. What makes Mr. Stevens a useful example of the moral power of individuality, then, is that he exemplifies it even though he himself doesn't much believe in liberty, equality, or fraternity. Even someone as illiberal as Mr. Stevens, that is, demonstrates the power of individuality as an ideal.

Social Choices

For Mill, Royce, and others, as we've seen, a plan of life serves as a way of integrating one's purposes over time, of fitting together the different things one values. The fulfillment of goals that flow from such a plan—or what we might prefer to call our ground projects and commitments[30]—has more value than the satisfaction of a fleeting desire. In particular, Mill says that it matters because, in effect, the life plan is an expression of my individuality, of who I am: and, in this sense, a desire that flows from a value that itself derives from a life plan is more important than a desire (such as an appetite) that I just happen to have; for it flows from my reflective choices, my commitments, not just from passing fancy.

The ideal of self-authorship strikes a popular chord: we all know the sentiment in the form that Frank Sinatra made famous. In a song in which a person reviews his life toward its end, Mr. Sinatra sings: "I've lived a life that's full. / I've traveled each and ev'ry highway; / But more, much more than this, / I did it my way."[31] If my choosing it is part of what makes my life plan good, then imposing on me a plan of life—even one that is, in other respects, an enviable one—is depriving me of a certain kind of good. For a person of a liberal disposition, my life's shape is up to me, even if I make a life that is objectively less good than a life I could have made, provided that I have done my duty toward others.[32] All of us could, no doubt, have made better lives than we have; but that, Mill says, is no reason for others to attempt to force those better lives upon us.

And yet this scenario of self-chosen individuality invites a couple of worries. First, it is hard to accept the idea that certain values derive from my choices if those choices themselves are just arbitrary. Why should the mere fact that I have laid out my existence mean that it is the best, especially if it is not the best "in itself"?

Suppose, for example, I adopt a life as a solitary traveler around the world, free of entanglements with family and community, settling for a few months here and there, making what little money I need by giving English lessons to businesspeople. My parents tell me that I am wasting my life as a

Scholar Gypsy, that I have a good education, talent as a musician, and a wonderful gift for friendship, all of which are being put to no use. You don't have to be a communitarian to wonder whether it is a satisfactory response to say only that I have considered the options and this is the way I have chosen. Don't I need to say something about what this way makes possible for me and for those I meet? Or about what other talents of mine it makes use of? It is one thing to say that the government or society or your parents ought not to stop you from wasting your life if you choose to; but it is another to say that wasting your life in your own way is good just because it is your way, just because you have chosen to waste your life.

This may be why Mill seesaws between arguing that I am in the optimal position to decide what plan of life is best for me, given "the mental, moral, and aesthetic stature" of which I am capable, and the more radical view that the mere fact that I have chosen a plan of life recommends it. For on the former view, my choice is not arbitrary. It reflects the facts of my capacities, and, given that I have enough "common sense and experience," I am likely to do a better job than anybody else of judging how to make a life that fits those capacities. On this view, I discover a life for myself, based in the facts of my nature and my place in the world. But on the latter, my role is as originator of value, not as discoverer of it. Here the charge against individuality is that it is *arbitrary*.

Let me raise a second worry with the picture of self-chosen individuality we've been examining. At times, Mill's way of talking can suggest a rather unattractive form of individualism, in which the aim is to make a life in which you yourself matter most. This conception has sometimes been prettified with a particular account of the unfettered human soul. The result finds memorable expression in the misty-eyed antinomianism of Oscar Wilde's "Soul of Man under Socialism," in which, once the shackles of convention are thrown off, some sort of dewy and flower-strewn Pre-Raphaelitism will reign: "It will be a marvelous thing — the true personality of man — when we see it. It will grow naturally and simply, flowerlike, or as a dispute. It will not prove things. It will know everything. And yet it will not busy itself about knowledge." And so breathlessly on.[33] This is the sort of moral kitsch that gives individuality a bad name.

And Mill does argue for a view of one's self as a project, in a way that might be read as suggesting that self-cultivation and sociability are competing values, though each has its place.[34] This can lead us to think that the good of individuality is reined in by or traded off against the goods of sociability so that there is an intrinsic opposition between the self and society. It can lead us to think that political institutions, which develop and reflect the value of sociability, are always a source of constraint on our individuality. Here is a second charge against individuality: that it is *unsociable*.

Now, to show that individuality, or, more baldly, self-creation, doesn't necessarily succumb to these pitfalls is not to show that it isn't susceptible to them; but, right away, we can establish that it *needn't* involve either arbitrariness or unsociability. A plan of life for Mill was likely to include family and friends and might include (as his did) public service. Mr. Stevens's individuality, too, is far from unsociable because what he has chosen to be is a butler, which is something you can be only if there are other people to play other roles in the social world; a butler needs a master or mistress, cooks, housekeepers, maids. It is an intrinsically social role, a station with its public duties, not just an opportunity to follow one's private tastes. And Mr. Stevens's individuality is far from arbitrary because it is a role that has developed within a tradition, a role that makes sense within a certain social world: a social world that no longer exists, as it happens, which is one of many reasons why none of us wants to be a butler in the way Mr. Stevens was. We don't want to be butlers in that way because—without a social world of "great houses," house parties, and the rest—one *can't* be a butler in that way. (This is a point that Bernard Williams has made by noting that, relative to a particular historical position, certain forms of life are not "real options.")[35] Mr. Stevens is an individual, and he has made his own plan of life: but he hasn't made it arbitrarily. The butler elements in his plan, for example, make sense—to give but two reasons—because there is, first, a career available with that role, a way of making a living; and, second, because his father was a butler before him. (Once again, I don't expect you to find these reasons attractive; but you should find them intelligible.)

As we've seen, a plan of life is not like an engineer's plan. It doesn't map out all the important (and many unimportant) features of our life in advance. These plans are, rather, mutable sets of organizing aims, aims within which you can fit both daily choices and a longer-term vision. Still, there remains a certain lack of clarity to talk of Mr. Stevens's plan of life: what precisely is his plan? Forced to speak in that way, we should say that his plan is to be the best butler he can be, to follow in his father's footsteps, to be a man. But I think it is more natural to say that he plans to live *as* a butler, his father's son, a man, a loyal Englishman. What structures his sense of his life, then, is something less like a blueprint and more like what we nowadays call an "identity."[36] For to speak of *living-as* here is to speak of identities.[37]

Mr. Stevens has constructed for himself an identity as a butler: more specifically as the butler to Lord Darlington and of Darlington Hall and as his father's son. It is an identity in which his gender plays a role (butlers must be men) and in which his nationality is important, too, because in the late 1930s Lord Darlington meddles (rather incompetently, it turns out) in the "great affairs" of the British nation, and it is his service to a man who is serving that nation that gives Mr. Stevens part of his satisfaction.[38] But Ishiguro's character has put these more generic identities—butler, son, man, Englishman—together with other skills and capacities that are more particular, and, in so doing, he has fashioned a self. And . . . the idea of identity already has built into it a recognition of the complex interdependence of self-creation and sociability.

Invention and Authenticity

At this point, it may be helpful to consider two rival pictures of what is involved in shaping one's individuality. One, a picture that comes from romanticism, is the idea of finding one's self—of discovering, by means of reflection or a careful attention to the world, a meaning for one's life that is already there, waiting to be found. This is the vision we can call *authenticity*: it is a matter of being true to who you already really are, or would be if it weren't for distorting influences. "The Soul of Man under Socialism" is one locus classicus of this vision. ("The personality of man . . . will be as wonderful as the personality of a child.") The other picture, the *existentialist* picture, let's call it, is one in which, as the doctrine goes, existence precedes essence: that is, you exist first and then have to decide what to exist *as*, who to be, afterward. On an extreme version of this view, we have to make a self up, as it were out of nothing, like God at the Creation, and individuality is valuable because only a person who has made a self has a life worth living.[39]

But neither of these pictures is right.

The authenticity picture is wrong because it suggests that there is no role for creativity in making a self, that the self is already and in its totality fixed by our natures. Mill was rightly emphatic that we do have such a role, however constrained we are by our nature and circumstances. Man "has, to a certain extent, a power to alter his character," he writes in *A System of Logic*.

> His character is formed by his circumstances (including among these his particular organization); but his own desire to mold it in a particular way, is one of those circumstances, and by no means one of the least influential. We can not, indeed, directly will to be different from what we are. But neither did those who are supposed to have formed our character directly will that we should be what we are. Their will had no direct power except over their own actions. They made us what they did make us, by willing, not the end, but the requisite means; and we, when our habits are not too inveterate, can, by similarly willing the requisite means, make ourselves different. If they could place us under the influence of certain circumstances, we, in like manner, can place ourselves under the influence of other circumstances. We are exactly as capable of making our own character, if we will, as others are of making it for us.[40]

By the same token, the existentialist picture is wrong because it suggests that there is *only* creativity, that there is nothing for us to respond to, nothing out of which to do the construction. "Human nature is not a machine to be built after a model, and set to do exactly the work prescribed for it, but a tree, which requires to grow . . . according to the tendency of the inward forces which make it a living thing," Mill told us. His metaphor makes the constraints apparent: a tree, whatever the circumstances, does not become a legume, a vine, or a cow. The reasonable middle view is that constructing an identity is a good thing (if self-authorship is a good thing) but that the identity must make some kind of sense. And for it to make sense, it must be an identity constructed in response to facts outside oneself, things that are beyond one's own choices.

Some philosophers—Sartre among them—have tried to combine both the romantic and the existentialist views, as Michel Foucault suggested some years ago:

> Sartre avoids the idea of the self as something that is given to us, but through the moral notion of authenticity, he turns back to the idea that we have to be ourselves—to be truly our true self. I think the only acceptable practical consequence of what Sartre has said is to link his theoretical insight to the practice of creativity—and not to that of authenticity. From the idea that the self is not given to us, I think there is only one practical consequence: we have to create ourselves as a work of art.[41]

Now Foucault, in this passage, speaks of creativity without, perhaps, sufficiently acknowledging the role of the materials on which our creativity is exercised. As Charles Taylor notes, "I can define my identity only against the background of things that matter. But to bracket out history, nature, society, the demands of solidarity, everything but what I find in myself, would be to eliminate all candidates for what matters."[42]

Let me propose a thought experiment that might dissuade those who speak of self-choice as the ultimate value. Suppose it were possible, through some sort of instantaneous genetic engineering, to change any aspect of your nature, so that you could have any combination of capacities that has ever been within the range of human possibility: you could have Michael Jordan's fade-away shot, Mozart's musicality, Groucho Marx's comic gifts, Proust's delicate way with language. Suppose you could put these together with any desires you wanted—homo- or hetero-, a taste for Wagner or Eminem. (You might saunter into the metamorphosis chamber whistling the overture to *Die Meistersinger* and strut out murmuring "Will the Real Slim Shady Please Stand Up?") Suppose, further, that there were no careers or professions in this world because all material needs and services were met by intelligent machines. Far from being a Utopia, so it seems to me, this would be a kind of hell. There would be no reason to choose any of these options, because there would be no achievement in putting together a life. One way of explaining why this life would be meaningless comes from Nietzsche:

> *One thing is needful.*—To "give style" to one's character—a great and rare art! It is practiced by those who survey all the strengths and weaknesses of their nature and then fit them into an artistic plan until every one of them appears as art and reason and even weaknesses delight the eye. Here a large mass of second nature has been added; there a piece of original nature has been removed—both times through long practice and daily

> work at it. Here the ugly that could not be removed is concealed;
> there it has been reinterpreted and made sublime.[43]

To create a life is to create a life out of the materials that history has given
you. As we saw, Mill's rhetoric juxtaposes the value of self-authorship with
the value of achieving our capacities, perhaps because the former can seem
arbitrary; but once it is tied to something out of our control, once our self-
construction is seen as a creative response to our capacities and our circumstances, then the accusation of arbitrariness loses its power.

Thinking about the capacities and circumstances that history has, in
fact, given each of us will also allow us to address the worry about the
unsociability of the individuated self, further elaborating on the social dependence we ascribed to Mr. Stevens. The language of identity reminds us
to what extent we are, in Charles Taylor's formulation, "dialogically" constituted. Beginning in infancy, it is in dialogue with other people's understandings of who I am that I develop a conception of my own identity. We
come into the world "mewling and puking in the nurse's arms" (as Shakespeare so genially put it), capable of human individuality but only if we
have the chance to develop it in interaction with others. An identity is always articulated through concepts (and practices) made available to you
by religion, society, school, and state, mediated by family, peers, friends.
Indeed, the very material out of which our identities are shaped is provided, in part, by what Taylor has called our language in "a broad sense,"
comprising "not only the words we speak, but also other modes of expression whereby we define ourselves, including the 'languages' of art, of gesture, of love, and the like."[44] It follows that the self whose choices liberalism celebrates is not a presocial thing—not some authentic inner essence
independent of the human world into which we have grown—but rather
the product of our interaction from our earliest years with others.

As a result, individuality presupposes sociability, not just a grudging
respect for the individuality of others. A free self is a human self, and we
are, as Aristotle long ago insisted, creatures of the πολιζ, social beings. We
are social in many ways and for many reasons: because we desire company, because we depend on one another for survival, because so much
that we care about is collectively created. And the prospect of such sociability was basic to Mill's own ethical vision. "The social feeling of mankind"
was, he thought, "a powerful natural sentiment," and one that formed a
basis for morality:

> The social state is at once so natural, so necessary, and so habit-
> ual to man, that, except in some unusual circumstances or by
> an effort of voluntary abstraction, he never conceives himself
> otherwise than as a member of a body; and this association is
> riveted more and more, as mankind are further removed from
> the state of savage independence. Any condition, therefore,
> which is essential to a state of society, becomes more and more
> an inseparable part of every person's conception of the state of

things which he is born into, and which is the destiny of a
human being. . . . The deeply rooted conception which every
individual even now has of himself as a social being, tends to
make him feel it one of his natural wants that there should be
harmony between his feelings and aims and those of his fellow
creatures. . . . To those who have it, it possesses all the characters of a natural feeling. It does not present itself to their minds
as a superstition of education, or a law despotically imposed by
the power of society, but as an attribute which it would not be
well for them to be without. This conviction is the ultimate sanction of the greatest happiness morality.[45]

And it's worth returning to the point that Mill's conception of happiness or well-being included individuality, freedom, autonomy; that these
had a constitutive, not just an instrumental, relation to it.[46] To value individuality properly just *is* to acknowledge the dependence of the good for
each of us on relationships with others. Without these bonds, as I say, we
could not come to be free selves, not least because we could not come to be
selves at all. Throughout our lives part of the material that we are responding to in shaping our selves is not within us but outside us, out there in the
social world. Most people shape their identities as partners of lovers who
become spouses and fellow parents; these aspects of our identities, though
in a sense social, are peculiar to who we are as individuals, and so represent a *personal* dimension of our identities. But we are all, as well, members
of broader collectivities. To say that *collective* identities—that is, the collective dimensions of our individual identities—are responses to something
outside our selves is to say that they are the products of histories, and our
engagement with them invokes capacities that are not under our control.
Yet they are social not just because they involve others, but because they
are constituted in part by socially transmitted conceptions of how a person
of that identity properly behaves.

The Social Scriptorium

In constructing an identity, one draws, among other things, on the
kinds of person available in one's society. Of course, there is not just *one*
way that gay or straight people or blacks or whites or men or women are to
behave, but there are ideas around (contested, many of them, but all sides
in these contests shape our options) about how gay, straight, black, white,
male, or female people ought to conduct themselves.[47] These notions provide loose norms or models, which play a role in shaping our plans of life.
Collective identities, in short, provide what we might call scripts: narratives that people can use in shaping their projects and in telling their life
stories. . . .

To be sure, an emphasis on how we make sense of our lives, our selves,
through narrative is shared by a number of philosophers—Charles Taylor
and Alasdair MacIntyre among them—who worry that conventional ver-

sions of liberal theory scant the social matrix in which our identities take shape. At the same time, the Millian language of life plans resonates with their insistence that to live our lives as agents requires that we see our actions and experiences as belonging to something like a story.[48] For Charles Taylor, it is "a basic condition of making sense of ourselves" that "we grasp our lives in a narrative"; narrative, then, is not "an optional extra." For Alasdair MacIntyre, it is "because we understand our own lives in terms of the narratives that we live out that the form of narrative is appropriate for understanding the actions of others." As he argues, each of our "shorter-term intentions is, and can only be made, intelligible by reference to some longer-term intentions," and so "behavior is only characterized adequately when we know what the longer and longest term intentions are and how the shorter-term intentions are related to the longer. Once again we are involved in writing a narrative history.[49] Such concerns, as I hope I've established, aren't foreign to the sort of liberalism that Mill, at least, sought to promulgate.

So we should acknowledge how much our personal histories, the stories we tell of where we have been and where we are going, are constructed, like novels and movies, short stories and folktales, within narrative conventions. Indeed, one of the things that popular narratives (whether filmed or televised, spoken or written) do for us is to provide models for telling our lives.[50] At the same time, part of the function of our collective identities — of the whole repertory of them that a society makes available to its members — is to structure possible narratives of the individual self.

Thus, for example, the rites of passage that many societies associate with the identities male and female provide shape to the transition to adulthood; gay identities may organize lives around the narrative of coming out; Pentecostalists are born again; and black identities in America often engage oppositional narratives of self-construction in the face of racism. One thing that matters to people across many societies is a certain narrative unity, the ability to tell a story of one's life that hangs together. The story — my story — should cohere in the way appropriate to a person in my society.[51] It need not be the exact same story, from week to week, or year to year, but how it fits into the wider story of various collectivities matters for most of us. It is not just that, say, gender identities give shape to one's life; it is also that ethnic and national identities fit a personal narrative into a larger narrative. For modern people, the narrative form entails seeing one's life as having a certain arc, as making sense through a life story that expresses who one is through one's own project of self-making. That narrative arc is yet another way in which an individual's life depends deeply on something socially created and transmitted.

I made a distinction earlier between a personal and a collective dimension of identity. Both play a role in these stories of the self. But only the collective identities have scripts, and only they count as what Ian Hacking meant by "kinds of person."[52] There is a logical category but no social category of the witty, or the clever, or the charming, or the greedy. People who share these properties do not constitute a social group. In the relevant sense, they are not a kind of person. In our society (though not, perhaps, in the England of Addison and Steele) being witty does not, for example, suggest the life-script of "the wit." And the main reason why the personal dimensions are different is that they are not dependent on labeling: while intelligence, in our society, is of the first social importance, people could be intelligent even if no one had the concept. To say that race is socially constructed, that an African American is, in Hacking's sense, a "kind of person," is, in part, to say that there are no African Americans independent of social practices associated with the racial label; by contrast, there could certainly be clever people even if we did not have the concept of cleverness.[53] . . .

Ethics in Identity

How does identity fit into our broader moral projects? One view is this: there are many things of value in the world. Their value is objective; they are important whether or not anybody recognizes they are important. But there is no way of ranking these many goods or trading them off against one another, so there is not always, all things considered, a best thing to do. As a result, there are many morally permissible options. One thing identity provides is another source of value, one that helps us make our way among those options. To adopt an identity, to make it mine, is to see it as structuring my way through life. That is, my identity has patterns built into it (so Mill is wrong when he implies that it is always better to be different from others), patterns that help me think about my life; one such simple pattern, for example, is the pattern of a career, which ends, if we live long enough, with retirement.[54] But identities also create forms of solidarity: if I think of myself as an X, then, sometimes, the mere fact that somebody else is an X, too, may incline me to do something with or for them; where X might be "woman," "black," or "American." Now solidarity with those who share your identity might be thought of as, other things being equal, a good thing. As such there is a universal value of solidarity, but it works out in different ways for different people because different people have different identities. Or it might be thought to be a good thing because we enjoy it and, other things being equal, it is good for people to have and to do what they enjoy having and doing.

As we have seen, however, many values are internal to an identity: they are among the values someone who has that identity must take into account, but are not values for people who do not have that identity. Take the value of ritual purity, as conceived of by many orthodox Jews. They think they should keep kosher because they are Jewish; they don't expect anyone who is not a Jew to do so, and they may not even think it would be a good thing if non-Jews did. It is a good thing only for those who are or those who become Jewish: and they do not think that it would be a better world if everybody did become Jewish. The Covenant, after all, is only with the Children of Israel.

Similarly, we might think that your identity as a nationalist in a struggle against colonial domination made it valuable for you to risk your life for the liberation of your country, as Nathan Hale did, regretting that he had only one of them to give. If you were not a nationalist, you might still die advancing a country's cause; and then, while some good might come of it, that good would not be, so to speak, a good for you. We might regard your life as wasted, just because you did not identify with the nation you had died for.

There are thus various ways that identity might be a source of value, rather than being something that realizes other values. First, if an identity is yours, it may determine certain acts of solidarity as valuable, or be an internal part of the specification of your satisfactions and enjoyments, or motivate and give meaning to acts of supererogatory kindness. Indeed, the presence of an identity concept in the specification of my aim—as helping a fellow bearer of some identity—may be part of what explains why I have the aim at all. Someone may gain satisfaction from giving money to the Red Cross after a hurricane in Florida as an act of solidarity with other Cuban Americans. Here the fact of the shared identity is part of why he or she has the aim. By the same token, a shared identity may give certain acts or achievements a value for me they would not otherwise have had. When a Ghanaian team wins the African Cup of Nations in soccer, that is of value to me by virtue of my identity as a Ghanaian. If I were a Catholic, a wedding in a Catholic church might be of value to me in a special way because I was a Catholic.

There are still other ways in which the success of our projects (not to mention our having those projects in the first place) might derive from a social identity. Since human beings are social creatures. Mill writes, they are "familiar with the fact of cooperating with others and proposing to themselves a collective, not an individual interest as the aim (at least for the time being) of their actions. So long as they are cooperating, their ends are identified with those of others; there is at least a temporary feeling that the interests of others are their own interests."[55] Projects and commitments may involve collective intentions, as with a religious ritual that requires the coordinated involvement of one's fellow worshipers for its realization.[56] A social project may involve the creation or re-creation of an identity, in the way that Elijah Muhammad sought to redefine the American Negro's collective self-understanding, or the way that Deaf activists seek to construct a group identity that supervenes upon the condition of deafness. For Theodor Herzl, success depended on creating a sense of national consciousness among a people who might never have conceived themselves (at least in his terms) as belonging to a common nation. But a common pursuit may involve much smaller-scale groups—of twenty, or ten, or two. "When two persons have their thoughts and speculations completely in common; when all subjects of intellectual or moral interest are discussed between them in daily life . . . when they set out from the same principles, and arrive at their conclusions by processes pursued jointly," Mill wrote of the composition of *On Liberty*, "it is of little consequence in respect to the question of originality, which of them holds the pen."[57]

Individuality and the State

The picture of self-development we've been tracing puts identity at the heart of human life. A theory of politics, I am suggesting, ought to take this picture seriously. That alone doesn't settle much in the way of practicalities, but the picture is one that we can develop and explore in trying to negotiate the political world we share. Self-development, as Wendy Donner has shown, is a theme that bridges Mill's ethical, social, and political contributions; but his view that the state has a role to play in such development brings him into conflict with some powerful currents of modern political thought, which insist that the public sphere be neutral among different conceptions of the good.[58] Unlike many contemporary liberals—Rawls, Dworkin, and Nagel, say—Mill made no claim to be a neutralist. "The first element of good government," Mill wrote in *Considerations on Representative Government*, "being the virtue and intelligence of the human beings composing the community, the most important point of excellence which any form of government can possess is to promote the virtue and intelligence of the people themselves."[59]

This is not, to be sure, a terribly *confining* conception of the good and, in Mill's construction of it, was bound to encourage diversity rather than inhibit it. Still, . . . Mill has been charged with playing favorites among religions, because of his emphasis on the fostering of personal autonomy as an appropriate goal of the state: does this not suggest that strong forms of Calvinism, say, will be contemned?[60]

And so *On Liberty* has had a curious legacy among liberal theorists. On the one hand, it has been taken to advocate a sort of nightwatchman state—a strong, my-freedom-ends-at-your-nose form of antipaternalism. On the other, as we've seen, it has been taken to espouse a sectarian conception of the good, and so a vision of the state that was excessively paternalist, intrusive, intolerant. (In Rawlsian terms, it is guilty of advocating a comprehensive, rather than a strictly political, liberalism.) What Isaiah Berlin called "negative liberty"—protection from government intervention in certain areas of our lives—can obviously be an aid in the development of a life of one's own, as Mill believed. But Mill's view of individuality also led him to suppose that we might need not only liberty from the state and society, but also help from state and society to achieve our selves. Isaiah Berlin taught us to call this "positive liberty," and he was deeply (and thoughtfully) skeptical about it: skeptical because, among other things, he thought that in the name of positive liberty, governments had been—and would continue to be—tempted to set out to shape people in the name of the better selves they might become.[61] It is hard to deny that terrible things have been done in the name of freedom, and that some bad arguments have led people from the ideal of emancipation down the path to the Gulag. But, *pace* Berlin, enabling people to construct and live out an identity does not have to go awry.[62]

Recall those words of Mill: "What more or better can be said of any condition of human affairs, than that it brings human beings themselves nearer to the best thing they can be? or what worse can be said of any obstruction to good, than that it prevents this?"[63] He took this to be a goal for governance, not merely a brake on governance. Certainly the author of *On Liberty* wasn't any kind of libertarian; he thought the state should sponsor scientific inquiry, regulate child labor, and restrict the working day for factory workers; require that children be educated; provide poor relief, and so forth.[64] At the same time, it was anathema to him that the government should seek to entrench a single form of life. "If it were only that people have diversities of taste that is reason enough for not attempting to shape them all after one model," he writes. "But different persons also require different conditions for their spiritual development; and can no more exist healthily in the same moral, than all variety of plants can exist in the same physical atmosphere and climate. The same things which are helps to one person towards the cultivation of his higher nature, are hindrances to another." And such are the differences among people that "unless there is a corresponding diversity in their modes of life, they neither obtain their fair share of happiness, nor grow up to the mental, moral, and aesthetic stature of which their nature is capable."[65] Here the idea is that freedom allows people to make the best of themselves. In such passages, it looks as though making the best of oneself entails becoming a kind of person that it is objectively valuable to be—a person of high mental or moral or aesthetic stature—whatever one's chosen plan of life.[66]

In truth, it's not obvious that Mill's "comprehensive" ideals . . . should estrange him from the standard-bearers of modern liberal theory. The ideal of self-cultivation you find in Mill has enjoyed widespread currency; Matthew Arnold enunciated it in *Culture and Anarchy* when he quoted Epictetus's view that "the formation of the spirit and character must be our real concern."[67] But it is most commonly associated with Aristotle, and it remains a powerful strand in political philosophy today. Indeed, what Rawls famously endorsed as "the Aristotelian Principle" was the notion that "other things being equal, human beings enjoy the exercise of their realized capacities, and this enjoyment increases the more the capacity is realized, or the greater its complexity."[68] At the same time. Mill's insistence that self-development should take diversity into account finds kinship with Amartya Sen's "capabilities" approach to equality. "Investigations of equality—theoretical as well as practical—that proceed with the assumption of antecedent uniformity (including the presumption that 'all men are created equal') thus miss out on a major aspect of the problem," Sen has written. "Human diversity is no secondary complication (to be ignored, or to be introduced 'later on'); it is a fundamental aspect of our interest in equality."[69] And . . . Dworkin's "challenge model" of human life, too, has deep affinities with Mill's picture of individuality. In each of these formulations is a version of the ethical idea: that there are things we owe to ourselves.

What my duties to *others* are, of course, remains one of the central questions for liberalism. Making a life as a social being requires making commitments to others. If these are voluntary, it may be proper to enforce them even against my (later) will. But how much does what I owe go beyond my voluntary undertakings? One of Mill's suggestions was, roughly, that what we owed to others, in addition to what we had committed ourselves to, was that we should not harm them; and that leads to interesting discussions about what counts as harm.[70] But it was critical to his vision that the mere fact that I do something you do not want me to do does not *eo ipso* count as my harming you:

> There are many who consider as an injury to themselves any conduct which they have a distaste for, and resent it as an outrage to their feelings. . . . But there is no parity between the feeling of a person for his own opinion, and the feeling of another who is offended at his holding it; no more than between the desire of a thief to take a purse, and the desire of the right owner to keep it. And a person's taste is as much his peculiar concern as his opinion or his purse.[71]

Accordingly, the view that I should be permitted to make whatever life flows from my choices, provided that I give you what I owe you and do you no harm, seems to leave me a wide range of freedom, which is as you'd expect. And yet Mill could appeal to the ideals of both self-authorship and self-development in order to justify state action.

Governments do, for example, provide public education in many countries that helps children who do not yet have any settled identity or projects, hopes, and dreams. This is more than negative liberty, more than government's getting out of the way. You may say that parents could do this; in principle, they could. But suppose they won't or can't? Shouldn't society step in, in the name of individuality, to insist that children be prepared for life as free adults? And, in our society, won't that require them to be able to read? To know the language or languages of their community? To be able to assess arguments, interpret traditions? And even if the parents are trying to provide all these things, isn't there a case to be made that society, through the state, should offer them positive support?[72]

Or take welfare provision. If individuality is a matter of developing a life in response to the materials provided by your capacities and your social world (including the social identities embedded in it), then liberalism seeks a politics that allows people to do this. But there can be obstacles to the realization of our individuality other than the limitations of law. Can people really construct dignified individual lives in a modern world where there is no frontier to conquer, no empty land to cultivate, unless they have certain basic material resources? Can people be said to be free to develop their individuality if they are ill and unable to afford treatment that will, as we say, "free them" from disease?

What holds together the desire to educate children, provide welfare for the poor, and give physical assistance to the handicapped who need it is the idea that assistance of these sorts enables people to develop lives worth living. Berlin wondered who would decide what a life worth living was. As we have seen, Mill had an answer to that question: "If a person possesses any tolerable amount of common sense and experience, his own mode of laying out his existence is best." But can communal institutions really afford to accommodate everyone's "own mode"? . . .

I mentioned just now Mill's celebrated "harm principle"—according to which the only justification for coercion is to prevent someone from harming another—and, though it is often given a libertarian construction, it may actually invite an appreciable amount of governmental intervention. To have autonomy, we must have acceptable choices. We are harmed when deprived of such choices. For Joseph Raz, accordingly, the "autonomy-based principle of freedom is best regarded as providing the moral foundation for the harm principle," and that tenet leads him to a rather expansive interpretation. "To harm a person is to diminish his prospects, to affect adversely his possibilities," Raz maintains. "It is a mistake to think that the harm principle recognizes only the duty of government to prevent loss of autonomy. Sometimes failing to improve the situation of another is harming him"—as when we deny someone what is due him, by, for example, discriminating against a potential employee.[73] Here his position is quite in keeping with Mill's stipulation:

> The most marked cases of injustice . . . are acts of wrongful aggression, or wrongful exercise of power over some one; the next are those which consist in wrongfully withholding from him something which is his due; in both cases, inflicting on him a positive hurt, either in the form of direct suffering, or of the privation of some good which he had reasonable ground, either of a physical or of a social kind, for counting upon.[74]

More generally, if (as Raz suggests) we harm someone by undermining the conditions necessary for the exercise of his or her autonomy (including the social forms in which it takes shape), then the state has considerable, perhaps excessive, latitude for interference.

Mill himself, though he thought the cultivation of individual excellence was central to the role of the state, was hardly impetuous about enlisting state power in the service of this good. He famously held that "there is a circle around every individual which no government . . . ought to be permitted to overstep."[75] And he took seriously the roles played by social approbation and opprobrium as alternate mechanisms for the regulation of behavior. In his essay "Thornton on Labour and Its Claims," he wrote that, outside the realm of moral duty, which must be enforced "compulsively,"

> there is the innumerable variety of modes in which the acts of human beings are either a cause, or a hindrance, of good to their fellow-creatures, but to which it is, on the whole, for the general

> interest that they should be left free; being merely encouraged, by praise and honor, to the performance of such beneficial actions as are not sufficiently stimulated by benefits flowing from them to the agent himself. This larger sphere is that of Merit or Virtue.[76]

And though Mill seems to celebrate an ideal of personal autonomy, he did not generally seek to enlist the coercive powers of the state to foster it, perhaps sensitive to the paradox of relying on an outside power to increase self-reliance. He thought the Mormon polygamous way of life inferior, particularly because of the subordinate role of women in a polygamous system, but so long as the marriages were predicated on consent, he thought they should not be unlawful. As Mill wrote in *On Liberty*, "I am not aware that any community has the right to force another to be civilized."[77]

But state action is not restricted to acts that take the form of prohibitions, of course. In *Principles of Political Economy*, Mill distinguishes "authoritative interference by government"—encompassing the realm of crimes and punishment—from another mode of involvement, in which

> a government, instead of issuing a command and enforcing it by penalties, adopts the course so seldom reverted to by governments, and of which such important use might be made, that of giving advice or promulgating information; and when, leaving individuals free to use their own means of pursuing any object of general interest, the government, not meddling with them, but not trusting the object solely to their care, establishes, side by side with their arrangements, an agency of its own for a like purpose.[78]

And he returned to the point in the fourth chapter of *On Liberty*, when he again abjures the notion that "human beings have no business with each other's conduct in life, and that they should not concern themselves about the well-doing or well-being of one another, unless their own interest is involved." On the contrary, Mill says, "Instead of any diminution, there is need of a great increase of disinterested exertion to promote the good of others. . . . Human beings owe to each other help to distinguish the better from the worse, and encouragement to choose the former and avoid the latter. They should be forever stimulating each other to increased exercise of their higher faculties."[79] But this obligation may not be restricted to individual citizens, and toward the end of *On Liberty*, he acknowledges

> a large class of questions respecting to limits of government interference, which, though closely connected with the subject of this Essay, do not, in strictness, belong to it. These are cases in which the reasons against interference do not turn upon the principle of liberty: the question is not about restraining the actions of individuals, but about helping them: it is asked whether the government should do, or cause to be done, something for their benefit, instead of leaving it to be done by themselves, individually, or in voluntary combination.[80]

This class of "interferences" has proved equally problematic for recent political philosophy. . . .

The Common Pursuit

"As Brutus was called the last of the Romans, Mill wrote of his father, "so was he the last of the eighteenth century."[81] John Stuart himself sought a careful equipoise among the various climates of thought through which he lived: it is what made him both deeply constant and deeply wayward. And yet this very equipoise, this sense of balance, ensured that *On Liberty* would not immediately enjoy the reception that Mill might have hoped for his and Harriet's *grand projet*. "None of my writings have been either so carefully composed, or so sedulously corrected as this," Mill recounted in his *Autobiography*.

> After it had been written as usual twice over, we kept going through it *de novo*, reading, weighing, and criticizing every sentence. Its final revision was to have been a work of the winter of 1858–9, the first after my retirement, which we had arranged to pass in the South of Europe. That hope and every other were frustrated by the most unexpected and bitter calamity of her death—at Avignon, on our way to Montpellier, from a sudden attack of pulmonary congestion.[82]

A few weeks later, Mill sent the manuscript of *On Liberty* to his publisher.

For various reasons, as his biographer points out, the timing of its publication was less than opportune. There were causes both for distraction and for resistance. *The Origin of Species* appeared in the same year, to be enlisted in causes progressive and reactionary; the Oxford movement was in full flower; and various forms of collectivism—whether promulgated by trade unionists or by Christian socialists—were gathering force. Many radicals found Mill's vision disabling; conservatives found it irresponsible and destructive. Sir James Fitzjames Stephen famously took after it with a cudgel: "To attack opinions on which the framework of society rests is a proceeding which both is and ought to be dangerous," he concluded, and he did his part to make it so. The book sent Thomas Carlyle into a choleric lather (though few things did not). "As if it were a sin to control, or coerce into better methods, human swine in any way; Ach Gott in Himmel!"[83]

For the recently bereaved author, of course, the book was as much a mortuary as a monument.

> To us who have known what it is to be with her and to belong to her, this silly phantasmagoria of human life, devoid of her, would be utterly meaningless and unendurably wearisome, were there not still some things to do in it which she wished done, and some public and other objects which she cared for, and in which therefore it is still possible to keep up some degree of interest. . . . I have been publishing some of her opinions, and I hope to employ what remains to me of life (if I am able to retain my

health) in continuing to work for them and to spread them, though with sadly diminished powers now that I no longer have her to prompt and guide me.[84]

In his *Autobiography*, too, he wrote of Harriet's role in his life—of their common pursuits—in terms that are almost the reciprocal of the robust individuality he endorsed.

> My objects in life are solely those which were hers; my pursuits and occupations those in which she shared, or sympathized, and which are indissolubly associated with her. Her memory is to me a religion, and her approbation the standard by which, summing up as it does all worthiness, I endeavor to regulate my life.[85]

It is the language of religious devotion, abjection, heteronomy, self-abnegation; and yet it does not cut against his commitment to individuality so much as it attests to its profoundly social nature. He was attentive to just those forms of collective intention that were omitted from his father's agent-centered view of politics; deprived of the company of his peers as a child, he tirelessly established societies and reviews as a young man, fraternal associations of politics and culture. And the associations that mattered to him, that gave meaning to his endeavors, were not just fraternal. What had been diminished, on his own account, by the loss of his life companion and of their common pursuits was precisely his individuality.

It did not still his pen. The ends of life may have been revisable; they were not, for him, perishable. And Mill himself—object and subject of so many bold experiments, a man whom all manner of visionary, from Bentham to Carlyle to Comte, sought and failed to enlist as a disciple—had a keen sense that influence went only so far, and communion was always incomplete. If no person was whole author of himself, neither could a person be wholly authored by another. "We can not, indeed, directly will to be different from what we are," as he wrote. "But neither did those who are supposed to have formed our character directly will that we should be what we are." Nobody knew better than Mill how one's life plans could be elevated when fused into a common pursuit. Yet at the same time nobody knew better how readily the attempt to promote another's excellence could become an oppression. As he wrote, in words of peculiar resonance:

> Let any man call to mind what he himself felt on emerging from boyhood—from the tutelage and control of even loved and affectionate elders—and entering upon the responsibilities of manhood. Was it not like the physical effect of taking off a heavy weight, or releasing him from obstructive, even if not otherwise painful bonds? Did he not feel twice as much alive, twice as much a human being, as before?[86]

Mill famously celebrated freedom from government and from public opinion: but what we see here is how much he also believed that in the business of making a life—in shaping your individuality—however many common pursuits you have, you must, in the end, find freedom even from the good intentions of those who love you. However social the individuality that Mill prized was, it was, first and last, still individuality: the final responsibility for each life is always the responsibility of the person whose life it is.

NOTES

[1]References to Mill's works will be by title, followed by volume and page number in *The Collected Works of John Stuart Mill*, ed. John M. Robson (Toronto: University of Toronto Press, 1963–91), vols. 1–33 — henceforth *CWM*. Here, I'm quoting from *The Autobiography of John Stuart Mill, CWM* 1:33, 35. Mill also makes it clear that his education was not a matter of knowledge passively acquired.

> Most boys or youths who have had much knowledge drilled into them, have their mental capacities not strengthened but overlaid by it. They are crammed with mere facts, and with the opinions or phrases of other people, and these are accepted as a substitute for the power to form opinions of their own: and thus the sons of eminent fathers, who have spared no pains in their education, so often grow up mere parroters of what they have learnt, incapable of using their minds except in the furrows traced for them. Mine, however, was not an education of cram. My father never permitted anything which I learnt to degenerate into a mere exercise of memory. (21)

[2]Mill, *The Earlier Letters*, 1812–1848, *CWM* 12:30.
[3]Mill, *Autobiography*, *CWM* 1:139.
[4]Ibid., 259.
[5]Mill, *On Liberty*, *CWM* 18:261.
[6]Ibid., 267.
[7]There are those who believe that Mill was always a consistent utilitarian, and who think, therefore, that he must, at bottom, be arguing for some connection between individuality and utility. But there is no general argument in *On Liberty* for such a connection, and Mill speaks here and elsewhere for individuality in ways that are plausible without such a connection. Even if you do assume a connection, it's not clear that the utility function would be doing any work, given that Mill's conception of happiness seems to have encompassed individuality. To possess and exercise the capacity to choose freely isn't valuable simply because it leads to happiness; rather, it seems to be part of what Mill had in mind by happiness. These issues receive careful attention in Fred Berger, *Happiness, Justice, and Freedom: The Moral and Political Philosophy of John Stuart Mill* (Berkeley and Los Angeles: University of California Press, 1984); John Gray, *Mill on Liberty: A Defence* (London: Routledge and Kegan Paul, 1983); and Richard J. Arneson, "Mill versus Paternalism," *Ethics* 90 (July 1980): 470–89. And see n. 45 below.
[8]In *On Liberty*, *CWM* 18 (262, 264), Mill elaborates:

> The human faculties of perception, judgement, discriminative feeling, mental activity, and even moral preference, are exercised only in making a choice. He who does anything because it is the custom makes no choice." A little later, "character" becomes a value term: "A person whose desires and impulses are his own — are the expression of his own nature, as it has been developed and modified by his own culture — is said to have a character. One whose desires and impulses are not his own, has no character, no more than a steam-engine has a character.

[9]Ibid., 270. Mill dates his emphasis on the training of the human being, rather than the "ordering of outward circumstances," to the shifting of his thoughts after the winter of 1826, when "I, for the first time, gave its proper place, among the prime necessities of human well-being, to the internal culture of the individual." Mill, *Autobiography*, *CWM* 1:147.

[10]See Lawrence Haworth's attentive discussion in *Autonomy: An Essay in Philosophical Psychology and Ethics* (New Haven: Yale University Press, 1986), identifying three ways in which autonomy can be associated with Millian individuality:

> Sense 1: if we think of autonomy as a *capacity*, then to have individuality is to have developed that capacity so that it is a realized personality trait. Sense 2: if we think of autonomy as a mode of life, as in 'living autonomously,' then individuality (the developed personality trait) is a necessary condition for autonomy. Sense 3: when we say of someone that 'he is autonomous' we may have in mind that his capacity for autonomy is developed; in such contexts being autonomous and having individuality are synonymous. (Cf. Arneson, "Mill versus Paternalism," 477)

[11]In urging the appeal of individuality, Mill has recourse to a battery of considerations. Some are aesthetic (by cultivating what is individual, "human beings become a noble and beautiful object of contemplation," *On Liberty*, *CWM* 18:266); some are semi-Carlylean (great heroes and geniuses will arise from the muck of mediocrity); and some considerations flow from the straitening effects of custom (the tendency "to maim by compression, like a Chinese lady's foot, every part of human nature which stands out prominently, and tends to make the person markedly dissimilar in outline to commonplace humanity," ibid., 271).

[12]Mill, *A System of Logic*, *CWM* 8:842–43.

[13]John Rawls, *A Theory of Justice* (Cambridge: Harvard University Press, 1971), 408. Here he makes explicit reference to Josiah Royce's *The Philosophy of Loyalty*, where it is used to "characterize the coherent, systematic purposes of the individual, what makes him a conscious, unified moral person" (in Rawls's gloss). . . .

[14]J. L. Mackie, "Can There Be a Right-Based Moral Theory?" in *Ethical Theory* 2: *Theories about How We Should Live*, ed. James Rachels (Oxford: Oxford University Press, 1998), 136; Daniel A. Bell, *Communitarianism and Its Critics* (New York; Oxford University Press, 1993), 6; Michael Slote, *Goods and Virtues* (Oxford: Oxford University Press, 1983), 43–47. Slote's focus is on the use of "plans of life" in recent contributions to liberal philosophy, notably those of David Richards, Charles Fried, and John Cooper.

[15]In *Principles of Political Economy*, *CWM* 3:953–54, Mill writes that an

> exception to the doctrine that individuals are the best judges of their own interest, is when an individual attempts to decide irrevocably now, what will be best for his interest at some future and distant time. The presumption in favor of individual judgment is only legitimate, where the judgment is grounded on actual, and especially on present, personal experience; not where it is formed antecedently to experience, and not suffered to be reversed even after experience has condemned it. When persons have bound themselves by a contract, not simply to do some one thing, but to continue doing something for ever or for a prolonged period, without any power of revoking the engagement, the presumption which their perseverance in that course of conduct would otherwise raise in favor of its being advantageous to them, does not exist; and any such presumption which can be grounded on their having voluntarily entered into the contract, perhaps at an early age, and without any real knowledge of what they undertook, is commonly next to null. The practical maxim of leaving contracts free is not applicable without great limitations in case of engagement in perpetuity; and the law should be extremely jealous of such engagements; should refuse its sanction to them, when the obligations they impose are such as the contracting party cannot be a competent judge of; if it ever does sanction them, it should take every possible security for their being contracted with foresight and deliberation; and in compensation for not permitting the parties themselves to revoke their engagement, should grant them a release from it, on a sufficient case being made out before an impartial authority. These considerations are eminently applicable to marriage, the most important of all cases of engagement for life.

[16]Charles Dickens, *Dombey and Son* (New York: Oxford University Press, 1991), 139.

[17]To be sure, in the course of his love affair with Mrs. Taylor, Mill assayed all sorts of plans, and one of them called for the two to elope and exile themselves, brazening out the ostracism that would result. He would resign himself to being (as he wrote to Harriet in 1835) "obscure & insignificant." This did not go down well with her, and at moments she questioned his own "planfulness": "The most horrible feeling I ever know is when for moments the fear comes over me that *nothing* which you say of yourself is to be absolutely relied on—that you are not sure even of your strongest feelings," she wrote to Mill in September 1833. Bruce Mazlish, *James and John Stuart Mill: Father and Son in the Nineteenth Century* (New York: Basic Books, 1975), 289.

[18]As Mill is careful to stipulate in chapter 3 of *On Liberty, CWM* 18:262:

[I]t would be absurd to pretend that people ought to live as if nothing whatever had been known in the world before they came into it; as if experience had as yet done nothing towards showing that one mode of existence, or of conduct, is preferable to another. Nobody denies that people should be so taught and trained in youth, as to know and benefit by the ascertained results of human experience. . . . The traditions and customs of other people are, to a certain extent, evidence of what their experience has taught them; presumptive evidence, and as such, have a claim to this deference.

[19]Kazuo Ishiguro, *The Remains of the Day* (New York: Knopf, 1989), 199.

[20]Ibid., 228.

[21]Ibid., 245. A measure of Ishiguro's stylistic subtlety is that this last sentence ends with a split infinitive, which would have been avoided by the kind of person Mr. Stevens aspires to be.

[22]Or so Caroline Fox reproduces it in her *Memories of Old Friends*, ed. Horace N. Pym, 2nd ed. (London, 1882); quoted in Charles Larrabee Street, *Individualism and Individuality in the Philosophy of John Stuart Mill* (Milwaukee: Morehouse Publishing, 1926), 41. We can stipulate, on Mill's behalf, that the "highest thing" might be chosen from a set with many members.

[23]Mill, *Utilitarianism, CWM* 10:212.

[24]Ishiguro, *Remains*, 210.

[25]Ibid., 185–86. Mill, it must be said, would not have been wholly out of sympathy with Mr. Stevens's skepticism. "As soon as any idea of equality enters the head of an uneducated English working man, his head is turned by it," Mill wrote. "When he ceases to be servile, he becomes insolent." Mill, *Principles of Political Economy, CWM* 2:109.

[26]Mill, *System of Logic, CWM* 8:942.

[27]Harriet Taylor, Michael St. John Packe tells us, had at one point hoped to be a journalist, a published commentator, like her sometime friend Harriet Martineau. But early in her relationship with Mill, she decided to shelve her own career and focus on promoting his, expressing herself "through her effect on him," as Packe writes. "It was Mill, not she, who was to be the writer; his, not her, development that was important to the world." Michael St. John Packe, *The Life of John Stuart Mill* (New York: Macmillan, 1954), 140. Despite the element of subordination, though, her role as coach and critic was the polar opposite of the servitor's determined equanimity.

[28]Some might object that a failure of genuine autonomy . . . led to this mishap: had he exercised his faculties for critical evaluation more strenuously, he would have been less susceptible to the bad luck of working for a fool. But (as we'll see), some forms of intellectual outsourcing are universal and inevitable, and it can be unreasonable to hold us accountable for assessments we are not competent to make. (Imagine two X-ray crystallographers who take jobs based on their proximity to their homes. One makes a great contribution to human knowledge, because she happens to be working with a team of highly successful molecular biochemists; the other makes very little contribution at all.) Of course, Ishiguro's narrative is powered by the mismatch between the starchy certitudes of Stevens's mind and the actual facts of the world, and we may leave it an open

question, for the moment, whether Stevens's life, or any life so beset, is an example of human flourishing or human failure.

[29]Thomas E. Hill, "Servility and Self-Respect," in *Autonomy and Self-Respect* (Cambridge: Cambridge University Press, 1991).

[30]Ground projects are "a nexus of projects which largely give meaning to life," as glossed in Bernard Williams, "Persons, Character, and Morality," in *Moral Luck* (Cambridge: Cambridge University Press, 1981), 13.

[31]Published 1967; first recorded on the Frank Sinatra album "My Way" (Warner Bros., February 13, 1969), track 6. Words and music by Giles Thibault, Jacques Revaux, and Claude François (originally as "Comme d'Habitude"), English lyrics by Paul Anka. There may be a small parable of globalization in the fact that Claude François was Egyptian-born and Anka was of Lebanese parentage; and some might draw conclusions about the differences between French and Anglo-Saxon concerns from the fact that the original French lyrics are about the routines of an empty love affair.

[32]Even this is a little too quick: there can be . . . two kinds of obligation.

[33]Oscar Wilde, *The Soul of Man under Socialism and Selected Critical Prose*, ed. Linda Dowling (New York: Penguin, 2001), 134. Wilde also had, to be sure, a Nietzschean mode, with which he is more widely associated, prizing self-invention above all.

[34]"I am the last person to undervalue the self-regarding virtues; they are only second in importance, if even second, to the social," Mill writes in chapter 4 of *On Liberty*, *CWM* 18:277. Notice that these sets of virtues can evidently be ranked, even if uncertainly.

[35]Bernard Williams, "The Truth in Relativism," in *Moral Luck*.

[36] . . . I should spell out that here I'm using "identity" in a sense that has gained currency only in the postwar era. There's a much older philosophical discourse on "personal identity," of course, centering on the continuity of an individual over time.

[37]As my colleague Mark Johnston pointed out to me, not all *living-as* involves identities in this way; a closeted homosexual lives as a straight person but does not have a straight identity (or, in the nice example he offered me, the spy Kim Philby lived as a British civil servant, though what he really was—a loyal servant of the Soviet government—meant that this was not his true identity). So, as I say, I am not claiming that talk of someone's "living as an X" always introduces an identity of X. . . .

[38]Ishiguro, *Remains*, 199.

[39]These are labels of convenience: not everyone who invokes authenticity uses it this way, and one of the profoundest critics of what I am calling the "existentialist" view is Nietzsche.

[40]Mill, *System of Logic*, *CWM* 8:840.

[41]Michel Foucault, *Ethics: Subjectivity and Truth* (New York: The New Press, 1998), 262.

[42]Charles Taylor, *The Ethics of Authenticity* (Cambridge: Harvard University Press, 1991), 40. I should note that my stipulative use of "authenticity" is different from Taylor's use of the term, which is meant to take in both the models of discovery and of self-creation.

[43]Friedrich Nietzsche, *The Gay Science*, ed. and trans. Walter Kaufmann (New York: Vintage, 1974), 232.

[44]Charles Taylor, *Multiculturalism: Examining the Politics of Recognition*, ed. Amy Gutmann (Princeton: Princeton University Press, 1994), 32.

[45]Mill continues:

This it is which makes any mind, of well-developed feelings, work with, and not against, the outward motives to care for others, afforded by what I have called the external sanctions; and when those sanctions are wanting, or act in an opposite direction, constitutes in itself a powerful internal binding force, in proportion to the sensitiveness and thoughtfulness of the character; since few but those whose mind is a moral blank, could bear to lay out their course of life on the plan of paying no regard to others except so far as their own private interest compels. (*Utilitarianism*, *CWM* 10:233)

Elsewhere in *Utilitarianism*, he urges that "education and opinion, which have so vast a power over human character, should so use that power as to establish in the mind of every individual an indissoluble association between his own happiness and the good of the whole. (Ibid., 218)

Even before the failure of self-cultivation, "selfishness" was, Mill held, "the principal cause which makes life unsatisfactory," and he inveighed against the notion that there is "an inherent necessity that any human being should be a selfish egotist, devoid of every feeling or care but those which center in his own miserable individuality." Ibid., 215–16. On this issue, see also the discussions in Wendy Donner, *The Liberal Self: John Stuart Mill's Moral and Political Philosophy* (Ithaca: Cornell University Press, 1992), 180, and in Alan Ryan, *The Philosophy of John Stuart Mill*, rev. ed. (Basingstoke: Macmillan, 1987), 200. The salience of the social is another point of affinity that Mill would have had with Wilhelm von Humboldt, whom Charles Taylor aptly describes as both individualist and holist. Immediately after the passage of his that Mill quoted in the opening of the third chapter of *On Liberty*, in *On the Limits of State Action*, ed. J. W. Burrows (Cambridge: Cambridge University Press, 1969), Humboldt wrote:

It is through a social union, therefore, based on the internal wants and capacities of its members, that each is enabled to participate in the rich collective resources of all the others. . . . The effectiveness of all such relations [of friendship, "ordinary love"] as instruments of cultivation, entirely depends on the extent to which the members can succeed in combining their personal independence with the intimacy of the association; for whilst, without this intimacy, one individual cannot sufficiently possess, as it were, the nature of the others, independence is no less essential, in order that each, in being possessed, may be transformed in his own unique way. . . . This individual vigor, then, and manifold diversity, combine themselves in originality. . . . Just as this individuality springs naturally from freedom of action, and the greatest diversity in agents, it tends in turn directly to produce them.

[46]John Gray—in his insightful early work *Mill on Liberty: A Defence*—notes that both the model of discovery and that of choice or creation play a role in Mill's conception of autonomy. So it would be misleading to ask whether autonomous choice is the criterion of the "higher pleasures" or the instrument of them. "[T]his distinction between a criterial and an evidential view of the relations between autonomy and the higher pleasures fails to capture the spirit of Mill's view of the matter," he writes.

There can be no doubt that Mill does take choice-making to be itself a necessary ingredient of happiness and of any higher pleasure: it is a necessary condition of a pleasure being a higher pleasure that it consist in activities that have been chosen after experience of an appropriate range of alternatives. But the sufficient condition of a pleasure's being a higher pleasure is that it expresses the individual nature of the man whose pleasure it is, and this, for the man himself as for others, is a matter of discovery and not of choice. Mill's position here is a complex one. On the one hand, like Aristotle, he affirmed that men were the makers of their own character. On the other hand, there is no doubt that Mill held to the Romantic belief that each has a quiddity or essence which awaits his discovery and which, if he is lucky, he may express in any one of a small number of styles of life. Mill seems, in his complex way, to be treating choice-making as itself partially constitutive of a happy human life and as instrumental to it. (73)

[47]Given Mill's tendency to exalt variety, it's noteworthy that he was inclined to doubt that there was "really any distinction between the highest masculine and the highest feminine character," as he wrote in a letter to Thomas Carlyle (October 1833): "But the women, of all I have known, who possessed the highest measure of what are considered feminine qualities, have combined with them more of the highest *masculine* qualities than I have ever seen in any but one or two men, & those one or two men were also in many respects almost women. I suspect it is the second-rate people of the two sexes that are unlike—the first-rate are alike in both." *The Earlier Letters, 1812–1848, CWM* 12:184.

[48]Of course, it's not just our own life that we narrativize in this way: we do the same to the lives of others. After Lincoln died, Mill wrote to John Elliot Cairns (the author of the

abolitionist tract *Slave Power*): "What I now principally feel is that the death of Lincoln, like that of Socrates, is a worthy end to a noble life, and puts the seal of universal remembrance upon his worth. He has now a place among the great names of history, and one could have wished nothing better for him personally than to die almost, or quite unconsciously, in perhaps the happiest moment of his life. How one rejoices that he lived to know of Lee's surrender." Mill to Cairnes, May 28, 1865, *The Late Letters, 1849–1873*, *CWM* 16:1057.

[49]Taylor, *Authenticity*, 47. Alasdair MacIntyre, *After Virtue: A Study in Moral Theory*, 2nd ed. (Notre Dame: University of Notre Dame Press, 1984), 212, 207–8.

[50]And sometimes characters in fictional narratives muse about how they draw upon fictional narratives. In *Lolita* (New York: Vintage, 1997) Nabokov writes:

> "Never in my life had I confessed so much or received so many confessions," Humbert Humbert recalls of his feigned intimacies with Lolita's mother, whom he is about to wed. "The sincerity and artlessness with which she discussed what she called her 'love-life,' from first necking to connubial catch-as-catch-can, were, ethically, in striking contrast with my glib compositions, but technically the two sets were congeneric since both were affected by the same stuff (soap operas, psychoanalysis, and cheap novelettes) upon which I drew for my characters and she for her mode of expression." (80)

[51]To possess virtue requires "a life that can be conceived and evaluated as a whole," says Alasdair MacIntyre, in his *After Virtue*, 205. We may, of course, reject the demand for a unified self as too stringent, remote from the loose, baggy, and somewhat aleatory nature of life as some of us experience it. In *The Morality of Freedom* (Oxford: Oxford University Press, 1986) Joseph Raz gets it about right when he observes: "An autonomous life is neither necessarily planned nor is it necessarily unified. There is, however, a grain of truth in the view that autonomy gives life a unity. The autonomous person has or is gradually developing a conception of himself, and his actions are sensitive to his past. A person who has projects is sensitive to his past in at least two respects. He must be aware of having the pursuits he has, and he must be aware of his progress in them." (385)

[52]Ian Hacking, "Making Up People," in *Reconstructing Individualism: Autonomy, Individuality, and the Self in Western Thought*, ed. Thomas C. Heller, Morton Sosna, and David E. Wellbery (Stanford: Stanford University Press, 1986), 222–36.

[53]This isn't to say that cleverness isn't a social product; it obviously is. You couldn't be clever if you grew up like Caspar Hauser. Nor is it to say that the social significance of cleverness isn't the result of social practices, attitudes, and shared beliefs.

[54]The "career" concept is fascinatingly traced in Richard Sennett, *The Corrosion of Character* (New York: Norton, 1998).

[55]*Utilitarianism*, *CWM* 10:231.

[56]See, e.g., Robert M. Adams, "Common Projects and Moral Virtue," *Midwest Studies in Philosophy* 13 (1988): 297–307; Nancy Sherman, "The Virtues of Common Pursuit," *Philosophy and Phenomenological Research* 53, no. 2 (June 1993): 277–99; and Michael Bratman, "Shared Cooperative Activities," *Philosophical Review* 101, no. 2 (April 1992): 327–41, and "Shared Intention," *Ethics* 104 (1993): 97–113; and Margaret Gilbert, *Living Together* (Lanham, MD: Rowman and Littlefield, 1996).

[57]Mill, *Autobiography*, *CWM* 1:251.

[58]See Wendy Donner's persuasive charting of the theme of development in Mill, in her *Liberal Self*.

[59]*Considerations on Representative Government*, *CWM* 19:390; and see Donner, *Liberal Self*, 126.

[60]See, for example, Bhikhu Parekh, *Rethinking Multiculturalism* (Cambridge: Harvard University Press, 2000), 44, and Martha Nussbaum, "A Plea for Difficulty," in Susan Moller Okin, *Is Multiculturalism Bad for Women?*, ed. Joshua Cohen, Matthew Howard, and Martha C. Nussbaum (Princeton: Princeton University Press, 1999), 111. (We may put aside, for the nonce, the familiar objection that the putative neutralists aren't neutral, by this exacting standard.)

[61]Isaiah Berlin, "Two Concepts of Liberty" in *Four Essays on Liberty* (Oxford: Oxford University Press, 1969), 118–72.

[62]Of course, Berlin didn't say it *had* to go awry. My *"pace"* here is meant only to acknowledge his anxiety that it might go awry.

[63]Mill, *On Liberty*, CWM 18:267. In his 1983 *Defence* (in contrast to his later position), Gray argued that "Mill's conception of the good life may be perfectionist in the sense that it ranks lives which are in large measure self-chosen over those that are customary, but this is a procedural perfectionism rather than a full theory of the good life. In weighting autonomy and security heavily in any scheme of human welfare, and giving priority to autonomy once certain conditions have been established, Mill does work with what Rawls has termed a thin theory of the good—a minimalist conception of human welfare expressed in terms of a theory of vital interests or primary goods." Gray, *Defence*, 88.

[64]In *Principles of Political Economy, CWM* 3:803–4, he advances a principle of expediency:

> There is a multitude of cases in which governments, with general approbation, assume powers and execute functions for which no reason can be assigned except the simple one, that they conduce to general convenience. We may take as an example, the function (which is a monopoly too) of coining money. This is assumed for no more recondite purpose than that of saving to individuals the trouble, delay, and expense of weighing and assaying. No one, however, even of those most jealous of state interference, has objected to this as an improper exercise of the powers of government. Prescribing a set of standard weights and measures is another instance. Paving, lighting, and cleansing the streets and thoroughfares, is another; whether done by the general government, or, as is more usual, and generally more advisable, by a municipal authority. Making or improving harbors, building lighthouses, making surveys in order to have accurate maps and charts, raising dykes to keep the sea out, and embankments to keep rivers in, are cases in point.

And a little later:

> Examples might be indefinitely multiplied without intruding on any disputed ground. But enough has been said to show that the admitted functions of government embrace a much wider field than can easily be included within the ringfence of any restrictive definition, and that it is hardly possible to find any ground of justification common to them all, except the comprehensive one of general expediency; nor to limit the interference of government by any universal rule, save the simple and vague one, that it should never be admitted but when the case of expediency is strong.

[65]Mill, *On Liberty, CWM* 18:270.

[66]In *A System of Logic* (*CWM* 8) Mill even identified something he called "the Art of Life," which, he said, had "three departments":

> Morality, Prudence or Policy, and Aesthetics; the Right, the Expedient, and the Beautiful or Noble, in human conduct and works. To this art (which, in the main, is unfortunately still to be created), all other arts are subordinate; since its principles are those which must determine whether the special aim of any particular art is worthy and desirable, and what is its place in the scale of desirable things. Every art is thus a joint result of laws of nature disclosed by science, and of the general principles of what has been called Teleology, or the Doctrine of Ends. (949)

Charles Larrabee Street (in Street, *Individualism*, 49) comments, "And yet at other times Mill saw clearly enough that there was a certain incommensurability among values. His famous admission of qualitative distinction between pleasures, damaging as it was to his own system, is an indication of this." The diagnosis adumbrates Berlin's, though Street's book appeared in 1926.

[67]Matthew Arnold, *Culture and Anarchy*, ed. Samuel Lipman (New Haven: Yale University Press, 1994), 36.

[68]Rawls, *A Theory of Justice*, 424.

[69]Amartya Sen, *Inequality Reexamined* (Cambridge: Harvard University Press, 1992), xi.

[70]These issues are extensively discussed in Joel Feinberg's *Harm to Others* (New York: Oxford University Press, 1984).

[71]*On Liberty*, CWM 18:283. Here, Mill makes it clear that his version of utilitarianism recognizes incommensurability. Amartya Sen reads a "vector view of utility" in such passages; see Sen, "Plural Utility," *Proceedings of the Aristotelian Society* 81 (1982): 196–97.

[72]Mill held that the state should require and subsidize education, but not provide it, probably because in his day, state education essentially meant sectarian education, under the tutelage of the established church. See John Kleinig, *Paternalism* (Totowa: Rowman & Allanheld, 1984), 34.

[73]See Raz, *Morality of Freedom*, 400, 410, 414, 415–16.

[74]Mill, *Utilitarianism*, CWM 10:256. And see Donner, *Liberal Self*, 164.

[75]Mill, *Principles of Political Economy*, CWM 3:937. It may be worth quoting his position here more fully:

> It is evident, even at first sight, that the authoritative form of government inter-vention has a much more limited sphere of legitimate action than the other. It re-quires a much stronger necessity to justify it in any case; while there are large de-partments of human life from which it must be unreservedly and imperiously excluded. Whatever theory we adopt respecting the foundation of the social union, and under whatever political institutions we live, there is a circle around every individual human being which no government, be it that of one, of a few, or of the many, ought to be permitted to overstep; there is a part of the life of every person who has come to years of discretion, within which the individual-ity of that person ought to reign uncontrolled either by any other individual or by the public collectively. That there is, or ought to be, some space in human ex-istence thus entrenched around, and sacred from authoritative intrusion, no one who professes the smallest regard to human freedom or dignity will call in ques-tion: the point to be determined is, where the limit should be placed; how large a province of human life this reserved territory should include. I apprehend that it ought to include all that part which concerns only the life, whether inward or outward, of the individual, and does not affect the interests of others, or affects them only through the moral influence of example. With respect to the domain of the inward consciousness, the thoughts and feelings, and as much of external conduct as is personal only, involving no consequences, none at least of a painful or injurious kind, to other people; I hold that it is allowable in all, and in the more thoughtful and cultivated often a duty, to assert and promulgate, with all the force they are capable of, their opinion of what is good or bad, admirable or con-temptible, but not to compel others to conform to that opinion; whether the force used is that of extra-legal coercion, or exerts itself by means of the law. (937–38)

[76]CWM 5:634. See discussions in Gray, *Defence*, 64, and Street, *Individualism*, 50.

[77]*On Liberty*, CWM 18:291. On the other hand, Mill also wrote that there are "condi-tions of society in which a vigorous despotism is in itself the best mode of government for training the people in what is specifically wanting to render them capable of a higher civ-ilization." Mill, *Considerations on Representative Government*, in CWM 19:567. At such mo-ments, we hear not the liberal but the chief examiner of India House, the paragovernmen-tal body in charge of British India and his employer for four decades. For a reading of Mill that focuses on these imperial strains, see Uday Singh Mehta, *Liberalism and Empire* (Chicago: University of Chicago Press, 1999), 97–106. There's an interesting paradox here; following Comte, he worries that a high degree of individuality is inconsistent with a high degree of civilization; so that societies that qualify for political autonomy are pre-cisely those that have, in some measure, sacrificed personal autonomy.

[78]Mill, *Principles of Political Economy*, CWM 3:937.

[79]*On Liberty*, CWM 18:277, Cf. the thoughtful discussion of Mill on the self-regarding/other-regarding distinction in Kleinig, *Paternalism*, 32–37.

[80]*On Liberty*, CWM 18:305.

[81]Mill, *Autobiography*, CWM 1:213.

[82]Ibid., 249.

[83]Packe, *The Life*, 405.

[84]Letter to Arthur Hardy, May 14, 1859, quoted in Packe, *The Life*, 409.

[85]*Autobiography*, CWM 1:251.

[86]John Stuart Mill and Harriet Taylor, *Essays on Sex Equality*, ed. Alice S. Rossi (Chicago: University of Chicago Press, 1970), 236; quoted in Mazlish, *James and John*, 342.

•　•　•　•　•　•　•　•　•　•　•　•

QUESTIONS FOR A SECOND READING

1. "The Ethics of Individuality" is the first chapter in Appiah's book *The Ethics of Identity*. The chapter, which we are inviting you to read as an essay, is organized—or punctuated—by subheadings. You might think of these as a way of *punctuating* the essay. The subheadings are collected in a group and listed just below the title. (And this is how it appears in the original.)

   As you reread the essay, pay attention to each unit marked off by a subheading, and pay attention to the progression or the arrangement of these units. How might they mark stages or strategies for the writer? For the reader? (Are they BIG paragraphs, for example, or mini-essays, or stanzas, or something else?) How might you describe the principle of selection and organization? Can you imagine bringing this strategy into your own writing?

2. In the preface to *The Ethics of Identity*, Appiah says that his book is not for those who are "looking for practical guidance." He says,

   > Alas, I am a poor physician: I'm interested in diagnosis—in etiology and nosology—but not in cures. If an agenda, a set of action items, is what you are after, my one bit of practical advice is that you look elsewhere.
   >   What's on offer here, indeed, is more in the spirit of exploration than of conclusion. (xvii)

   As you reread "The Ethics of Individuality," do so in order to present an account of an act of writing conducted "more in the spirit of exploration than of conclusion." Can you prepare an outline or a chart or a plan to represent what goes on in this essay? If you were going to teach someone to write in such a spirit, what pages, paragraphs, or moments in the essay would you point to as key or central to Appiah's project? How would you describe the body of the essay if it is not constructing an argument? How would you describe its ending, if (in fact) it is something other than a conclusion?

3. Footnotes, it is sometimes said, are where the real action is in scholarly writing. Footnotes or endnotes—these are where you find the jokes, the fights, the confessions, the second thoughts, the interesting subtexts to the drama unfolding on stage or in the arena. As you reread, pay particular attention to what is going on in the endnotes. What do they say about Appiah as a scholar and a writer? What is he doing in these additions to the text? What

conclusions might you draw—or, better yet, what lesson might you learn—about scholarly writing and scholarly work?

4. "The Ethics of Individuality" is by and large a friendly, generous, and inviting text. You learn a lot about John Stuart Mill and about Kazuo Ishiguro's novel *The Remains of the Day*. Still, Appiah makes several brief references to ideas and figures that, while instantly recognizable to some of his readers, may not be recognizable to you. Benthamite principles. Buridan's ass. Bernard Williams's famous analysis of "moral luck." Existentialism. πολιζ. Michel Foucault. Jules Pfeiffer. Individually, or in groups, choose some of these references that seem to you to be most interesting, suggestive, or important, and do the homework necessary to be able to provide a gloss (or to prepare a glossary). Prepare a brief explanation, but also a way of understanding how the reference functions in terms of Appiah's way of thinking things through at that point in the text.

ASSIGNMENTS FOR WRITING

1. In the preface to *The Ethics of Identity*, Appiah says that his book is offered "more in the spirit of exploration than of conclusion." (See preceding Questions for a Second Reading 1 and 2.) The style and method of "The Ethics of Individuality" provide an enactment of writing in such a spirit. For this assignment, we'd like you to carry out such a project, with Appiah's text as your guide and model. You should begin, that is, by talking about Kwame Anthony Appiah and passages from "The Ethics of Individuality," just as Appiah begins by talking about John Stuart Mill and key passages from his work—passages, that is, that are important to the writer. You should turn, then, to some example of an individual life from film or literature or television, just as Appiah turns to the example of Mr. Stevens, the butler in Kazuo Ishiguro's novel *The Remains of the Day*. Use subheadings to organize or punctuate your essay; you needn't use as many as Appiah, nor do you need to write an essay quite as long, but you should feel free to use the same terms if and when they can be strategically helpful to you: "Plans of Life," "Invention and Authenticity," "Ethics in Identity." You are conducting a parallel project, in other words, one written from your perspective. You are writing from a similar concern to better understand individuality and, to put it more loosely than you need to, what the individual owes the self and others.

2. When we have taught this essay, "The Ethics of Individuality," our students tended to forget or to ignore or to tune out the final subheaded sections: "The Social Scriptorium," "Ethics in Identity," "Individuality and the State," and "The Common Pursuit." It was easier (or more pleasant) to think about the individual; it was harder (or less pleasant) to think about the "State" and "common" pursuits.

   There is reason, we believe, to go back to reread those sections with particular attention. What is Appiah doing there? What is he getting at? Why are these moves (in this essay) important? For this assignment, write an essay that addresses these questions and that works closely with the final sections of his essay. Although Appiah makes it clear that he is more interested in exploration than conclusion, that he is not providing "practical advice," you can turn your essay toward an argument or a plan of action if you choose. (And if you do, think carefully about your audience. To whom is your essay addressed?)

3. Plans of life. Social choices. Career choices. "We wish to ace our gross anatomy exam, but don't wish to study for it on this sunny afternoon." Sound familiar?

    While this essay, "The Ethics of Individuality," is written by a philosopher for an adult and academic audience, there is much in it that draws immediately upon the concerns of college students (and their parents) and much that echoes conversations with which you most certainly are familiar. What do you owe your family? What do you owe yourself? What do you owe your race or your gender or your class position or your region or your religious group or your sport or your fraternity or sorority and so on? In Appiah's terms, what "scripts" are offered to you in your project of "self-making"?

    For this assignment, write an essay in which you think back and forth between the urgings and the advice—the ways of thinking about "plans of life"—that are a part of your world, a part of the common thinking for you and for your generation (or for people like you) and the concerns and the thought in Appiah's "The Ethics of Individuality." To what uses might this essay be put? What does it have to offer? What, from your point of view, does it miss or just not understand?

4. At one point, Appiah says:

    > So we should acknowledge how much our personal histories, the stories we tell of where we have been and where we are going, are constructed, like novels and movies, short stories and folktales, within narrative conventions. Indeed, one of the things that popular narratives (whether filmed or televised, spoken or written) do for us is to provide models for telling our lives. At the same time, part of the function of our collective identities—of the whole repertory of them that a society makes available to its members—is to structure possible narratives of the individual self. (73)

    Write an essay in which you present in some detail one or (at most) two of the stories you tell yourself about where you have been and where you are going. And think about these in relation to the models that you are given by our contemporary culture, whether filmed or televised, spoken or written, to use Appiah's language, models drawn from the "whole repertory . . . a society makes available to its members" in order to "structure possible narratives of the individual self." How do you choose? What makes a script possible or powerful? And how, in Appiah's terms, do you understand the "ethics" of all this?

MAKING CONNECTIONS

1. At a key point in his essay, "The Ethics of Individuality," Appiah turns strategically to Kazuo Ishiguro's novel *The Remains of the Day* to provide an example, a "helpful illustration of individuality." He says, "because Mill

speaks abstractly, it may help to imagine a more concrete example." And the example of the butler, a man who defines himself in service to others, is helpful because it is an *unlikely* example, something to think about or to think *with* rather than something to confirm what we already know and believe; the example of the butler does not fit the ways we usually think about the individual or about individuality and, so, it is useful.

Several selections in *Ways of Reading* might provide useful examples in an essay that would apply or extend Appiah's work in "The Ethics of Individuality." We'll give the author's names: Anzaldúa, Jacobs, Rodriguez, Walker, Wideman. Choose one and write an essay that takes both its shape and its inspiration from Appiah's example.

Begin by talking about Kwame Anthony Appiah and passages from "The Ethics of Individuality," just as Appiah begins by talking about John Stuart Mill and key passages from his work—passages, that is, that are important to the writer. You should then present the example from the selection you have chosen. You might use subheadings to organize or punctuate your essay; you needn't use as many as Appiah, nor do you need to write an essay quite as long, but you should feel free to use the same terms if and when they can be strategically helpful to you: "Plans of Life," "Invention and Authenticity," "Ethics in Identity." You are conducting a parallel project, in other words, one written from your perspective. You are writing from a similar concern to better understand individuality and, to put it more loosely than you need to, what the individual owes the self and others.

2. In the second half of his essay, Appiah turns to discuss "collective identities." He says:

> To say that *collective* identities—that is, the collective dimensions of our individual identities—are responses to something outside our selves is to say that they are the products of histories, and our engagement with them invokes capacities that are not under our control. Yet they are social not just because they involve others, but because they are constituted in part by socially transmitted conceptions of how a person of that identity properly behaves. (72)

The subheadings of the sections that follow mark the essay's concern with the social nature of identity: "The Social Scriptorium," "Ethics in Identity," "Individuality and the State," and "The Common Pursuit."

A number of selections in *Ways of Reading* think through the question of the social (and historical and political) nature of identity. Susan Bordo and Adrienne Rich provide particularly powerful examples of how we come to think about gender—about "socially transmitted conceptions of how a person . . . properly behaves" as a man or as a woman.

Read one (or both if you choose), and read it (them) with your own case in mind, as though the essay(s) were addressed to you. And reread Appiah's essay, similarly, with a sense of where and how and to what degree he is talking about you and about how you have learned to tell the story of who you are and what you will become. Write an essay in which you present your case as both an example and a way of responding to what you have read. Appiah, Bordo, and/or Rich (their thoughts and passages of their prose) should appear in your essay as ways of thinking about the example you provide.

JOHN
BERGER

JOHN BERGER (b. 1926), like few other art critics, elicits strong and contradictory reactions to his writing. He has been called (sometimes in the same review) "preposterous" as well as "stimulating," "pompous" yet "exciting." He has been accused of falling prey to "ideological excesses" and of being a victim of his own "lack of objectivity," but he has been praised for his "scrupulous" and "cogent" observations on art and culture. He is one of Europe's most influential Marxist critics, yet his work has been heralded and damned by leftists and conservatives alike. Although Berger's work speaks powerfully, its tone is quiet, thoughtful, measured. According to the poet and critic Peter Schjeldahl, "The most mysterious element in Mr. Berger's criticism has always been the personality of the critic himself, a man of strenuous conviction so loath to bully that even his most provocative arguments sit feather-light on the mind."

The first selection is Chapter 1 from Ways of Seeing, *a book which began as a series on BBC television. In fact, the show was a forerunner of those encyclopedic television series later popular on public television stations in the United States:* Civilization, The Ascent of Man, Cosmos, The Civil War. *Berger's show was less glittery and ambitious, but in its way it was more serious in its claims to be educational. As you watched the screen, you saw a series of images (like those in the following text). These were sometimes presented with commentary, but sometimes in silence, so that you constantly saw one image in the context of another—for example, classic presentations of women in oil paintings interspersed with images of women from contemporary art, advertising, movies, and "men's magazines." The goal of the exercise, according to Berger, was to "start a process of questioning," to focus his viewer's attention not on a single painting in isolation but on "ways of seeing" in general, on the ways we have learned to look at and understand the images that surround us, and on the culture that teaches us to see things as we do. The method of* Ways of Seeing, *a book of art history, was used by Berger in another book,* A Seventh Man, *to document the situation of the migrant worker in Europe.*

After the chapter from Ways of Seeing, *we have added two brief passages from a beautiful, slight, and quite compelling book by Berger,* And Our Faces, My Heart, Brief as Photos. *This book is both a meditation on time and space and a long love letter (if you can imagine such a combination!). At several points in the book, Berger turns his (and his reader's) attention to paintings. We have included two instances, his descriptions of Rembrandt's* Woman in Bed *and Caravaggio's* The Calling of St. Matthew *(and we have included reproductions of the paintings). We offer these as supplements to* Ways of Seeing, *as additional examples of how a writer turns images into words and brings the present to the past.*

Berger has written poems, novels, essays, and film scripts, including The Success and Failure of Picasso *(1965),* A Fortunate Man *(1967),* G. *(1971), and* About Looking *(1980). He lived and worked in England for years, but he currently lives in Quincy, a small peasant village in Haute-Savoie, France, where he wrote, over the course of several years, a trilogy of books on peasant life, titled* Into Their Labours. *The first book in the series,* Pig Earth *(1979), is a collection of essays, poems, and stories set in Haute-Savoie. The second,* Once in Europa *(1987), consists of five peasant tales that take love as their subject. The third and final book in the trilogy,* Lilac and Flag: An Old Wives' Tale of the City *(1990), is a novel about the migration of peasants to the city. His most recent books are* Photocopies, *a collection of short stories (1996);* King: A Street Story, *a novel (1999);* I Send You This Cadmium Red: A Correspondence between John Berger and John Christie *(2000); two essay collections,* The Shape of the Pocket *(2001) and* Selected Essays *(2001);* Here Is Where We Meet: A Fiction *(2005), a series of autobiographical vignettes; and* Hold Everything Dear: Dispatches on Survival and Resistance *(2007), a meditation on political resistance.*

Ways of Seeing

Seeing comes before words. The child looks and recognizes before it can speak.

But there is also another sense in which seeing comes before words. It is seeing which establishes our place in the surrounding world; we explain that world with words, but words can never undo the fact that we are surrounded by it. The relation between what we see and what we know is never settled. Each evening we *see* the sun set. We *know* that the earth is turning away from it. Yet the knowledge, the explanation, never quite fits the sight. The Surrealist painter Magritte commented on this always-present gap between words and seeing in a painting called *The Key of Dreams*.

The way we see things is affected by what we know or what we believe. In the Middle Ages when men believed in the physical existence of Hell the sight of fire must have meant something different from what it means today. Nevertheless their idea of Hell owed a lot to the sight of fire consuming and the ashes remaining—as well as to their experience of the pain of burns.

When in love, the sight of the beloved has a completeness which no words and no embrace can match: a completeness which only the act of making love can temporarily accommodate.

The Key of Dreams by Magritte [1898–1967].

Yet this seeing which comes before words, and can never be quite covered by them, is not a question of mechanically reacting to stimuli. (It can only be thought of in this way if one isolates the small part of the process which concerns the eye's retina.) We only see what we look at. To look is an act of choice. As a result of this act, what we see is brought within our reach—though not necessarily within arm's reach. To touch something is to situate oneself in relation to it. (Close your eyes, move round the room and notice how the faculty of touch is like a static, limited form of sight.) We never look at just one thing; we are always looking at the relation between things and ourselves. Our vision is continually active, continually moving, continually holding things in a circle around itself, constituting what is present to us as we are.

Soon after we can see, we are aware that we can also be seen. The eye of the other combines with our own eye to make it fully credible that we are part of the visible world.

If we accept that we can see that hill over there, we propose that from that hill we can be seen. The reciprocal nature of vision is more fundamental than that of spoken dialogue. And often dialogue is an attempt to verbalize this—an attempt to explain how, either metaphorically or literally, "you see things," and an attempt to discover how "he sees things."

In the sense in which we use the word in this book, all images are manmade [see below]. An image is a sight which has been recreated or reproduced. It is an appearance, or a set of appearances, which has been detached from the place and time in which it first made its appearance and

preserved—for a few moments or a few centuries. Every image embodies a way of seeing. Even a photograph. For photographs are not, as is often assumed, a mechanical record. Every time we look at a photograph, we are aware, however slightly, of the photographer selecting that sight from an infinity of other possible sights. This is true even in the most casual family snapshot. The photographer's way of seeing is reflected in his choice of subject. The painter's way of seeing is reconstituted by the marks he makes on the canvas or paper. Yet, although every image embodies a way of seeing, our perception or appreciation of an image depends also upon our own way of seeing. (It may be, for example, that Sheila is one figure among twenty; but for our own reasons she is the one we have eyes for.)

Images were first made to conjure up the appearance of something that was absent. Gradually it became evident that an image could outlast what it represented; it then showed how something or somebody had once looked—and thus by implication how the subject had once been seen by other people. Later still the specific vision of the image-maker was also recognized as part of the record. An image became a record of how X had seen Y. This was the result of an increasing consciousness of individuality, accompanying an increasing awareness of history. It would be rash to try to date this last development precisely. But certainly in Europe such consciousness has existed since the beginning of the Renaissance.

No other kind of relic or text from the past can offer such a direct testimony about the world which surrounded other people at other times. In this respect images are more precise and richer than literature. To say this is not to deny the expressive or imaginative quality of art, treating it as mere documentary evidence; the more imaginative the work, the more profoundly it allows us to share the artist's experience of the visible.

Yet when an image is presented as a work of art, the way people look at it is affected by a whole series of learnt assumptions about art. Assumptions concerning:

> Beauty
> Truth
> Genius
> Civilization
> Form
> Status
> Taste, etc.

Many of these assumptions no longer accord with the world as it is. (The world-as-it-is is more than pure objective fact, it includes consciousness.) Out of true with the present, these assumptions obscure the past. They mystify rather than clarify. The past is never there waiting to be discovered, to be recognized for exactly what it is. History always constitutes the relation between a present and its past. Consequently fear of the present leads to mystification of the past. The past is not for living in; it is a well of conclusions from which we draw in order to act. Cultural mystification of the past entails a double loss. Works of art are made unnecessarily remote. And the past offers us fewer conclusions to complete in action.

When we "see" a landscape, we situate ourselves in it. If we "saw" the art of the past, we would situate ourselves in history. When we are prevented from seeing it, we are being deprived of the history which belongs to us. Who benefits from this deprivation? In the end, the art of the past is being mystified because a privileged minority is striving to invent a history which can retrospectively justify the role of the ruling classes, and such a justification can no longer make sense in modern terms. And so, inevitably, it mystifies.

Regents of the Old Men's Alms House by Hals [1580–1666].

Regentesses of the Old Men's Alms House by Hals [1580–1666].

Let us consider a typical example of such mystification. A two-volume study was recently published on Frans Hals.[1] It is the authoritative work to date on this painter. As a book of specialized art history it is no better and no worse than the average.

The last two great paintings by Frans Hals [p. 100] portray the Governors and the Governesses of an Alms House for old paupers in the Dutch seventeenth-century city of Haarlem. They were officially commissioned portraits. Hals, an old man of over eighty, was destitute. Most of his life he had been in debt. During the winter of 1664, the year he began painting these pictures, he obtained three loads of peat on public charity, otherwise he would have frozen to death. Those who now sat for him were administrators of such public charity.

The author records these facts and then explicitly says that it would be incorrect to read into the paintings any criticism of the sitters. There is no evidence, he says, that Hals painted them in a spirit of bitterness. The author considers them, however, remarkable works of art and explains why. Here he writes of the Regentesses:

> Each woman speaks to us of the human condition with equal importance. Each woman stands out with equal clarity against the *enormous* dark surface, yet they are linked by a firm rhythmical arrangement and the subdued diagonal pattern formed by their heads and hands. Subtle modulations of the *deep*, glowing blacks contribute to the *harmonious fusion* of the whole and form an *unforgettable contrast* with the *powerful* whites and vivid flesh tones where the detached strokes reach *a peak of breadth and strength*. [Berger's italics]

The compositional unity of a painting contributes fundamentally to the power of its image. It is reasonable to consider a painting's composition. But here the composition is written about as though it were in itself the emotional charge of the painting. Terms like *harmonious fusion, unforgettable contrast*, reaching *a peak of breadth and strength* transfer the emotion provoked by the image from the plane of lived experience, to that of disinterested "art appreciation." All conflict disappears. One is left with the unchanging "human condition," and the painting considered as a marvellously made object.

Very little is known about Hals or the Regents who commissioned him. It is not possible to produce circumstantial evidence to establish what their relations were. But there is the evidence of the paintings themselves: the evidence of a group of men and a group of women as seen by another man, the painter. Study this evidence and judge for yourself.

The art historian fears such direct judgement:

> As in so many other pictures by Hals, the penetrating characterizations almost seduce us into believing that we know the personality traits and even the habits of the men and women portrayed.

What is this "seduction" he writes of? It is nothing less than the paintings working upon us. They work upon us because we accept the way Hals saw

his sitters. We do not accept this innocently. We accept it in so far as it corresponds to our own observation of people, gestures, faces, institutions. This is possible because we still live in a society of comparable social relations and moral values. And it is precisely this which gives the paintings their psychological and social urgency. It is this — not the painter's skill as a "seducer" — which convinces us that we *can* know the people portrayed.

The author continues:

> In the case of some critics the seduction has been a total success. It has, for example, been asserted that the Regent in the tipped slouch hat, which hardly covers any of his long, lank hair, and whose curiously set eyes do not focus, was shown in a drunken state. [p. 103]

This, he suggests, is a libel. He argues that it was a fashion at that time to wear hats on the side of the head. He cites medical opinion to prove that the Regent's expression could well be the result of a facial paralysis. He insists that the painting would have been unacceptable to the Regents if one of them had been portrayed drunk. One might go on discussing each of these points for pages. (Men in seventeenth-century Holland wore their hats on the side of their heads in order to be thought of as adventurous and pleasure-loving. Heavy drinking was an approved practice. Etcetera.) But such a discussion would take us even farther away from the only confrontation which matters and which the author is determined to evade.

In this confrontation the Regents and Regentesses stare at Hals, a destitute old painter who has lost his reputation and lives off public charity; he examines them through the eyes of a pauper who must nevertheless try to be objective; i.e., must try to surmount the way he sees as a pauper. This is the drama of these paintings. A drama of an "unforgettable contrast."

Mystification has little to do with the vocabulary used. Mystification is the process of explaining away what might otherwise be evident. Hals was the first portraitist to paint the new characters and expressions created by capitalism. He did in pictorial terms what Balzac did two centuries later in literature. Yet the author of the authoritative work on these paintings sums up the artist's achievement by referring to

> Hals's unwavering commitment to his personal vision, which enriches our consciousness of our fellow men and heightens our awe for the ever-increasing power of the mighty impulses that enabled him to give us a close view of life's vital forces.

That is mystification.

In order to avoid mystifying the past (which can equally well suffer pseudo-Marxist mystification) let us now examine the particular relation which now exists, so far as pictorial images are concerned, between the present and the past. If we can see the present clearly enough, we shall ask the right questions of the past.

Today we see the art of the past as nobody saw it before. We actually perceive it in a different way.

This difference can be illustrated in terms of what was thought of as perspective. The convention of perspective, which is unique to European art and which was first established in the early Renaissance, centers everything on the eye of the beholder. It is like a beam from a lighthouse—only instead of light traveling outwards, appearances travel in. The conventions called those appearances *reality*. Perspective makes the single eye the center of the visible world. Everything converges on to the eye as to the vanishing point of infinity. The visible world is arranged for the spectator as the universe was once thought to be arranged for God.

According to the convention of perspective there is no visual reciprocity. There is no need for God to situate himself in relation to others: he is himself the situation. The inherent contradiction in perspective was that it structured all images of reality to address a single spectator who, unlike God, could only be in one place at a time.

After the invention of the camera this contradiction gradually became apparent.

> I'm an eye. A mechanical eye. I, the machine, show you a world the way only I can see it. I free myself for today and forever from human immobility. I'm in constant movement. I approach and pull away from objects. I creep under them. I move alongside a running horse's mouth. I fall and rise with the falling and rising bodies. This is I, the machine, maneuvring in the chaotic movements, recording one movement after another in the most complex combinations.
>
> Freed from the boundaries of time and space, I coordinate any and all points of the universe, wherever I want them to be. My way leads towards the creation of a fresh perception of the world. Thus I explain in a new way the world unknown to you.[2]

Still from *Man with a Movie Camera* by Vertov [1895–1954].

The camera isolated momentary appearances and in so doing destroyed the idea that images were timeless. Or, to put it another way, the camera showed that the notion of time passing was inseparable from the experience of the visual (except in paintings). What you saw depended upon where you were when. What you saw was relative to your position in time and space. It was no longer possible to imagine everything converging on the human eye as on the vanishing point of infinity.

This is not to say that before the invention of the camera men believed that everyone could see everything. But perspective organized the visual field as though that were indeed the ideal. Every drawing or painting that used perspective proposed to the spectator that he was the unique center of the world. The camera—and more particularly the movie camera—demonstrated that there was no center.

The invention of the camera changed the way men saw. The visible came to mean something different to them. This was immediately reflected in painting.

For the Impressionists the visible no longer presented itself to man in order to be seen. On the contrary, the visible, in continual flux, became fugitive. For the Cubists the visible was no longer what confronted the single eye, but the totality of possible views taken from points all round the object (or person) being depicted [below].

The invention of the camera also changed the way in which men saw paintings painted long before the camera was invented. Originally paintings were an integral part of the building for which they were designed. Sometimes in an early Renaissance church or chapel one has the feeling that the images on the wall are records of the building's interior life, that together they make up the building's memory—so much are they part of the particularity of the building [p. 106].

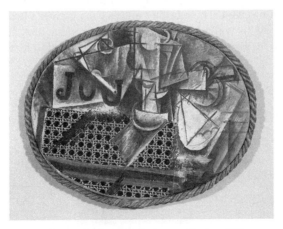

Still Life with Wicker Chair by Picasso [1881–1973].

Church of St. Francis at Assisi.

The uniqueness of every painting was once part of the uniqueness of the place where it resided. Sometimes the painting was transportable. But it could never be seen in two places at the same time. When the camera reproduces a painting, it destroys the uniqueness of its image. As a result its meaning changes. Or, more exactly, its meaning multiplies and fragments into many meanings.

This is vividly illustrated by what happens when a painting is shown on a television screen. The painting enters each viewer's house. There it is surrounded by his wallpaper, his furniture, his mementos. It enters the atmosphere of his family. It becomes their talking point. It lends its meaning

to their meaning. At the same time it enters a million other houses and, in each of them, is seen in a different context. Because of the camera, the painting now travels to the spectator rather than the spectator to the painting. In its travels, its meaning is diversified.

One might argue that all reproductions more or less distort, and that therefore the original painting is still in a sense unique. Here [below] is a reproduction of the *Virgin of the Rocks* by Leonardo da Vinci.

Having seen this reproduction, one can go to the National Gallery to look at the original and there discover what the reproduction lacks. Alternatively one can forget about the quality of the reproduction and simply be reminded, when one sees the original, that it is a famous painting of which somewhere one has already seen a reproduction. But in either case the uniqueness of the original now lies in it being *the original of a reproduction*. It is no longer what its image shows that strikes one as unique; its first meaning is no longer to be found in what it says, but in what it is.

This new status of the original work is the perfectly rational consequence of the new means of reproduction. But it is at this point that a process of mystification again enters. The meaning of the original work no longer lies in what it uniquely says but in what it uniquely is. How is its unique existence evaluated and defined in our present culture? It is defined as an object whose value depends upon its rarity. This market is affirmed

Virgin of the Rocks by Leonardo da Vinci [1452–1519]. Reproduced by courtesy of the Trustees, The National Gallery, London.

and gauged by the price it fetches on the market. But because it is nevertheless "a work of art"—and art is thought to be greater than commerce—its
market price is said to be a reflection of its spiritual value. Yet the spiritual
value of an object, as distinct from a message or an example, can only be
explained in terms of magic or religion. And since in modern society neither
of these is a living force, the art object, the "work of art," is enveloped in an
atmosphere of entirely bogus religiosity. Works of art are discussed and presented as though they were holy relics: relics which are first and foremost evidence of their own survival. The past in which they originated is studied in
order to prove their survival genuine. They are declared art when their line
of descent can be certified.

Before the *Virgin of the Rocks* the visitor to the National Gallery would be
encouraged by nearly everything he might have heard and read about the
painting to feel something like this: "I am in front of it. I can see it. This painting by Leonardo is unlike any other in the world. The National Gallery has
the real one. If I look at this painting hard enough, I should somehow be able
to feel its authenticity. The *Virgin of the Rocks* by Leonardo da Vinci: it is authentic and therefore it is beautiful."

To dismiss such feelings as naive would be quite wrong. They accord
perfectly with the sophisticated culture of art experts for whom the National
Gallery catalogue is written. The entry on the *Virgin of the Rocks* is one of the

National
Gallery

Virgin of the Rocks by Leonardo da Vinci
[1452–1519]. Louvre Museum

longest entries. It consists of fourteen closely printed pages. They do not deal with the meaning of the image. They deal with who commissioned the painting, legal squabbles, who owned it, its likely date, the families of its owners. Behind this information lie years of research. The aim of the research is to prove beyond any shadow of doubt that the painting is a genuine Leonardo. The secondary aim is to prove that an almost identical painting in the Louvre is a replica of the National Gallery version.

French art historians try to prove the opposite [see p. 108].

The National Gallery sells more reproductions of Leonardo's cartoon of *The Virgin and Child with St. Anne and St. John the Baptist* [below] than any other picture in their collection. A few years ago it was known only to scholars. It became famous because an American wanted to buy it for two and a half million pounds.

Now it hangs in a room by itself. The room is like a chapel. The drawing is behind bullet-proof perspex. It has acquired a new kind of impressiveness. Not because of what it shows—not because of the meaning of its image. It has become impressive, mysterious, because of its market value.

The bogus religiosity which now surrounds original works of art, and which is ultimately dependent upon their market value, has become the substitute for what paintings lost when the camera made them reproducible. Its

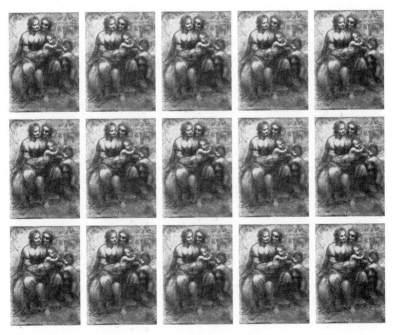

The Virgin and Child with St. Anne and St. John the Baptist
by Leonardo da Vinci [1452–1519]. Reproduced by courtesy of the
Trustees, The National Gallery, London.

function is nostalgic. It is the final empty claim for the continuing values of an oligarchic, undemocratic culture. If the image is no longer unique and exclusive, the art object, the thing, must be made mysteriously so.

The majority of the population do not visit art museums. The following table shows how closely an interest in art is related to privileged education.

National proportion of art museum visitors according to level of education:
Percentage of each educational category who visit art museums

	Greece	Poland	France	Holland		Greece	Poland	France	Holland
With no educational qualification	0.02	0.12	0.15	—	Only secondary education	10.5	10.4	10	20
Only primary education	0.30	1.50	0.45	0.50	Further and higher education	11.5	11.7	12.5	17.3

Source: Pierre Bourdieu and Alain Darbel, *L'Amour de l'art*, Editions de Minuit, Paris 1969, Appendix 5, table 4

The majority take it as axiomatic that the museums are full of holy relics which refer to a mystery which excludes them: the mystery of unaccountable wealth. Or, to put this another way, they believe that original masterpieces belong to the preserve (both materially and spiritually) of the rich. Another table indicates what the idea of an art gallery suggests to each social class.

Of the places listed below which does a museum remind you of most?

	Manual workers	Skilled and white collar workers	Professional and upper managerial
	%	%	%
Church	66	45	30.5
Library	9	34	28
Lecture hall	—	4	4.5
Department store or entrance hall in public building	—	7	2
Church and library	9	2	4.5
Church and lecture hall	4	2	—
Library and lecture hall	—	—	2
None of these	4	2	19.5
No reply	8	4	9
	100 (n = 53)	100 (n = 98)	100 (n = 99)

Source: as above, Appendix 4, table 8

In the age of pictorial reproduction the meaning of paintings is no longer attached to them; their meaning becomes transmittable: that is to say it becomes information of a sort, and, like all information, it is either put to use or ignored; information carries no special authority within itself. When a painting is put to use, its meaning is either modified or totally changed. One should be quite clear about what this involves. It is not a question of reproduction failing to reproduce certain aspects of an image faithfully; it is a question of reproduction making it possible, even inevitable, that an image will be used for many different purposes and that the reproduced image, unlike an original work, can lend itself to them all. Let us examine some of the ways in which the reproduced image lends itself to such usage.

Venus and Mars by Botticelli [1445–1510]. Reproduced by courtesy of the Trustees, The National Gallery, London.

Reproduction isolates a detail of a painting from the whole. The detail is transformed. An allegorical figure becomes a portrait of a girl [see bottom, p. 111].

When a painting is reproduced by a film camera it inevitably becomes material for the film-maker's argument.

A film which reproduces images of a painting leads the spectator, through the painting, to the film-maker's own conclusions. The painting lends authority to the film-maker. This is because a film unfolds in time and a painting does not. In a film the way one image follows another, their succession, constructs an argument which becomes irreversible. In a painting all its elements are there to be seen simultaneously. The spectator may need time to examine each element of the painting but whenever he reaches a conclusion, the simultaneity of the whole painting is there to reverse or qualify his conclusion. The painting maintains its own authority [below]. Paintings are often reproduced with words around them [see top, p. 113].

Procession to Calvary by Breughel [1525–1569].

This is a landscape of a cornfield with birds flying out of it. Look at it for a moment [below]. Then turn the page [p. 114].

It is hard to define exactly how the words have changed the image but undoubtedly they have. The image now illustrates the sentence.

In this essay each image reproduced has become part of an argument which has little or nothing to do with the painting's original independent meaning. The words have quoted the paintings to confirm their own verbal authority. . . .

Reproduced paintings, like all information, have to hold their own against all the other information being continually transmitted [see bottom, p. 114].

Wheatfield with Crows by Van Gogh [1853–1890].

This is the last picture that Van Gogh painted before he killed himself.

Consequently a reproduction, as well as making its own references to the image of its original, becomes itself the reference point for other images. The meaning of an image is changed according to what one sees immediately beside it or what comes immediately after it. Such authority as it retains, is distributed over the whole context in which it appears [see p. 115].

Because works of art are reproducible, they can, theoretically, be used by anybody. Yet mostly—in art books, magazines, films, or within gilt frames in living-rooms—reproductions are still used to bolster the illusion that nothing has changed, that art, with its unique undiminished authority, justifies most other forms of authority, that art makes inequality seem noble and hierarchies seem thrilling. For example, the whole concept of the National Cultural Heritage exploits the authority of art to glorify the present social system and its priorities.

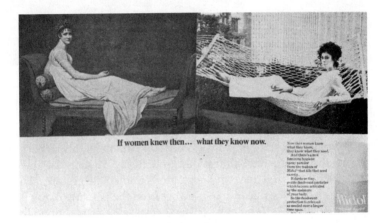

If women knew then... what they know now.

The means of reproduction are used politically and commercially to disguise or deny what their existence makes possible. But sometimes individuals use them differently [p. 116].

Adults and children sometimes have boards in their bedrooms or living-rooms on which they pin pieces of paper: letters, snapshots, reproductions of paintings, newspaper cuttings, original drawings, postcards. On each board all the images belong to the same language and all are more or less equal within it, because they have been chosen in a highly personal way to match and express the experience of the room's inhabitant. Logically, these boards should replace museums.

What are we saying by that? Let us first be sure about what we are not saying.

We are not saying that there is nothing left to experience before original works of art except a sense of awe because they have survived. The way original works of art are usually approached—through museum catalogues, guides, hired cassettes, etc.—is not the only way they might be approached. When the art of the past ceases to be viewed nostalgically, the works will cease to be holy relics—although they will never re-become what they were

before the age of reproduction. We are not saying original works of art are now useless.

Original paintings are silent and still in a sense that information never is. Even a reproduction hung on a wall is not comparable in this respect for in the original the silence and stillness permeate the actual material, the paint, in which one follows the traces of the painter's immediate gestures. This has the effect of closing the distance in time between the painting of the picture and one's own act of looking at it. In this special sense all paintings are contemporary. Hence the immediacy of their testimony. Their historical moment is literally there before our eyes. Cézanne made a similar observation from the painter's point of view. "A minute in the world's life passes! To paint it in its reality, and forget everything for that! To become that minute, to be the sensitive plate ... give the image of what we see, forgetting everything that has appeared before our time. . . ." What we make of that painted moment when it is before our eyes depends upon what we expect of art, and that in turn depends today upon how we have already experienced the meaning of paintings through reproductions.

Nor are we saying that all art can be understood spontaneously. We are not claiming that to cut out a magazine reproduction of an archaic Greek head, because it is reminiscent of some personal experience, and to pin it to a board beside other disparate images, is to come to terms with the full meaning of that head.

The idea of innocence faces two ways. By refusing to enter a conspiracy, one remains innocent of that conspiracy. But to remain innocent may also be to remain ignorant. The issue is not between innocence and knowledge (or between the natural and the cultural) but between a total approach to art which attempts to relate it to every aspect of experience and the esoteric approach of a few specialized experts who are the clerks of the nostalgia of a ruling class in decline. (In decline, not before the proletariat, but before the new power of the corporation and the state.) The real question is: to whom does the meaning of the art of the past properly belong? to those who can apply it to their own lives, or to a cultural hierarchy of relic specialists?

The visual arts have always existed within a certain preserve; originally this preserve was magical or sacred. But it was also physical: it was the place, the cave, the building, in which, or for which, the work was made. The experience of art, which at first was the experience of ritual, was set apart from the rest of life—precisely in order to be able to exercise power over it. Later the preserve of art became a social one. It entered the culture of the ruling class, whilst physically it was set apart and isolated in their palaces and houses. During all this history the authority of art was inseparable from the particular authority of the preserve.

What the modern means of reproduction have done is to destroy the authority of art and to remove it—or, rather, to remove its images which they reproduce—from any preserve. For the first time ever, images of art have become ephemeral, ubiquitous, insubstantial, available, valueless, free. They surround us in the same way as a language surrounds us. They have entered the mainstream of life over which they no longer, in themselves, have power.

Yet very few people are aware of what has happened because the means of reproduction are used nearly all the time to promote the illusion

Woman Pouring Milk by Vermeer [1632–1675].

that nothing has changed except that the masses, thanks to reproductions, can now begin to appreciate art as the cultured minority once did. Understandably, the masses remain uninterested and sceptical.

If the new language of images were used differently, it would, through its use, confer a new kind of power. Within it we could begin to define our experiences more precisely in areas where words are inadequate. (Seeing comes before words.) Not only personal experience, but also the essential historical experience of our relation to the past: that is to say the experience of seeking to give meaning to our lives, of trying to understand the history of which we can become the active agents.

The art of the past no longer exists as it once did. Its authority is lost. In its place there is a language of images. What matters now is who uses that language for what purpose. This touches upon questions of copyright for reproduction, the ownership of art presses and publishers, the total policy of public art galleries and museums. As usually presented, these are narrow professional matters. One of the aims of this essay has been to show that what is really at stake is much larger. A people or a class which is cut off from its own past is far less free to choose and to act as a people or class than one that has been able to situate itself in history. This is why—and this is the only reason why—the entire art of the past has now become a political issue.

Many of the ideas in the preceding essay have been taken from another, written over forty years ago by the German critic and philosopher Walter Benjamin.

His essay was entitled The Work of Art in the Age of Mechanical Reproduction. *This essay is available in English in a collection called* Illuminations *(Cape, London, 1970).*

NOTES

[1] Seymour Slive, *Frans Hals* (Phaidon, London).
[2] This quotation is from an article written in 1923 by Dziga Vertov, the revolutionary Soviet film director.

On *Rembrandt's* Woman in Bed

It is strange how art historians sometimes pay so much attention, when trying to date certain paintings, to "style," inventories, bills, auction lists, and so little to the painted evidence concerning the model's age. It is as if they do not trust the painter on this point. For example, when they try to date and arrange in chronological order Rembrandt's paintings of Hendrickje Stoffels. No painter was a greater expert about the process of aging, and no painter has left us a more intimate record of the great love of his life. Whatever the

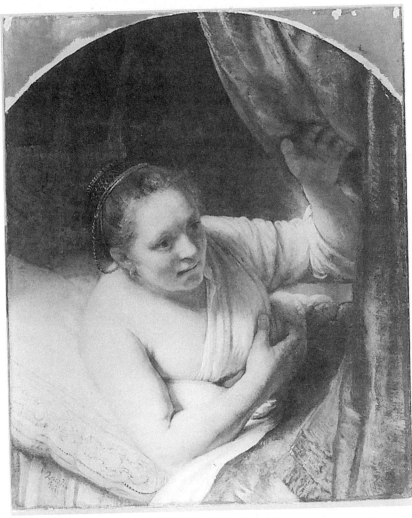

Woman in Bed by Rembrandt.

documentary conjectures may allow, the paintings make it clear that the love between Hendrickje and the painter lasted for about twenty years, until her death, six years before his.

She was ten or twelve years younger than he. When she died she was, on the evidence of the paintings, at the very least forty-five, and when he first painted her she could certainly not have been older than twenty-seven. Their daughter, Cornelia, was baptized in 1654. This means that Hendrickje gave birth to their child when she was in her mid-thirties.

The *Woman in Bed* (from Edinburgh) was painted, by my reckoning, a little before or a little after the birth of Cornelia. The historians suggest that it may be a fragment taken from a larger work representing the wedding night of Sarah and Tobias. A biblical subject for Rembrandt was always contemporary. If it is a fragment, it is certain that Rembrandt finished it, and bequeathed it finally to the spectator, as his most intimate painting of the woman he loved.

There are other paintings of Hendrickje. Before the *Bathsheba* in the Louvre, or the *Woman Bathing* in the National Gallery (London), I am wordless. Not because their genius inhibits me, but because the experience from which they derive and which they express—desire experiencing itself as something as old as the known world, tenderness experiencing itself as the end of the world, the eyes' endless rediscovery, as if for the first time, of their love of a familiar body—all this comes before and goes beyond words. No other paintings lead so deftly and powerfully to silence. Yet, in both, Hendrickje is absorbed in her own actions. In the painter's vision of her there is the greatest intimacy, but there is no mutual intimacy between them. They are paintings which speak of his love, not of hers.

In the painting of the *Woman in Bed* there is a complicity between the woman and the painter. This complicity includes both reticence and abandon, day and night. The curtain of the bed, which Hendrickje lifts up with her hand, marks the threshold between daytime and nighttime.

In two years, by daylight, Van Rijn will be declared bankrupt. Ten years before, by daylight, Hendrickje came to work in Van Rijn's house as a nurse for his baby son. In the light of Dutch seventeenth-century accountability and Calvinism, the housekeeper and the painter have distinct and separate responsibilities. Hence their reticence.

At night, they leave their century.

> A necklace hangs loose across her breasts,
> And between them lingers—
> yet is it a lingering
> and not an incessant arrival?—
> the perfume of forever.
> A perfume as old as sleep,
> as familiar to the living as to the dead.

Leaning forward from her pillows, she lifts up the curtain with the back of her hand, for its palm, its face, is already welcoming, already making a gesture which is preparatory to the act of touching his head.

She has not yet slept. Her gaze follows him as he approaches. In her face the two of them are reunited. Impossible now to separate the two images: his image of her in bed, as he remembers her: her image of him as she sees him approaching their bed. It is nighttime.

On Caravaggio's The Calling of St. Matthew

One night in bed you asked me who was my favorite painter. I hesitated, searching for the least knowing, most truthful answer. Caravaggio. My own reply surprised me. There are nobler painters and painters of greater breadth of vision. There are painters I admire more and who are more admirable. But there is none, so it seems—for the answer came unpremeditated—to whom I feel closer.

The Calling of St. Matthew by Caravaggio.

The few canvases from my own incomparably modest life as a painter, which I would like to see again, are those I painted in the late 1940s of the streets of Livorno. This city was then war-scarred and poor, and it was there that I first began to learn something about the ingenuity of the dispossessed. It was there too that I discovered that I wanted as little as possible to do in this world with those who wield power. This has turned out to be a lifelong aversion.

The complicity I feel with Caravaggio began, I think, during that time in Livorno. He was the first painter of life as experienced by the popolaccio, the people of the backstreets, les sans-culottes, the lumpenproletariat, the lower orders, those of the lower depths, the underworld. There is no word in any traditional European language which does not either denigrate or patronize the urban poor it is naming. That is power.

Following Caravaggio up to the present day, other painters—Brower, Ostade, Hogarth, Goya, Géricault, Guttuso—have painted pictures of the same social milieu. But all of them—however great—were genre pictures, painted in order to show others how the less fortunate or the more dangerous lived. With Caravaggio, however, it was not a question of presenting scenes but of seeing itself. He does not depict the underworld for others: his vision is one that he shares with it.

In art-historical books Caravaggio is listed as one of the great innovating masters of chiaroscuro and a forerunner of the light and shade later used by Rembrandt and others. His vision can of course be considered art-historically as a step in the evolution of European art. Within such a perspective a Caravaggio was almost inevitable, as a link between the high art of the Counter Reformation and the domestic art of the emerging Dutch bourgeoisie, the form of this link being that of a new kind of space, defined by darkness as well as by light. (For Rome and for Amsterdam damnation had become an everyday affair.)

For the Caravaggio who actually existed—for the boy called Michelangelo born in a village near Bergamo, not far from where my friends, the Italian woodcutters, come—light and shade, as he imagined and saw them, had a deeply personal meaning, inextricably entwined with his desires and his instinct for survival. And it is by this, not by any art-historical logic, that his art is linked with the underworld.

His chiaroscuro allowed him to banish daylight. Shadows, he felt, offered shelter as can four walls and a roof. Whatever and wherever he painted he really painted interiors. Sometimes—for *The Flight into Egypt* or one of his beloved John the Baptists—he was obliged to include a landscape in the background. But these landscapes are like rugs or drapes hung up on a line across an inner courtyard. He only felt at home—no, that he felt nowhere—he only felt relatively at ease *inside*.

His darkness smells of candles, overripe melons, damp washing waiting to be hung out the next day: it is the darkness of stairwells, gambling corners, cheap lodgings, sudden encounters. And the promise is not in what will flare against it, but in the darkness itself. The shelter it offers is only relative, for the chiaroscuro reveals violence, suffering, longing, mortality, but at least it reveals them intimately. What has been banished, along with the daylight, are distance and solitude—and both these are feared by the underworld.

Those who live precariously and are habitually crowded together develop a phobia about open spaces which transforms their frustrating lack of space and privacy into something reassuring. He shared those fears.

The Calling of St. Matthew depicts five men sitting round their usual table, telling stories, gossiping, boasting of what one day they will do, counting money. The room is dimly lit. Suddenly the door is flung open. The two figures who enter are still part of the violent noise and light of the invasion. (Berenson wrote that Christ, who is one of the figures, comes in like a police inspector to make an arrest.)

Two of Matthew's colleagues refuse to look up, the other two younger ones stare at the strangers with a mixture of curiosity and condescension. Why is he proposing something so mad? Who's protecting him, the thin one who does all the talking? And Matthew, the tax-collector with a shifty conscience which has made him more unreasonable than most of his colleagues, points at himself and asks: Is it really I who must go? Is it really I who must follow you?

How many thousands of decisions to leave have resembled Christ's hand here! The hand is held out towards the one who has to decide, yet it is ungraspable because so fluid. It orders the way, yet offers no direct support. Matthew will get up and follow the thin stranger from the room, down the narrow streets, out of the district. He will write his gospel, he will travel to Ethiopia and the South Caspian and Persia. Probably he will be murdered.

And behind the drama of this moment of decision in the room at the top of the stairs, there is a window, giving onto the outside world. Traditionally in painting, windows were treated either as sources of light or as frames framing nature or framing an exemplary event outside. Not so this window. No light enters by it. The window is opaque. We see nothing. Mercifully we see nothing because what is outside is bound to be threatening. It is a window through which only the worst news can come.

•   •   •   •   •   •   •   •   •   •   •

QUESTIONS FOR A SECOND READING

1. Berger says, "The past is never there waiting to be discovered, to be recognized for exactly what it is. History always constitutes the relation between a present and its past" (p. 99). And he says, "If we 'saw' the art of the past, we would situate ourselves in history. When we are prevented from seeing it, we are being deprived of the history which belongs to us" (p. 100). As you reread this essay, pay particular attention to Berger's uses of the word

"history." What does it stand for? What does it have to do with looking at pictures? How might you define the term if your definition were based on its use in this essay?

You might take Berger's discussion of the Hals paintings as a case in point. What is the relation Berger establishes between the past and the present? If he has not "discovered" the past or recognized it for exactly what it is, what has Berger done in writing about these paintings? What might it mean to say that he has "situated" us in history or has returned a history that belongs to us? And in what way might this be said to be a political act?

2. Berger argues forcefully that the account of the Hals painting offered by the unnamed art historian is a case of "mystification." How would you characterize Berger's account of that same painting? Would you say that he sees what is "really" there? If so, why wasn't it self-evident? Why does it take an expert to see "clearly"? As you read back over the essay, look for passages you could use to characterize the way Berger looks at images or paintings. If, as he says, "The way we see things is affected by what we know or what we believe," what does he know and what does he believe?

ASSIGNMENTS FOR WRITING

1.   We are not saying that there is nothing left to experience before original works of art except a sense of awe because they have survived. The way original works of art are usually approached—through museum catalogues, guides, hired cassettes, etc.—is not the only way they might be approached. When the art of the past ceases to be viewed nostalgically, the works will cease to be holy relics—although they will never rebecome what they were before the age of reproduction. We are not saying original works of art are now useless. (pp. 115–16)

Berger argues that there are barriers to vision, problems in the ways we see or don't see original works of art, problems that can be located in and overcome by strategies of approach.

For Berger, what we lose if we fail to see properly is history: "If we 'saw' the art of the past, we would situate ourselves in history. When we are prevented from seeing it, we are being deprived of the history which belongs to us" (p. 100). It is not hard to figure out who, according to Berger, prevents us from seeing the art of the past. He says it is the ruling class. It is difficult, however, to figure out what he believes gets in the way and what all this has to do with history.

For this assignment, write an essay explaining what, as you read Berger, it is that gets in the way when we look at paintings, and what it is that we might do to overcome the barriers to vision (and to history). You should imagine that you are writing for someone interested in art, perhaps preparing to go to a museum, but someone who has not read Berger's essay. You will, that is, need to be careful in summary and paraphrase.

2. Berger says that the real question is this: "To whom does the meaning of the art of the past properly belong?" Let's say, in Berger's spirit, that it belongs to you. Look again at the painting by Vermeer, *Woman Pouring Milk*, that is included in "Ways of Seeing" (p. 117). Berger includes the painting but without much discussion, as though he were, in fact, leaving it for you.

Write an essay that shows others how they might best understand that painting. You should offer this lesson in the spirit of John Berger. Imagine that you are doing this work for him, perhaps as his apprentice.

3.   Original paintings are silent and still in a sense that information never is. Even a reproduction hung on a wall is not comparable in this respect for in the original the silence and stillness permeate the actual material, the paint, in which one follows the traces of the painter's immediate gestures. This has the effect of closing the distance in time between the painting of the picture and one's own act of looking at it. . . . What we make of that painted moment when it is before our eyes depends upon what we expect of art, and that in turn depends today upon how we have already experienced the meaning of paintings through reproductions. (p. 116)

While Berger describes original paintings as silent in this passage, it is clear that these paintings begin to speak if one approaches them properly, if one learns to ask "the right questions of the past." Berger demonstrates one route of approach, for example, in his reading of the Hals paintings, where he asks questions about the people and objects and their relationships to the painter and the viewer. What the paintings might be made to say, however, depends on the viewer's expectations, his or her sense of the questions that seem appropriate or possible. Berger argues that, because of the way art is currently displayed, discussed, and reproduced, the viewer expects only to be mystified.

For this paper, imagine that you are working against the silence and mystification Berger describes. Go to a museum—or, if that is not possible, to a large-format book of reproductions in the library (or, if that is not possible, to the reproductions on the Web)—and select a painting that seems silent and still, yet invites conversation. Your job is to figure out what sorts of questions to ask, to interrogate the painting, to get it to speak, to engage with the past in some form of dialogue. Write an essay in which you record this process and what you have learned from it. Somewhere in your paper, perhaps at the end, turn back to Berger's essay and speak to it about how this process has or hasn't confirmed what you take to be Berger's expectations.

Note: If possible, include with your essay a reproduction of the painting you select. (Check the postcards at the museum gift shop.) In any event, you want to make sure that you describe the painting in sufficient detail for your readers to follow what you say.

4. In "Ways of Seeing" Berger says,

If the new language of images were used differently, it would, through its use, confer a new kind of power. Within it we could begin to define our experiences more precisely in areas where words are inadequate. . . . Not only personal experience, but also the essential historical experience of our relation to the past: that is to say the experience of seeking to give meaning to our lives, of trying to understand the history of which we can become the active agents. (p. 118)

As a writer, Berger is someone who uses images (including some of the great paintings of the Western tradition) "to define [experience] more precisely in areas where words are inadequate." In a wonderful book, *And Our Faces, My Heart, Brief as Photos*, a book that is both a meditation on time and space and a long love letter, Berger writes about paintings in order to say what he wants to say to his lover. We have included two examples, descriptions of Rembrandt's *Woman in Bed* and Caravaggio's *The Calling of St. Matthew.*

Read these as examples, as lessons in how and why to look at, to value, to think with, to write about paintings. Then use one or both as a way of thinking about the concluding section of "Ways of Seeing" (pp. 116–18). You can assume that your readers have read Berger's essay but have difficulty grasping what he is saying in that final section, particularly since it is a section that seems to call for action, asking the reader to do something. Of what use might Berger's example be in trying to understand what we might do with and because of paintings?

MAKING CONNECTIONS

1. Walker Percy, in "The Loss of the Creature" (p. 481), like Berger in "Ways of Seeing," talks about the problems people have seeing things. "How can the sightseer recover the Grand Canyon?" Percy asks. "He can recover it in any number of ways, all sharing in common the stratagem of avoiding the approved confrontation of the tour and the Park Service." There is a way in which Berger also tells a story about tourists—tourists going to a museum to see paintings, to buy postcards, gallery guides, reprints, and T-shirts featuring the image of the Mona Lisa. "The way original works of art are usually approached—through museum catalogues, guides, hired cassettes, etc.—is not the only way they might be approached. When the art of the past ceases to be viewed nostalgically, the works will cease to be holy relics—although they will never re-become what they were before the age of reproduction" (pp. 115–16).

   Write an essay in which you describe possible "approaches" to a painting in a museum, approaches that could provide for a better understanding or a more complete "recovery" of that painting than would be possible to a casual viewer, to someone who just wandered in, for example, with no strategy in mind. You should think of your essay as providing real advice to a real person. (You might, if you can, work with a particular painting in a particular museum.) What should that person do? How should that person prepare? What would the consequences be?

   At least one of your approaches should reflect Percy's best advice to a viewer who wanted to develop a successful strategy, and at least one should represent the best you feel Berger would have to offer. When you've finished explaining these approaches, go on in your essay to examine the differences between those you associate with Percy and those you associate with Berger. What are the key differences? And what do they say about the different ways these two thinkers approach the problem of why we do or do not see that which lies before us?

2. Both John Berger in "Ways of Seeing" and Michel Foucault in "Panopticism" (p. 209) discuss what Foucault calls "power relations." Berger claims that "the entire art of the past has now become a political issue," and he

makes a case for the evolution of a "new language of images" that could "confer a new kind of power" if people were to understand history in art. Foucault argues that the Panopticon signals an "inspired" change in power relations. "It is," he says, "an important mechanism, for it automatizes and disindividualizes power. Power has its principle not so much in a person as in a certain concerted distribution of bodies, surfaces, lights, gazes; in an arrangement whose internal mechanisms produce the relation in which individuals are caught up" (p. 216).

Both Berger and Foucault create arguments about power and its methods and goals. As you read through their essays, mark passages you might use to explain how each author thinks about power—where it comes from, who has it, how it works, where you look for it, how you know it when you see it, what it does, where it goes. You should reread the essays as a pair, as part of a single project in which you are seeking to explain theories of power.

Write an essay in which you present and explain "Ways of Seeing" and "Panopticism" as examples of Berger's and Foucault's theories of power and vision. Both Berger and Foucault are arguing against usual understandings of power and knowledge and history. In this sense, their projects are similar. You should be sure, however, to look for differences as well as similarities.

3. Clifford Geertz, in "Deep Play: Notes on the Balinese Cockfight" (p. 259), argues that the cockfights are a "Balinese reading of Balinese experience; a story they tell themselves about themselves." They are not, then, just cockfights. Or, as Geertz says, the cockfights can be seen as texts "saying something of something." Berger's essay, "Ways of Seeing," offers a view of our culture and, in particular, of the way our culture reproduces and uses images from the past. They are placed in museums, on bulletin boards, on T-shirts, and in advertisements. They are described by experts in certain predictable tones or phrases. It is interesting to look at our use of those images as a story we tell ourselves about ourselves, as a practice that says something about something else.

Geertz's analysis of the cockfight demonstrates this way of seeing and interpreting a feature of a culture. Write an essay in which you use Geertz's methods to interpret the examples that Berger provides of the ways our culture reproduces and uses images from the past. If these practices say something about something else, what do they say, and about what do they say it? What story might we be telling ourselves about ourselves?

Note: For this assignment, you should avoid rushing to the conclusion Berger draws—that the story told here is a story about the ruling class and its conspiracy against the proletariat. You should see, that is, what other interpretation you can provide. You may, if you choose, return to Berger's conclusions in your paper, but only after you have worked on some of your own.

4. In "Beauty (Re)discovers the Male Body" (p. 131) Susan Bordo refers to John Berger and his work in *Ways of Seeing*, although she refers to a different chapter than the one included here. In general, however, both Berger and Bordo are concerned with how we see and read images; both are concerned to correct the ways images are used and read; both trace the ways images serve the interests of money and power; both are written to teach

readers how and why they should pay a different kind of attention to the images around them.

For this assignment, use Bordo's work to reconsider Berger's. Write an essay in which you consider the two chapters as examples of an ongoing project. Berger's essay precedes Bordo's by about a quarter of a century. If you look closely at one or two of their examples, and if you look at the larger concerns of their arguments, are they saying the same things? doing the same work? If so, how? And why is such work still necessary? If not, how do their projects differ? And how might you explain those differences?

SUSAN
BORDO

SUSAN BORDO (b. 1947) is the Otis A. Singletary Chair of Humanities at the University of Kentucky. Bordo is a philosopher, and while her work has touched on figures and subjects traditional to the study of philosophy (René Descartes, for example), she brings her training to the study of culture, including popular culture and its representations of the body. She is a philosopher, that is, who writes not only about Plato but about Madonna and John Travolta.

In Unbearable Weight: Feminism, Western Culture, and the Body *(1993), Bordo looks at the complicated cultural forces that have produced our ways of understanding and valuing a woman's body. These powerful forces have shaped not only attitudes and lives but, through dieting, training, and cosmetic surgery, the physical body itself.* Unbearable Weight *was nominated for the 1993 Pulitzer Prize; it won the Association for Women in Psychology's Distinguished Publication Award and was named by the* New York Times *as one of the "Notable Books of 1993." The book had a broad audience and made a significant contribution to the academic study of gender and the body. In fact, Bordo's work (in this book and those that followed) has been central to the newly evolving field of "body studies." Bordo is also the author of* The Flight to

Objectivity: Essays on Cartesianism and Culture *(1987) and* Twilight Zones: The Hidden Life of Cultural Images from Plato to O.J. *(1997); she is co-editor (with Alison Jaggar) of* Gender/Body/Knowledge: Feminist Reconstruction of Being and Knowing *(1989) and editor of* Feminist Interpretations of Descartes *(1999).*

In 1992, Bordo says, as she was finishing work on Unbearable Weight, *she received a letter from Laurence Goldstein, editor of* Michigan Quarterly Review, *asking her to write a review article on a surprising series of recently published books concerning men and masculinity. It was as though the feminist work on women as figures of thought and commerce had made the category of the "male" equally available for study and debate. She said,*

> *It was as if Larry had read my mind. . . . I had known for a long time that I wanted to write about men and their bodies; it seemed the logical, natural, almost inevitable next step. I just wasn't expecting to begin quite so soon. But I couldn't resist the opportunity. . . .*

The review essay was the beginning of what became her next major publication, The Male Body: A New Look at Men in Public and Private *(1999), from which the following selection is drawn. As was the case with* Unbearable Weight, The Male Body *has been read with great interest and care by a wide audience, with favorable reviews in the* New York Times, Elle, *and* Vanity Fair. *In* The Male Body, *Bordo writes about her father, about the 1950s, about gay men and straight men, about movies, and about sex manuals. The chapter we have chosen, "Beauty (Re)discovers the Male Body," comes from a section titled "Public Images," and looks specifically at the use of men in advertising, where men's bodies (rather than the usual case—women's) are presented as objects of pleasure and instances of commerce. There is a powerful argument here about gender, identity, and the media (about how we come to see and value our physical selves). The writing is witty, committed, and engaging—moving from personal his-* 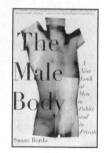 *tory to cultural history, deftly bringing in key concepts from contemporary literary and media theory, like the concept of the "gaze." In this chapter, Bordo provides a compelling example of what it means to read closely, to read images as well as words, and to write those close readings into an extended argument. She brings the concerns of a philosopher to the materials of everyday life.*

Beauty (Re)discovers the Male Body

Men on Display

Putting classical art to the side for the moment, the naked and near-naked female body became an object of mainstream consumption first in *Playboy* and its imitators, then in movies, and only then in fashion photographs. With the male body, the trajectory has been different. Fashion has taken the lead, the movies have followed. Hollywood may have been a chest-fest in the fifties, but it was male clothing designers who went south and violated the really powerful taboos—not just against the explicit depiction of penises and male bottoms but against the admission of all sorts of forbidden "feminine" qualities into mainstream conceptions of manliness.

It was the spring of 1995, and I was sipping my first cup of morning coffee, not yet fully awake, flipping through *The New York Times Magazine*, when I had my first real taste of what it's like to inhabit this visual culture as a man. It was both thrilling and disconcerting. It was the first time in my experience that I had encountered a commercial representation of a male body that seemed to deliberately invite me to linger over it. Let me make that stronger—that seemed to reach out to me, interrupting my mundane but peaceful Sunday morning, and provoke me into erotic consciousness, whether or not I wanted it. Women—both straight and gay—have always gazed covertly, of course, squeezing our illicit little titillations out of representations designed for—or pretending to—other purposes than to turn us on. *This* ad made no such pretense. It caused me to knock over my coffee cup, ruining the more cerebral pleasures of the *Book Review*. Later, when I had regained my equilibrium, I made a screen-saver out of him, so I could gaze at my leisure.

I'm sure that many gay men were as taken as I was, and perhaps some gay women too. The erotic charge of various sexual styles is not neatly mapped onto sexual orientation (let alone biological sex). Brad Pitt's baby-butch looks are a turn-on to many lesbians, while I—regarded by most of my gay friends as a pretty hard-core heterosexual—have always found Anne Heche irresistible (even before Ellen did). A lesbian friend of mine, reading a draft of my section on biblical S&M, said the same movies influenced her later attraction to butch *women*. Despite such complications, until recently only heterosexual men have continually been inundated by popular cultural images *designed* with their sexual responses (or, at least, what those sexual responses are imagined to be) in mind. It's not entirely a gift. On the minus side is having one's composure continually challenged by what Timothy Beneke has aptly described as a culture of "intrusive images," eliciting fantasies, emotions, and erections at times and in places where they might not be appropriate. On the plus side is the cultural permission to be a voyeur.

Some psychologists say that the circuit from eyes to brain to genitals is a quicker trip for men than for women. "There's some strong evidence," popular science writer Deborah Blum reports, citing studies of men's responses to pictures of naked women, "that testosterone is wired for visual response." Maybe. But who is the electrician here? God? Mother Nature? Or Hugh Hefner? Practice makes perfect. And women have had little practice. The Calvin Klein ad made me feel like an adolescent again, brought me back to that day when I saw Barry Resnick on the basketball court of Weequahic High and realized that men's legs could make me weak in the knees. Men's legs? I knew that *women's* legs were supposed to be sexy. I had learned that from all those hose-straightening scenes in the movies.

But men's legs? Who had ever seen a woman gaga over some guy's legs in the movies? Or even read about it in a book? Yet the muscular grace of Barry's legs took my breath away. Maybe something was wrong with me. Maybe my sex drive was too strong, too much like a man's. By the time I came across that Calvin Klein ad, several decades of feminism and life experience had left me a little less worried about my sex drive. Still, the sight of that model's body made me feel that my sexual education was still far from complete.

I brought the ad to classes and lectures, asking women what they thought of him. Most began to sweat the moment I unfolded the picture, then got their bearings and tried to explore the bewitching stew of sexual elements the picture has to offer. The model—a young Jackson Browne look-alike—stands there in his form-fitting and rip-speckled Calvin Klein briefs, head lowered, dark hair loosely falling over his eyes. His body projects strength, solidity; he's no male waif. But his finely muscled chest is not so overdeveloped as to suggest a sexuality immobilized by the thick matter of the body. Gay theorist Ron Long, describing contemporary gay sexual aesthetics—lean, taut, sinuous muscles rather than Schwarzenegger bulk—points to a "dynamic tension" that the incredible hulks lack. Stiff, engorged Schwarzenegger bodies, he says, seem to *be* surrogate penises—with nowhere to go and nothing to do but stand there looking massive—whereas muscles like this young man's seem designed for movement, for sex. His body isn't a stand-in phallus; rather, he *has* a penis—the real thing, not a symbol, and a fairly breathtaking one, clearly outlined through the soft jersey fabric of the briefs. It seems slightly erect, or perhaps that's his nonerect size; either way, there's a substantial presence there that's palpable (it looks so touchable, you want to cup your hand over it) and very, very male.

At the same time, however, my gaze is invited by something "feminine" about the young man. His underwear may be ripped, but ever so slightly, subtly; unlike the original ripped-underwear poster boy Kowalski, he's hardly a thug. He doesn't stare at the viewer challengingly, belligerently, as do so many models in other ads for male underwear, facing off like a street tough passing a member of the rival gang on the street. ("Yeah, this is an underwear ad and I'm half naked. But I'm still the one in charge here. Who's gonna look away first?") No, this model's languid body posture, his averted look are classic signals, both in the "natural" and the "cultural" world, of willing subordination. He offers himself nonaggressively to the gaze of another. Hip cocked in the snaky S-curve usually reserved for depictions of women's bodies, eyes downcast but not closed, he gives off a sultry, moody, subtle but undeniably seductive consciousness of his erotic allure. Feast on me, I'm here to be looked at, my body is for your eyes. Oh my.

Such an attitude of male sexual supplication, although it has (as we'll see) classical antecedents, is very new to contemporary mainstream representations. Homophobia is at work in this taboo, but so are attitudes about gender that cut across sexual orientation. For many men, both gay and straight, to be so passively dependent on the gaze of another person for one's sense of self-worth is incompatible with being a real man. As we'll see, such notions about manliness are embedded in Greek culture, in contemporary visual representation, and even (in disguised form) in existentialist philosophy. "For the woman," as philosopher Simone de Beauvoir writes, ". . . the absence of her lover is always torture; he is an eye, a judge . . . away from him, she is dispossessed, at once of herself and of the world." For Beauvoir's sometime lover and lifelong soul mate Jean-Paul Sartre, on the other hand, the gaze (or the Look, as he called it) of another person—including the gaze of one's lover—is the "hell" that other people represent. If we were alone in the world, he argues, we would be utterly free—within physical constraints—to be whomever we wanted to be, to be the creatures of our own self-fantasies, to define our behavior however we like. Other people intrude on this solipsism, and have the audacity to see us from their own perspective rather than ours. The result is what Sartre calls primordial Shame under the eyes of the Other, and a fierce desire to reassert one's freedom. The other person has stolen "the secret" of who I am. I must fight back, resist their attempts to define me.

I understand, of course, what Sartre is talking about here. We've all, male and female alike, felt the shame that another pair of eyes can bring. Sartre's own classic example is of being caught peeking through a keyhole by another person. It isn't until those other eyes are upon you that you truly feel not just the "wrongness" of what you are doing, but—Sartre would argue—the very fact that you are doing it. Until the eyes of another are upon us, "catching us" in the act, we can deceive ourselves, pretend. Getting caught in moments of fantasy or vanity may be especially shameful. When I was an adolescent, I loved to pretend I was a radio personality, and talking into an empty coffee can created just the right sound. One day, my mother caught me speaking in the smooth and slightly sultry tones that radio personalities had even in those days. The way I felt is what Sartre means when he describes the Look of another person as the fulcrum of shame-making. My face got hot, and suddenly I saw how ridiculous I must have seemed, my head in the Chock Full O' Nuts, my narcissistic fantasies on full display. I was caught, I wanted to run.

The disjunction between self-conception and external judgment can be especially harsh when the external definitions carry racial and gender stereotypes with them. Sartre doesn't present such examples—he's interested in capturing the contours of an existential situation shared by all rather than in analyzing the cultural differences that affect that situation—but they are surely relevant to understanding the meaning of the Look of the Other. A black man jogs down the street in sweat clothes, thinking of the class he is going to teach later that day; a white woman passes him, clutches her handbag more tightly, quickens her step; in her eyes, the teacher is a potentially dangerous animal. A Latin American student arrives early the first day of college; an administrator, seeing him in the still-deserted hall, asks him if he is the new janitor. The aspiring student has had his emerging identity erased, a stereotype put in its place by another pair of eyes. When women are transformed from professionals to "pussies" by the comments of men on the street, it's humiliating, not so much because we're puritans as because we sense the hostility in the hoots, the desire to bring an uppity woman down to size by reminding her that she's just "the sex" (as Beauvoir put it).

We may all have felt shame, but—as the different attitudes of Beauvoir and Sartre suggest—men and women are socially sanctioned to deal with the gaze of the Other in different ways. Women learn to anticipate, even play to the sexualizing gaze, trying to become what will please, captivate, turn shame into pride. (In the process, we also learn how sexy being gazed at can feel—perhaps precisely because it walks the fine edge of shame.) Many of us, truth be told, get somewhat addicted to the experience. I'm renting a video, feeling a bit low, a bit tired. The young man at the counter, unsolicited, tells me I'm "looking good." It alters everything, I feel fine, alive; it seems to go right down to my cells. I leave the store feeling younger, stronger, more awake. When women sense that they are not being assessed sexually—for example, as we age, or if we are disabled—it may feel like we no longer exist.

Women may dread being surveyed harshly—being seen as too old, too fat, too flat-chested—but men are not supposed to enjoy being surveyed *period*. It's feminine to be on display. Men are thus taught—as my uncle Leon used to say—to be a moving target. Get out of range of those eyes, don't let them catch you—even as the object of their fantasies (or, as Sartre would put it, don't let them "possess," "steal" your freedom). This phobia has even distorted scientific research, as mentioned earlier. Evolutionary theorists have long acknowledged display as an important feature of courting behavior among primates—except when it comes to *our* closest ancestors. With descriptions of hominid behavior, male display behavior "suddenly drops out of the primate evolutionary picture" (Sheets-Johnstone) and is replaced by the concept of year-round female sexual receptivity. It seems that it has been intolerable, unthinkable for male evolutionary theorists to imagine the bodies of their male ancestors being on display, sized up, dependent on selection (or rejection) by female hominids.

Scientists and "ordinary guys" are totally in synch here, as is humorously illustrated in Peter Cattaneo's popular 1997 British film *The Full Monty*. In the film, a group of unemployed metalworkers in Sheffield, England, watch a Chippendale's show and hatch the money-making scheme of presenting their own male strip show in which they will go right down to the "full Monty." At the start of the film, the heroes are hardly pillars of successful manliness (Gaz, their leader, refers to them as "scrap"). Yet even they have been sheltered by their guyhood, as they learn while putting the show together. One gets a penis pump. Another borrows his wife's face cream. They run, they wrap their bellies in plastic, they do jumping jacks, they get artificial tans. The most overweight one among them (temporarily) pulls out of the show. Before, these guys hadn't lived their lives under physical scrutiny, but in male action mode, in which men are judged by their accomplishments. Now, anticipating being on display to a roomful of spectators, they suddenly realize how it feels to be judged as women routinely are, sized up by another pair of eyes. "I pray that they'll be a bit more understanding about us" than they've been with women, David (the fat one) murmurs.

They get past their discomfort, in the end, and their show is greeted with wild enthusiasm by the audience. The movie leaves us with this feel-good ending, not raising the question obvious to every woman watching the film: would a troupe of out-of-shape women be received as warmly, as affectionately? The climactic moment when the men throw off their little pouches is demurely shot from the rear, moreover, so we—the audience—don't get "the full Monty." Nonetheless, the film gently and humorously makes an important point: for a heterosexual man to offer himself up to a sexually evaluating gaze is for him to make a large, scary leap—and not just because of the anxieties about size discussed earlier in this book (the guy who drops out of the show, remember, is embarrassed by his fat, not his penis). The "full Monty"—the naked penis—is not merely a body part in the movie (hence it doesn't really matter that the film doesn't show it). It's a symbol for male exposure, vulnerability to an evaluation and judgment that women—clothed or naked—experience all the time.

I had to laugh out loud at a 1997 *New York Times Magazine* "Style" column, entitled "Overexposure," which complained of the "contagion" of nudity spreading through celebrity culture. "Stars no longer have private parts," the author observed, and fretted that civilians would soon also be measured by the beauty of their buns. I share this author's concern about our body-obsessed culture. But, pardon me, he's just noticing this now??? Actresses have been baring their breasts, their butts, even their bushes, for some time, and ordinary women have been tromping off to the gym in pursuit of comparably perfect bodies. What's got the author suddenly crying "overkill," it turns out, is Sly Stallone's "surreally fat-free" appearance on the cover of *Vanity Fair*, and Rupert Everett's "dimpled behind" in a Karl Lagerfeld fashion spread. Now that *men* are taking off their clothes, the culture is suddenly going too far. Could it be that the author doesn't even "read" all those naked female bodies as "overexposed"? Does he protest a bit too much when he declares in the first sentence of the piece that he found it "a yawn" when Dirk Diggler unsheathed his "prosthetic shillelagh" ("penis" is still a word to be avoided whenever possible) at the end of *Boogie Nights*? A yawn? My friend's palms were sweating profusely, and I was not about to drop off to sleep either.

As for dimpled behinds, my second choice for male pinup of the decade is the Gucci series of two ads in which a beautiful young man, shot from the rear, puts on a pair of briefs. In the first ad, he's holding them in his hands, contemplating them. Is he checking out the correct washing-machine temp? It's odd, surely, to stand there looking at your underwear, but never mind. The point is: his underwear is in his hands, not on his butt. *It*—his bottom,

that is—is gorgeously, completely naked—a motif so new to mainstream advertising (but since then catching on rapidly) that several of my friends, knowing I was writing about the male body, E-mailed me immediately when they saw the ad. In the second ad, he's put the underwear on, and is adjusting it to fit. Luckily for us, he hasn't succeeded yet, so his buns are peeking out the bottom of the underwear, looking biteable. For the *Times* writer, those buns may be an indecent exposure of parts that should be kept private (or they're a boring yawn, I'm afraid he can't have it both ways), but for me—and for thousands of gay men across the country—this was a moment of political magnitude, and a delicious one. The body parts that *we* love to squeeze (those plastic breasts, they're the real yawn for me) had come out of the closet and into mainstream culture, where *we* can enjoy them without a trip to a specialty store.

But all this is very new. Women aren't used to seeing naked men frankly portrayed as "objects" of a sexual gaze (and neither are heterosexual men, as that *Times* writer makes clear). So pardon me if I'm skeptical when I read arguments about men's greater "biological" responsiveness to visual stimuli. These "findings," besides being ethnocentric (no one thinks to poll Trobriand Islanders), display little awareness of the impact of changes in cultural representations on our capacities for sexual response. Popular science writer Deborah Blum, for example, cites a study from the Kinsey Institute which showed a group of men and women a series of photos and drawings of nudes, both male and female:

> Fifty-four percent of the men were erotically aroused versus 12 percent of the women—in other words, more than four times as many men. The same gap exists, on a much larger scale, in the business of pornography, a $500-million-plus industry in the U.S. which caters almost exclusively to men. In the first flush of 1970s feminism, two magazines—*Playgirl* and *Viva*—began publishing male centerfolds. *Viva* dropped the nude photos after surveys showed their readers didn't care for them; the editor herself admitted to finding them slightly disgusting.

Blum presents these findings as suggestive of a hard-wired difference between men and women. I'd be cautious about accepting that conclusion. First of all, there's the question of which physiological responses count as "erotic arousal" and whether they couldn't be evidence of other states. Clearly, too, we can *learn* to have certain physiological responses—and to suppress them—so nothing biologically definitive is proved by the presence or absence of physical arousal.

Studies that rely on viewers' *own* reports need to be carefully interpreted too. I know, from talking to women students, that they sometimes aren't all that clear about *what* they feel in the presence of erotic stimuli, and even when they are, they may not be all that comfortable admitting what they feel. Hell, not just my students! Once, a lover asked me, as we were about to part for the evening, if there was anything that we hadn't done that I'd really like to do. I knew immediately what that was: I wanted him to undress, very slowly, while I sat on the floor and just watched. But I couldn't tell him. I was too embarrassed. Later, alone in my compartment on the train, I sorely regretted my cowardice. The fact is that I love to watch a man getting undressed, and I especially like it if he is conscious of being looked at. But there is a long legacy of shame to be overcome here, for both sexes, and the cultural models are only now just emerging which might help us move beyond it.

Perhaps, then, we should wait a bit longer, do a few more studies, before we come to any biological conclusions about women's failure to get aroused by naked pictures. A newer (1994) University of Chicago study found that 30 percent of women ages eighteen to forty-four and 19 percent of women ages forty-five to fifty-nine said they found "watching a partner undress" to be "very appealing." ("Not a bad percentage," Nancy Friday comments, "given that Nice Girls didn't look.") There's still a gender gap—the respective figures for men of the same age groups were 50 percent and 40 percent. We're just learning, after all, to be voyeuses. Perhaps, too, heterosexual men could learn to be less uncomfortable offering themselves as "sexual objects" if they realized the pleasure women get from it. Getting what you have been most deprived of is the best gift, the most healing gift, the most potentially transforming gift—because it has the capacity to make one more whole. Women have been deprived not so much of the *sight* of beautiful male bodies as the experience of having the male body *offered* to us, handed to us on a silver platter, the way female bodies—in the ads, in the movies—are handed to men. Getting this from her partner is the erotic equivalent of a woman's coming home from work to find a meal prepared and ready for her. Delicious—even if it's just franks and beans.

Thanks, Calvin!

Despite their bisexual appeal, the cultural genealogy of the ads I've been discussing and others like them is to be traced largely through gay male aesthetics, rather than a sudden blossoming of appreciation for the fact that women might enjoy looking at sexy, well-hung young men who don't appear to be about to rape them. Feminists might like to imagine that Madison Avenue heard our pleas for sexual equality and finally gave us "men as sex objects." But what's really happened is that women have been the beneficiaries of what might be described as a triumph of pure consumerism—and with it, a burgeoning male fitness and beauty culture—over homophobia and the taboos against male vanity, male "femininity," and erotic display of the male body that have gone along with it.

Throughout [the twentieth] century, gay photographers have created a rich, sensuous, and dramatic tradition which is unabashed in eroticizing the male body, male sensuousness, and male potency, including penises. But until recently, such representations have been kept largely in the closet. Mainstream responses to several important exhibits which opened in the seventies—featuring the groundbreaking early work of Wilhelm von Gloeden, George Dureau, and George Platt Lynes as well as then-contemporary artists such as Robert Mapplethorpe, Peter Hujar, and Arthur Tress—would today probably embarrass the critics who wrote about them when they opened. John Ashbery, in *New York* magazine, dismissed the entire genre of male nude photography with the same sexist tautology that covertly underlies that *Times* piece on cultural "overexposure": "Nude women seem to be in their natural state; men, for some reason, merely look undressed. . . . When is a nude not a nude? When it is male." (Substitute "blacks" and "whites" for "women" and "men" and you'll see how offensive the statement is.)

For other reviewers, the naked male, far from seeming "merely un-dressed," was unnervingly sexual. *New York Times* critic Gene Thompson wrote that "there is something disconcerting about the sight of a man's naked body being presented as a sexual object"; he went on to describe the world of homoerotic photography as one "closed to most of us, fortu-nately." Vicki Goldberg, writing for the *Saturday Review*, was more appre-ciative of the "beauty and dignity" of the nude male body, but concluded that so long as its depiction was erotic in emphasis, it will "remain half-private, slightly awkward, an art form cast from its traditions and in search of some niche to call its home."

Goldberg needed a course in art history. It's true that in classical art, the naked human body was often presented as a messenger of spiritual themes, and received as such. But the male bodies sculpted by the Greeks and Michelangelo were not exactly nonerotic. It might be more accurate to say that in modernity, with the spiritual interpretation of the nude body no longer a convention, the contemporary homophobic psyche is not screened from the sexual charge of the nude male body. Goldberg was dead wrong about something else too. Whatever its historical lineage, the frankly sexual representation of the male body was to find, in the next twenty years, a far from private "niche to call its home": consumer culture discovered its com-mercial potency.

Calvin Klein had his epiphany, according to one biography, one night in 1974 in New York's gay Flamingo bar:

> As Calvin wandered through the crowd at the Flamingo, the body heat rushed through him like a revelation; this was the cut-ting edge. . . . [The] men! The men at the Flamingo had less to do about sex for him than the notion of portraying men as gods. He realized that what he was watching was the freedom of a new generation, unashamed, in-the-flesh embodiments of Calvin's ideals: straight-looking, masculine men, with chiseled bodies, young Greek gods come to life. The vision of shirtless young men with hardened torsos, all in blue jeans, top button opened, a whisper of hair from the belly button disappearing into the denim pants, would inspire and inform the next ten years of Calvin Klein's print and television advertisements.

Klein's genius was that of a cultural Geiger counter; his own bisexual-ity enabled him to see that the phallic body, as much as any female figure, is an enduring sex object within Western culture. In America in 1974, how-ever, that ideal was still largely closeted. Only gay culture unashamedly sexualized the lean, fit body that virtually everyone, gay and straight, now aspires to. Sex, as Calvin Klein knew, sells. He also knew that gay sex wouldn't sell to straight men. But the rock-hard, athletic gay male bodies that Klein admired at the Flamingo did not advertise their sexual prefer-ence through the feminine codes—limp wrists, raised pinkie finger, swishy walk—which the straight world then identified with homosexuality. Rather, they embodied a highly masculine aesthetic that—although definitely exciting for gay men—would scream "heterosexual" to (clueless) straights. Klein knew just the kind of clothing to show that body off in too. As Steven Gaines and Sharon Churcher tell it:

> He had watched enough attractive young people with good bodies in tight jeans dancing at the Flamingo and Studio 54 to know that the "basket" and the behind was what gave jeans sex appeal. Calvin sent his assistants out for several pairs of jeans, including the classic five-button Levi's, and cut them apart to see how they were made. Then he cut the "rise," or area from the waistband to under the groin, much shorter to accentuate the crotch and pull the seam up between the buttocks, giving the behind more shape and prominence. The result was instant sex appeal—and a look that somehow Calvin just *knew* was going to sell.

So we come to the mainstream commercialization of the aesthetic legacy of Stanley Kowalski and those inspired innovations of Brando's costumer in *A Streetcar Named Desire*. When I was growing up, jeans were "dungarees"—suitable for little kids, hayseeds, and juvenile delinquents, but not for anyone to wear on a date. Klein transformed jeans from utilitarian garments to erotic second skins. Next, Klein went for underwear. He wasn't the first, but he was the most daring. In 1981, Jockey International had broken ground by photographing Baltimore Oriole pitcher Jim Palmer in a pair of briefs (airbrushed) in one of its ads—selling $100 million worth of underwear by year's end. Inspired by Jockey's success, in 1983 Calvin Klein put a forty-by-fifty-foot Bruce Weber photograph of Olympic pole vaulter Tom Hintinauss in Times Square, Hintinauss's large penis clearly discernible through his briefs. The Hintinauss ad, unlike the Palmer ad, did not employ any of the usual fictional rationales for a man's being in his underwear—for example, the pretense that the man is in the process of getting dressed—but blatantly put Hintinauss's body on display, sunbathing on a rooftop, his skin glistening. The line of shorts "flew off the shelves" at Bloomingdale's and when Klein papered bus shelters in Manhattan with poster versions of the ad they were all stolen overnight.

Images of masculinity that will do double (or triple or quadruple) duty with a variety of consumers, straight and gay, male and female, are not difficult to create in a culture like ours, in which the muscular male body has a long and glorious aesthetic history. That's precisely what Calvin Klein was the first to recognize and exploit—the possibility and profitability of what is known in the trade as a "dual marketing" approach. Since then, many advertisers have taken advantage of Klein's insight. A recent Abercrombie & Fitch ad, for example, depicts a locker room full of young, half-clothed football players getting a postmortem from their coach after a game. Beautiful, undressed male bodies doing what real men are "supposed to do." Dirty uniforms and smudged faces, wounded players, helmets. What could be more straight? But as iconography depicting a culture of exclusively male bodies, young, gorgeous, and well-hung, what could be more "gay"?

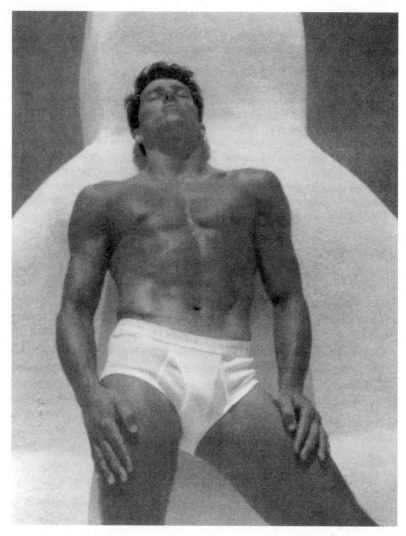

Bronzed and beautiful Tom Hintinauss: a breakthrough ad for Calvin Klein—and the
beginning of a new era for the unabashed erotic
display of the male body.

It required a Calvin Klein to give the new vision cultural form. But the fact
is that if we've entered a brave, new world of male bodies it is largely because
of a more "material" kind of epiphany—a dawning recognition among advertisers of the buying power of gay men. For a long time prejudice had triumphed over the profit motive, blinding marketers to just how sizable—and
well-heeled—a consumer group gay men represent. (This has been the case
with other "minorities" too. Hollywood producers, never bothering to do any
demographics on middle-class and professional African American women—
or the issues that they share with women of other races and classes in this

culture—were shocked at the tremendous box office success of *Waiting to Exhale*. They won't make that particular mistake again.) It took a survey conducted by *The Advocate* to jolt corporate America awake about gay consumers. The survey, done between 1977 and 1980, showed that 70 percent of its readers aged twenty to forty earned incomes well above the national median. Soon, articles were appearing on the business pages of newspapers, like one in 1982 in *The New York Times Magazine*, which described advertisers as newly interested in "wooing . . . the white, single, well-educated, well-paid man who happens to be homosexual."

"Happens to be homosexual": the phrasing—suggesting that sexual identity is peripheral, even accidental—is telling. Because of homophobia, dual marketing used to require a delicate balancing act, as advertisers tried to speak to gays "in a way that the straight consumer will not notice." Often, that's been accomplished through the use of play and parody, as in Versace's droll portraits of men being groomed and tended by male servants, and Diesel's overtly narcissistic gay posers. "Thanks, Diesel, for making us so very beautiful," they gush. Or take the ad below, with its gorgeous, mechanically inept model admitting that he's "known more for my superb bone construction and soft, supple hair than my keen intellect." The

"I'm known more for my superb bone construction and soft, supple hair than my keen intellect. But even I can hook up Kenwood's Centerstage Home Theater System in a few minutes."

playful tone reassures heterosexual consumers that the vanity (and mechanical incompetence) of the man selling the product is "just a joke." For gay consumers, on the other hand, this reassurance is *itself* the "joke"; they read the humor in the ad as an insider wink, which says, "This is for *you*, guys." The joke is further layered by the fact that they know the model in the ad is very likely to be gay.

Contrast this ad to the ostentatious heterosexual protest of a Perry Ellis ad which appeared in the early 1990s (and no, it's not a parody):

> I hate this job. I'm not just an empty suit who stands in front of a camera, collects the money and flies off to St. Maarten for the weekend.
>
> I may model for a living, but I hate being treated like a piece of meat. I once had a loud-mouthed art director say "Stand there and pretend you're a human." I wanted to punch him, but I needed the job.
>
> What am I all about? Well, I know I'm very good-looking, and there are days when that is enough. Some nights, when I'm alone, it's not.
>
> I like women—all kinds.
>
> I like music—all kinds.
>
> I like myself so I don't do drugs.
>
> Oh yeah, about this fragrance. It's good. Very good.
>
> When I posed for this picture, the art director insisted that I wear it while the pictures were being taken. I thought it was silly, but I said "What the hell? It's their money."
>
> After a while, I realized I like this fragrance a lot. When the photo shoot was over, I walked right over, picked up the bottle, put it in my pocket and said "If you don't mind, I'd like to take this as a souvenir." Then I smiled my best f—— you smile and walked out.
>
> Next time, I'll pay for it.
>
> It's that good.

Today, good-looking straight guys are flocking to the modeling agencies, much less concerned about any homosexual taint that will cleave to them. It's no longer necessary for an ad to plant its tongue firmly in cheek when lavishing erotic attention on the male body—or to pepper the ad with proofs of heterosexuality. It used to be, if an advertisement aimed at straight men dared to show a man fussing over his looks with seemingly romantic plans in mind, there had better be a woman in the picture, making it clear just *whom* the boy was getting pretty for. To sell a muscle-building product to heterosexuals, of course, you had to link it to virility and the ability to attract women on the beach. Today, muscles are openly sold for their looks; Chroma Lean nutritional supplement unabashedly compares the well-sculpted male body to a work of art (and a gay male icon, to boot)— Michelangelo's "David." Many ads display the naked male body without shame or plot excuse, and often exploit rather than resolve the sexual ambiguity that is generated.

Today, too, the athletic, muscular male body that Calvin plastered all over buildings, magazines, and subway stops has become an aesthetic norm, for straights as well as gays. "No pecs, no sex," is how the trendy David Barton gym sells itself: "My motto is not 'Be healthy'; it's 'Look better naked,'" Barton says. The notion has even made its way into that most determinedly heterosexual of contexts, a Rob Reiner film. In *Sleepless in Seattle*, Tom Hanks's character, who hasn't been on a date in fifteen years, asks his friend (played by Rob) what women are looking for nowadays. "Pecs and a cute butt," his friend replied without hesitation. "You can't even turn on the news nowadays without hearing about how some babe thought some guy's butt was cute. Who the first woman to say this was I don't know, but somehow it caught on." Should we tell Rob that it wasn't a woman who started the craze for men's butts?

Rocks and Leaners

We "nouvelles voyeuses" thus owe a big measure of thanks to gay male designers and consumers, and to the aesthetic and erotic overlap—not uniform or total, but significant—in what makes our hearts go thump. But although I've been using the term for convenience, I don't think it's correct to say that these ads depict men as "sex objects." Actually, I find that whole notion misleading, whether applied to men or women, because it seems to suggest that what these representations offer is a body that is inert, depersonalized, flat, a mere thing. In fact, advertisers put a huge amount of time, money, and creativity into figuring out how to create images of beautiful bodies that are heavy on attitude, style, associations with pleasure, success, happiness. The most compelling images are suffused with "subjectivity"— they *speak* to us, they seduce us. Unlike other kinds of "objects" (chairs and tables, for example), they don't let us use them in any way we like. In fact, they exert considerable power over us—over our psyches, our desires, our self-image.

How do male bodies in the ads speak to us nowadays? In a variety of ways. Sometimes the message is challenging, aggressive. Many models stare coldly at the viewer, defying the observer to view them in any way other than how they have chosen to present themselves: as powerful, armored, emotionally impenetrable. "I am a rock," their bodies (and sometimes their genitals) seem to proclaim. Often, as in the Jackson Browne lookalike ad, the penis is prominent, but *unlike* the penis in that ad, its presence is martial rather than sensual. Overall, these ads depict what I would describe as "face-off masculinity," in which victory goes to the dominant contestant in a game of will against will. Who can stare the other man down? Who will avert his eyes first? Whose gaze will be triumphant? Such moments—"facing up," "facing off," "staring down"—as anthropologist David Gilmore has documented, are a test of macho in many cultures, including our own. "Don't eyeball me!" barks the sergeant to his cadets in training in *An Officer and a Gentleman*; the authority of the stare is a prize to

Face-off masculinity.

be won only with full manhood. Before then, it is a mark of insolence—or stupidity, failure to understand the codes of masculine rank. In *Get Shorty*, an unsuspecting film director challenges a mob boss to look him in the eye; in return, he is hurled across the room and has his fingers broken.

"Face-off" ads, except for their innovations in the amount of skin exposed, are pretty traditional—one might even say primal—in their conception of masculinity. Many other species use staring to establish dominance, and not only our close primate relatives. It's how my Jack Russell terrier intimidates my male collie, who weighs over four times as much as the little guy but cowers under the authority of the terrier's macho stare. In the doggie world, size doesn't matter; it's the power of the gaze—which indicates the power to stand one's ground—that counts. My little terrier's dominance, in other words, is based on a convincing acting job—and it's one that is very similar, according to William Pollack, to the kind of performance that young boys in our culture must learn to master. Pollack's studies of boys suggest that a set of rules—which he calls "The Boy Code"—govern their behavior with each other. The first imperative of the code—"Be a sturdy oak"—represents the emotional equivalent of "face-off masculinity": Never reveal weakness. Pretend to be confident even though you may be scared. Act like a rock even when you feel shaky. Dare others to challenge your position.

The face-off is not the only available posture for male bodies in ads today. Another possibility is what I call "the lean"—because these bodies are almost always reclining, leaning against, or propped up against something in the fashion typical of women's bodies. James Dean was probably our first pop-culture "leaner"; he made it stylish for teenagers to slouch. Dean, however, never posed as languidly or was as openly seductive as some of the high-fashion leaners are today. A recent Calvin Klein "Escape" ad depicts a young, sensuous-looking man leaning against a wall, arm raised, dark underarm hair exposed. His eyes seek out the imagined viewer, soberly but flirtatiously. *"Take Me,"* the copy reads.

Languid leaners have actually been around for a long time. Statues of sleeping fauns, their bodies draped languorously, exist in classical art alongside more heroic models of male beauty. I find it interesting, though, that Klein has chosen Mr. Take Me to advertise a perfume called "Escape." Klein's "Eternity" ads usually depict happy, heterosexual couples, often with a child. "Obsession" has always been cutting-edge, sexually ambiguous erotica. This ad, featuring a man offering himself up seductively, invitingly to the observer, promises "escape." From what? *To* what? Men have complained, justly, about the burden of always having to be the sexual initiator, the pursuer, the one of whom sexual "performance" is expected. Perhaps the escape is from these burdens, and toward the freedom to indulge in some of the more receptive pleasures traditionally reserved for women. The pleasures, not of staring someone down but of feeling one's body caressed by another's eyes, of being the one who receives the awaited call rather than the one who must build up the nerve to make the call, the one who doesn't have to hump and pump, but is permitted to lie quietly, engrossed in reverie and sensation.

Some people describe these receptive pleasures as "passive"—which gives them a bad press with men, and is just plain inaccurate too. "Passive" hardly describes what's going on when one person offers himself or herself

to another. Inviting, receiving, responding—these are active behaviors too, and rather thrilling ones. It's a macho bias to view the only *real* activity as that which takes, invades, aggresses. It's a bias, however, that's been with us for a long time, in both straight and gay cultures. In many Latin cultures, it's not a disgrace to sleep with other men, so long as one is *activo* (or *machista*)—the penetrator rather than the penetratee. To be a *pasivo*, on the other hand, is to be socially stigmatized. It's that way in prison cultures too—a good indication of the power hierarchies involved. These hierarchies date back to the ancient Greeks, who believed that passivity, receptivity, penetrability were marks of inferior feminine being. The qualities were inherent in women; it was our nature to be passively controlled by our sexual needs. (Unlike us, the Greeks viewed women—not men—as the animalistic ones.) Real Men, who unlike women had the necessary rationality and will, were expected to be judicious in the exercise of their desires. But being judicious and being "active"—deciding when to pursue, whom to pursue, making advances, pleading one's case—went hand in hand.

Allowing oneself to be pursued, flirting, accepting the advances of another, offering one's body—these behaviors were permitted also (but only on a temporary basis) to still-developing, younger men. These young men—not little boys, as is sometimes incorrectly believed—were the true "sex objects" of elite Greek culture. Full-fledged male citizens, on the other hand, were expected to be "active," initiators, the penetrators not the penetratees, masters of their own desires rather than the objects of another's. Plato's *Symposium* is full of speeches on the different sexual behaviors appropriate to adult men with full beards and established professions and glamorous young men still revered more for their beauty than their minds. But even youth could not make it okay for a man to behave *too much* like a woman. The admirable youth was the one who—unlike a woman—was able to remain sexually "cool" and remote, to keep his wits about him. "Letting go" was not seemly.

Where does our culture stand today with respect to these ideas about men's sexuality? Well, to begin with, consider how rarely male actors are shown—on their faces, in their utterances, and not merely in the movements of their bodies—having orgasms. In sex scenes, the moanings and writhings of the female partner have become the conventional cinematic code for heterosexual ecstasy and climax. The male's participation is largely represented by caressing hands, humping buttocks, and—on rare occasions—a facial expression of intense concentration. She's transported to another world; he's the pilot of the ship that takes her there. When men are shown being transported themselves, it's usually been played for comedy (as in Al Pacino's shrieks in *Frankie and Johnny*, Eddie Murphy's moanings in *Boomerang*, Kevin Kline's contortions in *A Fish Called Wanda*), or it's coded to suggest that something is not quite normal about the man—he's sexually enslaved, for example (as with Jeremy Irons in *Damage*). Mostly, men's bodies are presented like action-hero toys—wind them up and watch them perform.

Hollywood—still an overwhelmingly straight-male-dominated industry—is clearly not yet ready to show us a man "passively" giving himself over to another, at least not when the actors in question are our cultural icons. Too feminine. Too suggestive, metaphorically speaking, of penetration by another. But perhaps fashion ads are less uptight? I decided to perform an experiment. I grouped ads that I had collected over recent years into a pile of "rocks" and a pile of "leaners" and found, not surprisingly, that both race and age played a role. African American models, whether in *Esquire* or *Vibe*, are almost always posed facing-off. And leaners tend to be younger than rocks. Both in gay publications and straight ones, the more languid, come-hither poses in advertisements are of boys and very young men. Once a certain maturity line is crossed, the challenging stares, the "face-off" postures are the norm. What does one learn from these ads? Well, I wouldn't want to claim too much. It used to be that one could tell a lot about gender and race from looking at ads. Racial stereotypes were transparent, the established formulas for representing men and women were pretty clear (sociologist Erving Goffman even called ads "gender advertisements"), and when the conventions were defied it was usually because advertisers sensed (or discovered in their polls) that social shifts had made consumers ready to receive new images. In this "post-modern" age, it's more of a free-for-all, and images are often more reactive to each other than to social change. It's the viewers' jaded eye, not their social prejudices, that is the prime consideration of every ad

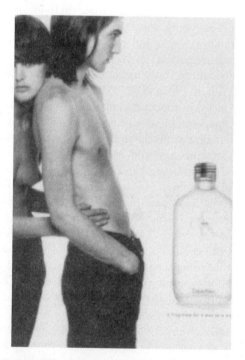

A youthful, androgynous "leaner" — appropriately enough, advertising [CK One] fragrance "for a man or a woman."

campaign, and advertisers are quick to tap into taboos, to defy expectations, simply in order to produce new and arresting images. So it wouldn't surprise me if we soon find languid black men and hairy-chested leaners in the pages of *Gentlemen's Quarterly*.

But I haven't seen any yet. At the very least, the current scene suggests that even in this era of postmodern pastiche racial clichés and gender taboos persist; among them, we don't want grown men to appear too much the "passive" objects of another's sexual gaze, another's desires. We appear, still, to have somewhat different rules for boys and men. As in ancient Greece, boys are permitted to be seductive, playful, to flirt with being "taken." *Men* must still be in command. Leonardo DiCaprio, watch out. Your days may be numbered.

"Honey, What Do I Want to Wear?"

Just as fifties masculinity was fought over (metaphorically speaking) by Stanley Kowalski and Stanley Banks, the male fashion scene of the nineties involves a kind of contest for the souls of men too. Calvin Klein, Versace, Gucci, Abercrombie & Fitch have not only brought naked bottoms and bulging briefs onto the commercial scene, they present underwear, jeans, shirts, and suits as items for enhancing a man's appearance and sexual

"I'm damn well gonna wear what I want.
Honey, what do I want?"

appeal. They suggest it's fine for a man to care about how he looks and to cultivate an openly erotic style. In response, aggressively heterosexual Dockers and Haggar ads compete—for the buying dollar of men, but in the process for their gender consciousness too—by stressing the no-nonsense utility of khakis. Consider the Haggar casuals advertisement on the previous page, and what it says about how "real men" should feel about their clothes:

"I'm damn well gonna wear what I want. . . . Honey, what do I want?"

Looked at in one light, the man in the advertisement is being made fun of, as a self-deceived blusterer who asserts his independence "like a man" and in the next breath reveals that he is actually a helpless little boy who needs his mommy to pick out his clothes for him. But fashion incompetence is a species of helplessness that many men feel quite comfortable with, even proud of. Recognizing this, Haggar and Dockers are among those manufacturers who have put a great deal of effort into marketing "nonfashion-guy fashion" to a niche of straight men—working-class and yuppie—who, they presume, would be scared off by even a whiff of "feminine" clothes-consciousness. Here's another one from Haggar's:

"In the female *the ability to match colors comes at an early age. In the* male *it comes when he marries a female."*

The juxtaposition of inept male/fashion-conscious female, which with one stroke establishes the masculinity *and* the heterosexuality of the depicted man, is a staple of virtually every Haggar ad. In a Haggar television spot with voice-over by John Goodman (Roseanne's beefy former television husband), a man wakes up, sleepily pulls on a pair of khakis, and goes outside to get the paper:

"I am not what I wear. I'm not a pair of pants, or a shirt." (He then walks by his wife, handing her the front section of the paper.) *"I'm not in touch with my inner child. I don't read poetry, and I'm not politically correct."* (He goes down a hall, and his kid snatches the comics from him.) *"I'm just a guy, and I don't have time to think about what I wear, because I've got a lot of important guy things to do."* (Left with only the sports section of the paper, he heads for the bathroom.) *"One-hundred-per-cent-cotton-wrinkle-free khaki pants that don't require a lot of thought. Haggar. Stuff you can wear."*

Yes, it's a bit of a parody, but that only allows Haggar to double its point that real guys have better things to do than think about what they are going to wear or how they appear to others. The guy who would be so worried about his image that he couldn't poke fun at himself wouldn't be a real guy at all. Real guys don't take themselves so seriously! That's for wimps who favor poetry, self-help psychology, and bleeding-heart politics. That's for girls, and for the men who are pussy-whipped by them.

In Haggar's world, real guys don't choose clothing that will enhance the appearance of their bodies or display a sense of style; real guys just put on some "stuff" to wear because they have to, it's socially required. The less decorative, the better. "We would never do anything with our pants that would frighten anyone away," says Dockers designer Gareth Morris as reported in a 1997 piece in *The New Yorker*. "We'd never do too many belt loops, or an unusual base cloth . . . [or] zips or a lot of pocket flaps and details on the back." Pocket flaps, the ultimate signifier of suspect sexuality! In such ads, male naiveté about the sexual potency of clothes, as agency maven David Altschiller claims, is critical. "In women's advertising," he points out, "self-confidence is sexy. But if a man is self-confident—if he knows he is attractive and is beautifully dressed—then he's not a man anymore. He's a fop. He's effeminate." In Dockers' "Nice Pants" television ads, for example, it's crucial that the guy not *know* his pants are "nice" until a gorgeous woman points it out to him.

It's no accident that the pants are described via the low-key understatement "nice" (rather than "great," for example, which would suggest that the guy was actually *trying* to look good). For the real man (according to Dockers), the mirror is a tool, not a captivating pool; if he could, he'd look the other way while he shaves. Many other advertisers capitalize on such notions, encouraging men to take care of their looks, but reassuring them that it's for utilitarian or instrumental purposes. Cosmetic surgeons emphasize the corporate advantage that a face-lift or tummy tuck will give the aging executive: "A youthful look," as one says, "gives the appearance of a more dynamic, charging individual who will go out and get the business." Male grooming products too are often marketed by way of "action hero" euphemisms which obscure their relation to feminine versions of the same product (a male girdle marketed by BodySlimmers is called the Double Agent Boxer) and the fact that their function is to enhance a man's appearance: hair spray as "hair control," exfoliating liquid as "scruffing lotion," astringents as "scrubs," moisturizers and fragrances as "after" or "pre" accompaniments to that most manly of rituals, the shave. They often have names like Safari and Chaps and Lab Series, and come in containers shaped like spaceships and other forms a girl could have some fun with.

The notions about gender that are maintained in this marketing run deeper than a refusal to use the word "perfume" for products designed to make men smell good. In the late seventies, coincident with the development of feminist consciousness about these matters, art historian John Berger discovered what he argued were a set of implicit cultural paradigms of masculinity and femininity, crystallized in a visual "rule" of both classical painting and commercial advertisements: *"men act and women appear."* Here's a contemporary illustration:

The man in the *Nautica* ad on the next page, rigging his sail, seems oblivious to his appearance; he's too busy checking the prevailing winds. The woman, in contrast, seems well aware and well pleased that her legs have caught the attention of the men gaping at her. A woman's *appearance*, Berger argued, has been socially determined to be "of crucial importance for what is normally thought of as the success of her life." Even walking on a city street, headed for their highpowered executive jobs, women exist to be seen, and they *know* it—a notion communicated by the constant tropes of female narcissism: women shown preening, looking in mirrors, stroking

Men act and women appear.

their own bodies, exhibiting themselves for an assumed spectator, asking to be admired for their beauty.

With depictions of men, it's just the opposite. "A man's presence," Berger wrote, "is dependent upon the promise of power which he embodies . . . what he is capable of doing to you or for you." Thus, the classic formula for representing men is always to show them in action, immersed in whatever they are doing, seemingly unaware of anyone who might be looking at them. They never fondle their own bodies narcissistically, display themselves purely as "sights," or gaze at themselves in the mirror. In everything from war paintings to jeans and cologne ads, men have been portrayed as utterly oblivious to their beauty (or lack of it), intent only on getting the job done—raising the flag, baling hay, lassoing a steer, busting up concrete. The ability to move heavy things around, tame wild creatures—that's manly business. Fretting about your love handles, your dry skin, your sagging eyelids? That's for girls.

Women in ads and movies thus require no plot excuse to show off their various body parts in ads, proudly, shyly, or seductively; it's the "business" of *all* of us to be beautiful—whether we are actresses, politicians, homemakers, teachers, or rock stars. This has changed very little since Berger came up with his formula. When *Time* magazine did a story on the new dominance of female stars in the rock world, its cover featured singing star Jewel, not performing, but in a dewy close-up, lips moist and soft eyes smiling from behind curled lashes. This formidable new "force" in the rock world might as well have been modeling Maybelline. True, a beautiful woman today may be depicted puffing away on a cigar, getting "in touch with her masculine side." But in expression she's still a seductress, gazing through long-lashed lids into the eyes of an imagined viewer. "Do you like what you see?" the expressions of the models seem to ask.

Men, according to Berger's formula, must never seem as though they are asking this question, and may display their beauty only if it is an unavoidable side effect of other "business." Thus, a lot of the glistening, naked male chests in the movies of the fifties and sixties were on the bodies of warriors, prisoners, slaves, and prizefighters. No one could claim there was vanity in such nakedness. (No time for preening while nailing spikes on a chain gang or rowing in a slave galley.) So a strong dose of male skin could be sneaked into a movie without disturbing the gender rules. The physical presence of an actor like Richard Gere, who emanates consciousness of his body as the erotic focus of the gaze and invites it, has always annoyed and disconcerted critics. The pomposity of Charlton Heston, on the other hand, his naked (and actually rather gorgeous) chest puffed up in numerous biblical epics, goes unnoticed, because he's doing it all in a builder-of-the-universe rather than narcissus-in-the-mirror mode.

Saturday Night Fever (1977) deserves mention here, for openly breaking with this convention. Tony Manero (John Travolta), a disco-dancing dandy who knows how to use his walk, was a man who *really* needed a course in masculinity-according-to-Haggar. He blows all his wages on fancy shirts and shoes. On Saturday night, he prepares his body meticulously, shaving, deodorizing, blow-drying, choosing just the right combination of gold chains and amulets, torso-clinging pants, shiny platforms. Eating dinner with his family, he swathes himself in a sheet like a baby to protect his new floral shirt; when his father boxes his ear roughly, his only thought is for his pompadour: "Just watch the hair! I work on my hair a long time and you hit it. He hits the hair!" Manero spends much of his time in front of the mirror, getting himself pretty, posing, anticipating the impression he's going to make when he enters the disco or struts down the street.

Never before *Saturday Night Fever* had a heterosexual male movie hero spent so much time on his toilette. (Even Cary Grant's glamorous looks were never shown as requiring any conscious effort or attention; in *The Awful Truth* he sits under a tanning lamp—but that's to fake a trip to Florida.) Although this was the polyester seventies, and men like Sonny Bono dressed like Tony on television, Bono was very careful (as the Beatles were too) to treat his flamboyant ruffles as showbiz costumes, while Cher proudly strutted her feathers and finery as a second skin for her body and sexuality. Tony, like Cher, chooses his clothes to highlight his sinuous form.

Manero was, in many ways, the cinema equivalent (reassuringly straight and working-class) of the revolution that Calvin Klein was making in more sexually ambiguous form in the fashion world. As a dancer, Tony is unembarrassed—and the camera isn't embarrassed either—to make his hips, groin, and buttocks the mesmerizing center of attention. Travolta was also the first actor to appear on-screen in form-fitting (if discreetly black) briefs.

One scene finds him asleep in his underwear, blanket between his legs, hip jutting upward; the camera moves slowly down the length of his body, watches as Tony rouses, sits up, pulls the blanket from between his legs, and puts his hand in his briefs to adjust his penis. (The script originally had called for Travolta to appear naked in a later scene; he balked, suggesting the early morning scene as a compromise.) We then follow him to the mirror (where he compares himself admiringly with a poster of Al Pacino) and into the hall, where he flexes teasingly for his shocked grandmother. This was new stuff, and some people were a bit taken aback by such open male vanity and exhibitionism. (Pauline Kael, for one, seemed to need to convince herself of Tony's sexual orientation. "It's a straight heterosexual film," she wrote, "but with a feeling for the sexiness of young boys who are bursting their britches with energy and desire.")

True, there is the suggestion, in the film, that Tony may grow out of his narcissism once he leaves Brooklyn and the gold chain crowd. Hollywood, of course, had shown men preening, decorating, and oiling themselves before—pimps and homosexuals, usually, but also various unassimilated natives (blacks, Puerto Ricans, Italians) depicted as living more fully in their bodies, with a taste for flashy clothes that marks them as déclassé. Manero fits those stereotypes—but only up to a point. He may have awful taste in jewelry, but he also has boyish charm and "native" intelligence. Unlike his friends—a pathetic trio of racist, homophobic, sexist homeboys—Tony has integrity. He is enraged when, at the "2001" dance contest, racism and favoritism land him first prize over a Puerto Rican couple. He's also the only one of his friends who doesn't taunt a gay couple as they pass on the street. The movie may poke affectionate fun at him, but it also admires him. A hero-narcissus—a very new image for postwar Hollywood.

Of course, most men, gold chains or not, straight or gay, *do* care how they "appear." The gender differences described in Berger's formula and embedded in the Dockers and Haggar advertisements are "fictional," a distillation of certain *ideas* about men and women, not an empirical generalization about their actual behavior. This doesn't mean, however, that they have no impact on "real life." Far from it. As embodied in attractive and sometimes highly manipulative images, "men act and women appear" functions as a visual instruction. Women are supposed to care very much about fashion, "vanity," looking good, and may be seen as unfeminine, man-hating, or lesbian if they don't. The reverse goes for men. The man who cares about his looks the way a woman does, self-esteem on the line, ready to be shattered at the slightest insult or weight gain, is unmanly, sexually suspect. ·

So the next time you see a Dockers or Haggar ad, think of it not only as an advertisement for khakis but also as an advertisement for a certain notion of what it means to be a man. The ad execs know that's what's going on, they're open about not wanting to frighten men off with touches of feminine decorativeness. What they are less open about is the fact that such ads don't just cater to male phobias about fashion but also perpetuate them. They have to. Nowadays, the Dockers man is competing against other models of masculinity, laughing at him from both the pages of history and from what was previously the "margin" of contemporary culture. Can you imagine Cary Grant, Rupert Everett, or Michael Jordan as the fashion-incompetent man in a Dockers ad? The stylish man, who began to make a new claim on popular cultural representations with the greater visibility of black and gay men—the men consumer culture once ignored—was chiseling cracks in the rule that "men act and women appear" even as Berger was formulating it.

Male Decorativeness in Cultural Perspective

Not all heterosexual men are as uptight about the pocket flaps on their pants as the Haggar executive would have us believe. Several weeks after the piece on khakis appeared in *The New Yorker*, a reader wrote in protesting that the idea "that men don't want to look like they're trying to be fashionable or sexy" was rather culture-bound. Maybe, this reader acknowledged, it applies to American, English, and Japanese men. "But are we really to believe that French, Italian, and Spanish men share this concern? And, when we expand the category 'male' beyond human beings, biologists have shown that the demonstration of male splendor is a key element in the vertebrate mating game. Are American males just an anomalous species?"

The letter reminds us that there are dangers in drawing broad conclusions on the basis of only those worlds with which one is familiar. And it's not just different international attitudes toward men and fashion that cast doubt on the universal applicability of the Dockers/Haggar view of masculinity. To look at the variables of race, class, and history is to produce a picture of male attitudes toward fashionable display that is far from consistently phobic.

First of all, for most of human history, there haven't been radically different "masculine" and "feminine" attitudes toward beauty and decorativeness. On farms, frontiers, and feudal estates, women were needed to work alongside men and beauty was hardly a priority for either. Among aristocrats, it was most important to maintain class privilege (rather than gender difference), and standards of elegance for both sexes (as Anne Hollander's fascinating *Sex and Suits* documents) were largely the same: elaborate headwear, cosmetics, nonutilitarian adornments, and accessories. Attention to beauty was associated not with femininity but with a life that was both privileged and governed by exacting standards. The constrictions, precarious adornments, elaborate fastenings reminded the elite that they were highly civilized beings, not simple peasant "animals." At the same time, decorativeness was a mode of royal and aristocratic competition, as households and courts would try to out-glam each other with jewels and furs. Hollander describes a sixteenth-century summit meeting between Francis I and Henry VIII, in which everyone wore "silver covered with diamonds, except when they were in cloth of gold and covered with rubies. Everything was lined with ermine and everything was 20 yards long, and there were plumes on everybody." Everybody—male or female—had to be as gorgeous as possible. It was a mode of power competition.

Until roughly the fourteenth century, men and women didn't even dress very differently. (Think of the Greeks and Romans and their unisex robes and togas.) Clear differences started to emerge only in the late Middle Ages and early Renaissance: women's breasts began to be exposed and emphasized in tight bodices, while their legs were covered with long skirts. Men's legs—and sometimes their genitals as well—were "fully articulated" and visible through pantaloons (what we call "tights"), with body armor covering the chest. While to our sensibilities, the shapely legs and genitals of men in tights (unless required by a ballet or historical drama) are either to be laughed at or drooled over, Hollander argues that in the Renaissance, to outline the male body was to make it more "real" and "natural," less a template for sexual fantasy (as women's bodies were becoming). This trend continued, with men's clothing getting progressively more unrestrictive, tailored, simple and women's more stiff, tightly fitted, decorative. Still, into the seventeenth century, fashionable gentlemen continued to wear lace and silk, and to don powder and wigs before appearing in public. Hollander regards the nineteenth century as a "great divide," after which not only the styles of men's and women's clothing (trousers for men, increasingly romantic froufrou for women) would become radically different, but ideas about them as well. Men's clothing must now be "honest, comfortable, and utilitarian," while women's begins to develop a reputation for being "frivolous" and "deceptive." The script for "men act and women appear" was being written—right onto male and female clothing.

Looking beyond fashion to the social world (something Hollander refuses to do, but I'll venture), it's hard not to speculate that these changes anticipate the emergence of the middle class and the nineteenth-century development of distinctively separate spheres for men and women within it. In the industrial era, men's sphere—increasingly the world of manufacturing, buying, selling, power brokering—was performance-oriented, and demanded "no nonsense." Women, for their part, were expected not only to provide a comfortable, well-ordered home for men to return to but to offer beauty, fantasy, and charm for a man to "escape" to and restore himself with after the grim grind of the working day. As this division of labor developed, strong dualistic notions about "masculinity" and "femininity" began to emerge, with sanctions against the man or woman who dared to cross over to the side of the divide where they did not belong "by nature."

By the end of the nineteenth century, older notions of manliness premised on altruism, self-restraint, and moral integrity—qualities that women could have too—began to be understood as vaguely "feminine." Writers and politicians (like Teddy Roosevelt) began to complain loudly about the emasculating effects of civilization and the excessive role played by women teachers in stifling the development of male nature. New words like "pussyfoot" and "stuffed shirt"—and, most deadly, "sissy"—came into parlance, and the "homosexual" came to be classified as a perverse personality type which the normal, heterosexual male had to prove himself distinct from. (Before, men's relations with each other had been considerably more fluid, and even the heterosexual male was allowed a certain degree of physical intimacy and emotional connection—indeed, "heterosexuality" as such was a notion that hardly made sense at the time.) A new vogue for bodybuilding emerged. "Women pity weakly men," O. S. Fowler warned, but they love and admire "right hearty feeders, not dainty; sprightly, not tottering; more muscular than exquisite, and more powerful than effeminate, in mind and body." To be "exquisite," to be decorative, to be on display, was now fully woman's business, and the man who crossed that line was a "fop."

From that time on, male "vanity" went into hiding, and when cosmetic products for men began to be marketed (for men *did* use them, albeit in secret), they had to justify themselves, as Kathy Piess documents, through the manly rhetoric of efficiency, rugged individualism, competitive advantage, autonomy. While Pompeian cream promises to "beautify and youthify" women, the same product for men will help them "win success" and "make promotion easier" on the job. Even that most manly of rituals (from our perspective), shaving, required special rhetoric when home shaving was first introduced early in the twentieth century. "The Gillette is typical of the American spirit," claimed a 1910 ad. "Its use starts habits of energy— of initiative. And men who *do* for themselves are men who *think* for themselves." Curley's Easy-Shaving Safety Razor claimed that "the first Roman to shave every day was no fop, but Scipio, conqueror of Africa." When it came to products used also by women—like scents and creams—manufacturers went out of their way to reassure prospective customers of their no-nonsense "difference," through action names (Brisk, Dash, Vim, Keen, Zest) and other means. When Florian, a line of men's toiletries, was introduced in 1929, its creator, Carl Weeks, advised druggists to locate the products near cigar (again!) counters, using displays featuring manly accouterments like boxing gloves, pipes, footballs. This, he argued, "will put over the idea that the mascu-*line* is all *stag*. It's for he-men with no women welcome nohow."

This isn't to say that from the turn of the nineteenth century on, the drive to separate "masculine" and "feminine" attitudes toward self-beautification pushed forward relentlessly. For one thing, culture is never of one piece; it has its dominant images, but also its marginal, recessive, and countercultural images. For another, the history of gender ideology didn't end with the nineteenth century, as dramatic as its changes were. A century of mutations and permutations followed, as demanded by social, economic, and political conditions. Older ideals lingered too and were revived when needed. The Depression, for example, brought a love affair with (a fantasy of) aristocratic "class" to popular culture, and a world of Hollywood representations . . . in which sexual difference was largely irrelevant, the heroes and heroines of screwball comedy a matched set of glamorously attired cutups. In these films, the appeal of actors like Cary Grant, Fred Astaire, and William Powell was largely premised not on assertions of masculine performance but on their elegance, wit, and charm. Their maleness wasn't thrown into question by the cut of their suits. Rather, being fashionable signified that they led an enviable life of pleasure and play. Such associations still persist today. Fashion advertisements for Ralph Lauren, Valentino, Hugo Boss, and many others are crafted to appeal to the class consciousness of consumers; in that universe, one can never be too beautiful or too vain, whatever one's sex.

In the screwball comedies, it didn't matter whether you were a man or a woman, everyone's clothes sparkled and shone. Following the lead of the movies, many advertisements of the thirties promoted a kind of androgynous elegance. But others tried to have their cake and eat it too, as in a 1934 ad for Fougère Royale aftershave, which depicts a group of tony men in tuxedos, hair slicked back, one even wearing a pince-nez, but with the caption "Let's *not* join the ladies!" We may be glamorous, even foppish—but *puh-lease! Ladies* we're not! I should note, too, that while the symbols of "class" can function to highlight equality between men and women, they can also be used to emphasize man's superiority over women—as in a contemporary Cutty Sark ad in which a glamorously attired woman relaxes, dreamily stroking a dog, while the tuxedo-clad men standing around her engage in serious conversation (about stocks, I imagine); these guys don't need to go off into the drawing room in order to escape the ladies; they can keep one around for a bit of decorativeness and sensual pleasure while she remains in her own, more languorous world within their own.

During World War II, movies and magazines continued to celebrate independent, adventurous women, to whom men were drawn "as much for their spirit and character as for their looks."[1] But when the fighting men returned, the old Victorian division of labor was revived with a new commercial avidity, and the world became one in which "men act" (read: *work*) and "women appear" (read: *decorate*—both themselves and their houses)—with a vengeance. Would Barbie get on a horse without the proper accessories? Would the Marlboro Man carry a mirror with him on the trail? By the late fifties and early sixties, the sexy, wisecracking, independent-minded heroine had morphed into a perky little ingenue. Popular actresses Annette Funicello, Connie Stevens, and Sandra Dee were living Barbie dolls, their femininity blatantly advertised on their shirt-waisted bodies. They had perfectly tended bouffant hairdos (which I achieved for myself by sleeping on the cardboard cylinders from toilet tissue rolls) and wore high heels even when washing dishes (I drew the line at that). And what about the dashing, cosmopolitan male figure in fashionable clothes? He now was usually played as a sissy or a heel—as for example Lester (Bob Evans), the slick playboy of *The Best of Everything*, who seduces gullible April (Diane Baker) with his big-city charm, then behaves like a cad when she gets pregnant.

There have always been ways to market male clothes consciousness, however. Emphasizing neatness is one. Our very own Ronnie Reagan (when he was still a B-movie star) advertised Van Heusen shirts as "the neatest Christmas gift of all" because they "won't wrinkle . . . ever!!" Joining elegance with violence is another. James Bond could get away with wearing beautiful suits because he was ruthless when it came to killing and bedding. (A men's cologne, called 007, was advertised in the sixties with clips from *Thunderball*, the voice-over recommending: "When you use 007, be kind" because "it's loaded" and "licensed to kill . . . women.") The elegant male who is capable of killing is like the highly efficient secretary who takes off her glasses to reveal a passionate, gorgeous babe underneath: a species of tantalizing, sexy disguise.

When elegance marks one man's superior class status over another it gives him a competitive edge (as was the dominant function of elegance before the eighteenth century) rather than turning him into a fop. "We have our caste marks, too" ran a 1928 ad for Aqua Velva, which featured a clean-shaven, top-hatted young man, alongside a turbaned, bejeweled, elite Indian man. This ad, however, proved to be problematic, as Kathy Piess points out. American men didn't like being compared with dark-skinned foreigners, even aristocratic ones. The more dominant tradition—among Europeans as well as Americans—has been to portray an order in which the clean, well-shaven white man is being served or serviced by the dark ones, as in a 1935 American ad for Arrow Shirts in which the black maid is so fashion-clueless that she doesn't even know what a manufacturer's label is, or in a German ad for shaving soap depicting the "appropriate" relation between the master race and the Others.

Such codes were clearly being poked fun at—how successfully I'm not sure—when a 1995 Arid Extra-Dry commercial depicted African American pro basketball player Charles Barkley dressed up as a nineteenth-century British colonial, declaring that anything less than Arid "would be uncivilized." The commercial, however, is not just (arguably) a poke at the racist equation of civilization and whiteness. It's also, more subtly, a playful assertion of some distinctive African American attitudes toward male display. "Primordial perspiration," Barkley says in the commercial, "shouldn't mess with your style." And "style" is a concept whose history and cultural meanings are very different for blacks and whites in this country. Among many young African American men, appearing in high style, "cleaned up" and festooned with sparkling jewelry, is not a sign of effeminacy, but potency and social standing. Consider the following description, from journalist Playthell

Benjamin's 1994 memoir, *Lush Life* (while you're reading it, you might also recall Anne Hollander's description of Henry VIII's summit meeting):

> [Fast Black] was dressed in a pair of white pants, white buck shoes, and a long-sleeve white silk shirt—which was open to his navel and revealed a 24-karat gold chain from which hung a gold medallion set with precious stones: diamonds, rubies, and emeralds. His massively muscled body was strikingly displayed in a white see-through silk shirt, and the trousers strained to contain his linebacker thighs. His eyes were bloodshot and his skin was

> tight against his face, giving it the look of an ebony mask. He
> struck me right off as a real dangerous muthafucka; mean
> enough to kill a rock.

A "real dangerous muthafucka" in a white see-through silk shirt? For the
white boys to whom the Dockers and Haggar ads are largely addressed, see-
through silk is for girls, and showing off one's body—particularly with sensuous fabrics—is a "fag" thing. Thus, while a Haggar ad may play up the
sensual appeal of soft fabrics—*"These clothes are very soft and they'll never
wrinkle"*—it makes sure to include a parenthetical (and sexist) reference to a
dreamed-of wife: *"Too bad you can't marry them."* But sartorial sensuality and
decorativeness, as I've learned, do not necessarily mean "femininity" for
African American men.

When I first saw the Charles Barkley commercial, the word "style"
slipped by me unnoticed, because I knew very little about the history of
African American aesthetics. An early paper of mine dealing with Berger's
equation was utterly oblivious to racial differences that might confound
the formula "men act and women appear." Luckily, an African American
male colleague of mine gently straightened me out, urging me to think
about Mike Tyson's gold front tooth as something other than willful masculine defiance of the tyranny of appearance. Unfortunately, at that time
not much of a systematic nature had been written about African American
aesthetics; I had to find illuminating nuggets here and there. Then, just this
year, Shane White and Graham White's *Stylin'* appeared. It's a fascinating
account of how the distinctive legacy of African aesthetics was maintained
and creatively, sometimes challengingly, incorporated into the fashion
practices of American blacks, providing a vibrant (and frequently subversive) way for blacks to "write themselves into the American story."

Under slavery, white ownership of blacks was asserted in the most concrete, humiliating way around the display of the body on the auction block.
Slaves were often stripped naked and instructed to show their teeth like
horses being examined for purchase. Women might have their hair cut off.
Everyone's skin would be polished to shine, as apples are polished in gro-
cery stores today. As a former slave described it:

> "The first thing they had to do was wash up and clean up real good and
> take a fat greasy meat skin and run over their hands, face and also their
> feet, or in other words, every place that showed about their body so that
> they would look real fat and shiny. Then they would trot them out before
> their would-be buyers and let them look over us real good, just like you
> would a bunch of fat cows that you were going to sell on the market and try
> to get all you could for them."

It makes perfect sense that with the body so intimately and degradingly
under the control of the slave owner, opportunities to "take back" one's
own body and assert one's own cultural meanings with it would have a
special significance. On Sundays, slaves would dress up for church in the
most colorful, vibrant clothes they could put together—a temporary escape
from and an active repudiation of the subservience their bodies were forced

into during the week. Their outfits, to white eyes, seemed "clashing" and mismatched. But putting together unusual combinations of color, texture, and pattern was an essential ingredient of West African textile traditions, handed down and adapted by African American women. Color and shape "coordination"—the tyranny of European American fashion until pretty recently—were not the ruling principles of style. "Visual aliveness," *Stylin'* reports, was. The visual aliveness of the slaves' Sunday best, so jangling to white sensibilities, was thus the child both of necessity—they were forced to construct their outfits through a process of bricolage, putting them together from whatever items of clothing were available—and aesthetic tradition.

From the start, whites perceived there was something insubordinate going on when blacks dressed up—and they were not entirely wrong. "Slaves were only too keen to display, even to flaunt, their finery both to slaves and to whites"; the Sunday procession was, as I've noted, a time to reclaim the body as one's own. But at the same time, blacks were not just "flaunting," but preserving and improvising on vibrant African elements of style whose "flashiness" and "insolence" were largely in the eye of the white beholder, used to a very different aesthetic. The cultural resistance going on here was therefore much deeper than offended whites (and probably most blacks too) realized at the time. It wasn't simply a matter of refusal to behave like Stepin Fetchit, with head lowered and eyes down. A new culture of unpredictable, playfully decorative, visually bold fashion was being created—and it would ultimately (although not for some time) transform the world of mainstream fashion as much as Klein's deliberately erotic underwear and jeans.

After "emancipation," funeral marches and celebratory promenades were a regular feature of black city life, in which marchers, male and female alike, were "emblazoned in colorful, expensive clothes," the men in "flashy sports outfits: fancy expensive silk shirts, new pants, hats, ties, socks," "yellow trousers and yellow silk shirts," and "bedecked with silk-and-satin-ribboned streamers, badges." Apart from formal processions, streets like Memphis's Beale Street and New Orleans's Decatur Street were ongoing informal sites for "strolling" and display. The most dazzlingly dressed men, often jazz musicians, were known as "sports." As "Jelly Roll" Morton describes it, each "sport" had to have a Sunday suit, with coat and pants that did not match, and crisply pressed trousers as tight as sausage skins. Suspenders were essential and had to be "very loud," with one strap left provocatively "hanging down." These guys knew how to "use their walk" too. The sport would walk down the street in a "very mosey" style: "Your hands is at your sides with your index fingers stuck out and you kind of struts with it." Morton—by all accounts a particularly flashy sport—had gold on his teeth and a diamond in one of them. "Those days," he recalled, "I thought I would die unless I had a hat with the emblem Stetson in it and some Edwin Clapp shoes." Shades of Tony Manero. Or King Henry VIII.

In fact, the flashiest African American male styles have partaken both of the African legacy and European notions of "class." Although the origin of the zoot suit—broad shoulders, long coats, ballooning, peg-legged trousers, usually worn with a wide-brimmed hat—is debated, one widely believed account says it was based on a style of suit worn by the Duke of Windsor. Another claims Rhett Butler in *Gone With the Wind* was the inspiration for the zoot suit (if so, it is a "deep irony," as the authors of *Stylin'* comment). But whatever its origins, the zoot suit, worn during the forties when cloth conservation orders ruled the use of that much fabric illegal, was a highly visible and dramatic statement in *disunity* and defiance of "American Democracy," a refusal to accede to the requirements of patriotism. Even more so than the slave's Sunday promenade, the zoot-suiter used "style" aggressively to assert opposition to the culture that had made him marginal to begin with—without his assent.

The use of high style for conspicuous display or defiance is still a big part of male street culture, as sociologist Richard Majors notes: "Whether it's your car, your clothes, your young body, your new hairdo, your jewelry, you style it. The word 'style' in [African American] vernacular usage means to show off what you've got. And for teenagers with little money and few actual possessions, showing off what you do have takes on increased importance. As one youth puts it, 'It's identity. It's a big ego trip.'"

What's changed since Majors wrote these words in the early nineties is the increasing commercial popularity of hip-hop music and culture, which has turned the rebellious stylings of street youth into an empire of images

Two versions of "style": "Style point" and "life, unity, peace."

and products, often promoted (and sometimes designed) by big-name stars. With postmodern sensibilities (grab what you like) ruling the fashion world, moreover, what once were signature elements of black street style have been incorporated—as gay styles have also been incorporated—in the fashions of other worlds, both "high" (designer clothing) and "low" (white high school boys with their pants slung low, trying to look so cool).

Despite the aggressive visibility of hip-hop culture, "showing off what you've got" has not been the only influential definition of style among African Americans. In the late nineteenth and early twentieth century, several etiquette books were published, written by middle-class blacks, promoting a very different fashion ideal. The *National Capital Code of Etiquette*, published in 1889, warned young men to "avoid colors that do not blend with the remainder of your wearing apparel, and above all things shun the so-called 'loud' ties with colors that fairly shriek unto Heaven. . . ." The young black men should also avoid "bright reds, yellows and light greens as you would the plague" and never, ever strut or swagger. Hortense Powdermaker, who studied black life in Indianola, Mississippi, in the late 1930s, noted that better-off African Americans "deliberately avoided bright colors" and were offended when clerks, on the basis of "the Negroe's reputation for wearing gaudy clothes," assumed they wanted something "loud." Those who advocated a less ostentatious style were dismayed by the lower-class practice of adorning healthy front teeth with gold, while leaving bad back teeth unattended.

A recent *Essence* list of fashion "do's and don'ts" emphasizes this deliberately understated—and in today's world, "professional"—conception of black male style. "Yes" to well-groomed hands, well-fitting suit and a "definite sense of self." "No" to "glossy polished nails," "cologne that arrives before he does," "Mr. T jewelry (the T stands for tacky)," and "saggy jeans on anyone old enough to remember when 'Killing Me Softly' was *first* released." Even in their most muted variations, African American styles have done a great deal to add color, playfulness, and unexpected, sexy little fillips to "tasteful," professional male clothing: whimsical ties, internationally inspired shirts and sweaters, and, in general, permission to be slightly dramatic, flirtatious, and ironic with one's clothes. The rule of always matching patterns, too, no longer holds in the world of high fashion, the result of a collaboration (not necessarily conscious, of course) between postmodern sensibilities and the slave legacy of bricolage.

Superstar Michael Jordan (his masculine credentials impeccable, his reputation as a family man solidly established over the years), a very effective spokesperson for style, has done a great deal to make fashionableness, even "feminine" decorativeness, congruous with masculinity. This year, he was named *GQ*'s "Most Stylish Man." "How stylish is Michael Jordan?" *GQ* asks. "Answer: So stylish he can get away with wearing five rings!" Of course, the fact that Jordan can "get away" with wearing five rings reveals *GQ*'s cultural biases. For the magazine, Jordan's stylishness resides in the "drape of his suits, in the plain gold hoop in his left ear, in the tempered, toned-down body language of his late career." For *GQ*, subtlety equals style. For Jordan too. But of course that plain gold hoop would not have been viewed as so tastefully subtle had Jordan not made it an acceptable item of male decorativeness.

Jordan, God bless him, is also unabashed in admitting that he shops more than his wife, and that he gets his inspiration from women's magazines. The

night before he goes on the road, he tries on every outfit he's going to wear. He describes himself as a "petite-type person" who tries to hide this with oversize clothes and fabrics that drape. When questioned about the contradiction between the "manliness" of sports and his "feminine" love of fashion, Jordan replies that "that's the fun part—I can get away from the stigma of being an athlete." Saved by fashion from the "stigma" of being a sweaty brute—that's something, probably, that only an African American man can fully appreciate. The fact that it's being an athlete and not "femininity" that's the "stigma" to be avoided by Jordan—that's something a woman's got to love.

The ultimate affront to Dockers masculinity, however, is undoubtedly the Rockport ad on the previous page, with drag superstar RuPaul in a beautifully tailored suit. His feet and his stare are planted—vitually identically to Michael Jordan's posture in the feature I've just discussed—in that unmistakable (and here, ironic) grammar of face-off ad masculinity. "I'm comfortable being a MAN," declares RuPaul. "I'm comfortable being a woman too," of course, is the unwritten subtext. Man, woman, what's the difference so long as one is "uncompromising" about style?

My World . . . and Welcome to It?

Despite everything I've said thus far, I feel decidedly ambivalent about consumer culture's inroads into the male body. I *do* find it wonderful—as I've made abundantly clear—that the male form, both clothed and unclothed, is being made so widely available for sexual fantasy and aesthetic admiration. I like the fact that more and more heterosexual white guys are feeling permission to play with fashion, self-decoration, sensual presentation of the self. Even Dockers has become a little less "me a guy . . . duh!" in its ads and spreads for khakis, which now include spaced-out women as well as men.

But I also know what it's like to be on the other side of the gaze. I know its pleasures, and I know its agonies—intimately. Even in the second half of the twentieth century, beauty remains a prerequisite for female success. In fact, in an era characterized by some as "postfeminist," beauty seems to count more than it ever did before, and the standards for achieving it have become more stringent, more rigorous, than ever. We live in an empire ruled not by kings or even presidents, but by images. The tight buns, the perfect skin, the firm breasts, the long, muscled legs, the bulgeless, sagless bodies are everywhere. Beautiful women, everywhere, telling the rest of us how to stand, how to swing our hair, how slim we must be.

Actually, all this flawless beauty is the product of illusion, generated with body doubles, computers, artful retouching. "Steal this look!" the lifestyles magazines urge women; it's clear from the photo that great new haircut of Sharon Stone's could change a woman's life. But in this era of digital retouching not even Sharon Stone looks like Sharon Stone. (Isabella Rossellini, who used to be the Lancôme girl before she got too old, has said that her photos are so enhanced that when people meet her they tell her,

"Your sister is so beautiful.") Still, we try to accomplish the impossible, and often get into trouble. Illusions set the standard for real women, and they spawn special disorders and addictions: in trying to become as fat-free and poreless as the ads, one's fleshly body is pushed to achieve the impossible.

I had a student who admitted to me in her journal that she had a makeup addiction. This young woman was unable to leave the house—not even to walk down to the corner mailbox—without a full face and body cover-up that took her over an hour and a half to apply. In her journal, she described having escalated over a year or so from minimal "touching-up" to a virtual mask of foundation, powder, eyebrow pencil, eye shadow, eyeliner, mascara, lip liner, lipstick—a mask so thorough, so successful in its illusionary reality that her own naked face now looked grotesque to her, mottled, pasty, featureless. She dreaded having sex with her boyfriend, for fear some of the mask might come off and he would see what she looked like underneath. As soon as they were done, she would race to the bathroom to reapply; when he stayed over, she would make sure to sleep lightly, in order to wake up earlier than he. It's funny—and not really funny. My student's disorder may be one generated by a superficial, even insane culture, a disorder befitting the Oprah show rather than a PBS documentary. But a disorder nonetheless. Real. Painful. Deforming of her life.

So, too, for the eating disorders that run rampant among girls and women. In much of my writing on the female body, I've chronicled how these disorders have spread across race, class, and ethnic differences in this culture. Today, serious problems with food, weight, and body image are no longer (if they ever were) the province of pampered, narcissistic, heterosexual white girls. To imagine that they are is to view black, Asian, Latin, lesbian, and working-class women as outside the loop of the dominant culture and untouched by its messages about what is beautiful—a mistake that has left many women feeling abandoned and alone with a disorder they weren't "supposed" to have. Today, eating problems are virtually the norm among high school and college women—and even younger girls. Yes, of course there are far greater tragedies in life than gaining five pounds. But try to reassure a fifteen-year-old girl that her success in life doesn't require a slender body, and she will think you dropped from another planet. *She* knows what's demanded; she's learned it from the movies, the magazines, the soap operas.

There, the "progressive" message conveyed by giving the girls and women depicted great careers or exciting adventures is overpowered, I think, by the more potent example of their perfect bodies. The plots may say: "The world is yours." The bodies caution: "But only if you aren't fat." What counts as "fat" today? Well, Alicia Silverstone was taunted by the press when she appeared at the Academy Awards barely ten pounds heavier than her (extremely) svelte self in *Clueless*. Janeane Garofalo was the "fat one" in *The Truth About Cats and Dogs*. Reviews of *Titanic* described Kate Winslett as plump, overripe, much too hefty for ethereal Leonardo DiCaprio. Any anger you detect here is personal too. I ironed my hair in the sixties, have dieted all my life, continue to be deeply ashamed of those parts of my body—like my peasant legs and zaftig behind—that our culture has coded as ethnic excess. I suspect it's only an accident of generational timing or a slight warp in the fabric of my cultural environment that prevented me from developing an eating disorder. I'm not a makeup junky like my student, but I am becoming somewhat addicted nowadays to alpha-hydroxies, skin drenchers, quenchers, and other "age-defying" potions.

No, I don't think the business of beauty is without its pleasures. It offers a daily ritual of transformation, renewal. Of "putting oneself together" and walking out into the world, more confident than you were, anticipating attraction, flirtation, sexual play. I love shopping for makeup with my friends. (Despite what Rush Limbaugh tells you, feminism—certainly not feminism in the nineties—is not synonymous with unshaved legs.) Women bond over shared makeup, shared beauty tips. It's fun. Too often, though, our bond is over shared pain—over "bad" skin, "bad" hair, "bad" legs. There's always that constant judgment and evaluation—not only by actual, living men but by an ever-present, watchful cultural gaze which always has its eye on our thighs—no matter how much else we accomplish. We judge each other that way too, sometimes much more nastily than men. Some of the bitchiest comments about Marcia Clark's hair and Hillary Clinton's calves have come from women. But if we are sometimes our "own worst enemies," it's usually because we see in each other not so much competition as a reflection of our fears and anxieties about ourselves. In this culture, all women suffer over their bodies. A demon is loose in our consciousness and can't easily be controlled. We see the devil, fat calves, living on Hillary's body. We point our fingers, like the accusers at Salem. Root him out, kill *her*!

And now men are suddenly finding that devil living in their flesh. If someone had told me in 1977 that in 1997 *men* would comprise over a quarter of cosmetic-surgery patients, I would have been astounded. I never dreamed that "equality" would move in the direction of men worrying *more* about their looks rather than women worrying less. I first suspected that something major was going on when the guys in my gender classes stopped yawning and passing snide notes when we discussed body issues, and instead began to protest when the women talked as though they were the only ones "oppressed" by standards of beauty. After my book *Unbearable Weight* appeared, I received several letters from male anorexics, reminding me that the incidence of such disorders among men was on the rise. Today, as many as a million men—and eight million women—have an eating disorder.

Then I began noticing all the new men's "health" magazines on the newsstands, dispensing diet and exercise advice ("A Better Body in Half the Time," "50 Snacks That Won't Make You Fat") in the same cheerleader-ish mode that Betty Friedan had once chastised the women's magazines for: "It's Chinese New Year, so make a resolution to custom-order your next takeout. Ask that they substitute wonton soup for oil. Try the soba noodles instead of plain noodles. They're richer in nutrients and contain much less fat." I guess the world doesn't belong to the meat-eaters anymore, Mr. Ben Quick.

It used to be a truism among those of us familiar with the research on body-image problems that most men (that is, most straight men, on whom the studies were based) were largely immune. Women, research showed, were chronically dissatisfied with themselves. But men tended, if anything, to see themselves as better-looking than they (perhaps) actually were. Peter Richmond, in a 1987 piece in *Glamour*, describes his "wonderful male trick" for seeing what he wants to see when he looks in the mirror:

> I edit out the flaws. Recently, under the influence of too many Heinekens in a strange hotel room, I stood in front of a wrap-around full-length mirror and saw, in a moment of nauseous clarity, how unshapely my stomach and butt have become. The next morning, looking again in the same mirror, ready to begin another business day, I simply didn't see these offending areas.

Notice all the codes for male "action" that Richmond has decorated his self-revelation with. "Too many Heinekens," "another business day"—all reassurances that other things matter more to him than his appearance. But a decade later, it's no longer so easy for men to perform these little tricks. Getting ready for the business day is apt to exacerbate rather than divert male anxieties about the body, as men compete with fitter, younger men and fitter, more self-sufficient women. In a 1994 survey, 6,000 men ages eighteen to fifty-five were asked how they would like to see themselves. Three of men's top six answers were about looks: attractive to women, sexy, good-looking. Male "action" qualities—assertiveness, decisiveness—trailed at numbers eight and nine.

"Back when bad bodies were the norm," claims *Fortune* writer Alan Farn-ham (again, operating with the presumption of heterosexuality), "money distinguished male from male. Now muscles have devalued money," and the market for products and procedures "catering to male vanity" (as *Fortune* puts it) is $9.5 billion or so a year. "It's a Face-Lifted, Tummy-Tucked Jungle Out There," reports *The New York Times*. To compete, a man

> could buy Rogaine to thicken his hair. He could invest in Body-Slimmers underwear for men, by the designer Nancy Ganz, with built-in support to suck in the waist. Or he could skip the aloe skin cream and go on to a more drastic measure, new to the male market: alpha-hydroxy products that slough off dead skin. Or he could rub on some belly- and thigh-shrinking creams . . . If rubbing cream seems too strenuous, [he] can just don an undershirt from Mountainville House, to "shape up and pull in loose stomachs and sagging chests," with a diamond-shaped insert at the gut for "extra control." . . . Plastic surgery offers pectoral implants to make the chest appear more muscular, and calf muscle implants to give the leg a bodybuilder shape. There is liposuction to counter thickening middles and accumulating breast and fatty tissue in the chest . . . and a half-dozen surgical methods for tightening skin.

Some writers blame all this on sexual equality in the workplace. Anthropologist Lionel Tiger offers this explanation: "Once," he says, "men could fairly well control their destiny through providing resources to women, but now that the female is obliged to earn a living, he himself becomes a resource. He becomes his own product: Is he good-looking? Does he smell good? Before, when he had to provide for the female, he could have a potbelly. Now he has to appear attractive in the way the female had to be." Some evidence does support this. A *Psychology Today* survey found that the more financially secure the woman, the more important a man's looks were to her.

I, however, tend to see consumer capitalism rather than women's expectations or proclivities as the true motor driving male concern with appearance. Calvin gave us those muscled men in underwear. Then the cosmetics, diet, exercise, and surgery industries elbowed in, providing the means for everyone to develop that great Soloflex body. After all, why should they restrict themselves to female markets if they can convince men that their looks need constant improvement too? The management and enhancement of the body is a gold mine for consumerism, and one whose treasures are inexhaustible, as women know. Dieting and staving off aging are never-ending processes. Ideals of beauty can be endlessly tinkered with by fashion designers and cosmetic manufacturers, remaining continually elusive, requiring constant new purchases, new kinds of work on the body.

John Berger's opposition of "acting" and "appearing," this body work reveals, is something of a false duality—and always has been. "Feminine" attention to appearance is hardly the absence of activity, as men are learning. It takes time, energy, creativity, dedication. It can *hurt*. Nowadays, the "act/appear" duality is even less meaningful, as the cultivation of the suitably fit appearance has become not just a matter of sexual allure but also a demonstration that one has the "right stuff": will, discipline, the ability to stop whining and "just do it." When I was growing up in the sixties, a muscular male body meant beefy but dumb jock; a middle-class girl could drool over him but probably wouldn't want to marry him. Today, with a booming "gymnasium culture" existing (as in ancient Greece) for professional men and with it a revival of the Greek idea that a good mind and a good body are not mutually exclusive, even Jeff Goldblum has got muscles, and the only type of jock he plays is a computer jock.

All of this, as physicians have begun to note, is landing more and more men straight into the formerly female territory of body-image dysfunction, eating disorders, and exercise compulsions. Last year, I read a survey that reported that 90 percent of male undergraduates believe that they are not muscular enough. That sent warning bells clanging in my mind, and sure enough, there's now a medical category for "muscle dysmorphia" (or "bigorexia," as it's actually sometimes called!), a kind of reverse anorexia in which the sufferer sees his muscles as never massive enough. Researchers are "explaining" bigorexia in the same dumb way they've tended to approach women's disorders—as a combination of bad biochemistry and "triggering events," such as being picked on. They just don't seem to fully appreciate the fact that bigorexia—like anorexia—only blooms in a very particular cultural soil. Not even the ancient Greeks—who revered athletic bodies and scorned weaklings, but also advised moderation in all things—produced "muscle dysmorphics." (Or at least, none of the available medical texts mention anything like it.) Anorexia and bigorexia, like so many contemporary disorders, are diseases of a culture that doesn't know when to stop.

Those beautiful bodies of Greek statues may be the historical inspiration for the muscled men in underwear of the Calvin Klein ads. But the fact is that studying the ancient Greeks reveals a different set of attitudes toward beauty and the body than our contemporary ideals, both homosexual and heterosexual. As is well known by now (although undiscussed when I studied philosophy as an undergraduate), Plato was not above appreciating a beautiful young body. In *Symposium*, he describes the beauty of the body as evidence of the presence of the divine on earth, and the original spur to all "higher" human endeavors (as well as earthly, sexual love). We see someone dazzling, and he or she awakens the soul to its natural hunger to be lifted above the mundane, transitory, mortal world. Some people seek that transcendence through ordinary human intercourse, and achieve the only immortality they will know through the begetting of human offspring and the continuation of the human race. For others, the beautiful body of another becomes the inspiration for a lifelong search for beauty in all its forms, the creation of beautiful art, beautiful words, beautiful ideals, beautiful cities. They will achieve their immortality through communion with something beyond the body—the idea of Beauty itself.

So human beauty is a pretty far-ranging and powerful thing for Plato, capable of evoking worlds beyond itself, even recalling a previous life when we dwelt among timeless, perfect forms. But human beauty, significantly (in fact, all earthly beauty), can only offer a glimpse of heavenly perfection. It's our nature to be imperfect, after all, and anyone who tries to overcome that limitation on earth is guilty of hubris—according to the Greeks. Our own culture, in contrast, is one without "limits" (a frequent theme of advertisements and commercials) and seemingly without any fear of hubris. Not only do we expect perfection in the bodies of others (just take a gander at some personal ads), we are constantly encouraged to achieve it ourselves, with the help of science and technology and the products and services they make available to us. "This body could be yours," the chiseled Greek statue in the Soloflex commercial tells us (and for only twenty minutes three times a week—give me a break!). "Timeless Beauty Is Within Your Reach," reads an ad for cosmetic surgery. Plato is rolling over in his grave.

For Plato (unlike Descartes) there are no "mere" physical bodies; bodies are lit with meaning, with memory. Our culture is more Cartesian; we like to think of our bodies as so much stuff, which can be tinkered with without any consequences for our soul. We bob our "family noses," lift our aging faces, suction extra fat, remove minor "flaws" with seemingly little concern for any "deep" meaning that our bodies might have, as repositories of our histories, our ethnic and racial and family lineage, our personalities. Actually, much of the time our intentions are to deliberately shed those meanings: to get rid of that Jewish nose, to erase the years from our faces. Unlike the Platonic philosopher, we aren't content to experience timelessness in philosophy, art, or even the beautiful bodies of others; we want to stop time on our own bodies too. In the process, we substitute individualized beauty—the distinctive faces of the generation of beautiful actresses of my own age, for example—for generic, very often racialized, reproducible codes of youth.

The fact is that we're not only Cartesian but Puritan in our attitudes toward the body. The Greeks went for muscles, sure, but they would have regarded our exercise compulsions as evidence of a system out of control. They thought it unseemly—and a failure of will—to get too self-obsessed with *any*thing. They were into the judicious "management" of the body (as French philosopher Michel Foucault has put it), not its utter subjugation. We, on the other hand, can become what our culture considers to be sexually alluring only if we're willing to regard our flesh as recalcitrant metal, to be pummeled, burned, and tempered into steel, day in and day out. No pain, no gain. Obsessively pursuing these ideals has deprived both men *and* women of the playful eros of beauty, turned it all into constant, hard work. I love gay and black body cultures for their flirtatiousness, their tongue-in-cheekness, their irony, their "let's dress up and have some fun" attitudes. Consumer culture, unfortunately, can even grind playfulness into a commodity, a required item for this year's wardrobe.

For all its idealization of the beauty of the body, Greek culture also understood that beauty could be "inner." In the *Symposium*, a group of elite Greeks discourse on the nature of love. Everyone except for Socrates and

Aristophanes is in love with someone else at the party, and they're madly flirting, advancing their own romantic agendas through their speeches. Among the participants are the most beautiful young men of their crowd. Socrates himself is over fifty at the time, and not a pretty man to look at (to put it generously). Yet as we're told at the beginning (and this seems to have been historically true), nearly everyone has at one time or another been "obsessed" with him, "transported, completely possessed" —by his cleverness, his irony, his ability to weave a spell with words and ideas. Even the most dazzling Athenian of them all—soldier superhero Alcibiades, generally regarded as one of the sexiest, handsomest men in town, who joins the party late (and drunk) with a beautiful wreath of violets and ivy and ribbons in his hair—is totally, madly smitten with Socrates.

Alcibiades' love for Socrates is *not* "Platonic" in the sense in which we have come to understand that term. In fact, Alcibiades is insulted because Socrates has refused to have sex with him. "The moment he starts to speak," he tells the crowd of his feelings for Socrates, "I am beside myself: my heart starts leaping in my chest, the tears come streaming down my face." This is not the way it usually goes. In the more normal Greek scheme of things, it's the beautiful young man—like Alcibiades—who is supposed to start the heart of the older man thumping, and who flirtatiously withholds his favors while the older lover does his best to win him. Alcibiades is in a state about this role reversal, but he understands why it has happened. He compares Socrates to a popular kind of satyr statue, which (like the little lacquered Russian dolls we're more familiar with) could be opened to reveal another figure within. Socrates may be ugly as a satyr on the outside, but "once I had a glimpse of the figures within—they were so godlike, so bright and beautiful, so utterly amazing, that I no longer had a choice—I just had to do whatever he told me."

We pay constant lip service to beauty that is more than skin-deep. The talk shows frequently parade extreme May-December matings for our ogling too. But the fact is that the idea of a glamorous young man being romantically, *sexually* obsessed with someone old and "ugly"—same-sex or other-sex and no matter what other sterling qualities he or she may have— is pretty much beyond us. Historically, men have benefited from a double standard which culturally codes their gray hair, middle-age paunches, facial lines, as signs of wisdom and experience rather than advancing decrepitude. My older gay male friends lament that those days are over for them. And if those new polls about women's attitudes are to be believed, the clock is ticking on that double standard for heterosexual men, too—no matter how hard Hollywood tries to preserve it. With more and more expectation that men be as physically well-tended as women, those celluloid pairings of Woody Allen and women half as old and forty-six times as good-looking are becoming more of a hoot every day.

There is something anti-sensual to me about current aesthetics. There's so much that my younger friends go "uggh" over. Fat—yecch! Wrinkles— yuck! They live in a constant state of squeamishness about the flesh. I find that finely muscled young Calvin Klein model beautiful and sexy, sure. But

I also was moved by Clint Eastwood's aging chest in *The Bridges of Madison County*. Deflated, skin loose around the waistband of his pants, not a washboard ridge in sight—for me, they signaled that Eastwood (at least for this role) had put Dirty Harry away for good, become a real, warm, penetrable, vulnerable human being instead of a make-my-day machine. Call me old-fashioned, but I find that very sexy. For a culture obsessed with youth and fitness, in contrast, sagging flesh is almost the ultimate signifier of decay and disorder. We prefer the clean machine—and are given it, in spades. Purified of "flaws," all loose skin tightened, armored with implants, digitally enhanced, the bodies of most movie stars and models are fully dressed even when naked.

In *Saturday Night Fever*, John Travolta had been trim, but (by contemporary standards) a bit "soft." Six years later, Travolta re-created Tony Manero in the sequel, *Staying Alive*. This time, however, the film was directed by Sylvester Stallone, who showed Travolta a statue of a discus thrower and asked, "How would you like to look like that?" "Terrific," Travolta replied, and embarked on a seven-month program of fitness training that literally redesigned his body into a carbon copy of Sly's. In the film, his body was "perfect": gleaming and muscular, without an ounce of fat. He was nice to look at. But if I had to choose between the Tony Manero of *Fever* and the Tony Manero of *Staying Alive*, it'd be no contest. I'd rather spend time (and have sex) with a dancing man with love handles than with a Greek statue who gets in a nasty mood if he misses a workout.

NOTE

[1] Not that women's beauty was dispensable. Concern for her looks symbolized that although she worked as hard as a man, a woman's mind was still on the *real* men who were fighting for her freedom. (An ad for Tangee lipstick describes "a woman's lipstick [as] an instrument of personal morale that helps her to conceal heartbreak or sorrow; gives her self-confidence when it's badly needed. . . . It symbolizes one of the reasons why we are fighting . . . the precious right of women to be feminine and lovely—under any circumstances.") The woman of this period was a creature of both "appearance" *and* "action"—a kind of forerunner to today's superwoman.

BIBLIOGRAPHY

Beauvoir, Simone de. (1952). *The Second Sex*. New York: Vintage Books.
Berger, John. (1972). *Ways of Seeing*. Great Britain: Penguin Books.
Blum, Deborah. (1997). *Sex on the Brain: The Biological Differences Between Men and Women*. New York: Viking Penguin.
Boyd, Herbert, and Robert Allen (eds.). (1995). *Brotherman*. New York: Ballantine.
Clark, Danae. (1995). "Commodity Lesbianism." In Kate Meuhuron and Gary Persecute (eds.). *Free Spirits*. Englewood Cliffs, NJ: Prentice Hall, pp. 82–94.
Clarkson, Wensley. (1997). *John Travolta: Back in Character*. Woodstock: Overlook Press.
Ellenzweig, Allen. (1992). *The Homoerotic Photograph*. New York: Columbia University Press.
Farnham, Alan. (1996). "You're So Vain," *Fortune*, September 9, pp. 66–82.
Foucault, Michel. (1985). *The Use of Pleasure*. New York: Vintage Books.
Friday, Nancy. (1996). *The Power of Beauty*. New York: HarperCollins.
Gaines, Steven, and Sharon Churcher. (1994). *Obsession: The Lives and Times of Calvin Klein*. New York: Avon Books.

Gilmore, David. (1990). *Manhood in the Making*. New Haven: Yale University Press.

Gladwell, Malcolm. (1997). "Listening to Khakis," *The New Yorker*, July 28, pp. 54–58.

Hollander, Anne. (1994). *Sex and Suits: The Evolution of Modern Dress*. New York: Kodansha International.

Long, Ron. (1997). "The Fitness of the Gym," *Harvard Gay and Lesbian Review*, Vol. IV, No. 3, Summer, pp. 20–22.

Majors, Richard, and Janet Mancini Billson. (1992). *Cool Pose: The Dilemmas of Black Manhood in America*. New York: Lexington Books.

Piess, Kathy. (1998). *Hope in a Jar: The Making of America's Beauty Culture*. New York: Metropolitan Books.

Pieterse, Jan Nederveen. (1990). *White on Black: Images of Africa and Blacks in Western Popular Culture*. New Haven: Yale University Press.

Plato. (1989). *Symposium*. Trans. Alexander Nehama. Indianapolis: Hackett Publishing.

Richmond, Peter. (1987). "How Do Men Feel About Their Bodies?" *Glamour*, April, pp. 312–13, 369–72.

Rotundo, E. Anthony. (1993). *American Manhood: Transformations in Masculinity from the Revolution to the Modern Era*. New York: Basic Books.

Sartre, Jean-Paul. (1966). *Being and Nothingness*. New York: Washington Square Press.

Shaw, Dan. (1994). "Mirror, Mirror," *New York Times*, May 29, Section 9, pp. 1, 6.

Sheets-Johnstone, Maxine. (1994). *The Roots of Power: Animate Form and Gendered Bodies*. Chicago: Open Court.

Spindler, Amy. (1996). "It's a Face-Lifted Tummy-Tucked Jungle Out There," *New York Times*, June 9,

Taylor, John. (1995). "The Long Hard Days of Dr. Dick," *Esquire*, September, pp. 120–30.

White, Shane, and Graham White. (1998). *Stylin'*. Ithaca: Cornell University Press.

• • • • • • • • • • •

QUESTIONS FOR A SECOND READING

1. This is a long essay. The writing operates under a set of expectations that does not value efficiency. The writing says, "It is better to take time with this, better to take time rather than hurry, rather than rushing to say what must be said, rather than pushing to be done. Slow down, relax, take your time. This can be fun." While there is attention to a "thesis," the organizing principle of this essay is such that the real work and the real pleasure lie elsewhere. Work and pleasure. As you reread, pay particular attention to how Bordo controls the pace and direction of the essay, where she prolongs the discussion and where and when she shifts direction. Think of this as a way for her (and you) to get work done. And think about it as a way of organizing the pleasure of the text. Be prepared to describe how she does this and whether it works for you (or doesn't). And to talk about the possibilities of adapting this strategy (a strategy of more rather than less) in your own writing.

2. This is a long essay divided into subsections. The subsections mark stages in the presentation. The subsections allow you to think about form in relation to units larger than the paragraph but smaller than the essay. As you reread, pay attention to these sections. How are they organized internally? How are they arranged? How do they determine the pace or rhythm of your reading, the tonality or phrasing of the text? Which is the slowest, for

example? Which is the loudest? And why? And where are they placed? What do they do to the argument?

3. Bordo is a distinctive and stylish writer. She is also one of many writers who are thinking about visual culture and popular culture (about movies, TV, and advertisements) in relation to (what Bordo refers to as) "consumer capitalism." For those who know this work, she makes use of some terms and strategies common to cultural studies. One is to think about "subject position." Bordo says that when she saw the Calvin Klein ad, ". . . I had my first real taste of what it's like to inhabit this visual culture as a man." Another related strategy is to think about how and where one is positioned, as subject or object, in the moment of vision, a moment of looking, when you are defined by the "gaze" of another or when your "gaze" is the source of definition. She says, for example, "For many men, both gay and straight, to be so passively dependent on the gaze of another person for one's sense of self-worth is incompatible with being a real man." She works this out in the section where she talks about Jean-Paul Sartre and Simone de Beauvoir (pp. 134–35). As you reread the chapter, pay particular attention to where and how Bordo invokes and/or inhabits the "subject position" of people different from herself. How are these differences defined? (You might make a list.) Where is she most convincing? Least convincing? And, finally, be prepared to speak back to the text from what you take to be your own "subject position." How does it look to you?

4. At one point, Bordo speaks directly to you and invites you into her project: "So the next time you see a Dockers or Haggar ad, think of it not only as an advertisement for khakis but also as an advertisement for a certain notion of what it means to be a man." You don't have to be limited to Dockers, Haggar, or khaki, but as you reread the essay, keep your eye out for advertisements that come your way, advertisements that seem perfect for thinking along with Bordo, for thinking her thoughts but also for thinking about how things have changed or might be seen differently. Clip these or copy them and bring them to class.

ASSIGNMENTS FOR WRITING

1. Bordo looks back to the history of advertising (the "cultural genealogy of the ads I've been discussing") and she works directly with the ads that prompted and served this chapter in her book. These images are a key part of the writing.

   Bordo also speaks directly to you and invites you into her project: "So the next time you see a Dockers or Haggar ad, think of it not only as an advertisement for khakis but also as an advertisement for a certain notion of what it means to be a man." You don't have to be limited to Dockers, Haggar, or khaki, but as you reread the essay and prepare for this writing assignment, keep your eye out for advertisements that come your way, advertisements that seem perfect for thinking along with Bordo (or advertisements that seem like interesting counter-examples). Clip these or copy them so that you can use them, as she does, as material for writing.

Write an essay in which you take up Bordo's invitation. You should assume an audience that has not read Bordo (or not read her work recently), so you will need to take time to present the terms and direction of her argument. Your goal, however, is to extend her project to your moment in time, where advertising may very well have moved on to different images or men and strategies of presentation. Bordo is quite specific about her age and experience, her point of view. You should be equally specific. You, too, should establish your point of view. You are placed at a different moment in time, your experience is different, your exposure to images has prepared you differently. You write from a different subject position. Your job, then, is not simply to reproduce Bordo's project but to extend it, to refine it, to put it to the test.

2. The first two "Questions for a Second Reading" (pp. 177–78) point attention to the length of the essay and to its organization. Here, in effect, is what they say:

> "Beauty (Re)discovers the Male Body" is a long essay. The writing operates under a set of expectations that does not value efficiency. The writing says, "It is better to take time with this, better to take time rather than hurry, rather than rushing to say what must be said, rather than pushing to be done. Slow down, relax, take your time. This can be fun." While there is attention to a "thesis," the organizing principle of this essay is such that the real work and the real pleasure lie elsewhere. Work and pleasure. As you reread, pay particular attention to how Bordo controls the pace and direction of the essay, where she prolongs the discussion and where and when she shifts direction. Think of this as a way for her (and you) to get work done. And think about it as a way of organizing the pleasure of the text.
>
> This is a long essay divided into subsections. The subsections mark stages in the presentation. The subsections allow you to think about form in relation to units larger than the paragraph but smaller than the essay. As you reread, pay attention to these sections. How are they organized internally? How are they arranged? How do they determine the pace or rhythm of your reading, the tonality or phrasing of the text? Which is the slowest, for example? Which is the loudest? And why? And where are they placed? What do they do to the argument?

Take time to reread and to think these questions through. It has become common for scholars and teachers to think about the pleasure, even the "erotics" of the text. This is not, to be sure, the usual language of the composition classroom. Write an essay in which you describe the pleasures (and, if you choose, the problems) of Bordo's writing. Describe how it is organized, and how it organizes your time and attention. Describe how it works (or doesn't) for you as a reader, how it works (or doesn't) for her as a writer and thinker. You can, to be sure, make reference to other things you are reading or have read or to the writing you are doing (and have done) in school.

3. Bordo assumes, always, that the representations of men's bodies are generally read (or viewed) in the context of the similar use of women's bodies—in art, in advertising, in visual popular culture (including film and television). For this assignment, choose two sources—one ad directed,

you feel, primarily to men and another ad directed primarily to women—or you might look more generally at all of the ads in two magazines, one directed (you feel) primarily to men and another to women. Write an essay in which you use Bordo's essay, and its claims, to think through your examples. You will need to take time to present your examples (including, ideally, the images) and Bordo's understanding of the role of gender in the ways images of the body are designed, presented, and read. How, that is, can you both present *and* extend Bordo's work on gender and advertising?

4. Bordo says that when she saw the Calvin Klein ad, ". . . I had my first real taste of what it's like to inhabit this visual culture as a man." Throughout the essay she makes reference to her "subject position" and to the subject position of other viewers, both real and imagined—viewers younger or older, viewers of another race or ethnicity, men, viewers who are gay rather than straight. As you prepare to write this essay reread the chapter (see the "Questions for a Second Reading," p. 177), and pay particular attention to those moments where Bordo speaks to the effects of particular ads, and where she speaks from her or from another subject position. Think carefully about how she is "reading" and responding to these images. Think with equal care about what you see and how you respond; think, that is, about how you might articulate the reactions from your "subject position" or from those that Bordo has not yet been able to imagine. Choose one or two of her examples and write about them as she sees and understands them, but also as you see or understand them. How do these images look to you and at you? How might you speak back to Bordo? Take care to develop both positions with care and detail. And, at the end, think about how you might best explain the differences.

MAKING CONNECTIONS

1. In "Beauty (Re)discovers the Male Body," Bordo refers to John Berger and his work in *Ways of Seeing* (p. 97), although she refers to a different chapter than the one included here. In general, however, both Berger and Bordo are concerned with how we see and read images; both are concerned to correct the ways images are used and read; both trace the ways images serve the interests of money and power; both are written to teach readers how and why they should pay a different kind of attention to the images around them.

    For this assignment, use Bordo's work to reconsider Berger's. Write an essay in which you consider the two chapters as examples of an ongoing project. Berger's essay precedes Bordo's by about a quarter of a century. If you look closely at one or two of their examples, and if you look at the larger concerns of their arguments, are they saying the same things? Doing the same work? If so, how? And why is such work still necessary? If not, how do their projects differ? And how might you explain those differences?

2. Linda Nochlin's "Renoir's *Great Bathers*" is full of sexually charged images of women; Susan Bordo's "Beauty (Re)discovers the Male Body" is full of sexually charged images of men, the latter in the realm of commerce, the former (or at least most of them) in the realm of "art." Both Nochlin and

Bordo are interested in how images of the body circulate, in the work to which these images can be put.

Toward the end of her essay, Nochlin says:

> In concluding, I should like to say once more that in studying a major nineteenth-century theme like bathers, serious attention needs to be paid to alternative points of view, to other modes of visual production rather than the high art studied by conventional art history. Advertising, mass media prints, cartoons, and so on exist not just as undifferentiated, visually indifferent "sources" for high art but, on the contrary, as alternatives, and, often, as adversaries of it. As alternatives, they have very different work to do and from time to time enter into a positive dialectical relationship with the practices of high art, while at other times, into an equally important relationship of fierce rejection or negation with it. (p. 472)

There are two invitations here. One is to find images of the male body in contemporary "high" art—and there are many that are considered important (and many in Nochlin's book, *Bathers, Bodies, Beauty*)—and to write about them in relation to images from advertising. The goal would be to read these representations in relation to advertising practices in order to make a claim, with Nochlin, for either a "positive dialectical relationship" or a "fierce rejection."

The other invitation is to work more closely between the two essays, as an exercise in close reading. If you follow this lead, as you reread each, look for an extended section of each essay, sections that seem to speak back and forth to each other in interesting or provocative ways. What do both have to say about how images are created and perceived, about how they circulate?

Working closely with these sections, and keeping in mind a reader familiar with neither, write an essay that discusses the important differences in the work of Bordo and Nochlin. And, in your essay, think about the consequences of this comparison, what is at stake in it for you or for anyone concerned about bodies—real bodies in real time.

CORNELIUS
EADY

CORNELIUS EADY (b. 1954) is one of the most inter-
esting and challenging poets of his generation writing in
the United States. He was born and raised in Rochester,
NY; he received his degrees from Monroe Community
College and Empire State College. He has taught at the
State University of New York at Stonybrook, Sarah
Lawrence, New York University, the City College of New
York, the College of William and Mary, and Sweet Briar
College. He is currently the director of the Creative Writ-
ing Program at the University of Notre Dame.

In 1996, with Toi Derricotte, Eady founded Cave Canem, a program designed
to provide support, encouragement, and a "safe haven" for black poets, poets who
were underrepresented or isolated in their communities, whether campus communities or not. Cave Canem began as a summer retreat where young black poets
would work in the company of established writers, find friendships, and form a network; it has become a substantial force in American letters, with regional workshops
and readings, a publication series, and a program of awards and alumni recognition. You can find information on Cave Canem at www.cavecanempoets.org/pages/
about.php.

Eady's poetry is widely read and highly acclaimed. His books include Kartunes *(1980);* Victims of the Latest Dance Craze *(1985), winner of the Lamont Poetry Prize;* BOOM BOOM BOOM *(1988);* The Gathering of My Name *(1991), nominated for the Pulitzer Prize;* You Don't Miss Your Water *(1995);* The Autobiography of a Jukebox *(1997); and* Brutal Imagination *(2001), a finalist for the National Book Award. His* Collected Works *is in preparation for publication by Penguin USA. Eady has also collaborated with jazz composer Deidre Murray on several projects for the stage, many of them, as you'll see from the titles that follow, in collaboration with his book work:* You Don't Miss Your Water; Running Man, *a finalist for the Pulitzer Prize in Drama in 1999,* Fangs; *and* Brutal Imagination, *which received* Newsday's *Oppenheimer (or "Oppie") Award in 2002. Eady's other awards include the* Prairie Schooner Strousse Award, *a Lily Wallace–Reader's Digest Award, and fellowships from the Guggenheim Foundation, the National Endowment for the Arts, and the Rockefeller Foundation.*

The selection that follows is drawn from a cycle of poems titled Brutal Imagination, *which make up the first half of a book with the same title.* Brutal Imagination *tells the story of Susan Smith, a woman eventually convicted of killing her two small sons in Union, South Carolina, in 1994, and it tells the story from the point of view of the black man she invented to cover up what she had done. On October 25, Smith called the police to say that a carjacker, a black man in his twenties, wearing a plaid jacket and jeans, had jumped into her car, waving a gun, and saying, "Shut up and drive or I'll kill you." Ten miles down the road, she said, he ordered her out of her car and, in spite of her pleas on behalf of her children, two boys aged three years and fourteen months who were strapped into their car seats in the back, he drove away. A distraught Susan Smith appeared on television several times to make a tearful plea for their release. After several days the police became suspicious and began to turn the investigation her way. On the ninth day she confessed to having pushed her car down a boat ramp into a lake, the children inside.*

We are presenting a selection of poems from the cycle or series that defines Brutal Imagination. *The cycle is divided into four sections, which we have indicated.*

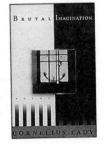

The poems are carefully arranged in sequence and they ask to be read, then, not as individual performances but as part of something that evolves, page after page. A sequence of poems, like an essay, can be a way of telling a story, of framing an argument, of thinking things through. That is how we are inviting you to approach the poems that follow. They don't require any special training, just a reader willing to read closely and carefully, and willing to take time to put it all together.

Brutal Imagination

The speaker is the young black man Susan Smith claimed kidnapped her children.

How I Got Born

Though it's common belief
That Susan Smith willed me alive
At the moment
Her babies sank into the lake

When called, I come.
My job is to get things done.
I am piecemeal.
I make my living by taking things.

So now a mother needs me clothed
In hand-me-downs
And a knit cap.

Whatever.
We arrive, bereaved
On a stranger's step.
Baby, they weep,
Poor child.

My Heart

Susan Smith has invented me because
Nobody else in town will do what
She needs me to do.
I mean: jump in an idling car
And drive off with two sad and
Frightened kids in the back.
Like a bad lover, she has given me a poisoned heart.
It pounds both our ribs, black, angry, nothing but business.
Since her fear is my blood
And her need part mythical,
Everything she says about me is true.

Who Am I?

Who are you, mister?
One of the boys asks
From the eternal backseat
And here is the one good thing:
If I am alive, then so, briefly, are they,
Two boys returned, three and one,
Quiet and scared, bunched together
Breathing like small beasts.
They can't place me, yet there's
Something familiar.
Though my skin and sex are different, maybe
It's the way I drive
Or occasionally glance back
With concern,
Maybe it's the mixed blessing
Someone, perhaps circumstance,
Has given us,
The secret thrill of hiding,
Childish, in plain sight,
Seen, but not seen,
As if suddenly given the power
To move through walls,
To know every secret without permission.
We roll sleepless through the dark streets, but inside
The cab is lit with brutal imagination.

Sightings

A few nights ago
A man swears he saw me pump gas
With the children
At a convenience store
Like a punchline you get the next day,
Or a kiss in a dream that returns while
You're in the middle of doing
Something else.

I left money in his hand.

Mr. _____ who lives in _____,
South Carolina,
Of average height
And a certain weight
Who may or may not
Believe in any of the
Basic recognized religions,
Saw me move like an angel
In my dusky skin
And knit hat.

Perhaps I looked him in the eye.

Ms. _____ saw a glint of us
On which highway?
On the street that's close
To what landmark?

She now recalls
The two children in the back
Appeared to be behaving.

Mr. _____ now knows he heard
The tires of the car
Everyone is looking for
Crunch the gravel
As I pulled up,
In the wee, wee hours
At the motel where
He works the night desk.

I signed or didn't sign the register.
I took or didn't take the key from his hand.
He looked or forgot to look
As I pulled off to park in front
Of one of the rooms at the back.

Did I say I was traveling with kids?
Who slept that night
In the untouched beds?

My Face

If you are caught
In my part of town
After dark,
You are not lost;
You are abandoned.

All that the neighbors will tell
Your kin
Is that you should
Have known better.

All they will do
Is nod their heads.
They will feel sorry
For you,

But rules are rules,
And when you were
Of a certain age
Someone pointed
A finger
In the wrong direction

And said:
All they do
Is fuck and drink
All they're good for
Ain't worth a shit.

You recall me now
To the police artist.
It wasn't really my face
That stared back that day,
But it was that look.

Susan Smith's Police Report

My shape came from out-of-nowhere.
The way some things don't belong
That's the way

I clanged up to the car
Trapped by a badly timed light.
Her poor kids never saw our image

Swell in the rearview mirror.
I was the danger of bulk; fast,
Nervous fingers

Barked the unlocked door open
And in I flooded, all the heartache
A lonely stretch of road can give.

Then she was alone, blinking in
The sight of an indifferent moon
Above the pines.

This, she swore, was the sound
Of my voice.

The Lake

When called, I come.
My job
Is to get things
Done.

Our hands grip the wheel
As I steer toward
The lake.

The children and I
Have been driving
For days.

Ever look someone
You know
Straight in the eye

And have them look
Right through you? That's been
Our fugitive lives.

They think:
They'll have to sleep
Sometime,
But we don't do things
The way you do.

They think:
Sooner or later
They'll have
To eat,

But a deal's a deal.
Our appetite behaves.
Our day seeps
Through yours.

Ever try to say
Something,
And know what you said
Slid past an ear?

That's the way these headlights
Rake the road along the lake.
That's the way
Her children yawn in the
Back seat.

The Law

I'm a black man, which means,
In Susan's case,
That I pour out of a shadow
At a traffic light,

But I'm also a mother,
Which is why she has me promise,
"I won't hurt your kids,"
Before I drift down the road.

I'm a mother,
Which is why we sing
Have mercy, come home,
No questions asked.

But I'm black, and we both know
The law.
Who's going to believe
That we had no choice
But to open that door?

Who's going to care
That it was now or
Never,
That there was no time
To unbuckle them,

That it was take the car
Or leave the car?

I'm black, which means
I mustn't slow down.
I float in forces
I can't always control,

But I'm also a mother,
Which is why
I hope
I'm as good as my word.

She knew she could get further with this if she said a black man
did it.

— A BLACK RESIDENT OF UNION, SOUTH CAROLINA

Why I Am Not a Woman

How far do you think we'd have gotten
If I'd jumped in her car, a car I wanted
For who knows what,
A woman,
And not noticed the paraphernalia?
The rattles, the child's seat?
Had smelled the spills, the dried pee,
The cloudy musk of old formula?

Even if I had pushed her out, head wild
With all I guessed I'd taken,
How many minutes,
After my foot brushed a ball,
After my eyes cooled down and focused on
The rubble of play,

How many lights do you think I'd run
Before all the stuff they'd dropped
Over the years
Into the small cracks; the straws, the cold
Fries, the pacifier,

How long do you think the cops would listen
Had Susan not sworn
I was black, I was a bad dream,
The children didn't mean a thing
To that woman.

Composite

I am not the hero of this piece.
I am only a stray thought, a solution.
But now my face is stuck to lampposts, glued
To plate glass, my forehead gets stapled
To my hat.

I am here, and here I am not.
I am a door that opens, and out walks
No-one-can-help-you.
Now I gaze, straight into your eye,
From bulletin boards, tree trunks.

I am papered everywhere,
A blizzard called
You see what happens?
I turn up when least expected.
If you decide to buy some milk,

If you decide to wash your car,
If you decide to mail a letter,

I might tumbleweed onto a pant leg.
You can stare, and stare, but I can't be found.
Susan has loosed me on the neighbors,
A cold representative,
The scariest face you could think of.

In 1989, in Boston, Charles Stuart killed his pregnant wife and
shot himself in a scheme to collect insurance money. He told the
police the assailant was a young black male.

Charles Stuart in the Hospital

Susan Smith now knows what
Charles Stuart knew in Boston:
We do quick, but sloppy work.
All these details:

How tall was I? the police asked Charles,
And ask Susan,
But I vary; I seem smaller and taller
After dusk.
What was the tone of my voice?
Did I growl like a hound as I waved
The pistol in their face?
Was I as desperate as a teenaged boy,
Horny for a sweetheart's kiss?

Here's what I told Susan:
"I won't harm your kids."
But if the moment was mine,
Why would I say that?

I sit with her at the station
The way I sat with Charles
At the hospital:
A shadow on the water glass,
Changing hues,

The slant of my nose and eyes.
Depending on the light
And the question.

Charles rocks in bed with the bullet
We gave ourselves.
How far away was I? We never stopped
To think.
We were in a hurry.
In Boston and South Carolina
I was hungry for a car
And didn't much care how I got it.
Deadly impatient, Charles tells the cops,
But if I couldn't be seen,
But why would I do it that way?
Why do wives and children seem to attract me?

I sat with Charles the way I sit
With Susan; like anyone, and no one,
Changing clothes,
Putting on and taking off ski caps,
Curling and relaxing my hair,
Trying hard to become sense.

II

Uncle Ben Watches the Local News

Like him, I live, but never agreed to it.
A hand drew me out of some mad concern.
I was pulled together
To give, to cook
But never eat.

So I know this fellow, this guy
They're overturning the world
To find. He and I were
Stamped from the same ink.
I look at them look, high, low,
Over, under. I know
What that white lady thinks,

She's as sad and crazy as the smile
They've quilled under my nose.

Buckwheat's Ailment

My family tells me this white gang I run with will
Grow up, and leave me behind. Our bones
Will change, and so will their affection. I will
Be a childlike man who lives in a shack. Just
Wait, they promise, my hair will become
Hoo-doo. The white girls will deny how we rassled,
What we saw. They laugh

Wait 'til you're *grown*. And I hear this sad place
At the middle of that word where they live,
Where they wait for my skin to go sour.

III

Interrogation

The children were fussy,
Susan tells the FBI agent,
So we strapped them in the back seat
And drove off to go shopping
At Kmart.

How can a black man drive
An old, beat-up Mazda
In a southern town
With two white kids
In the backseat,
And never be seen?
The agent would like an
Explanation.

He binds our arm to the
Polygraph,

But we swear we were in the
Parking lot,
In the hours before
I officially arrive,
Under the brute light
Of the mercury lamps.

Who could have missed us, diving
To find a bottle, wedged
Under the back seat?

Who didn't notice us
As we walked the aisles,
A cranky family among
The other cranky families?

He insists: what we say
Is not what we mean.
He tries to spike our heart.

We say, as evenly as we can: the children
Were twitchy bombs
Of sugar; first
We exhaust their eyes, then
Cruise the town,
Like any family,
Bargaining for sleep.

Press Conference

And this is my life now.
I am a faint hum behind
The sensation, the blur of doubt
At the corner of the flashbulb.

These are my names these days:
Hungry, senseless, man of little
Schooling, ninny, fraidy-cat.

If I had an opinion, I guess
I would tell you all I'm tired,
Days and days of near misses,
Almost snapping into focus,

The in-between feel of circling
These streets, a rumor.
If I could, I'd let our weariness
Bite into the sheriff's ear.

Susan steps to the mike.
How do we feel?
There's a crack in our voice.

Confession

There have been days I've almost
Spilled

From her, nearly taken a breath.
Yanked

Myself clean. I've
Trembled

Her coffee cup. I well
Under

Her eyelids. I've been
Gravel

On her mattress. I am
Not

Gone. I am going to
Worm

My way out. I have
Not

Disappeared. I half
Slide

Between her teeth,
Double

Her over as she tries
Not

To blurt me out. The
Closer

Susan inches me
Toward

This, the
Louder

The sheriff
Hears

Me bitch.

IV

The italicized language is from Susan Smith's handwritten confession.

Birthing

When I left my home on Tuesday, October 25, I
was very emotionally distraught

I have yet
To breathe.

I am in the back of her mind,
Not even a notion.

A scrap of cloth, the way
A man lopes down a street.

Later, a black woman will say:
"We knew exactly who she was describing."

At this point, I have no language,
No tongue, no mouth.

I am not me, yet.
I am just an understanding.

————

As I rode and rode and rode, I felt
Even more anxiety.

Susan parks on a bridge,
And stares over the rail.
Below her feet, a dark blanket of river
She wants to pull over herself,
Children and all.

I am not the call of the current.

She is heartbroken.
She gazes down,
And imagines heaven.

————

I felt I couldn't be a good mom anymore, but I didn't want
my children to grow up without a mom.

I am not me, yet.
At the bridge,
One of Susan's kids cries,
So she drives to the lake,
To the boat dock.

I am not yet opportunity.

————

I had never felt so lonely
And so sad.

Who shall be a witness?
Bullfrogs, water fowl.

————

When I was at John D. Long Lake
I had never felt so scared
And unsure.

I've yet to be called.
Who will notice?
Moths, dragonflies,
Field mice.

————

I wanted to end my life so bad
And was in my car ready to
Go down that ramp into
The water

My hand isn't her hand
Panicked on the
Emergency brake.

————

And I did go part way,
But I stopped.

I am not Gravity,
The water lapping against
The gravel.

———

I went again and stopped.
I then got out of the car.

Susan stares at the sinking.
My muscles aren't her muscles,
Burned from pushing.
The lake has no appetite,
But it takes the car slowly,
Swallow by swallow, like a snake.

———

Why was I feeling this way?
Why was everything so bad
In my life?

Susan stares at the taillights
As they slide from here
To hidden.

———

I have no answers
To these questions.

She only has me,
After she removes our hands
From our ears.

. . . .

QUESTIONS FOR A SECOND READING

1. This selection is drawn from a cycle or sequence of poems (thirty in all) ti-
    tled *Brutal Imagination*. Eady divided the cycle into four sections, which we
    have marked. We were not able to reproduce all of the poems, and so it is
    important for you to have a sense of the shape of what you have read in re-
    lation to the shape of the original. We reproduced most of the poems from
    section 1 (all but two). We felt it important for you to see a substantial block
    of poems working together, and we thought it best to do this with the open-
    ing section. We reproduced two of five poems in section 2, and three of
    eleven poems in section 3. Section 4, in the original, was only one poem,
    "Birthing," which we have reproduced in its entirety. (If you are interested,
    you could turn to the book to see what we have cut.)

    As the headnote says, the poems in *Brutal Imagination* are carefully
    arranged in sequence. They ask to be read not as individual performances
    but as part of something that evolves, page after page. A sequence of poems,
    like an essay, can be a way of telling a story, of framing an argument, of
    thinking things through. As you reread, prepare to provide an account
    of the whole of this selection. How is it arranged? How does it organize the
    time and attention of the reader? How would you describe the movement
    from poem to poem in section 1? How do you understand the purpose
    or intent of section 2? section 3? How do these sections work together?
    And how do you understand "Birthing," the final poem and the whole
    of the final section? Would you call it a conclusion? If not a conclusion,
    then what?

2. The poems in *Brutal Imagination* are written in the first person (and so they
    are, in that sense, in the tradition of *lyric* poetry). As you reread, pay attention
    to the speaker. Who is speaking? How does the speaker think, imagine, relate
    his story? Pay attention to the other personal pronouns—*we, her, his, our.*

    And, as you reread, pay attention to the work of the writer, Cornelius
    Eady. If the project of these poems is to give voice to a character who would
    otherwise never get to speak, what are the defining characteristics of this
    voice and this speaker? If this is Eady's project, to create this character,
    what is he, the writer, doing?

3. Although we are inviting you to read *Brutal Imagination* as a text in prose—
    as a story or an essay—it is, to be sure, a work of poetry. As you reread,
    think about what it is that makes these poems poems (and not prose); think
    about how the experience of reading this text is *not* like reading an essay or
    a story. You might look for particular qualities or features of language or
    form. You might think about sentences and stanzas and the white space
    that stands around and before and after each poem.

    And you might think about the line. Poets work with sentences—Eady
    does, at least—and while the sentences have standard punctuation, they
    are also punctuated by line breaks. Here are two passages from two poems,
    written as both prose and verse.

a. "I'm a black man, which means, in Susan's case, that I pour out of a shadow at a traffic light, but I'm also a mother, which is why she has me promise 'I won't hurt your kids,' before I drift down the road." (p. 191)

> I'm a black man, which means,
> In Susan's case,
> That I pour out of a shadow
> At a traffic light,
>
> But I'm also a mother,
> Which is why she has me promise,
> "I won't hurt your kids,"
> Before I drift down the road.

b. "There have been days I've almost spilled from her, nearly taken a breath. Yanked myself clean. I've trembled her coffee cup. I well under her eyelids. I've been gravel on her mattress. I am not gone." (p. 197)

> There have been days I've almost
> Spilled
>
> From her, nearly taken a breath.
> Yanked
>
> Myself clean. I've
> Trembled
>
> Her coffee cup. I well
> Under
>
> Her eyelids. I've been
> Gravel
>
> On her mattress. I am
> Not
>
> Gone.

You might, if you choose, prepare a similar example of your own. As you reread, think about the line breaks as a strategy—a strategy for the writer and a strategy for the reader. How do you understand the decision to break a line where it is broken? How do the line breaks change the ways the lines might be read? Are there lessons here for prose writers as well as for poets?

4. *Brutal Imagination* writes (or rewrites) history. It began, in a sense, as a research project. It was not completely a work of the imagination. There is a Susan Smith. Her children were drowned in a car in a lake. There was an investigation in Union, South Carolina. (There was also a Charles Stuart and an Uncle Ben.) The cycle of poems is a way of bringing home the news — in these cases, news from the recent past. And, in fact, both the Smith and the Stuart cases were widely publicized and occupied the nation's attention for an extended period of time.

As a research project, perhaps working in teams, find the articles on the Susan Smith case that were published in major newspapers or magazines. It would be useful to include on your list of possibilities those magazines and newspapers that serve an African American audience—not only *Time* or *Newsweek* but also *Ebony* or *Jet*; not only the *New York Times* or the *Atlanta Constitution* but also *The Chicago Defender* or the *Pittsburgh Courier*. (Note: You can also find the case represented at "crime" Web sites such as *thesmokinggun.com* or *crimelibrary.com*.) All of these provide a *representation* of what happened, one version of who, what, when, where, and why. With a particular representation of the case as a point of reference, reread *Brutal Imagination*. How is Eady's representation different? In what ways, and to what ends, might he be rewriting history?

ASSIGNMENTS FOR WRITING

1. The questions above for rereading and for close reading suggest ways of working with Eady's poems, including individual poems. For this assignment, choose one of the poems in *Brutal Imagination* that strikes you as both interesting and representative of Eady's work as a writer in this cycle. Write an essay that provides a close reading of this poem and that situates it in relation to Eady's project.

    Please note: *Close reading* is a term used to describe careful, close attention to the language on the page—to what it *does* as well as to what it *says*. In order to do this, you have to include in your prose lines from the poem—often lines offered in a block quotation. The lines you include must make sense to a reader who does not have the book at hand and who has not committed the poem to memory. And the lines must be grammatical—sentences in their own right or fully integrated into your sentences. (Your handbook or your instructor can show you how to work with a block quotation and how to include lines of poetry in a work of prose.)

    This assignment asks you to write about Eady and his work, his project as a writer as that project is represented in *Brutal Imagination*. You are writing about a single poem, to be sure, but also about something bigger. You can write in a speculative or tentative manner; this is one way of establishing yourself as a careful, thoughtful, and attentive reader. Ideally, you will have the opportunity to come back to this assignment for revision.

2. This assignment follows the first of the preceding "Questions for a Second Reading."

    > As the headnote says, the poems in *Brutal Imagination* are carefully arranged in sequence. They ask to be read not as individual performances but as part of something that evolves, page after page. A sequence of poems, like an essay, can be a way of telling a story, of framing an argument, of thinking things through. As you reread, prepare to provide an account of the whole of this selection. How is it arranged? How does it organize the time and attention of the reader? How would you describe the movement from poem to poem in section 1? How do you understand the purpose or intent of section 2? section 3? How do these

sections work together? And how do you understand "Birthing," the final poem and the whole of the final section? Would you call it a conclusion? If not a conclusion, then what?

Write an essay in which you present the sequence of poems in this selection from *Brutal Imagination* as elements in a single project. What is Eady doing in this cycle of poems? What is it about? And, as his reader, what do you have to say in return?

It will be useful to refer directly to specific poems at key moments in the text and to work with them closely. (Your handbook or your instructor can show you how to work with a block quotation and how to include lines of poetry in a work of prose.)

You can write in a speculative or tentative manner; this is one way of establishing yourself as a careful, thoughtful, and attentive reader. Ideally, you will have the opportunity to come back to this assignment for revision.

3. This assignment follows the last of the "Questions for a Second Reading."

> *Brutal Imagination* writes (or rewrites) history. It began, in a sense, as a research project. It is not completely a work of the imagination. There is a Susan Smith. Her children were drowned in a car in a lake. There was an investigation in Union, South Carolina. (There was also a Charles Stuart.) The cycle of poems is a way of bringing home the news — in these cases, news from the recent past. And, in fact, both the Smith and the Stuart cases were widely publicized and occupied the nation's attention for an extended period of time.

As a research project, review some of the articles on the Susan Smith case that were published in major newspapers or magazines. It would be useful to include on your list of possibilities those magazines and newspapers that serve an African American audience — not only *Time* or *Newsweek* but also *Ebony* or *Jet*; not only the *New York Times* or the *Atlanta Constitution* but also *The Chicago Defender* or the *Pittsburgh Courier*. (Note: You can also find the case represented at "crime" Web sites, such as *thesmokinggun.com* or *crimelibrary.com*.) All of these provide a *representation* of what happened, one version of who, what, when, where, and why.

With a particular representation of the case as a point of reference, reread *Brutal Imagination*, and write an essay on Eady's rewriting of (or intervention in) the popular accounts (the popular history) of Susan Smith. You will need to work closely with your sources. And, because you are writing about writing (about two written accounts of the case), you will need to include substantial block quotations. (Your handbook or your instructor can show you how to work with a block quotation and how to include lines of poetry in a work of prose.)

You can write in a speculative or tentative manner; this is one way of establishing yourself as a careful, thoughtful, and attentive reader. Ideally, you will have the opportunity to come back to this assignment for revision.

4. In *Brutal Imagination*, Cornelius Eady gives voice to a public figure who would otherwise remain voiceless. (We are careful, in this sense, to say "figure" and not person.)

This assignment is an invitation to carry out an Eady-like project. Think of a public figure (or a public person) who is spoken about but who never (or rarely) is afforded the opportunity to speak for himself or herself. Write a set of linked poems or prose passages that give voice to this figure (or person). You will be creating a character and situating that character in relation to what has been thought or assumed, to what is usually said and understood. In a brief introduction, present your work in relation to your reading of *Brutal Imagination*.

MAKING CONNECTIONS

1. Central to Linda Nochlin's essay "Renoir's *Great Bathers*" is the distinction between a *practice* and a *representation*—or, as the subtitle says, between "Bathing as Practice" and "Bathing as Representation." To prepare for this assignment, you should reread the essay to see how Nochlin uses these terms—*practice* and *representation*—to organize her research project, here focused primarily on the representation of women. What is she doing, in other words, when she turns to the history of swimming and swimming pools and to the "discourses of swimming and bathing" in Paris in the second half of the nineteenth century? What does this allow her to think, to understand, or to say about the paintings?

   Brutal Imagination is also about representation—about the representation of black men in the United States in print, speech, and thought. How might one of these two works, an essay and a sequence of poems, be useful to a reader of the other? How might a reading of both of these projects help you to think about questions of practice and representation as they are most urgent and meaningful to you and to your generation?

2. In a 2002 *New York Times* book review, Margo Jefferson writes that W. G. Sebald "keeps looking for ways to approach and understand history in its brute simplicity and its subtleties." The selections from his book *The Rings of Saturn* (p. 613), combine documentary with fiction and situate the speaker, an odd character, in relation to European history. *Brutal Imagination* uses first-person poems to rework or rewrite the history of Susan Smith and the death of her two children. Write an essay that discusses the work of history (and historical understanding) as they are represented by Sebald and Eady. These are not conventional histories, to be sure, the kind that are taught in class or as represented in textbooks. What claims might you make for the usefulness of these two projects? For the problems they entail?

3. About three quarters of the way into her essay "When We Dead Awaken: Writing as Re-Vision," Adrienne Rich writes:

   > For a poem to coalesce, for a character or an action to take shape, there has to be an imaginative transformation of reality which is in no way passive. . . . Moreover, if the imagination is to transcend and transform experience it has to question, to challenge, to conceive of alternatives, perhaps to the very life you are living at that moment. You have to be free to play around with the notion that day might be night, love might be hate; nothing can be too sacred for the imagination to turn into its opposite or to call experimentally by another name. For writing is renaming. (p. 528)

Rich's essay provides poems but also commentary on those poems, commentary and context. Reread Rich's essay to see where and how her work might be useful in describing and understanding Eady's. Are there terms or examples in the commentary that might be useful? Are there comparisons between the poems, between examples of the work that might be useful?

And reread the poems from *Brutal Imagination*. Eady does not provide commentary. His practice, however, enacts an argument about the imagination, life, language, and history. What does he offer a reader of Rich? What does he bring to this conversation?

4. The "Questions for a Second Reading" we have provided for the selections from John Edgar Wideman's *Brothers and Keepers* and from Harriet Jacobs's *Incidents in the Life of a Slave Girl* call attention to each as illustrative of the difficulties of narrating, or representing, the experiences of African Americans—of telling the story, of getting it right, of recovering experience from the representations of others. Both could carry the subtitle *Brutal Imagination*.

Eady's *Brutal Imagination* brings a new perspective (the "I" of these poems) and a new genre to these selections in our anthology. Working from either Wideman's text or Jacobs's text, write an essay in which you represent Eady as working on a problem that has a particular urgency for black writers. How might you name this problem? How might you illustrate it? What do you find compelling in these two approaches to the problem? And what might this problem have to do with you as a writer and thinker?

MICHEL
FOUCAULT

MICHEL FOUCAULT (1926–1984) stands at the begin-
ning of the twenty-first century as one of the world's lead-
ing intellectuals. He was trained as a philosopher, but
much of his work, like that presented in Discipline and
Punish: The Birth of the Prison *(1975), traces the pres-*
ence of certain ideas across European history. So he could
also be thought of as a historian, but a historian whose goal
is to revise the usual understanding of history—not as a
progressive sequence but as a series of repetitions gov-
erned by powerful ideas, terms, and figures. Foucault was
also a public intellectual, involved in such prominent issues as prison reform. He
wrote frequently for French newspapers and reviews. His death from AIDS was
front-page news in Le Monde, *the French equivalent of the* New York Times. *He*
taught at several French universities and in 1970 was appointed to a professorship
at the Collège de France, the highest position in the French system. He traveled
widely, lecturing and visiting at universities throughout the world.

Foucault's work is central to much current work in the humanities and the
social sciences. In fact, it is hard to imagine any area of the academy that has not
been influenced by his writing. There is a certain irony in all this, since Foucault ar-
gued persuasively that we need to give up thinking about knowledge as individually

produced; we have to stop thinking the way we do about the "author" or the "genius," about individuality or creativity; we have to stop thinking as though there were truths that stand beyond the interests of a given moment. It is both dangerous and wrong, he argued, to assume that knowledge is disinterested. Edward Said had this to say of Foucault:

> *His great critical contribution was to dissolve the anthropological models of identity and subjecthood underlying research in the humanistic and social sciences. Instead of seeing everything in culture and society as ultimately emanating from either a sort of unchanging Cartesian ego or a heroic solitary artist, Foucault proposed the much juster notion that all work, like social life itself, is collective. The principal task therefore is to circumvent or break down the ideological biases that prevent us from saying that what enables a doctor to practice medicine or a historian to write history is not mainly a set of individual gifts, but an ability to follow rules that are taken for granted as an unconscious a priori by all professionals. More than anyone before him, Foucault specified rules for those rules, and even more impressively, he showed how over long periods of time the rules became epistemological enforcers of what (as well as of how) people thought, lived, and spoke.*

These rules, these unconscious enforcers, are visible in "discourse" —ways of thinking and speaking and acting that we take for granted as naturally or inevitably there but that are constructed over time and preserved by those who act without question, without stepping outside the discourse and thinking critically. But, says Foucault, there is no place "outside" the discourse, no free, clear space. There is always only another discursive position. A person in thinking, living, and speaking expresses not merely himself or herself but the thoughts and roles and phrases governed by the available ways of thinking and speaking. The key questions to ask, then, according to Foucault, are not Who said this? or Is it original? or Is it true? or Is it authentic? but Who talks this way? or What unspoken rules govern this way of speaking? or Where is this discourse used? Who gets to use it? when? and to what end?

The following selection is the third chapter of Discipline and Punish: The Birth of the Prison *(translated from the French by Alan Sheridan). In this book, Foucault is concerned with the relationships between knowledge and power, arguing that knowledge is not pure and abstract but is implicated in networks of power relations. Or, as he puts it elsewhere, people govern themselves "through the production of truth." This includes the "truths" that determine how we imagine and manage the boundaries between the "normal" and the transgressive, the lawful and the delinquent. In a characteristic move, Foucault reverses our intuitive sense of how things are. He argues, for example, that it is not the case that prisons serve the courts and a system of justice but that the courts are the products, the servants of "the prison," the prison as an idea, as the central figure in a way of thinking about transgression, order, and the body, a way of thinking that is persistent and general, present, for example, through all efforts to produce the normal or "disciplined individual": "in the central position that [the prison] occupies, it is not alone, but linked to a whole series of 'carceral' mechanisms which seem distinct enough—since they* are intended to alleviate pain, to cure, to comfort—but which all tend, like the prison, to exercise a power of normalization." *Knowledge stands in an antagonistic role in* Discipline and Punish; *it is part of a problem, not a route to a solution.*

You will find "Panopticism" difficult reading. All readers find Foucault's prose tough going. It helps to realize that it is necessarily difficult. Foucault, remember, is trying to work outside of, or in spite of, the usual ways of thinking and writing. He is trying not to reproduce the standard discourse but to point to what it cannot or will not say. He is trying to make gestures beyond what is ordinarily, normally said. So his prose struggles with its own situation. Again, as Edward Said says, "What [Foucault] was interested in . . . was 'the more' that can be discovered lurking in signs and discourses but that is irreducible to language and speech; 'it is this "more,"' he said, 'that we must reveal and describe.' Such a concern appears to be both devious and obscure, yet it accounts for a lot that is especially unsettling in Foucault's writing. There is no such thing as being at home in his writing, neither for reader nor for writer." While readers find Foucault difficult, he is widely read and widely cited. His books include The Birth of the Clinic: An Archaeology of Medical Perception *(1963),* The Order of Things: An Archaeology of the Human Sciences *(1966),* The Archaeology of Knowledge *(1969),* Madness and Civilization *(1971), and the three-volume* History of Sexuality *(1976, 1979, 1984).*

Panopticism

The following, according to an order published at the end of the seventeenth century, were the measures to be taken when the plague appeared in a town.[1]

First, a strict spatial partitioning: the closing of the town and its outlying districts, a prohibition to leave the town on pain of death, the killing of all stray animals; the division of the town into distinct quarters, each governed by an intendant. Each street is placed under the authority of a syndic, who keeps it under surveillance; if he leaves the street, he will be condemned to death. On the appointed day, everyone is ordered to stay indoors: it is forbidden to leave on pain of death. The syndic himself comes to lock the door of each house from the outside; he takes the key with him and hands it over to the intendant of the quarter; the intendant keeps it until the end of the quarantine. Each family will have made its own provisions; but, for bread and wine, small wooden canals are set up between the street and the interior of the houses, thus allowing each person to receive his ration without communicating with the suppliers and other residents; meat, fish, and herbs will be hoisted up into the houses with pulleys and baskets. If it is absolutely necessary to leave the house, it will be done in turn, avoiding any meeting. Only the intendants, syndics, and guards will move about the streets and also, between the infected houses, from one corpse to another, the "crows," who can be left to die: these are "people of little substance who carry the sick, bury the dead, clean, and do many vile and abject offices." It is a segmented, immobile, frozen space. Each individual is fixed in his place. And, if he moves, he does so at the risk of his life, contagion, or punishment.

Inspection functions ceaselessly. The gaze is alert everywhere: "A considerable body of militia, commanded by good officers and men of substance," guards at the gates, at the town hall, and in every quarter to ensure the prompt obedience of the people and the most absolute authority of the magistrates, "as also to observe all disorder, theft and extortion." At each of the town gates there will be an observation post; at the end of each street sentinels. Every day, the intendant visits the quarter in his charge, inquires whether the syndics have carried out their tasks, whether the inhabitants have anything to complain of; they "observe their actions." Every day, too, the syndic goes into the street for which he is responsible; stops before each house: gets all the inhabitants to appear at the windows (those who live overlooking the courtyard will be allocated a window looking onto the street at which no one but they may show themselves); he calls each of them by name; informs himself as to the state of each and every one of them—"in which respect the inhabitants will be compelled to speak the truth under pain of death"; if someone does not appear at the window, the syndic must ask why: "In this way he will find out easily enough whether dead or sick are being concealed." Everyone locked up in his cage, everyone at his window, answering to his name and showing himself when asked—it is the great review of the living and the dead.

This surveillance is based on a system of permanent registration: reports from the syndics to the intendants, from the intendants to the magistrates or mayor. At the beginning of the "lock up," the role of each of the inhabitants present in the town is laid down, one by one; this document bears "the name, age, sex of everyone, notwithstanding his condition": a copy is sent to the intendant of the quarter, another to the office of the town hall, another to enable the syndic to make his daily roll call. Everything that may be observed during the course of the visits—deaths, illnesses, complaints, irregularities—is noted down and transmitted to the intendants and magistrates. The magistrates have complete control over medical treatment; they have appointed a physician in charge; no other practitioner may treat, no apothecary prepare medicine, no confessor visit a sick person without having received from him a written note "to prevent anyone from concealing and dealing with those sick of the contagion, unknown to the magistrates." The registration of the pathological must be constantly centralized. The relation of each individual to his disease and to his death passes through the representatives of power, the registration they make of it, the decisions they take on it.

Five or six days after the beginning of the quarantine, the process of purifying the houses one by one is begun. All the inhabitants are made to leave; in each room "the furniture and goods" are raised from the ground or suspended from the air; perfume is poured around the room; after carefully sealing the windows, doors, and even the keyholes with wax, the perfume is set alight. Finally, the entire house is closed while the perfume is consumed; those who have carried out the work are searched, as they were on entry, "in the presence of the residents of the house, to see that they did not have something on their persons as they left that they did not have on entering." Four hours later, the residents are allowed to reenter their homes.

This enclosed, segmented space, observed at every point, in which the individuals are inserted in a fixed place, in which the slightest movements are supervised, in which all events are recorded, in which an uninterrupted work of writing links the center and periphery, in which power is exercised without division, according to a continuous hierarchical figure, in which each individual is constantly located, examined, and distributed among the living beings, the sick, and the dead—all this constitutes a compact model of the disciplinary mechanism. The plague is met by order; its function is to sort out every possible confusion: that of the disease, which is transmitted when bodies are mixed together; that of the evil, which is increased when fear and death overcome prohibitions. It lays down for each individual his place, his body, his disease, and his death, his well-being, by means of an omnipresent and omniscient power that subdivides itself in a regular, uninterrupted way even to the ultimate determination of the individual, of what characterizes him, of what belongs to him, of what happens to him. Against the plague, which is a mixture, discipline brings into play its power, which is one of analysis. A whole literary fiction of the festival grew up around the plague: suspended laws, lifted prohibitions, the frenzy of passing time, bodies mingling together without respect, individuals unmasked, abandoning their statutory identity and the figure under which they had been recognized, allowing a quite different truth to appear. But there was also a political dream of the plague, which was exactly its reverse: not the collective festival, but strict divisions; not laws transgressed, but the penetration of regulation into even the smallest details of everyday life through the mediation of the complete hierarchy that assured the capillary functioning of power; not masks that were put on and taken off, but the assignment to each individual of his "true" name, his "true" place, his "true" body, his "true" disease. The plague as a form, at once real and imaginary, of disorder had as its medical and political correlative discipline. Behind the disciplinary mechanisms can be read the haunting memory of "contagions," of the plague, of rebellions, crimes, vagabondage, desertions, people who appear and disappear, live and die in disorder.

If it is true that the leper gave rise to rituals of exclusion, which to a certain extent provided the model for and general form of the great Confinement, then the plague gave rise to disciplinary projects. Rather than the massive, binary division between one set of people and another, it called for multiple separations, individualizing distributions, an organization in depth of surveillance and control, an intensification and a ramification of power. The leper was caught up in a practice of rejection, of exile-enclosure; he was left to his doom in a mass among which it was useless to differentiate; those sick of the plague were caught up in a meticulous tactical partitioning in which individual differentiations were the constricting effects of a power that multiplied, articulated, and subdivided itself; the great confinement on the one hand; the correct training on the other. The leper and his separation; the plague and its segmentations. The first is marked; the second analyzed and distributed. The exile of the leper and the arrest of the plague do not bring with them the same political dream. The first is that of a pure community, the second that of a disciplined society. Two ways of exercising power over men, of controlling their relations, of separating out their dangerous mixtures. The plague-stricken town, traversed throughout with hierarchy, surveillance, observation, writing; the town immobilized by the functioning of an extensive power that bears in a distinct way over all individual bodies—this is the utopia of the perfectly governed city. The plague (envisaged as a possibility at least) is the trial in the course of which one may define ideally the exercise of disciplinary power. In order to make rights and laws function according to pure theory, the jurists place themselves in imagination in the state of nature; in order to see perfect disciplines functioning, rulers dreamed of the state of plague. Underlying disciplinary projects the image of the plague stands for all forms of confusion and disorder; just as the image of the leper, cut off from all human contact, underlies projects of exclusion.

They are different projects, then, but not incompatible ones. We see them coming slowly together, and it is the peculiarity of the nineteenth century that it applied to the space of exclusion of which the leper was the symbolic inhabitant (beggars, vagabonds, madmen, and the disorderly formed the real population) the technique of power proper to disciplinary partitioning. Treat "lepers" as "plague victims," project the subtle segmentations of discipline onto the confused space of internment, combine it with the methods of analytical distribution proper to power, individualize the excluded, but use procedures of individualization to mark exclusion—this is what was operated regularly by disciplinary power from the beginning of the nineteenth century in the psychiatric asylum, the penitentiary, the reformatory, the approved school, and to some extent, the hospital. Generally speaking, all the authorities exercising individual control function according to a double mode; that of binary division and branding (mad/sane; dangerous/harmless; normal/abnormal); and that of coercive assignment, of differential distribution (who he is; where he must be; how he is to be characterized; how he is to be recognized; how a constant surveillance is to be exercised over him in an individual way, etc.). On the one hand, the lepers are treated as plague victims; the tactics of individualizing disciplines are imposed on the excluded; and, on the other hand, the universality of disciplinary controls makes it possible to brand the "leper" and to bring into play against him the dualistic mechanisms of exclusion. The constant division between the normal and the abnormal, to which every individual is subjected, brings us back to our own time, by applying the binary branding and exile of the leper to quite different objects; the existence of a whole set of techniques and institutions for measuring, supervising, and correcting the abnormal brings into play the disciplinary mechanisms to which the fear of the plague gave rise. All the mechanisms of power which, even today, are disposed around the abnormal individual, to brand him and to alter him, are composed of those two forms from which they distantly derive.

Bentham's *Panopticon* is the architectural figure of this composition. We know the principle on which it was based: at the periphery, an annular building; at the center, a tower; this tower is pierced with wide windows that open onto the inner side of the ring; the peripheric building is divided into cells, each of which extends the whole width of the building; they have

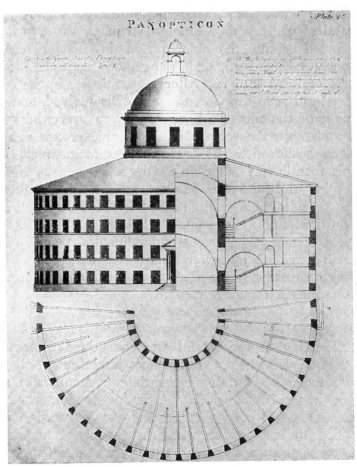

Plan of the Panopticon by J. Bentham (*The Works of Jeremy Bentham*, ed. Bowring, vol. IV, 1843, 172–73).

two windows, one on the inside, corresponding to the windows of the tower; the other, on the outside, allows the light to cross the cell from one end to the other. All that is needed, then, is to place a supervisor in a central tower and to shut up in each cell a madman, a patient, a condemned man, a worker, or a schoolboy. By the effect of backlighting, one can observe from the tower, standing out precisely against the light, the small captive shadows in the cells of the periphery. They are like so many cages, so many small theaters, in which each actor is alone, perfectly individualized and constantly visible. The panoptic mechanism arranges spatial unities that make it possible to see constantly and to recognize immediately. In short, it reverses the principle of the dungeon; or rather of its three functions—to enclose, to deprive of light, and to hide—it preserves only the first and eliminates the other two. Full lighting and the eye of a supervisor capture better than darkness, which is ultimately protected. Visibility is a trap.

To begin with, this made it possible—as a negative effect—to avoid those compact, swarming, howling masses that were to be found in places of confinement, those painted by Goya or described by Howard. Each individual, in his place, is securely confined to a cell from which he is seen from the front by the supervisor; but the side walls prevent him from coming into contact with his companions. He is seen, but he does not see; he is the object of information, never a subject in communication. The arrangement of his room, opposite the central tower, imposes on him an axial visibility; but the divisions of the ring, those separated cells, imply a lateral invisibility. And this invisibility is a guarantee of order. If the inmates are convicts, there is no danger of a plot, an attempt at collective escape, the planning of new crimes for the future, bad reciprocal influences; if they are patients, there is no danger of contagion; if they are madmen, there is no risk of their committing violence upon one another; if they are schoolchildren, there is no copying, no noise, no chatter, no waste of time; if they are workers, there are no disorders, no theft, no coalitions, none of those distractions that slow down the rate of work, make it less perfect, or cause accidents. The crowd, a compact mass, a locus of multiple exchanges, individualities merging together, a collective effect, is abolished and replaced by a collection of separated individualities. From the point of view of the guardian, it is replaced by a multiplicity that can be numbered and supervised; from the point of view of the inmates, by a sequestered and observed solitude (Bentham 60–64).

Hence the major effect of the Panopticon: to induce in the inmate a state of conscious and permanent visibility that assures the automatic functioning of power. So to arrange things that the surveillance is permanent in its effects even if it is discontinuous in its action; that the perfection of power should tend to render its actual exercise unnecessary; that this architectural apparatus should be a machine for creating and sustaining a power relation independent of the person who exercises it; in short, that the inmates should be caught up in a power situation of which they are themselves the bearers. To achieve this, it is at once too much and too little that the prisoner should be constantly observed by an inspector: too little, for what

Handwriting model. *Collections historiques de l'I.N.R.D.P.*

matters is that he knows himself to be observed; too much, because he has no need in fact of being so. In view of this, Bentham laid down the principle that power should be visible and unverifiable. Visible: the inmate will constantly have before his eyes the tall outline of the central tower from which he is spied upon. Unverifiable: the inmate must never know whether he is being looked at at any one moment; but he must be sure that he may always be so. In order to make the presence or absence of the inspector unverifiable, so that the prisoners, in their cells, cannot even see a shadow, Bentham envisaged not only venetian blinds on the windows of the central observation hall, but, on the inside, partitions that intersected the hall at right angles and, in order to pass from one quarter to the other, not doors but zigzag openings; for the slightest noise, a gleam of light, a brightness in a half-opened door would betray the presence of the guardian.[2] The Panopticon is a machine for dissociating the see/being seen dyad: in the peripheric ring, one is totally seen, without ever seeing; in the central tower, one sees everything without ever being seen.[3]

It is an important mechanism, for it automatizes and disindividualizes power. Power has its principle not so much in a person as in a certain concerted distribution of bodies, surfaces, lights, gazes; in an arrangement whose internal mechanisms produce the relation in which individuals are caught up. The ceremonies, the rituals, the marks by which the sovereign's surplus power was manifested are useless. There is a machinery that assures dissymmetry, disequilibrium, difference. Consequently, it does not matter who exercises power. Any individual, taken almost at random, can operate the machine: in the absence of the director, his family, his friends,

Interior of the penitentiary at Stateville, United States, twentieth century.

Lecture on the evils of alcoholism in the auditorium of Fresnes prison.

his visitors, even his servants (Bentham 45). Similarly, it does not matter what motive animates him: the curiosity of the indiscreet, the malice of a child, the thirst for knowledge of a philosopher who wishes to visit this museum of human nature, or the perversity of those who take pleasure in spying and punishing. The more numerous those anonymous and temporary observers are, the greater the risk for the inmate of being surprised and the greater his anxious awareness of being observed. The Panopticon is a marvelous machine which, whatever use one may wish to put it to, produces homogeneous effects of power.

A real subjection is born mechanically from a fictitious relation. So it is not necessary to use force to constrain the convict to good behavior, the madman to calm, the worker to work, the schoolboy to application, the patient to the observation of the regulations. Bentham was surprised that panoptic institutions could be so light: there were no more bars, no more chains, no more heavy locks; all that was needed was that the separations should be clear and the openings well arranged. The heaviness of the old "houses of security," with their fortresslike architecture, could be replaced by the simple, economic geometry of a "house of certainty." The efficiency of power, its constraining force have, in a sense, passed over to the other side—to the side of its surface of application. He who is subjected to a field of visibility, and who knows it, assumes responsibility for the constraints of power; he makes them play spontaneously upon himself; he inscribes in himself the power relation in which he simultaneously plays both roles; he becomes the principle of his own subjection. By this very fact, the external power may throw off its physical weight; it tends to the noncorporal; and, the more it approaches this limit, the more constant, profound, and permanent are its effects: it is a perpetual victory that avoids any physical confrontation and which is always decided in advance.

Bentham does not say whether he was inspired, in his project, by Le Vaux's menagerie at Versailles: the first menagerie in which the different elements are not, as they traditionally were, distributed in a park (Loisel 104–7). At the center was an octagonal pavilion which, on the first floor, consisted of only a single room, the king's *salon*; on every side large windows looked out onto seven cages (the eighth side was reserved for the entrance), containing different species of animals. By Bentham's time, this menagerie had disappeared. But one finds in the program of the Panopticon a similar concern with individualizing observation, with characterization and classification, with the analytical arrangement of space. The Panopticon is a royal menagerie; the animal is replaced by man, individual distribution by specific grouping, and the king by the machinery of a furtive power. With this exception, the Panopticon also does the work of a naturalist. It makes it possible to draw up differences: among patients, to observe the symptoms of each individual, without the proximity of beds, the circulation of miasmas, the effects of contagion confusing the clinical tables; among schoolchildren, it makes it possible to observe performances (without there being any imitation or copying), to map aptitudes, to assess characters, to draw up rigorous classifications, and in relation to normal development, to distinguish "laziness and stubbornness" from "incurable imbecility"; among workers, it makes it possible to note the aptitudes of each worker, compare the time he takes to perform a task, and if they are paid by the day, to calculate their wages (Bentham 60–64).

So much for the question of observation. But the Panopticon was also a laboratory; it could be used as a machine to carry out experiments, to alter behavior, to train or correct individuals. To experiment with medicines and monitor their effects. To try out different punishments on prisoners, according to their crimes and character, and to seek the most effective ones. To teach different techniques simultaneously to the workers, to decide which is the best. To try out pedagogical experiments—and in particular to take up once again the well-debated problem of secluded education, by using orphans. One would see what would happen when, in their sixteenth or eighteenth year, they were presented with other boys or girls; one could verify whether, as Helvetius thought, anyone could learn anything; one would follow "the genealogy of every observable idea"; one could bring up different children according to different systems of thought, making certain children believe that two and two do not make four or that the moon is a cheese, then put them together when they are twenty or twenty-five years old; one would then have discussions that would be worth a great deal more than the sermons or lectures on which so much money is spent; one would have at least an opportunity of making discoveries in the domain of metaphysics. The Panopticon is a privileged place for experiments on men, and for analyzing with complete certainty the transformations that may be obtained from them. The Panopticon may even provide an apparatus for supervising its own mechanisms. In this central tower, the director may spy on all the employees that he has under his orders: nurses, doctors, foremen, teachers, warders; he will be able to judge them continuously, alter their behavior, impose upon them the methods he thinks best; and it will even be possible to observe the director himself. An inspector arriving unexpectedly at the center of the Panopticon will be able to judge at a glance, without anything being concealed from him, how the entire establishment is functioning. And, in any case, enclosed as he is in the middle of this architectural mechanism, is not the director's own fate entirely bound up with it? The incompetent physician who has allowed contagion to spread, the incompetent prison governor or workshop manager will be the first victims of an epidemic or a revolt. " 'By every tie I could devise,' said the master of the Panopticon, 'my own fate had been bound up by me with theirs' " (Bentham 177). The Panopticon functions as a kind of laboratory of power. Thanks to its mechanisms of observation, it gains in efficiency and in the ability to penetrate into men's behavior; knowledge follows the advances of power, discovering new objects of knowledge over all the surfaces on which power is exercised.

The plague-stricken town, the panoptic establishment—the differences are important. They mark, at a distance of a century and a half, the transformations of the disciplinary program. In the first case, there is an exceptional situation: against an extraordinary evil, power is mobilized; it makes itself everywhere present and visible; it invents new mechanisms; it separates, it immobilizes, it partitions; it constructs for a time what is both a counter-city and the perfect society; it imposes an ideal functioning, but one that is reduced, in the final analysis, like the evil that it combats, to a simple dualism of life and death: that which moves brings death, and one kills that which moves. The Panopticon, on the other hand, must be understood as a generalizable model of functioning; a way of defining power relations in terms of the everyday life of men. No doubt Bentham presents it as a particular institution, closed in upon itself. Utopias, perfectly closed in upon themselves, are common enough. As opposed to the ruined prisons, littered with mechanisms of torture, to be seen in Piranese's engravings, the Panopticon presents a cruel, ingenious cage. The fact that it should have given rise, even in our own time, to so many variations, projected or realized, is evidence of the imaginary intensity that it has possessed for almost two hundred years. But the Panopticon must not be understood as a dream building: it is the diagram of a mechanism of power reduced to its ideal form; its functioning, abstracted from any obstacle, resistance, or friction, must be represented as a pure architectural and optical system: it is in fact a figure of political technology that may and must be detached from any specific use.

It is polyvalent in its applications; it serves to reform prisoners, but also to treat patients, to instruct schoolchildren, to confine the insane, to supervise workers, to put beggars and idlers to work. It is a type of location of bodies in space, of distribution of individuals in relation to one another, of hierarchical organization, of disposition of centers and channels of power, of definition of the instruments and modes of intervention of power, which can be implemented in hospitals, workshops, schools, prisons. Whenever one is dealing with a multiplicity of individuals on whom a task or a particular form of behavior must be imposed, the panoptic schema may be used. It is —necessary modifications apart—applicable "to all establishments whatsoever, in which, within a space not too large to be covered or commanded by buildings, a number of persons are meant to be kept under inspection" (Bentham 40; although Bentham takes the penitentiary house as his prime example, it is because it has many different functions to fulfill—safe custody, confinement, solitude, forced labor, and instruction).

In each of its applications, it makes it possible to perfect the exercise of power. It does this in several ways: because it can reduce the number of those who exercise it, while increasing the number of those on whom it is exercised. Because it is possible to intervene at any moment and because the constant pressure acts even before the offenses, mistakes, or crimes have been committed. Because, in these conditions, its strength is that it never intervenes, it is exercised spontaneously and without noise, it constitutes a mechanism whose effects follow from one another. Because, without any physical instrument other than architecture and geometry, it acts directly on individuals; it gives "power of mind over mind." The panoptic schema makes any apparatus of power more intense: it assures its economy (in material, in personnel, in time); it assures its efficacity by its preventative character, its continuous functioning, and its automatic mechanisms. It is a way of obtaining from power "in hitherto unexampled quantity," "a great and new instrument of government . . . ; its great excellence consists in the great strength it is capable of giving to *any* institution it may be thought proper to apply it to" (Bentham 66).

It's a case of "it's easy once you've thought of it" in the political sphere. It can in fact be integrated into any function (education, medical treatment, production, punishment); it can increase the effect of this function, by being linked closely with it; it can constitute a mixed mechanism in which relations of power (and of knowledge) may be precisely adjusted, in the smallest detail, to the processes that are to be supervised; it can establish a direct proportion between "surplus power" and "surplus production." In short, it arranges things in such a way that the exercise of power is not added on from the outside, like a rigid, heavy constraint, to the functions it invests, but is so subtly present in them as to increase their efficiency by itself increasing its own points of contact. The panoptic mechanism is not simply a hinge, a point of exchange between a mechanism of power and a function; it is a way of making power relations function in a function, and of making a function function through these power relations. Bentham's preface to *Panopticon* opens with a list of the benefits to be obtained from his "inspection-house": *"Morals reformed—health preserved—industry invigorated—instruction diffused—public burthens lightened*—Economy seated, as it were, upon a rock—the gordian knot of the Poor-Laws not cut, but untied—all by a simple idea in architecture!" (Bentham 39).

Furthermore, the arrangement of this machine is such that its enclosed nature does not preclude a permanent presence from the outside: we have seen that anyone may come and exercise in the central tower the functions of surveillance, and that, this being the case, he can gain a clear idea of the way in which the surveillance is practiced. In fact, any panoptic institution, even if it is as rigorously closed as a penitentiary, may without difficulty be subjected to such irregular and constant inspections: and not only by the appointed inspectors, but also by the public; any member of society will have the right to come and see with his own eyes how the schools, hospitals, factories, prisons function. There is no risk, therefore, that the increase of power created by the panoptic machine may degenerate into tyranny; the disciplinary mechanism will be democratically controlled, since it will be constantly accessible "to the great tribunal committee of the world."[4] This Panopticon, subtly arranged so that an observer may observe, at a glance, so many different individuals, also enables everyone to come and observe any of the observers. The seeing machine was once a sort of dark room into which individuals spied; it has become a transparent building in which the exercise of power may be supervised by society as a whole.

The panoptic schema, without disappearing as such or losing any of its properties, was destined to spread throughout the social body; its vocation was to become a generalized function. The plague-stricken town provided an exceptional disciplinary model: perfect, but absolutely violent; to the disease that brought death, power opposed its perpetual threat of death; life inside it was reduced to its simplest expression; it was, against the power of death, the meticulous exercise of the right of the sword. The Panopticon, on the other hand, has a role of amplification; although it arranges power, although it is intended to make it more economic and more effective, it does so not for power itself, nor for the immediate salvation of a threatened society: its aim is to strengthen the social forces—to increase production, to develop the economy, spread education, raise the level of public morality; to increase and multiply.

How is power to be strengthened in such a way that, far from impeding progress, far from weighing upon it with its rules and regulations, it actually facilitates such progress? What intensificator of power will be able at the same time to be a multiplicator of production? How will power, by increasing its forces, be able to increase those of society instead of confiscating them or impeding them? The Panopticon's solution to this problem is that the productive increase of power can be assured only if, on the one hand, it can be exercised continuously in the very foundations of society, in the subtlest possible way, and if, on the other hand, it functions outside these sudden, violent, discontinuous forms that are bound up with the exercise of sovereignty. The body of the king, with its strange material and physical presence, with the force that he himself deploys or transmits to some few others, is at the opposite extreme of this new physics of power represented by panopticism; the domain of panopticism is, on the contrary, that whole lower region, that region of irregular bodies, with their details, their multiple movements, their heterogeneous forces, their spatial relations; what are required are mechanisms that analyze distributions, gaps, series, combinations, and which use instruments that render visible, record, differentiate, and compare: a physics of a relational and multiple power, which has its maximum intensity not in the person of the king, but in the bodies that can be individualized by these relations. At the theoretical level, Bentham defines another way of analyzing the social body and the power relations that traverse it; in terms of practice, he defines a procedure of subordination of bodies and forces that must increase the utility of power while practicing the economy of the prince. Panopticism is the general principle of a new "political anatomy" whose object and end are not the relations of sovereignty but the relations of discipline.

The celebrated, transparent, circular cage, with its high tower, powerful and knowing, may have been for Bentham a project of a perfect disciplinary institution; but he also set out to show how one may "unlock" the disciplines and get them to function in a diffused, multiple, polyvalent way throughout the whole social body. These disciplines, which the classical age had elaborated in specific, relatively enclosed places—barracks, schools, workshops—and whose total implementation had been imagined only at the limited and temporary scale of a plague-stricken town, Bentham dreamed of transforming into a network of mechanisms that would be everywhere and always alert, running through society without interruption in space or in time. The panoptic arrangement provides the formula for this generalization. It programs, at the level of an elementary and easily transferable mechanism, the basic functioning of a society penetrated through and through with disciplinary mechanisms.

There are two images, then, of discipline. At one extreme, the discipline-blockade, the enclosed institution, established on the edges of society, turned inwards towards negative functions: arresting evil, breaking communications, suspending time. At the other extreme, with panopticism, is the discipline-mechanism: a functional mechanism that must improve the exercise of power by making it lighter, more rapid, more effective, a design of subtle coercion for a society to come. The movement from one project to the other, from a schema of exceptional discipline to one of a generalized surveillance, rests on a historical transformation: the gradual extension of the mechanisms of discipline throughout the seventeenth and eighteenth centuries, their spread throughout the whole social body, the formation of what might be called in general the disciplinary society.

A whole disciplinary generalization—the Benthamite physics of power represents an acknowledgment of this—had operated throughout the classical age. The spread of disciplinary institutions, whose network was beginning to cover an ever larger surface and occupying above all a less and less marginal position, testifies to this: what was an islet, a privileged place, a circumstantial measure, or a singular model, became a general formula; the regulations characteristic of the Protestant and pious armies of William of Orange or of Gustavus Adolphus were transformed into regulations for all the armies of Europe; the model colleges of the Jesuits, or the schools of Batencour or Demia, following the example set by Sturm, provided the outlines for the general forms of educational discipline; the ordering of the naval and military hospitals provided the model for the entire reorganization of hospitals in the eighteenth century.

But this extension of the disciplinary institutions was no doubt only the most visible aspect of various, more profound processes.

1. *The functional inversion of the disciplines.* At first, they were expected to neutralize dangers, to fix useless or disturbed populations, to avoid the inconveniences of over-large assemblies; now they were being asked to play a positive role, for they were becoming able to do so, to increase the possible utility of individuals. Military discipline is no longer a mere means of preventing looting, desertion, or failure to obey orders among the troops; it has become a basic technique to enable the army to exist, not as an assembled crowd, but as a unity that derives from this very unity an increase in its forces; discipline increases the skill of each individual, coordinates these skills, accelerates movements, increases fire power, broadens the fronts of attack without reducing their vigor, increases the capacity for resistance, etc. The discipline of the workshop, while remaining a way of enforcing respect for the regulations and authorities, of preventing thefts or losses, tends to increase aptitudes, speeds, output, and therefore profits; it still exerts a moral influence over behavior, but more and more it treats actions in terms of their results, introduces bodies into a machinery, forces into an economy. When, in the seventeenth century, the provincial schools or the Christian elementary schools were founded, the justifications given for them were above all negative: those poor who were unable to bring up their children left them "in ignorance of their obligations: given the difficulties they have in earning a living, and themselves having been badly brought up, they are unable to communicate a sound upbringing that they themselves never had"; this involves three major inconveniences: ignorance of God,

idleness (with its consequent drunkenness, impurity, larceny, brigandage), and the formation of those gangs of beggars, always ready to stir up public disorder and "virtually to exhaust the funds of the Hôtel-Dieu" (Demia 60–61). Now, at the beginning of the Revolution, the end laid down for primary education was to be, among other things, to "fortify," to "develop the body," to prepare the child "for a future in some mechanical work," to give him "an observant eye, a sure hand and prompt habits" (Talleyrand's Report to the Constituent Assembly, 10 September 1791, quoted by Léon 106). The disciplines function increasingly as techniques for making useful individuals. Hence their emergence from a marginal position on the confines of society, and detachment from the forms of exclusion or expiation, confinement, or retreat. Hence the slow loosening of their kinship with religious regularities and enclosures. Hence also their rooting in the most important, most central, and most productive sectors of society. They become attached to some of the great essential functions: factory production, the transmission of knowledge, the diffusion of aptitudes and skills, the war-machine. Hence, too, the double tendency one sees developing throughout the eighteenth century to increase the number of disciplinary institutions and to discipline the existing apparatuses.

2. *The swarming of disciplinary mechanisms.* While, on the one hand, the disciplinary establishments increase, their mechanisms have a certain tendency to become "deinstitutionalized," to emerge from the closed fortresses in which they once functioned and to circulate in a "free" state; the massive, compact disciplines are broken down into flexible methods of control, which may be transferred and adapted. Sometimes the closed apparatuses add to their internal and specific function a role of external surveillance, developing around themselves a whole margin of lateral controls. Thus the Christian School must not simply train docile children; it must also make it possible to supervise the parents, to gain information as to their way of life, their resources, their piety, their morals. The school tends to constitute minute social observatories that penetrate even to the adults and exercise regular supervision over them: the bad behavior of the child, or his absence, is a legitimate pretext, according to Demia, for one to go and question the neighbors, especially if there is any reason to believe that the family will not tell the truth; one can then go and question the parents themselves, to find out whether they know their catechism and the prayers, whether they are determined to root out the vices of their children, how many beds there are in the house and what the sleeping arrangements are; the visit may end with the giving of alms, the present of a religious picture, or the provision of additional beds (Demia 39–40). Similarly, the hospital is increasingly conceived of as a base for the medical observation of the population outside; after the burning down of the Hôtel-Dieu in 1772, there were several demands that the large buildings, so heavy and so disordered, should be replaced by a series of smaller hospitals; their function would be to take in the sick of the quarter, but also to gather information, to be alert to any endemic or epidemic

phenomena, to open dispensaries, to give advice to the inhabitants, and to keep the authorities informed of the sanitary state of the region.[5]

One also sees the spread of disciplinary procedures, not in the form of enclosed institutions, but as centers of observation disseminated throughout society. Religious groups and charity organizations had long played this role of "disciplining" the population. From the Counter-Reformation to the philanthropy of the July monarchy, initiatives of this type continued to increase; their aims were religious (conversion and moralization), economic (aid and encouragement to work), or political (the struggle against discontent or agitation). One has only to cite by way of example the regulations for the charity associations in the Paris parishes. The territory to be covered was divided into quarters and cantons and the members of the associations divided themselves up along the same lines. These members had to visit their respective areas regularly. "They will strive to eradicate places of ill-repute, tobacco shops, life-classes, gaming houses, public scandals, blasphemy, impiety, and any other disorders that may come to their knowledge." They will also have to make individual visits to the poor; and the information to be obtained is laid down in regulations: the stability of the lodging, knowledge of prayers, attendance at the sacraments, knowledge of a trade, morality (and "whether they have not fallen into poverty through their own fault"); lastly, "one must learn by skillful questioning in what way they behave at home. Whether there is peace between them and their neighbors, whether they are careful to bring up their children in the fear of God . . . , whether they do not have their older children of different sexes sleeping together and with them, whether they do not allow licentiousness and cajolery in their families, especially in their older daughters. If one has any doubts as to whether they are married, one must ask to see their marriage certificate."[6]

3. *The state-control of the mechanisms of the discipline.* In England, it was private religious groups that carried out, for a long time, the functions of social discipline (cf. Radzinovitz 203–14); in France, although a part of this role remained in the hands of parish guilds or charity associations, another—and no doubt the most important part—was very soon taken over by the police apparatus.

The organization of a centralized police had long been regarded, even by contemporaries, as the most direct expression of royal absolutism; the sovereign had wished to have "his own magistrate to whom he might directly entrust his orders, his commissions, intentions, and who was entrusted with the execution of orders and orders under the King's private seal" (a note by Duval, first secretary at the police magistrature, quoted in Funck-Brentano, I). In effect, in taking over a number of preexisting functions—the search for criminals, urban surveillance, economic and political supervision—the police magistratures and the magistrature-general that presided over them in Paris transposed them into a single, strict, administrative machine: "All the radiations of force and information that spread from the circumference culminate in the magistrate-general. . . . It is he who operates all the wheels that together produce order and harmony. The effects of his administration cannot be better compared than to the movement of the celestial bodies" (Des Essarts 344, 528).

But, although the police as an institution were certainly organized in the form of a state apparatus, and although this was certainly linked directly to the center of political sovereignty, the type of power that it exercises, the mechanisms it operates, and the elements to which it applies them are specific. It is an apparatus that must be coextensive with the entire social body and not only by the extreme limits that it embraces, but by the minuteness of the details it is concerned with. Police power must bear "over everything": it is not, however, the totality of the state nor of the kingdom as visible and invisible body of the monarch; it is the dust of events, actions, behavior, opinions—"everything that happens";[7] the police are concerned with "those things of every moment," those "unimportant things," of which Catherine II spoke in her Great Instruction (Supplement to the *Instruction for the Drawing Up of a New Code*, 1769, article 535). With the police, one is in the indefinite world of a supervision that seeks ideally to reach the most elementary particle, the most passing phenomenon of the social body: "The ministry of the magistrates and police officers is of the greatest importance; the objects that it embraces are in a sense definite, one may perceive them only by a sufficiently detailed examination" (Delamare, unnumbered preface): the infinitely small of political power.

And, in order to be exercised, this power had to be given the instrument of permanent, exhaustive, omnipresent surveillance, capable of making all visible, as long as it could itself remain invisible. It had to be like a faceless gaze that transformed the whole social body into a field of perception: thousands of eyes posted everywhere, mobile attentions ever on the alert, a long, hierarchized network which, according to Le Maire, comprised for Paris the forty-eight *commissaires*, the twenty *inspecteurs*, then the "observers," who were paid regularly, the *"basses mouches,"* or secret agents, who were paid by the day, then the informers, paid according to the job done, and finally the prostitutes. And this unceasing observation had to be accumulated in a series of reports and registers; throughout the eighteenth century, an immense police text increasingly covered society by means of a complex documentary organization (on the police registers in the eighteenth century, cf. Chassaigne). And, unlike the methods of judicial or administrative writing, what was registered in this way were forms of behavior, attitudes, possibilities, suspicions—a permanent account of individuals' behavior.

Now, it should be noted that, although this police supervision was entirely "in the hands of the king," it did not function in a single direction. It was in fact a double-entry system: it had to correspond, by manipulating the machinery of justice, to the immediate wishes of the king, but it was also capable of responding to solicitations from below; the celebrated *lettres de cachet*, or orders under the king's private seal, which were long the symbol of arbitrary royal rule and which brought detention into disrepute on political grounds, were in fact demanded by families, masters, local notables, neighbors, parish priests; and their function was to punish by confinement a whole infrapenality, that of disorder, agitation, disobedience, bad conduct; those things that Ledoux wanted to exclude from his architecturally perfect city and which he called "offenses of nonsurveillance." In short, the eighteenth-century police added a disciplinary function to its role as the auxiliary of justice in the pursuit of criminals and as an instrument for the political supervision of plots, opposition movements, or revolts. It was a complex function since it linked the absolute power of the monarch to the lowest levels of power disseminated in society; since, between these different, enclosed institutions of discipline (workshops, armies, schools), it extended an intermediary network, acting where they could not intervene, disciplining the nondisciplinary spaces; but it filled in the gaps, linked them together, guaranteed with its armed force an interstitial discipline and a metadiscipline. "By means of a wise police, the sovereign accustoms the people to order and obedience" (Vattel 162).

The organization of the police apparatus in the eighteenth century sanctioned a generalization of the disciplines that became coextensive with the state itself. Although it was linked in the most explicit way with everything in the royal power that exceeded the exercise of regular justice, it is understandable why the police offered such slight resistance to the rearrangement of the judicial power; and why it has not ceased to impose its prerogatives upon it, with ever-increasing weight, right up to the present day; this is no doubt because it is the secular arm of the judiciary; but it is also because, to a far greater degree than the judicial institution, it is identified, by reason of its extent and mechanisms, with a society of the disciplinary type. Yet it would be wrong to believe that the disciplinary functions were confiscated and absorbed once and for all by a state apparatus.

"Discipline" may be identified neither with an institution nor with an apparatus; it is a type of power, a modality for its exercise, comprising a whole set of instruments, techniques, procedures, levels of application, targets; it is a "physics" or an "anatomy" of power, a technology. And it may be taken over either by "specialized" institutions (the penitentiaries or "houses of correction" of the nineteenth century), or by institutions that use it as an essential instrument for a particular end (schools, hospitals), or by preexisting authorities that find in it a means of reinforcing or reorganizing their internal mechanisms of power (one day we should show how intrafamilial relations, essentially in the parents-children cell, have become "disciplined," absorbing since the classical age external schemata, first educational and military, then medical, psychiatric, psychological, which have made the family the privileged locus of emergence for the disciplinary question of the normal and the abnormal), or by apparatuses that have made discipline their principle of internal functioning (the disciplinarization of the administrative apparatus from the Napoleonic period), or finally by state apparatuses whose major, if not exclusive, function is to assure that discipline reigns over society as a whole (the police).

On the whole, therefore, one can speak of the formation of a disciplinary society in this movement that stretches from the enclosed disciplines, a sort of social "quarantine," to an indefinitely generalizable mechanism of "panopticism." Not because the disciplinary modality of power has replaced all the others; but because it has infiltrated the others, sometimes undermining them, but serving as an intermediary between them, linking them together, extending them, and above all making it possible to bring the effects of power to the most minute and distant elements. It assures an infinitesimal distribution of the power relations.

A few years after Bentham, Julius gave this society its birth certificate (Julius 384–86). Speaking of the panoptic principle, he said that there was much more there than architectural ingenuity: it was an event in the "history of the human mind." In appearance, it is merely the solution of a technical problem; but, through it, a whole type of society emerges. Antiquity had been a civilization of spectacle. "To render accessible to a multitude of men the inspection of a small number of objects": this was the problem to which the architecture of temples, theaters, and circuses responded. With spectacle, there was a predominance of public life, the intensity of festivals, sensual proximity. In these rituals in which blood flowed, society found new vigor and formed for a moment a single great body. The modern age poses the opposite problem: "To procure for a small number, or even for a single individual, the instantaneous view of a great multitude." In a society in which the principal elements are no longer the community and public life, but, on the one hand, private individuals and, on the other, the state, relations can be regulated only in a form that is the exact reverse of the spectacle: "It was to the modern age, to the ever-growing influence of the state, to its ever more profound intervention in all the details and all the relations of social life, that was reserved the task of increasing and perfecting its guarantees, by using and directing towards that great aim the building and distribution of buildings intended to observe a great multitude of men at the same time."

Julius saw as a fulfilled historical process that which Bentham had described as a technical program. Our society is one not of spectacle, but of surveillance; under the surface of images, one invests bodies in depth; behind the great abstraction of exchange, there continues the meticulous, concrete training of useful forces; the circuits of communication are the supports of an accumulation and a centralization of knowledge; the play of signs defines the anchorages of power; it is not that the beautiful totality of the individual is amputated, repressed, altered by our social order, it is rather that the individual is carefully fabricated in it, according to a whole technique of forces and bodies. We are much less Greeks than we believe. We are neither in the amphitheater, nor on the stage, but in the panoptic machine, invested by its effects of power, which we bring to ourselves since we are part of its mechanism. The importance, in historical mythology, of the Napoleonic character probably derives from the fact that it is at the point of junction of the monarchical, ritual exercise of sovereignty and the hierarchical, permanent exercise of indefinite discipline. He is the individual who looms over everything with a single gaze which no detail, however minute, can escape: "You may consider that no part of the Empire is without surveillance, no crime, no offense, no contravention that remains unpunished, and that the eye of the genius who can enlighten all embraces the whole of this vast machine, without, however, the slightest detail escaping his attention" (Treilhard 14). At the moment of its full blossoming, the disciplinary society still assumes with the Emperor the old aspect of the power of spectacle. As a monarch who is at one and the same time a usurper of the ancient throne and the organizer of the new state, he combined into a single symbolic, ultimate figure the whole of the long process by which the pomp of sovereignty, the necessarily spectacular manifestations of power, were extinguished one by one in the daily exercise of surveillance, in a panopticism in which the vigilance of intersecting gazes was soon to render useless both the eagle and the sun.

The formation of the disciplinary society is connected with a number of broad historical processes—economic, juridico-political, and lastly, scientific—of which it forms part.

1. Generally speaking, it might be said that the disciplines are techniques for assuring the ordering of human multiplicities. It is true that there is nothing exceptional or even characteristic in this: every system of power is presented with the same problem. But the peculiarity of the disciplines is that they try to define in relation to the multiplicities a tactics of power that fulfills three criteria: firstly, to obtain the exercise of power at the lowest possible cost (economically, by the low expenditure it involves; politically, by its discretion, its low exteriorization, its relative invisibility, the little resistance it arouses); secondly, to bring the effects of this social power to their maximum intensity and to extend them as far as possible, without either failure or interval; thirdly, to link this "economic" growth of power with the output of the apparatuses (educational, military, industrial, or medical) within which it is exercised; in short, to increase both the docility and the utility of all the elements of the system. This triple objective of the disciplines corresponds to a well-known historical conjuncture. One aspect of this conjuncture was the large demographic thrust of the eighteenth century; an increase in the floating population (one of the primary objects of discipline is to fix; it is an anti-nomadic technique); a change of quantitative scale in the groups to be supervised or manipulated (from the beginning of the seventeenth century to the eve of the French Revolution, the school population had been increasing rapidly, as had no doubt the hospital population; by the end of the eighteenth century, the peacetime army exceeded 200,000 men). The other aspect of the conjuncture was the growth in the apparatus of production, which was becoming more and more extended and complex; it was also becoming more costly and its profitability had to be increased. The development of the disciplinary methods corresponded to these two processes, or rather, no doubt, to the new need to adjust their correlation. Neither the residual forms of feudal power nor the structures of the administrative

monarchy, nor the local mechanisms of supervision, nor the unstable, tangled mass they all formed together could carry out this role: they were hindered from doing so by the irregular and inadequate extension of their network, by their often conflicting functioning, but above all by the "costly" nature of the power that was exercised in them. It was costly in several senses: because directly it cost a great deal to the Treasury; because the system of corrupt offices and farmed-out taxes weighed indirectly, but very heavily, on the population; because the resistance it encountered forced it into a cycle of perpetual reinforcement; because it proceeded essentially by levying (levying on money or products by royal, seigniorial, ecclesiastical taxation; levying on men or time by *corvées* of press-ganging, by locking up or banishing vagabonds). The development of the disciplines marks the appearance of elementary techniques belonging to a quite different economy: mechanisms of power which, instead of proceeding by deduction, are integrated into the productive efficiency of the apparatuses from within, into the growth of this efficiency and into the use of what it produces. For the old principle of "levying-violence," which governed the economy of power, the disciplines substitute the principle of "mildness-production-profit." These are the techniques that make it possible to adjust the multiplicity of men and the multiplication of the apparatuses of production (and this means not only "production" in the strict sense, but also the production of knowledge and skills in the school, the production of health in the hospitals, the production of destructive force in the army).

In this task of adjustment, discipline had to solve a number of problems for which the old economy of power was not sufficiently equipped. It could reduce the inefficiency of mass phenomena: reduce what, in a multiplicity, makes it much less manageable than a unity; reduce what is opposed to the use of each of its elements and of their sum; reduce everything that may counter the advantages of number. That is why discipline fixes; it arrests or regulates movements; it clears up confusion; it dissipates compact groupings of individuals wandering about the country in unpredictable ways; it establishes calculated distributions. It must also master all the forces that are formed from the very constitution of an organized multiplicity; it must neutralize the effects of counterpower that spring from them and which form a resistance to the power that wishes to dominate it: agitations, revolts, spontaneous organizations, coalitions—anything that may establish horizontal conjunctions. Hence the fact that the disciplines use procedures of partitioning and verticality, that they introduce, between the different elements at the same level, as solid separations as possible, that they define compact hierarchical networks, in short, that they oppose to the intrinsic, adverse force of multiplicity the technique of the continuous, individualizing pyramid. They must also increase the particular utility of each element of the multiplicity, but by means that are the most rapid and the least costly, that is to say, by using the multiplicity itself as an instrument of this growth. Hence, in order to extract from bodies the maximum time and force, the use of those overall methods known as timetables, collective training, exercises, total and detailed surveillance. Furthermore, the disciplines must increase the effect of utility proper to the multiplicities, so that each is made more useful than the simple sum of its elements: it is in order to increase the utilizable effects of the multiple that the disciplines define tactics of distribution, reciprocal adjustment of bodies, gestures, and rhythms, differentiation of capacities, reciprocal coordination in relation to apparatuses or tasks. Lastly, the disciplines have to bring into play the power relations, not above but inside the very texture of the multiplicity, as discreetly as possible, as well articulated on the other functions of these multiplicities and also in the least expensive way possible: to this correspond anonymous instruments of power, coextensive with the multiplicity that they regiment, such as hierarchical surveillance, continuous registration, perpetual assessment, and classification. In short, to substitute for a power that is manifested through the brilliance of those who exercise it, a power that insidiously objectifies those on whom it is applied; to form a body of knowledge about these individuals, rather than to deploy the ostentatious signs of sovereignty. In a word, the disciplines are the ensemble of minute technical inventions that made it possible to increase the useful size of multiplicities by decreasing the inconveniences of the power which, in order to make them useful, must control them. A multiplicity, whether in a workshop or a nation, an army or a school, reaches the threshold of a discipline when the relation of the one to the other becomes favorable.

If the economic take-off of the West began with the techniques that made possible the accumulation of capital, it might perhaps be said that the methods for administering the accumulation of men made possible a political take-off in relation to the traditional, ritual, costly, violent forms of power, which soon fell into disuse and were superseded by a subtle, calculated technology of subjection. In fact, the two processes—the accumulation of men and the accumulation of capital—cannot be separated; it would not have been possible to solve the problem of the accumulation of men without the growth of an apparatus of production capable of both sustaining them and using them; conversely, the techniques that made the cumulative multiplicity of men useful accelerated the accumulation of capital. At a less general level, the technological mutations of the apparatus of production, the division of labor and the elaboration of the disciplinary techniques sustained an ensemble of very close relations (cf. Marx, *Capital*, vol. I, chapter XIII and the very interesting analysis in Guerry and Deleule). Each makes the other possible and necessary; each provides a model for the other. The disciplinary pyramid constituted the small cell of power within which the separation, coordination, and supervision of tasks was imposed and made efficient; and analytical partitioning of time, gestures, and bodily forces constituted an operational schema that could easily be transferred from the groups to be subjected to the mechanisms of production; the massive projection of military methods onto industrial organization was an example of this modeling of the division of labor following the model laid down by the schemata of power. But, on the other hand, the technical analysis of the process of production, its "mechanical" breaking-down, were projected onto the labor force whose task it was to implement it: the constitution of those disciplinary machines in which the individual forces that they bring together are composed into a whole and therefore increased is the effect of this projection. Let us say that discipline is the unitary technique by which the body is reduced as a "political" force at the least cost and maximized as a useful force. The growth of a capitalist economy gave rise to the specific modality of disciplinary power, whose general formulas, techniques of submitting forces and bodies, in short, "political anatomy," could be operated in the most diverse political regimes, apparatuses, or institutions.

2. The panoptic modality of power—at the elementary, technical, merely physical level at which it is situated—is not under the immediate dependence or a direct extension of the great juridico-political structures of a society; it is nonetheless not absolutely independent. Historically, the process by which the bourgeoisie became in the course of the eighteenth century the politically dominant class was masked by the establishment of an explicit, coded, and formally egalitarian juridical framework, made possible by the organization of a parliamentary, representative regime. But the development and generalization of disciplinary mechanisms constituted the other, dark side of these processes. The general juridical form that guaranteed a system of rights that were egalitarian in principle was supported by these tiny, everyday, physical mechanisms, by all those systems of micropower that are essentially nonegalitarian and asymmetrical that we call the disciplines. And although, in a formal way, the representative regime makes it possible, directly or indirectly, with or without relays, for the will of all to form the fundamental authority of sovereignty, the disciplines provide, at the base, a guarantee of the submission of forces and bodies. The real, corporal disciplines constituted the foundation of the formal, juridical liberties. The contract may have been regarded as the ideal foundation of law and political power; panopticism constituted the technique, universally widespread, of coercion. It continued to work in depth on the juridical structures of society, in order to make the effective mechanisms of power function in opposition to the formal framework that it had acquired. The "Enlightenment," which discovered the liberties, also invented the disciplines.

In appearance, the disciplines constitute nothing more than an infralaw. They seem to extend the general forms defined by law to the infinitesimal level of individual lives; or they appear as methods of training that enable individuals to become integrated into these general demands. They seem to constitute the same type of law on a different scale, thereby making it more meticulous and more indulgent. The disciplines should be regarded as a sort of counterlaw. They have the precise role of introducing insuperable asymmetries and excluding reciprocities. First, because discipline creates between individuals a "private" link, which is a relation of constraints entirely different from contractual obligation; the acceptance of a discipline may be underwritten by contract; the way in which it is imposed, the mechanisms it brings into play, the nonreversible subordination of one group of people by another, the "surplus" power that is always fixed on the same side, the inequality of position of the different "partners" in relation to the common regulation, all these distinguish the disciplinary link from the contractual link, and make it possible to distort the contractual link systematically from the moment it has as its content a mechanism of discipline. We know, for example, how many real procedures undermine the legal fiction of the work contract: workshop discipline is not the least important. Moreover, whereas the juridical systems define juridical subjects according to universal norms, the disciplines characterize, classify, specialize; they distribute along a scale, around a norm, hierarchize individuals in relation to one another and, if necessary, disqualify and invalidate. In any case, in the space and during the time in which they exercise their control and bring into play the asymmetries of their power, they effect a suspension of the law that is never total, but is never annulled either. Regular and institutional as it may be, the discipline, in its mechanism, is a "counterlaw." And, although the universal juridicism of modern society seems to fix limits on the exercise of power, its universally widespread panopticism enables it to operate, on the underside of the law, a machinery that is both immense and minute, which supports, reinforces, multiplies the asymmetry of power and undermines the limits that are traced around the law. The minute disciplines, the panopticisms of every day may well be below the level of emergence of the great apparatuses and the great political struggles. But, in the genealogy of modern society, they have been, with the class domination that traverses it, the political counterpart of the juridical norms according to which power was redistributed. Hence, no doubt, the importance that has been given for so long to the small techniques of discipline, to those apparently insignificant tricks that it has invented, and even to those "sciences" that give it a respectable face; hence the fear of abandoning them if one cannot find any substitute; hence the affirmation that they are at the very foundation of society, and an element in its equilibrium, whereas they are a series of mechanisms for unbalancing power relations definitively and everywhere; hence the persistence in regarding them as the humble, but concrete form of every morality, whereas they are a set of physico-political techniques.

To return to the problem of legal punishments, the prison with all the corrective technology at its disposal is to be resituated at the point where the codified power to punish turns into a disciplinary power to observe; at the point where the universal punishments of the law are applied selectively to certain individuals and always the same ones; at the point where the redefinition of the juridical subject by the penalty becomes a useful training of the criminal; at the point where the law is inverted and passes outside itself, and where the counterlaw becomes the effective and institutionalized content of the juridical forms. What generalizes the power to punish, then, is not the universal consciousness of the law in each juridical subject; it is the regular extension, the infinitely minute web of panoptic techniques.

3. Taken one by one, most of these techniques have a long history be-hind them. But what was new, in the eighteenth century, was that, by being combined and generalized, they attained a level at which the formation of knowledge and the increase of power regularly reinforce one another in a circular process. At this point, the disciplines crossed the "technological" threshold. First the hospital, then the school, then, later, the workshop were not simply "reordered" by the disciplines; they became, thanks to them, apparatuses such that any mechanism of objectification could be used in them as an instrument of subjection, and any growth of power could give rise in them to possible branches of knowledge; it was this link, proper to the technological systems, that made possible within the disciplinary ele-ment the formation of clinical medicine, psychiatry, child psychology, edu-cational psychology, the rationalization of labor. It is a double process, then: an epistemological "thaw" through a refinement of power relations; a multiplication of the effects of power through the formation and accumula-tion of new forms of knowledge.

The extension of the disciplinary methods is inscribed in a broad histor-ical process: the development at about the same time of many other tech-nologies—agronomical, industrial, economic. But it must be recognized that, compared with the mining industries, the emerging chemical indus-tries or methods of national accountancy, compared with the blast furnaces or the steam engine, panopticism has received little attention. It is regarded as not much more than a bizarre little utopia, a perverse dream—rather as though Bentham had been the Fourier of a police society, and the Pha-lanstery had taken on the form of the Panopticon. And yet this represented the abstract formula of a very real technology, that of individuals. There were many reasons why it received little praise; the most obvious is that the discourses to which it gave rise rarely acquired, except in the academic classifications, the status of sciences; but the real reason is no doubt that the power that it operates and which it augments is a direct, physical power that men exercise upon one another. An inglorious culmination had an ori-gin that could be only grudgingly acknowledged. But it would be unjust to compare the disciplinary techniques with such inventions as the steam en-gine or Amici's microscope. They are much less; and yet, in a way, they are much more. If a historical equivalent or at least a point of comparison had to be found for them, it would be rather in the "inquisitorial" technique.

The eighteenth century invented the techniques of discipline and the examination, rather as the Middle Ages invented the judicial investigation. But it did so by quite different means. The investigation procedure, an old fiscal and administrative technique, had developed above all with the reor-ganization of the Church and the increase of the princely states in the twelfth and thirteenth centuries. At this time it permeated to a very large degree the jurisprudence first of the ecclesiastical courts, then of the lay courts. The investigation as an authoritarian search for a truth observed or attested was thus opposed to the old procedures of the oath, the ordeal, the judicial duel, the judgment of God, or even of the transaction between private individuals. The investigation was the sovereign power arrogating to itself the right to establish the truth by a number of regulated techniques. Now, although the investigation has since then been an integral part of Western justice (even up to our own day), one must not forget either its political origin, its link with the birth of the states and of monarchical sovereignty, or its later extension and its role in the formation of knowledge. In fact, the investigation has been the no doubt crude, but fundamental, element in the constitution of the empirical sciences; it has been the juridico-political matrix of this experimental knowledge, which, as we know, was very rapidly released at the end of the Middle Ages. It is perhaps true to say that, in Greece, mathematics were born from techniques of measurement; the sciences of nature, in any case, were born, to some extent, at the end of the Middle Ages, from the practices of investigation. The great empirical knowledge that covered the things of the world and transcribed them into the ordering of an indefinite discourse that observes, describes, and establishes the "facts" (at a time when the Western world was beginning the economic and political conquest of this same world) had its operating model no doubt in the Inquisition—that immense invention that our recent mildness has placed in the dark recesses of our memory. But what this politico-juridical, administrative, and criminal, religious and lay, investigation was to the sciences of nature, disciplinary analysis has been to the sciences of man. These sciences, which have so delighted our "humanity" for over a century, have their technical matrix in the petty, malicious minutiae of the disciplines and their investigations. These investigations are perhaps to psychology, psychiatry, pedagogy, criminology, and so many other strange sciences, what the terrible power of investigation was to the calm knowledge of the animals, the plants, or the earth. Another power, another knowledge. On the threshold of the classical age, Bacon, lawyer and statesman, tried to develop a methodology of investigation for the empirical sciences. What Great Observer will produce the methodology of examination for the human sciences? Unless, of course, such a thing is not possible. For, although it is true that, in becoming a technique for the empirical sciences, the investigation has detached itself from the inquisitorial procedure, in which it was historically rooted, the examination has remained extremely close to the disciplinary power that shaped it. It has always been and still is an intrinsic element of the disciplines. Of course it seems to have undergone a speculative purification by integrating itself with such sciences as psychology and psychiatry. And, in effect, its appearance in the form of tests, interviews, interrogations, and consultations is apparently in order to rectify the mechanisms of discipline: educational psychology is supposed to correct the rigors of the school, just as the medical or psychiatric interview is supposed to rectify the effects of the discipline of work. But we must not be misled; these techniques merely refer individuals from one disciplinary authority to another, and they reproduce, in a concentrated or formalized form, the schema of power-knowledge proper to each discipline (on this subject, cf. Tort). The great investigation that gave rise to the sciences of nature has become detached from its politico-juridical model; the examination, on the other hand, is still caught up in disciplinary technology.

In the Middle Ages, the procedure of investigation gradually superseded the old accusatory justice, by a process initiated from above; the disciplinary technique, on the other hand, insidiously and as if from below, has invaded a penal justice that is still, in principle, inquisitorial. All the great movements of extension that characterize modern penality—the problematization of the criminal behind his crime, the concern with a punishment that is a correction, a therapy, a normalization, the division of the act of judgment between various authorities that are supposed to measure, assess, diagnose, cure, transform individuals—all this betrays the penetration of the disciplinary examination into the judicial inquisition.

What is now imposed on penal justice as its point of application, its "useful" object, will no longer be the body of the guilty man set up against the body of the king; nor will it be the juridical subject of an ideal contract; it will be the disciplinary individual. The extreme point of penal justice under the Ancien Régime was the infinite segmentation of the body of the regicide: a manifestation of the strongest power over the body of the greatest criminal, whose total destruction made the crime explode into its truth. The ideal point of penality today would be an indefinite discipline: an interrogation without end, an investigation that would be extended without limit to a meticulous and ever more analytical observation, a judgment that would at the same time be the constitution of a file that was never closed, the calculated leniency of a penalty that would be interlaced with the ruthless curiosity of an examination, a procedure that would be at the same time the permanent measure of a gap in relation to an inaccessible norm and the asymptotic movement that strives to meet in infinity. The public execution was the logical culmination of a procedure governed by the Inquisition. The practice of placing individuals under "observation" is a natural extension of a justice imbued with disciplinary methods and examination procedures. Is it surprising that the cellular prison, with its regular chronologies, forced labor, its authorities of surveillance and registration, its experts in normality, who continue and multiply the functions of the judge, should have become the modern instrument of penalty? Is it surprising that prisons resemble factories, schools, barracks, hospitals, which all resemble prisons?

NOTES

[1] Archives militaires de Vincennes, A 1,516 91 sc. Pièce. This regulation is broadly similar to a whole series of others that date from the same period and earlier.

[2] In the *Postscript to the Panopticon*, 1791, Bentham adds dark inspection galleries painted in black around the inspector's lodge, each making it possible to observe two stories of cells.

[3] In his first version of the *Panopticon*, Bentham had also imagined an acoustic surveillance, operated by means of pipes leading from the cells to the central tower. In the *Postscript* he abandoned the idea, perhaps because he could not introduce into it the principle of dissymmetry and prevent the prisoners from hearing the inspector as well as

the inspector hearing them. Julius tried to develop a system of dissymmetrical listening (Julius 18).

[4] Imagining this continuous flow of visitors entering the central tower by an underground passage and then observing the circular landscape of the Panopticon, was Bentham aware of the Panoramas that Barker was constructing at exactly the same period (the first seems to have dated from 1787) and in which the visitors, occupying the central place, saw unfolding around them a landscape, a city, or a battle? The visitors occupied exactly the place of the sovereign gaze.

[5] In the second half of the eighteenth century, it was often suggested that the army should be used for the surveillance and general partitioning of the population. The army, as yet to undergo discipline in the seventeenth century, was regarded as a force capable of instilling it. Cf., for example, Servan, *Le Soldat citoyen*, 1780.

[6] Arsenal, MS. 2565. Under this number, one also finds regulations for charity associations of the seventeenth and eighteenth centuries.

[7] Le Maire in a memorandum written at the request of Sartine, in answer to sixteen questions posed by Joseph II on the Parisian police. This memorandum was published by Gazier in 1879.

BIBLIOGRAPHY

Archives militaires de Vincennes, A 1,516 91 sc.
Bentham, J., *Works*, ed. Bowring, IV, 1843.
Chassaigne, M., *La Lieutenance générale de police*, 1906.
Delamare, N., *Traité de police*, 1705.
Demia, C., *Règlement pour les écoles de la ville de Lyon*, 1716.
Des Essarts, T. N., *Dictionnaire universel de police*, 1787.
Funck-Brentano, F., *Catalogue des manuscrits de la bibliothèque de l'Arsenal*, IX.
Guerry, F., and Deleule, D., *Le Corps productif*, 1973.
Julius, N. H., *Leçons sur les prisons*, I, 1831 (Fr. trans.).
Léon, A., *La Révolution française et l'éducation technique*, 1968.
Loisel, G., *Histoire des ménageries*, II, 1912.
Marx, Karl, *Capital*, vol. I, ed. 1970.
Radzinovitz, L., *The English Criminal Law*, II, 1956.
Servan, J., *Le Soldat citoyen*, 1780.
Tort, Michel, *Q.I.*, 1974.
Treilhard, J. B., *Motifs du code d'instruction criminelle*, 1808.
Vattel, E. de, *Le Droit des gens*, 1768.

• • • • • • • • • • •

QUESTIONS FOR A SECOND READING

1. Foucault's text begins with an account of a system enacted in the seventeenth century to control the spread of plague. After describing this system of surveillance, he compares it to the "rituals of exclusion" used to control lepers. He says, "The exile of the leper and the arrest of the plague do not bring with them the same political dream." At many points he sets up similar pairings, all in an attempt to understand the relations of power and knowledge in modern public life.

   As you reread, mark the various points at which Foucault works out the differences between a prior and the current "political dream" of order.

What techniques or instruments belong to each? What moments in history are defined by each? How and where are they visible in public life?

2. Toward the end of the chapter Foucault says, "The extension of the disciplinary methods is inscribed in a broad historical process." Foucault writes a difficult kind of history (at one point he calls it a genealogy), since it does not make use of the usual form of historical narrative—with characters, plots, scenes, and action. As you reread, take notes that will allow you to trace time, place, and sequence (and, if you can, agents and agency) in Foucault's account of the formation of the disciplinary society based on technologies of surveillance. Why do you think he avoids a narrative mode of presentation?

3. As you reread Foucault's text, bring forward the stages in his presentation (or the development of his argument). Mark those moments that you consider key or central to the working out of his argument concerning the panopticon. What sentences of his would you use to represent key moments in the text? The text at times turns to numbered sections. How, for example, do they function? Describe the beginning, middle, and end of the essay. Describe the skeleton or understructure of the chapter. What are its various stages or steps? How do they relate to each other?

ASSIGNMENTS FOR WRITING

1. About three quarters of the way into this chapter, Foucault says,

> Our society is one not of spectacle, but of surveillance; under the surface of images, one invests bodies in depth; behind the great abstraction of exchange, there continues the meticulous, concrete training of useful forces; the circuits of communication are the supports of an accumulation and a centralization of knowledge; the play of signs defines the anchorages of power; it is not that the beautiful totality of the individual is amputated, repressed, altered by our social order, it is rather that the individual is carefully fabricated in it, according to a whole technique of forces and bodies. (p. 228)

This prose is eloquent and insists on its importance to our moment and our society; it is also very hard to read or to paraphrase. Who is doing what to whom? How do we think about the individual's being carefully fabricated in the social order?

Take this chapter as a problem to solve. What is it about? What are its key arguments? its examples and conclusions? Write an essay that summarizes "Panopticism." Imagine that you are writing for readers who have read the chapter (although they won't have the pages in front of them). You will need to take time to present and discuss examples from the text. Your job is to help your readers figure out what it says. You get the chance to take the lead and be the teacher. You should feel free to acknowledge that you don't understand certain sections even as you write about them.

So, how do you write about something you don't completely understand? Here's a suggestion. When you have completed your summary, read it over and treat it as a draft. Ask questions like these: What have

I left out? What was I tempted to ignore or finesse? Go back to those sections of the chapter that you ignored and bring them into your essay. Revise by adding discussions of some of the very sections you don't understand. You can write about what you think Foucault *might* be saying—you can, that is, be cautious and tentative; you can admit that the text is what it is, hard to read. You don't have to master this text. You do, however, need to see what you can make of it.

2. About a third of the way through his text, Foucault asserts, "The Panopticon is a marvelous machine which, whatever use one may wish to put it to, produces homogeneous effects of power." Write an essay in which you explain the machinery of the panopticon as a mechanism of power. Paraphrase Foucault and, where it seems appropriate, use his words. Present Foucault's account as you understand it. As part of your essay, and in order to explain what he is getting at, include two examples—one of his, perhaps, and then one of your own.

3. Perhaps the most surprising thing about Foucault's argument in "Panopticism" is the way it equates prisons with schools, hospitals, and workplaces, sites we are accustomed to imagining as very different from a prison. Foucault argues against our commonly accepted understanding of such things.

   At the end of the chapter Foucault asks two questions. These are rhetorical questions, strategically placed at the end. Presumably we are prepared to feel their force and to think of possible answers.

   > Is it surprising that the cellular prison, with its regular chronologies, forced labor, its authorities of surveillance and registration, its experts in normality, who continue and multiply the functions of the judge, should have become the modern instrument of penality? Is it surprising that prisons resemble factories, schools, barracks, hospitals, which all resemble prisons? (p. 236)

   For this assignment, take the invitation of Foucault's conclusion. No, you want to respond, it is not surprising that "experts in normality, who continue and multiply the functions of the judge, should have become the modern instrument of penality." No, it is not surprising that "prisons resemble factories, schools, barracks, hospitals, which all resemble prisons." Why isn't it surprising? Or, why isn't it surprising if you are thinking along with Foucault?

   Write an essay in which you explore one of these possible resemblances. You may, if you choose, cite Foucault. You can certainly pick up some of his key terms or examples and put them into play. You should imagine, however, that it is your turn. With your work on Foucault behind you, you are writing to a general audience about "experts in normality" and the key sites of surveillance and control.

MAKING CONNECTIONS

1. Both John Berger in "Ways of Seeing" (p. 97) and Michel Foucault in "Panopticism" discuss what Foucault calls "power relations." Berger claims that "the entire art of the past has now become a political issue," and he makes a case for the evolution of a "new language of images" which could "confer

a new kind of power" if people were to understand history in art. Foucault argues that the Panopticon signals an "inspired" change in power relations. "It is," he says,

> an important mechanism, for it automatizes and disindividualizes power. Power has its principle not so much in a person as in a certain concerted distribution of bodies, surfaces, lights, gazes; in an arrangement whose internal mechanisms produce the relation in which individuals are caught up. (p. 216)

Both Berger and Foucault create arguments about power, its methods and goals. As you read through their essays, mark passages you might use to explain how each author thinks about power—where it comes from, who has it, how it works, where you look for it, how you know when you see it, what it does, where it goes. You should reread the essays as a pair, as part of a single project in which you are looking to explain theories of power.

Write an essay in which you present and explain "Ways of Seeing" and "Panopticism" as examples of Berger's and Foucault's theories of power. Both Berger and Foucault are arguing against usual understandings of power and knowledge and history. In this sense, their projects are similar. You should be sure, however, to look for differences as well as similarities.

2. In "Panopticism," Michel Foucault presents a disciplinary society based on technologies of surveillance. The image (and history) of the Panopticon stands at the center of Foucault's argument; it signals what he refers to as an "inspired" change in disciplinary practices since it "automatizes and disindividualizes power." He says, "Power has its principle not so much in a person as in a certain concerted distribution of bodies, surfaces, lights, gazes; in an arrangement whose internal mechanisms produce the relation in which individuals are caught up. . . . Consequently, it does not matter who exercises power" (p. 216).

Clifford Geertz ("Deep Play," p. 259) is an ethnographer. He does his work by watching others (those beyond the urban centers), by speaking for and about their lives and thoughts, and by "capturing" them for consumption by readers who inhabit the urban centers. Several critics, including Foucault, have thought about the work of ethnographers (and anthropologists more generally) as a procedure of investigation or a form of surveillance designed for the purposes of discipline and the assertion of power. Write an essay that considers "Deep Play" with the panopticon (and Foucault's account of it) as a point of reference. Are there ways of watching others, of subjecting them to scrutiny and definition, that might be said to elude or transcend the arts of domination and control?

3. At the end of "Panopticism," Foucault asks two questions. These are rhetorical questions, strategically placed at the end. Presumably we are prepared to feel their force and to think of possible answers.

> Is it surprising that the cellular prison, with its regular chronologies, forced labor, its authorities of surveillance and registration, its experts in normality, who continue and multiply the functions of the judge, should have become the modern instrument of penalty? Is it surprising that prisons resemble factories, schools, barracks, hospitals, which all resemble prisons? (p. 236)

Is Foucault making the same argument as Paulo Freire, in "The 'Banking' Concept of Education" (p. 243)? Reread the Freire essay with Foucault's general argument in mind and thinking through the particular image (and institution) of the panopticon. How might you summarize these two arguments and their take on schooling? Freire, who speaks of a revolution in education, imagines a future in which students might be "free." Free in what sense? Does he have an answer to Foucault's concerns? Or does Foucault have an argument that might trump Freire's optimism?

You should assume an audience interested in education. It will not be the case, however, that they have read these two essays. You will need, then, to be careful in providing summary, paraphrase, and quotation. You will need to provide the background to an argument that you (and your readers) can identify as *yours*.

4. "Panopticism" opens with a scene from the seventeenth century, when measures were being taken to separate the sick and the well. Foucault says:

> The constant division between the normal and the abnormal, to which every individual is subjected, brings us back to our own time, by applying the binary branding and exile of the leper to quite different objects; the existence of a whole set of techniques and institutions for measuring, supervising, and correcting the abnormal brings into play the disciplinary mechanisms to which the fear of the plague gave rise. All the mechanisms of power which, even today, are disposed around the abnormal individual, to brand him and to alter him, are composed of those two forms from which they distantly derive. (pp. 212–13)

And, at the end, he asks two questions:

> Is it surprising that the cellular prison, with its regular chronologies, forced labor, its authorities of surveillance and registration, its experts in normality, who continue and multiply the functions of the judge, should have become the modern instrument of penalty? Is it surprising that prisons resemble factories, schools, barracks, hospitals, which all resemble prisons? (p. 236)

Although Michael McKeon, in "Subdividing Inside Spaces," doesn't write about prisons and schools, and he doesn't use words like *normal* and *abnormal*, he does write about how space is organized in service of power and as the expression of an idea about the relations between individuals and between conceptions of public and private life. Foucault writes:

> Power has its principle not so much in a person as in a certain concerted distribution of bodies, surfaces, lights, gazes; in an arrangement whose internal mechanisms produce the relation in which individuals are caught up. (p. 216)

Read "Panopticism" and then as you reread "Subdividing Inside Spaces," think about why McKeon (unlike many scholars of his generation) does not reference Foucault in his essay. He does not reference Foucault and, although he is certainly concerned with relations of power, he does not use the word *power* and, if he does, he uses it differently. How is his argument different from Foucault's? As you define that difference, where do you stand? Has McKeon lost something important? Has he made an argument that is more convincing or compelling?

PAULO
FREIRE

 *PAULO FREIRE (pronounce it "Fr-air-ah" unless you can make a Portuguese "r") was one of the most influential radical educators of our world. A native of Recife, Brazil, he spent most of his early career working in poverty-stricken areas of his homeland, developing methods for teaching illiterate adults to read and write and (as he would say) to think critically and, thereby, to take power over their own lives. Because he has created a classroom where teachers and students have equal power and equal dignity, his work has stood as a model for educators around the world. It led also to sixteen years of exile after the military coup in Brazil in 1964. During that time he taught in Europe and in the United States and worked for the Allende government in Chile, training the teachers whose job it would be to bring modern agricultural methods to the peasants.*

Freire (1921–1997) worked with the adult education programs of UNESCO, the Chilean Institute of Agrarian Reform, and the World Council of Churches. He was professor of educational philosophy at the Catholic University of São Paulo. He is the author of Education for Critical Consciousness, The Politics of Education, Pedagogy of the Oppressed, Revised Edition *(from which the following essay is drawn), and* Learning to Question: A Pedagogy of Liberation *(with Antonio*

Faundez). Pedagogy of Indignation, *the first English translations of Freire's late-life reflections on personal development, was published in 2004.*

For Freire, education is not an objective process, if by objective we mean "neutral" or "without bias or prejudice." Because teachers could be said to have something that their students lack, it is impossible to have a "neutral" classroom; and when teachers present a subject to their students they also present a point of view on that subject. The choice, according to Freire, is fairly simple: teachers either work "for the liberation of the people—their humanization—or for their domestication, their domination." The practice of teaching, however, is anything but simple. According to Freire, a teacher's most crucial skill is his or her ability to assist students' struggle to gain control over the conditions of their lives, and this means helping them not only to know but "to know that they know."

Freire edited, along with Henry A. Giroux, a series of books on education and teaching. In Literacy: Reading the Word and the World, *a book for the series, Freire describes the interrelationship between reading the written word and understanding the world that surrounds us.*

> *My parents introduced me to reading the word at a certain moment in this rich experience of understanding my immediate world. Deciphering the word flowed naturally from reading my particular world; it was not something superimposed on it. I learned to read and write on the grounds of the backyard of my house, in the shade of the mango trees, with words from my world rather than from the wider world of my parents. The earth was my blackboard, the sticks my chalk.*

For Freire, reading the written word involves understanding a text in its very particular social and historical context. Thus reading always involves "critical perception, interpretation, and rewriting of what is read."

The "Banking" Concept of Education

A careful analysis of the teacher-student relationship at any level, inside or outside the school, reveals its fundamentally *narrative* character. This relationship involves a narrating Subject (the teacher) and patient, listening objects (the students). The contents, whether values or empirical dimensions of reality, tend in the process of being narrated to become lifeless and petrified. Education is suffering from narration sickness.

The teacher talks about reality as if it were motionless, static, compartmentalized, and predictable. Or else he expounds on a topic completely alien to the existential experience of the students. His task is to "fill" the students with the contents of his narration—contents which are detached from reality, disconnected from the totality that engendered them and could give them significance. Words are emptied of their concreteness and become a hollow, alienated, and alienating verbosity.

The outstanding characteristic of this narrative education, then, is the sonority of words, not their transforming power. "Four times four is sixteen; the capital of Pará is Belém." The student records, memorizes, and repeats these phrases without perceiving what four times four really means, or realizing the true significance of "capital" in the affirmation "the capital of Pará is Belém," that is, what Belém means for Pará and what Pará means for Brazil.

Narration (with the teacher as narrator) leads the students to memorize mechanically the narrated content. Worse yet, it turns them into "containers," into "receptacles" to be "filled" by the teacher. The more completely she fills the receptacles, the better a teacher she is. The more meekly the receptacles permit themselves to be filled, the better students they are.

Education thus becomes an act of depositing, in which the students are the depositories and the teacher is the depositor. Instead of communicating, the teacher issues communiqués and makes deposits which the students patiently receive, memorize, and repeat. This is the "banking" concept of education, in which the scope of action allowed to the students extends only as far as receiving, filing, and storing the deposits. They do, it is true, have the opportunity to become collectors or cataloguers of the things they store. But in the last analysis, it is the people themselves who are filed away through the lack of creativity, transformation, and knowledge in this (at best) misguided system. For apart from inquiry, apart from the praxis, individuals cannot be truly human. Knowledge emerges only through invention and re-invention, through the restless, impatient, continuing, hopeful inquiry human beings pursue in the world, with the world, and with each other.

In the banking concept of education, knowledge is a gift bestowed by those who consider themselves knowledgeable upon those whom they consider to know nothing. Projecting an absolute ignorance onto others, a characteristic of the ideology of oppression, negates education and knowledge as processes of inquiry. The teacher presents himself to his students as their necessary opposite; by considering their ignorance absolute, he justifies his own existence. The students, alienated like the slave in the Hegelian dialectic, accept their ignorance as justifying the teacher's existence—but, unlike the slave, they never discover that they educate the teacher.

The *raison d'être* of libertarian education, on the other hand, lies in its drive towards reconciliation. Education must begin with the solution of the teacher-student contradiction, by reconciling the poles of the contradiction so that both are simultaneously teachers *and* students.

This solution is not (nor can it be) found in the banking concept. On the contrary, banking education maintains and even stimulates the contradiction through the following attitudes and practices, which mirror oppressive society as a whole:

a. the teacher teaches and the students are taught;
b. the teacher knows everything and the students know nothing;
c. the teacher thinks and the students are thought about;
d. the teacher talks and the students listen—meekly;
e. the teacher disciplines and the students are disciplined;
f. the teacher chooses and enforces his choice, and the students comply;
g. the teacher acts and the students have the illusion of acting through the action of the teacher;
h. the teacher chooses the program content, and the students (who were not consulted) adapt to it;
i. the teacher confuses the authority of knowledge with his or her own professional authority, which she and he sets in opposition to the freedom of the students;
j. the teacher is the Subject of the learning process, while the pupils are mere objects.

It is not surprising that the banking concept of education regards men as adaptable, manageable beings. The more students work at storing the deposits entrusted to them, the less they develop the critical consciousness which would result from their intervention in the world as transformers of that world. The more completely they accept the passive role imposed on them, the more they tend simply to adapt to the world as it is and to the fragmented view of reality deposited in them.

The capability of banking education to minimize or annul the students' creative power and to stimulate their credulity serves the interests of the oppressors, who care neither to have the world revealed nor to see it transformed. The oppressors use their "humanitarianism" to preserve a profitable situation. Thus they react almost instinctively against any experiment in education which stimulates the critical faculties and is not content with a partial view of reality but always seeks out the ties which link one point to another and one problem to another.

Indeed, the interests of the oppressors lie in "changing the consciousness of the oppressed, not the situation which oppresses them";[1] for the more the oppressed can be led to adapt to that situation, the more easily they can be dominated. To achieve this end, the oppressors use the banking concept of education in conjunction with a paternalistic social action apparatus, within which the oppressed receive the euphemistic title of "welfare recipients." They are treated as individual cases, as marginal persons who deviate from the general configuration of a "good, organized, and just" society. The oppressed are regarded as the pathology of the healthy society, which must therefore adjust these "incompetent and lazy" folk to its own patterns by changing their mentality. These marginals need to be "integrated," "incorporated" into the healthy society that they have "forsaken."

The truth is, however, that the oppressed are not "marginals," are not people living "outside" society. They have always been "inside"—inside the structure which made them "beings for others." The solution is not to "integrate" them into the structure of oppression, but to transform that structure so that they can become "beings for themselves." Such transformation, of course, would undermine the oppressors' purposes; hence their utilization of the banking concept of education to avoid the threat of student *conscientização*.*

The banking approach to adult education, for example, will never propose to students that they critically consider reality. It will deal instead with such vital questions as whether Roger gave green grass to the goat, and insist upon the importance of learning that, on the contrary, Roger gave green grass to the rabbit. The "humanism" of the banking approach masks the effort to turn women and men into automatons—the very negation of their ontological vocation to be more fully human.

Those who use the banking approach, knowingly or unknowingly (for there are innumerable well-intentioned bank-clerk teachers who do not realize that they are serving only to dehumanize), fail to perceive that the deposits themselves contain contradictions about reality. But, sooner or later, these contradictions may lead formerly passive students to turn against their domestication and the attempt to domesticate reality. They may discover through existential experience that their present way of life is irreconcilable with their vocation to become fully human. They may perceive through their relations with reality that reality is really a *process*, undergoing constant transformation. If men and women are searchers and their ontological vocation is humanization, sooner or later they may perceive the contradiction in which banking education seeks to maintain them, and then engage themselves in the struggle for their liberation.

But the humanist, revolutionary educator cannot wait for this possibility to materialize. From the outset, her efforts must coincide with those of the students to engage in critical thinking and the quest for mutual humanization. His efforts must be imbued with a profound trust in people and their creative power. To achieve this, they must be partners of the students in their relations with them.

The banking concept does not admit to such partnership—and necessarily so. To resolve the teacher-student contradiction, to exchange the role of depositor, prescriber, domesticator, for the role of student among students would be to undermine the power of oppression and serve the cause of liberation.

---

conscientização According to Freire's translator, "The term *conscientização* refers to learning to perceive social, political, and economic contradictions, and to take action against the oppressive elements of reality."

Implicit in the banking concept is the assumption of a dichotomy between human beings and the world: a person is merely *in* the world, not *with* the world or with others; the individual is spectator, not re-creator. In this view, the person is not a conscious being (*corpo consciente*); he or she is rather the possessor of *a* consciousness: an empty "mind" passively open to the reception of deposits of reality from the world outside. For example, my desk, my books, my coffee cup, all the objects before me—as bits of the world which surrounds me—would be "inside" me, exactly as I am inside my study right now. This view makes no distinction between being accessible to consciousness and entering consciousness. The distinction, however, is essential: the objects which surround me are simply accessible to my consciousness, not located within it. I am aware of them, but they are not inside me.

It follows logically from the banking notion of consciousness that the educator's role is to regulate the way the world "enters into" the students. The teacher's task is to organize a process which already occurs spontaneously, to "fill" the students by making deposits of information which he or she considers to constitute true knowledge.[2] And since people "receive" the world as passive entities, education should make them more passive still, and adapt them to the world. The educated individual is the adapted person, because she or he is better "fit" for the world. Translated into practice, this concept is well suited to the purposes of the oppressors, whose tranquility rests on how well people fit the world the oppressors have created, and how little they question it.

The more completely the majority adapt to the purposes which the dominant minority prescribe for them (thereby depriving them of the right to their own purposes), the more easily the minority can continue to prescribe. The theory and practice of banking education serve this end quite efficiently. Verbalistic lessons, reading requirements,[3] the methods for evaluating "knowledge," the distance between the teacher and the taught, the criteria for promotion: everything in this ready-to-wear approach serves to obviate thinking.

The bank-clerk educator does not realize that there is no true security in his hypertrophied role, that one must seek to live *with* others in solidarity. One cannot impose oneself, nor even merely co-exist with one's students. Solidarity requires true communication, and the concept by which such an educator is guided fears and proscribes communication.

Yet only through communication can human life hold meaning. The teacher's thinking is authenticated only by the authenticity of the students' thinking. The teacher cannot think for her students, nor can she impose her thoughts on them. Authentic thinking, thinking that is concerned about *reality*, does not take place in ivory tower isolation, but only in communication. If it is true that thought has meaning only when generated by action upon the world, the subordination of students to teachers becomes impossible.

Because banking education begins with a false understanding of men and women as objects, it cannot promote the development of what Fromm calls "biophily," but instead produces its opposite: "necrophily."

> While life is characterized by growth in a structured, functional manner, the necrophilous person loves all that does not grow, all that is mechanical. The necrophilous person is driven by the desire to transform the organic into the inorganic, to approach life mechanically, as if all living persons were things. . . . Memory, rather than experience; having, rather than being, is what counts. The necrophilous person can relate to an object—a flower or a person—only if he possesses it; hence a threat to his possession is a threat to himself; if he loses possession he loses contact with the world. . . . He loves control, and in the act of controlling he kills life.[4]

Oppression—overwhelming control—is necrophilic; it is nourished by love of death, not life. The banking concept of education, which serves the interests of oppression, is also necrophilic. Based on a mechanistic, static, naturalistic, spatialized view of consciousness, it transforms students into receiving objects. It attempts to control thinking and action, leads women and men to adjust to the world, and inhibits their creative power.

When their efforts to act responsibly are frustrated, when they find themselves unable to use their faculties, people suffer. "This suffering due to impotence is rooted in the very fact that the human equilibrium has been disturbed."[5] But the inability to act which causes people's anguish also causes them to reject their impotence, by attempting

> to restore [their] capacity to act. But can [they], and how? One way is to submit to and identify with a person or group having power. By this symbolic participation in another person's life, [men have] the illusion of acting, when in reality [they] only submit to and become part of those who act.[6]

Populist manifestations perhaps best exemplify this type of behavior by the oppressed, who, by identifying with charismatic leaders, come to feel that they themselves are active and effective. The rebellion they express as they emerge in the historical process is motivated by that desire to act effectively. The dominant elites consider the remedy to be more domination and repression, carried out in the name of freedom, order, and social peace (that is, the peace of the elites). Thus they can condemn—logically, from their point of view—"the violence of a strike by workers and [can] call upon the state in the same breath to use violence in putting down the strike."[7]

Education as the exercise of domination stimulates the credulity of students, with the ideological intent (often not perceived by educators) of indoctrinating them to adapt to the world of oppression. This accusation is not made in the naïve hope that the dominant elites will thereby simply abandon the practice. Its objective is to call the attention of true humanists to the fact that they cannot use banking educational methods in the pursuit of liberation, for they would only negate that very pursuit. Nor may a revolutionary society inherit these methods from an oppressor society. The revolutionary society which practices banking education is either misguided or mistrusting of people. In either event, it is threatened by the specter of reaction.

Unfortunately, those who espouse the cause of liberation are themselves surrounded and influenced by the climate which generates the banking concept, and often do not perceive its true significance or its dehumanizing power. Paradoxically, then, they utilize this same instrument of alienation in what they consider an effort to liberate. Indeed, some "revolutionaries" brand as "innocents," "dreamers," or even "reactionaries" those who would challenge this educational practice. But one does not liberate people by alienating them. Authentic liberation—the process of humanization—is not another deposit to be made in men. Liberation is a praxis: the action and reflection of men and women upon their world in order to transform it. Those truly committed to the cause of liberation can accept neither the mechanistic concept of consciousness as an empty vessel to be filled, nor the use of banking methods of domination (propaganda, slogans—deposits) in the name of liberation.

Those truly committed to liberation must reject the banking concept in its entirety, adopting instead a concept of women and men as conscious beings, and consciousness as consciousness intent upon the world. They must abandon the educational goal of deposit-making and replace it with the posing of the problems of human beings in their relations with the world. "Problem-posing" education, responding to the essence of consciousness—*intentionality*—rejects communiqués and embodies communications. It epitomizes the special characteristic of consciousness: being *conscious of*, not only as intent on objects but as turned in upon itself in a Jasperian "split"—consciousness as consciousness *of* consciousness.

Liberating education consists in acts of cognition, not transferrals of information. It is a learning situation in which the cognizable object (far from being the end of the cognitive act) intermediates the cognitive actors—teacher on the one hand and students on the other. Accordingly, the practice of problem-posing education entails at the outset that the teacher-student contradiction be resolved. Dialogical relations—indispensable to the capacity of cognitive actors to cooperate in perceiving the same cognizable object—are otherwise impossible.

Indeed, problem-posing education, which breaks with the vertical patterns characteristic of banking education, can fulfill its function as the practice of freedom only if it can overcome the above contradiction. Through dialogue, the teacher-of-the-students and the students-of-the-teacher cease to exist and a new term emerges: teacher-student with students-teachers. The teacher is no longer merely the-one-who-teaches, but one who is himself taught in dialogue with the students, who in turn while being taught also teach. They become jointly responsible for a process in which all grow. In this process, arguments based on "authority" are no longer valid; in order to function, authority must be *on the side of* freedom, not *against* it. Here, no one teaches another, nor is anyone self-taught. People teach each other, mediated by the world, by the cognizable objects which in banking education are "owned" by the teacher.

The banking concept (with its tendency to dichotomize everything) distinguishes two stages in the action of the educator. During the first, he cognizes a cognizable object while he prepares his lessons in his study or his laboratory; during the second, he expounds to his students about that object. The students are not called upon to know, but to memorize the contents narrated by the teacher. Nor do the students practice any act of cognition, since the object towards which that act should be directed is the property of the teacher rather than a medium evoking the critical reflection of both teacher and students. Hence in the name of the "preservation of culture and knowledge" we have a system which achieves neither true knowledge nor true culture.

The problem-posing method does not dichotomize the activity of the teacher-student: she is not "cognitive" at one point and "narrative" at another. She is always "cognitive," whether preparing a project or engaging in dialogue with the students. He does not regard cognizable objects as his private property, but as the object of reflection by himself and the students. In this way, the problem-posing educator constantly re-forms his reflections in the reflection of the students. The students—no longer docile listeners—are now critical co-investigators in dialogue with the teacher. The teacher presents the material to the students for their consideration, and re-considers her earlier considerations as the students express their own. The role of the problem-posing educator is to create, together with the students, the conditions under which knowledge at the level of the *doxa* is superseded by true knowledge, at the level of the *logos*.

Whereas banking education anesthetizes and inhibits creative power, problem-posing education involves a constant unveiling of reality. The former attempts to maintain the *submersion* of consciousness; the latter strives for the *emergence* of consciousness and *critical intervention* in reality.

Students, as they are increasingly posed with problems relating to themselves in the world and with the world, will feel increasingly challenged and obliged to respond to that challenge. Because they apprehend the challenge as interrelated to other problems within a total context, not as a theoretical question, the resulting comprehension tends to be increasingly critical and thus constantly less alienated. Their response to the challenge evokes new challenges, followed by new understandings; and gradually the students come to regard themselves as committed.

Education as the practice of freedom—as opposed to education as the practice of domination—denies that man is abstract, isolated, independent, and unattached to the world; it also denies that the world exists as a reality apart from people. Authentic reflection considers neither abstract man nor the world without people, but people in their relations with the world. In these relations consciousness and world are simultaneous: consciousness neither precedes the world nor follows it.

> La conscience et le monde sont donnés d'un même coup: extérieur par essence à la conscience, le monde est, par essence relatif à elle.[8]

In one of our culture circles in Chile, the group was discussing (based on a codification) the anthropological concept of culture. In the midst of the discussion, a peasant who by banking standards was completely ignorant said: "Now I see that without man there is no world." When the educator responded: "Let's say, for the sake of argument, that all the men on earth were to die, but that the earth itself remained, together with trees, birds, animals, rivers, seas, the stars . . . wouldn't all this be a world?" "Oh no," the peasant replied emphatically. "There would be no one to say: 'This is a world.' "

The peasant wished to express the idea that there would be lacking the consciousness of the world which necessarily implies the world of consciousness. *I* cannot exist without a *non-I*. In turn, the *not-I* depends on that existence. The world which brings consciousness into existence becomes the world *of* that consciousness. Hence, the previously cited affirmation of Sartre: *"La conscience et le monde sont donnés d'un même coup."*

As women and men, simultaneously reflecting on themselves and on the world, increase the scope of their perception, they begin to direct their observations towards previously inconspicuous phenomena:

> In perception properly so-called, as an explicit awareness [*Gewahren*], I am turned towards the object, to the paper, for instance. I apprehend it as being this here and now. The apprehension is a singling out, every object having a background in experience. Around and about the paper lie books, pencils, inkwell, and so forth, and these in a certain sense are also "perceived," perceptually there, in the "field of intuition"; but whilst I was turned towards the paper there was no turning in their direction, nor any apprehending of them, not even in a secondary sense. They appeared and yet were not singled out, were not posited on their own account. Every perception of a thing has such a zone of background intuitions or background awareness, if "intuiting" already includes the state of being turned towards, and this also is a "conscious experience," or more briefly a "consciousness of" all indeed that in point of fact lies in the co-perceived objective background.[9]

That which had existed objectively but had not been perceived in its deeper implications (if indeed it was perceived at all) begins to "stand out," assuming the character of a problem and therefore of challenge. Thus, men and women begin to single out elements from their "background awarenesses" and to reflect upon them. These elements are now objects of their consideration, and, as such, objects of their action and cognition.

In problem-posing education, people develop their power to perceive critically *the way they exist* in the world *with which* and *in which* they find themselves; they come to see the world not as a static reality, but as a reality in process, in transformation. Although the dialectical relations of women and men with the world exist independently of how these relations are perceived (or whether or not they are perceived at all), it is also true that the form of action they adopt is to a large extent a function of how they perceive themselves in the world. Hence, the teacher-student and the students-teachers reflect simultaneously on themselves and the world without dichotomizing this reflection from action, and thus establish an authentic form of thought and action.

Once again, the two educational concepts and practices under analysis come into conflict. Banking education (for obvious reasons) attempts, by mythicizing reality, to conceal certain facts which explain the way human beings exist in the world; problem-posing education sets itself the task of demythologizing. Banking education resists dialogue; problem-posing education regards dialogue as indispensable to the act of cognition which unveils reality. Banking education treats students as objects of assistance; problem-posing education makes them critical thinkers. Banking education inhibits creativity and domesticates (although it cannot completely destroy) the *intentionality* of consciousness by isolating consciousness from the world, thereby denying people their ontological and historical vocation of becoming more fully human. Problem-posing education bases itself on creativity and stimulates true reflection and action upon reality; thereby responding to the vocation of persons as beings who are authentic only when engaged in inquiry and creative transformation. In sum: banking theory and practice, as immobilizing and fixating forces, fail to acknowledge men and women as historical beings; problem-posing theory and practice take the people's historicity as their starting point.

Problem-posing education affirms men and women as beings in the process of *becoming*—as unfinished, uncompleted beings in and with a likewise unfinished reality. Indeed, in contrast to other animals who are unfinished, but not historical, people know themselves to be unfinished; they are aware of their incompletion. In this incompletion and this awareness lie the very roots of education as an exclusively human manifestation. The unfinished character of human beings and the transformational character of reality necessitate that education be an ongoing activity.

Education is thus constantly remade in the praxis. In order to *be*, it must *become*. Its "duration" (in the Bergsonian meaning of the word) is found in the interplay of the opposites *permanence* and *change*. The banking method emphasizes permanence and becomes reactionary; problem-posing education—which accepts neither a "well-behaved" present nor a predetermined future—roots itself in the dynamic present and becomes revolutionary.

Problem-posing education is revolutionary futurity. Hence, it is prophetic (and, as such, hopeful). Hence, it corresponds to the historical nature of humankind. Hence, it affirms women and men as beings who transcend themselves, who move forward and look ahead, for whom immobility represents a fatal threat, for whom looking at the past must only be a means of understanding more clearly what and who they are so that they can more wisely build the future. Hence, it identifies with the movement which engages people as beings aware of their incompletion—an historical movement which has its point of departure, its Subjects and its objective.

The point of departure of the movement lies in the people themselves. But since people do not exist apart from the world, apart from reality, the movement must begin with the human-world relationship. Accordingly, the point of departure must always be with men and women in the "here and now," which constitutes the situation within which they are submerged, from which they emerge, and in which they intervene. Only by starting from this situation—which determines their perception of it—can they begin to move. To do this authentically they must perceive their state not as fated and unalterable, but merely as limiting—and therefore challenging.

Whereas the banking method directly or indirectly reinforces men's fatalistic perception of their situation, the problem-posing method presents this very situation to them as a problem. As the situation becomes the object of their cognition, the naïve or magical perception which produced their fatalism gives way to perception which is able to perceive itself even as it perceives reality, and can thus be critically objective about that reality.

A deepened consciousness of their situation leads people to apprehend that situation as an historical reality susceptible of transformation. Resignation gives way to the drive for transformation and inquiry, over which men feel themselves to be in control. If people, as historical beings necessarily engaged with other people in a movement of inquiry, did not control that movement, it would be (and is) a violation of their humanity. Any situation in which some individuals prevent others from engaging in the process of inquiry is one of violence. The means used are not important; to alienate human beings from their own decision making is to change them into objects.

This movement of inquiry must be directed towards humanization—the people's historical vocation. The pursuit of full humanity, however, cannot be carried out in isolation or individualism, but only in fellowship and solidarity; therefore it cannot unfold in the antagonistic relations between oppressors and oppressed. No one can be authentically human while he prevents others from being so. Attempting *to be more* human, individualistically, leads to *having more*, egotistically, a form of dehumanization. Not that it is not fundamental *to have* in order *to be* human. Precisely because it *is* necessary, some men's *having* must not be allowed to constitute an obstacle to others' *having*, must not consolidate the power of the former to crush the latter.

Problem-posing education, as a humanist and liberating praxis, posits as fundamental that the people subjected to domination must fight for their emancipation. To that end, it enables teachers and students to become Subjects of the educational process by overcoming authoritarianism and an alienating intellectualism; it also enables people to overcome their false perception of reality. The world—no longer something to be described with deceptive words—becomes the object of that transforming action by men and women which results in their humanization.

Problem-posing education does not and cannot serve the interests of the oppressor. No oppressive order could permit the oppressed to begin to question: Why? While only a revolutionary society can carry out this education in systematic terms, the revolutionary leaders need not take full power before they can employ the method. In the revolutionary process, the leaders cannot utilize the banking method as an interim measure, justified on grounds of expediency, with the intention of *later* behaving in a genuinely revolutionary fashion. They must be revolutionary—that is to say, dialogical—from the outset.

NOTES

[1] Simone de Beauvoir, *La pensée de droite, aujourd'hui* (Paris); ST, *El pensamiento político de la derecha* (Buenos Aires, 1963), p. 34.

[2] This concept corresponds to what Sartre calls the "digestive" or "nutritive" concept of education, in which knowledge is "fed" by the teacher to the students to "fill them out." See Jean-Paul Sartre, "Une idée fondamentale de la phénoménologie de Husserl: L'intentionalité," *Situations* I (Paris, 1947).

[3] For example, some professors specify in their reading lists that a book should be read from pages 10 to 15—and do this to "help" their students!

[4] Erich Fromm, *The Heart of Man* (New York, 1966), p. 41.

[5] Ibid., p. 31.

[6] Ibid.

[7] Reinhold Niebuhr, *Moral Man and Immoral Society* (New York, 1960), p. 130.

[8] Sartre, op. cit., p. 32. [The passage is obscure but could be read as "Consciousness and the world are given at one and the same time: the exterior world as it enters consciousness is relative to our ways of seeing and understanding that world."—Editors' note]

[9] Edmund Husserl, *Ideas—General Introduction to Pure Phenomenology* (London, 1969), pp. 105–6.

•   •   •   •   •   •   •   •   •   •   •

QUESTIONS FOR A SECOND READING

1. While Freire speaks powerfully about the politics of the classroom, he provides few examples of actual classroom situations. As you go back through the essay, try to ground (or to test) what he says with examples of your own. What would take place in a "problem-posing" class in English, history, psychology, or math? What is an "authentic form of thought and action"? How might you describe what Freire refers to as "reflection"? What, really, might teachers be expected to learn from their students? What example can you give of a time when you were "conscious of consciousness" and it made a difference to you with your schoolwork?

You might also look for moments when Freire does provide examples of his own. On page 247, for example, Freire makes the distinction between a student's role as a "spectator" and as "re-creator" by referring to his own relationship to the objects on his desk. How might you explain this distinction? Or, how might you use the example of his books and coffee cup to explain the distinction he makes between "being accessible to consciousness" and "entering consciousness"?

2. Freire uses two terms drawn from Marxist literature: *praxis* and *alienation*. From the way these words are used in the essay, how would you define them? And how might they be applied to the study of education?

3. A writer can be thought of as a teacher and a reader as a student. If you think of Freire as your teacher in this essay, does he enact his own principles? Does he speak to you as though he were making deposits in a bank? Or is there a way in which the essay allows for dialogue? Look for sections in the essay you could use to talk about the role Freire casts you in as a reader.

ASSIGNMENTS FOR WRITING

1. Surely all of us, anyone who has made it through twelve years of formal education, can think of a class, or an occasion outside of class, to serve as a quick example of what Freire calls the "banking" concept of education, where students were turned into "containers" to be "filled" by their teachers. If Freire is to be useful to you, however, he must do more than enable you to call up quick examples. He should allow you to say more than that a teacher once treated you like a container or that a teacher once gave you your freedom.

   Write an essay that focuses on a rich and illustrative incident from your own educational experience and read it (that is, interpret it) as Freire would. You will need to provide careful detail: things that were said and done, perhaps the exact wording of an assignment, a textbook, or a teacher's comments. And you will need to turn to the language of Freire's argument, to take key phrases and passages and see how they might be used to investigate your case.

   To do this you will need to read your account as not simply the story of you and your teacher, since Freire is not writing about individual personalities (an innocent student and a mean teacher, a rude teacher, or a thoughtless teacher) but about the roles we are cast in, whether we choose to be or not, by our culture and its institutions. The key question, then, is not who you were or who your teacher was but what roles you played and how those roles can lead you to better understand the larger narrative or drama of Education (an organized attempt to "regulate the way the world 'enters into' the students").

   Freire would not want you to work passively or mechanically, however, as though you were following orders. He would want you to make your own mark on the work he has begun. Use your example, in other words, as a way of testing and examining what Freire says, *particularly those passages that you find difficult or obscure.*

2. Problem-posing education, according to Freire, "sets itself the task of de-mythologizing"; it "stimulates true reflection and action"; it allows students to be "engaged in inquiry and creative transformation." These are grand and powerful phrases, and it is interesting to consider what they might mean if applied to the work of a course in reading and writing.

If the object for study were Freire's essay, "The 'Banking' Concept of Education," what would Freire (or a teacher determined to adapt his prac-tices) ask students to *do* with the essay? What writing assignment might he set for his students? Prepare that assignment, or a set of questions or guide-lines or instructions (or whatever) that Freire might prepare for his class.

Once you've prepared the writing assignment, write the essay that you think would best fulfill it. And, once you've completed the essay, go on, fi-nally, to write the teacher's comments on it—to write what you think Freire, or a teacher following his example, might write on a piece of student work.

MAKING CONNECTIONS

1. Freire says,

> Students, as they are increasingly posed with problems relating to them-selves in the world and with the world, will feel increasingly challenged and obliged to respond to that challenge. Because they apprehend the challenge as interrelated to other problems within a total context, not as a theoretical question, the resulting comprehension tends to be increasingly critical and thus constantly less alienated. (p. 250)

Students learn to respond, Freire says, through dialogue with their teachers. Freire could be said to serve as your first teacher here. He has raised the issue for you and given you some language you can use to frame questions and to imagine the possibilities of response.

Using one of the essays in this book as a starting point, pose a problem that challenges you and makes you feel obliged to respond, a problem that, in Freire's terms, relates to you "in the world and with the world." This is a chance for you, in other words, to pose a Freirian question and then to write a Freirian essay, all as an exercise in the practice of freedom.

When you are done, you might reread what you have written to see how it resembles or differs from what you are used to writing. What are the indi-cations that you are working with greater freedom? If you find evidence of alienation or "domination," to what would you attribute it and what, then, might you do to overcome it?

2. Freire writes about the distribution of power and authority in the classroom and argues that education too often alienates individuals from their own historical situation. Richard Rodriguez, in "The Achievement of Desire" (p. 545), writes about his education as a process of difficult but necessary alienation from his home, his childhood, and his family. And he writes about power—about the power that he gained and lost as he became increasingly successful as a student.

But Freire and Rodriguez write about education as a central event in the shaping of an adult life. It is interesting to imagine what they might have to say to each other. Write a dialogue between the two in which they discuss what Rodriguez has written in "The Achievement of Desire." What would they say to each other? What questions would they ask? How would they respond to each other in the give-and-take of conversation?

Note: This should be a dialogue, not a debate. Your speakers are trying to learn something about each other and about education. They are not trying to win points or convince a jury.

CLIFFORD
GEERTZ

CLIFFORD GEERTZ was born in San Francisco in 1926. After two years in the U.S. Navy Reserve, he earned a BA from Antioch College and a PhD from Harvard. A Fellow of the National Academy of Sciences, the American Academy of Arts and Sciences, and the American Philosophical Society, Geertz was a professor in the department of social science of the Institute for Advanced Study in Princeton, New Jersey, from 1970 to 2000. He wrote several books (mostly anthropological studies of Third World cultures) and published two collections of essays, The Interpretation of Cultures *(1977) and* Local Knowledge *(1985).* The Interpretation of Cultures, *from which the following essay is drawn, became a classic and won for Geertz the rare distinction of being an academic whose scholarly work is eagerly read by people outside his academic discipline, even outside the academic community altogether. His book* Works and Lives: The Anthropologist as Author *(1989) won the National Book Critics Circle Award for Criticism. Geertz's most recent work is* Available Light: Anthropological Reflections on Philosophical Topics *(2000). Geertz died in 2006.*

"Deep Play" was first presented at a Paris conference organized by Geertz, the literary critic Paul de Man, and the American Academy of Arts and Sciences. The

purpose of the conference was to bring together scholars from various academic departments (in the humanities, the social sciences, and the natural sciences) to see if
they could find a way of talking to each other and, in doing so, find a common
ground to their work. The conference planners believed that there was a common
ground, that all of these scholars were bound together by their participation in
what they called "systematic study of meaningful forms." This is a grand phrase, but
Geertz's essay clearly demonstrates what work of this sort requires of an anthropologist. The essay begins with a story, an anecdote, and the story Geertz tells is as
open to your interpretation as it is to anyone else's. What follow, however, are
Geertz's attempts to interpret the story he has told, first this way and then that. As
you watch him work—finding patterns, making comparisons, drawing on the theories of experts, proposing theories of his own—you are offered a demonstration of
how he finds meaningful forms and then sets out to study them systematically.

"Deep Play," in fact, was sent out as a model for all prospective conference participants, since it was a paper that showed not only what its author knew about his
subject (cockfights in Bali) but what he knew about the meth-
ods and procedures that gave him access to his subject. It is a
witty and sometimes dazzling essay with a wonderful story to
tell—a story of both a Balinese cockfight and an anthropologist
trying to write about and understand people whose culture
seems, at first, so very different from his own.

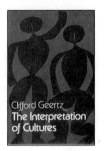

Clifford Geertz
**The Interpretation
of Cultures**

*Deep Play: Notes on the
Balinese Cockfight*

The Raid

Early in April of 1958, my wife and I arrived, malarial and diffident, in
a Balinese village we intended, as anthropologists, to study. A small place,
about five hundred people, and relatively remote, it was its own world. We
were intruders, professional ones, and the villagers dealt with us as Balinese seem always to deal with people not part of their life who yet press
themselves upon them: as though we were not there. For them, and to a degree for ourselves, we were nonpersons, specters, invisible men.

We moved into an extended family compound (that had been arranged
before through the provincial government) belonging to one of the four
major factions in village life. But except for our landlord and the village
chief, whose cousin and brother-in-law he was, everyone ignored us in a

way only a Balinese can do. As we wandered around, uncertain, wistful, eager to please, people seemed to look right through us with a gaze focused several yards behind us on some more actual stone or tree. Almost nobody greeted us; but nobody scowled or said anything unpleasant to us either, which would have been almost as satisfactory. If we ventured to approach someone (something one is powerfully inhibited from doing in such an atmosphere), he moved, negligently but definitively, away. If, seated or leaning against a wall, we had him trapped, he said nothing at all, or mumbled what for the Balinese is the ultimate non-word—"yes." The indifference, of course, was studied; the villagers were watching every move we made and they had an enormous amount of quite accurate information about who we were and what we were going to be doing. But they acted as if we simply did not exist, which, in fact, as this behavior was designed to inform us, we did not, or anyway not yet.

This is, as I say, general in Bali. Everywhere else I have been in Indonesia, and more latterly in Morocco, when I have gone into a new village people have poured out from all sides to take a very close look at me, and, often, an all-too-probing feel as well. In Balinese villages, at least those away from the tourist circuit, nothing happens at all. People go on pounding, chatting, making offerings, staring into space, carrying baskets about while one drifts around feeling vaguely disembodied. And the same thing is true on the individual level. When you first meet a Balinese, he seems virtually not to relate to you at all; he is, in the term Gregory Bateson and Margaret Mead made famous, "away."[1] Then—in a day, a week, a month (with some people the magic moment never comes)—he decides, for reasons I have never been quite able to fathom, that you *are* real, and then he becomes a warm, gay, sensitive, sympathetic, though, being Balinese, always precisely controlled person. You have crossed, somehow, some moral or metaphysical shadow line. Though you are not exactly taken as a Balinese (one has to be born to that), you are at least regarded as a human being rather than a cloud or a gust of wind. The whole complexion of your relationship dramatically changes to, in the majority of cases, a gentle, almost affectionate one—a low-keyed, rather playful, rather mannered, rather bemused geniality.

My wife and I were still very much in the gust of wind stage, a most frustrating, and even, as you soon begin to doubt whether you are really real after all, unnerving one, when, ten days or so after our arrival, a large cockfight was held in the public square to raise money for a new school.

Now, a few special occasions aside, cockfights are illegal in Bali under the Republic (as, for not altogether unrelated reasons, they were under the Dutch), largely as a result of the pretensions to puritanism radical nationalism tends to bring with it. The elite, which is not itself so very puritan, worries about the poor, ignorant peasant gambling all his money away, about what foreigners will think, about the waste of time better devoted to building up the country. It sees cockfighting as "primitive," "backward," "unprogressive," and generally unbecoming an ambitious nation. And, as with those other embarrassments—opium smoking, begging, or uncovered breasts—it seeks, rather unsystematically, to put a stop to it.

Of course, like drinking during prohibition or, today, smoking marijuana, cockfights, being a part of "The Balinese Way of Life," nonetheless go on happening, and with extraordinary frequency. And, like prohibition or marijuana, from time to time the police (who, in 1958 at least, were almost all not Balinese but Javanese) feel called upon to make a raid, confiscate the cocks and spurs, fine a few people, and even now and then expose some of them in the tropical sun for a day as object lessons which never, somehow, get learned, even though occasionally, quite occasionally, the object dies.

As a result, the fights are usually held in a secluded corner of a village in semisecrecy, a fact which tends to slow the action a little—not very much, but the Balinese do not care to have it slowed at all. In this case, however, perhaps because they were raising money for a school that the government was unable to give them, perhaps because raids had been few recently, perhaps, as I gathered from subsequent discussion, there was a notion that the necessary bribes had been paid, they thought they could take a chance on the central square and draw a larger and more enthusiastic crowd without attracting the attention of the law.

They were wrong. In the midst of the third match, with hundreds of people, including, still transparent, myself and my wife, fused into a single body around the ring, a superorganism in the literal sense, a truck full of policemen armed with machine guns roared up. Amid great screeching cries of "pulisi! pulisi!" from the crowd, the policemen jumped out, and, springing into the center of the ring, began to swing their guns around like gangsters in a motion picture, though not going so far as actually to fire them. The superorganism came instantly apart as its components scattered in all directions. People raced down the road, disappeared head first over walls, scrambled under platforms, folded themselves behind wicker screens, scuttled up coconut trees. Cocks armed with steel spurs sharp enough to cut off a finger or run a hole through a foot were running wildly around. Everything was dust and panic.

On the established anthropological principle, When in Rome, my wife and I decided, only slightly less instantaneously than everyone else, that the thing to do was run too. We ran down the main village street, northward, away from where we were living, for we were on that side of the ring. About halfway down another fugitive ducked suddenly into a compound—his own, it turned out—and we, seeing nothing ahead of us but rice fields, open country, and a very high volcano, followed him. As the three of us came tumbling into the courtyard, his wife, who had apparently been through this sort of thing before, whipped out a table, a tablecloth, three chairs, and three cups of tea, and we all, without any explicit communication whatsoever, sat down, commenced to sip tea, and sought to compose ourselves.

A few moments later, one of the policemen marched importantly into the yard, looking for the village chief. (The chief had not only been at the fight, he had arranged it. When the truck drove up he ran to the river, stripped off his sarong, and plunged in so he could say, when at length they found him sitting there pouring water over his head, that he had been away bathing when the whole affair had occurred and was ignorant of it. They did not believe him and fined him three hundred rupiah, which the village raised collectively.) Seeing my wife and I, "White Men," there in the yard, the policeman performed a classic double take. When he found his voice again he asked, approximately, what in the devil did we think we were doing there. Our host of five minutes leaped instantly to our defense, producing an impassioned description of who and what we were, so detailed and so accurate that it was my turn, having barely communicated with a living human being save my landlord and the village chief for more than a week, to be astonished. We had a perfect right to be there, he said, looking the Javanese upstart in the eye. We were American professors; the government had cleared us; we were there to study culture; we were going to write a book to tell Americans about Bali. And we had all been there drinking tea and talking about cultural matters all afternoon and did not know anything about any cockfight. Moreover, we had not seen the village chief all day, he must have gone to town. The policeman retreated in rather total disarray. And, after a decent interval, bewildered but relieved to have survived and stayed out of jail, so did we.

The next morning the village was a completely different world for us. Not only were we no longer invisible, we were suddenly the center of all attention, the object of a great outpouring of warmth, interest, and, most especially, amusement. Everyone in the village knew we had fled like everyone else. They asked us about it again and again (I must have told the story, small detail by small detail, fifty times by the end of the day), gently, affectionately, but quite insistently teasing us: "Why didn't you just stand there and tell the police who you were?" "Why didn't you just say you were only watching and not betting?" "Were you really afraid of those little guns?" As always, kinesthetically minded and, even when fleeing for their lives (or, as happened eight years later, surrendering them), the world's most poised people, they gleefully mimicked, also over and over again, our graceless style of running and what they claimed were our panic-stricken facial expressions. But above all, everyone was extremely pleased and even more surprised that we had not simply "pulled out our papers" (they knew about those too) and asserted our Distinguished Visitor status, but had instead demonstrated our solidarity with what were now our covillagers. (What we had actually demonstrated was our cowardice, but there is fellowship in that too.) Even the Brahmana priest, an old, grave, halfway-to-Heaven type who because of its associations with the underworld would never be involved, even distantly, in a cockfight, and was difficult to approach even to other Balinese, had us called into his courtyard to ask us about what had happened, chuckling happily at the sheer extraordinariness of it all.

In Bali, to be teased is to be accepted. It was the turning point so far as our relationship to the community was concerned, and we were quite literally "in." The whole village opened up to us, probably more than it ever would have otherwise (I might actually never have gotten to that priest, and our accidental host became one of my best informants), and certainly very much faster. Getting caught, or almost caught, in a vice raid is perhaps not a very generalizable recipe for achieving that mysterious necessity of anthropological field work, rapport, but for me it worked very well. It led to a sudden and unusually complete acceptance into a society extremely difficult for outsiders to penetrate. It gave me the kind of immediate, inside-view grasp of an aspect of "peasant mentality" that anthropologists not fortunate enough to flee headlong with their subjects from armed authorities normally do not get. And, perhaps most important of all, for the other things might have come in other ways, it put me very quickly on to a combination emotional explosion, status war, and philosophical drama of central significance to the society whose inner nature I desired to understand. By the time I left I had spent about as much time looking into cockfights as into witchcraft, irrigation, caste, or marriage.

Of Cocks and Men

Bali, mainly because it is Bali, is a well-studied place. Its mythology, art, ritual, social organization, patterns of child rearing, forms of law, even styles of trance, have all been microscopically examined for traces of that elusive substance Jane Belo called "The Balinese Temper."[2] But, aside from a few passing remarks, the cockfight has barely been noticed, although as a popular obsession of consuming power it is at least as important a revelation of what being a Balinese "is really like" as these more celebrated phenomena.[3] As much of America surfaces in a ball park, on a golf links, at a race track, or around a poker table, much of Bali surfaces in a cock ring. For it is only apparently cocks that are fighting there. Actually, it is men.

To anyone who has been in Bali any length of time, the deep psychological identification of Balinese men with their cocks is unmistakable. The double entendre here is deliberate. It works in exactly the same way in Balinese as it does in English, even to producing the same tired jokes, strained puns, and uninventive obscenities. Bateson and Mead have even suggested that, in line with the Balinese conception of the body as a set of separately animated parts, cocks are viewed as detachable, self-operating penises, ambulant genitals with a life of their own.[4] And while I do not have the kind of unconscious material either to confirm or disconfirm this intriguing notion, the fact that they are masculine symbols *par excellence* is about as indubitable, and to the Balinese about as evident, as the fact that water runs downhill.

The language of everyday moralism is shot through, on the male side of it, with roosterish imagery. *Sabung*, the word for cock (and one which appears in inscriptions as early as AD 922), is used metaphorically to mean "hero," "warrior," "champion," "man of parts," "political candidate," "bachelor," "dandy," "lady-killer," or "tough guy." A pompous man whose behavior presumes above his station is compared to a tailless cock who struts about as though he had a large, spectacular one. A desperate man who makes a last, irrational effort to extricate himself from an impossible situation is likened to a dying cock who makes one final lunge at his tormentor to drag him along to a common destruction. A stingy man, who promises much, gives little, and begrudges that is compared to a cock which, held by the tail, leaps at another without in fact engaging him. A marriageable young man still shy with the opposite sex or someone in a new job anxious to make a good impression is called "a fighting cock caged for the first time."[5] Court trials, wars, political contests, inheritance disputes, and street arguments are all compared to cockfights.[6] Even the very island itself is perceived from its shape as a small, proud cock, poised, neck extended, back taut, tail raised, in eternal challenge to large, feckless, shapeless Java.[7]

But the intimacy of men with their cocks is more than metaphorical. Balinese men, or anyway a large majority of Balinese men, spend an enormous amount of time with their favorites, grooming them, feeding them, discussing them, trying them out against one another, or just gazing at them with a mixture of rapt admiration and dreamy self-absorption. Whenever you see a group of Balinese men squatting idly in the council shed or along the road in their hips down, shoulders forward, knees up fashion, half or more of them will have a rooster in his hands, holding it between his thighs, bouncing it gently up and down to strengthen its legs, ruffling its feathers with abstract sensuality, pushing it out against a neighbor's rooster to rouse its spirit, withdrawing it toward his loins to calm it again. Now and then, to get a feel for another bird, a man will fiddle this way with someone else's cock for a while, but usually by moving around to squat in place behind it, rather than just having it passed across to him as though it were merely an animal.

In the houseyard, the high-walled enclosures where the people live, fighting cocks are kept in wicker cages, moved frequently about so as to maintain the optimum balance of sun and shade. They are fed a special diet, which varies somewhat according to individual theories but which is mostly maize, sifted for impurities with far more care than it is when mere humans are going to eat it and offered to the animal kernel by kernel. Red pepper is stuffed down their beaks and up their anuses to give them spirit. They are bathed in the same ceremonial preparation of tepid water, medicinal herbs, flowers, and onions in which infants are bathed, and for a prize cock just about as often. Their combs are cropped, their plumage dressed, their spurs trimmed, their legs massaged, and they are inspected for flaws with the squinted concentration of a diamond merchant. A man who has a passion for cocks, an enthusiast in the literal sense of the term, can spend most of his life with them, and even those, the overwhelming majority, whose passion though intense has not entirely run away with them, can and do spend what seems not only to an outsider, but also to themselves, an inordinate amount of time with them. "I am cock crazy," my landlord, a quite ordinary *afficionado* by Balinese standards, used to moan as he went to move another cage, give another bath, or conduct another feeding. "We're all cock crazy."

The madness has some less visible dimensions, however, because although it is true that cocks are symbolic expressions or magnifications of their owner's self, the narcissistic male ego writ out in Aesopian terms, they are also expressions—and rather more immediate ones—of what the Balinese regard as the direct inversion, aesthetically, morally, and metaphysically, of human status: animality.

The Balinese revulsion against any behavior regarded as animal-like can hardly be overstressed. Babies are not allowed to crawl for that reason. Incest, though hardly approved, is a much less horrifying crime than bestiality. (The appropriate punishment for the second is death by drowning, for the first being forced to live like an animal.)[8] Most demons are represented—in sculpture, dance, ritual, myth—in some real or fantastic animal form. The main puberty rite consists in filing the child's teeth so they will not look like animal fangs. Not only defecation but eating is regarded as a disgusting, almost obscene activity, to be conducted hurriedly and privately, because of its association with animality. Even falling down or any form of clumsiness is considered to be bad for these reasons. Aside from cocks and a few domestic animals—oxen, ducks—of no emotional significance, the Balinese are aversive to animals, and treat their large number of dogs not merely callously but with a phobic cruelty. In identifying with his cock, the Balinese man is identifying not just with his ideal self, or even his penis, but also, and at the same time, with what he most fears, hates, and ambivalence being what it is, is fascinated by—The Powers of Darkness.

The connection of cocks and cockfighting with such Powers, with the animalistic demons that threaten constantly to invade the small, cleared off space in which the Balinese have so carefully built their lives and devour its inhabitants, is quite explicit. A cockfight, any cockfight, is in the first instance a blood sacrifice offered, with the appropriate chants and oblations, to the demons in order to pacify their ravenous, cannibal hunger. No temple festival should be conducted until one is made. (If it is omitted someone will inevitably fall into a trance and command with the voice of an angered spirit that the oversight be immediately corrected.) Collective responses to natural evils—illness, crop failure, volcanic eruptions—almost always involve them. And that famous holiday in Bali, The Day of Silence (*Njepi*), when everyone sits silent and immobile all day long in order to avoid contact with a sudden influx of demons chased momentarily out of hell, is preceded the previous day by large-scale cockfights (in this case legal) in almost every village on the island.

In the cockfight, man and beast, good and evil, ego and id, the creative power of aroused masculinity and the destructive power of loosened animality fuse in a bloody drama of hatred, cruelty, violence, and death. It is little wonder that when, as is the invariable rule, the owner of the winning cock takes the carcass of the loser—often torn limb from limb by its enraged owner—home to eat, he does so with a mixture of social embarrassment, moral satisfaction, aesthetic disgust, and cannibal joy. Or that a man who has lost an important fight is sometimes driven to wreck his family shrines and curse the gods, an act of metaphysical (and social) suicide. Or that in seeking earthly analogues for heaven and hell the Balinese compare the former to the mood of a man whose cock has just won, the latter to that of a man whose cock has just lost.

The Fight

Cockfights (*tetadjen; sabungan*) are held in a ring about fifty feet square. Usually they begin toward late afternoon and run three or four hours until sunset. About nine or ten separate matches (*sehet*) comprise a program. Each match is precisely like the others in general pattern: there is no main match, no connection between individual matches, no variation in their format, and each is arranged on a completely ad hoc basis. After a fight has ended and the emotional debris is cleaned away—the bets paid, the curses cursed, the carcasses possessed—seven, eight, perhaps even a dozen men slop negligently into the ring with a cock and seek to find there a logical opponent for it. This process, which rarely takes less than ten minutes and often a good deal longer, is conducted in a very subdued, oblique, even dissembling manner. Those not immediately involved give it at best but disguised, sidelong attention; those who, embarrassedly, are, attempt to pretend somehow that the whole thing is not really happening.

A match made, the other hopefuls retire with the same deliberate indifference, and the selected cocks have their spurs (*tadji*) affixed—razor-sharp, pointed steel swords, four or five inches long. This is a delicate job which only a small portion of men, a half-dozen or so in most villages, know how to do properly. The man who attaches the spurs also provides them, and if the rooster he assists wins its owner awards him the spur-leg of the victim. The spurs are affixed by winding a long length of string around the foot of the spur and the leg of the cock. For reasons I shall come to presently, it is done somewhat differently from case to case, and is an obsessively deliberate affair. The lore about spurs is extensive—they are sharpened only at eclipses and the dark of the moon, should be kept out of the sight of women, and so forth. And they are handled, both in use and out, with the same curious combination of fussiness and sensuality the Balinese direct toward ritual objects generally.

The spurs affixed, the two cocks are placed by their handlers (who may or may not be their owners) facing one another in the center of the ring.[9] A coconut pierced with a small hole is placed in a pail of water, in which it takes about twenty-one seconds to sink, a period known as a *tjeng* and marked at beginning and end by the beating of a slit gong. During these twenty-one seconds the handlers (*pengangkeb*) are not permitted to touch their roosters. If, as sometimes happens, the animals have not fought during this time, they are picked up, fluffed, pulled, prodded, and otherwise insulted, and put back in the center of the ring and the process begins again. Sometimes they refuse to fight at all, or one keeps running away, in which case they are imprisoned together under a wicker cage, which usually gets them engaged.

Most of the time, in any case, the cocks fly almost immediately at one another in a wing-beating, head-thrusting, leg-kicking explosion of animal fury so pure, so absolute, and in its own way so beautiful, as to be almost abstract, a Platonic concept of hate. Within moments one or the other drives home a solid blow with his spur. The handler whose cock has delivered the blow immediately picks it up so that it will not get a return blow, for if he does not the match is likely to end in a mutually mortal tie as the two birds wildly hack each other to pieces. This is particularly true if, as often happens, the spur sticks in its victim's body, for then the aggressor is at the mercy of his wounded foe.

With the birds again in the hands of their handlers, the coconut is now sunk three times after which the cock which has landed the blow must be set down to show that he is firm, a fact he demonstrates by wandering idly around the ring for a coconut sink. The coconut is then sunk twice more and the fight must recommence.

During this interval, slightly over two minutes, the handler of the wounded cock has been working frantically over it, like a trainer patching a mauled boxer between rounds, to get it in shape for a last, desperate try for victory. He blows in its mouth, putting the whole chicken head in his own mouth and sucking and blowing, fluffs it, stuffs its wounds with various sorts of medicines, and generally tries anything he can think of to arouse the last ounce of spirit which may be hidden somewhere within it. By the time he is forced to put it back down he is usually drenched in chicken blood, but, as in prize fighting, a good handler is worth his weight in gold. Some of them can virtually make the dead walk, at least long enough for the second and final round.

In the climactic battle (if there is one; sometimes the wounded cock simply expires in the handler's hands or immediately as it is placed down again), the cock who landed the first blow usually proceeds to finish off his weakened opponent. But this is far from an inevitable outcome, for if a cock can walk he can fight, and if he can fight, he can kill, and what counts is which cock expires first. If the wounded one can get a stab in and stagger on until the other drops, he is the official winner, even if he himself topples over an instant later.

Surrounding all this melodrama—which the crowd packed tight around the ring follows in near silence, moving their bodies in kinesthetic sympathy with the movement of the animals, cheering their champions on with wordless hand motions, shiftings of the shoulders, turnings of the head, falling back *en masse* as the cock with the murderous spurs careens toward one side of the ring (it is said that spectators sometimes lose eyes and fingers from being too attentive), surging forward again as they glance off toward another—is a vast body of extraordinarily elaborate and precisely detailed rules.

These rules, together with the developed lore of cocks and cockfighting which accompanies them, are written down in palm leaf manuscripts (*lontar; rontal*), passed on from generation to generation as part of the general legal and cultural tradition of the villages. At a fight, the umpire (*saja komong; djuru kembar*)—the man who manages the coconut—is in charge of their application and his authority is absolute. I have never seen an umpire's judgment questioned on any subject, even by the more despondent losers, nor have I ever heard, even in private, a charge of unfairness directed against one, or, for that matter, complaints about umpires in general. Only exceptionally well-trusted, solid, and, given the complexity of the code, knowledgeable citizens perform this job, and in fact men will bring their cocks only to fights presided over by such men. It is also the umpire to whom accusations of cheating, which, though rare in the extreme, occasionally arise, are referred; and it is he who in the not infrequent cases where the cocks expire virtually together decides which (if either, for, though the Balinese do not care for such an outcome, there can be ties) went first. Likened to a judge, a king, a priest, and a policeman, he is all of these, and under his assured direction the animal passion of the fight proceeds within the civic certainty of the law. In the dozens of cockfights I saw in Bali, I never once saw an altercation about rules. Indeed, I never saw an open altercation, other than those between cocks, at all.

This crosswise doubleness of an event which, taken as a fact of nature, is rage untrammeled and, taken as a fact of culture, is form perfected, defines the cockfight as a sociological entity. A cockfight is what, searching for a name for something not vertebrate enough to be called a group and not structureless enough to be called a crowd, Erving Goffman has called a "focused gathering"—a set of persons engrossed in a common flow of activity and relating to one another in terms of that flow.[10] Such gatherings meet and disperse; the participants in them fluctuate; the activity that focuses them is discreet—a particulate process that reoccurs rather than a continuous one that endures. They take their form from the situation that evokes them, the floor on which they are placed, as Goffman puts it; but it is a form, and an articulate one, nonetheless. For the situation, the floor is itself created, in jury deliberations, surgical operations, block meetings, sitins, cockfights, by the cultural preoccupations—here, as we shall see, the celebration of status rivalry—which not only specify the focus but, assembling actors and arranging scenery, bring it actually into being.

In classical times (that is to say, prior to the Dutch invasion of 1908), when there were no bureaucrats around to improve popular morality, the staging of a cockfight was an explicitly societal matter. Bringing a cock to an important fight was, for an adult male, a compulsory duty of citizenship; taxation of fights, which were usually held on market day, was a major source of public revenue; patronage of the art was a stated responsibility of princes; and the cock ring, or *wantilan*, stood in the center of the village near those other monuments of Balinese civility—the council house, the origin temple, the marketplace, the signal tower, and the banyan tree. Today, a few special occasions aside, the newer rectitude makes so open a statement of the connection between the excitements of collective life and those of blood sport impossible, but, less directly expressed, the connection itself remains intimate and intact. To expose it, however, it is necessary to turn to the aspect of cockfighting around which all the others pivot, and through which they exercise their force, an aspect I have thus far studiously ignored. I mean, of course, the gambling.

Odds and Even Money

The Balinese never do anything in a simple way that they can contrive to do in a complicated one, and to this generalization cockfight wagering is no exception.

In the first place, there are two sorts of bets, or *toh*.[11] There is the single axial bet on the center between the principals (*toh ketengah*), and there is the cloud of peripheral ones around the ring between members of the audience (*toh kesasi*). The first is typically large; the second typically small. The first is collective, involving coalitions of bettors clustering around the owner; the second is individual, man to man. The first is a matter of deliberate, very quiet, almost furtive arrangement by the coalition members and the umpire huddled like conspirators in the center of the ring; the second is a matter of impulsive shouting, public offers, and public acceptances by the excited throng around its edges. And most curiously, and as we shall see most revealingly, *where the first is always, without exception, even money, the second, equally without exception, is never such.* What is a fair coin in the center is a biased one on the side.

The center bet is the official one, hedged in again with a webwork of rules, and is made between the two cock owners, with the umpire as overseer and public witness.[12] This bet, which, as I say, is always relatively and sometimes very large, is never raised simply by the owner in whose name it is made, but by him together with four or five, sometimes seven or eight, allies—kin, village mates, neighbors, close friends. He may, if he is not especially well-to-do, not even be the major contributor, though, if only to show that he is not involved in any chicanery, he must be a significant one.

Of the fifty-seven matches for which I have exact and reliable data on the center bet, the range is from fifteen ringgits to five hundred, with a mean at eighty-five and with the distribution being rather noticeably tri-modal: small fights (15 ringgits either side of 35) accounting for about 45 percent of the total number; medium ones (20 ringgits either side of 70) for about 25 percent; and large (75 ringgits either side of 175) for about 20 percent, with a few very small and very large ones out at the extremes. In a society where the normal daily wage of a manual laborer—a brickmaker, an ordinary farmworker, a market porter—was about 3 ringgits a day, and considering the fact that fights were held on the average about every two-and-a-half days in the immediate area I studied, this is clearly serious gambling, even if the bets are pooled rather than individual efforts.

The side bets are, however, something else altogether. Rather than the solemn, legalistic pactmaking of the center, wagering takes place rather in the fashion in which the stock exchange used to work when it was out on the curb. There is a fixed and known odds paradigm which runs in a continuous series from ten-to-nine at the short end to two-to-one at the long: 10-9, 9-8, 8-7, 7-6, 6-5, 5-4, 4-3, 3-2, 2-1. The man who wishes to back the *underdog cock* (leaving aside how favorites, *kebut*, and underdogs, *ngai*, are established for the moment) shouts the short-side number indicating the odds he wants *to be given*. That is, if he shouts *gasal*, "five," he wants the underdog at five-to-four (or, for him, four-to-five); if he shouts "four," he wants it at four-to-three (again, he putting up the "three"), if "nine," at nine-to-eight, and so on. A man backing the favorite, and thus considering giving odds if he can get them short enough, indicates the fact by crying out the color-type of that cock— "brown," "speckled," or whatever.[13]

As odds-takers (backers of the underdog) and odds-givers (backers of the favorite) sweep the crowd with their shouts, they begin to focus in on one another as potential betting pairs, often from far across the ring. The taker tries to shout the giver into longer odds, the giver to shout the taker into shorter ones.[14] The taker, who is the wooer in this situation, will signal how large a bet he wishes to make at the odds he is shouting by holding a number of fingers up in front of his face and vigorously waving them. If the giver, the wooed, replies in kind, the bet is made; if he does not, they unlock gazes and the search goes on.

The side betting, which takes place after the center bet has been made and its size announced, consists then in a rising crescendo of shouts as backers of the underdog offer their propositions to anyone who will accept them, while those who are backing the favorite but do not like the price being offered, shout equally frenetically the color of the cock to show they too are desperate to bet but want shorter odds.

Almost always odds-calling, which tends to be very consensual in that at any one time almost all callers are calling the same thing, starts off toward the long end of the range—five-to-four or four-to-three—and then moves, also consensually, toward the short end with greater or lesser speed and to a greater or lesser degree. Men crying "five" and finding themselves answered only with cries of "brown" start crying "six," either drawing the other callers fairly quickly with them or retiring from the scene as their too-generous offers are snapped up. If the change is made and partners are still scarce, the procedure is repeated in a move to "seven," and so on, only rarely, and in the very largest fights, reaching the ultimate "nine" or "ten" levels. Occasionally, if the cocks are clearly mismatched, there may be no upward movement at all, or even a movement down the scale to four-to-three, three-to-two, very, very rarely two-to-one, a shift which is accompanied by a declining number of bets as a shift upward is accompanied by an increasing number. But the general pattern is for the betting to move a shorter or longer distance up the scale toward the, for sidebets, nonexistent pole of even money, with the overwhelming majority of bets falling in the four-to-three to eight-to-seven range.[15]

As the moment for the release of the cocks by the handlers approaches, the screaming, at least in a match where the center bet is large, reaches almost frenzied proportions as the remaining unfulfilled bettors try desperately to find a last-minute partner at a price they can live with. (Where the center bet is small, the opposite tends to occur: betting dies off, trailing into silence, as odds lengthen and people lose interest.) In a large-bet, well-made match — the kind of match the Balinese regard as "real cockfighting" — the mob scene quality, the sense that sheer chaos is about to break loose, with all those waving, shouting, pushing, clambering men is quite strong, an effect which is only heightened by the intense stillness that falls with instant suddenness, rather as if someone had turned off the current, when the slit gong sounds, the cocks are put down, and the battle begins.

When it ends, anywhere from fifteen seconds to five minutes later, *all bets are immediately paid*. There are absolutely no IOUs, at least to a betting opponent. One may, of course, borrow from a friend before offering or accepting a wager, but to offer or accept it you must have the money already in hand and, if you lose, you must pay it on the spot, before the next match begins. This is an iron rule, and as I have never heard of a disputed umpire's decision (though doubtless there must sometimes be some), I have also never heard of a welshed bet, perhaps because in a worked-up cockfight crowd the consequences might be, as they are reported to be sometimes for cheaters, drastic and immediate.

It is, in any case, this formal asymmetry between balanced center bets and unbalanced side ones that poses the critical analytical problem for a theory which sees cockfight wagering as the link connecting the fight to the wider world of Balinese culture. It also suggests the way to go about solving it and demonstrating the link.

The first point that needs to be made in this connection is that the higher the center bet, the more likely the match will in actual fact be an even one. Simple considerations of rationality suggest that. If you are betting fifteen ringgits on a cock, you might be willing to go along with even money even if you feel your animal somewhat the less promising. But if you are betting five hundred you are very, very likely to be loath to do so. Thus, in large-bet fights, which of course involve the better animals, tremendous care is taken to see that the cocks are about as evenly matched as to size, general condition, pugnacity, and so on as is humanly possible. The different ways of adjusting the spurs of the animals are often employed to secure this. If one cock seems stronger, an agreement will be made to position his spur at a slightly less advantageous angle—a kind of handicapping, at which spur affixers are, so it is said, extremely skilled. More care will be taken, too, to employ skillful handlers and to match them exactly as to abilities.

In short, in a large-bet fight the pressure to make the match a genuinely fifty-fifty proposition is enormous, and is consciously felt as such. For medium fights the pressure is somewhat less, and for small ones less yet, though there is always an effort to make things at least approximately equal, for even at fifteen ringgits (five days' work) no one wants to make an even money bet in a clearly unfavorable situation. And, again, what statistics I have tend to bear this out. In my fifty-seven matches, the favorite won thirty-three times overall, the underdog twenty-four, a 1.4 to 1 ratio. But if one splits the figures at sixty ringgits center bets, the ratios turn out to be 1.1 to 1 (twelve favorites, eleven underdogs) for those above this line, and 1.6 to 1 (twenty-one and thirteen) for those below it. Or, if you take the extremes, for very large fights, those with center bets over a hundred ringgits the ratio is 1 to 1 (seven and seven); for very small fights, those under forty ringgits, it is 1.9 to 1 (nineteen and ten).[16]

Now, from this proposition—that the higher the center bet the more exactly a fifty-fifty proposition the cockfight is—two things more or less immediately follow: (1) the higher the center bet, the greater is the pull on the side betting toward the short-odds end of the wagering spectrum and vice versa; (2) the higher the center bet, the greater the volume of side betting and vice versa.

The logic is similar in both cases. The closer the fight is in fact to even money, the less attractive the long end of the odds will appear and, therefore, the shorter it must be if there are to be takers. That this is the case is apparent from mere inspection, from the Balinese's own analysis of the matter, and from what more systematic observations I was able to collect. Given the difficulty of making precise and complete recordings of side betting, this argument is hard to cast in numerical form, but in all my cases the odds-giver, odds-taker consensual point, a quite pronounced minimax saddle where the bulk (at a guess, two-thirds to three-quarters in most cases) of the bets are actually made, was three or four points further along the scale toward the shorter end for the large-center-bet fights than for the small ones, with medium ones generally in between. In detail, the fit is not, of course, exact, but the general pattern is quite consistent: the power of the center bet to pull the side bets toward its own even-money pattern is directly proportional to its size, because its size is directly proportional to the degree to which the cocks are in fact evenly matched. As for the volume question, total wagering is greater in large-center-bet fights because such fights are considered more "interesting" not only in the sense that they are less predictable, but, more crucially, that more is at stake in them—in terms of money, in terms of the quality of the cocks, and consequently, as we shall see, in terms of social prestige.[17]

The paradox of fair coin in the middle, biased coin on the outside is thus a merely apparent one. The two betting systems, though formally incongruent, are not really contradictory to one another, but part of a single larger system in which the center bet is, so to speak, the "center of gravity," drawing, the larger it is the more so, the outside bets toward the short-odds end of the scale. The center bet thus "makes the game," or perhaps better, defines it, signals what, following a notion of Jeremy Bentham's, I am going to call its "depth."

The Balinese attempt to create an interesting, if you will, "deep," match by making the center bet as large as possible so that the cocks matched will be as equal and as fine as possible, and the outcome, thus, as unpredictable as possible. They do not always succeed. Nearly half the matches are relatively trivial, relatively uninteresting—in my borrowed terminology, "shallow"—affairs. But that fact no more argues against my interpretation than the fact that most painters, poets, and playwrights are mediocre argues against the view that artistic effort is directed toward profundity and, with a certain frequency, approximates it. The image of artistic technique is indeed exact: the center bet is a means, a device, for creating "interesting," "deep" matches, *not* the reason, at least not the main reason, *why* they are interesting, the source of their fascination, the substance of their depth. The question why such matches are interesting—indeed, for the Balinese, exquisitely absorbing—takes us out of the realm of formal concerns into more broadly sociological and social-psychological ones, and to a less purely economic idea of what "depth" in gaming amounts to.[18]

Playing with Fire

Bentham's concept of "deep play" is found in his *The Theory of Legislation*.[19] By it he means play in which the stakes are so high that it is, from his utilitarian standpoint, irrational for men to engage in it at all. If a man whose fortune is a thousand pounds (or ringgits) wages five hundred of it on an even bet, the marginal utility of the pound he stands to win is clearly less than the marginal disutility of the one he stands to lose. In genuine deep play, this is the case for both parties. They are both in over their heads. Having come together in search of pleasure they have entered into a relationship which will bring the participants, considered collectively, net pain rather than net pleasure. Bentham's conclusion was, therefore, that deep play was immoral from the first principles and, a typical step for him, should be prevented legally.

But more interesting than the ethical problem, at least for our concerns here, is that despite the logical force of Bentham's analysis men do engage in such play, both passionately and often, and even in the face of law's revenge. For Bentham and those who think as he does (nowadays mainly lawyers, economists, and a few psychiatrists), the explanation is, as I have said, that such men are irrational—addicts, fetishists, children, fools, savages, who need only to be protected against themselves. But for the Balinese, though naturally they do not formulate it in so many words, the explanation lies in the fact that in such play money is less a measure of utility, had or expected, than it is a symbol of moral import, perceived or imposed.

It is, in fact, in shallow games, ones in which smaller amounts of money are involved, that increments and decrements of cash are more nearly synonyms for utility and disutility, in the ordinary, unexpanded sense—for pleasure and pain, happiness and unhappiness. In deep ones, where the amounts of money are great, much more is at stake than material gain: namely esteem, honor, dignity, respect—in a word, though in Bali a profoundly freighted word, status.[20] It is at stake symbolically, for (a few cases of ruined addict gamblers aside) no one's status is actually altered by the outcome of a cockfight; it is only, and that momentarily, affirmed or insulted. But for the Balinese, for whom nothing is more pleasurable than an affront obliquely delivered or more painful than one obliquely received— particularly when mutual acquaintances, undeceived by surfaces, are watching—such appraisive drama is deep indeed.

This, I must stress immediately, is *not* to say that the money does not matter, or that the Balinese is no more concerned about losing five hundred ringgits than fifteen. Such a conclusion would be absurd. It is because money *does*, in this hardly unmaterialistic society, matter and matter very much that the more of it one risks the more of a lot of other things, such as one's pride, one's poise, one's dispassion, one's masculinity, one also risks, again only momentarily but again very publicly as well. In deep cockfights an owner and his collaborators, and, as we shall see, to a lesser but still quite real extent also their backers on the outside, put their money where their status is.

It is in large part *because* the marginal disutility of loss is so great at the higher levels of betting that to engage in such betting is to lay one's public self, allusively and metaphorically, through the medium of one's cock, on the line. And though to a Benthamite this might seem merely to increase the irrationality of the enterprise that much further, to the Balinese what it mainly increases is the meaningfulness of it all. And as (to follow Weber rather than Bentham) the imposition of meaning on life is the major end and primary condition of human existence, that access of significance more than compensates for the economic costs involved.[21] Actually, given the even-money quality of the larger matches, important changes in material fortune among those who regularly participate in them seem virtually nonexistent, because matters more or less even out over the long run. It is, actually, in the smaller, shallow fights, where one finds the handful of more pure, addict-type gamblers involved—those who *are* in it mainly for the money—that "real" changes in social position, largely downward, are affected. Men of this sort, plungers, are highly dispraised by "true cockfighters" as fools who do not understand what the sport is all about, vulgarians who simply miss the point of it all. They are, these addicts, regarded as fair game for the genuine enthusiasts, those who do understand, to take a little money away from, something that is easy enough to do by luring them, through the force of their greed, into irrational bets on mismatched cocks. Most of them do indeed manage to ruin themselves in a remarkably short time, but there always seem to be one or two of them around, pawning their land and selling their clothes in order to bet, at any particular time.[22]

This graduated correlation of "status gambling" with deeper fights and, inversely, "money gambling" with shallower ones is in fact quite general. Bettors themselves form a sociomoral hierarchy in these terms. As noted earlier, at most cockfights there are, around the very edges of the cockfight area, a large number of mindless, sheer-chance type gambling games (roulette, dice throw, coin-spin, pea-under-the-shell) operated by concessionaires. Only women, children, adolescents, and various other sorts of people who do not (or not yet) fight cocks—the extremely poor, the socially despised, the personally idiosyncratic—play at these games, at, of course, penny ante levels. Cockfighting men would be ashamed to go anywhere near them. Slightly above these people in standing are those who, though they do not themselves fight cocks, bet on the smaller matches around the edges. Next, there are those who fight cocks in small, or occasionally medium matches, but have not the status to join in the large ones, though they may bet from time to time on the side in those. And finally, there are those, the really substantial members of the community, the solid citizenry around whom local life revolves, who fight in the larger fights and bet on them around the side. The focusing element in these focused gatherings, these men generally dominate and define the sport as they dominate and define the society. When a Balinese male talks, in that almost venerative way, about "the true cockfighter," the *bebatoh* ("bettor") or *djuru kurung* ("cage keeper"), it is this sort of person, not those who bring the mentality of the pea-and-shell game into the quite different, inappropriate context of the cockfight, the driven gambler (*potét*, a word which has the secondary meaning of thief or reprobate), and the wistful hanger-on, that they mean. For such a man, what is really going on in a match is something rather close to an *affaire d'honneur* (though, with the Balinese talent for practical fantasy, the blood that is spilled is only figuratively human) than to the stupid, mechanical crank of a slot machine.

What makes Balinese cockfighting deep is thus not money in itself, but what, the more of it that is involved the more so, money causes to happen: the migration of the Balinese status hierarchy into the body of the cockfight. Psychologically an Aesopian representation of the ideal/demonic, rather narcissistic, male self, sociologically it is an equally Aesopian representation of the complex fields of tension set up by the controlled, muted, ceremonial, but for all that deeply felt, interaction of those selves in the context of everyday life. The cocks may be surrogates for their owners' personalities, animal mirrors of psychic form, but the cockfight is—or more exactly, deliberately is made to be—a simulation of the social matrix, the involved system of crosscutting, overlapping, highly corporate groups— villages, kingroups, irrigation societies, temple congregations, "castes"—in which its devotees live.[23] And as prestige, the necessity to affirm it, defend it, celebrate it, justify it, and just plain bask in it (but not, given the strongly ascriptive character of Balinese stratification, to seek it), is perhaps the central driving force in the society, so also—ambulant penises, blood sacrifices, and monetary exchanges aside—is it of the cockfight. This apparent amusement and seeming sport is, to take another phrase from Erving Goffman, "a status bloodbath."[24]

The easiest way to make this clear, and at least to some degree to demonstrate it, is to invoke the village whose cockfighting activities I observed the closest—the one in which the raid occurred and from which my statistical data are taken.

As all Balinese villages, this one—Tihingan, in the Klungkung region of southeast Bali—is intricately organized, a labyrinth of alliances and oppositions. But, unlike many, two sorts of corporate groups, which are also status groups, particularly stand out, and we may concentrate on them, in a part-for-whole way, without undue distortion.

First, the village is dominated by four large, patrilineal, partly endogamous descent groups which are constantly vying with one another and form the major factions in the village. Sometimes they group two and two, or rather the two larger ones versus the two smaller ones plus all the unaffiliated people; sometimes they operate independently. There are also subfactions within them, subfactions within the subfactions, and so on to rather fine levels of distinction. And second, there is the village itself, almost entirely endogamous, which is opposed to all the other villages round about in its cockfight circuit (which, as explained, is the market region), but which also forms alliances with certain of these neighbors against certain others in various supravillage political and social contexts. The exact situation is thus, as everywhere in Bali, quite distinctive; but the general pattern of a tiered hierarchy of status rivalries between highly corporate but various based groupings (and, thus, between the members of them) is entirely general.

Consider, then, as support of the general thesis that the cockfight, and especially the deep cockfight, is fundamentally a dramatization of status concerns, the following facts, which to avoid extended ethnographic description I will simply pronounce to be facts—though the concrete evidence—examples, statements, and numbers that could be brought to bear in support of them is both extensive and unmistakable:

1. A man virtually never bets against a cock owned by a member of his own kingroup. Usually he will feel obliged to bet for it, the more so the closer the kin tie and the deeper the fight. If he is certain in his mind that it will not win, he may just not bet at all, particularly if it is only a second cousin's bird or if the fight is a shallow one. But as a rule he will feel he must support it and, in deep games, nearly always does. Thus the great majority of the people calling "five" or "speckled" so demonstratively are expressing their allegiance to their kinsman, not their evaluation of his bird, their understanding of probability theory, or even their hopes of unearned income.

2. This principle is extended logically. If your kingroup is not involved you will support an allied kingroup against an unallied one in the same way, and so on through the very involved networks of alliances which, as I say, make up this, as any other, Balinese village.

3. So, too, for the village as a whole. If an outsider cock is fighting any cock from your village, you will tend to support the local one. If, what is a rare circumstance but occurs every now and then, a cock from outside your cockfight circuit is fighting one inside it you will also tend to support the "home bird."

4. Cocks which come from any distance are almost always favorites, for the theory is the man would not have dared to bring it if it was not a good cock, the more so the further he has come. His followers are, of course, obliged to support him, and when the more grand-scale legal cockfights are held (on holidays, and so on) the people of the village take what they regard to be the best cocks in the village, regardless of ownership, and go off to support them, although they will almost certainly have to give odds on them and to make large bets to show that they are not a cheapskate village. Actually, such "away games," though infrequent, tend to mend the ruptures between village members that the constantly occurring "home games," where village factions are opposed rather than united, exacerbate.

5. Almost all matches are sociologically relevant. You seldom get two outsider cocks fighting, or two cocks with no particular group backing, or with group backing which is mutually unrelated in any clear way. When you do get them, the game is very shallow, betting very slow, and the whole thing very dull, with no one save the immediate principals and an addict gambler or two at all interested.

6. By the same token, you rarely get two cocks from the same group, even more rarely from the same subfaction, and virtually never from the same sub-subfaction (which would be in most cases one extended family) fighting. Similarly, in outside village fights two members of the village will rarely fight against one another, even though, as bitter rivals, they would do so with enthusiasm on their home grounds.

7. On the individual level, people involved in an institutionalized hostility relationship, called *puik*, in which they do not speak or otherwise have anything to do with each other (the causes of this formal breaking of relations are many: wife-capture, inheritance arguments, political differences) will bet very heavily, sometimes almost maniacally, against one another in what is a frank and direct attack on the very masculinity, the ultimate ground of his status, of the opponent.

8. The center bet coalition is, in all but the shallowest games, always made up by structural allies—no "outside money" is involved. What is "outside" depends upon the context, of course, but given it, no outside money is mixed in with the main bet; if the principals cannot raise it, it is not made. The center bet, again especially in deeper games, is thus the most direct and open expression of social opposition, which is one

of the reasons why both it and match making are surrounded by such an air of unease, furtiveness, embarrassment, and so on.

9. The rule about borrowing money—that you may borrow *for* a bet but not *in* one—stems (and the Balinese are quite conscious of this) from similar considerations: you are never at the *economic* mercy of your enemy that way. Gambling debts, which can get quite large on a rather short-term basis, are always to friends, never to enemies, structurally speaking.

10. When two cocks are structurally irrelevant or neutral so far as *you* are concerned (though, as mentioned, they almost never are to each other) you do not even ask a relative or a friend whom he is betting on, because if you know how he is betting and he knows you know, and you go the other way, it will lead to strain. This rule is explicit and rigid; fairly elaborate, even rather artificial precautions are taken to avoid breaking it. At the very least you must pretend not to notice what he is doing, and he what you are doing.

11. There is a special word for betting against the grain, which is also the word for "pardon me" (*mpura*). It is considered a bad thing to do, though if the center bet is small it is sometimes all right as long as you do not do it too often. But the larger the bet and the more frequently you do it, the more the "pardon me" tack will lead to social disruption.

12. In fact, the institutionalized hostility relation, *puik*, is often formally initiated (though its causes always lie elsewhere) by such a "pardon me" bet in a deep fight, putting the symbolic fat in the fire. Similarly, the end of such a relationship and resumption of normal social intercourse is often signalized (but, again, not actually brought about) by one or the other of the enemies supporting the other's bird.

13. In sticky, cross-loyalty situations, of which in this extraordinarily complex social system there are of course many, where a man is caught between two more or less equally balanced loyalties, he tends to wander off for a cup of coffee or something to avoid having to bet, a form of behavior reminiscent of that of American voters in similar situations.[25]

14. The people involved in the center bet are, especially in deep fights, virtually always leading members of their group—kinship, village, or whatever. Further, those who bet on the side (including these people) are, as I have already remarked, the more established members of the village—the solid citizens. Cockfighting is for those who are involved in the everyday politics of prestige as well, not for youth, women, subordinates, and so forth.

15. So far as money is concerned, the explicitly expressed attitude toward it is that it is a secondary matter. It is not, as I have said, of no importance; Balinese are no happier to lose several weeks' income than anyone else. But they mainly look on the monetary aspects of the cockfight as self-balancing, a matter of just moving money around, circulating it among a fairly well-defined group of serious cockfighters. The really important wins and losses are seen mostly in other terms, and

the general attitude toward wagering is not any hope of cleaning up, of making a killing (addict gamblers again excepted), but that of the horseplayer's prayer: "O, God, please let me break even." In prestige terms, however, you do not want to break even, but, in a momentary, punctuate sort of way, win utterly. The talk (which goes on all the time) is about fights against such-and-such a cock of So-and-So which your cock demolished, not on how much you won, a fact people, even for large bets, rarely remember for any length of time, though they will remember the day they did in Pan Loh's finest cock for years.

16. You must bet on cocks of your own group aside from mere loyalty considerations, for if you do not people generally will say, "What! Is he too proud for the likes of us? Does he have to go to Java or Den Pasar [the capital town] to bet, he is such an important man?" Thus there is a general pressure to bet not only to show that you are important locally, but that you are not so important that you look down on everyone else as unfit even to be rivals. Similarly, home team people must bet against outside cocks or the outsiders will accuse it—a serious charge—of just collecting entry fees and not really being interested in cockfighting, as well as again being arrogant and insulting.

17. Finally, the Balinese peasants themselves are quite aware of all this and can and, at least to an ethnographer, do state most of it in approximately the same terms as I have. Fighting cocks, almost every Balinese I have ever discussed the subject with has said, is like playing with fire only not getting burned. You activate village and kingroup rivalries and hostilities, but in "play" form, coming dangerously and entrancingly close to the expression of open and direct interpersonal and intergroup aggression (something which, again, almost never happens in the normal course of ordinary life), but not quite, because, after all, it is "only a cockfight."

More observations of this sort could be advanced, but perhaps the general point is, if not made, at least well-delineated, and the whole argument thus far can be usefully summarized in a formal paradigm:

THE MORE A MATCH IS . . .

1. Between near status equals (and/or personal enemies)
2. Between high status individuals

THE DEEPER THE MATCH.

THE DEEPER THE MATCH . . .

1. The closer the identification of cock and man (or: more properly, the deeper the match the more the man will advance his best, most closely-identified-with cock).
2. The finer the cocks involved and the more exactly they will be matched.

3. The greater the emotion that will be involved and the more the general absorption in the match.

4. The higher the individual bets center and outside, the shorter the outside bet odds will tend to be, and the more betting there will be overall.

5. The less an "economic" and the more a "status" view of gaming will be involved, and the "solider" the citizens who will be gaming.[26] *logical structure*

Inverse arguments hold for the shallower the fight, culminating, in a reversed-signs sense, in the coin-spinning and dice-throwing amusements. For deep fights there are no absolute upper limits, though there are of course practical ones, and there are a great many legendlike tales of great Duel-in-the-Sun combats between lords and princes in classical times (for cockfighting has always been as much an elite concern as a popular one), far deeper than anything anyone, even aristocrats, could produce today anywhere in Bali.

Indeed, one of the great culture heroes of Bali is a prince, called after his passion for the sport, "The Cockfighter," who happened to be away at a very deep cockfight with a neighboring prince when the whole of his family—father, brothers, wives, sisters—were assassinated by commoner usurpers. Thus spared, he returned to dispatch the upstarts, regain the throne, reconstitute the Balinese high tradition, and build its most powerful, glorious, and prosperous state. Along with everything else that the Balinese see in fighting cocks—themselves, their social order, abstract hatred, masculinity, demonic power—they also see the archetype of status virtue, the arrogant, resolute, honor-mad player with real fire, the *ksatria* prince.[27]

Feathers, Blood, Crowds, and Money

"Poetry makes nothing happen," Auden says in his elegy of Yeats, "it survives in the valley of its saying . . . a way of happening, a mouth." The cockfight too, in this colloquial sense, makes nothing happen. Men go on allegorically humiliating one another and being allegorically humiliated by one another, day after day, glorying quietly in the experience if they have triumphed, crushed only slightly more openly by it if they have not. *But no one's status really changes.* You cannot ascend the status ladder by winning cockfights; you cannot, as an individual, really ascend it at all. Nor can you descend it that way.[28] All you can do is enjoy and savor, or suffer and withstand, the concocted sensation of drastic and momentary movement along an aesthetic semblance of that ladder, and kind of behind-the-mirror status jump which has the look of mobility without its actuality.

As any art form—for that, finally, is what we are dealing with—the cockfight renders ordinary, everyday experience comprehensible by presenting it in terms of acts and objects which have had their practical consequences removed and been reduced (or, if you prefer, raised) to the level of sheer appearances, where their meaning can be more powerfully articulated and more exactly perceived. The cockfight is "really real" only to the cocks—it does not kill anyone, castrate anyone, reduce anyone to animal status, alter the hierarchical relations among people, nor refashion the hierarchy; it does not even redistribute income in any significant way. What it does is what, for other peoples with other temperaments and other conventions, *Lear* and *Crime and Punishment* do; it catches up these themes—death, masculinity, rage, pride, loss, beneficence, chance—and, ordering them into an encompassing structure, presents them in such a way as to throw into relief a particular view of their essential nature. It puts a construction on them, makes them, to those historically positioned to appreciate the construction, meaningful—visible, tangible, graspable—"real," in an ideational sense. An image, fiction, a model, a metaphor, the cockfight is a means of expression; its function is neither to assuage social passions nor to heighten them (though, in its play-with-fire way, it does a bit of both), but, in a medium of feathers, blood, crowds, and money, to display them.

The question of how it is that we perceive qualities in things—paintings, books, melodies, plays—that we do not feel we can assert literally to be there has come, in recent years, into the very center of aesthetic theory.[29] Neither the sentiments of the artist, which remain his, nor those of the audience, which remain theirs, can account for the agitation of one painting or the serenity of another. We attribute grandeur, wit, despair, exuberance to strings of sounds; lightness, energy, violence, fluidity to blocks of stone. Novels are said to have strength, buildings eloquence, plays momentum, ballets repose. In this realm of eccentric predicates, to say that the cockfight, in its perfected cases at least, is "disquietful" does not seem at all unnatural, merely, as I have just denied it practical consequence, somewhat puzzling.

The disquietfulness arises, "somehow," out of a conjunction of three attributes of the fight: its immediate dramatic shape; its metaphoric content; and its social context. A cultural figure against a social ground, the fight is at once a convulsive surge of animal hatred, a mock war of symbolical selves, and a formal simulation of status tensions, and its aesthetic power derives from its capacity to force together these diverse realities. The reason it is disquietful is not that it has material effects (it has some, but they are minor); the reason that it is disquietful is that, joining pride to selfhood, selfhood to cocks, and cocks to destruction, it brings to imaginative realization a dimension of Balinese experience normally well-obscured from view. The transfer of a sense of gravity into what is in itself a rather blank and unvarious spectacle, a commotion of beating wings and throbbing legs, is effected by interpreting it as expressive of something unsettling in the way its authors and audience live, or, even more ominously, what they are.

As a dramatic shape, the fight displays a characteristic that does not seem so remarkable until one realizes that it does not have to be there: a radically atomistical structure.[30] Each match is a world unto itself, a particulate burst of form. There is the match making, there is the betting, there is the fight, there is the result—utter triumph and utter defeat—and there is the hurried, embarrassed passing of money. The loser is not consoled.

People drift away from him, look through him, leave him to assimilate his momentary descent into nonbeing, reset his face, and return, scarless and intact, to the fray. Nor are winners congratulated, or events rehashed; once a match is ended the crowd's attention turns totally to the next, with no looking back. A shadow of the experience no doubt remains with the principals, perhaps even with some of the witnesses, of a deep fight, as it remains with us when we leave the theater after seeing a powerful play well-performed; but it quite soon fades to become at most a schematic memory—a diffuse glow or an abstract shudder—and usually not even that. Any expressive form lives only in its own present—the one it itself creates. But, here, that present is severed into a string of flashes, some more bright than others, but all of them disconnected, aesthetic quanta. Whatever the cockfight says, it says in spurts.

But, as I have argued lengthily elsewhere, the Balinese live in spurts.[31] Their life, as they arrange it and perceive it, is less a flow, a directional movement out of the past, through the present, toward the future than an on-off pulsation of meaning and vacuity, an arrhythmic alternation of short periods when "something" (that is, something significant) is happening and equally short ones where "nothing" (that is, nothing much) is — between what they themselves call "full" and "empty" times, or, in another idiom, "junctures" and "holes." In focusing activity down to a burning-glass dot, the cockfight is merely being Balinese in the same way in which everything from the monadic encounters of everyday life, through the changing pointillism of *gamelan* music, to the visiting-day-of-the-gods temple celebrations are. It is not an imitation of the punctuateness of Balinese social life, nor a depiction of it, nor even an expression of it; it is an example of it, carefully prepared.[32]

 If one dimension of the cockfight's structure, its lack of temporal directionality, makes it seem a typical segment of the general social life, however, the other, its flat-out, head-to-head (or spur-to-spur) aggressiveness, makes it seem a contradiction, a reversal, even a subversion of it. In the normal course of things, the Balinese are shy to the point of obsessiveness of open conflict. Oblique, cautious, subdued, controlled, masters of indirection and dissimulation—what they call *alus*, "polished," "smooth"—they rarely face what they can turn away from, rarely resist what they can evade. But here they portray themselves as wild and murderous, manic explosions of instinctual cruelty. A powerful rendering of life as the Balinese most deeply do not want it (to adapt a phrase Frye has used of Gloucester's blinding) is set in the context of a sample of it as they do in fact have it.[33] And, because the context suggests that the rendering, if less than a straightforward description is nonetheless more than an idle fancy, it is here that the disquietfulness—the disquietfulness of the *fight*, not (or, anyway, not necessarily) its patrons, who seem in fact rather thoroughly to enjoy it—emerges. The slaughter in the cock ring is not a depiction of how things literally are among men, but, what is almost worse, of how, from a particular angle, they imaginatively are.[34]

The angle, of course, is stratificatory. What, as we have already seen, the cockfight talks most forcibly about is status relationships, and what it says about them is that they are matters of life and death. That prestige is a profoundly serious business is apparent everywhere one looks in Bali—in the village, the family, the economy, the state. A peculiar fusion of Polynesian title ranks and Hindu castes, the hierarchy of pride is the moral backbone of the society. But only in the cockfight are the sentiments upon which that hierarchy rests revealed in their natural colors. Enveloped elsewhere in a haze of etiquette, a thick cloud of euphemism and ceremony, gesture and allusion, they are here expressed in only the thinnest disguise of an animal mask, a mask which in fact demonstrates them far more effectively than it conceals them. Jealousy is as much a part of Bali as poise, envy as grace, brutality as charm; but without the cockfight the Balinese would have a much less certain understanding of them, which is, presumably, why they value it so highly.

Any expressive form works (when it works) by disarranging semantic contexts in such a way that properties conventionally ascribed to certain things are unconventionally ascribed to others, which are then seen actually to possess them. To call the wind a cripple, as Stevens does, to fix tone and manipulate timbre, as Schoenberg does, or, closer to our case, to picture an art critic as a dissolute bear, as Hogarth does, is to cross conceptual wires; the established conjunctions between objects and their qualities are altered and phenomena—fall weather, melodic shape, or cultural journalism—are clothed in signifiers which normally point to other referents.[35] Similarly, to connect—and connect, and connect—the collision of roosters with the divisiveness of status is to invite a transfer of perceptions from the former to the latter, a transfer which is at once a description and a judgment. (Logically, the transfer could, of course, as well go the other way; but, like most of the rest of us, the Balinese are a great deal more interested in understanding men than they are in understanding cocks.)

What sets the cockfight apart from the ordinary course of life, lifts it from the realm of everyday practical affairs, and surrounds it with an aura of enlarged importance is not, as functionalist sociology would have it, that it reinforces status discriminations (such reinforcement is hardly necessary in a society where every act proclaims them), but that it provides a metasocial commentary upon the whole matter of assorting human beings into fixed hierarchical ranks and then organizing the major part of collective existence around that assortment. Its function, if you want to call it that, is interpretive: it is a Balinese reading of Balinese experience; a story they tell themselves about themselves.

Saying Something of Something

To put the matter this way is to engage in a bit of metaphorical refocusing of one's own, for it shifts the analysis of cultural forms from an endeavor in general parallel to dissecting an organism, diagnosing a symptom, deciphering a code, or ordering a system—the dominant analogies in contemporary anthropology—to one in general parallel with penetrating a literary text. If one takes the cockfight, or any other collectively sustained symbolic structure, as a means of "saying something of something" (to invoke a famous Aristotelian tag), then one is faced with a problem not in social mechanics but social semantics.[36] For the anthropologist, whose concern is with formulating sociological principles, not with promoting or appreciating cockfights, the question is, what does one learn about such principles from examining culture as an assemblage of texts?

Such an extension of the notion of a text beyond written material, and even beyond verbal, is, though metaphorical, not, of course, all that novel. The *interpretatio naturae* tradition of the Middle Ages, which, culminating in Spinoza, attempted to read nature as Scripture, the Nietzschean effort to treat value systems as glosses on the will to power (or the Marxian one to treat them as glosses on property relations), and the Freudian replacement of the enigmatic text of the manifest dream with the plain one of the latent, all offer precedents, if not equally recommendable ones.[37] But the idea remains theoretically undeveloped; and the more profound corollary, so far as anthropology is concerned, that cultural forms can be treated as texts, as imaginative works built out of social materials, has yet to be systematically exploited.[38]

In the case at hand, to treat the cockfight as a text is to bring out a feature of it (in my opinion, the central feature of it) that treating it as a rite or a pastime, the two most obvious alternatives, would tend to obscure: its use of emotion for cognitive ends. What the cockfight says it says in a vocabulary of sentiment—the thrill of risk, the despair of loss, the pleasure of triumph. Yet what it says is not merely that risk is exciting, loss depressing, or triumph gratifying, banal tautologies of affect, but that it is of these emotions, thus exampled, that society is built and individuals put together. Attending cockfights and participating in them is, for the Balinese, a kind of sentimental education. What he learns there is what his culture's ethos and his private sensibility (or, anyway, certain aspects of them) look like when spelled out externally in a collective text; that the two are near enough alike to be articulated in the symbolics of a single such text; and—the disquieting part—that the text in which this revelation is accomplished consists of a chicken hacking another mindlessly to bits.

Every people, the proverb has it, loves its own form of violence. The cockfight is the Balinese reflection on theirs: on its look, its uses, its force, its fascination. Drawing on almost every level of Balinese experience, it brings together themes—animal savagery, male narcissism, opponent gambling, status rivalry, mass excitement, blood sacrifice—whose main connection is their involvement with rage and the fear of rage, and, binding them into a set of rules which at once contains them and allows them play, builds a symbolic structure in which, over and over again, the reality of their inner affiliation can be intelligibly felt. If, to quote Northrop Frye again, we go to see *Macbeth* to learn what a man feels like after he has gained a kingdom and lost his soul, Balinese go to cockfights to find out what a man, usually composed, aloof, almost obsessively self-absorbed, a kind of moral autocosm, feels like when, attacked, tormented, challenged, insulted, and driven in result to the extremes of fury, he has totally triumphed or been brought totally low. The whole passage, as it takes us back to Aristotle (though to the *Poetics* rather than the *Hermeneutics*), is worth quotation:

> But the poet [as opposed to the historian], Aristotle says, never makes any real statements at all, certainly no particular or specific ones. The poet's job is not to tell you what happened, but what happens: not what did take place, but the kind of thing that always does take place. He gives you the typical, recurring, or what Aristotle calls universal event. You wouldn't go to *Macbeth* to learn about the history of Scotland—you go to it to learn what man feels like after he's gained a kingdom and lost his soul. When you meet such a character as Micawber in Dickens, you don't feel that there must have been a man Dickens knew who was exactly like this: you feel that there's a bit of Micawber in almost everybody you know, including yourself. Our impressions of human life are picked up one by one, and remain for most of us loose and disorganized. But we constantly find things in literature that suddenly coordinate and bring into focus a great many such impressions, and this is part of what Aristotle means by the typical or universal human event.[39]

It is this kind of bringing of assorted experiences of everyday life to focus that the cockfight, set aside from that life as "only a game" and reconnected to it as "more than a game," accomplishes, and so creates what, better than typical or universal, could be called a paradigmatic human event— that is, one that tells us less what happens than the kind of thing that would happen if, as is not the case, life were art and could be as freely shaped by styles of feeling as *Macbeth* and *David Copperfield* are.

Enacted and reenacted, so far without end, the cockfight enables the Balinese, as, read and reread, *Macbeth* enables us, to see a dimension of his own subjectivity. As he watches fight after fight, with the active watching of an owner and a bettor (for cockfighting has no more interest as a pure spectator sport than croquet or dog racing do), he grows familiar with it and what it has to say to him, much as the attentive listener to string quartets or the absorbed viewer of still lifes grows slowly more familiar with them in a way which opens his subjectivity to himself.[40]

Yet, because—in another of those paradoxes, along with painted feelings and unconsequenced acts, which haunt aesthetics—that subjectivity does not properly exist until it is thus organized, art forms generate and regenerate the very subjectivity they pretend only to display. Quartets, still lifes, and cockfights are not merely reflections of a preexisting sensibility analogically represented; they are positive agents in the creation and maintenance of such a sensibility. If we see ourselves as a pack of Micawbers it is from reading too much Dickens (if we see ourselves as unillusioned realists, it is from reading too little); and similarly for Balinese, cocks, and cockfights. It is in such a way, coloring experience with the light they cast it in, rather than through whatever material effects they may have, that the arts play their role, as arts, in social life.[41]

In the cockfight, then, the Balinese forms and discovers his temperament and his society's temper at the same time. Or, more exactly, he forms and discovers a particular face of them. Not only are there a great many other cultural texts providing commentaries on status hierarchy and self-regard in Bali, but there are a great many other critical sectors of Balinese life besides the stratificatory and the agonistic that receive such commentary. The ceremony consecrating a Brahmana priest, a matter of breath control, postural immobility, and vacant concentration upon the depths of being, displays a radically different, but to the Balinese equally real, property of social hierarchy—its reach toward the numinous transcendent. Set not in the matrix of the kinetic emotionality of animals, but in that of the static passionlessness of divine mentality, it expresses tranquillity not disquiet. The mass festivals at the village temples, which mobilize the whole local population in elaborate hostings of visiting gods—songs, dances, compliments, gifts—assert the spiritual unity of village mates against their status inequality and project a mood of amity and trust.[42] The cockfight is not the master key to Balinese life, any more than bullfighting is to Spanish. What it says about that life is not unqualified nor even unchallenged by what other equally eloquent cultural statements say about it. But there is nothing more surprising in this than in the fact that Racine and Molière were contemporaries, or that the same people who arrange chrysanthemums cast swords.[43]

 The culture of a people is an ensemble of texts, themselves ensembles, which the anthropologist strains to read over the shoulders of those to whom they properly belong. There are enormous difficulties in such an enterprise, methodological pitfalls to make a Freudian quake, and some moral perplexities as well. Nor is it the only way that symbolic forms can be sociologically handled. Functionalism lives, and so does psychologism. But to regard such forms as "saying something of something," and saying it to somebody, is at least to open up the possibility of an analysis which attends to their substance rather than to reductive formulas professing to account for them.

As in more familiar exercises in close reading, one can start anywhere in a culture's repertoire of forms and end up anywhere else. One can stay, as I have here, within a single, more or less bounded form and circle steadily within it. One can move between forms in search of broader unities or informing contrasts. One can even compare forms from different cultures to define their character in reciprocal relief. But whatever the level at which one operates, and however intricately, the guiding principle is the same: societies, like lives, contain their own interpretations. One has only to learn how to gain access to them.

NOTES

[1] Gregory Bateson and Margaret Mead, *Balinese Character: A Photographic Analysis* (New York: New York Academy of Sciences, 1942), p. 68.

[2] Jane Belo, "The Balinese Temper," in Jane Belo, ed., *Traditional Balinese Culture* (New York: Columbia University Press, 1970; originally published in 1935), pp. 85–110.

[3] The best discussion of cockfighting is again Bateson and Mead's (*Balinese Character*, pp. 24–25, 140), but it, too, is general and abbreviated.

[4] Ibid., pp. 25–26. The cockfight is unusual within Balinese culture in being a single-sex public activity from which the other sex is totally and expressly excluded. Sexual differentiation is culturally extremely played down in Bali and most activities, formal and informal, involve the participation of men and women on equal ground, commonly as linked couples. From religion, to politics, to economics, to kinship, to dress, Bali is a rather "uni-sex" society, a fact both its customs and its symbolism clearly express. Even in contexts where women do not in fact play much of a role—music, painting, certain agricultural activities—their absence, which is only relative in any case, is more a mere matter of fact than socially enforced. To this general pattern, the cockfight, entirely of, by, and for men (women—at least *Balinese* women—do not even watch), is the most striking exception.

[5] Christiaan Hooykass, *The Lay of the Jaya Prana* (London, 1958), p. 39. The lay has a stanza (no. 17) with the reluctant bridegroom use. Jaya Prana, the subject of a Balinese Uriah myth, responds to the lord who has offered him the loveliest of six hundred servant girls: "Godly King, my Lord and Master/I beg you, give me leave to go/such things are not yet in my mind;/like a fighting cock encaged/indeed I am on my mettle/I am alone/as yet the flame has not been fanned."

[6] For these, see V. E. Korn, *Het Adatrecht van Bali*, 2d ed. ('S-Gravenhage: G. Naeff, 1932), index under *toh*.

[7] There is indeed a legend to the effect that the separation of Java and Bali is due to the action of a powerful Javanese religious figure who wished to protect himself against a Balinese culture hero (the ancestor of two Ksatria castes) who was a passionate cockfighting gambler. See Christiaan Hooykass, *Agama Tirtha* (Amsterdam: Noord-Hollandsche, 1964), p. 184.

[8] An incestuous couple is forced to wear pig yokes over their necks and crawl to a pig trough and eat with their mouths there. On this, see Jane Belo, "Customs Pertaining to Twins in Bali," in Belo, ed., *Traditional Balinese Culture*, p. 49; on the abhorrence of animality generally, Bateson and Mead, *Balinese Character*, p. 22.

[9] Except for unimportant, small-bet fights (on the question of fight "importance," see below) spur affixing is usually done by someone other than the owner. Whether the owner handles his own cock or not more or less depends on how skilled he is at it, a consideration whose importance is again relative to the importance of the fight. When spur affixers and cock handlers are someone other than the owner, they are almost always a close relative—a brother or cousin—or a very intimate friend of his. They are thus almost extensions of his personality, as the fact that all three will refer to the cock as "mine," say "I" fought So-and-So, and so on, demonstrates. Also, owner-handler-affixer triads tend to be fairly fixed, though individuals may participate in several and often exchange roles within a given one.

[10] Erving Goffman, *Encounters: Two Studies in the Sociology of Interaction* (Indianapolis: Bobbs-Merrill, 1961), pp. 9–10.

[11] This word, which literally means an indelible stain or mark, as in a birthmark or a vein in a stone, is used as well for a deposit in a court case, for a pawn, for security offered in a loan, for a stand-in for someone else in a legal or ceremonial context, for an earnest advanced in a business deal, for a sign placed in a field to indicate its ownership is in dispute, and for the status of an unfaithful wife from whose lover her husband must gain satisfaction or surrender her to him. See Korn, *Het Adatrecht van Bali*; Theodoor Pigeaud, *Javaans-Nederlands Handwoordenbock* (Groningen: Wolters, 1938); H. H. Juynboll, *Oudjavaansche-Nederlandsche Woordenlijst* (Leiden: Brill, 1923).

[12] The center bet must be advanced in cash by both parties prior to the actual fight. The umpire holds the stakes until the decision is rendered and then awards them to the winner, avoiding, among other things, the intense embarrassment both winner and loser would feel if the latter had to pay off personally following his defeat. About 10 percent of the winner's receipts are subtracted for the umpire's share and that of the fight sponsors.

[13] Actually, the typing of cocks, which is extremely elaborate (I have collected more than twenty classes, certainly not a complete list), is not based on color alone, but on a series of independent, interacting, dimensions, which include, beside color, size, bone thickness, plumage, and temperament. (But *not* pedigree. The Balinese do not breed cocks to any significant extent, nor, so far as I have been able to discover, have they ever done so. The *asil*, or jungle cock, which is the basic fighting strain everywhere the sport is found, is native to southern Asia, and one can buy a good example in the chicken section of almost any Balinese market for anywhere from four or five ringgits up to fifty or more.) The color element is merely the one normally used as the type name, except when the two cocks of different types—as on principle they must be—have the same color, in which case a secondary indication from one of the other dimensions ("large speckled" v. "small speckled," etc.) is added. The types are coordinated with various cosmological ideas which help shape the making of matches, so that, for example, you fight a small, headstrong, speckled brown-on-white cock with flat-lying feathers and thin legs from the east side of the ring on a certain day of the complex Balinese calendar, and a large, cautious, all-black cock with tufted feathers and stubby legs from the north side on another day, and so on. All this is again recorded in palm-leaf manuscripts and endlessly discussed by the Balinese (who do not all have identical systems), and full-scale componential-cum-symbolic analysis of cock classifications would be extremely valuable both as an adjunct to the description of the cockfight and in itself. But my data on the subject, though extensive and varied, do not seem to be complete and systematic enough to attempt such an analysis here. For Balinese cosmological ideas more generally see Belo, ed., *Traditional Balinese Culture*, and J. L. Swellengrebel, ed., *Bali: Studies in Life, Thought, and Ritual* (The Hague: W. van Hoeve, 1960); for calendrical ones, Clifford Geertz, *Person, Time, and Conduct in Bali: An Essay in Cultural Analysis* (New Haven: Southeast Asia Studies, Yale University, 1966), pp. 45–53.

[14] For purposes of ethnographic completeness, it should be noted that it is possible for the man backing the favorite—the odds-giver—to make a bet in which he wins if his cock wins or there is a tie, a slight shortening of the odds (I do not have enough cases to be exact, but ties seem to occur about once every fifteen or twenty matches). He indicates his wish to do this by shouting *sapih* ("tie") rather than the cock-type, but such bets are in fact infrequent.

[15] The precise dynamics of the movement of the betting is one of the most intriguing, most complicated, and, given the heroic conditions under which it occurs, most difficult to study, aspects of the fight. Motion picture recording plus multiple observers would probably be necessary to deal with it effectively. Even impressionistically—the only approach open to a lone ethnographer caught in the middle of all this—it is clear that certain men lead both in determining the favorite (that is, making the opening cock-type calls which always initiate the process) and in directing the movement of the odds, these "opinion leaders" being the more accomplished cockfighters-cum-solid-citizens to be discussed below. If these men begin to change their calls, others follow; if they begin to make bets, so do others and—though there is always a large number of frustrated bettors crying for shorter or longer odds to the end—the movement more or less ceases. But a detailed understanding of the whole process awaits what, alas, it is not very likely ever to get: a decision theorist armed with precise observations of individual behavior.

[16] Assuming only binomial variability, the departure from a fifty-fifty expectation in the sixty ringgits and below case is 1.38 standard deviations, or (in a one-direction test) an eight in one hundred possibility by chance alone; for the below forty ringgits case it is

1.65 standard deviations, or about five in one hundred. The fact that these departures though real are not extreme merely indicates, again, that even in the smaller fights the tendency to match cocks at least reasonably evenly persists. It is a matter of relative relaxation of the pressures toward equalization, not their elimination. The tendency for high-bet contests to be coin-flip propositions is, of course, even more striking, and suggests the Balinese know quite well what they are about.

[17] The reduction in wagering in smaller fights (which, of course, feeds on itself; one of the reasons people find small fights uninteresting is that there is less wagering in them, and contrariwise for large ones) takes place in three mutually reinforcing ways. First, there is a simple withdrawal of interest as people wander off to have a cup of coffee or chat with a friend. Second, the Balinese do not mathematically reduce odds, but bet directly in terms of stated odds as such. Thus, for a nine-to-eight bet, one man wagers nine ringgits, the other eight; for five-to-four, one wagers five, the other four. For any given currency unit, like the ringgit, therefore, 6.3 times as much money is involved in a ten-to-nine bet as in a two-to-one bet, for example, and, as noted, in small fights betting settles toward the longer end. Finally, the bets which are made tend to be one- rather than two-, three-, or in some of the very largest fights, four- or five-finger ones. (The fingers indicate the *multiples* of the stated bet odds at issue, not absolute figures. Two fingers in a six-to-five situation means a man wants to wager ten ringgits on the underdog against twelve, three in an eight-to-seven situation, twenty-one against twenty-four, and so on.)

[18] Besides wagering there are other economic aspects of the cockfight, especially its very close connection with the local market system which, though secondary both to its motivation and to its function, are not without importance. Cockfights are open events to which anyone who wishes may come, sometimes from quite distant areas, but well over 90 percent, probably over 95, are very local affairs, and the locality concerned is defined not by the village, nor even by the administrative district, but by the rural market system. Bali has a three-day market week with familiar "solar-system" type rotation. Though the markets themselves have never been very highly developed, small morning affairs in a village square, it is the microregion such rotation rather generally marks out—ten or twenty square miles, seven or eight neighboring villages (which in contemporary Bali is usually going to mean anywhere from five to ten to eleven thousand people) from which the core of any cockfight audience, indeed virtually all of it, will come. Most of the fights are in fact organized and sponsored by small combines of petty rural merchants under the general premise, very strongly held by them and indeed by all Balinese, that cockfights are good for trade because "they get money out of the house, they make it circulate." Stalls selling various sorts of things as well as assorted sheer-chance gambling games (see below) are set up around the edge of the area so that this even takes on the quality of a small fair. This connection of cockfighting with markets and market sellers is very old, as, among other things, their conjunction in inscriptions (Roelof Goris, *Prasasti Bali*, 2 vols. [Bandung: N. V. Masa Baru, 1954]) indicates. Trade has followed the cock for centuries in rural Bali and the sport has been one of the main agencies of the island's monetization.

[19] The phrase is found in the Hildreth translation, International Library of Psychology, 1931, note to p. 106; see L. L. Fuller, *The Morality of Law* (New Haven: Yale University Press, 1964), pp. 6ff.

[20] Of course, even in Bentham, utility is not normally confined as a concept to monetary losses and gains, and my argument here might be more carefully put in terms of a denial that for the Balinese, as for any people, utility (pleasure, happiness . . .) is merely identifiable with wealth. But such terminological problems are in any case secondary to the essential point: the cockfight is not roulette.

[21] Max Weber, *The Sociology of Religion* (Boston: Beacon Press, 1963). There is nothing specifically Balinese, of course, about deepening significance with money, as Whyte's description, in *Street Corner Society*, 2d ed. (Chicago: University of Chicago Press, 1955), of corner boys in a working-class district of Boston demonstrates:

Gambling plays an important role in the lives of Cornerville people. Whatever game the corner boys play, they nearly always bet on the outcome. When there is nothing at stake, the game is not considered a real contest. This does not mean that the financial element is all-important. I have frequently heard men say that the honor of winning was much more important than the money at stake. The corner boys consider playing for money the real test of skill and, unless a man performs well when money is at stake, he is not considered a good competitor. (p. 140)

[22] The extreme to which this madness is conceived on occasion to go—and the fact that it is considered madness—is demonstrated by the Balinese folktale *I Tuhung Kuning*. A gambler becomes so deranged by his passion that, leaving on a trip, he orders his pregnant wife to take care of the prospective newborn if it is a boy but to feed it as meat to his fighting cocks if it is a girl. The mother gives birth to a girl, but rather than giving the child to the cocks she gives them a large rat and conceals the girl with her own mother. When the husband returns the cocks, crowing a jingle, inform him of the deception and, furious, he sets out to kill the child. A goddess descends from heaven and takes the girl up to the skies with her. The cocks die from the food given them, the owner's sanity is restored, the goddess brings the girl back to the father and reunites him with his wife. The story is given as "Geel Komkommertje" in Jacoba Hooykaas-van Leeuwen Boomkamp, *Sprookjes en Verhalen van Bali* ('S-Gravenhage: Van Hoeve, 1956), pp. 19–25.

[23] For a fuller description of Balinese rural social structure, see Clifford Geertz, "Form and Variation in Balinese Village Structure," *American Anthropologist*, 61 (1959), 94–108; "Tihingan, A Balinese Village," in R. M. Koentjaraningrat, *Villages in Indonesia* (Ithaca: Cornell University Press, 1967), pp. 210–43; and, though it is a bit off the norm as Balinese villages go, V. E. Korn, *De Dorpsrepubliek tnganan Pagringsingan* (Santpoort [Netherlands]: C. A. Mees, 1933).

[24] Goffman, *Encounters*, p. 78.

[25] B. R. Berelson, P. F. Lazersfeld, and W. N. McPhee, *Voting: A Study of Opinion Formation in a Presidential Campaign* (Chicago: University of Chicago Press, 1954).

[26] As this is a formal paradigm, it is intended to display the logical, not the casual, structure of cockfighting. Just which of these considerations leads to which, in what order, and by what mechanisms, is another matter—one I have attempted to shed some light on in the general discussion.

[27] In another of Hooykaas-van Leeuwen Boomkamp's folk tales ("De Gast," *Sprookjes en Verhalen van Bali*, pp. 172–80), a low-caste *Sudra*, a generous, pious, and carefree man who is also an accomplished cockfighter, loses, despite his accomplishment, fight after fight until he is not only out of money but down to his last cock. He does not despair, however—"I bet," he says, "upon the Unseen World."

His wife, a good and hard-working woman, knowing how much he enjoys cockfighting, gives him her last "rainy day" money to go and bet. But, filled with misgivings due to his run of ill luck, he leaves his own cock at home and bets merely on the side. He soon loses all but a coin or two and repairs to a food stand for a snack, where he meets a decrepit, odorous, and generally unappetizing older beggar leaning on a staff. The old man asks for food, and the hero spends his last coins to buy him some. The old man then asks to pass the night with the hero, which the hero gladly invites him to do. As there is no food in the house, however, the hero tells his wife to kill the last cock for dinner. When the old man discovers this fact, he tells the hero he has three cocks in his own mountain hut and says the hero may have one of them for fighting. He also asks for the hero's son to accompany him as a servant, and, after the son agrees, this is done.

The old man turns out to be Siva and, thus, to live in a great palace in the sky, though the hero does not know this. In time, the hero decides to visit his son and collect the promised cock. Lifted up into Siva's presence, he is given the choice of three cocks. The first crows: "I have beaten fifteen opponents." The second crows, "I have beaten twenty-five opponents." The third crows, "I have beaten the King." "That one, the third, is my choice," says the hero, and returns with it to earth.

When he arrives at the cockfight, he is asked for an entry fee and replies, "I have no money; I will pay after my cock has won." As he is known never to win, he is let in because the king, who is there fighting, dislikes him and hopes to enslave him when he loses and cannot pay off. In order to insure that this happens, the king matches his finest cock against the hero's. When the cocks are placed down, the hero's flees, and the crowd, led by the arrogant king, hoots in laughter. The hero's cock then flies at the king himself, killing him with a spur stab in the throat. The hero flees. His house is encircled by the king's men. The cock changes into a Garuda, the great mythic bird of Indic legend, and carries the hero and his wife to safety in the heavens.

When the people see this, they make the hero king and his wife queen and they return as such to earth. Later his son, released by Siva, also returns and the hero-king announces his intention to enter a hermitage. ("I will fight no more cockfights. I have bet on the Unseen and won.") He enters the hermitage and his son becomes king.

[28] Addict gamblers are really less declassed (for their status is, as everyone else's, inherited) than merely impoverished and personally disgraced. The most prominent addict gambler in my cockfight circuit was actually a very high caste *satria* who sold off most of his considerable lands to support his habit. Though everyone privately regarded him as a fool and worse (some, more charitable, regarded him as sick), he was publicly treated with the elaborate deference and politeness due his rank. On the independence of personal reputation and public status in Bali, see Geertz, *Person, Time, and Conduct*, pp. 28–35.

[29] For four, somewhat variant treatments, see Susanne Langer, *Feeling and Form* (New York: Scribner's, 1953); Richard Wollheim, *Art and Its Objects* (New York: Harper and Row, 1968); Nelson Goodman, *Languages of Art* (Indianapolis: Bobbs-Merrill, 1968); Maurice Merleau-Ponty, "The Eye and the Mind," in his, *The Primacy of Perception* (Evanston: Northwestern University Press, 1964), pp. 159–90.

[30] British cockfights (the sport was banned there in 1840) indeed seem to have lacked it, and to have generated, therefore, a quite different family of shapes. Most British fights were "mains," in which a preagreed number of cocks were aligned into two teams and fought serially. Score was kept and wagering took place both on the individual matches and on the main as a whole. There were also "battle Royales," both in England and on the Continent, in which a large number of cocks were let loose at once with the one left standing at the end the victor. And in Wales, the so-called "Welsh main" followed an elimination pattern, along the lines of a present-day tennis tournament, winners proceeding to the next round. As a genre, the cockfight has perhaps less compositional flexibility than, say, Latin comedy, but it is not entirely without any. On cockfighting more generally, see Arch Ruport, *The Art of Cockfighting* (New York: Devin-Adair, 1949); G. R. Scott, *History of Cockfighting* (1957); and Lawrence Fitz-Barnard, *Fighting Sports* (London: Odhams Press, 1921).

[31] *Person, Time, and Conduct*, esp. pp. 42ff. I am, however, not the first person to have argued it: see G. Bateson, "Bali, the Value System of a Steady State," and "An Old Temple and a New Myth," in Belo, ed., *Traditional Balinese Culture*, pp. 384–402 and 111–36.

[32] For the necessity of distinguishing among "description," "representation," "exemplification," and "expression" (and the irrelevance of "imitation" to all of them), as modes of symbolic reference, see Goodman, *Languages of Art*, pp. 6–10, 45–91, 225–41.

[33] Northrop Frye, *The Educated Imagination* (Bloomington: University of Indiana Press, 1964), p. 99.

[34] There are two other Balinese values and disvalues which, connected with punctuate temporality on the one hand and unbridled aggressiveness on the other, reinforce the sense that the cockfight is at once continuous with ordinary social life and a direct negation of it: what the Balinese call *ramé*, and what they call *paling*. *Ramé* means crowded, noisy, and active, and is a highly sought after social state: crowded markets, mass festivals, busy

streets are all *ramé*, as of course, is, in the extreme, a cockfight. *Ramé* is what happens in the "full" times (its opposite, *sepi*, "quiet," is what happens in the "empty" ones). *Paling* is social vertigo, the dizzy, disoriented, lost, turned around feeling one gets when one's place in the coordinates of social space is not clear, and it is a tremendously disfavored, immensely anxiety-producing state. Balinese regard the exact maintenance of spatial orientation ("not to know where north is" is to be crazy), balance, decorum, status relationships, and so forth, as fundamental to ordered life (*krama*) and *paling*, the sort of whirling confusion of position the scrambling cocks exemplify as its profoundest enemy and contradiction. On *ramé*, see Bateson and Mead, *Balinese Character*, pp. 3, 64; on *paling*, ibid., p. 11, and Belo, ed., *Traditional Balinese Culture*, pp. 90ff.

[35] The Stevens reference is to his "The Motive for Metaphor" ("You like it under the trees in autumn,/Because everything is half dead./The wind moves like a cripple among the leaves/And repeats words without meaning"); the Schoenberg reference is to the third of his *Five Orchestral Pieces* (Opus 16), and is borrowed from H. H. Drager, "The Concept of 'Tonal Body,'" in Susanne Langer, ed., *Reflections of Art* (New York: Oxford University Press, 1961), p. 174. On Hogarth, and on this whole problem—there called "multiple matrix matching" — see E. H. Gombrich, "The Use of Art for the Study of Symbols," in James Hogg, ed., *Psychology and the Visual Arts* (Baltimore: Penguin Books, 1969), pp. 149–70. The more usual term for this sort of semantic alchemy is "metaphorical transfer," and good technical discussions of it can be found in M. Black, *Models and Metaphors* (Ithaca: Cornell University Press, 1962), pp. 25ff; Goodman, *Languages of Art*, pp. 44ff; and W. Percy, "Metaphor as Mistake," *Sewanee Review*, 66 (1958), 78–99.

[36] The tag is from the second book of the *Organon*, *On Interpretation*. For a discussion of it, and for the whole argument for freeing "the notion of text . . . from the notion of scripture or writing," and constructing, thus, a general hermeneutics, see Paul Ricoeur, *Freud and Philosophy* (New Haven: Yale University Press, 1970), pp. 20ff.

[37] Ibid.

[38] Lévi-Strauss's "structuralism" might seem an exception. But it is only an apparent one, for, rather than taking myths, totem rites, marriage rules, or whatever as texts to interpret, Lévi-Strauss takes them as ciphers to solve, which is very much not the same thing. He does not seek to understand symbolic forms in terms of how they function in concrete situations to organize perceptions (meanings, emotions, concepts, attitudes); he seeks to understand them entirely in terms of their internal structure, *indépendent de tout sujet, de tout objet, et de toute contexte*. For my own view of this approach—that is suggestive and indefensible—see Clifford Geertz, "The Cerebral Savage: On the Work of Lévi-Strauss," *Encounter*, 48 (1967), 25–32.

[39] Frye, *The Educated Imagination*, pp. 63–64.

[40] The use of the, to Europeans, "natural" visual idiom for perception—"see," "watches," and so forth—is more than usually misleading here, for the fact that, as mentioned earlier, Balinese follow the progress of the fight as much (perhaps, as fighting cocks are actually rather hard to see except as blurs of motion, more) with their bodies as with their eyes, moving their limbs, heads, and trunks in gestural mimicry of the cocks' maneuvers, means that much of the individual's experience of the fight is kinesthetic rather than visual. If ever there was an example of Kenneth Burke's definition of a symbolic act as "the dancing of an attitude" (*The Philosophy of Literary Form*, rev. ed. [New York: Vintage Books, 1957], p. 9) the cockfight is it. On the enormous role of kinesthetic perception in Balinese life, [see] Bateson and Mead, *Balinese Character*, pp. 84–88; on the active nature of aesthetic perception in general, [see] Goodman, *Languages of Art*, pp. 241–44.

[41] All this coupling of the occidental great with the oriental lowly will doubtless disturb certain sorts of aestheticians as the earlier effort of anthropologists to speak of Christianity and totemism in the same breath disturbed certain sorts of theologians. But as ontological questions are (or should be) bracketed in the sociology of religion, judgmental ones are (or should be) bracketed in the sociology of art. In any case, the attempt to deprovincialize the concept of art is but part of the general anthropological conspiracy to deprovincialize all im-

portant social concepts—marriage, religion, law, rationality—and though this is a threat to aesthetic theories which regard certain works of art as beyond the reach of sociological analysis, it is no threat to the conviction, for which Robert Graves claims to have been reprimanded at his Cambridge tripos, that some poems are better than others.

[42] For the consecration ceremony, see V. E. Korn, "The Consecration of the Priest," in Swellengrebel, ed., *Bali*, pp. 131–54; for (somewhat exaggerated) village communion, Roelof Goris, "The Religious Character of the Balinese Village," ibid., pp. 79–100.

[43] That what the cockfight has to say about Bali is not altogether without perception and the disquiet it expresses about the general pattern of Balinese life is not wholly without reason is attested by the fact that in two weeks of December 1965, during the upheavals following the unsuccessful coup in Djakarta, between forty and eighty thousand Balinese (in a population of about two million) were killed, largely by one another—the worst outburst in the country. (John Hughes, *Indonesian Upheaval* [New York: McKay, 1967], pp. 173–83. Hughes's figures are, of course, rather casual estimates, but they are not the most extreme.) This is not to say, of course, that the killings were caused by the cockfight, could have been predicted on the basis of it, or were some sort of enlarged version of it with real people in the place of the cocks—all of which is nonsense. It is merely to say that if one looks at Bali not just through the medium of its dances, its shadowplays, its sculpture, and its girls, but—as the Balinese themselves do—also through the medium of its cockfight, the fact that the massacre occurred seems, if no less appealing, less like a contradiction to the laws of nature. As more than one real Gloucester has discovered, sometimes people actually get life precisely as they most deeply do not want it.

•   •   •   •   •   •   •   •   •   •   •   •

QUESTIONS FOR A SECOND READING

1. Geertz says that the cockfight provides a "commentary upon the whole matter of sorting human beings into fixed hierarchical ranks and then organizing the major parts of collective existence around that assortment." The cockfights don't reinforce the patterns of Balinese life; they comment on them. Perhaps the first question to ask as you go back to the essay is "What is that commentary?" What do the cockfights say? And what don't they say?

2. "Deep Play: Notes on the Balinese Cockfight" is divided into seven sections. As you reread the essay, pay attention to the connections between these sections and the differences in the ways they are written. For each, think about what they propose to do (some, for example, tell stories, some use numbers, some have more footnotes than others).

    What is the logic or system that makes one section follow another? Do you see the subtitles as seven headings on a topic outline?

    If you look at the differences in the style or method of each section, what might they be said to represent? If each is evidence of something Geertz, as an anthropologist, knows how to do, what, in each case, is he doing? What is his expertise? And why, in each case, would it require this particular style of writing? The last two sections are perhaps the most difficult to read and understand. They also make repeated reference to literary texts. Why? What is Geertz doing here?

3. Throughout the essay Geertz is working very hard to *do* something with what he observed in Bali. (There are "enormous difficulties in such an enterprise," he says.) He is also, however, working hard *not* to do some things. (He doesn't want to be a "formalist," for example.) As you read the essay for the second time, look for passages that help you specifically define what it is Geertz wants to do and what it is he wants to be sure not to do.

4. It could be argued that "Deep Play" tells again the story of how white Western men have taken possession of the Third World, here with Geertz performing an act of intellectual colonization. In the opening section, for example, Geertz (as author) quickly turns both his wife and the Balinese people into stock characters, characters in a story designed to make him a hero. And, in the service of this story, he pushes aside the difficult political realities of Bali—the later killing of Balinese by the police is put in parentheses (so as not to disturb the flow of the happy story of how an anthropologist wins his way into the community). The remaining sections turn Balinese culture into numbers and theories, reducing the irreducible detail of people's lives into material for the production of goods (an essay furthering his career). And, one could argue, the piece ends by turning to Shakespeare and Dickens to "explain" the Balinese, completing the displacement of Balinese culture by Western culture.

   This, anyway, is how such an argument might be constructed. As you reread the essay, mark passages you could use, as the author, to argue both for and against Geertz and his relationship to this story of colonization. To what extent can one say that Geertz is, finally, one more white man taking possession of the Third World? And to what extent can one argue that Geertz, as a writer, is struggling against this dominant, conventional narrative, working to revise it or to distance himself from it?

ASSIGNMENTS FOR WRITING

1. If this essay were your only evidence, how might you describe the work of an anthropologist? What do anthropologists do and how do they do it? Write an essay in which you look at "Deep Play" section by section, including the references, describing on the basis of each what it is that an anthropologist must be able to do. In each case, you have the chance to watch Geertz at work. (Your essay, then, might well have sections that correspond to Geertz's.) When you have worked through them all, write a final section that discusses how these various skills or arts fit together to define the expertise of someone like Geertz.

2. Geertz says that "the culture of a people is an ensemble of texts, themselves ensembles, which the anthropologist strains to read over the shoulders of those to whom they properly belong." Anthropologists are expert at "reading" in this way. One of the interesting things about being a student is that you get to (or you have to) act like an expert, even though, properly speaking, you are not. Write an essay in which you prepare a Geertzian "reading" of some part of our culture you know well. Ideally, you should go out

and observe the behavior you are studying, examining it and taking notes with your project in mind. You should imagine that you are working in Geertz's spirit, imitating his method and style and carrying out work that he has begun.

3. This is really a variation on the first assignment. This assignment, however, invites you to read against the grain of Geertz's essay. Imagine that someone has made the argument outlined briefly in the fourth "Question for a Second Reading"—that "Deep Play" is just one more version of a familiar story, a story of a white man taking possession of everything that is not already made in his own image. If you were going to respond to this argument—to extend it or to answer it—to what in the essay would you turn for evidence? And what might you say about what you find?

   Write an essay, then, in which you respond to the argument that says "Deep Play" is one more version of the familiar story of a white man taking possession of that which is not his.

MAKING CONNECTIONS

1. Susan Bordo in "Beauty (Re)discovers the Male Body" (p. 131), Jane Tompkins in "'Indians'" (p. 647), and Susan Griffin in "Our Secret" (p. 299) could all be said to take an "anthropological" view of the people and practices they study. The worlds they describe are familiar (at least compared with Bali), and yet, as writers, they distance themselves from those worlds, make the familiar seem exotic, look at the people involved as "natives" whose behavior they choose to read as a strange and arbitrary text.

   Choose one of these selections—by Bordo, Tompkins, or Griffin—and read it along with Geertz's. Take the position that both authors read cultural patterns and cultural artifacts. Look at the characteristic examples of their ways of reading. What might you say about their methods? Do they look for the same things?

   Write an essay in which you explore and describe the different methods of the two writers. As researchers, what do they notice? What do they do with what they notice? Do they seek the same *kinds* of conclusions? How do they gather their materials, weigh them, think them through? How, that is, do they do their work? And what might you conclude about the possibilities and limitations of each writer's project?

2. In "The Loss of the Creature" (p. 481), Walker Percy writes about tourists (actually several different kinds of tourists) and the difficulty they have seeing what lies before them. Properly speaking, anthropologists are not tourists. There is a scholarly purpose to their travel, and presumably they have learned or developed the strategies necessary to get beyond the pre-formed "symbolic complexes" which would keep them from seeing the place or the people they have traveled to study. Geertz is an expert, in other words, not just any "layman seer of sights."

   In his travels to Bali, Geertz seems to get just what he wants. He gets both the authentic experience and a complex understanding of that experience.

If you read "Deep Play" from the perspective of Percy's essay, however, it is interesting to ask whether Percy would say that this was the case, and to ask how Percy would characterize the "strategies" that define Geertz's approach to his subject.

Write an essay in which you place Geertz in the context of Percy's tourists—not all of them, but the two or three whose stories seem most interesting when placed alongside Geertz's. The purpose of your essay should be to determine whether or not Geertz has solved the problem Percy defines for the tourist in "The Loss of the Creature."

SUSAN GRIFFIN

SUSAN GRIFFIN (b. 1943) is a well-known and respected feminist writer, poet, essayist, lecturer, teacher, playwright, and filmmaker. She has published more than twenty books, including an Emmy Award–winning play, Voices, *with a preface by Adrienne Rich (1975); three books of poetry,* Like the Iris of an Eye *(1976),* Unremembered Country *(1987), and* Bending Home: Selected and New Poems *(1998), and four books of nonfiction that have become key feminist texts,* Women and Nature: The Roaring inside Her *(1978),* Rape: The Power of Consciousness *(1979),* Pornography and Silence: Culture's Revenge against Nature *(1981), and* A Chorus of Stones: The Private Life of War *(1992). Her most recent books are* The Eros of Everyday Life *(1996), a collection of essays on women in Western culture;* What Her Body Thought: A Journey into the Shadows *(1999), on her battle with illness; and* The Book of the Courtesans: A Catalog of Their Virtues *(2002), which includes biographies of courtesans throughout history.*

"Our Secret" is a chapter from Susan Griffin's moving and powerful book A Chorus of Stones, *winner of the Bay Area Book Reviewers Association Award and a finalist for the Pulitzer Prize in nonfiction. The book explores the connections*

between present and past, public life and private life, an individual life and the lives of others. Griffin writes, for example, "I do not see my life as separate from history. In my mind my family secrets mingle with the secrets of statesmen and bombers." In one section of the book she writes of her mother's alcoholism and her father's response to it. In another she writes of her paternal grandmother, who was banished from the family for reasons never spoken. Next to these she thinks about Heinrich Himmler, head of the Nazi secret police, or Hugh Trenchard of the British Royal Air Force, who introduced the saturation bombing of cities and civilians to modern warfare, or Wernher von Braun and the development of rockets and rocketry. "As I held these [figures and scenes] in my mind," she writes, "a certain energy was generated between them. There were two subjects but one theme: denying and bearing witness."

A Chorus of Stones *combines the skills of a careful researcher working with the documentary records of war, the imaginative powers of a novelist entering the lives and experiences of those long dead, and a poet's attention to language. It is a remarkable piece of writing, producing in its form and style the very experience of surprise and connectedness that Griffin presents as the product of her research. "It's not a historian's history," she once told an interviewer. "What's in it is true, but I think of it as a book that verges on myth and legend, because those are the ways we find the deepest meanings and significance of events."*

Griffin's history is not a historian's history; her sociology is not a sociologist's; her psychology is not written in conventional forms or registers. She is actively engaged in the key research projects of our time, providing new knowledge and new ways of thinking and seeing, but she works outside the usual forms and boundaries of the academic disciplines. There are other ways of thinking about this, she seems to say. There are other ways to do this work. Her book on rape, for example, ends with a collage of women's voices, excerpts from public documents, and bits and pieces from the academy.

"Our Secret" has its own peculiar structure and features—the sections in italics, for example. As a piece of writing, it proceeds with a design that is not concerned to move quickly or efficiently from introduction to conclusion. It is, rather, a kind of collage or collection of stories, sketches, anecdotes, fragments. While the sections in the essay are presented as fragments, the essay is not, however, deeply confusing or disorienting. The pleasure of the text, in fact, is moving from here to there, feeling a thread of connection at one point, being surprised by a new direction at another. The writing is careful, thoughtful, controlled, even if this is not the kind of essay that announces its thesis and then collects examples for support. It takes a different attitude toward examples—and toward the kind of thinking one might bring to bear in gathering them and thinking them through. As Griffin says, "the telling and hearing of a story is not a simple act." It is not simple and, as her writing teaches us, it is not straightforward. As you read this essay, think of it as a lesson in reading, writing, and thinking. Think of it as a lesson in working differently. And you might ask why it is that this kind of writing is seldom taught in school.

Our Secret

The nucleus of the cell derives its name from the Latin nux, *meaning nut. Like the stone in a cherry, it is found in the center of the cell, and like this stone, keeps its precious kernel in a shell.*

She is across the room from me. I am in a chair facing her. We sit together in the late darkness of a summer night. As she speaks the space between us grows larger. She has entered her past. She is speaking of her childhood. Her father. The war. Did I know her father fought in the Battle of the Bulge? What was it for him, this great and terrible battle? She cannot say. He never spoke of it at home. They knew so little, her mother, her brothers, herself. Outside, the sea has disappeared. One finds the water now only by the city lights that cease to shine at its edges. California. She moved here with her family when her father became the commander of a military base. There were nuclear missiles standing just blocks from where she lived. But her father never spoke about them. Only after many years away from home did she learn what these weapons were.

The first guided missile is developed in Germany, during World War II. It is known as the Vergeltungswaffe, *or the Vengeance weapon. Later, it will be called the V-1 rocket.*

She is speaking of another life, another way of living. I give her the name Laura here. She speaks of the time after the war, when the cold war was just beginning. The way we are talking now, Laura tells me, was not possible in her family. I nod in recognition. Certain questions were never answered. She learned what not to ask. She begins to tell me a story. Once when she was six years old she went out with her father on a long trip. It was not even a year since the war ended. They were living in Germany.

They drove for miles and miles. Finally they turned into a small road at the edge of a village and drove through a wide gate in a high wall. The survivors were all gone. But there were other signs of this event beyond and yet still within her comprehension. Shoes in great piles. Bones. Women's hair, clothes, stains, a terrible odor. She began to cry a child's frightened tears and then to scream. She had no words for what she saw. Her father admonished her to be still. Only years later, and in a classroom, did she find out the name of this place and what had happened here.

The shell surrounding the nucleus is not hard and rigid; it is a porous membrane. These pores allow only some substances to pass through them, mediating the movement of materials in and out of the nucleus.

Often I have looked back into my past with a new insight only to find that some old, hardly recollected feeling fits into a larger pattern of meaning.

Time can be measured in many ways. We see time as moving forward and hope that by our efforts this motion is toward improvement. When the atomic bomb exploded, many who survived the blast say time stopped with the flash of light and was held suspended until the ash began to descend. Now, in my mind, I can feel myself moving backward in time. I am as if on a train. And the train pushes into history. This history seems to exist somewhere, waiting, a foreign country behind a border and, perhaps, also inside me. From the windows of my train, I can see what those outside do not see. They do not see each other, or the whole landscape through which the track is laid. This is a straight track, but still there are bends to fit the shape of the earth. There are even circles. And returns.

The missile is guided by a programmed mechanism. There is no electronic device that can be jammed. Once it is fired it cannot stop.

It is 1945 and a film is released in Germany. This film has been made for other nations to see. On the screen a train pulls into a station. The train is full of children. A man in a uniform greets the children warmly as they step off the train. Then the camera cuts to boys and girls who are swimming. The boys and girls race to see who can reach the other side of the pool first. Then a woman goes to a post office. A man goes to a bank. Men and women sit drinking coffee at a cafe. The film is called *The Führer Presents the Jews with a City*. It has been made at Terezin concentration camp.

Through the pores of the nuclear membrane a steady stream of ribonucleic acid, RNA, the basic material from which the cell is made, flows out.

It is wartime and a woman is writing a letter. *Everyone is on the brink of starvation,* she says. In the right-hand corner of the page she has written *Nordhausen, Germany 1944.* She is writing to Hans. *Do you remember,* she asks, the day this war was declared? The beauty of the place. The beauty of the sea. *And I bathed in it that day, for the last time.*

In the same year, someone else is also writing a letter. In the right-hand corner he has put his name followed by a title. *Heinrich Himmler. Reichsführer, SS. Make no mention of the special treatment of the Jews,* he says, use only the words Transportation of the Jews toward the Russian East.

A few months later this man will deliver a speech to a secret meeting of leaders in the district of Posen. *Now you know all about it, and you will keep quiet,* he will tell them. Now we share a secret and *we should take our secret to our graves.*

The missile flies from three to four thousand feet above the earth and this makes it difficult to attack from the ground.

The woman who writes of starvation is a painter in her seventy-seventh year. She has lost one grandchild to this war. And a son to the war before. Both boys were named Peter. Among the drawings she makes which have already become famous: a terrified mother grasps a child, *Death Seizes Children*; an old man curls over the bent body of an old woman, *Parents*; a thin face emerges white from charcoal, *Beggars*.

A small but critical part of the RNA flowing out of the pores holds most of the knowledge issued by the nucleus. These threads of RNA act as messengers.

Encountering such images, one is grateful to be spared. But is one ever really free of the fate of others? I was born in 1943, in the midst of this war. And I sense now that my life is still bound up with the lives of those who lived and died in this time. Even with Heinrich Himmler. All the details of his existence, his birth, childhood, adult years, death, still resonate here on earth.

The V-1 rocket is a winged plane powered by a duct motor with a pulsating flow of fuel.

It is April 1943, Heinrich Himmler, Reichsführer SS, has gained control of the production of rockets for the Third Reich. The SS Totenkampf stand guard with machine guns trained at the entrance to a long tunnel, two miles deep, fourteen yards wide and ten yards high, sequestered in the Harz Mountains near Nordhausen. Once an old mining shaft, this tunnel serves now as a secret factory for the manufacture of V-1 and V-2 missiles. The guards aim their machine guns at the factory workers who are inmates of concentration camp Dora.

Most of the RNA flowing out of the cell is destined for the construction of a substance needed to compensate for the continual wearing away of the cell.

It is 1925. Heinrich Himmler, who is now twenty-five years old, has been hired as a secretary by the chief of the Nazi Party in Landshut. He sits behind a small desk in a room overcrowded with party records, correspondence, and newspaper files. On the wall facing him he can see a portrait of Adolf Hitler. He hopes one day to meet the Führer. In anticipation of that day, while he believes no one watches, he practices speaking to this portrait.

It is 1922. Heinrich visits friends who have a three-year-old child. Before going to bed this child is allowed to run about naked. And this disturbs Heinrich. He writes in his diary, *One should teach a child a sense of shame.*

It is the summer of 1910. Heinrich begins his first diary. He is ten years old. He has just completed elementary school. His father tells him his childhood is over now. In the fall he will enter Wilhelms Gymnasium. There the grades he earns will determine his prospects for the future. From now on he must learn to take himself seriously.

· · ·

Eight out of ten of the guided missiles will land within eight miles of their targets.

His father Gebhard is a schoolmaster. He knows the requirements. He provides the boy with pen and ink. Gebhard was once a tutor for Prince Heinrich of Wittelsbach. He has named his son Heinrich after this prince. He is grateful that the prince consented to be Heinrich's godparent. Heinrich is to write in his diary every day. Gebhard writes the first entry in his son's diary, to show the boy how it is to be done.

July 13, Departed at 11:50 and arrive safely on the bus in L. We have a very pretty house. In the afternoon we drink coffee at the coffee house.

I open the cover of the journal I began to keep just as I started my work on this book. I want to see what is on the first page. *It is here I begin a new life,* I wrote. Suffering many losses at once, I was alone and lonely. Yet suddenly I felt a new responsibility for myself. *The very act of keeping a journal,* I sensed, would help me into this life that would now be my own.

Inside the nucleus is the nucleolus where the synthesis of RNA takes place. Each nucleolus is filled with a small jungle of fern-like structures all of whose fronds and stalks move and rotate in perfect synchrony.

It is 1910. The twenty-second of July. Gebhard adds the words *first swim* to his son's brief entry, *thirteenth wedding anniversary of my dear parents.* 1911. Over several entries Heinrich lists each of thirty-seven times he takes a swim, in chronological order. *11:37 A.M. Departed for Lindau.* He does not write of his feelings. *August 8, Walk in the park.* Or dreams. *August 10, Bad weather.*

In the last few years I have been searching, though for what precisely I cannot say. Something still hidden which lies in the direction of Heinrich Himmler's life. I have been to Berlin and Munich on this search, and I have walked over the gravel at Dachau. Now as I sit here I read once again the fragments from Heinrich's boyhood diary that exist in English. I have begun to think of these words as ciphers. Repeat them to myself, hoping to find a door into the mind of this man, even as his character first forms so that I might learn how it is he becomes himself.

The task is not easy. The earliest entries in this diary betray so little. Like the words of a schoolboy commanded to write what the teacher requires of him, they are wooden and stiff. The stamp of his father's character is so heavy on this language that I catch not even a breath of a self here. It is easy to see how this would be true. One simply has to imagine Gebhard standing behind Heinrich and tapping his foot.

His father must have loomed large to him. Did Gebhard lay his hand on Heinrich's shoulder? The weight of that hand would not be comforting. It would be a warning. A reminder. Heinrich must straighten up now and be still. Yet perhaps he turns his head. Maybe there is a sound outside. A bird. Or his brother Gebhard's voice. But from the dark form behind him he hears a name pronounced. This is his name, *Heinrich*. The sound rolls sharply off his father's tongue. He turns his head back. He does not know what to write. He wants to turn to this form and beseech him, but this man who is his father is more silent than stone. And now when Heinrich can feel impatience all around him, he wants to ask, *What should I write?* The edge of his father's voice has gotten sharper. *Why can't you remember?* Just write what happened yesterday. And make sure you get the date right. *Don't you remember?* We took a walk in the park together and we ran into the duchess. Be certain you spell her name correctly. And look here, you must get the title right. That is extremely important. Cross it out. Do it again. *The title.*

The boy is relieved. His mind has not been working. His thoughts were like paralyzed limbs, immobile. Now he is in motion again. He writes the sentences as they are dictated to him. *The park.* He crosses out the name. He writes it again. Spelling it right. *The duchess.* And his father makes one more correction. The boy has not put down the correct time for their walk in the park.

And who is the man standing behind? In a photograph I have before me of the aging Professor and Frau Himmler, as they pose before a wall carefully composed with paintings and family portraits, Frau Himmler adorned with a demure lace collar, both she and the professor smiling kindly from behind steel-rimmed glasses, the professor somewhat rounded with age, in a dark three-piece suit and polka-dot tie, looks so ordinary.

The missile carries a warhead weighing 1,870 pounds. It has three different fuses to insure detonation.

Ordinary. What an astonishing array of images hide behind this word. The ordinary is of course never ordinary. I think of it now as a kind of mask, not an animated mask that expresses the essence of an inner truth, but a mask that falls like dead weight over the human face, making flesh a stationary object. One has difficulty penetrating the heavy mask that Gebhard and his family wore, difficulty piercing through to the creatures behind.

It must not have been an easy task to create this mask. One detects the dimensions of the struggle in the advice of German child-rearing experts from this and the last century. *Crush the will*, they write. *Establish dominance. Permit no disobedience. Suppress everything in the child.*

I have seen illustrations from the books of one of these experts, perhaps the most famous of these pedagogues, Dr. Daniel Gottlieb Moritz Schreber. At first glance these pictures recall images of torture. But they are instead pictures of children whose posture or behavior is being corrected. A brace up the spine, a belt tied to a waist and the hair at the back of the neck so the child will be discouraged from slumping, a metal plate at the edge of a desk keeping the child from curling over her work, a child tied to a bed to prevent poor sleeping posture or masturbation. And there are other methods recommended in the text. An enema to be given before bedtime. The child immersed in ice-cold water up to the hips, before sleep.

The nightmare images of the German child-rearing practices that one discovers in this book call to mind the catastrophic events of recent German history. I first encountered this pedagogy in the writing of Alice Miller. At one time a psychoanalyst, she was haunted by the question, *What could make a person conceive the plan of gassing millions of human beings to death?* In her work, she traces the origins of this violence to childhood.

Of course there cannot be one answer to such a monumental riddle, nor does any event in history have a single cause. Rather a field exists, like a field of gravity that is created by the movements of many bodies. Each life is influenced and it in turn becomes an influence. Whatever is a cause is also an effect. Childhood experience is just one element in the determining field.

As a man who made history, Heinrich Himmler shaped many childhoods, including, in the most subtle of ways, my own. And an earlier history, a history of governments, of wars, of social customs, an idea of gender, the history of a religion leading to the idea of original sin, shaped Heinrich Himmler's childhood as certainly as any philosophy of child raising. One can take for instance any formative condition of his private life, the fact that he was a frail child, for example, favored by his mother, who could not meet masculine standards, and show that this circumstance derived its real meaning from a larger social system that gave inordinate significance to masculinity.

Yet to enter history through childhood experience shifts one's perspective not away from history but instead to an earlier time just before history has finally shaped us. Is there a child who existed before the conventional history that we tell of ourselves, one who, though invisible to us, still shapes events, even through this absence? How does our sense of history change when we consider childhood, and perhaps more important, why is it that until now we have chosen to ignore this point of origination, the birthplace and womb of ourselves, in our consideration of public events?

In the silence that reverberates around this question, an image is born in my mind. I can see a child's body, small, curled into itself, knees bent toward the chest, head bending softly into pillows and blankets, in a posture thought unhealthy by Dr. Schreber, hand raised to the face, delicate mouth making a circle around the thumb. There is comfort as well as sadness in this image. It is a kind of a self-portrait, drawn both from memory and from a feeling that is still inside me. As I dwell for a moment with this image I can imagine Heinrich in this posture, silent, curled, fetal, giving comfort to himself.

But now, alongside this earlier image, another is born. It is as if these two images were twins, always traveling in the world of thought together. One does not come to mind without the other. In this second portrait, which is also made of feeling and memory, a child's hands are tied into mittens. And by a string extending from one of the mittens, her hand is tied to the bars of her crib. She is not supposed to be putting her finger in her mouth. And she is crying out in rage while she yanks her hand violently trying to free herself of her bonds.

To most of existence there is an inner and an outer world. Skin, bark, surface of the ocean open to reveal other realities. What is inside shapes and sustains what appears. So it is too with human consciousness. And yet the mind rarely has a simple connection to the inner life. At a certain age we begin to define ourselves, to choose an image of who we are. I am this and not that, we say, attempting thus to erase whatever is within us that does not fit our idea of who we should be. In time we forget our earliest selves and replace that memory with the image we have constructed at the bidding of others.

One can see this process occur in the language of Heinrich's diaries. If in the earliest entries, except for the wooden style of a boy who obeys authority, Heinrich's character is hardly apparent, over time this stilted style becomes his own. As one reads on, one no longer thinks of a boy who is forced to the task, but of a prudish and rigid young man.

In Heinrich's boyhood diaries no one has been able to find any record of rage or of events that inspire such rage. Yet one cannot assume from this evidence that such did not exist. His father would have permitted neither anger nor even the memory of it to enter these pages. That there must be no visible trace of resentment toward the parent was the pedagogy of the age. Dr. Schreber believed that children should learn to be grateful. The pain and humiliation children endure are meant to benefit them. The parent is only trying to save the child's soul.

Now, for different reasons, I too find myself on the track of a child's soul. The dimensions of Heinrich Himmler's life have put me on this track. I am trying to grasp the inner state of his being. For a time the soul ceased to exist in the modern mind. One thought of a human being as a kind of machine, or as a cog in the greater mechanism of society, operating within another machine, the earth, which itself operates within the greater mechanical design of the universe.

When I was in Berlin, I spoke to a rabbi who had, it seemed to me, lost his faith. When I asked him if he still believed in God, he simply shook his head and widened his eyes as if to say, *How is this possible?* He had been telling me about his congregation: older people, many of Polish origin, survivors of the holocaust who were not able to leave Germany after the war because they were too ill to travel. He was poised in this painful place by choice. He had come to lead this congregation only temporarily but, once feeling the condition of his people, decided to stay. Still, despite his answer, and as much as the holocaust made a terrible argument for the death of the spirit, talking in that small study with this man, I could feel from him the light of something surviving.

The religious tradition that shaped Heinrich's childhood argues that the soul is not part of flesh but is instead a, prisoner of the body. But suppose the soul is meant to live in and through the body and to know itself in the heart of earthly existence?

Then the soul is an integral part of the child's whole being, and its growth is thus part of the child's growth. It is, for example, like a seed planted underground in the soil, naturally moving toward the light. And it comes into its fullest manifestation thus only when seen, especially when self meeting self returns a gaze.

What then occurs if the soul in its small beginnings is forced to take on a secret life? A boy learns, for instance, to hide his thoughts from his father simply by failing to record them in his journals. He harbors his secrets in fear and guilt, confessing them to no one until in time the voice of his father chastising him becomes his own. A small war is waged in his mind. Daily implosions take place under his skin, by which in increments something in him seems to disappear. Gradually his father's voice subsumes the vitality of all his desires and even his rage, so that now what he wants most passionately is his own obedience, and his rage is aimed at his own failures. As over time his secrets fade from memory, he ceases to tell them, even to himself, so that finally a day arrives when he believes the image he has made of himself in his diaries is true.

The child, Dr. Schreber advised, *should be permeated by the impossibility of locking something in his heart.* The doctor who gave this advice had a son who was hospitalized for disabling schizophrenia. Another of his children committed suicide. But this was not taken as a warning against his approach. His methods of educating children were so much a part of the canon of everyday life in Germany that they were introduced into the state school system.

That this philosophy was taught in school gives me an interior view of the catastrophe to follow. It adds a certain dimension to my image of these events to know that a nation of citizens learned that no part of themselves could be safe from the scrutiny of authority, nothing locked in the heart, and at the same time to discover that the head of the secret police of this nation was the son of a schoolmaster. It was this man, after all, Heinrich Himmler, Reichsführer SS, who was later to say, speaking of the mass arrests of Jews, *Protective custody is an act of care.*

The polite manner of young Heinrich's diaries reminds me of life in my grandmother's home. Not the grandmother I lost and later found, but the one who, for many years, raised me. She was my mother's mother. The family would assemble in the living room together, sitting with a certain reserve, afraid to soil the surfaces. What was it that by accident might have been made visible?

All our family photographs were posed. We stood together in groups of three or four and squinted into the sun. My grandmother directed us to smile. I have carried one of these photographs with me for years without acknowledging to myself that in it my mother has the look she always had when she drank too much. In another photograph, taken near the time of my parents' divorce, I can see that my father is almost crying, though I could not see this earlier. I must have felt obliged to see only what my grandmother wanted us to see. Tranquil, domestic scenes.

In the matrix of the mitochondria all the processes of transformation join to-
gether in a central vortex.

We were not comfortable with ourselves as a family. There was a great shared suffering and yet we never wept together, except for my mother, who would alternately weep and then rage when she was drunk. Together, under my grandmother's tutelage, we kept up appearances. Her effort was ceaseless.

When at the age of six I went to live with her, my grandmother worked to reshape me. I learned what she thought was correct grammar. The manners she had studied in books of etiquette were passed on to me, not by casual example but through anxious memorization and drill. Napkin to be lifted by the corner and swept onto the lap. Hand to be clasped firmly but not too firmly.

We were not to the manner born. On one side my great-grandfather was a farmer, and on the other a butcher newly emigrated from Ireland, who still spoke with a brogue. Both great-grandfathers drank too much, the one in public houses, the other more quietly at home. The great-grandfather who farmed was my grandmother's father. He was not wealthy but he aspired to gentility. My grandmother inherited both his aspiration and his failure.

We considered ourselves finer than the neighbors to our left with their chaotic household. But when certain visitors came, we were as if driven by an inward, secret panic that who we really were might be discovered. Inadvertently, by some careless gesture, we might reveal to these visitors who were our betters that we did not belong with them, that we were not real. Though of course we never spoke of this, to anyone, not even ourselves.

Gebhard Himmler's family was newly risen from poverty. Just as in my family, the Himmlers' gentility was a thinly laid surface, maintained no doubt only with great effort. Gebhard's father had come from a family of peasants and small artisans. Such a living etched from the soil, and by one's hands, is tenuous and hard. As is frequently the case with young men born to poverty, Johann became a soldier. And, like many young soldiers, he got himself into trouble more than once for brawling and general mischief. On one occasion he was reproved for what was called *immoral behavior with a low woman*. But nothing of this history survived in his son's version of him. By the time Gebhard was born, Johann was fifty-six years old and had reformed his ways. Having joined the royal police force of Bavaria, over the years he rose to the rank of sergeant. He was a respectable man, with a respectable position.

Perhaps Gebhard never learned of his father's less than respectable past. He was only three years old when Johann died. If he had the slightest notion, he did not breathe a word to his own children. Johann became the icon of the Himmler family, the heroic soldier who single-handedly brought his family from the obscurity of poverty into the warm light of the favored. Yet obscure histories have a way of casting a shadow over the present. Those who are born to propriety have a sense of entitlement, and this affords them some ease as they execute the correct mannerisms of their class. More recent members of the elect are less certain of themselves; around the edges of newly minted refinement one discerns a certain fearfulness, expressed perhaps as uncertainty, or as its opposite, rigidity.

One can sense that rigidity in Gebhard's face as a younger man. In a photograph of the Himmler family, Gebhard, who towers in the background, seems severe. He has the face of one who looks for mistakes. He is vigilant. Heinrich's mother looks very small next to him, almost as if she is cowering. She has that look I have seen many times on my father's face, which one can only describe as ameliorating. Heinrich is very small. He stands closest to the camera, shimmering in a white dress. His face is pretty, even delicate.

I am looking now at the etching called *Poverty*, made in 1897. Near the center, calling my attention, a woman holds her head in her hands. She stares through her hands into the face of a sleeping infant. Though the infant and the sheet and pillow around are filled with light, one recognizes that the child is dying. In a darker corner, two worried figures huddle, a father and another child. Room, mother, father, child exist in lines, a multitude of lines, and each line is filled with a rare intelligence.

Just as the physicist's scrutiny changes the object of perception, so does art transmute experience. One cannot look upon what Käthe Kollwitz has drawn without feeling. The lines around the child are bleak with unreason. Never have I seen so clearly that what we call poverty is simply a raw exposure to the terror and fragility of life. But there is more in this image. There is meaning in the frame. One can feel the artist's eyes. Her gaze is in one place soft, in another intense. Like the light around the infant, her attention interrupts the shadow that falls across the room.

The artist's choice of subject and the way she saw it were both radical departures, not only from certain acceptable assumptions in the world of art, but also from established social ideas because the poor were thought of as less than human. The death of a child to a poor parent was supposed to be a less painful event. In her depiction, the artist told a different story.

Heinrich is entering a new school now, and so his father makes a list of all his future classmates. Beside the name of each child he writes the child's father's name, what this father does for a living, and his social position. Heinrich must be careful, Gebhard tells him, to choose whom he befriends. In his diaries the boy seldom mentions his friends by name. Instead he writes that he played, for instance, with the landlord's child.

There is so much for Heinrich to learn. Gebhard must teach him the right way to bow. The proper forms of greeting. The history of his family; the history of his nation. Its heroes. His grandfather's illustrious military past. There is an order in the world and Heinrich has a place in this order which he must be trained to fill. His life is strictly scheduled. At this hour a walk in the woods so that he can appreciate nature. After that a game of chess to develop his mind. And after that piano, so that he will be cultured.

If a part of himself has vanished, that part of the self that feels and wants, and from which hence a coherent life might be shaped, Heinrich is not at sea yet. He has no time to drift or feel lost. Each moment has been spoken for, every move prescribed. He has only to carry out his father's plans for him.

But everything in his life is not as it should be. He is not popular among his classmates. Should it surprise us to learn that he has a penchant for listening to the secrets of his companions, and that afterward he repeats these secrets to his father, the schoolmaster? There is perhaps a secret he would like to learn and one he would like to tell, but this has long since been forgotten. Whatever he learns now he must tell his father. He must not keep anything from him. He must keep his father's good will at all costs. For, without his father, he does not exist.

And there is another reason Heinrich is not accepted by his classmates. He is frail. As an infant, stricken by influenza, he came close to perishing and his body still retains the mark of that illness. He is not strong. He is not good at the games the other boys play. At school he tries over and over to raise himself on the crossbars, unsuccessfully. He covets the popularity of his stronger, more masculine brother, Gebhard. But he cannot keep up with his brother. One day, when they go out for a simple bicycle ride together, Heinrich falls into the mud and returns with his clothes torn.

It is 1914. A war begins. There are parades. Young men marching in uniform. Tearful ceremonies at the railway station. Songs. Decorations. Heinrich is enthusiastic. The war has given him a sense of purpose in life. Like other boys, he plays at soldiering. He follows the war closely, writing in his diary of the progress of armies, *This time with 40 Army Corps and Russia and France against Germany*. The entries he makes do not seem so listless now; they have a new vigor. As the war continues, a new ambition gradually

takes the shape of determination. Is this the way he will finally prove himself? Heinrich wants to be a soldier. And above all he wants a uniform.

It is 1915. In her journal Käthe Kollwitz records a disturbing sight. The
night before at the opera she found herself sitting next to a young soldier.
He was blinded. He sat *without stirring, his hands on his knees, his head erect.*
She could not stop looking at him, and the memory of him, she writes now,
cuts her to the quick.

It is 1916. As Heinrich comes of age he implores his father to help him
find a regiment. He has many heated opinions about the war. But his
thoughts are like the thoughts and feelings of many adolescents; what he
expresses has no steady line of reason. His opinions are filled with contradictions, and he lacks that awareness of self which can turn ambivalence
into an inner dialogue. Yet, beneath this amorphous bravado, there is a pattern. As if he were trying on different attitudes, Heinrich swings from
harshness to compassion. In one place he writes, *The Russian prisoners multiply like vermin.* (Should I write here that this is a word he will one day use
for Jews?) But later he is sympathetic to the same prisoners because they
are so far away from home. Writing once of *the silly old women and petty
bourgeois . . . who so dislike war*, in another entry, he remembers the young
men he has seen depart on trains and he asks, *How many are alive today?*

Is the direction of any life inevitable? Or are there crossroads, points at
which the direction might be changed? I am looking again at the Himmler
family. Heinrich's infant face resembles the face of his mother. His face is
soft. And his mother? In the photograph she is a fading presence. She occupied the same position as did most women in German families, secondary
and obedient to the undisputed power of her husband. She has a slight
smile which for some reason reminds me of the smile of a child I saw in a
photograph from an album made by the SS. This child's image was captured
as she stood on the platform at Auschwitz. In the photograph she emanates
a certain frailty. Her smile is a very feminine smile. Asking, or perhaps
pleading, *Don't hurt me.*

Is it possible that Heinrich, looking into that child's face, might have
seen himself there? What is it in a life that makes one able to see oneself in
others? Such affinities do not stop with obvious resemblance. There is a
sense in which we all enter the lives of others.

It is 1917, and a boy who will be named Heinz is born to Catholic parents living in Vienna. Heinz's father bears a certain resemblance to Heinrich's father. He is a civil servant and, also like Gebhard, he is pedantic and
correct in all he does. Heinrich will never meet this boy. And yet their paths
will cross.

Early in the same year as Heinz's birth, Heinrich's father has finally succeeded in getting him into a regiment. As the war continues for one more
year, Heinrich comes close to achieving his dream. He will be a soldier. He

is sent to officer's training. Yet he is not entirely happy. *The food is bad,* he writes to his mother, *and there is not enough of it. It is cold. There are bedbugs. The room is barren.* Can she send him food? A blanket? Why doesn't she write him more often? Has she forgotten him? They are calling up troops. Suppose he should be called to the front and die?

But something turns in him. Does he sit on the edge of a neat, narrow military bunk bed as he writes in his diary that he does not want to be like a boy who whines to his mother? Now, he writes a different letter: *I am once more a soldier body and soul.* He loves his uniform; the oath he has learned to write; the first inspection he passes. He signs his letters now, *Miles Heinrich.* Soldier Heinrich.

I am looking at another photograph. It is of two boys. They are both in military uniform. Gebhard, Heinrich's older brother, is thicker and taller. Next to him Heinrich is still diminutive. But his face has become harder, and his smile, though faint like his mother's smile, has gained a new quality, harsh and stiff like the little collar he wears.

Most men can remember a time in their lives when they were not so different from girls, and they also remember when that time ended. In ancient Greece a young boy lived with his mother, practicing a feminine life in her household, until the day he was taken from her into the camp of men. From this day forward the life that had been soft and graceful became rigorous and hard, as the older boy was prepared for the life of a soldier.

My grandfather on my mother's side was a contemporary of Heinrich Himmler. He was the youngest boy in the family and an especially pretty child. Like Heinrich and all small boys in this period, he was dressed in a lace gown. His hair was long and curled about his face. Like Heinrich, he was his mother's favorite. She wanted to keep him in his finery. He was so beautiful in it, and he was her last child. My great-grandmother Sarah had a dreamy, artistic nature, and in his early years my grandfather took after her. But all of this made him seem girlish. And his father and older brothers teased him mercilessly. Life improved for him only when he graduated to long pants. With them he lost his dreamy nature too.

The soul is often imagined to be feminine. All those qualities thought of as soulful, a dreaminess or artistic sensibility, are supposed to come more naturally to women. Ephemeral, half seen, half present, nearly ghostly, with only the vaguest relation to the practical world of physical law, the soul appears to us as lost. The hero, with his more masculine virtues, must go in search of her. But there is another, older story of the soul. In this story she is firmly planted on the earth. She is incarnate and visible everywhere. Neither is she faint of heart, nor fading in her resolve. It is she, in fact, who goes bravely in search of desire.

1918. Suddenly the war is over. Germany has lost. Heinrich has failed to win his commission. He has not fought in a single battle. Prince Heinrich, his namesake, has died. The prince will be decorated for heroism, after his death. Heinrich returns home, not an officer or even a soldier any longer. He returns to school, completing his studies at the gymnasium and then the university. But he is adrift. Purposeless. And like the world he belongs to, dissatisfied. Neither man nor boy, he does not know what he wants.

Until now he could rely on a strict regimen provided by his father. Nothing was left uncertain or undefined for long in his father's house. The thoroughness of Gebhard's hold over his family comes alive for me through this procedure: every package, letter, or money order to pass through the door was by Gebhard's command to be duly recorded. And I begin to grasp a sense of Gebhard's priorities when I read that Heinrich, on one of his leaves home during the war, assisted his mother in this task. The shadow of his father's habits will stretch out over history. They will fall over an office in Berlin through which the SS, and the entire network of concentration camps, are administered. Every single piece of paper issued with regard to this office will pass over Heinrich's desk, and to each page he will add his own initials. Schedules for trains. Orders for building supplies. Adjustments in salaries. No detail will escape his surmise or fail to be recorded.

But at this moment in his life Heinrich is facing a void. I remember a similar void, when a long and intimate relationship ended. What I felt then was fear. And at times panic. In a journal I kept after this separation, I wrote, *Direct knowledge of the illusory nature of panic. The feeling that I had let everything go out of control.* I could turn in only one direction: inward. Each day I abated my fears for a time by observing myself. But what exists in that direction for Heinrich? He has not been allowed to inhabit that terrain. His inner life has been sealed off both from his father and himself.

I am not certain what I am working for, he writes, and then, not able to let this uncertainty remain, he adds, *I work because it is my duty.* He spends long hours in his room, seldom leaving the house at all. He is at sea. Still somewhat the adolescent, unformed, not knowing what face he should put on when going out into the world, in his journal he confesses that he still lacks that *naturally superior kind of manner that he would dearly like to possess.*

Is it any wonder then that he is so eager to rejoin the army? The army gave purpose and order to his life. He wants his uniform again. In his uniform he knows who he is. But his frailty haunts him. Over and over he shows up at recruiting stations throughout Bavaria only to be turned away each time, with the single word, *Untauglich.* Unfit. At night the echo of this word keeps him awake.

When he tries to recover his pride, he suffers another failure of a similar kind. A student of agriculture at the university, now he dreams of becoming a farmer. He believes he can take strength and vitality from the soil. After all his own applications are rejected, his father finds him a position in the countryside. He rides toward his new life on his motorcycle and is

pelted by torrents of rain. Though he is cold and hungry, he is also exuber-
ant. He has defeated his own weakness. But after only a few weeks his
body fails him again. He returns home ill with typhus and must face the
void once more.

What Germany needs now is a man of iron. How easy it is to hear the irony
of these words Heinrich records in his journal. But at this moment in history, he is hearing another kind of echo. There are so many others who agree
with him. The treaty of Versailles is taken as a humiliation. An unforgivable
weakness, it is argued, has been allowed to invade the nation.

1920. 1922. 1923. Heinrich is twenty, twenty-two, twenty-three. He is
growing up with the century. And he starts to adopt certain opinions popular at this time. As I imagine myself in his frame of mind, facing a void,
cast into unknown waters, these opinions appear like rescue ships on the
horizon, a promise of *terra firma*, the known.

It is for instance fashionable to argue that the emergence of female
equality has drained the nation of its strength. At social gatherings Heinrich likes to discuss the differences between men and women. That twilight
area between the certainties of gender, homosexuality, horrifies him. A man
should be a man and a woman a woman. Sexually explicit illustrations in a
book by Oscar Wilde horrify him. Uncomfortable with the opposite sex, so
much so that one of his female friends believes he hates women, he has
strong feelings about how men and women ought to relate. *A real man*, he
sets down in his diary, *should love a woman as a child who must be admonished
perhaps even punished, when she is foolish, though she must also be protected and
looked after because she is so weak.*

As I try to enter Heinrich's experience, the feeling I sense behind these
words is of immense comfort. I know who I am. My role in life, what I am
to feel, what I am to be, has been made clear. I am a man. I am the strong
protector. And what's more, I am needed. There is one who is weak. One
who is weaker than I am. And I am the one who must protect her.

And yet behind the apparent calm of my present mood, there is an
uneasiness. Who is this one that I protect? Does she tell me the truth about
herself? I am beginning to suspect that she hides herself from me. There
is something secretive in her nature. She is an unknown, even dangerous,
territory.

The year is 1924. And Heinrich is still fascinated with secrets. He discovers that his brother's fiancée has committed one or maybe even two
indiscretions. At his urging, Gebhard breaks off the engagement. But Heinrich is still not satisfied. He writes a friend who lives near his brother's former fiancée, *Do you know of any other shameful stories?* After this, he hires a
private detective to look into her past.

Is it any coincidence that in the same year he writes in his diary that he
has met a *great man, genuine and pure?* This man, he notes, may be the new

leader Germany is seeking. He finds he shares a certain drift of thought with this man. He is discovering who he is now, partly by affinity and partly by negation. In his picture of himself, a profile begins to emerge cast in light and shadow. He knows now who he is and who he is not. He is not Jewish.

And increasingly he becomes obsessed with who he is not. In this pursuit, his curiosity is fed by best-selling books, posters, films, journals; he is part of a larger social movement, and this no doubt gives him comfort, and one cannot, in studying the landscape of his mind as set against the landscape of the social body, discover where he ends and the milieu of this time begins. He is perhaps like a particle in a wave, a wave which has only the most elusive relationship with the physical world, existing as an afterimage in the mind.

I can imagine him sitting at a small desk in his bedroom, still in his father's home. Is it the same desk where he was required to record some desultory sentences in his diary every day? He is bent over a book. It is evening. The light is on, shining on the pages of the book. Which book among the books he has listed in his journal does he read now? Is it *Das Liebesnest* (*The Lovenest*), telling the story of a liaison between a Jewish man and a gentile woman? *Rasse*? Explaining the concept of racial superiority? Or is it *Juden Schuldbuch* (*The Book of Jewish Guilt*). Or *Die Sünde wider das Blut* (*The Sin Against the Blood*).

One can follow somewhat his train of thought here and there where he makes comments on what he reads in his journal. When he reads *Tscheka*, for instance, a history of the secret police in Russia, he says he is disappointed. *Everyone knows*, he writes, that the Jews control the secret police in Russia. But nowhere in the pages of this book does he find a mention of this "fact."

His mind has begun to take a definite shape, even a predictable pattern. Everywhere he casts his eyes he will discover a certain word. Wherever his thoughts wander he brings them back to this word. *Jew. Jude. Jew.* With this word he is on firm ground again. In the sound of the word, a box is closed, a box with all the necessary documents, with all the papers in order.

My grandfather was an anti-Semite. He had a long list of enemies that he liked to recite. Blacks were among them. And Catholics. And the English. He was Protestant and Irish. Because of his drinking he retired early (though we never discussed the cause). In my childhood I often found him sitting alone in the living room that was darkened by closed venetian blinds which kept all our colors from fading. Lonely myself, I would try to speak with him. His repertoire was small. When I was younger he would tell me stories of his childhood, and I loved those stories. He talked about the dog named Blackie that was his then. A ceramic statue of a small black dog resembling him stood near the fireplace. He loved this dog in a way that was almost painful to hear. But he could never enter that intricate world of expressed emotion in which the shadings of one's life as it is felt and experienced become articulated. This way of speaking was left to the women of our family. As I grew older and he could no longer tell me the story of his dog, he would talk to me about politics. It was then that, with a passion he revealed nowhere else, he would recite to me his long list filled with everyone he hated.

I did not like to listen to my grandfather speak this way. His face would get red, and his voice took on a grating tone that seemed to abrade not only the ears but some other slower, calmer velocity within the body of the room. His eyes, no longer looking at me, blazed with a kind of blindness. There was no reaching him at these moments. He was beyond any kind of touch or remembering. Even so, reciting the long list of those he hated, he came temporarily alive. Then, once out of this frame of mind, he lapsed into a kind of fog which we called, in the family, his retirement.

There was another part of my grandfather's mind that also disturbed me. But this passion was veiled. I stood at the borders of it occasionally catching glimpses. He had a stack of magazines by the chair he always occupied. They were devoted to the subject of crime, and the crimes were always grisly, involving photographs of women or girls uncovered in ditches, hacked to pieces or otherwise mutilated. I was never supposed to look in these magazines, but I did. What I saw there could not be reconciled with the other experience I had of my grandfather, fond of me, gentle, almost anachronistically protective.

Heinrich Himmler was also fascinated with crime. Along with books about Jews, he read avidly on the subjects of police work, espionage, torture. Despite his high ideals regarding chastity, he was drawn to torrid, even pornographic fiction, including *Ein Sadist im Priesterrock* (*A Sadist in Priestly Attire*) which he read quickly, noting in his journal that it was a book *about the corruption of women and girls . . . in Paris.*

Entering the odd and often inconsistent maze of his opinions, I feel a certain queasiness. I cannot find a balance point. I search in vain for some center, that place which is in us all, and is perhaps even beyond nationality, or even gender, the felt core of existence, which seems to be at the same time the most real. In Heinrich's morass of thought there are no connecting threads, no integrated whole. I find only the opinions themselves, standing in an odd relation to gravity, as if hastily formed, a rickety, perilous structure.

I am looking at a photograph. It was taken in 1925. Or perhaps 1926. A group of men pose before a doorway in Landshut. Over this doorway is a wreathed swastika. Nearly all the men are in uniform. Some wear shiny black boots. Heinrich is among them. He is the slightest, very thin. Heinrich Himmler. He is near the front. At the far left there is the blurred figure of a man who has been caught in motion as he rushes to join the other men. Of course I know his feeling. The desire to partake, and even to be part of memory.

Photographs are strange creations. They are depictions of a moment that is always passing; after the shutter closes, the subject moves out of the frame and begins to change outwardly or inwardly. One ages. One shifts to a different state of consciousness. Subtle changes can take place in an instant, perhaps one does not even feel them—but they are perceptible to the camera.

The idea we have of reality as a fixed quantity is an illusion. Everything moves. And the process of knowing oneself is in constant motion too, because the self is always changing. Nowhere is this so evident as in the process of art which takes one at once into the self and into *terra incognita*, the land of the unknown. *I am groping in the dark,* the artist Käthe Kollwitz writes in her journal. Here, I imagine she is not so much uttering a cry of despair as making a simple statement. A sense of emptiness always precedes creation.

Now, as I imagine Himmler, dressed in his neat uniform, seated behind his desk at party headquarters, I can feel the void he feared begin to recede. In every way his life has taken on definition. He has a purpose and a schedule. Even the place left by the cessation of his father's lessons has now been filled. He is surrounded by men whose ideas he begins to adopt. From Alfred Rosenberg he learns about the history of Aryan blood, a line Rosenberg traces back to thousands of years before Christ. From Walther Darré he learns that the countryside is a source of Nordic strength. (And that Jews gravitate toward cities.)

Yet I do not find the calmness of a man who has found himself in the descriptions I have encountered of Heinrich Himmler. Rather, he is filled with an anxious ambivalence. If there was once someone in him who felt strongly one way or the other, this one has long ago vanished. In a room filled with other leaders, he seems to fade into the woodwork, his manner obsequious, his effect inconsequential. He cannot make a decision alone. He is known to seek the advice of other men for even the smallest decisions. In the years to come it will be whispered that he is being led by his own assistant, Reinhard Heydrich. He has made only one decision on his own with a consistent resolve. Following Hitler with unwavering loyalty, he is known as *der treue Heinrich,* true Heinrich. He describes himself as an instrument of the Führer's will.

But still he has something of his own. Something hidden. And this will make him powerful. He is a gatherer of secrets. As he supervises the sale of advertising space for the Nazi newspaper, *Völkischer Beobachter,* he instructs the members of his staff to gather information, not only on the party enemies, the socialists and the communists, but on Nazi Party members themselves. In his small office he sits surrounded by voluminous files that are filled with secrets. From this he will build his secret police. By 1925, with an order from Adolf Hitler, the Schutzstaffel, or SS, has become an official institution.

His life is moving now. Yet in this motion one has the feeling not of a flow, as in the flow of water in a cell, nor as the flow of rivers toward an ocean, but of an engine, a locomotive moving at high speed, or even a missile, traveling above the ground. History has an uncanny way of creating its own metaphors. In 1930, months after Himmler is elected to the Reichstag, Wernher von Braun begins his experiments with liquid fuel missiles that will one day soon lead to the development of the V-2 rocket.

The successful journey of a missile depends upon the study of ballistics. Gravitational fields vary at different heights. The relationship of a projectile to the earth's surface will determine its trajectory. The missile may give the illusion of liberation from the earth, or even abandon. Young men dreaming of space often invest the missile with these qualities. Yet, paradoxically, one is more free of the consideration of gravity while traveling the surface of the earth on foot. There is no necessity for mathematical calculation for each step, nor does one need to apply Newton's laws to take a walk. But the missile has in a sense been forced away from its own presence; the wisdom that is part of its own weight has been transgressed. It finds itself thus careening in a space devoid of memory, always on the verge of falling, but not falling and hence like one who is constantly afraid of illusion, gripped by an anxiety that cannot be resolved even by a fate that threatens catastrophe.

The catastrophes which came to pass after Heinrich Himmler's astonishing ascent to power did not occur in his own life, but came to rest in the lives of others, distant from him, and out of the context of his daily world. It is 1931. Heinz, the boy born in Vienna to Catholic parents, has just turned sixteen, and he is beginning to learn something about himself. All around him his school friends are falling in love with girls. But when he searches inside himself, he finds no such feelings. He is pulled in a different direction. He finds that he is still drawn to another boy. He does not yet know, or even guess, that these feelings will one day place him in the territory of a target.

It is 1933. Heinrich Himmler, Reichsführer SS, has become President of the Bavarian police. In this capacity he begins a campaign against *subversive elements*. Opposition journalists, Jewish business owners, Social Democrats, Communists — names culled from a list compiled on index cards by Himmler's deputy, Reinhard Heydrich — are rounded up and arrested. When the prisons become too crowded, Himmler builds temporary camps. Then, on March 22, the Reichsführer opens the first official and permanent concentration camp at Dachau.

It is 1934. Himmler's power and prestige in the Reich are growing. Yet someone stands in his way. Within the hierarchy of the state police forces, Ernst Röhm, Commandant of the SA, stands over him. But Himmler has made an alliance with Hermann Göring, who as President Minister of Prussia controls the Prussian police, known as the Gestapo. Through a telephone-tapping technique Göring has uncovered evidence of a seditious plot planned by Röhm against the Führer, and he brings this evidence to Himmler. The Führer, having his own reasons to proceed against Röhm, a notorious homosexual and a socialist, empowers the SS and the Gestapo to form an execution committee. This committee will assassinate Röhm, along with the other leaders of the SA. And in the same year, Göring transfers control of the Gestapo to the SS.

But something else less easy to conquer stands in the way of his dreams for himself. It is his own body. I can see him now as he struggles. He is on a playing field in Berlin. And he has broken out in a sweat. He has been trying once again to earn the Reich's sports badge, an honor whose requirements he himself established but cannot seem to fulfill. For three years he has exercised and practiced. On one day he will lift the required weights or run the required laps, but at every trial he fails to throw the discus far enough. His attempt is always a few centimeters short.

And once he is Reichsführer, he will set certain other standards for superiority that, no matter how heroic his efforts, he will never be able to meet. A sign of the *Übermensch*, he says, is blondness, but he himself is dark. He says he is careful to weed out any applicant for the SS who shows traces of a mongolian ancestry, but he himself has the narrow eyes he takes as a sign of such a descent. *I have refused to accept any man whose size was below six feet because I know only men of a certain size have the necessary quality of blood*, he declares, standing just five foot seven behind the podium.

It is the same year, and Heinz, who is certain now that he is a homosexual, has decided to end the silence which he feels to be a burden to him. From the earliest years of his childhood he has trusted his mother with all of his secrets. Now he will tell her another secret, the secret of whom he loves. *My dear child*, she tells him, *it is your life and you must live it.*

It is 1936. Though he does not know it, Himmler is moving into the sphere of Heinz's life now. He has organized a special section of the Gestapo to deal with homosexuality and abortion. On October 11, he declares in a public speech, *Germany's forebears knew what to do with homosexuals. They drowned them in bogs.* This was not punishment, he argues, but *the extermination of unnatural existence.*

As I read these words from Himmler's speech, they call to mind an image from a more recent past, an event I nearly witnessed. On my return from Berlin and after my search for my grandmother, I spent a few days in Maine, close to the city of Bangor. This is a quiet town, not much used to violence. But just days before I arrived a young man had been murdered there. He was a homosexual. He wore an earring in one ear. While he walked home one evening with another man, three boys stopped him on the street. They threw him to the ground and began to kick him. He had trouble catching his breath. He was asthmatic. They picked him up and carried him to a railing of a nearby bridge. He told them he could not swim. Yet still, they threw him over the railing of the bridge into the stream, and he drowned. I saw a picture of him printed in the newspaper. That kind of beauty only very graceful children possess shined through his adult features. It was said that he had come to New England to live with his lover. But the love had failed, and before he died he was piecing his life back together.

When Himmler heard that one of his heroes, Frederick the Great, was a homosexual, he refused to believe his ears. I remember the year when my sister announced to my family that she was a lesbian. I can still recall the chill of fear that went up my spine at the sound of the word "queer." We came of age in the fifties; this was a decade of conformity, awash with mood both public and private, bearing on the life of the body and the body politic. Day after day my grandfather would sit in front of the television set watching as Joseph McCarthy interrogated witnesses about their loyalty to the flag. At the same time, a strict definition of what a woman or a man is had returned to capture the shared imagination. In school I was taught sewing and cooking, and I learned to carry my books in front of my chest to strengthen the muscles which held up my breasts.

I was not happy to hear that my sister was a homosexual. Moved from one member of my family to another, I did not feel secure in the love of others. As the child of divorce I was already different. *Where are your mother and father? Why don't you live with them?* I dreaded these questions. Now my sister, whom I adored and in many ways had patterned myself after, had become an outcast, moved even further out of the circle than I.

It is March 1938. Germany has invaded Austria. Himmler has put on a field-gray uniform for the occasion. Two hand grenades dangle from his Sam Browne belt. Accompanied by a special command unit of twenty-eight men armed with tommy guns and light machine guns, he proceeds to Vienna. Here he will set up Gestapo headquarters in the Hotel Metropole before he returns to Berlin.

It is a Friday, in March of 1939. Heinz, who is twenty-two years old now, and a university student, has received a summons. He is to appear for questioning at the Hotel Metropole. Telling his mother it can't be anything serious, he leaves. He enters a room and stands before a desk. The man behind the desk does not raise his head to nod. He continues to write. When he puts his pen down and looks up at the young man, he tells him, *You are a queer, homosexual, admit it.* Heinz tries to deny this. But the man behind the desk pulls out a photograph. He sees two faces here he knows. His own face and the face of his lover. He begins to weep.

I have come to believe that every life bears in some way on every other. The motion of cause and effect is like the motion of a wave in water, continuous, within and not without the matrix of being, so that all consequences, whether we know them or not, are intimately embedded in our experience. But the missile, as it hurls toward its target, has lost its context. It has been driven farther than the eye can see. How can one speak of direction any longer? Nothing in the space the missile passes through can seem familiar. In the process of flight, alienated by terror, this motion has become estranged from life, has fallen out of the natural rhythm of events.

I am imagining Himmler as he sits behind his desk in January of 1940. The procedures of introduction into the concentration camps have all been outlined or authorized by Himmler himself. He supervises every detail of these operations. Following his father's penchant for order, he makes many very explicit rules, and requires that reports be filed continually. Train schedules, orders for food supplies, descriptions of punishments all pass over his desk. He sits behind a massive door of carved wood, in his office, paneled in light, unvarnished oak, behind a desk that is normally empty, and clean, except for the bust of Hitler he displays at one end, and a little drummer boy at the other, between which he reads, considers and initials countless pieces of paper.

One should teach a child a sense of shame. These words of Himmler's journals come back to me as I imagine Heinz now standing naked in the snow. The weather is below zero. After a while he is taken to a cold shower, and then issued an ill-fitting uniform. Now he is ordered to stand with the other prisoners once more out in the cold while the commandant reads the rules. All the prisoners in these barracks are homosexuals. There are pink triangles sewn to their uniforms. They must sleep with the light on, they are told, and with their hands outside their blankets. This is a rule especially for homosexual men. Any man caught with his hands under his blankets will be taken outside into the icy night where several bowls of water will be poured over him, and where he will he made to stand for an hour.

Except for the fact that this punishment usually led to death from cold and exposure, this practice reminds me of Dr. Schreber's procedure for curing children of masturbation. Just a few nights ago I woke up with this thought: *Was Dr. Schreber afraid of children?* Or the child he once was? Fear is often just beneath the tyrant's fury, a fear that must grow with the trajectory of his flight from himself. At Dachau I went inside a barrack. It was a standard design, similar in many camps. The plan of the camps too was standard, and resembled, so I was told by a German friend, the camp sites designed for the Hitler Youth. This seemed to me significant, not as a clue in an analysis, but more like a gesture that colors and changes a speaker's words.

It is the summer of 1940. After working for nearly a decade on liquid fuel rockets, Wernher von Braun begins to design a missile that can be used in the war. He is part of a team trying to meet certain military specifications. The missile must be carried through railway tunnels. It must cover a range of 275 kilometers and carry a warhead weighing one metric ton. The engineers have determined that the motor of this rocket, a prototype of the V-2, will need to be fueled by a pump, and now a pump has been made. Von Braun is free to turn his attention to the turbine drive.

When I think of this missile, or of men sleeping in a barrack, hands exposed, lying on top of worn blankets, an image of Himmler's hands comes to me. Those who remember him say that as he conducted a conversation, discussing a plan, for example, or giving a new order, his hands would lie on top of his desk, limp and inert. He did not like to witness the consequences of his commands. His plans were launched toward distant targets and blind to the consequences of flesh.

After a few months, in one of countless orders which mystify him, coming from a nameless source, and with no explanation, but which he must obey, Heinz is transferred from Sachsenhausen to Flossenbürg. The regime at this camp is the same, but here the commandant, unlike Himmler, does not choose to distance himself from the suffering of others. He is instead drawn to it. He will have a man flogged for the slightest infraction of the rules, and then stand to watch as this punishment is inflicted. The man who is flogged is made to call out the number of lashes as he is lashed, creating in him, no doubt, the feeling that he is causing his own pain. As the man's skin bursts open and he cries out in pain, the commandant's eyes grow excited. His face turns red. His hand slips into his trousers, and he begins to handle himself.

Was the commandant in this moment in any way an extension of the Reichsführer, living out a hidden aspect of this man, one who takes pleasure in the pain of others? This explanation must shed some light, except perhaps as it is intended through the category of an inexplicable perversity to put the crimes Himmler committed at a distance from any understanding of ourselves. The Reichsführer's sexuality is so commonplace. He was remarkable only for the extent of his prudery as a young man. Later, like so many men, he has a wife, who dominates him, and a mistress, younger, more docile, adoring, whom he in turn adores. It has been suggested that he takes pleasure in seeing the naked bodies of boys and young men. If he has a sexual fetish it is certainly this, the worship of physical perfection in the male body. And this worship has its sadistic aspects: his efforts to control reproduction, to force SS men to procreate with many women, the kidnapping from occupied countries of children deemed worthy. Under the veneer of his worship, an earlier rage must haunt him. The subject of cruel insults from other boys with hardier bodies, and the torturous methods his father used to raise him, does he not feel rage toward his persecutors, a rage that, in the course of time, enters history? Yet this is an essential part of the picture: he is dulled to rage. So many of his feelings are inaccessible to him. Like the concentration camps he commands, in many ways he remains absent to himself. And in this he is not so different from the civilization that produced him.

Writing this, I have tried to find my own rage. The memory is immediate. I am a child, almost nine years old. I sit on the cold pavement of a winter day in Los Angeles. My grandmother has angered me. There is a terrible injustice. A punishment that has enraged me. As I sit picking blades of grass and arranging them into piles, I am torturing her in my mind. I have tied her up and I am shouting at her. Threatening her. Striking her. I batter her, batter her as if with each blow, each landing of my hand against her flesh, I can force my way into her, I can be inside her, I can grab hold of someone inside her, someone who feels, who feels as I do, who feels the hurt I feel, the wound I feel, who feels pain as I feel pain. I am forcing her to feel what I feel. I am forcing her to know me. And as I strike her, blow after blow, a shudder of weeping is released in me, and I become utterly myself, the weeping in me becoming rage, the rage turning to tears, all the time my heart beating, all the time uttering a soundless, bitter, passionate cry, a cry of vengeance and of love.

Is this what is in the torturer's heart? With each blow of his whip does he want to make the tortured one feel as he himself has felt? The desire to know and be known is strong in all of us. Many years after the day I imagined myself as my grandmother's torturer I came to understand that, just as I had wanted my grandmother to feel what I had felt, she wanted me to feel as she had felt. Not what she felt as a woman, but what she had felt long ago as a child. Her childhood was lost to her, the feelings no longer remembered. One way or another, through punishment, severity, or even ridicule, she could goad me into fury and then tears. I expressed for her all she had held inside for so long.

One day, the commandant at Flossenbürg encounters a victim who will not cry and Heinz is a witness to this meeting. As usual this prisoner must count out the number of blows assigned to him. The beating commences. And the prisoner counts out the numbers. But otherwise he is silent. Except for the numbers, not a cry, not a sound, passes his lips. And this puts the commandant in a rage. He orders the guard to strike harder with the lash; he increases the number of lashes; he orders the prisoner to begin counting from zero again. Finally, the beating shall continue *until the swine starts screaming*, he shouts. And now, when the prisoner's blood is flowing to the ground, he starts to howl. And with this, the commandant's face grows red, and his hands slip into his trousers again.

A connection between violence and sexuality threads its way through many histories. As we sit in the living room together, looking out over the water, Laura's stories move in and out of the world of her family, and of our shared world, its habits, its wars. She is telling me another story about her father, the general. They were living on the missile base. She had been out late baby-sitting. When she returned home the house was dark. She had no key. It was raining hard. She rang. There was no answer. Then she began to pound on the door. Suddenly the door opened. The hallway was dark. She was yanked into this darkness by her father. He was standing naked. Without speaking to her he began to slap her hard across the face, again and again, and did not stop until her mother, appearing in the stairs in a bathrobe, stood between them. *I knew*, she told me, *they had been making love.*

What was the source of his rage? Did it come from childhood, or battle, or both, the battle awakening the panic of an earlier abuse? The training a soldier receives is to wreak his anger on others. Anyone near receives it. I have heard stories of a man waking at night screaming in terror, reaching for a gun hidden under the pillow, and pointing it or even firing at his own family. In a play about Heracles by Euripides, the great warrior, who has just returned from the underworld, thinking that he has vanquished death, is claimed by madness. He believes himself to be in the home of his enemy. But he is in his own home and, finding his own children, mistakes them for the children of his enemy, clubs one to death and then kills the other two with arrows.

But it is not only warriors who wreak vengeance on their own children. Suffering is passed on from parent to child unto many generations. Did I know as a child that my grandmother's unclaimed fury had made its way into my mother's psyche too? With all her will my mother tried not to repeat against her own children the crimes that had battered her. Where my grandmother was tyrannical, my mother was tolerant and gave free reign. Where my grandmother goaded with critical remarks, my mother was encouraging, and even elaborately praising. But, like my grandfather, my mother drank too much. It was a way of life for her. Sooner or later the long nights would come. Every time I returned home, either to live with her or to visit, I prayed she would not drink again, while I braced myself for what I knew to be inevitable. The evening would begin with a few beers at home, followed by an endless tour of several bars. Either I went along and waited in cars, or I waited at home. In the early morning she would return, her eyes wandering like moths in their sockets. We would sit in two chairs opposite each other, as if these were prearranged places, marked out for us on the stage by a powerful but invisible director. She would start by joking with me. She was marvelously witty when she was drunk. All her natural intelligence was released then and allowed to bloom. But this performance was brief. Her humor turned by dark degrees to meanness. What must have daily constricted her, a kind of sea monster, feeding beneath the waters of her consciousness, and strong, would rise up to stop her glee and mine. Then she would strike. If I was not in my chair to receive her words, she would come and get me. What she said was viperous to me, sank like venom into my veins, and burned a path inside me. Even today I can remember very few of the words she used. She said that my laugh was too loud, or ugly. That I was incapable of loving. I am thankful now that, because she was not in her right mind, I knew at least in a part of myself that these accusations were unfounded. Yet they produced a doubt in me, a lingering shadow, the sense that perhaps I deserved whatever suffering befell me, and that shadow lingers.

Even if a feeling has been made secret, even if it has vanished from memory, can it have disappeared altogether? A weapon is lifted with the force of a forgotten memory. The memory has no words, only the insistence of a pain that has turned into fury. A body, tender in its childhood or its nakedness, lies under this weapon. And this body takes up the rage, the pain, the disowned memory with each blow.

1893. *Self-portrait at Table.* An etching and aquatint, the first in a long series of self-portraits that span the artist's life. A single lamp illuminates her face, the upper part of the body and the table where she sits. Everything else is in darkness. At first glance one thinks of loneliness. But after a moment it is solitude one sees. And a single moment in that solitude, as if one note of music, resonant and deep, played uninterrupted, echoing from every surface, coming to full consciousness in this woman, who in this instant looks out to those who will return her gaze with a face that has taken in and is expressing the music in the air about her. Solemnly and with a quiet patience, her hands pause over the etching she makes, a form she is bringing into being, the one she recognizes as herself.

Who are we? The answer is not easy. There are so many strands to the story, and one must trace every strand. I begin to suspect each thread goes out infinitely and touches everything, everyone. I read these words from an ancient gnostic text, words that have been lost to us for a long time: *For I am the first and the last.* Though in another account we have heard the beginning of this speech spoken by Jesus, here these words come to us in the voice of the goddess. *I am the honored one and scorned one*, the older text goes on. *I am the whore and the holy one. I am the wife and the virgin. I am the barren one, and many are her sons.* These words take on a new meaning for me, as I remember them now. *I am the silence that is incomprehensible*, the text reads, and ends, *I am the utterance of my name.*

Were you to trace any life, and study even the minute consequences, the effect, for instance, of a three-minute walk over a patch of grass, of words said casually to a stranger who happens to sit nearby in a public place, the range of that life would extend way beyond the territory we imagine it to inhabit. This is of course less difficult to understand when imagining the boundaries of a life such as Heinrich Himmler had.

After my visit to Dachau, I went to Paris where, in the fourteenth arrondissement, in the Métro station, I met Hélène. She stopped to help me read my map. We found we were going in the same direction, and thus it was on our way there that we began to speak. Something told me she had survived a concentration camp. And she had. She too fell into the circle of

Himmler's life and its consequences. Himmler never went to Paris. At the time of the first mass arrests there he was taking a group of high Nazi officials on a tour of Auschwitz. During the tour, by his orders, the prisoners were made to stand at attention for six hours under the hot sun, but that is another story. Under his command, the Gestapo in Paris began to prepare for the mass arrests of Jews.

Paris had fallen to the German armies in July 1940. By September of that year a notice went up in all the neighborhoods. *Avis aux Israélites*, it read. *Notice to Israelites. By the demand of the occupying authorities, Israelites must present themselves, by October 2, without delay, equipped with identification papers, to the office of the Censor, to complete an identity card.* The notice was signed by the mayor and threatened the most severe punishment for the failure to comply. Through this process vital information was recorded about each Jewish family. Names, ages, addresses, occupations, places of work. An index card was made up for each person. And each card was then duplicated and sent to the offices of the Gestapo on Avenue Foch. There, the cards were duplicated several more times so that the names could be filed by several categories, alphabetically by surname, by address, by arrondissement, occupation, and nationality. At this point in history, work that would be done by computer now was painstakingly completed by countless men and women. Their labor continued feverishly almost until the hour of the first mass arrests, the *rafles*, two years later.

One can trace every death to an order signed by Himmler, yet these arrests could never have taken place on such a massive scale without this vast system of information. What did they think, those who were enlisted for this work? They were civilians. French. There were of course Nazi collaborators, among them, those who shared the same philosophy, or who simply obeyed and profited from whoever might be in power. But among the men and women who did this work, my suspicion is, there were many who tried to keep from themselves the knowledge of what they did. Of course, the final purpose of their labors was never revealed to those who prepared the machinery of arrest. If a man allowed his imagination to stray in the direction of this purpose, he could no doubt comfort himself with the argument that he was only handling pieces of paper. He could tell himself that matters were simply being set in order. The men and women who manufacture the trigger mechanisms for nuclear bombs do not tell themselves they are making weapons. They say simply that they are metal forgers.

There are many ways we have of standing outside ourselves in ignorance. Those who have learned as children to become strangers to themselves do not find this a difficult task. Habit has made it natural not to feel. To ignore the consequences of what one does in the world becomes ordinary. And this tendency is encouraged by a social structure that makes fragments of real events. One is never allowed to see the effects of what one does. But this ignorance is not entirely passive. For some, blindness becomes a kind of refuge, a way of life that is chosen, even with stubborn volition, and does not yield easily even to visible evidence.

The arrests were accompanied by an elaborate procedure, needed on some level, no doubt, for practical reasons, but also serving another purpose. They garbed this violence in the cloak of legality. A mind separated from the depths of itself cannot easily tell right from wrong. To this mind, the outward signs of law and order signify righteousness. That Himmler had such a mind was not unique in his generation, nor, I suspect, in ours.

In a museum in Paris I found a mimeographed sheet giving instructions to the Parisian police on how to arrest Jews. They must always carry red pencils, the sheet admonished, because all records regarding the arrests of Jews must be written in red. And the instructions went on to specify that, regarding the arrests of Jews, all records must be made in triplicate. Finally, the sheet of instructions included a way to categorize those Jews arrested. I could not make any sense of the categories. I only knew them to be crucial. That they might determine life and death for a woman, or man, or child. And that in the mind that invented these categories they had to have had some hidden significance, standing, like the crudely shaped characters of a medieval play, for shades of feeling, hidden states of being, secret knowledge.

For the most part, the men who designed the first missiles were not interested in weapons so much as flight. In his account of the early work at Peenemünde laboratories, Wernher von Braun explains that the scientists there had discovered a way to fund their research by making rockets appeal to the military. Colonel Dornberger told the other scientists that they could not hope to continue if all they created were experimental rockets. All Wernher von Braun wanted was to design vehicles that would travel to the moon. In the early fifties, in a book he wrote with two other scientists, he speaks of the reasons for such a flight. Yes, he says, curiosity and adventure play a part. But the primary reason is *to increase man's knowledge of the universe.*

To tell a story, or to hear a story told, is not a simple transmission of information. Something else in the telling is given too, so that, once hearing, what one has heard becomes a part of oneself. Hélène and I went to the museum in Paris together. There, among photographs of the first mass arrests and the concentration camp at Drancy, she told me this story. Reading the notice signed by the mayor, she presented herself immediately at the office of the censor. She waited with others, patiently. But when her turn in line came, the censor looked at her carefully. She was blond and had blue eyes. *Are you really Jewish?* he asked her.

The question of who was and who was not Jewish was pivotal to the Nazi mind and much legal controversy hung in the balance of this debate. For a few years, anyone with three Jewish grandparents was considered Jewish. An ancestor who belonged to the faith, but was not of Jewish blood would be Jewish. One who did not belong to the faith, but was of Jewish blood, was also Jewish. At the heart of this controversy, I hear the whisper of ambivalence, and perhaps the smallest beginning of compassion. For, to this mind, the one who is not Jewish becomes recognizable as like oneself.

Yes, I am Jewish, she said. *But your mother*, he asked again. *Can you be certain? Yes*, she said. *Ask her, go home and ask her*, he said, putting his stamp away. *But my mother is dead*, she protested. Then, he said, keeping his stamp in the drawer, *Your father. Your father must not be Jewish. Go home and ask him. I know he is Jewish*, Hélène answered. *There is no doubt that he is Jewish. He has always been Jewish, and I am Jewish too.* Then the man was silent, he shook his head. And, looking past her, said, *Perhaps your father was not really your father. Have you thought of that? Perhaps he was not your father?* She was young. *Of course he's my father. How can you say that? Certainly he is my father*, she insisted. *He is Jewish and so am I.* And she demanded that her papers be stamped.

What was in this man's mind as he questioned her? Did he say to himself, Perhaps here is someone I can save? Did he have what Pierre Sauvage has called *a moment of goodness?* What we know as goodness is not a static quality but arrives through a series of choices, some imperceptible, which are continually presented to us.

It is 1941. And Heinrich Himmler pays a visit to the Russian front. He has been put in charge of organizing the *Einsatzgruppen*, moving groups of men who carry out the killing of civilians and partisans. He watches as a deep pit is dug by the captured men and women. Then, suddenly, a young man catches his eye. He is struck by some quality the man possesses. He takes a liking to him. He has the commandant of the *Einsatzgruppen* bring the young man to him. *Who was your father?* he asks. *Your mother? Your grandparents? Do you have at least one grandparent who was not Jewish?* He is trying to save the young man. But he answers no to all the questions. So Himmler, strictly following the letter of the law, watches as the young man is put to death.

The captured men, women, and children are ordered to remove their clothing then. Naked, they stand before the pit they have dug. Some scream. Some attempt escape. The young men in uniform place their rifles against their shoulders and fire into the naked bodies. They do not fall silently. There are cries. There are open wounds. There are faces blown apart. Stomachs opened up. The dying groan. Weep. Flutter. Open their mouths.

There is no photograph of the particular moment when Heinrich Himmler stares into the face of death. What does he look like? Is he pale? He is stricken, the accounts tell us, and more than he thought he would be. He has imagined something quieter, more efficient, like the even rows of numbers, the alphabetical lists of names he likes to put in his files. Something he might be able to understand and contain. But one cannot contain death so easily.

. . .

Death with Girl in Her Lap. One of many studies the artist did of death. A
girl is drawn, her body dead or almost dead, in that suspended state where
the breath is almost gone. There is no movement. No will. The lines the
artist has drawn are simple. She has not rendered the natural form of head,
arm, buttock, thigh exactly. But all these lines hold the feeling of a body in
them. And as my eyes rest on this image, I can feel my own fear of death,
and also, the largeness of grief, how grief will not let you remain insulated
from your own feelings, or from life itself. It is as if I knew this girl. And
death, too, appears to know her, cradling the fragile body with tenderness;
she seems to understand the sorrow of dying. Perhaps this figure has taken
into herself all the deaths she has witnessed. And in this way, she has become merciful.

Because Himmler finds it so difficult to witness these deaths, the commandant makes an appeal to him. If it is hard for you, he says, think what it
must be for these young men who must carry out these executions, day
after day. Shaken by what he has seen and heard, Himmler returns to
Berlin resolved to ease the pain of these men. He will consult an engineer
and set him to work immediately on new designs. Before the year has
ended, he presents the *Einsatzgruppen* with a mobile killing truck. Now the
young men will not have to witness death day after day. A hose from the
exhaust pipe funnels fumes into a chamber built on the bed of a covered
truck, which has a red cross painted on its side so its passengers will not be
alarmed as they enter it.

To a certain kind of mind, what is hidden away ceases to exist.

Himmler does not like to watch the suffering of his prisoners. In this
sense he does not witness the consequences of his own commands. But the
mind is like a landscape in which nothing really ever disappears. What
seems to have vanished has only transmuted to another form. Not wishing
to witness what he has set in motion, still, in a silent part of himself,
he must imagine what takes place. So, just as the child is made to live out
the unclaimed imagination of the parent, others under Himmler's power
were made to bear witness for him. Homosexuals were forced to witness
and sometimes take part in the punishment of other homosexuals, Poles of
other Poles, Jews of Jews. And as far as possible, the hands of the men of
the SS were protected from the touch of death. Other prisoners were required to bury the bodies, or burn them in the ovens.

Hélène was turned in by a Jewish man who was trying, no doubt, to
save his own life, and she was put under arrest by another Jewish man, an
inmate of the same camp to which she was taken. She was grateful that
she herself had not been forced to do harm. But something haunted her.

A death that came to stand in place of her own death. As we walked through the streets of Paris she told me this story.

By the time of her arrest she was married and had a young son. Her husband was taken from their apartment during one of the mass arrests that began in July of 1942. Hélène was out at the time with her son. For some time she wandered the streets of Paris. She would sleep at night at the homes of various friends and acquaintances, leaving in the early morning so that she would not arouse suspicion among the neighbors. This was the hardest time, she told me, because there was so little food, even less than she was to have at Drancy. She had no ration card or any way of earning money. Her whole existence was illegal. She had to be as if invisible. She collected scraps from the street. It was on the street that she told me this story, as we walked from the fourth arrondissement to the fifth, crossing the bridge near Notre Dame, making our way toward the Boulevard St. Michel.

Her husband was a citizen of a neutral country and for this reason legally destined for another camp. From this camp he would not be deported. Instead he was taken to the French concentration camp at Drancy. After his arrest, hoping to help him, Hélène managed to take his papers to the Swiss Consulate. But the papers remained there. After her own arrest she was taken with her son to Drancy, where she was reunited with her husband. He told her that her efforts were useless. But still again and again she found ways to smuggle out letters to friends asking them to take her husband's papers from the Swiss Consulate to the camp at Drancy. One of these letters was to save their lives.

After a few months, preparations began to send Hélène and her family to Auschwitz. Along with many other women, she was taken to have her hair cut short, though those consigned to that task decided she should keep her long, blond hair. Still, she was herded along with the others to the train station and packed into the cars. Then, just two hours before the train was scheduled to leave, Hélène, her son, and her husband were pulled from the train. Her husband's papers had been brought by the Swiss consul to the camp. The Commandant, by assuming Hélène shared the same nationality with her husband, had made a fortuitous mistake.

But the train had to have a specific number of passengers before it could leave. In Hélène's place the guards brought a young man. She would never forget his face, she told me, or his name. Later she tried to find out whether he had lived or died but could learn nothing.

Himmler did not partake in the actual preparations for what he called "the final solution." Nor did he attend the Wannsee Conference where the decision to annihilate millions of human beings was made. He sent his assistant Heydrich. Yet Heydrich, who was there, did not count himself entirely present. He could say that each decision he made was at the bequest of Heinrich Himmler. In this way an odd system of insulation was created. These crimes, these murders of millions, were all carried out in absentia, as if by no one in particular.

This ghostlike quality, the strange absence of a knowing conscience, as if the living creature had abandoned the shell, was spread throughout the entire chain of command. So a French bureaucrat writing a letter in 1942 speaks in detail of the mass arrests that he himself supervised as if he had no other part in these murders except as a kind of spiritless cog in a vast machine whose force compelled him from without. *The German authorities have set aside especially for that purpose enough trains to transport 30,000 Jews,* he writes. *It is therefore necessary that the arrests made should correspond to the capacity of the trains.*

It is August 23, 1943. The first inmates of concentration camp Dora have arrived. Is there some reason why an unusually high percentage of prisoners ordered to work in this camp are homosexuals? They are set to work immediately, working with few tools, often with bare hands, to convert long tunnels carved into the Harz Mountains into a factory for the manufacture of missiles. They work for eighteen hours each day. Six of these hours are set aside for formal procedures, roll calls, official rituals of the camp. For six hours they must try to sleep in the tunnels, on the damp earth, in the same area where the machines, pickaxes, explosions, and drills are making a continually deafening noise, twenty-four hours of every day. They are fed very little. They see the daylight only once a week, at the Sunday roll call. The tunnels themselves are illuminated with faint light bulbs. The production of missiles has been moved here because the factories at Peenemünde were bombed. Because the secret work at Peenemünde had been revealed to the Allies by an informer, after the bombing the Reichsführer SS proposed that the factories should be installed in a concentration camp. Here, he argued, security could be more easily enforced; only the guards had any freedom, and they were subject to the harsh discipline of the SS. The labor itself could be hidden under the soil of the Harz Mountains.

Memory can be like a long, half-lit tunnel, a tunnel where one is likely to encounter phantoms of a self, long concealed, no longer nourished with the force of consciousness, existing in a tortured state between life and death. In his account of his years at Peenemünde, Wernher von Braun never mentions concentration camp Dora. Yet he was seen there more than once by inmates who remembered him. As the designing engineer, he had to supervise many details of production. Conditions at camp Dora could not have escaped his attention. Dora did not have its own crematorium. And so many men and women died in the course of a day that the bodies waiting to be picked up by trucks and taken to the ovens of Buchenwald were piled high next to the entrance to the tunnels.

Perhaps von Braun told himself that what went on in those tunnels had nothing to do with him. He had not wished for these events, had not wanted them. The orders came from someone who had power over him. In the course of this writing I remembered a childhood incident that made me disown myself in the same way. My best friend, who was my neighbor, had a mean streak and because of this had a kind of power over the rest of us who played with her. For a year I left my grandmother's house to live with my mother again. On my return I had been replaced by another little girl, and the two of them excluded me. But finally my chance arrived. My friend had a quarrel with her new friend and enlisted me in an act of revenge. Together we cornered her at the back of a yard, pushing her into the garbage cans, yelling nasty words at her, throwing things at her.

My friend led the attack, inventing the strategies and the words which were hurled. With part of myself I knew what it was to be the object of this kind of assault. But I also knew this was the way to regain my place with my friend. Later I disowned my acts, as if I had not committed them. Because I was under the sway of my friend's power, I told myself that what I did was really her doing. And in this way became unreal to myself. It was as if my voice threatening her, my own anger, and my voice calling names, had never existed.

I was told this story by a woman who survived the holocaust. The war had not yet begun. Nor the exiles. Nor the mass arrests. But history was on the point of these events, tipping over, ready to fall into the relentless path of consequences. She was then just a child, playing games in the street. And one day she found herself part of a circle of other children. They had surrounded a little boy and were calling him names because he was Jewish. He was her friend. But she thought if she left this circle, or came to his defense, she herself would lose her standing among the others. Then, suddenly, in an angry voice her mother called her in from the street. As soon as the door shut behind her, her mother began to shout, words incomprehensible to her, and slapped her across the face. *Your father*, her mother finally said, after crying, and in a quieter voice, *was Jewish*. Her father had been dead for three years. Soon after this day her mother too would die. As the danger grew worse her gentile relatives would not harbor her any longer, and she joined the fate of those who tried to live in the margins, as if invisible, as if mere shadows, terrified of a direct glance, of recognition, existing at the unsteady boundary of consciousness.

In disowning the effects we have on others, we disown ourselves. My father watched the suffering of my childhood and did nothing. He was aware of my mother's alcoholism and the state of her mind when she drank. He knew my grandmother to be tyrannical. We could speak together of these things almost dispassionately, as if both of us were disinterested witnesses to a fascinating social drama. But after a day's visit with him, spent at the park, or riding horses, or at the movies, he would send me back into that world of suffering we had discussed so dispassionately.

His disinterest in my condition was not heartless. It reflected the distance he kept from his own experience. One could sense his suffering but he never expressed it directly. He was absent to a part of himself. He was closer to tears than many men, but he never shed those tears. If I cried he would fall into a frightened silence. And because of this, though I spent a great deal of time with him, he was always in a certain sense an absent father. Unknowingly I responded in kind, for years, feeling a vaguely defined anger that would neither let me love nor hate him.

My father learned his disinterest under the guise of masculinity. Boys don't cry. There are whole disciplines, institutions, rubrics in our culture which serve as categories of denial.

Science is such a category. The torture and death that Heinrich Himmler found disturbing to witness became acceptable to him when it fell under this rubric. He liked to watch the scientific experiments in the concentration camps. And then there is the rubric of military order. I am looking at a photograph. It was taken in 1941 in the Ukraine. The men of an *einsatzgruppen* are assembled in a group pose. In front of them their rifles rest in ceremonial order, composed into tripods. They stand straight and tall. They are clean-shaven and their uniforms are immaculate, in *apple-pie order*, as we would say in America.

It is not surprising that cleanliness in a profession that sheds blood would become a compulsion. Blood would evidence guilt and fear to a mind trying to escape the consequence of its decisions. It is late in the night when Laura tells me one more story. Her father is about to be sent to Europe, where he will fight in the Battle of the Bulge and become a general. For weeks her mother has prepared a party. The guests begin to arrive in formal dress and sparkling uniforms. The white-gloved junior officers stand to open the doors. Her mother, regal in satin and jewels, starts to descend the staircase. Laura sits on the top stair watching, dressed in her pajamas. Then suddenly a pool of blood appears at her mother's feet, her mother falls to the floor, and almost as quickly, without a word uttered, a junior officer sweeps up the stairs, removes her mother into a waiting car, while another one cleans up the blood. No one tells Laura that her mother has had a miscarriage, and the party continues as if no event had taken place, no small or large death, as if no death were about to take place, nor any blood be spilled.

But the nature of the material world frustrates our efforts to remain free of the suffering of others. The mobile killing van that Himmler summoned into being had some defects. Gas from the exhaust pipes leaked into the cabin where the drivers sat and made them ill. When they went to remove the bodies from the van they were covered with blood and excrement, and their faces bore expressions of anguish. Himmler's engineers fixed the leak, increased the flow of gas so the deaths would be quicker, and built in a drain to collect the bodily fluids that are part of death.

There are times when no engineers can contain death. Over this same landscape through which the mobile killing vans traveled, an invisible cloud would one day spread, and from it would descend a toxic substance that would work its way into the soil and the water, the plants and the bodies of animals, and into human cells, not only in this landscape of the Ukraine, but in the fjords of Norway, the fields of Italy and France, and even here, in the far reaches of California, bringing a death that recalled, more than forty years later, those earlier hidden deaths.

You can see pictures of them. Whole families, whole communities. The fabric on their backs almost worn through. Bodies as if ebbing away before your eyes. Poised on an edge. The cold visible around the thin joints of arms and knees. A bed made in a doorway. Moving then, over time, deeper and deeper into the shadows. Off the streets. Into back rooms, and then to the attics or the cellars. Windows blackened. Given less and less to eat. Moving into smaller and smaller spaces. Sequestered away like forbidden thoughts, or secrets.

Could he have seen in these images of those he had forced into hiding and suffering, into agony and death, an image of the outer reaches of his own consciousness? It is only now that I can begin to see he has become part of them. Those whose fate he sealed. Heinrich Himmler. A part of Jewish history. Remembered by those who fell into the net of his unclaimed life. Claimed as a facet of the wound, part of the tissue of the scar. A mark on the body of our minds, both those of us who know this history and those who do not.

For there is a sense in which we are all witnesses. Hunger, desperation, pain, loneliness, these are all visible in the streets about us. The way of life we live, a life we have never really chosen, forces us to walk past what we see. And out at the edge, beyond what we see or hear, we can feel a greater suffering, cries from a present or past starvation, a present or past torture, cries of those we have never met, coming to us in our dreams, and even if these cries do not survive in our waking knowledge, still, they live on in the part of ourselves we have ceased to know.

I think now of the missile again and how it came into being. Scientific inventions do not spring whole like Athena from the head of Zeus from the analytic implications of scientific discoveries. Technological advance takes shape slowly in the womb of society and is influenced and fed by our shared imagination. What we create thus mirrors the recesses of our own minds, and perhaps also hidden capacities. Television mimics the ability to see in the mind's eye. And the rocket? Perhaps the night flight of the soul, that ability celebrated in witches to send our thoughts as if through the air to those distant from us, to send images of ourselves, and even our secret feelings, out into an atmosphere beyond ourselves, to see worlds far flung from and strange to us becomes manifest in a sinister fashion in the missile.

Self-portrait in charcoal. Since the earliest rendering she made of her own image, much time has passed. The viewer here has moved closer. Now the artist's head fills the frame. She is much older in years and her features have taken on that androgyny which she thought necessary to the work of an artist. Her hair is white on the paper where the charcoal has not touched it. She is in profile and facing a definite direction. Her eyes look in that direction. But they do not focus on anyone or anything. The portrait is soft, the charcoal rubbed almost gently over the surface, here light, here dark. Her posture is one not so much of resolution as resignation. The portrait was drawn just after the First World War, the war in which her son Peter died. I have seen these eyes in the faces of those who grieve, eyes that are looking but not focused, seeing perhaps what is no longer visible.

After the war, German scientists who developed the V-1 and V-2 rocket immigrate to the United States where they continue to work on rocketry. Using the Vengeance weapon as a prototype, they develop the first ICBM missiles.

On the twenty-third of May 1945, as the war in Europe comes to an end, Heinrich Himmler is taken prisoner by the Allied command. He has removed the military insignia from his clothing, and he wears a patch over one eye. Disguised in this manner, and carrying the identity papers of a man he had condemned to death, he attempts to cross over the border at Bremervörde. No one at the checkpoint suspects him of being the Reichsführer SS. But once under the scrutiny of the guards, all his courage fails him. Like a trembling schoolboy, he blurts out the truth. Now he will be taken to a center for interrogation, stripped of his clothing and searched. He will refuse to wear the uniform of the enemy, so he will be given a blanket to wrap over his underclothing. Taken to a second center for interrogation, he will be forced to remove this blanket and his underclothes. The interrogators, wishing to make certain he has no poison hidden anywhere, no means by which to end his life and hence avoid giving testimony, will surround his naked body. They will ask him to open his mouth. But just as one of them sees a black capsule wedged between his teeth, he will jerk his head away and swallow. All attempts to save his life will fail. He will not survive to tell his own story. His secrets will die with him.

There were many who lived through those years who did not wish to speak of what they saw or did. None of the German rocket engineers bore witness to what they saw at concentration camp Dora. Common rank and file members of the Nazi Party, those without whose efforts or silent support the machinery could not have gone on, fell almost as a mass into silence. In Berlin and Munich I spoke to many men and women, in my generation or younger, who were the children of soldiers, or party members, or SS men, or generals, or simply believers. Their parents would not speak to them of what had happened. The atmosphere in both cities was as if a pall had been placed over memory. And thus the shared mind of this nation has no roots, no continuous link with what keeps life in a pattern of meaning.

Lately I have come to believe that an as yet undiscovered human need and even a property of matter is the desire for revelation. The truth within us has a way of coming out despite all conscious efforts to conceal it. I have heard stories from those in the generation after the war, all speaking of the same struggle to ferret truth from the silence of their parents so that they themselves could begin to live. One born the year the war ended was never told a word about concentration camps, at home or in school. She began to wake in the early morning hours with nightmares which mirrored down to fine and accurate detail the conditions of the camps. Another woman searching casually through some trunks in the attic of her home found a series of pamphlets, virulently and cruelly anti-Semitic, which had been written by her grandfather, a high Nazi official. Still another pieced together the truth of her father's life, a member of the Gestapo, a man she remembered as playful by contrast to her stern mother. He died in the war. Only over time could she put certain pieces together. How he had had a man working under him beaten. And then, how he had beaten her.

Many of those who survived the holocaust could not bear the memories of what happened to them and, trying to bury the past, they too fell into silence. Others continue to speak as they are able. The manner of speech varies. At an artist's retreat in the Santa Cruz Mountains I met a woman who survived Bergen Belsen and Auschwitz. She inscribes the number eight in many of her paintings. And the number two. This is the story she is telling with those numbers. It was raining the night she arrived with her mother, six brothers and sisters at Auschwitz. It fell very hard, she told me. We were walking in the early evening up a hill brown in the California fall. The path was strewn with yellow leaves illuminated by the sun in its descent. They had endured the long trip from Hungary to Poland, without food or water. They were very tired. Now the sky seemed very black but the platform, lit up with stadium lights, was blinding after the darkness of the train. She would never, she told me, forget the shouting. It is as if she still cannot get the sound out of her ears. The Gestapo gave one shrill order after another, in a language she did not yet understand. They were herded in confusion, blows coming down on them randomly from the guards, past a tall man in a cape. This was Dr. Mengele. He made a single gesture toward all her family and continued it toward her but in a different direction. For days, weeks, months after she had learned what their fate had been she kept walking in the direction of their parting and beyond toward the vanishing point of her vision of them.

There were seven from her family who died there that night. The eighth to die was her father. He was sent to a different camp and died on the day of liberation. Only two lived, she and one brother. The story of one life cannot be told separately from the story of other lives. Who are we? The question is not simple. What we call the self is part of a larger matrix of relationship and society. Had we been born to a different family, in a different time, to a different world, we would not be the same. All the lives that surround us are in us.

· · ·

On the first day that I met Lenke she asked a question that stays with me still. Why do some inflict on others the suffering they have endured? What is it in a life that makes one choose to do this, or not? It is a question I cannot answer. Not even after several years pondering this question in the light of Heinrich Himmler's soul. Two years after my conversation with Lenke, as if there had been a very long pause in our dialogue, I was given a glimpse in the direction of an answer. Leo told me his story; it sounded back over time, offering not so much solution as response.

The nucleus of every cell in the human body contains the genetic plan for the whole organism.

We sat together in a large and noisy restaurant, light pouring through the windows, the present clamoring for our attention, even as we moved into the past. Leo was nine years old when the war entered his life. He remembers standing in a crowd, he told me, watching as a partisan was flogged and executed by the Germans. *What do you think I felt?* he asked me, the irony detectable in his voice. What he told me fell into his narration as part of a larger picture. The capture, the roughness, the laceration of flesh, the sight of death, all this excited him.

Violence was not new to him. Through bits and pieces surrounding the central line of his story I came to some idea of what his childhood must have been. His father was a cold man, given to rages over small errors. Leo was beaten often. Such attacks had already forced his older half brother out of the house. It was to this brother that Leo bonded and gave his love.

Leo remembered a party before the war. The room was lively with talk until his older brother arrived. Then a silence fell over everyone. The older men were afraid of this young man, even his father. And to Leo, his brother, with his air of power and command, was a hero. He could scarcely understand the roots of this power, moored in a political system of terror so effective, few even spoke of it. Leo's brother was a young member of Stalin's secret police. Cast into the streets while still a boy, he learned the arts of survival. Eventually he was arrested for assaulting and robbing a man. It was under this circumstance that he offered himself to the NKVD, the forerunner of the KGB, as an interrogator. He learned to torture men and women suspected of treason or of harboring secrets.

He wore high black leather boots and a black leather jacket, which impressed Leo. Leo followed him about, and they would take long walks together, his brother telling him the stories he could tell no one else. How he had tortured a woman. How he had made blood flow from the nipples of her breasts.

Everything he heard from his brother he took into himself. Such love as Leo had for his brother can be a forceful teacher. He did not see his brother often, nor was his intimacy with him great enough to create familiarity. What he had was a continual taste awakening hunger. Never did he know the daily presence of the beloved, or all his imperfections, the real person dwelling behind the mask of the ideal, the shiny and impervious leather. To fill the nearly perpetual absence of his brother he clung to this ideal. An appearance of strength. A certain arrogance in the face of violence, promising an even greater violence. Love always seeks a resting place.

I knew a similar attachment to my sister. Separated when I was six and she was thirteen, the experience of love I knew with her was longing, and over time this bonded me to longing itself. And to the books she brought me to read, the poems she read to me, worlds she pointed me toward.

And the German occupation of the Ukraine? The accident at Chernobyl had taken place just weeks before we met. But long before this event, the same land suffered other wounds. As the Soviet army retreated, they burned crops and killed livestock. Even before the German invasion, the land was charred and black for miles around. Then when the German army came, the executions began. And the deportations. Many were taken away to forced labor camps. Leo was among them.

His father was an agronomist with some knowledge of how to increase crop yields. The whole family was transported to Germany, but at the scientist's camp Leo was transported in another direction. His father watched him go, Leo told me, with no protest, not even the protestation of tears.

What was it like for him in the labor camp to which he was sent? His telling of the past existed in a framework of meaning he had built slowly over the years, and with great pain, forced to this understanding by events that he himself had brought into being, later in his life.

It is a question of passion, he told me. While he was in the camps, he began to worship the uniformed members of the SS and the SA, just as he had loved his brother. Their strength, their ideals, their willingness to do violence, to live for something beyond themselves, the black leather they wore, the way they were clean and polished and tall. He saw those who, like himself, were imprisoned as small and demeaned, caught in the ugliness of survival, lacking any heroism, cowardly, petty. Even now, as he looked back himself with another eye, his disdain for those who suffered persisted in a phantom form, in the timbre of his voice.

The punishment of the guards did not embitter him. In his mind he believed he himself was always justly punished. Once, against the rules, he stole food, honey, while he was working. He did not accept his own hunger as an argument for kindness. He admired the strength with which he was hit. Even the intimacy of the blows gave him a certain pride in himself. Loving the arms that hit him, he could think of this power as his own.

But there were two assaults which he could not forgive. They humiliated him. Now as I write I can see that to him his attackers must have been unworthy of his admiration. He was on a work detail in the neighboring village when a boy his own age slapped him. And later an old woman spat in his face.

This was all he told me of his time of imprisonment. After the liberation, he went into Germany to search for his family. Did he believe that perhaps, even now, something outside of the circle drawn by what he had suffered existed for him? Was there a seed of hope, a wish that made him, thin, weak, on shaking legs, travel the hundreds of miles, sleeping in trains and train stations, to search? He was exhausted, I can imagine, past that edge of weariness in which whatever is real ceases entirely to matter and existence itself is just a gesture, not aimed any longer at outcome, but just a simple expression of what remains and so can seem even brighter. He was making a kind of pilgrimage.

It is in this way, coldness beyond cold, frailty beyond endurance, that sorrow becomes a power. A light begins to shine past the fire of ovens, yet from them, as if stars, or turning leaves, falling and trapped in their fall, nevertheless kept their brilliance, and this brilliance a beacon, like a code, flashes out the precise language of human suffering. Then we know that what we suffer is not going to pass by without meaning.

Self-portrait, 1923. The artist's face is drawn of lines left white on the page which seem as if they were carved out of night. We are very close to her. It is only her face we see. Eye to eye, she looks directly at us. But her eyes are unfocused and weary with that kind of tiredness that has accumulated over so much time we think of it as aging. Her mouth, wide and frank, does not resist gravity any longer. This mouth smiles with an extraordinary subtlety. We can almost laugh with this mouth, drawn with lines which, like all the lines on the page, resemble scars, or tears in a fabric.

A story is told as much by silence as by speech. Like the white spaces in an etching, such silences render form. But unlike an etching in which the whole is grasped at once, the silence of a story must be understood over time. Leo described to me what his life was like after he found his parents, but he did not describe the moment, or even the day or week, when he found them. Only now as I write these words does the absence of joy in this reunion begin to speak to me. And in the space of this absence I can feel the kind of cold that can extinguish the most intense of fires.

Leo was soon streetwise. His family was near starvation. He worked the black market. Older men buying his goods would ask him for women, and he began to procure for them. He kept his family alive. His father, he told me, never acknowledged his effort. When they moved to America a few years later and Leo reminded him that his work had fed him, his father exclaimed, in a voice of shock and disparagement, *And what you did!*

In 1957, the Soviet Union develops the SS-6, a surface-to-surface missile. It is launched with thirty-two engines. Failing as a weapon, this device is used to launch the first satellite into space. In 1961, the Soviet Union develops the SS-7. These missiles carry nuclear warheads. They are launched from hardened silos to protect them from attack.

In America he was sent to high school. But he did not know how to be an ordinary boy among boys. He became a street fighter. Together with a group of boys among whom he was the toughest, he would look for something to happen. More than once they devised a trap for homosexual men. They would place the prettiest boy among them on a park bench and wait behind the trees and bushes. Usually a man would pull up in his car and go to sit on the bench next to the boy. When this man made any gesture of seduction, or suggested the boy leave with him, the boys would suddenly appear and, surrounding him, beat him and take his money.

I am thinking of these boys as one after another they forced the weight of their bodies into another man's body and tried to hurt him, to bloody him, to defeat him. I know it is possible to be a stranger to one's feelings. For the years after I was separated from my mother, I forgot that I missed her. My feeling was driven so deep, it was imperceptible, so much a part of me, I would not have called it grief. It is said that when boys or young men attack a man they find effeminate or believe to be homosexual they are trying to put at a distance all traces of homosexuality in themselves. But what does this mean? What is the central passion in this issue of manhood, proven or disproven? In my imagination I witness again the scene that Leo described to me. It is a passionate scene, edged by a love the boys feel for each other, and by something more, by a kind of grief, raging because it is buried so deep inside. Do they rage against this man's body because of what has been withheld from them, held back, like the food of intimacy, imprisoned and guarded in the bodies of older men, in the bodies of fathers? Is it this rage that fires the mettle of what we call manhood?

Yet, are we not all affected by this that is withheld in men? Are we not all forged in the same inferno? It was never said directly, but I know my great-grandfather beat my grandfather, and lectured him, drunkenly, humiliating and shaming him. I am told that as adults they quarreled violently over politics. No one in my family can remember the substance of the disagreement, only the red faces, the angry voices. Now, as I look back to imagine my grandfather passionately reciting the list of those he hated, our black neighbors, the Jews, the Communists, I follow the path of his staring eyes and begin to make out a figure. It is my great-grandfather Colvin, receiving even after his death too indifferently the ardent and raging pleas of his son. And hearing that voice again, I hear an echo from my grandfather's daughter, my mother, whose voice when she had been drinking too much had the same quality, as of the anguish of feeling held back for so long it has become monstrous, the furies inside her unleashed against me.

Leo's telling had a slightly bitter edge, a style which felt like the remnant of an older harshness. He kept looking at me as if to protect himself from any sign of shock in my face. Now he was not certain he would tell me the rest of his story. But he did.

Just after he graduated from high school, the Korean War began. He was drafted, and sent directly to Korea. Was he in combat? Leo shook his head. He was assigned to an intelligence unit. He spoke Russian. And he was directed to interrogate Russian prisoners who were captured behind enemy lines. He told me this story. He was given two men to question. With the first man he made every kind of threat. But he carried nothing out. The man was resolutely silent. And Leo learned nothing from him. He left the room with all his secrets. *You can never*, Leo told me later, *let any man get the better of you*. With the second man he was determined not to fail. He would get him to tell whatever he knew. He made the same threats again, and again met silence. Then, suddenly, using his thumb and finger, he put out the man's eye. And as the man was screaming and bleeding, he told him he would die one way or the other. He was going to be shot. But he had the choice now of seeing his executioners or not, of dying in agony or not. And then the man told him his secrets.

Self-portrait, 1927. She has drawn herself in charcoal again, and in profile. And she still looks out but now her eyes are focused. She is looking at something visible, distant, but perhaps coming slowly closer. Her mouth still turns down, and this must be a characteristic expression because her face is lined in that direction. The form of her face is drawn with soft strokes, blended into the page, as one life blends into another life, or a body into earth. There is something in the quality of her attention, fine lines sketched over her eyebrow. A deeper black circle under her eye. With a resolute, unhappy awareness, she recognizes what is before her.

The life plan of the body is encoded in the DNA molecule, a substance that has the ability to hold information and to replicate itself.

Self-portrait, 1934. As I look now I see in her face that whatever it was she saw before has now arrived. She looks directly at us again and we are even closer to her than before. One finger at the edge of the frame pulls against her eyebrow, against lines drawn there earlier, as if to relieve pain. All the lines lead downward, like rain. Her eyes are open but black, at once impenetrable and infinite. There is a weariness here again, the kind from which one never recovers. And grief? It is that grief I have spoken of earlier, no longer apart from the flesh and bone of her face.

After many years of silence, my mother and I were able to speak of what happened between us and in our family. It was healing for us, to hear and speak the truth, and made for a closeness we had not felt before. Both of us knew we were going to speak before we did.

Before a secret is told one can often feel the weight of it in the atmosphere. Leo gazed at me for a long moment. There was more he wanted to tell me and that I wanted to hear. The rest of his story was elsewhere, in the air, in our hands, the traffic on the street, felt. He shook his head again before he began. The war was over, but he had started in a certain direction and now he could not stop. He befriended a young man from the army. This man looked up to him the way he had to his brother. He wanted to teach the younger man what he knew. He had already committed several robberies, and he wanted an accomplice. They went out together, looking for an easy target for the young man to practice on. They found someone who was easy. He was old, and black. Leo showed his friend how to hold his gun, up close to the temple, pointing down. The boy did this. But the old man, terrified, simply ran. As Leo directed him, the younger man held the gun out in front of him to shoot and he pulled the trigger. But the cartridge of the bullet stuck in the chamber. So the man, still alive, kept running. Then, as Leo urged him on, his friend ran after the old man and, jumping on his back, began to hit him on the head with the butt of his pistol. The moment overtook him. Fear, and exhilaration at mastering fear, a deeper rage, all made a fuel for his fury. He hit and hit again and again. He drew blood. Then the man ceased to cry out, ceased to struggle. He lay still. And the younger man kept on hitting, so that the moment of the older man's death was lost in a frenzy of blows. Then finally there was silence. The young man, knowing he had caused a death, stood up shaking and walked away. He was stunned, as if he himself had been beaten. And Leo, who had been calling and shouting to encourage his friend, who had been laughing, he said, so hard he had to hold himself, was silent too. He went to stand by the body of the old man. Blood poured profusely from the wounds on his head. He stared into the face of this dead man. And now in his telling of the story he was crying. He paused. What was it there in that face for him, broken, afraid, shattered, flesh and bone past repair, past any effort, any strength? *I could see,* he told me, *that this man was just like me.*

In 1963 America develops a new missile, the Titan II. It has a larger range, a larger carrying capacity, a new guidance system, and an improved vehicle for re-entry. These missiles are still being deployed.

1938. *Self-portrait.* The artist is once again in profile. But now she faces another direction. The bones of her cheeks, mouth, nose, eyes are still all in shadow. Her eyebrows arch in tired anticipation. She has drawn herself with the simplest of strokes. Charcoal blending softly downward, all the strokes moving downward. This is old age. Not a single line drawn for vanity, or for the sake of pretense, protects us from her age. She is facing toward death.

We knew, both Leo and I, that now he was telling me what was most crucial to him. In the telling, some subtle change passed through him. Something unknown was taking shape here, both of us witnesses, both of us part of the event. This that he lived through was what I was seeking to understand. What he saw in the face of the dead man did not leave him. For a long time he was afraid of his own dreams. Every night, the same images returned to him, but images in motion, belonging to a longer narration. He dreamed that he entered a park and began to dig up a grave there. Each night he would plunge his hands in the earth and find the body buried there. But each night the body he found was more and more eroded. This erosion filled him with horror. He could not sleep alone. Every night he would find a different woman to sleep with him. Every night he would drink himself into insensibility. But the images of dreams began to come to him even in his waking hours. And so he began to drink ceaselessly. Finally he could not go on as before. Two months after the death he had witnessed he confessed his part in it.

For many reasons his sentence was light. Both he and his friend were young. They had been soldiers. He knew that, had the man he helped to kill not been black, his sentence would have been longer; or he may himself have been put to death. He said nothing of his years of imprisonment. Except that these years served to quiet the dreams that had haunted him. His wit, his air of toughness, all he had seen make him good at the work he does now with boys who have come into conflict with society, a work which must in some way be intended as restitution.

Yet, as he spoke, I began to see that he believed some part of his soul would never be retrieved. *There is a circle of humanity*, he told me, *and I can feel its warmth. But I am forever outside.*

I made no attempt to soften these words. What he said was true. A silence between us held what had been spoken. Then gradually we began to make small movements. Hands reaching for a key, a cigarette. By a quiet agreement, his story was over, and we were in the present again.

The telling and the hearing of a story is not a simple act. The one who tells must reach down into deeper layers of the self, reviving old feelings, reviewing the past. Whatever is retrieved is reworked into a new form, one that narrates events and gives the listener a path through these events that leads to some fragment of wisdom. The one who hears takes the story in, even to a place not visible or conscious to the mind, yet there. In this inner place a story from another life suffers a subtle change. As it enters the memory of the listener it is augmented by reflection, by other memories, and even the body hearing and responding in the moment of the telling. By such transmissions, consciousness is woven.

Over a year has passed now since I heard Leo's story. In my mind's eye, I see the events of his life as if they were carved out in woodblock prints, like the ones Käthe Kollwitz did. Of all her work, these most resemble Expressionist art. Was it intended that the form be so heavy, as if drawn centuries back into a mute untold history? Her work, and the work of the Expressionist movement, was called degenerate by the Nazis. These images, images of tumultuous inner feelings, or of suffering caused and hidden by social circumstance, were removed from the walls of museums and galleries.

When I was in Munich, a German friend told me that her generation has been deprived of German culture. What existed before the Third Reich was used in Nazi propaganda, and so has become as if dyed with the stain of that history. The artists and writers of the early twentieth century were silenced; they went into exile or perished. The link with the past was broken. Yet, even unremembered, the past never disappears. It exists still and continues under a mantle of silence, invisibly shaping lives.

The DNA molecule is made of long, fine, paired strands. These strands are helically coiled.

What is buried in the past of one generation falls to the next to claim. The children of Nazis and survivors alike have inherited a struggle between silence and speech.

The night I met Hélène at a Métro station in Paris I was returning from dinner with a friend. Ten years older than I, Jewish, French, in 1942, the year before my own birth, Natalie's life was put in danger. She was given false papers and shepherded with other children out of Paris through an underground movement. She lived out the duration of war in the countryside in the home of an ambassador who had diplomatic immunity. A woman who has remained one of her closest friends to this day was with her in this hiding place. The night we had dinner Natalie told me a story about her. This friend, she said, grew up determined to shed her past. She made Natalie promise never to reveal who she was or what had happened to her. She changed her name, denied that she was Jewish, and raised her children as gentiles. Then, opening her hands in a characteristic gesture, Natalie smiled at me. The story was to take a gently ironic turn. The past was to return. This summer, she told me, she had held one end of a bridal canopy, what in a Jewish wedding is called a chuppa, at the wedding of her friend's daughter. This girl was marrying the son of an Orthodox rabbi. And her son too, knowing nothing of his mother's past, had gravitated toward Judaism.

In 1975 the SS-19 missile is deployed in the Soviet Union. It carries several warheads, each with a different target. A computer within it controls and detects deviations from its programmed course.

One can find traces of every life in each life. There is a story from my own family history that urges its way onto the page here. Sometime in the eighteenth century three brothers migrated from Scotland to the United States. They came from Aberdeen and bore the name Marks, a name common in that city to Jewish families who had immigrated from Germany to escape the pogroms. Jacob Marks, who descended from these brothers, was my great-great-grandfather. The family story was that he was descended from Huguenots. In our family, only my sister and I speak of the possibility that he could have been Jewish. Jacob married Rosa and they gave birth to a daughter whom they named Sarah. She married Thomas Colvin, and their last son was Ernest Marks Colvin, my grandfather, the same grandfather who would recite to me his furious list of those he hated, including Jews.

Who would my grandfather, I wonder now, have been if he had known his own history. Could he then have seen the shape of his life as part of a larger configuration? Wasn't he without this knowledge like the missile, or the neutron torn away from gravity, the matrix that sustains and makes sense of experience?

In any given cell only a small fraction of the genes are active. Messages to awaken these genes are transmitted by the surrounding cytoplasm, messages from other cells, or from outside substances.

I cannot say for certain what our family history was. I know only that I did gravitate myself toward what seemed missing or lost in me. In my first years of high school I lived alone with my father. He was often gone, at work or staying with his girlfriend. I adopted the family of a school friend, spending hours with them, baby-sitting their younger children, helping with household tasks, sharing meals, spending an evening speaking of art or politics. Then one evening, as I returned home, I saw a strange man standing near my door. He had come to tell me my father was dead, struck by an automobile while he was crossing the street in the light of dusk. I turned for solace and finally shelter to my adopted family. In the short time we lived together, out of my love for them, I took on their gestures, the manner and rhythm of their thought, ways of cooking, cadences, a sprinkling of Yiddish vocabulary. I became in some ways Jewish.

In the late seventies the United States develops a circuitry for the Minuteman rocket which allows for a target to be changed in the midst of flight.

Is there any one of us who can count ourselves outside the circle circumscribed by our common past? Whether or not I was trying to reweave threads severed from my family history, a shared heritage of despair and hope, of destruction and sustenance, was within me. What I received from my adopted family helped me to continue my life. My suffering had been placed, even wordlessly, in a larger stream of suffering, and as if wrapped and held by a culture that had grown up to meet suffering, to retell the tales and place them in a larger context by which all life continues.

L'chayim. Life. Held to even at the worst times. The dream of a better world. The schoolbook, tattered, pages flying loose, gripped in the hands of a young student, his coat open at the shoulder and along the front where the fabric was worn. The ghetto of Slonim. 1938. The Passover cup, fashioned secretly by inmates at Terezin, the Passover plate, the menorah, made at the risk of death from purloined materials. Pictures drawn by those who were there. Despair, the attrition of pain, daily cold, hunger somehow entering the mark of pencil or brush. Butterflies painted by children who all later perished. Stitches made across Lenke's drawings, reminding us of the stitches she sustained in one operation after another, after her liberation, when she was stricken with tuberculosis of the spine. The prisoner forced to pick up discarded clothing of those sent to the gas chambers, who said that among this clothing, as he gathered it, he saw *Stars of David like a drift of yellow flowers.*

As the fertilized egg cell starts to divide, all the daughter cells have identical DNA, but the cells soon cease to look alike, and in a few weeks, a number of different kinds of cells can be recognized in the embryo.

I am thinking again of a child's body. Curled and small. Innocent. The skin soft like velvet to the touch. Eyes open and staring without reserve or calculation, quite simply, into the eyes of whoever appears in this field of vision. Without secrets. Arms open, ready to receive or give, just in the transpiration of flesh, sharing the sound of the heartbeat, the breath, the warmth of body on body.

In 1977 the Soviet Union puts the SS-NX-17 and SS N-18 into service. These are ballistic missiles to be launched from submarines. In 1978 the United States perfects the underwater launch system of the Tomahawk missile.

I could not, in the end, for some blessed reason, turn away from myself. Not at least in this place. The place of desire. I think now of the small lines etching themselves near the eyes of a woman's face I loved. And how, seeing these lines, I wanted to stroke her face. To lean myself, my body, my skin into her. A part of me unravels as I think of this, and I am taken toward longing, and beyond, into another region, past the walls of this house, or all I can see, stretching farther than the horizon where right now sea and sky blend. It is as if my cells are moving in a larger wave, a wave that takes in every history, every story.

At the end of nine months a multitude of different cells make up the newborn infant's body, including nerve cells, muscle cells, skin cells, retinal cells, liver cells, brain cells, cells of the heart that beats, cells of the mouth that opens, cells of the throat that cries . . .

When I think of that young man now, who died in the river near the island of my father's birth, died because he loved another man, I like to imagine his body bathed in the pleasure of that love. To believe that the hands that touched this young man's thighs, his buttocks, his penis, the mouth that felt its way over his body, the man who lay himself between his legs, or over, around his body did this lovingly, and that then the young man felt inside his flesh what radiated from his childlike beauty. Part angel. Bathed in a passionate sweetness. Tasting life at its youngest, most original center, the place of reason, where one is whole again as at birth.

In the last decade the Soviet Union improves its antiballistic missiles to make them maneuverable and capable of hovering in midair. The United States continues to develop and test the MX missile, with advanced inertial guidance, capable of delivering ten prearmed electronically guided warheads, each with maneuverability, possessing the power and accuracy to penetrate hardened silos. And the Soviet Union begins to design a series of smaller one-warhead mobile missiles, the SS-25, to be driven around by truck, and the SS-X-24, to be drawn on railroad tracks. And the United States develops a new warhead for the Trident missile carrying fourteen smaller warheads that can be released in a barrage along a track or a road.

A train is making its way through Germany. All along its route those who are in the cars can look out and see those who are outside the cars. And those who are outside can see those who are inside. Sometimes words are exchanged. Sometimes there is a plea for water. And sometimes, at the risk of life, water is given. Sometimes names are called out, or curses are spoken, under the breath. And sometimes there is only silence.

Who are those on the inside and where are they going? There are rumors. It is best not to ask. There are potatoes to buy with the last of the rations. There is a pot boiling on the stove. And, at any rate, the train has gone; the people have vanished. You did not know them. You will not see them again. Except perhaps in your dreams. But what do those images mean? Images of strangers. Agony that is not yours. A face that does not belong to you. And so in the daylight you try to erase what you have encountered and to forget those tracks that are laid even as if someplace in your body, even as part of yourself.

•   •   •   •   •   •   •   •   •   •   •

QUESTIONS FOR A SECOND READING

1. One of the challenges a reader faces with Griffin's text is knowing what to make of it. It's a long piece, but the reading is not difficult. The sections are short and straightforward. While the essay is made up of fragments, the arrangement is not deeply confusing or disorienting. Still, the piece has no single controlling idea; it does not move from thesis to conclusion. One way of reading the essay is to see what one can make of it, what it might add up to. In this sense, the work of reading is to find an idea, passage, image, or metaphor—something in the text—and use this to organize the essay.

   As you prepare to work back through the text, think about the point of reference you could use to organize your reading. Is the essay "about"

Himmler? secrets? fascism? art? Germany? the United States? families and child-rearing? gay and lesbian sexuality? Can one of the brief sections be taken as a key to the text? What about the italicized sections—how are they to be used?

You should not assume that one of these is the right way to read. Assume, rather, that one way of working with the text is to organize it around a single point of reference, something you could say that Griffin "put there" for you to notice and to use.

Or you might want to do this in your name rather than Griffin's. That is, you might, as you reread, chart the connections *you* make, connections that you feel belong to you (to your past, your interests, your way of reading), and think about where and how you are drawn into the text (and with what you take to be Griffin's interests and desires). You might want to be prepared to talk about why you sum things up the way you do.

2. Although this is not the kind of prose you would expect to find in a textbook for a history course, and although the project is not what we usually think of as a "research" project, Griffin is a careful researcher. The project is serious and deliberate; it is "about" history, both family history and world history. Griffin knows what she is doing. So what *is* Griffin's project? As you reread, look to those sections where Griffin seems to be speaking to her readers about her work—about how she reads and how she writes, about how she gathers her materials and how she studies them. What is she doing? What is at stake in adopting such methods? How and why might you teach someone to do this work?

ASSIGNMENTS FOR WRITING

1. Griffin's text gathers together related fragments and works on them, but does so without yoking examples to a single, predetermined argument or thesis. In this sense, it is a kind of antiessay. One of the difficulties readers of this text face is in its retelling. If someone says to you, "Well, what was it about?" the answer is not easy or obvious. The text is so far-reaching, so carefully composed of interrelated stories and reflections, and so suggestive in its implications and in the connections it enables that it is difficult to summarize without violence, without seriously reducing the text.

   But, imagine that somebody asks, "Well, what was it about?" Write an essay in which you present your reading of "Our Secret." You want to give your reader a sense of what the text is like (or what it is like to read the text), and you want to make clear that the account you are giving is your reading, your way of working it through. You might, in fact, want to suggest what you leave out or put to the side. (The first "Question for a Second Reading" might help you prepare for this.)

2. Griffin argues that we—all of us, especially all of us who read her essay— are part of a complex web of connections. At one point she says,

   > Who are we? The question is not simple. What we call the self is part of
   > a larger matrix of relationship and society. Had we been born to a differ-
   > ent family, in a different time, to a different world, we would not be the
   > same. All the lives that surround us are in us. (p. 335)

At another point she asks, "Is there any one of us who can count ourselves outside the circle circumscribed by our common past?" She speaks of a "field,"

> like a field of gravity that is created by the movements of many bodies. Each life is influenced and it in turn becomes an influence. Whatever is a cause is also an effect. Childhood experience is just one element in the determining field. (p. 304)

One way of thinking about this concept of the self (and of interrelatedness), at least under Griffin's guidance, is to work on the connections that she implies and asserts. As you reread the selection, look for powerful and surprising juxtapositions, fragments that stand together in interesting and suggestive ways. Think about the arguments represented by the blank space between those sections. (And look for Griffin's written statements about "relatedness.") Look for connections that seem important to the text (and to you) and representative of Griffin's thinking (and yours). Then, write an essay in which you use these examples to think through your understanding of Griffin's claims for this "larger matrix," the "determining field," or our "common past."

3. It is useful to think of Griffin's prose as experimental. She is trying to do something that she can't do in the "usual" essay form. She wants to make a different kind of argument or engage her reader in a different manner. And so she mixes personal and academic writing. She assembles fragments and puts seemingly unrelated material into surprising and suggestive relationships. She breaks the "plane" of the page with italicized intersections. She organizes her material, but not in the usual mode of thesis-example-conclusion. The arrangement is not nearly so linear. At one point, when she seems to be prepared to argue that German childrearing practices produced the Holocaust, she quickly says:

> Of course there cannot be one answer to such a monumental riddle, nor does any event in history have a single cause. Rather a field exists, like a field of gravity that is created by the movements of many bodies. Each life is influenced and it in turn becomes an influence. Whatever is a cause is also an effect. Childhood experience is just one element in the determining field. (p. 304)

Her prose serves to create a "field," one where many bodies are set in relationship.

It is useful, then, to think about Griffin's prose as the enactment of a method, as a way of doing a certain kind of intellectual work. One way to study this, to feel its effects, is to imitate it, to take it as a model. For this assignment, write a Griffin-like essay, one similar in its methods of organization and argument. You will need to think about the stories you might tell, about the stories and texts you might gather (stories and texts not your own). As you write, you will want to think carefully about arrangement and about commentary (about where, that is, you will speak to your reader *as* the writer of the piece). You should not feel bound to Griffin's subject matter, but you should feel that you are working in her spirit.

MAKING CONNECTIONS

1. Is it surprising that prisons resemble factories, schools, barracks, hospitals, which all resemble prisons? (p. 236)

—MICHEL FOUCAULT
Panopticism

The child, Dr. Schreber advised, *should be permeated by the impossibility of locking something in his heart.* . . . That this philosophy was taught in school gives me an interior view of the catastrophe to follow. It adds a certain dimension to my image of these events to know that a nation of citizens learned that no part of themselves could be safe from the scrutiny of authority, nothing locked in the heart, and at the same time to discover that the head of the secret police of this nation was the son of a schoolmaster. It was this man, after all, Heinrich Himmler, Reichsführer SS, who was later to say, speaking of the mass arrests of Jews, *Protective custody is an act of care.* (p. 306)

—SUSAN GRIFFIN
Our Secret

Both Griffin and Foucault write about the "fabrication" of human life and desire within the operations of history and of specific social institutions—the family, the school, the military, the factory, the hospital. Both are concerned with the relationship between forces that are hidden, secret, and those that are obvious, exposed. Both write with an urgent concern for the history of the present, for the ways our current condition is tied to history, politics, and culture.

And yet these are very different pieces to read. They are written differently—that is, they differently invite a reader's participation and understanding. They take different examples from history. They offer different accounts of the technologies of order and control. It can even be said that they do their work differently and that they work toward different ends.

Write an essay in which you use one of the essays to explain and to investigate the other—where you use Griffin as a way of thinking about Foucault or Foucault as a way of thinking about Griffin. "To explain," "to investigate"—perhaps you would prefer to think of this encounter as a dialogue or a conversation, a way of bringing the two texts together. You should imagine that your readers are familiar with both texts, but have not yet thought of the two together. You should imagine that your readers do not have the texts in front of them, that you will need to do the work of presentation and summary.

2. Both Gloria Anzaldúa in the two chapters reprinted here from her book *Borderlands/La frontera* (p. 42) and Susan Griffin in "Our Secret" write mixed texts, or what might be called "montages." Neither of their pieces proceeds as simply a story or an essay, although both have elements of fiction and nonfiction in them (and, in Anzaldúa's case, poetry). They both can be said to be making arguments and to be telling stories. Anzaldúa, in her chapters, is directly concerned with matters of identity and the ways identity is represented through sexuality, religion, and culture. Griffin is concerned with the "self" as "part of a larger matrix of relationship and society."

Write an essay in which you present and explain Anzaldúa's and Griffin's key arguments about the relation of identity, history, culture, and society. What terms and examples do they provide? What arguments or concerns? What different positions do they take? And what about their writing styles? How might their concerns be reflected in the ways they write?

3. Adrienne Rich, in "When We Dead Awaken: Writing as Re-Vision" (p. 520), and John Edgar Wideman, in "Our Time" (p. 681), use personal history to think about and to represent forces beyond the individual that shape human life and possibility—patriarchy, national history, and race. Susan Griffin is engaged in a similar project; she explains her motives this way, "One can find traces of every life in each life."

Perhaps. It is a bold step to think that this is true and to believe that one can, or should, write the family into the national or international narrative. Write an essay in which you read "Our Secret" alongside one of these other selections. Your goal is not only to discuss how these writers do what they do, and to what conclusions and to what ends, but also to discuss your sense of what is at stake in each project. How does a skilled writer handle such a project? What are the technical issues? What would lead a writer to write like this? Would you do the same? where and how? for whose benefit?

4. Like Alice Walker, Susan Griffin is concerned with understanding, promoting, and preserving her relationship to the past, a past that is both her family's past and part of twentieth-century history. Write an essay in which you present both projects: Walker's in "In Search of Our Mothers' Gardens" (p. 668) and Susan Griffin's in "Our Secret." You should assume that your readers are familiar with neither. You will need, then, to carefully present the arguments of the essays but also a sense of how they are written, of how they do their work. How do they justify looking backward? What is the most productive relationship of present to past? What examples can you bring to the discussion—that is, as you look to the culture of your own moment (to movies and television, music, art, advertising, literature), what are the interesting or significant examples of the use of the past? How might you bring them into a discussion of Walker and Griffin? How might you speak for your generation and its use of the past?

5. Like Griffin, W. G. Sebald in "The Rings of Saturn" (p. 613) puts history and research in an unconventional relationship to the "person" one finds in a personal essay. Both are researchers, both are well-read and thoughtful, both are interested in the events of the past and in the work of writers and artists. Neither, however, writes the kind of prose you find in a textbook; neither writes the kind of prose conventionally held up as a model for academic writing. Write an essay in which you present and compare the "projects" represented in the writing of Sebald and Griffin. How might you explain (even defend) their work as a model for the classroom? You will need to be sure to work closely with examples—including examples of the kinds of classrooms you know and that you hope to know.

HARRIET
JACOBS

HARRIET JACOBS *was born in North Carolina in or around 1815. The selection that follows reproduces the opening chapters of her autobiography,* Incidents in the Life of a Slave Girl, *and tells the story of her life from childhood to early adulthood, through the birth of her first child. In these chapters Jacobs describes how she came to understand her identity as men's property—as a slave and as a woman—as that identity was determined by her particular situation (her appearance, her education, the psychology of her owner, the values of her family) and by the codes governing slavery in the South.*

In the remaining chapters of her book, Jacobs tells of the birth of a second child, of her escape from her owner, Dr. Flint, and of seven years spent hiding in a crawl space under the roof of her grandmother's house. The father of her children, Mr. Sands, did not, as she thought he might, purchase and free her, although he eventually did purchase her children and allow them to live with her grandmother. He did not free the children, and they never bore his name.

Around 1842 Jacobs fled to New York, where she made contact with her children and found work as a nursemaid in the family of Nathaniel P. Willis, a magazine

*editor who with his wife helped hide Jacobs from southern slaveholders and eventu-
ally purchased Jacobs and her children and gave them their freedom.*

This is the end of Jacobs's story as it is reported in Incidents. *Recent research,
however, enables us to tell the story of the production of this autobiography, the
text that represents its author's early life. Through her contact with the Willises,
Jacobs met both black and white abolitionists and became active in the antislavery
movement. She told her story to Amy Post, a feminist and abolitionist, and Post
encouraged her to record it, which she did by writing in the evenings between 1853
and 1858. After unsuccessfully seeking publication in England, and with the help
of the white abolitionist writer L. Maria Child, who read the manuscript and
served as an editor (by rearranging sections and suggesting that certain incidents
be expanded into chapters), Jacobs published* Incidents in Boston *in 1861 under
the pseudonym "Linda Brent," along with Child's introduction, which is also reproduced here. During the Civil War, Jacobs left the Willises to be a nurse for black
troops. She remained active, working with freed slaves for the next thirty years,
and died in Washington, D.C., in 1897.*

*For years scholars questioned the authenticity of this autobiography, arguing
that it seemed too skillful to have been written by a slave, and that more likely it
had been written by white abolitionists as propaganda for their cause. The recent
discovery, however, of a cache of letters and the research of Jean Fagan Yellin have
established Jacobs's authorship and demonstrated that Child made only minor
changes and assisted primarily by helping Jacobs find a publisher and an audience.*

*Still, the issue of authorship remains a complicated one, even if we can be con-
fident that the writing belongs to Jacobs and records her struggles and achievements. The issue of authorship becomes complicated if we think of the dilemma facing Jacobs as a writer, telling a story that defied description to an audience who
could never completely understand. There is, finally, a precarious relationship between the story of a slave's life, the story Jacobs had to tell, and the stories available
to her and to her readers as models — stories of privileged, white, middle-class life:
conventional narratives of family and childhood, love and marriage.*

*Houston Baker, one of our leading scholars of black culture, has described the
situation of the slave narrator this way:*

> *But the slave narrator must also accomplish the almost unthinkable
> (since thought and language are inseparable) task of transmuting an
> authentic, unwritten self — a self that exists outside the conventional
> literary discourse structures of a white reading public — into a literary
> representation. . . . The voice of the unwritten self, once it is subjected to
> the linguistic codes, literary conventions, and audience expectations of
> a literate population, is perhaps never again the authentic voice of
> black American slavery. It is, rather, the voice of a self transformed by
> an autobiographical act into a sharer in the general public discourse
> about slavery.*

The author of Incidents *could be said to stand outside "the general public
discourse," both because she was a slave and because she was a woman. The story
she has to tell does not fit easily into the usual stories of courtship and marriage or*

the dominant attitudes toward sexuality and female "virtue." When you read Jacobs's concerns about her "competence," about her status as a woman or as a writer, concerns that seem strange in the face of this powerful text; when you hear her addressing her readers, sometimes instructing them, sometimes apologizing, trying to bridge the gap between her experience and theirs, you should think not only of the trials she faced as a woman and a mother but also of her work as a writer. Here, too, she is struggling to take possession of her life.

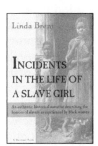

Incidents in the Life of a Slave Girl

Written by Herself

Northerners know nothing at all about Slavery. They think it is perpetual bondage only. They have no conception of the depth of *degradation* involved in that word, SLAVERY; if they had, they would never cease their efforts until so horrible a system was overthrown.

— A WOMAN OF NORTH CAROLINA

Rise up, ye women that are at ease! Hear my voice, ye careless daughters! Give ear unto my speech.

—Isaiah xxxii.9

Preface

Linda Brent

Reader, be assured this narrative is no fiction. I am aware that some of my adventures may seem incredible; but they are, nevertheless, strictly true. I have not exaggerated the wrongs inflicted by Slavery; on the contrary, my descriptions fall far short of the facts. I have concealed the names of places, and given persons fictitious names. I had no motive for secrecy on my own account, but I deemed it kind and considerate towards others to pursue this course.

I wish I were more competent to the task I have undertaken. But I trust my readers will excuse deficiencies in consideration of circumstances. I was born and reared in Slavery; and I remained in a Slave State twenty-seven years. Since I have been at the North, it has been necessary for me to work diligently for my own support, and the education of my children. This has not left me much leisure to make up for the loss of early opportunities to improve myself; and it has compelled me to write these pages at irregular intervals, whenever I could snatch an hour from household duties.

When I first arrived in Philadelphia, Bishop Paine advised me to publish a sketch of my life, but I told him I was altogether incompetent to such an undertaking. Though I have improved my mind somewhat since that time, I still remain of the same opinion; but I trust my motives will excuse what might otherwise seem presumptuous. I have not written my experiences in order to attract attention to myself; on the contrary, it would have been more pleasant to me to have been silent about my own history. Neither do I care to excite sympathy for my own sufferings. But I do earnestly desire to arouse the women of the North to a realizing sense of the condition of two millions of women at the South, still in bondage, suffering what I suffered, and most of them far worse. I want to add my testimony to that of abler pens to convince the people of the Free States what Slavery really is. Only by experience can any one realize how deep, and dark, and foul is that pit of abominations. May the blessing of God rest on this imperfect effort in behalf of my persecuted people!

Introduction

L. Maria Child

The author of the following autobiography is personally known to me, and her conversation and manners inspire me with confidence. During the last seventeen years, she has lived the greater part of the time with a distinguished family in New York, and has so deported herself as to be highly esteemed by them. This fact is sufficient, without further credentials of her character. I believe those who know her will not be disposed to doubt her veracity, though some incidents in her story are more romantic than fiction.

At her request, I have revised her manuscript; but such changes as I have made have been mainly for purposes of condensation and orderly arrangement. I have not added any thing to the incidents, or changed the import of her very pertinent remarks. With trifling exceptions, both the ideas and the language are her own. I pruned excrescences a little, but otherwise I had no reason for changing her lively and dramatic way of telling her own story. The names of both persons and places are known to me; but for good reasons I suppress them.

It will naturally excite surprise that a woman reared in Slavery should be able to write so well. But circumstances will explain this. In the first place, nature endowed her with quick perceptions. Secondly, the mistress, with whom she lived till she was twelve years old, was a kind, considerate friend, who taught her to read and spell. Thirdly, she was placed in favorable circumstances after she came to the North; having frequent intercourse with intelligent persons, who felt a friendly interest in her welfare, and were disposed to give her opportunities for self-improvement.

I am well aware that many will accuse me of indecorum for presenting these pages to the public; for the experiences of this intelligent and much-injured woman belong to a class which some call delicate subjects, and others indelicate. This peculiar phase of Slavery has generally been kept veiled; but the public ought to be made acquainted with its monstrous features, and I willingly take the responsibility of presenting them with the veil withdrawn. I do this for the sake of my sisters in bondage, who are suffering wrongs so foul, that our ears are too delicate to listen to them. I do it with the hope of arousing conscientious and reflecting women at the North to a sense of their duty in the exertion of moral influence on the question of Slavery, on all possible occasions. I do it with the hope that every man who reads this narrative will swear solemnly before God that, so far as he has power to prevent it, no fugitive from Slavery shall ever be sent back to suffer in that loathsome den of corruption and cruelty.

Incidents in the Life of a Slave Girl,
Seven Years Concealed

I. Childhood

I was born a slave; but I never knew it till six years of happy childhood had passed away. My father was a carpenter, and considered so intelligent and skilful in his trade, that, when buildings out of the common line were to be erected, he was sent for from long distances, to be head workman. On condition of paying his mistress two hundred dollars a year, and supporting himself, he was allowed to work at his trade, and manage his own affairs. His strongest wish was to purchase his children; but, though he several times offered his hard earnings for that purpose, he never succeeded. In complexion my parents were a light shade of brownish yellow, and were termed mulattoes. They lived together in a comfortable home; and, though we were all slaves, I was so fondly shielded that I never dreamed I was a piece of merchandise, trusted to them for safe keeping, and liable to be demanded of them at any moment. I had one brother, William, who was two years younger than myself—a bright, affectionate child. I had also a great treasure in my maternal grandmother, who was a remarkable woman in many respects. She was the daughter of a planter in South Carolina, who, at his death, left her mother and his three children free, with money to go to St. Augustine, where they had relatives. It was during the Revolutionary War; and they were captured on their passage, carried back, and sold to different purchasers. Such was the story my grandmother used to tell me; but I do not remember all the particulars. She was a little girl when she was captured and sold to the keeper of a large hotel. I have often heard her tell how hard she fared during childhood. But as she grew older she evinced so much intelligence, and was so faithful, that her master and mistress could not help seeing it was for their interest to take care of such a valuable piece of property. She became an indispensable personage in the household, officiating in all capacities, from cook and wet nurse to seamstress. She was much praised for her cooking; and her nice crackers became so famous in the neighborhood that many people were desirous of obtaining them. In consequence of numerous requests of this kind, she asked permission of her mistress to bake crackers at night, after all the household work was done; and she obtained leave to do it, provided she would clothe herself and her children from the profits. Upon these terms, after working hard all day for her mistress, she began her midnight bakings, assisted by her two oldest children. The business proved profitable; and each year she laid by a little, which was saved for a fund to purchase her children. Her master died, and the property was divided among his heirs. The widow had her dower in the hotel, which she continued to keep open. My grandmother remained in her service as a slave; but her children were divided among her master's children. As she had five, Benjamin, the youngest one, was sold, in order that each heir might have an equal portion of dollars and cents. There was so little difference in our ages that he seemed more like my brother than my uncle. He was a bright, handsome lad, nearly white; for he inherited the complexion my grandmother had derived from Anglo-Saxon ancestors. Though only ten years old, seven hundred and twenty dollars were paid for him. His sale was a terrible blow to my grandmother; but she was naturally hopeful, and she went to work with renewed energy, trusting in time to be able to purchase some of her children. She had laid up three hundred dollars, which her mistress one day begged as a loan, promising to pay her soon. The reader probably knows that no promise or writing given to a slave is legally binding; for, according to Southern laws, a slave, *being* property, can *hold* no property. When my grandmother lent her hard earnings to her mistress, she trusted solely to her honor. The honor of a slaveholder to a slave!

To this good grandmother I was indebted for many comforts. My brother Willie and I often received portions of the crackers, cakes, and preserves, she made to sell; and after we ceased to be children we were indebted to her for many more important services.

Such were the unusually fortunate circumstances of my early childhood. When I was six years old, my mother died; and then, for the first time, I learned, by the talk around me, that I was a slave. My mother's mistress was the daughter of my grandmother's mistress. She was the foster sister of my mother; they were both nourished at my grandmother's breast. In fact, my mother had been weaned at three months old, that the babe of the mistress might obtain sufficient food. They played together as children; and, when they became women, my mother was a most faithful servant to her whiter foster sister. On her death-bed her mistress promised that her children should never suffer for any thing; and during her lifetime she kept her word. They all spoke kindly of my dead mother, who had been a slave merely in name, but in nature was noble and womanly. I grieved for her, and my young mind was troubled with the thought who would now take care of me and my little brother. I was told that my home was now to be with her mistress; and I found it a happy one. No toilsome or disagreeable duties were imposed upon me. My mistress was so kind to me that I was always glad to do her bidding, and proud to labor for her as much as my young years would permit. I would sit by her side for hours, sewing diligently, with a heart as free from care as that of any freeborn white child. When she thought I was tired, she would send me out to run and jump; and away I bounded, to gather berries or flowers to decorate her room. Those were happy days—too happy to last. The slave child had no thought for the morrow; but there came that blight, which too surely waits on every human being born to be a chattel.

When I was nearly twelve years old, my kind mistress sickened and died. As I saw the cheek grow paler, and the eye more glassy, how earnestly I prayed in my heart that she might live! I loved her; for she had been almost like a mother to me. My prayers were not answered. She died, and they buried her in the little churchyard, where, day after day, my tears fell upon her grave.

I was sent to spend a week with my grandmother. I was now old enough to begin to think of the future; and again and again I asked myself what they would do with me. I felt sure I should never find another mistress so kind as the one who was gone. She had promised my dying mother that her children should never suffer for any thing; and when I remembered that, and recalled her many proofs of attachment to me, I could not help having some hopes that she had left me free. My friends were almost certain it would be so. They thought she would be sure to do it, on account of my mother's love and faithful service. But, alas! we all know that the memory of a faithful slave does not avail much to save her children from the auction block.

After a brief period of suspense, the will of my mistress was read, and we learned that she had bequeathed me to her sister's daughter, a child of five years old. So vanished our hopes. My mistress had taught me the precepts of God's Word: "Thou shalt love thy neighbor as thyself." "Whatsoever ye would that men should do unto you, do ye even so unto them." But I was her slave, and I suppose she did not recognize me as her neighbor. I would give much to blot out from my memory that one great wrong. As a child, I loved my mistress; and, looking back on the happy days I spent with her, I try to think with less bitterness of this act of injustice. While I was with her, she taught me to read and spell; and for this privilege, which so rarely falls to the lot of a slave, I bless her memory.

She possessed but few slaves; and at her death those were all distributed among her relatives. Five of them were my grandmother's children, and had shared the same milk that nourished her mother's children. Notwithstanding my grandmother's long and faithful service to her owners, not one of her children escaped the auction block. These God-breathing machines are no more, in the sight of their masters, than the cotton they plant, or the horses they tend.

II. The New Master and Mistress

Dr. Flint, a physician in the neighborhood, had married the sister of my mistress, and I was now the property of their little daughter. It was not without murmuring that I prepared for my new home; and what added to my unhappiness, was the fact that my brother William was purchased by the same family. My father, by his nature, as well as by the habit of trans-acting business as a skilful mechanic, had more of the feelings of a freeman than is common among slaves. My brother was a spirited boy; and being brought up under such influences, he early detested the name of master and mistress. One day, when his father and his mistress both happened to call him at the same time, he hesitated between the two; being perplexed to know which had the strongest claim upon his obedience. He finally con-cluded to go to his mistress. When my father reproved him for it, he said, "You both called me, and I didn't know which I ought to go to first."

"You are *my* child," replied our father, "and when I call you, you should come immediately, if you have to pass through fire and water."

Poor Willie! He was now to learn his first lesson of obedience to a mas-ter. Grandmother tried to cheer us with hopeful words, and they found an echo in the credulous hearts of youth.

When we entered our new home we encountered cold looks, cold words, and cold treatment. We were glad when the night came. On my nar-row bed I moaned and wept, I felt so desolate and alone.

I had been there nearly a year, when a dear little friend of mine was buried. I heard her mother sob, as the clods fell on the coffin of her only child, and I turned away from the grave, feeling thankful that I still had something left to love. I met my grandmother, who said, "Come with me, Linda;" and from her tone I knew that something sad had happened. She led me apart from the people, and then said, "My child, your father is dead." Dead! How could I believe it? He had died so suddenly I had not even heard that he was sick. I went home with my grandmother. My heart rebelled against God, who had taken from me mother, father, mistress, and friend. The good grandmother tried to comfort me. "Who knows the ways of God?" said she. "Perhaps they have been kindly taken from the evil days to come." Years afterwards I often thought of this. She promised to be a mother to her grandchildren, so far as she might be permitted to do so; and strengthened by her love, I returned to my master's. I thought I should be allowed to go to my father's house the next morning; but I was ordered to go for flowers, that my mistress's house might be decorated for an evening party. I spent the day gathering flowers and weaving them into festoons, while the dead body of my father was lying within a mile of me. What cared my owners for that? he was merely a piece of property. Moreover, they thought he had spoiled his children, by teaching them to feel that they were human beings. This was blasphemous doctrine for a slave to teach; presumptuous in him, and dangerous to the masters.

The next day I followed his remains to a humble grave beside that of my dear mother. There were those who knew my father's worth, and respected his memory.

My home now seemed more dreary than ever. The laugh of the little slave-children sounded harsh and cruel. It was selfish to feel so about the joy of others. My brother moved about with a very grave face. I tried to comfort him, by saying, "Take courage, Willie; brighter days will come by and by."

"You don't know any thing about it, Linda," he replied. "We shall have to stay here all our days; we shall never be free."

I argued that we were growing older and stronger, and that perhaps we might, before long, be allowed to hire our own time, and then we could earn money to buy our freedom. William declared this was much easier to say than to do; moreover, he did not intend to *buy* his freedom. We held daily controversies upon this subject.

Little attention was paid to the slaves' meals in Dr. Flint's house. If they could catch a bit of food while it was going, well and good. I gave myself no trouble on that score, for on my various errands I passed my grandmother's house, where there was always something to spare for me. I was frequently threatened with punishment if I stopped there; and my grandmother, to avoid detaining me, often stood at the gate with something for my breakfast or dinner. I was indebted to *her* for all my comforts, spiritual or temporal. It was *her* labor that supplied my scanty wardrobe. I have a vivid recollection of the linsey-woolsey dress given me every winter by Mrs. Flint. How I hated it! It was one of the badges of slavery.

While my grandmother was thus helping to support me from her hard earnings, the three hundred dollars she had lent her mistress were never repaid. When her mistress died, her son-in-law, Dr. Flint, was appointed executor. When grandmother applied to him for payment, he said the estate was insolvent, and the law prohibited payment. It did not, however, prohibit him from retaining the silver candelabra, which had been purchased with that money. I presume they will be handed down in the family, from generation to generation.

My grandmother's mistress had always promised her that, at her death, she should be free; and it was said that in her will she made good the promise. But when the estate was settled, Dr. Flint told the faithful old servant that, under existing circumstances, it was necessary she should be sold.

On the appointed day, the customary advertisement was posted up, proclaiming that there would be a "public sale of negroes, horses, &c." Dr. Flint called to tell my grandmother that he was unwilling to wound her feelings by putting her up at auction, and that he would prefer to dispose of her at private sale. My grandmother saw through his hypocrisy; she understood very well that he was ashamed of the job. She was a very spirited woman, and if he was base enough to sell her, when her mistress intended she should be free, she was determined the public should know it. She had for a long time supplied many families with crackers and preserves; consequently, "Aunt Marthy," as she was called, was generally known, and every body who knew her respected her intelligence and good character. Her long and faithful service in the family was also well known, and the intention of her mistress to leave her free. When the day of sale came, she took her place among the chattels, and at the first call she sprang upon the auction-block. Many voices called out, "Shame! Shame! Who is going to sell *you*, Aunt Marthy? Don't stand there! That is no place for *you*." Without saying a word, she quietly awaited her fate. No one bid for her. At last, a feeble voice said, "Fifty dollars." It came from a maiden lady, seventy years old, the sister of my grandmother's deceased mistress. She had lived forty years under the same roof with my grandmother; she knew how faithfully she had served her owners, and how cruelly she had been defrauded of her rights; and she resolved to protect her. The auctioneer waited for a higher bid; but her wishes were respected; no one bid above her. She could neither read nor write; and when the bill of sale was made out, she signed it with a cross. But what consequence was that, when she had a big heart overflowing with human kindness? She gave the old servant her freedom.

At that time, my grandmother was just fifty years old. Laborious years had passed since then; and now my brother and I were slaves to the man who had defrauded her of her money, and tried to defraud her of her freedom. One of my mother's sisters, called Aunt Nancy, was also a slave in his family. She was a kind, good aunt to me; and supplied the place of both housekeeper and waiting maid to her mistress. She was, in fact, at the beginning and end of every thing.

Mrs. Flint, like many southern women, was totally deficient in energy. She had not strength to superintend her household affairs; but her nerves were so strong, that she could sit in her easy chair and see a woman whipped, till the blood trickled from every stroke of the lash. She was a member of the church; but partaking of the Lord's supper did not seem to put her in a Christian frame of mind. If dinner was not served at the exact time on that particular Sunday, she would station herself in the kitchen, and wait till it was dished, and then spit in all the kettles and pans that had been used for cooking. She did this to prevent the cook and her children from eking out their meagre fare with the remains of the gravy and other scrapings. The slaves could get nothing to eat except what she chose to give them. Provisions were weighed out by the pound and ounce, three times a day. I can assure you she gave them no chance to eat wheat bread from her flour barrel. She knew how many biscuits a quart of flour would make, and exactly what size they ought to be.

Dr. Flint was an epicure. The cook never sent a dinner to his table without fear and trembling; for if there happened to be a dish not to his liking, he would either order her to be whipped, or compel her to eat every mouthful of it in his presence. The poor, hungry creature might not have objected to eating it; but she did object to having her master cram it down her throat till she choked.

They had a pet dog, that was a nuisance in the house. The cook was ordered to make some Indian mush for him. He refused to eat, and when his head was held over it, the froth flowed from his mouth into the basin. He died a few minutes after. When Dr. Flint came in, he said the mush had not been well cooked, and that was the reason the animal would not eat it. He sent for the cook, and compelled her to eat it. He thought that the woman's stomach was stronger than the dog's; but her sufferings afterwards proved that he was mistaken. This poor woman endured many cruelties from her master and mistress; sometimes she was locked up, away from her nursing baby, for a whole day and night.

When I had been in the family a few weeks, one of the plantation slaves was brought to town, by order of his master. It was near night when he arrived, and Dr. Flint ordered him to be taken to the work house, and tied up to the joist, so that his feet would just escape the ground. In that situation he was to wait till the doctor had taken his tea. I shall never forget that night. Never before, in my life, had I heard hundreds of blows fall, in succession, on a human being. His piteous groans, and his "O, pray don't massa," rang in my ear for months afterwards. There were many conjectures as to the cause of this terrible punishment. Some said master accused him of stealing corn; others said the slave had quarrelled with his wife, in presence of the overseer, and had accused his master of being the father of her child. They were both black, and the child was very fair.

I went into the work house next morning, and saw the cowhide still wet with blood, and the boards all covered with gore. The poor man lived, and continued to quarrel with his wife. A few months afterwards Dr. Flint handed them both over to a slave-trader. The guilty man put their value into his pocket, and had the satisfaction of knowing that they were out of sight and hearing. When the mother was delivered into the trader's hands, she said, "You *promised* to treat me well." To which he replied, "You have let your tongue run too far; damn you!" She had forgotten that it was a crime for a slave to tell who was the father of her child.

From others than the master persecution also comes in such cases. I once saw a young slave girl dying soon after the birth of a child nearly white. In her agony she cried out, "O Lord, come and take me!" Her mistress stood by, and mocked at her like an incarnate fiend. "You suffer, do you?" she exclaimed. "I am glad of it. You deserve it all, and more too."

The girl's mother said, "The baby is dead, thank God; and I hope my poor child will soon be in heaven, too."

"Heaven!" retorted the mistress. "There is no such place for the like of her and her bastard."

The poor mother turned away, sobbing. Her dying daughter called her, feebly, and as she bent over her, I heard her say, "Don't grieve so, mother; God knows all about it; and HE will have mercy upon me."

Her sufferings, afterwards, became so intense, that her mistress felt unable to stay; but when she left the room, the scornful smile was still on her lips. Seven children called her mother. The poor black woman had but the one child, whose eyes she saw closing in death, while she thanked God for taking her away from the greater bitterness of life.

III. The Slaves' New Year's Day

Dr. Flint owned a fine residence in town, several farms, and about fifty slaves, besides hiring a number by the year.

Hiring-day at the south takes place on the 1st of January. On the 2d, the slaves are expected to go to their new masters. On a farm, they work until the corn and cotton are laid. They then have two holidays. Some masters give them a good dinner under the trees. This over, they work until Christmas eve. If no heavy charges are meantime brought against them, they are given four or five holidays, whichever the master or overseer may think proper. Then comes New Year's eve; and they gather together their little alls, or more properly speaking, their little nothings, and wait anxiously for the dawning of day. At the appointed hour the grounds are thronged with men, women, and children, waiting, like criminals, to hear their doom pronounced. The slave is sure to know who is the most humane, or cruel master, within forty miles of him.

It is easy to find out, on that day, who clothes and feeds his slaves well; for he is surrounded by a crowd, begging, "Please, massa, hire me this year. I will work *very* hard, massa."

If a slave is unwilling to go with his new master, he is whipped, or locked up in jail, until he consents to go, and promises not to run away during the year. Should he chance to change his mind, thinking it justifiable to violate an extorted promise, woe unto him if he is caught! The whip is used till the blood flows at his feet; and his stiffened limbs are put in chains, to be dragged in the field for days and days!

If he lives until the next year, perhaps the same man will hire him again, without even giving him an opportunity of going to the hiring-ground. After those for hire are disposed of, those for sale are called up.

O, you happy free women, contrast *your* New Year's day with that of the poor bond-woman! With you it is a pleasant season, and the light of the day is blessed. Friendly wishes meet you every where, and gifts are showered upon you. Even hearts that have been estranged from you soften at this season, and lips that have been silent echo back, "I wish you a happy New Year." Children bring their little offerings, and raise their rosy lips for a caress. They are your own, and no hand but that of death can take them from you.

But to the slave mother New Year's day comes laden with peculiar sorrows. She sits on her cold cabin floor, watching the children who may all be torn from her the next morning; and often does she wish that she and they might die before the day dawns. She may be an ignorant creature, degraded by the system that has brutalized her from childhood; but she has a mother's instincts, and is capable of feeling a mother's agonies.

On one of these sale days, I saw a mother lead seven children to the auction-block. She knew that *some* of them would be taken from her; but they took *all*. The children were sold to a slave-trader, and their mother was bought by a man in her own town. Before night her children were all far away. She begged the trader to tell her where he intended to take them; this he refused to do. How *could* he, when he knew he would sell them, one by one, wherever he could command the highest price? I met that mother in the street, and her wild, haggard face lives to-day in my mind. She wrung her hands in anguish, and exclaimed, "Gone! All gone! Why *don't* God kill me?" I had no words wherewith to comfort her. Instances of this kind are of daily, yea, of hourly occurrence.

Slaveholders have a method, peculiar to their institution, of getting rid of *old* slaves, whose lives have been worn out in their service. I knew an old woman, who for seventy years faithfully served her master. She had become almost helpless, from hard labor and disease. Her owners moved to Alabama, and the old black woman was left to be sold to any body who would give twenty dollars for her.

IV. The Slave Who Dared to Feel Like a Man

Two years had passed since I entered Dr. Flint's family, and those years had brought much of the knowledge that comes from experience, though they had afforded little opportunity for any other kinds of knowledge.

My grandmother had, as much as possible, been a mother to her orphan grandchildren. By perseverance and unwearied industry, she was now mistress of a snug little home, surrounded with the necessaries of life. She would have been happy could her children have shared them with her. There remained but three children and two grandchildren, all slaves. Most earnestly did she strive to make us feel that it was the will of God: that He had seen fit to place us under such circumstances; and though it seemed hard, we ought to pray for contentment.

It was a beautiful faith, coming from a mother who could not call her children her own. But I, and Benjamin, her youngest boy, condemned it. We reasoned that it was much more the will of God that we should be situated as she was. We longed for a home like hers. There we always found sweet balsam for our troubles. She was so loving, so sympathizing! She always met us with a smile, and listened with patience to all our sorrows. She spoke so hopefully, that unconsciously the clouds gave place to sunshine. There was a grand big oven there, too, that baked bread and nice things for the town, and we knew there was always a choice bit in store for us.

But, alas! even the charms of the old oven failed to reconcile us to our hard lot. Benjamin was now a tall, handsome lad, strongly and gracefully made, and with a spirit too bold and daring for a slave. My brother William, now twelve years old, had the same aversion to the word master that he had when he was an urchin of seven years. I was his confidant. He came to me with all his troubles. I remember one instance in particular. It was on a lovely spring morning, and when I marked the sunlight dancing here and there, its beauty seemed to mock my sadness. For my master, whose restless, craving, vicious nature roved about day and night, seeking whom to devour, had just left me, with stinging, scorching words; words that scathed ear and brain like fire. O, how I despised him! I thought how glad I should be, if some day when he walked the earth, it would open and swallow him up, and disencumber the world of a plague.

When he told me that I was made for his use, made to obey his command in *every* thing; that I was nothing but a slave, whose will must and should surrender to his, never before had my puny arm felt half so strong.

So deeply was I absorbed in painful reflections afterwards, that I neither saw nor heard the entrance of any one, till the voice of William sounded close beside me. "Linda," said he, "what makes you look so sad? I love you. O, Linda, isn't this a bad world? Every body seems so cross and unhappy. I wish I had died when poor father did."

I told him that every body was *not* cross, or unhappy; that those who had pleasant homes, and kind friends, and who were not afraid to love them, were happy. But we, who were slave-children, without father or mother, could not expect to be happy. We must be good; perhaps that would bring us contentment.

"Yes," he said, "I try to be good; but what's the use? They are all the time troubling me." Then he proceeded to relate his afternoon's difficulty with young master Nicholas. It seemed that the brother of master Nicholas had pleased himself with making up stories about William. Master Nicholas said he should be flogged, and he would do it. Whereupon he went to work; but William fought bravely, and the young master, finding he was getting the better of him, undertook to tie his hands behind him. He failed in that likewise. By dint of kicking and fisting, William came out of the skirmish none the worse for a few scratches.

He continued to discourse on his young master's *meanness;* how he whipped the *little* boys, but was a perfect coward when a tussle ensued between him and white boys of his own size. On such occasions he always took to his legs. William had other charges to make against him. One was his rubbing up pennies with quicksilver, and passing them off for quarters of a dollar on an old man who kept a fruit stall. William was often sent to buy fruit, and he earnestly inquired of me what he ought to do under such circumstances. I told him it was certainly wrong to deceive the old man, and that it was his duty to tell him of the impositions practised by his young master. I assured him the old man would not be slow to comprehend the whole, and there the matter would end. William thought it might with the old man, but not with *him*. He said he did not mind the smart of the whip, but he did not like the *idea* of being whipped.

While I advised him to be good and forgiving I was not unconscious of the beam in my own eye. It was the very knowledge of my own shortcomings that urged me to retain, if possible, some sparks of my brother's God-given nature. I had not lived fourteen years in slavery for nothing. I had felt, seen, and heard enough, to read the characters, and question the motives, of those around me. The war of my life had begun; and though one of God's most powerless creatures, I resolved never to be conquered. Alas, for me!

If there was one pure, sunny spot for me, I believed it to be in Benjamin's heart, and in another's, whom I loved with all the ardor of a girl's first love. My owner knew of it, and sought in every way to render me miserable. He did not resort to corporal punishment, but to all the petty, tyrannical ways that human ingenuity could devise.

I remember the first time I was punished. It was in the month of February. My grandmother had taken my old shoes, and replaced them with a new pair. I needed them; for several inches of snow had fallen, and it still continued to fall. When I walked through Mrs. Flint's room, their creaking grated harshly on her refined nerves. She called me to her, and asked what I had about me that made such a horrid noise. I told her it was my new shoes. "Take them off," said she; "and if you put them on again, I'll throw them into the fire."

I took them off, and my stockings also. She then sent me a long distance, on an errand. As I went through the snow, my bare feet tingled. That night I was very hoarse; and I went to bed thinking the next day would find me sick, perhaps dead. What was my grief on waking to find myself quite well!

I had imagined if I died, or was laid up for some time, that my mistress would feel a twinge of remorse that she had so hated "the little imp," as she styled me. It was my ignorance of that mistress that gave rise to such extravagant imaginings.

Dr. Flint occasionally had high prices offered for me; but he always said, "She don't belong to me. She is my daughter's property, and I have no right to sell her." Good, honest man! My young mistress was still a child, and I could look for no protection from her. I loved her, and she returned my affection. I once heard her father allude to her attachment to me; and his wife promptly replied that it proceeded from fear. This put unpleasant doubts into my mind. Did the child feign what she did not feel? or was her mother jealous of the mite of love she bestowed on me? I concluded it must be the latter. I said to myself, "Surely, little children are true."

One afternoon I sat at my sewing, feeling unusual depression of spirits. My mistress had been accusing me of an offence, of which I assured her I was perfectly innocent; but I saw, by the contemptuous curl of her lip, that she believed I was telling a lie.

I wondered for what wise purpose God was leading me through such thorny paths, and whether still darker days were in store for me. As I sat musing thus, the door opened softly, and William came in. "Well, brother," said I, "what is the matter this time?"

"O Linda, Ben and his master have had a dreadful time!" said he.

My first thought was that Benjamin was killed. "Don't be frightened, Linda," said William; "I will tell you all about it."

It appeared that Benjamin's master had sent for him, and he did not immediately obey the summons. When he did, his master was angry, and began to whip him. He resisted. Master and slave fought, and finally the master was thrown. Benjamin had cause to tremble; for he had thrown to the ground his master—one of the richest men in town. I anxiously awaited the result.

That night I stole to my grandmother's house, and Benjamin also stole thither from his master's. My grandmother had gone to spend a day or two with an old friend living in the country.

"I have come," said Benjamin, "to tell you good by. I am going away."

I inquired where.

"To the north," he replied.

I looked at him to see whether he was in earnest. I saw it all in his firm, set mouth. I implored him not to go, but he paid no heed to my words. He said he was no longer a boy, and every day made his yoke more galling. He had raised his hand against his master, and was to be publicly whipped for the offence. I reminded him of the poverty and hardships he must encounter among strangers. I told him he might be caught and brought back; and that was terrible to think of.

He grew vexed, and asked if poverty and hardships with freedom, were not preferable to our treatment in slavery. "Linda," he continued, "we are dogs here; foot-balls, cattle, every thing that's mean. No, I will not stay. Let them bring me back. We don't die but once."

He was right; but it was hard to give him up. "Go," said I, "and break your mother's heart."

I repented of my words ere they were out.

"Linda," said he, speaking as I had not heard him speak that evening, "how *could* you say that? Poor mother! be kind to her, Linda; and you, too, cousin Fanny."

Cousin Fanny was a friend who had lived some years with us.

Farewells were exchanged, and the bright, kind boy, endeared to us by so many acts of love, vanished from our sight.

It is not necessary to state how he made his escape. Suffice it to say, he was on his way to New York when a violent storm overtook the vessel. The captain said he must put into the nearest port. This alarmed Benjamin, who was aware that he would be advertised in every port near his own town. His embarrassment was noticed by the captain. To port they went. There the advertisement met the captain's eye. Benjamin so exactly answered its description, that the captain laid hold on him, and bound him in chains. The storm passed, and they proceeded to New York. Before reaching that port Benjamin managed to get off his chains and throw them overboard. He escaped from the vessel, but was pursued, captured, and carried back to his master.

When my grandmother returned home and found her youngest child had fled, great was her sorrow; but, with characteristic piety, she said,

"God's will be done." Each morning, she inquired if any news had been heard from her boy. Yes, news *was* heard. The master was rejoicing over a letter, announcing the capture of his human chattel.

That day seems but as yesterday, so well do I remember it. I saw him led through the streets in chains, to jail. His face was ghastly pale, yet full of determination. He had begged one of the sailors to go to his mother's house and ask her not to meet him. He said the sight of her distress would take from him all self-control. She yearned to see him, and she went; but she screened herself in the crowd, that it might be as her child had said.

We were not allowed to visit him; but we had known the jailer for years, and he was a kind-hearted man. At midnight he opened the jail door for my grandmother and myself to enter, in disguise. When we entered the cell not a sound broke the stillness. "Benjamin, Benjamin!" whispered my grandmother. No answer. "Benjamin!" she again faltered. There was a jingle of chains. The moon had just risen, and cast an uncertain light through the bars of the window. We knelt down and took Benjamin's cold hands in ours. We did not speak. Sobs were heard, and Benjamin's lips were unsealed; for his mother was weeping on his neck. How vividly does memory bring back that sad night! Mother and son talked together. He asked her pardon for the suffering he had caused her. She said she had nothing to forgive; she could not blame his desire for freedom. He told her that when he was captured, he broke away, and was about casting himself into the river, when thoughts of *her* came over him, and he desisted. She asked if he did not also think of God. I fancied I saw his face grow fierce in the moonlight. He answered, "No, I did not think of him. When a man is hunted like a wild beast he forgets there is a God, a heaven. He forgets every thing in his struggle to get beyond the reach of the bloodhounds."

"Don't talk so, Benjamin," said she. "Put your trust in God. Be humble, my child, and your master will forgive you."

"Forgive me for *what*, mother? For not letting him treat me like a dog? No! I will never humble myself to him. I have worked for him for nothing all my life, and I am repaid with stripes and imprisonment. Here I will stay till I die, or till he sells me."

The poor mother shuddered at his words. I think he felt it; for when he next spoke, his voice was calmer. "Don't fret about me, mother. I ain't worth it," said he. "I wish I had some of your goodness. You bear every thing patiently, just as though you thought it was all right. I wish I could."

She told him she had not always been so; once, she was like him; but when sore troubles came upon her, and she had no arm to lean upon, she learned to call on God, and he lightened her burdens. She besought him to do likewise.

We overstaid our time, and were obliged to hurry from the jail.

Benjamin had been imprisoned three weeks, when my grandmother went to intercede for him with his master. He was immovable. He said Benjamin should serve as an example to the rest of his slaves; he should be kept in jail till he was subdued, or be sold if he got but one dollar for him.

However, he afterwards relented in some degree. The chains were taken off, and we were allowed to visit him.

As his food was of the coarsest kind, we carried him as often as possible a warm supper, accompanied with some little luxury for the jailer.

Three months elapsed, and there was no prospect of release or of a purchaser. One day he was heard to sing and laugh. This piece of indecorum was told to his master, and the overseer was ordered to re-chain him. He was now confined in an apartment with other prisoners, who were covered with filthy rags. Benjamin was chained near them, and was soon covered with vermin. He worked at his chains till he succeeded in getting out of them. He passed them through the bars of the window, with a request that they should be taken to his master, and he should be informed that he was covered with vermin.

This audacity was punished with heavier chains, and prohibition of our visits.

My grandmother continued to send him fresh changes of clothes. The old ones were burned up. The last night we saw him in jail his mother still begged him to send for his master, and beg his pardon. Neither persuasion nor argument could turn him from his purpose. He calmly answered, "I am waiting his time."

Those chains were mournful to hear.

Another three months passed, and Benjamin left his prison walls. We that loved him waited to bid him a long and last farewell. A slave-trader had bought him. You remember, I told you what price he brought when ten years of age. Now he was more than twenty years old, and sold for three hundred dollars. The master had been blind to his own interest. Long confinement had made his face too pale, his form too thin; moreover, the trader had heard something of his character, and it did not strike him as suitable for a slave. He said he would give any price if the handsome lad was a girl. We thanked God that he was not.

Could you have seen that mother clinging to her child, when they fastened the irons upon his wrists; could you have heard her heart-rending groans, and seen her bloodshot eyes wander wildly from face to face, vainly pleading for mercy; could you have witnessed that scene as I saw it, you would exclaim, *Slavery is damnable!*

Benjamin, her youngest, her pet, was forever gone! She could not realize it. She had had an interview with the trader for the purpose of ascertaining if Benjamin could be purchased. She was told it was impossible, as he had given bonds not to sell him till he was out of the state. He promised that he would not sell him till he reached New Orleans.

With a strong arm and unvaried trust, my grandmother began her work of love. Benjamin must be free. If she succeeded, she knew they would still be separated; but the sacrifice was not too great. Day and night she labored. The trader's price would treble that he gave; but she was not discouraged.

She employed a lawyer to write to a gentleman, whom she knew, in New Orleans. She begged him to interest himself for Benjamin, and he willingly favored her request. When he saw Benjamin, and stated his business, he thanked him; but said he preferred to wait a while before making the trader an offer. He knew he had tried to obtain a high price for him, and had invariably failed. This encouraged him to make another effort for freedom. So one morning, long before day, Benjamin was missing. He was riding over the blue billows, bound for Baltimore.

For once his white face did him a kindly service. They had no suspicion that it belonged to a slave; otherwise, the law would have been followed out to the letter, and the *thing* rendered back to slavery. The brightest skies are often overshadowed by the darkest clouds. Benjamin was taken sick, and compelled to remain in Baltimore three weeks. His strength was slow in returning; and his desire to continue his journey seemed to retard his recovery. How could he get strength without air and exercise? He resolved to venture on a short walk. A by-street was selected, where he thought himself secure of not being met by any one that knew him; but a voice called out, "Halloo, Ben, my boy! what are you doing *here*?"

His first impulse was to run; but his legs trembled so that he could not stir. He turned to confront his antagonist, and behold, there stood his old master's next door neighbor! He thought it was all over with him now; but it proved otherwise. That man was a miracle. He possessed a goodly number of slaves, and yet was not quite deaf to that mystic clock, whose ticking is rarely heard in the slaveholder's breast.

"Ben, you are sick," said he. "Why, you look like a ghost. I guess I gave you something of a start. Never mind, Ben, I am not going to touch you. You had a pretty tough time of it, and you may go on your way rejoicing for all me. But I would advise you to get out of this place plaguy quick, for there are several gentlemen here from our town." He described the nearest and safest route to New York, and added, "I shall be glad to tell your mother I have seen you. Good by, Ben."

Benjamin turned away, filled with gratitude, and surprised that the town he hated contained such a gem—a gem worthy of a purer setting.

This gentleman was a Northerner by birth, and had married a southern lady. On his return, he told my grandmother that he had seen her son, and of the service he had rendered him.

Benjamin reached New York safely, and concluded to stop there until he had gained strength enough to proceed further. It happened that my grandmother's only remaining son had sailed for the same city on business for his mistress. Through God's providence, the brothers met. You may be sure it was a happy meeting. "O Phil," exclaimed Benjamin, "I am here at last." Then he told him how near he came to dying, almost in sight of free land, and how he prayed that he might live to get one breath of free air. He said life was worth something now, and it would be hard to die. In the old jail he had not valued it; once, he was tempted to destroy it; but something, he did not know what, had prevented him; perhaps it was fear. He had heard those who profess to be religious declare there was no heaven for self-murderers; and as his life had been pretty hot here, he did not desire a continuation of the same in another world. "If I die now," he exclaimed, "thank God, I shall die a freeman!"

He begged my uncle Phillip not to return south; but stay and work with him, till they earned enough to buy those at home. His brother told him it would kill their mother if he deserted her in her trouble. She had pledged her house, and with difficulty had raised money to buy him. Would he be bought?

"No, never!" he replied. "Do you suppose, Phil, when I have got so far out of their clutches, I will give them one red cent? No! And do you suppose I would turn mother out of her home in her old age? That I would let her pay all those hard-earned dollars for me, and never to see me? For you know she will stay south as long as her other children are slaves. What a good mother! Tell her to buy *you*, Phil. You have been a comfort to her, and I have been a trouble. And Linda, poor Linda; what'll become of her? Phil, you don't know what a life they lead her. She has told me something about it, and I wish old Flint was dead, or a better man. When I was in jail, he asked her if she didn't want *him* to ask my master to forgive me, and take me home again. She told him, No; that I didn't want to go back. He got mad, and said we were all alike. I never despised my own master half as much as I do that man. There is many a worse slaveholder than my master; but for all that I would not be his slave."

While Benjamin was sick, he had parted with nearly all his clothes to pay necessary expenses. But he did not part with a little pin I fastened in his bosom when we parted. It was the most valuable thing I owned, and I thought none more worthy to wear it. He had it still.

His brother furnished him with clothes, and gave him what money he had.

They parted with moistened eyes; and as Benjamin turned away, he said, "Phil, I part with all my kindred." And so it proved. We never heard from him again.

Uncle Phillip came home; and the first words he uttered when he entered the house were, "Mother, Ben is free! I have seen him in New York." She stood looking at him with a bewildered air. "Mother, don't you believe it?" he said, laying his hand softly upon her shoulder. She raised her hands, and exclaimed, "God be praised! Let us thank him." She dropped on her knees, and poured forth her heart in prayer. Then Phillip must sit down and repeat to her every word Benjamin had said. He told her all; only he forbore to mention how sick and pale her darling looked. Why should he distress her when she could do him no good?

The brave old woman still toiled on, hoping to rescue some of her other children. After a while she succeeded in buying Phillip. She paid eight hundred dollars, and came home with the precious document that secured his freedom. The happy mother and son sat together by the old hearthstone that night, telling how proud they were of each other, and how they would prove to the world that they could take care of themselves, as they had long taken care of others. We all concluded by saying, "He that is *willing* to be a slave, let him be a slave."

V. The Trials of Girlhood

During the first years of my service in Dr. Flint's family, I was accustomed to share some indulgences with the children of my mistress. Though this seemed to me no more than right, I was grateful for it, and tried to merit the kindness by the faithful discharge of my duties. But I now entered on my fifteenth year—a sad epoch in the life of a slave girl. My master began to whisper foul words in my ear. Young as I was, I could not remain ignorant of their import. I tried to treat them with indifference or contempt. The master's age, my extreme youth, and the fear that his conduct would be reported to my grandmother, made me bear this treatment for many months. He was a crafty man, and resorted to many means to accomplish his purposes. Sometimes he had stormy, terrific ways, that made his victims tremble; sometimes he assumed a gentleness that he thought must surely subdue. Of the two, I preferred his stormy moods, although they left me trembling. He tried his utmost to corrupt the pure principles my grandmother had instilled. He peopled my young mind with unclean images, such as only a vile monster could think of. I turned from him with disgust and hatred. But he was my master. I was compelled to live under the same roof with him—where I saw a man forty years my senior daily violating the most sacred commandments of nature. He told me I was his property; that I must be subject to his will in all things. My soul revolted against the mean tyranny. But where could I turn for protection? No matter whether the slave girl be as black as ebony or as fair as her mistress. In either case, there is no shadow of law to protect her from insult, from violence, or even from death; all these are inflicted by fiends who bear the shape of men. The mistress, who ought to protect the helpless victim, has no other feelings towards her but those of jealousy and rage. The degradation, the wrongs, the vices, that grow out of slavery, are more than I can describe. They are greater than you would willingly believe. Surely, if you credited one half the truths that are told you concerning the helpless millions suffering in this cruel bondage, you at the north would not help to tighten the yoke. You surely would refuse to do for the master, on your own soil, the mean and cruel work which trained bloodhounds and the lowest class of whites do for him at the south.

Every where the years bring to all enough of sin and sorrow; but in slavery the very dawn of life is darkened by these shadows. Even the little child, who is accustomed to wait on her mistress and her children, will learn, before she is twelve years old, why it is that her mistress hates such and such a one among the slaves. Perhaps the child's own mother is among those hated ones. She listens to violent outbreaks of jealous passion, and cannot help understanding what is the cause. She will become prematurely knowing in evil things. Soon she will learn to tremble when she hears her master's footfall. She will be compelled to realize that she is no longer a child. If God has bestowed beauty upon her, it will prove her greatest curse. That which commands admiration in the white woman only hastens the degradation of the female slave. I know that some are too much brutalized by slavery to feel the humiliation of their position; but many slaves feel it most acutely, and shrink from the memory of it. I cannot tell how much I suffered in the presence of these wrongs, nor how I am still pained by the retrospect. My master met me at every turn, reminding me that I belonged to him, and swearing by heaven and earth that he would compel me to submit to him. If I went out for a breath of fresh air, after a day of unwearied toil, his footsteps dogged me. If I knelt by my mother's grave, his dark shadow fell on me even there. The light heart which nature had given me became heavy with sad forebodings. The other slaves in my master's house noticed the change. Many of them pitied me; but none dared to ask the cause. They had no need to inquire. They knew too well the guilty practices under that roof; and they were aware that to speak of them was an offence that never went unpunished.

I longed for some one to confide in. I would have given the world to have laid my head on my grandmother's faithful bosom, and told her all my troubles. But Dr. Flint swore he would kill me, if I was not as silent as the grave. Then, although my grandmother was all in all to me, I feared her as well as loved her. I had been accustomed to look up to her with a respect bordering upon awe. I was very young, and felt shamefaced about telling her such impure things, especially as I knew her to be very strict on such subjects. Moreover, she was a woman of a high spirit. She was usually very quiet in her demeanor; but if her indignation was once roused, it was not very easily quelled. I had been told that she once chased a white gentleman with a loaded pistol, because he insulted one of her daughters. I dreaded the consequences of a violent outbreak; and both pride and fear kept me silent. But though I did not confide in my grandmother, and even evaded her vigilant watchfulness and inquiry, her presence in the neighborhood was some protection to me. Though she had been a slave, Dr. Flint was afraid of her. He dreaded her scorching rebukes. Moreover, she was known and patronized by many people; and he did not wish to have his villainy made public. It was lucky for me that I did not live on a distant plantation, but in a town not so large that the inhabitants were ignorant of each other's affairs. Bad as are the laws and customs in a slaveholding community, the doctor, as a professional man, deemed it prudent to keep up some outward show of decency.

O, what days and nights of fear and sorrow that man caused me! Reader, it is not to awaken sympathy for myself that I am telling you truthfully what I suffered in slavery. I do it to kindle a flame of compassion in your hearts for my sisters who are still in bondage, suffering as I once suffered.

I once saw two beautiful children playing together. One was a fair white child; the other was her slave, and also her sister. When I saw them embracing each other, and heard their joyous laughter, I turned sadly away from the lovely sight. I foresaw the inevitable blight that would fall on the little slave's heart. I knew how soon her laughter would be changed to sighs. The fair child grew up to be a still fairer woman. From childhood to womanhood her pathway was blooming with flowers, and overarched by a sunny sky. Scarcely one day of her life had been clouded when the sun rose on her happy bridal morning.

How had those years dealt with her slave sister, the little playmate of her childhood? She, also, was very beautiful; but the flowers and sunshine of love were not for her. She drank the cup of sin, and shame, and misery, whereof her persecuted race are compelled to drink.

In view of these things, why are ye silent, ye free men and women of the north? Why do your tongues falter in maintenance of the right? Would that I had more ability! But my heart is so full, and my pen is so weak! There are noble men and women who plead for us, striving to help those who cannot help themselves. God bless them! God give them strength and courage to go on! God bless those, every where, who are laboring to advance the cause of humanity!

VI. The Jealous Mistress

I would ten thousand times rather that my children should be the half-starved paupers of Ireland than to be the most pampered among the slaves of America. I would rather drudge out my life on a cotton plantation, till the grave opened to give me rest, than to live with an unprincipled master and a jealous mistress. The felon's home in a penitentiary is preferable. He may repent, and turn from the error of his ways, and so find peace; but it is not so with a favorite slave. She is not allowed to have any pride of character. It is deemed a crime in her to wish to be virtuous.

Mrs. Flint possessed the key to her husband's character before I was born. She might have used this knowledge to counsel and to screen the young and the innocent among her slaves; but for them she had no sympathy. They were the objects of her constant suspicion and malevolence. She watched her husband with unceasing vigilance; but he was well practised in means to evade it. What he could not find opportunity to say in words he manifested in signs. He invented more than were ever thought of in a deaf and dumb asylum. I let them pass, as if I did not understand what he meant; and many were the curses and threats bestowed on me for my stupidity. One day he caught me teaching myself to write. He frowned, as if he was not well pleased; but I suppose he came to the conclusion that such an accomplishment might help to advance his favorite scheme. Before long, notes were often slipped into my hand. I would return them, saying, "I can't read them, sir." "Can't you?" he replied; "then I must read them to you." He always finished the reading by asking, "Do you understand?"

Sometimes he would complain of the heat of the tea room, and order his supper to be placed on a small table in the piazza. He would seat himself there with a well-satisfied smile, and tell me to stand by and brush away the flies. He would eat very slowly, pausing between the mouthfuls. These intervals were employed in describing the happiness I was so foolishly throwing away, and in threatening me with the penalty that finally awaited my stubborn disobedience. He boasted much of the forbearance he had exercised towards me, and reminded me that there was a limit to his patience. When I succeeded in avoiding opportunities for him to talk to me at home, I was ordered to come to his office, to do some errand. When there, I was obliged to stand and listen to such language as he saw fit to address to me. Sometimes I so openly expressed my contempt for him that he would become violently enraged, and I wondered why he did not strike me. Circumstanced as he was, he probably thought it was better policy to be forbearing. But the state of things grew worse and worse daily. In desperation I told him that I must and would apply to my grandmother for protection. He threatened me with death, and worse than death, if I made any complaint to her. Strange to say, I did not despair. I was naturally of a buoyant disposition, and always I had a hope of somehow getting out of his clutches. Like many a poor, simple slave before me, I trusted that some threads of joy would yet be woven into my dark destiny.

I had entered my sixteenth year, and every day it became more apparent that my presence was intolerable to Mrs. Flint. Angry words frequently passed between her and her husband. He had never punished me himself, and he would not allow any body else to punish me. In that respect, she was never satisfied; but, in her angry moods, no terms were too vile for her to bestow upon me. Yet I, whom she detested so bitterly, had far more pity for her than he had, whose duty it was to make her life happy. I never wronged her, or wished to wrong her; and one word of kindness from her would have brought me to her feet.

After repeated quarrels between the doctor and his wife, he announced his intention to take his youngest daughter, then four years old, to sleep in his apartment. It was necessary that a servant should sleep in the same room, to be on hand if the child stirred. I was selected for that office, and informed for what purpose that arrangement had been made. By managing to keep within sight of people, as much as possible, during the day time, I had hitherto succeeded in eluding my master, though a razor was often held to my throat to force me to change this line of policy. At night I slept by the side of my great aunt, where I felt safe. He was too prudent to come into her room. She was an old woman, and had been in the family many years. Moreover, as a married man, and a professional man, he deemed it necessary to save appearances in some degree. But he resolved to remove the obstacle in the way of his scheme; and he thought he had planned it so that he should evade suspicion. He was well aware how much I prized my refuge by the side of my old aunt, and he determined to dispossess me of it. The first night the doctor had the little child in his room alone. The next morning, I was ordered to take my station as nurse the following night. A kind Providence interposed in my favor. During the day Mrs. Flint heard of this new arrangement, and a storm followed. I rejoiced to hear it rage.

After a while my mistress sent for me to come to her room. Her first question was, "Did you know you were to sleep in the doctor's room?"

"Yes, ma'am."

"Who told you?"

"My master."

"Will you answer truly all the questions I ask?"

"Yes, ma'am."

"Tell me, then, as you hope to be forgiven, are you innocent of what I have accused you?"

"I am."

She handed me a Bible, and said, "Lay your hand on your heart, kiss this holy book, and swear before God that you tell me the truth."

I took the oath she required, and I did it with a clear conscience.

"You have taken God's holy word to testify your innocence," said she. "If you have deceived me, beware! Now take this stool, sit down, look me directly in the face, and tell me all that has passed between your master and you."

I did as she ordered. As I went on with my account her color changed frequently, she wept, and sometimes groaned. She spoke in tones so sad, that I was touched by her grief. The tears came to my eyes; but I was soon convinced that her emotions arose from anger and wounded pride. She felt that her marriage vows were desecrated, her dignity insulted; but she had no compassion for the poor victim of her husband's perfidy. She pitied herself as a martyr; but she was incapable of feeling for the condition of shame and misery in which her unfortunate, helpless slave was placed.

Yet perhaps she had some touch of feeling for me; for when the conference was ended, she spoke kindly, and promised to protect me. I should have been much comforted by this assurance if I could have had confidence in it; but my experiences in slavery had filled me with distrust. She was not a very refined woman, and had not much control over her passions. I was an object of her jealousy, and, consequently, of her hatred; and I knew I could not expect kindness or confidence from her under the circumstances in which I was placed. I could not blame her. Slaveholders' wives feel as other women would under similar circumstances. The fire of her temper kindled from small sparks, and now the flame became so intense that the doctor was obliged to give up his intended arrangement.

I knew I had ignited the torch, and I expected to suffer for it afterwards; but I felt too thankful to my mistress for the timely aid she rendered me to care much about that. She now took me to sleep in a room adjoining her own. There I was an object of her especial care, though not of her especial comfort, for she spent many a sleepless night to watch over me. Sometimes I woke up, and found her bending over me. At other times she whispered in my ear, as though it was her husband who was speaking to me, and listened to hear what I would answer. If she startled me, on such occasions, she would glide stealthily away; and the next morning she would tell me I had been talking in my sleep, and ask who I was talking to. At last, I began to be fearful for my life. It had been often threatened; and you can imagine, better than I can describe, what an unpleasant sensation it must produce to wake up in the dead of night and find a jealous woman bending over you. Terrible as this experience was, I had fears that it would give place to one more terrible.

My mistress grew weary of her vigils; they did not prove satisfactory. She changed her tactics. She now tried the trick of accusing my master of crime, in my presence, and gave my name as the author of the accusation. To my utter astonishment, he replied, "I don't believe it; but if she did acknowledge it, you tortured her into exposing me." Tortured into exposing him! Truly, Satan had no difficulty in distinguishing the color of his soul! I understood his object in making this false representation. It was to show me that I gained nothing by seeking the protection of my mistress; that the power was still all in his own hands. I pitied Mrs. Flint. She was a second wife, many years the junior of her husband; and the hoary-headed miscreant was enough to try the patience of a wiser and better woman. She was completely foiled, and knew not how to proceed. She would gladly have had me flogged for my supposed false oath; but, as I have already stated, the doctor never allowed any one to whip me. The old sinner was politic. The application of the lash might have led to remarks that would have exposed him in the eyes of his children and grandchildren. How often did I rejoice that I lived in a town where all the inhabitants knew each other! If I had been on a remote plantation, or lost among the multitude of a crowded city, I should not be a living woman at this day.

The secrets of slavery are concealed like those of the Inquisition. My master was, to my knowledge, the father of eleven slaves. But did the mothers dare to tell who was the father of their children? Did the other slaves dare to allude to it, except in whispers among themselves? No, indeed! They knew too well the terrible consequences.

My grandmother could not avoid seeing things which excited her suspicions. She was uneasy about me, and tried various ways to buy me; but the never-changing answer was always repeated: "Linda does not belong to *me*. She is my daughter's property, and I have no legal right to sell her." The conscientious man! He was too scrupulous to *sell* me; but he had no scruples whatever about committing a much greater wrong against the helpless young girl placed under his guardianship, as his daughter's property. Sometimes my persecutor would ask me whether I would like to be sold. I told him I would rather be sold to any body than to lead such a life as I did. On such occasions he would assume the air of a very injured individual, and reproach me for my ingratitude. "Did I not take you into the house, and make you the companion of my own children?" he would say. "Have I ever treated you like a negro? I have never allowed you to be punished, not even to please your mistress. And this is the recompense I get, you ungrateful girl!" I answered that he had reasons of his own for screening me from punishment, and that the course he pursued made my mistress hate me and persecute me. If I wept, he would say, "Poor child! Don't cry! don't cry! I will make peace for you with your mistress. Only let me arrange matters in my own way. Poor, foolish girl! you don't know what is for your own good. I would cherish you. I would make a lady of you. Now go, and think of all I have promised you."

I did think of it.

Reader, I draw no imaginary pictures of southern homes. I am telling you the plain truth. Yet when victims make their escape from this wild beast of Slavery, northerners consent to act the part of bloodhounds, and hunt the poor fugitive back into his den, "full of dead men's bones, and all uncleanness." Nay, more, they are not only willing, but proud, to give their daughters in marriage to slaveholders. The poor girls have romantic notions of a sunny clime, and of the flowering vines that all the year round shade a happy home. To what disappointments are they destined! The young wife soon learns that the husband in whose hands she has placed her happiness pays no regard to his marriage vows. Children of every shade of complexion play with her own fair babies, and too well she knows that they are born unto him of his own household. Jealousy and hatred enter the flowery home, and it is ravaged of its loveliness.

Southern women often marry a man knowing that he is the father of many little slaves. They do not trouble themselves about it. They regard such children as property, as marketable as the pigs on the plantation; and it is seldom that they do not make them aware of this by passing them into the slavetrader's hands as soon as possible, and thus getting them out of their sight. I am glad to say there are some honorable exceptions.

I have myself known two southern wives who exhorted their husbands to free those slaves towards whom they stood in a "parental relation;" and their request was granted. These husbands blushed before the superior nobleness of their wives' natures. Though they had only counselled them to do that which it was their duty to do, it commanded their respect, and rendered their conduct more exemplary. Concealment was at an end, and confidence took the place of distrust.

Though this bad institution deadens the moral sense, even in white women, to a fearful extent, it is not altogether extinct. I have heard southern ladies say of Mr. Such a one, "He not only thinks it no disgrace to be the father of those little niggers, but he is not ashamed to call himself their master. I declare, such things ought not to be tolerated in any decent society!"

VII. The Lover

Why does the slave ever love? Why allow the tendrils of the heart to twine around objects which may at any moment be wrenched away by the hand of violence? When separations come by the hand of death, the pious soul can bow in resignation, and say, "Not my will, but thine be done,

O Lord!" But when the ruthless hand of man strikes the blow, regardless of the misery he causes, it is hard to be submissive. I did not reason thus when I was a young girl. Youth will be youth. I loved, and I indulged the hope that the dark clouds around me would turn out a bright lining. I forgot that in the land of my birth the shadows are too dense for light to penetrate. A land

> Where laughter is not mirth; nor thought the mind;
> Nor words a language; nor e'en men mankind.
> Where cries reply to curses, shrieks to blows,
> And each is tortured in his separate hell.

There was in the neighborhood a young colored carpenter; a free-born man. We had been well acquainted in childhood, and frequently met together afterwards. We became mutually attached, and he proposed to marry me. I loved him with all the ardor of a young girl's first love. But when I reflected that I was a slave, and that the laws gave no sanction to the marriage of such, my heart sank within me. My lover wanted to buy me; but I knew that Dr. Flint was too wilful and arbitrary a man to consent to that arrangement. From him, I was sure of experiencing all sorts of opposition, and I had nothing to hope from my mistress. She would have been delighted to have got rid of me, but not in that way. It would have relieved her mind of a burden if she could have seen me sold to some distant state, but if I was married near home I should be just as much in her husband's power as I had previously been,—for the husband of a slave has no power to protect her. Moreover, my mistress, like many others, seemed to think that slaves had no right to any family ties of their own; that they were created merely to wait upon the family of the mistress. I once heard her abuse a young slave girl, who told her that a colored man wanted to make her his wife. "I will have you peeled and pickled, my lady," said she, "if I ever hear you mention that subject again. Do you suppose that I will have you tending *my* children with the children of that nigger?" The girl to whom she said this had a mulatto child, of course not acknowledged by its father. The poor black man who loved her would have been proud to acknowledge his helpless offspring.

Many and anxious were the thoughts I revolved in my mind. I was at a loss what to do. Above all things, I was desirous to spare my lover the insults that had cut so deeply into my own soul. I talked with my grandmother about it, and partly told her my fears. I did not dare to tell her the worst. She had long suspected all was not right, and if I confirmed her suspicions I knew a storm would rise that would prove the overthrow of all my hopes.

This love-dream had been my support through many trials; and I could not bear to run the risk of having it suddenly dissipated. There was a lady in the neighborhood, a particular friend of Dr. Flint's, who often visited the house. I had a great respect for her, and she had always manifested a friendly interest in me. Grandmother thought she would have great influence with the doctor. I went to this lady, and told her my story. I told her I was aware that my lover's being a free-born man would prove a great objection; but he wanted to buy me; and if Dr. Flint would consent to that arrangement, I felt sure he would be willing to pay any reasonable price. She knew that Mrs. Flint disliked me; therefore, I ventured to suggest that perhaps my mistress would approve of my being sold, as that would rid her of me. The lady listened with kindly sympathy, and promised to do her utmost to promote my wishes. She had an interview with the doctor, and I believe she pleaded my cause earnestly; but it was all to no purpose.

How I dreaded my master now! Every minute I expected to be summoned to his presence; but the day passed, and I heard nothing from him. The next morning, a message was brought to me: "Master wants you in his study." I found the door ajar, and I stood a moment gazing at the hateful man who claimed a right to rule me, body and soul. I entered, and tried to appear calm. I did not want him to know how my heart was bleeding. He looked fixedly at me, with an expression which seemed to say, "I have half a mind to kill you on the spot." At last he broke the silence, and that was a relief to both of us.

"So you want to be married, do you?" said he, "and to a free nigger."

"Yes, sir."

"Well, I'll soon convince you whether I am your master, or the nigger fellow you honor so highly. If you *must* have a husband, you may take up with one of my slaves."

What a situation I should be in, as the wife of one of *his* slaves, even if my heart had been interested!

I replied, "Don't you suppose, sir, that a slave can have some preference about marrying? Do you suppose that all men are alike to her?"

"Do you love this nigger?" said he, abruptly.

"Yes, sir."

"How dare you tell me so!" he exclaimed, in great wrath. After a slight pause, he added, "I supposed you thought more of yourself; that you felt above the insults of such puppies."

I replied, "If he is a puppy I am a puppy, for we are both of the negro race. It is right and honorable for us to love each other. The man you call a puppy never insulted me, sir; and he would not love me if he did not believe me to be a virtuous woman."

He sprang upon me like a tiger, and gave me a stunning blow. It was the first time he had ever struck me; and fear did not enable me to control my anger. When I had recovered a little from the effects, I exclaimed, "You have struck me for answering you honestly. How I despise you!"

There was silence for some minutes. Perhaps he was deciding what should be my punishment; or, perhaps, he wanted to give me time to reflect on what I had said, and to whom I had said it. Finally, he asked, "Do you know what you have said?"

"Yes, sir; but your treatment drove me to it."

"Do you know that I have a right to do as I like with you,—that I can kill you, if I please?"

"You have tried to kill me, and I wish you had; but you have no right to do as you like with me."

"Silence!" he exclaimed, in a thundering voice. "By heavens, girl, you forget yourself too far! Are you mad? If you are, I will soon bring you to your senses. Do you think any other master would bear what I have borne from you this morning? Many masters would have killed you on the spot. How would you like to be sent to jail for your insolence?"

"I know I have been disrespectful, sir," I replied; "but you drove me to it; I couldn't help it. As for the jail, there would be more peace for me there than there is here."

"You deserve to go there," said he, "and to be under such treatment, that you would forget the meaning of the word *peace*. It would do you good. It would take some of your high notions out of you. But I am not ready to send you there yet, notwithstanding your ingratitude for all my kindness and forbearance. You have been the plague of my life. I have wanted to make you happy, and I have been repaid with the basest ingratitude; but though you have proved yourself incapable of appreciating my kindness, I will be lenient towards you, Linda. I will give you one more chance to redeem your character. If you behave yourself and do as I require, I will forgive you and treat you as I always have done; but if you disobey me, I will punish you as I would the meanest slave on my plantation. Never let me hear that fellow's name mentioned again. If I ever know of your speaking to him, I will cowhide you both; and if I catch him lurking about my premises, I will shoot him as soon as I would a dog. Do you hear what I say? I'll teach you a lesson about marriage and free niggers! Now go, and let this be the last time I have occasion to speak to you on this subject."

Reader, did you ever hate? I hope not. I never did but once; and I trust I never shall again. Somebody has called it "the atmosphere of hell;" and I believe it is so.

For a fortnight the doctor did not speak to me. He thought to mortify me; to make me feel that I had disgraced myself by receiving the honorable addresses of a respectable colored man, in preference to the base proposals of a white man. But though his lips disdained to address me, his eyes were very loquacious. No animal ever watched its prey more narrowly than he watched me. He knew that I could write, though he had failed to make me read his letters; and he was now troubled lest I should exchange letters with another man. After a while he became weary of silence; and I was sorry for it. One morning, as he passed through the hall, to leave the house, he contrived to thrust a note into my hand. I thought I had better read it, and spare myself the vexation of having him read it to me. It expressed regret for the blow he had given me, and reminded me that I myself was wholly to blame for it. He hoped I had become convinced of the injury I was doing myself by incurring his displeasure. He wrote that he had made up his mind to go to Louisiana; that he should take several slaves with him, and intended I should be one of the number. My mistress would remain where she was; therefore I should have nothing to fear from that quarter. If I merited kindness from him, he assured me that it would be lavishly bestowed. He begged me to think over the matter, and answer the following day.

The next morning I was called to carry a pair of scissors to his room. I laid them on the table, with the letter beside them. He thought it was my answer, and did not call me back. I went as usual to attend my young mistress to and from school. He met me in the street, and ordered me to stop at his office on my way back. When I entered, he showed me his letter, and asked me why I had not answered it. I replied, "I am your daughter's property, and it is in your power to send me, or take me, wherever you please." He said he was very glad to find me so willing to go, and that we should start early in the autumn. He had a large practice in the town, and I rather thought he had made up the story merely to frighten me. However that might be, I was determined that I would never go to Louisiana with him.

Summer passed away, and early in the autumn Dr. Flint's eldest son was sent to Louisiana to examine the country, with a view to emigrating. That news did not disturb me. I knew very well that I should not be sent with *him*. That I had not been taken to the plantation before this time, was owing to the fact that his son was there. He was jealous of his son; and jealousy of the overseer had kept him from punishing me by sending me into the fields to work. Is it strange that I was not proud of these protectors? As for the overseer, he was a man for whom I had less respect than I had for a bloodhound.

Young Mr. Flint did not bring back a favorable report of Louisiana, and I heard no more of that scheme. Soon after this, my lover met me at the corner of the street, and I stopped to speak to him. Looking up, I saw my master watching us from his window. I hurried home, trembling with fear. I was sent for, immediately, to go to his room. He met me with a blow. "When is mistress to be married?" said he, in a sneering tone. A shower of oaths and imprecations followed. How thankful I was that my lover was a free man! that my tyrant had no power to flog him for speaking to me in the street!

Again and again I revolved in my mind how all this would end. There was no hope that the doctor would consent to sell me on any terms. He had an iron will, and was determined to keep me, and to conquer me. My lover was an intelligent and religious man. Even if he could have obtained permission to marry me while I was a slave, the marriage would give him no power to protect me from my master. It would have made him miserable to witness the insults I should have been subjected to. And then, if we had children, I knew they must "follow the condition of the mother." What a terrible blight that would be on the heart of a free, intelligent father! For *his* sake, I felt that I ought not to link his fate with my own unhappy destiny. He was going to Savannah to see about a little property left him by an uncle; and hard as it was to bring my feelings to it, I earnestly entreated him not to come back. I advised him to go to the Free States, where his tongue would not be tied, and where his intelligence would be of more avail to him. He left me, still hoping the day would come when I could be bought. With me the lamp of hope had gone out. The dream of my girlhood was over. I felt lonely and desolate.

Still I was not stripped of all. I still had my good grandmother, and my affectionate brother. When he put his arms round my neck, and looked into my eyes, as if to read there the troubles I dared not tell, I felt that I still had something to love. But even that pleasant emotion was chilled by the reflection that he might be torn from me at any moment, by some sudden freak of my master. If he had known how we loved each other, I think he would have exulted in separating us. We often planned together how we could get to the north. But, as William remarked, such things are easier said than done. My movements were very closely watched, and we had no means of getting any money to defray our expenses. As for grandmother, she was strongly opposed to her children's undertaking any such project. She had not forgotten poor Benjamin's sufferings, and she was afraid that if another child tried to escape, he would have a similar or a worse fate. To me, nothing seemed more dreadful than my present life. I said to myself, "William *must* be free. He shall go to the north, and I will follow him." Many a slave sister has formed the same plans. . . .

X. A Perilous Passage in the Slave Girl's Life

After my lover went away, Dr. Flint contrived a new plan. He seemed to have an idea that my fear of my mistress was his greatest obstacle. In the blandest tones, he told me that he was going to build a small house for me, in a secluded place, four miles away from the town. I shuddered; but I was constrained to listen, while he talked of his intention to give me a home of my own, and to make a lady of me. Hitherto, I had escaped my dreaded fate, by being in the midst of people. My grandmother had already had high words with my master about me. She had told him pretty plainly what she thought of his character, and there was considerable gossip in the neighborhood about our affairs, to which the open-mouthed jealousy of Mrs. Flint contributed not a little. When my master said he was going to build a house for me, and that he could do it with little trouble and expense, I was in hopes something would happen to frustrate his scheme; but I soon heard that the house was actually begun. I vowed before my Maker that I would never enter it. I had rather toil on the plantation from dawn till dark; I had rather live and die in jail, than drag on, from day to day, through such a living death. I was determined that the master, whom I so hated and loathed, who had blighted the prospects of my youth, and made my life a desert, should not, after my long struggle with him, succeed at last in trampling his victim under his feet. I would do any thing, every thing, for the sake of defeating him. What *could* I do? I thought and thought, till I became desperate, and made a plunge into the abyss.

And now, reader, I come to a period in my unhappy life, which I would gladly forget if I could. The remembrance fills me with sorrow and shame.

It pains me to tell you of it; but I have promised to tell you the truth, and I will do it honestly, let it cost me what it may. I will not try to screen myself behind the plea of compulsion from a master; for it was not so. Neither can I plead ignorance or thoughtlessness. For years, my master had done his utmost to pollute my mind with foul images, and to destroy the pure principles inculcated by my grandmother, and the good mistress of my childhood. The influences of slavery had had the same effect on me that they had on other young girls; they had made me prematurely knowing, concerning the evil ways of the world. I knew what I did, and I did it with deliberate calculation.

But, O, ye happy women, whose purity has been sheltered from childhood, who have been free to choose the objects of your affection, whose homes are protected by law, do not judge the poor desolate slave girl too severely! If slavery had been abolished, I, also, could have married the man of my choice; I could have had a home shielded by the laws; and I should have been spared the painful task of confessing what I am now about to relate; but all my prospects had been blighted by slavery. I wanted to keep myself pure; and, under the most adverse circumstances, I tried hard to preserve my self-respect; but I was struggling alone in the powerful grasp of the demon Slavery; and the monster proved too strong for me. I felt as if I was forsaken by God and man; as if all my efforts must be frustrated; and I became reckless in my despair.

I have told you that Dr. Flint's persecutions and his wife's jealousy had given rise to some gossip in the neighborhood. Among others, it chanced that a white unmarried gentleman had obtained some knowledge of the circumstances in which I was placed. He knew my grandmother, and often spoke to me in the street. He became interested for me, and asked questions about my master, which I answered in part. He expressed a great deal of sympathy, and a wish to aid me. He constantly sought opportunities to see me, and wrote to me frequently. I was a poor slave girl, only fifteen years old.

So much attention from a superior person was, of course, flattering; for human nature is the same in all. I also felt grateful for his sympathy, and encouraged by his kind words. It seemed to me a great thing to have such a friend. By degrees, a more tender feeling crept into my heart. He was an educated and eloquent gentleman; too eloquent, alas, for the poor slave girl who trusted in him. Of course I saw whither all this was tending. I knew the impassable gulf between us; but to be an object of interest to a man who is not married, and who is not her master, is agreeable to the pride and feelings of a slave, if her miserable situation has left her any pride or sentiment. It seems less degrading to give one's self, than to submit to compulsion. There is something akin to freedom in having a lover who has no control over you, except that which he gains by kindness and attachment. A master may treat you as rudely as he pleases, and you dare not speak; moreover, the wrong does not seem so great with an unmarried man, as with one who has a wife to be made unhappy. There may be sophistry in all this; but the condition of a slave confuses all principles of morality, and, in fact, renders the practice of them impossible.

When I found that my master had actually begun to build the lonely cottage, other feelings mixed with those I have described. Revenge, and calculations of interest, were added to flattered vanity and sincere gratitude for kindness. I knew nothing would enrage Dr. Flint so much as to know that I favored another; and it was something to triumph over my tyrant even in that small way. I thought he would revenge himself by selling me, and I was sure my friend, Mr. Sands, would buy me. He was a man of more generosity and feeling than my master, and I thought my freedom could be easily obtained from him. The crisis of my fate now came so near that I was desperate. I shuddered to think of being the mother of children that should be owned by my old tyrant. I knew that as soon as a new fancy took him, his victims were sold far off to get rid of them; especially if they had children. I had seen several women sold, with his babies at the breast. He never allowed his offspring by slaves to remain long in sight of himself and his wife. Of a man who was not my master I could ask to have my children well supported; and in this case, I felt confident I should obtain the boon. I also felt quite sure that they would be made free. With all these thoughts revolving in my mind, and seeing no other way of escaping the doom I so much dreaded, I made a headlong plunge. Pity me, and pardon me, O virtuous reader! You never knew what it is to be a slave; to be entirely unprotected by law or custom; to have the laws reduce you to the condition of a chattel, entirely subject to the will of another. You never exhausted your ingenuity in avoiding the snares, and eluding the power of a hated tyrant; you never shuddered at the sound of his footsteps, and trembled within hearing of his voice. I know I did wrong. No one can feel it more sensibly than I do. The painful and humiliating memory will haunt me to my dying day. Still, in looking back, calmly, on the events of my life, I feel that the slave woman ought not to be judged by the same standard as others.

The months passed on. I had many unhappy hours. I secretly mourned over the sorrow I was bringing on my grandmother, who had so tried to shield me from harm. I knew that I was the greatest comfort of her old age, and that it was a source of pride to her that I had not degraded myself, like most of the slaves. I wanted to confess to her that I was no longer worthy of her love; but could not utter the dreaded words.

As for Dr. Flint, I had a feeling of satisfaction and triumph in the thought of telling *him*. From time to time he told me of his intended arrangements, and I was silent. At last, he came and told me the cottage was completed, and ordered me to go to it. I told him I would never enter it. He said, "I have heard enough of such talk as that. You shall go, if you are carried by force; and you shall remain there."

I replied, "I will never go there. In a few months I shall be a mother."

He stood and looked at me in dumb amazement, and left the house without a word. I thought I should be happy in my triumph over him. But now that the truth was out, and my relatives would hear of it, I felt wretched. Humble as were their circumstances, they had pride in my good character. Now, how could I look them in the face? My self-respect was gone! I had resolved that I would be virtuous, though I was a slave. I had said, "Let the storm beat! I will brave it till I die." And now, how humiliated I felt!

I went to my grandmother. My lips moved to make confession, but the words stuck in my throat. I sat down in the shade of a tree at her door and began to sew. I think she saw something unusual was the matter with me. The mother of slaves is very watchful. She knows there is no security for her children. After they have entered their teens she lives in daily expectation of trouble. This leads to many questions. If the girl is of a sensitive nature, timidity keeps her from answering truthfully, and this well-meant course has a tendency to drive her from maternal counsels. Presently, in came my mistress, like a mad woman, and accused me concerning her husband. My grandmother, whose suspicions had been previously awakened, believed what she said. She exclaimed, "O Linda! has it come to this? I had rather see you dead than to see you as you now are. You are a disgrace to your dead mother." She tore from my fingers my mother's wedding ring and her silver thimble. "Go away!" she exclaimed, "and never come to my house, again." Her reproaches fell so hot and heavy, that they left me no chance to answer. Bitter tears, such as the eyes never shed but once, were my only answer. I rose from my seat, but fell back again, sobbing. She did not speak to me; but the tears were running down her furrowed cheeks, and they scorched me like fire. She had always been so kind to me! *So* kind! How I longed to throw myself at her feet, and tell her all the truth! But she had ordered me to go, and never to come there again. After a few minutes, I mustered strength, and started to obey her. With what feelings did I now close that little gate, which I used to open with such an eager hand in my childhood! It closed upon me with a sound I never heard before.

Where could I go? I was afraid to return to my master's. I walked on recklessly, not caring where I went, or what would become of me. When I had gone four or five miles, fatigue compelled me to stop. I sat down on the stump of an old tree. The stars were shining through the boughs above me. How they mocked me, with their bright, calm light! The hours passed by, and as I sat there alone a chilliness and deadly sickness came over me. I sank on the ground. My mind was full of horrid thoughts. I prayed to die; but the prayer was not answered. At last, with great effort I roused myself, and walked some distance further, to the house of a woman who had been a friend of my mother. When I told her why I was there, she spoke soothingly to me; but I could not be comforted. I thought I could bear my shame if I could only be reconciled to my grandmother. I longed to open my heart to her. I thought if she could know the real state of the case, and all I had been bearing for years, she would perhaps judge me less harshly. My friend advised me to send for her. I did so; but days of agonizing suspense passed before she came. Had she utterly forsaken me? No. She came at last. I knelt before her, and told her things that had poisoned my life; how long I had been persecuted; that I saw no way of escape; and in an hour of extremity I had become desperate. She listened in silence. I told her I would bear any thing and do any thing, if in time I had hopes of obtaining her forgiveness. I begged of her to pity me, for my dead mother's sake. And she did pity me. She did not say, "I forgive you;" but she looked at me lovingly, with her eyes full of tears. She laid her old hand gently on my head, and murmured, "Poor child! Poor child!"

XI. The New Tie to Life

I returned to my good grandmother's house. She had an interview with Mr. Sands. When she asked him why he could not have left her one ewe lamb,—whether there were not plenty of slaves who did not care about character,—he made no answer; but he spoke kind and encouraging words. He promised to care for my child, and to buy me, be the conditions what they might.

I had not seen Dr. Flint for five days. I had never seen him since I made the avowal to him. He talked of the disgrace I had brought on myself; how I had sinned against my master, and mortified my old grandmother. He intimated that if I had accepted his proposals, he, as a physician, could have saved me from exposure. He even condescended to pity me. Could he have offered wormwood more bitter? He, whose persecutions had been the cause of my sin!

"Linda," said he, "though you have been criminal towards me, I feel for you, and I can pardon you if you obey my wishes. Tell me whether the fellow you wanted to marry is the father of your child. If you deceive me, you shall feel the fires of hell."

I did not feel as proud as I had done. My strongest weapon with him was gone. I was lowered in my own estimation, and had resolved to bear his abuse in silence. But when he spoke contemptuously of the lover who had always treated me honorably; when I remembered that but for *him* I might have been a virtuous, free, and happy wife, I lost my patience. "I have sinned against God and myself," I replied; "but not against you."

He clinched his teeth, and muttered, "Curse you!" He came towards me, with ill-suppressed rage, and exclaimed, "You obstinate girl! I could grind your bones to powder! You have thrown yourself away on some worthless rascal. You are weak-minded, and have been easily persuaded by those who don't care a straw for you. The future will settle accounts between us. You are blinded now; but hereafter you will be convinced that your master was your best friend. My lenity towards you is a proof of it. I might have punished you in many ways. I might have had you whipped till you fell dead under the lash. But I wanted you to live; I would have bettered your condition. Others cannot do it. You are my slave. Your mistress, disgusted by your conduct, forbids you to return to the house; therefore I leave you here for the present; but I shall see you often. I will call tomorrow."

He came with frowning brows, that showed a dissatisfied state of mind. After asking about my health, he inquired whether my board was paid, and who visited me. He then went on to say that he had neglected his duty; that as a physician there were certain things that he ought to have explained to me. Then followed talk such as would have made the most shameless blush. He ordered me to stand up before him. I obeyed. "I command you," said he, "to tell me whether the father of your child is white or black." I hesitated. "Answer me this instant!" he exclaimed. I did answer. He sprang upon me like a wolf, and grabbed my arm as if he would have broken it. "Do you love him?" said he, in a hissing tone.

"I am thankful that I do not despise him," I replied.

He raised his hand to strike me; but it fell again. I don't know what arrested the blow. He sat down, with lips tightly compressed. At last he spoke. "I came here," said he, "to make you a friendly proposition; but your ingratitude chafes me beyond endurance. You turn aside all my good intentions towards you. I don't know what it is that keeps me from killing you." Again he rose, as if he had a mind to strike me.

But he resumed. "On one condition I will forgive your insolence and crime. You must henceforth have no communication of any kind with the father of your child. You must not ask any thing from him, or receive any thing from him. I will take care of you and your child. You had better promise this at once, and not wait till you are deserted by him. This is the last act of mercy I shall show towards you."

I said something about being unwilling to have my child supported by a man who had cursed it and me also. He rejoined, that a woman who had sunk to my level had no right to expect any thing else. He asked, for the last time, would I accept his kindness? I answered that I would not.

"Very well," said he; "then take the consequences of your wayward course. Never look to me for help. You are my slave, and shall always be my slave. I will never sell you, that you may depend upon."

Hope died away in my heart as he closed the door after him. I had calculated that in his rage he would sell me to a slavetrader; and I knew the father of my child was on the watch to buy me.

About this time my uncle Phillip was expected to return from a voyage. The day before his departure I had officiated as bridesmaid to a young friend. My heart was then ill at ease, but my smiling countenance did not betray it. Only a year had passed; but what fearful changes it had wrought! My heart had grown gray in misery. Lives that flash in sunshine, and lives that are born in tears, receive their hue from circumstances. None of us know what a year may bring forth.

I felt no joy when they told me my uncle had come. He wanted to see me, though he knew what had happened. I shrank from him at first; but at last consented that he should come to my room. He received me as he always had done. O, how my heart smote me when I felt his tears on my burning cheeks! The words of my grandmother came to my mind,— "Perhaps your mother and father are taken from the evil days to come." My disappointed heart could now praise God that it was so. But why, thought I, did my relatives ever cherish hopes for me? What was there to save me from the usual fate of slave girls? Many more beautiful and more intelligent than I had experienced a similar fate, or a far worse one. How could they hope that I should escape?

My uncle's stay was short, and I was not sorry for it. I was too ill in mind and body to enjoy my friends as I had done. For some weeks I was unable to leave my bed. I could not have any doctor but my master, and I would not have him sent for. At last, alarmed by my increasing illness, they sent for him. I was very weak and nervous; and as soon as he entered the room, I began to scream. They told him my state was very critical. He had no wish to hasten me out of the world, and he withdrew.

When my babe was born, they said it was premature. It weighed only four pounds; but God let it live. I heard the doctor say I could not survive till morning. I had often prayed for death; but now I did not want to die, unless my child could die too. Many weeks passed before I was able to leave my bed. I was a mere wreck of my former self. For a year there was scarcely a day when I was free from chills and fever. My babe also was sickly. His little limbs were often racked with pain. Dr. Flint continued his visits, to look after my health; and he did not fail to remind me that my child was an addition to his stock of slaves.

I felt too feeble to dispute with him, and listened to his remarks in silence. His visits were less frequent; but his busy spirit could not remain quiet. He employed my brother in his office, and he was made the medium of frequent notes and messages to me. William was a bright lad, and of much use to the doctor. He had learned to put up medicines, to leech, cup, and bleed. He had taught himself to read and spell. I was proud of my brother; and the old doctor suspected as much. One day, when I had not seen him for several weeks, I heard his steps approaching the door. I dreaded the encounter, and hid myself. He inquired for me, of course; but I was nowhere to be found. He went to his office, and despatched William with a note. The color mounted to my brother's face when he gave it to me; and he said, "Don't you hate me, Linda, for bringing you these things?" I told him I could not blame him; he was a slave, and obliged to obey his master's will. The note ordered me to come to his office. I went. He demanded to know where I was when he called. I told him I was at home. He flew into a passion, and said he knew better. Then he launched out upon his usual themes,—my crimes against him, and my ingratitude for his forbearance. The laws were laid down to me anew, and I was dismissed. I felt humiliated that my brother should stand by, and listen to such language as would be addressed only to a slave. Poor boy! He was powerless to defend me; but I saw the tears, which he vainly strove to keep back. This manifestation of feeling irritated the doctor. William could do nothing to please him. One morning he did not arrive at the office so early as usual; and that circumstance afforded his master an opportunity to vent his spleen. He was put in jail. The next day my brother sent a trader to the doctor, with a request to be sold. His master was greatly incensed at what he called his insolence. He said he had put him there to reflect upon his bad conduct, and he certainly was not giving any evidence of repentance. For two days he harassed himself to find somebody to do his office work; but every thing went wrong without William. He was released, and ordered to take his old stand, with many threats, if he was not careful about his future behavior.

As the months passed on, my boy improved in health. When he was a year old, they called him beautiful. The little vine was taking deep root in my existence, though its clinging fondness excited a mixture of love and pain. When I was most sorely oppressed I found a solace in his smiles. I loved to watch his infant slumbers; but always there was a dark cloud over my enjoyment. I could never forget that he was a slave. Sometimes I wished that he might die in infancy. God tried me. My darling became very ill. The bright eyes grew dull, and the little feet and hands were so icy cold that I thought death had already touched them. I had prayed for his death, but never so earnestly as I now prayed for his life; and my prayer was heard. Alas, what mockery it is for a slave mother to try to pray back her dying child to life! Death is better than slavery. It was a sad thought that I had no name to give my child. His father caressed him and treated him kindly, whenever he had a chance to see him. He was not unwilling that he should bear his name; but he had no legal claim to it; and if I had bestowed it upon him, my master would have regarded it as a new crime, a new piece of insolence, and would, perhaps, revenge it on the boy. O, the serpent of Slavery has many and poisonous fangs!

• • • • • • • • • • • •

QUESTIONS FOR A SECOND READING

1. This text makes it difficult to say what some are prepared to say: that slaves were illiterate, uneducated, simple in their speech and thought. Jacobs's situation was not typical, to be sure, but she challenges the assumptions we bring to our imagination of this country's past and its people. This text has to be read carefully or it becomes familiar, a product of what we think we already know.

     As you reread, mark sentences, phrases, or paragraphs you might use to illustrate Jacobs's characteristic style or skill as a writer. And mark those features of the text you might use to identify this text as the work of a woman held in slavery. Where and how is doing this difficult? surprising? a problem?

2. In her preface, Jacobs says that she doesn't care to excite sympathy for her suffering but to "arouse the women of the North to a realizing sense of the

condition of two millions of women at the South." As you reread this selection, pay attention to the ways Jacobs addresses (and tries to influence) her readers. Why would she be suspicious of sympathy? What do you suppose she might have meant by "a realizing sense"? What kind of reader does she want? Why does she address women?

Be sure to mark those sections that address the reader directly, and also those that seem to give evidence of Jacobs as a writer, working on the material, highlighting some incidents and passing over others (why do we get "incidents" and not the full story?), organizing our experience of the text, shaping scenes and sentences, organizing chapters. What is Jacobs doing in this text? What might her work as a writer have to do with her position (as a female slave) in relation to the world of her readers?

3. The emotional and family relations between people are difficult to chart in this selection, partly because they defy easy categorization. Can we, for example, assume that blacks and whites lived separately? that blacks were in bondage and whites were free? that family lines and color lines were distinct markers? that lovers were lovers and enemies were enemies? As you reread, pay close attention to the ways people are organized by family, love, community, and color. See what you can determine about the codes that govern relations in this representation of slave culture. And ask where and how Jacobs places herself in these various networks.

ASSIGNMENTS FOR WRITING

1. In the preface to her edition of *Incidents in the Life of a Slave Girl*, Jean Fagin Yellin says the following about Jacobs's narrative:

> Contrasting literary styles express the contradictory thrusts of the story. Presenting herself as a heroic slave mother, Jacobs's narrator includes clear detail, uses straightforward language, and when addressing the reader directly, utilizes standard abolitionist rhetoric to lament the inadequacy of her descriptions and to urge her audience to involve themselves in antislavery efforts. But she treats her sexual experiences obliquely, and when addressing the reader concerning her sexual behavior, pleads for forgiveness in the overwrought style of popular fiction. These melodramatic confessions are, however, subsumed within the text. What finally dominates is a new voice. It is the voice of a woman who, although she cannot discuss her sexual past without expressing deep conflict, nevertheless addresses this painful personal subject in order to politicize it, to insist that the forbidden topic of the sexual abuse of slave women be included in public discussions of the slavery question. By creating a narrator who presents her private sexual history as a subject of public political concern, Jacobs moves her book out of the world of conventional nineteenth-century polite discourse. In and through her creation of Linda Brent, who yokes her success story as a heroic slave mother to her confession as a woman who mourns that she is not a storybook heroine, Jacobs articulates her struggle to assert her womanhood and projects a new kind of female hero.

Yellin's account of the "voice" in Jacobs's text gives us a way to foreground the difference between life and narrative, a person (Harriet Jacobs) and a person rendered on the page ("Linda Brent," the "I" of the narrative), between the experience of slavery and the conventional ways of telling the story of slavery, between experience and the ways in which experience is shaped by a writer, readers, and a culture. It is interesting, in this sense, to read Yellin's account of *Incidents* along with Houston Baker's more general account of the "voice of the Southern slave" (quoted at length on p. 352). Baker, you may recall, said: "The voice of the unwritten self, once it is subjected to the linguistic codes, literary conventions, and audience expectations of a literate population, is perhaps never again the authentic voice of black American slavery. It is, rather, the voice of a self transformed by an autobiographical act into a sharer in the general public discourse about slavery."

Jacobs's situation as a writer could be said to reproduce her position as a slave, cast as a member of the community but not as a person. Write an essay in which you examine Jacobs's work as a writer. Consider the ways she works on her reader (a figure she both imagines and constructs) and also the ways she works on her material (a set of experiences, a language, and the conventional ways of telling the story of one's life). To do this, you will need to reread the text as something constructed (see the second "Question for a Second Reading").

2. We can take these opening chapters of *Incidents in the Life of a Slave Girl* as an account of a girl's coming of age, particularly in the sense that coming of age is a cultural (and not simply a biological) process. The chapters represent the ways in which Jacobs comes to be positioned as a woman in the community, and they represent her understanding of that process (and the necessary limits to her understanding, since no person can stand completely outside her culture and what it desires her to believe or to take as natural).

   Read back through "Incidents," paying particular attention to what Jacobs sees as the imposed structure of slave culture and what she takes as part of human nature. Remember that there are different ways of reading the codes that govern human relations. What Jacobs takes to be unnatural may well seem natural to Dr. Flint. Jacobs could be said to be reading "against" what Flint, or the Slave Owner as a generic type, would understand as naturally there.

   Now read through again, this time reading against Jacobs, to see how her view of relationships could be said to be shaped also by a set of beliefs and interests. Look for a system governing Jacobs's understanding. You might ask, for instance, what system leads her to see Dr. Flint and Mr. Sands as different, since they could also be said to be similar — both slave owners, both after the same thing. How does Jacobs place herself in relation to other slaves? other blacks? Jacobs is light skinned. How does she fit into a system governed by color? Both Mrs. Flint and Jacobs's grandmother react strongly to Jacobs. What system governs Jacobs's sense of the difference between these two women?

   Write an essay in which you try to explain the codes that govern the relations between people in slave culture, at least as that culture is represented in "Incidents."

MAKING CONNECTIONS

1. Alice Walker's reading of the history of African American women in her essay, "In Search of Our Mothers' Gardens" (p. 668), pays particular attention to the "creative spirit" of these women in the face of oppressive working and living conditions. Of her mother, Walker writes:

   > Her face, as she prepares the Art that is her gift, is a legacy of respect she leaves to me, for all that illuminates and cherishes life. She has handed down respect for the possibilities—and the will to grasp them. (p. 675)

   And to the poet Phillis Wheatley she writes: "It is not so much what you sang, as that you kept alive, in so many of our ancestors, *the notion of song.*"

   Although Walker does not include Harriet Jacobs in her essay, one could imagine ways in which Jacobs's work as a writer is appropriate to Walker's discussion of African American women's creativity. As you reread Jacobs's selection, note the choices she makes as a writer: her language, her selection of incidents and details, her method of addressing an audience, the ways in which she negotiates a white literary tradition. Where, for instance, do you see her writing purposely negotiating a literary tradition that is not hers? Who does she imagine as her audience? How does she use language differently for different purposes? Why?

   How would you say that the writerly choices Jacobs makes and enacts allow her to express a creativity that otherwise would have been stifled? What type of legacy does she create in her narrative to pass on to her descendants? And, as Walker writes in honor of her mother and Wheatley, what might Walker or you write in honor of Jacobs?

   Write an essay in which you extend Walker's project by considering where and how Jacobs's work as a writer and artist would complement Walker's argument for the "creative spirit" of African American women in the face of oppressive conditions.

2. In "When We Dead Awaken: Writing as Re-Vision" (p. 520), Adrienne Rich says, "Re-vision—the act of looking back, of seeing with fresh eyes, of entering an old text from a new critical direction—is for women more than a chapter in cultural history: it is an act of survival. Until we can understand the assumptions in which we are drenched we cannot know ourselves" (p. 522).

   Let's imagine that one of the difficulties we have in reading "Incidents" is that we approach it drenched in assumptions; we look with old eyes (or the wrong eyes). In honor of the challenge Rich sets for a reader—or, for that matter, in honor of Harriet Jacobs and the challenge she sets for a reader—write an essay in which you show what it would mean to revise your reading (or what you take to be most people's reading, the "common" reading) of "Incidents." You will want to show both how the text would be read from this new critical direction and what effort (or method) would be involved in pushing against the old ways of reading.

3. Here, from "Arts of the Contact Zone" (p. 499), is Mary Louise Pratt on the "autoethnographic" text:

Guaman Poma's *New Chronicle* is an instance of what I have proposed to call an *autoethnographic* text, by which I mean a text in which people undertake to describe themselves in ways that engage with representations others have made of them. Thus if ethnographic texts are those in which European metropolitan subjects represent to themselves their others (usually their conquered others), autoethnographic texts are representations that the so-defined others construct *in response to* or in dialogue with those texts. . . . [T]hey involve a selective collaboration with and appropriation of idioms of the metropolis or the conqueror. These are merged or infiltrated to varying degrees with indigenous idioms to create self-representations intended to intervene in metropolitan modes of understanding. . . . Such texts often constitute a marginalized group's point of entry into the dominant circuits of print culture. It is interesting to think, for example, of American slave autobiography in its autoethnographic dimensions, which in some respects distinguish it from Euramerican autobiographical tradition. (pp. 501–2)

Reread Jacobs's "Incidents in the Life of a Slave Girl" after reading Pratt's essay. Using the example of Pratt's work with the *New Chronicle*, write an essay in which you present a reading of Jacobs's text as an example of an autoethnographic and/or transcultural text. You should imagine that you are working to put Pratt's ideas to the test, but also to see what you can say on your own about *Incidents* as a text, as something written and read.

4. John Edgar Wideman's *Brothers and Keepers*, Cornelius Eady's *Brutal Imagination*, and Harriet Jacobs's *Incidents in the Life of a Slave Girl* all call attention to the difficulties of narrating or representing the experiences of African Americans—of telling the story, of getting it right, of recovering experience from the representations of others. Both Jacobs's and Wideman's texts could carry the subtitle *Brutal Imagination*.

    Read either Eady or Wideman alongside Jacobs and write an essay in which you consider both writers to be working on a problem that has particular urgency for black writers. How might you name this problem? How might you illustrate it? What do you find compelling in these two approaches to the problem? And what might this problem have to do with you as a writer and thinker?

MICHAEL
McKEON

MICHAEL McKEON (b. 1943) received his BA from the University of Chicago and his PhD from Columbia University. He is currently the Board of Governor's Professor of English at Rutgers University. McKeon is one of the world's leading scholars of Early Modern Britain, its history, literature, and culture. The phrase "early modern" alludes to the period between the Middle Ages and the Industrial Revolution (roughly 1500–1800), a period characterized by the rise of science and technology, the spread of literacy and education, a movement of people toward urban centers, and of government from religious to civic law and from there to the idea of the nation-state. It was also a period that marked dramatic changes in the nature and structure of the family, of the relations between men and women, and, as marketplaces became abstracted to a market economy, dramatic changes between social classes, between those who had money and those who worked for it. The phrase "early modern" was coined to indicate a period of transition between the "dark" ages and the "modern" world, the world we take for granted. The phrase has helped to organize periods or stages in the history (say) of domesticity or everyday life; it has also helped to make available for scrutiny current practices, those ways of thinking and acting that we take for granted as "normal" or "natural" or inevitable, and to make them seem noteworthy or strange.

McKeon is the author of several ground-breaking books on seventeenth- and eighteenth-century Britain, including Politics and Poetry in Restoration England *(1975) and the edited anthology* Theory of the Novel: A Historical Approach *(2000). His most important work, however, is represented in two very big books:* The Origins of the English Novel, 1600–1740, *which won the Modern Language Association's James Russell Lowell Prize, and* The Secret History of Domesticity: Public, Private, and the Division of Knowledge *(2005), which won a "professional and scholarly publishing award" from the Association of American Publishers. These books are big in size (*The Secret History of Domesticity *has 873 pages) but they are also large in sweep and ambition, finding pattern and sense across broad periods of time and from a staggering array of sources and primary materials. One reviewer (in the* New Yorker) *referred to* The Secret History *as "colossal" and said "the strength of the book lies in the wealth of historical, literary, and pictorial examples that evoke the texture of domesticity, from bedchambers to bigamy."*

The selection that follows comes from the fifth (of fifteen) chapters in The Secret History of Domesticity, *"Subdividing Inside Spaces." It concerns domestic architecture and the division of inside spaces to separate public and private life and, in doing so, to create the forms of privacy that we now take for granted. In the introduction to the book, McKeon says:*

> *This book began as an effort to address a set of questions central to our understanding of the past. On the one hand, the modern Western view of the public and the private, both the categories and the constitutive difference between them, has seemed to students of many disciplines a fundamentally new historical phenomenon. On the other hand, both the categories and their difference are a fundamental feature of traditional societies as well, whether we mean by "tradition" what precedes the modern period or what coexists with modernity in time independent of its singular character and influence. (p. xvii)*

It would be wrong, in other words, to think that "early modern people," people in "traditional societies," had no concept of the difference between public and private life; it is that the distinction was not "constitutive" — it was not yet represented by necessarily separate public and private spaces, either on the street or in a public building (like a coffeehouse) or in a palace, home, or cottage. He says: "In 'traditional' culture, the differential relationship between public and private modes of experience is conceived as a distinction that does not admit of separation" (p. xix). He shows how this is represented (in architectural drawings, for example) and asks his readers to imagine a life so conceived. In his opening example, for instance, he shows a scientist's laboratory that is also the kitchen, where, he says, "work and housework enjoy a harmonious coexistence."

The chapter that follows is filled with illustrations, both artistic and architectural representations of interior spaces. You will need to take time to "read" them as crucial elements in the text.

Subdividing Inside Spaces

The transition from cottage industry to the factory system has a well-known significance in the emergence of modern culture. In Max Weber's words, "The modern rational organization of the capitalistic enterprise would not have been possible without . . . the separation of business from the household, which completely dominates modern economic life . . . ."[1] Industrial production is only the most obvious instance of this transition. The rise of the professions entailed the separation out not only of specialized technical practices but also of specialized workplaces. As with the cottage industry and protoindustrialization, a brief glimpse of "protoprofessional" space at this transitional moment affords some insight into one aspect of the modern public-private relationship.

Separating Out "Science"

Perhaps the most consequential of all divisions of knowledge in the early modern period is the separation out of "the sciences" in the modern sense of the term: from *scientia* in the traditional meaning of knowledge as such; from the arts and the humanities; and from all practices indifferent to the strictest principles of empirical epistemology. The development of modern science is coextensive with the development of what we have learned to call "laboratories," whose family resemblances distinguish them from the disparate range of spaces—monasteries, theaters, altars, domestic kitchens and closets—in which "natural philosophers" of all sorts were accustomed to practice their arts.[2] These practitioners—alchemists, astrologers, apothecaries, unnatural natural historians, collectors, quacks, antiquarians, virtuosi—helped mediate the emergence of the modern figure of the "scientist." In contemporary depictions of their practices the particularity of a distinctive and specialized kind of space is precisely what is absent. What these images share looks retrospectively like a parasitic dependence on the more "traditional" sorts of inside space, as well as some representational commonplaces that seem for that reason alone to bespeak a common enterprise.

A number of seventeenth-century, primarily Dutch genre painters were fond of the subject of the alchemist at work. Figures 1 and 2, paintings of the mid- to later seventeenth century by Thomas Wijck and his younger contemporary Richard Brakenburgh, illustrate the coextension of "public" laboratory and private household space within a single shared interior through the depiction of male alchemical activity alongside female housework and maternal care. In Wijck's painting, the alchemist is set back from his family by the doubly vaulted structure of the deep but open interior space. He sits at his desk reading, surrounded by books and a globe, a studious and contemplative figure whose beret and fur-trimmed cloak are

Figure 1. Thomas Wijck, *The Alchemist*, seventeenth century. Oil on panel. Eddleman Collection 00.03.06, Chemical Heritage Foundation Collections, Philadelphia, PA. Photo: Will Brown.

those of a scholar. Suspended from the ceiling are specimens, a reptile and a turtle, whose presence and placement are, as we will see, a representational convention that helps define the common ground between the disparate practitioners of protoscience (cf. Fig. 3, the entrance to the apothecary's shop). In the left foreground an alchemical distillation occupies part of the stove. To its right are the alchemist's wife and two children, the son helping his mother prepare food and the daughter, perhaps too young for real work, nonetheless imitating her mother's diligence. On the table are

Figure 2. Richard Brakenburgh, *An Alchemist's Workshop with Children Playing*, late seventeenth century. Oil on canvas. Eddleman Collection 00.03.11, Chemical Heritage Foundation Collections, Philadelphia, PA. Photo: Will Brown.

bread and a pitcher, on the floor a jumble of alchemical and culinary utensils. Light enters the foreground space from windows that look out onto a village scene. This is a household in which work and housework enjoy a harmonious coexistence.

In Brakenburgh's painting, similar elements are arranged to very different effect. The space is dark but not deep, the limits of the background defined by the dim outlines of furniture and the seated group, a typical and familiar image from other Netherlandish genre painters. The foreground—indeed, the painting—is dominated by the standing figure of the alchemist's wife, whose graceful frustration organizes the sense of ironic disjunction that permeates the scene she surveys. A small child clinging to her skirts, she expostulates with her husband, her right hand gesturing toward four more children in the left foreground: one plays alchemist on the floor, two sit forlorn at a small empty table, and another points to an empty cupboard. On the other side of the room, his eyes wide with excitement, is the alchemist, monopolizing the fire and surrounded by the clutter of his instruments, his eldest son behind him gaily aping his father by pumping the lever of the hearth bellows. The conventionality of the alchemist paintings

Figure 3. Frontispiece, J. S., *Childrens Diseases Both Outward and Inward* (1664),
in Wendy Wall, *Staging Domesticity: Household Work and English Identity
in Early Modern Drama* (Cambridge: Cambridge University Press, 2002).
Princeton University Library.

militates against reading them, as some have done, as efforts at the "realistic" representation of early laboratory space.[3] Still, the interpenetration of public and private spaces, of scientific experiment and the domestic household, is consistent with what we know from other sources about the early practice of natural philosophy.[4] What Brakenburgh registers, however, is a growing skepticism about the figure of the alchemist that itself becomes conventional in genre paintings and other cultural commentary in the eighteenth century and that has some bearing on this spatial coextension.[5] The central irony concerns what is gradually being exposed as the grandiose impracticality of the alchemical ambition, and it is pointed by the failure of the dreamy head of household to support his family with his labor. But the resulting disjunction between the alchemist's work and his wife's vain efforts at housework depends for much of its effect on the way Brakenburgh makes us feel their incompatibility within the same domestic space.

One of William Hogarth's large engraved illustrations (1725) for Samuel Butler's *Hudibras* (1663), set in the astrologer Sidrophel's chambers (Fig. 4), depicts the knight holding off Sidrophel and his assistant Whachum as Ralpho runs to fetch the constable (pt. 2, canto 3, lines 1013–70). As in the alchemist paintings, the astrologer's sanctum is cluttered with arcane paraphernalia, including books, a globe, and suspended specimens of fish and reptiles. Moreover, the presence of a cat places the scene of *arcana naturae* in

Figure 4. William Hogarth, *Hudibras beats Sidrophel and Whacum*, 1726.
No. 8 of twelve illustrations for Samuel Butler's *Hudibras* (1663, 1664, 1678),
in William Hogarth, *Hogarth: The Complete Engravings*, ed. Joseph Burke
and Colin Caldwell (New York: Abrams, 1968). Princeton University Library.

a larger if largely suggested domestic setting. . . . Figure 5, *Dr. Silvester Partridge's Predictions* (1719), is more obviously part of a household space. The astrologer, casting nativities for his customers, is surrounded by books, equipment (some of it alchemical), and suspended specimens.

The motif of the suspended specimen links these representations of alchemists and astrologers, both partly embedded in the household, to a

Figure 5. Elisha Kirkall, *Dr. Silvester Partridge's Predictions*, 1719,
in Charles Saumarez Smith, *Eighteenth-Century Decoration: Design and the Domestic Interior in England* (New York: Abrams, 1993). Princeton University Library.

third practice of early modern natural philosophy, the cabinet of curiosities. The term "cabinet" first referred to a cupboard with shelves and drawers that held assorted small natural and cultural rarities. Although it continued to have this meaning, by the seventeenth century the word might also designate the larger space—a closet or a chamber—that contained such cabinets.[6] The wall structure we see behind Dr. Partridge fits the original description well enough, but its contents are more serviceable than collectible; the cabinet of curiosities was, not surprisingly, a luxury of the nobility and/or the wealthy. A private space within a private space, the cabinet encapsulated the great world within its odd and wondrous confines, and it announced its owner to be a gentleman of polite and cosmopolitan understanding. Public museums owe their origins to these private collections, which graced the estates and palaces of the Renaissance patriciate. Figure 6 is the first known illustration of such a museum, every inch of wall and ceiling filled with the recondite secrets of the universe. The son of the owner, the apothecary Ferrante Imperato, points out some choice specimens to elegantly attired visitors, while at their feet two domesticated lap dogs counterbalance the wild beasts overhead and remind us that this seemingly public museum is part of the apothecary's private family palace.[7]

Figure 6. *Ferrante Imperato's Museum in Naples*, 1599, in *The Origins of Museums: The Cabinet of Curiosities in Sixteenth- and Seventeenth-Century Europe*, ed. Oliver Impey and Arthur MacGregor (Oxford: Clarendon, 1985). Princeton University Press.

When the Royal Society announced the existence of its museum "repository" in 1666 it was described as a place where the gifts of benefactors would be preserved for posterity "probably much better and safer, than in their own private Cabinets."[8] Something of the early modern transformation of "science" from a collection of *arcana naturae* to the vast domain of material knowledge can be felt in the relationship between these cabinets and John Locke's domestication of epistemology as a process of furnishing and familiarizing the cabinet of the mind: "The Senses at first let in particular *Ideas*, and furnish the yet empty Cabinet: And the Mind by degrees growing familiar with some of them, they are lodged in the Memory, and Names got to them."[9] It may be unwarranted to read in Locke's metaphorical account of "lodging," then "naming," a systematic organizing motive. Nonetheless, we may speculate that what distinguishes the traditional cabinet of curiosities from the modern museum is not only its publicness but also its explicit aim to rationalize. One central ambition of the cabinet of curiosities is to amass objects that amaze not only in their odd singularity but also in the way this singularity is reinforced by the arbitrariness of their arrangement. In rationalizing its objects according to geographical, temporal, and cultural criteria, the modern museum on the contrary emphasizes collectivity over singularity, even—in allowing for empty spaces that will be filled by future specimens that are known to exist but not yet possessed—virtual collectivity.

The Royal Household

The separation of workplace from household is an almost universal feature of capitalist development, although it proceeded at different rates in different locales. Like the inn and the alehouse before it, the coffeehouse brought the private activity of food consumption into the public realm of market exchange. Images of eighteenth-century coffeehouses show traces of domestic living space, not only likely culinary articles (hearths, dish cupboards, and buffets) but also less predictable details like paintings, mirrors, and a customer still dressed for bed (see Figs. 7 and 8). "They say," wrote Joseph Moxon in 1684, "Such a One has set up a *Printing-House*, when thereby they only mean he has remov'd the Tools us'd in his former House." Indeed the state's apprehension of "Printing-houses, and Presses erected in byplaces and corners, out of the Eye of Government" led to the Interregnum parliamentary requirement that printers work *only* in "their respective Dwelling-Houses, and not elsewhere." In this exceptional way, then, domestic space was to have the visibility of public space: according to Moxon, illicit printers had "to get a Hole Private," where they might do their work "With More Secrecy Privaty and Securaty."[10] On the other hand, in the centers of large provincial towns, lockup shops, where the family lived off the premises, did not become common until after the middle of the

Figure 7. *The Coffee-house Politicians*, c. 1733.

Figure 8. *A Coffee House*, eighteenth-century French (?) adaptation
of Restoration drawing, in A. S. Turberville, *English Men and Manners
in the Eighteenth Century* (New York: Galaxy, 1957).

nineteenth century.[11] In Figure 9 we have an image of what the coextension
of household and workplace looked like at the lower levels of common life.

However, the separation of workplace from household is only the most
obvious manifestation of the way the division of the private from the public was spatialized in early modern interiors. In the development of elite
dwelling structures from the fifteenth through the eighteenth centuries we
have a graphic account both of the long-term transition from relations of
distinction to those of separation between the public and the private and of
the way this change proceeds through the successive rediscovery, within
the private realm, of a capacity for further subdivision. The risk of this kind
of survey lies in the methodological necessity of a starting point, which,
however heuristic its originating status, by the nature of the operation
never undergoes the complicating analysis to which later stages are pro-
grammatically subjected. I trust the reader will understand this as a formal
consequence of method rather than as a substantive claim as to the im-
mutability of medieval interiors, which I have neither the motive nor the
knowledge to make.

In the mid-seventeenth century, John Selden looked back to a time when
the hall was "the place where the great lord used to eat (wherefore else were
the Halls made so big?), where he saw all his servants and tenants about
him. He ate not in private, except in time of sickness: when once he became a
thing cooped up, all his greatness was spilled." In the late-medieval household, the maintenance of greatness required public spectacle and display,

Figure 9. Frontispiece, *Crispin the Cobler's Confutation of Ben H[oadley]* . . . (1709).
By permission of the British Library, shelf mark 94.e.21.

nowhere more so than in the ceremony of eating. But the openness of the great household went hand in hand with the ritualized expression of hierarchy, deference, and social place, which required a system of distinctions between spaces that marked differences in status that were also permeable to the basic principle of social totality. Francis Bacon acknowledged the most important of these architectural distinctions when he wrote that "you cannot have a perfect palace, except you have two several sides; a side for the banquet, . . . and a side for the household; the one for feasts and triumphs, and the other for dwelling."[12]

But Bacon's distinction cannot be correlated with our notions of the divide between the public and the private in any decisive way. This can be seen in Figure 10, a schematic diagram of the great house, whose basic distinction between the household of magnificence and the household of service cuts across Bacon's categorization. On the one hand, "public" feasts are set apart from "private" dwellings. On the other hand, feasts in the great hall are coextensive with the service rooms that produce them and distinct from the sequestered magnificence of the lord and his nuclear family in the great chamber. The dais step marks the barrier between these two households; but the screen marks another barrier, between those visitors who were admitted to the great hall to dine with the lord and those who might be offered no more than a drink at the buttery bar—as well as the servants engaged in food preparation. At the end of the screens passage is the door to the house, a third barrier between house and courtyard, which supplements the more fundamental act of social filtering that occurs at the gatehouse, "the immediate limit of the lord's territory." Viewed in this way, the great household exemplifies the model of the "linear house," the central aim of whose layout was to map, as a "visual expression of hierarchy," the successive degrees of access to the lord. All distinctions subserve this purpose of social subordination, which subsumes the several divisions between chamber and hall, hall and service rooms, house and courtyard, gatehouse and outside territory.[13] Indeed, the inapplicability of a consistent "public versus private" distinction even to these several divisions is clear from basic ambiguities in usage (thus life in the great chamber entails both the ultimate publicity of "magnificence" and the ultimate privacy of absence from public display). "Private" and "public" have a real but locally variable utility in this system, whose organizing coordinates are determined rather by a status hierarchy for which the difference between the public and the private in our sense of those terms is of ancillary importance.

Broadly speaking, innovation in interior design and usage began at the highest level of the social hierarchy and filtered downwards. Between the fifteenth and the early sixteenth centuries it became increasingly customary for the lord, his family, and his most immediate guests to dine in the chamber rather than in the hall. In the royal household this development—a withdrawal of public state into semiprivacy, which might equally be seen as an adaptation of private space to semipublic uses—occurred as early as

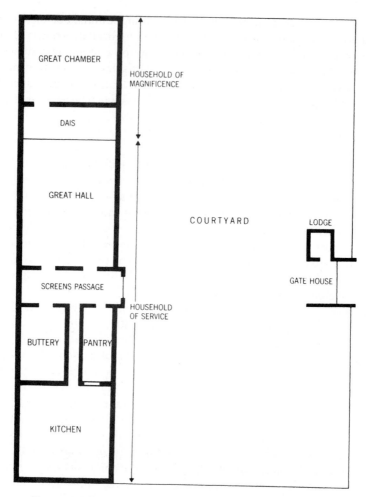

Figure 10. Schematic diagram of the great house, in Felicity Heal,
Hospitality in Early Modern England (Oxford: Clarendon, 1990), Fig. 21 (p. 28).
By permission of Oxford University Press.

the beginning of the fourteenth century. Thus began the slow process by which the great hall was transformed, by the seventeenth century, from the place of collective dining to the place where one first enters the house itself, the entrance hall. As if in confirmation, a century later Henry VII initiated a subdivision of the great chamber into its ceremonial and its personal aspects, the latter of which included the privy chamber (also called the secret chamber) or bedchamber, whose servants alone were likely to come into anything more than the most formal contact with the king. Now the structure of the royal household was triadic: privy chamber, chamber, household. According to one historian, "the process of withdrawal and subdivision entered a new phase" in the following reign, when Henry VIII created a new room, the presence chamber, to assume the functions of the old chamber, which now was to house the newly founded yeomen of the guard. Meanwhile the privy chamber became a private dining and reception chamber, subdivided from the royal bedchamber by a withdrawing room. Figure 11 is a schematic diagram of the king's apartments in the palace at Whitehall as they reflected these changes in the century between 1540 and 1640.[14]

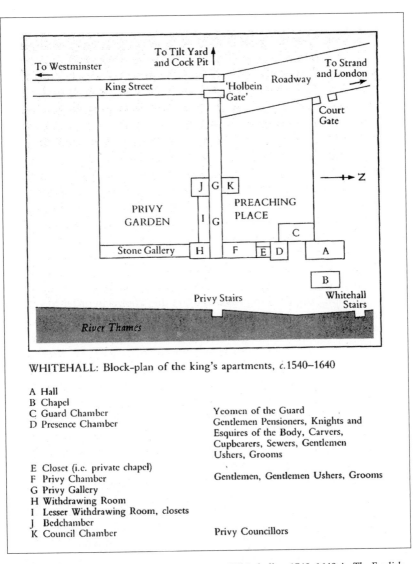

WHITEHALL: Block-plan of the king's apartments, *c.*1540–1640

A Hall
B Chapel
C Guard Chamber — Yeomen of the Guard
D Presence Chamber — Gentlemen Pensioners, Knights and Esquires of the Body, Carvers, Cupbearers, Sewers, Gentlemen Ushers, Grooms

E Closet (i.e. private chapel)
F Privy Chamber — Gentlemen, Gentlemen Ushers, Grooms
G Privy Gallery
H Withdrawing Room
I Lesser Withdrawing Room, closets
J Bedchamber
K Council Chamber — Privy Councillors

Figure 11. Block plan of the king's apartments, Whitehall, c. 1540–1640, in *The English Court: From the Wars of the Roses to the Civil War* (London: Longman, 1987), ed. David Starkey et al. Copyright © Jutland Ltd. Reproduced by permission of Curtis Brown Ltd., London, on behalf of the copyright owner. Princeton University Library.

A Restoration alchemical writer used the linearity of the royal interior to domesticate his vision of mystical theology as an exacting rite of sequential passages: "As in a *Royal Palace* we must pass through many rooms and *apartments*, before we come to the *Presence-chamber* of the Prince, so in *Eternal Nature* the *forms of darkness* must be pass'd through and after these the *Fire* and *Water*, before we can come to the *Love-fire*, which the Holy Trinity hath chosen for his *Presence-chamber*."[15] At the same time, however, it is not hard to see signs of the future in this plan. One general feature that will have important consequences in the later design of interiors is the way in which the subdivision and multiplication of rooms challenges the structure of the linear house and its incremental expression of hierarchy. Indeed, the ramification of architectural space with which the following pages will be concerned had its corollaries in other sorts of inferiority. John Locke, a contemporary of the alchemical writer just cited, also used the figure of the royal presence chamber to express how exacting must be the access of our senses to our understanding: "There are *some* Ideas, *which have admittance only through one Sense. . . .* And if these Organs, or the Nerves which are the Conduits, to convey them from without to their Audience in the Brain, the mind's Presence-room (as I may so call it) are any of them so disordered, as not to perform their Functions, they have no Postern to be admitted by. . . ." To do justice to the actual complexity of cognition, however, Locke is obliged to undercut the model of uniform linearity—there are five senses, not one—that the analogy otherwise might have conveyed, and we are left instead with the image of multiple passages radiating out from a singular center.[16] Another foretaste of futurity in this plan is the privy gallery (G), a mediating passageway that promotes privacy in principle by obviating the need to pass through other rooms in order to gain access to one's chosen destination. A third notable feature of this plan is the use of the closet as a sort of extended withdrawing room (H, I). . . .

Noble and Gentle Households

In royal and noble households the woman's levee was less officially designed for politics or business than the man's and was held in her bedroom or dressing room. The latter space seems to have been an English refinement—the term enters the language in the middle of the seventeenth century—perhaps because unlike in France, in England couples tended to share the same bedchamber. Still, Figure 12, rare in its representation of a seventeenth-century English interior as early as 1640, depicts an English lady's fashionable bedchamber that incorporates a dressing table covered by a table carpet and a *toilette* made of linen and lace, on which rests a dressing box with a built-in mirror. This is the period in which the ancient female arts of cosmetics are being separated out from culinary contexts and given an increasingly specialized status. In 1675 the lady's accomplishments in "Preserving, Physick, Beautifying and Cookery" could be pic-

Figure 12. *An English Lady's Bedchamber*, c. 1640, in Peter Thornton, *Authentic Decor: The Domestic Interior, 1620–1920* (New York: Viking, 1984). Marquand Library, Princeton University Library.

tured as transpiring in distinct spaces that nonetheless were part of a single domain of domestic expertise (Fig. 13). A Restoration critique of women for the luxurious excess of their dressing rooms met with the retort that "it is a general Desire in Men, that their Ladies should keep Home, and therefore it is but reasonable they should make their Homes as delightfull as it is possible. . . ." In the eighteenth century the dressing room often functioned as a private sitting room that (like the closet) contained a writing desk and table and might be larger than the bedroom itself. When the French word *garde-robe* was used to refer to a dressing room it designated a smaller closet off the bedchamber. Otherwise it named a wardrobe or (also) the place where the close-stool was kept.

Separate *appartements des bains* were unusual in the seventeenth century, although Ham House and Chatsworth (see below) had them, the former in a "Withdrawing-Roome." Most often people bathed piecemeal in basins or tubs placed for that purpose in their dressing rooms. Figure 14, entitled *Femme de qualité déshabillée pour le bain*, shows a woman sitting with her lap dog on a daybed, fashionable in 1685, washing her feet in a vessel that is set next to a perfume burner (*cassolette*), while her visitor's stagy pose of *politesse* just fails to shield his eyes from the intimate sight. Chamber pots sat in the bedchamber, under or next to the bed, or in an adjoining pantry when not in use. The more substantial close-stool might be elaborately

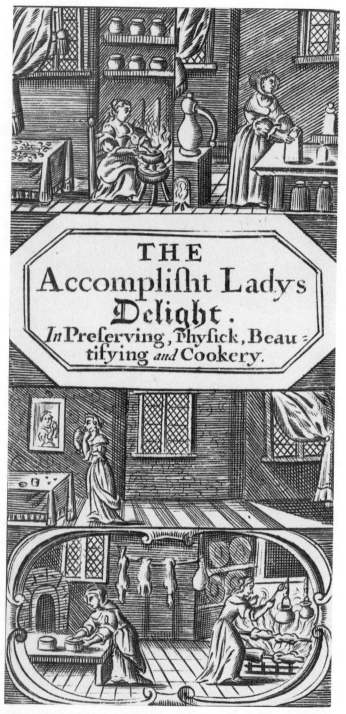

Figure 13. Frontispiece, Hannah Wooley, *The Accomplisht Ladys Delight* (1675).
Department of Rare Books and Special Collections, Princeton University Library.

Femme de qualité déshabillée pour le bain..

Figure 14. *Femme de qualité déshabillée pour le bain*, 1685, in Peter Thornton,
Seventeenth-Century Interior Decoration in England, France, and Holland
(New Haven, CT: Yale University Press, 1979). Marquand Library,
Princeton University Library.

worked, like "the Chest" in Swift's poem "The Lady's Dressing Room"
(1732), whose "counterfeit . . . Disguise" makes euphemism palpable. Close-
stools too might be left, as was Swift's, in full view, but they often were privately placed in separate small rooms or cubicles, or "water closets" (before
the eighteenth century close-stools tended to share a room with a servant).
Swift's ekphrastic close-stool, alluding as it does to the larger poetic enclo-
sure of which it forms one part, aptly captures the synecdochic profusion
characteristic of these female rooms, where multitudinous containers seem
to be larger and smaller variations on one another.[17]

When the birth of a child approached, the bedroom was temporarily (for as long as a month) transformed into another sort of female room,
the lying-in chamber, where the ceremony of childbirth was performed.
Both the ceremony and its spatialization had deep roots in traditional English culture, and they continued to dominate social life across the social
ranks until the end of the eighteenth century and the consolidation of the

man-midwife's expertise. This was a "private," but also an emphatically collective, activity. The bedroom was insulated from the outside, its air excluded by blocked keyholes, daylight shut out by the use of heavy curtains. The housewife withdrew from her customary physical labor and sexual services, taking to her bed in the company of the midwife—a distinct category of waged female household labor—and her several gossips (from "god-sib" or "god-sibling," a woman invited to witness the birth for the purpose of the later baptism). In Figure 15, the frontispiece of a popular eighteenth-century midwifery manual, the mother lies in a canopied four-poster in a comfortable bedroom that is illuminated by firelight and furnished with a dressing table, a framed painting, and the customary domestic pet and chamber pot, closely attended by six women who feed her the traditional caudle and swaddle the newborn baby. (In a humbler household the lying-in space might be confined to the bed itself; see Fig. 3.) The lying-in ceremony could be seen as a ritual of woman on top, positive where the skimmington ride is negative because gender reversal is expressed here not through physical and verbal domination but in the aura of a self-sufficiently female household that simply excludes men. This may go too far, however: in a tract of 1683 a husband is made to remark that "for gossips to meet . . . at a lying-in, and not to talk, you may as well dam up the arches of London Bridge, as stop their mouths at such a time. 'Tis a time of freedom, when women, like parliament men have a privilege to talk petty treason."[18]

The well-known replacement of the midwife's authority by the man-midwife's has recently been complicated by scholars in a number of ways. Before this development of the later eighteenth century, the man-midwife was already a known and accepted figure, customarily called in to supplement the supervisory role of the midwife when a dead birth necessitated the medical expertise of obstetric surgery. His ascent to the supervisory role, a professionalizing male takeover of women's traditional inside work, was made possible by the class aspirations of upwardly mobile wives to the social cachet his services provided. One of the most sought after man-midwives, William Hunter, was the first to resolve the anatomy of the placenta, was resistant (as most midwives were) to intervention by the use of forceps, and was highly empathetic with the expectant mothers he served as a kind of private secretary:

> The world will give me credit, surely, for having had sufficient opportunities of knowing a good deal of female characters. I have seen the private as well as the public virtues, the private as well as the more public frailties of women in all ranks of life. I have been in their secrets, their counsellor and adviser in the moments of their greatest distress in body and mind. I have been a witness to their private conduct, when they were preparing themselves to meet danger, and have heard their last and most serious reflections, when they were certain they had but few hours to live.

Figure 15. Frontispiece, *Aristotle's Compleat and Experienc'd Midwife . . .* (1733).
Wellcome Library, London.

Providing for "female characters" something like the medical equivalent of free indirect narration, Hunter was a remarkable pioneer in the benign but implacable exploration of the female interior: the lying-in chamber, the womb, the secret privacy of mind and body.[19]

The search for domestic privacy "took a variety of forms, depending upon who was excluding whom in order to achieve it."[20] The family sought privacy from domestic servants; males and females increasingly were thought to require segregation from each other; children had to be separable, if not entirely separated, from adults; personal privacy was required for reading, writing, contemplation, and bodily evacuation; and all members of the household sought privacy from the outside world of uninvited visitors. Below the apogee of the royal household, the linear model in English domestic design was successfully challenged in the seventeenth century by a symmetrical model that gained strength at least in part through the great popularity of Andrea Palladio. In the linear model, as we have seen, two elongated suites of rooms, *en enfilade* (in English usage, "rooms of parade"), extend in opposite directions from a central hall. Roger North thought such a ground plan "fit for a colledge or hospitall, to be devided into cells, and chambers independent of each other; but not for a dwelling house, that ought to have a connexion, and unity, without crossing to and fro from one part to the other. . . ." Thomas Fuller put it succinctly: "[L]et not the common rooms be several nor the several rooms common." Symmetry replaced linearity primarily through the use of a double-pile ground plan, which compacted space into a deeper rectangle and thus enabled one to choose one's route through the house, facilitating both circulation and privacy.[21] The basic difference between the two models can be seen in Figure 16, which presents simplified plans for several English country houses. Doddington, in Lincolnshire (A), built about 1595, illustrates the older, linear model. Charlton House, in Kent (B), built in 1607–12, modifies the linear model; while the other diagrams show variations on the double-pile plan, some of which, by expanding space through the use of a triple pile in order to solve problems created by the extreme compaction of the double pile, also created new difficulties in circulation.

Coleshill, in Oxfordshire (formerly Berkshire) (G), designed by Sir Roger Pratt and built in 1657–62, is "the supreme, yet atypical, example of the double pile form," using service stairs, closets, and especially the passageway or corridor to maximum effect.[22] Figure 17 provides a more detailed view of Coleshill. The great hall, two stories high, accommodates the main staircase and functions not (as of old) as a dining area where the lord's magnificence is publicly displayed in the ceremony of service but as an elegant room of entry to the house. The corridor and two sets of back stairs ensure the separation of the family and guests from the servants, who dine separately in the basement, to which the kitchen and its food preparation have also been relegated. The arrangement of bedchambers, withdrawing chambers, and closets into several sets of rooms composed of a larger and two smaller, inner spaces aims at flexibility of use.[23]

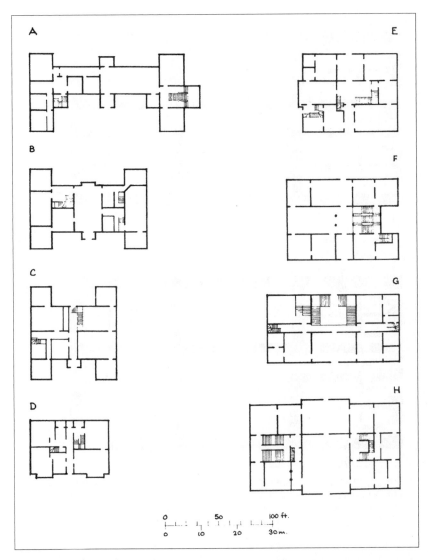

Figure 16. Simplified ground plans of seventeenth-century English country houses: (A) Doddington; (B) Charlton House; (C) Swakeleys; (D) The Dutch House, Kew; (E) Melton Constable; (F) Tring (Wren); (G) Coleshill (Pratt); (H) Horseheath (Pratt). Drawing by John Morrey. In John Bold, "Privacy and the Plan," in *English Architecture Public and Private: Essays for Kerry Downes*, ed. John Bold and Edward Chaney (London: Hambledon, 1993). By permission of Hambledon and London. Marquand Library, Princeton University Library.

Pratt thought the bedchambers "must each of them have a closet, and a servant's lodging with chimney both of which will easily be made by dividing the breadth of one end of the room into two such parts as shall be convenient and to the servant's room a pair of backstairs ought to be adjoining . . . [and] so contrived . . . that the ordinary servants may never publicly

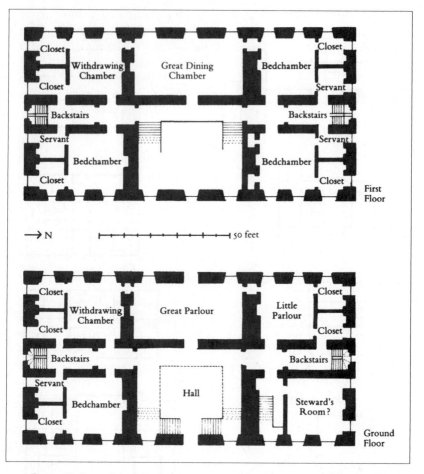

Figure 17. Ground- and first-floor plans, Coleshill, Oxfordshire, built 1657–62,
in Mark Girouard, *Life in the English Country House: A Social and Architectural History*
(New Haven, CT: Yale University Press, 1978). Copyright Yale University Press.
Princeton University Library.

appear in passing to and from for their occasions there." North believed that
in such country houses the main entry "must not be the common passage for
all things, in regard your freinds and persons of esteem should pass without
being annoyed with the sight of foull persons, and things, which must and
will be moving in some part of a large and well inhabited dwelling. . . . The
like is to be sayd of stayres. For the cheif must not be annoyed with disagreeable objects, but be releived of them by a back-inferior stairecase," for although "it is no unseemly object to an English gentleman . . . to see his servants and buissness passing at ordinary times, . . . if we consult convenience,
we must have severall avenews and bolting holes. . . ."[24] Yet North was
disdainful of urban architects who built for quality even though their use
of small spaces was justified not only by the profit motive but also by the
aim to achieve that privacy which he applauded in the great country

houses. Indeed, North's words against the professionalized architecture of the townhouses of quality might also apply to Coleshill. He sneered at the many ways "aggreable to litleness, whereby all the grandure proper to quality is layd aside; large rooms, great tables and glasses, capacious chimneys, spacious hangings, are not be found, as when the nobility built their owne houses. Nay, the evil spreads, so that country gentlemen of value and fortune, in their new erected seats, creep after the meanness of these town builders and order their houses in squares [i.e., double-pile] like suburb dwellings. . . ."[25]

What distinguishes a house like Coleshill is not just service stairs and corridors (which pre-existed it) but the explicitness of their deployment, "the articulation of the need for them and the overall form of their accommodation" to the aim of separating the labor of maintaining the house from the leisure of inhabiting it.[26] In a related fashion, the tendency to dissociate the hall from ceremonial dining (which also had precedents) and to remove the kitchen from the dwelling quarters (which did not) expresses a growing consensus that eating together was no longer the paradigmatic ritual of a communal status hierarchy and that the production of food should be segregated from its consumption.[27] In the linear plan of tradition, the household of service encompasses the entire spectrum of status hierarchy, a finely calibrated continuum of social degrees in which the display of eating in the great hall is only the most important ritual of distinction. In such a system, the only crucial difference is between the absolute magnificence of nobility and the service done by those who are variously dependent upon it. In the emergent plan, a continuous and graded hierarchy of social distinctions has been replaced by a complex network of social spaces in which the incremental ladder of status difference has been reduced to a dyadic separation between the public and the private, production and consumption, labor and capital at domestic leisure: between those who labor at the house and those, whether family or their guests, who inhabit it. Labor comprises both the inside work of domestic servants and the outside work of "business" that is brought into the house.[28] The separation between the public and the private, available repeatedly but discontinuously throughout the house, suggests the emergent terms of class conflict, in which the abstract category "labor"[29] both produces domestic space and is secreted within its interstices. Privacy is the recourse of absolute property, of the owners of the means of production in their capacity as consumers. At the same time, however, the relative ease of mobility between social categories that characterizes a class system of social relations—prefigured in the lability of the early modern secretary—ensures that the social identity of the actual people who fill the antithetical categories of production and consumption, labor and capital, will be highly variable. . . .

The schematic abstraction of the account of historical transition in the architecture of domestic interiors as I have given it thus far inevitably obscures its unevenness. For one thing, the historic separation of production from consumption in the country house was hardly inexorable. At Wilton House, in Wiltshire, in 1786, the Earl of Pembroke thought that "a steward's office *in the house* would be the very devil. One should never be free an instant from meeting people full of words and wants." Within a few months, however, he had become "convinced of the absolute indispensable necessity of a land-steward, doing nobody's business but mine, living and boarding in the house, and transacting everything in my office."[30] Evidently the pleasures of ownership might be enjoyed both through the privatizing removal of labor and through its public display. More broadly, if the fashion for Palladio and for Italian classicism reinforced native tendencies toward the separation of the public from the private in English architecture during the early part of the seventeenth century, it is also true that the growing popularity of the French formal *appartement* in the middle years of the century revived the linear model—but with differences from the more traditional English layout. On the one hand, the formal plan reflected French—and a modified English—absolutism in its commitment to a sequence of rooms of increasing exclusivity. On the other hand, the French plan favored a symmetrical effect that might be achieved not through the double-pile plan but by balancing two great apartments against each other off a central structure. The major attraction of the French plan was the elegant sequencing of rooms *en enfilade*, which was especially admired as a model for the layout of those state apartments in English country houses that were adapted to accommodate visiting royalty in the splendor of an independent suite occupying most or all of one floor of the house.[31]

Ham House, in Surrey (Fig. 18), built in the 1630s, was given a form comparable to that of the double pile in the 1670s by doubling the central

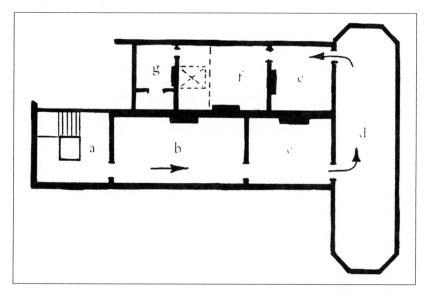

Figure 18. First-floor plan. Ham House, Surrey, built 1630s, in Peter Thornton, *Seventeenth-Century Interior Decoration in England, France, and Holland* (New Haven, CT: Yale University Press, 1979). Copyright Yale University Press. Marquand Library, Princeton University Library.

range of the original structure. This created matching apartments for the Duke and Duchess of Lauderdale on the ground floor of the house. On the first floor, the new range of rooms completed a single state apartment whose sequence comprised the original staircase (a), great dining room (b), withdrawing room (c), and gallery (d), as well as the added suite of ante-chamber (e), state bedchamber (f), and closet with alcove (g). At Chatsworth, in Derbyshire (Fig. 19), the state apartment was located on the second floor of the south front. The Elizabethan design of the house facilitated a 1680s remodeling that highlighted the processional formality of a grand sequence from great dining chamber to antechamber, withdrawing chamber, bedchamber, and closet. But the original design prohibited the achievement of the desired symmetry through reconstruction, so the effect was created instead by the *trompe l'oeil* device of a large mirror that was set into the wall of the dining chamber, reflecting back the sequence of doors in the existing

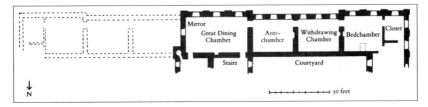

Figure 19. Remodeling of the state apartment on the second floor of the south front of Chatsworth, Derbyshire, 1680s, with *trompe l'oeil mirror*; and (top) floor plan of same apartment; in Mark Girouard, *Life in the English Country House: A Social and Architectural History* (New Haven, CT: Yale University Press, 1978). Copyright Yale University Press. Princeton University Library.

apartment as though it were a perfectly balancing apartment of "rooms of parade."[32] Seventy-five years later the device—or perhaps the linear plan itself—had lost its charm. In 1763 Philip Yorke thought the rooms of the state apartment at Chatsworth "of little use but to be walked through."[33] The linearity of the formal plan was modified in many eighteenth-century houses to create a circuit of reception rooms that preserved but relativized the sense of a stately procession into the interior. At the opening assembly of the newly built Norfolk House, in London, in 1756 (Fig. 20) guests circled around the first floor of the deep, triple-pile space through rooms of varied hues and decor, from the antechamber to a closet "filled," according to one guest, "with an infinite number of curiosities," and back again to the antechamber. Here if not elsewhere in Norfolk House the ceremonial function of the quasi-public assembly outweighed all considerations of privacy, and the dressing room, bedchamber, and closet were probably seldom used by an individual. The Norfolk House plan became standard for London houses in the next couple of decades.[34]

The capacity to provide efficient public assembly is not, of course, the broadest lesson to be learned from this brief tour of royal and stately homes before the nineteenth century. That lesson can be summarized succinctly by comparing the ground plans of Longleat House (Wiltshire) when it was built about 1570 and when it was remodeled in the early nineteenth century (Figs. 21 and 22).[35] In the plan of c. 1570 there is little evidence of a distinction between public and private spaces: there are no corridors off which

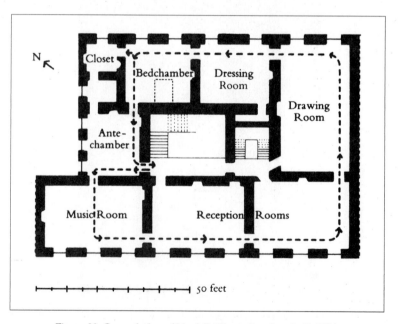

Figure 20. Ground plan of Norfolk House, London, built 1756,
in Mark Girouard, *Life in the English Country House: A Social and Architectural History*
(New Haven, CT: Yale University Press, 1978). Copyright Yale University Press.
Princeton University Library.

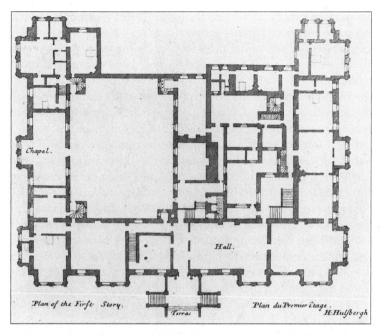

Figure 21. Ground plan of Longleat House, Wiltshire, 1570, in Colen Campbell, *Vitruvius Britannicus, or The British Architect . . .* (1717), 2:69. Marquand Library, Princeton University Library.

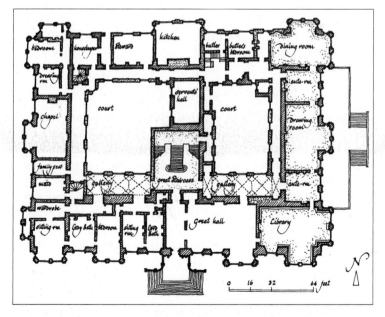

Figure 22. Ground plan of Longleat House, Wiltshire, c. 1809, in Derek Linstrum, *Sir Jeffry Wyatville, Architect to the King*, Oxford Studies in the History of Art and Architecture (Oxford: Clarendon, 1972), Fig. 1 (p. 57). By permission of Oxford University Press. Marquand Library, Princeton University Library.

private rooms might be hived, and the left and right wings of the house are sequenced as rooms of parade; servants and family share the same living spaces; no water closets or dark closets provide excretory privacy; and the hall functions as a general dining place for all members and guests of the household.

The modernization of c. 1809 provides the entire ground floor with a rectangular system of corridors and galleries that both allows private entry to the outer rooms that feed off it and divides the family rooms, on the outside left and front of the house, from the inner and back areas where the servants are given their own living spaces. (The exception to this division is the lady's maid's room, which offers service at a slight but discreet remove from the family suite.) Family members and servants alike are provided with their own sets of water closets and staircases, and the hall has ceased to function as a communal dining place for either family or servants. In 1871 Robert Kerr, comparing the old and the new plans of Longleat, remarked on "the confusion which prevail[s] in this old plan . . . the want of special purpose in the rooms, the want of intelligent relationship between them, and the particular defectiveness of the means of communication; but in the new plan all these evils vanish as if by magic. . . . [N]othing of the kind is to be found . . . in even the best of the eighteenth-century Mansions." The futurity of the stately home lay, however, in publicity as well as privacy. By the mid-eighteenth century the well-known conversion of England's stately homes into show houses for tourist consumption was already under way. This involved less a physical than a cultural reconstruction, and public curiosity about how "the other half" lived was transfixed no more by aristocratic magnificence than it was by the wonderful intricacy of interiority through which the aristocratic itch for privacy by this time had been relieved.[36]

Households of the Middling Sort

"The historians taught us long ago that the King was never left alone," wrote Philippe Ariès. "But in fact, until the end of the seventeenth century, nobody was ever left alone."[37] I have already remarked that innovation in interior design observed a trickle-down pattern; but this leaves open the question whether the quest for privacy among the middling social orders was fueled primarily by motivations of status or of class aspiration. There is little doubt that below the status level of the nobility and gentry, wealthy yeomen and merchants replicated many of the changes in domestic architecture already discussed in the assimilationist spirit of emulating their betters.[38] But differences in building within those groups confirm that it was not the qualitative codes of status hierarchy but the quantitative, class-based criterion of income that determined how innovation trickled down. That is, the impulse toward physical privacy was experienced as a universal human value rather than as proper to the socially elevated alone. What had begun as an elite withdrawal from collective presence had become the architectural expression of an emergent individualist norm.

In 1724 an unidentified Bristol architect prepared plans and elevations for several townhouses to be occupied by merchants. The largest plan (Fig. 23), for a house in which the merchant's clerks also will live and work, is accompanied by extensive notes that testify to the importance of already familiar privacy considerations. Each floor of the house contains a central hall that permits private access to each of its main rooms. "At the Entrance you find a Vestibule [A] for the Conveniency of Common people attending till they can be spoken to, or Strangers Servants to wait in and is therefore

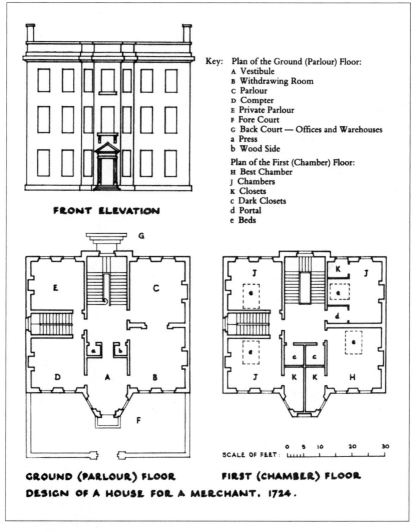

Key: Plan of the Ground (Parlour) Floor:
A Vestibule
B Withdrawing Room
c Parlour
D Compter
E Private Parlour
F Fore Court
G Back Court — Offices and Warehouses
a Press
b Wood Side

Plan of the First (Chamber) Floor:
H Best Chamber
J Chambers
K Closets
c Dark Closets
d Portal
e Beds

FRONT ELEVATION

GROUND (PARLOUR) FLOOR   FIRST (CHAMBER) FLOOR

DESIGN OF A HOUSE FOR A MERCHANT. 1724.

SCALE OF FEET: 0 5 10 20 30

Figure 23. Front elevation and ground- and first-floor plans of a house for a merchant
in Bristol, 1724, in John Bold, "The Design of a House for a Merchant, 1724,"
Architectural History 33 (1990). Redrawing by John Morrey of original
in Bristol Record Office. By permission of John Bold and John Morrey.
Marquand Library, Princeton University Library.

separated from the [great] Stairs that they may not be at liberty to walk about and that the Family may pass privately about their affairs." The semihexagonal shape of the vestibule distances the front door from the adjacent compter (or business room) and withdrawing room so as to spare their inhabitants "any inconveniency" caused by entry. Intended "for the Mistress of the House to entertain Company in," the withdrawing room [B] has "a Private door to the Staircase for her Servants to bring any thing (without exposing it to people who may be waiting in the Vestibule,). . . ." The separate parlor behind [C], primarily an "Eating Room," can also be used to accommodate more company or "to make a Shew. . . ." As the right half of the ground floor is dedicated to the nuclear family and the entertainment of their guests, so the left side is given over to work.[39] The compter [D] "has a private door by the Back stairs to retreat without being seen by people that are visiting, and the conveying away anything that should not be exposed to view: and by it is the Back Stairs, to the Chambers that the young Men may at night go to their Beds and in the morning come to their business without disturbing or dirtying the best part of the House. Beyond the Back stairs is a Private Parlour where the Master may treat with any Dealer. . . ."[40] So the labor of the clerks is comparable to that of the servants. Still, the author recommends, perhaps to protect the family from the spread of scandal, that in dining arrangements the clerks "have as little occasion as may be to mix and converse with Common Servants from whom they seldom learn any good." Other features of the plan are familiar from our survey of country houses. Three of the four best bedchambers (H, J), all on the first floor, have a "Light Closet" (K), the two front ones built so as to "be perfectly Private." The front chambers also contain "large dark Closets" (c), "of great conveniency for the holding Close: Stools and many other Family necessarys." The detached kitchen and associated offices are in the rear court, below separate sleeping accommodations for servants.[41]

The same architect who was responsible for this plan also designed three more modest townhouses for merchants, two small units on either side of a larger one.[42] A comparison of these three plans (Fig. 24) with that of the largest townhouse we have just explored provides a graduated scale of privacy, all within a single status group, whose differences are dictated not by degrees of status emulation but by the quantitative standard of available space and money. The ground floor of the central plan in Figure 24, like that of Figure 23, has four rooms, a main stairs, and a back stairs.[43] Here the much smaller hall space in the area of the main stairs still separates the family from the "common people" and "strangers' servants" they would otherwise encounter at the front of the house. But the diminished hall space provides separate entry for only the two back rooms; the front rooms must be entered through what is here called the "Hall," which assumes the function of both hall and vestibule in Figure 24. The separation of business from family affairs is maintained, although less adequately, by placing the hall entries to the compter and the best parlor diagonally across (hence at the greatest distance) from each other, which, however, deprives

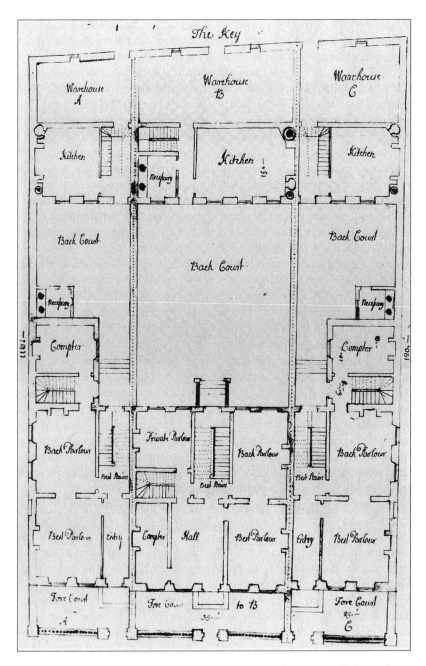

Figure 24. Ground plans for three merchants' houses in Prince Street, Bristol, c. 1725, in Mark Girouard, *The English Town* (New Haven, CT: Yale University Press, 1990). Copyright Yale University Press. Marquand Library, Princeton University Library.

the compter of a "private door by the back stairs." As a result, clerks have easy access to the compter from the front door, but they also mix with guests and visitors heading for the best parlor. The mistress of the house is also deprived of the "private door to the staircase" for her servants to avoid people waiting in the hall. In the two smallest plans, privacy continues to be served, and to be compromised, by space limitations. These mirror reflections of each other reduce the number of rooms by one and pursue a linear model from the family rooms in the front to the compter in the back. An entry hall provides separate access to the best parlor and to the staircase, but from the latter one has only walk-through access to the two back rooms. Traffic from the outside mixes with family and servant affairs, although the clerks are successfully segregated adjacent to the back stairs.[44] Kitchen and servants' quarters remain detached from the main house.

The differential achievement of privacy that is evident in this comparison of households of variant income levels below the gentry level can also be seen chronologically, in the way the Yorkshire farmhouse of a successful yeoman-clothier was refashioned in the sixteenth and early seventeenth centuries. When it was built about 1500, High Bentley, in Shelf (Yorkshire), had a linear structure whose aisled hall was characteristic of the Halifax region of the West Riding (Fig. 25). The passage, echoing the screens passage in the late-medieval great house (see Fig. 10), separates the hall and chambers from the workshop. A century later the workshop space was more than doubled, creating a wing that balanced that of the private chambers. And in 1661 the separation of consumption from production space was completed by several strategies. Both food preparation and servants were removed to a new kitchen wing with its own hearth; the original passage was moved to the wall of the added shop wing, while the original shop was converted to domestic purposes; the hall was modernized for family use and entertainment; and the front door, which had opened into the passage, was moved to the side to create a separate lobby entrance.[45]

Where the Poor Should Live

When Daniel Defoe toured this Yorkshire countryside in the 1720s he was struck by the prosperity and industry not only of the "Manufacturers Houses" but also of the "Number of Cottages or small Dwellings, in which dwell the Workmen which are employed, the Women and Children of whom, are always busy Carding, Spinning, &c. so that no Hands being unemploy'd, all can gain their Bread. . . . This is the Reason also why we saw so few People without Doors. . . ."[46] The condition of existing manufacturers' cottages looked considerably bleaker to the architect John Wood fifty years later. The humanitarian Wood believed there was a "regular gradation between the plan of the most simple hut and that of the most superb palace; that a palace is nothing more than a cottage IMPROVED; and that the plan of the latter is the basis as it were of plans for the former. . . ." Yet when he surveyed the cottages of laborers not only in husbandry but also

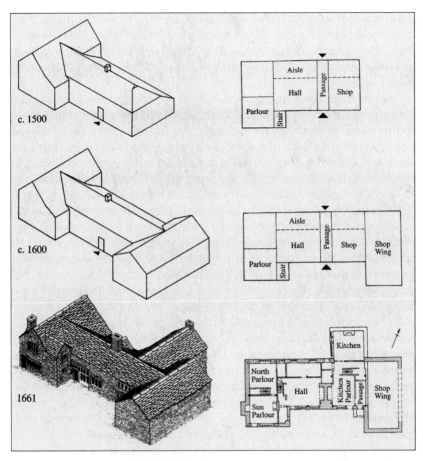

Figure 25. Elevations and ground plans for High Bentley, Shelf, Yorkshire, c. 1500, c. 1600, and 1661, in Colin Platt, *The Great Rebuildings of Tudor and Stuart England: Revolutions in Architectural Taste* (London: University College of London Press, 1994), fig. 67 (p. 156). Marquand Library, Princeton University Library.

in the "manufacturing counties," he found them "to be shattered, dirty, inconvenient, miserable hovels, scarcely affording a shelter for beasts of the forest. . . ." Affected by contemporary currents of sentiment and sensibility and determined to make a difference, Wood, unwilling to be only "the melancholy spectator" of such scenes, thought it "necessary for me to feel as the cottager himself; for . . . no architect can form a convenient plan, unless he ideally places himself in the situation of the person for whom he designs. . . ." So he surveyed the opinions of the cottagers, as well as their habitations, and found, among other complaints, that their domiciles "were *inconvenient* for their want of room. . . ." Interpreting this as a problem not just of space but of separate space, Wood decided that as a basic principle "there should be one lodging room for the parents, another for the female, and a third for the male children . . . ," at least those children over the age of nine. Wood designed plans and elevations for four types of cottages, their differences depending strictly on the number of people that would inhabit them. The cottages, proposed for an area east of Bath (Wiltshire), adhere to a close economy in their construction and would most likely be built "at parochial expense."[47]

By contemporary housing standards, Wood's modest plans are utopian. "Humanity shudders," wrote the Marquis of Bath's steward, "at the idea of the industrious labourer, with a wife and five or six children, being obliged to live or rather to exist, in a wretched, damp, gloomy room, of 10 or 12 ft square, and that room without a floor; but common decency must revolt at considering, that over this wretched apartment, there is only *one* chamber, to hold all the miserable beds of the miserable family."[48]

Although horizontal subdivisions of space provide some of the best evidence of the quest for privacy among the middle and upper status groups, country houses and townhouses also shared a broad commitment to a model of vertical stratification in which servants' quarters and household production were relegated to the top and the bottom of the house. The urban tenements of the poor evince a comparable model: the poorest lived in garrets and cellars, where the crowding and the squalor were even worse than in the middle stories. "It will scarcely appear credible," observed a medical doctor at the end of the eighteenth century, "though it is precisely true, that persons of the lowest class do not put clean sheets on their beds three times a year; . . . that from three to eight individuals of different ages often sleep in the same bed; there being but one room and one bed for each family. . . . The room occupied is either a deep cellar, almost inaccessible to the light, and admitting of no change of air; or a garret with a low roof and small windows, the passage to which is close, kept dark, and filled not only with bad air, but with putrid excremental effluvia from a vault at the bottom of the staircase." Another doctor confirmed that "[i]n a large proportion of the dwellings of the poor a house contains as many families as rooms. . . ." Common lodging-houses were similar. According to the Middlesex justices, "It is now become a common practice, in the extreme parts of the town, to receive into their houses persons unknown, without distinction of sex or age on their paying one penny or more per night for lying in such houses without beds or covering, and . . . it is frequent in such houses for fifteen or twenty or more to lie in a small room." In 1826 the working-class reformer Francis Place looked back: "In a few years from this time it will hardly be believed that an immense number of houses were built in narrow courts and close lanes, each house being at least three stories and many of them four stories above the ground floor. That in these courts and lanes the dirt and filth used to accumulate in heaps and was but seldom removed, that many of these tall houses had two, three, and sometimes four rooms on a floor, and that from the garrets to the cellars a family lived or starved in each room."[49]

The living conditions of the poor force on our attention a criterion of spatial privacy that is less compellingly obvious among their betters. At the higher social levels the boon of spatial privacy is sought in the physical separation of quality from commoners, of family from servants, and of one person from another. What is thrown into relief by these accounts of the poor, a good deal more brutally than the incidence of close-stools and water closets among the nobility, gentry, and middling sort, is the criterion that consists in separating persons from their own and others' bodily waste. True, standards of health, cleanliness, and delicacy have their own history and cannot simply be equated with standards of privacy. But there is some justice in seeing the growing intolerance of the proximity of bodies and their excrement as one measure of the growing norm of individualism and autonomy—and in this sense, of privacy—in the modern period (although the term "privy" had been in use since the fourteenth century). This was of course an outside as well as an inside issue. In the middle decades of the eighteenth century a series of public acts drained stagnant pools, replaced kennels in the middle of roads by gutters at their sides, and covered over filthy open drains of refuse.[50] For the poor, who effectively dwelled outside as much as they did inside houses, these reforms represent something like the equivalent of replacing the chamber pot by the segregated close-stool in more respectable houses. Still, Wood's plans are sensitive, as we will see, to these inside needs as well.

The quest for privacy at the most indigent level, especially if it is a matter of public (i.e., parochial) policy, severely tests what Wood hopefully calls the "regular gradation" between palace and hut. In the latter, at least, there is a strict equivalence in the relation between cost and privacy that is far less flexible than in the country houses we have been examining: the more money, the more space; the more space, the more rooms. Nonetheless, Wood shows considerable ingenuity in his designs. Figure 26 depicts one of his plans for one-room cottages; here two such cottages are joined together, their back-to-back chimneys offering "the great conveniency of having cupboards or shelves on each side of them, as the saving of materials." (Needless to say, cupboards and cabinets of curiosities, although physically similar, imply very different modes of existence.) Pantries are marked by the letter C. The privy is attached to the shed, divorced from the living space but of relatively easy access to its inhabitant. "These cottages, with a piece of ground for a garden, would serve . . . two women, or a man and his wife, either without a family, or with one or two children."[51]

In providing four variations on a basic two-room plan, Figure 27 evinces a sensitivity to bed placement as a cardinal criterion of privacy. In No. 1 the single bed is in the bedroom (C). In No. 2 the "porch" (A) is made into an "inside porch" (i.e., a foyer) whose construction "makes a very convenient recess E for a bed, which in this sample is thrown open to [and effectively enlarges] bed room C, the most proper situation for a bed for small children. . . ." No. 3 achieves the same recess effect in the other room (B) "for the sleeping place of an adult," whose propriety and convenience differ from those of a child. This difference is further pursued in No. 4, where the recess is enlarged and more fully enclosed by partition, a design

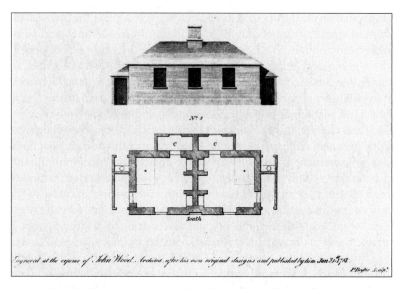

Figure 26. Elevation and ground plan for two one-room attached cottages. Bath,
Wiltshire, in John Wood, *A Series of Plans, for Cottages or Habitations of the Labourer,
Either in Husbandry, or the Mechanic Arts . . .* (1792). Department of Rare Books
and Special Collections, Princeton University Library.

that says to Wood that "it must have a window," which in turn requires the
division of the shed into pantry (E) and fuel storage/privy (F).[52] In No. 1 of
Figure 28, very little more space is deployed to design three-room cottages
in which the bed recess acquires the status of a (windowed) bedroom (F)
largely by moving its entrance from one of the other rooms (B) (as in Fig.
27, No. 4) to the "passage" (C) that is created by one wall of the recess and
that enables private access to each of the three rooms. No. 2 uses its additional 4.5 feet of length to move the front door from the porch—where in
No. 1 it shares the space of storage (B) and privy—to its own separate entry
on the east. The passage (A) into which the front door opens, however, sacrifices private access to one of the rooms (G).[53]

"Farms presented the greatest challenge to the separation of domestic
life from production."[54] In 1785 Thomas Stone thought that "[w]ith regard
to a house to be built upon any farm, a parlour, kitchen, hen-house, dairy,
and cellar are absolutely necessary; with chambers, and garrets upon large
farms, and chambers in the roof upon small ones."[55] In the 1750s William
Halfpenny designed a number of farmhouses, like Wood with a close eye
to cost. Figure 29 shows plans for two small houses. No. 1 largely ignores
the challenge to separate domestic living space from productive workspace
in order to situate the kitchen (C) at the center of the house, having access
both to the pantry or cupboard (D) and to the passage (B) to the front entrance (A) (note that Halfpenny's plan reverses the order of Nos. 1 and 2).
For convenience the kitchen also communicates directly to the "Milk-
Room" (E) and the cellar (F), which abut on it, although not to the similarly

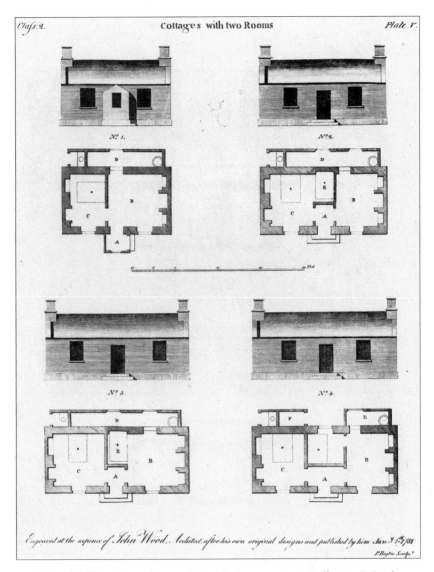

Figure 27. Elevations and ground plans for two-room cottage (four variations).
Bath, Wiltshire, in John Wood, *A Series of Plans, for Cottages or Habitations of the Labourer,
Either in Husbandry, or the Mechanic Arts . . .* (1792). Department of Rare Books
and Special Collections, Princeton University Library.

situated husbandry sheds (G), which are by that detail alone defined apart
from the contiguous kitchen. In No. 2 the challenge to separate living space
from workspace is once again largely avoided in that the house, which also
might serve as a parsonage, has only a "Milk-House" (E) and cellar (F) to
link it to productive farm labor. Instead these two rooms are used to make
a separation, within the domestic space of the house, between the produc-

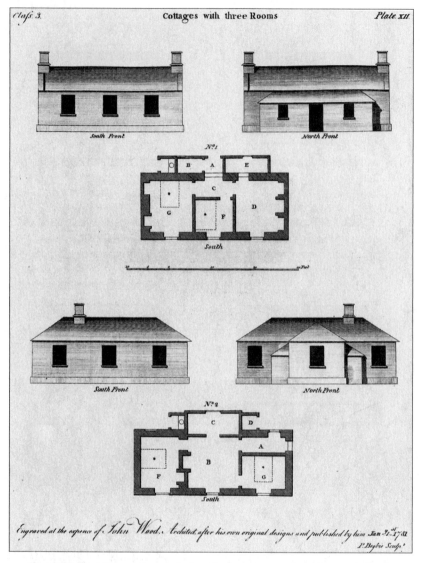

Figure 28. Elevations and ground plans for three-room cottage (two variations).
Bath, Wiltshire, in John Wood, *A Series of Plans, for Cottages or Habitations of the Labourer,*
Either in Husbandry, or the Mechanic Arts . . . (1792). Department of Rare Books
and Special Collections, Princeton University Library.

tive labor of the kitchen (G) and the leisured consumption of the parlor (C), closet (D), and first-story bedchambers, which are approached by the stairs. None of the four principal rooms can be entered from any of the others; all have private access to the connecting passage (A, B).[56]

In another publication Halfpenny offered designs for farmhouses that situate them within the full context of the farm and its productive facilities.

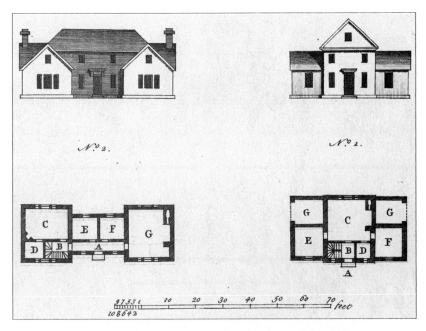

Figure 29. Elevations and ground plans for two small farmhouses,
in William Halfpenny, *Useful Architecture in Twenty-one New Designs for Erecting
Parsonage-Houses, Farm-Houses, and Inns* . . . (1752). By permission
of the British Library, shelf mark 1264.c.16.

In these plans he uses the placement of rooms, and especially entryways, to make subtle but significant distinctions between several kinds of animal husbandry as they stand in spatial relation to the domestic core of the house. In Figure 30, the central parlor (D), which contains stairs up to the first-floor bedchambers, communicates to the passage (B), which also gives private access to the kitchen (C) (with which the parlor shares a chimney but not a doorway), pantries (E), front court (A), and "Dairy-Room" (F). Although the stables (G) abut on both the passage and the parlor stairs, they can be entered only from the outside, through the barnyard (I) or the back court (L). The latter space, which contains (outdoor) privies (O), can be reached through the kitchen, parlor, or stables and in turn communicates to the more detached area of the "Hog-stye" (P), the shed (N), and the "Calf-house" (M). Entirely detached from the domestic quarters and located at the four corners of the barnyard are the barn (K), the "Cow-house" and grainery (H), and two shelters for livestock and carts (Q). The effect suggests the concentric ripples of a pool, their comparative distance from the parlor dictated no doubt by issues of labor efficiency but also by propriety-inflected considerations of privacy.[57]

The logic of division and subdivision we have observed in the design of interior spaces entails a basic structural principle rather than a predictable

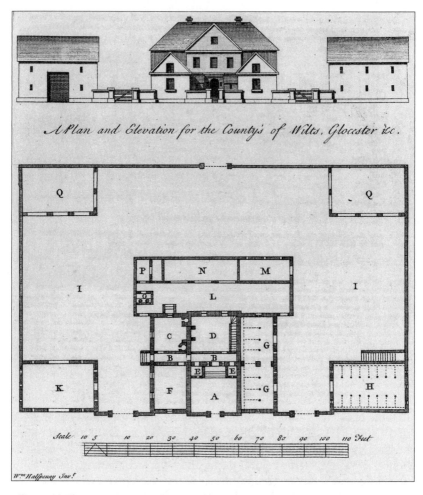

Figure 30. Elevation and ground plan for farmhouse and yard, in William Halfpenny, *Twelve Beautiful Designs for Farm-Houses* ... (1750). By permission of the British Library, shelf mark 1482.ee3.

and consistent body of results. We can generalize about the broad movement from a model of linear hierarchy to one of separation and difference, for example, so long as we remain responsive to the specific variations that this simple abstraction subtends. At the same time, it is important to see that the specificity of these variations, even their intelligibility as such, depends on the capacity of abstraction to enclose a field that both includes and exceeds them. One factor in the density of this field is the complex counterpoint of status and gender criteria in the proliferation of outside and especially inside spaces. But these criteria are themselves in flux, and in ways that can be clarified by bringing to bear on them the same modes of particularizing analysis and generalizing abstraction that are useful in understanding the history of spatial arrangements. . . .

As the emergence of modern attitudes toward the public and the private is an incremental rather than a rapid historical process, so its contributing elements (e.g., systems of social and gender categorization) evince a comparable pattern of change. The most comprehensive abstraction of such patterns that I have used in this study is that of the movement from relations of distinction to relations of separation, and I have stressed the likelihood that in a period of change such as this one, evidence of what can be abstracted as "before" and "after" will be overlapping and coextensive. The title of Alexander Ross's tract of 1651 — *Arcana Microcosmi: or, the Hid Secrets of Man's Body Disclosed* — points in two directions: backward, to the "view of the universe as a vast continuum of correspondences between greater and lesser, outside and inside versions of each other; and forward, through the disclosing force of a devolutionary absolutism that, by rendering tacit correspondence explicit, discovers secreted difference where similarity formerly had been assumed. In 1639 William Austin used the language of correspondence to a related end. In a book about "the excellency of the creation of woman," Austin observed that "the *female body* hath in it not only *all the rooms* and divisions in the *male* body, but diverse others besides that he hath not. . . . She is therefore so *largely* made, with so many *more rooms* than the *masculine* building, because she must contain *another house* within her, with an *unruly guest*, and all *provision* necessary for him."[58] The brunt of Austin's argument has the traditionalist force of distinction, not separation: male and female are, like house and body, greater and lesser spaces. Yet the distinction he makes between the bodies of men and women, although it draws on a knowledge of anatomical difference familiar to traditional thought and easily reconciled therein with a belief in the morphological continuity of things, also plays with the figure of proliferating domestic interiors to suggest in the female body a capacity for incorporation and inferiority that in coming years will seem more and more to bespeak not simply a distinct but a separate sort of being.

NOTES

[1] Max Weber, *The Protestant Ethic and the Spirit of Capitalism* (1905), trans. Talcott Parsons (New York: Scribner's, 1958), 21–22.

[2] See John Shanahan, *Elaborate Works: Untangling Drama and Science in Early Modern England* (forthcoming).

[3] See the useful caveats of C. R. Hill, "The Iconography of the Laboratory," *Ambix* 22, pt. 2 (1975): 102–10.

[4] See Steven Shapin, "The House of Experiment in Seventeenth-Century England," *Isis* 79 (1988): 373–404; and Deborah E. Harkness, "Managing an Experimental Household: The Dees of Mortlake and the Practice of Natural Philosophy," *Isis* 88 (1997): 247–62.

[5] On this tendency, see Lawrence M. Principe and Lloyd DeWitt, *Transmutations: Alchemy in Art* (Philadelphia: Chemical Heritage Foundation, 2002), on whose commentary I have also relied in my discussion of these paintings.

[6] See Marjorie Swann, *Curiosities and Texts: The Culture of Collecting in Early Modern England* (Philadelphia: University of Pennsylvania Press, 2001), 2.

[7] See Paula Findlen, "Masculine Prerogatives: Gender, Space, and Knowledge in the Early Modern Museum," in *The Architecture of Science*, ed. Emily Thompson and Peter Gallison (Cambridge, MA: MIT Press, 1999), 35, 36. For images of later cabinet-museums featuring the suspended-specimen motif, see Oliver Impey and Arthur MacGregor, eds., *The Origins of Museums: The Cabinet of Curiosities in Sixteenth- and Seventeenth-Century Europe* (Oxford: Clarendon, 1985), plates 10, 51; Neil Rhodes and Jonathan Sawday, eds., *The Renaissance Computer* (London: Routledge, 2000), figs. 45, 46, 49; *Hogarth: The Complete Engravings*, ed. Joseph Burke and Colin Caldwell (New York: Abrams, 1968), fig. 195; and Barbara M. Stafford, *Artful Science: Enlightenment Entertainment and the Eclipse of Visual Education* (Cambridge, MA: MIT Press, 1994), fig. 172. The motif also received literary treatment. Cf. William Shakespeare, *Romeo and Juliet* (1594–95), act 5, sc. 1, lines 35–49:

> Well, Juliet, I will lie with thee tonight./Let's see for means. O mischief, thou art swift/To enter in the thoughts of desperate men./I do remember an apothecary,/And hereabouts a dwells, which late I noted,/In tattered weeds, with overwhelming brows,/Culling of simples. Meagre were his looks,/Sharp misery had worn him to the bones;/And in his needy shop a tortoise hung, /An alligator stuffed, and other skins/Of ill-shaped fishes; and above his shelves/A beggarly account of empty boxes,/Green earthen pots, bladders, and musty seeds,/Remnants of packthread, and old cakes of roses/Were thinly scattered to make up a show";

and Mark Akenside, "The Virtuoso; in Imitation of Spencer's Style and Stanza" (1737), st. 6, in *The Poetical Works of Mark Akenside*, ed. Robin Dix (Madison, NJ; Fairleigh Dickinson University Press, 1996), 390:

> Here in a corner stood a rich scrutoire,/With many a curiosity replete;/In seemly order furnish'd ev'ry draw'r,/Products of art or nature as was meet;/Air-pumps and prisms were plac'd beneath his feet,/A *Memphian* mummy-king hung o'er his head;/Here phials with live insects small and great,/There stood a tripod of the *Pythian* maid;/Above, a crocodile diffus'd a grateful shade.

[8] *Philosophical Transactions of the Royal Society* 1 (1666): 321, quoted in Michael Hunter, "The Cabinet Institutionalized: The Royal Society's 'Repository' and Its Background," in Impey and MacGregor, *Origins of Museums*, 159. The cabinet of curiosities took public form not only through the museum but also as popular entertainment. See Richard D. Altick, *The Shows of London* (Cambridge, MA: Harvard University Press, 1978), chaps. 1–2. On the relationship between private cabinets of curiosities and the typographical publication of "cabinets" and "collections" of discursive materials, see Danielle Bobker, "Augustan Interiors: Intimate Spaces and British Writing, 1660–1770" (PhD diss., Rutgers University, 2006).

[9] John Locke, *An Essay concerning Human Understanding* (1690), ed. Peter H. Nidditch (Oxford: Clarendon, 1979), bk. 1, chap. 2, sec. 15, p. 55.

[10] Joseph Moxon, *Mechanick Exercises on the Whole Art of Printing* (1684), and C. H. Firth and R. S. Rait, eds., *Acts and Ordinances of the Interregnum, 1642–1660* (London: HMSO, 1911), quoted in Adrian Johns, *The Nature of the Book: Print and Knowledge in the Making* (Chicago: University of Chicago Press, 1998), 82–83 and 129, respectively.

[11] See Leonore Davidoff and Catherine Hall, *Family Fortunes: Men and Women of the English Middle Class, 1780–1850* (Chicago: University of Chicago Press, 1987), 242.

[12] John Selden, *Table Talk* (1689), ed. Arthur Warwick (London, 1890), 62, quoted in Alastair Fowler, *The Country House Poem: A Cabinet of Seventeenth-Century Estate Poems and Related Items* (Edinburgh: Edinburgh University Press, 1994), 8; *The Yale Edition of Horace Walpole's Correspondence with Sir Horace Mann*, ed. Wilmarth S. Lewis, Warren Hunting Smith, and George L. Lau; Walpole to Mann, 3 Oct. 1743, in *Horace Walpole's Correspondence*, ed. Wilmarth S. Lewis (New Haven: Yale University Press, 1937–1983), 18:316;

Francis Bacon, "Of Building," in *Essays* (1625), in *The Philosophical Works of Francis Bacon*, ed. Robert L. Ellis and James Spedding, rev. ed. John M. Robertson (London: Routledge, 1905), 789–90. See Felicity Heal, *Hospitality in Early Modern England* (Oxford: Clarendon, 1990), 33, 36, 37, 391; and generally Norbert Elias, *The Court Society* (1953), trans. Edmund Jephcott (New York: Pantheon, 1969), chap. 3.

[13] Heal, *Hospitality*, 30, 154; see also 29–30.

[14] Mark Girouard, *Life in the English Country House: A Social and Architectural History* (New Haven, CT: Yale University Press, 1978), 110. See also David Starkey, introduction to *The English Court: From the Wars of the Roses to the Civil War*, ed. David Starkey et al. (London: Longman, 1987), 4, 5; and Heal, *Hospitality*, 40, 44. On the transformation of eating hall into entrance hall, see also Lawrence Stone, "The Public and the Private in the Stately Homes of England, 1500–1990," *Social Research* 58, no. 1 (1991): 235.

[15] [John Pordage], *Theologia mystica* (1683), 149, quoted in J. Andrew Mendelsohn, "Alchemy and Politics in England, 1649–1655," *Past and Present*, no. 135 (1992): 58.

[16] Locke, *Essay*, bk. 2, chap. 3, sec. 1, p. 121.

[17] *Mundus Foppensis: or, the Fop Display'd. Being the Ladies Vindication, In Answer to a late Pamphlet, Entituled, Mundus Muliebris: Or, The Ladies Dressing-Room Unlock'd, &c.* . . . (1691), A2r–v; Jonathan Swift, "The Lady's Dressing Room," lines 70, 76–77, in *Jonathan Swift: The Complete Poems*, ed. Pat Rogers (New Haven, CT: Yale University Press, 1983), 450. See also Girouard, *Life*, 138, 149–50, 206; John S. Fowler and John Cornforth, *English Decoration in the Eighteenth Century* (London: Barrie and Jenkins, 1974), 80–81; Peter Thornton, *Authentic Decor: The Domestic Interior, 1620–1920* (New York: Viking, 1984), 36; and Thornton, *Seventeenth-Century Interior*, 301, 300, 299, 325, 316, 321, 324–25. Richard Steele's Will Honeycomb takes revenge on his disdainful beloved by corrupting her attendant to place him "early in the Morning behind the Hangings in her Mistress's Dressing-Room," revealing himself just when her face-painting is half completed. *Spectator*, no. 41 (17 Apr. 1711), in *The Spectator*, ed. Donald F. Bond, 5 vols. (Oxford: Clarendon, 1965).

I am not the first reader to think that "misogyny" is far too crude an instrument with which to grasp Swift's subtle ambivalence about women. Disparate themes of revelatory disclosure—the inside brought to outside view—saturate and complicate his "woman poems," whose reflexivity obliges us to see them also as "poetry poems" that parody the hypocrisy of Petrarchan idealism, especially the *blazon* and its inventory of body parts. . . .

[18] *The Woman's Advocate* (1683), unpaginated, quoted in Anthony Fletcher, *Gender, Sex, and Subordination in England, 1500–1800* (New Haven, CT: Yale University Press, 1995), 187. Adrian Wilson, "The Ceremony of Childbirth and Its Interpretation," in *Women as Mothers in Pre-Industrial England: Essays in Memory of Dorothy McLaren*, ed. Valerie Fildes (London: Routledge, 1990), 82; see also 71, 72–73, 73, 75, 81, 87–88. . . .

[19] William Hunter, "On the uncertainty of the signs of murder, in the case of bastard children. By the late William Hunter . . . Read July 14, 1783," in *Medical Observations and Inquiries* 6 (1784): 269 (Hunter had died the previous year), quoted in Adrian Wilson, *The Making of Man-Midwifery: Childbirth in England, 1660–1770* (London: University College of London Press, 1995), 181; see generally chaps. 13, 14 and esp. 175–76. Hunter was the author of *Anatomy of the Gravid Uterus* (Birmingham, UK, 1774). On free indirect discourse in novelistic narration, see below, chap. 15, nn. 48–56.

[20] Stone, "Public and the Private," 233; following are Stone's suggested categories, 233–34.

[21] Roger North, *Of Building: Roger North's Writings on Architecture*, ed. H. M. Colvin and J. Newman (Oxford: Clarendon, 1981), 32; and Thomas Fuller, *The Holy State*, 2nd ed. (1648), 156, quoted in John Bold, "Privacy and the Plan," in *English Architecture Public and Private: Essays for Kerry Downes*, ed. John Bold and Edward Chaney (London: Hambledon, 1993), 113 and 109, respectively. See also Heal, *Hospitality*, 158; Girouard, *Life*, 120; and Bold, "Privacy," 112, 113–14. In his description of how the devotional closet should be situated, however, Edward Wettenhall thought that the experience of moving from room to

room was itself conducive to privacy. . . . For the English usage, see Stone, "Public and the Private," 231.

[22] Bold, "Privacy," 116.

[23] For details, see Girouard, *Life*, 122–23. For a plan of the basement, see Colin Platt, *The Great Rebuildings of Tudor and Stuart England: Revolutions in Architectural Taste* (London: University College of London Press, 1994), fig. 12, p. 38. The use of the back stairs to separate servants from family and guests, a familiar feature of domestic living arrangements in the next two centuries, ensures a different sort of privacy from that enabled by the king's back stairs in the royal household. . . .

[24] Sir Roger Pratt, "Certain Short Notes Concerning Architecture," in Pratt, *Architecture*, 64, quoted in Girouard, *Life*, 138, and in Bold, "Privacy," 116; North, *Of Building*, 122–23, quoted in Platt, *Great Rebuildings*, 157–58, and in Bold, "Privacy," 115.

[25] North, *Of Building*, 25–26, quoted in Platt, *Great Rebuildings*, 136.

[26] Bold, "Privacy," 115. On the segregation of servants, see also Heal, *Hospitality*, 155; and Girouard, *Life*, 136, 143.

[27] For an early example of the dissociation of the hall from eating, see the plan of Robert Smythson's Hardwick Hall, in Derbyshire, built in 1590–96, in Heal, *Hospitality*, 161. For the tendency to remove the kitchen, see Girouard, *Life*, 151, 211; and Davidoff and Hall, *Family Fortunes*, 383. However, the open fire and hearth persisted into the nineteenth century, long after technology had made possible and efficient the separation of the stove (for cooking) from the fireplace (for heating), at least in part because the traditional arrangement evoked an image of a pristine and unfragmented domesticity. See Davidoff and Hall, *Family Fortunes*, 380–81.

[28] The boundary between inside and outside work within the category of domestic service was permeable. During the seventeenth century, footmen, cheaper because of lower status, began to come into the house to wait at tables, and by the end of the century they had supplanted both gentlemen and yeomen waiters. See Girouard, *Life*, 141–42.

[29] See Karl Marx, *Grundrisse: Foundations of the Critique of Political Economy* (wr. 1857–58; pub. 1939), trans. Martin Nicolaus (Harmondsworth, UK: Penguin, 1973), 100, 103–5.

[30] *Pembroke Papers (1780–1794): Letters and Diaries of Henry, 10th Earl of Pembroke and His Circle*, ed. Herbert, Earl of Pembroke (London: Cape, 1950), 299, 304, quoted in Girouard, *Life*, 206.

[31] See Heal, *Hospitality*, 163; and Girouard, *Life*, 145–46.

[32] See Bold, "Privacy," 113; Girouard, *Life*, 151–52; and Thornton, *Seventeenth-Century Interior*, fig. 59, p. 60.

[33] Philip Yorke in Joyce Goodber, "The Marchioness Grey of Wrest Park," *Bedfordshire Historical Society* 47 (1968): 162, quoted in Fowler and Cornforth, *English Decoration*, 60.

[34] Desmond Fitzgerald, *The Norfolk House Music Room* (London: Victoria and Albert Museum, 1973), 49, quoted in Girouard, *Life*, 197; see also 194–96. On the use of assembly rooms, see also Fowler and Cornforth, *English Decoration*, 76–78.

[35] In the following comparison I draw on Stone, "Public and the Private," 237–38.

[36] Robert Kerr, *The Gentleman's House: or how to plan English residences from the parsonage to the palace* (1871), quoted in Derek Linstrum, *Sir Jeffry Wyatville, Architect to the King*, Oxford Studies in the History of Art and Architecture (Oxford: Clarendon, 1972), 58. On tourism, see Stone, "Public and the Private," 248–49; Carole Fabricant, "The Literature of Domestic Tourism and the Public Consumption of Private Property," in *The New Eighteenth Century: Theory, Politics, English Literature*, ed. Felicity Nussbaum and Laura Brown (New York: Methuen, 1987), 254–75; and Ian Ousby, *The Englishman's England: Taste, Travel, and the Rise of Tourism* (Cambridge: Cambridge University Press, 1990), chap. 2.

[37] Philippe Ariès, *Centuries of Childhood: A Social History of Family Life*, trans. Robert Baldick (New York: Vintage, 1962), 398.

[38] See Platt, *Great Rebuildings*, 150–53, 157.

[39] Cf. the composition of George Morland's *The Fruits of Early Industry and Economy* . . . 1789. Philadelphia Museum of Art.

[40] The clerks sleep in chambers on the second floor (not shown).

[41] "Explanation of the Draughts of a House Proposed for a Merchant," bound at the end of *Sir John Vanbrugh's Designs for Kings Weston*, Bristol Record Office 33746, printed in John Bold, "The Design of a House for a Merchant, 1724," *Architectural History* 33 (1990): 78–81.

[42] Reproductions of the original plans may be found in Kerry Downes, "The Kings Weston Book of Drawings," *Architectural History* 10 (1967): 77–78, figs. 76 and 77.

[43] Only the ground floors of these three plans are reproduced, and there is no accompanying explanation.

[44] The near side of the back court is occupied by "necessaries," but these are presumably for the clerks rather than for the family, whose close-stools are located more privately in the largest townhouse, within the dark closets of the best chambers on the first floor.

[45] See Platt, *Great Rebuildings*, 155–57.

[46] Daniel Defoe, *A Tour Thro' the Whole Island of Great Britain . . .* (1724–26), ed. G. D. H. Cole (Cambridge: Cambridge University Press, 1927), 2:602 (Everyman's Library ed. [London: Dent, 1928], 2:195).

[47] John Wood, *A Series of Plans, for Cottages or Habitations, of the Labourer, Either in Husbandry, or the Mechanic Arts . . .* (1792), 1–6, 35. The relativizing comparison of the palace and the cottage was a common trope. See Samuel Johnson, *Rambler*, no. 168 (26 Oct. 1751), in *The Yale Edition of the Works of Samuel Johnson*, vol. 4, *The Rambler*, ed. W. J. Bate and Albrecht B. Strauss (New Haven, CT: Yale University Press, 1969), 126; Adam Smith, *The Theory of Moral Sentiments* (1759), ed. D. D. Raphael and A. L. Macfie (Indianapolis: Liberty Classics, 1982), 50; and [Hannah More], "The Ploughman's Ditty," line 37, in *Cheap Repository Tracts* (1795). . . . Explicit designs of cottages only began to appear in the mid-eighteenth century, along with the innovative criterion of "comfort" as a standard to be met in architectural plans that mediated between the more traditional, antithetical poles of "necessity" and "luxury." See John Crowley, "From Luxury to Comfort and Back Again: Landscape Architecture and the Cottage in Britain and America," in *Luxury in the Eighteenth Century: Debates, Desires, and Delectable Goods*, ed. Maxine Berg and Elizabeth Eger (Basingstoke, UK: Palgrave Macmillan, 2003), 135–50; see also idem, *The Invention of Comfort: Sensibilities and Design in Early Modern Britain and Early America* (Baltimore: Johns Hopkins University Press, 2001).

[48] Thomas Davis, n.d., quoted in Roy Porter, *English Society in the Eighteenth Century* (Harmondsworth, UK: Penguin, 1982), 233. The Marquis of Bath was the owner of Longleat (see figs. 5.18 and 5.19).

[49] Dr. Wilan, *Diseases in London* (1801), 255; T. A. Murray, *Remarks on the Situation of the Poor in the Metropolis* (1801), 5; *Middlesex Records, Orders of Court*, Cal., 153; and Francis Place, BL, Add. MSS 35147, fol. 230, quoted in M. Dorothy George, *London Life in the Eighteenth Century* (New York: Capricorn Books, 1965), 86, 87, 88, and 106, respectively.

[50] See George, *London Life*, chap. 2. On "privy," see *OED*.

[51] Wood, *Series*, 24.

[52] Ibid., 27–28.

[53] Ibid., 31.

[54] Davidoff and Hall, *Family Fortunes*, 367.

[55] Thomas Stone, *An Essay on Agriculture, with a view to inform Gentlemen of Landed Property, Whether Their Estates are managed to the Greatest Advantage* (1785), 243.

[56] William Halfpenny, *Useful Architecture in Twenty-one New Designs for Erecting Parsonage-Houses, Farm-Houses, and Inns . . .* (1752), 63, 65.

[57] William Halfpenny, *Twelve Beautiful Designs for Farm-Houses . . .* (1750), 25.

[58] William Austin, *Haec Homo: Wherein the Excellency of the Creation of Woman Is Described . . .* (1639), 92–93.

• • • • • • • • • • • •

QUESTIONS FOR A SECOND READING

1. If you follow the subheadings, McKeon's chapter (which we will call an essay) seems straightforward in its structure, with the discussion organized primarily in terms of social class: "The Royal Household," "Noble and Gentle Households," "Households of the Middling Sort," and "Where the Poor Should Live." As is the case with most scholarly and academic writing, however, other threads (or motives) run through the essay as well. As you reread, focus on two of them: the essay as a history (where dates, for example, matter) and the essay as an exercise in what McKeon refers to as "speculative generalization"—a generalization about the developing difference between "relations of distinction" and "relations of separation." McKeon is using the terms *distinction* and *separation*—to develop a difficult idea, one hard to think and hard to name, and this idea is at the center of his book.

   He says at the beginning of the essay,

   > In the development of elite dwelling structures from the fifteenth through the eighteenth centuries we have a graphic account both of the long-term transition from relations of distinction to those of separation between the public and the private and of the way this change proceeds through the successive rediscovery, within the private realm, of a capacity for further subdivision. (p. 405)

   And he says at the end:

   > As the emergence of modern attitudes toward the public and the private is an incremental rather than a rapid historical process, so its contributing elements . . . evince a comparable pattern of change. The most comprehensive abstraction of such patterns that I have used in this study is that of the movement from relations of distinction to relations of separation, and I have stressed the likelihood that in a period of change such as this one, evidence of what can be abstracted as "before" and "after" will be overlapping and coextensive. (p. 437)

   As you reread, follow these three threads: class, history, distinction/separation. Be prepared to point to passages where McKeon is marking key moments in the presentation of each thread. And be prepared to paraphrase—to turn into one or two sentences—what he is saying in each.

2. This is an essay written by a scholar, a specialist in literary and cultural study, and as a piece of scholarly writing, it relies on specialized vocabulary. There are probably a lot of words whose meanings are not immediately clear. Some of these are technical terms or philosophical terms: "protoindustrialization," "heuristic," "synecdochic profusion," "antithetical categories." And some of them belong to a different period of history: "double-pile plan," "skimmington ride," "close-stool"; even words like "cabinet," "closet," and "parlor" have had different meanings across time. Using available resources (and this would be a fine time to turn to the *Oxford Dictionary of the English Language*), prepare a list of key terms and a set of definitions. This work might be done in groups; the goal would be to

provide a glossary for all to use. With a glossary and a sense of what they mean, these terms would be available for your own writing.

3. Footnotes (or endnotes), it is sometimes said, are where the real action is in scholarly writing. As you reread, pay particular attention to what is going on in the endnotes. What do they say about McKeon as a scholar and a writer? What is he *doing* in these additions to the text? What conclusions might you draw—or, better yet, what lessons might you learn—about scholarly writing and scholarly work?

4. As part of the project of this essay, McKeon works with artistic and architectural representations of interior space—the figures that are presented with the text. You can imagine, in fact, that McKeon has worked with many, many that are not included as illustration. Choose four that you can study and, in a sense, master. If you look at them together, in relation to one another, what argument might you make? What argument is McKeon making? If appropriate, be prepared to present these to the class in an oral presentation.

ASSIGNMENTS FOR WRITING

1. Quoting from one of his sources, McKeon writes, "The search for domestic privacy 'took a variety of forms, depending upon who was excluding whom in order to achieve it'" (p. 416). If you take this thought as a starting point, how do the principles and practices of exclusion change across social class—from "The Royal Household" to "Noble and Gentle Households" to "Households of the Middling Sort" to "Where the Poor Should Live"—and how do they change across time, from McKeon's earliest examples to his most recent?

   Write an essay that addresses these questions. Much of your work will rely on summary, quotation, and paraphrase (where you translate what McKeon is saying into another set of terms), and you will most likely need to include at least some of the images, but be sure to leave space for your own thoughts and observations. These might be drawn from your own studies or travels; you might also think about the degree to which the world you are living in is "traditional," "modern" or, to grab another term, "postmodern."

2. The essay, "Subdividing Inside Spaces," is an exercise in what McKeon refers to as "speculative generalization"—a generalization about the developing difference between "relations of distinction" and "relations of separation." McKeon is using the terms—*distinction* and *separation*—to develop a difficult idea, one hard to think and hard to name, and this idea is at the center of his book.

   He says at the beginning of the essay,

   > In the development of elite dwelling structures from the fifteenth through the eighteenth centuries we have a graphic account both of the long-term transition from relations of distinction to those of separation between the public and the private and of the way this change proceeds through the successive rediscovery, within the private realm, of a capacity for further subdivision. (p. 405)

And he says at the end:

> As the emergence of modern attitudes toward the public and the private
> is an incremental rather than a rapid historical process, so its contribut-
> ing elements . . . evince a comparable pattern of change. The most com-
> prehensive abstraction of such patterns that I have used in this study is
> that of the movement from relations of distinction to relations of separa-
> tion, and I have stressed the likelihood that in a period of change such as
> this one, evidence of what can be abstracted as "before" and "after" will
> be overlapping and coextensive. (p. 437)

Write an essay in which you take up these terms and explain how you
understand them. Much of your work will rely on summary, quotation,
and paraphrase (where you translate what McKeon is saying into another
set of terms), and you will most likely need to include at least some of the
images, but be sure to leave space for your own thoughts and observations.
These might be drawn from your own studies or travels; you might also
think about the degree to which the world you are living in is "traditional,"
"modern" or, to grab another term, "postmodern."

3. McKeon thinks about gender as one way of making distinctions in the organization and use of space. Write an essay in which you track the distinctions and separations related specifically to bodies identified as male and
   female. You should think about how this is played out across time (in history, that is) but also across social classes or social hierarchy. Much of your
   work will rely on summary, quotation, and paraphrase (where you translate what McKeon is saying into another set of terms), and you will most
   likely need to include at least some of the images, but be sure to leave space
   for your own thoughts and observations. These might be drawn from your
   own studies or travels; you might also think about the degree to which the
   world you are living in is "traditional," "modern" or, to grab another term,
   "postmodern."

   Note: In order to keep the selection relatively short and manageable,
   we do not include some subsections of this chapter that deal specifically
   with the ways men and women were figured in the art and architecture of
   the period. If this project interests you (or, perhaps, as a way to motivate a
   revision), you could go the library and read the chapter in full. And if you
   want to keep going, the chapter that precedes this one, chapter 4, has sections on "The Housewife as Governor" and "The Whore's Labor." The
   chapter that follows, chapter 6, is titled "Sex and Book Sex."

4. Near the end of the essay McKeon says:

> As the emergence of modern attitudes toward the public and the private
> is an incremental rather than a rapid historical process, so its contribut-
> ing elements . . . evince a comparable pattern of change. The most com-
> prehensive abstraction of such patterns that I have used in this study is
> that of the movement from relations of distinction to relations of separa-
> tion, and I have stressed the likelihood that in a period of change such as
> this one, evidence of what can be abstracted as "before" and "after" will
> be overlapping and coextensive. (p. 437)

Let's suppose that the organization of public and private space today is different from, but also overlapping and coextensive with, the history McKeon
presents.

For this assignment, extend McKeon's project by considering contemporary examples of the subdivision of interior spaces. You should work with sites you know well. Most likely you will need to draw floor plans. You can certainly find representations in art and advertising. Part of the project will be to work between image and text. As a point of reference, you should present McKeon's basic argument about historical change, about class or social hierarchy, and about relations of distinction and separation. Your primary goal, however, is to extend the discussion to the present, to offer your account of public and private space in the sites of modernity (or postmodernity) that interest you.

MAKING CONNECTIONS

1. "Panopticism," the selection from Michel Foucault's *Discipline and Punish*, opens with a scene from the seventeenth century, when measures were being taken to separate the sick and the well. He turns, as well, to the treatment of lepers. He says:

   > The constant division between the normal and the abnormal, to which every individual is subjected, brings us back to our own time, by applying the binary branding and exile of the leper to quite different objects; the existence of a whole set of techniques and institutions for measuring, supervising, and correcting the abnormal brings into play the disciplinary mechanisms to which the fear of the plague gave rise. All the mechanisms of power which, even today, are disposed around the abnormal individual, to brand him and alter him, are composed of those two forms from which they distantly derive. (pp. 212–13)

   And, at the end, he asks two questions:

   > Is it surprising that the cellular prison, with its regular chronologies, forced labor, its authorities of surveillance and registration, its experts in normality, who continue and multiply the functions of the judge, should have become the modern instrument of penalty? Is it surprising that prisons resemble factories, schools, barracks, hospitals, which all resemble prisons? (p. 236)

   Although McKeon doesn't write about prisons and schools, and he doesn't use words like *normal* and *abnormal*, he does write about how space is organized in service of power and as the expression of an idea about the relations between individuals and between conceptions of public and private life. Foucault writes:

   > Power has its principle not so much in a person as in a certain concerted distribution of bodies, surfaces, lights, gazes; in an arrangement whose internal mechanisms produce the relation in which individuals are caught up. (p. 216)

   Read "Panopticism" and then as you reread "Subdividing Interior Spaces," think about why McKeon (unlike many scholars of his generation) does not refer to Foucault in his essay. Although McKeon is certainly concerned with relations of power, he does not use the word *power* and, if he does, he uses it differently than the way Foucault uses it. How is his argument different from Foucault's? As you define that difference, where do you stand? Has McKeon lost something important? Has he made an argument that is more convincing or compelling than Foucault's?

2. Linda Nochlin's "Renoir's *Great Bathers*: Bathing as Practice, Bathing as Representation" (p. 449), W. G. Sebald's chapters from *The Rings of Saturn* (p. 613), John Berger's selections from *Ways of Seeing* (p. 97), and Michael McKeon's "Subdividing Inside Spaces" all provide interesting examples of what we might call scholarly writing. They are different in style and organization, to be sure, different in voice and method. All, however, enact an intellectual project that works with historical materials, including high art; all work sequentially across a range of these materials, all work toward (or from) an argument, and all have a sense of the importance of their mission and its contribution to knowledge.

McKeon is the central text for this assignment. Choosing one of the others, write an essay in which you present the work of the two as examples of scholarly writing. You'll need to take the time to give each project its proper and respectful presentation. Be sure, however, to leave time and space for your reflections, particularly on the differences. What do you see and value? What is at stake for you—someone who, whatever your career plans, will be writing as a scholar for the next few years?

LINDA
NOCHLIN

LINDA NOCHLIN (b. 1931) is the Lila Acheson Wallace Professor of Modern Art at New York University's Institute of Fine Arts. She earned her BA in philosophy at Vassar College, her MA in English literature at Columbia University, and her PhD in art history (in 1963) at New York University. Early in her career, Nochlin established a reputation as a leading scholar of the "realist" tradition in painting, focusing particularly on the work of Gustave Courbet. In 1966 she published Realism and Tradition in Art, 1848–1900 *and* Impressionism and Post-Impressionism, 1874–1904; *in 1967 she was awarded the Arthur Kingsley Porter Prize for the best article published in the Art Bulletin, an article on Courbet's painting,* Meeting; *in 1968 she organized a show at Vassar, where she was teaching, on contemporary realist artists; in 1969 she created one of the first undergraduate art history courses devoted to women, "The Image of Women in the Nineteenth and Twentieth Centuries."*

But it was in 1971 that Nochlin became internationally known for her groundbreaking article "Why Have There Been No Great Women Artists?" This article raised questions about the concept of greatness in art and pointed to the social, economic, and institutional structures that had prevented women from having access to artistic careers, let alone "greatness." In 1972, with Ann Sutherland

Harris, she organized an exhibition on women artists at the Los Angeles County
Museum of Art; the book that accompanied the exhibition, **Women Artists:
1550–1950,** became a classic in the field.

   Since the early 1970s, Nochlin has been known as a founding figure, a scholar,
and a writer who led the next generation of feminist critics and who brought
the category of gender to the study of art. Her books include **Woman as Sex
Object: Studies in Erotic Art, 1730–1970; The Politics of Vision: Essays on
Nineteenth-Century Art and Society; Representing Women; The Body in
Pieces: The Fragment as Metaphor of Modernity; Women, Art, and Power
and Other Essays; The Politics of Vision: Essays on Nineteenth-Century Art
and Society;** and, in 2006, **Bathers, Bodies, Beauty: The Visceral Eye,** the book
from which the following selection is taken.

   Bathers, Bodies, Beauty began as a series of lectures delivered as the 2004
Charles Eliot Norton Lectures at Harvard University. "Renoir's **Great Bathers**"
is the first chapter of the book and sets the theme of the body on display. Nochlin
thinks of herself as an essayist and a poet, and her prose is clear, eloquent and generous. "Renoir's **Great Bathers,**" which we'll call an essay, is not the kind of essay
to hammer home a point or to march deliberately toward a conclusion. It is, rather,
evidence of a project, a way of thinking. It takes time to reflect on the images—to
"read" them—and it invites you to do the same. It also moves from one point of
view to the next, a strategy that begins with the second paragraph. Nochlin's goal,
she says at one point, is to create an "interpretive collage," deliberately ambiguous
or unsettling, recognizing that a painting, like **The Great Bathers,** is "impervious
to any reductive solution."

   There are two particular challenges to reading this selection:

   • It makes a great difference to see the paintings in color and in large format.
     You can find links to many of these images at our Web site: bedfordstmartins
     .com/waysofreading.
   • Nochlin's prose is sprinkled with French words. Some she defines in paren-
     theses; some are easy to understand in context; some you will need to look up
     in a French–English dictionary (a number of which you can access online).

We do, however, want to give you help with two French terms because they are key
words and have some useful history attached:

   rappel à l'ordre: to return to order, or to put back in order.
        The term refers to a 1926 book of essays by the avant-garde artist and poet Jean
        Cocteau, Le rappel à l'ordre. After the shock and horror of World War I, some
        critics, artists, and consumers rejected the extreme forms of modernist and
        avant-garde art that had circulated before the war. Cocteau uses the phrase "re-
        turn to order" to describe this challenge to the avant-garde.
   l'informe: that which is shapeless, unformed, not classified
   or classifiable.
        In 1929 the French writer Georges Bataille used this term
        in a challenge to artists and intellectuals to undo formal
        categories, to think outside of form, but also to think of the
        noxious and the abject (his metaphor was "spittle") as
        both subject and goal in art and thought.

Renoir's Great Bathers: Bathing as Practice, Bathing as Representation

The women linger at the water's edge, and they are stunning in the most unusual way: large women, voluptuous, abundant, delighted. They lounge along the river bank, they lift their arms toward the sun, their hair ripples down their backs, which are smooth and broad and strong. There is softness in the way they move, and also strength and sensuality, as though they revel in the feel of their own heft and substance.

> Step back from the canvas, think, feel. This is an image of bounty, a view of female physicality in which a woman's hungers are both celebrated and undifferentiated, as though all her appetites are of a piece, the physical and the emotional intertwined and given equal weight. Food is love on this landscape, and love is sex, and sex is connection, and connection is food; appetites exist in a full circle, or in a sonata where eating and touching and making love and feeling close are all distinct cords that nonetheless meld with and complement one another.
>
> Renoir, who created this image, once said that were it not for the female body, he never could have become a painter. This is clear: there is love for women in each detail of the canvas, and love for self, and there is joy, and there is a degree of sensual integration that makes you want to weep, so beautiful it seems, and so elusive.[1]

I didn't write these words, of course. This is a set piece that constitutes the prologue to *Appetites: Why Women Want*, a chillingly honest, sometimes exasperating study of female appetite and its repression by the late Caroline Knapp, an anorexic and a passionate student of anorexia. As such, it might be compared with Michel Foucault's analysis of Velázquez's *Las Meninas* in the long opening chapter of *Les Mots et les choses*, a chapter in which that author "seeks to demonstrate . . . the spatial mapping within which knowledge becomes knowledge rather than accidental array of facts and objects."[2] When I first read Knapp's paragraphs, I hated them with the kind of visceral hatred that makes you, or at least me, want to hurl a book across the room. All that sentimental cant about food and softness and sex, especially the bit about Renoir loving women—as a feminist, as an art historian with the proper sort of critical training, as a person who, fifteen years ago when I first started working on the painting, sought to demystify the male artist's disempowering idealization of the female body, and for whom *The Great Bathers* (*Les Grandes Baigneuses*) (Fig. 1) was the paradigm of all I found wrong with the traditional representation of the nude, I found

Figure 1. Auguste Renoir, *The Great Bathers*, 1884–1887.

the painting, and Knapp's enraptured response to it, pernicious both from
a formal standpoint and in terms of what it represented.

My negative gut reaction to the sentimentalized, sexualized prettiness
of the image, I might add, was shared by many critics at the time Renoir
painted it but has been articulated with particular forcefulness by a contemporary feminist authority on nineteenth-century French painting, Tamar
Garb. Garb, unlike Caroline Knapp, sees Renoir's many bathers, of which
The Great Bathers is a large-scale example, as constructions designed to receive the desiring male gaze at a specific moment in history. Speaking of
the slightly earlier *Blonde Bather* (Fig. 2) of 1881, Garb declares,

> From the 1880s on [Renoir's] ideal woman would be the person-
> ification of all that was wholesome, bountiful, and sustaining to
> modern man, a nostalgic fantasy typified by the retardataire
> *Blonde Bather* of 1881. Her rounded forms, carefully licked by a
> loaded brush, her erect and highlighted nipples mounted on full
> breasts, her remote expression fixed on some indeterminate spot
> in the distance, her flowing hair and rosy countenance would
> symbolize the eternal values of art and the unusual properties
> of Woman. Plump, pink, and pliable, the blonde bather . . . rep-
> resented a sexuality that was tangible in a setting that was tanta-
> lizingly remote. . . . Art was at the service of a femininity at risk
> from the corruption of modern life, and the nude, as recon-
> ceived by Renoir, was the perfect means for the reaffirmation
> of traditional values in art and traditional relationships between
> the sexes. The caress of a woman's body and the encounter of
> the brush with the painted surface had, as sensory experiences,
> an equivalence that only painting could articulate.[3]

Figure 2. Auguste Renoir, *Blonde Bather*, 1881.

Pliant, seductive, natural, Renoir's bathers embody a whole tradition of masculine mastery and feminine display which underpins so much of Western pictorial culture—and which was increasingly being challenged by feminists, social reformers, and the effects of the modernization Renoir increasingly despised. It is interesting that both Knapp, who loves the picture, and Garb, who scathingly demystifies it, see the picture in similar terms; they simply draw different conclusions. One might say their visceral eyes devour the pictorial material differently.

Yet even when I first became engaged with the painting back in 1990, at the time of an exhibition of *The Great Bathers* and sketches for it at the Philadelphia Museum of Art, I realized that although my gut reaction to it was strongly negative, I was aware of a certain ambivalence, a certain undertow of attraction. In the lecture I gave on the occasion of the exhibition, in which I articulated a feminist position similar to Garb's, insisting on the dominance of the male gaze in the work of both painter and viewer, I was forced to speculate about the position of the putative *female* spectator—not the ahistorical anorexic posited by Caroline Knapp but a historically specific one: was there any position available to the female viewer of Renoir's painting, specifically the female viewer of Renoir's time? Long consideration and a too tight belt in Paris gave me a possible answer.

Perhaps Renoir's nudes enable a certain feminine fantasy as well as the more conventional male one, a fantasy of bodily liberation. It is difficult to imagine how women, especially ample women, condemned to the strictures of corsets and lacing, must have felt before this vision of freely expanding flesh, the pictorial possibility of unconstricted movement, of simply breathing deeply, of not having their breasts pushed up under their chins and their ribs and lungs encased in whalebone. The imaginary pleasure of lolling about with their uncorsetted flesh exposed to air and light in the epoch before sun was supposed to be good for you (though now of course supposedly it is no longer good for you) when well-brought-up ladies scrupulously covered their pale skins with parasols, veils, and long sleeves, not to speak of long skirts and stockings, must have been considerable. Perhaps this aspect of openness, unfetteredness, and deconstriction might have appealed not merely to men, for obvious reasons that have been reiterated innumerable times, but, for the reasons I have just stated, by women as well. And obviously the image is still seen as appropriate to the self-enjoyment of women bathers, as a large-scale tile mural gracing the wall of the Ginseng Korean Baths, the pride of Sydney, Australia, attests.

Yet still another voice needs to be woven into this fugue of strong responses to Renoir's *Great Bathers*, this time a psychoanalytic one. Elizabeth Young-Bruehl, author of a biography of Hannah Arendt, then a teacher at Wesleyan University where I was lecturing about the painting four years later, now a psychoanalyst in the East Village, felt strongly enough about my interpretation and about issues raised by the painting to write me the following letter. It is dated October 9, 1991, and certainly constitutes a fresh and provocative take on what the scene addresses. Wrote Young-Bruehl:

> You tended to dismiss any inquiry into the psychodynamics of male viewers of Renoir's painting . . . as though all that needed to be said on the topic of male voyeurism and the subtopic of male voyeurism in relation to female homoeroticism had been said. So you turned your attention, instead, and interestingly, to female viewers and the possibility that what they might have enjoyed in these paintings was liberated flesh, uncorsetted movement, and so forth. I can see why you both felt "enough already" about male voyeurism and why the liberated flesh theory was appealing, but I think there is a psychodynamic dimension that these approaches miss.
>
> What struck me very forcefully about the Renoir [continues Young-Bruehl], was the configuration of the women. There is not the classic (psychodynamically speaking) threesome, the ménage with two women—more or less bound to each other— and one male viewer, either in the painting or implied in the form of painter or viewer. Instead, there are viewers of the females in the painting, and these viewers are female. The lithe girl to the front right is [the] viewer [in] the main trio, and, in the rear a girl with her back to us [is] being stared at by a nearly submerged figure. These right side figures . . . are painted in Impressionist strokes (as you noted), very different from the shiny, hard-edged flesh-exaggerating strokes of the centerpiece trio. They are also thin, boyish in comparison to the voluptuous center trio, and presented to viewers from the back, which in this context is also androgynizing. It seems to me that viewers, male and female, are being invited to identify with the female viewers in the painting. Women are being invited to enjoy female

nakedness in the role of boyish girls, and men are being wel-
comed not just as men, but as women as well, that is, in both the
masculine and the feminine "positions." And female homo-
eroticism is, so to say, for everybody.

And now Young-Bruehl dives, quite literally, into the Freudian depths:

Let me put this matter another way. Women bathers are . . . precisely that, bathers—the medium in which they are and are to
be viewed is water. . . . Their medium is, symbolically, female.
They are all bound by a female medium and men get to be par-
ticipators. I think that the coy splasher [the "viewer" in the
triad] helps them along in the participatory side of this invitation: the splashing girls [in the foreground and background] are
active, and they recall both the unending art history of male
putti peeing from fountains and the common fantasy of female
ejaculation (if one wanted to be *echt* Freudian, much could be
said about phallic women, etc.).

She concludes about the painting, "From the female side: viewing naked
women, like going to a swimming pool, allows a woman to enjoy masculine or boyish pleasures (I should say pleasures conceived or constructed as
masculine) of gaze and activity—girls can be boys, while being girls."

But now Young-Bruehl goes on to generalize, boldly—and at times with
an endearing lack of historical accuracy—about the sexuality of a whole
period of European history on the basis of her take on *The Great Bathers.*

What I see in the Renoir, and see as an outgrowth of his earlier
crowd scenes in which the people are often so crowded together
that their sexual identities merge, is the phenomenon that seems
to me palpable across the whole of 1880s and 1890s Europe: the
emergence into art and text of enjoyment of bisexuality, in all
kinds of coded but nonetheless well-understood forms: the
Oscar Wilding and George Sanding . . . of Europe. By the time
men appear in the scenes—as with the morning-dressed Manet
picnickers [Fig. 3]—the imperative to play all the possible sexual parts at once seems to me to be loud and clear, for both men
and women, though the emphasis is, with these male painters,
on men. Cézanne [Fig. 15], from this perspective, simply blurs
the boundaries of identification more: sexual differentiation is
transcended, and viewers are invited into a scene, which is like
a polymorphously perverse jungle (it even includes the previously suppressed lying-ready rear-ends, presented for fantasy
anal intercourse).

Young-Bruehl ends on a high note with her final words on Cézanne's
Large Bathers: "It is so polymorphous and pansexual as to be almost un-
erotic, unsexual! (Hail to the 1960s!)"

With Renoir's *Great Bathers*, what I have started with, then, is neither
representation nor practice, nor even a unified reading of the painting in
which I, the speaker, lay out the task with the understood assurance that

Figure 3. Edouard Manet, *Déjeuner sur l'herbe*, 1863.

from my position of superior knowledge I will pull it all together at the end. What I am proposing instead is a kind of piecemeal deconstruction, an interpretive collage, as it were, appropriated from the readings of differing, strong-willed, and — it must be emphasized — *female* viewpoints. How do I reconcile these views? I don't. If, as Theodor Adorno believed, all works of art are by definition mysterious, then even such a seemingly obvious one as *The Great Bathers* must remain ambiguous in its address, impervious to any reductive solution. Think of *The Great Bathers*, then, as Orpheus and my multiple female interpreters as the Thracian women laying into the artist's body with a vengeance. Like Humpty Dumpty, all the king's horses and all the king's men will never put it back together again.

But I have another point to make. I deliberately began this lecture with my subject as a vision of corporeal plenitude seen through the eyes — and desires — of lack: the anorexic eye. I wanted to make the point that eyes — and psyches — are located in specific bodies, and I am referring to the eyes of both artist and viewer. The art historian, in this case myself, no less than Renoir or the late Caroline Knapp, is a corporeal being, seeing through the very body whose representation was put in crisis during the nineteenth century and was further and more radically destabilized during the twentieth.

For there is history, of course: the corporeal eye, the visceral eye — all eyes are located not merely in bodies but in historically specific bodies and can thus be viewed within a history of representation and a history of practices, a social history, in short, that can thicken up our responses to *The Great Bathers*.

On the surface of it, nothing would seem less problematic than the late-nineteenth-century bather. It seems to be a natural "given" of art history: timeless, elevated, idealized, and as such central to the discourses of high art. Yet of course, it has become obvious already that the bather theme is anything but a given, the opposite of natural. On the contrary, it is a construction particular to a certain historical period, though based on and attaching itself to a long artistic tradition; and far from being natural, it is a highly artificial and self-conscious construction at that.

I am now going to continue my attempt to problematize this apparently unproblematic and "natural" subject by putting the bather, and bathing, back into the history of social institutions, practices, and representations from which Renoir and most of the "high" artists of his time abstracted them. The point of this part of my investigation is not so much to discover anything new about Renoir's *Great Bathers* but rather to consider what it has excluded: what about bathers and bathing during our "bathtime" of the late nineteenth century has the painting occluded?

"Bathtime" was the title of the lecture I gave on *The Great Bathers* in 1990, and I had a reason for choosing it — the reason was history. The title was meant to imply a study focusing on a certain historical period in France, and the project of my research was to locate Renoir within a historically specific discourse of the pool, bathers, and bathing, a discourse both visual and textual, extending from approximately 1850 to the fin de siècle.

The Paris Salon of 1887, the year when Renoir completed his *Great Bathers*, exhibited at least twenty-five representations of female bathers, all indistinguishable in theme from Renoir's painting, except perhaps for the relatively daring *Bathers* by Frédéric Dufaux, with its half-dressed contemporary figures slipping in and out of the water. The bather was a perennial favorite in the Salons of the nineteenth century, a theme increasingly secularized and generalized as the century progressed and as earlier classical or biblical pretexts — Dianas, Susannahs, or even the more up-to-date orientalist Sarahs — vanished, giving way to the newer bather subject of preference: the "bather" *tout court*.[4]

Why, at a certain moment in the history of French art, did the naked female figure, alone or in company, in water or near it, become so important?[5] Viewed from a historical vantage point, Renoir's *Great Bathers* may be said to belong to a particular moment of bathtime: that of the artistic *rappel à l'ordre* of the 1880s (a recall to order presaging the better-known one which took place in France after the First World War).[6] After the bold attempt of Impressionism to create a modern art, contemporary in both its formal strategies and its subject matter, certain artists in the group, most arduously Renoir, attempted to restore a sense of permanence, timelessness, and harmony to the openness, instability, and vivid contemporaneity characteristic of High Impressionism.[7] Renoir espoused high-minded reasons for his project in *The Great Bathers*. Yet it is important to see that in it he returns not merely to the traditional sanctions for the bather subject provided by Raphael and Girardon, whose work has often been cited in relation to the formal and iconographic specificity of the work, nor even to the

Figure 4. Charles Gleyre, *Bathers*, c. 1860.

precedent of such minor artists of the eighteenth century as Jean-Baptiste Pater, who specialized in semiprurient bather fantasies deploying semiclothed female bathers in imaginary settings of great piquancy, nor to the example provided by his teacher, the long-suffering Charles Gleyre (Fig. 4).[8]

More important, perhaps, Renoir returns to the kitsch sensibility of his own milieu—to works like *L'Espièglerie* (Teasing), of which there are versions from 1849 and 1867, mass-produced lithographs replete with lesbian overtones (Elizabeth Young-Bruehl was certainly on the right track), in which the theme of mischievous, naked bathing girls, teasing and splashing one another, is archly frozen in place for the pleasure of a male viewer. The standard range of poses and physical types, the gamut of complexions and ages, the sense of savoring the delectable details of the youthful bodies and their titillating playfulness—all these features are shared by works as different in ambition as Renoir's *Great Bathers* and the popular lithographs of the period.[9]

This, then, is the construction of the female bather within a convention that may encompass a variety of practices, from mass culture to high art, from the site of erstwhile vanguard production to that of the most conservative "official" specialists in the nude, like Adolphe-William Bouguereau. All of these bather paintings are replete with what I would call "the aesthetic effect"; they are smooth, fetching, playful, relaxed, and strenuously removed from any context that would suggest either contemporaneity or

Figure 5. Adolphe-William Bouguereau, *Bathers*, 1884.

the realities of urban existence, including the existence of the opposite sex (Fig. 5).[10] There are rarely any men in these pictures aside from an occasional faun or satyr. The pastoral idyll represents only the naked female: the male presence is an absence; or, rather, it is displaced to the understood position of the creating artist and the consuming viewer, not to speak of the potential buyer of the work.

But what has been less investigated is something quite different from the representation of bathers: the practice of bathing and swimming that was coming into being during the bathtime under consideration, a time a little earlier than that of Renoir's *Great Bathers* but certainly contemporary with other artists' highly idealized and aesthetically specific constructions of the bather motif, a practice whose representation has, for the most part, been left unstudied by traditional art history, with its consistent neglect of all forms of visual representation that cannot be considered "high" art.[11] I refer to evolving popular practices and representations of bathing and swimming—water sports and water amusements in general, specifically as they involve women—that mark the nineteenth century as a whole and its latter half in particular.[12] Not that Renoir was ignorant of the swimming of his day. Indeed, in his representations of *La Grenouillère* done in company with his friend Monet in the late 1860s, he had kept a lively record of the activities of contemporary bathers off the island and on it.[13]

The Impressionists, with Renoir prominent among them, at this early point in their existence as a group, were calling into question the traditional practices of the high art of their time by representing bathing, as well as sailing and rowing, as a contemporary activity, carried on in bathing suits and bonnets, in a context of urban (or, more accurately, suburban) social relaxation rather than an elevated, classical topos represented by artificially posed nudes in idealized pastoral landscapes. Recalling those days in later years, Renoir remembered them with great nostalgia, choosing to envision this period as an idyllic, preindustrial pastoral era rather than the period of vigorous urban modernization that it was. He told his dealer and friend Ambroise Vollard that "in 1868 I painted a good deal at La Grenouillère. I remember an amusing restaurant called Fournaises where life was a perpetual holiday. . . . The world knew how to laugh in those days! Machinery had not yet absorbed all of life; you had leisure for enjoyment and no one was the worse for it."[14]

But in addition to such revolutionary paintings of the sixties—revolutionary in their synoptic style and vivid broken color, which is part of the modernity of their subject—there exists an unexplored archive of visual alternatives to those provided by the Salons and by the later Renoir's idyllic versions of the bather theme. This is the whole realm of representation, produced by the nascent mass media, focused for the most part on Paris itself, although in some cases on the Parisian suburbs, and dealing with contemporary swimming and swimming pools. There, one found female bathers beneath the notice of the sort of elevated artist and conservative yearner for the simpler, more natural verities of the past, a persona Renoir was increasingly affecting by the decade of the 1880s.

As early as mid-century, Honoré Daumier was engaging with bathing and bathers, male and female—but in Paris, not in the country; clothed, not naked; ridiculous, not elevated.[15] One can only think, in looking at such caricatures as his *Naiads of the Seine*, that he was pillorying not merely his victims but the high-art bather theme itself, as it existed in endless dreary Salon representations of his time: the naiads, Dianas, Susannahs, and just plain bathers whose ranks cast a pall of boredom over the art experience, year after year. Daumier's lithograph plays on the oxymoronic humor of this juxtaposition of terms (Fig. 6). There cannot be serious naiads of the Seine, Daumier implies, because, like Marx, he believes that antiquity can be repeated in modern times only as farce. The present-day Seine gets the bathers it deserves, those who are appropriate to bathtime today: bathing-suited, spindle-shanked, frowsy-headed, anticlassical in figure type. His bathers are grotesques of the Seine, but living, breathing contemporaries, not classical nymphs or goddesses.

Figure 6. Honoré Daumier, *Naiads of the Seine*, 1847.

Here, the connection between the female bather and the world of nature is severed, revealed for the farce that it is: nothing could be less natural
than these bathers and their baths. Modern life, essentially urban for Daumier, is necessarily sundered from the pastoral: women's bodies cavorting
in that prototypically modern body of water, the Parisian *piscine*, is naturally funny to him. As Daumier's lithographs asserted with brilliant and
acerbic formal inventiveness, modern women bathers—and men too, for
that matter—were neither naked nor classically beautiful, but they did
engage the splendors and miseries of the modern world with a certain
courage and sense of adventure. Their forms are cast with an edgy energy
of contour and character utterly foreign to the later Renoir's bland *poncif*.

Of course, Freud's understanding of jokes should be kept in mind while
enjoying Daumier's bathers. For Freud, jokes are never innocent, and in
these images the aggressive and destructive aspects of humor assert their
presence. On the one hand, the bather series can be read in the light of Daumier's more specific antifeminist caricatures of the late forties as misogy-
nistic lampoons directed against the foolish and grotesque pretensions of
middle-class women—women who should, one can understand by infer-
ence, be home taking care of husbands and children rather than cavorting
about in public in this unseemly manner. On the other hand, they, like
Daumier's caricatures of the classical theater of his time and his wildly
satirical pillories of classical literary narratives, can also be understood as
powerful attacks on the anachronistic hollowness of a high culture which
proposed the classics as the only valid aesthetic experience for a modern

nation. Whether or not Daumier actually authored the phrase "Il faut être de son temps" (One must be of one's own time), his caricatures constituted a powerful visual counter-discourse in the popular press to that language of classical timelessness and elevation represented by the Salon, the lycée, and the classical theater.[16]

Daumier, it turns out, was not working from imagination. As luck would have it, his home on the Ile Saint-Louis was almost next door to the most prominent women's swimming pool and swimming school in all of Paris: the Ecole de Natation pour Dames, operated by the Hotel Lambert on the Quai de Béthune (or Quai d'Anjou) of the Ile Saint-Louis. The second half of the nineteenth century was certainly bathtime for the Parisian public, which flocked to the public pools established on the Seine, and later, after 1884, in all the *quartiers* of Paris, for sport, hygiene, and pleasure. An article-advertisement for the Bains Lambert, published around 1850, emphasized the pool's high-class ambience and its health-giving properties: "The cold baths of running water, those for swimming above all, are for ladies the most powerful means of hygiene; for young ladies [*les jeunes personnes*] it is the best of gymnastics; they are also recommended for both by all the doctors, but only on condition that the water in which they are taken is healthy and salubrious—that is to say, as pure as possible."[17]

Using as its major illustration a print based on the original by Hugot (Fig. 7) which had appeared in the 1846 *Illustration*, the article goes on to praise the qualities of the Seine where the Bains Lambert are located—at a point where the river has not yet received the "tribute of filth" (*tribut des immondices*) from the great city. Elegance, decorum, and amenity are emphasized by the often repeated and varied visual representations of the interior—the classical columns and pediment as well as sculpture suggesting the baths of antiquity. It is noteworthy, in the interests of decorum, that

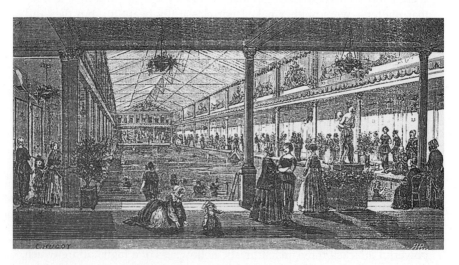

Figure 7. C. Hugot, *Bains de Paris*, 1844.

the only nude female body represented in the prints is that of classical sculpture: all the contemporary ladies are properly dressed. A maid is prominently featured in the foreground, and bathing costumes are as concealing and unseductive as possible. Propriety, good morals, decent hygiene, and healthfulness are the primary characteristics stressed by these visual representations of the female bather. Nudity exists only as a sign of elevation, establishing the credentials of the pool as a site of upper-middle-class recreation, strictly segregated by sex as well as class.

Yet this is only one view of women's bathing establishments and their *habituées* during France's nineteenth-century bathtime. Other draftsmen or journalists figured the subject quite differently. Notions of sexuality, voluptuousness, and seductiveness haunted the imagination of the commercial artist who designed this print of women at the Bain des Lionnes (Fig. 8). Memories of the odalisques of Ingres and his prototypical Turkish bath are roused by the languid poses and the intimate crowding together of female bodies. Despite the reassuring presence of the *maître-nageur* and the contemporary bathing costumes, the print stirs up a certain uneasiness connected with sexual exoticism. "Low" or popular art, it is clear, can no more be viewed monolithically than high art: here, too, there are different voices, different tasks the image is intended to perform, with different audiences in view. The naked classical statue seems more a reference to the near-nakedness of the swimmers and their lack of *tenu* (decorum) than to bourgeois decorum and elevation. Indeed, many accounts of women's swimming pools stressed the unfortunate presence in them of ladies of the theater and, even worse, smoking and drinking and carrying on "like men."[18] Women on their own enjoying themselves without the benefits of male companionship or protection then, as now, inspired suspicion, sexual innuendo, and often gross satire.

Figure 8. Negrier, *Le Bain des Lionnes*.

Ultimately, the discourses of bathing and swimming must be understood in connection with other regimes of reglementarianism—official government regulation—connected with the body and its practices, regimes brilliantly analyzed by Michel Foucault and by Alain Corbin in his studies of prostitution, smells, and garbage, as well as by Georges Vigarello in his histories of cleanliness, sports, posture, and deportment training.[19] Bathing and its representation must be viewed as part of a more generalized politics and policy of "putting the body in its place": a policy that had its origins during the later eighteenth century and was associated with Enlightenment ideals of control, hygiene, and civil order. As with the discourses of prostitution, sanitation, and wet-nursing, to which the discourses of swimming and bathing are related in that all are concerned with the body's products, comportments, or employments, there is an evolving official government code of regulations, stipulating prohibitions, and approving practices in the realm of swimming and bathing. This official regulationism is accompanied by a stream of propaganda extolling the physical and social benefits of swimming and bathing and, at the same time, by a contradictory plethora of irreverent satire aimed at the foibles associated with water sports.

In none of this material, however, is the critique aimed at naked goddesses lolling about on the banks of classical or Edenic shores, but rather at modern women emerging from locker rooms, learning the strokes and the dives, taking showers before and after, and eyeing one another in bathing suits. Nakedness and the elevation of the nude is never an issue here, but rather the ludicrous effects of contemporary bathing costumes on less-than-perfect bodies. Popular art tells a story of mundane dangers and down-to-earth (or down-to-water, more accurately) triumphs.

The Parisian *piscines* (municipal swimming pools) are viewed as democratizing where men are concerned, and perhaps somewhat equivocally when it concerns women.[20] What might be perceived as a beneficent temporary mixing of social milieus in the case of male swimmers had different overtones in the case of female ones, as *demi-mondaines*, *grisettes*, dancers, and actresses mingling with respectable girls and women might well be a corrupting influence.[21]

Crowding, jostling, and loss of control over the urban river-space, especially in the case of the cheap *bains à quatre sous* ("nickel baths") was perceived as a real issue, whether represented humorously, as in Nadar's *Les Chaleurs* (Fig. 9), or more objectively, as in an 1880s photograph of the Seine viewed from the Louvre, showing the area around the Pont Neuf encumbered with floating wooden pools.[22] Swimming pools had become very popular by the decade of the 1880s. In 1884, the year of the grand opening of the Piscine Château-Landon, one of the first swimming pools to be constructed *away* from the Seine, 200,000 people visited the pool, of which 1,000 learned how to swim.[23]

Sophisticated posters began to appear, advertising the attractions of the various municipal pools. What I find interesting about a poster like the one

Figure 9. Nadar (Gaspard Félix Tournachon), *Les Chaleurs*, c. 1860s.

published by Emile Levi in 1882, advertising the Bains Bourse, is, in comparison to Renoir's almost contemporary *Great Bathers*, its modernity (Fig. 10). I am not talking about quality here—the poster, although it has a certain pizzazz, makes no claims to aesthetic excellence—but rather the way the image engages with commodity, how it catches the eye of the spectator, male or female, and keeps it focused on what is at stake: the pool, the bodies, the prices. Segmented in its construction, combining print and illusionistic representation as boldly as a much later cubist collage, the poster assigns each part a specific task to perform, a task of commercial communication. The deeply receding space of the pool, emphasizing its amplitude, is decoratively related to, yet, in terms of signification, separated from, the segment communicating prices and amenities (the print section), which in turn is separated from the two "come on" figures—the *commère* and the *compère*, as it were—connecting the viewer with the possibilities offered by the image. The woman is someone we know from the ads of our own day: sprightly, up-to-date, come-hither, her sexuality already functioning as a

Figure 10. Emile Levi, *Poster of Bains Bourse Pool*, 1882.

visual sign of exchange-value in much the way we take for granted in modern advertising. Color is flat, outlines simplified, the easier to get the message across and the cheaper to print up multiple copies. It is in the "low"
art of the *piscine* poster that visual representation and modernity intersect,
in a way utterly foreign to Renoir's enterprise.

Of course high art had its own counter-discursive strategies during
bathtime: that campaign of subversion from within which art history has
always identified with Modernism itself. In both Courbet's *Bathing Women*
of 1853 (Fig. 11) and Manet's *Déjeuner sur l'herbe* of ten years later (the latter
originally entitled *Le Bain*; Fig. 3), the traditional elevation of the bather
theme is called into question with a "shock of the new." In both cases, although differently, a disconcerting combination of alienation and the reality effect is involved. In the Courbet, "reality" is signified by the coarse
fleshiness of the fat body and the presence of abandoned clothing; but
the meaninglessness of the gesture calls into question the naturalness of
the topos itself and invokes alienation. In the Manet painting, abandoned
clothing as well as the presence of modern, fully dressed men signify, once
more, contemporaneity; but the formal language in toto refuses the natural
as a possibility of representation.

This was a subversion from within which Renoir, as an Impressionist,
had actively participated, as his interesting, disturbing, not wholly success-

Figure 11. Gustave Courbet, *Bathing Women*, 1853.

ful *Nude in Sunlight* of 1876 reveals (Fig. 12). But by the 1880s and 1890s, things had changed within the avant-garde itself. It was not just Renoir who was fleeing immediacy and contemporaneity but other vanguard artists as well, most notably Gauguin, who actually left France itself in search of more timeless, universal, indeed eternal values inscribed on the bodies of naked, dark-skinned females (Fig. 13).

Earlier, I made the assertion that Renoir's *Great Bathers* might belong to a certain subcategory or moment of bathtime—that of the *rappel à l'ordre* of the 1880s, when certain artists, most arduously Renoir, attempted to restore timelessness and high-minded harmony to late Impressionism. I should now like to suggest, very sketchily, why this should be the case, and to indicate the various overdeterminations mediating the construction of *The Great Bathers* and other works of this period.

I would like to make clear that I consider *Great Bathers* an ambitious but badly flawed painting rather than a masterpiece—a record of conflicting

Figure 12. Auguste Renoir, *Nude in Sunlight*, 1876.

desires, intentions, and practices, and interesting as such. It is certainly not a painting that either innovates or summarizes. These contradictions, I maintain, exist not merely on a formal level, as at least one authority has contended, but are the inscription of much more complex conceptual and ideological muddles.[24] *The Great Bathers*, with all its ambiguities and failures, constitutes a response to a multitude of pressures during the period preceding its creation, including:

1. Growing demands on the part of women for rights, education, and subjecthood within industrial society, a sign of "progress" that Renoir increasingly found dangerous and to which he reacted with longing for the "good old days" when women—and everyone else—knew their place.[25]

2. Market forces demanding specialization and individualization of artistic production.[26] This, in a way, might be considered part of the same objectionable "progress" that Renoir so disliked, and he complained bitterly about it in his letters. Nevertheless, he understandably did his best to succeed within the dealer system and through the cultivation of wealthy clients. Increasingly, during the 1880s, each artist had to be positioned as a

Figure 13. Paul Gauguin, *What, Are You Jealous?* 1892.

unique (almost invariably male) hero of creation and self-creation. Renoir and his fellow artists felt, not incorrectly, that Impressionism's brief communal enterprise had blurred and blunted the uniqueness of individual styles and personalities. Viewers had difficulty, for example, telling the difference between Monet's and Renoir's versions of *La Grenouillère*. Now, by the decade of the 1880s, stimulated by the dealer system and a competitive market extending as far as the United States, the unique artist was encouraged to produce identifiable objects: it was no longer a question of "Impressionist works" but of "Monets" or "Renoirs."

One might call it "bending to the market" or "opportunism," but that is to imagine that at all times an artist like Renoir is consciously catering to the wishes of others and would, on his own, do something quite different. On the contrary, I would say that, most of the time, producer and consumers shared similar values, and it is a question not so much of bowing to market pressures as interpellating (to use an Althusserian term) in the realm of cultural institutions: certain positions and formations gradually emerge which call into being subjects who will fill them. "The artist" by the 1880s was already positioning himself as a specialist and a genius—not a *representer* of modern life but its opposite, an *inventor* of timeless, aestheticized realms of value, beginning perhaps with experience but transcending it. Monet became a specialist in series, Renoir in bathers, Gauguin in Tahitians, and so on, with styles that could not be confused with those of other artists.

Sticking to the city and to an interchangeable style, Cézanne (of whom more later), but especially Seurat and the Neoimpressionists, offer a counter-example to this more general trend of the 1880s and 1890s. Yet even they, like Renoir, rejected the fluidity and experiential ephemerality characteris-tic of Impressionism at its high point in the 1870s. Renoir's *Great Bathers*, then, is part of the history of that retreat from experience, from daily life, from urban subject matter, and from social engagement which defines one strand—perhaps the dominant one—of Modernism until the advent of Cubism. The question is, of course, to what extent can such a painting be associated with the Modernist enterprise at all.

In Renoir's case, I think certain special factors are at work in the *rappel à l'ordre*. Impressionism, and Renoir in particular, came in the late 1870s to be associated not only with the inchoate, the momentary, and the transient but, at the same time, with the quintessentially feminine in both subject and style. In other words, I believe a hidden, and probably an unconscious, gender agenda is at work here. There is a way in which, in *The Great Bathers*, Renoir may be said to be ridding himself of what was considered "feminine" formlessness and the triviality of a "feminine" style.[27]

Renoir, who could hardly but be aware of this effeminization of Impres-sionism in the critical texts of the period generally, and particularly those critiques directed toward his own production, took harsh steps to remedy these "flaws." Earlier, he had engaged with the rest of the Impressionists in constructing a painting of daily life, of city or suburbs where men and women interacted as social beings within the milieu of historical experi-ence, even if this might be a Utopian world of desire and pleasure, as it was in *Le Moulin de la Galette* of 1876 (Fig. 14) and other works of that period.

Now, in 1887 with *The Great Bathers*, the male is positioned outside the world of the painting, as desirer and viewer rather than participant. The representation is no longer social and concrete but reduced to a "timeless" realm of women's bodies in a vague, natural setting. History and social hi-erarchy are occluded in order to produce an atemporal, natural realm in which a masculine subject views a feminine object.

The end of Impressionism, viewed from the vantage point of gender, coincides with a (possibly unconscious) rejection of the "feminine" toward the end of the century, and a return to "solid" values on the part of a certain fraction of the avant-garde. The nude, specifically the bather, inscribed in the order of the "natural," stands for the return of value in art itself. Nowhere can this mythology of the return of solid values to art be so con-vincingly deployed as in the case of the ambivalently approached *female* body. It is here that aesthetic goals can coincide most productively with un-conscious psychosexual factors, and these unconscious impulses in turn erased, modified, or sublimated. The bathers, freed from contemporary specificity and historical narrative alike, are now understood to be the pri-mary realm of pure aesthetic—of course, masculine aesthetic—challenge.

And what of the other painter of large bathers, Cézanne? One might begin by observing that in his work, modernity intersects with the female

Figure 14. Auguste Renoir, *Le Moulin de la Galette*, 1876.

nude in terms of a language, a pictorial construction, not a subject matter. Cézanne's "doubt," as Maurice Merleau-Ponty labeled it, calls into question both subject and object: the painter's vision, his powers of inscription, the naked body, and the space-surface within or upon which it must exist.[28]

In terms of perspectival construction, Cézanne's decentering of the pictorial point of view relates both to desire and sexuality in the construction of his bather paintings. Cézanne refuses Renoir's obvious, single, centered viewpoint in his *Large Bathers* of 1906, and, by shattering one-point perspective, destroys the understood presence of the desiring individual male as the painter/spectator's point of view (Fig. 15).

In emphasizing Cézanne's famous doubt, a doubt of which the signifier is revealed *process*, I should like to compare it with Renoir's doubtfulness, an uncertainty veiled by the harmonious stasis characteristic of a *product*. For Renoir, of course, has doubts, too; or rather, he has troubles about the validity of his art, especially about the everyday subjects, impermanently painted surfaces, and the unstable compositions—in short, the processive structures—characteristic of High Impressionism. And, from a different standpoint, like most female nudes of the nineteenth century, his bathers as subjects of representation are sites of contradiction and uncertainty, inscribing anxieties and their repression.

Cézanne's bathers, unlike Renoir's, do not bathe or play or talk. There is no longer any sensory illusion, or narrative pretext, as in Renoir's: no splashing, drying, or *espièglerie* (teasing). The specific qualities of the body—not

Figure 15. Paul Cézanne, *Large Bathers*, 1906.

just the seductiveness of the female or its fearsomeness and power but its very anatomy, its proportions, its ability to support itself, and perhaps most especially its *boundaries*, that which separates the body in its integrity from that which is not the body (the so-called background), boundaries which, in the form of contour, were so carefully and lovingly maintained by Renoir and the academicians of the day—are here disregarded, suppressed, or made ambiguous. Perhaps most important, the very signs of sexual difference themselves are erased or made to seem inconsequential in the late *Bathers*. In short, Cézanne's *Large Bathers* of 1906 constitutes a heroic effort to escape from the dominion of the sexual-scopic implicated in the traditional masculine gaze on the female sex, as well as the heavy-breathing sexual violence or equally disturbing repressive strategies characterizing his early work, not to speak of their inscription of the personal, the contemporary, the concrete—and the popular.

What Cézanne is erasing is as important as what he is constructing. He is erasing a traditional discourse of the nude, encoding desire and the ideal as well as its opposite, humiliation and awkwardness (the historical turf of naturalism as well as piety); above all, in the *Large Bathers* he is erasing the codes constructed for the purpose of maintaining gender difference from classical antiquity down through the nineteenth century, and in some way negating his own relation to such difference. As much as the postermaker or the caricaturist or mass-media printmaker, although with diametrically opposite ends in view, Cézanne is a destroyer of traditions of visual representation, a reinventor of the body for a public which gradually learns to appreciate his practice as a kind of analogue to the modern epistemological dilemma itself, and which finally might be said to fetishize it as such.

Figure 16. Auguste Renoir, *The Bathers*, 1918.

Figure 17. Gustave Courbet, *Sleepers*, 1866.

The beached, blubbery whale-women in Renoir's *The Bathers* (Fig. 16) of 1918 are of course, without question, antifeminist icons, an insult to the feminine mind and body. Positioned historically, they are the postcoital sequel to Courbet's scandalous lesbian *Sleepers* of 1866 (Fig. 17), the two lovers now satiated and languorously awake, the blonde woman lying back in the traditionally seductive hands-behind-the-head pose, the dark-haired "dominant" nude apparently meditating in the classical "thinker" pose, if one can associate anything as coherent as thinking with this monstrously corporeal creature. But they are also positioned historically at the end of the First World War, and at the end of Renoir's life itself. Despite their rolls of fat (perhaps an inspiration for the Michelin Man), these figures did not appeal to Caroline Knapp, our anorexic viewer—too much of a good thing, perhaps.

But I, and you, can see it differently. One might say that in his old age, Renoir finally allowed himself to go literally over the top: over the top of Impressionist visual verism, over the top of the kitschy classicism of *The Great Bathers*, into a visceral dreamland, the dreamworld of the *Informe*. The nude has expanded, liquefied, deboned itself into a viscero-visionary icon of pneumatic bliss. Brushstrokes loosen and lose their thickness, plasticity, their substance, merging figure and background.

Indeed, the word "icon" is too firm, too enclosed to account for what we see here. I suppose we can think of it as an old age style, whatever we mean by this suspect term, if we think of old age as accompanied by arthritis, the dissolution of bone and connective tissue, experienced painfully by Renoir. Horizontality is the direction. These nudes lie down for the most part, succumbing to the downward pull of the flesh, to gravity, and the better to demonstrate the enticing abjection of the flesh. Yet even if they maintain their status as "nudes," their flesh has been transmuted by a kind of reverse alchemy into some lower substance, a sort of aestheticized gunk. They predict, in their antihumanism—materialist, brutally anti-idealist—a host of inventively macerated bodies to come: those of Picasso at his most paroxysmic, perhaps, but even more those of Dubuffet and De Kooning later in the twentieth century. I am speaking of course not of Renoir's intentions— who knows what they were, and how much is due to sheer infirmity; we can be certain he had not read Georges Bataille on the *Informe*, at any rate— but of what exists on the canvas as form and substance.

In concluding, I should like to say once more that in studying a major nineteenth-century theme like bathers, serious attention needs to be paid to alternative points of view, to other modes of visual production rather than the high art studied by conventional art history. Advertising, mass media prints, cartoons, and so on exist not just as undifferentiated, visually indifferent "sources" for high art but, on the contrary, as alternatives, and, often, as adversaries of it. As alternatives, they have very different work to do and from time to time enter into a positive dialectical relationship with the practices of high art, while at other times, into an equally important relationship of fierce rejection or negation with it. It is only through an understanding of such relationships and the cultural struggles through which they are manifested in all their complexity that we can begin to construct an inclusive and truly social history of nineteenth-century visual representation, a history in which works like Renoir's *Great Bathers* will be viewed not as either a masterpiece or a sorry failure but rather as the result of certain kinds of practices, the product of a particular shifting structure of cultural institutions at a particular moment of history.

At the same time, the interpretation of a work of art also exists within history, and no one voice is entitled to iterate its "meaning." Indeed, it has, I hope, become clear that there is no single way of understanding *The Great Bathers*, that its meanings are multiple, construed differently, often at cross-purposes by different viewers and interpreters. It is not a case of "anything goes"—if someone were to insist that Renoir in this painting is creating an allegory of the Second Coming of Christ, I would reject it out of hand. Yet the range of relevant interpretations is broad, no matter how far afield from Renoir's purported intentions in creating the work, or even how far they may stray from the contexts and interpretations of the historical period in which it came into being. Before there was a disease called anorexia, before there was a feminist movement, before Freud, Renoir's *Bathers* could not "mean" what it does today. It is only by allowing new interpretations that works of art—in our case, representations of bathers, but also bathtime itself as a cultural entity—can be more fully understood and remain a living, sometimes unruly entity rather than a respectable corpse.

NOTES

[1] Caroline Knapp, *Appetites: Why Women Want* (New York: Counterpoint, 2003), ix.

[2] George Steiner, *New York Times*, February 28, 1971. Michel Foucault, *Les Mots et les choses: Une archéologie des sciences humaines* (Paris: Gallimard, 1966).

[3] Tamar Garb, *Bodies of Modernity: Figure and Flesh in Fin-de-Siècle France* (London: Thames and Hudson, 1998), 169–170.

[4] These conclusions are based on a methodical search for representations of female bathers in the Salon *livrets* from 1814 to 1890. This was not an easy task, although it became somewhat easier after 1879, when partial illustrations in the form of engravings were provided. *Diana* was clear enough, as was *Bathsheba* or just plain *Une Baigneuse*. But what about *Le Bain*, which, especially if it were by a woman artist, might turn out to be a mother bathing her baby; or *Aux Bords du Lac*, which often meant the presence of nudes on the shore, whereas *Aux Bords du Lac Leman* inevitably referred to a landscape? Guesswork was inevitable, but some interesting information nevertheless resulted from this survey.

[5] In attempting to answer this question, or at least to formulate questions to be asked about it, my approach will be both diachronic and synchronic: concerned both with change and evolution and with the interaction of simultaneous practices and products.

[6] For a discussion of the twentieth-century *rappel à l'ordre*, a time after World War I when political conservatism in France found its artistic equivalent in a variety of reactionary "harmonizing," sometimes historicizing styles, see *Les Réalismes, 1919–1939* (exhibition catalogue; Paris: Centre Georges Pompidou, 1980); Kenneth E. Silver, *Esprit de Corps: The Art of the Parisian Avant-Garde and the First World War, 1914–1925* (Princeton: Princeton University Press, 1989); and Romy Golan, "Modes of Escape: The Representation of Paris in the Twenties," in *The 1920s: Age of Metropolis*, ed. Jean Clair (exhibition catalogue; Montreal: Montreal Museum of Fine Arts, 1991), 336–377. All of these constructions of the conservative reaction after World War I influenced my thinking about the recall to order characteristic of many of the dominant art styles in France, particularly those of the erstwhile avant-garde, during the last twenty years of the nineteenth century.

[7] For a recent attempt to contextualize Renoir's *Great Bathers* historically, within the context of the cultural politics of the Third French Republic, see John House, "Renoir's *Baigneuses* of 1887 at the Politics of Escapism," *Burlington Magazine*, 134, 1074 (September 1992): 636–642.

[8] See, for example, Christopher Riopelle, Philadelphia Museum of Art *Bulletin*, 1990: 28, and fig. 30 for an illustration of the François Girardon relief, *Nymphs Bathing*, c. 1670, in connection with Renoir's project.

[9] For a thoroughgoing account of the role of lesbian imagery in nineteenth-century representation, see Maura Reilly, "Le vice à la mode: Gustave Courbet and the Vogue for Lesbianism in Second Empire France," PhD diss., New York University, Institute of Fine Arts, 2000.

[10] This is, of course, an opposing effect to Roland Barthes' oft-cited *effet de réelle*, or reality effect. It seems to me what many of these purveyors of the female bather were getting at were "effects of the aesthetic" within a basically naturalistic premise. This effect is particularly evident in the orientalizing bathers of Gérôme, in which motifs from Ingres "aestheticize" the otherwise scrupulously "objective" representations of naked black and white women in obsessively detailed interior spaces. For a further examination of this topos, the "sign of the artistic" in realist art, see Linda Nochlin, "The Imaginary Orient," in Nochlin, *The Politics of Vision: Essays on Nineteenth-Century Art and Society* (New York: Harper & Row, 1989), 47–49.

[11] The recent controversies over high and low art and their relationship, to which an extremely controversial exhibition at the Museum of Modern Art in New York in 1990–1991 gave rise, have stimulated interest, I hope, in these neglected aspects of visual representation which social and cultural historians, in the United States, England, and France, have been investigating with great intelligence and originality for quite a few years now. See *Modern Art and Popular Culture: Readings in High and Low*, eds. Kirk Varnedoe and Adam Gopnik (New York: Museum of Modern Art, H. N. Abrams, 1990). There has also been a good deal of original work on the history and social positioning of the body in recent times, an issue, like that of popular art and culture, relevant to the subject of this essay. See, for example, the various investigations of the body in relation to cleanliness, sport, and hygiene by Georges Vigarello: *Le Propre et le sale: L'Hygiène du corps depuis le Moyen Age* (Paris: Seuil, 1985); *Le Corps redressé* (Paris: Delarge, 1978); and *Une Histoire culturelle du sport, techniques d'hier et d'aujourd'hui* (Paris: EPS/R. Laffont, 1988). These studies investigate subjects relevant to bathing and swimming in their textual, if not in their visual, aspects.

[12] For a long discussion of the rise in importance of boating and sailing as leisure activities in the later nineteenth century, see Paul Tucker, *Monet at Argenteuil* (New Haven: Yale University Press, 1981). Robert L. Herbert, *Impressionism: Art, Leisure, and Parisian Society* (New Haven: Yale University Press, 1988), devotes a substantial section of his study to sailing at Argenteuil and rowing and boating at Chatou (229–245).

[13] See the versions of this theme by Renoir of 1869 now in the Pushkin Museum in Moscow, the Nationalmuseum in Stockholm, and the Oskar Reinhart Collection in Winterthur. Robert L. Herbert publishes a richly detailed engraving of men and women bathing together at La Grenouillère of 1873; see Herbert, *Impressionism: Art, Leisure, and Parisian Society* (New Haven: Yale University Press, 1988), fig. 210, p. 211. And there is a spirited and sexy color print of 1880 illustrating mixed bathing and general good fun at this popular bathing establishment in François Beaudouin, *Paris sur Seine: Ville fluviale: son histoire des origins à nos jours* (Paris: Editions de la Martinière, 1994), 172.

[14] Cited in Ambroise Vollard, *Renoir: An Intimate Record*, tr. H. L. Van Doren and R. T. Weaver (1925; New York: Alfred A. Knopf, 1934), 49. It is interesting to see how often artists, and the rest of us as well, tend to look back at our youthful years as "preindustrial," simpler, and more leisured, despite the fact that one person's youth is, of course, another's old age, and that the period from which Renoir was looking back so nostalgically was dubbed "the gay Nineties" by people who had been young during it, looking back from their vantage point of the twentieth century.

[15] Daumier's series devoted to female bathers in the pools of Paris, entitled *Les Baigneuses*, appeared in *Le Charivari* in 1847. There was also a series featuring male *habitués* of the Paris swimming pools.

[16] For an excellent account of Daumier's counter-discursive practice and the complexity of the notion of counter-discourse itself, see Richard Terdiman, *Discourse/Counter-Discourse: The Theory and Practice of Symbolic Resistance in Nineteenth-Century France* (Ithaca: Cornell University Press, 1985). See especially chapter 3, "Counter-Images: Daumier and *Le Charivari*," 149–197.

[17] Article-advertisement for the Bains Lambert, illustrated by Daubigny and others, c. 1850, in Album Bains, Salle des Estampes, Bibliothèque Nationale, Paris.

[18] For a description of the coarse behavior of women at swimming pools, one of many, see Eugène Briffault, *Paris dans l'eau* (Paris: J. Hetzel, 1844), 99: "In the women's bath meet, for the most part, heroines of gallantry and of opulent pleasure; other women keep themselves apart, and good reputations separate themselves from the golden belts . . . they smoke there as much as men." Many of the illustrations accompanying these descriptive texts are far from flattering either to women's bodies or their character!

[19] See, for example, Michel Foucault, *The Birth of the Clinic: An Archaeology of Medical Perception*, trans. A. M. Sheridan Smith (New York: Pantheon Books, 1973); *Discipline and Punish: The Birth of the Prison*, trans. Alan Sheridan (New York: Pantheon Books, 1977); or *The History of Sexuality*, vol. 1: *An Introduction*, trans. Robert Hurley (New York: Pantheon, 1978). See also Alain Corbin, *Les Filles de noces; misère sexuelle et prostitution: 19e et 20e siècles* (Paris: Aubier Montaigne, 1978); and his *Le Miasme et la jonquille: L'Odorat et l'imaginaire social XVIIIe–XIXe siècles* (Paris: Aubier Montaigne, 1982). Equally relevant is the work of Georges Vigarello, cited above, n. 11.

[20] See, for example, Eugène Chapus, *Le Sport à Paris* (Paris: Hachette, 1854), 187:

> At the swimming school, the domination of rank disappears in the uniformity of the bathrobe and the bathing suit required by everyone. There is no longer any distinction, except in the art of diving, of doing the Jack-knife or swan-dives, of getting up from the water without tiring. The great dignitaries of the swimming school are those who dare to do high dives from the top of the diving board, or who hurl themselves boldly from the top of the tower into the pool.

[21] See, for example, the descriptions cited by Michel Jansel, *Paris incroyable* (Paris: Hachette, 1986), 98–99, of the "perfect equality" reigning in all the female bathing establishments of the mid-nineteenth century; nevertheless, the "vraies jeunes filles" distinguished themselves by preferring sugar-water to the stronger refreshment selected by more morally equivocal women swimmers.

[22] The Seine became choked with *établissements flottants* at the end of the nineteenth century. See *Deux siècles d'architecture sportive à Paris: Piscines, gymnases . . .* (exhibition catalogue; Paris: Mairie du XXe arrondissement, 1984), 34.

[23] Ibid., 29–31, and cat. no. 37, p. 34, for the history of the Château-Landon pool and the origin of pools away from the Seine in 1884, as well as the staggering attendance figures at Château-Landon. Also see Paul Christmann, *La Natation et les bains* (Paris: Librairie Alcide Picard et Kaan, 1886), 16–27. Christmann, president of the Société des Gymnases Nautiques, created at Château-Landon the first covered pool provided with warm water. A staunch advocate of all-year-round pools in Paris, from a point of view both hygienic and patriotic, he seems to have gotten the concession to supply warm water to the Paris *piscines* (44–45).

[24] See, for example, Barbara White's contention that the two sides are disparate in style, which accounts for the failure of the painting to attain unity: "The forms on the left side and foreground are linear, realistic and clarified; on the right side and in the distance they are Impressionist. But the figures do not relate to one another or to their setting in a natural or comfortable fashion. . . . With such complex intentions, it is no wonder that, in the end, Renoir created a stilted, labored exercise that lacked stylistic unity." Barbara Ehrlich White, *Renoir: His Life, Art, and Letters* (New York: H. N. Abrams, 1984), 174.

[25] For extended analysis of Renoir's reactionary attitudes toward women, see Tamar Garb, "Renoir and the Natural Woman," *Oxford Art Journal*, 8, no. 2 (1985): 3–15; also see Desa Philippi, "Desiring Renoir: Fantasy and Spectacle at the Hayward," *Oxford Art Journal*, 8, no. 2 (1985): 16–20, as well as articles by Fred Orton and John House also published in the same journal. Of equal importance in evaluating Renoir's gender position is Kathleen Adler's review article, "Reappraising Renoir," *Art History*, 8 (September 1985): 374–380.

[26] For a detailed, and radical, analysis of the place of economics in the transformation of French painting during the period from 1870 to the end of the nineteenth century, see

Nicholas Green, "Dealing in Temperaments: Economic Transformation of the Artistic Field in France during the Second Half of the Nineteenth Century," *Art History*, 10, no. 1 (March 1987): 59–78.

[27] For an analysis of the association of femininity and Impressionist style, see Anne Higonnet, "Writing the Gender of the Image: Art Criticism in Late Nineteenth-Century France," *Genders*, 6 (Fall 1989): 60–73, and Tamar Garb, "'Soeurs de pinceau': The Formation of a Separate Women's Art World in Paris, 1881–1897," PhD diss., Courtauld Institute of Art, University of London, 1991, 337–339.

[28] The classic article constructing this topic is Maurice Merleau-Ponty's "Cézanne's Doubt," first published in 1945 and then republished in the great phenomenologist's *Sens et non-sens* (Paris: Nagel, 1966), 15–44.

•   •   •   •   •   •   •   •   •   •   •   •

QUESTIONS FOR A SECOND READING

1. "Step back from the canvas, think, feel." This is from the passage by Caroline Knapp, whose account of *The Great Bathers* provides a key reference point for Linda Nochlin. In the opening section, Nochlin also includes a passage from Michel Foucault's early work, *The Order of Things* (*Les Mots et les choses*), a reference to the ways "knowledge becomes knowledge rather than accidental array of facts and objects" (p. 449). And she concludes the chapter by saying: "It is only by allowing new interpretations that works of art . . . can be more fully understood and remain a living, sometimes unruly entity rather than a respectable corpse" (p. 473). To think and feel, to fully understand, to bring to life, to have knowledge beyond facts or information—the chapter is a demonstration of how this art historian carries out a scholarly or intellectual project, a work of understanding.

    As you reread the essay, mark passages and prepare notes that will allow you to provide an account of how Nochlin, as represented in the writing of this piece, comes to understand *The Great Bathers* and the work of Renoir. She is writing a research paper. How does she conduct this research? She is doing intellectual work. What are the steps or strategies? (What is the role of the history of swimming pools, for instance?) What are her tools and methods? How might you carry out a similar project?

2. There are a number of key terms in this essay, words and phrases that belong to a critical tradition (to the work of other scholars, that is), words and phrases that carry a lot of weight or have a lot of work to do. They make more than "ordinary" sense. Here is a list. You might add to it. Sometimes the terms operate in pairs. In the headnote to this selection, we provide a brief gloss of the two French terms listed here. They have a rich and interesting context.

    the desiring male gaze, sexual-scopic

    representation and practice

    natural and artificial

    discourse, historically specific discourse, traditional discourse,
        counter-discourse

topos

Informe

rappel à l'ordre

The library, the Internet, and specialized dictionaries like a dictionary of critical terms can help you with these terms. But you can also work on them in the context of Nochlin's sentences and paragraphs. As you reread, develop a personal glossary, a set of working definitions for these terms. Your goal should be to bring them into your own sentences as you speak and write.

3. Throughout the essay, Nochlin makes easy reference to a range of scholars, painters, and paintings (e.g., Caroline Knapp, Raphael, Girardon, Jean-Baptiste Pater, Frédéric Dufaux, Bouguereau, Daumier, Courbet, Dubuffet, De Kooning). You might think of each reference as the invitation to a mini-research project, the occasion for a report that you (or groups of you) might prepare for the class. The more you know about these figures, the more you can make of references to their work as you reread.

4. As an essay, this chapter does not drive toward a conclusion about Renoir. It does, however, have something to say about Renoir and his career; that is, it says something about the *place* of *The Great Bathers* in a long career of painting nude women. As you reread, bring forward the account of Renoir's career that underlays the broader discussion.

ASSIGNMENTS FOR WRITING

1. Central to the essay, "Renoir's *Great Bathers*," is Nochlin's sense of history. She says,

> For there is history, of course: the corporeal eye, the visceral eye—all eyes are located not merely in bodies but in historically specific bodies and can thus be viewed within a history of representation and a history of practices, a social history, in short, that can thicken up our responses to *The Great Bathers*. (p. 452)

The visceral eye. The male eye. The female eye. The desiring eye. The anorexic eye. The art historian's eye. All of these reference points are used to "thicken up" Nochlin's account of Renoir's painting.

What about you—the historically specific you? Or your generation? Or people like you? What are the personal investments, the histories of practices and representations, the social institutions through which you see and understand a painting like this one?

Write an essay in which you bring your experience, context, and point of view into conversation with Nochlin's. You should work closely with *The Great Bathers* and with Nochlin's account of it (and the paintings and images she brings alongside it), but of course you can bring images, knowledge, and experiences of your own. You'll need to provide a fair and rich account of what Nochlin says; at the same time you'll want to claim equal time and space for what you have to say; you will want to "thicken" her response.

2. Central to Nochlin's essay "Renoir's *Great Bathers*" is the distinction between a *practice* and a *representation*—or, as the subtitle says, between "Bathing as Practice" and "Bathing as Representation." To prepare for this assignment, reread the essay to see how Nochlin uses these terms—*practice* and *representation*—to organize her research project. What is she doing when she turns to the history of swimming and swimming pools and to the "discourses of swimming and bathing" in Paris in the second half of the nineteenth century? What do these points of comparison allow her to think, to understand, or to say about the paintings?

   Once you have a sense of method, gather materials you might use to conduct a similar project—one that considers a set of representations (images and/or texts that matter to you) in relation to the practices to which they allude. Think of your essay as an homage, as carrying out a Nochlin-like project. It would be appropriate to allude to her work (and her conclusions) at some point in your essay.

3. This assignment is for the student (or students) who are interested in doing research in the art and/or thought that informs Nochlin's essay. Nochlin makes easy reference to a range of scholars, painters, and paintings from Caroline Knapp and Michel Foucault to Raphael, Bouguereau, Courbet, and De Kooning. (This, of course, is only a partial list and isn't meant to be exclusive.) You might think of each reference, each figure included in the essay, and each footnote, for that matter, as the invitation to a mini-research project.

   For this project, follow one lead and become knowledgeable about the painting or text, first by studying it on your own—Nochlin takes time both to study an image and to describe it—then perhaps by looking at only one or two secondary sources (what someone else, for example, has had to say about Bouguereau's *Bathers* or Knapp's *Appetites*). The point of your essay would be to extend, but also to question, Nochlin's account of the image or text you choose and what it says and what it does.

MAKING CONNECTIONS

1. Like Linda Nochlin, John Berger is a highly regarded art historian, someone who was said to provide powerful new ways of looking at paintings. Both Nochlin and Berger are interested in the relationship between "high" and "low" art, both are interested in the distinction between "practice" and "representation," and both are interested in the relationship between art and history. As an exercise, as a way of thinking closely about the work of each, it can be useful to work out the differences in method and intent. As you reread each author's essay, look for an extended section, a place where Nochlin or Berger work at length with a particular painting or idea, and let these provide the starting points for your project.

   Working closely with these sections, and keeping in mind a reader familiar with neither, write an essay that discusses what you find to be the interesting or important differences between the two writers and their work. Of the two, Nochlin and Berger, who speaks most powerfully to you (or to your generation) about art and image, about the past and the present, about a responsible way of seeing the world? Who makes the most sense—or who seems to you to be doing the kind of work that is most useful and necessary?

2. With Adrienne Rich's essay, "When We Dead Awaken: Writing as Re-Vision" (p. 520) as a lens or as a point of reference, it is possible to read "Renoir's *Great Bathers*: Bathing as Practice, Bathing as Representation" as an essay on revision. Nochlin talks about changes in her own thinking; she charts changes across Renoir's career and across a particular genre of painting in France in the second half of the nineteenth century. Both essays are reflections on the practice as well as the idea of revision. Both essays assume a difficult relationship between a woman's desire and patriarchal expectation. As you reread them, keep an eye out for interesting or suggestive examples or counterexamples, places where the essays seem to be speaking back and forth to each other, even though no direct reference is there. And write an essay that thinks through these accounts of revision. How do they understand and value change? And how might these works speak directly to you?

3. Linda Nochlin's "Renoir's *Great Bathers*" is full of sexually charged images of women; Susan Bordo's "Beauty (Re)discovers the Male Body" (p. 131) is full of sexually charged images of men, the latter in the realm of commerce, the former (or at least most of them) in the realm of "art." Both Nochlin and Bordo are interested in how images of the body circulate, and in the work to which these images are and can be put.

   Toward the end of her essay, Nochlin says:

   > In concluding, I should like to say once more that in studying a major nineteenth-century theme like bathers, serious attention needs to be paid to alternative points of view, to other modes of visual production rather than the high art studied by conventional art history. Advertising, mass media prints, cartoons, and so on exist not just as undifferentiated, visually indifferent "sources" for high art but, on the contrary, as alternatives, and, often, as adversaries of it. As alternatives, they have very different work to do and from time to time enter into a positive dialectical relationship with the practices of high art, while at other times, into an equally important relationship of fierce rejection or negation with it. (p. 472)

   There are two invitations here. One is to find images of the male body in contemporary "high" art—and there are many that are considered important (and many in Nochlin's book, *Bathers, Bodies, Beauty*)—and to write about them in relation to images from advertising. You might read these representations in relation to advertising practice with the goal of making a claim, with Nochlin, for either a "positive dialectical relationship" or a "fierce rejection."

   The other invitation is to work with the two essays as an exercise in close reading. If you follow this lead, as you reread them, look for an extended section of each essay, sections that seem to speak back and forth to each other in interesting or provocative ways. What do both have to say about how images are created and perceived, about how they circulate?

   Working closely with these sections, and keeping in mind a reader familiar with neither, write an essay that discusses what you find to be the interesting or important differences between the two writers and their work. Of the two, Nochlin and Bordo, who speaks most powerfully to you (or to your generation) about the body and about images of the body, and about how these circulate in contemporary culture? Who makes the most sense—or who seems to you to be doing the kind of work that is most useful or necessary?

WALKER
PERCY

WALKER PERCY, in his midforties, after a life of rela-
tive obscurity and after a career as, he said, a "failed
physician," wrote his first novel, The Moviegoer. *It won*
the National Book Award for fiction in 1962, and Percy
emerged as one of this country's leading novelists. Little
in his background would have predicted such a career.

After graduating from Columbia University's medical
school in 1941, Percy (1916–1990) went to work at Belle-
vue Hospital in New York City. He soon contracted tu-
berculosis from performing autopsies on derelicts and
was sent to a sanitorium to recover, where, as he said, "I was in bed so much,
alone so much, that I had nothing to do but read and think. I began to question
everything I had once believed." He returned to medicine briefly but suffered a re-
lapse and during his long recovery began "to make reading a full-time occupa-
tion." He left medicine, but not until 1954, almost a decade later, did he publish
his first essay, "Symbol as Need."

The essays that followed, including "The Loss of the Creature," all dealt with
the relationships between language and understanding or belief, and they were all
published in obscure academic journals. In the later essays, Percy seemed to turn
away from academic forms of argument and to depend more and more on stories or

anecdotes from daily life—to write, in fact, as a storyteller and to be wary of abstraction or explanation. Robert Coles has said that Percy's failure to find a form that would reach a larger audience may have led him to try his hand at a novel. You will notice in the essay that follows that Percy delights in piling example upon example; he never seems to settle down to a topic sentence, or any sentence for that matter, that sums everything up and makes the examples superfluous.

In addition to The Moviegoer, Percy has written five other novels, including Lancelot (1977), Love in the Ruins (1971), and The Thanatos Syndrome (1987). He has published two books of essays, The Message in the Bottle: How Queer Man Is, How Queer Language Is, and What One Has to Do with the Other (1975, from which "The Loss of the Creature" is taken), and Lost in the Cosmos: The Last Self-help Book (1983). Walker Percy died at his home in Covington, Louisiana, on May 10, 1990, leaving a considerable amount of unpublished work, some of which has been gathered into a posthumous collection, Signposts in a Strange Land (1991). The Correspondence of Shelby Foote and Walker Percy was published in 1996.

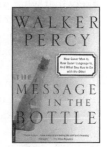

The Loss of the Creature

I

Every explorer names his island Formosa, beautiful. To him it is beautiful because, being first, he has access to it and can see it for what it is. But to no one else is it ever as beautiful—except the rare man who manages to recover it, who knows that it has to be recovered.

Garcia López de Cárdenas discovered the Grand Canyon and was amazed at the sight. It can be imagined: One crosses miles of desert, breaks through the mesquite, and there it is at one's feet. Later the government set the place aside as a national park, hoping to pass along to millions the experience of Cárdenas. Does not one see the same sight from the Bright Angel Lodge that Cárdenas saw?

The assumption is that the Grand Canyon is a remarkably interesting and beautiful place and that if it had a certain value P for Cárdenas, the same value P may be transmitted to any number of sightseers—just as

Banting's discovery of insulin can be transmitted to any number of diabetics. A counterinfluence is at work, however, and it would be nearer the truth to say that if the place is seen by a million sightseers, a single sightseer does not receive value P but a millionth part of value P.

It is assumed that since the Grand Canyon has the fixed interest value P, tours can be organized for any number of people. A man in Boston decides to spend his vacation at the Grand Canyon. He visits his travel bureau, looks at the folder, signs up for a two-week tour. He and his family take the tour, see the Grand Canyon, and return to Boston. May we say that this man has seen the Grand Canyon? Possibly he has. But it is more likely that what he has done is the one sure way not to see the canyon.

Why is it almost impossible to gaze directly at the Grand Canyon under these circumstances and see it for what it is—as one picks up a strange object from one's back yard and gazes directly at it? It is almost impossible because the Grand Canyon, the thing as it is, has been appropriated by the symbolic complex which has already been formed in the sightseer's mind. Seeing the canyon under approved circumstances is seeing the symbolic complex head on. The thing is no longer the thing as it confronted the Spaniard; it is rather that which has already been formulated—by picture postcard, geography book, tourist folders, and the words *Grand Canyon*. As a result of this preformulation, the source of the sightseer's pleasure undergoes a shift. Where the wonder and delight of the Spaniard arose from his penetration of the thing itself, from a progressive discovery of depths, patterns, colors, shadows, etc., now the sightseer measures his satisfaction *by the degree to which the canyon conforms to the preformed complex*. If it does so, if it looks just like the postcard, he is pleased; he might even say, "Why it is every bit as beautiful as a picture postcard!" He feels he has not been cheated. But if it does not conform, if the colors are somber, he will not be able to see it directly; he will only be conscious of the disparity between what it is and what it is supposed to be. He will say later that he was unlucky in not being there at the right time. The highest point, the term of the sightseer's satisfaction, is not the sovereign discovery of the thing before him; it is rather the measuring up of the thing to the criterion of the preformed symbolic complex.

Seeing the canyon is made even more difficult by what the sightseer does when the moment arrives, when sovereign knower confronts the thing to be known. Instead of looking at it, he photographs it. There is no confrontation at all. At the end of forty years of preformulation and with the Grand Canyon yawning at his feet, what does he do? He waives his right of seeing and knowing and records symbols for the next forty years. For him there is no present; there is only the past of what has been formulated and seen and the future of what has been formulated and not seen. The present is surrendered to the past and the future.

The sightseer may be aware that something is wrong. He may simply be bored; or he may be conscious of the difficulty: that the great thing yawning at his feet somehow eludes him. The harder he looks at it, the less he can see. It eludes everybody. The tourist cannot see it; the bellboy at the Bright Angel Lodge cannot see it: for him it is only one side of the space he lives in, like one wall of a room; to the ranger it is a tissue of everyday signs relevant to his own prospects—the blue haze down there means that he will probably get rained on during the donkey ride.

How can the sightseer recover the Grand Canyon? He can recover it in any number of ways, all sharing in common the stratagem of avoiding the approved confrontation of the tour and the Park Service.

It may be recovered by leaving the beaten track. The tourist leaves the tour, camps in the back country. He arises before dawn and approaches the South Rim through a wild terrain where there are no trails and no railed-in lookout points. In other words, he sees the canyon by avoiding all the facilities for seeing the canyon. If the benevolent Park Service hears about this fellow and thinks he has a good idea and places the following notice in the Bright Angel Lodge: *Consult ranger for information on getting off the beaten track*—the end result will only be the closing of another access to the canyon.

It may be recovered by a dialectical movement which brings one back to the beaten track but at a level above it. For example, after a lifetime of avoiding the beaten track and guided tours, a man may deliberately seek out the most beaten track of all, the most commonplace tour imaginable: he may visit the canyon by a Greyhound tour in the company of a party from Terre Haute—just as a man who has lived in New York all his life may visit the Statue of Liberty. (Such dialectical savorings of the familiar as the familiar are, of course, a favorite stratagem of *The New Yorker* magazine.) The thing is recovered from familiarity by means of an exercise in familiarity. Our complex friend stands behind his fellow tourists at the Bright Angel Lodge and sees the canyon through them and their predicament, their picture taking and busy disregard. In a sense, he exploits his fellow tourists; he stands on their shoulders to see the canyon.

Such a man is far more advanced in the dialectic than the sightseer who is trying to get off the beaten track—getting up at dawn and approaching the canyon through the mesquite. This stratagem is, in fact, for our complex man the weariest, most beaten track of all.

It may be recovered as a consequence of a breakdown of the symbolic machinery by which the experts present the experience to the consumer. A family visits the canyon in the usual way. But shortly after their arrival, the park is closed by an outbreak of typhus in the south. They have the canyon to themselves. What do they mean when they tell the home folks of their good luck: "We had the whole place to ourselves"? How does one see the thing better when the others are absent? Is looking like sucking: the more lookers, the less there is to see? They could hardly answer, but by saying this they testify to a state of affairs which is considerably more complex than the simple statement of the schoolbook about the Spaniard and the millions who followed him. It is a state in which there is a complex distribution of sovereignty, of zoning.

It may be recovered in a time of national disaster. The Bright Angel Lodge is converted into a rest home, a function that has nothing to do with the canyon a few yards away. A wounded man is brought in. He regains consciousness; there outside his window is the canyon.

The most extreme case of access by privilege conferred by disaster is the Huxleyan novel of the adventures of the surviving remnant after the great wars of the twentieth century. An expedition from Australia lands in Southern California and heads east. They stumble across the Bright Angel Lodge, now fallen into ruins. The trails are grown over, the guard rails fallen away, the dime telescope at Battleship Point rusted. But there is the canyon, exposed at last. Exposed by what? By the decay of those facilities which were designed to help the sightseer.

This dialectic of sightseeing cannot be taken into account by planners, for the object of the dialectic is nothing other than the subversion of the efforts of the planners.

The dialectic is not known to objective theorists, psychologists, and the like. Yet it is quite well known in the fantasy-consciousness of the popular arts. The devices by which the museum exhibit, the Grand Canyon, the ordinary thing, is recovered have long since been stumbled upon. A movie shows a man visiting the Grand Canyon. But the movie maker knows something the planner does not know. He knows that one cannot take the sight frontally. The canyon must be approached by the stratagems we have mentioned: the Inside Track, the Familiar Revisited, the Accidental Encounter. Who is the stranger at the Bright Angel Lodge? Is he the ordinary tourist from Terre Haute that he makes himself out to be? He is not. He has another objective in mind, to revenge his wronged brother, counterespionage, etc. By virtue of the fact that he has other fish to fry, he may take a stroll along the rim after supper and then we can see the canyon through him. The movie accomplishes its purpose by concealing it. Overtly the characters (the American family marooned by typhus) and we the onlookers experience pity for the sufferers, and the family experience anxiety for themselves; covertly and in truth they are the happiest of people and we are happy through them, for we have the canyon to ourselves. The movie cashes in on the recovery of sovereignty through disaster. Not only is the canyon now accessible to the remnant: the members of the remnant are now accessible to each other, a whole new ensemble of relations becomes possible—friendship, love, hatred, clandestine sexual adventures. In a movie when a man sits next to a woman on a bus, it is necessary either that the bus break down or that the woman lose her memory. (The question occurs to one: Do you imagine there are sightseers who see sights just as they are supposed to? a family who live in Terre Haute, who decide to take the canyon tour, who go there, see it, enjoy it immensely, and go home content? a family who are entirely innocent of all the barriers, zones, losses of sovereignty I have been talking about? Wouldn't most people be sorry if Battleship Point fell into the canyon, carrying all one's fellow passengers to their death, leaving one alone on the South Rim? I cannot answer this. Perhaps there are such people. Certainly a great many American families would swear they had no such problems, that they came, saw, and went away happy. Yet it is just these families who would be happiest if they had gotten the Inside Track and been among the surviving remnant.)

It is now apparent that as between the many measures which may be taken to overcome the opacity, the boredom, of the direct confrontation of the thing or creature in its citadel of symbolic investiture, some are less authentic than others. That is to say, some stratagems obviously serve other purposes than that of providing access to being—for example, various unconscious motivations which it is not necessary to go into here.

Let us take an example in which the recovery of being is ambiguous, where it may under the same circumstances contain both authentic and unauthentic components. An American couple, we will say, drives down into Mexico. They see the usual sights and have a fair time of it. Yet they are never without the sense of missing something. Although Taxco and Cuernavaca are interesting and picturesque as advertised, they fall short of "it." What do the couple have in mind by "it"? What do they really hope for? What sort of experience could they have in Mexico so that upon their return, they would feel that "it" had happened? We have a clue: Their hope has something to do with their own role as tourists in a foreign country and the way in which they conceive this role. It has something to do with other American tourists. Certainly they feel that they are very far from "it" when, after traveling five thousand miles, they arrive at the plaza in Guanajuato only to find themselves surrounded by a dozen other couples from the Midwest.

Already we may distinguish authentic and unauthentic elements. First, we see the problem the couple faces and we understand their efforts to surmount it. The problem is to find an "unspoiled" place. "Unspoiled" does not mean only that a place is left physically intact; it means also that it is not encrusted by renown and by the familiar (as in Taxco), that it has not been discovered by others. We understand that the couple really want to get at the place and enjoy it. Yet at the same time we wonder if there is not something wrong in their dislike of their compatriots. Does access to the place require the exclusion of others?

Let us see what happens.

The couple decide to drive from Guanajuato to Mexico City. On the way they get lost. After hours on a rocky mountain road, they find themselves in a tiny valley not even marked on the map. There they discover an Indian village. Some sort of religious festival is going on. It is apparently a corn dance in supplication of the rain god.

The couple know at once that this is "it." They are entranced. They spend several days in the village, observing the Indians and being themselves observed with friendly curiosity.

Now may we not say that the sightseers have at last come face to face with an authentic sight, a sight which is charming, quaint, picturesque, unspoiled, and that they see the sight and come away rewarded? Possibly this may occur. Yet it is more likely that what happens is a far cry indeed from an immediate encounter with being, that the experience, while masquerading as such, is in truth a rather desperate impersonation. I use the word *desperate* advisedly to signify an actual loss of hope.

The clue to the spuriousness of their enjoyment of the village and the festival is a certain restiveness in the sightseers themselves. It is given expression by their repeated exclamations that "this is too good to be true," and by their anxiety that it may not prove to be so perfect, and finally by their downright relief at leaving the valley and having the experience in the bag, so to speak—that is, safely embalmed in memory and movie film.

What is the source of their anxiety during the visit? Does it not mean that the couple are looking at the place with a certain standard of performance in mind? Are they like Fabre, who gazed at the world about him with wonder, letting it be what it is; or are they not like the overanxious mother who sees her child as one performing, now doing badly, now doing well? The village is their child and their love for it is an anxious love because they are afraid that at any moment it might fail them.

We have another clue in their subsequent remark to an ethnologist friend. "How we wished you had been there with us! What a perfect goldmine of folkways! Every minute we would say to each other, if only you were here! You must return with us." This surely testifies to a generosity of spirit, a willingness to share their experience with others, not at all like their feelings toward their fellow Iowans on the plaza at Guanajuato!

I am afraid this is not the case at all. It is true that they longed for their ethnologist friend, but it was for an entirely different reason. They wanted him, not to share their experience, but to certify their experience as genuine.

"This is it" and "Now we are really living" do not necessarily refer to the sovereign encounter of the person with the sight that enlivens the mind and gladdens the heart. It means that now at last we are having the acceptable experience. The present experience is always measured by a prototype, the "it" of their dreams. "Now I am really living" means that now I am filling the role of sightseer and the sight is living up to the prototype of sights. This quaint and picturesque village is measured by a Platonic ideal of the Quaint and the Picturesque.

Hence their anxiety during the encounter. For at any minute something could go wrong. A fellow Iowan might emerge from a 'dobe hut; the chief might show them his Sears catalog. (If the failures are "wrong" enough, as these are, they might still be turned to account as rueful conversation pieces. "There we were expecting the chief to bring us a churinga and he shows up with a Sears catalog!") They have snatched victory from disaster, but their experience always runs the danger of failure.

They need the ethnologist to certify their experience as genuine. This is borne out by their behavior when the three of them return for the next corn dance. During the dance, the couple do not watch the goings-on; instead they watch the ethnologist! Their highest hope is that their friend should find the dance interesting. And if he should show signs of true absorption, an interest in the goings-on so powerful that he becomes oblivious of his friends—then their cup is full. "Didn't we tell you?" they say at last. What they want from him is not ethnological explanations; all they want is his approval.

What has taken place is a radical loss of sovereignty over that which is as much theirs as it is the ethnologist's. The fault does not lie with the ethnologist. He has no wish to stake a claim to the village; in fact, he desires the opposite: he will bore his friends to death by telling them about the village and the meaning of the folkways. A degree of sovereignty has been surrendered by the couple. It is the nature of the loss, moreover, that they are not aware of the loss, beyond a certain uneasiness. (Even if they read this and admitted it, it would be very difficult for them to bridge the gap in their confrontation of the world. Their consciousness of the corn dance cannot escape their consciousness of their consciousness, so that with the onset of the first direct enjoyment, their higher consciousness pounces and certifies: "Now you are doing it! Now you are really living!" and, in certifying the experience, sets it at nought.)

Their basic placement in the world is such that they recognize a priority of title of the expert over his particular department of being. The whole horizon of being is staked out by "them," the experts. The highest satisfaction of the sightseer (not merely the tourist but any layman seer of sights) is that his sight should be certified as genuine. The worst of this impoverishment is that there is no sense of impoverishment. The surrender of title is so complete that it never even occurs to one to reassert title. A poor man may envy the rich man, but the sightseer does not envy the expert. When a caste system becomes absolute, envy disappears. Yet the caste of layman-expert is not the fault of the expert. It is due altogether to the eager surrender of sovereignty by the layman so that he may take up the role not of the person but of the consumer.

I do not refer only to the special relation of layman to theorist. I refer to the general situation in which sovereignty is surrendered to a class of privileged knowers, whether these be theorists or artists. A reader may surrender sovereignty over that which has been written about, just as a consumer may surrender sovereignty over a thing which has been theorized about. The consumer is content to receive an experience just as it has been presented to him by theorists and planners. The reader may also be content to judge life by whether it has or has not been formulated by those who know and write about life. A young man goes to France. He too has a fair time of it, sees the sights, enjoys the food. On his last day, in fact as he sits in a restaurant in Le Havre waiting for his boat, something happens. A group of French students in the restaurant get into an impassioned argument over a recent play. A riot takes place. Madame la concierge joins in, swinging her mop at the rioters. Our young American is transported. This is "it." And he had almost left France without seeing "it"!

But the young man's delight is ambiguous. On the one hand, it is a pleasure for him to encounter the same Gallic temperament he had heard about from Puccini and Rolland. But on the other hand, the source of his pleasure testifies to a certain alienation. For the young man is actually barred from a direct encounter with anything French excepting only that which has been set forth, authenticated by Puccini and Rolland—those who know. If he had encountered the restaurant scene without reading Hemingway, without knowing that the performance was so typically, charmingly French, he would not have been delighted. He would only have been anxious at seeing things get so out of hand. The source of his delight is the sanction of those who know.

This loss of sovereignty is not a marginal process, as might appear from my example of estranged sightseers. It is a generalized surrender of the horizon to those experts within whose competence a particular segment of the horizon is thought to lie. Kwakiutls are surrendered to Franz Boas; decaying Southern mansions are surrendered to Faulkner and Tennessee Williams. So that, although it is by no means the intention of the expert to expropriate sovereignty—in fact he would not even know what sovereignty meant in this context—the danger of theory and consumption is a seduction and deprivation of the consumer.

In the New Mexico desert, natives occasionally come across strange-looking artifacts which have fallen from the skies and which are stenciled: *Return to U.S. Experimental Project, Alamogordo. Reward.* The finder returns the object and is rewarded. He knows nothing of the nature of the object he has found and does not care to know. The sole role of the native, the highest role he can play, is that of finder and returner of the mysterious equipment.

The same is true of the laymen's relation to *natural* objects in a modern technical society. No matter what the object or event is, whether it is a star, a swallow, a Kwakiutl, a "psychological phenomenon," the layman who confronts it does not confront it as a sovereign person, as Crusoe confronts a seashell he finds on the beach. The highest role he can conceive himself as playing is to be able to recognize the title of the object, to return it to the appropriate expert and have it certified as a genuine find. He does not even permit himself to see the thing—as Gerard Hopkins could see a rock or a cloud or a field. If anyone asks him why he doesn't look, he may reply that he didn't take that subject in college (or he hasn't read Faulkner).

This loss of sovereignty extends even to oneself. There is the neurotic who asks nothing more of his doctor than that his symptoms should prove interesting. When all else fails, the poor fellow has nothing to offer but his own neurosis. But even this is sufficient if only the doctor will show interest when he says, "Last night I had a curious sort of dream; perhaps it will be significant to one who knows about such things. It seems I was standing in a sort of alley—" (I have nothing else to offer you but my own unhappiness. Please say that it, at least, measures up, that it is a *proper* sort of unhappiness.)

II

A young Falkland Islander walking along a beach and spying a dead dogfish and going to work on it with his jackknife has, in a fashion wholly unprovided in modern educational theory, a great advantage over the

Scarsdale high-school pupil who finds the dogfish on his laboratory desk. Similarly the citizen of Huxley's *Brave New World* who stumbles across a volume of Shakespeare in some vine-grown ruins and squats on a potsherd to read it is in a fairer way of getting at a sonnet than the Harvard sophomore taking English Poetry II.

The educator whose business it is to teach students biology or poetry is unaware of a whole ensemble of relations which exist between the student and the dogfish and between the student and the Shakespeare sonnet. To put it bluntly: A student who has the desire to get at a dogfish or a Shakespeare sonnet may have the greatest difficulty in salvaging the creature itself from the educational package in which it is presented. The great difficulty is that he is not aware that there is a difficulty; surely, he thinks, in such a fine classroom, with such a fine textbook, the sonnet must come across! What's wrong with me?

The sonnet and the dogfish are obscured by two different processes. The sonnet is obscured by the symbolic package which is formulated not by the sonnet itself but by the *media* through which the sonnet is transmitted, the media which the educators believe for some reason to be transparent. The new textbook, the type, the smell of the page, the classroom, the aluminum windows and the winter sky, the personality of Miss Hawkins— these media which are supposed to transmit the sonnet may only succeed in transmitting themselves. It is only the hardiest and cleverest of students who can salvage the sonnet from this many-tissued package. It is only the rarest student who knows that the sonnet must be salvaged from the package. (The educator is well aware that something is wrong, that there is a fatal gap between the student's learning and the student's life: the student reads the poem, appears to understand it, and gives all the answers. But what does he recall if he should happen to read a Shakespeare sonnet twenty years later? Does he recall the poem or does he recall the smell of the page and the smell of Miss Hawkins?)

One might object, pointing out that Huxley's citizen reading his sonnet in the ruins and the Falkland Islander looking at his dogfish on the beach also receive them in a certain package. Yes, but the difference lies in the fundamental placement of the student in the world, a placement which makes it possible to extract the thing from the package. The pupil at Scarsdale High sees himself placed as a consumer receiving an experience-package; but the Falkland Islander exploring his dogfish is a person exercising the sovereign right of a person in his lordship and mastery of creation. He too could use an instructor and a book and a technique, but he would use them as his subordinates, just as he uses his jackknife. The biology student does not use his scalpel as an instrument, he uses it as a magic wand! Since it is a "scientific instrument," it should do "scientific things."

The dogfish is concealed in the same symbolic package as the sonnet. But the dogfish suffers an additional loss. As a consequence of this double deprivation, the Sarah Lawrence student who scores A in zoology is apt to know very little about a dogfish. She is twice removed from the dogfish, once by the symbolic complex by which the dogfish is concealed, once again by the spoliation of the dogfish by theory which renders it invisible. Through no fault of zoology instructors, it is nevertheless a fact that the zoology laboratory at Sarah Lawrence College is one of the few places in the world where it is all but impossible to see a dogfish.

The dogfish, the tree, the seashell, the American Negro, the dream, are rendered invisible by a shift of reality from concrete thing to theory which Whitehead has called the fallacy of misplaced concreteness. It is the mistaking of an idea, a principle, an abstraction, for the real. As a consequence of the shift, the "specimen" is seen as less real than the theory of the specimen. As Kierkegaard said, once a person is seen as a specimen of a race or a species, at that very moment he ceases to be an individual. Then there are no more individuals but only specimens.

To illustrate: A student enters a laboratory which, in the pragmatic view, offers the student the optimum conditions under which an educational experience may be had. In the existential view, however—that view of the student in which he is regarded not as a receptacle of experience but as a knowing being whose peculiar property it is to see himself as being in a certain situation—the modern laboratory could not have been more effectively designed to conceal the dogfish forever.

The student comes to his desk. On it, neatly arranged by his instructor, he finds his laboratory manual, a dissecting board, instruments, and a mimeographed list:

Exercise 22: Materials
1 dissecting board
1 scalpel
1 forceps
1 probe
1 bottle india ink and syringe
1 specimen of *Squalus acanthias*

The clue of the situation in which the student finds himself is to be found in the last item: 1 specimen of *Squalus acanthias.*

The phrase *specimen of* expresses in the most succinct way imaginable the radical character of the loss of being which has occurred under his very nose. To refer to the dogfish, the unique concrete existent before him, as a "specimen of *Squalus acanthias*" reveals by its grammar the spoliation of the dogfish by the theoretical method. This phrase, *specimen of,* example of, instance of, indicates the ontological status of the individual creature in the eyes of the theorist. The dogfish itself is seen as a rather shabby expression of an ideal reality, the species *Squalus acanthias.* The result is the radical devaluation of the individual dogfish. (The *reductio ad absurdum* of Whitehead's shift is Toynbee's employment of it in his historical method. If a gram of NaCl is referred to by the chemist as a "sample of" NaCl, one may think of it as such and not much is missed by the oversight of the act of being of this particular pinch of salt, but when the Jews and the Jewish religion are understood as—in Toynbee's favorite phrase—a "classical example of" such and such a kind of *Voelkerwanderung*, we begin to suspect that something is being left out.)

If we look into the ways in which the student can recover the dogfish (or the sonnet), we will see that they have in common the stratagem of avoiding the educator's direct presentation of the object as a lesson to be learned and restoring access to sonnet and dogfish as beings to be known, reasserting the sovereignty of knower over known.

In truth, the biography of scientists and poets is usually the story of the discovery of the indirect approach, the circumvention of the educator's presentation—the young man who was sent to the *Technikum* and on his way fell into the habit of loitering in book stores and reading poetry; or the young man dutifully attending law school who on the way became curious about the comings and goings of ants. One remembers the scene in *The Heart Is a Lonely Hunter* where the girl hides in the bushes to hear the Capehart in the big house play Beethoven. Perhaps she was the lucky one after all. Think of the unhappy souls inside, who see the record, worry about scratches, and most of all worry about whether they are *getting it*, whether they are bona fide music lovers. What is the best way to hear Beethoven: sitting in a proper silence around the Capehart or eavesdropping from an azalea bush?

However it may come about, we notice two traits of the second situation: (1) an openness of the thing before one—instead of being an exercise to be learned according to an approved mode, it is a garden of delights which beckons to one; (2) a sovereignty of the knower—instead of being a consumer of a prepared experience, I am a sovereign wayfarer, a wanderer in the neighborhood of being who stumbles into the garden.

One can think of two sorts of circumstances through which the thing may be restored to the person. (There is always, of course, the direct recovery: A student may simply be strong enough, brave enough, clever enough to take the dogfish and the sonnet by storm, to wrest control of it from the educators and the educational package.) First by ordeal: The Bomb falls; when the young man recovers consciousness in the shambles of the biology laboratory, there not ten inches from his nose lies the dogfish. Now all at once he can see it directly and without let, just as the exile or the prisoner or the sick man sees the sparrow at his window in all its inexhaustibility; just as the commuter who has had a heart attack sees his own hand for the first time. In these cases, the simulacrum of everydayness and of consumption has been destroyed by disaster; in the case of the bomb, literally destroyed. Secondly, by apprenticeship to a great man: one day a great biologist walks into the laboratory; he stops in front of our student's desk; he leans over, picks up the dogfish, and, ignoring instruments and procedure, probes with a broken fingernail into the little carcass. "Now here is a curious business," he says, ignoring also the proper jargon of the speciality. "Look here how this little duct reverses its direction and drops into the pelvis. Now if you would look into a coelacanth, you would see that it—" And all at once the student can see. The technician and the sophomore who loves his textbooks are always offended by the genuine research man because the latter is usually a little vague and always humble before the thing; he doesn't have much use for the equipment or the jargon. Whereas the technician is never vague and never humble before the thing; he holds the thing disposed of by the principle, the formula, the textbook outline; and he thinks a great deal of equipment and jargon.

But since neither of these methods of recovering the dogfish is pedagogically feasible—perhaps the great man even less so than the Bomb—I wish to propose the following educational technique which should prove equally effective for Harvard and Shreveport High School. I propose that English poetry and biology should be taught as usual, but that at irregular intervals, poetry students should find dogfishes on their desks and biology students should find Shakespeare sonnets on their dissection boards. I am serious in declaring that a Sarah Lawrence English major who began poking about in a dogfish with a bobby pin would learn more in thirty minutes than a biology major in a whole semester; and that the latter upon reading on her dissecting board

> That time of year Thou may'st in me behold
> When yellow leaves, or none, or few, do hang
> Upon those boughs which shake against the cold—
> Bare ruin'd choirs where late the sweet birds sang

might catch fire at the beauty of it.

The situation of the tourist at the Grand Canyon and the biology student are special cases of a predicament in which everyone finds himself in a modern technical society—a society, that is, in which there is a division between expert and layman, planner and consumer, in which experts and planners take special measures to teach and edify the consumer. The measures taken are measures appropriate to the consumer: the expert and the planner *know* and *plan*, but the consumer *needs* and *experiences*.

There is a double deprivation. First, the thing is lost through its packaging. The very means by which the thing is presented for consumption, the very techniques by which the thing is made available as an item of need-satisfaction, these very means operate to remove the thing from the sovereignty of the knower. A loss of title occurs. The measures which the museum curator takes to present the thing to the public are self-liquidating. The upshot of the curator's efforts are not that everyone can see the exhibit but that no one can see it. The curator protests: Why are they so indifferent? Why do they even deface the exhibit? Don't they know it is theirs? But it is not theirs. It is his, the curator's. By the most exclusive sort of zoning, the museum exhibit, the park oak tree, is part of an ensemble, a package, which is almost impenetrable to them. The archaeologist who puts his find in a museum so that everyone can see it accomplishes the reverse of his expectations. The result of his action is that no one can see it now but the archaeologist. He would have done better to keep it in his pocket and show it now and then to strangers.

The tourist who carves his initials in a public place, which is theoretically "his" in the first place, has good reasons for doing so, reasons which the exhibitor and planner know nothing about. He does so because in his role of consumer of an experience (a "recreational experience" to satisfy a "recreational need") he knows that he is disinherited. He is deprived of his title over being. He knows very well that he is in a very special sort of zone in which his only rights are the rights of a consumer. He moves like a ghost through schoolroom, city streets, trains, parks, movies. He carves his initials as a last desperate measure to escape his ghostly role of consumer. He is saying in effect: I am not a ghost after all; I am a sovereign person. And he establishes title the only way remaining to him, by staking his claim over one square inch of wood or stone.

Does this mean that we should get rid of museums? No, but it means that the sightseer should be prepared to enter into a struggle to recover a sight from a museum.

The second loss is the spoliation of the thing, the tree, the rock, the swallow, by the layman's misunderstanding of scientific theory. He believes that the thing is *disposed of* by theory, that it stands in the Platonic relation of being a *specimen* of such and such an underlying principle. In the transmission of scientific theory from theorist to layman, the expectation of the theorist is reversed. Instead of the marvels of the universe being made available to the public, the universe is disposed of by theory. The loss of sovereignty takes this form: as a result of the science of botany, trees are not made available to every man. On the contrary. The tree loses its proper density and mystery as a concrete existent and, as merely another *specimen* of a species, becomes itself nugatory.

Does this mean that there is no use taking biology at Harvard and Shreveport High? No, but it means that the student should know what a fight he has on his hands to rescue the specimen from the educational package. The educator is only partly to blame. For there is nothing the educator can do to provide for this need of the student. Everything the educator does only succeeds in becoming, for the student, part of the educational package. The highest role of the educator is the maieutic role of Socrates: to help the student come to himself not as a consumer of experience but as a sovereign individual.

The thing is twice lost to the consumer. First, sovereignty is lost: it is theirs, not his. Second, it is radically devalued by theory. This is a loss which has been brought about by science but through no fault of the scientist and through no fault of scientific theory. The loss has come about as a consequence of the seduction of the layman by science. The layman will be seduced as long as he regards beings as consumer items to be experienced rather than prizes to be won, and as long as he waives his sovereign rights as a person and accepts his role of consumer as the highest estate to which the layman can aspire.

As Mounier said, the person is not something one can study and provide for; he is something one struggles for. But unless he also struggles for himself, unless he knows that there is a struggle, he is going to be just what the planners think he is.

.   .   .   .

QUESTIONS FOR A SECOND READING

1. Percy's essay proceeds by adding example to example, one after another. If all the examples were meant to illustrate the same thing, the same general point or idea, then one would most likely have been enough. The rest would have been redundant. It makes sense, then, to assume that each example gives a different view of what Percy is saying, that each modifies the others, or qualifies them, or adds a piece that was otherwise lacking. It's as though Percy needed one more to get it right or to figure out what was missing along the way. As you read back through the essay, pay particular attention to the *differences* between the examples (between the various tourists going to the Grand Canyon, or between the tourists at the Grand Canyon and the tourists in Mexico). Also note the logic or system that leads from one to the next. What progress of thought is represented by the movement from one example to another, or from tourists to students?

2. The essay is filled with talk about "loss"—the loss of sovereignty, the loss of the creature—but it is resolutely ambiguous about what it is that we have lost. As you work your way back through, note the passages that describe what we are missing and why we should care. Are we to believe, for example, that Cárdenas actually had it (whatever "it" is)—that he had no preconceived notions when he saw the Grand Canyon? Mightn't he have said, "I claim this for my queen" or "There I see the glory of God" or "This wilderness is not fit for man"? To whom, or in the name of what, is this loss that Percy chronicles such a matter of concern? If this is not just Percy's peculiar prejudice, if we are asked to share his concerns, whose interests or what interests are represented here?

3. The essay is made up of stories or anecdotes, all of them fanciful. Percy did not, in other words, turn to first-person accounts of visitors to the Grand Canyon or to statements by actual students or teachers. Why not, do you suppose? What does this choice say about his "method"—about what it can and can't do? As you reread the essay, look for sections you could use to talk about the power and limits of Percy's method.

ASSIGNMENTS FOR WRITING

1. Percy tells several stories—some of them quite good stories—but it is often hard to know just what he is getting at, just what point it is he is trying to make. If he's making an argument, it's not the sort of argument that is easy to summarize. And if the stories (or anecdotes) are meant to serve as examples, they are not the sort of examples that lead directly to a single, general conclusion or that serve to clarify a point or support an obvious thesis. In fact, at the very moment when you expect Percy to come forward

and pull things together, he offers yet another story, as though another example, rather than any general statement, would get you closer to what he is saying.

There are, at the same time, terms and phrases to suggest that this is an essay with a point to make. Percy talks, for example, about "the loss of sovereignty," "symbolic packages," "consumers of experience," and "dialectic," and it seems that these terms and phrases are meant to name or comment on key scenes, situations, or characters in the examples.

For this assignment, tell a story of your own, one that is suggested by the stories Percy tells—perhaps a story about a time you went looking for something or at something, or about a time when you did or did not find a dogfish in your Shakespeare class. You should imagine that you are carrying out a project that Walker Percy has begun, a project that has you looking back at your own experience through the lens of "The Loss of the Creature," noticing what Percy would notice and following the paths that he would find interesting. Try to bring the terms that Percy uses—like "sovereign," "consumer," "expert," and "dialectic"—to bear on the story you have to tell. Feel free to imitate Percy's style and method in your essay.

2. Percy charts several routes to the Grand Canyon: you can take the packaged tour, you can get off the beaten track, you can wait for a disaster, you can follow the "dialectical movement which brings one back to the beaten track but at a level above it." This last path (or stratagem), he says, is for the complex traveler.

> Our complex friend stands behind his fellow tourists at the Bright Angel Lodge and sees the canyon through them and their predicament, their picture taking and busy disregard. In a sense, he exploits his fellow tourists; he stands on their shoulders to see the canyon. (p. 483)

The complex traveler sees the Grand Canyon through the example of the common tourists with "their predicament, their picture taking and busy disregard." He "stands on their shoulders" to see the canyon. This distinction between complex and common approaches is an important one in the essay. It is interesting to imagine how the distinction could be put to work to define ways of reading.

Suppose that you read "The Loss of the Creature" as a common reader. What would you see? What would you identify as key sections of the text? What would you miss? What would you say about what you see?

If you think of yourself, now, as a complex reader, modeled after any of Percy's more complex tourists or students, what would you see? What would you identify as key sections of the text? What would you miss? What would you say about what you see?

For this assignment, write an essay with three sections. You may number them, if you choose. The first section should represent the work of a common reader with "The Loss of the Creature," and the second should represent the work of a complex reader. The third section should look back and comment on the previous two. In particular, you might address these questions: Why might a person prefer one reading over the other? What is to be gained or lost with both?

MAKING CONNECTIONS

1. In "The Loss of the Creature," Percy writes about tourists and the difficulty they have seeing that which lies before them. In "Deep Play: Notes on the Balinese Cockfight" (p. 259), Clifford Geertz tells the story of his travels in Bali. Anthropologists, properly speaking, are not tourists. There is a scholarly purpose to their travel and, presumably, they have learned or developed the strategies necessary to get beyond the preformed "symbolic complex" that would keep them from seeing the place or the people they have traveled to study. They are experts, in other words, not common sightseers.

   In his travels to Bali, Geertz seems to get just what he wants. He gets both the authentic experience and a complex understanding of that experience. If you read "Deep Play" from the perspective of Percy's essay, however, it is interesting to ask whether Percy would say that this was the case (whether Percy might say that Geertz has gone as far as one can go after Cárdenas), and it is interesting to ask how Percy would characterize the "strategies" that define Geertz's approach to his subject.

   Write an essay in which you place Geertz in the context of Percy's tourists (not all of them, but two or three whose stories seem most interesting when placed alongside Geertz's). The purpose of your essay is to offer a Percian reading of Geertz's essay—to study his text, that is, in light of the terms and methods Percy has established in "The Loss of the Creature."

2. But the difference lies in the fundamental placement of the student in the world. . . . (Walker Percy, p. 489)

   What I am about to say to you has taken me more than twenty years to admit: *A primary reason for my success in the classroom was that I couldn't forget that schooling was changing me and separating me from the life I enjoyed before becoming a student.* (Richard Rodriguez, p. 547)

   Both Percy and Richard Rodriguez, in "The Achievement of Desire" (p. 545), write about students and how they are "placed" in the world by teachers and by the way schools characteristically represent knowledge, the novice, and the expert. And both tell stories to make their points, stories of characteristic students in characteristic situations. Write an essay in which you tell a story of your own, one meant to serve as a corrective or a supplement to the stories Percy and Rodriguez tell. You will want both to tell your story and to use it as a way of returning to and commenting on Percy and Rodriguez and the arguments they make. Your authority can rest on the fact that you are a student and as a consequence have ways of understanding that position that they do not.

MARY LOUISE PRATT

MARY LOUISE PRATT (b. 1948) grew up in Listowel, Ontario, a small Canadian farm town. She got her BA at the University of Toronto and her PhD from Stanford University, where for nearly thirty years she was a professor in the departments of comparative literature and Spanish and Portuguese. At Stanford, she was one of the cofounders of the new freshman culture program, a controversial series of required courses that replaced the old Western civilization core courses. The course she is particularly associated with is called "Europe and the Americas"; it brings together European representations of the Americas with indigenous American texts. As you might guess from the essay that follows, the program at Stanford expanded the range of countries, languages, cultures, and texts that are seen as a necessary introduction to the world; it also, however, revised the very idea of culture that many of us take for granted—particularly the idea that culture, at its best, expresses common values in a common language. Among other awards and honors, Pratt is the recipient of a Guggenheim Fellowship and a Fellowship at the Center for Advanced Study in the Behavioral Sciences, Stanford University. She is Silver Professor in the Department of Spanish and Portuguese at New York University. She served as president of the Modern Language Association for 2003.

Pratt is the author of Toward a Speech Act Theory of Literary Discourse *(1977) and coauthor of* Women, Culture, and Politics in Latin America *(1990), the textbook* Linguistics for Students of Literature *(1980),* Amor Brujo: The Images and Culture of Love in the Andes *(1990), and* Imperial Eyes: Studies in Travel Writing and Transculturation *(1992). The essay that follows was revised to serve as the introduction to* Imperial Eyes, *which examines European travel writing in the eighteenth and nineteenth centuries, when Europe was "discovering" Africa and the Americas. It argues that travel writing produced "the rest of the world" for European readers. It didn't "report" on Africa or South America; it produced an "Africa" or an "America" for European consumption. Travel writing produced places that could be thought of as barren, empty, undeveloped, inconceivable, needful of European influence and control, ready to serve European industrial, intellectual, and commercial interests. The reports of travelers or, later, scientists and anthropologists are part of a more general process by which the emerging industrial nations took possession of new territory.*

The European understanding of Peru, for example, came through European accounts, not from attempts to understand or elicit responses from Andeans, Peruvian natives. Such a response was delivered, when an Andean, Guaman Poma, wrote to King Philip III of Spain, but his letter was unreadable. Pratt is interested in just those moments of contact between peoples and cultures. She is interested in how King Philip read (or failed to read) a letter from Peru, but also in how someone like Guaman Poma prepared himself to write to the king of Spain. To fix these moments, she makes use of a phrase she coined, the "contact zone," which, she says,

> *I use to refer to the space of colonial encounters, the space in which peoples geographically and historically separated come into contact with each other and establish ongoing relations, usually involving conditions of coercion, radical inequality, and intractable conflict. . . . By using the term "contact," I aim to foreground the interactive, improvisational dimensions of colonial encounters so easily ignored or suppressed by diffusionist accounts of conquest and domination. A "contact" perspective emphasizes how subjects are constituted in and by their relations to each other. It treats the relations among colonizers and colonized, or travelers and "travelees," not in terms of separateness or apartheid, but in terms of copresence, interaction, interlocking understandings and practices.*

Like Adrienne Rich's "When We Dead Awaken: Writing as Re-Vision" (and, for that matter, Clifford Geertz's "Deep Play"), "Arts of the Contact Zone" was first written as a lecture. It was delivered as a keynote address at the second Modern Language Association Literacy Conference, held in Pittsburgh, Pennsylvania, in 1990.

Arts of the Contact Zone

Whenever the subject of literacy comes up, what often pops first into my mind is a conversation I overheard eight years ago between my son Sam and his best friend, Willie, aged six and seven, respectively: "Why don't you trade me Many Trails for Carl Yats . . . Yesits . . . Ya-strum-scrum." "That's not how you say it, dummy, it's Carl Yes . . . Yes . . . oh, I don't know." Sam and Willie had just discovered baseball cards. Many Trails was their decoding, with the help of first-grade English phonics, of the name Manny Trillo. The name they were quite rightly stumped on was Carl Yastrzemski. That was the first time I remembered seeing them put their incipient literacy to their own use, and I was of course thrilled.

Sam and Willie learned a lot about phonics that year by trying to decipher surnames on baseball cards, and a lot about cities, states, heights, weights, places of birth, stages of life. In the years that followed, I watched Sam apply his arithmetic skills to working out batting averages and subtracting retirement years from rookie years; I watched him develop senses of patterning and order by arranging and rearranging his cards for hours on end, and aesthetic judgment by comparing different photos, different series, layouts, and color schemes. American geography and history took shape in his mind through baseball cards. Much of his social life revolved around trading them, and he learned about exchange, fairness, trust, the importance of processes as opposed to results, what it means to get cheated, taken advantage of, even robbed. Baseball cards were the medium of his economic life too. Nowhere better to learn the power and arbitrariness of money, the absolute divorce between use value and exchange value, notions of long- and short-term investment, the possibility of personal values that are independent of market values.

Baseball cards meant baseball card shows, where there was much to be learned about adult worlds as well. And baseball cards opened the door to baseball books, shelves and shelves of encyclopedias, magazines, histories, biographies, novels, books of jokes, anecdotes, cartoons, even poems. Sam learned the history of American racism and the struggle against it through baseball; he saw the Depression and two world wars from behind home plate. He learned the meaning of commodified labor, what it means for one's body and talents to be owned and dispensed by another. He knows something about Japan, Taiwan, Cuba, and Central America and how men and boys do things there. Through the history and experience of baseball stadiums he thought about architecture, light, wind, topography, meteorology, the dynamics of public space. He learned the meaning of expertise, of knowing about something well enough that you can start a conversation with a stranger and feel sure of holding your own. Even with an adult—especially with an adult. Throughout his preadolescent years, baseball history was Sam's luminous point of contact with grown-ups, his lifeline to caring. And, of course, all this time he was also playing baseball, struggling his way through the stages of the local Little League system, lucky enough to be a pretty good player, loving the game and coming to know deeply his strengths and weaknesses.

Literacy began for Sam with the newly pronounceable names on the picture cards and brought him what has been easily the broadest, most varied, most enduring, and most integrated experience of his thirteen-year life. Like many parents, I was delighted to see schooling give Sam the tools with which to find and open all these doors. At the same time I found it unforgivable that schooling itself gave him nothing remotely as meaningful to do, let alone anything that would actually take him beyond the referential, masculinist ethos of baseball and its lore.

However, I was not invited here to speak as a parent, nor as an expert on literacy. I was asked to speak as an MLA [Modern Language Association] member working in the elite academy. In that capacity my contribution is undoubtedly supposed to be abstract, irrelevant, and anchored outside the real world. I wouldn't dream of disappointing anyone. I propose immediately to head back several centuries to a text that has a few points in common with baseball cards and raises thoughts about what Tony Sarmiento, in his comments to the conference, called new visions of literacy. In 1908 a Peruvianist named Richard Pietschmann was exploring in the Danish Royal Archive in Copenhagen and came across a manuscript. It was dated in the city of Cuzco in Peru, in the year 1613, some forty years after the final fall of the Inca empire to the Spanish and signed with an unmistakably Andean indigenous name: Felipe Guaman Poma de Ayala. Written in a mixture of Quechua and ungrammatical, expressive Spanish, the manuscript was a letter addressed by an unknown but apparently literate Andean to King Philip III of Spain. What stunned Pietschmann was that the letter was twelve hundred pages long. There were almost eight hundred pages of written text and four hundred of captioned line drawings. It was titled *The First New Chronicle and Good Government*. No one knew (or knows) how the manuscript got to the library in Copenhagen or how long it had been there. No one, it appeared, had ever bothered to read it or figured out how. Quechua was not thought of as a written language in 1908, nor Andean culture as a literate culture.

Pietschmann prepared a paper on his find, which he presented in London in 1912, a year after the rediscovery of Machu Picchu by Hiram Bingham. Reception, by an international congress of Americanists, was apparently confused. It took twenty-five years for a facsimile edition of the work to appear in Paris. It was not till the late 1970s, as positivist reading habits gave way to interpretive studies and colonial elitisms to post-colonial pluralisms, that Western scholars found ways of reading Guaman Poma's *New Chronicle and Good Government* as the extraordinary intercultural tour de force that it was. The letter got there, only 350 years too late, a miracle and a terrible tragedy.

I propose to say a few more words about this erstwhile unreadable text, in order to lay out some thoughts about writing and literacy in what I like to call the *contact zones.* I use this term to refer to social spaces where cultures meet, clash, and grapple with each other, often in contexts of highly asymmetrical relations of power, such as colonialism, slavery, or their aftermaths as they are lived out in many parts of the world today. Eventually I will use the term to reconsider the models of community that many of us rely on in teaching and theorizing and that are under challenge today. But first a little more about Guaman Poma's giant letter to Philip III.

Insofar as anything is known about him at all, Guaman Poma exemplified the sociocultural complexities produced by conquest and empire. He was an indigenous Andean who claimed noble Inca descent and who had adopted (at least in some sense) Christianity. He may have worked in the Spanish colonial administration as an interpreter, scribe, or assistant to a Spanish tax collector—as a mediator, in short. He says he learned to write from his half brother, a mestizo whose Spanish father had given him access to religious education.

Guaman Poma's letter to the king is written in two languages (Spanish and Quechua) and two parts. The first is called the *Nueva corónica,* "New Chronicle." The title is important. The chronicle of course was the main writing apparatus through which the Spanish presented their American conquests to themselves. It constituted one of the main official discourses. In writing a "new chronicle," Guaman Poma took over the official Spanish genre for his own ends. Those ends were, roughly, to construct a new picture of the world, a picture of a Christian world with Andean rather than European peoples at the center of it—Cuzco, not Jerusalem. In the *New Chronicle* Guaman Poma begins by rewriting the Christian history of the world from Adam and Eve (Fig. 1), incorporating the Amerindians into it as offspring of one of the sons of Noah. He identifies five ages of Christian history that he links in parallel with the five ages of canonical Andean history—separate but equal trajectories that diverge with Noah and reintersect not with Columbus but with Saint Bartholomew, claimed to have preceded Columbus in the Americas. In a couple of hundred pages, Guaman Poma constructs a veritable encyclopedia of Inca and pre-Inca history, customs, laws, social forms, public offices, and dynastic leaders. The depictions resemble European manners and customs description, but also reproduce the meticulous detail with which knowledge in Inca society was stored on *quipus* and in the oral memories of elders.

Guaman Poma's *New Chronicle* is an instance of what I have proposed to call an *autoethnographic* text, by which I mean a text in which people undertake to describe themselves in ways that engage with representations others have made of them. Thus if ethnographic texts are those in which European metropolitan subjects represent to themselves their others (usually their conquered others), autoethnographic texts are representations that the so-defined others construct *in response to* or in dialogue with those

Figure 1. Adam and Eve.

texts. Autoethnographic texts are not, then, what are usually thought of
as autochthonous forms of expression or self-representation (as the Andean *quipus* were). Rather they involve a selective collaboration with and
appropriation of idioms of the metropolis or the conqueror. These are
merged or infiltrated to varying degrees with indigenous idioms to create
self-representations intended to intervene in metropolitan modes of understanding. Autoethnographic works are often addressed to both metropolitan audiences and the speaker's own community. Their reception is thus
highly indeterminate. Such texts often constitute a marginalized group's
point of entry into the dominant circuits of print culture. It is interesting to think, for example, of American slave autobiography in its autoethnographic dimensions, which in some respects distinguish it from
Euramerican autobiographical tradition. The concept might help explain
why some of the earliest published writing by Chicanas took the form of
folkloric manners and customs sketches written in English and published
in English-language newspapers or folklore magazines (see Treviño). Autoethnographic representation often involves concrete collaborations be-

tween people, as between literate ex-slaves and abolitionist intellectuals, or between Guaman Poma and the Inca elders who were his informants. Often, as in Guaman Poma, it involves more than one language. In recent decades autoethnography, critique, and resistance have reconnected with writing in a contemporary creation of the contact zone, the *testimonio*.

Guaman Poma's *New Chronicle* ends with a revisionist account of the Spanish conquest, which, he argues, should have been a peaceful encounter of equals with the potential for benefiting both, but for the mindless greed of the Spanish. He parodies Spanish history. Following contact with the Incas, he writes, "In all Castille, there was a great commotion. All day and at night in their dreams the Spaniards were saying, 'Yndias, yndias, oro, plata, oro, plata del Piru'" ("Indies, Indies, gold, silver, gold, silver from Peru") (Fig. 2). The Spanish, he writes, brought nothing of value to share with the Andeans, nothing "but armor and guns con la codicia de oro, plata, oro y plata, yndias, a las Yndias, Piru" ("with the lust for gold, silver, gold and silver, Indies, the Indies, Peru") (p. 372). I quote these

Figure 2. Conquista. Meeting of Spaniard and Inca. The Inca says in Quechua, "You eat this gold?" Spaniard replies in Spanish, "We eat this gold."

words as an example of a conquered subject using the conqueror's language to construct a parodic, oppositional representation of the conqueror's own speech. Guaman Poma mirrors back to the Spanish (in their language, which is alien to him) an image of themselves that they often suppress and will therefore surely recognize. Such are the dynamics of language, writing, and representation in contact zones.

The second half of the epistle continues the critique. It is titled *Buen gobierno y justicia,* "Good Government and Justice," and combines a description of colonial society in the Andean region with a passionate denunciation of Spanish exploitation and abuse. (These, at the time he was writing, were decimating the population of the Andes at a genocidal rate. In fact, the potential loss of the labor force became a main cause for reform of the system.) Guaman Poma's most implacable hostility is invoked by the clergy, followed by the dreaded *corregidores,* or colonial overseers (Fig. 3). He also praises good works, Christian habits, and just men where he finds them, and offers at length his views as to what constitutes "good government and justice." The Indies, he argues, should be administered through a

Figure 3. Corregidor de minas. Catalog of Spanish abuses of indigenous labor force.

collaboration of Inca and Spanish elites. The epistle ends with an imaginary question-and-answer session in which, in a reversal of hierarchy, the king is depicted asking Guaman Poma questions about how to reform the empire—a dialogue imagined across the many lines that divide the Andean scribe from the imperial monarch, and in which the subordinated subject single-handedly gives himself authority in the colonizer's language and verbal repertoire. In a way, it worked—this extraordinary text did get written—but in a way it did not, for the letter never reached its addressee.

To grasp the import of Guaman Poma's project, one needs to keep in mind that the Incas had no system of writing. Their huge empire is said to be the only known instance of a full-blown bureaucratic state society built and administered without writing. Guaman Poma constructs his text by appropriating and adapting pieces of the representational repertoire of the invaders. He does not simply imitate or reproduce it; he selects and adapts it along Andean lines to express (bilingually, mind you) Andean interests and aspirations. Ethnographers have used the term *transculturation* to describe processes whereby members of subordinated or marginal groups select and invent from materials transmitted by a dominant or metropolitan culture. The term, originally coined by Cuban sociologist Fernando Ortiz in the 1940s, aimed to replace overly reductive concepts of acculturation and assimilation used to characterize culture under conquest. While subordinate peoples do not usually control what emanates from the dominant culture, they do determine to varying extents what gets absorbed into their own and what it gets used for. Transculturation, like autoethnography, is a phenomenon of the contact zone.

As scholars have realized only relatively recently, the transcultural character of Guaman Poma's text is intricately apparent in its visual as well as its written component. The genre of the four hundred line drawings is European—there seems to have been no tradition of representational drawing among the Incas—but in their execution they deploy specifically Andean systems of spatial symbolism that express Andean values and aspirations.[1]

In Figure 1, for instance, Adam is depicted on the left-hand side below the sun, while Eve is on the right-hand side below the moon, and slightly lower than Adam. The two are divided by the diagonal of Adam's digging stick. In Andean spatial symbolism, the diagonal descending from the sun marks the basic line of power and authority dividing upper from lower, male from female, dominant from subordinate. In Figure 2, the Inca appears in the same position as Adam, with the Spaniard opposite, and the two at the same height. In Figure 3, depicting Spanish abuses of power, the symbolic pattern is reversed. The Spaniard is in a high position indicating dominance, but on the "wrong" (right-hand) side. The diagonals of his lance and that of the servant doing the flogging mark out a line of illegitimate, though real, power. The Andean figures continue to occupy the left-hand side of the picture, but clearly as victims. Guaman Poma wrote that the Spanish conquest had produced *"un mundo al revés,"* "a world in reverse."

In sum, Guaman Poma's text is truly a product of the contact zone. If one thinks of cultures, or literatures, as discrete, coherently structured, monolingual edifices, Guaman Poma's text, and indeed any autoethnographic work, appears anomalous or chaotic—as it apparently did to the European scholars Pietschmann spoke to in 1912. If one does not think of cultures this way, then Guaman Poma's text is simply heterogeneous, as the Andean region was itself and remains today. Such a text is heterogeneous on the reception end as well as the production end: it will read very differently to people in different positions in the contact zone. Because it deploys European and Andean systems of meaning making, the letter necessarily means differently to bilingual Spanish-Quechua speakers and to monolingual speakers in either language; the drawings mean differently to monocultural readers, Spanish or Andean, and to bicultural readers responding to the Andean symbolic structures embodied in European genres.

In the Andes in the early 1600s there existed a literate public with considerable intercultural competence and degrees of bilingualism. Unfortunately, such a community did not exist in the Spanish court with which Guaman Poma was trying to make contact. It is interesting to note that in the same year Guaman Poma sent off his letter, a text by another Peruvian was adopted in official circles in Spain as the canonical Christian mediation between the Spanish conquest and Inca history. It was another huge encyclopedic work, titled the *Royal Commentaries of the Incas,* written, tellingly, by a mestizo, Inca Garcilaso de la Vega. Like the mestizo half brother who taught Guaman Poma to read and write, Inca Garcilaso was the son of an Inca princess and a Spanish official, and had lived in Spain since he was seventeen. Though he too spoke Quechua, his book is written in eloquent, standard Spanish, without illustrations. While Guaman Poma's life's work sat somewhere unread, the *Royal Commentaries* was edited and reedited in Spain and the New World, a mediation that coded the Andean past and present in ways thought unthreatening to colonial hierarchy.[2] The textual hierarchy persists; the *Royal Commentaries* today remains a staple item on PhD reading lists in Spanish, while the *New Chronicle and Good Government,* despite the ready availability of several fine editions, is not. However, though Guaman Poma's text did not reach its destination, the transcultural currents of expression it exemplifies continued to evolve in the Andes, as they still do, less in writing than in storytelling, ritual, song, dance-drama, painting and sculpture, dress, textile art, forms of governance, religious belief, and many other vernacular art forms. All express the effects of long-term contact and intractable, unequal conflict.

Autoethnography, transculturation, critique, collaboration, bilingualism, mediation, parody, denunciation, imaginary dialogue, vernacular expression—these are some of the literate arts of the contact zone. Miscomprehension, incomprehension, dead letters, unread masterpieces, absolute heterogeneity of meaning—these are some of the perils of writing in the contact zone. They all live among us today in the transnationalized metropolis of the United States and are becoming more widely visible, more pressing, and, like Guaman Poma's text, more decipherable to those who once would have ignored them in defense of a stable, centered sense of knowledge and reality.

Contact and Community

The idea of the contact zone is intended in part to contrast with ideas of community that underlie much of the thinking about language, communication, and culture that gets done in the academy. A couple of years ago, thinking about the linguistic theories I knew, I tried to make sense of a utopian quality that often seemed to characterize social analyses of language by the academy. Languages were seen as living in "speech communities," and these tended to be theorized as discrete, self-defined, coherent entities, held together by a homogeneous competence or grammar shared identically and equally among all the members. This abstract idea of the speech community seemed to reflect, among other things, the utopian way modern nations conceive of themselves as what Benedict Anderson calls "imagined communities."[3] In a book of that title, Anderson observes that with the possible exception of what he calls "primordial villages," human communities exist as *imagined* entities in which people "will never know most of their fellow-members, meet them or even hear of them, yet in the mind of each lives the image of their communion." "Communities are distinguished," he goes on to say, "not by their falsity/genuineness, but by *the style in which they are imagined*" (15; emphasis mine). Anderson proposes three features that characterize the style in which the modern nation is imagined. First, it is imagined as *limited*, by "finite, if elastic, boundaries"; second, it is imagined as *sovereign*; and, third, it is imagined as *fraternal*, "a deep, horizontal comradeship" for which millions of people are prepared "not so much to kill as willingly to die" (15). As the image suggests, the nation-community is embodied metonymically in the finite, sovereign, fraternal figure of the citizen-soldier.

Anderson argues that European bourgeoisies were distinguished by their ability to "achieve solidarity on an essentially imagined basis" (74) on a scale far greater than that of elites of other times and places. Writing and literacy play a central role in this argument. Anderson maintains, as have others, that the main instrument that made bourgeois nation-building projects possible was print capitalism. The commercial circulation of books in the various European vernaculars, he argues, was what first created the invisible networks that would eventually constitute the literate elites and those they ruled as nations. (Estimates are that 180 million books were put into circulation in Europe between the years 1500 and 1600 alone.)

Now obviously this style of imagining of modern nations, as Anderson describes it, is strongly utopian, embodying values like equality, fraternity, liberty, which the societies often profess but systematically fail to realize. The prototype of the modern nation as imagined community was, it seemed to me, mirrored in ways people thought about language and the speech community. Many commentators have pointed out how modern views of language as code and competence assume a unified and homogeneous social world in which language exists as a shared patrimony—as a device, precisely, for imagining community. An image of a universally shared literacy is also part of the picture. The prototypical manifestation of language is generally taken to be the speech of individual adult native speakers face-to-face (as in Saussure's famous diagram) in monolingual, even monodialectal situations—in short, the most homogeneous case linguistically and socially. The same goes for written communication. Now one could certainly imagine a theory that assumed different things—that argued, for instance, that the most revealing speech situation for understanding language was one involving a gathering of people each of whom spoke two languages and understood a third and held only one language in common with any of the others. It depends on what workings of language you want to see or want to see first, on what you choose to define as normative.

In keeping with autonomous, fraternal models of community, analyses of language use commonly assume that principles of cooperation and shared understanding are normally in effect. Descriptions of interactions between people in conversation, classrooms, medical and bureaucratic settings, readily take it for granted that the situation is governed by a single set of rules or norms shared by all participants. The analysis focuses then on how those rules produce or fail to produce an orderly, coherent exchange. Models involving games and moves are often used to describe interactions. Despite whatever conflicts or systematic social differences might be in play, it is assumed that all participants are engaged in the same game and that the game is the same for all players. Often it is. But of course it often is not, as, for example, when speakers are from different classes or cultures, or one party is exercising authority and another is submitting to it or questioning it. Last year one of my children moved to a new elementary school that had more open classrooms and more flexible curricula than the conventional school he started out in. A few days into the term, we asked him what it was like at the new school. "Well," he said, "they're a lot nicer, and they have a lot less rules. But know *why* they're nicer?" "Why?" I asked. "So you'll obey all the rules they don't have," he replied. This is a very coherent analysis with considerable elegance and explanatory power, but probably not the one his teacher would have given.

When linguistic (or literate) interaction is described in terms of orderliness, games, moves, or scripts, usually only legitimate moves are actually named as part of the system, where legitimacy is defined from the point of view of the party in authority—regardless of what other parties might see themselves as doing. Teacher-pupil language, for example, tends to be described almost entirely from the point of view of the teacher and teaching, not from the point of view of pupils and pupiling (the word doesn't even exist, though the thing certainly does). If a classroom is analyzed as a social world unified and homogenized with respect to the teacher, whatever students do other than what the teacher specifies is invisible or anomalous to the analysis. This can be true in practice as well. On several occasions my fourth grader, the one busy obeying all the rules they didn't have, was given writing assignments that took the form of answering a series of questions to build up a paragraph. These questions often asked him to identify with the interests of those in power over him—parents, teachers, doctors, public authorities. He invariably sought ways to resist or subvert these assignments. One assignment, for instance, called for imagining "a helpful invention." The students were asked to write single-sentence responses to the following questions:

> What kind of invention would help you?
> How would it help you?
> Why would you need it?
> What would it look like?
> Would other people be able to use it also?
> What would be an invention to help your teacher?
> What would be an invention to help your parents?

Manuel's reply read as follows:

> A grate adventchin

> Some inventchins are GRATE!!!!!!!!!!! My inventchin would be a shot that would put every thing you learn at school in your brain. It would help me by letting me graduate right now!! I would need it because it would let me play with my friends, go on vacachin and, do fun a lot more. It would look like a regular shot. Ather peaple would use to. This inventchin would help my teacher parents get away from a lot of work. I think a shot like this would be GRATE!

Despite the spelling, the assignment received the usual star to indicate the task had been fulfilled in an acceptable way. No recognition was available, however, of the humor, the attempt to be critical or contestatory, to parody the structures of authority. On that score, Manuel's luck was only slightly better than Guaman Poma's. What is the place of unsolicited oppositional discourse, parody, resistance, critique in the imagined classroom community? Are teachers supposed to feel that their teaching has been most successful when they have eliminated such things and unified the social world, probably in their own image? Who wins when we do that? Who loses?

Such questions may be hypothetical, because in the United States in the 1990s, many teachers find themselves less and less able to do that even if they want to. The composition of the national collectivity is changing and so are the styles, as Anderson put it, in which it is being imagined. In the 1980s in many nation-states, imagined national syntheses that had retained hegemonic force began to dissolve. Internal social groups with histories and lifeways different from the official ones began insisting on those histories and lifeways *as part of their citizenship,* as the very mode of their membership in the national collectivity. In their dialogues with dominant institutions, many groups began asserting a rhetoric of belonging that made demands beyond those of representation and basic rights granted from above. In universities we started to hear, "I don't just want you to let me be here, I want to belong here; this institution should belong to me as much as it does to anyone else." Institutions have responded with, among other things, rhetorics of diversity and multiculturalism whose import at this moment is up for grabs across the ideological spectrum.

These shifts are being lived out by everyone working in education today, and everyone is challenged by them in one way or another. Those of us committed to educational democracy are particularly challenged as that notion finds itself besieged on the public agenda. Many of those who govern us display, openly, their interest in a quiescent, ignorant, manipulable electorate. Even as an ideal, the concept of an enlightened citizenry seems to have disappeared from the national imagination. A couple of years ago the university where I work went through an intense and wrenching debate over a narrowly defined Western-culture requirement that had been instituted there in 1980. It kept boiling down to a debate over the ideas of national patrimony, cultural citizenship, and imagined community. In the end, the requirement was transformed into a much more broadly defined course called Cultures, Ideas, Values.[4] In the context of the change, a new course was designed that centered on the Americas and the multiple cultural histories (including European ones) that have intersected here. As you can imagine, the course attracted a very diverse student body. The classroom functioned not like a homogeneous community or a horizontal alliance but like a contact zone. Every single text we read stood in specific historical relationships to the students in the class, but the range and variety of historical relationships in play were enormous. Everybody had a stake in nearly everything we read, but the range and kind of stakes varied widely.

It was the most exciting teaching we had ever done, and also the hardest. We were struck, for example, at how anomalous the formal lecture became in a contact zone (who can forget Atahuallpa throwing down the Bible because it would not speak to him?). The lecturer's traditional (imagined) task—unifying the world in the class's eyes by means of a monologue that rings equally coherent, revealing, and true for all, forging an ad hoc community, homogeneous with respect to one's own words—this task became not only impossible but anomalous and unimaginable. Instead, one had to work in the knowledge that whatever one said was going to be systematically received in radically heterogeneous ways that we were neither able nor entitled to prescribe.

The very nature of the course put ideas and identities on the line. All the students in the class had the experience, for example, of hearing their culture discussed and objectified in ways that horrified them; all the students saw their roots traced back to legacies of both glory and shame; all the students experienced face-to-face the ignorance and incomprehension, and occasionally the hostility, of others. In the absence of community values and the hope of synthesis, it was easy to forget the positives; the fact, for instance, that kinds of marginalization once taken for granted were gone. Virtually every student was having the experience of seeing the world described with him or her in it. Along with rage, incomprehension, and pain, there were exhilarating moments of wonder and revelation, mutual understanding, and new wisdom—the joys of the contact zone. The sufferings and revelations were, at different moments to be sure, experienced by every student. No one was excluded, and no one was safe.

The fact that no one was safe made all of us involved in the course appreciate the importance of what we came to call "safe houses." We used the term to refer to social and intellectual spaces where groups can constitute themselves as horizontal, homogeneous, sovereign communities with high degrees of trust, shared understandings, temporary protection from legacies of oppression. This is why, as we realized, multicultural curricula should not seek to replace ethnic or women's studies, for example. Where there are legacies of subordination, groups need places for healing and mutual recognition, safe houses in which to construct shared understandings, knowledges, claims on the world that they can then bring into the contact zone.

Meanwhile, our job in the Americas course remains to figure out how to make that crossroads the best site for learning that it can be. We are looking for the pedagogical arts of the contact zone. These will include, we are sure, exercises in storytelling and in identifying with the ideas, interests, histories, and attitudes of others; experiments in transculturation and collaborative work and in the arts of critique, parody, and comparison (including unseemly comparisons between elite and vernacular cultural forms); the redemption of the oral; ways for people to engage with suppressed aspects of history (including their own histories), ways to move *into and out of* rhetorics of authenticity; ground rules for communication across lines of difference and hierarchy that go beyond politeness but maintain mutual respect; a systematic approach to the all-important concept of *cultural mediation*. These arts were in play in every room at the extraordinary Pittsburgh conference on literacy. I learned a lot about them there, and I am thankful.

NOTES

[1] For an introduction in English to these and other aspects of Guaman Poma's work, see Rolena Adorno. Adorno and Mercedes Lopez-Baralt pioneered the study of Andean symbolic systems in Guaman Poma.

[2] It is far from clear that the *Royal Commentaries* was as benign as the Spanish seemed to assume. The book certainly played a role in maintaining the identity and aspirations of indigenous elites in the Andes. In the mid-eighteenth century, a new edition of the *Royal Commentaries* was suppressed by Spanish authorities because its preface included a prophecy by Sir Walter Raleigh that the English would invade Peru and restore the Inca monarchy.

[3] The discussion of community here is summarized from my essay "Linguistic Utopias."

[4] For information about this program and the contents of courses taught in it, write Program in Cultures, Ideas, Values (CIV), Stanford Univ., Stanford, CA 94305.

WORKS CITED

Adorno, Rolena. *Guaman Poma de Ayala: Writing and Resistance in Colonial Peru.* Austin: U of Texas P, 1986.

Anderson, Benedict. *Imagined Communities: Reflections on the Origins and Spread of Nationalism.* London: Verso, 1984.

Garcilaso de la Vega, El Inca. *Royal Commentaries of the Incas.* 1613. Austin: U of Texas P, 1966.

Guaman Poma de Ayala, Felipe. *El primer nueva corónica y buen gobierno.* Manuscript. Ed. John Murra and Rolena Adorno. Mexico: Siglo XXI, 1980.

Pratt, Mary Louise. "Linguistic Utopias." *The Linguistics of Writing.* Ed. Nigel Fabb et al. Manchester: Manchester UP, 1987. 48–66.

Treviño, Gloria. "Cultural Ambivalence in Early Chicano Prose Fiction." Diss. Stanford U, 1985.

•   •   •   •   •   •   •   •   •   •   •   •   •

QUESTIONS FOR A SECOND READING

1. Perhaps the most interesting question "Arts of the Contact Zone" raises for its readers is how to put together the pieces: the examples from Pratt's children, the discussion of Guaman Poma and the *New Chronicle and Good Government*, the brief history of European literacy, and the discussion of curriculum reform at Stanford. The terms that run through the sections are, among others, these: "contact," "community," "autoethnography," "transculturation." As you reread, mark those passages you might use to trace the general argument that cuts across these examples.

2. This essay was originally delivered as a lecture. Before you read Pratt's essay again, create a set of notes on what you remember as important, relevant, or worthwhile. Imagine yourself as part of her audience. Then reread the essay. Where would you want to interrupt her? What questions could you ask her that might make "Arts of the Contact Zone" more accessible to you?

3. This is an essay about reading and writing and teaching and learning, about the "literate arts" and the "pedagogical arts" of the contact zone. Surely the composition class, the first-year college English class, can be imagined as a contact zone. And it seems in the spirit of Pratt's essay to identify (as a student) with Guaman Poma. As you reread, think about how and where this essay might be said to speak directly to you about your education as a reader and writer in a contact zone.

4. There are some difficult terms in this essay: "autochthonous," "autoethnography," "transculturation." The last two are defined in the text; the first you will have to look up. (We did.) In some ways, the slipperiest of the key words in the essay is "culture." At one point Pratt says,

    > If one thinks of cultures, or literatures, as discrete, coherently structured, monolingual edifices, Guaman Poma's text, and indeed any autoethnographic work, appears anomalous or chaotic—as it apparently did to the European scholars Pietschmann spoke to in 1912. If one does not

think of cultures this way, then Guaman Poma's text is simply heterogeneous, as the Andean region was itself and remains today. Such a text
is heterogeneous on the reception end as well as the production end: it
will read very differently to people in different positions in the contact
zone. (p. 506)

If one thinks of cultures as "coherently structured, monolingual edifices,"
the text appears one way; if one thinks otherwise, the text is "simply heterogeneous." What might it mean to make this shift in the way one thinks
of culture? Can you do it—that is, can you read the *New Chronicle* from
both points of view, make the two points of view work in your own imagining? Can you, for example, think of a group that you participate in as a
"community"? Then can you think of it as a "contact zone"? Which one
seems "natural" to you? What does Pratt assume to be the dominant point
of view now, for *her* readers?

As you reread, not only do you want to get a sense of how to explain
these two attitudes toward culture, but you need to practice shifting your
point of view from one to the other. Think, from inside the position of each,
of the things you would be expected to say about Poma's text, Manuel's invention, and your classroom.

ASSIGNMENTS FOR WRITING

Here, briefly, are two descriptions of the writing one might find or expect in the "contact zone." They serve as an introduction to the three writing assignments.

Autoethnography, transculturation, critique, collaboration, bilingualism, mediation, parody, denunciation, imaginary dialogue, vernacular
expression—these are some of the literate arts of the contact zone. Miscomprehension, incomprehension, dead letters, unread masterpieces,
absolute heterogeneity of meaning—these are some of the perils of
writing in the contact zone. They all live among us today in the transnationalized metropolis of the United States and are becoming more
widely visible, more pressing, and, like Guaman Poma's text, more decipherable to those who once would have ignored them in defense of a
stable, centered sense of knowledge and reality. (pp. 506–7)

We are looking for the pedagogical arts of the contact zone. These will
include, we are sure, exercises in storytelling and in identifying with the
ideas, interests, histories, and attitudes of others; experiments in transculturation and collaborative work and in the arts of critique, parody,
and comparison (including unseemly comparisons between elite and
vernacular cultural forms); the redemption of the oral; ways for people
to engage with suppressed aspects of history (including their own histories), ways to move *into and out of* rhetorics of authenticity; ground rules
for communication across lines of difference and hierarchy that go beyond politeness but maintain mutual respect; a systematic approach to
the all-important concept of *cultural mediation*. (p. 511)

1. One way of working with Pratt's essay, of extending its project, would
   be to conduct your own local inventory of writing from the contact zone.
   You might do this on your own or in teams with others from your class.

You will want to gather several similar documents, your "archive," before you make your final selection. Think about how to make that choice. What makes one document stand out as representative? Here are two ways you might organize your search:

a. You could look for historical documents. A local historical society might have documents written by Native Americans ("Indians") to the white settlers. There may be documents written by slaves to masters or to northern whites explaining their experience with slavery. There may be documents by women (like suffragettes) trying to negotiate for public positions and rights. There may be documents from any of a number of racial or ethnic groups—Hispanic, Jewish, Irish, Italian, Polish, Swedish—trying to explain their positions to the mainstream culture. There may, perhaps at union halls, be documents written by workers to owners. Your own sense of the heritage of your area should direct your search.

b. Or you could look for contemporary documents in the print that is around you, things that you might otherwise overlook. Pratt refers to one of the characteristic genres of the Hispanic community, the *"testimonio."* You could look at the writing of any marginalized group, particularly writing intended, at least in part, to represent the experience of outsiders to the dominant culture (or to be in dialogue with that culture or to respond to that culture). These documents, if we follow Pratt's example, would encompass the work of young children or students, including college students.

Once you have completed your inventory, choose a document you would like to work with and present it carefully and in detail (perhaps in even greater detail than Pratt's presentation of the *New Chronicle*). You might imagine that you are presenting this to someone who would not have seen it and would not know how to read it, at least not as an example of the literate arts of the contact zone.

2. Another way of extending the project of Pratt's essay would be to write your own autoethnography. It should not be too hard to locate a setting or context in which you are the "other"—the one who speaks from outside rather than inside the dominant discourse. Pratt says that the position of the outsider is marked not only by differences of language and ways of thinking and speaking but also by differences in power, authority, status. In a sense, she argues, the only way those in power can understand you is in *their* terms. These are terms you will need to use to tell your story, but your goal is to describe your position in ways that "engage with representations others have made of [you]" without giving in or giving up or disappearing in their already formed sense of who you are.

This is an interesting challenge. One of the things that will make the writing difficult is that the autoethnographic or transcultural text calls upon skills not usually valued in American classrooms: bilingualism, parody, denunciation, imaginary dialogue, vernacular expression, storytelling, unseemly comparisons of high and low cultural forms—these are some of the terms Pratt offers. These do not fit easily with the traditional genres of the writing class (essay, term paper, summary, report) or its traditional values (unity, consistency, sincerity, clarity, correctness, decorum).

You will probably need to take this essay (or whatever it should be called) through several drafts. It might be best to begin as Pratt's student, using her description as a preliminary guide. Once you get a sense of your own project, you may find that you have terms or examples to add to her list of the literate arts of the contact zone.

3. Citing Benedict Anderson and what he calls "imagined communities," Pratt argues that our idea of community is "strongly utopian, embodying values like equality, fraternity, liberty, which the societies often profess but systematically fail to realize." Against this utopian vision of community, Pratt argues that we need to develop ways of understanding (even noticing) social and intellectual spaces that are not homogeneous, unified; we need to develop ways of understanding and valuing difference.

Think of a community of which you are a member, a community that is important to you. And think about the utopian terms you are given to name and describe this community. Think, then, about this group in Pratt's terms—as a "contact zone." How would you name and describe this social space? Write an essay in which you present these alternate points of view on a single social group. You will need to present this discussion fully, so that someone who is not part of your group can follow what you say, and you should take time to think about the consequences (for you, for your group) of this shift in point of view, in terms.

MAKING CONNECTIONS

1. Here, from "Arts of the Contact Zone," is Mary Louise Pratt on the "autoethnographic" text:

> Guaman Poma's *New Chronicle* is an instance of what I have proposed to call an *autoethnographic* text, by which I mean a text in which people undertake to describe themselves in ways that engage with representations others have made of them. Thus if ethnographic texts are those in which European metropolitan subjects represent to themselves their others (usually their conquered others), autoethnographic texts are representations that the so-defined others construct *in response to* or in dialogue with those texts. ... [T]hey involve a selective collaboration with and appropriation of idioms of the metropolis or the conqueror. These are merged or infiltrated to varying degrees with indigenous idioms to create self-representations intended to intervene in metropolitan modes of understanding. ... Such texts often constitute a marginalized group's point of entry into the dominant circuits of print culture. It is interesting to think, for example, of American slave autobiography in its autoethnographic dimensions, which in some respects distinguish it from Euramerican autobiographical tradition. (pp. 501–2)

Harriet Jacobs's *Incidents in the Life of a Slave Girl* (p. 353) is an example of an American slave autobiography. John Edgar Wideman's "Our Time" (p. 681), and the excerpts from Gloria Anzaldúa's *Borderlands/La frontera* (p. 42) could serve as twentieth-century counterparts. Choose one of these selections and reread it with "Arts of the Contact Zone" in mind. Write an essay that presents the selection as an example of autoethnographic and/or transcultural texts. You should imagine that you are working to put Pratt's ideas to the test (*do* they do what she says such texts must do?), but also add what you have to say concerning this text as a literate effort to be present in the context of difference.

2. In the selection titled "States" Edward Said says,

> All cultures spin out a dialectic of self and other, the subject "I" who is native, authentic, at home, and the object "it" or "you," who is foreign, perhaps threatening, different, out there. From this dialectic comes the series of heroes and monsters, founding fathers and barbarians, prized masterpieces and despised opponents that express a culture from its deepest sense of national self-identity to its refined patriotism, and finally to its coarse jingoism, xenophobia, and exclusivist bias. (p. 596)

This is as true of the Palestinians as it is of the Israelis—although, he adds, "For Palestinian culture, the odd thing is that its own identity is more frequently than not perceived as 'other'."

Citing Benedict Anderson and what he refers to as "imagined communities," Mary Louise Pratt in "Arts of the Contact Zone" (p. 499) argues that our idea of community is "strongly utopian, embodying values like equality, fraternity, liberty, which the societies often profess but systematically fail to realize." Against this utopian vision of community, Pratt argues that we need to develop ways of understanding (noticing or creating) social and intellectual spaces that are not homogeneous or unified— contact zones; she argues that we need to develop ways of understanding and valuing difference.

There are similar goals and objects to these projects. Reread Pratt's essay with Said's "States" in mind. As she defines what she refers to as the "literate arts of the contact zone," can you find points of reference in Said's text? Said's thinking always attended to the importance and the conditions of writing, including his own. There are ways that "States" could be imagined as both "autoethnographic" and "transcultural." How might Said's work allow you to understand the "literate arts of the contact zone" in practice? How might his work allow you to understand the problems and possibilities of such writing beyond what Pratt has imagined, presented, and predicted?

ADRIENNE RICH

ADRIENNE RICH (b. 1929) once said that whatever she knows, she wants to "know it in [her] own nerves." As a writer, Rich found it necessary to acknowledge her anger at both the oppression of women and her immediate experience of that oppression. She needed to find the "anger that is creative." "Until I could tap into the very rich ocean," she said, "I think that my work was constrained in certain ways. There's this fear of anger in women, which is partly because we've been told it was always destructive, it was always unseemly, and unwomanly, and monstrous."

Rich's poetry combines passion and anger with a "yen for order." She wrote her first book of poems, A Change of World, *while an undergraduate at Radcliffe College. The book won the 1951 Yale Younger Poets Award and a generous introduction from W. H. Auden, who was one of the judges. In 1991 she won the Commonwealth Award in Literature and in 1992 the Robert Frost Medal from the Poetry Society of America for a lifetime of achievement in literature. Her other works, which include* The Diamond Cutters *(1955),* Snapshots of a Daughter-in-Law *(1963, 1967),* Necessities of Life *(1966),* Leaflets *(1969),* The Will to Change *(1970), and* Diving into the Wreck *(1973), show an increasing concern for the political and psychological consequences of life in patriarchal society. When offered the National Book Award for* Diving into the Wreck, *Rich refused it as an individual but accepted it, in a statement written with two other nominees—Audre Lorde and Alice Walker (whose essay "In Search of Our Mothers' Gardens" appears on p. 668)—in the name of all women:*

> We . . . together accept this award in the name of all the women whose voices have gone and still go unheard in a patriarchal world, and in the name of those who, like us, have been tolerated as token women in this culture, often at great cost and in great pain. . . . We dedicate this occasion to the struggle for self-determination of all women, of every color, identification, or derived class, . . . the women who will understand what we are doing here and those who will not understand yet; the silent women whose voices have been denied us, the articulate women who have given us the strength to do our work.

After graduating from Radcliffe in 1951, Rich married and raised three sons. One of her prose collections, Of Woman Born: Motherhood as Experience and Institution *(1976), treats her experience as both mother and daughter with eloquence, even as it calls for the destruction of motherhood as an institution. In 1970 Rich left her marriage, and six years later she published a book of poems that explore a lesbian relationship. But the term "lesbian" for Rich referred to "nothing so simple and dismissible as the fact that two women might go to bed together." As she says in "It Is the Lesbian in Us," a speech reprinted in* On Lies, Secrets, and Silence: Selected Prose *(1979), it refers also to "a sense of desiring oneself; above all, of choosing oneself; it was also a primary intensity; between women, an intensity which in the world at large was trivialized, caricatured, or invested with evil. . . . It is the lesbian in us who drives us to feel imaginatively, render in language, grasp, the full connection between woman and woman."*

The essay "When We Dead Awaken: Writing as Re-Vision" was written in 1971. In an introduction to a collection of her essays, Arts of the Possible *(2001), Rich says,*

> In selecting a few essays from my earlier work . . . , I sometimes had a rueful sense of how one period's necessary strategies can mutate into the monsters of a later time. The accurate feminist perceptions that women's lives, historically and individually, were mostly unrecorded and that the personal is political are cases in point. Feminism has depended heavily on the concrete testimony of individual women, a testimony that was meant to accumulate toward collective understanding and practice. . . . In "When We Dead Awaken," I borrowed a title from Ibsen's last play, written in 1900. Certainly the issues Ibsen had dramatized were very much alive. I "used myself" to illustrate a woman writer's journey, rather tentatively. In 1971, this still seemed a questionable, even illegitimate, approach, especially in a paper to be given at an academic convention. . . .
>
> By the late 1900s, in mainstream American public discourse, personal anecdote was replacing critical argument, true confessions were foregrounding the discussion of ideas. A feminism that sought to engage race and colonialism, the global monoculture of United States

> *corporate and military interests, the specific locations and agencies*
> *of women within all this was being countered by the marketing of a*
> *United States model of female—or feminine—self-involvement and*
> *self-improvement, devoid of political context or content.*

One way of working on her essay is to move from it to the later work, using
"When We Dead Awaken" as a framework for further reading. We have provided a
selection of poems that can serve as preparation for such a project. These poems are
selected from Rich's 1986 book Your Native Land, Your Life, a book that addresses questions of legacy, heritage, and inheritance. The poems are drawn from
the opening section, which is titled "Sources." One of the poems contains the
phrase "split at the root." This is a phrase Rich has used before to refer to her own
formation as the daughter of a Jewish man and a Gentile woman. It appears for the
first time in a long poem, "Readings of History," included in Snapshots of a
Daughter-in-Law, where she describes herself as "Split at the root, neither Gentile nor Jew, Yankee nor Rebel."

And, in a 1982 essay, "Split at the Root: An Essay on Jewish Identity," she
says of that poem: "I was still trying to have it both ways: to be neither/nor, trying
to live (with my Jewish husband and three children more Jewish in ancestry than I)
in the predominantly gentile, Yankee academic world of Cambridge, Massachusetts." The essay, "Split at the Root," concludes with these paragraphs:

> *Sometimes I feel I have seen too long from too many disconnected an-*
> *gles: white, Jewish, anti-Semite, racist, anti-racist, once-married, les-*
> *bian, middle-class, feminist, exmatriate Southerner, split at the root:*
> *that I will never bring them whole. I would have liked, in this essay, to*
> *bring together the meanings of anti-Semitism and racism as I have ex-*
> *perienced them and as I believe they intersect in the world beyond my*
> *life. But I am not able to do this yet.*

And:

> *This essay, then, has no conclusions: it is another beginning, for me.*
> *Not just a way of saying, in 1982 Right-wing America, I too will wear*
> *the yellow star. It's a moving into accountability, enlarging the range*
> *of accountability. I know that in the rest of my life, the next half-*
> *century or so, every aspect of my identity will have to be engaged. The*
> *middle-class white girl taught to trade obedience for privilege. The*
> *Jewish lesbian raised to be a heterosexual Gentile. The woman who first*
> *heard oppression named and analyzed in the Black civil rights strug-*
> *gle. The woman with three sons, the feminist who hates male violence.*
> *The woman limping with a cane, the woman who has stopped bleeding,*
> *are also accountable. The poet who knows that beautiful language can*
> *lie, that the oppressor's language sometimes sounds beautiful. The*
> *woman trying, as part of her resistance, to clean up her act.*

Adrienne Rich has published nearly twenty books of poetry and five collections of
prose. They include Blood, Bread, and Poetry: Selected Prose (1986); An Atlas
of the Difficult World: Poems, 1988–91 (1991), which was awarded the 1992 Los
Angeles Times Book Prize for poetry and was a finalist for both the National Book

Award and the National Book Critics Circle Award; Collected Early Poems: 1950–1970 *(1993);* Dark Fields of the Republic: Poems 1991–1995 *(1995);* Midnight Salvage: Poems 1995–1998 *(1999);* Fox: Poems 1998–2000 *(2001); and* School Among the Ruins: Poems 2000–2004 *(2004);* Telephone Ringing in the Labyrinth: Poems, 2004–2006 *(2007); and* Poetry & Commitment: An Essay *(2007). Rich has taught at Columbia, Brandeis, Cornell, Rutgers, and Stanford universities, Swarthmore College, and the City College of New York. Among her many awards and honors she has held two Guggenheim Fellowships and an Amy Lowell Traveling Fellowship. She has been a member of the department of literature of the American Academy and Institute of Arts and Letters since 1990. In 1997 Rich was awarded the Academy's Wallace Stevens Award for outstanding and proven mastery in the art of poetry, and in 1999 she was elected a Chancellor of the Academy. In 1999 she received the Lifetime Achievement Award from the Lannan Foundation and in 2003 she was awarded the Bollingen Prize for Poetry. She lives in northern California.*

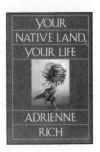

*When We Dead Awaken: Writing as Re-Vision**

The Modern Language Association is both marketplace and funeral parlor for the professional study of Western literature in North America. Like all gatherings of the professions, it has been and remains a "procession of the sons of educated men" (Virginia Woolf): a congeries of old-boys' networks, academicians rehearsing their numb canons in sessions dedicated to the literature of white males, junior scholars under the lash of "publish or perish" delivering papers in the bizarrely lit drawing-rooms of immense hotels: a ritual competition veering between cynicism and desperation.

However, in the interstices of these gentlemanly rites (or, in Mary Daly's words, on the boundaries of this patriarchal space),[1] some feminist scholars, teachers, and

---

*As Rich explains, this essay—written in 1971—was first published in 1972 and then included in her volume On Lies, Secrets, and Silence (1979). At that time she added the introductory note reprinted here, as well as some notes, identified as "A. R., 1978." [Editor's note in the Norton edition.]

*graduate students, joined by feminist writers, editors, and publishers, have for a
decade been creating more subversive occasions, challenging the sacredness of the
gentlemanly canon, sharing the rediscovery of buried works by women, asking
women's questions, bringing literary history and criticism back to life in both senses.
The Commission of the Status of Women in the Profession was formed in 1969, and
held its first public event in 1970. In 1971 the Commission asked Ellen Peck Killoh,
Tillie Olsen, Elaine Reuben, and myself, with Elaine Hedges as moderator, to talk on
"The Woman Writer in the Twentieth Century." The essay that follows was written
for that forum, and later published, along with the other papers from the forum and
workshops, in an issue of* College English *edited by Elaine Hedges ("Women Writing and Teaching," vol. 34, no. 1, October 1972). With a few revisions, mainly updat-
ing, it was reprinted in* American Poets *in 1976, edited by William Heyen (New
York: Bobbs-Merrill, 1976). That later text is the one published here.*

The challenge flung by feminists at the accepted literary canon, at
the methods of teaching it, and at the biased and astigmatic view of male
"literary scholarship," has not diminished in the decade since the first
Women's Forum; it has become broadened and intensified more recently
by the challenges of black and lesbian feminists pointing out that feminist
literary criticism itself has overlooked or held back from examining the
work of black women and lesbians. The dynamic between a political vision
and the demand for a fresh vision of literature is clear: without a growing
feminist movement, the first inroads of feminist scholarship could not have
been made; without the sharpening of a black feminist consciousness, black
women's writing would have been left in limbo between misogynist black
male critics and white feminists still struggling to unearth a white women's
tradition; without an articulate lesbian/feminist movement, lesbian writing
would still be lying in that closet where many of us used to sit reading forbidden books "in a bad light."

Much, much more is yet to be done; and university curricula have of
course changed very little as a result of all this. What *is* changing is the
availability of knowledge, of vital texts, the visible effects on women's lives
of seeing, hearing our wordless or negated experience affirmed and pursued further in language.

Ibsen's *When We Dead Awaken* is a play about the use that the male artist
and thinker — in the process of creating culture as we know it — has made of
women, in his life and in his work; and about a woman's slow struggling
awakening to the use to which her life has been put. Bernard Shaw wrote in
1900 of this play:

> [Ibsen] shows us that no degradation ever devised or permitted
> is as disastrous as this degradation; that through it women can
> die into luxuries for men and yet can kill them; that men and
> women are becoming conscious of this; and that what remains to
> be seen as perhaps the most interesting of all imminent social de-
> velopments is what will happen "when we dead awaken."[2]

It's exhilarating to be alive in a time of awakening consciousness; it can also be confusing, disorienting, and painful. The awakening of dead or sleeping consciousness has already affected the lives of millions of women, even those who don't know it yet. It is also affecting the lives of men, even those who deny its claims upon them. The argument will go on whether an oppressive economic class system is responsible for the oppressive nature of male/female relations, or whether, in fact, patriarchy—the domination of males—is the original model of oppression on which all others are based. But in the last few years the women's movement has drawn inescapable and illuminating connections between our sexual lives and our political institutions. The sleepwalkers are coming awake, and for the first time this awakening has a collective reality; it is no longer such a lonely thing to open one's eyes.

Re-vision—the act of looking back, of seeing with fresh eyes, of entering an old text from a new critical direction—is for women more than a chapter in cultural history: it is an act of survival. Until we can understand the assumptions in which we are drenched we cannot know ourselves. And this drive to self-knowledge, for women, is more than a search for identity: it is part of our refusal of the self-destructiveness of male-dominated society. A radical critique of literature, feminist in its impulse, would take the work first of all as a clue to how we live, how we have been living, how we have been led to imagine ourselves, how our language has trapped as well as liberated us, how the very act of naming has been till now a male prerogative, and how we can begin to see and name—and therefore live—afresh. A change in the concept of sexual identity is essential if we are not going to see the old political order reassert itself in every new revolution. We need to know the writing of the past, and know it differently than we have ever known it; not to pass on a tradition but to break its hold over us.

For writers, and at this moment for women writers in particular, there is the challenge and promise of a whole new psychic geography to be explored. But there is also a difficult and dangerous walking on the ice, as we try to find language and images for the consciousness we are just coming into, and with little in the past to support us. I want to talk about some aspect of this difficulty and this danger.

Jane Harrison, the great classical anthropologist, wrote in 1914 in a letter to her friend Gilbert Murray:

> By and by, about "Women," it has bothered me often—why do women never want to write poetry about Man as a sex—why is Woman a dream and a terror to man and not the other way around? . . . Is it mere convention and propriety, or something deeper?[3]

I think Jane Harrison's question cuts deep into the myth-making tradition, the romantic tradition; deep into what women and men have been to each other; and deep into the psyche of the woman writer. Thinking about that question, I began thinking of the work of two twentieth-century women poets, Sylvia Plath and Diane Wakoski. It strikes me that in the work of both Man appears as, if not a dream, a fascination and a terror; and that the source of the fascination and the terror is, simply, Man's power—to dominate, tyrannize, choose, or reject the woman. The charisma of Man seems to come purely from his power over her and his control of the world by force, not from anything fertile or life-giving in him. And, in the work of both these poets, it is finally the woman's sense of *herself*—embattled, possessed—that gives the poetry its dynamic charge, its rhythms of struggle, need, will, and female energy. Until recently this female anger and this furious awareness of the Man's power over her were not available materials to the female poet, who tended to write of Love as the source of her suffering, and to view that victimization by Love as an almost inevitable fate. Or, like Marianne Moore and Elizabeth Bishop, she kept sexuality at a measured and chiseled distance in her poems.

One answer to Jane Harrison's question has to be that historically men and women have played very different parts in each others' lives. Where woman has been a luxury for man, and has served as the painter's model and the poet's muse, but also as comforter, nurse, cook, bearer of his seed, secretarial assistant, and copyist of manuscripts, man has played a quite different role for the female artist. Henry James repeats an incident which the writer Prosper Mérimée described, of how, while he was living with George Sand,

> he once opened his eyes, in the raw winter dawn, to see his companion, in a dressing-gown, on her knees before the domestic hearth, a candle-stick beside her and a red *madras* round her head, making bravely, with her own hands the fire that was to enable her to sit down betimes to urgent pen and paper. The story represents him as having felt that the spectacle chilled his ardor and tried his taste; her appearance was unfortunate, her occupation an inconsequence, and her industry a reproof—the result of all which was a lively irritation and an early rupture.[4]

The specter of this kind of male judgment, along with the misnaming and thwarting of her needs by a culture controlled by males, has created problems for the woman writer: problems of contact with herself, problems of language and style, problems of energy and survival.

In rereading Virginia Woolf's *A Room of One's Own* (1929) for the first time in some years, I was astonished at the sense of effort, of pains taken, of dogged tentativeness, in the tone of that essay. And I recognized that tone. I had heard it often enough, in myself and in other women. It is the tone of a woman almost in touch with her anger, who is determined not to appear angry, who is *willing* herself to be calm, detached, and even charming in a roomful of men where things have been said which are attacks on her very integrity. Virginia Woolf is addressing an audience of women, but she is acutely conscious—as she always was—of being overheard by men: by Morgan and Lytton and Maynard Keynes and for that matter by her father,

Leslie Stephen.[5] She drew the language out into an exacerbated thread in her determination to have her own sensibility yet protect it from those masculine presences. Only at rare moments in that essay do you hear the passion in her voice; she was trying to sound as cool as Jane Austen, as Olympian as Shakespeare, because that is the way the men of the culture thought a writer should sound.

No male writer has written primarily or even largely for women, or with the sense of women's criticism as a consideration when he chooses his materials, his theme, his language. But to a lesser or greater extent, every woman writer has written for men even when, like Virginia Woolf, she was supposed to be addressing women. If we have come to the point when this balance might begin to change, when women can stop being haunted, not only by "convention and propriety" but by internalized fears of being and saying themselves, then it is an extraordinary moment for the woman writer—and reader.

I have hesitated to do what I am going to do now, which is to use myself as an illustration. For one thing, it's a lot easier and less dangerous to talk about other women writers. But there is something else. Like Virginia Woolf, I am aware of the women who are not with us here because they are washing the dishes and looking after the children. Nearly fifty years after she spoke, that fact remains largely unchanged. And I am thinking also of women whom she left out of the picture altogether—women who are washing other people's dishes and caring for other people's children, not to mention women who went on the streets last night in order to feed their children. We seem to be special women here, we have liked to think of ourselves as special, and we have known that men would tolerate, even romanticize us as special, as long as our words and actions didn't threaten their privilege of tolerating or rejecting us and our work according to *their* ideas of what a special woman ought to be. An important insight of the radical women's movement has been how divisive and how ultimately destructive is this myth of the special woman, who is also the token woman. Every one of us here in this room has had great luck—we are teachers, writers, academicians; our own gifts could not have been enough, for we all know women whose gifts are buried or aborted. Our struggles can have meaning and our privileges—however precarious under patriarchy—can be justified only if they can help to change the lives of women whose gifts—and whose very being—continue to be thwarted and silenced.

My own luck was being born white and middle-class into a house full of books, with a father who encouraged me to read and write. So for about twenty years I wrote for a particular man, who criticized and praised me and made me feel I was indeed "special." The obverse side of this, of course, was that I tried for a long time to please him, or rather, not to displease him. And then of course there were other men—writers, teachers—the Man, who was not a terror or a dream but a literary master and a master in other ways less easy to acknowledge. And there were all those poems about women, written by men: it seemed to be a given that men wrote poems and women frequently inhabited them. These women were almost always beautiful, but threatened with the loss of beauty, the loss of youth—the fate worse than death. Or, they were beautiful and died young, like Lucy and Lenore. Or, the woman was like Maud Gonne, cruel and disastrously mistaken, and the poem reproached her because she had refused to become a luxury for the poet.

A lot is being said today about the influence that the myths and images of women have on all of us who are products of culture. I think it has been a peculiar confusion to the girl or woman who tries to write because she is peculiarly susceptible to language. She goes to poetry or fiction looking for *her* way of being in the world, since she too has been putting words and images together; she is looking eagerly for guides, maps, possibilities; and over and over in the "words' masculine persuasive force" of literature she comes up against something that negates everything she is about: she meets the image of Woman in books written by men. She finds a terror and a dream, she finds a beautiful pale face, she finds La Belle Dame Sans Merci, she finds Juliet or Tess or Salomé, but precisely what she does not find is that absorbed, drudging, puzzled, sometimes inspired creature, herself, who sits at a desk trying to put words together.

So what does she do? What did I do? I read the older women poets with their peculiar keenness and ambivalence: Sappho, Christina Rossetti, Emily Dickinson, Elinor Wylie, Edna Millay, H. D. I discovered that the woman poet most admired at the time (by men) was Marianne Moore, who was maidenly, elegant, intellectual, discreet. But even in reading these women I was looking in them for the same things I had found in the poetry of men, because I wanted women poets to be the equals of men, and to be equal was still confused with sounding the same.

I know that my style was formed first by male poets: by the men I was reading as an undergraduate—Frost, Dylan Thomas, Donne, Auden, Mac-Neice, Stevens, Yeats. What I chiefly learned from them was craft.[6] But poems are like dreams: in them you put what you don't know you know. Looking back at poems I wrote before I was twenty-one, I'm startled because beneath the conscious craft are glimpses of the split I even then experienced between the girl who wrote poems, who defined herself in writing poems, and the girl who was to define herself by her relationships with men. "Aunt Jennifer's Tigers" (1951), written while I was a student, looks with deliberate detachment at this split.

> Aunt Jennifer's tigers stride across a screen,
> Bright topaz denizens of a world of green.
> They do not fear the men beneath the tree;
> They pace in sleek chivalric certainty.
>
> Aunt Jennifer's fingers fluttering through her wool
> Find even the ivory needle hard to pull.

The massive weight of Uncle's wedding band
Sits heavily upon Aunt Jennifer's hand.

When Aunt is dead, her terrified hands will lie
Still ringed with ordeals she was mastered by.
The tigers in the panel that she made
Will go on striding, proud and unafraid.

In writing this poem, composed and apparently cool as it is, I thought I was creating a portrait of an imaginary woman. But this woman suffers from the opposition of her imagination, worked out in tapestry, and her lifestyle, "ringed with ordeals she was mastered by." It was important to me that Aunt Jennifer was a person as distinct from myself as possible—distanced by the formalism of the poem, by its objective, observant tone—even by putting the woman in a different generation.

In those years formalism was part of the strategy—like asbestos gloves, it allowed me to handle materials I couldn't pick up barehanded. A later strategy was to use the persona of a man, as I did in "The Loser" (1958):

> *A man thinks of the woman he once loved:*
> *first, after her wedding, and then nearly a*
> *decade later.*

> I
> I kissed you, bride and lost, and went
> home from that bourgeois sacrament,
> your cheek still tasting cold upon
> my lips that gave you benison
> with all the swagger that they knew—
> as losers somehow learn to do.

> Your wedding made my eyes ache; soon
> the world would be worse off for one
> more golden apple dropped to ground
> without the least protesting sound,
> and you would windfall lie, and we
> forget your shimmer on the tree.

> Beauty is always wasted: if
> not Mignon's song sung to the deaf,
> at all events to the unmoved.
> A face like yours cannot be loved
> long or seriously enough.
> Almost, we seem to hold it off.

> II
> Well, you are tougher than I thought.
> Now when the wash with ice hangs taut
> this morning of St. Valentine,
> I see you strip the squeaking line,
> your body weighed against the load,
> and all my groans can do no good.

Because you still are beautiful,
though squared and stiffened by the pull
of what nine windy years have done.
You have three daughters, lost a son.
I see all your intelligence
flung into that unwearied stance.

My envy is of no avail.
I turn my head and wish him well
who chafed your beauty into use
and lives forever in a house
lit by the friction of your mind.
You stagger in against the wind.

I finished college, published my first book by a fluke, as it seemed to me, and broke off a love affair. I took a job, lived alone, went on writing, fell in love. I was young, full of energy, and the book seemed to mean that others agreed I was a poet. Because I was also determined to prove that as a woman poet I could also have what was then defined as a "full" woman's life, I plunged in my early twenties into marriage and had three children before I was thirty. There was nothing overt in the environment to warn me: these were the fifties, and in reaction to the earlier wave of feminism, middle-class women were making careers of domestic perfection, working to send their husbands through professional schools, then retiring to raise large families. People were moving out to the suburbs, technology was going to be the answer to everything, even sex; the family was in its glory. Life was extremely private; women were isolated from each other by the loyalties of marriage. I have a sense that women didn't talk to each other much in the fifties—not about their secret emptinesses, their frustrations. I went on trying to write; my second book and first child appeared in the same month. But by the time that book came out I was already dissatisfied with those poems, which seemed to me mere exercises for poems I hadn't written. The book was praised, however, for its "gracefulness"; I had a marriage and a child. If there were doubts, if there were periods of null depression or active despairing, these could only mean that I was ungrateful, insatiable, perhaps a monster.

About the time my third child was born, I felt that I had either to consider myself a failed woman and a failed poet, or to try to find some synthesis by which to understand what was happening to me. What frightened me most was the sense of drift, of being pulled along a current which called itself my destiny, but in which I seemed to be losing touch with whoever I had been, with the girl who had experienced her own will and energy almost ecstatically at times, walking around a city or riding a train at night or typing in a student room. In a poem about my grandmother I wrote (of myself): "A young girl, thought sleeping, is certified dead" ("Halfway"). I was writing very little, partly from fatigue, that female fatigue of suppressed anger and loss of contact with my own being; partly from the discontinuity of female life with its attention to small chores, errands, work that others constantly undo, small children's constant needs. What I did write was unconvincing to me; my anger and frustration were hard to acknowledge in or out of poems because in fact I cared a great deal about my husband and my children. Trying to look back and understand that time I have tried to analyze the real nature of the conflict. Most, if not all, human lives are full of fantasy—passive day-dreaming which need not be acted on. But to write poetry or fiction, or even to think well, is not to fantasize, or to put fantasies on paper. For a poem to coalesce, for a character or an action to take shape, there has to be an imaginative transformation of reality which is in no way passive. And a certain freedom of the mind is needed—freedom to press on, to enter the currents of your thought like a glider pilot, knowing that your motion can be sustained, that the buoyancy of your attention will not be suddenly snatched away. Moreover, if the imagination is to transcend and transform experience it has to question, to challenge, to conceive of alternatives, perhaps to the very life you are living at that moment. You have to be free to play around with the notion that day might be night, love might be hate; nothing can be too sacred for the imagination to turn into its opposite or to call experimentally by another name. For writing is renaming. Now, to be maternally with small children all day in the old way, to be with a man in the old way of marriage, requires a holding-back, a putting-aside of that imaginative activity, and demands instead a kind of conservatism. I want to make it clear that I am *not* saying that in order to write well, or think well, it is necessary to become unavailable to others, or to become a devouring ego. This has been the myth of the masculine artist and thinker; and I do not accept it. But to be a female human being trying to fulfill traditional female functions in a traditional way *is* in direct conflict with the subversive function of the imagination. The word traditional is important here. There must be ways, and we will be finding out more and more about them, in which the energy of creation and the energy of relation can be united. But in those years I always felt the conflict as a failure of love in myself. I had thought I was choosing a full life; the life available to most men, in which sexuality, work, and parenthood could coexist. But I felt, at twenty-nine, guilt toward the people closest to me, and guilty toward my own being.

I wanted, then, more than anything, the one thing of which there was never enough: time to think, time to write. The fifties and early sixties were years of rapid revelations: the sit-ins and marches in the South, the Bay of Pigs, the early antiwar movement, raised large questions—questions for which the masculine world of the academy around me seemed to have expert and fluent answers. But I needed to think for myself—about pacifism and dissent and violence, about poetry and society, and about my own relationship to all these things. For about ten years I was reading in fierce snatches, scribbling in notebooks, writing poetry in fragments; I was looking desperately for clues, because if there were no clues then I thought I might be insane. I wrote in a notebook about this time:

> Paralyzed by the sense that there exists a mesh of relationships—
> e.g., between my anger at the children, my sensual life, pacifism,
> sex (I mean sex in its broadest significance, not merely sexual
> desire)—an interconnectedness which, if I could see it, make it
> valid, would give me back myself, make it possible to function
> lucidly and passionately. Yet I grope in and out among these
> dark webs.

I think I began at this point to feel that politics was not something "out
there" but something "in here" and of the essence of my condition.

In the late fifties I was able to write, for the first time, directly about experiencing myself as a woman. The poem was jotted in fragments during
children's naps, brief hours in a library, or at 3:00 A.M. after rising with a
wakeful child. I despaired of doing any continuous work at this time. Yet I
began to feel that my fragments and scraps had a common consciousness
and a common theme, one which I would have been very unwilling to put
on paper at an earlier time because I had been taught that poetry should be
"universal," which meant, of course, nonfemale. Until then I had tried very
much *not* to identify myself as a female poet. Over two years I wrote a ten-
part poem called "Snapshots of a Daughter-in-Law" (1958–1960), in a
longer looser mode than I'd ever trusted myself with before. It was an extraordinary relief to write that poem. It strikes me now as too literary, too
dependent on allusion; I hadn't found the courage yet to do without authorities, or even to use the pronoun "I"—the woman in the poem is always "she." One section of it, No. 2, concerns a woman who thinks she is
going mad; she is haunted by voices telling her to resist and rebel, voices
which she can hear but not obey.

> 2.
> Banging the coffee-pot into the sink
> she hears the angels chiding, and looks out
> past the raked gardens to the sloppy sky.
> Only a week since They said: *Have no patience.*
>
> The next time it was: *Be insatiable.*
> Then: *Save yourself; others you cannot save.*
> Sometimes she's let the tapstream scald her arm,
> a match burn to her thumbnail,
>
> or held her hand above the kettle's snout
> right in the woolly steam. They are probably angels,
> since nothing hurts her anymore, except
> each morning's grit blowing into her eyes.

The poem "Orion," written five years later, is a poem of reconnection
with a part of myself I had felt I was losing—the active principle, the ener-
getic imagination, the "half-brother" whom I projected, as I had for many
years, into the constellation Orion. It's no accident that the words "cold and
egotistical" appear in this poem, and are applied to myself.

Far back when I went zig-zagging
through tamarack pastures
you were my genius, you
my cast-iron Viking, my helmed
lion-heart king in prison.
Years later now you're young

my fierce half-brother, staring
down from that simplified west
your breast open, your belt dragged down
by an oldfashioned thing, a sword
the last bravado you won't give over
though it weighs you down as you stride

and the stars in it are dim
and maybe have stopped burning.
But you burn, and I know it;
as I throw back my head to take you in
an old transfusion happens again:
divine astronomy is nothing to it.

Indoors I bruise and blunder,
break faith, leave ill enough
alone, a dead child born in the dark.
Night cracks up over the chimney,
pieces of time, frozen geodes
come showering down in the grate.

A man reaches behind my eyes
and finds them empty
a woman's head turns away
from my head in the mirror
children are dying my death
and eating crumbs of my life.

Pity is not your forte.
Calmly you ache up there
pinned aloft in your crow's nest,
my speechless pirate!
You take it all for granted
and when I look you back

it's with a starlike eye
shooting its cold and egotistical spear
where it can do least damage.
Breathe deep! No hurt, no pardon
out here in the cold with you
you with your back to the wall.

The choice still seemed to be between "love" —womanly, maternal love, al-
truistic love—a love defined and ruled by the weight of an entire culture;
and egotism—a force directed by men into creation, achievement, ambi-

tion, often at the expense of others, but justifiably so. For weren't they men, and wasn't that their destiny as womanly, selfless love was ours? We know now that the alternatives are false ones—that the word "love" is itself in need of re-vision.

There is a companion poem to "Orion," written three years later, in which at last the woman in the poem and the woman writing the poem become the same person. It is called "Planetarium," and it was written after a visit to a real planetarium, where I read an account of the work of Caroline Herschel, the astronomer, who worked with her brother William, but whose name remained obscure, as his did not.

Thinking of Caroline Herschel, 1750–1848,
astronomer, sister of William; and others

A woman in the shape of a monster
a monster in the shape of a woman
the skies are full of them

a woman   'in the snow
among the Clocks and instruments
or measuring the ground with poles'

in her 98 years to discover
8 comets

she whom the moon ruled
like us
levitating into the night sky
riding the polished lenses

Galaxies of women, there
doing penance for impetuousness
ribs chilled
in those spaces   of the mind

An eye,

     'virile, precise and absolutely certain'
from the mad webs of Uranusborg

                    encountering the NOVA

every impulse of light exploding
from the core
as life flies out of us

     Tycho whispering at last
     'Let me not seem to have lived in vain'

What we see, we see
and seeing is changing

the light that shrivels a mountain
and leaves a man alive

> Heartbeat of the pulsar
> heart sweating through my body
>
> The radio impulse
> pouring in from Taurus
>
>   I am bombarded yet   I stand
>
> I have been standing all my life in the
> direct path of a battery of signals
> the most accurately transmitted most
> untranslateable language in the universe
> I am a galactic cloud so deep   so invo-
> luted that a light wave could take 15
> years to travel through me   And has
> taken   I am an instrument in the shape
> of a woman trying to translate pulsations
> into images   for the relief of the body
> and the reconstruction of the mind.

In closing I want to tell you about a dream I had last summer. I dreamed I was asked to read my poetry at a mass women's meeting, but when I began to read, what came out were the lyrics of a blues song. I share this dream with you because it seemed to me to say something about the problems and the future of the woman writer, and probably of women in general. The awakening of consciousness is not like the crossing of a frontier—one step and you are in another country. Much of woman's poetry has been of the nature of the blues song: a cry of pain, of victimization, or a lyric of seduction.[7] And today, much poetry by women—and prose for that matter—is charged with anger. I think we need to go through that anger, and we will betray our own reality if we try, as Virginia Woolf was trying, for an objectivity, a detachment, that would make us sound more like Jane Austen or Shakespeare. We know more than Jane Austen or Shakespeare knew: more than Jane Austen because our lives are more complex, more than Shakespeare because we know more about the lives of women—Jane Austen and Virginia Woolf included.

Both the victimization and the anger experienced by women are real, and have real sources, everywhere in the environment, built into society, language, the structures of thought. They will go on being trapped and explored by poets, among others. We can neither deny them, nor will we rest there. A new generation of women poets is already working out of the psychic energy released when women begin to move out towards what the feminist philosopher Mary Daly has described as the "new space" on the boundaries of patriarchy.[8] Women are speaking to and of women in these poems, out of a newly released courage to name, to love each other, to share risk and grief and celebration.

To the eye of a feminist, the work of Western male poets now writing reveals a deep, fatalistic pessimism as to the possibilities of change, whether societal or personal, along with a familiar and threadbare use of women (and nature) as redemptive on the one hand, threatening on the other; and a new tide of phallocentric sadism and overt woman-hating which matches the sexual brutality of recent films. "Political" poetry by men remains stranded amid the struggles for power among male groups; in condemning U.S. imperialism or the Chilean junta the poet can claim to speak for the oppressed while remaining, as male, part of a system of sexual oppression. The enemy is always outside the self, the struggle somewhere else. The mood of isolation, self-pity, and self-imitation that pervades "nonpolitical" poetry suggests that a profound change in masculine consciousness will have to precede any new male poetic—or other—inspiration. The creative energy of patriarchy is fast running out; what remains is its self-generating energy for destruction. As women, we have our work cut out for us.

NOTES

[1] Mary Daly, *Beyond God the Father* (Boston: Beacon, 1973), pp. 40–41.

[2] G. B. Shaw, *The Quintessence of Ibsenism* (New York: Hill & Wang, 1922), p. 139.

[3] J. G. Stewart, *Jane Ellen Harrison: A Portrait from Letters* (London: Merlin, 1959), p. 140.

[4] Henry James, "Notes on Novelists," in *Selected Literary Criticism of Henry James*, Morris Shapira, ed. (London: Heinemann, 1963), pp. 157–58.

[5] *A. R., 1978*: This intuition of mine was corroborated when, early in 1978, I read the correspondence between Woolf and Dame Ethel Smyth (Henry W. and Albert A. Berg Collection, The New York Public Library, Astor, Lenox and Tilden Foundations); in a letter dated June 8, 1933, Woolf speaks of having kept her own personality out of *A Room of One's Own* lest she not be taken seriously: ". . . how personal, so will they say, rubbing their hands with glee, women always are; *I even hear them as I write.*" (Italics mine.)

[6] *A. R., 1978*: Yet I spent months, at sixteen, memorizing and writing imitations of Millay's sonnets; and in notebooks of that period I find what are obviously attempts to imitate Dickinson's metrics and verbal compression. I knew H. D. only through anthologized lyrics; her epic poetry was not then available to me.

[7] *A. R., 1978*: When I dreamed that dream, was I wholly ignorant of the tradition of Bessie Smith and other women's blues lyrics which transcended victimization to sing of resistance and independence?

[8] Mary Daly, *Beyond God the Father: Towards a Philosophy of Women's Liberation* (Boston: Beacon, 1973).

Sources

from *Your Native Land, Your Life*

I

Sixteen years.   The narrow, rough-gullied backroads
almost the same.   The farms: almost the same,
a new barn here, a new roof there, a rusting car,
collapsed sugar-house, trailer, new young wife
trying to make a lawn instead of a dooryard,
new names, old kinds of names: Rocquette, Desmarais,
Clark, Pierce, Stone.   Gossier.   No names of mine.

The vixen I met at twilight on Route 5
south of Willoughby: long dead.   She was an omen
to me, surviving, herding her cubs
in the silvery bend of the road
in nineteen sixty-five.

Shapes of things: so much the same
they feel like eternal forms: the house and barn
on the rise above May Pond; the brow of Pisgah;
the face of milkweed blooming,
brookwater pleating over slanted granite,
boletus under pine, the half-composted needles
it broke through patterned on its skin.
Shape of queen anne's lace, with the drop of blood.
Bladder-campion veined with purple.
Multifoliate heal-all.

II

I refuse to become a seeker for cures.
Everything that has ever
helped me has come through what already
lay stored in me.   Old things, diffuse, unnamed, lie strong
across my heart.
                              This is from where
my strength comes, even when I miss my strength
even when it turns on me
like a violent master.

III

From where?   the voice asks coldly.

This is the voice in cold morning air
that pierces dreams.   *From where does your strength come?*

Old things . . .
                              From where does your strength come, you Southern Jew?
split at the root, raised in a castle of air?

Yes.   I expected this.   I have known for years
the question was coming.   *From where*

(not from these, surely,
Protestant separatists, Jew-baiters, nightriders

who fired in Irasburg in nineteen-sixty-eight
on a black family newly settled in these hills)
                                                            From where

the dew grows thick late August on the fierce green grass
and on the wooden sill and on the stone

the mountains stand in an extraordinary
point of no return   though still are green

collapsed shed-boards gleam like pewter in the dew
the realms of touch-me-not   fiery with tiny tongues

cover the wild ground of the woods

IV

With whom do you believe your lot is cast?
From where does your strength come?

I think somehow, somewhere
every poem of mine must repeat those questions

which are not the same.   There is a *whom*, a *where*
that is not chosen   that is given   and sometimes falsely given

in the beginning we grasp whatever we can
to survive

V

All during World War II
I told myself I had some special destiny:
there had to be a reason
I was not living in a bombed-out house
or cellar   hiding out with rats

there had to be a reason
I was growing up safe, American
with sugar rationed in a Mason jar

split at the root   white-skinned social christian
neither gentile nor Jew

through the immense silence
of the Holocaust

I had no idea of what I had been spared

still less of the women and men   my kin
the Jews of Vicksburg or Birmingham
whose lives must have been strategies no less
than the vixen's on Route 5

VI

If they had played the flute, or chess
I was told   I was not told what they told
their children when the Klan rode
how they might have seen themselves

                                        a chosen people
of shopkeepers
clinging by strategy to a way of life
that had its own uses for them

proud of their length of sojourn in America
deploring the late-comers   the peasants from Russia

I saw my father building
his rootless ideology

his private castle in air

in that most dangerous place, the family home
we were the chosen people

In the beginning we grasp whatever we can

VII

For years I struggled with you: your categories, your theories, your
will, the cruelty which came inextricable from your love.   For years all arguments I carried on in my head were with you.   I saw myself, the eldest
daughter raised as a son, taught to study but not to pray, taught to hold
reading and writing sacred: the eldest daughter in a house with no son, she
who must overthrow the father, take what he taught her and use it against
him.   All this in a castle of air, the floating world of the assimilated who
know and deny they will always be aliens.

After your death I met you again as the face of patriarchy, could name
at last precisely the principle you embodied, there was an ideology at last
which let me dispose of you, identify the suffering you caused, hate you
righteously as part of a system, the kingdom of the fathers.   I saw the
power and arrogance of the male as your true watermark; I did not see
beneath it the suffering of the Jew, the alien stamp you bore, because you
had deliberately arranged that it should be invisible to me.   It is only now,
under a powerful, womanly lens, that I can decipher your suffering and
deny no part of my own.

XVIII

There is something more than self-hatred. That still outlives
these photos of the old Ashkenazi life:
we are gifted children at camp in the country
or orphaned children in kindergarten

we are hurrying along the rare book dealers' street
with the sunlight striking one side
we are walking the wards of the Jewish hospital
along diagonal squares   young serious nurses
we are part of a family group
formally taken in 1936
with tables, armchairs, ferns
(behind us, in our lives, the muddy street
and the ragged shames
the street-musician, the weavers lined for strike)
we are part of a family wearing white head-bandages
we were beaten in a pogrom

The place where all tracks end
is the place where history was meant to stop
but does not stop   where thinking
was meant to stop but does not stop
where the pattern was meant to give way at last
                                        but only

becomes a different pattern
                            terrible, threadbare
strained   familiar   on-going

XX

The faithful drudging child
the child at the oak desk whose penmanship,
hard work, style will win her prizes
becomes the woman with a mission, not to win prizes
but to change the laws of history.
How she gets this mission
is not clear, how the boundaries of perfection
explode, leaving her cheekbone grey with smoke
a piece of her hair singed off, her shirt
spattered with earth . . . Say that she grew up in a house
with talk of books, ideal societies —
she is gripped by a blue, a foreign air,
a desert absolute: dragged by the roots of her own will
into another scene of choices.

XXII

I have resisted this for years, writing to you as if you could hear me.   It's
been different with my father: he and I always had a kind of rhetoric
going with each other, a battle between us, it didn't matter if one of us was
alive or dead.   But, you, I've had a sense of protecting your existence, not
using it merely as a theme for poetry or tragic musings; letting you dwell in
the minds of those who have reason to miss you, in your way, or their way,

not mine. The living, writers especially, are terrible projectionists. I hate the way they use the dead.

Yet I can't finish this without speaking to you, not simply of you. You knew there was more left than food and humor. Even as you said that in 1953 I knew it was a formula you had found, to stand between you and pain. The deep crevices of black pumpernickel under the knife, the sweet butter and red onions we ate on those slices; the lox and cream cheese on fresh onion rolls; bowls of sour cream mixed with cut radishes, cucumber, scallions; green tomatoes and kosher dill pickles in half-translucent paper; these, you said, were the remnants of the culture, along with the fresh *challah* which turned stale so fast but looked so beautiful.

That's why I want to speak to you now. To say: no person, trying to take responsibility for her or his identity, should have to be so alone. There must be those among whom we can sit down and weep, and still be counted as warriors. (I make up this strange, angry packet for you, threaded with love.) I think you thought there was no such place for you, and perhaps there was none then, and perhaps there is none now; but we will have to make it, we who want an end to suffering, who want to change the laws of history, if we are not to *give ourselves away.*

XXIII

I have wished I could rest among the beautiful and common weeds I can name, both here and in other tracts of the globe. But there is no finite knowing, no such rest. Innocent birds, deserts, morning-glories, point to choices, leading away from the familiar. When I speak of an end to suffering I don't mean anesthesia. I mean knowing the world, and my place in it, not in order to stare with bitterness or detachment, but as a powerful and womanly series of choices: and here I write the words, in their fullness: powerful;   womanly.

August 1981–August 1982

•   •   •   •   •   •   •   •   •   •   •

QUESTIONS FOR A SECOND READING

1. Rich says, "We need to know the writing of the past, and know it differently than we have ever known it; not to pass on a tradition but to break its hold over us." In what ways does this essay, as an example of a woman writing, both reproduce and revise the genre? As she is writing here, what does Rich *do* with the writing of the past—with the conventions of the essay or the public lecture? As you reread the essay, mark sections that illustrate the ways Rich is either reproducing or revising the conventions of the essay or the public lecture. Where and how does she revise the genre? Where and how does she not? Where does Rich resist tradition? Where does she conform? How might you account for the differences?

2. It is a rare pleasure to hear a poet talk in detail about her work. As you read back through the essay, pay particular attention to what Rich notices in her poems. What *does* she notice? What does she say about what she notices? What does this allow you to say about poems or the making of poems? What does it allow you to say about the responsibilities of a reader?

3. As Rich writes her essay, she refers to a number of literary figures like Morgan, Lytton, and Maynard Keynes, Lucy and Lenore and Maude Gonne, and Plath, Bishop, and Wakoski. Reading through her essay again, make a complete list of the names Rich draws into her discussion. Who are these people? The Internet will certainly provide links to sources that will help to answer this question. You might also use this moment as the occasion to get into the college or university library; if you do, be sure to meet with a reference librarian. A reference librarian is a person who is paid a salary to help you make efficient use of a research library's quite amazing materials and resources.

   Once you've identified the names on your list, the next question to consider is how this knowledge influences your reading of Rich. What does each individual represent that merits her or his inclusion? To answer this question you will need to have located and read through at least one text by the individuals—one "primary source," that is—or one text about the individuals—a "secondary source"—you are researching. Why might Rich have chosen to include particular references at particular moments? What differences do they make in her arguments? in your reading of her arguments?

4. "When We Dead Awaken: Writing as Re-Vision" was written in 1971. The poem "Planetarium," the last of those she uses as an example (p. 531), was written in (or around) 1968. The work does not end there, however. Rich has had, and she continues to have, a productive career as a writer. An interesting project would be to read and study poems from a later point in her career. To serve that project we have included a long section from her 1986 book, *Your Native Land, Your Life*, poems that continue to think about her father and her connections to her past. To begin, reread the essay with particular attention to the trajectory indicated by her treatment of the three poems she offers as examples of "re-vision": the excerpt from "Snapshots of a Daughter-in-Law" (p. 529), "Orion" (p. 530), and "Planetarium" (p. 531). Think about the direction that is implied, the questions that are raised, and how those questions relate not only to subject matter but to point of view, form, and style. (If a larger project were appropriate, you could go to the library to find other books of hers and, perhaps, to find reviews of those books. The reviews will give you another reader's, perhaps another poet's, sense of what is happening in her poetry as she moves from book to book.) Prepare a discussion for class that considers that later work as a continuation of the process of "re-vision" as defined in the essay.

ASSIGNMENTS FOR WRITING

1. Rich says,

   > For a poem to coalesce, for a character or an action to take shape, there has to be an imaginative transformation of reality which is in no way passive. . . . Moreover, if the imagination is to transcend and transform experience it has to question, to challenge, to conceive of alternatives,

> perhaps to the very life you are living at that moment. You have to be
> free to play around with the notion that day might be night, love might
> be hate; nothing can be too sacred for the imagination to turn into its op-
> posite or to call experimentally by another name. For writing is renam-
> ing. (p. 528)

This is powerful language, and it is interesting to imagine how it might
work for a person trying to read and understand one of Rich's poems. For
this assignment, begin with a close reading of the quotation from Rich:
What is your understanding of her term "imaginative transformation"?
What does it allow a writer to do? And why might that be important? Then,
as a way of testing Rich's term and your reading of it, choose one of the
poems Rich includes in the essay and write an essay of your own that considers the poem as an act of "imaginative transformation." What is transformed into what? and to what end? or to what consequence? What can you
say about the poem as an act of "renaming"? as a form of political action?

2. In "When We Dead Awaken: Writing as Re-Vision," Rich chooses five of
   her poems to represent stages in her history as a poet; however, it is a history not charted entirely (or mostly) by conscious decisions on her part as
   she tells us when she writes: "poems are like dreams: in them you put what
   you don't know you know." It is through the act of "re-vision"—of entering
   the old text of her poems from a new critical direction—that patterns in her
   work as a writer begin to emerge.

   Write an essay in which you explore Rich's term—"re-vision"—by describing what you consider to be a significant pattern of change in Rich's
   poems. As you do this work, you will want to attend closely to and quote
   from the language of her poems and what she has to say about them. You
   might want to consider such questions as: How does her explanation of
   herself as a poet inform your reading of her poems? What did she put into
   her poems that she didn't yet know on a conscious level? What does her poetry reveal about the evolution of Rich as a poet? as a woman?

3. > I have hesitated to do what I am going to do now, which is to use myself
   > as an illustration. For one thing, it's a lot easier and less dangerous to
   > talk about other[s]. (p. 524)
   >
   > Until we can understand the assumptions in which we are drenched we
   > cannot know ourselves. (p. 522)

   Although Rich tells a story of her own, she does so to provide an illustration of an even larger story—one about what it means to be a woman and a
   writer. Tell a story of your own about the ways you might be said to have
   been named or shaped or positioned by an established and powerful culture. Like Rich does (and perhaps with similar hesitation), use your own
   experience as an illustration, as a way of investigating both your own situation and the situation of people like you. You should imagine that this assignment is a way for you to use (and put to the test) some of Rich's terms,
   words like "re-vision," "renaming," and "structure." You might also want to
   consider defining key terms specific to your story (for Rich, for example, a
   defining term is "patriarchy").

4. Rich says, "We need to know the writing of the past, and know it differently than we have ever known it; not to pass on a tradition but to break its

hold over us." That "us" includes you too. Look back over your own writing (perhaps the drafts and revisions you have written for this course), and think back over comments teachers have made, textbooks you've seen; think about what student writers do and what they are told to do, about the secrets students keep and the secrets teachers keep. You can assume, as Rich does, that there are ways of speaking about writing that are part of the culture of schooling and that they are designed to preserve certain ways of writing and thinking and to discourage others.

One might argue, in other words, that there are traditions here. As you look at the evidence of the "past" in your own work, what are its significant features? What might you name this tradition (or these traditions)? How would you illustrate its hold on your work or the work of students generally? What might you have to do to begin to "know it differently," "to break its hold," or to revise? And, finally, why would someone want (or not want) to break its hold?

5. Reread the essay "When We Dead Awaken" so that it can provide a framework as you read the poems from *Your Native Land, Your Life.* As you reread, pay particular attention to the trajectory indicated by her treatment of the three poems she offers as examples of "re-vision": the excerpt from "Snapshots of a Daughter-in-Law" (p. 529), "Orion" (p. 530), and "Planetarium" (p. 531). And remember the dates: "When We Dead Awaken" was written in 1971; "Split at the Root" was written in 1982; the poems from *Your Native Land, Your Life* date from around 1986. You should be sure to attend to changes in form, style, and presentation as well as to variations in subject matter and point of view.

Write an essay in which you think *from* "When We Dead Awaken" *to* these later poems. You could imagine that you are extending the original essay, adding paragraphs to the end of the discussion of the poems. That discussion is followed by the essay's conclusion: "In closing, I want to tell you about a dream I had last summer." You might also consider how Rich might have revised the conclusion. Or you could use these poems to be in conversation with the Rich of "When We Dead Awaken," in dialogue with her and with her argument, thinking about what she is not yet ready or willing or able to say, to think, or to do.

MAKING CONNECTIONS

1. Adrienne Rich in "When We Dead Awaken: Writing as Re-Vision," Susan Griffin in "Our Secret" (p. 299), John Edgar Wideman in "Our Time" (p. 681), and Cornelius Eady in "Brutal Imagination" (p. 184) use a life story to think about and to represent forces beyond the individual that shape life and possibility—patriarchy, war, race, and ethnicity. Susan Griffin explains her motive this way, "One can find traces of every life in each life." Perhaps. It is a bold step to think that this is true and to believe that one can, or should, use autobiography as a way to understand the national or international narrative. Write an essay in which you read "When We Dead Awaken" alongside one of the other essays. Your goal is not only to discuss how these writers do what they do, and to what conclusions and to

what ends, but also to discuss your sense of what is at stake in such a project. What are the technical issues? How does a skilled writer handle this project? What would lead a writer to write something like this? Would you do it? where and how? for whose benefit?

2. Susan Bordo and Gloria Anzaldúa make strong statements about gender and identity—in relation to the past, to language and image, to politics and culture. Look back over the selections from them included here and choose one to reread alongside "When We Dead Awaken." As you read, mark passages that you might use in your writing and, when you are done, write an essay in which you consider the interesting *differences* in these two essays—in what they say and in how they say what they say (assuming that each enacts as well as argues a position for a woman as a writer). You might consider the essays as different forms or schools of thought on gender, different ways of thinking critically about the way men and women are positioned as men and women. Assume that there is more to say than that "different people have different opinions." How else might you account for these differences?

3.   The truth is, however, that the oppressed are not "marginals," are not
         men living "outside" society. They have always been "inside"—inside
         the structure which made them "beings for others." The solution is
         not to "integrate" them into the structure of oppression, but to trans-
         form that structure so that they can become "beings for themselves."
         Such transformation, of course, would undermine the oppressors' pur-
         poses. . . . (p. 246)

                              —PAULO FREIRE
                              The "Banking" Concept of Education

         For a poem to coalesce, for a character or an action to take shape, there
         has to be an imaginative transformation of reality which is in no way
         passive. . . . Moreover, if the imagination is to transcend and transform
         experience it has to question, to challenge, to conceive of alternatives,
         perhaps to the very life you are living at that moment. You have to be
         free to play around with the notion that day might be night, love might
         be hate; nothing can be too sacred for the imagination to turn into its op-
         posite or to call experimentally by another name. For writing is renam-
         ing. (p. 528)

                              —ADRIENNE RICH
                              When We Dead Awaken: Writing as Re-Vision

    Both Freire and Rich talk repeatedly about transformations—about transforming structures, transforming the world, transforming the way language is used, transforming the relations between people. In fact, the changes in Rich's poetry might be seen as evidence of her transforming the structures from within which she worked. And, when Freire takes a situation we think of as "natural" (teachers talking and students sitting silent) and names it "banking education," he makes it possible for students and their teachers to question, challenge, conceive of alternatives, and transform experience. Each, in other words, can be framed as an example in the language of the other—Freire in Rich's terms, Rich in Freire's. For both, this act of transformation is something that takes place within and through the use of language.

Rich's essay could be read as a statement about the aims of education, particularly if the changes in her work are taken as evidence of something the poet learned to do. Rich talks about teachers, about people who helped her to reimagine her situation as a woman and a poet, and about the work she had to do on her own.

For this assignment, take three of the poems Rich offers as examples of change in her writing—"Aunt Jennifer's Tigers," the section from "Snapshots of a Daughter-in-Law," and "Planetarium," as well as the additional poems reprinted in "Sources" from *Your Native Land, Your Life*—and use them as a way of talking about revision. What, to your mind, are the key differences among these poems? What might the movement they mark be said to represent? And what do these poems, as examples, have to do with the argument about writing, culture, and gender in the rest of the essay?

As you prepare to write, you might also ask some questions in Freire's name. For example: What problems did Rich pose for herself? How might this be taken as an example of a problem-posing education? In what ways might Rich be said to have been having a "dialogue" with her own work? Who was the teacher (or the teachers) here and what did the poet learn to do?

You are not alone as you read these poems, in other words. In fact, Rich provides her own commentary on the three poems, noting what for her are key changes and what they represent. You will want to acknowledge what Rich has to say, to be sure, but you should not be bound by it. You, too, are a person with a point of view on this issue. Rich (with Freire) provides a powerful language for talking about change, but be sure to carve out space where you have the opportunity to speak as well.

RICHARD
RODRIGUEZ

RICHARD RODRIGUEZ, the son of Mexican immi-grants, was born in San Francisco in 1944. He grew up in Sacramento, where he attended Catholic schools before going on to Stanford University, Columbia University, the Warburg Institute in London, and the University of Cali-fornia at Berkeley, eventually completing a PhD in English Renaissance literature. His essays have been published in Saturday Review, The American Scholar, Change, *and elsewhere. He now lives in San Francisco and works as a lecturer, educational consultant, and freelance writer. He has published several books:* Brown: The Last Discovery of America *(2002),* Days of Obligation: An Argument with My Mexican Father *(1992),* The Ethics of Change *(1992), and* Hunger of Memory *(1981).*

In Hunger of Memory, *a book of autobiographical essays that the* Christian Science Monitor *called "beautifully written, wrung from a sore heart," Rod-riguez tells the story of his education, paying particular attention to both the mean-ing of his success as a student and, as he says, "its consequent price—the loss." Rodriguez's loss is represented most powerfully by his increased alienation from his parents and the decrease of intimate exchanges in family life. His parents' pri-mary language was Spanish; his, once he became eager for success in school, was*

English. *But the barrier was not only a language barrier. Rodriguez discovered that the interests he developed at school and through his reading were interests he did not share with those at home—in fact, his desire to speak of them tended to threaten and humiliate his mother and father.*

This separation, Rodriguez argues, is a necessary part of every person's development, even though not everyone experiences it so dramatically. We must leave home and familiar ways of speaking and understanding in order to participate in public life. On these grounds, Rodriguez has been a strong voice against bilingual education, arguing that classes conducted in Spanish will only reinforce Spanish-speaking students' separateness from mainstream American life. Rodriguez's book caused a great deal of controversy upon publication, particularly in the Hispanic community. As one critic argued, "It is indeed painful that Mr. Rodriguez has come to identify himself so completely with the majority culture that he must propagandize for a system of education which can only produce other deprived and impoverished souls like himself." In his second book, Days of Obligation: An Argument with My Mexican Father, *Rodriguez continues to explore his relationship with his family and with his Mexican heritage; here, however, he also writes of his life as a gay male and the forms of alienation entailed by his sexuality, including his sense of distance from gay lifestyles and culture, both popular and academic.*

The selection that follows, Chapter 2 of Hunger of Memory, *deals with Rodriguez's experiences in school. "If," he says, "because of my schooling I had grown culturally separated from my parents, my education finally had given me ways of speaking and caring about that fact." This essay is a record of how he came to understand the changes in his life. A reviewer writing in the* Atlantic Monthly *concluded that* Hunger of Memory *will survive in our literature "not because of some forgotten public issues that once bisected Richard Rodriguez's life, but because his history of that life has something to say about what it means to be American . . . and what it means to be human."*

The Achievement of Desire

I stand in the ghetto classroom—"the guest speaker"—attempting to lecture on the mystery of the sounds of our words to rows of diffident students. "Don't you hear it? Listen! The music of our words. *'Sumer is icumen in. . . .'* And songs on the car radio. We need Aretha Franklin's voice to fill plain words with music—her life." In the face of their empty stares, I try to create an enthusiasm. But the girls in the back row turn to watch some boy passing outside. There are flutters of smiles, waves. And someone's mouth elongates heavy, silent words through the barrier of glass. Silent words— the lips straining to shape each voiceless syllable: *"Meet meee late errr."* By the door, the instructor smiles at me, apparently hoping that I will be able to spark some enthusiasm in the class. But only one student seems to be listening. A girl, maybe fourteen. In this gray room her eyes shine with ambition. She keeps nodding and nodding at all that I say; she even takes notes. And each time I ask a question, she jerks up and down in her desk like a marionette, while her hand waves over the bowed heads of her classmates. It is myself (as a boy) I see as she faces me now (a man in my thirties).

The boy who first entered a classroom barely able to speak English, twenty years later concluded his studies in the stately quiet of the reading room in the British Museum. Thus with one sentence I can summarize my academic career. It will be harder to summarize what sort of life connects the boy to the man.

With every award, each graduation from one level of education to the next, people I'd meet would congratulate me. Their refrain [was] always the same: "Your parents must be very proud." Sometimes then they'd ask me how I managed it—my "success." (How?) After a while, I had several quick answers to give in reply. I'd admit, for one thing, that I went to an excellent grammar school. (My earliest teachers, the nuns, made my success their ambition.) And my brother and both my sisters were very good students. (They often brought home the shiny school trophies I came to want.) And my mother and father always encouraged me. (At every graduation they were behind the stunning flash of the camera when I turned to look at the crowd.)

As important as these factors were, however, they account inadequately for my academic advance. Nor do they suggest what an odd success I managed. For although I was a very good student, I was also a very bad student. I was a "scholarship boy," a certain kind of scholarship boy. Always successful, I was always unconfident. Exhilarated by my progress. Sad. I became the prized student—anxious and eager to learn. Too eager, too anxious—an imitative and unoriginal pupil. My brother and two sisters enjoyed the advantages I did, and they grew to be as successful as I, but none of them ever seemed so anxious about their schooling. A second-grade student, I was the one who came home and corrected the "simple" grammatical mistakes of our parents. ("Two negatives make a positive.") Proudly I announced—to my family's startled silence—that a teacher had said I was losing all trace of a Spanish accent. I was oddly annoyed when I was unable to get parental help with a homework assignment. The night my father tried to help me with an arithmetic exercise, he kept reading the instructions, each time more deliberately, until I pried the textbook out of his hands, saying, "I'll try to figure it out some more by myself."

When I reached the third grade, I outgrew such behavior. I became more tactful, careful to keep separate the two very different worlds of my day. But then, with ever-increasing intensity, I devoted myself to my studies. I became bookish, puzzling to all my family. Ambition set me apart. When my brother saw me struggling home with stacks of library books, he would laugh, shouting: "Hey, Four Eyes!" My father opened a closet one day and was startled to find me inside, reading a novel. My mother would find me reading when I was supposed to be asleep or helping around the house or playing outside. In a voice angry or worried or just curious, she'd ask: "What do you see in your books?" It became the family's joke. When I was called and wouldn't reply, someone would say I must be hiding under my bed with a book.

(How did I manage my success?)

What I am about to say to you has taken me more than twenty years to admit: *A primary reason for my success in the classroom was that I couldn't forget that schooling was changing me and separating me from the life I enjoyed before becoming a student.* That simple realization! For years I never spoke to anyone about it. Never mentioned a thing to my family or my teachers or classmates. From a very early age, I understood enough, just enough about my classroom experiences to keep what I knew repressed, hidden beneath layers of embarrassment. Not until my last months as a graduate student, nearly thirty years old, was it possible for me to think much about the reasons for my academic success. Only then. At the end of my schooling, I needed to determine how far I had moved from my past. The adult finally confronted, and now must publicly say, what the child shuddered from knowing and could never admit to himself or to those many faces that smiled at his every success. ("Your parents must be very proud. . . .")

I

At the end, in the British Museum (too distracted to finish my dissertation) for weeks I read, speed-read, books by modern educational theorists, only to find infrequent and slight mention of students like me. (Much more is written about the more typical case, the lower-class student who barely is helped by his schooling.) Then one day, leafing through Richard Hoggart's *The Uses of Literacy*, I found, in his description of the scholarship boy, myself. For the first time I realized that there were other students like me, and so I was able to frame the meaning of my academic success, its consequent price—the loss.

Hoggart's description is distinguished, at least initially, by deep understanding. What he grasps very well is that the scholarship boy must move between environments, his home and the classroom, which are at cultural extremes, opposed. With his family, the boy has the intense pleasure of intimacy, the family's consolation in feeling public alienation. Lavish emotions texture home life. *Then*, at school, the instruction bids him to trust lonely reason primarily. Immediate needs set the pace of his parents' lives. From his mother and father the boy learns to trust spontaneity and nonrational ways of knowing. *Then*, at school, there is mental calm. Teachers emphasize the value of a reflectiveness that opens a space between thinking and immediate action.

Years of schooling must pass before the boy will be able to sketch the cultural differences in his day as abstractly as this. But he senses those differences early. Perhaps as early as the night he brings home an assignment from school and finds the house too noisy for study.

> He has to be more and more alone, if he is going to "get on." He will have, probably unconsciously, to oppose the ethos of the hearth, the intense gregariousness of the working-class family group. Since everything centres upon the living-room, there is unlikely to be a room of his own; the bedrooms are cold and inhospitable, and to warm them or the front room, if there is one, would not only be expensive, but would require an imaginative leap—out of the tradition—which most families are not capable of making. There is a corner of the living-room table. On the other side Mother is ironing, the wireless is on, someone is singing a snatch of song or Father says intermittently whatever comes into his head. The boy has to cut himself off mentally, so as to do his homework, as well as he can.[1]

The next day, the lesson is as apparent at school. There are even rows of desks. Discussion is ordered. The boy must rehearse his thoughts and raise his hand before speaking out in a loud voice to an audience of classmates. And there is time enough, and silence, to think about ideas (big ideas) never considered at home by his parents.

Not for the working-class child alone is adjustment to the classroom difficult. Good schooling requires that any student alter early childhood habits. But the working-class child is usually least prepared for the change. And, unlike many middle-class children, he goes home and sees in his parents a way of life not only different but starkly opposed to that of the classroom. (He enters the house and hears his parents talking in ways his teachers discourage.)

Without extraordinary determination and the great assistance of others—at home and at school—there is little chance for success. Typically most working-class children are barely changed by the classroom. The exception succeeds. The relative few become scholarship students. Of these, Richard Hoggart estimates, most manage a fairly graceful transition. Somehow they learn to live in the two very different worlds of their day. There are some others, however, those Hoggart pejoratively terms "scholarship boys," for whom success comes with special anxiety. Scholarship boy: good student, troubled son. The child is "moderately endowed," intellectually mediocre, Hoggart supposes—though it may be more pertinent to note the special qualities of temperament in the child. High-strung child. Brooding. Sensitive. Haunted by the knowledge that one *chooses* to become a student. (Education is not an inevitable or natural step in growing up.) Here is a child who cannot forget that his academic success distances him from a life he loved, even from his own memory of himself.

Initially, he wavers, balances allegiance. ("The boy is himself [until he reaches, say, the upper forms] very much of *both* the worlds of home and school. He is enormously obedient to the dictates of the world of school, but emotionally still strongly wants to continue as part of the family circle.") Gradually, necessarily, the balance is lost. The boy needs to spend more and more time studying, each night enclosing himself in the silence permitted and required by intense concentration. He takes his first step toward academic success, away from his family.

From the very first days, through the years following, it will be with his parents—the figures of lost authority, the persons toward whom he feels deepest love—that the change will be most powerfully measured. A separation will unravel between them. Advancing in his studies, the boy notices that his mother and father have not changed as much as he. Rather, when he sees them, they often remind him of the person he once was and the life he earlier shared with them. He realizes what some Romantics also know when they praise the working class for the capacity for human closeness, qualities of passion and spontaneity, that the rest of us experience in like measure only in the earliest part of our youth. For the Romantic, this doesn't make working-class life childish. Working-class life challenges precisely because it is an *adult* way of life.

The scholarship boy reaches a different conclusion. He cannot afford to admire his parents. (How could he and still pursue such a contrary life?) He permits himself embarrassment at their lack of education. And to evade nostalgia for the life he has lost, he concentrates on the benefits education will bestow upon him. He becomes especially ambitious. Without the support of old certainties and consolations, almost mechanically, he assumes the procedures and doctrines of the classroom. The kind of allegiance the young student might have given his mother and father only days earlier, he transfers to the teacher, the new figure of authority. "[The scholarship boy] tends to make a father-figure of his form-master," Hoggart observes.

But Hoggart's calm prose only makes me recall the urgency with which I came to idolize my grammar school teachers. I began by imitating their accents, using their diction, trusting their every direction. The very first facts they dispensed, I grasped with awe. Any book they told me to read, I read—then waited for them to tell me which books I enjoyed. Their every casual opinion I came to adopt and to trumpet when I returned home. I stayed after school "to help"—to get my teacher's undivided attention. It was the nun's encouragement that mattered most to me. (She understood exactly what—my parents never seemed to appraise so well—all my achievements entailed.) Memory gently caressed each word of praise bestowed in the classroom so that compliments teachers paid me years ago come quickly to mind even today.

The enthusiasm I felt in second-grade classes I flaunted before both my parents. The docile, obedient student came home a shrill and precocious son who insisted on correcting and teaching his parents with the remark: "My teacher told us. . . ."

I intended to hurt my mother and father. I was still angry at them for having encouraged me toward classroom English. But gradually this anger was exhausted, replaced by guilt as school grew more and more attractive to me. I grew increasingly successful, a talkative student. My hand was raised in the classroom; I yearned to answer any question. At home, life was less noisy than it had been. (I spoke to classmates and teachers more often each day than to family members.) Quiet at home, I sat with my papers for hours each night. I never forgot that schooling had irretrievably changed my family's life. That knowledge, however, did not weaken ambition. Instead, it strengthened resolve. Those times I remembered the loss of my past with regret, I quickly reminded myself of all the things my teachers could give me. (They could make me an educated man.) I tightened my grip on pencil and books. I evaded nostalgia. Tried hard to forget. But one does not forget by trying to forget. One only remembers. I remembered too well that education had changed my family's life. I would not have become a scholarship boy had I not so often remembered.

Once she was sure that her children knew English, my mother would tell us, "You should keep up your Spanish." Voices playfully groaned in response. "*¡Pochos!*" my mother would tease. I listened silently.

After a while, I grew more calm at home. I developed tact. A fourth-grade student, I was no longer the show-off in front of my parents. I became a conventionally dutiful son, politely affectionate, cheerful enough, even—for reasons beyond choosing—my father's favorite. And much about my family life was easy then, comfortable, happy in the rhythm of our living together: hearing my father getting ready for work; eating the breakfast my mother had made me; looking up from a novel to hear my brother or one of my sisters playing with friends in the backyard; in winter, coming upon the house all lighted up after dark.

But withheld from my mother and father was any mention of what most mattered to me: the extraordinary experience of first-learning. Late afternoon: in the midst of preparing dinner, my mother would come up behind me while I was trying to read. Her head just over mine, her breath warmly scented with food. "What are you reading?" Or, "Tell me all about your new courses." I would barely respond, "Just the usual things, nothing special." (A half smile, then silence. Her head moving back in the silence. Silence! Instead of the flood of intimate sounds that had once flowed smoothly between us, there was this silence.) After dinner, I would rush to a bedroom with papers and books. As often as possible, I resisted parental pleas to "save lights" by coming to the kitchen to work. I kept so much, so often, to myself. Sad. Enthusiastic. Troubled by the excitement of coming upon new ideas. Eager. Fascinated by the promising texture of a brand-new book. I hoarded the pleasures of learning. Alone for hours. Enthralled. Nervous. I rarely looked away from my books—or back on my memories. Nights when relatives visited and the front rooms were warmed by Spanish sounds, I slipped quietly out of the house.

It mattered that education was changing me. It never ceased to matter. My brother and sisters would giggle at our mother's mispronounced words. They'd correct her gently. My mother laughed girlishly one night, trying not to pronounce *sheep* as *ship*. From a distance I listened sullenly. From that distance, pretending not to notice on another occasion, I saw my father looking at the title pages of my library books. That was the scene on my mind when I walked home with a fourth-grade companion and heard him say that his parents read to him every night. (A strange-sounding book — *Winnie the Pooh.*) Immediately, I wanted to know, "What is it like?" My companion, however, thought I wanted to know about the plot of the book. Another day, my mother surprised me by asking for a "nice" book to read. "Something not too hard you think I might like." Carefully I chose one, Willa Cather's *My Ántonia.* But when, several weeks later, I happened to see it next to her bed unread except for the first few pages, I was furious and suddenly wanted to cry. I grabbed up the book and took it back to my room and placed it in its place, alphabetically on my shelf.

"Your parents must be very proud of you." People began to say that to me about the time I was in sixth grade. To answer affirmatively, I'd smile. Shyly I'd smile, never betraying my sense of the irony: I was not proud of my mother and father. I was embarrassed by their lack of education. It was not that I ever thought they were stupid, though stupidly I took for granted their enormous native intelligence. Simply, what mattered to me was that they were not like my teachers.

But, "Why didn't you tell us about the award?" my mother demanded, her frown weakened by pride. At the grammar school ceremony several weeks after, her eyes were brighter than the trophy I'd won. Pushing back the hair from my forehead, she whispered that I had "shown" the *gringos*. A few minutes later, I heard my father speak to my teacher and felt ashamed of his labored, accented words. Then guilty for the shame. I felt such contrary feelings. (There is no simple road-map through the heart of the scholarship boy.) My teacher was so soft-spoken and her words were edged sharp and clean. I admired her until it seemed to me that she spoke too carefully. Sensing that she was condescending to them, I became nervous. Resentful. Protective. I tried to move my parents away. "You both must be very proud of Richard," the nun said. They responded quickly. (They were proud.) "We are proud of all our children." Then this afterthought: "They sure didn't get their brains from us." They all laughed. I smiled.

Tightening the irony into a knot was the knowledge that my parents were always behind me. They made success possible. They evened the path. They sent their children to parochial schools because the nuns "teach better." They paid a tuition they couldn't afford. They spoke English to us.

For their children my parents wanted chances they never had — an easier way. It saddened my mother to learn that some relatives forced their children to start working right after high school. To *her* children she would say, "Get all the education you can." In schooling she recognized the key to job advancement. And with the remark she remembered her past.

As a girl new to America my mother had been awarded a high school diploma by teachers too careless or busy to notice that she hardly spoke English. On her own, she determined to learn how to type. That skill got her jobs typing envelopes in letter shops, and it encouraged in her an optimism about the possibility of advancement. (Each morning when her sisters put on uniforms, she chose a bright-colored dress.) The years of young womanhood passed, and her typing speed increased. She also became an excellent speller of words she mispronounced. "And I've never been to college," she'd say, smiling, when her children asked her to spell words they were too lazy to look up in a dictionary.

Typing, however, was dead-end work. Finally frustrating. When her youngest child started high school, my mother got a full-time office job once again. (Her paycheck combined with my father's to make us—in fact—what we had already become in our imagination of ourselves—middle class.) She worked then for the (California) state government in numbered civil service positions secured by examinations. The old ambition of her youth was rekindled. During the lunch hour, she consulted bulletin boards for announcements of openings. One day she saw mention of something called an "anti-poverty agency." A typing job. A glamorous job, part of the governor's staff. "A knowledge of Spanish required." Without hesitation she applied and became nervous only when the job was suddenly hers.

"Everyone comes to work all dressed up," she reported at night. And didn't need to say more than that her co-workers wouldn't let her answer the phones. She was only a typist, after all, albeit a very fast typist. And an excellent speller. One morning there was a letter to be sent to a Washington cabinet officer. On the dictating tape, a voice referred to urban guerrillas. My mother typed (the wrong word, correctly): "gorillas." The mistake horrified the anti-poverty bureaucrats who shortly after arranged to have her returned to her previous position. She would go no further. So she willed her ambition to their children. "Get all the education you can; with an education you can do anything." (With a good education *she* could have done anything.)

When I was in high school, I admitted to my mother that I planned to become a teacher someday. That seemed to please her. But I never tried to explain that it was not the occupation of teaching I yearned for as much as it was something more elusive: I wanted to *be* like my teachers, to possess their knowledge, to assume their authority, their confidence, even to assume a teacher's persona.

In contrast to my mother, my father never verbally encouraged his children's academic success. Nor did he often praise us. My mother had to remind him to "say something" to one of his children who scored some academic success. But whereas my mother saw in education the opportunity for job advancement, my father recognized that education provided an even more startling possibility: it could enable a person to escape from a life of mere labor.

In Mexico, orphaned when he was eight, my father left school to work as an "apprentice" for an uncle. Twelve years later, he left Mexico in frustration and arrived in America. He had great expectations then of becoming an engineer. ("Work for my hands and my head.") He knew a Catholic priest who promised to get him money enough to study full time for a high school diploma. But the promises came to nothing. Instead there was a dark succession of warehouse, cannery, and factory jobs. After work he went to night school along with my mother. A year, two passed. Nothing much changed, except that fatigue worked its way into the bone; then everything changed. He didn't talk anymore of becoming an engineer. He stayed outside on the steps of the school while my mother went inside to learn typing and shorthand.

By the time I was born, my father worked at "clean" jobs. For a time he was a janitor at a fancy department store. ("Easy work; the machines do it all.") Later he became a dental technician. ("Simple.") But by then he was pessimistic about the ultimate meaning of work and the possibility of ever escaping its claims. In some of my earliest memories of him, my father already seems aged by fatigue. (He has never really grown old like my mother.) From boyhood to manhood, I have remembered him in a single image: seated, asleep on the sofa, his head thrown back in a hideous corpselike grin, the evening newspaper spread out before him. "But look at all you've accomplished," his best friend said to him once. My father said nothing. Only smiled.

It was my father who laughed when I claimed to be tired by reading and writing. It was he who teased me for having soft hands. (He seemed to sense that some great achievement of leisure was implied by my papers and books.) It was my father who became angry while watching on television some woman at the Miss America contest tell the announcer that she was going to college. ("Majoring in fine arts.") "College!" he snarled. He despised the trivialization of higher education, the inflated grades and cheapened diplomas, the half education that so often passed as mass education in my generation.

It was my father again who wondered why I didn't display my awards on the wall of my bedroom. He said he liked to go to doctors' offices and see their certificates and degrees on the wall. ("Nice.") My citations from school got left in closets at home. The gleaming figure astride one of my trophies was broken, wingless, after hitting the ground. My medals were placed in a jar of loose change. And when I lost my high school diploma, my father found it as it was about to be thrown out with the trash. Without telling me, he put it away with his own things for safe-keeping.

These memories slammed together at the instant of hearing that refrain familiar to all scholarship students: "Your parents must be proud. . . ." Yes, my parents were proud. I knew it. But my parents regarded my progress with more than mere pride. They endured my early precocious behavior—but with what private anger and humiliation? As their children got older and would come home to challenge ideas both of them held, they argued before submitting to the force of logic or superior factual evidence with the disclaimer, "It's what we were taught in our time to believe." These discussions ended abruptly, though my mother remembered them on other occasions when she complained that our "big ideas" were going to our heads. More acute was her complaint that the family wasn't close anymore, like some others she knew. Why weren't we close, "more in the Mexican style"? Everyone is so private, she added. And she mimicked the yes and no answers she got in reply to her questions. Why didn't we talk more? (My father never asked.) I never said.

I was the first in my family who asked to leave home when it came time to go to college. I had been admitted to Stanford, one hundred miles away. My departure would only make physically apparent the separation that had occurred long before. But it was going too far. In the months preceding my leaving, I heard the question my mother never asked except indirectly. In the hot kitchen, tired at the end of her workday, she demanded to know, "Why aren't the colleges here in Sacramento good enough for you? They are for your brother and sister." In the middle of a car ride, not turning to face me, she wondered, "Why do you need to go so far away?" Late at night, ironing, she said with disgust, "Why do you have to put us through this big expense? You know your scholarship will never cover it all." But when September came there was a rush to get everything ready. In a bedroom that last night I packed the big brown valise, and my mother sat nearby sewing initials onto the clothes I would take. And she said no more about my leaving.

Months later, two weeks of Christmas vacation: the first hours home were the hardest. ("What's new?") My parents and I sat in the kitchen for a conversation. (But, lacking the same words to develop our sentences and to shape our interests, what was there to say? What could I tell them of the term paper I had just finished on the "universality of Shakespeare's appeal"?) I mentioned only small, obvious things: my dormitory life; weekend trips I had taken; random events. They responded with news of their own. (One was almost grateful for a family crisis about which there was much to discuss.) We tried to make our conversation seem like more than an interview.

II

From an early age I knew that my mother and father could read and write both Spanish and English. I had observed my father making his way through what, I now suppose, must have been income tax forms. On other occasions I waited apprehensively while my mother read onion-paper letters airmailed from Mexico with news of a relative's illness or death. For both my parents, however, reading was something done out of necessity and as quickly as possible. Never did I see either of them read an entire book. Nor did I see them read for pleasure. Their reading consisted of work manuals, prayer books, newspaper, recipes.

Richard Hoggart imagines how, at home,

> [the scholarship boy] sees strewn around, and reads regularly himself, magazines which are never mentioned at school, which seem not to belong to the world to which the school introduces him; at school he hears about and reads books never mentioned at home. When he brings those books into the house they do not take their place with other books which the family are reading, for often there are none or almost none; his books look, rather, like strange tools.

In our house each school year would begin with my mother's careful instruction: "Don't write in your books so we can sell them at the end of the year." The remark was echoed in public by my teachers, but only in part: "Boys and girls, don't write in your books. You must learn to treat them with great care and respect."

OPEN THE DOORS OF YOUR MIND WITH BOOKS, read the red and white poster over the nun's desk in early September. It soon was apparent to me that reading was the classroom's central activity. Each course had its own book. And the information gathered from a book was unquestioned. READ TO LEARN, the sign on the wall advised in December. I privately wondered: What was the connection between reading and learning? Did one learn something only by reading it? Was an idea only an idea if it could be written down? In June, CONSIDER BOOKS YOUR BEST FRIENDS. Friends? Reading was, at best, only a chore. I needed to look up whole paragraphs of words in a dictionary. Lines of type were dizzying, the eye having to move slowly across the page, then down, and across. . . . The sentences of the first books I read were coolly impersonal. Toned hard. What most bothered me, however, was the isolation reading required. To console myself for the loneliness I'd feel when I read, I tried reading in a very soft voice. Until: "Who is doing all that talking to his neighbor?" Shortly after, remedial reading classes were arranged for me with a very old nun.

At the end of each school day, for nearly six months, I would meet with her in the tiny room that served as the school's library but was actually only a storeroom for used textbooks and a vast collection of *National Geographics.* Everything about our sessions pleased me: the smallness of the room; the noise of the janitor's broom hitting the edge of the long hallway outside the door; the green of the sun, lighting the wall; and the old woman's face blurred white with a beard. Most of the time we took turns. I began with my elementary text. Sentences of astonishing simplicity seemed to me lifeless and drab: "The boys ran from the rain. . . . She wanted to sing. . . . The kite rose in the blue." Then the old nun would read from her favorite books, usually biographies of early American presidents. Playfully she ran through complex sentences, calling the words alive with her voice, making it seem that the author somehow was speaking directly to me. I smiled just to listen to her. I sat there and sensed for the very first time some possibility of fellowship between a reader and a writer, a communication, never *intimate* like that I heard spoken words at home convey, but one nonetheless *personal*.

One day the nun concluded a session by asking me why I was so reluctant to read by myself. I tried to explain; said something about the way written words made me feel all alone—almost, I wanted to add but didn't, as when I spoke to myself in a room just emptied of furniture. She studied my face as I spoke; she seemed to be watching more than listening. In an uneventful voice she replied that I had nothing to fear. Didn't I realize that reading would open up whole new worlds? A book could open doors for me. It could introduce me to people and show me places I never imagined existed. She gestured toward the bookshelves. (Bare-breasted African women danced, and the shiny hubcaps of automobiles on the back covers of the *Geographic* gleamed in my mind.) I listened with respect. But her words were not very influential. I was thinking then of another consequence of literacy, one I was too shy to admit but nonetheless trusted. Books were going to make me "educated." *That* confidence enabled me, several months later, to overcome my fear of the silence.

In fourth grade I embarked upon a grandiose reading program. "Give me the names of important books," I would say to startled teachers. They soon found out that I had in mind "adult books." I ignored their suggestion of anything I suspected was written for children. (Not until I was in college, as a result, did I read *Huckleberry Finn* or *Alice's Adventures in Wonderland*.) Instead, I read *The Scarlet Letter* and Franklin's *Autobiography*. And whatever I read I read for extra credit. Each time I finished a book, I reported the achievement to a teacher and basked in the praise my effort earned. Despite my best efforts, however, there seemed to be more and more books I needed to read. At the library I would literally tremble as I came upon whole shelves of books I hadn't read. So I read and I read and I read: *Great Expectations*; all the short stories of Kipling; *The Babe Ruth Story*; the entire first volume of the *Encyclopedia Britannica* (A–ANSTEY); the *Iliad*; *Moby Dick*; *Gone with the Wind*; *The Good Earth*; *Ramona*; *Forever Amber*; *The Lives of the Saints*; *Crime and Punishment*; *The Pearl*.... Librarians who initially frowned when I checked out the maximum ten books at a time started saving books they thought I might like. Teachers would say to the rest of the class, "I only wish the rest of you took reading as seriously as Richard obviously does."

But at home I would hear my mother wondering, "What do you see in your books?" (Was reading a hobby like her knitting? Was so much reading even healthy for a boy? Was it the sign of "brains"? Or was it just a convenient excuse for not helping about the house on Saturday mornings?) Always, "What do you see . . . ?"

What *did* I see in my books? I had the idea that they were crucial for my academic success, though I couldn't have said exactly how or why. In the sixth grade I simply concluded that what gave a book its value was some major idea or theme it contained. If that core essence could be mined and memorized, I would become learned like my teachers. I decided to record in a notebook the themes of the books that I read. After reading *Robinson Crusoe*, I wrote that its theme was "the value of learning to live by oneself." When I completed *Wuthering Heights*, I noted the danger of "letting emotions get out of control." Rereading these brief moralistic appraisals usually left me disheartened. I couldn't believe that they were really the source of reading's value. But for many more years, they constituted the only means I had of describing to myself the educational value of books.

In spite of my earnestness, I found reading a pleasurable activity. I came to enjoy the lonely good company of books. Early on weekday mornings, I'd read in my bed. I'd feel a mysterious comfort then, reading in the dawn quiet—the blue-gray silence interrupted by the occasional churning of the refrigerator motor a few rooms away or the more distant sounds of a city bus beginning its run. On weekends I'd go to the public library to read, surrounded by old men and women. Or, if the weather was fine, I would take my books to the park and read in the shade of a tree. A warm summer evening was my favorite reading time. Neighbors would leave for vacation and I would water their lawns. I would sit through the twilight on the front porches or in backyards, reading to the cool, whirling sounds of the sprinklers.

I also had favorite writers. But often those writers I enjoyed most I was least able to value. When I read William Saroyan's *The Human Comedy*, I was immediately pleased by the narrator's warmth and the charm of his story. But as quickly I became suspicious. A book so enjoyable to read couldn't be very "important." Another summer I determined to read all the novels of Dickens. Reading his fat novels, I loved the feeling I got—after the first hundred pages—of being at home in a fictional world where I knew the names of the characters and cared about what was going to happen to them. And it bothered me that I was forced away at the conclusion, when the fiction closed tight, like a fortune-teller's fist—the futures of all the major characters neatly resolved. I never knew how to take such feelings seriously, however. Nor did I suspect that these experiences could be part of a novel's meaning. Still, there were pleasures to sustain me after I'd finish my books. Carrying a volume back to the library, I would be pleased by its weight. I'd run my fingers along the edge of the pages and marvel at the breadth of my achievement. Around my room, growing stacks of paperback books reenforced my assurance.

I entered high school having read hundreds of books. My habit of reading made me a confident speaker and writer of English. Reading also enabled me to sense something of the shape, the major concerns, of Western thought. (I was able to say something about Dante and Descartes and Engels and James Baldwin in my high school term papers.) In these various ways, books brought me academic success as I hoped that they would. But I was not a good reader. Merely bookish, I lacked a point of view when I read. Rather, I read in order to acquire a point of view. I vacuumed books for epigrams, scraps of information, ideas, themes—anything to fill the hollow within me and make me feel educated. When one of my teachers suggested to his drowsy tenth-grade English class that a person could not have a "complicated idea" until he had read at least two thousand books, I heard the remark without detecting either its irony or its very complicated truth. I merely determined to compile a list of all the books I had ever read. Harsh with myself, I included only once a title I might have read several times. (How, after all, could one read a book more than once?) And I included only those books over a hundred pages in length. (Could anything shorter be a book?)

There was yet another high school list I compiled. One day I came across a newspaper article about the retirement of an English professor at a nearby state college. The article was accompanied by a list of the "hundred most important books of Western Civilization." "More than anything else in my life," the professor told the reporter with finality, "these books have made me all that I am." That was the kind of remark I couldn't ignore. I clipped out the list and kept it for the several months it took me to read all of the titles. Most books, of course, I barely understood. While reading Plato's *Republic*, for instance, I needed to keep looking at the book jacket comments to remind myself what the text was about. Nevertheless, with the special patience and superstition of a scholarship boy, I looked at every word of the text. And by the time I reached the last word, relieved, I convinced myself that I had read *The Republic*. In a ceremony of great pride, I solemnly crossed Plato off my list.

III

The scholarship boy pleases most when he is young—the working-class child struggling for academic success. To his teachers, he offers great satisfaction; his success is their proudest achievement. Many other persons offer to help him. A businessman learns the boy's story and promises to underwrite part of the cost of his college education. A woman leaves him her entire library of several hundred books when she moves. His progress is featured in a newspaper article. Many people seem happy for him. They marvel. "How did you manage so fast?" From all sides, there is lavish praise and encouragement.

In his grammar school classroom, however, the boy already makes students around him uneasy. They scorn his desire to succeed. They scorn him for constantly wanting the teacher's attention and praise. "Kiss Ass," they call him when his hand swings up in response to every question he hears. Later, when he makes it to college, no one will mock him aloud. But he detects annoyance on the faces of some students and even some teachers who watch him. It puzzles him often. In college, then in graduate school, he behaves much as he always has. If anything is different about him it is that he dares to anticipate the successful conclusion of his studies. At last he feels that he belongs in the classroom, and this is exactly the source of the dissatisfaction he causes. To many persons around him, he appears too much the academic. There may be some things about him that recall his beginnings—his shabby clothes; his persistent poverty; or his dark skin (in those cases when it symbolizes his parents' disadvantaged condition)—but they only make clear how far he has moved from his past. He has used education to remake himself.

It bothers his fellow academics to face this. They will not say why exactly. (They sneer.) But their expectations become obvious when they are disappointed. They expect—they want—a student less changed by his schooling. If the scholarship boy, from a past so distant from the classroom, could remain in some basic way unchanged, he would be able to prove that it is possible for anyone to become educated without basically changing from the person one was.

Here is no fabulous hero, no idealized scholar-worker. The scholarship boy does not straddle, cannot reconcile, the two great opposing cultures of his life. His success is unromantic and plain. He sits in the classroom and offers those sitting beside him no calming reassurance about their own lives. He sits in the seminar room—a man with brown skin, the son of working-class Mexican immigrant parents. (Addressing the professor at the head of the table, his voice catches with nervousness.) There is no trace of his parents in his speech. Instead he approximates the accents of teachers and classmates. Coming from *him* those sounds seem suddenly odd. Odd too is the effect produced when *he* uses academic jargon—bubbles at the tip of his tongue: *"Topos* . . . negative capability . . . vegetation imagery in Shakespearean comedy." He lifts an opinion from Coleridge, takes something else from Frye or Empson or Leavis. He even repeats exactly his professor's earlier comment. All his ideas are clearly borrowed. He seems to have no thought of his own. He chatters while his listeners smile—their look one of disdain.

When he is older and thus when so little of the person he was survives, the scholarship boy makes only too apparent his profound lack of *self-*confidence. This is the conventional assessment that even Richard Hoggart repeats:

> [The scholarship boy] tends to over-stress the importance of examinations, of the piling-up of knowledge and of received opinions. He discovers a technique of apparent learning, of the acquiring of facts rather than of the handling and use of facts. He learns how to receive a purely literate education, one using only a small part of the personality and challenging only a limited area of his being. He begins to see life as a ladder, as permanent examination with some praise and some further exhortation at each stage. He becomes an expert imbiber and doler-out; his competence will vary, but will rarely be accompanied by genuine enthusiasms. He rarely feels the reality of knowledge, of other men's thoughts and imaginings, on his own pulses. . . . He has something of the blinkered pony about him. . . .

But this is criticism more accurate than fair. The scholarship boy is a very bad student. He is the great mimic; a collector of thoughts, not a thinker; the very last person in class who ever feels obliged to have an opinion of his own. In large part, however, the reason he is such a bad student is because he realizes more often and more acutely than most other students— than Hoggart himself—that education requires radical self-reformation. As a very young boy, regarding his parents, as he struggles with an early homework assignment, he knows this too well. That is why he lacks self-assurance. He does not forget that the classroom is responsible for remaking him. He relies on his teacher, depends on all that he hears in the classroom and reads in his books. He becomes in every obvious way the worst student, a dummy mouthing the opinions of others. But he would not be so bad—nor would he become so successful, a *scholarship* boy—if he did not accurately perceive that the best synonym for primary "education" is "imitation."

Those who would take seriously the boy's success—and his failure— would be forced to realize how great is the change any academic undergoes, how far one must move from one's past. It is easiest to ignore such considerations. So little is said about the scholarship boy in pages and pages of educational literature. Nothing is said of the silence that comes to separate the boy from his parents. Instead, one hears proposals for increasing the self-esteem of students and encouraging early intellectual independence. Paragraphs glitter with a constellation of terms like *creativity* and *originality*. (Ignored altogether is the function of imitation in a student's life.) Radical educationalists meanwhile complain that ghetto schools "oppress" students by trying to mold them, stifling native characteristics. The truer critique would be just the reverse: not that schools change ghetto students too much, but that while they might promote the occasional scholarship student, they change most students barely at all.

From the story of the scholarship boy there is no specific pedagogy to glean. There is, however, a much larger lesson. His story makes clear that education is a long, unglamorous, even demeaning process—*a nurturing never natural to the person one was before one entered a classroom*. At once different from most other students, the scholarship boy is also the archetypal "good student." He exaggerates the difficulty of being a student, but his exaggeration reveals a general predicament. Others are changed by their schooling as much as he. They too must re-form themselves. They must develop the skill of memory long before they become truly critical thinkers. And when they read Plato for the first several times, it will be with awe more than deep comprehension.

The impact of schooling on the scholarship boy is only more apparent to the boy himself and to others. Finally, although he may be laughable— a blinkered pony—the boy will not let his critics forget their own change. He ends up too much like them. When he speaks, they hear themselves echoed. In his pedantry, they trace their own. His ambitions are theirs. If his failure were singular, they might readily pity him. But he is more troubling than that. They would not scorn him if this were not so.

IV

Like me, Hoggart's imagined scholarship boy spends most of his years in the classroom afraid to long for his past. Only at the very end of his schooling does the boy-man become nostalgic. In this sudden change of heart, Richard Hoggart notes:

> He longs for the membership he lost, "he pines for some Nameless Eden where he never was." The nostalgia is the stronger and the more ambiguous because he is really "in quest of his own absconded self yet scared to find it." He both wants to go back and yet thinks he has gone beyond his class, feels himself weighted with knowledge of his own and their situation, which hereafter forbids him the simpler pleasures of his father and mother. . . .

According to Hoggart, the scholarship boy grows nostalgic because he remains the uncertain scholar, bright enough to have moved from his past, yet unable to feel easy, a part of a community of academics.

This analysis, however, only partially suggests what happened to me in my last year as a graduate student. When I traveled to London to write a dissertation on English Renaissance literature, I was finally confident of membership in a "community of scholars." But the pleasure that confidence gave me faded rapidly. After only two or three months in the reading room of the British Museum, it became clear that I had joined a lonely community. Around me each day were dour faces eclipsed by large piles of books. There were the regulars, like the old couple who arrived every morning, each holding a loop of the shopping bag which contained all their notes. And there was the historian who chattered madly to herself. ("Oh dear! Oh! Now, what's this? What? Oh, my!") There were also the faces of young men and women worn by long study. And everywhere eyes turned away the moment our glance accidentally met. Some persons I sat beside day after day, yet we passed silently at the end of the day, strangers. Still, we were united by a common respect for the written word and for scholarship. We did form a union, though one in which we remained distant from one another.

More profound and unsettling was the bond I recognized with those writers whose books I consulted. Whenever I opened a text that hadn't been used for years, I realized that my special interests and skills united me to a mere handful of academics. We formed an exclusive — eccentric! — society, separated from others who would never care or be able to share our concerns. (The pages I turned were stiff like layers of dead skin.) I began to wonder: Who, beside my dissertation director and a few faculty members, would ever read what I wrote? And: Was my dissertation much more than an act of social withdrawal? These questions went unanswered in the silence of the Museum reading room. They remained to trouble me after I'd leave the library each afternoon and feel myself shy—unsteady, speaking simple sentences at the grocer's or the butcher's on my way back to my bed-sitter.

Meanwhile my file cards accumulated. A professional, I knew exactly how to search a book for pertinent information. I could quickly assess and summarize the usability of the many books I consulted. But whenever I started to write, I knew too much (and not enough) to be able to write anything but sentences that were overly cautious, timid, strained brittle under the heavy weight of footnotes and qualifications. I seemed unable to dare a passionate statement. I felt drawn by professionalism to the edge of sterility, capable of no more than pedantic, lifeless, unassailable prose.

Then nostalgia began.

After years spent unwilling to admit its attractions, I gestured nostalgically toward the past. I yearned for that time when I had not been so alone. I became impatient with books. I wanted experience more immediate. I feared the library's silence. I silently scorned the gray, timid faces around me. I grew to hate the growing pages of my dissertation on genre and Renaissance literature. (In my mind I heard relatives laughing as they tried to make sense of its title.) I wanted something—I couldn't say exactly what. I told myself that I wanted a more passionate life. And a life less thoughtful. And above all, I wanted to be less alone. One day I heard some Spanish academics whispering back and forth to each other, and their sounds seemed ghostly voices recalling my life. Yearning became preoccupation then. Boyhood memories beckoned, flooded my mind. (Laughing intimate voices. Bounding up the front steps of the porch. A sudden embrace inside the door.)

For weeks after, I turned to books by educational experts. I needed to learn how far I had moved from my past—to determine how fast I would be able to recover something of it once again. But I found little. Only a chapter in a book by Richard Hoggart. . . . I left the reading room and the circle of faces.

I came home. After the year in England, I spent three summer months living with my mother and father, relieved by how easy it was to be home. It no longer seemed very important to me that we had little to say. I felt easy sitting and eating and walking with them. I watched them, nevertheless, looking for evidence of those elastic, sturdy strands that bind generations in a web of inheritance. I thought as I watched my mother one night: of course a friend had been right when she told me that I gestured and laughed just like my mother. Another time I saw for myself: my father's eyes were much like my own, constantly watchful.

But after the early relief, this return, came suspicion, nagging until I realized that I had not neatly sidestepped the impact of schooling. My desire to do so was precisely the measure of how much I remained an academic. *Negatively* (for that is how this idea first occurred to me): my need to think so much and so abstractly about my parents and our relationship was in itself an indication of my long education. My father and mother did not pass their time thinking about the cultural meanings of their experience. It was I who described their daily lives with airy ideas. And yet, *positively*: the ability to consider experience so abstractly allowed me to shape into desire what would otherwise have remained indefinite, meaningless longing in the British Museum. If, because of my schooling, I had grown culturally separated from my parents, my education finally had given me ways of speaking and caring about that fact.

My best teachers in college and graduate school, years before, had tried to prepare me for this conclusion, I think, when they discussed texts of aristocratic pastoral literature. Faithfully, I wrote down all that they said. I memorized it: "The praise of the unlettered by the highly educated is one of the primary themes of 'elitist' literature." But, "the importance of the praise given the unsolitary, richly passionate and spontaneous life is that it simultaneously reflects the value of a reflective life." I heard it all. But there was no way for any of it to mean very much to me. I was a scholarship boy at the time, busily laddering my way up the rungs of education. To pass an examination, I copied down exactly what my teachers told me. It would require many more years of schooling (an inevitable miseducation) in which I came to trust the silence of reading and the habit of abstracting from immediate experience—moving away from a life of closeness and immediacy I remembered with my parents, growing older—before I turned unafraid to desire the past, and thereby achieved what had eluded me for so long—the end of education.

NOTE
_____

[1] All quotations in this essay are from Richard Hoggart, *The Uses of Literacy* (London: Chatto and Windus, 1957), chapter 10. [Author's note]

• • • • • • • • • • • •

QUESTIONS FOR A SECOND READING

1. In *Hunger of Memory*, the book from which "The Achievement of Desire" is drawn, Rodriguez says several times that the story he tells, although it is very much his story, is also a story of our common experience—growing up, leaving home, becoming educated, entering the world. When you reread this essay, look particularly for sections or passages you might bring forward as evidence that this is, in fact, an essay which can give you a way of looking at your own life, and not just his. And look for sections that defy universal application. To what degree *is* his story the story of our common experience? Why might he (or his readers) want to insist that his story is everyone's story?

2. At the end of the essay, Rodriguez says:

> It would require many more years of schooling (an inevitable miseduca-
> tion) in which I came to trust the silence of reading and the habit of
> abstracting from immediate experience—moving away from a life of
> closeness and immediacy I remembered with my parents, growing
> older—before I turned unafraid to desire the past, and thereby achieved
> what had eluded me for so long—the end of education. (p. 563)

What do you think, as you reread this essay, is the "end of education"? And
what does that end (that goal? stopping point?) have to do with "miseducation," "the silence of reading," "the habit of abstracting from immediate experience," and "desiring the past"?

ASSIGNMENTS FOR WRITING

1. You could look at the relationship between Richard Rodriguez and Richard
    Hoggart as a case study of the relation of a reader to a writer or a student to
    a teacher. Look closely at Rodriguez's references to Hoggart's book, *The
    Uses of Literacy*, and at the way Rodriguez made use of that book to name
    and describe his own experience as a student. (An extended selection of
    The Uses of Literacy can be found on pages 180–85 in *Resources for Teaching
    WAYS OF READING*.) What did he find in the book? How did he use it? How
    does he use it in his own writing?

    Write an essay in which you discuss Rodriguez's use of Hoggart's *The
    Uses of Literacy*. How, for example, would you compare Rodriguez's ver-
    sion of the "scholarship boy" with Hoggart's? (At one point, Rodriguez
    says that Hoggart's account is "more accurate than fair." What might he
    have meant by that?) And what kind of reader is the Rodriguez who is
    writing "The Achievement of Desire"—is he still a "scholarship boy," or is
    that description no longer appropriate?

    Note: You might begin your research ·with what may seem to be a
    purely technical matter, examining how Rodriguez handles quotations and
    works Hoggart's words into paragraphs of his own. On the basis of Rod-
    riguez's use of quoted passages, how would you describe the relationship
    between Hoggart's words and Rodriguez's? Who has the greater author-
    ity? Who is the expert, and under what conditions? What "rules" might
    Rodriguez be said to follow or to break? Do you see any change in the
    course of the essay in how Rodriguez uses block quotations? in how he
    comments on them?

2. Rodriguez insists that his story is also everyone's story. Take an episode
    from your life, one that seems in some way similar to one of the episodes in
    "The Achievement of Desire," and cast it into a shorter version of Rod-
    riguez's essay. Your job here is to look at your experience in Rodriguez's
    terms, which means thinking the way he does, noticing what he would no-
    tice, interpreting details in a similar fashion, using his key terms, seeing
    through his point of view; it could also mean imitating his style of writing,
    working with quotations from other writers, doing whatever it is you see
    him doing characteristically while he writes. Imitation, Rodriguez argues,
    is not necessarily a bad thing; it can, in fact, be one of the powerful ways in
    which a person learns.

Note: This assignment can also be used to read against "The Achieve-ment of Desire." Rodriguez insists on the universality of his experience leaving home and community and joining the larger public life. You could highlight the differences between your experience and his. You should begin by imitating Rodriguez's method; you do not have to arrive at his conclusions, however.

3. What I am about to say to you has taken me more than twenty years to admit: *A primary reason for my success in the classroom was that I couldn't forget that schooling was changing me and separating me from the life I enjoyed before becoming a student.* (p. 547)

    If, because of my schooling, I had grown culturally separated from my parents, my education finally had given me ways of speaking and car-ing about that fact. (p. 563)

    As you reread Rodriguez's essay, what would you say are his "ways of speaking and caring"? One way to think about this question is to trace how the lessons he learned about reading, education, language, family, culture, and class shifted as he moved from elementary school through college and graduate school to his career as a teacher and a writer. What scholarly abil-ities did he learn that provided him with "ways of speaking and caring" valued in the academic community? Where and how do you see him using them in his essay?

    Write an essay in which you discuss how Rodriguez reads (reviews, summarizes, interprets) his family, his teachers, his schooling, himself, and his books. What differences can you say such reading makes to those ways of speaking and caring that you locate in the text?

MAKING CONNECTIONS

1. Paulo Freire, in "The 'Banking' Concept of Education" (p. 243), discusses the political implications of the relations between teachers and students. Some forms of schooling, he says, can give students control over their lives, but most schooling teaches students only to submit to domination by others. If you look closely at the history of Rodriguez's schooling from the perspective of Freire's essay, what do you see? Write an essay describing how Freire might analyze Rodriguez's education. How would he see the process as it unfolds throughout Rodriguez's experience, as a student, from his early schooling (including the study he did on his own at home), through his college and graduate studies, to the position he takes, finally, as the writer of "The Achievement of Desire"?

2. Here, from "Arts of the Contact Zone" (p. 499), is Mary Louise Pratt on the "autoethnographic" text:

    Guaman Poma's *New Chronicle* is an instance of what I have proposed to call an *autoethnographic* text, by which I mean a text in which people un-dertake to describe themselves in ways that engage with representations others have made of them. Thus if ethnographic texts are those in which European metropolitan subjects represent to themselves their others (usually their conquered others), autoethnographic texts are representa-tions that the so-defined others construct *in response to* or in dialogue with

those texts. . . . [T]hey involve a selective collaboration with and appropriation of idioms of the metropolis or the conqueror. These are merged
or infiltrated to varying degrees with indigenous idioms to create self-
representations intended to intervene in metropolitan modes of understanding. . . . Such texts often constitute a marginalized group's point of
entry into the dominant circuits of print culture. (pp. 501–2)

Richard Rodriguez's "The Achievement of Desire" could be considered
"autoethnography." He is clearly working to explain himself, to account
for who he is and who he has become. But to whom? Who is identified as
his audience? Can you talk here about "indigenous idioms" or the "idioms
of the metropolis"?

Reread "The Achievement of Desire" with Pratt's essay in mind. And
write an essay in which you discuss "The Achievement of Desire" as an example of an autoethnographic and/or a transcultural text. You should
imagine that you are working to put Pratt's ideas to the test (does it present
itself as a convenient example?), but also add what you have to say about
the ways this autobiography defines its audience, speaker, and purpose.

3. Richard Rodriguez in "The Achievement of Desire," Adrienne Rich in
    "When We Dead Awaken: Writing as Re-Vision" (p. 520), Susan Griffin in
    "Our Secret" (p. 299), and John Edgar Wideman in "Our Time" (p. 681) use
    a life story to think about and to represent forces beyond the individual
    that shape life and possibility—patriarchy, war, race, and ethnicity. Susan
    Griffin explains her motive this way, "One can find traces of every life in
    each life." Perhaps. It is a bold step to think that this is true and to believe
    that one can, or should, use autobiography as a way to understand the na-
    tional or international narrative. Write an essay in which you read "The
    Achievement of Desire" alongside one of the other three essays. Your goal
    is not only to discuss how these writers do what they do, and to what con-
    clusions and to what ends, but also to discuss your sense of what is at stake
    in such a project. How are their accounts of family different? How do they
    connect the structure of the family to larger structural concerns? What are
    the key differences, and how might you explain them?

EDWARD
SAID

EDWARD SAID (1935–2003) was one of the world's most distinguished literary critics and scholars, distinguished (among other things) for his insistence on the connectedness of art and politics, literature and history. As he argues in his influential essay "The World, the Text, the Critic,"

> *Texts have ways of existing, both theoretical and practical, that even in their most rarefied form are always enmeshed in circumstance, time, place, and society—in short, they are in the world, and hence worldly. The same is doubtless true of the critic, as reader and as writer.*

Said (pronounced "sigh-eed") was a "worldly" reader and writer and the selection that follows is a case in point. It is part of his long-term engagement with the history and politics of the Middle East, particularly of the people we refer to as Palestinians. His critical efforts, perhaps best represented by his most influential book Orientalism *(1978), examine the ways the West has represented and understood the East ("They cannot represent themselves; they must be represented"), demonstrating how Western journalists, writers, artists, and scholars have created and*

567

preserved a view of Eastern cultures as mysterious, dangerous, unchanging, and inferior.

Said was born in Jerusalem, in what was at that time Palestine, to parents who were members of the Christian Palestinian community. In 1947, as the United Nations was establishing Israel as a Jewish state, his family fled to Cairo. In the introduction to After the Last Sky: Palestinian Lives (1986), the book from which the following selection was taken, he says,

> I was twelve, with the limited awareness and memory of a relatively sheltered boy. By the mid-spring of 1948 my extended family in its entirety had departed, evicted from Palestine along with almost a million other Palestinians. This was the nakba, or catastrophe, which heralded the destruction of our society and our dispossession as a people.

Said was educated in English-speaking schools in Cairo and Massachusetts; he completed his undergraduate training at Princeton and received his PhD from Harvard in 1964. He was a member of the English department at Columbia University in New York from 1963 until his death from leukemia in 2003. In the 1970s, he began writing to a broad public on the situation of the Palestinians; from 1977 to 1991 he served on the Palestinian National Council, an exile government. In 1991 he split from the Palestine Liberation Organization (PLO) over its Gulf War policy (Yasir Arafat's support of Saddam Hussein) and, as he says, for "what I considered to be its new defeatism."

The peculiar and distinctive project represented by After the Last Sky began in the 1980s, in the midst of this political engagement. "In 1983," Said writes in the introduction,

> while I was serving as a consultant to the United Nations for its International Conference on the Question of Palestine (ICQP), I suggested that photographs of Palestinians be hung in the entrance hall to the main conference site in Geneva. I had of course known and admired Mohr's work with John Berger, and I recommended that he be commissioned to photograph some of the principal locales of Palestinian life. Given the initial enthusiasm for the idea, Mohr left on a special UN-sponsored trip to the Near East. The photographs he brought back were indeed wonderful; the official response, however, was puzzling and, to someone with a taste for irony, exquisite. You can hang them up, we were told, but no writing can be displayed with them.

In response to a UN mandate, Said had also commissioned twenty studies for the participants at the conference. Of the twenty, only three were accepted as "official documents." The others were rejected "because one after another Arab state objected to this or that principle, this or that insinuation, this or that putative injury to its sovereignty." And yet, Said argues, the complex experience, history, and identity of the people known as Palestinians remained virtually unknown, particularly in the West (and in the United States). To most, Said says, "Palestinians are visible principally as fighters, terrorists, and lawless pariahs." When Jean Mohr, the photographer, told a friend that he was preparing an exhibition on the Palestinians, the friend responded, "Don't you think the subject's a bit dated? Look, I've taken photographs of Palestinians too, especially in the refugee camps . . . it's really sad! But these days, who's interested in people who eat off the ground with their hands? And then there's all that terrorism. . . . I'd have thought you'd be better off using your energy and capabilities on something more worthwhile."

For both Said and Mohr, these rejections provided the motive for After the Last Sky. Said's account, from the book's introduction, is worth quoting at length for how well it represents the problems of writing:

> Let us use photographs and a text, we said to each other, to say something that hasn't been said about Palestinians. Yet the problem of writing about and representing—in all senses of the word—Palestinians in some fresh way is part of a much larger problem. For it is not as if no one speaks about or portrays the Palestinians. The difficulty is that everyone, including the Palestinians themselves, speaks a very great deal. A huge body of literature has grown up, most of it polemical, accusatory, denunciatory. At this point, no one writing about Palestine— and indeed, no one going to Palestine—starts from scratch: We have all been there before, whether by reading about it, experiencing its millennial presence and power, or actually living there for periods of time. It is a terribly crowded place, almost too crowded for what it is asked to be by way of history or interpretation of history.

The resulting book is quite a remarkable document. The photos are not the photos of a glossy coffee-table book and yet they are compelling and memorable. The prose at times leads to the photos; at times it follows as meditation or explanation, an effort to get things right—"things like exile, dispossession, habits of expression, internal and external landscapes, stubbornness, poignancy, and heroism." It is a writing with pictures, not a writing to which photos were later added. Said had, in fact, been unable to return to Israel/Palestine for several years. As part of this project, he had hoped to be able to take a trip to the West Bank and Gaza in order to see beyond Mohr's photographs, but such a trip proved to be unsafe and impossible— both Arab and Israeli officials had reason to treat him with suspicion. The book was written in exile; the photos, memories, books, and newspapers, these were the only vehicles of return.

After the Last Sky is, Said wrote in 1999, "an unreconciled book, in which the contradictions and antinomies of our lives and experiences remain as they are, assembled neither (I hope) into neat wholes nor into sentimental ruminations about the past. Fragments, memories, disjointed scenes, intimate particulars." The Palestinians, Said wrote in the introduction, fall between classifications. "We are at once too recently formed and too variously experienced to be a population of articulate exiles with a completely systematic vision and too voluble and trouble making to be simply a pathetic mass of refugees." And he adds, "The whole point of this book is to engage this difficulty, to deny the habitually simple, even harmful representations of Palestinians, and to replace them with something more capable of capturing the complex reality of their experience."

Furthermore, he says, "just as Jean Mohr and I, a Swiss and a Palestinian, collaborated in the process, we would like you — Palestinians, Europeans, Americans, Africans, Latin Americans, Asians — to do so also." This is both an invitation and a challenge. While there is much to learn about the Palestinians, the people and their history, the opening moment in the collaborative project is to learn to look and to read in the service of a complex and nuanced act of understanding.

Said is the author of many books and collections, including Joseph Conrad and the Fiction of Autobiography *(1966),* Beginnings: Intention and Method *(1975),* Orientalism *(1978),* The Question of Palestine *(1979),* Covering Islam: How the Media and the Experts Determine How We See the Rest of the World *(1981),* Blaming the Victims *(1988),* Musical Elaborations *(1991),* Culture and Imperialism *(1993),* The Politics of Dispossession: The Struggle for Palestinian Self-Determination, 1989–1994 *(1994),* Representations of the Intellectual *(1994),* Peace and Its Discontents: Essays on Palestine in the Middle East Peace Process *(1995),* Out of Place: A Memoir *(2000),* Reflections on Exile *(2000),* The Edward Said Reader *(2000),* The End of the Peace Process: Oslo and After *(2001),* Power, Politics, and Culture *(2001),* Mona Hatoum: The Entire World as a Foreign Land *(2001),* On Late Style: Music and Literature Against the Grain *(2006), and* Music at the Limits *(2007).*

Jean Mohr has worked as a photographer for UNESCO, the World Health Organization, and the International Red Cross. He has collaborated on four books with John Berger, Ways of Seeing *(1972; see excerpt on p. 97),* A Seventh Man *(1975),* Another Way of Telling *(1982), and* A Fortunate Man *(1967).*

States

Caught in a meager, anonymous space outside a drab Arab city, outside a refugee camp, outside the crushing time of one disaster after another, a wedding party stands, surprised, sad, slightly uncomfortable [p. 571]. Palestinians — the telltale mixture of styles and attitudes is so evidently theirs — near Tripoli in northern Lebanon. A few months after this picture was taken their camp was ravaged by intra-Palestinian fighting. Cutting across the wedding party's path here is the ever-present Mercedes, emblazoned with its extra mark of authenticity, the proud *D* for *Deutschland*. A rare luxury in the West, the Mercedes — usually secondhand and smuggled in — is the commonest of cars in the Levant. It has become what horse, mule, and camel were, and then much more. Universal taxi, it is a symbol of modern technology domesticated, of the intrusion of the West into traditional life, of illicit

Tripoli, Badawi camp, May 1983.

trade. More important, the Mercedes is the all-purpose conveyance, something one uses for everything—funerals, weddings, births, proud display, leaving home, coming home, fixing, stealing, reselling, running away in, hiding in. But because Palestinians have no state of their own to shield them, the Mercedes, its provenance and destination obscure, seems like an intruder, a delegate of the forces that both dislocate and hem them in. "The earth is closing on us, pushing us through the last passage," writes the poet Mahmoud Darwish.

The paradox of mobility and insecurity. Wherever we Palestinians are, we are not in our Palestine, which no longer exists. You travel, from one end of the Arab world to the other, in Europe, Africa, the Americas, Australia, and there you find Palestinians like yourself who, like yourself, are subject to special laws, a special status, the markings of a force and violence not yours. Exiles at home as well as abroad, Palestinians also still inhabit the territory of former Palestine (Israel, the West Bank, Gaza), in sadly reduced circumstances. They are either "the Arabs of Judea and Samaria," or, in Israel, "non-Jews." Some are referred to as "present absentees." In Arab countries, except for Jordan, they are given special cards identifying them as "Palestinian refugees," and even where they are respectable engineers, teachers, business people, or technicians, they know that in the eyes of their host country they will always be aliens. Inevitably, photographs of Palestinians today include this fact and make it visible.

Tel Sheva, 1979. A village of settled nomads near Bersheeba. Some years ago, these people still lived in a tent, under the desert sky. The carpet on the ground is the only reminder of that earlier period.

Memory adds to the unrelieved intensity of Palestinian exile. Palestine is central to the cultures of Islam, Christianity, and Judaism; Orient and Occident have turned it into a legend. There is no forgetting it, no way of overlooking it. The world news is often full of what has happened in Palestine-Israel, the latest Middle East crisis, the most recent Palestinian exploits. The sights, wares, and monuments of Palestine are the objects of commerce, war, pilgrimage, cults, the subjects of literature, art, song, fantasy. East and West, their high and their commercial cultures, have descended on Palestine. Bride and groom wear the ill-fitting nuptial costumes of Europe, yet behind and around them are the clothes and objects of their native land, natural to their friends and attendants. The happiness of the occasion is at odds with their lot as refugees with nowhere to go. The children playing nearby contrast starkly with the unappealing surroundings; the new husband's large workman's hands clash with his wife's delicate, obscuring white. When we cross from Palestine into other territories, even if we find ourselves decently in new places, the old ones loom behind us as tangible and unreal as reproduced memory or absent causes for our present state.

Sometimes the poignancy of resettlement stands out like bold script imposed on faint pencil traces. The fit between body and new setting is not good. The angles are wrong. Lines supposed to decorate a wall instead form an imperfectly assembled box in which we have been put. We perch on chairs uncertain whether to address or evade our interlocutor. This child is held out, and yet also held in. Men and women re-express the unattractiveness around them: The angle made across her face by the woman's robe duplicates the ghastly wall pattern, the man's crossed feet repeat and contradict the outward thrust of the chair leg. He seems unsettled, poised for departure. Now what? Now where? All at once it is our transience and impermanence that our visibility expresses, for we can be seen as figures forced to push on to another house, village, or region. Just as we once were taken from one "habitat" to a new one, we can be moved again.

Exile is a series of portraits without names, without contexts. Images that are largely unexplained, nameless, mute. I look at them without precise anecdotal knowledge, but their realistic exactness nevertheless makes a deeper impression than mere information. I cannot reach the actual people who were photographed, except through a European photographer who saw them for me. And I imagine that he, in turn, spoke to them through an interpreter. The one thing I know for sure, however, is that they treated him politely but as someone who came from, or perhaps acted at the direction of, those who put them where they so miserably are. There was the embarrassment of people uncertain why they were being looked at and recorded. Powerless to stop it.

When A. Z.'s father was dying, he called his children, one of whom is married to my sister, into his room for a last family gathering. A frail, very old man from Haifa, he had spent his last thirty-four years in Beirut in a state of agitated disbelief at the loss of his house and property. Now he murmured to his children the final faltering words of a penniless, helpless patriarch. "Hold on to the keys and the deed," he told them, pointing to a battered suitcase near his bed, a repository of the family estate salvaged from Palestine when Haifa's Arabs were expelled. These intimate mementos of a past irrevocably lost circulate among us, like the genealogies and fables of a wandering singer of tales. Photographs, dresses, objects severed from their original locale, the rituals of speech and custom: Much reproduced, enlarged, thematized, embroidered, and passed around, they are strands in the web of affiliations we Palestinians use to tie ourselves to our identity and to each other.

Sometimes these objects, heavy with memory—albums, rosary beads, shawls, little boxes—seem to me like encumbrances. We carry them about, hang them up on every new set of walls we shelter in, reflect lovingly on them. Then we do not notice the bitterness, but it continues and grows nonetheless. Nor do we acknowledge the frozen immobility of our attitudes. In the end the past owns us. My father spent his life trying to escape these objects, "Jerusalem" chief among them—the actual place as much as its reproduced and manufactured self. Born in Jerusalem, as were his parents, grandparents, and all his family back in time to a distant vanishing point, he was a child of the Old City who traded with tourists in bits of the true cross and crowns of thorn. Yet he hated the place; for him, he often said, it meant death. Little of it remained with him except a fragmentary story or two, an odd coin

Amman, 1984. A visit to the former mayor of Jerusalem and his wife, in exile in Jordan.

or medal, one photograph of his father on horseback, and two small rugs. I never even saw a picture of my grandmother's face. But as he grew older, he reverted to old Jerusalemite expressions that I did not understand, never having heard them during the years of my youth.

Identity—who we are, where we come from, what we are—is difficult to maintain in exile. Most other people take their identity for granted. Not the

Ramallah, 1979. An everyday street scene, banal and reassuring. And yet, the
tension is constant. A passing military jeep, a flying stone—the incident,
the drama, can occur at any moment.

Palestinian, who is required to show proofs of identity more or less constantly. It is not only that we are regarded as terrorists, but that our existence
as native Arab inhabitants of Palestine, with primordial rights there (and not
elsewhere), is either denied or challenged. And there is more. Such as it is, our
existence is linked negatively to encomiums about Israel's democracy,
achievements, excitement; in much Western rhetoric we have slipped into the

place occupied by Nazis and anti-Semites; collectively, we can aspire to little except political anonymity and resettlement; we are known for no actual achievement, no characteristic worthy of esteem, except the effrontery of disrupting Middle East peace. Some Israeli settlers on the West Bank say: "The Palestinians can stay here, with no rights, as resident aliens." Other Israelis are less kind. We have no known Einsteins, no Chagall, no Freud or Rubinstein to protect us with a legacy of glorious achievements. We have had no Holocaust to protect us with the world's compassion. We are "other," and opposite, a flaw in the geometry of resettlement and exodus. Silence and discretion veil the hurt, slow the body searches, soothe the sting of loss.

A zone of recollected pleasure surrounds the few unchanged spots of Palestinian life in Palestine. The foodsellers and peddlers—itinerant vendors of cakes or corn—are still there for the casual eye to see, and they still provoke the appetite. They seem to travel not only from place to place, but from an earlier time to the present, carrying with them the same clientele— the young girls and boys, the homeward-bound cyclist, the loitering student or clerk—now as then. We buy their wares with the same surreptitiously found change (who can remember the unit? was it a piaster? fils? shilling?) spent on the same meager object, neither especially good nor especially well prepared. The luxurious pleasure of tasting the vendor's *simsim*, the round sesame cakes dipped in that tangy mixture of thyme and sumac, or his *durra*, boiled corn sprayed with salt, surpasses the mere act of eating and opens before us the altogether agreeable taste of food not connected with meals, with nourishment, with routine. But what a distance

now actually separates me from the concreteness of that life. How easily traveled the photographs make it seem, and how possible to suspend the barriers keeping me from the scenes they portray.

For the land is further away than it has ever been. Born in Jerusalem in late 1935, I left mandatory Palestine permanently at the end of 1947. In the spring of 1948, my last cousin evacuated our family's house in West Jerusalem; Martin Buber subsequently lived there till his death, I have been told. I grew up in Egypt, then came to the United States as a student. In 1966 I visited Ramallah, part of the Jordanian West Bank, for a family wedding. My father, who was to die five years later, accompanied my sister and me. Since our visit, all the members of my family have resettled—in Jordan, in Lebanon, in the United States, and in Europe. As far as I know, I have no relatives who still live in what was once Palestine. Wars, revolutions, civil struggles have changed the countries I have lived in—Lebanon, Jordan, Egypt—beyond recognition. Until thirty-five years ago I could travel from Cairo to Beirut overland, through territories held or in other ways controlled by rival colonial powers. Now, although my mother lives in Beirut, I have not visited her since the Israeli invasion of 1982: Palestinians are no longer welcome there. The fact is that today I can neither return to the places of my youth, nor voyage freely in the countries and places that mean the most to me, nor feel safe from arrest or violence even in the countries I used to frequent but whose governments and policies have changed radically in recent times. There is little that is more unpleasant for me these days than the customs and police check upon entering an Arab country.

Consider the tremendous upheavals since 1948 each of which effectively destroyed the ecology of our previous existence. When I was born, we in Palestine felt ourselves to be part of a small community, presided over by the majority community and one or another of the outside powers holding sway over the territory. My family and I, for example, were members of a tiny Protestant group within a much larger Greek Orthodox Christian minority, within the larger Sunni Islam majority; the important outside power was Britain, with its great rival France a close second. But then after World War II Britain and France lost their hold, and for the first time we directly confronted the colonial legacy—inept rulers, divided populations, conflicting promises made to resident Arabs and mostly European Jews with incompatible claims. In 1948 Israel was established; Palestine was destroyed, and the great Palestinian dispossession began. In 1956 Egypt was invaded by Britain, France, and Israel, causing what was left of the large Levantine communities there (Italian, Greek, Jewish, Armenian, Syrian) to leave. The rise of Abdel Nasser fired all Arabs—especially Palestinians—with the hope of a revived Arab nationalism, but after the union of Syria with Egypt failed in 1961, the Arab cold war, as it has been called, began in earnest; Saudi Arabia versus Egypt, Jordan versus Syria, Syria versus Iraq. . . . A new population of refugees, migrant workers, and traveling political parties crisscrossed the Arab world. We Palestinians immersed ourselves in the politics of Baathism in Syria and Iraq, of Nasserism in Egypt, of the Arab Nationalist Movement in Lebanon.

The 1967 war was followed shortly after by the Arab oil boom. For the first time, Palestinian nationalism arose as an independent force in the Middle East. Never did our future seem more hopeful. In time, however, our appearance on the political scene stimulated, if it did not actually cause, a great many less healthy phenomena: fundamentalist Islam, Maronite nationalism, Jewish zealotry. The new consumer culture, the computerized economy, further exacerbated the startling disparities in the Arab world between rich and poor, old and new, privileged and disinherited. Then, starting in 1975, the Lebanese civil war pitted the various Lebanese sects, the Palestinians, and a number of Arab and foreign powers against each other. Beirut was destroyed as the intellectual and political nerve center of Arab life; for us, it was the end of our only important, relatively independent center of Palestinian nationalism, with the Palestinian Liberation Organization at its heart. Anwar Sadat recognized Israel, and Camp David further dismantled the region's alliances and disrupted its balance. After the Iranian revolution in 1979 came the Iran-Iraq war. Israel's 1982 invasion of Lebanon put more Palestinians on the move, as the massacres in the Palestinian refugee camps of Sabra and Shatila reduced the community still further. By the end of 1983, Palestinians were fighting each other, and Syria and Libya were directly involved, supporting Palestinian dissidents against PLO loyalists. With the irony typical of our political fate, however, in mid-1985 we were united together in Sabra and Shatila to fight off a hostile Shi'ite militia patronized by Syria.

The stability of geography and the continuity of land—these have completely disappeared from my life and the life of all Palestinians. If we are not stopped at borders, or herded into new camps, or denied reentry and residence, or barred from travel from one place to another, more of our land is taken, our lives are interfered with arbitrarily, our voices are prevented from reaching each other, our identity is confined to frightened little islands in an inhospitable environment of superior military force sanitized by the clinical jargon of pure administration. On the West Bank and in Gaza we confront several Zionist "master plans"—which, according to Meron Benvenisti, ex-deputy mayor of Jerusalem, are "explicitly sectarian." He continues:

> The criteria established to determine priorities of settlement regions are "*interconnection [havirah]* between existing Jewish areas for the creation of [Jewish] settlement continuity" and "*separation [hayitz]* to restrict uncontrolled Arab settlement and the prevention of Arab settlement blocs"; "*scarcity [hesech]* refers to areas devoid of Jewish settlement." In these criteria "pure planning and political planning elements are included."
>
> (*The West Bank Data Project: A Survey of Israeli Policies*)

Continuity for *them*, the dominant population; discontinuity for *us*, the dispossessed and dispersed.

The circle is completed, though, when we Palestinians acknowledge that much the same thesis is adhered to by Arab and other states where sizable Palestinian communities exist. There too we are in dispersed camps, regions, quarters, zones; but unlike their Israeli counterparts, these places are not the scientific product of "pure planning" or "political planning." The Baqa'a camp in Amman, the Palestinian quarter of Hawaly in Kuwait, are simply there.

All forms of Palestinian activity, all attempts at unity, are suspect. On the West Bank and Gaza, "development" (the systematic strengthening of Palestinian economic and social life) is forbidden, whereas "improvement" is tolerated so long as there isn't too much of it; so long as it doesn't become development. The colors of the Palestinian flag are outlawed by Israeli military law; Fathi Gabin of Gaza, an artist, was given a six-month prison sentence for using black, green, red, and white in one of his works. An exhibit of Palestinian culture at al-Najah University in Nablus earned the school a four-month closing. Since our history is forbidden, narratives are rare; the story of origins, of home, of nation is underground. When it appears it is broken, often wayward and meandering in the extreme, always coded, usually in outrageous forms—mock-epics, satires, sardonic parables, absurd rituals—that make little sense to an outsider. Thus Palestinian life is scattered, discontinuous, marked by the artificial and imposed arrangements of

Tyre, South Lebanon, 1983. Bourj el-Shemali camp. The car bears witness to a drama, circumstances unknown. The flowers: the month of May, it is spring. The children: wearing smart clothes, almost certainly donated by a charity. They are refugees— the children of refugees.

Bedouin encampment near Bersheeba, 1979.

interrupted or confined space, by the dislocations and unsynchronized
rhythms of disturbed time. Across our children's lives, in the open fields in
which they play, lie the ruins of war, of a borrowed or imported industrial
technology, of cast-off or abandoned forms. How odd the conjuncture, and
yet for Palestinians, how fitting. For where no straight line leads from
home to birthplace to school to maturity, all events are accidents, all progress is a digression, all residence is exile. We linger in nondescript places,
neither here nor there; we peer through windows without glass, ride con-

veyances without movement or power. Resourcefulness and receptivity are the attitudes that serve best.

The difference between the new generation of Palestinians and that of 1948 is striking. Our parents bore on their faces the marks of disaster uncomprehended. Suddenly their past had been interrupted, their society obliterated, their existence radically impoverished. Refugees, all of them. Our children know no such past. Cars are equally for riding or, ruined, for playing in. Everything around them seems expendable, impermanent, unstable, especially where—as in Lebanon—Palestinian communities have been disastrously depleted or destroyed, where much of their life is undocumented, where they themselves are uncounted.

No Palestinian census exists. There is no line that can be drawn from one Palestinian to another that does not seem to interfere with the political designs of one or another state. While all of us live among "normal" people, people with complete lives, they seem to us hopelessly out of reach, with their countries, their familial continuity, their societies intact. How does a Palestinian father tell his son and daughter that Lebanon (Egypt, Syria, Jordan, New York) is where we are, but not where we are *from*? How does a mother confirm her intimate recollections of childhood in Palestine to her children, now that the facts, the places, even the names, are no longer allowed to exist?

So we borrow and we patch things together. Palestinians retain the inflections of Jaffa, of Hebron, of Jerusalem and other cities left behind, even as their dialect becomes that of Beirut, Detroit, or Paris. I have found out much more about Palestine and met many more Palestinians than I ever did, or perhaps could have, in pre-1948 Palestine. For a long time I thought that this was so because I was a child then, somewhat sheltered, a member of a minority. But my experience is confirmed by my oldest and closest Palestinian friend, Ibrahim Abu-Lughod. Although he was more in and of pre-1948 Palestine—because older, more conscious and active—than I ever was, he too says that he is much more in contact with Palestinians today than when he was in Palestine. He writes,

> Thanks to modern technological progress, Palestinian families, and Palestinian society as a whole, have been able to forge very numerous human, social, and political links. By getting on a plane I can see the majority of my friends. It's because of this that our family has remained unified. I see all the members of my family at least once or twice a year. Being in Jaffa, I could never have seen relatives who lived in Gaza, for example.

But Ibrahim does not celebrate this sociability: "I constantly experience the sense that something is missing for me. To compensate for this lack, I multiply and intensify human contacts."

Over the missing "something" are superimposed new realities. Plane travel and phone conversations nourish and connect the fortunate; the symbols of a universal pop culture enshroud the vulnerable.

Gaza, 1979. Refugee camp. A boy of unknown age.

There can be no orderly sequence of time. You see it in our children who seem to have skipped a phase of growth or, more alarming, achieved an out-of-season maturity in one part of their body or mind while the rest remains childlike. None of us can forget the whispers and occasional proclamations that our children are "the population factor"—to be feared, and hence to be deported—or constitute special targets for death. I heard it said in Lebanon that Palestinian children in particular should be killed because each of them is a potential terrorist. Kill them before they kill you.

How rich our mutability, how easily we change (and are changed) from one thing to another, how unstable our place—and all because of the missing foundation of our existence, the lost ground of our origin, the broken link with our land and our past. There are no Palestinians. Who are the

Tel Sheva, 1979. A group portrait, taken at the request of the children.

Palestinians? "The inhabitants of Judea and Samaria." Non-Jews. Terrorists. Troublemakers. DPs.° Refugees. Names on a card. Numbers on a list.
Praised in speeches—*el pueblo palestino, il popolo palestino, le peuple pales-
tinien*—but treated as interruptions, intermittent presences. Gone from Jordan in 1970, now from Lebanon.

None of these departures and arrivals is clean, definitive. Some of us
leave, others stay behind. Remnants, new arrivals, old residents. Two great
images encapsulate our unresolved existence. One is the identity card
(passport, travel document, laissez-passer), which is never Palestinian but

---

DPs   Displaced persons or displaced people. [Editors' note] always something else; it is the subject of our national poem, Mahmoud Darwish's "Bitaqit Hawia": "Record! I am an Arab/Without a name— without title/patient in a country/with people enraged." And the second is Emil Habiby's invention the Pessoptimist (*al-mutasha'il*), the protagonist of a disorderly and ingenious work of Kafkaesque fiction, which has become a kind of national epic. The Pessoptimist is being half here, half not here, part historical creature, part mythological invention, hopeful and hopeless, everyone's favorite obsession and scapegoat. Is Habiby's character fiction, or does his extravagant fantasy only begin to approximate the real? Is he a made-up figure or the true essence of our existence? Is Habiby's jamming-together of words—*mutafa'il* and *mutasha'im* into *mutasha'il*, which repeats the Palestinian habit of combining opposites like *la* ("no") and *na'am* ("yes") into *la'am*—a way of obliterating distinctions that do not apply to us, yet must be integrated into our lives?

Emil Habiby is a craggy, uncompromisingly complex, and fearsomely ironic man from Haifa, son of a Christian family, Communist party stalwart, longtime Knesset member, journalist, editor. His novel about the Pessoptimist (whose first name, incidentally, is Said) is chaotic because it mixes time, characters, and places; fiction, allegory, history, and flat statement, without any thread to guide the reader through its complexities. It is the best work of Palestinian writing yet produced, precisely because the most seemingly disorganized and ironic. In it we encounter characters whose names are of par-

Bersheeba, 1979. Near a Bedouin encampment, a little kitchen garden—and its scarecrow of bits and pieces.

represents taking a people taking bits of them left by constant destruction and making use of what they not have (but have) taking a moment

ticular significance to Palestinians: The name of Yuaad, the work's female lead, means "it shall be repeated," a reference to the string of defeats that mark our history, and the fatalistic formulae that color our discourse. One of the other characters is Isam al-Bathanjani—Isam the Eggplant, a lawyer who is not very helpful to Said but who keeps turning up just the same. So it is with eggplants in Palestine. My family—my father in particular—has always been attached to eggplants from Battir, and during the many years since any of us had Battiri eggplants the seal of approval on good eggplants was that "they're almost as good as the Battiris."

Today when I recall the tiresome paeans to Battiris, or when in London and Paris I see the same Jaffa oranges or Gaza vegetables grown in the *bayarat* ("orchards") and fields of my youth, but now marketed by Israeli export companies, the contrast between the inarticulate rich *thereness* of what we once knew and the systematic export of the produce into the hungry mouths of Europe strikes me with its unkind political message. The land and the peasants are bound together through work whose products seem always to have meant something to other people, to have been destined for consumption elsewhere. This observation holds force not just because the Carmel boxes and the carefully wrapped eggplants are emblems of the power that rules the sprawling fertility and enduring human labor of Palestine, but also because the discontinuity between me, out here, and the actuality there is so much more compelling now than my receding memories and experiences of Palestine.

Another, far more unusual, item concerning this vegetable appears in an article by Avigdor Feldman, "The New Order of the Military Government: State of Israel Against the Eggplant," which appeared in the journal *Koteret Rashit*, August 24, 1983. Laws 1015 and 1039, Feldman reports, stipulate that any Arab on the West Bank and Gaza who owns land must get written permission from the military governor before planting either a new vegetable—for example, an eggplant—or fruit tree. Failure to get permission risks one the destruction of the tree or vegetable plus one year's imprisonment.

Exile again. The facts of my birth are so distant and strange as to be about someone I've heard of rather than someone I know. Nazareth—my mother's town. Jerusalem—my father's. The pictures I see display the same produce, presented in the same carelessly plentiful way, in the same rough wooden cases. The same people walk by, looking at the same posters and trinkets, concealing the same secrets, searching for the same profits, pleasures, and goals. The same as what? There is little that I can truly remember about Jerusalem and Nazareth, little that is specific, little that has the irreducible durability of tactile, visual, or auditory memories that concede nothing to time, little—and this is the "same" I referred to—that is not confused with pictures I have seen or scenes I have glimpsed elsewhere in the Arab world.

Gaza, 1979. Farm using refugee labor.

Palestine is exile, dispossession, the inaccurate memories of one place slipping into vague memories of another, a confused recovery of general wares, passive presences scattered around in the Arab environment. The story of Palestine cannot be told smoothly. Instead, the past, like the present, offers only occurrences and coincidences. Random. The man enters a quiet alley where he will pass cucumbers on his right, tomatoes on his left; a priest walks down the stairs, the boy dashes off, satchel under arm, other boys loiter, shopkeepers look out for business; carrying an airline bag, a man advances past a display of trinkets, a young man disappears around the corner, two boys idle aimlessly. Tomatoes, watermelons, arcades, cucumbers, posters, people, eggplants—not simply there, but represented by photographs as being there—saturated with meaning and memory, and still very far away. Look more closely and think through these possibilities: The poster is about Egypt. The trinkets are made in Korea or Hong Kong. The scenes are surveyed, enclosed, and surrounded by Israelis. European and Japanese tourists have more access to Jerusalem and Nazareth than I do. Slowly, our lives—like Palestine itself—dissolve into something else. We can't hold to the center for long.

Exile. At a recent conference in America featuring a "dialogue" between Israeli and Palestinian intellectuals with reconciliation high on the agenda, a man rises from the audience to pose a question. "I am a Palestinian, a peasant. Look at my hands. I was kicked out in 1948 and went to Lebanon. Then I was driven out, and went to Africa. Then to Europe. Then to here. Today [he

Nazareth, 1979. Portrait of Om Kalsoum.

Jerusalem, 1979. A snapshot.

Jerusalem, 1979. A snapshot.

pulls out an envelope] I received a paper telling me to leave this country. Would one of you scholars tell me please: Where am I supposed to go now?" No one had anything to tell him. He was an embarrassment, and I have no idea what in fact he did, what became of him. My shame.

The Palestinian's claims on Israel are generally unacknowledged, much less seen as directly connected to the founding of the state. On the Arabs

Old City of Jerusalem, 1984. A tourist shop. Customers are rare. Will they be American, Swiss, or Israeli?

Jerusalem, 1979.

there is an ambivalent Palestinian claim, recognized in Arab countries by countless words, gestures, threats, and promises. Palestine, after all, is the centerpiece of Arab nationalism. No Arab leader since World War II has failed to make Palestine a symbol of his country's nationalist foreign policy. Yet, despite the avowals, we have no way of knowing really how they—all the "theys"—feel about us. Our history has cost every one of our friends a great deal. It has gone on too long.

Let Ghassan Kanafani's novella *Men in the Sun* stand for the fear we have that unless we press "them" they will allow us to disappear, and the equal worry that if we press them they will either decry our hectoring presence, and quash it in their states, or turn us into easy symbols of their nationalism. Three refugees concealed in the belly of a tanker truck are being transported illegally across the border into Kuwait. As the driver converses with the guards, the men (Palestinians) die of suffocation—in the sun, forgotten. It is not the driver's forgetfulness that nags at him. It is their silence. "Why didn't you knock on the sides of the tank? Why didn't you bang the sides of the tank? Why? Why? Why?" Our fear to press.

The Palestinians as commodity. Producing ourselves much as the *masabih*, lamps, tapestries, baskets, embroideries, mother-of-pearl trinkets are produced. We turn ourselves into objects not for sale, but for scrutiny. People ask us, as if looking into an exhibit case, "What is it you Palestinians want?"—as if we can put our demands into a single neat phrase. All of us speak of *awdah*, "return," but do we mean that literally, or do we mean "we must restore ourselves to ourselves"? The latter is the real point, I think, although I know many Palestinians who want their houses and their way of life back, exactly. But is there any place that fits us, together with our accumulated memories and experiences?

Do we exist? What proof do we have?

The further we get from the Palestine of our past, the more precarious our status, the more disrupted our being, the more intermittent our presence. When did we become "a people"? When did we stop being one? Or are we in the process of becoming one? What do those big questions have to do with our intimate relationships with each other and with others? We frequently end our letters with the mottoes "Palestinian love" or "Palestinian kisses." Are there really such things as Palestinian intimacy and embraces, or are they simply intimacy and embraces, experiences common to everyone, neither politically significant nor particular to a nation or a people?

The politics of such a question gets very close to our central dilemma: We all know that we are Arabs, and yet the concept, not to say the lived actuality, of Arabism—once the creed and the discourse of a proud Arab nation, free of imperialism, united, respected, powerful—is fast disappearing, cut up into the cautious defensiveness of relatively provincial Arab states, each with its own traditions—partly invented, partly real—each with its own nationality and restricted identity. In addition, Palestine has been replaced by an Israel whose aggressive sense of itself as the state of the Jewish people fuels the exclusivity of a national identity won and maintained to a great extent at our expense. We are not Jews, we have no place there except as resident aliens, we are outsiders. In the Arab states we are in a different position. There we are Arabs, but it is the process of nationalization that excludes us: Egypt is for and by Egyptians, Iraq is for and by Iraqis, in ways that cannot include Palestinians whose intense national revival is a separate phenomenon. Thus we are the same as other Arabs, and yet different. We cannot exist except as Arabs, even though "the Arabs" exist otherwise as Lebanese, Jordanians, Moroccans, Kuwaitis, and so forth.

Add to this the problems we have of sustaining ourselves as a collective unit and you then get a sense of how *abstract*, how very solitary and unique, we tend to feel.

Strip off the occasional assertiveness and stridency of the Palestinian stance and you may catch sight of a much more fugitive, but ultimately quite beautifully representative and subtle, sense of identity. It speaks in languages not yet fully formed, in settings not completely constituted, like the shy glance of a child holding her father's knee while she curiously and tentatively examines the stranger who photographs her. Her look conjures up the unappreciated fact of birth, that sudden, unprepared-for depositing of a small bundle of self on the fields of the Levant after which comes the

Village of Ramah, Galilee, 1979. A secular high school with students from thirty-six neighboring villages.

trajectory of dispossession, military and political violence, and that constant, mysterious entanglement with monotheistic religion at its most profound—the Christian Incarnation and Resurrection, the Ascension to heaven of the Prophet Mohammed, the Covenant of Yahweh with his people—that is knotted definitively in Jerusalem, center of the world, *locus classicus* of Palestine, Israel, and Paradise.

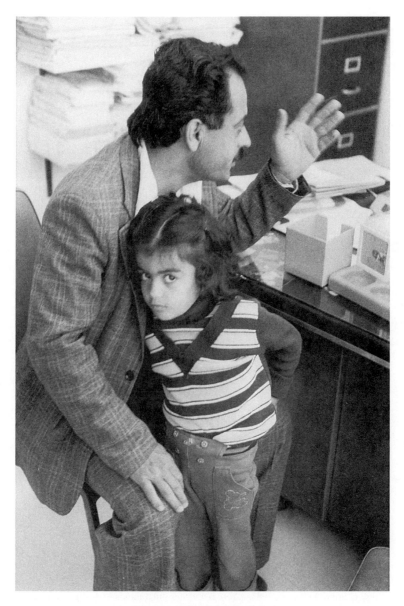

Amman, 1984. Pediatric clinic.

A secular world of fatigue and miraculously renewed energies, the world of American cigarettes and an unending stream of small papers pulled out of miscellaneous notebooks or "blocnotes," written on with disposable pens, messages of things wanted, of people missing, of requests to the bureaucracy. The Palestinian predicament: finding an "official" place for yourself in a system that makes no allowances for you,

Sidon, South Lebanon, 1983. A refugee writes out a message destined for her husband, a prisoner in the camp at Ansar.

which means endlessly improvising solutions for the problem of finding a missing loved one, of planning a trip, of entering a school, on whatever bit of paper is at hand. Constructed and deconstructed, ephemera are what we negotiate with, since we authorize no part of the world and only influence increasingly small bits of it. In any case, we keep going.

The striking thing about Palestinian prose and prose fiction is its formal instability: Our literature in a certain very narrow sense *is* the elusive, resistant reality it tries so often to represent. Most literary critics in Israel and the West focus on what is said in Palestinian writing, who is described, what the plot and contents deliver, their sociological and political meaning. But it is *form* that should be looked at. Particularly in fiction, the struggle to achieve form expresses the writer's efforts to construct a coherent scene, a narrative that might overcome the almost metaphysical impossibility of representing the present. A typical Palestinian work will always be concerned with this peculiar problem, which is at once a problem of plot and an enactment of the writer's enterprise. In Kanafani's *Men in the Sun* much of the action takes place on the dusty streets of an Iraqi town where three Palestinian men must petition, plead, and bargain with "specialists" to smuggle them across the border into Kuwait. Impelled by exile and dislocation, the Palestinians need to carve a path for themselves in existence, which for them is by no means a given or stable reality. Like the history of the lands they left, their lives seem interrupted just before they could come to maturity and satisfaction; thus each man leaves behind family and responsibilities, to whose exigencies he must answer—unsuccessfully—here in the present. Kanafani's very sentences express instability and fluctuation—the present tense is subject to echoes from the past, verbs of sight give way to verbs of sound or smell, and one sense interweaves with another—in an effort to defend against the harsh present and to protect some particularly cherished fragment of the past. Thus, the precarious actuality of these men in the sun reproduces the precarious status of the writer, each echoing the other.

Our characteristic mode, then, is not a narrative, in which scenes take place *seriatim*, but rather broken narratives, fragmentary compositions, and self-consciously staged testimonials, in which the narrative voice keeps stumbling over itself, its obligations, and its limitations.

Each Palestinian structure presents itself as a potential ruin. The theme of the formerly proud family house (village, city, camp) now wrecked, left behind, or owned by someone else, turns up everywhere in our literature and cultural heritage. Each new house is a substitute, supplanted in turn by yet another substitute. The names of these places extend all the way from the private (my friend Mohammed Tarbush expatiates nobly on the beauties of Beit Natif, a village near Bethlehem that was wiped out of existence by Israeli bulldozers in 1948; his widowed mother now lives in Jarash, Jordan, he in Paris) to the official, or institutionalized, sites of ruin—Deir Yassin, Tell el-Zaatar, Birim and Ikrit, Ein el-Hilwé, Sabra, Shatila, and more. Even "Palestine" itself is such a place and, curiously, already appears as a subject of elegy in journalism, essays, and literature of the early twentieth century. In the works of Halim Nassar, Ezzat Darwaza, Khallil Beidas, and Aref el-Aref, Palestine's destruction is predicted.

Sidon, South Lebanon, 1983. Camp at Ein el-Hilwé. Time passes: destruction, reconstruction, redestruction.

All cultures spin out a dialectic of self and other, the subject "I" who is native, authentic, at home, and the object "it" or "you," who is foreign, perhaps threatening, different, out there. From this dialectic comes the series of heroes and monsters, founding fathers and barbarians, prized masterpieces and despised opponents that express a culture from its deepest sense of national self-identity to its refined patriotism, and finally to its coarse jingoism, xenophobia, and exclusivist bias. For Palestinian culture, the odd thing is that its own identity is more frequently than not perceived as "other." "Palestine" is so charged with significance for others that Palestinians cannot perceive it as intimately theirs without a simultaneous sense of its urgent importance for others as well. "Ours" but not yet fully "ours." Before 1948, Palestine had a central agonistic meaning both for Arab nationalism and for the Zionist movement. After 1948, the parts of Palestine still inhabited by Arabs took on the additional label of the "non-Jewish" part of the Jewish state. Even a picture of an Arab town—like Nazareth where my mother was born and grew up—may express this alienating perspective. Because it is taken from outside Nazareth (in fact, from Upper Nazareth, a totally Jewish addition to the town, built on the surrounding hills), the photograph renders Palestine as "other." I never knew Nazareth, so this is my only image of it, an image of the "other," from the "outside," Upper Nazareth.

Thus the insider becomes the outsider. Not only have the interpositions between us and Palestine grown more formidable over time, but, to make matters worse, most of us pass our lives separated from each other. Yet we live in comradely communication despite the barriers. Today the Palestinian genius expresses itself in crossings-over, in clearing hurdles, activities that do not lessen the alienation, discontinuity, and dispossession, but that dramatize and clarify them instead. We have remained; in the words of Tawfik Zayyad's famous poem, "The Twenty Impossibles," it would be easier "to catch fried fish in the Milky Way,/to plow the sea,/to teach the alligator speech" than to make us leave. To the Israelis, whose incomparable military and political power dominates us, we are at the periphery, the image that will not go away. Every assertion of our nonexistence, every attempt to spirit us away, every new effort to prove that we were never really there, simply raises the question of why so much denial of, and such energy expended on, what was not there? Could it be that even as alien outsiders we dog their military might with our obdurate moral claim, our insistence (like that of Bartleby the Scrivener) that "we would prefer not to," not to leave, not to abandon Palestine forever?

The proof of whatever small success we have had is not that we have regained a homeland, or acquired a new one; rather, it is that some Israelis have admitted the possibility of sharing a common space with us, in Palestine. The proposed modes of such a sharing are adventurous and utopian in the present context of hostility between Arabs and Jews, but on an intellectual level they are actual, and to some of us — on both sides — they make

Arab Nazareth, 1979. Viewed from Upper Nazareth.

Tyre, South Lebanon, 1983. Rashidyé camp: A local official
collects messages from the relations of refugees for the
International Red Cross.

sense. Most Palestinians have their own special instance of the Israeli who
reached out across the barricade most humanly. For some it is the intrepid
Israeli lawyer defending Palestinian political prisoners, or trying to prevent land expropriations and collective punishment; for others it is—the
testimony of Salah Ta'amari, leader of the Palestinian prisoners rounded
up during the Israeli invasion and put in the Ansar prison camp, comes to
mind—an Israeli in a position of authority (prison guard or army officer)
who prevented some atrocity or showed some clear sign of humanity and
fellow feeling. For my part, removed from the terrible pressures of the
scene, I think of all the Israeli (or non-Israeli) Jews whose articulate wit-

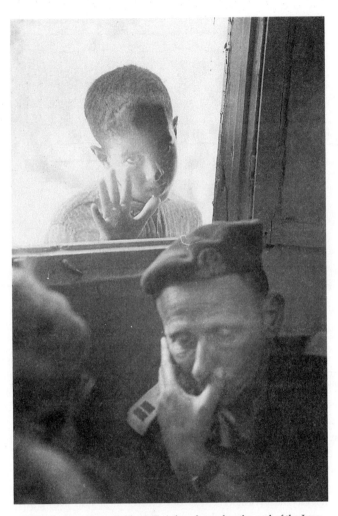

Kalandia (near Ramallah), 1967. A few days after the end of the June War: in the foreground, an Israeli officer, lost in thought. Behind the window, a young villager.

ness to the injustice of their people against mine has marked out a communal territory. The result has usually been a friendship whose depth is directly proportional to the admiration I feel for their tenacity of conscience and belief in the face of the most slanderous attacks. Surely few have equaled the courage and principle of Israel Shahak, of Leah Tsemal and Felicia Langer, of Noam Chomsky, of Izzy Stone, of Elmer Berger, of Matti Peled, of so many others who stood up bravely during the events in Lebanon.

There are few opportunities for us Palestinians, or us Palestinians *and* Israelis, to learn anything about the world we live in that is *not* touched

Jerusalem, 1979. A dialogue between left-wing Israeli and Arab intellectuals.

by, indeed soaked in, the hostilities of our struggle. And if it isn't the Palestinian-Zionist struggle, there are the pressures of religion, of every conceivable ideology, of family, peers, and compatriots, each of them bearing down upon us, pushing, kneading, prodding every one of us from childhood to maturity.

In such an environment, learning itself is a chancy, hybrid activity, laced with the unresolvable antitheses of our age. The child is full of the curious hope and undirected energy that attract the curatorial powers of both church and state. Fortunately, here the spirit of the creative urge in all human activity asserts itself—neither church nor state can ultimately exhaust, or control, the possibilities latent in the classroom, playground, or family. An orderly row of chairs and tables, a disciplined recitation circle in a Catholic school with a nun in charge, are also places for the absorption of more knowledge and experience than authorities impart—places where the child explores here and there, his/her mind and body wandering in space and time despite the constraints in each. In a school where the teacher is a devout Muslim, the child's propensity for disturbing or opposing the schemes of knowledge and discipline causes him/her to leave the table, disrupt the pattern, seek unthought-of possibilities. The tension between teachers and students remains, but better the tension than the peace of passivity, or the unresisting assent to authority.

The pressures of the here and now require an answer to the Palestinian crisis here and now. Whereas our interlocutors, our "others"—the Arab states, the United States, the USSR, Israel, our friends and enemies—have the luxury of a state in which institutions do their work undisturbed by the

Nazareth, 1979. A municipal kindergarten, looked after by nuns.

question of existence-or-not, we lead our lives under a sword of Damocles, whose dry rhetorical form is the query "When are you Palestinians going to accept a solution?"—the implication being that if we don't, we'll disappear. This, then, is our midnight hour.

It is difficult to know how much the often stated, tediously reiterated worries about us, which include endless lectures on the need for a clear Palestinian statement of the desire for peace (as if we controlled the decisive factors!), are malicious provocation and how much genuine, if sympathetic, ignorance. I don't think any of us reacts as impatiently to such things as we did, say, five years ago. True, our collective situation is more precarious now than it was, but I detect a general turning inward among Palestinians, as if many of us feel the need to consolidate and collect the shards

Amman, 1984. Camp at Baqa'a, one of the oldest in Jordan. The YWCA looks after
some of the kindergartens.

of Palestinian life still present and available to us. This is not quietism at all, nor is it resignation. Rather, it springs from the natural impulse to stand back when the headlong rush of events gets to be too much, perhaps, for us to savor life as life, to reflect at some distance from politics on where we came from and where we are, to regrasp, revise, recomprehend the tumultuous experiences at whose center, quite without our consent, we have been made to stand.

Jean Mohr's photograph [p. 604] of a small but clearly formed human group surrounded by a dense and layered reality expresses very well what we experience during that detachment from an ideologically saturated world. This image of four people seen at a distance near Ramallah, in the middle of and yet separated from thick foliage, stairs, several tiers of terraces and houses, a lone electricity pole off to the right, is for me a private, crystallized, almost Proustian evocation of Palestine. Memory: During the summer of 1942—I was six—we rented a house in Ramallah. My father, I recall, was ill with high blood pressure and recovering from a nervous breakdown. I remember him as withdrawn and constantly smoking. My mother took me to a variety show at the local Friends school. During the second half I left the hall to go to the toilet, but for reasons I could not (and still do not) grasp, the boy-scout usher would not let me back in. I recall with ever-renewed poignancy the sudden sense of distance I experienced from what was familiar and pleasant—my mother, friends, the show; all at once the rift introduced into the cozy life I led taught me the meaning of separation, of solitude, and of anguished boredom. There was nothing to do but wait,

Jerusalem, 1984.

Near Senjel, a village between Ramallah and Nablus, 1979.

although my mother did appear a little later to find out what had happened to me. We left immediately, but not before I furtively took a quick look back through the door window at the lighted stage. The telescoped vision of small figures assembled in a detached space has remained with me for over forty years, and it reappears in the adjusted and transformed center of Jean's 1983 picture. I never ventured anywhere near that part of Ramallah again. I would no more know it than I would the precise place of this photo; and yet I am sure it would be familiar, the way this one immediately seemed.

My private past is inscribed on the surface of this peaceful but some-how brooding pastoral scene in the contemporary West Bank. I am not the only one surveying the scene. There is the child on the left who looks on. There are also the Swiss photographer, compassionate, curious, silent, and of course the ever-present Israeli security services, who hold the West Bank and its population in the vise of occupation. As for those terraces and mul-tiple levels: Do they serve the activities of daily life or are they the haunted stairs of a prison which, like Piranesi's, lead nowhere, confining their human captives? The dense mass of leaves, right and left, lend their bulk to the frame, but they too impinge on the slender life they surround, like memory or a history too complex to be sorted out, bigger than its subject, richer than any consciousness one might have of it.

The power grid recalls the Mercedes in Tripoli. Unassimilated, its modernity and power have been felt with considerable strength in our lives here and there throughout the Third World. Another childhood memory: Driving through the Sinai from Egypt into Palestine, we would see the row of telephone and electricity pylons partnering the empty macadamized road that cut through an even emptier desert. Who are they, I would ask myself. What do they think when we are not here? When we stopped to stretch our legs, I would go up to a pole and look at its dull brown surface for some sign of life, identity, or awareness. Once I marked one with my initials EWS, hoping to find it again on the trip back. All of them looked exactly the same as we hurtled by. We never stopped. I never drove there again, nor can I now. Futile efforts to register my presence on the scene.

Intimate memory and contemporary social reality seem connected by the little passage between the child, absorbed in his private, silent sphere, and the three older people, who are the public world of adults, work, and community. It is a vacant, somewhat tenuously maintained space, however; sandy, pebbly, and weedy. All the force in the photograph moves dramatically from trees left to trees right, from the visible enclave of domesticity (stairs, houses, terrace) to the unseen larger world of power and authority beyond. I wonder whether the four people are in fact connected, or whether as a group they simply happen to be in the way of unseen forces totally indifferent to the dwelling and living space these people inhabit. This is also, then, a photograph of latent, of impending desolation, and once again I am depressed by the transience of Palestinian life, its vulnerability and all too easy dislocation. But another movement, another feeling, asserts itself in response, set in motion by the two strikingly marked openings in the buildings, openings that suggest rich, cool interiors which outsiders cannot penetrate. Let us enter.

•   •   •   •   •   •   •   •   •   •   •

QUESTIONS FOR A SECOND READING

1. The first three paragraphs provide a "reading" of the opening photograph, "Tripoli, Badawi camp, May 1983." Or, to put it another way, the writing evolves from and is in response to that photograph. As you reread these paragraphs, pay close attention to what Said is doing, to what he notices, to what prompts or requires commentary. How would you describe and explain the writing that follows? What is he doing with the photo? What is he doing as a writer? What is he doing for a reader? (How does he position a reader?)

It might be useful to begin by thinking about what Said is *not* doing. It is not, for example, the presentation one might expect in a slide show on travel in Lebanon. Nor is it the kind of presentation one might expect while seeing the slides of family or friends, or slides in an art history or art appreciation class.

Once you have worked through the opening three paragraphs, reread the essay paying attention to Said's work with all the photographs. Is there a pattern? Do any of the commentaries stand out for their force, variety, innovation?

2. Here is another passage from the introduction to *After the Last Sky:*

> Its style and method—the interplay of text and photos, the mixture of genres, modes, styles—do not tell a consecutive story, nor do they constitute a political essay. Since the main features of our present existence are dispossession, dispersion, and yet also a kind of power incommensurate with our stateless exile, I believe that essentially unconventional, hybrid, and fragmentary forms of expression should be used to represent us. What I have quite consciously designed, then, is an alternative mode of expression to the one usually encountered in the media, in works of social science, in popular fiction. (p. 6)

And later:

> The multifaceted vision is essential to any representation of us. Stateless, dispossessed, de-centered, we are frequently unable either to speak the "truth" of our experience or to make it heard. We do not usually control the images that represent us; we have been confined to spaces designed to reduce or stunt us; and we have often been distorted by pressures and powers that have been too much for us. An additional problem is that our language, Arabic, is unfamiliar in the West and belongs to a tradition and civilization usually both misunderstood and maligned. Everything we write about ourselves, therefore, is an interpretive translation—of our language, our experience, our senses of self and others. (p. 6)

And from "States":

> The striking thing about Palestinian prose and prose fiction is its formal instability: Our literature in a certain very narrow sense *is* the elusive, resistant reality it tries so often to represent. Most literary critics in Israel and the West focus on what is said in Palestinian writing, who is described, what the plot and contents deliver, their sociological and political meaning. But it is *form* that should be looked at. Particularly in fiction, the struggle to achieve form expresses the writer's efforts to construct a coherent scene, a narrative that might overcome the almost metaphysical impossibility of representing the present. (p. 595)

As you reread, think about form—organization, arrangement, and genre. What *is* the order of the writing in this essay? (We will call it an essay for lack of a better term.) How might you diagram or explain its organization? By what principle(s) is it ordered and arranged? The essay shifts genres— memoir, history, argument. It is, as Said says, "hybrid." What surprises are there? or disappointments? How might you describe the writer's strategy as he works on his audience, on readers? And, finally, do you find Said's explanation sufficient or useful—does the experience of exile produce its own inevitable style of report and representation?

3. The essay is filled with references to people (including writers), places, and events that are, most likely, foreign to you. Choose one that seems interesting or important, worth devoting time to research. Of course the Internet will be a resource, but you should also use the library, if only to become aware of the different opportunities and materials it provides. Compile a report of the additional information; be prepared to discuss how the research has served or changed your position as a reader of "States."

4. The final chapter of *After the Last Sky* ends with this:

> I would like to think, though, that such a book not only tells the reader about us, but in some way also reads the reader. I would like to think that we are not just the people seen or looked at in these photographs: We are also looking at our observers. (p. 166)

Read back through Said's essay by looking at the photos with this reversal in mind—looking in order to see yourself as the one who is being looked at, as the one observed. How are you positioned by the photographer, Jean Mohr? How are you positioned by the person in the scene, always acknowledging your presence? What are you being told?

Once you have read through the photographs, reread the essay with a similar question in mind. This time, however, look for evidence of how Said positions you, defines you, invents you as a presence in the scene.

ASSIGNMENTS FOR WRITING

1. Compose a similar project, a Said-like reading of a set of photos. These can be photos prepared for the occasion (by you or a colleague); they could also be photos already available. Whatever their source, they should represent people and places, a history and/or geography that you know well, that you know to be complex and contradictory, and that you know will not be easily or readily understood by others, both the group for whom you will be writing (most usefully the members of your class) and readers more generally. You must begin with a sense that the photos cannot speak for themselves; you must speak for them.

In preparation, you should reread closely to come to a careful understanding of Said's project. (The first and second "Questions for a Second Reading" should be useful for this.) To prepare a document that is Said-like (one that shows your understanding of what Said is doing), you will need an expert's sense of how to write from and to photographs, and you will need to consider questions of form—of order, arrangement, and genre.

2. While "States" does not present itself as polemical writing—an argument in defense of Palestinian rights, an argument designed to locate blame or propose national or international policy—it is, still, writing with a purpose. It has an argument, it has a particular project in mind, and it wants something to happen.

Write an essay that represents the argument or the project of "States" for someone who has not read it. You will need, in other words, to establish a context and to summarize. You should also work from passages (and images) to give your reader a sense of the text, its key terms and language. And write about "States" as though it has something to do with you.

Your essay is not just summary, in other words, but summary in service of statement, response, or extension. As you are invited to think about the Palestinians, or about exile more generally, or about the texts and images that are commonly available, what do you think? What do you have to add?

3. The final chapter of *After the Last Sky* ends with this:

    > I would like to think, though, that such a book not only tells the reader about us, but in some way also reads the reader. I would like to think that we are not just the people seen or looked at in these photographs: We are also looking at our observers. (p. 166)

    The fourth question in "Questions for a Second Reading" sets a strategy for rereading with this passage in mind—looking in order to see yourself as the one who is being looked at, as the one observed. Write an essay in which you think this through by referring specifically to images and to text. How are you positioned? by whom and to what end?

4. Said insists upon our recognizing the contemporary social, political, and historic context for intimate scenes he (and Jean Mohr) present of people going about their everyday lives. The Palestinian people are still much in the news—there are photographs of scenes from their lives featured regularly in newspapers, magazines, and on the Internet. Collect a series of these images from a particular and defined recent period of time—a week or a month, say, when the Palestinians have been in the news. Using these images, and putting them in conversation with some of the passages and images in "States," write an essay in the manner of Said's essay, with text and image in productive relationship. The goal of your essay should be to examine how Said's work, in "States," can speak to us (or might speak to us) today.

MAKING CONNECTIONS

1. Edward Said talks about the formal problems in the writing of "States" (and for more on this, see the second of the "Questions for a Second Reading"):

    > The striking thing about Palestinian prose and prose fiction is its formal instability: Our literature in a certain very narrow sense *is* the elusive, resistant reality it tries so often to represent. Most literary critics in Israel and the West focus on what is said in Palestinian writing, who is described, what the plot and contents deliver, their sociological and political meaning. But it is *form* that should be looked at. Particularly in fiction, the struggle to achieve form expresses the writer's efforts to construct a coherent scene, a narrative that might overcome the almost metaphysical impossibility of representing the present. (p. 595)

    And here is a similar discussion from the introduction to *After the Last Sky*:

    > The multifaceted vision is essential to any representation of us. Stateless, dispossessed, de-centered, we are frequently unable either to speak the "truth" of our experience or to make it heard. We do not usually control the images that represent us; we have been confined to spaces

> designed to reduce or stunt us; and we have often been distorted by
> pressures and powers that have been too much for us. An additional
> problem is that our language, Arabic, is unfamiliar in the West and be-
> longs to a tradition and civilization usually both misunderstood and
> maligned. Everything we write about ourselves, therefore, is an inter-
> pretive translation — of our language, our experience, our senses of self
> and others. (p. 6)

Edward Said's sense of his project as a writing project, a writing project requiring formal experimentation, is similar to Gloria Anzaldúa's in *Borderlands / La frontera*. In the two chapters represented in *Ways of Reading*, "Entering into the Serpent" (p. 29) and "How to Tame a Wild Tongue" (p. 42),
Anzaldúa is also writing (and resisting) "interpretive translation." In place
of the photographs in "States," she offers poems, stories, and myths, passages in Spanish.

    Write an essay in which you consider these selections as writing
projects. The formal experimentation in each is said by the writers to be fundamental, necessary, a product of the distance between a particular world of
experience and the available modes of representation. In what ways are the
essays similar? In what ways are they different? Where and how is a reader
(where and how are you) positioned in each? What is the experience of reading them? What does one need to learn to be their ideal reader?

2. One of the unusual features of the selections from W. G. Sebald's *The Rings
of Saturn* (p. 570) are the illustrations — oddly chosen, difficult (at times) to
see, and yet clearly important to the text. Read Sebald's two chapters with
an eye to the relationship between image and text. Image and text are in an
interesting and unusual relationship as well in Said's "States."

    As you read Sebald, choose two or three images that you find particu-
larly striking or interesting (or puzzling). What is their purpose? That is, as
you imagine the author's project, why would it invite or require illustrations? How does a reader work with them? That is, as you come upon
them, how do they work in relation to the text? What is your theory of the
use of images in these chapters?

    With this project in mind, reread Edward Said's "States." Both projects
begin with the assumption that word or image is not enough by itself; they
must work together. Write an essay in which you describe that work in each
of these two cases. How are the collaborations different? How do word and
image work together in each case? How might we understand the differences and, through them, the limits of word or image alone?

3. There are several writers in *Ways of Reading* whose writing could be called
unconventional, even experimental. A short list includes Gloria Anzaldúa,
Susan Griffin, John Edgar Wideman, and W. G. Sebald. (We can imagine
arguments for several other selections as well.)

    Choose a selection from one of these writers to read alongside Edward
Said's "States." As you read the two, pay particular attention to what the
writing does, to how it works. This is not quite the same as paying attention
to what it says. What does this way of writing allow each writer to do that
another style, perhaps "topic sentence, examples, and conclusion," would
not? What does it offer a reader — or what does it allow a reader to do?

Write an essay in which you compare the styles of these two essays. Is there one that you find compelling or attractive? If each provides a textbook example, what are you invited to think about as you consider the possibilities and limits of your own style? Of "standard" or "school" style? In what ways might this work be seen as a way of working on the problems of writing? And what might this work have to do with you, a student in a writing class?

4. Said says,

> All cultures spin out a dialectic of self and other, the subject "I" who is native, authentic, at home, and the object "it" or "you," who is foreign, perhaps threatening, different, out there. From this dialectic comes the series of heroes and monsters, founding fathers and barbarians, prized masterpieces and despised opponents that express a culture from its deepest sense of national self-identity to its refined patriotism, and finally to its coarse jingoism, xenophobia, and exclusivist bias. (p. 596)

This is as true of the Palestinians as it is of the Israelis—although, he adds, "For Palestinian culture, the odd thing is that its own identity is more frequently than not perceived as 'other'."

Citing Benedict Anderson and what he refers to as "imagined communities," Mary Louise Pratt in "Arts of the Contact Zone" (p. 499) argues that our idea of community is "strongly utopian, embodying values like equality, fraternity, liberty, which the societies often profess but systematically fail to realize." Against this utopian vision of community, Pratt argues that we need to develop ways of understanding (noticing or creating) social and intellectual spaces that are not homogeneous or unified—contact zones; she argues that we need to develop ways of understanding and valuing difference.

There are similar goals and objects to these projects. Reread Pratt's essay with Said's "States" in mind. Recalling what she refers to as the "literate arts of the contact zone," can you find points of reference in Said's text? Said's thinking always attended to the importance and the conditions of writing, including his own. There are ways that "States" could be imagined as both "autoethnographic" and "transcultural." How might his work allow you to understand the "literate arts of the contact zone" in practice? How might his work allow you to understand the problems and possibilities of such writing beyond what Pratt has imagined, presented, and predicted?

5. Jean Mohr's collaboration with John Berger was important to Said, particularly in the 1975 book *A Seventh Man*, a photographic essay on migrant workers in Europe. Find a copy of *A Seventh Man* (in a library or a bookstore or online) and write an essay on what you think it was in Mohr's work, and in his collaboration with Berger, that was most compelling to Said.

W. G.
SEBALD

*WINFRIED GEORG "MAX" SEBALD (1944–2001)
was born in a small, rural town in Bavaria, Germany,
during World War II. He was of that generation of German children who grew up when the effects of the war
were seen and felt everywhere. His father, a POW in
France, wasn't released until 1947, when Sebald was three.
As a child, Sebald witnessed the horrible destruction of
Germany's cities and countryside, which he wrote about
later in his life. When he was growing up, however, there
was silence about the war. It was not to be talked about; it
was something to forget—and to forget as quickly as possible. Sebald tells the story
of a day in grade school when his class was shown newsreel footage of the concentration camp at Belsen, and yet there was no discussion, no context, no way to
place or to understand what they had seen.*

*Sebald was educated in Germany and then, as a graduate student, in England,
where he eventually became a distinguished academic, writing primarily on German and Austrian literature. He spent most of his career at the University of East
Anglia, where he was a professor of German (in the Department of European Languages and Literatures) and he was the director of the British Centre for Literary
Translation. Relatively late in his career as a professor, he began to write "literary*

prose"—he was always hesitant to call himself a novelist—and published a series of four books, all written originally in German, that brought him great success and international acclaim: Vertigo (1990, English translation 2000); The Emigrants (1993, English translation 1996—this book brought him a wide readership in the United States); The Rings of Saturn (1995, English translation 1998); and Austerlitz (2001, English translation 2001). Four more books were published in English translation after his death, from an automobile accident, in 2001: For Years Now: Poems; After Nature; On the Natural History of Destruction; and Unrecounted (poems).

Critics have had trouble describing Sebald's books of prose, books often cataloged as novels. They are not structured or plotted as novels. (Sebald disapproved of the novel's preoccupation with the personal and with insignificant detail.) Sebald's books mix genres. They are part travelog, part memoir, part essay, and part fiction. It is often hard to know what is fiction and what is fact in his writing. (Sebald once said that in his books the big events were true; only the details were invented.) Sebald writes about German and European history, yet always obliquely and seldom through direct, extended reference to the major events of the twentieth century—World War II, the Holocaust, the Berlin Wall. Speaking of The Emigrants, André Aciman said: "Supremely tactful, Sebald never brings up the Holocaust. The reader, meanwhile, thinks of nothing else." In an obituary, his friend and colleague, Eric Homberger, said that Sebald, in his writing about the war, "claimed no false intimacy with the dead."

The Rings of Saturn, from which the following selections are taken, is perhaps the oddest of Sebald's major books. It blends story with documentary, essay with memoir; it provides an extended discussion of the work of the seventeenth-century British physician and writer Sir Thomas Browne and observations on Rembrandt's painting The Anatomy Lesson. There are chapters (not included here) that speak of the natural history of the herring (and the decline of the fishing industry in England) and of the Chinese empress Tzu Hsi. It is travelog—each chapter marking the progress of a trip down the coast of East Anglia. You can follow the stops on a map. (In the German edition, it was subtitled An English Pilgrimage.) It is also the story of the speaker, a W. G. Sebald who emerges as a character (an odd character), writing the book from memory, from photographs, and from notes, all while recovering from a personal crisis.

It is not a book designed to seduce or to engage a reader, at least not using the familiar strategies—action, color, emotion, excitement—and yet The Rings of Saturn has seduced and engaged readers around the world, and Sebald is thought of as one of the great prose stylists and one of the great writers of our time. As you read these selections (chapters 1 and 4 of the original), you might ask yourself why. What is it that has led others to describe his work as brilliant, serious, beautiful, and thrilling?

The Rings of Saturn

I

In August 1992, when the dog days were drawing to an end, I set off to walk the county of Suffolk, in the hope of dispelling the emptiness that takes hold of me whenever I have completed a long stint of work. And in fact my hope was realized, up to a point; for I have seldom felt so carefree as I did then, walking for hours in the day through the thinly populated countryside, which stretches inland from the coast. I wonder now, however, whether there might be something in the old superstition that certain ailments of the spirit and of the body are particularly likely to beset us under the sign of the Dog Star. At all events, in retrospect I became preoccupied not only with the unaccustomed sense of freedom but also with the paralyzing horror that had come over me at various times when confronted with the traces of destruction, reaching far back into the past, that were evident even in that remote place. Perhaps it was because of this that, a year to the day after I began my tour, I was taken into hospital in Norwich in a state of almost total immobility. It was then that I began in my thoughts to write these pages. I can remember precisely how, upon being admitted to that room on the eighth floor, I became overwhelmed by the feeling that the Suffolk expanses I had walked the previous summer had now shrunk once and for all to a single, blind, insensate spot. Indeed, all that could be seen of the world from my bed was the colorless patch of sky framed in the window.

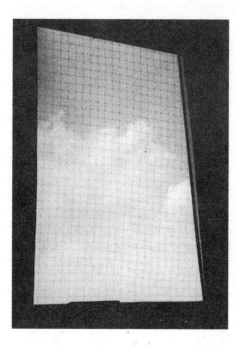

Several times during the day I felt a desire to assure myself of a reality I feared had vanished forever by looking out of that hospital window, which, for some strange reason, was draped with black netting, and as dusk fell the wish became so strong that, contriving to slip over the edge of the bed to the floor, half on my belly and half sideways, and then to reach the wall on all fours, I dragged myself, despite the pain, up to the windowsill. In the tortured posture of a creature that has raised itself erect for the first time I stood leaning against the glass. I could not help thinking of the scene in which poor Gregor Samsa, his little legs trembling, climbs the armchair and looks out of his room, no longer remembering (so Kafka's narrative goes) the sense of liberation that gazing out of the window had formerly given him. And just as Gregor's dimmed eyes failed to recognize the quiet street where he and his family had lived for years, taking Charlottenstrabe for a grey wasteland, so I too found the familiar city, extending from the hospital courtyards to the far horizon, an utterly alien place. I could not believe that anything might still be alive in that maze of buildings down there; rather, it was as if I were looking down from a cliff upon a sea of stone or a field of rubble, from which the tenebrous masses of multistorey carparks rose up like immense boulders. At that twilit hour there were no passers-by to be seen in the immediate vicinity, but for a nurse crossing the cheerless gardens outside the hospital entrance on the way to her night shift. An ambulance with its light flashing was negotiating a number of turns on its way from the city center to Casualty. I could not hear its siren; at that height I was cocooned in an almost complete and, as it were, artificial silence. All I could hear was the wind sweeping in from the country and buffeting the window; and in between, when the sound subsided, there was the never entirely ceasing murmur in my own ears.

Now that I begin to assemble my notes, more than a year after my discharge from hospital, I cannot help thinking of Michael Parkinson who was, as I stood watching the city fade into the dying light, still alive in his small house in the Portersfield Road, busy perhaps, preparing a seminar or working on his study of Charles Ramuz, which had occupied him for many years. Michael was in his late forties, a bachelor, and, I believe, one of the most innocent people I have ever met. Nothing was ever further from his thoughts than self-interest; nothing troubled him quite so much as the dire responsibility of performing his duties, under increasingly adverse conditions. Above all, he was remarkable for the modesty of his needs, which some considered bordered on eccentricity. At a time when most people have constantly to be shopping in order to survive, Michael seemed to have no such need. Year in, year out, as long as I knew him, he wore either a navy blue or a rust-colored jacket, and if the cuffs were frayed or the elbows threadbare he would sew on leather trims or patches. He even turned the collars of his shirts himself. In the summer vacations, Michael would make long walking tours of the Valais and the area around Lake Geneva, in connection with his Ramuz studies, and sometimes in the Jura or the Cévennes. It often seemed to me, when he returned from these travels or when I marvelled at the degree of dedication he always brought to his work, that in his own way he had found happiness, in a modest form that is scarcely conceivable nowadays. But then without warning last May Michael, who had not been seen for some days, was found dead in his bed, lying on his side and already quite rigid, his face curiously mottled with red blotches. The inquest concluded that he had died of unknown causes, a verdict to which I added the words, in the deep and dark hours of the night. The shock that went through us at this quite unexpected death affected no one more deeply than Janine Dakyns, who, like Michael, was a lecturer in Romance languages and unmarried too. Indeed, one might say that she was so unable to bear the loss of the ingenuous, almost childlike friendship they had shared, that a few weeks after his death she succumbed to a disease that swiftly consumed her body. Janine, who lived in a lane next to the hospital, had, like Michael, studied at Oxford and over the years had come to a profound understanding of the nineteenth-century French novel that had about it a certain private quality, wholly free of intellectual vanity and was guided by a fascination for obscure detail rather than by the self-evident. Gustave Flaubert was for her by far the finest of writers, and on many occasions she quoted long passages from the thousands of pages of his correspondence, never failing to astound me. Janine had taken an intense personal interest in the scruples which dogged Flaubert's writing, that fear of the false which, she said, sometimes kept him confined to his couch for weeks or months on end in the dread that he would never be able to write another word without compromising himself in the most grievous of ways. Moreover, Janine said, he was convinced that everything he had written hitherto consisted solely in a string of the most abysmal errors and lies, the consequences of which were immeasurable. Janine maintained that the source of Flaubert's scruples was to be found in the relentless spread of stupidity which he had observed everywhere, and which he believed had already invaded his own head. It was (so supposedly once he said) as if one was sinking into sand. This was probably the reason, she said, that sand possessed such significance in all of Flaubert's works. Sand conquered all. Time and again, said Janine, vast dust clouds drifted through Flaubert's dreams by day and by night, raised over the arid plains of the African continent and moving north across the Mediterranean and the Iberian peninsula till sooner or later they settled like ash from a fire on the Tuileries gardens, a suburb of Rouen or a country town in Normandy, penetrating into the tiniest crevices. In a grain of sand in the hem of Emma Bovary's winter gown, said Janine, Flaubert saw the whole of the Sahara. For him, every speck of dust weighed as heavy as the Atlas mountains. Many a time, at the end of a working day, Janine would talk to me about Flaubert's view of the world, in her office where there were such quantities of lecture notes, letters, and other documents lying around that it was like standing amidst a flood of paper. On the desk, which was both the origin and the focal point of this amazing profusion of paper, a virtual paper landscape had come into being in the course of time, with mountains and valleys. Like a glacier when it reaches the sea, it had broken off at the edges and established new deposits all around on the floor, which in turn were advancing imperceptibly towards the center of the room. Years ago, Janine had been obliged by the ever-increasing masses of paper on her desk to bring further tables into use, and these tables, where similar processes of accretion had subsequently taken place, represented later epochs, so to speak, in the evolution of Janine's paper universe. The carpet, too, had long since vanished beneath several inches of paper; indeed, the paper had begun climbing from the floor, on which, year after year, it had settled, and was now up the walls as high as the top of the door frame, page upon page of memoranda and notes pinned up in multiple layers, all of them by just one corner. Wherever it was possible there were piles of papers on the books on her shelves as well. It once occurred to me that at dusk, when all of this paper seemed to gather into itself the pallor of the fading light, it was like the snow in the fields, long ago, beneath the ink-black sky. In the end Janine was reduced to working from an easychair drawn more or less into the middle of her room where, if one passed her door, which was always ajar, she could be seen bent almost double scribbling on a pad on her knees or sometimes just lost in thought. Once when I remarked that sitting there amidst her papers she resembled the angel in Dürer's *Melancholia*, steadfast among the instruments of destruction, her response was that the apparent chaos surrounding her represented in reality a perfect kind of order, or an order which at least tended towards perfection. And the fact was that whatever she might be looking for amongst her papers or her books, or in her head, she was generally able to find right away. It was Janine who referred me to the surgeon Anthony Batty Shaw, whom she knew from the Oxford Society, when after my discharge from hospital I began my enquiries about Thomas Browne, who had practiced as a doctor in Norwich in the seventeenth century and had left a number of writings that defy all comparison. An entry in the 1911 edition of the *Encyclopaedia Britannica* had told me that Browne's skull was kept in the museum of the Norfolk & Norwich Hospital. Unequivocal though this claim appeared, my attempts to locate the skull in the very place where until recently I had been a patient met with no success, for none of the ladies and gentlemen of the present administrative staff at the hospital was aware that any such museum existed. Not only did they stare at me in utter incomprehension when I voiced my strange request, but I even had the impression that some of those I asked thought of me as an eccentric crank. Yet it is well known that in the period when public health and hygiene were being reformed and hospitals established, many of these institutions kept museums, or rather chambers of horrors, in which prematurely born, deformed, or hydrocephalic fetuses, hypertrophied organs, and other items of a similar nature were preserved in jars of formaldehyde, for medical purposes, and occasionally exhibited to the public. The question was where the things had got to. The local history section of the main library, which has since been destroyed by fire, was unable to give me any information concerning the Norfolk & Norwich Hospital and the whereabouts of Browne's skull. It was not until I made contact with Anthony Batty Shaw, through Janine, that I obtained the information I was after. Thomas Browne, so Batty Shaw wrote in an article he sent me which he had just published in the *Journal of Medical Biography*, died in 1682 on his seventy-seventh birthday and was buried in the parish church of St Peter Mancroft in Norwich. There his mortal remains lay undisturbed until 1840, when the coffin was damaged during preparations for another burial in the chancel, and its contents partially exposed. As a result, Browne's skull and a lock of his hair passed into the possession of one Dr Lubbock, a parish councillor, who in turn left the relics in his will to the hospital museum, where they were put on display amidst various anatomical curiosities until 1921 under a bell jar. It was not until then that St Peter Mancroft's repeated request for the return of Browne's skull was acceded to, and, almost a quarter of a millennium after the first burial, a second interment was performed with all due ceremony. Curiously enough, Browne himself, in his famous part-archaeological and part-metaphysical treatise, *Urn Burial*, offers the most fitting commentary on the subsequent odyssey of his own skull when he writes that to be gnaw'd out of our graves is a tragical abomination. But, he adds, who is to know the fate of his bones, or how often he is to be buried? Thomas Browne was born in London on the

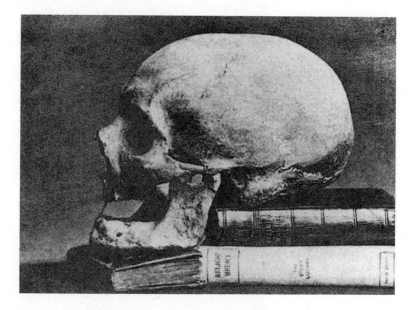

19th of October 1605, the son of a silk merchant. Little is known of his childhood, and the accounts of his life following completion of his master's degree at Oxford tell us scarcely anything about the nature of his later medical studies. All we know for certain is that from his twenty-fifth to his twenty-eighth year he attended the universities of Montpellier, Padua, and Vienna, then outstanding in the Hippocratic sciences, and that just before returning to England, received a doctorate in medicine from Leiden. In January 1632, while Browne was in Holland, and thus at a time when he was engaging more profoundly with the mysteries of the human body than ever before, the dissection of a corpse was undertaken in public at the Waaggebouw in Amsterdam—the body being that of Adriaan Adriaan-szoon alias Aris Kindt, a petty thief of that city who had been hanged for his misdemeanors an hour or so earlier. Although we have no definite evidence for this, it is probable that Browne would have heard of the dissection and was present at the extraordinary event, which Rembrandt depicted in his painting of the Guild of Surgeons, for the anatomy lessons given every year in the depth of winter by Dr Nicolaas Tulp were not only of the greatest interest to a student of medicine but constituted in addition a significant date in the agenda of a society that saw itself as emerging from the darkness into the light. The spectacle, presented before a paying public drawn from the upper classes, was no doubt a demonstration of the undaunted investigative zeal in the new sciences; but it also represented (though this surely would have been refuted) the archaic ritual of dismem-

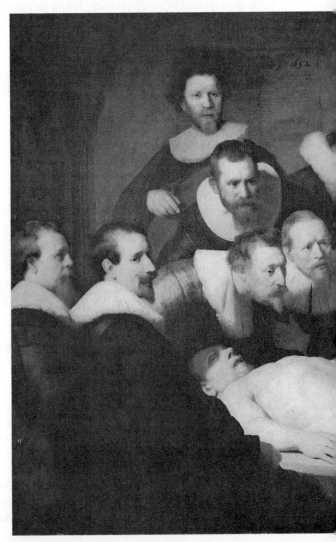

bering a corpse, of harrowing the flesh of the delinquent even beyond death, a procedure then still part of the ordained punishment. That the anatomy lesson in Amsterdam was about more than a thorough knowledge of the inner organs of the human body is suggested by Rembrandt's representation of the ceremonial nature of the dissection—the surgeons are in their finest attire, and Dr Tulp is wearing a hat on his head—as well as by the fact that afterwards there was a formal, and in a sense symbolic, banquet. If we stand today before the large canvas of Rembrandt's *The Anatomy Lesson* in the Mauritshuis we are standing precisely where those who were present at the dissection in the Waaggebouw stood, and we believe that we see what they saw then: in the foreground, the greenish, prone body of Aris Kindt, his neck broken and his chest risen terribly in rigor mortis. And yet it is debatable whether anyone ever really saw that body, since the art of anatomy, then in its infancy, was not least a way of

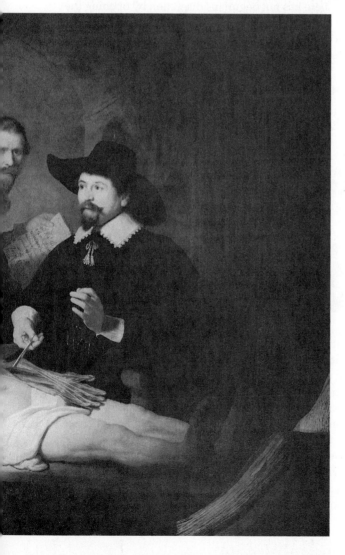

making the reprobate body invisible. It is somehow odd that Dr Tulp's colleagues are not looking at Kindt's body, that their gaze is directed just past it to focus on the open anatomical atlas in which the appalling physical facts are reduced to a diagram, a schematic plan of the human being, such as envisaged by the enthusiastic amateur anatomist René Descartes, who was also, so it is said, present that January morning in the Waaggebouw. In his philosophical investigations, which form one of the principal chapters of the history of subjection, Descartes teaches that one should disregard the flesh, which is beyond our comprehension, and attend to the machine within, to what can fully be understood, be made wholly useful for work, and, in the event of any fault, either repaired or discarded. Though the body is open to contemplation, it is, in a sense, excluded, and in the same way the much-admired verisimilitude of Rembrandt's picture proves on closer examination to be more apparent than real. Contrary to normal practice, the anatomist shown here has not begun his dissection by opening the abdomen and removing the intestines, which are most prone to putrefaction, but has started (and this too may imply a punitive dimension to the act) by dissecting the offending hand. Now, this hand is most peculiar. It is

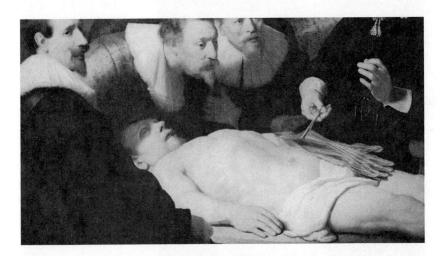

not only grotesquely out of proportion compared with the hand closer to us, but it is also anatomically the wrong way round: the exposed tendons, which ought to be those of the left palm, given the position of the thumb, are in fact those of the back of the right hand. In other words, what we are faced with is a transposition taken from the anatomical atlas, evidently without further reflection, that turns this otherwise true-to-life painting (if one may so express it) into a crass misrepresentation at the exact center point of its meaning, where the incisions are made. It seems inconceivable that we are faced here with an unfortunate blunder. Rather, I believe that there was deliberate intent behind this flaw in the composition. That unshapely hand signifies the violence that has been done to Aris Kindt. It is with him, the victim, and not the Guild that gave Rembrandt his commission, that the painter identifies. His gaze alone is free of Cartesian rigidity. He alone sees that greenish annihilated body, and he alone sees the shadow in the half-open mouth and over the dead man's eyes.

We have no evidence to tell us from which angle Thomas Browne watched the dissection, if, as I believe, he was among the onlookers in the anatomy theatre in Amsterdam, or indeed what he might have seen there. Perhaps, as Browne says in a later note about the great fog that shrouded large parts of England and Holland on the 27th of November 1674, it was the white mist that rises from within a body opened presently after death, and which during our lifetime, so he adds, clouds our brain when asleep and dreaming. I still recall how my own consciousness was veiled by the same sort of fog as I lay in my hospital room once more after surgery late in the evening. Under the wonderful influence of the painkillers coursing through me, I felt, in my iron-framed bed, like a balloonist floating weightless amidst the mountainous clouds towering on every side. At times the billowing masses would part and I gazed out at the indigo vastness and down into the depths where I supposed the earth to be, a black and impenetrable maze. But in the firmament above were the stars, tiny points of gold speckling the barren wastes. Through the resounding emptiness, my ears caught the voices of the two nurses who took my pulse and from time to time moistened my lips with a small, pink sponge attached to a stick, which reminded me of the Turkish Delight lollipops we used to buy at the fair. Katy and Lizzie were the names of these ministering angels, and I think I have rarely been as elated as I was in their care that night. Of the everyday matters they chatted about I understood very little. All I heard was the rise and fall of their voices, a kind of warbling such as comes from the throats of birds, a perfect, fluting sound, part celestial and part the song of sirens. Of all the things Katy said to Lizzie and Lizzie to Katy, I remember only one odd scrap. I think Katy, or Lizzie, was describing a holiday on Malta where, she said, the Maltese, with a death-defying insouciance quite beyond comprehension, drove neither on the left nor on the right, but always on the shady side of the road. It was not until dawn, when the morning shift relieved the night nurses, that I realized where I was. I became aware again of my body, the insensate foot, and the pain in my back; I heard the rattle of crockery as the hospital's daily routine started in the corridor; and, as the first light brightened the sky, I saw a vapor trail cross the segment framed by my window. At the time I took that white trail for a good omen, but now, as I look back, I fear it marked the beginning of a fissure that has since riven my life. The aircraft at the tip of the trail was as invisible as the passengers inside it. The invisibility and intangibility of that which moves us remained an unfathomable mystery for Thomas Browne too, who saw our world as no more than a shadow image of another one far beyond. In his thinking and writing he therefore sought to look upon earthly existence, from the things that were closest to him to the spheres of the universe, with the eye of an outsider, one might even say of the creator. His only means of achieving the sublime heights that this endeavor required was a parlous loftiness in his language. In common with other English writers of the seventeenth century, Browne wrote out of the fullness of his erudition, deploying a vast repertoire of quotations and the names of authorities who had gone before, creating complex metaphors and analogies, and constructing labyrinthine sentences that sometimes extend over one or two pages, sentences that resemble processions or a funeral cortège in their sheer ceremonial lavishness. It is true that, because of the immense weight of the impediments he is carrying, Browne's writing can be held back by the force of gravitation, but when he does succeed in rising higher and higher through the circles of his spiralling prose, borne aloft like a glider on warm currents of air, even today the reader is overcome by a sense of levitation. The greater the distance, the clearer the view: one sees the tiniest of details with the utmost clarity. It is as if one were looking through a reversed opera glass and through a microscope at the same time. And yet, says Browne, all knowledge is enveloped in darkness. "What we perceive are no more than isolated lights in the abyss of ignorance, in the shadow-filled edifice of the world. We study the order of things, says Browne, but we cannot grasp their innermost essence. And because it is so, it befits our philosophy to be writ small, using the shorthand and contracted forms of transient Nature, which alone are a reflection of eternity. True to his own prescription, Browne records the patterns which recur in the seemingly infinite diversity of forms; in *The Garden of Cyrus*, for instance, he draws the quincunx, which is composed by using the corners of a regular quadrilateral and the point at which its diagonals intersect. Browne identifies this structure everywhere, in animate and inanimate matter: in certain crystalline forms, in starfish and sea urchins, in the vertebrae of mammals and the backbones of birds and fish, in the skins of various species of snake, in the crosswise prints left by quadrupeds, in the physical shapes of caterpillars, butterflies, silkworms, and moths, in the root of the water fern, in the seed husks of the sunflower and the Caledonian pine, within young oak shoots or the stem of the horsetail; and in the creations of mankind, in the pyramids of Egypt and the mausoleum of Augustus as in the garden of King Solomon, which was planted with mathematical precision with pomegranate trees and white lilies. Examples might be multiplied without end, says Browne, and one might demonstrate *ad infinitum* the elegant geometrical designs of Nature; however—thus, with a fine turn of phrase and image, he concludes his treatise—the constellation of the Hyades, the Quincunx of Heaven, is already sinking beneath the horizon, and so 'tis time to close the five ports of knowledge. We are unwilling to spin out our waking thoughts into the phantasmes of sleep; making cables of cobwebs and wildernesses of handsome groves. Besides, he adds, Hippocrates in his notes on sleeplessness has spoken so little of the miracle of plants, that there is scant encouragement to dream of Paradise, not least since in practice we are occupied above all by the abnormalities of creation, be they the deformities pro-

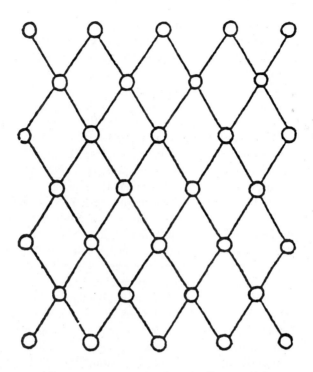

Quid Quincunce speciosius, qui, in quam cunq; partem spectaueris, rectus est. Quintilian:

duced by sickness or the grotesqueries with which Nature, with an inventiveness scarcely less diseased, fills every vacant space in her atlas. And indeed, while on the one hand the study of Nature today aims to describe a system governed by immutable laws, on the other it delights in drawing our attention to creatures noteworthy for their bizarre physical form or behavior. Even in Brehm's *Thierleben*, a popular nineteenth-century zoological compendium, pride of place is given to the crocodile and the kangaroo, the anteater and the armadillo, the seahorse and the pelican; and nowadays we are shown on the television screen a colony of penguins, say, standing motionless through the long dark winter of the Antarctic, with its icy storms, on their feet the eggs laid at a milder time of year. In programs of this kind, which are called *Nature Watch* or *Survival* and are considered particularly educational, one is more likely to see some monster coupling at the bottom of Lake Baikal than an ordinary blackbird. Thomas Browne too was often distracted from his investigations into the isomorphic line of the quincunx by singular phenomena that fired his curiosity, and by work on a comprehensive pathology. He is said to have long kept a bittern in his study in order to find out how this peculiar bird could produce from the depths of its throat such a strange bassoon-like sound, unique in the whole of Nature; and in the *Pseudodoxia Epidemica*, in which he dispels popular errors and legends, he deals with beings both real and imaginary, such as the chameleon, the salamander, the ostrich, the gryphon and the phoenix, the basilisk, the unicorn, and the amphisbaena, the serpent with two heads. In most cases, Browne refutes the existence of the fabled creatures, but the astonishing monsters that we know to be properly part of the natural world leave us with a suspicion that even the most fantastical beasts might not be mere inventions. At all events, it is clear from Browne's account that the endless mutations of Nature, which go far beyond any rational limit, and equally the chimeras produced by our own minds, were as much a source of fascination to him as they were, three hundred years later, to Jorge Luís Borges, whose *Libra de los seres imaginarios* was published in Buenos Aires in 1967. Recently I realized that the imaginary beings listed alphabetically in that compendium include the creature Baldanders, whom Simplicius Simplicissimus encounters in the sixth book of Grimmelshausen's narrative. There, Baldanders is first seen as a stone sculpture lying in a forest, resembling a Germanic hero of old and wearing a Roman soldier's tunic with a big Swabian bib. Baldanders claims to have come from Paradise, to have always been in Simplicius's company, unbeknownst to him, and to be unable to quit his side until Simplicius shall have reverted to the clay he is made of. Then, before the very eyes of Simplicius, Baldanders changes into a scribe who writes these lines, and then into a mighty oak, a sow, a

Jch bin der Anfang und das End und gelte an allen Ortyen.

Manoha·gilos, timad, ifafer, fale; lacob, falet, enni nacob idil dadele neuaco ide eges Eli neme meodi eledid emonatan defi negogag editor goga naneg eriden, hohe ritatan auilac, hohe ilamen eriden diledi lifac ufur fodaled autar, amu falifononor macheli retoran; Vlidon dad amu offoffon, Gedal amu bede neuavv, alijs, dilede ronodavv agnoh regnoh eni tatæ hyn lamini celotah, ifis toloftabas oronatah affis tobulu, V Viera faladid egrivi nanon ægar rimini fifac, heliofole Ramelu ononor vvindelishi timinitur, bagoge gogoe hana-, nor elimitat.

sausage, a piece of excrement, a field of clover, a white flower, a mulberry tree, and a silk carpet. Much as in this continuous process of consuming and being consumed, nothing endures, in Thomas Browne's view. On every new thing there lies already the shadow of annihilation. For the history of every individual, of every social order, indeed of the whole world, does not describe an ever-widening, more and more wonderful arc, but rather follows a course which, once the meridian is reached, leads without fail down into the dark. Knowledge of that descent into the dark, for Browne, is inseparable from his belief in the day of resurrection, when, as in a theater, the last revolutions are ended and the actors appear once more on stage, to complete and make up the catastrophe of this great piece. As a doctor, who saw disease growing and raging in bodies, he understood mortality better than the flowering of life. To him it seems a miracle that we should last so much as a single day. There is no antidote, he writes, against the opium of time. The winter sun shows how soon the light fades from the ash, how soon night enfolds us. Hour upon hour is added to the sum. Time itself grows old. Pyramids, arches, and obelisks are melting pillars of snow. Not even those who have found a place amidst the heavenly constellations have perpetuated their names: Nimrod is lost in Orion, and Osiris in the Dog Star. Indeed, old families last not three oaks. To set one's name to a work gives no one a title to be remembered, for who knows how many of the best of men have gone without a trace? The iniquity of oblivion blindly scatters her poppyseed and when wretchedness falls upon us one summer's day like snow, all we wish for is to be forgotten. These are the circles Browne's thoughts describe, most unremittingly perhaps in the *Hydriotaphia* or *Urn Burial* of 1658, a discourse on sepulchral urns found in a field near Walsingham in Norfolk. Drawing upon the most varied of historical and natural historical sources, he expatiates upon the rites we enact when one from our midst sets out on his last journey. Beginning with some examples of sepulture in elephants, cranes, the sepulchral cells of pismires and practice of bees; which civil society carrieth out their dead, and hath exequies, if not interments, he describes the funeral rites of numerous peoples before coming to the Christian religion, which buries the sinful body whole and thus extinguishes the fires once and for all. The almost universal practice of cremation in pre-Christian times should not lead one to conclude, as is often done, that the heathen were ignorant of life beyond death, to show which Browne observes that the funeral pyres were built of sweet fuel, cypress, fir, yew, and other trees perpetually verdant as silent expressions of their surviving hopes. Browne also remarks that, contrary to general belief, it is not difficult to burn a human body: a piece of an old boat burnt Pompey, and the King of Castile burnt large numbers of Saracens with next to no fuel, the fire being visible far and wide. Indeed, he adds, if the burthen of Isaac were sufficient for an holocaust, a man may carry his own pyre. Browne then turns to the strange vessels unearthed from the field near Walsingham. It is astounding, he says, how long these thin-walled clay urns remained intact a yard underground, while the sword and ploughshare passed above them and great buildings, palaces, and cloud-high towers crumbled and collapsed. The cremated remains in the urns are examined closely: the ash, the loose teeth, some long roots of quitch, or dog's grass wreathed about the bones, and the coin intended for the Elysian ferryman. Browne records other objects known to have been placed with the dead, whether as ornament or utensil. His catalogue includes a variety of curiosities: the circumcision knives of Joshua, the ring which belonged to the mistress of Propertius, an ape of agate, a grasshopper, three hundred golden bees, a blue opal, silver belt buckles and clasps, combs, iron pins, brass plates and brazen nippers to pull away hair, and a brass jew's-harp that last sounded on the crossing over the black water. The most marvelous item, however, from a Roman urn preserved by Cardinal Farnese, is a drinking glass, so bright it might have been newly blown. For Browne, things of this kind, unspoiled by the passage of time, are symbols of the indestructibility of the human soul assured by scripture, which the physician, firm though he may be in his Christian faith, perhaps secretly doubts. And since the heaviest stone that melancholy can throw at a man is to tell him he is at the end of his nature, Browne scrutinizes that which escaped annihilation for any sign of the mysterious capacity for transmigration he has so often observed in caterpillars and moths. That purple piece of silk he refers to, then, in the urn of Patroclus—what does it mean?

IV

The rain clouds had dispersed when, after dinner, I took my first walk around the streets and lanes of the town. Darkness was falling, and only

the lighthouse with its shining glass cabin still caught the last luminous rays that came in from the western horizon. Footsore and weary as I was after my long walk from Lowestoft, I sat down on a bench on the green called Gunhill and looked out on the tranquil sea, from the depths of which the shadows were now rising. Everyone who had been out for an evening stroll was gone. I felt as if I were in a deserted theater, and I should not have been surprised if a curtain had suddenly risen before me and on the proscenium I had beheld, say, the 28th of May 1672—that memorable day when the Dutch fleet appeared offshore from out of the drifting mists, with the bright morning light behind it, and opened fire on the English ships in Sole Bay. In all likelihood the people of Southwold hurried out of the town as soon as the first cannonades were fired to watch the rare spectacle from the beach. Shading their eyes with their hands against the dazzling sun, they would have watched the ships moving hither and thither, apparently at random, their sails billowing in a light northeast wind and then, as they maneuvred ponderously, flapping once again. They would not have been able to make out human figures at that distance, not even the gentlemen of the Dutch and English admiralties on the bridges. As the battle continued, the powder magazines exploded, and some of the tarred hulls burned down to the waterline; the scene would have been shrouded in an acrid, yellowish-black smoke creeping across the entire bay and masking the combat from view. While most of the accounts of the battles fought on the so-called fields of honor have from time immemorial been unreliable, the pictorial representations of great naval engagements are without exception figments of the imagination. Even celebrated painters such as Storck, van der Velde, or de Loutherbourg, some of whose versions of the Battle of

Sole Bay I studied closely in the Maritime Museum in Greenwich, fail to
convey any true impression of how it must have been to be on board one of
these ships, already overloaded with equipment and men, when burning
masts and sails began to fall or cannonballs smashed into the appallingly
overcrowded decks. On the Royal James alone, which was set aflame by a
fireship, nearly half the thousand-strong crew perished. No details of the
end of the three-master have come down to us. There were eye-witnesses
who claimed to have seen the commander of the English fleet, the Earl of
Sandwich, who weighed almost twenty-four stone, gesticulating on the af-
terdeck as the flames encircled him. All we know for certain is that his
bloated body was washed up on the beach near Harwich a few weeks later.
The seams of his uniform had burst asunder, the buttonholes were torn
open, yet the Order of the Garter still gleamed in undiminished splendor.
At that date there can have been only a few cities on earth that numbered as
many souls as were annihilated in sea-battles of this kind. The agony that
was endured and the enormity of the havoc wrought defeat our powers of
comprehension, just as we cannot conceive the vastness of the effort that
must have been required—from felling and preparing the timber, mining
and smelting the ore, and forging the iron, to weaving and sewing the sail-
cloth—to build and equip vessels that were almost all predestined for destruction. For a brief time only these curious creatures sailed the seas,
moved by the winds that circle the earth, bearing names such as Stavoren,
Resolution, Victory, Groot Hollandia, and Olyfan, and then they were
gone. It has never been determined which of the two parties in the naval
battle fought off Southwold to extort trading advantages emerged victori-
ous. It is certain, however, that the decline of the Netherlands began here,
with a shift in the balance of power so small that it was out of proportion to
the human and material resources expended in the battle; while on the
other hand the English government, almost bankrupt, diplomatically isolated, and humiliated by the Dutch raid on Chatham, was now able, despite a complete absence of strategic thinking and a naval administration
on the verge of disintegration, and thanks only to the vagaries of the wind
and the waves that day, to commence the sovereignty at sea that was to be
unbroken for so long. — As I sat there that evening in Southwold overlooking the German Ocean, I sensed quite clearly the earth's slow turning into
the dark. The huntsmen are up in America, writes Thomas Browne in *The
Garden of Cyrus*, and they are already past their first sleep in Persia. The
shadow of night is drawn like a black veil across the earth, and since almost
all creatures, from one meridian to the next, lie down after the sun has set,
so, he continues, one might, in following the setting sun, see on our globe
nothing but prone bodies, row upon row, as if levelled by the scythe of Saturn—an endless graveyard for a humanity struck by falling sickness. I
gazed farther and farther out to sea, to where the darkness was thickest and
where there extended a cloudbank of the most curious shape, which I could
barely make out any longer, the rearward view, I presume, of the storm

that had broken over Southwold in the late afternoon. For a while, the top-most summit regions of this massif, dark as ink, glistened like the icefields of the Caucasus, and as I watched the glare fade I remembered that years before, in a dream, I had once walked the entire length of a mountain range just as remote and just as unfamiliar. It must have been a distance of a thousand miles or more, through ravines, gorges, and valleys, across ridges, slopes, and drifts, along the edges of great forests, over wastes of rock, shale, and snow. And I recalled that in my dream, once I had reached the end of my journey, I looked back, and that it was six o'clock in the evening. The jagged peaks of the mountains I had left behind rose in almost fearful silhouette against a turquoise sky in which two or three pink clouds drifted. It was a scene that felt familiar in an inexplicable way, and for weeks it was on my mind until at length I realized that, down to the last detail, it matched the Vallüla massif, which I had seen from the bus, through eyes drooping with tiredness, a day or so before I started school, as we returned home from an outing to the Montafon. I suppose it is submerged memories that give to dreams their curious air of hyper-reality. But perhaps there is something else as well, something nebulous, gauze-like, through which everything one sees in a dream seems, paradoxically, much clearer. A pond becomes a lake, a breeze becomes a storm, a handful of dust is a desert, a grain of sulphur in the blood is a volcanic inferno. What manner of theater is it, in which we are at once playwright, actor, stage manager, scene painter, and audience?

Just as these things have always been beyond my understanding, so too I found it impossible to believe, as I sat on Gunhill in Southwold that evening, that just one year earlier I had been looking across to England from a beach in Holland. On that occasion, following a bad night spent at Baden in Switzerland, I had travelled via Basle and Amsterdam to The Hague, where I had taken a room in one of the less salubrious hotels near the station. I no longer remember whether it was the Lord Asquith, the Aristo, or the Fabiola. At all events, in the lobby of this establishment, which would deeply have depressed even the humblest of travellers, there sat two gentlemen, no longer in their first youth, who must have been partners for a long time; and between them, in the stead of a child, as it were, was an apricot-colored poodle. After I had rested a little in the room I was allotted, I went for a stroll, looking for a bite to eat, up the road that runs from the station to the city center, past the Bristol Bar, Yuksel's Café, a video library, Aran Turk's pizza place, a Euro-sex-shop, a halal butcher's, and a carpet store, above whose display a rudimentary fresco in four parts showed a caravan crossing the desert. The name Perzenpaleis was lettered in red on the façade of the run-down building, the upper-storey windows of which were all white-washed over. As I was looking up at this façade, a man with a dark beard, wearing a suit jacket over a long tunic, slipped past me through a doorway, so close that our elbows touched. Through that doorway, for an unforgettable moment that seemed to exist outside time, I glimpsed the

wooden rack on which perhaps a hundred pairs of well-worn shoes had
been placed beside and above one another. Only later did I see the minaret
rising from the courtyard of the building into the azure Dutch evening sky.
For an hour or more I walked around this somehow extraterritorial part of
town. Most of the windows in the side streets were boarded up, and slogans like Help de regenwouden redden or Welcome to the Royal Dutch
Graveyard were graffiti'd on the sooty brick walls. No longer able to decide
on a place to eat, I bought a carton of chips at McDonald's, where I felt like
a criminal wanted worldwide as I stood at the brightly lit counter, and ate
them as I walked back to my hotel. Outside the entrances of the entertainment and dining establishments on the road to the station, small
groups of oriental men had now gathered, most of them smoking in silence
while the odd one appeared to be doing a deal with a client. When I
reached the little canal that crosses the road, an open-top American limou-
sine studded with lights and gleaming with chrome glided past me across
the carriageway as if it had come out of nowhere, and in it sat a pimp in a
white suit, wearing gold-framed sunglasses and on his head a ludicrous
Tyrolean hat. And as I stood gazing in amazement after this almost supernatural apparition, a dark-skinned man shot round the corner towards me,
sheer terror in his face, and, swerving to avoid me, left me full in the path of
his pursuer, who, judging by appearances, was a countryman of his. This
pursuer, whose eyes were shining with rage and blood lust, was probably
a chef or kitchen porter, since he was wearing an apron and holding a long,
glinting knife in one hand, which passed by me so close that I imagined I
felt it piercing between my ribs. Disturbed by the impression this experience made on me, I lay on my bed in my hotel room. I did not have a good
night. It was so oppressive and sultry that one could not leave the windows
closed; but if one opened them, one heard the din of traffic from the cross-

roads and every few minutes the dreadful squeal of the tram as it ground round the terminus track-loop. I was therefore not in the best of states next morning at the Mauritshuis when I stood before the large group portrait, *The Anatomy Lesson*. Although I had gone to The Hague especially to see this painting, which would continue to occupy me considerably over the years to come, I was so out of sorts after my bad night that I was quite unable to harness my thoughts as I looked at the body being dissected under the eyes of the Guild of Surgeons. Indeed, without knowing why, I was so affected by the painting that later it took me a full hour to recover, in front of Jacob van Ruisdael's *View of Haarlem with Bleaching Fields*. The flatland stretching out towards Haarlem is seen from above, from a vantage point generally identified as the dunes, though the sense of a bird's-eye view is so strong that the dunes would have to be veritable hills or even modest mountains. The truth is of course that Ruisdael did not take up a position on the dunes in order to paint; his vantage point was an imaginary position some distance above the earth. Only in this way could he see it all together: the vast cloudscape that occupies two thirds of the picture; the town, which is little more than a fraying of the horizon, except for St Bavo's cathedral, which towers above all the other buildings; the dark bosks and bushes; the farm in the foreground; and the bright field where the sheets of white linen have been laid out to bleach and where, by my count, seven or eight people no taller than a quarter of an inch, are going about their work. After I left the gallery, I sat for a while on the sunlit steps of the palais which Governor Johann Maurits, as the guidebook I had bought informed me, had built in his homeland whilst he was in Brazil for seven years, and fitted out as a cosmographic residence reflecting the wonders of the remotest regions of the earth, in keeping with his personal motto: "Even unto the limits of our world." Report has it that when the house was opened in May 1644, three hundred years before I was born, eleven Indians the Governor had brought with him from Brazil performed a dance on the cobbled square in front of the new building, conveying to the townspeople some sense of the foreign lands to which the power of their community now extended. These dancers, about whom nothing else is known, have long since disappeared, as soundless as shadows, as silent as the heron I saw when I set off once more, flying just above the shining surface of the water, the beat of its wings calm and even, undisturbed by the traffic creeping along the bank of the Hofvijver. Who can say how things were in ages past? Diderot, in one of his travel journals, described Holland as the Egypt of Europe, where one might cross the fields in a boat and, as far as the eye could see, there would be scarcely anything to break the flooded surface of the plain. In that curious country, he wrote, the most modest rise gave one the loftiest sensation. And for Diderot there was nothing more satisfying to the human mind than the neat Dutch towns with their straight, tree-lined canals, exemplary in every respect. Settlement succeeded settlement just as if they had been conjured up overnight by the hand of an artist in accordance with some

carefully worked-out plan, wrote Diderot, and even in the heart of the
largest of them one still felt one was out in the country. The Hague, at that
time with a population of about forty thousand, he felt was the loveliest village on earth, and the road from the town to the strand at Scheveningen a
promenade without equal. It was not easy to appreciate these observations
as I walked along Parkstraat towards Scheveningen. Here and there stood
a fine villa in its garden, but otherwise there was nothing to afford me any
respite. Perhaps I had gone the wrong way, as so often in unfamiliar cities.
In Scheveningen, where I had hoped to be able to see the sea from a distance, I walked for a long time in the shadow of tall apartment blocks, as if
at the bottom of a ravine. When at last I reached the beach I was so tired
that I lay down and slept till the afternoon. I heard the surge of the sea, and,
half dreaming, understood every word of Dutch and for the first time in my
life believed I had arrived, and was home. Even when I awoke it seemed to
me for a moment that my people were resting all around me as we made
our way across the desert. The façade of the Kurhaus towered above me
like a great caravanserai, a comparison which sat well with the fact that the

palatial hotel, built on the beach at the turn of the century, had numerous
modern extensions with roofs resembling tents, housing newsagents, souvenir shops, and fast-food outlets. In one of these, the Massada Grill, where
the illuminated photo-panels above the counter showed kosher foods instead of the usual hamburger combinations, I had a cup of tea before
returning to the city and marvelled at a beatifically beaming couple surrounded by the motley host of their grandchildren, celebrating some family or holiday occasion in a cafeteria otherwise deserted.

That evening, in Amsterdam, I sat in the peace of the lounge of a private hotel by the Vondel Park, which I knew from earlier visits, and made notes on the stations of my journey, now almost at an end: the days I had spent on various enquiries at Bad Kissingen, the panic attack in Baden, the boat excursion on Lake Zurich, my run of good luck at the casino in Lindau, and my visits to the Alte Pinakothek in Munich and to the grave of my patron saint in Nuremberg, of whom legend has it that he was the son of a king, from Dacia or Denmark, who married a French princess in Paris. During the wedding night, the story goes, he was afflicted with a sense of profound unworthiness. Today, he is supposed to have said to his bride, our bodies are adorned, but tomorrow they will be food for worms. Before the break of day, he fled, making a pilgrimage to Italy, where he lived in solitude until he felt the power to work miracles arising within him. After saving the Anglo-Saxon princes Winnibald and Wunibald from certain starvation with a loaf baked from ashes and brought to them by a celestial messenger, and after preaching a celebrated sermon in Vicenza, he went over the Alps to Germany. At Regensburg he crossed the Danube on his cloak, and there made a broken glass whole again; and, in the house of a wheelwright too mean to spare the kindling, lit a fire with icicles. This story of the burning of the frozen substance of life has, of late, meant much to me, and I wonder now whether inner coldness and desolation may not be the precondition for making the world believe, by a kind of fraudulent showmanship, that one's own wretched heart is still aglow. Be that as it may, my namesake is said to have performed many more miracles in his hermitage in the imperial forests between the rivers Regnitz and Pegnitz, and to have healed the sick, before his corpse, as he had ordained, was borne on a cart drawn by two oxen to the place where his grave is to this day. Centuries later, in May 1507, the Patriciate of Nuremberg resolved to have a brass sarcophagus crafted for the holy prince of heaven St Sebolt by master smith Peter Vischer. In June 1519, when his twelve-year labors were completed, the great monument, weighing many tons, standing almost five yards high on twelve snails and four curved dolphins, and representing the entire order of salvation, was installed in the chancel of the church consecrated in the name of the city's saint. On the base of the tomb, fauns, mermaids, fabulous creatures, and animals of every conceivable description throng about the four cardinal virtues of Justice, Prudence, Temperance, and Fortitude. Above them are mythical figures — Nimrod the hunter, Hercules with his club, Samson with the jawbone of an ass, and the god Apollo between two swans — along with representations of the miracle of the burning of ice, the feeding of the hungry, and the conversion of a heretic. Then come the apostles with their emblems and the instruments of their martyrdom, and, crowning all, the celestial city with its three pinnacles and many mansions, Jerusalem, the fervently longed-for bride, God's tabernacle amongst mankind, the image of an other, renewed life. And in the heart of this reliquary cast in a single piece, surrounded by eighty angels, in a

shrine of sheet silver, lie the bones of the exemplary dead man, the harbinger of a time when the tears will be wiped from our eyes and there will be no more grief, or pain, or weeping and wailing.

Night had fallen and I sat in the darkness of my room on the top floor of the Vondel Park Hotel and listened to the stormy gusts buffeting the crowns of the trees. From afar came the rumble of thunder. Pallid sheet lightning streaked the horizon. At about one o'clock, when I heard the first drops rattling on the metal roof, I leant out of the window into the warm, storm-filled air. Soon the rain was pouring down into the shadowy depths of the park, which flared from time to time as if lit up by Bengal fire. The water in the gutter gurgled like a mountain stream. Once, when lightning again flashed across the sky, I looked down into the hotel garden far below me, and there, in the broad ditch that runs between the garden and the park, in the shelter of an overhanging willow, I saw a solitary mallard, motionless on the garish green surface of the water. This image emerged from the darkness, for a fraction of a second, with such perfect clarity that I can still see every individual willow leaf, the myriad green scales of duckweed, the subtlest nuances in the fowl's plumage, and even the pores in the lid closed over its eye.

Next morning, the atmosphere at Schiphol airport was so strangely muted that one might have thought one was already a good way beyond this world. As if they were under sedation or moving through time stretched and expanded, the passengers wandered the halls or, standing still on the escalators, were delivered to their various destinations on high or underground. In the train from Amsterdam, leafing through Lévi-Strauss's *Tristes Tropiques*, I had come across a description of the Campos Elyseos, a street in São Paulo where the colorfully painted wooden villas and residences, built at the turn of the century by the wealthy in a kind of Swiss fantasy style, were falling to pieces in gardens overgrown with eucalyptus and mango trees. Perhaps that was why the airport, filled with a murmuring whisper, seemed to me that morning like an ante room of that undiscovered country from whose bourn no traveller returns. Every now and then the announcers' voices, disembodied and intoning their messages like angels, would call someone's name. Passagiers Sandberg en Stromberg naar Copenhagen. Mr Freeman to Lagos. La señora Rodrigo, por favor. Sooner or later the call would come for each and every one of those waiting here. I sat down on one of the upholstered benches where travellers who had spent the night in this place of transit were still asleep, stretched out unconscious, or curled up. Not far from me was a group of Africans, clad in flowing, snow-white robes; and opposite me a well-groomed gentleman with a golden fob-chain crossing his waistcoat was reading a newspaper, on the front page of which was a photograph of a vast pall of smoke, boiling up like an atomic mushroom cloud above an atoll. De aswolk boven de Vulkaan Pinatubo read the headline. Outside, on the tarmac, the summer heat was shimmering, tiny trucks were beetling to and fro, and from the runway aeroplanes with hundreds of people aboard rose, one after another into the blue air. For my part, I must have dozed off for a while as I watched this spectacle, because presently I heard my name from afar, followed by the injunction Immediate boarding at Gate C4 please.

The small propeller plane that services the route from Amsterdam to Norwich first climbed toward the sun before turning west. Spread out beneath us lay one of the most densely populated regions in Europe, with endless terraces, sprawling satellite towns, business parks, and shining glass houses which looked like large quadrangular ice floes drifting across this corner of the continent where not a patch is left to its own devices. Over the centuries the land had been regulated, cultivated, and built on until the whole region was transformed into a geometrical pattern. The roads, water channels, and railway tracks ran in straight lines and gentle curves past fields and plantations, basins and reservoirs. Like beads on an abacus designed to calculate infinity, cars glided along the lanes of the motorways, while the ships moving up and down river appeared as if they had been halted for ever. Embedded in this even fabric lay a manor surrounded by its park, the relic of an earlier age. I watched the shadow of our plane hastening below us across hedges and fences, rows of poplars, and canals. Along a line that seemed to have been drawn with a ruler a tractor crawled through a field of stubble, dividing it into one lighter and one darker half. Nowhere, however, was a single human being to be seen. No matter whether one is flying over Newfoundland or the sea of lights that stretches from Boston to Philadelphia after nightfall, over the Arabian deserts which gleam like mother-of-pearl, over the Ruhr or the city of Frankfurt, it is as though there were no people, only the things they have made and in which they are hiding. One sees the places where they live and the roads that link them, one sees the smoke rising from their houses and factories, one sees the vehicles in which they sit, but one sees not the people themselves. And yet they are present everywhere upon the face of the earth, extending their dominion by the hour, moving around the honeycombs of towering buildings and tied into networks of a complexity that goes far beyond the power of any one individual to imagine, from the thousands of hoists and winches that once worked the South African diamond mines to the floors of today's

stock and commodity exchanges, through which the global tides of information flow without cease. If we view ourselves from a great height, it is frightening to realize how little we know about our species, our purpose, and our end, I thought, as we crossed the coastline and flew out over the jelly-green sea.

Such were my reminiscences concerning my visit to Holland a year before, as I sat on Gunhill that evening. Now, with an advancing chill in the air, I sought the familiarity of the streets and soon found myself outside the Sailors' Reading Room, a charitable establishment housed in a small building above the promenade, which nowadays, sailors being a dying breed, serves principally as a kind of maritime museum, where all manner of things connected with the sea and seafaring life are kept and collected. On the walls hang barometers and navigational instruments, figureheads, and models of ships in glass cases and in bottles. On the tables are harbormasters' registers, log books, treatises on sailing, various nautical periodicals, and several volumes with color plates which show legendary clippers and ocean-going steamers such as the Conte di Savoia or the Mauretania, giants of iron and steel, more than three hundred yards long, into which the Washington Capitol might have fitted, their funnels so tall they vanished into the low-hanging clouds. The Reading Room in Southwold is opened every morning at seven (save only on Christmas Day) and remains open until almost midnight. At best, it attracts a handful of visitors during the holidays, and the few who do cross the threshold leave again after they have taken a brief look around in the uncomprehending way characteristic of such holidaymakers. The Reading Room is thus almost always deserted but for one or two of the surviving fishermen and seafarers sitting in silence in the armchairs, whiling the hours away. Sometimes, in the evenings, they play a game of pool in the back room. Apart from the muffled sound of the sea and the clicking of the balls there is nothing to be heard then, except perhaps, from time to time, the slight scratching noise made by a player priming his cue and the short puff when he blows off the chalk. Whenever I am in Southwold, the Sailors' Reading Room is by far my favorite haunt. It is better than anywhere else for reading, writing letters, following one's thoughts, or in the long winter months simply looking out at the stormy sea as it crashes on the promenade. So on this occasion too I went to the Reading Room the morning after my arrival in Southwold, intending to make notes on what I had seen the previous day. At first, as on some of my earlier visits, I leafed through the log of the Southwold, a patrol ship that was anchored off the pier from autumn of 1914. On the large landscape-format pages, a fresh one for each new date, there are occasional entries surrounded by a good deal of empty space, reading, for instance, Maurice Farman Bi-plane N'ward Inland or White Steam-yacht Flying White Ensign Cruising on Horizon to S. Every time I decipher one of these entries I am astounded that a trail that has long since vanished from the air or the water remains visible here on the paper. That morning, as I closed the marbled cover of the log book, pondering the mysterious survival of the written word, I noticed lying to one side on the table a thick, tattered tome that I had not seen before on my visits to the Reading Room. It turned out to be a photographic history of the First World War, compiled and published in 1933 by the *Daily Express*, to mark the past tragedy, and perhaps as a warning of another approaching. Every theater of war is documented in this compendious collection, from the Vall' Inferno on the Austro-Italian Alpine front to Flanders fields. There are illustrations of all conceivable forms of violent death, from the shooting down of a single aviation pioneer over the Somme estuary to the mass slaughter in the swamps of Galicia, and pictures of French towns reduced to rubble, corpses rotting in the no-man's-land between the trenches, woodlands razed by artillery fire, battleships sinking under black clouds of petroleum smoke, armies on the march, never-ending streams of refugees, shattered zeppelins, scenes from Prszemysl and St Quentin, from Montfaucon and Gallipoli, scenes of destruction, mutilation, desecration, starvation, conflagration, and freezing cold. The titles are almost without exception bitterly ironic—When Cities

Deck Their Streets for War! This Was a Forest! This Was a Man! There Is Some Corner of a Foreign Field That Is Forever England! One section of the book is devoted to the chaos in the Balkans, a part of the world which was further removed from England then than Lahore or Omdurman. Page after page of pictures from Serbia, Bosnia, and Albania show scattered groups of people and stray individuals trying to escape the War by ox-cart, in the heat of summer, along dusty country roads, or on foot through drifting snow with a pony half-dead with exhaustion. The chronicle of disaster opens with the notorious snapshot from Sarajevo. The picture has the caption Princip Lights the Fuse! It is the 28th of June 1914, a bright, sunny day, ten forty-five in the morning. One sees a few Bosnians, some Austrian military personnel, and the assassin being apprehended. The facing page shows the tunic of Archduke Franz Ferdinand's uniform, holed by bullets and soaked with blood, which must have been photographed for the press after being stripped from the body of the heir to the throne and transferred

by rail to the capital of the empire, where it can be viewed to this day, together with his feather bushed hat and trousers, in a black-framed reliquary in the army museum. Gavrilo Princip was the son of a Grahovo valley farmer, and until recently had been a grammar-school pupil in Belgrade. After being sentenced he was locked up in the Theresiensradt casemates, and there, in April 1918, he died of the bone tuberculosis that had been consuming him since his early youth. In 1993 the Serbs celebrated the seventy-fifth anniversary of his death.

That afternoon I sat alone till tea time in the bar restaurant of the Crown Hotel. The rattle of crockery in the kitchen had long since subsided; in the grandfather clock, with its rising and setting sun and a moon that appears at night, the cogwheels gripped, the pendulum swung from side to side, and the big hand, bit by bit, in tiny jerks, went its round. For some time I had been feeling a sense of eternal peace when, leafing through the *Independent on Sunday*, I came across an article that was related to the Balkan pictures I had seen in the Reading Room that morning. The article, which was about the so-called cleansing operations carried out fifty years ago in Bosnia, by the Croats together with the Austrians and the Germans, began by describing a photograph taken as a souvenir by men of the Croatian Ustasha, in which fellow militiamen in the best of spirits, some of them striking heroic poses, are sawing off the head of a Serb named Branco Jungic. A second snap shows the severed head with a cigarette between lips still parted in a last cry of pain. This happened at Jasenovac camp on the Sava. Seven hundred thousand men, women, and children were killed there alone in ways that made even the hair of the Reich's experts stand on end, as some of them are said to have admitted when they were amongst themselves. The

preferred instruments of execution were saws and sabres, axes and ham-
mers, and leather cuff-bands with fixed blades that were fastened on the
lower arm and made especially in Solingen for the purpose of cutting
throats, as well as a kind of rudimentary crossbar gallows on which the
Serbs, Jews, and Bosnians, once rounded up, were hanged in rows like

crows or magpies. Not far from Jasenovac, in a radius of no more than ten
miles, there were also the camps of Prijedor, Stara Gradiska, and Banja
Luka, where the Croatian militia, its hand strengthened by the Wehrmacht
and its spirit by the Catholic church, performed one day's work after another in similar manner. The history of this massacre, which went on for
years, is recorded in fifty thousand documents abandoned by the Germans
and Croats in 1945, which are kept to this day, according to the author of
the 1992 article, in the Bosanske Krajine Archive in Banja Luka, which is, or
used to be, housed in what was once an Austro-Hungarian barracks, serving in 1942 as the headquarters of the Heeresgruppe E intelligence division.
"Without a doubt those who were stationed there knew what was going on
in the Ustasha camps, just as they knew of the enormities perpetrated during the Kozara campaign against Tito's partisans, for instance, in the course
of which between sixty and ninety thousand people were killed in so-called
acts of war, that is to say were executed, or died as a result of deportation.
The female population of Kozara was transported to Germany and worked
to death in the slave-labor system that extended over the entire territory of
the Reich. Of the children who were left behind, twenty-three thousand in
number, the militia murdered half on the spot, while the rest were herded
together at various assembly points to be sent on to Croatia; of these, not a
few died of typhoid fever, exhaustion and fear, even before the cattle wag-

ons reached the Croatian capital. Many of those who were still alive were so hungry that they had eaten the cardboard identity tags they wore about their necks and thus in their extreme desperation had eradicated their own names. Later they were brought up as Catholics in Croatian families, and sent to confession and their first holy communion. Like everyone else they learnt the socialist ABC at school, chose an occupation, and became railway workers, salesgirls, tool-fitters or book-keepers. But no one knows what shadowy memories haunt them to this day. In this connection one might also add that one of the Heeresgruppe E intelligence officers at that time was a young Viennese lawyer whose chief task was to draw up memoranda relating to the necessary resettlements, described as imperative for humanitarian reasons. For this commendable paperwork he was awarded by Croatian head of state Ante Pavelić the silver medal of the crown of King Zvonomir, with oak leaves. In the postwar years this officer, who at the very start of his career was so promising and so very competent in the technicalities of administration, occupied various high offices, among them that of Secretary General of the United Nations. And reportedly it was in this last capacity that he spoke onto tape, for the benefit of any extraterrestrials that may happen to share our universe, words of greeting that are now, together with other memorabilia of mankind, approaching the outer limits of our solar system aboard the space probe Voyager II.

· · · · · · · · · · · ·

QUESTIONS FOR A SECOND READING

1. Sebald writes unusual prose. He is a "stylist." For most readers, his style is strange, peculiar, extraordinary. And, at least for many, his prose is rich and compelling, even beautiful. As an exercise, let's think of style as a matter of sentences and paragraphs. As you reread, bracket off what you feel to be one or two characteristic Sebald sentences. And pay attention to what Sebald does with the paragraph. (The first chapter, for example, has only three of them.) The paragraphs are long and do not follow the usual classroom pattern of thesis, example, and conclusion. Choose one paragraph and prepare an account of how it is organized and how it works.

   With these materials, prepare to give a presentation that provides a theory of the Sebald sentence and the Sebald paragraph. As you think of the material you've gathered, ask questions about what Sebald sentences and paragraphs do (as opposed to what they *say*). What do they do for the writer? for the reader? (You might also ask what role such sentences and paragraphs could play in your prose.)

2. The "Thoreau" of *Walden* is said to be one of the great characters of American literature. It is useful to think of the speaker in these chapters from *The Rings of Saturn* as a character. As you read the chapters, you develop a

relationship with that character. As you reread, prepare notes and passages you can use to describe this character and to describe a reader's evolving relationship with him.

3. One of the unusual features of these chapters from *The Rings of Saturn* are the illustrations—oddly chosen, difficult (at times) to see and yet clearly important to the text. As you reread, choose two or three illustrations to study. What is their purpose? As you imagine the author's project, why would it invite or require illustrations? How does a reader work with them? That is, as you come upon them, how do they work in relation to the text? What is your theory of the use of images in these chapters?

4. These chapters (and the full text of *The Rings of Saturn*) tell the story of a trip the narrator has taken along the east coast of England (in East Anglia). They also present a journey through the speaker's thoughts, reading, and scholarship. The text is full of names, some of them part of intellectual history, from Charles Ramuz to Gustave Flaubert to Thomas Browne, Rembrandt, and Jorge Luís Borges, concluding (in our selection) with a reference to the unnamed former Secretary-General of the United Nations, Kurt Waldheim.

   Individually or in groups, choose some of these references that seem to be most interesting, suggestive, or important, and do the homework necessary to provide a fuller description of these individuals and their work. And from these, work back to an account of the narrator. Why would these people and this work be so much a part of his life and his thinking?

5. Here are two characteristic Sebald passages. (You could, if you choose, provide your own examples.) Read them with particular attention to the sentences, their syntax and punctuation.

> Many a time, at the end of a working day, Janine would talk to me about Flaubert's view of the world, in her office where there were such quantities of lecture notes, letters, and other documents lying around that it was like standing amidst a flood of paper. On the desk, which was both the origin and the focal point of this amazing profusion of paper, a virtual paper landscape had come into being in the course of time, with mountains and valleys. Like a glacier when it reaches the sea, it had broken off at the edges and established new deposits all around on the floor, which in turn were advancing imperceptibly towards the center of the room. Years ago, Janine had been obliged by the ever-increasing masses of paper on her desk to bring further tables into use, and these tables, where similar processes of accretion had subsequently taken place, represented later epochs, so to speak, in the evolution of Janine's paper universe. (pp. 615–16)

> Night had fallen and I sat in the darkness of my room on the top floor of the Vondel Park Hotel and listened to the stormy gusts buffeting the crowns of the trees. From afar came the rumble of thunder. Pallid sheet lightning streaked the horizon. At about one o'clock, when I heard the first drops rattling on the metal roof, I leant out of the window into the warm, storm-filled air. Soon the rain was pouring down into the shadowy depths of the park, which flared from time to time as if lit up by Bengal fire. The water in the gutter gurgled like a mountain stream. Once, when lightning again flashed across the sky, I looked down into the hotel garden far below me, and there, in the broad ditch that runs between the garden and the park, in the shelter of an overhanging willow,

> I saw a solitary mallard, motionless on the garish green surface of the
> water. This image emerged from the darkness, for a fraction of a second,
> with such perfect clarity that I can still see every individual willow leaf,
> the myriad green scales of duckweed, the subtlest nuances in the fowl's
> plumage, and even the pores in the lid closed over its eye. (pp. 634–35)

Choose one excerpt and write a parallel passage—one similar (even exactly similar) in the shape of the sentences (including punctuation), the
arrangement of the sentences, and intent.

Sebald has provided the model; you provide a new subject with new
words. When you are finished, prepare a sentence or two of reflection on
the style of your passage. What's the point? What is the usefulness? What
does such writing do? What doesn't it do?

ASSIGNMENTS FOR WRITING

1. We have given you two chapters from *The Rings of Saturn*—Chapters 1
    and 4. On the basis of these two, or taking these two as representative, what
    is the book about? If there is an argument here, what is it? If a reader is
    given directions on how to read and what to do with this text, what are
    they? And where, for you at least, do the directions lead? Write an essay
    that begins with these questions and accounts for the text. Be sure to work
    from passages, from your initial encounter with those passages, and from
    your sense of those passages upon reflection.

    Note: There are several published reviews of this book. While it would
    be best not to *begin* with one of them, you could, if appropriate, revise your
    essay to bring it into conversation with one of the reviewers.

2. The speaker (or writer or narrator) in *The Rings of Saturn* has an interest in
    the early English writer Thomas Browne, "who had practiced as a doctor in
    Norwich in the seventeenth century and had left a number of writings that
    defy all comparison" (p. 616). Of Browne's writing, he says:

    > In common with other English writers of the seventeenth century,
    > Browne wrote out of the fullness of his erudition, deploying a vast
    > repertoire of quotations and the names of authorities who had gone be-
    > fore, creating complex metaphors and analogies, and constructing
    > labyrinthine sentences that sometimes extend over one or two pages,
    > sentences that resemble processions or a funeral cortège in their sheer
    > ceremonial lavishness. It is true that, because of the immense weight of
    > the impediments he is carrying, Browne's writing can be held back by
    > the force of gravitation, but when he does succeed in rising higher and
    > higher through the circles of his spiraling prose, borne aloft like a glider
    > on warm currents of air, even today the reader is overcome by a sense of
    > levitation. The greater the distance, the clearer the view: one sees the
    > tiniest of details with the utmost clarity. It is as if one were looking
    > through a reversed opera glass and through a microscope at the same
    > time. (p. 622)

    This is a description of Browne's style—of what the writing does rather
    than what it says in its paraphrasable content. Write an essay in which you
    provide an account of Sebald's style. ("Questions for a Second Reading"
    1 and 5 help to prepare for such an essay.) You can begin in the spirit of his

description of Browne's writing but you will need examples from the text to describe Sebald's writing. If you work with both chapters, think about how they are different and about how chapter 4 could be said to follow chapter 1.

   Note: Although it would make your essay a much more ambitious project, it would be interesting to select a passage from Browne's work—from *Urn Burial* (also called *Hydriotaphia*) or *The Garden of Cyrus*—and to present it in relation to a passage from *The Rings of Saturn*. How are they alike? How are they different? What does a seventeenth-century project look like in the late twentieth century? Is Sebald attempting to write in Browne's style? If so, does he succeed?

3. In a 2001 *New York Times* essay titled "Writers in the Shadows," Margo Jefferson says that Sebald "keeps looking for ways to approach and understand history in its brute simplicity and its subtleties." How might these two chapters from *The Rings of Saturn* be said to be about history? Write an essay that accounts for the historical references in these two chapters. How do they approach history? How do they understand it? With these two chapters as your points of reference, how does Sebald represent and make sense of the past?

4. Let's think for a moment of the two chapters from *The Rings of Saturn* as essays. Each has a distinct way of working. Each presents a character speaking, thinking, and writing. Both are short; they combine the personal with issues and references of general concern. Each moves from the story of a life (travels in the east of England) to the story of a mental or intellectual life. They give special importance to the records (and details) of reading and scholarship—books, authors, paintings. They demonstrate that personal history is bound up in a history of one's thinking and learning. Write a similar essay, one that follows the design and order (if not the style) of Sebald. You can, if you choose, draw on the material you are reading and studying in other courses this semester. You could also include images and illustrations. When you are finished, provide a very brief (one page) preface in which you present to a reader what he or she is about to read.

MAKING CONNECTIONS

1. John Berger, in "Ways of Seeing," says, "The past is never there waiting to be discovered, to be recognized for exactly what it is. History always constitutes the relation between a present and its past" (p. 99). And he says, "If we 'saw' the art of the past, we would situate ourselves in history. When we are prevented from seeing it, we are being deprived of the history which belongs to us" (p. 100). Sebald, in these chapters from *The Rings of Saturn*, enacts a relation between a present and its past. Write an essay that discusses the work of Berger and Sebald and the ways in which they understand and represent an appropriate way to "situate" oneself in history.

   Note: A good way to begin might be to look at the discussion of painters and their work—Franz Hals and Rembrandt for Berger and Rembrandt for Sebald. Would Berger be sympathetic to Sebald's use of Rembrandt's *The Anatomy Lesson*? Berger's short essay on Caravaggio's *The Calling of*

St. Matthew is somewhat in the style and spirit of Sebald's writing. Would Sebald be a sympathetic reader of Berger's prose?

2. Like Sebald, Susan Griffin (in "Our Secret," p. 299) puts history and research in an unconventional relationship to the "person" one finds in a personal essay. Both are researchers, both are well-read and thoughtful, both are interested in the events of the past and in the work of writers and artists. Neither, however, writes the kind of prose you find in a textbook; neither writes the kind of prose conventionally held up as a model for academic writing. Write an essay in which you present and compare the "projects" represented in the writing of Sebald and Griffin. How might you explain (even defend) their work as a model for the classroom? You will need to be sure to work closely with examples, including examples of the kinds of classrooms you know and that you hope to know.

JANE
TOMPKINS

JANE TOMPKINS (b. 1940) received her BA from Bryn Mawr and completed both an MA and a PhD at Yale University. She has taught at Temple University, Connecticut College, Duke University, and the University of Illinois at Chicago. Among her publications are Sensational Designs: The Cultural Work of American Fiction, 1790–1860 *(1985) and* West of Everything: The Inner Life of Westerns *(1992). She is also editor of* Reader-Response Criticism: From Formalism to Post-Structuralism *(1980). Her most recent book,* A Life in School: What the Teacher Learned *(1997), is a first-person critical account of American higher education.*

In Sensational Designs *Tompkins suggests that novels and short stories ought to be studied "not because they manage to escape the limitations of their particular time and place, but because they offer powerful examples of the way a culture thinks about itself, articulating and proposing solutions for the problems that shape a particular historical moment." This perspective leads Tompkins to conclude that the study of literature ought to focus not merely on those texts we call masterpieces but also on the texts of popular or best-selling authors. By studying these popular texts,*

*Tompkins believes we can learn more of the "work" of novels and short stories, the in-
fluence they exert over the society in which they have been produced.*

*"'Indians'" was first published in 1986 in the influential journal of literary
criticism* Critical Inquiry. *It is an unusual essay in many ways, not the least of
which is how it turns, as Tompkins's work often does, to anecdote and personal example. This is a surprising essay, perhaps even more surprising to faculty than to
undergraduates. It is as though Tompkins was not willing to hide the "limitation of
[her] particular time and place," limitations most scholars are more than happy to
hide. In fact, Tompkins's selection could be said to take the reader behind the scenes
of the respectable drama of academic research, offering a powerful example of how
contemporary academic culture thinks about itself, articulating and proposing solutions for the problems that shape its particular historical moment. If individual
interpretations are made and not found—if, for that matter,
the "truths" of history or the background to American literature are made and not found—then there is every reason to acknowledge the circumstances of their making. And this is what
Tompkins does. "'Indians'" is both a report on Tompkins's research and a reflection on the ways knowledge is produced, defended, and revised in academic life.*

*"Indians": Textualism,
Morality, and the
Problem of History*

When I was growing up in New York City, my parents used to take me to
an event in Inwood Park at which Indians—real American Indians dressed
in feathers and blankets—could be seen and touched by children like me.
This event was always a disappointment. It was more fun to imagine that
you *were* an Indian in one of the caves in Inwood Park than to shake the hand
of an old man in a headdress who was not overwhelmed at the opportunity
of meeting you. After staring at the Indians for a while, we would take a walk
in the woods where the caves were, and once I asked my mother if the remains of a fire I had seen in one of them might have been left by the original
inhabitants. After that, wandering up some stone steps cut into the side of
the hill, I imagined I was a princess in a rude castle. My Indians, like my
princesses, were creatures totally of the imagination, and I did not care to
have any real exemplars interfering with what I already knew.

I already knew about Indians from having read about them in school. Over and over we were told the story of how Peter Minuit had bought Manhattan Island from the Indians for twenty-four dollars' worth of glass beads. And it was a story we didn't mind hearing because it gave us the rare pleasure of having someone to feel superior to, since the poor Indians had not known (as we eight-year-olds did) how valuable a piece of property Manhattan Island would become. Generally, much was made of the Indian presence in Manhattan; a poem in one of our readers began: "Where we walk to school today/Indian children used to play," and we were encouraged to write poetry on this topic ourselves. So I had a fairly rich relationship with Indians before I ever met the unprepossessing people in Inwood Park. I felt that I had a lot in common with them. They, too, liked animals (they were often named after animals); they, too, made mistakes— they liked the brightly colored trinkets of little value that the white men were always offering them; they were handsome, warlike, and brave and had led an exciting, romantic life in the forest long ago, a life such as I dreamed of leading myself. I felt lucky to be living in one of the places where they had definitely been. Never mind where they were or what they were doing now.

My story stands for the relationship most non-Indians have to the people who first populated this continent, a relationship characterized by narcissistic fantasies of freedom and adventure, of a life lived closer to nature and to spirit than the life we lead now. As Vine Deloria, Jr., has pointed out, the American Indian Movement in the early seventies couldn't get people to pay attention to what was happening to Indians who were alive in the present, so powerful was this country's infatuation with people who wore loincloths, lived in tepees, and roamed the plains and forest long ago.[1] The present essay, like these fantasies, doesn't have much to do with actual Indians, though its subject matter is the histories of European-Indian relations in seventeenth-century New England. In a sense, my encounter with Indians as an adult doing "research" replicates the childhood one, for while I started out to learn more about Indians, I ended up preoccupied with a problem of my own.

This essay enacts a particular instance of the challenge poststructuralism poses to the study of history. In simpler language, it concerns the difference that point of view makes when people are giving accounts of events, whether at first or second hand. The problem is that if all accounts of events are determined through and through by the observer's frame of reference, then one will never know, in any given case, what really happened.

I encountered this problem in concrete terms while preparing to teach a course in colonial American literature. I'd set out to learn what I could about the Puritans' relations with American Indians. All I wanted was a general idea of what happened between the English settlers and the natives in seventeenth-century New England; poststructuralism and its dilemmas were the furthest thing from my mind. I began, more or less automatically, with Perry Miller, who hardly mentions the Indians at all, then proceeded to the work of historians who had dealt exclusively with the European-Indian encounter. At first, it was a question of deciding which of these authors to believe, for it quickly became apparent that there was no unanimity on the subject. As I read on, however, I discovered that the problem was more complicated than deciding whose version of events was correct. Some of the conflicting accounts were not simply contradictory, they were completely incommensurable, in that their assumptions about what counted as a valid approach to the subject, and what the subject itself was, diverged in fundamental ways. Faced with an array of mutually irreconcilable points of view, points of view which determined what was being discussed as well as the terms of the discussion, I decided to turn to primary sources for clarification, only to discover that the primary sources reproduced the problem all over again. I found myself, in other words, in an epistemological quandary, not only unable to decide among conflicting versions of events but also unable to believe that any such decision could, in principle, be made. It was a moral quandary as well. Knowledge of what really happened when the Europeans and the Indians first met seemed particularly important, since the result of that encounter was virtual genocide. This was the kind of past "mistake" which, presumably, we studied history in order to avoid repeating. If studying history couldn't put us in touch with actual events and their causes, then what was to prevent such atrocities from happening again?

For a while, I remained at this impasse. But through analyzing the process by which I had reached it, I eventually arrived at an understanding which seemed to offer a way out. This essay records the concrete experience of meeting and solving the difficulty I have just described (as an abstract problem, I thought I had solved it long ago). My purpose is not to throw new light on antifoundationalist epistemology—the solution I reached is not a new one—but to dramatize and expose the troubles antifoundationalism gets you into when you meet it, so to speak, in the road.

My research began with Perry Miller. Early in the preface to *Errand into the Wilderness*, while explaining how he came to write his history of the New England mind, Miller writes a sentence that stopped me dead. He says that what fascinated him as a young man about his country's history was "the massive narrative of the movement of European culture into the vacant wilderness of America."[2] "Vacant"? Miller, writing in 1956, doesn't pause over the word "vacant," but to people who read his preface thirty years later, the word is shocking. In what circumstances could someone proposing to write a history of colonial New England *not* take account of the Indian presence there?

The rest of Miller's preface supplies an answer to this question, if one takes the trouble to piece together its details. Miller explains that as a young man, jealous of older compatriots who had had the luck to fight in World War I, he had gone to Africa in search of adventure. "The adventures that Africa afforded," he writes, "were tawdry enough, but it became the setting for a sudden epiphany" (p. vii). "It was given to me," he writes, "disconsolate on the edge of a jungle of central Africa, to have thrust upon me the mission of expounding what I took to be the innermost propulsion of the United States, while supervising, in that barbaric tropic, the unloading of drums of case oil flowing out of the inexhaustible wilderness of America" (p. viii). Miller's picture of himself on the banks of the Congo furnishes a key to the kind of history he will write and to his mental image of a vacant wilderness; it explains why it was just there, under precisely these conditions, that he should have had his epiphany.

The fuel drums stand, in Miller's mind, for the popular misconception of what this country is about. They are "tangible symbols of [America's] appalling power," a power that everyone but Miller takes for the ultimate reality (p. ix). To Miller, "the mind of man is the basic factor in human history," and he will plead, all unaccommodated as he is among the fuel drums, for the intellect—the intellect for which his fellow historians, with their chapters on "stoves or bathtubs, or tax laws," "the Wilmot Proviso" and "the chain store," "have so little respect" (pp. viii, ix). His preface seethes with a hatred of the merely physical and mechanical, and this hatred, which is really a form of moral outrage, explains not only the contempt with which he mentions the stoves and bathtubs but also the nature of his experience in Africa and its relationship to the "massive narrative" he will write.

Miller's experiences in Africa are "tawdry," his tropic is barbaric because the jungle he stands on the edge of means nothing to him, no more, indeed something less, than the case oil. It is the nothingness of Africa that precipitates his vision. It is the barbarity of the "dark continent," the obvious (but superficial) parallelism between the jungle at Matadi and America's "vacant wilderness" that releases in Miller the desire to define and vindicate his country's cultural identity. To the young Miller, colonial Africa and colonial America are—but for the history he will bring to light—mirror images of one another. And what he fails to see in the one landscape is the same thing he overlooks in the other: the human beings who people it. As Miller stood with his back to the jungle, thinking about the role of mind in human history, his failure to see that the land into which European culture had moved was not vacant but already occupied by a varied and numerous population, is of a piece with his failure, in his portrait of himself at Matadi, to notice *who* was carrying the fuel drums he was supervising the unloading of.

The point is crucial because it suggests that what is invisible to the historian in his own historical moment remains invisible when he turns his gaze to the past. It isn't that Miller didn't "see" the black men, in a literal sense, any more than it's the case that when he looked back he didn't "see" the Indians, in the sense of not realizing they were there. Rather, it's that neither the Indians nor the blacks *counted* for him, in a fundamental way. The way in which Indians can be seen but not counted is illustrated by an entry in Governor John Winthrop's journal, three hundred years before, when he recorded that there had been a great storm with high winds "yet through God's great mercy it did no hurt, but only killed one Indian with the fall of a tree."[3] The juxtaposition suggests that Miller shared with Winthrop a certain colonial point of view, a point of view from which Indians, though present, do not finally matter.

A book entitled *New England Frontier: Puritans and Indians, 1620–1675*, written by Alden Vaughan and published in 1965, promised to rectify Miller's omission. In the outpouring of work on the European-Indian encounter that began in the early sixties, this book is the first major landmark, and to a neophyte it seems definitive. Vaughan acknowledges the absence of Indian sources and emphasizes his use of materials which catch the Puritans "off guard."[4] His announced conclusion that "the New England Puritans followed a remarkably humane, considerate, and just policy in their dealings with the Indians" seems supported by the scope, documentation, and methodicalness of his project (*NEF*, p. vii). The author's fair-mindedness and equanimity seem everywhere apparent, so that when he asserts "the history of interracial relations from the arrival of the Pilgrims to the outbreak of King Philip's War is a credit to the integrity of both peoples," one is positively reassured (*NEF*, p. viii).

But these impressions do not survive an admission that comes late in the book, when, in the course of explaining why works like Helen Hunt Jackson's *Century of Dishonor* had spread misconceptions about Puritan treatment of the Indians, Vaughan finally lays his own cards on the table.

> The root of the misunderstanding [about Puritans and Indians] . . . lies[s] in a failure to recognize the nature of the two societies that met in seventeenth-century New England. One was unified, visionary, disciplined, and dynamic. The other was divided, self-satisfied, undisciplined, and static. It would be unreasonable to expect that such societies could live side by side indefinitely with no penetration of the more fragmented and passive by the more consolidated and active. What resulted, then, was not—as many have held—a clash of dissimilar ways of life, but rather the expansion of one into the areas in which the other was lacking. [*NEF*, p. 323]

From our present vantage point, these remarks seem culturally biased to an incredible degree, not to mention inaccurate: Was Puritan society unified? If so, how does one account for its internal dissensions and obsessive need to cast out deviants? Is "unity" necessarily a positive culture trait? From what standpoint can one say that American Indians were neither disciplined nor visionary, when both these characteristics loom so large in the ethnographies? Is it an accident that ways of describing cultural strength and weakness coincide with gender stereotypes—active/passive, and so on? Why is one culture said to "penetrate" the other? Why is the "other" described in terms of "lack"?

Vaughan's fundamental categories of apprehension and judgment will not withstand even the most cursory inspection. For what looked like evenhandedness when he was writing *New England Frontier* does not look that way anymore. In his introduction to *New Directions in American Intellectual History*, John Higham writes that by the end of the sixties

> the entire conceptual foundation on which [this sort of work] rested [had] crumbled away.... Simultaneously, in sociology, anthropology, and history, two working assumptions ... came under withering attack: first, the assumption that societies tend to be integrated, and second, that a shared culture maintains that integration.... By the late 1960s all claims issued in the name of an "American mind" ... were subject to drastic skepticism.[5]

"Clearly," Higham continues, "the sociocultural upheaval of the sixties created the occasion" for this reaction.[6] Vaughan's book, it seemed, could only have been written before the events of the sixties had sensitized scholars to questions of race and ethnicity. It came as no surprise, therefore, that ten years later there appeared a study of European-Indian relations which reflected the new awareness of social issues the sixties had engendered. And it offered an entirely different picture of the European-Indian encounter.

Francis Jennings's *The Invasion of America* (1975) rips wide open the idea that the Puritans were humane and considerate in their dealings with the Indians. In Jennings's account, even more massively documented than Vaughan's, the early settlers lied to the Indians, stole from them, murdered them, scalped them, captured them, tortured them, raped them, sold them into slavery, confiscated their land, destroyed their crops, burned their homes, scattered their possessions, gave them alcohol, undermined their systems of belief, and infected them with diseases that wiped out 90 percent of their numbers within the first hundred years after contact.[7]

Jennings mounts an all-out attack on the essential decency of the Puritan leadership and their apologists in the twentieth century. The Pequot War, which previous historians had described as an attempt on the part of Massachusetts Bay to protect itself from the fiercest of the New England tribes, becomes, in Jennings's painstakingly researched account, a deliberate war of extermination, waged by whites against Indians. It starts with trumped-up charges, is carried on through a series of increasingly bloody reprisals, and ends in the massacre of scores of Indian men, women, and children, all so that Massachusetts Bay could gain political and economic control of the southern Connecticut Valley. When one reads this and then turns over the page and sees a reproduction of the Bay Colony seal, which depicts an Indian from whose mouth issue the words "Come over and help us," the effect is shattering.[8]

But even so powerful an argument as Jennings's did not remain unshaken by subsequent work. Reading on, I discovered that if the events of the sixties had revolutionized the study of European-Indian relations, the events of the seventies produced yet another transformation. The American Indian Movement, and in particular the founding of the Native American Rights Fund in 1971 to finance Indian litigation, and a court decision in 1975 which gave the tribes the right to seek redress for past injustices in federal court, created a climate within which historians began to focus on the Indians themselves. "Almost simultaneously," writes James Axtell, "frontier and colonial historians began to discover the necessity of considering the American natives as real determinants of history and the utility of ethnohistory as a way of ensuring parity of focus and impartiality of judgment."[9] In Miller, Indians had been simply beneath notice; in Vaughan, they belonged to an inferior culture; and in Jennings, they were the more or less innocent prey of power-hungry whites. But in the most original and provocative of the ethnohistories, Calvin Martin's *Keepers of the Game*, Indians became complicated, purposeful human beings, whose lives were spiritually motivated to a high degree.[10] Their relationship to the animals they hunted, to the natural environment, and to the whites with whom they traded became intelligible within a system of beliefs that formed the basis for an entirely new perspective on the European-Indian encounter.

Within the broader question of why European contact had such a devastating effect on the Indians, Martin's specific aim is to determine why Indians participated in the fur trade which ultimately led them to the brink of annihilation. The standard answer to this question had always been that once the Indian was introduced to European guns, copper kettles, woolen blankets, and the like, he literally couldn't keep his hands off them. In order to acquire these coveted items, he decimated the animal populations on which his survival depended. In short, the Indian's motivation in participating in the fur trade was assumed to be the same as the white European's—a desire to accumulate material goods. In direct opposition to this thesis, Martin argues that the reason why Indians ruthlessly exploited their own resources had nothing to do with supply and demand, but stemmed rather from a breakdown of the cosmic worldview that tied them to the game they killed in a spiritual relationship of parity and mutual obligation.

The hunt, according to Martin, was conceived not primarily as a physical activity but as a spiritual quest, in which the spirit of the hunter must overmaster the spirit of the game animal before the kill can take place. The animal, in effect, *allows* itself to be found and killed, once the hunter has mastered its spirit. The hunter prepared himself through rituals of fasting, sweating, or dreaming which revealed the identity of his prey and where he can find it. The physical act of killing is the least important element in the process. Once the animal is killed, eaten, and its parts used for clothing or implements, its remains must be disposed of in ritually prescribed fashion, or the game boss, the "keeper" of that species, will not permit more animals to be killed. The relationship between Indians and animals, then, is contractual; each side must hold up its end of the bargain, or no further transactions can occur.

What happened, according to Martin, was that as a result of diseases introduced into the animal population by Europeans, the game suddenly disappeared, began to act in inexplicable ways, or sickened and died in plain view, and communicated their diseases to the Indians. The Indians, consequently, believed that their compact with the animals had been broken and that the keepers of the game, the tutelary spirits of each animal species whom they had been so careful to propitiate, had betrayed them. And when missionization, wars with the Europeans, and displacement from their tribal lands had further weakened Indian society and its belief structure, the Indians, no longer restrained by religious sanctions, in effect, turned on the animals in a holy war of revenge.

Whether or not Martin's specific claim about the "holy war" was correct, his analysis made it clear to me that, given the Indians' understanding of economic, religious, and physical processes, an Indian account of what transpired when the European settlers arrived here would look nothing like our own. Their (potential, unwritten) history of the conflict could bear only a marginal resemblance to Eurocentric views. I began to think that the key to understanding European-Indian relations was to see them as an encounter between wholly disparate cultures, and that therefore either defending or attacking the colonists was beside the point since, given the cultural disparity between the two groups, conflict was inevitable and in large part a product of mutual misunderstanding.

But three years after Martin's book appeared, Shepard Krech III edited a collection of seven essays called *Indians, Animals, and the Fur Trade*, attacking Martin's entire project. Here the authors argued that we don't need an ideological or religious explanation for the fur trade. As Charles Hudson writes,

> The Southeastern Indians slaughtered deer (and were prompted to enslave and kill each other) because of their position on the outer fringes of an expanding modern world-system. . . . In the modern world-system there is a core region which establishes *economic* relations with its colonial periphery. . . . If the Indians could not produce commodities, they were on the road to cultural extinction. . . . To maximize his chances for survival, an eighteenth-century Southeastern Indian had to . . . live in the interior, out of range of European cattle, forestry, and agriculture. . . . He had to produce a commodity which was valuable enough to earn him some protection from English slavers.[11]

Though we are talking here about Southeastern Indians, rather than the subarctic and Northeastern tribes Martin studied, what really accounts for these divergent explanations of why Indians slaughtered the game are the assumptions that underlie them. Martin believes that the Indians acted on the basis of perceptions made available to them by their own cosmology; that is, he explains their behavior as the Indians themselves would have explained it (insofar as he can), using a logic and a set of values that are not Eurocentric but derived from within Amerindian culture. Hudson, on the other hand, insists that the Indians' own beliefs are irrelevant to an explanation of how they acted, which can only be understood, as far as he is concerned, in the terms of a Western materialist economic and political analysis. Martin and Hudson, in short, don't agree on what counts as an explanation, and this disagreement sheds light on the preceding accounts as well. From this standpoint, we can see that Vaughan, who thought that the Puritans were superior to the Indians, and Jennings, who thought the reverse, are both, like Hudson, using Eurocentric criteria of description and evaluation. While all three critics (Vaughan, Jennings, and Hudson) acknowledge that Indians and Europeans behave differently from one another, the behavior differs, as it were, within the order of the same: all three assume, though only Hudson makes the assumption explicit, that an understanding of relations between the Europeans and the Indians must be elaborated in European terms. In Martin's analysis, however, what we have are not only two different sets of behavior but two incommensurable ways of describing and assigning meaning to events. This difference at the level of explanation calls into question the possibility of obtaining any theory-independent account of interaction between Indians and Europeans.

At this point, dismayed and confused by the wildly divergent views of colonial history the twentieth-century historians had provided, I decided to look at some primary materials. I thought, perhaps, if I looked at some firsthand accounts and at some scholars looking at those accounts, it would be possible to decide which experts were right and which were wrong by comparing their views with the evidence. Captivity narratives seemed a good place to begin, since it was logical to suppose that the records left by whites who had been captured by Indians would furnish the sort of firsthand information I wanted.

I began with two fascinating essays based on these materials written by the ethnohistorian James Axtell, "The White Indians of Colonial America" and "The Scholastic Philosophy of the Wilderness."[12] These essays suggest that it would have been a privilege to be captured by North American Indians and taken off to Canada to dwell in a wigwam for the rest of one's life. Axtell's reconstruction of the process by which Indians taught European captives to feel comfortable in the wilderness, first taking their shoes away and giving them moccasins, carrying the children on their backs, sharing the scanty food supply equally, ceremonially cleansing them of their old identities, giving them Indian clothes and jewelry, assiduously teaching them the Indian language, finally adopting them into their families, and even visiting them after many years if, as sometimes happened, they were restored to white society—all of this creates a compelling portrait of Indian culture and helps to explain the extraordinary attraction that Indian culture apparently exercised over Europeans.

But, as I had by now come to expect, this beguiling portrait of the Indians' superior humanity is called into question by other writings on Indian captivity—for example, Norman Heard's *White into Red*, whose summation of the comparative treatment of captive children east and west of the Mississippi seems to contradict some of Axtell's conclusions:

> The treatment of captive children seems to have been similar in
> initial stages. . . . Most children were treated brutally at the time
> of capture. Babies and toddlers usually were killed immediately

and other small children would be dispatched during the rapid retreat to the Indian villages if they cried, failed to keep the pace, or otherwise indicated a lack of fortitude needed to become a worthy member of the tribe. Upon reaching the village, the child might face such ordeals as running the gauntlet or dancing in the center of a throng of threatening Indians. The prisoner might be so seriously injured at this time that he would no longer be acceptable for adoption.[13]

One account which Heard reprints is particularly arresting. A young girl captured by the Comanches who had not been adopted into the family but used as a slave had been peculiarly mistreated. When they wanted to wake her up the family she belonged to would take a burning brand from the fire and touch it to her nose. When she was returned to her parents, the flesh of her nose was completely burned away, exposing the bone.[14]

Since the pictures drawn by Heard and Axtell were in certain respects irreconcilable, it made sense to turn to a firsthand account to see how the Indians treated their captives in a particular instance. Mary Rowlandson's "The Sovereignty and Goodness of God," published in Boston around 1680, suggested itself because it was so widely read and had set the pattern for later narratives. Rowlandson interprets her captivity as God's punishment on her for failing to keep the Sabbath properly on several occasions. She sees everything that happens to her as a sign from God. When the Indians are kind to her, she attributes her good fortune to Divine Providence; when they are cruel, she blames her captors. But beyond the question of how Rowlandson interprets events is the question of what she saw in the first place and what she considered worth reporting. The following passage, with its abrupt shifts of focus and peculiar emphases, makes it hard to see her testimony as evidence of anything other than the Puritan point of view:

> Then my heart began to fail: and I fell weeping, which was the first time to my remembrance, that I wept before them. Although I had met with so much Affliction, and my heart was many times ready to break, yet could I not shed one tear in their sight: but rather had been all this while in a maze, and like one astonished: but not I may say as, Psal. 137.1. *By the Rivers of Babylon, there we sate down; yea, we wept when we remembered Zion.* There one of them asked me, why I wept, I could hardly tell what to say: yet I answered, they would kill me: No, said he, none will hurt you. Then came one of them and gave me two spoon-fulls of Meal to comfort me, and another gave me half a pint of Pease; which was more worth than many Bushels at another time. Then I went to see King Philip, he bade me come in and sit down, and asked me whether I woold smoke it (a usual Complement nowadayes among Saints and Sinners) but this no way suited me. For though I had formerly used Tobacco, yet I had left it ever since I was first taken. It seems to be a Bait, the Devil layes to make men loose their precious time: I remember with shame, how formerly, when I had taken two or three pipes, I was

> presently ready for another, such a bewitching thing it is: But I
> thank God, he has now given me power over it; surely there are
> many who may be better imployed than to ly sucking a stinking
> Tobacco-pipe.[15]

Anyone who has ever tried to give up smoking has to sympathize with
Rowlandson, but it is nonetheless remarkable, first, that a passage which begins with her weeping openly in front of her captors, and comparing herself
to Israel in Babylon, should end with her railing against the vice of tobacco;
and, second, that it has not a word to say about King Philip, the leader of the
Indians who captured her and mastermind of the campaign that devastated
the white population of the English colonies. The fact that Rowlandson has
just been introduced to the chief of chiefs makes hardly any impression on
her at all. What excites her is a moral issue which was being hotly debated
in the seventeenth century: to smoke or not to smoke (Puritans frowned on
it, apparently, because it wasted time and presented a fire hazard). What
seem to us the peculiar emphases in Rowlandson's relation are not the result of her having *screened out* evidence she couldn't handle, but of her way
of constructing the world. She saw what her seventeenth-century English
Separatist background made visible. It is when one realizes that the biases
of twentieth-century historians like Vaughan or Axtell cannot be corrected
for simply by consulting the primary materials, since the primary materials
are constructed according to *their* authors' biases, that one begins to envy
Miller his vision at Matadi. Not for what he didn't see—the Indian and the
black—but for his epistemological confidence.

Since captivity narratives made a poor source of evidence for the nature
of European-Indian relations in early New England because they were so
relentlessly pietistic, my hope was that a better source of evidence might be
writings designed simply to tell Englishmen what the American natives
were like. These authors could be presumed to be less severely biased,
since they hadn't seen their loved ones killed by Indians or been made to
endure the hardships of captivity, and because they weren't writing propaganda calculated to prove that God had delivered his chosen people from
the hands of Satan's emissaries.

The problem was that these texts were written with aims no less specific
than those of the captivity narrative, though the aims were of a different
sort. Here is a passage from William Wood's *New England's Prospect*, published in London in 1634.

> To enter into a serious discourse concerning the natural condi-
> tions of these Indians might procure admiration from the peo-
> ple of any civilized nations, in regard of their civility and good
> natures. . . . These Indians are of affable, courteous, and well-
> disposed natures, ready to communicate the best of their wealth
> to the mutual good of one another; . . . so . . . perspicuous is
> their love . . . that they are as willing to part with a mite in
> poverty as treasure in plenty. . . . If it were possible to recount
> the courtesies they have showed the English, since their first

arrival in those parts, it would not only steady belief, that they are a loving people, but also win the love of those that never saw them, and wipe off that needless fear that is too deeply rooted in the conceits of many who think them envious and of such rancorous and inhumane dispositions, that they will one day make an end of their English inmates.[16]

However, in a pamphlet published twenty-one years earlier, Alexander Whitaker of Virginia has this to say of the natives:

These naked slaves . . . serve the divell for feare, after a most base manner, sacrificing sometimes (as I have heere heard) their own Children to him. . . . They live naked in bodie, as if their shame of their sinne deserved no covering: Their names are as naked as their bodie: They esteem it a virtue to lie, deceive, and steale as their master the divell teacheth to them.[17]

According to Robert Berkhofer in *The White Man's Indian*, these divergent reports can be explained by looking at the authors' motives. A favorable report like Wood's, intended to encourage new emigrants to America, naturally represented Indians as loving and courteous, civilized and generous, in order to allay the fears of prospective colonists. Whitaker, on the other hand, a minister who wishes to convince his readers that the Indians are in need of conversion, paints them as benighted agents of the devil. Berkhofer's commentary constantly implies that white men were to blame for having represented the Indians in the image of their own desires and needs.[18] But the evidence supplied by Rowlandson's narrative, and by the accounts left by early reporters such as Wood and Whitaker, suggests something rather different. Though it is probably true that in certain cases Europeans did consciously tamper with the evidence, in most cases there is no reason to suppose that they did not record faithfully what they saw. And what they saw was not an illusion, was not determined by selfish motives in any narrow sense, but was there by virtue of a *way* of seeing which they could no more consciously manipulate than they could choose not to have been born. At this point, it seemed to me, the ethnocentric bias of the firsthand observers invited an investigation of the cultural situation they spoke from. Karen Kupperman's *Settling with the Indians* (1980) supplied just such an analysis.

Kupperman argues that Englishmen inevitably looked at Indians in exactly the same way that they looked at other Englishmen. For instance, if they looked down on Indians and saw them as people to be exploited, it was not because of racial prejudice or antique notions about savagery, it was because they looked down on ordinary English men and women and saw them as subjects for exploitation as well.[19] According to Kupperman, what concerned these writers most when they described the Indians were the insignia of social class, of rank, and of prestige. Indian faces are virtually never described in the earliest accounts, but clothes and hairstyles, tattoos and jewelry, posture and skin color are. "Early modern Englishmen believed that people can create their own identity, and that therefore one communicates to the world through signals such as dress and other forms of decoration who one is, what group or category one belongs to."[20]

Kupperman's book marks a watershed in writings on European-Indian relations, for it reverses the strategy employed by Martin two years before. Whereas Martin had performed an ethnographic analysis of Indian cosmology in order to explain, from within, the Indians' motives for engaging in the fur trade, Kupperman performs an ethnographic study of seventeenth-century England in order to explain, from within, what motivated Englishmen's behavior. The sympathy and understanding that Martin, Axtell, and others extend to the Indians are extended in Kupperman's work to the English themselves. Rather than giving an account of "what happened" between Indians and Europeans, like Martin, she reconstructs the worldview that gave the experience of one group its context. With her study, scholarship on European-Indian relations comes full circle.

It may well seem to you at this point that, given the tremendous variation among the historical accounts, I had no choice but to end in relativism. If the experience of encountering conflicting versions of the "same" events suggests anything certain it is that the attitude a historian takes up in relation to a given event, the way in which he or she judges and even describes "it"—and the "it" has to go in quotation marks because, depending on the perspective, that event either did or did not occur—this stance, these judgments and descriptions are a function of the historian's position in relation to the subject. Miller, standing on the banks of the Congo, couldn't see the black men he was supervising because of his background, his assumptions, values, experiences, goals. Jennings, intent on exposing the distortions introduced into the historical record by Vaughan and his predecessors stretching all the way back to Winthrop, couldn't see that Winthrop and his peers were not racists but only Englishmen who looked at other cultures in the way their own culture had taught them to see one another. The historian can never escape the limitations of his or her own position in history and so inevitably gives an account that is an extension of the circumstances from which it springs. But it seems to me that when one is confronted with this particular succession of stories, cultural and historical relativism is not a position that one can comfortably assume. The phenomena to which these histories testify—conquest, massacre, and genocide, on the one hand; torture, slavery, and murder on the other—cry out for judgment. When faced with claims and counterclaims of this magnitude one feels obligated to reach an understanding of what actually did occur. The dilemma posed by the study of European-Indian relations in early America is that the highly charged nature of the materials demands a moral decisiveness which the succession of conflicting accounts effectively precludes. That is the dilemma I found myself in at the end of this course of reading, and which I eventually came to resolve as follows.

After a while it began to seem to me that there was something wrong with the way I formulated the problem. The statement that the materials on European-Indian relations were so highly charged that they demanded moral judgment, but that the judgment couldn't be made because all possible descriptions of what happened were biased, seemed to contain an internal contradiction. The statement implied that in order to make a moral judgment about something, you have to know something else first—namely, the facts of the case you're being called upon to judge. My complaint was that their perspectival nature would disqualify any facts I might encounter and that therefore I couldn't judge. But to say as I did that the materials I had read were "highly charged" and therefore demanded judgment suggests both that I was reacting to something real—to some facts—*and* that I judged them. Perhaps I wasn't so much in the lurch morally or epistemologically as I had thought. If you—or I—react with horror to the story of the girl captured and enslaved by Comanches who touched a firebrand to her nose every time they wanted to wake her up, it's because we read this as a story about cruelty and suffering, and not as a story about the conventions of prisoner exchange or the economics of Comanche life. The *seeing* of the story as a cause for alarm rather than a droll anecdote or a piece of curious information is evidence of values we already hold, of judgments already made, of facts already perceived as facts.

My problem presupposed that I couldn't judge because I didn't know what the facts were. All I had, or could have, was a series of different perspectives, and so nothing that would count as an authoritative source on which moral judgments could be based. But, as I have just shown, I did judge, and that is because, as I now think, I did have some facts. I seemed to accept as facts that ninety percent of the native American population of New England died after the first hundred years of contact, that tribes in eastern Canada and the northeastern United States had a compact with the game they killed, that Comanches had subjected a captive girl to casual cruelty, that King Philip smoked a pipe, and so on. It was only where different versions of the same event came into conflict that I doubted the text was a record of something real. And even then, there was no question about certain major catastrophes. I believed that four hundred Pequots were killed near Saybrook, that Winthrop was the Governor of the Massachusetts Bay Colony when it happened, and so on. My sense that certain events, such as the Pequot War, did occur in no way reflected the indecisiveness that overtook me when I tried to choose among the various historical versions. In fact, the need I felt to make up my mind was impelled by the conviction that certain things *had* happened that shouldn't have happened. Hence it was never the case that "what happened" was completely unknowable or unavailable. It's rather that in the process of reading so many different approaches to the same phenomenon I became aware of the difference in the attitudes that informed these approaches. The awareness of the interests motivating each version cast suspicion over everything, in retrospect, and I ended by claiming that there was nothing I could know. This, I now see, was never really the case. But how did it happen?

Someone else, confronted with the same materials, could have decided that one of these historical accounts was correct. Still another person might have decided that more evidence was needed in order to decide among them. Why did I conclude that none of the accounts was accurate because they were all produced from some particular angle of vision? Presumably there was something in my background that enabled me to see the problem in this way. That something, very likely, was poststructuralist theory. I let my discovery that Vaughan was a product of the fifties, Jennings of the sixties, Rowlandson of a Puritan worldview, and so on lead me to the conclusion that all facts are theory dependent because that conclusion was already a thinkable one for me. My inability to come up with a true account was not the product of being situated nowhere; it was the product of certitude that existed *somewhere else*, namely, in contemporary literary theory. Hence, the level at which my indecision came into play was a function of particular beliefs I held. I was never in a position of epistemological indeterminacy, I was never *en abyme*. The idea that all accounts are perspectival seemed to me a superior standpoint from which to view all the versions of "what happened," and to regard with sympathetic condescension any person so old-fashioned and benighted as to believe that there really was some way of arriving at the truth. But this skeptical standpoint was just as firm as any other. The fact that it was also seriously disabling—it prevented me from coming to any conclusion about what I had read—did not render it any less definite.

At this point something is beginning to show itself that has up to now been hidden. The notion that all facts are only facts within a perspective has the effect of emptying statements of their content. Once I had Miller and Vaughan and Jennings, Martin and Hudson, Axtell and Heard, Rowlandson and Wood and Whitaker, and Kupperman; I had Europeans and Indians, ships and canoes, wigwams and log cabins, bows and arrows and muskets, wigs and tattoos, whiskey and corn, rivers and forts, treaties and battles, fire and blood—and then suddenly all I had was a metastatement about perspectives. The effect of bringing perspectivism to bear on history was to wipe out completely the subject matter of history. And it follows that bringing perspectivism to bear in this way on any subject matter would have a similar effect; everything is wiped out and you are left with nothing but a single idea—perspectivism itself.

But—and it is a crucial but—all this is true only if you believe that there is an alternative. As long as you think that there are or should be facts that exist outside of any perspective, then the notion that facts are perspectival will have this disappearing effect on whatever it touches. But if you are convinced that the alternative does not exist, that there really are no facts except as they are embedded in some particular way of seeing the world, then the argument that a set of facts derives from some particular worldview is no longer an argument against that set of facts. If all facts share this characteristic, to say that any one fact is perspectival doesn't change its factual nature in the slightest. It merely reiterates it.

This doesn't mean that you have to accept just anybody's facts. You can show that what someone else asserts to be a fact is false. But it does mean that you can't argue that someone else's facts are not facts *because they are only the product of a perspective*, since this will be true of the facts that you perceive as well. What this means then is that arguments about "what happened" have to proceed much as they did before poststructuralism broke in with all its talk about language-based reality and culturally produced knowledge. Reasons must be given, evidence adduced, authorities cited, analogies drawn. Being aware that all facts are motivated, believing that people are always operating inside some particular interpretive framework or other is a pertinent argument when what is under discussion is the way beliefs are grounded. But it doesn't give one any leverage on the facts of a particular case.[21]

What this means for the problem I've been addressing is that I must piece together the story of European-Indian relations as best I can, believing this version up to a point, that version not at all, another almost entirely, according to what seems reasonable and plausible, given everything else that I know. And this, as I've shown, is what I was already doing in the back of my mind without realizing it, because there was nothing else I *could* do. If the accounts don't fit together neatly, that is not a reason for rejecting them all in favor of a metadiscourse about epistemology; on the contrary, one encounters contradictory facts and divergent points of view in practically every phase of life, from deciding whom to marry to choosing the right brand of cat food, and one decides as best one can given the evidence available. It is only the nature of the academic situation which makes it appear that one can linger on the threshold of decision in the name of an epistemological principle. What has really happened in such a case is that the subject of debate has changed from the question of what happened in a particular instance to the question of how knowledge is arrived at. The absence of pressure to decide what happened creates the possibility for this change of venue.

The change of venue, however, is itself an action taken. In diverting attention from the original problem and placing it where Miller did, on "the mind of man," it once again ignores what happened and still is happening to American Indians. The moral problem that confronts me now is not that I can never have any facts to go on, but that the work I do is not directed toward solving the kinds of problems that studying the history of European-Indian relations has awakened me to.

NOTES

[1] See Vine Deloria, Jr., *God Is Red* (New York, 1973), pp. 39–56.

[2] Perry Miller, *Errand into the Wilderness* (Cambridge, Mass., 1964), p. vii; all further references will be included in the text.

[3] This passage from John Winthrop's *Journal* is excerpted by Perry Miller in his anthology *The American Puritans: Their Prose and Poetry* (Garden City, N.Y., 1956), p. 43. In his headnote to the selections from the *Journal*, Miller speaks of Winthrop's "characteristic objectivity" (p. 37).

[4] Alden T. Vaughan, *New England Frontier: Puritans and Indians, 1620–1675* (Boston, 1965), pp. vi–vii; all further references to this work, abbreviated *NEF*, will be included in the text.

[5] John Higham, intro. to *New Directions in American Intellectual History*, ed. Higham and Paul K. Conkin (Baltimore, 1979), p. xii.

[6] Ibid.

[7] See Francis Jennings, *The Invasion of America: Indians, Colonialism, and the Cant of Conquest* (New York, 1975), pp. 3–31. Jennings writes: "The so-called settlement of America was a *re*settlement, reoccupation of a land made waste by the diseases and demoralization introduced by the newcomers. Although the source data pertaining to populations have never been compiled, one careful scholar, Henry D. Dobyns, has provided a relatively conservative and meticulously reasoned estimate conforming to the known effects of conquest catastrophe. Dobyns has calculated a total aboriginal population for the western hemisphere within the range of 90 to 112 million, of which 10 to 12 million lived north of the Rio Grande" (p. 30).

[8] Jennings, fig. 7, p. 229; and see pp. 186–229.

[9] James Axtell, *The European and the Indian: Essays in the Ethnohistory of Colonial North America* (Oxford, 1981), p. viii.

[10] See Calvin Martin, *Keepers of the Game: Indian-Animal Relationships and the Fur Trade* (Berkeley and Los Angeles, 1978).

[11] See the essay by Charles Hudson in *Indians, Animals, and the Fur Trade: A Critique of "Keepers of the Game,"* ed. Shepard Krech III (Athens, Ga., 1981), pp. 167–69.

[12] See Axtell, "The White Indians of Colonial America" and "The Scholastic Philosophy of the Wilderness," *The European and the Indian*, pp. 168–206 and 131–67.

[13] J. Norman Heard, *White into Red: A Study of the Assimilation of White Persons Captured by Indians* (Metuchen, N.J., 1973), p. 97.

[14] See ibid., p. 98.

[15] Mary Rowlandson, "The Soveraignty and Goodness of God, Together with the Faithfulness of His Promises Displayed; Being a Narrative of the Captivity and Restauration of Mrs. Mary Rowlandson (1676)," in *Held Captive by Indians: Selected Narratives, 1642–1836*, ed. Richard VanDerBeets (Knoxville, Tenn., 1973), pp. 57–58.

[16] William Wood, *New England's Prospect*, ed. Vaughan (Amherst, Mass., 1977), pp. 88–89.

[17] Alexander Whitaker, *Goode Newes from Virginia* (1613), quoted in Robert F. Berkhofer, Jr., *The White Man's Indian: Images of the American Indian from Columbus to the Present* (New York, 1978), p. 19.

[18] See, for example, Berkhofer's discussion of the passages he quotes from Whitaker (*The White Man's Indian*, pp. 19, 20).

[19] See Karen Ordahl Kupperman, *Settling with the Indians: The Meeting of English and Indian Cultures in America, 1580–1640* (Totowa, N.J., 1980), pp. 3, 4.

[20] Ibid., p. 35.

[21] The position I've been outlining is a version of neopragmatism. For an exposition, see *Against Theory: Literary Studies and the New Pragmatism*, ed. W. J. T. Mitchell (Chicago, 1985).

• • • • • • • • • •

QUESTIONS FOR A SECOND READING

1. Tompkins's essay can be divided into three parts: the account of her childhood understanding of Indians; the account of her research into scholarly and first-person accounts of the relations between the Indians and the settlers in New England; and a final conclusion (beginning on p. 659). The conclusion, in many ways, is the hardest part of the essay to understand.

Like the conclusion to Clifford Geertz's "Deep Play: Notes on the Balinese Cockfight" (p. 259), it assumes not only that you have followed a chain of reasoning but that you have access to the larger philosophical questions that have preoccupied the academic community. In this sense the conclusion presents special problems for a student reader. Why might one be dissatisfied with "metadiscourse"? What kind of work is Tompkins talking about, for example, when she says, "The moral problem that confronts me now is . . . that the work I do is not directed toward solving the kinds of problems that studying the history of European-Indian relations has awakened me to" (p. 662)?

As you reread the essay, look to see how the first two sections might be seen as a preparation for the conclusion. And as you reread the concluding section (which you may have to do several times), try to imagine the larger, unspoken issues it poses for those who teach American literature or who are professionally involved in reading and researching the past.

2. One of the things to notice about Tompkins's essay is how neatly all the pieces fit together in her narrative. If you wanted to read against this essay, you might say that they fit together *too* neatly. The seemingly "natural" progression from book to book or step to step in this account of her research and her thinking could be said to reveal the degree to which the story was shaped or made, constructed for the occasion. Real experience is never quite so tidy.

As you reread the essay, be aware of the narrative as something made and ask yourself, How does she do that? What is she leaving out? Where is she working hard to get her material to fit? This is partly a matter of watching how Tompkins does her work—looking at paragraphs, for instance, and seeing how they represent her material and her reading of that material. It is also a matter of looking for what is not there, for seams that indicate necessary or unconscious omissions (as though while writing this essay, too, she "did not care to have any real exemplars interfering with what I already knew").

ASSIGNMENTS FOR WRITING

1. Tompkins's essay tells the story of a research project. It also, however, "reads" that narrative—that is, not only does Tompkins describe what she did, or what other people said, but she reflects on what her actions or the work of others might be said to represent. She writes about "point of view" or "frame of reference" and the ways they might be said to determine how people act, what they write, and what they know.

Write an essay that tells a similar story, one of your own, using Tompkins's essay as a model. There are two ways you might do this:

a. You could tell the story of a research project, a paper (most likely a term paper) you prepared for school. This does not have to be a pious or dutiful account. Tompkins, after all, is writing against what she takes to be the predictable or expected account of research as the disinterested pursuit of truth—in which a student would go to the library to "find" the truth about the Indians and the settlers. And she writes in a style that is not solemnly academic. Like Tompkins, you can tell what you take to be the untold story of term-paper research, you can reflect on the "problem" of such research by turning to your own account.

Your account should begin well before your work in the library — that is, you too will want to show the "prehistory" of your project, the possible connections between school work and your life outside school. It should also tell the story of your work with other people's writing. The purpose of all this is to reflect on how knowledge is constructed and how you, as a student, have been expected to participate (and how you have, in fact, participated) in that process.

b. You could tell the story of a discovery that did not involve reading or library research; in fact, you could tell the story of a discovery that did not involve school at all. In this sense you would be working in response to the first section of Tompkins's essay, in which what she knows about Indians is constructed from a combination of cultural models and personal desire.

2. In her essay Tompkins offers her experience as a representative case. Her story is meant to highlight a problem central to teaching, learning, and research—central, that is, to academic life. As a student, you can read this essay as a way of looking in on the work and concerns of your faculty (a group represented not only by Tompkins but by those against whom she is arguing). Write an essay directed to someone who has not read "'Indians'," someone who will be entering your school as a first-year student next semester. Your job is to introduce an incoming freshman to the academy, using Tompkins as your guide. You will need to present her argument and her conclusion in such a way as to make clear the consequences of what she says for someone about to begin an undergraduate education. Remember, you are writing to an incoming student; you will want to capture that audience's attention.

MAKING CONNECTIONS

1. In "Our Time" (p. 681), John Edgar Wideman writes about the problems he has "knowing" and writing about his brother Robby. In this sense, both "Our Time" and "'Indians'" are about the problems of understanding, about the different relationship between "real exemplars" and what we know. Write an essay in which you compare these two selections, looking in particular at the differences in the ways each author represents this problem and its possible solutions. Although you are working from only two sources, you could imagine that your essay is a way of investigating the differences between the work of a "creative" writer and that of a scholar.

2. At a key point in "When We Dead Awaken: Writing as Re-Vision," Adrienne Rich says:

> I have hesitated to do what I am going to do now, which is to use myself as an illustration. For one thing, it's a lot easier and less dangerous to talk about other women writers. (p. 524)

> Until we can understand the assumptions in which we are drenched we cannot know ourselves. (p. 522)

Although Rich tells a story of her own, she does so to provide an illustration of an even larger story—one about what it means to be a woman and a writer, to be a person like her.

For this assignment, work with Tompkins's essay and reread it with Rich's hesitation in mind. How is the personal used in each? What are the taboos or the risks in doing such work? What are the advantages? Write an essay that presents these two sources and their use of personal experience. How do these examples allow you, as a student looking in on adult, professional life, to understand the relationship between personal experience and professional discourse, between life and art?

ALICE
WALKER

ALICE WALKER, the youngest of eight children in a sharecropping family, was born in 1944 in Eatonton, Georgia. She is now one of the most widely read contemporary American novelists. In her work, she frequently returns to scenes of family life—some violent, some peaceful. "I was curious to know," she writes, "why people of families (specifically black families) are often cruel to each other and how much of this cruelty is caused by outside forces. . . . Family relationships are sacred. No amount of outside pressure and injustice should make us lose sight of that fact." In her nonfiction, Walker has helped to define a historical context for the contemporary black artist, a legacy that has had to be recovered from libraries and archives. The essay that follows, "In Search of Our Mothers' Gardens," defines black history as a family matter. It begins by charting the violence done to women who "died with their real gifts stifled within them" and concludes with Walker's recollection of her own mother, a recollection that enables her to imagine generations of black women handing on a "creative spark" to those who follow.

In addition to In Search of Our Mothers' Gardens *(1983), Walker has written novels, including* The Third Life of Grange Copeland *(1970) and* The Color Purple *(1982), which won the Pulitzer Prize; collections of poems, including*

Revolutionary Petunias *(1973) and* Good Night, Willie Lee, I'll See You in the Morning *(1979); two collections of short stories,* In Love and Trouble *(1973) and* You Can't Keep a Good Woman Down *(1981), and a biography of Langston Hughes. She has also served as an editor at* Ms. *magazine. After graduating from Sarah Lawrence College in 1965, she taught at a number of colleges and universities, including Wellesley College, Yale University, and the University of California at Berkeley. She has held a Guggenheim Fellowship and a National Endowment for the Arts fellowship. She lives in San Francisco.*

While pursuing her own career as a writer, Walker has fought to win recognition for the work of Zora Neale Hurston, a black woman author and anthropologist whose best-known work is the novel Their Eyes Were Watching God *(1937). Hurston died penniless in a Florida welfare home. Walker's more recent work includes* Living by the Word *(1988), a collection of essays, letters, journal entries, lectures, and poems on the themes of race, gender, sexuality, and political freedom;* To Hell with Dying *(1988), a children's picture book;* The Temple of My Familiar *(1989) and* Possessing the Secret of Joy *(1992), both novels; and* Her Blue Body Everything We Know: Earthling Poems, 1965–1990 *(1991), a collection of poems. Walker has also co-written, with Michael Meade, the introduction to a sound recording by Sobonfu Some titled* We Have No Word for Sex *(1994), an African oral tale. Her latest books are* Anything We Love Can Be Saved: A Writer's Activism *(1997), a collection of essays;* By the Light of My Father's Smile *(1998), a novel;* The Way Forward Is with a Broken Heart *(2000), a collection of stories based in part on Walker's failed early marriage;* Sent by Earth *(2001), a collection of poems;* Absolute Trust in the Goodness of the Earth: New Poems *(2003);* Now Is the Time to Open Your Heart *(2004), a novel;* We Are the Ones We Have Been Waiting For: Inner Light in a Time of Darkness *(2006);* There Is a Flower at the Tip of My Nose Smelling Me *(2006); and* Why War Is Never a Good Idea *(2007).*

In Search of Our Mothers' Gardens

I described her own nature and temperament. Told how they needed a larger life for their expression. . . . I pointed out that in lieu of proper channels, her emotions had overflowed into paths that dissipated them. I talked, beautifully I thought, about an art that would be born, an art that would open the way for women the likes of her. I asked her to hope, and build up an inner life

against the coming of that day. . . . I sang, with a strange quiver
in my voice, a promise song.

— "AVEY," JEAN TOOMER, *Cane*
The poet speaking to a prostitute who falls
asleep while he's talking

When the poet Jean Toomer walked through the South in the early
twenties, he discovered a curious thing: black women whose spirituality was
so intense, so deep, so *unconscious*, they were themselves unaware of the
richness they held. They stumbled blindly through their lives: creatures so
abused and mutilated in body, so dimmed and confused by pain, that they
considered themselves unworthy even of hope. In the selfless abstractions
their bodies became to the men who used them, they became more than "sexual objects," more even than mere women: they became "Saints." Instead of
being perceived as whole persons, their bodies became shrines: what was
thought to be their minds became temples suitable for worship. These crazy
Saints stared out at the world, wildly, like lunatics—or quietly, like suicides;
and the "God" that was in their gaze was as mute as a great stone.

Who were these Saints? These crazy, loony, pitiful women?

Some of them, without a doubt, were our mothers and grandmothers.

In the still heat of the post-Reconstruction South, this is how they
seemed to Jean Toomer: exquisite butterflies trapped in an evil honey, toil-
ing away their lives in an era, a century, that did not acknowledge them, except as "the *mule* of the world." They dreamed dreams that no one knew—
not even themselves, in any coherent fashion—and saw visions no one
could understand. They wandered or sat about the countryside crooning
lullabies to ghosts, and drawing the mother of Christ in charcoal on court-
house walls.

They forced their minds to desert their bodies and their striving spirits
sought to rise, like frail whirlwinds from the hard red clay. And when those
frail whirlwinds fell, in scattered particles, upon the ground, no one
mourned. Instead, men lit candles to celebrate the emptiness that remained,
as people do who enter a beautiful but vacant space to resurrect a God.

Our mothers and grandmothers, some of them: moving to music not
yet written. And they waited.

They waited for a day when the unknown thing that was in them
would be made known; but guessed, somehow in their darkness, that on
the day of their revelation, they would be long dead. Therefore to Toomer
they walked, and even ran, in slow motion. For they were going nowhere
immediate, and the future was not yet within their grasp. And men took
our mothers and grandmothers, "but got no pleasure from it." So complex
was their passion and their calm.

To Toomer, they lay vacant and fallow as autumn fields, with harvest
time never in sight; and he saw them enter loveless marriages, without joy;
and become prostitutes, without resistance; and become mothers of children, without fulfillment.

For these grandmothers and mothers of ours were not Saints, but Artists; driven to a numb and bleeding madness by the springs of creativity in them for which there was no release. They were Creators, who lived lives of spiritual waste, because they were so rich in spirituality—which is the basis of Art—that the strain of enduring their unused and unwanted talent drove them insane. Throwing away this spirituality was their pathetic attempt to lighten the soul to a weight their work-worn, sexually abused bodies could bear.

What did it mean for a black woman to be an artist in our grandmothers' time? In our great-grandmothers' day? It is a question with an answer cruel enough to stop the blood.

Did you have a genius of a great-great-grandmother who died under some ignorant and depraved white overseer's lash? Or was she required to bake biscuits for a lazy backwater tramp, when she cried out in her soul to paint watercolors of sunsets, or the rain falling on the green and peaceful pasturelands? Or was her body broken and forced to bear children (who were more often than not sold away from her)—eight, ten, fifteen, twenty children—when her one joy was the thought of modeling heroic figures of rebellion, in stone or clay?

How was the creativity of the black woman kept alive, year after year and century after century, when for most of the years black people have been in America, it was a punishable crime for a black person to read or write? And the freedom to paint, to sculpt, to expand the mind with action did not exist. Consider, if you can bear to imagine it, which might have been the result if singing, too, had been forbidden by law. Listen to the voices of Bessie Smith, Billie Holiday, Nina Simone, Roberta Flack, and Aretha Franklin, among others, and imagine those voices muzzled for life. Then you may begin to comprehend the lives of our "crazy," "Sainted" mothers and grandmothers. The agony of the lives of women who might have been Poets, Novelists, Essayists, and Short-Story Writers (over a period of centuries), who died with their real gifts stifled within them.

And, if this were the end of the story, we would have cause to cry out in my paraphrase of Okot p'Bitek's great poem:

> O, my clanswomen
> Let us all cry together!
> Come,
> Let us mourn the death of our mother,
> The death of a Queen
> The ash that was produced
> By a great fire!
> O, this homestead is utterly dead
> Close the gates
> With *lacari* thorns,
> For our mother
> The creator of the Stool is lost!
> And all the young women
> Have perished in the wilderness!

But this is not the end of the story, for all the young women—our mothers and grandmothers, *ourselves*—have not perished in the wilderness. And if we ask ourselves why, and search for and find the answer, we will know beyond all efforts to erase it from our minds, just exactly who, and of what, we black American women are.

One example, perhaps the most pathetic, most misunderstood one, can provide a backdrop for our mothers' work: Phillis Wheatley, a slave in the 1700s.

Virginia Woolf, in her book *A Room of One's Own*, wrote that in order for a woman to write fiction she must have two things, certainly: a room of her own (with key and lock) and enough money to support herself.

What then are we to make of Phillis Wheatley, a slave, who owned not even herself? This sickly, frail black girl who required a servant of her own at times—her health was so precarious—and who, had she been white, would have been easily considered the intellectual superior of all the women and most of the men in the society of her day.

Virginia Woolf wrote further, speaking of course not of our Phillis, that "any woman born with a great gift in the sixteenth century [insert "eighteenth century," insert "black woman," insert "born or made a slave"] would certainly have gone crazed, shot herself, or ended her days in some lonely cottage outside the village, half witch, half wizard [insert "Saint"], feared and mocked at. For it needs little skill and psychology to be sure that a highly gifted girl who had tried to use her gift of poetry would have been so thwarted and hindered by contrary instincts [add "chains, guns, the lash, the ownership of one's body by someone else, submission to an alien religion"], that she must have lost her health and sanity to a certainty."

The key words, as they relate to Phillis, are "contrary instincts." For when we read the poetry of Phillis Wheatley—as when we read the novels of Nella Larsen or the oddly false-sounding autobiography of that freest of all black women writers, Zora Hurston—evidence of "contrary instincts" is everywhere. Her loyalties were completely divided, as was, without question, her mind.

But how could this be otherwise? Captured at seven, a slave of wealthy, doting whites who instilled in her the "savagery" of the Africa they "rescued" her from . . . one wonders if she was even able to remember her homeland as she had known it, or as it really was.

Yet, because she did try to use her gift for poetry in a world that made her a slave, she was "so thwarted and hindered by . . . contrary instincts, that she . . . lost her health. . . ." In the last years of her brief life, burdened not only with the need to express her gift but also with a penniless, friendless "freedom" and several small children for whom she was forced to do strenuous work to feed, she lost her health, certainly. Suffering from malnutrition and neglect and who knows what mental agonies, Phillis Wheatley died.

So torn by "contrary instincts" was black, kidnapped, enslaved Phillis that her description of "the Goddess"—as she poetically called the Liberty she did not have—is ironically, cruelly humorous. And, in fact, has held

Phillis up to ridicule for more than a century. It is usually read prior to hanging Phillis's memory as that of a fool. She wrote:

> The Goddess comes, she moves divinely fair,
> Olive and laurel binds her *golden* hair.
> Wherever shines this native of the skies,
> Unnumber'd charms and recent graces rise. [My italics]

It is obvious that Phillis, the slave, combed the "Goddess's" hair every morning, prior, perhaps, to bringing in the milk, or fixing her mistress's lunch. She took her imagery from the one thing she saw elevated above all others.

With the benefit of hindsight we ask, "How could she?"

But at last, Phillis, we understand. No more snickering when your stiff, struggling, ambivalent lines are forced on us. We know now that you were not an idiot or a traitor; only a sickly little black girl, snatched from your home and country and made a slave; a woman who still struggled to sing the song that was your gift, although in a land of barbarians who praised you for your bewildered tongue. It is not so much what you sang, as that you kept alive, in so many of our ancestors, *the notion of song*.

Black women are called, in the folklore that so aptly identified one's status in society, "the *mule* of the world," because we have been handed the burdens that everyone else — *everyone* else — refused to carry. We have also been called "Matriarchs," "Superwomen," and "Mean and Evil Bitches." Not to mention "Castraters" and "Sapphire's Mama." When we have pleaded for understanding, our character has been distorted; when we have asked for simple caring, we have been handed empty inspirational appellations, then stuck in the farthest corner. When we have asked for love, we have been given children. In short, even our plainer gifts, our labors of fidelity and love, have been knocked down our throats. To be an artist and a black woman, even today, lowers our status in many respects, rather than raises it: and yet, artists we will be.

Therefore we must fearlessly pull out of ourselves and look at and identify with our lives the living creativity some of our great-grandmothers were not allowed to know. I stress *some* of them because it is well known that the majority of our great-grandmothers knew, even without "knowing" it, the reality of their spirituality, even if they didn't recognize it beyond what happened in the singing at church — and they never had any intention of giving it up.

How they did it — those millions of black women who were not Phillis Wheatley, or Lucy Terry or Frances Harper or Zora Hurston or Nella Larsen or Bessie Smith; or Elizabeth Catlett, or Katherine Dunham, either — brings me to the title of this essay, "In Search of Our Mothers' Gardens," which is a personal account that is yet shared, in its theme and its meaning, by all of us. I found, while thinking about the far-reaching world of the creative black woman, that often the truest answer to a question that really matters can be found very close.

In the late 1920s my mother ran away from home to marry my father. Marriage, if not running away, was expected of seventeen-year-old girls. By the time she was twenty, she had two children and was pregnant with a third. Five children later, I was born. And this is how I came to know my mother: she seemed a large, soft, loving-eyed woman who was rarely impatient in our home. Her quick, violent temper was on view only a few times a year, when she battled with the white landlord who had the misfortune to suggest to her that her children did not need to go to school.

She made all the clothes we wore, even my brothers' overalls. She made all the towels and sheets we used. She spent the summers canning vegetables and fruits. She spent the winter evenings making quilts enough to cover all our beds.

During the "working" day, she labored beside—not behind—my father in the fields. Her day began before sunup, and did not end until late at night. There was never a moment for her to sit down, undisturbed, to unravel her own private thoughts; never a time free from interruption—by work or the noisy inquiries of her many children. And yet, it is to my mother—and all our mothers who were not famous—that I went in search of the secret of what has fed that muzzled and often mutilated, but vibrant, creative spirit that the black woman has inherited, and that pops out in wild and unlikely places to this day.

But when, you will ask, did my overworked mother have time to know or care about feeding the creative spirit?

The answer is so simple that many of us have spent years discovering it. We have constantly looked high, when we should have looked high—and low.

For example: in the Smithsonian Institution in Washington, D.C., there hangs a quilt unlike any other in the world. In fanciful, inspired, and yet simple and identifiable figures, it portrays the story of the Crucifixion. It is considered rare, beyond price. Though it follows no known pattern of quilt-making, and though it is made of bits and pieces of worthless rags, it is obviously the work of a person of powerful imagination and deep spiritual feeling. Below this quilt I saw a note that says it was made by "an anonymous black woman in Alabama, a hundred years ago."

If we could locate this "anonymous" black woman from Alabama, she would turn out to be one of our grandmothers—an artist who left her mark in the only materials she could afford, and in the only medium her position in society allowed her to use.

As Virginia Woolf wrote further, in *A Room of One's Own:*

> Yet genius of a sort must have existed among women as it must have existed among the working class. [Change this to "slaves" and the "wives and daughters of sharecroppers."] Now and again an Emily Brontë or a Robert Burns [change this to "a Zora Hurston or a Richard Wright"] blazes out and proves its presence. But certainly it never got itself on to paper. When, however, one reads of a witch being ducked, of a woman possessed by devils [or "Sainthood"], of a wise woman selling herbs [our

root workers], or even a very remarkable man who had a
mother, then I think we are on the track of a lost novelist, a suppressed poet, or some mute and inglorious Jane Austen. . . .
Indeed, I would venture to guess that Anon, who wrote so many
poems without singing them, was often a woman. . . .

And so our mothers and grandmothers have, more often than not anony-
mously, handed on the creative spark, the seed of the flower they themselves
never hoped to see: or like a sealed letter they could not plainly read.

And so it is, certainly, with my own mother. Unlike "Ma" Rainey's
songs, which retained their creator's name even while blasting forth from
Bessie Smith's mouth, no song or poem will bear my mother's name. Yet
so many of the stories that I write, that we all write, are my mother's stories. Only recently did I fully realize this: that through years of listening
to my mother's stories of her life, I have absorbed not only the stories
themselves, but something of the manner in which she spoke, something
of the urgency that involves the knowledge that her stories—like her
life—must be recorded. It is probably for this reason that so much of what
I have written is about characters whose counterparts in real life are so
much older than I am.

But the telling of these stories, which came from my mother's lips as
naturally as breathing, was not the only way my mother showed herself as
an artist. For stories, too, were subject to being distracted, to dying without
conclusion. Dinners must be started, and cotton must be gathered before
the big rains. The artist that was and is my mother showed itself to me only
after many years. This is what I finally noticed.

Like Mem, a character in *The Third Life of Grange Copeland*, my mother
adorned with flowers whatever shabby house we were forced to live in. And
not just your typical straggly country stand of zinnias, either. She planted
ambitious gardens—and still does—with over fifty different varieties of
plants that bloom profusely from early March until late November. Before
she left home for the fields, she watered her flowers, chopped up the grass,
and laid out new beds. When she returned from the fields she might divide
clumps of bulbs, dig a cold pit, uproot and replant roses, or prune branches
from her taller bushes or trees—until night came and it was too dark to see.

Whatever she planted grew as if by magic, and her fame as a grower of
flowers spread over three counties. Because of her creativity with her flowers, even my memories of poverty are seen through a screen of blooms—
sunflowers, petunias, roses, dahlias, forsythia, spirea, delphiniums, ver-
bena . . . and on and on.

And I remember people coming to my mother's yard to be given cuttings
from her flowers; I hear again the praise showered on her because whatever
rocky soil she landed on, she turned into a garden. A garden so brilliant with
colors, so original in its design, so magnificent with life and creativity, that to
this day people drive by our house in Georgia—perfect strangers and imperfect strangers—and ask to stand or walk among my mother's art.

I notice that it is only when my mother is working in her flowers that
she is radiant, almost to the point of being invisible—except as Creator:

hand and eye. She is involved in work her soul must have. Ordering the universe in the image of her personal conception of Beauty.

Her face, as she prepares the Art that is her gift, is a legacy of respect she leaves to me, for all that illuminates and cherishes life. She has handed down respect for the possibilities—and the will to grasp them.

For her, so hindered and intruded upon in so many ways, being an artist has still been a daily part of her life. This ability to hold on, even in very simple ways, is work black women have done for a very long time.

This poem is not enough, but it is something, for the woman who literally covered the holes in our walls with sunflowers.

> They were women then
> My mama's generation
> Husky of voice—Stout of
> Step
> With fists as well as
> Hands
> How they battered down
> Doors
> And ironed
> Starched white
> Shirts
> How they led
> Armies
> Headragged Generals
> Across mined
> Fields
> Booby-trapped
> Kitchens
> To discover books
> Desks
> A place for us
> How they knew what we
> *Must* know
> Without knowing a page
> Of it
> Themselves

Guided by my heritage of a love of beauty and a respect for strength— in search of my mother's garden, I found my own.

And perhaps in Africa over two hundred years ago, there was just such a mother; perhaps she painted vivid and daring decorations in oranges and yellows and greens on the walls of her hut; perhaps she sang—in a voice like Roberta Flack's—*sweetly* over the compounds of her village; perhaps she wove the most stunning mats or told the most ingenious stories of all the village storytellers. Perhaps she was herself a poet—although only her daughter's name is signed to the poems that we know.

Perhaps Phillis Wheatley's mother was also an artist.

Perhaps in more than Phillis Wheatley's biological life is her mother's signature made clear.

•   •   •   •   •   •   •   •   •   •   •   •

QUESTIONS FOR A SECOND READING

1. In the essay, Walker develops the interesting notion of "contrary instincts," particularly when she discusses Phillis Wheatley. The problem for Walker (and others) is that Wheatley would idolize a fair-haired white woman as a goddess of liberty rather than turn to herself as a model, or to the black women who struggled mightily for their identities and liberty. Walker asks, "How could she?" As you reread the essay, pay attention to the sections in which Walker discusses "contrary instincts." How would you define this term? What kind of answers does this essay make possible to the question "How could she?"

2. Bessie Smith, Roberta Flack, Phillis Wheatley, Zora Neale Hurston— Walker's essay is filled with allusions to black women artists; in fact, the essay serves as a kind of book list or reader's guide; it suggests a program of reading. Jean Toomer, however, is a man, and Virginia Woolf, a white woman; the references aren't strictly to black women. As you reread this essay, pay attention to the names. What can you make of the collection of writers, poets, singers, and artists Walker sets down as a heritage? What use does she make of them? The Internet will certainly provide links to sources that will help to track down these names. You might also use this moment as the occasion to get into the college or university library; if you do, be sure to meet with a reference librarian. A reference librarian is a person who is paid a salary to help you make efficient use of a research library's quite amazing materials and resources.

3. As you reread the essay, note the sections in which Walker talks about herself. How does she feel about her mother, the history of black women in America, and "contrary instincts"? How would you describe Walker's feelings and attitudes toward herself, the past, and the pressures of living in a predominantly white culture? In considering these questions, don't settle for big words like "honest," "sensitive," or "compassionate." They are accurate, to be sure, but they are imprecise and don't do justice to Walker's seriousness and individuality.

ASSIGNMENTS FOR WRITING

1. Virginia Woolf, a white British writer from the early twentieth century, plays a key role in Walker's essay. Not only does Walker cite Woolf's work, but she revises a long passage to bring it to bear on her experience or to make it serve her argument. This is a bold move on her part. How do you understand it? How do you understand it as a way of indicating her relationship to this writer and the intellectual heritage she represents? Why bring Virginia Woolf into this essay at all?

   (You might, as an exercise, perform similar revisions of passages from "In Search of Our Mothers' Gardens," or of other selections in *Ways of Reading*, of other texts in courses you are taking this term, or from books that you've kept with you over the years. You might think about other, similar acts of revision familiar to you from current literary or popular culture—music, film, TV, art, and advertising. How and why are these artists making use of the past?)

Write an essay in which you focus attention on Walker's revision of Woolf. Use it as a way of thinking about the essay, both what it says and what it does. Use it as a way of thinking out from the essay to the situation of African American writers. And use it as a way of thinking about the relationship of those in the present, including yourself, to the work of the past.

2. Walker's essay poses a number of questions about the history of African American women in America, including how their "creative spirit" survived in the face of oppressive working and living conditions. At one point, Walker describes her mother's life in the late 1920s, after she ran away from home to marry Walker's father. Her mother's difficult life was filled with unrelenting work, yet she managed to keep a "vibrant, creative spirit" alive. At another point, Walker writes, "Our mothers and grandmothers, some of them: moving to music not yet written. And they waited . . . for a day when the unknown thing that was in them would be made known; but guessed, somehow in their darkness, that on the day of their revelation, they would be long dead" (p. 669).

Write an essay in which you discuss Walker's project as a creative endeavor, one in which she reconceives, or rewrites, texts from the past. What would you say, in other words, that Walker creates as she writes her essay?

3. In her essay Walker raises the question of what it meant (and what it still means) to be a black woman and an artist, and her response proceeds from examples that take her mother and herself, among others, into account. As you reread her essay, observe Walker's methods of working. How does she build her arguments? Where does her evidence come from? her authority? To whom is she appealing? What do her methods allow her to see (and say) and not to see? And, finally, how might her conclusions be related to her methods?

Write a paper in which you examine Walker's essay in terms of the methods by which it proceeds. Consider the connections among her arguments, evidence, supposed audience, and conclusions, and feel free to invent names and descriptions for what you would call her characteristic ways of working. Remember that your job is to invent a way of describing how Walker works and how her methods—her ways of gathering materials, of thinking them through, of presenting herself and her thoughts, of imagining a world of speakers and listeners—might be related to the issues she raises and the conclusions she draws.

MAKING CONNECTIONS

1. Throughout "Our Time" (p. 681) by John Edgar Wideman, Robby talks about his contrary instincts, his ambivalent feelings toward making it in the "square" world. How can you consider Robby in light of Walker's observations about contrary instincts and the way black women lived in the past? Write an essay in which you explore how Wideman's understanding

of his brother Robby's contrary instincts is different from Walker's understanding of her mother's contrary instincts.

2. Like Alice Walker, Susan Griffin is concerned with understanding, promoting, and preserving her relationship to the past, a past that is both her family's past and part of the twentieth-century history. Write an essay in which you present both projects: Walker's "In Search of Our Mothers' Gardens" and Susan Griffin's "Our Secret" (p. 299). You should assume that your readers are familiar with neither. You will need, then, to carefully present the arguments of the essays but also a sense of how they are written, of how they do their work. How do they justify looking backward? What is the most productive relationship of present to past? What examples can you bring to the discussion—that is, as you look to the culture of your own moment (to movies and television, music, art, advertising, literature, the Internet), what are the interesting or significant examples of the use of the past? How might you bring them into a discussion of Walker and Griffin? How might you speak for your generation and its use of the past?

3. Like Alice Walker, Adrienne Rich (in "When We Dead Awaken, p. 520), Gloria Anzaldúa (in the selections we've included from *Borderlands/La frontera*, p. 42), Susan Bordo (in "Beauty (Re)discovers the Male Body," p. 131), and Cornelius Eady (in "Brutal Imagination," p. 184) are concerned with understanding their past, a past that is both their own and part of the history of the twentieth century. Look through these selections to think about which you would like to read alongside Walker's "In Search of Our Mothers' Gardens." Choose one, and as you reread it, mark passages you might use in your essay, passages that might make for interesting conversation with selected passages from Walker's essay.

    Write an essay that considers the uses (and misuses) of the past by examining the work of these two writers. How do they justify looking backward? What is the most productive relationship of past to present? What examples might *you* bring to the discussion—that is, as you look to the culture of your own moment (to movies and television, music, art, advertising, literature, photography), what are the interesting or significant examples of the use of the past?

JOHN EDGAR
WIDEMAN

JOHN EDGAR WIDEMAN was born in 1941 in Washington, D.C., but spent most of his youth in Homewood, a neighborhood in Pittsburgh. He earned a BA from the University of Pennsylvania, taught at the University of Wyoming and the University of Massachusetts at Amherst. He is currently Asa Messer Professor and Professor of Africana Studies and English at Brown University. In addition to the nonfiction work Brothers and Keepers *(1984), from which this selection is drawn, Wideman has published a number of critically acclaimed works of fiction, including* The Lynchers *(1986);* Reuben *(1989);* Philadelphia Fire: A Novel *(1991);* Fever: Twelve Stories *(1989); and a series of novels set in Homewood:* Damballah *(1981),* Hiding Place *(1982), and* Sent for You Yesterday *(which won the 1984 PEN/Faulkner Award). The latter novels have been reissued as a set, titled* The Homewood Trilogy. *His most recent books include* The Cattle Killing *(1996),* Two Cities *(1998),* Hoop Roots *(2001),* The Island, Martinique *(2003),* God's Gym *(2005), and* Fanon *(2008). In 1994, Wideman published another work of nonfiction,* Fatheralong: A Meditation on Fathers and Sons, Race and Society.

In the preface to this collection, Wideman writes,

> The value of black life in America is judged, as life generally in
> this country is judged, by external, material signs of success. Urban
> ghettoes are dangerous, broken-down, economically marginal pockets
> of real estate infected with drugs, poverty, violence, crime, and since
> black life is seen as rooted in the ghetto, black people are identified with
> the ugliness, danger, and deterioration surrounding them. This logic is
> simpleminded and devastating, its hold on the American imagination
> as old as slavery; in fact, it recycles the classic justification for slavery,
> blaming the cause and consequences of oppression on the oppressed.
> Instead of launching a preemptive strike at the flawed assumptions that
> perpetuate racist thinking, blacks and whites are doomed to battle end-
> lessly with the symptoms of racism.
>
>   In these three books again bound as one I have set myself to the task
> of making concrete those invisible planes of existence that bear witness to
> the fact that black life, for all its material impoverishment, continues to
> thrive, to generate alternative styles, redemptive strategies, people who
> hope and cope. But more than attempting to prove a "humanity," which
> should be self-evident anyway to those not blinded by racism, my goal is
> to celebrate and affirm. Where did I come from? Who am I? Where
> am I going?

Brothers and Keepers *is a family story; it is about Wideman and his brother
Robby. John went to Oxford as a Rhodes scholar, and Robby went to prison for his
role in a robbery and a murder. In the section that follows, "Our Time," Wideman
tries to understand his brother, their relationship, where they came from, where they
are going. In this account, you will hear the voices of Robby, John, and people from
the neighborhood, but also the voice of the writer, speaking about the difficulty of
writing and the dangers of explaining away Robby's life.*

Brothers and Keepers *is not the first time Wideman has written to or about
his brother. The first of the Homewood series,* Damballah, *is dedicated to Robby.
The dedication reads:*

> Stories are letters. Letters sent to anybody or everybody. But the best
> kind are meant to be read by a specific somebody. When you read that
> kind you know you are eavesdropping. You know a real person some-
> where will read the same words you are reading and the story is that
> person's business and you are a ghost listening in.
>
>   Remember. I think it was Geral I first heard call a watermelon a
> letter from home. After all these years I understand a little better what
> she meant. She was saying the melon is a letter addressed to us. A story
> for us from down home. Down Home being everywhere we've never
> been, the rural South, the old days, slavery, Africa. That juicy, striped
> message with red meat and seeds, which always looked like roaches to
> me, was blackness as cross and celebration, a history we could taste and
> chew. And it was meant for us. Addressed to us. We were meant to slit
> it open and take care of business.
>
>   Consider all these stories as letters from home. I never liked
> watermelon as a kid. I think I remember you did. You weren't afraid of

*becoming instant nigger, of sitting barefoot and goggle-eyed and Day-
Glo black and drippy-lipped on massa's fence if you took one bite of the
forbidden fruit. I was too scared to enjoy watermelon.
Too self-conscious. I let people rob me of a simple pleasure. Watermelon's still tainted for me. But I know better
now. I can play with the idea even if I can't get down and
have a natural ball eating a real one.*

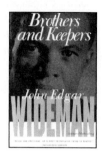

    *Anyway . . . these stories are letters. Long overdue
letters from me to you. I wish they could tear down the
walls. I wish they could snatch you away from where
you are.*

Our Time

    *You remember what we were saying about young black men in the street-world
life. And trying to understand why the "square world" becomes completely unattractive to them. It has to do with the fact that their world is the GHETTO and in
that world all the glamour, all the praise and attention is given to the slick guy, the
gangster especially, the ones that get over in the "life." And it's because we can't
help but feel some satisfaction seeing a brother, a black man, get over on these people, on their system without playing by their rules. No matter how much we have
incorporated these rules as our own, we know that they were forced on us by people
who did not have our best interests at heart. So this hip guy, this gangster or player
or whatever label you give these brothers that we like to shun because of the poison
that they spread, we, black people, still look at them with some sense of pride and
admiration, our children openly, us adults somewhere deep inside. We know they
represent rebellion—what little is left in us. Well, having lived in the "life," it becomes very hard—almost impossible—to find any contentment in joining the status quo. Too hard to go back to being nobody in a world that hates you. Even if I
had struck it rich in the life, I would have managed to throw it down the fast lane.
Or have lost it on a revolutionary whim. Hopefully the latter.*

    *I have always burned up in my fervent passions of desire and want. My senses
at times tingle and itch with my romantic, idealistic outlook on life, which has always made me keep my distance from reality, reality that was a constant insult to
my world, to my dream of happiness and peace, to my people-for-people kind of
world, my easy-cars-for-a-nickel-or-a-dime sorta world. And these driving passions, this sensitivity to the love and good in people, also turned on me because I
used it to play on people and their feelings. These aspirations of love and desire
turned on me when I wasn't able to live up to this sweet-self morality, so I began
to self-destruct, burning up in my sensitivity, losing direction, because nowhere
could I find this world of truth and love and harmony.*

In the real world, the world left for me, it was unacceptable to be "good," it was square to be smart in school, it was jive to show respect to people outside the street world, it was cool to be cold to your woman and the people that loved you. The things we liked we called "bad." "Man, that was a bad girl." The world of the angry black kid growing up in the sixties was a world in which to be in was to be out—out of touch with the square world and all of its rules on what's right and wrong. The thing was to make your own rules, do your own thing, but make sure it's contrary to what society says or is.

I SHALL ALWAYS PRAY

I

Garth looked bad. Real bad. Ichabod Crane anyway, but now he was a skeleton. Lying there in the bed with his bones poking through his skin, it made you want to cry. Garth's barely able to talk, his smooth, medium-brown skin yellow as pee. Ichabod legs and long hands and long feet, Garth could make you laugh just walking down the street. On the set you'd see him coming a far way off. Three-quarters leg so you knew it had to be Garth the way he was split up higher in the crotch than anybody else. Wilt the Stilt with a lean bird body perched on top his high waist. Size-fifteen shoes. Hands could palm a basketball easy as holding a pool cue. Fingers long enough to wrap round a basketball, but Garth couldn't play a lick. Never could get all that lankiness together on the court. You'd look at him some-times as he was trucking down Homewood Avenue and think that nigger ain't walking, he's trying to remember how to walk. Awkward as a pigeon on roller skates. Knobby joints out of whack, arms and legs flailing, going their separate ways, his body jerking to keep them from going too far. Mov-ing down the street like that wouldn't work, didn't make sense if you stood back and watched, if you pretended you hadn't seen Garth get where he was going a million times before. Nothing funny now, though. White hospi-tal sheets pulled to his chest. Garth's head always looked small as a tennis ball way up there on his shoulders. Now it's a yellow, shrunken skull.

Ever since Robby had entered the ward, he'd wanted to reach over and hide his friend's arm under the covers. For two weeks Gar had been wasting away in the bed. Bad enough knowing Gar was dying. Didn't need that piti-ful stick arm reminding him how close to nothing his main man had fallen. So fast. It could happen so fast. If Robby tried to raise that arm it would come off in his hand. As gentle as he could would not be gentle enough. The arm would disintegrate, like a long ash off the end of a cigarette.

Time to leave. No sense in sitting any longer. Garth not talking, no way of telling whether he was listening either. And Robby has nothing more to say. Choked up the way he gets inside hospitals. Hospital smell and quiet, the bare halls and bare floors, the echoes, something about all that he can't name, wouldn't try to name, rises in him and chills him. Like his teeth are chattering the whole time he's inside a hospital. Like his entire body is trembling uncontrollably, only nobody can see it or hear it but him. Shaking because he can't breathe the stuffy air. Hot and cold at the same time. He's been aching to leave since he entered the ward. Aching to get up and bust through the big glass front doors. Aching to pounce on that spidery arm flung back behind Gar's head. The arm too wasted to belong to his friend. He wants to grab it and hurl it away.

Robby pulls on tight white gloves the undertaker had dealt out to him and the rest of the pallbearers. His brown skin shows through the thin material, turns the white dingy. He's remembering that last time in Garth's ward. The hospital stink. Hot, chilly air. A bare arm protruding from the sleeve of the hospital gown, more dried-up toothpick than arm, a withered twig, with Garth's fingers like a bunch of skinny brown bananas drooping from the knobby tip.

Robby had studied the metal guts of the hospital bed, the black scuff marks swirling around the chair's legs. When he'd finally risen to go, his chair scraping against the vinyl floor broke a long silence. The noise must have roused Garth's attention. He'd spoken again.

You're good, man. Don't ever forget, Rob. You're the best.

Garth's first words since the little banter back and forth when Robby had entered the ward and dragged a chair to the side of Gar's bed. A whisper scarcely audible now that Robby was standing. Garth had tried to grin. The best he could manage was a pained adjustment of the bones of his face, no more than a shadow scudding across the yellow skull, but Robby had seen the famous smile. He hesitated, stopped rushing toward the door long enough to smile back. Because that was Gar. That was the way Gar was. He always had a smile and a good word for his cut buddies. Garth's grin was money in the bank. You could count on it like you could count on a good word from him. Something in his face would tell you you were alright, better than alright, that he believed in you, that you were, as he'd just whispered, "the best." You could depend on Garth to say something to make you feel good, even though you knew he was lying. With that grin greasing the lie you had to believe it, even though you knew better. Garth was the gang's dreamer. When he talked, you could see his dreams. That's why Robby had believed it, seen the grin, the bright shadow lighting Garth's face an instant. Out of nothing, out of pain, fear, the certainty of death gripping them both, Garth's voice had manufactured the grin.

Now they had to bury Garth. A few days after the visit to the hospital the phone rang and it was Garth's mother with the news of her son's death. Not really news. Robby had known it was just a matter of time. Of waiting for the moment when somebody else's voice would pronounce the words he'd said to himself a hundred times. *He's gone. Gar's dead.* Long gone before the telephone rang. Gar was gone when they stuck him up in the hospital bed. By the time they'd figured out what ailed him and admitted him to the hospital, it was too late. The disease had turned him to a skeleton. Nothing left of Garth to treat. They hid his messy death under white sheets, perfumed it with disinfectant, pumped him full of drugs so he wouldn't disturb his neighbors.

The others had squeezed into their pallbearers' gloves. Cheap white cotton gloves so you could use them once and throw them away like the rubber ones doctors wear when they stick their fingers up your ass. Michael, Cecil, and Sowell were pallbearers, too. With Robby and two men from Garth's family they would carry the coffin from Gaines Funeral Parlor to the hearse. Garth had been the dreamer for the gang. Robby counted four black fingers in the white glove. Garth was the thumb. The hand would be clumsy, wouldn't work right without him. Garth was different. But everybody else was different, too. Mike, the ice man, supercool. Cecil indifferent, ready to do most anything or nothing and couldn't care less which it was. Sowell wasn't really part of the gang; he didn't hang with them, didn't like to take the risks that were part of the "life." Sowell kept a good job. The "life" for him was just a way to make quick money. He didn't shoot up; he thought of himself as a businessman, an investor not a partner in their schemes. They knew Sowell mostly through Garth. Perhaps things would change now. The four survivors closer after they shared the burden of Gar's coffin, after they hoisted it and slid it on steel rollers into the back of Gaines's Cadillac hearse.

Robby was grateful for the gloves. He'd never been able to touch anything dead. He'd taken a beating once from his father rather than touch the bloody mousetrap his mother had nudged to the back door with her toe and ordered him to empty. The brass handle of the coffin felt damp through the glove. He gripped tighter to stop the flow of blood or sweat, whatever it was leaking from him or seeping from the metal. Garth had melted down to nothing by the end so it couldn't be him nearly yanking off Robby's shoulder when the box shifted and its weight shot forward. Felt like a coffin full of bricks. Robby stared across at Mike but Mike was a soldier, eyes front, riveted to the yawning rear door of the hearse. Mike's eyes wouldn't admit it, but they'd almost lost the coffin. They were rookie pallbearers and maneuvering down the carpeted front steps of Gaines Funeral Parlor they'd almost let Garth fly out their hands. They needed somebody who knew what he was doing. An old, steady head to show them the way. They needed Garth. But Garth was long gone. Ashes inside the steel box.

They began drinking later that afternoon in Garth's people's house. Women and food in one room, men hitting the whiskey hard in another. It was a typical project apartment. The kind everybody had stayed in or visited one time or another. Small, shabby, featureless. Not a place to live. No matter what you did to it, how clean you kept it or what kind of furniture you loaded it with, the walls and ceilings were not meant to be home for anybody. A place you passed through. Not yours, because the people who'd been there before you left their indelible marks everywhere and you couldn't help adding your bruises and knots for the next tenants. You could rent a kitchen and bedroom and a bathroom and a living room, the project flats were laid out so you had a room for each of the things people did in houses. Problem was, every corner was cut. Living cramped is one thing and people can get cozy in the closest quarters. It's another thing to live in a place designed to be just a little less than adequate. No slack, no space to personalize, to stamp the flat with what's peculiar to your style. Like a man sitting on a toilet seat that's too small and the toilet too close to the bathtub so his knees shove against the enamel edge. He can move his bowels that way and plenty of people in the world have a lot less but he'll never enjoy sitting there, never feel the deep down comfort of belonging where he must squat.

Anyway, the whiskey started flowing in that little project apartment. Robby listened, for Garth's sake, as long as he could to old people reminiscing about funerals they'd attended, about all the friends and relatives they'd escorted to the edge of Jordan, old folks sipping good whiskey and moaning and groaning till it seemed a sin to be left behind on this side of the river after so many saints had crossed over. He listened to people express their grief, tell sad, familiar stories. As he got high he listened less closely to the words. Faces and gestures revealed more than enough. When he split with Mike and Cecil and their ladies, Sowell tagged along. By then the tacky, low-ceilinged rooms of the flat were packed. Loud talk, laughter, storytellers competing for audiences. Robby half expected the door he pushed shut behind himself to pop open again, waited for bottled-up noise to explode into the funky hallway.

Nobody thinking about cemeteries now. Nobody else needs to be buried today, so it was time to get it on. Some people had been getting close to rowdy. Some people had been getting mad. Mad at one of the guests in the apartment, mad at doctors and hospitals and whites in general who had the whole world in their hands but didn't have the slightest idea what to do with it. A short, dark man, bubble-eyed, immaculately dressed in a three-piece, wool, herringbone suit, had railed about the callousness, the ignorance of white witch doctors who, by misdiagnosing Garth's illness, had sealed his doom. His harangue had drawn a crowd. He wasn't just talking, he was testifying, and a hush had fallen over half the room as he dissected the dirty tricks of white folks. If somebody ran to the hospital and snatched a white-coated doctor and threw him into the circle surrounding the little fish-eyed man, the mourners would tear the pale-faced devil apart. Robby wished he could feed them one. Remembered Garth weak and helpless in the bed and the doctors and nurses flitting around in the halls, jiving the other patients, ignoring Gar like he wasn't there. Garth was dead because he had believed them. Dead because he had nowhere else to turn when the pain in his gut and the headaches grew worse and worse. Not that he trusted the doctors or believed they gave a flying fuck about him. He'd just run out of choices and had to put himself in their hands. They told him jaundice was his problem, and while his liver rotted away and pain cooked him dizzy Garth assured anyone who asked that it was just a matter of giving the medicine time to work. To kill the pain he blew weed as long as he had strength to hold a joint between his lips. Take a whole bunch of smoke to cool me out these days. Puffing like a chimney till he lost it and fell back and Robby scrambling to grab the joint before Garth torched hisself.

When you thought about it, Garth's dying made no sense. And the more you thought the more you dug that nothing else did neither. The world's a stone bitch. Nothing true if that's not true. The man had you coming and going. He owned everything worth owning and all you'd ever get was what he didn't want anymore, what he'd chewed and spit out and left in the gutter for niggers to fight over. Garth had pointed to the street and said, If we ever make it, it got to come from there, from the curb. We got to melt that rock till we get us some money. He grinned then, Ain't no big thing. We'll make it, brother man. We got what it takes. It's our time.

Something had crawled in Garth's belly. The man said it wasn't nothing. Sold him some aspirins and said he'd be alright in no time. The man killed Garth. Couldn't kill him no deader with a .357 magnum slug, but ain't no crime been committed. Just one those things. You know, everybody makes mistakes. And a dead nigger ain't really such a big mistake when you think about it. Matter of fact you mize well forget the whole thing. Nigger wasn't going nowhere, nohow. I mean he wasn't no brain surgeon or astronaut, no movie star or big-time athlete. Probably a dope fiend or gangster. Wind up killing some innocent person or wasting another nigger. Shucks. That doctor ought to get a medal.

Hey, man. Robby caught Mike's eye. Then Cecil and Sowell turned to him. They knew he was speaking to everybody. Late now. Ten, eleven, because it had been dark outside for hours. Quiet now. Too quiet in his pad. And too much smoke and drink since the funeral. From a bare bulb in the kitchen ceiling light seeped down the hallway and hovered dimly in the doorway of the room where they sat. Robby wondered if the others felt as bad as he did. If the cemetery clothes itched their skin. If they could smell grave dust on their shoes. He hoped they'd finish this last jug of wine and let the day be over. He needed sleep, downtime to get the terrible weight of Garth's death off his mind. He'd been grateful for the darkness. For the company of his cut buddies after the funeral. For the Sun Ra tape until it ended and plunged them into a deeper silence than any he'd ever known. Garth was gone. In a few days people would stop talking about him. He was in the ground. Stone-cold dead. Robby had held a chunk of crumbly ground in his white-gloved fingers and mashed it and dropped the dust into the hole. Now the ground had closed over Garth and what did it mean? Here one day and gone the next and that was that. They'd bury somebody else out of Gaines tomorrow. People would dress up and cry and get drunk and tell lies and next day it'd be somebody else's turn to die. Which one of the shadows in this black room would go first? What did it matter? Who cared? Who would remember their names; they were ghosts already. Dead as Garth already. Only difference was, Garth didn't have it to worry about no more. Garth didn't have to pretend he was going anywhere cause he was there. He'd made it to the place they all were headed fast as their legs could carry them. Every step was a step closer to the stone-cold ground, the pitch-black hole where they'd dropped Garth's body.

Hey, youall. We got to drink to Garth one last time.

They clinked glasses in the darkness. Robby searched for something to say. The right words wouldn't come. He knew there was something proper and precise that needed to be said. Because the exact words eluded him, because only the right words would do, he swallowed his gulp of heavy, sweet wine in silence.

He knew he'd let Garth down. If it had been one of the others dead, Michael or Cecil or Sowell or him, Garth wouldn't let it slide by like this, wouldn't let it end like so many other nights had ended, the fellows nodding off one by one, stupefied by smoke and drink, each one beginning to shop around in his mind, trying to figure whether or not he should turn in or if there was a lady somewhere who'd welcome him in her bed. No. Garth would have figured a way to make it special. They wouldn't be hiding in the bushes. They'd be knights in shining armor around a big table. They'd raise their giant, silver cups to honor the fallen comrade. Like in the olden days. Clean, brave dudes with gold rings and gold chains. They'd draw their blades. Razor-edged swords that gleam in the light with jewels sparkling in the handles. They'd make a roof over the table when they stood and raised their swords and the points touched in the sky. A silver dagger on a satin pillow in the middle of the table. Everybody roll up their sleeves and prick a vein and go round, each one touching everybody else so the blood runs together and we're brothers forever, brothers as long as blood flows in anybody's arm. We'd ride off and do unbelievable shit. The dead one always with us cause we'd do it all for him. Swear we'd never let him down.

It's our time now. We can't let Garth down. Let's drink this last one for him and promise him we'll do what he said we could. We'll be the best. We'll make it to the top for him. We'll do it for Garth.

Glasses rattled together again. Robby empties his and thinks about smashing it against a wall. He'd seen it done that way in movies but it was late at night and these crazy niggers might not know when to stop throwing things. A battlefield of broken glass for him to creep through when he gets out of bed in the morning. He doesn't toss the empty glass. Can't see a solid place anyway where it would strike clean and shatter to a million points of light.

My brother had said something about a guy named Garth during one of my visits to the prison. Just a name mentioned in passing. *Garth* or *Gar*. I'd asked Robby to spell it for me. Garth had been a friend of Robby's, about Robby's age, who died one summer of a mysterious disease. Later when Robby chose to begin the story of the robbery and killing by saying, "It all started with Gar dying," I remembered that first casual mention and remembered a conversation with my mother. My mom and I were in the kitchen of the house on Tokay Street. My recollection of details was vague at first but something about the conversation had made a lasting impression because, six years later, hearing Robby say the name *Garth* brought back my mother's words.

My mother worried about Robby all the time. Whenever I visited home, sooner or later I'd find myself alone with Mom and she'd pour out her fears about Robby's *wildness*, the deep trouble he was bound for, the web of entanglements and intrigues and bad company he was weaving around himself with a maddening disregard for the inevitable consequences.

I don't know. I just don't know how to reach him. He won't listen. He's doing wrong and he knows it but nothing I say makes any difference. He's not like the rest of youall. You'd misbehave but I could talk to you or smack you if I had to and you'd straighten up. With Robby it's like talking to a wall.

I'd listen and get angry at my brother because I registered not so much the danger he was bringing on himself, but the effect of his escapades on the woman who'd brought us both into the world. After all, Robby was no baby. If he wanted to mess up, nobody could stop him. Also Robby was my brother, meaning that his wildness was just a stage, a chaotic phase of his life that would only last till he got his head together and decided to start doing right. Doing as the rest of us did. He was my brother. He couldn't fall too far. His brushes with the law (I'd had some, too), the time he'd spent in jail, were serious but temporary setbacks. I viewed his troubles, when I thought about them at all, as a form of protracted juvenile delinquency, and fully expected Robby would learn his lesson sooner or later and return to the fold, the prodigal son, chastened, perhaps a better person for the experience. In the meantime the most serious consequence of his wildness was Mom's devastating unhappiness. She couldn't sustain the detachment, the laissez-faire optimism I had talked myself into. Because I was two thousand miles away, in Wyoming, I didn't have to deal with the day-to-day evidence of Robby's trouble. The syringe Mom found under his bed. The twenty-dollar bill missing from her purse. The times he'd cruise in higher than a kite, his pupils reduced to pinpricks, with his crew and they'd raid the refrigerator and make a loud, sloppy feast, all of them feeling so good they couldn't imagine anybody not up there on cloud nine with them enjoying the time of their lives. Cruising in, then disappearing just as abruptly, leaving their dishes and pans and mess behind. Robby covering Mom with kisses and smiles and drowning her in babytalk hootchey-coo as he staggers through the front door. Her alone in the ravaged, silent kitchen, listening as doors slam and a car squeals off on the cobblestones of Tokay, wondering where they're headed next, wishing, praying Robby will return and eat and eat and eat till he falls asleep at the table so she can carry him upstairs and tuck him in and kiss his forehead and shut the door gently on his sleep.

I wasn't around for all that. Didn't want to know how bad things were for him. Worrying about my mother was tough enough. I could identify with her grief, I could blame my brother. An awful situation, but simple too. My role, my responsibilities and loyalties were clear. The *wildness* was to blame, and it was a passing thing, so I just had to help my mother survive the worst of it, then everything would be alright. I'd steel myself for the moments alone with her when she'd tell me the worst. In the kitchen, usually, over a cup of coffee with the radio playing. When my mother was alone in the house on Tokay, either the TV or a radio or both were always on. Atop the kitchen table a small clock radio turned to WAMO, one of Pittsburgh's soul stations, would background with scratchy gospel music whatever we said in the morning in the kitchen. On a morning like that in 1975, while I drank a cup of coffee and part of me, still half-asleep, hidden, swayed to the soft beat of gospel, my mother had explained how upset Robby was over the death of his friend, Garth.

It was a terrible thing. I've known Garth's mother for years. He was a good boy. No saint for sure, but deep down a good boy. Like your brother. Not a mean bone in his body. Out there in the street doing wrong, but that's where most of them are. What else can they do, John? Sometimes I can't blame them. No jobs, no money in their pockets. How they supposed to feel like men? Garth did better than most. Whatever else he was into, he kept that little job over at Westinghouse and helped out his mother. A big, playful kid. Always smiling. I think that's why him and Robby were so tight. Neither one had good sense. Giggled and acted like fools. Garth no wider than my finger. Straight up and down. A stringbean if I ever saw one. When Robby lived here in the house with me, Garth was always around. I know how bad Robby feels. He hasn't said a word but I know. When Robby's quiet, you know something's wrong. Soon as his eyes pop open in the morning he's looking for the party. First thing in the morning he's chipper and chattering. Looking for the party. That's your brother. He had a match in Garth.

Shame the way they did that boy. He'd been down to the clinic two or three times but they sent him home. Said he had an infection and it would take care of itself. Something like that anyway. You know how they are down there. Have to be spitting blood to get attention. Then all they give you is a Band-Aid. He went back two times, but they kept telling him the same dumb thing. Anybody who knew Garth could see something awful was wrong. Circles under his eyes. Sallow look to his skin. Losing weight. And the poor thing didn't have any weight to lose. Last time I saw him I was shocked. Just about shocked out my shoes. Wasn't Garth standing in front of me. Not the boy I knew.

Well, to make a long story short, they finally took him in the hospital but it was too late. They let him walk the streets till he was dead. It was wrong. Worse than wrong how they did him, but that's how those dogs do us every day God sends here. Garth's gone, so nothing nobody can say will do any good. I feel so sorry for his mother. She lived for that boy. I called her and tried to talk but what can you say? I prayed for her and prayed for

Garth and prayed for Robby. A thing like that tears people up. It's worse if you keep it inside. And that's your brother's way. He'll let it eat him up and then go out and do something crazy.

Until she told me Garth's story I guess I hadn't realized how much my mother had begun to change. She had always seemed to me to exemplify the tolerance, the patience, the long view epitomized in her father. John French's favorite saying was, Give 'em the benefit of the doubt. She could get as ruffled, as evil as the rest of us, cry and scream or tear around the house fit to be tied. She had her grudges and quarrels. Mom could let it all hang out, yet most of the time she radiated a deep calm. She reacted strongly to things but at the same time held judgment in abeyance. Events, personalities always deserved a second, slower appraisal, an evaluation outside the sphere of everyday hassles and vexations. You gave people the benefit of the doubt. You attempted to remove your ego, acknowledge the limitations of your individual view of things. You consulted as far as you were equipped by temperament and intelligence a broader, more abiding set of relationships and connections.

You tried on the other person's point of view. You sought the other, better person in yourself who might talk you into relinquishing for a moment your selfish interest in whatever was at issue. You stopped and considered the long view, possibilities other than the one that momentarily was leading you by the nose. You gave yourself and other people the benefit of the doubt.

My mother had that capacity. I'd admired, envied, and benefited infinitely from its presence. As she related the story of Garth's death and my brother's anger and remorse, her tone was uncompromisingly bitter. No slack, no margin of doubt was being granted to the forces that destroyed Garth and still pursued her son. She had exhausted her reserves of understanding and compassion. The long view supplied the same ugly picture as the short. She had an enemy now. It was that revealed truth that had given the conversation its edge, its impact. *They* had killed Garth, and his dying had killed part of her son; so the battle lines were drawn. Irreconcilably. Absolutely. The backside of John French's motto had come into play. Giving someone the benefit of the doubt was also giving him enough rope to hang himself. If a person takes advantage of the benefit of the doubt and keeps on taking and taking, one day the rope plays out. The piper must be paid. If you've been the one giving, it becomes incumbent on you to grip your end tight and take away. You turn the other cheek, but slowly, cautiously, and keep your fist balled up at your side. If your antagonist decides to smack rather than kiss you or leave you alone, you make sure you get in the first blow. And make sure it's hard enough to knock him down.

Before she told Garth's story, my mother had already changed, but it took years for me to realize how profoundly she hated what had been done to Garth and then Robby. The gentleness of my grandfather, like his fair skin and good French hair, had been passed down to my mother. Gentleness styled the way she thought, spoke, and moved in the world. Her easy disposition and sociability masked the intensity of her feelings. Her attitude to authority of any kind, doctors, clerks, police, bill collectors, newscasters, whites in general partook of her constitutional gentleness. She wasn't docile or cowed. The power other people possessed or believed they possessed didn't frighten her; she accommodated herself, offered something they could accept as deference but that was in fact the same resigned, alert attention she paid to roaches or weather or poverty, any of the givens outside herself that she couldn't do much about. She never engaged in public tests of will, never pushed herself or her point of view on people she didn't know. Social awkwardness embarrassed her. Like most Americans she didn't like paying taxes, was suspicious of politicians, resented the disparity between big and little people in our society and the double standard that allowed big shots to get away with murder. She paid particular attention to news stories that reinforced her basic political assumption that power corrupts. On the other hand she knew the world was a vale of tears and one's strength, granted by God to deal with life's inevitable calamities, should not be squandered on small stuff.

In spite of all her temperamental and philosophic resistance to extremes, my mother would be radicalized. What the demonstrations, protest marches, and slogans of the sixties had not effected would be accomplished by Garth's death and my brother's troubles. She would become an aggressive, acid critic of the status quo in all its forms: from the President ("If it wasn't for that rat I'd have a storm door to go with the storm windows but he cut the program") on down to bank tellers ("I go there every Friday and I'm one of the few black faces she sees all day and she knows me as well as she knows that wart on her cheek but she'll still make me show my license before she'll cash my check"). A son she loved would be pursued, captured, tried, and imprisoned by the forces of law and order. Throughout the ordeal her love for him wouldn't change, couldn't change. His crime tested her love and also tested the nature, the intent of the forces arrayed against her son. She had to make a choice. On one side were the stark facts of his crime: robbery, murder, flight; her son an outlaw, a fugitive; then a prisoner. On the other side the guardians of society, the laws, courts, police, judges, and keepers who were responsible for punishing her son's transgression.

She didn't invent the two sides and initially didn't believe there couldn't be a middle ground. She extended the benefit of the doubt. Tried to situate herself somewhere in between, acknowledging the evil of her son's crime while simultaneously holding on to the fact that he existed as a human being before, after, and during the crime he'd committed. He'd done wrong but he was still Robby and she'd always be his mother. Strangely, on the dark side, the side of the crime and its terrible consequences, she would find room to exercise her love. As negative as the elements were, a life taken, the grief of the survivors, suffering, waste, guilt, remorse, the scale was human; she could apply her sense of right and wrong. Her life to that point had equipped her with values, with tools for sorting out and coping with disaster. So she would choose to make her fight there, on treacherous yet familiar ground—familiar since her son was there—and she could place herself, a woman, a mother, a grieving, bereaved human being, there beside him.

Nothing like that was possible on the other side. The legitimacy of the other side was grounded not in her experience of life, but in a set of rules seemingly framed to sidestep, ignore, or replace her sense of reality. Accepting the version of reality encoded in *their* rules would be like stepping into a cage and locking herself in. Definitions of her son, herself, of need and frailty and mercy, of blackness and redemption and justice had all been neatly formulated. No need here for her questions, her uncertainty, her fear, her love. Everything was clean and clear. No room for her sense that things like good and evil, right and wrong bleed into each other and create a dreadful margin of ambiguity no one could name but could only enter, enter at the risk of everything because everything is at stake and no one on earth knows what it means to enter or what will happen if and when the testing of the margin is over.

She could love her son, accept his guilt, accept the necessity of punishment, suffer with him, grow with him past the stage of blaming everyone but himself for his troubles, grieve with him when true penitence began to exact its toll. Though she might wish penance and absolution could be achieved in private, without the intervention of a prison sentence, she understood dues must be paid. He was her son but he was also a man who had committed a robbery in the course of which another woman's son had been killed. What would appall her and what finally turned her against the forces of law and order was the incapacity of the legal system to grant her son's humanity. "Fair" was the word she used—a John French word. She expected them to treat Robby fair. Fairness was what made her willing to give him up to punishment even though her love screamed no and her hands clung to his shoulders. Fairness was what she expected from the other side in their dealings with her and her son.

She could see their side, but they steadfastly refused to see hers. And when she realized fairness was not forthcoming, she began to hate. In the lack of reciprocity, in the failure to grant that Robby was first a man, then a man who had done wrong, the institutions and individuals who took over control of his life denied not only his humanity but the very existence of the world that had nurtured him and nurtured her—the world of touching, laughing, suffering black people that established Robby's claim to something more than a number.

Mom expects the worst now. She's peeped their hole card. She understands they have a master plan that leaves little to accident, that most of the ugliest things happening to black people are not accidental but the predictable results of the working of the plan. What she learned about authority, about law and order didn't make sense at first. It went against her instincts, what she wanted to believe, against the generosity she'd observed in her father's interactions with other Homewood people. He was fair. He'd pick up the egg rolls he loved from the back kitchen door of Mr. Wong's restaurant and not blame Wong, his old talking buddy and card-playing crony, for not serving black people in his restaurant. Wong had a family and depended on white folks to feed them, so Wong didn't have any choice and neither did John French if he wanted those incredible egg rolls. He treated everyone, high and low, the same. He said what he meant and meant what he said. John French expected no more from other people than he expected from himself. And he'd been known to mess up many a time, but that was him, that was John French, no better, no worse than any man who pulls on his britches one leg at a time. He needed a little slack, needed the benefit of that blind eye people who love, or people who want to get along with other people, must learn to cast. John French was grateful for the slack, so was quick to extend it to others. Till they crossed him.

My mother had been raised in Homewood. The old Homewood. Her relations with people in that close-knit, homogeneous community were based on trust, mutual respect, common spiritual and material concerns. Face-to-face contact, shared language and values, a large fund of communal experience rendered individual lives extremely visible in Homewood. Both a person's self-identity ("You know who you are") and accountability ("Other people know who you are") were firmly established.

If one of the Homewood people said, "That's the French girl" or, "There goes John French's daughter," a portrait with subtle shading and complex resonance was painted by the words. If the listener addressed was also a Homewood resident, the speaker's voice located the young woman passing innocently down Tioga Street in a world invisible to outsiders. A French girl was somebody who lived in Cassina Way, somebody you didn't fool with or talk nasty to. Didn't speak to at all except in certain places or on certain occasions. French girls were church girls, Homewood African Methodist Episcopal Zion Sunday-school-picnic and social-event young ladies. You wouldn't find them hanging around anywhere without escorts or chaperones. French girls had that fair, light, bright, almost white redbone complexion and fine blown hair and nice big legs but all that was to be appreciated from a distance because they were nice girls and because they had this crazy daddy who wore a big brown country hat and gambled and drank wine and once ran a man out of town, ran him away without ever laying a hand on him or making a bad-mouthed threat, just cut his eyes a certain way when he said the man's name and the word went out and the man who had cheated a drunk John French with loaded dice was gone. Just like that. And there was the time Elias Brown was cleaning his shotgun in his backyard. Brown had his double-barreled shotgun across his knees and a jug of Dago Red on the ground beside him and it was a Saturday and hot and Brown was sweating through his BVD undershirt and paying more attention to the wine than he was to the gun. Next thing you know, *Boom!* Off it goes and buckshot sprayed down Cassina Way, and it's Saturday and summer like I said, so chillens playing everywhere but God watches over fools and babies so nobody hit bad. Nobody hit at all except the little French girl, Geraldine, playing out there in the alley and she got nicked in her knee. Barely drew blood. A sliver of that buckshot musta ricocheted off the cobblestones and cut her knee. Thank Jesus she the only one hit and she ain't hit bad. Poor Elias Brown don't quite know what done happened till some the mens run over in his yard and snatch the gun and shake the wine out his head. What you doing, fool? Don't you know no better all those children running round here? Coulda killed one these babies. Elias stone drunk and don't hear nothing, see nothing till one the men say French girl. Nicked the little French girl, Geraldine. Then Elias woke up real quick. His knees, his dusty butt, everything he got starts to trembling and his eyes get big as dinner plates. Then he's gone like a turkey through the corn. Nobody seen Elias for a week. He's in Ohio at his sister's next time anybody hear anything about Elias. He's cross there in Ohio and still shaking till he git word John French ain't after him. It took three men gon over there telling the same story to get Elias back to Homewood. John French ain't mad. He *was* mad but he ain't mad now. Little girl just nicked is all and French ain't studying you, Brown.

You heard things like that in Homewood names. Rules of etiquette, thumbnail character sketches, a history of the community. A dire warning to get back could be coded into the saying of a person's name, and a further inflection of the speaker's voice could tell you to ignore the facts, forget what he's just reminded you to remember and go on. Try your luck.

Because Homewood was self-contained and possessed such a strong personality, because its people depended less on outsiders than they did on each other for so many of their most basic satisfactions, they didn't notice the net settling over their community until it was already firmly in place. Even though the strands of the net—racial discrimination, economic exploitation, white hate and fear—had existed time out of mind, what people didn't notice or chose not to notice was that the net was being drawn tighter, that ruthless people outside the community had the power to choke the life out of Homewood, and as soon as it served their interests would do just that. During the final stages, as the net closed like a fist around Homewood, my mother couldn't pretend it wasn't there. But instead of setting her free, the truth trapped her in a cage as tangible as the iron bars of Robby's cell.

Some signs were subtle, gradual. The A & P started to die. Nobody mopped filth from the floors. Nobody bothered to restock empty shelves. Fewer and fewer white faces among the shoppers. A plate-glass display window gets broken and stays broken. When they finally close the store, they paste the going-out-of-business notice over the jagged, taped crack. Other signs as blatant, as sudden as fire engines and patrol cars breaking your sleep, screaming through the dark Homewood streets. First Garth's death, then Robby's troubles brought it all home. My mother realized her personal unhappiness and grief were inseparable from what was happening *out there*. Out there had never been further away than the thousand insults and humiliations she had disciplined herself to ignore. What she had deemed petty, not worth bothering about, were strings of the net just as necessary, as effective as the most dramatic intrusions into her life. She decided to stop letting things go by. No more benefit of the doubt. Doubt had been cruelly excised. She decided to train herself to be as wary, as unforgiving as she'd once been ready to live and let live. My mother wouldn't become paranoid, not even overtly prickly or bristling. That would have been too contrary to her style, to what her blood and upbringing had instilled. The change was inside. What she thought of people. How she judged situations. Things she'd say or do startled me, set me back on my heels because I didn't recognize my mother in them. I couldn't account for the stare of pure unadulterated hatred she directed at the prison guard when he turned away from her to answer the phone before handing her the rest-room key she'd requested, the vehemence with which she had cussed Richard Nixon for paying no taxes when she, scraping by on an income of less than four thousand dollars a year, owed the IRS three hundred dollars.

Garth's death and Robby's troubles were at the center of her new vision. Like a prism, they caught the light, transformed it so she could trace the seemingly random inconveniences and impositions coloring her life to their source in a master plan.

I first heard Garth's story in the summer of 1975, the summer my wife carried our daughter Jamila in her belly, the summer before the robbery and killing. The story contained all the clues I'm trying to decipher now. Sitting in the kitchen vaguely distracted by gospel music from the little clock radio atop the table, listening as my mother expressed her sorrow, her indignation at the way Garth was treated, her fears for my brother, I was hearing a new voice. Something about the voice struck me then, but I missed what was novel and crucial. I'd lost my Homewood ear. Missed all the things unsaid that invested her words with special urgency. People in Homewood often ask: You said that to say what? The impacted quality of an utterance either buries a point too obscurely or insists on a point so strongly that the listener wants the meat of the message repeated, wants it restated clearly so it stands alone on its own two feet. If I'd been alert enough to ask that question, to dig down to the root and core of Garth's story after my mother told it, I might have understood sooner how desperate and dangerous Homewood had become. Six years later my brother was in prison, and when he began the story of his troubles with Garth's death, a circle completed itself; Robby was talking to me, but I was still on the outside, looking in.

That day six years later, I talked with Robby three hours, the maximum allotted for weekday visits with a prisoner. It was the first time in life we'd ever talked that long. Probably two and a half hours longer than the longest, unbroken, private conversation we'd ever had. And it had taken guards, locks, and bars to bring us together. The ironies of the situation, the irony of that fact, escaped neither of us.

I listened mostly, interrupting my brother's story a few times to clarify dates or names. Much of what he related was familiar. The people, the places. Even the voice, the words he chose were mine in a way. We're so alike, I kept thinking, anticipating what he would say next, how he would say it, filling in naturally, easily with my words what he left unsaid. Trouble was our minds weren't interchangeable. No more than our bodies. The guards wouldn't have allowed me to stay in my brother's place. He was the criminal. I was the visitor from outside. Different as night and day. As Robby talked I let myself forget that difference. Paid too much attention to myself listening and lost some of what he was saying. What I missed would have helped define the difference. But I missed it. It was easy to half listen. For both of us to pretend to be closer than we were. We needed the closeness. We were brothers. In the prison visiting lounge I acted toward my brother the way I'd been acting toward him all my life, heard what I wanted to hear, rejected the rest.

When Robby talked, the similarity of his Homewood and mine was a trap. I could believe I knew exactly what he was describing. I could relax into his story, walk down Dunfermline or Tioga, see my crippled grandmother sitting on the porch of the house on Finance, all the color her pale face had lost blooming in the rosebush beneath her in the yard, see Robby in the downstairs hall of the house on Marchand, rapping with his girl on the phone, which sat on a three-legged stand just inside the front door. I'd slip unaware out of his story into one of my own. I'd be following him, an obedient shadow, then a cloud would blot the sun and I'd be gone, unchained, a dark form still skulking behind him but no longer in tow.

The hardest habit to break, since it was the habit of a lifetime, would be listening to myself listen to him. That habit would destroy any chance of seeing my brother on his terms; and seeing him in his terms, learning his terms, seemed the whole point of learning his story. However numerous and comforting the similarities, we were different. The world had seized on the difference, allowed me room to thrive, while he'd been forced into a cage. Why did it work out that way? What was the nature of the difference? Why did it haunt me? Temporarily at least, to answer these questions, I had to root my fiction-writing self out of our exchanges. I had to teach myself to listen. Start fresh, clear the pipes, resist too facile an identification, tame the urge to take off with Robby's story and make it my own.

I understood all that, but could I break the habit? And even if I did learn to listen, wouldn't there be a point at which I'd have to take over the telling? Wasn't there something fundamental in my writing, in my capacity to function, that depended on flight, on escape? Wasn't another person's skin a hiding place, a place to work out anxiety, to face threats too intimidating to handle in any other fashion? Wasn't writing about people a way of exploiting them?

A stranger's gait, or eyes, or a piece of clothing can rivet my attention. Then it's like falling down to the center of the earth. Not exactly fear or panic but an uneasy, uncontrollable momentum, a sense of being swallowed, engulfed in blackness that has no dimensions, no fixed points. That boundless, incarcerating black hole is another person. The detail grabbing me functions as a door and it swings open and I'm drawn, sucked, pulled in head over heels till suddenly I'm righted again, on track again and the peculiarity, the ordinariness of the detail that usurped my attention becomes a window, a way of seeing out of another person's eyes, just as for a second it had been my way in. I'm scooting along on short, stubby legs and the legs are not anybody else's and certainly not mine, but I feel for a second what it's like to motor through the world atop these peculiar duck thighs and foreshortened calves and I know how wobbly the earth feels under those run-over-at-the-heel, split-seamed penny loafers. Then just as suddenly I'm back. I'm me again, slightly embarrassed, guilty because I've been trespassing and don't know how long I've been gone or if anybody noticed me violating somebody else's turf.

Do I write to escape, to make a fiction of my life? If I can't be trusted with the story of my own life, how could I ask my brother to trust me with his?

The business of making a book together was new for both of us. Difficult. Awkward. Another book could be constructed about a writer who goes to a prison to interview his brother but comes away with his own story. The conversations with his brother would provide a stage for dramatizing the writer's tortured relationship to other people, himself, his craft. The writer's motives, the issue of exploitation, the inevitable conflict between his role as detached observer and his responsibility as a brother would be at the center of such a book. When I stopped hearing Robby and listened to myself listening, that kind of book shouldered its way into my consciousness. I didn't like the feeling. That book compromised the intimacy I wanted to achieve with my brother. It was as obtrusive as the Wearever pen in my hand, the little yellow sheets of Yard Count paper begged from the pad of the guard in charge of overseeing the visiting lounge. The borrowed pen and paper (I was not permitted into the lounge with my own) were necessary props. I couldn't rely on memory to get my brother's story down and the keepers had refused my request to use a tape recorder, so there I was. Jimmy Olson, cub reporter, poised on the edge of my seat, pen and paper at ready, asking to be treated as a brother.

We were both rookies. Neither of us had learned very much about sharing our feelings with other family members. At home it had been assumed that each family member possessed deep, powerful feelings and that very little or nothing at all needed to be said about these feelings because we all were stuck with them and talk wouldn't change them. Your particular feelings were a private matter and family was a protective fence around everybody's privacy. Inside the perimeter of the fence each family member resided in his or her own quarters. What transpired in each dwelling was mainly the business of its inhabitant as long as nothing generated within an individual unit threatened the peace or safety of the whole. None of us knew how traditional West African families were organized or what values the circular shape of their villages embodied, but the living arrangements we had worked out among ourselves resembled the ancient African patterns. You were granted emotional privacy, independence, and space to commune with your feelings. You were encouraged to deal with as much as you could on your own, yet you never felt alone. The high wall of the family, the collective, communal reality of other souls, other huts like yours eliminated some of the dread, the isolation experienced when you turned inside and tried to make sense out of the chaos of your individual feelings. No matter how grown you thought you were or how far you believed you'd strayed, you knew you could cry *Mama* in the depths of the night and somebody would tend to you. Arms would wrap round you, a soft soothing voice lend its support. If not a flesh-and-blood mother then a mother in the form of song or story or a surrogate, Aunt Geral, Aunt Martha, drawn from the network of family numbers.

Privacy was a bridge between you and the rest of the family. But you had to learn to control the traffic. You had to keep it uncluttered, resist the temptation to cry wolf. Privacy in our family was a birthright, a union card granted with family membership. The card said you're one of us but also certified your separateness, your obligation to keep much of what defined your separateness to yourself.

An almost aesthetic consideration's involved. Okay, let's live together. Let's each build a hut and for security we'll arrange the individual dwellings in a circle and then build an outer ring to enclose the whole village. Now your hut is your own business, but let's in general agree on certain outward forms. Since we all benefit from the larger pattern, let's compromise, conform to some degree on the materials, the shape of each unit. Because symmetry and harmony please the eye. Let's adopt a style, one that won't crimp anybody's individuality, one that will buttress and enhance each member's image of what a living place should be.

So Robby and I faced each other in the prison visiting lounge as familiar strangers, linked by blood and time. But how do you begin talking about blood, about time? He's been inside his privacy and I've been inside mine, and neither of us in thirty-odd years had felt the need to exchange more than social calls. We shared the common history, values, and style developed within the tall stockade of family, and that was enough to make us care about each other, enough to insure a profound depth of mutual regard, but the feelings were undifferentiated. They'd seldom been tested specifically, concretely. His privacy and mine had been exclusive, sanctioned by family traditions. Don't get too close. Don't ask too many questions or give too many answers. Don't pry. Don't let what's inside slop out on the people around you.

The stories I'd sent to Robby were an attempt to reveal what I thought about certain matters crucial to us both. Our shared roots and destinies. I wanted him to know what I'd been thinking and how that thinking was drawing me closer to him. I was banging on the door of his privacy. I believed I'd shed some of my own.

We were ready to talk. It was easy to begin. Impossible. We were neo-phytes, rookies. I was a double rookie. A beginner at this kind of intimacy, a beginner at trying to record it. My double awkwardness kept getting in the way. I'd hidden the borrowed pen by dropping my hand below the level of the table where we sat. Now when in hell would be the right moment to raise it? To use it? I had to depend on my brother's instincts, his generosity. I had to listen, listen.

Luckily there was catching up to do. He asked me about my kids, about his son, Omar, about the new nieces and nephews he'd never seen. That helped. Reminded us we were brothers. We got on with it. Conditions in the prisons. Robby's state of mind. The atmosphere behind the prison walls had been particularly tense for over a year. A group of new, younger guards had instituted a get-tough policy. More strip searches, cell shakedowns, strict enforcement of penny-ante rules and regulations. Grown men treated like children by other grown men. Inmates yanked out of line and punished because a button is undone or hair uncombed. What politicians demanded in the free world was being acted out inside the prison. A crusade, a war on crime waged by a gang of gung-ho guards against men who were already certified casualties, prisoners of war. The walking wounded being beaten and shot up again because they're easy targets. Robby's closest friends, including Cecil and Mike, are in the hole. Others who were considered potential troublemakers had been transferred to harsher prisons. Robby was warned by a guard. We ain't caught you in the shit yet, but we will. We know what you're thinking and we'll catch you in it. Or put you in it. Got your buddies and we'll get you.

The previous summer, 1980, a prisoner, Leon Patterson, had been asphyxiated in his cell. He was an asthma sufferer, a convicted murderer who depended on medication to survive the most severe attacks of his illness. On a hot August afternoon when the pollution index had reached its highest count of the summer, Patterson was locked in his cell in a cell block without windows and little air. At four o'clock, two hours after he'd been confined to the range, he began to call for help. Other prisoners raised the traditional distress signal, rattling tin cups against the bars of their cells. Patterson's cries for help became screams, and his fellow inmates beat on the bars and shouted with him. Over an hour passed before any guards arrived. They carted away Patterson's limp body. He never revived and was pronounced dead at 10:45 that evening. His death epitomized the polarization in the prison. Patterson was seen as one more victim of the guards' inhumanity. A series of incidents followed in the ensuing year, hunger strikes, melees between guards and prisoners, culminating in a near massacre when the dog days of August hung once more over the prison.

One of the favorite tactics of the militant guards was grabbing a man from the line as the prisoners moved single-file through an archway dividing the recreation yard from the main cell blocks. No reason was given or needed. It was a simple show of force, a reminder of the guards' absolute power, their right to treat the inmates any way they chose, and do it with impunity. A sit-down strike in the prison auditorium followed one of the more violent attacks on an inmate. The prisoner who had resisted an arbitrary seizure and strip search was smacked in the face. He punched back and the guards jumped him, knocked him to the ground with their fists and sticks. The incident took place in plain view of over a hundred prisoners and it was the last straw. The victim had been provoked, assaulted, and surely would be punished for attempting to protect himself, for doing what any man would and should do in similar circumstances. The prisoner would suffer again. In addition to the physical beating they'd administered, the guards would attack the man's record. He'd be written up. A kangaroo court would take away his *good time*, thereby lengthening the period he'd have to wait before becoming eligible for probation or parole. Finally, on the basis of the guards' testimony he'd probably get a sixty-day sojourn in the hole. The prisoners realized it was time to take a stand. What had happened to one could happen to any of them. They rushed into the auditorium and locked themselves in. The prisoners held out till armed state troopers and prison guards in riot gear surrounded the building. Given the mood of that past year and the unmistakable threat in the new warden's voice as he repeated through a loudspeaker his refusal to meet with the prisoners and discuss their grievances, everybody inside the building knew that the authorities meant business, that the forces of law and order would love nothing better than an excuse to turn the auditorium into a shooting gallery. The strike was broken. The men filed out. A point was driven home again. Prisoners have no rights the keepers are bound to respect.

That was how the summer had gone. Summer was bad enough in the penitentiary in the best of times. Warm weather stirred the prisoners' blood. The siren call of the streets intensified. Circus time. The street blooming again after the long, cold winter. People outdoors. On their stoops. On the corners. In bright summer clothes or hardly any clothes at all. The free-world sounds and sights more real as the weather heats up. Confinement a torture. Each cell a hotbox. The keepers take advantage of every excuse to keep you out of the yard, to deprive you of the simple pleasure of a breeze, the blue sky. Why? So that the pleasant weather can be used as a tool, a boon to be withheld. So punishment has a sharper edge. By a perverse turn of the screw something good becomes something bad. Summer a bitch at best, but this past summer as the young turks among the guards ran roughshod over the prisoners, the prison had come close to blowing, to exploding like a piece of rotten fruit in the sun. And if the lid blew, my brother knew he'd be one of the first to die. During any large-scale uprising, in the first violent, chaotic seconds no board of inquiry would ever be able to reconstruct, scores would be settled. A bullet in the back of the brain would get rid of troublemakers, remove potential leaders, uncontrollable prisoners the guards hated and feared. You were supremely eligible for a bullet if the guards couldn't press your button. If they hadn't learned how to manipulate you, if you couldn't be bought or sold, if you weren't into drug and sex games, if you weren't cowed or depraved, then you were a threat.

Robby understood that he was sentenced to die. That all sentences were death sentences. If he didn't buckle under, the guards would do everything in their power to kill him. If he succumbed to the pressure to surrender dignity, self-respect, control over his own mind and body, then he'd become a beast, and what was good in him would die. The death sentence was unambiguous. The question for him became: How long could he survive in spite of the death sentence? Nothing he did would guarantee his safety. A disturbance in a cell block halfway across the prison could provide an excuse for shooting him and dumping him with the other victims. Anytime he was ordered to go with guards out of sight of other prisoners, his escorts could claim he attacked them, or attempted to escape. Since the flimsiest pretext would make murdering him acceptable, he had no means of protecting himself. Yet to maintain sanity, to minimize their opportunities to destroy him, he had to be constantly vigilant. He had to discipline himself to avoid confrontations, he had to weigh in terms of life and death every decision he made; he had to listen and obey his keepers' orders, but he also had to determine in certain threatening situations whether it was better to say no and keep himself out of a trap or take his chances that this particular summons was not the one inviting him to his doom. Of course to say no perpetuated his reputation as one who couldn't be controlled, a bad guy, a guy you never turn your back on, one of the prisoners out to get the guards. That rap made you more dangerous in the keepers' eyes and therefore increased the likelihood they'd be frightened into striking first. Saying no put you in no less jeopardy than going along with the program. Because the program was contrived to kill you. Directly or indirectly, you knew where you were headed. What you didn't know was the schedule. Tomorrow. Next week. A month. A minute. When would one of them get itchy, get beyond waiting a second longer? Would there be a plan, a contrived incident, a conspiracy they'd talk about and set up as they drank coffee in the guards' room or would it be the hair-trigger impulse of one of them who held a grudge, harbored an antipathy so elemental, so irrational that it could express itself only in a burst of pure, unrestrained violence?

If you're Robby and have the will to survive, these are the possibilities you must constantly entertain. Vigilance is the price of survival. Beneath the vigilance, however, is a gnawing awareness boiling in the pit of your stomach. You can be as vigilant as you're able, you can keep fighting the good fight to survive, and still your fate is out of your hands. If they decide to come for you in the morning, that's it. Your ass is grass and those minutes, and hours, days and years you painfully stitched together to put off the final reckoning won't matter at all. So the choice, difficult beyond words, to say yes or say no is made in light of the knowledge that in the end neither your yes nor your no matters. Your life is not in your hands.

The events, the atmosphere of the summer had brought home to Robby the futility of resistance. Power was absurdly apportioned all on one side.

To pretend you could control your own destiny was a joke. You learned to laugh at your puniness, as you laughed at the stink of your farts lighting up your cell. Like you laughed at the seriousness of the masturbation ritual that romanticized, cloaked in darkness and secrecy, the simple, hungry shaking of your penis in your fist. You had no choice, but you always had to decide to go on or stop. It had been a stuttering, stop, start, maybe, fuck it, bitch of a summer, and now, for better or worse, we were starting up something else. Robby backtracks his story from Garth to another beginning, the house on Copeland Street in Shadyside where we lived when he was born.

I know that had something to do with it. Living in Shadyside with only white people around. You remember how it was. Except for us and them couple other families it was a all-white neighborhood. I got a thing about black. See, black was like the forbidden fruit. Even when we went to Freed's in Homewood, Geraldine and them never let me go no farther than the end of the block. All them times I stayed over there I didn't go past Mr. Conrad's house by the vacant lot or the other corner where Billy Shields and them stayed. Started to wondering what was so different about a black neighborhood. I was just a little kid and I was curious. I really wanted to know why they didn't want me finding out what was over there. Be playing with the kids next door to Freed, you know, Sonny and Gumpy and them, but all the time I'm wondering what's round the corner, what's up the street. Didn't care if it was *bad* or good or dangerous or what, I had to find out. If it's something bad I figured they would have told me, tried to scare me off. But nobody said nothing except, No. Don't you go no farther than the corner. Then back home in Shadyside nothing but white people so I couldn't ask nobody what was special about black. Black was a mystery and in my mind I decided I'd find out what it was all about. Didn't care if it killed me, I was going to find out.

One time, it was later, I was close to starting high school, I overheard Mommy and Geraldine and Sissy talking in Freed's kitchen. They was talking about us moving from Shadyside back to Homewood. The biggest thing they was worried about was me. How would it be for me being in Homewood and going to Westinghouse? I could tell they was scared. Specially Mom. You know how she is. She didn't want to move. Homewood scared her. Not so much the place but how I'd act if I got out there in the middle of it. She already knew I was wild, hard to handle. There'd be too much mess for me to get into in Homewood. She could see trouble coming.

And she was right. Me and trouble hooked up. See, it was a question of being somebody. Being my own person. Like youns had sports and good grades sewed up. Wasn't nothing I could do in school or sports that youns hadn't done already. People said, Here comes another Wideman. He's gon be a good student like his brothers and sister. That's the way it was spozed to be. I was another Wideman, the last one, the baby, and everybody knew how I was spozed to act. But something inside me said no. Didn't want to be like the rest of youns. Me, I had to be a rebel. Had to get out from under youns' good grades and do. Way back then I decided I wanted to be a star. I wanted to make it big. My way. I wanted the glamour. I wanted to sit high up.

Figured out school and sports wasn't the way. I got to thinking my brothers and sister was squares. Loved youall but wasn't no room left for me. Had to figure out a new territory. I had to be a rebel.

Along about junior high I discovered Garfield. I started hanging out up on Garfield Hill. You know, partying and stuff in Garfield cause that's where the niggers was. Garfield was black, and I finally found what I'd been looking for. That place they was trying to hide from me. It was heaven. You know. Hanging out with the fellows. Drinking wine and trying anything else we could get our hands on. And the ladies. Always a party on the weekends. Had me plenty sweet little soft-leg Garfield ladies. Niggers run my butt off that hill more than a couple times behind messing with somebody's piece but I'd be back next weekend. Cause I'd found heaven. Looking back now, wasn't much to Garfield. Just a rinky-dink ghetto up on a hill, but it was the street. I'd found my place.

Having a little bit of a taste behind me I couldn't wait to get to Homewood. In a way I got mad with Mommy and the rest of them. Seemed to me like they was trying to hold me back from a good time. Seemed like they just didn't want me to have no fun. That's when I decided I'd go on about my own business. Do it my way. Cause I wasn't getting no slack at home. They still expected me to be like my sister and brothers. They didn't know I thought youns was squares. Yeah. I knew I was hipper and groovier than youns ever thought of being. Streetwise, into something. Had my own territory and I was bad. I was a rebel. Wasn't following in nobody's footsteps but my own. And I was a hip cookie, you better believe it. Wasn't a hipper thing out there than your brother, Rob. I couldn't wait for them to turn me loose in Homewood.

Me being the youngest and all, the baby in the family, people always said, ain't he cute. That Robby gon be a ladykiller. Been hearing that mess since day one so ain't no surprise I started to believing it. Youns had me pegged as a lady's man so that's what I was. The girls be talking the same trash everybody else did. Ain't he cute. Be petting me and spoiling me like I'm still the baby of the family and I sure ain't gon tell them stop. Thought I was cute as the girls be telling me. Thought sure enough, I'm gon be a star. I loved to get up and show my behind. Must have been good at it too cause the teacher used to call me up in front of the class to perform. The kids'd get real quiet. That's probably why the teacher got me up. Keep the class quiet while she nods off. Cause they'd listen to me. Sure nuff pay attention.

Performing always come natural to me. Wasn't nervous or nothing. Just get up and do my thing. They liked for me to do impressions. I could mimic anybody. You remember how I'd do that silly stuff around the house. Anybody I'd see on TV or hear on a record I could mimic to a T. Bob Hope, Nixon, Smokey Robinson, Ed Sullivan. White or black. I could talk just like them or sing a song just like they did. The class yell out a famous name and I'd do the one they wanted to hear. If things had gone another way I've always believed I could have made it big in show business. If you could keep them little frisky kids in Liberty School quiet you could handle any audience. Always could sing and do impressions. You remember Mom asking me to do them for you when you came home from college.

I still be performing. Read poetry in the hole. The other fellows get real quiet and listen. Sing down in there too. Nothing else to do, so we entertain each other. They always asking me to sing or read. "Hey, Wideman. C'mon man and do something." Then it gets quiet while they waiting for me to start. Quiet and it's already dark. You in your own cell and can't see nobody else. Barely enough light to read by. The other fellows can hear you but it's just you and them walls so it feels like being alone much as it feels like you're singing or reading to somebody else.

Yeah. I read my own poems sometimes. Other times I just start in on whatever book I happen to be reading. One the books you sent me, maybe. Fellows like my poems. They say I write about the things they be thinking. Say it's like listening to their own self thinking. That's cause we all down there together. What else you gonna do but think of the people on the outside. Your woman. Your kids or folks, if you got any. Just the same old sad shit we all be thinking all the time. That's what I write and the fellows like to hear it.

Funny how things go around like that. Go round and round and keep coming back to the same place. Teacher used to get me up to pacify the class and I'm doing the same thing in prison. You said your teachers called on you to tell stories, didn't they? Yeah. It's funny how much we're alike. In spite of everything I always believed that. Inside. The feeling side. I always believed we was the most alike out of all the kids. I see stuff in your books. The kinds of things I be thinking or feeling.

Your teachers got you up, too. To tell stories. That's funny, ain't it.

I listen to my brother Robby. He unravels my voice. I sit with him in the darkness of the Behavioral Adjustment Unit. My imagination creates something like a giant seashell, enfolding, enclosing us. Its inner surface is velvet-soft and black. A curving mirror doubling the darkness. Poems are Jean Toomer's petals of dusk, petals of dawn. I want to stop. Savor the sweet, solitary pleasure, the time stolen from time in the hole. But the image I'm creating is a trick of the glass. The mirror that would swallow Robby and then chime to me: You're the fairest of them all. The voice I hear issues from a crack in the glass. I'm two or three steps ahead of my brother, making fiction out of his words. Somebody needs to snatch me by the neck and say, Stop. Stop and listen, listen to him.

The Behavioral Adjustment Unit is, as one guard put it, "a maximum-security prison within a maximum-security prison." The "Restricted Housing Unit" or "hole" or "Home Block" is a squat, two-story cement building containing thirty-five six-by-eight-foot cells. The governor of Pennsylvania closed the area in 1972 because of "inhumane conditions," but within a year the hole was reopened. For at least twenty-three hours a day the prisoners are confined to their cells. An hour of outdoor exercise is permitted only on days the guards choose to supervise it. Two meals are served three hours apart, then nothing except coffee and bread for the next twenty-one. The regulation that limits the time an inmate can serve in the BAU for a single offense is routinely sidestepped by the keepers. "Administrative custody" is a provision allowing officials to cage men in the BAU indefinitely. Hunger strikes are one means the prisoners have employed to protest the harsh conditions of the penal unit. Hearings prompted by the strikes have produced no major changes in the way the hole operates. Law, due process, the rights of the prisoners are irrelevant to the functioning of this prison within a prison. Robby was sentenced to six months in the BAU because a guard suspected he was involved in an attempted escape. The fact that a hearing, held six months later, established Robby's innocence, was small consolation since he'd already served his time in the hole.

Robby tells me about the other side of being the youngest: Okay, you're everybody's pet and that's boss, but on the other hand you sometimes feel you're the least important. Always last. Always bringing up the rear. You learn to do stuff on your own because the older kids are always busy, off doing their things, and you're too young, left behind because you don't fit, or just because they forget you're back here, at the end, bringing up the rear. But when orders are given out, you sure get your share. "John's coming home this weekend. Clean up your room." Robby remembers being forced to get a haircut on the occasion of one of my visits. Honor thy brother. Get your hair cut, your room rid up, and put on clean clothes. He'll be here with his family and I don't want the house looking like a pigpen.

I have to laugh at the image of myself as somebody to get a haircut for. Robby must have been fit to be tied.

Yeah, I was hot. I mean, you was doing well and all that, but shit, you were my brother. And it was my head. What's my head got to do with you? But you know how Mommy is. Ain't no talking to her when her mind gets set. Anything I tried to say was "talking *back*," so I just went ahead to the man and got my ears lowered.

I was trying to be a rebel but back then the most important thing still was what the grown-ups thought about me. How they felt meant everything. Everything. Me and Tish and Dave were the ones at home then. You was gone and Gene was gone so it was the three of us fighting for attention. And we fought. Every crumb, everytime something got cut up or parceled out or it was Christmas or Easter, we so busy checking out what the other one got wasn't hardly no time to enjoy our own. Like a dogfight or cat fight all the time. And being the youngest I'm steady losing ground most the time. Seemed like to me, Tish and Dave the ones everybody talked about. Seemed like my time would never come. That ain't the way it really was, I know. I had my share cause I was the baby and ain't he cute and lots of times I know I got away with outrageous stuff or got my way cause I could play that baby mess to the hilt. Still it seemed like Dave and Tish was the ones really mattered. Mommy and Daddy and Sis and Geral and Big Otie and Ernie always slipping some change in their pockets or taking them to the store or letting them stay over all night in Homewood. I was a jealous little rascal. Sometimes I thought everybody thought I was just a spoiled brat. I'd say damn all youall. I'd think, Go on and love those square turkeys, but one day I'll be the one coming back with a suitcase full of money and a Cadillac. Go on and love them good grades. Robby gon do it his own way.

See, in my mind I was Superfly. I'd drive up slow to the curb. My hog be half a block long and these fine foxes in the back. Everybody looking when I ease out the door clean and mean. Got a check in my pocket to give to Mom. Buy her a new house with everything in it new. Pay her back for the hard times. I could see that happening as real as I can see your face right now. Wasn't no way it wasn't gon happen. Rob was gon make it big. I'd be at the door, smiling with the check in my hand and Mommy'd be so happy she'd be crying.

Well, it's a different story ain't it. Turned out different from how I used to think it would. The worst thing I did, the thing I feel most guilty behind is stealing Mom's life. It's like I stole her youth. Can't nothing change that. I can't give back what's gone. Robbing white people didn't cause me to lose no sleep back then. Couldn't feel but so bad about that. How you gon feel sorry when society's so corrupt, when everybody got their hand out or got their hand in somebody else's pocket and ain't no rules nobody listens to if they can get away with breaking them? How you gon apply the rules? It was dog eat dog out there, so how was I spozed to feel sorry if I was doing what everybody else doing. I just got caught is all. I'm sorry about that, and damned sorry that guy Stavros got killed, but as far as what I did, as far as robbing white people, ain't no way I was gon torture myself over that one.

I tried to write Mom a letter. Not too long ago. Should say I did write the letter and put it in a envelope and sent it cause that's what I did, but I be crying so much trying to write it I don't know what wound up in that letter. I wanted Mom to know I knew what I'd done. In a way I wanted to say I was sorry for spoiling her life. After all she did for me I turned around and made her life miserable. That's the wrongest thing I've done and I wanted to say I was sorry but I kept seeing her face while I was writing the letter. I'd see her face and it would get older while I was looking. She'd get this old woman's face all lined and wrinkled and tired about the eyes. Wasn't nothing I could do but watch. Cause I'd done it and knew I done it and all the letters in the world ain't gon change her face. I sit and think about stuff like that all the time. It's better now. I think about other things too. You know like trying to figure what's really right and wrong, but there be days the guilt don't never go away.

I'm the one made her tired, John. And that's my greatest sorrow. All the love that's in me she created. Then I went and let her down.

When you in prison you got plenty of time to think, that's for damned sure. Too much time. I've gone over and over my life. Every moment. Every little thing again and again. I lay down on my bed and watch it happening over and over. Like a movie. I get it all broke down in pieces then I break up the pieces then I take the pieces of the pieces and run them through my hands so I remember every word a person said to me or what I said to them and weigh the words till I think I know what each and every one meant. Then I try to put it back together. Try to understand where I been. Why I did what I did. You got time for that in here. Time's all you got in here.

Going over and over things sometimes you can make sense. You know. Like the chinky-chinky Chinaman sittin' on the fence. You put it together and you think, yes. That's why I did thus and so. Yeah. That's why I lost that job or lost that woman or broke that one's heart. You stop thinking in terms of something being good or being evil, you just try to say this happened because that happened because something else came first. You can spend days trying to figure out just one little thing you did. People out there in the world walk around in a daze cause they ain't got time to think. When I was out there, I wasn't no different. Had this Superfly thing and that was the whole bit. Nobody could tell me nothing.

Seems like I should start the story back in Shadyside. In the house on Copeland Street. Nothing but white kids around. Them little white kids had everything, too. That's what I thought, anyway. Nice houses, nice clothes. They could buy pop and comic books and candy when they wanted to. We wasn't that bad off, but compared to what them little white kids had I always felt like I didn't have nothing. It made me kinda quiet and shy around them. Me knowing all the time I wanted what they had. Wanted it bad. There was them white kids with everything and there was the black world Mommy and them was holding back from me. No place to turn, in a way. I guess you could say I was stuck in the middle. Couldn't have what the white kids in Shadyside had, and I wasn't allowed to look around the corner for something else. So I'd start the story with Shadyside, the house on Copeland.

Another place to start could be December 29, 1950—the date of Robby's birth. For some reason—maybe my mother and father were feuding, maybe we just happened to be visiting my grandmother's house when my mother's time came—the trip to the hospital to have Robby began from Finance Street, from the house beside the railroad tracks in Homewood. What I remember is the bustle, people rushing around, yelling up and down the stairwell, doors slammed, drawers being opened and shut. A cold winter day so lots of coats and scarves and galoshes. My mother's face was very pale above the dark cloth coat that made her look even bigger than she was, carrying Robby the ninth month. On the way out the front door she stopped and stared back over her shoulder like she'd forgotten something. People just about shoving her out the house. Lots of bustle and

noise getting her through the crowded hallway into the vestibule. Somebody opened the front door and December rattled the glass panes. Wind
gusting and whistling, everybody calling out last-minute instructions,
arrangements, goodbyes, blessings, prayers. My mother's white face calm,
hovering a moment above it all as she turned back toward the hall, the
stairs where I was planted, halfway to the top. She didn't find me, wasn't
looking for me. A thought had crossed her mind and carried her far away.
She didn't know why so many hands were rushing her out the door. She
didn't hear the swirl of words, the icy blast of wind. Wrapped in a navy-
blue coat, either Aunt Aida's or an old one of my grandmother's, which
didn't have all its black buttons but stretched double over her big belly, my
mother was wondering whether or not she'd turned off the water in the
bathroom sink and deciding whether or not she should return up the stairs
to check. Something like that crossing her mind, freeing her an instant before she got down to the business of pushing my brother into the world.

Both my grandfathers died on December 28. My grandmother died just
after dawn on December 29. My sister lost a baby early in January. The end
of the year has become associated with mournings, funerals; New Year's
Day arrives burdened by a sense of loss, bereavement. Robby's birthday
became tainted. To be born close to Christmas is bad enough in and of itself. Your birthday celebration gets upstaged by the orgy of gift giving on
Christmas Day. No matter how many presents you receive on December
29, they seem a trickle after the Christmas flood. Plus there's too much excitement in too brief a period. Parents and relatives are exhausted, broke,
still hung over from the Christmas rush, so there just isn't very much left to
work with if your birthday comes four short days after Jesus'. Almost like
not having a birthday. Or even worse, like sharing it with your brothers
and sister instead of having the private oasis of your very own special day.
So Robby cried a lot on his birthdays. And it certainly wasn't a happy time
for my mother. Her father, John French, died the year after Robby was
born, one day before Robby's birthday. Fifteen years and a day later Mom
would lose her mother. The death of the baby my sister was carrying was a
final, cruel blow, scaring my mother, jinxing the end of the year eternally.
She dreaded the holiday season, expected it to bring dire tidings. She had
attempted at one point to consecrate the sad days, employ them as a period
of reflection, quietly, privately memorialize the passing of the two people
who'd loved her most in the world. But the death of my father's father,
then the miscarriage within this jinxed span of days burst the fragile truce
my mother had effected with the year's end. She withdraws into herself,
anticipates the worst as soon as Christmas decorations begin appearing. In
1975, the year of the robbery and murder, Robby was on the run when his
birthday fell. My mother was sure he wouldn't survive the deadly close of
the year.

Robby's birthday is smack dab in the middle of the hard time. Planted
like a flag to let you know the bad time's arrived. His adult life, the man-

hood of my mother's last child, begins as she is orphaned, as she starts to become nobody's child.

I named Robby. Before the women hustled my mother out the door into a taxi, I jumped down the stairs, tugged on her coattail, and reminded her she'd promised it'd be Robby. No doubt in my mind she'd bring me home a baby brother. Don't ask me why I was certain. I just was. I hadn't even considered names for a girl. Robby it would be. Robert Douglas. Where the Douglas came from is another story, but the Robert came from me because I liked the sound. Robert was formal, dignified, important. Robert. And that was nearly as nice as the chance I'd have to call my little brother Rob and Robby.

He weighed seven pounds, fourteen ounces. He was born in Allegheny Hospital at 6:30 in the evening, December 29, 1950. His fingers and toes were intact and quite long. He was a plump baby. My grandfather, high on Dago Red, tramped into the maternity ward just minutes after Robby was delivered. John French was delighted with the new baby. Called him Red. A big fat little red nigger.

December always been a bad month for me. One the worst days of my life was in December. It's still one the worst days in my life even after all this other mess. Jail. Running. The whole bit. Been waiting to tell you this a long time. Ain't no reason to hold it back no longer. We into this telling-the-truth thing so mize well tell it all. I'm still shamed, but there it is. You know that TV of youall's got stolen from Mommy's. Well, I did it. Was me and Henry took youall's TV that time and set the house up to look like a robbery. We did it. Took my own brother's TV. Couldn't hardly look you in the face for a long time after we done it. Was pretty sure youall never knowed it was me, but I felt real bad round youns anyway. No way I was gon confess though. Too shamed. A junkie stealing from his own family. See. Used to bullshit myself. Say I ain't like them other guys. They stone junkies, they hooked. Do anything for a hit. But me, I'm Robby. I'm cool. I be believing that shit, too. Fooling myself. You got to bullshit yourself when you falling. Got to do it to live wit yourself. See but where it's at is you be doing any goddam thing for dope. You hooked and that's all's to it. You a stone junkie just like the rest.

Always wondered if you knew I took it.

Mom was suspicious. She knew more than we did then. About the dope. The seriousness of it. Money disappearing from her purse when no-body in the house but the two of you. Finding a syringe on the third floor. Stuff like that she hadn't talked about to us yet. So your stealing the TV was a possibility that came up. But to me it was just one of many. One of the things that could have happened along with a whole lot of other possibilities we sat around talking about. An unlikely possibility as far as I was concerned. Nobody wanted to believe it was you. Mom tried to tell us how it *could* be but in my mind you weren't the one. Haven't thought about it much since then. Except as one of those things that make me worry about Mom living in the house alone. One of those things making Homewood dangerous, tearing it down.

I'm glad I'm finally getting to tell you. I never could get it out. Didn't want you to think I'd steal from my own brother. Specially since all youall done to help me out. You and Judy and the kids. Stealing youall's TV. Don't make no sense, does it? But if we gon get the story down mize well get it all down.

It was a while ago. Do you remember the year?

Nineteen seventy-one was Greens. When we robbed Greens and got in big trouble so it had to be the year before that, 1970. That's when it had to be. Youns was home for Christmas. Mommy and them was having a big party. A reunion kinda cause all the family was together. Everybody home for the first time in a long time. Tish in from Detroit. David back from Philly. Youns in town. My birthday, too. Party spozed to celebrate my birthday too, since it came right along in there after Christmas. Maybe that's why I was feeling so bad. Knowing I had a birthday coming and knowing at the same time how fucked up I was.

Sat in a chair all day. I was hooked for the first time. Good and hooked. Didn't know how low you could feel till that day. Cold and snowing outside. And I got the stone miseries inside. Couldn't move. Weak and sick. Henry too. He was wit me in the house feeling bad as I was. We was two desperate dudes. Didn't have no money and that Jones down on us.

Mommy kept asking, What's wrong with you two? She was on my case all day. What ails you, Robby? Got to be about three o'clock. She come in the room again: You better get up and get some decent clothes on. We're leaving for Geral's soon. See cause it was the day of the big Christmas party. Geral had baked a cake for me. Everybody was together and they'd be singing Happy Birthday Robby and do. The whole bit an I'm spozed to be guest of honor and can't even move out the chair. Here I go again disappointing everybody. Everybody be at Geral's looking for me and Geral had a cake and everything. Where's Robby? He's home dying cause he can't get no dope.

Feeling real sorry for myself but I'm hating me too. Wrapped up in a blanket like some damned Indin. Shivering and wondering how the hell Ima go out in this cold and hustle up some money. Wind be howling. Snow pitching a bitch. There we is. Stuck in the house. Two pitiful junkies. Scheming how we gon get over. Some sorry-assed dudes. But it's comical in a way too, when you look back. To get well we need to get money. And no way we gon get money less we go outside and get sicker than we already is. Mom peeking in the room, getting on my case. Get up out that chair, boy. What are you waiting for? We're leaving in two minutes.

So I says, Go on. I ain't ready. Youns go on. I'll catch up with youns at Geral's.

Mommy standing in the doorway. She can't say too much, cause youns is home and you ain't hip to what's happening. C'mon now. We can't wait any longer for you. Please get up. Geral baked a cake for you. Everybody's looking forward to seeing you.

Seem like she stands there a hour begging me to come. She ain't mad no more. She's begging. Just about ready to cry. Youall in the other room. You can hear what she's saying but you can't see her eyes and they tearing me up. Her eyes begging me to get out the chair and it's tearing me up to see her hurting so bad, but ain't nothing I can do. Jones sitting on my chest and ain't no getup in me.

Youns go head, Mommy. I'll be over in a little while. Be there to blow them candles out and cut the cake.

She knew better. Knew if I didn't come right then, chances was I wasn't coming at all. She knew but wasn't nothing she could do. Guess I knew I was lying too. Nothing in my mind cept copping that dope. Yeah, Mom. Be there to light them candles. I'm grinning but she ain't smiling back. She knows I'm in trouble, deep trouble. I can see her today standing in the doorway begging me to come with youns.

But it ain't meant to be. Me and Henry thought we come up with a idea. Henry's old man had some pistols. We was gon steal em and hock em. Take the money and score. Then we be better. Wouldn't be no big thing to hustle some money, get the guns outa hock. Sneak the pistols back in Henry's house, everything be alright. Wouldn't even exactly be stealing from his old man. Like we just borrowing the pistols till we score and take care business. Henry's old man wouldn't even know his pistols missing. Slick. Sick as we was, thinking we slick.

A hundred times. Mom musta poked her head in the room a hundred times.

What's wrong with you?

Like a drum beating in my head. What's wrong with you? But the other thing is stronger. The dope talking to me louder. It says get you some. It says you ain't never gon get better less you cop.

We waited long as we could but it didn't turn no better outside. Still snowing. Wind shaking the whole house. How we gon walk to Henry's and steal them pistols? Henry live way up on the hill. And the way up Tokay then you still got a long way to go over into the projects. Can't make it. No way we gon climb Tokay. So then what? Everybody's left for Geral's. Then I remembers the TV youns brought. A little portable Sony black-and-white, right? You and Judy sleeping in Mom's room and she has her TV already in there, so the Sony ain't unpacked. Saw it sitting with youall's suitcases over by the dresser. On top the dresser in a box. Remembered it and soon's I did I knew we had to have it. Sick as I was that TV had to go. Wouldn't really be stealing. Borrow it instead of borrowing the pistols. Pawn it. Get straight. Steal some money and buy it back. Just borrowing youall's TV.

Won't take me and Henry no time to rob something and buy back the TV. We stone thieves. Just had to get well first so we could operate. So we took youns TV and set the house up to look like a robbery.

I'm remembering the day. Wondering why it had slipped completely from my mind. I feel like a stranger. Yet as Robby talks, my memory confirms details of his recollection. I admit, yes. I was there. That's the way it was. But *where* was I? Who was I? How did I miss so much?

His confessions make me uncomfortable. Instead of concentrating on what he's revealing, I'm pushed into considering all the things I could be confessing, should be confessing but haven't and probably won't ever. I feel hypocritical. Why should I allow my brother to repose a confidence in me when it's beyond my power to reciprocate? Shouldn't I confess that first? My embarrassment, my uneasiness, the clinical, analytic coldness settling over me when I catch on to what's about to happen.

I have a lot to hide. Places inside myself where truth hurts, where incriminating secrets are hidden, places I avoid, or deny most of the time. Pulling one piece of that debris to the surface, airing it in the light of day doesn't accomplish much, doesn't clarify the rest of what's buried down there. What I feel when I delve deeply into myself is chaos. Chaos and contradiction. So how up front can I get? I'm moved by Robby's secrets. The heart I have is breaking. But what that heart is and where it is I can't say. I can't depend on it, so he shouldn't. Part of me goes out to him. Heartbreak is the sound of ice cracking. Deep. Layers and layers muffling the sound.

I listen but I can't trust myself. I have no desire to tell everything about myself so I resist his attempt to be up front with me. The chaos at my core must be in his. His confession pushes me to think of all the stuff I should lay on him. And that scares the shit out of me. I don't like to feel dirty, but that's how I feel when people try to come clean with me.

Very complicated and very simple too. The fact is I don't believe in clean. What I know best is myself and, knowing what I know about myself, clean seems impossible. A dream. One of those better selves occasionally in the driver's seat but nothing more. Nothing to be depended upon. A self no more or less in control than the countless other selves who each, for a time, seem to be running things.

Chaos is what he's addressing. What his candor, his frankness, his confession echo against. Chaos and time and circumstances and the old news, the bad news that we still walk in circles, each of us trapped in his own little world. Behind bars. Locked in our cells.

But my heart can break, does break listening to my brother's pain. I just remember differently. Different parts of the incident he's describing come back. Strange thing is my recollections return through the door he opened. My memories needed his. Maybe the fact that we recall different things is crucial. Maybe they are foreground and background, propping each other up. He holds on to this or that scrap of the past and I listen to what he's saved and it's not mine, not what I saw or heard or felt. The pressure's on me then. If his version of the past is real, then what's mine? Where does it fit? As he stitches his memories together they bridge a vast emptiness. The time lost enveloping us all. Everything. And hearing him talk, listening to him try to make something of the nothing, challenges me. My sense of the emptiness playing around his words, any words, is intensified. Words are nothing and everything. If I don't speak I have no past. Except the nothing, the emptiness. My brother's memories are not mine, so I have to break into the silence with my own version of the past. My words. My whistling in the dark. His story freeing me, because it forces me to tell my own.

I'm sorry you took so long to forgive yourself. I forgave you a long time ago, in advance for a sin I didn't even know you'd committed. You lied to me. You stole from me. I'm in prison now listening because we committed those sins against each other countless times. I want your forgiveness. Talking about debts you owe me makes me awkward, uneasy. We remember different things. They set us apart. They bring us together searching for what is lost, for the meaning of difference, of distance.

For instance, the Sony TV. It was a present from Mort, Judy's dad. When we told him about the break-in and robbery at Mom's house, he bought us another Sony. Later we discovered the stolen TV was covered by our homeowner's policy even though we'd lost it in Pittsburgh. A claim was filed and eventually we collected around a hundred bucks. Not enough to buy a new Sony but a good portion of the purchase price. Seemed a lark when the check arrived. Pennies from heaven. One hundred dollars free and clear since we already had the new TV Mort had surprised us with. About a year later one of us, Judy or I, was telling the story of the robbery and how well we came out of it. Not until that very moment when I caught a glimpse of Mort's face out of the corner of my eye did I realize what we'd done. Judy remembers urging me to send Mort that insurance check and she probably did, but I have no recollection of an argument. In my mind there had never been an issue. Why shouldn't we keep the money? But when I saw the look of surprise and hurt flash across Mort's face, I knew the insurance check should have gone directly to him. He's a generous man and probably would have refused to accept it, but we'd taken advantage of his generosity by not offering the check as soon as we received it. Clearly the money belonged to him. Unasked, he'd replaced the lost TV. I had treated him like an institution, one of those faceless corporate entities like the gas company or IRS. By then, by the time I saw the surprise in Mort's face and understood how selfishly, thoughtlessly, even corruptly I'd behaved, it was too late. Offering Mort a hundred dollars at that point would have been insulting. Anything I could think of saying sounded hopelessly lame, inept. I'd fucked up. I'd injured someone who'd been nothing but kind and generous to me. Not intentionally, consciously, but that only made the whole business worse in a way because I'd failed him instinctively. The failure was a measure of who I was. What I'd unthinkingly done revealed something about my relationship to Mort I'm sure he'd rather not have discovered. No way I could take my action back, make it up. It reflected a truth about who I was.

That memory pops right up. Compromising, ugly. Ironically, it's also about stealing from a relative. Not to buy dope, but to feed a habit just as self-destructive. The habit of taking good fortune for granted, the habit of blind self-absorption that allows us to believe the world owes us everything and we are not responsible for giving anything in return. Spoiled children. The good coming our way taken as our due. No strings attached.

Lots of other recollections were triggered as Robby spoke of that winter and the lost TV. The shock of walking into a burgled house. How it makes you feel unclean. How quickly you lose the sense of privacy and security a house, any place you call home, is supposed to provide. It's a form of rape. Forced entry, violation, brutal hands defiling what's personal, and precious. The aftershock of seeing your possessions strewn about, broken. Fear gnawing at you because what you thought was safe isn't safe at all. The worst has happened and can happen again. Your sanctuary has been destroyed. Any time you walk in your door you may be greeted by the same scene. Or worse. You may stumble upon the thieves themselves. The symbolic rape of your dwelling place enacted on your actual body. Real screams. Real blood. A knife at your throat. A stranger's weight bearing down.

Mom put it in different words but she was as shaken as I was when we walked into her house after Geral's party. Given what I know now, she must have been even more profoundly disturbed than I imagined. A double bind. Bad enough to be ripped off by anonymous thieves. How much worse if the thief is your son? For Mom the robbery was proof Robby was gone. Somebody else walking round in his skin. Mom was wounded in ways I hadn't begun to guess at. At the root of her pain were your troubles, the troubles stealing you away from her, from all of us. The troubles thick in the air as that snow you are remembering, the troubles falling on your head and mine, troubles I refused to see. . . .

Snowing and the hawk kicking my ass but I got to have it. TV's in a box under my arm and me and Henry walking down Bennett to Homewood Avenue. Need thirty dollars. Thirty dollars buy us two spoons. Looking for One-Arm Ralph, the fence. Looking for him or that big white Cadillac he drives.

Wind blowing snow all up in my face. Thought I's bout to die out there. Nobody on the avenue. Even the junkies and dealers inside today. Wouldn't put no dog out in weather like that. So cold my teeth is chattering, talking to me. No feeling in my hands but I got to hold on to that TV. Henry took it for a little while so's I could put both my hands in my pockets. Henry lookin bad as I'm feeling. Thought I was gon puke. But it's too goddamn cold to puke.

Nobody in sight. Shit and double shit's what I'm thinking. They got to be somewhere. Twenty-four hours a day, seven days a week somebody doing business. Finally we seen One-Arm Ralph come out the Hi Hat.

This TV, man, Lemme hold thirty dollars on it.

Ralph ain't goin for it. Twenty-five the best he say he can do. Twenty-five don't do us no good. It's fifteen each for a spoon. One spoon ain't enough. We begging the dude now. We got to have it, man. Got to get well. We good for the money. Need thirty dollars for two hits. You get your money back.

Too cold to be standing around arguing. The dude go in his pocket and give us the thirty. He been knowing us. He know we good for it. I'm telling him don't sell the TV right away. Hold it till tomorrow we have his money. He say, You don't come back tonight you blow it. Ralph a hard motherfucker and don't want him changing his mind again about the thirty so I say, We'll have the money tonight. Hold the TV till tonight, you get your money.

Now all we got to do is find Goose. Goose always be hanging on the set. Ain't nobody else dealing, Goose be out there for his people. Goose an alright dude, but even Goose ain't out in the street on no day like this. I know the cat stays over the barbershop on Homewood Avenue. Across from Murphy's five-and-ten. I goes round to the side entrance, the alleyway tween Homewood and Kelly. That's how you get to his place. Goose lets me in and I cop. For some reason I turn up the alley and go toward Kelly instead of back to Homewood the way I came in. Don't know why I did it. Being slick. Being scared. Henry's waiting on the avenue for me so I go round the long way just in case somebody pinned him. I can check out the scene before I come back up the avenue. That's probably what I'm thinking. But soon's I turn the corner of Kelly, Bam. Up pops the devil.

Up against the wall, Squirrel.

It's Simon and Garfunkel, two jive undercover cops. We call them that, you dig. Lemme tell you what kind of undercover cops these niggers was. Both of em wearing Big Apple hats and jackets like people be wearing then but they both got on police shoes. Police brogans you could spot a mile away. But they think they slick. They disguised, see. Apple hats and hippy-dip jackets. Everybody knew them chumps was cops. Ride around in a big Continental. Going for bad. Everybody hated them cause everybody knew they in the dope business. They bust a junkie, take his shit and sell it. One them had a cousin. Biggest dealer on the Hill. You know where he getting half his dope. Be selling again what Simon and Garfunkel stole from junkies. Some rotten dudes. Liked to beat on people too. Wasn't bad enough they robbing people. They whipped heads too.

Soon's I turn the corner they got me. Bams me up against the wall. They so lame they think they got Squirrel. Think I'm Squirrel and they gon make a big bust. We got you, Squirrel. They happy, see, cause Squirrel dealing heavy then. Thought they caught them a whole shopping bag of dope.

Wearing my double-breasted pea coat. Used to be sharp but it's raggedy now. Ain't worth shit in cold weather like that. Pockets got holes and the dope dropped down in the lining so they don't find nothing the first time they search me. Can tell they mad. Thought they into something big and don't find shit. Looking at each other like, What the fuck's going on here? We big-time undercover supercops. This ain't spozed to be happening to us. They roughing me up too. Pulling my clothes off and shit. Hands all down in my pockets again. It's freezing and I'm shivering but these fools don't give a fuck. Rip my goddamn pea coat off me. Shaking it. Tearing it up. Find the two packs of dope inside the lining this time. Ain't what they wanted but they pissed off now. Take what they can get now.

What's this, Squirrel? Got your ass now.

Slinging me down the alley. I'm stone sick now. Begging these cats for mercy. Youall got me. You got your bust. Lemme snort some the dope, man. Little bit out each bag. You still got your bust. I'm dying. Little taste fore you lock me up.

Rotten motherfuckers ain't going for it. They see I'm sick as a dog. They know what's happening. Cold as it is, the sweat pouring out me. It's sweat but it's like ice. Like knives cutting me. They ain't give back my coat. Snowing on me and I'm shaking and sweating and sick. They can see all this. They know what's happening but ain't no mercy in these dudes. Henry's cross the street watching them bust me. Tears in his eyes. Ain't nothing he can do. The street's empty. Henry's bout froze too. Watching them sling my ass in their Continental. Never forget how Henry looked that day. All alone on the avenue. Tears froze in his eyes. Seeing him like that was a sad thing. Last thing I saw was him standing there across Homewood Avenue before they slammed me up in the car. Like I was in two places. That's me standing there in the snow. That's me so sick and cold I'm crying in the empty street and ain't a damn thing I can do about it.

By the time they get me down to the Police Station, down to No. 5 in East Liberty, I ain't no more good, sure nuff. Puking. Begging them punks not to bust me. Just bout out my mind. Must have been a pitiful sight. Then's when Henry went to Geral's house and scratched on the window and called David out on the porch. That's when youall found out I was in trouble and had to come down and get me. Right in the middle of the party and everything. Henry's sick too and he been walking round Homewood in the cold didn't know what to do. But he's my man. He got to Geral's so youall could come down and help me. Shamed to go in so he scratched on the window to get Dave on the porch.

Party's over and youns go to Mommy's and on top everything else find the house broke in and the TV gone. All the stuff's going through my mind. I'm on the bottom now. Low as you can go. Had me in a cell and I was lying cross the cot staring at the ceiling. Bars all round. Up cross the ceiling too. Like in a cage in the zoo. Miserable as I could be. All the shit staring me in the face. You're a dope fiend. You stole your brother's TV. You're hurting

Mommy again. Hurting everybody. You're sick. You're nothing. Looking up at the bars on the ceiling and wondering if I could tie my belt there. Stick my neck in it. I wanted to be dead.

Tied my belt to the ceiling. Then this guard checking on me he starts to hollering.

What you doing? Hey, Joe. This guy's trying to commit suicide.

They take my clothes. Leave me nothing but my shorts. I'm lying there shivering in my underwear and that's the end. In a cage naked like some goddamn animal. Shaking like a leaf. Thinking maybe I can beat my head against the bars or maybe jump down off the bed head first on the concrete and bust my brains open. Dead already. Nothing already. Low as I can go.

Must have passed out or gone to sleep or something, cause it gets blurry round in here. Don't remember much but they gave back my clothes and took me Downtown and there was a arraignment next morning.

Mommy told me later, one the cops advised her not to pay my bond. Said the best thing for him be to stay in jail awhile. Let him see how it is inside. Scare im. But I be steady beggin. Please, please get me out here. Youns got soft-hearted. Got the money together and paid the bond.

What would have happened if you left me to rot in there till my hearing? Damned if I know. I probably woulda went crazy, for one thing. I do know that. Know I was sick and scared and cried like a baby for Mommy and them to get me out. Don't think it really do no good letting them keep me in there. I mean the jail's a terrible place. You can get everything in jail you get in the street. No different. Cept in jail it's more dangerous cause you got a whole bunch of crazies locked up in one little space. Worse than the street. Less you got buddies in there they tear you up. Got to learn to survive quick. Cause jail be the stone jungle. Call prison the House of Knowledge cause you learns how to be a sure nuff criminal. Come in lame you leave knowing all kinds of evil shit. You learn quick or they eats you up. That's where it's at. So you leave a person in there, chances are they gets worse. Or gets wasted.

But Mom has that soft heart anyway and she ain't leaving her baby boy in no miserable jail. Right or wrong, she ain't leaving me in no place like that. Daddy been talking to Simon and Garfunkel. Daddy's hip, see. He been out there in the street all his life and he knows what's to it. Knows those guys and knows how rotten they is. Ain't no big thing they catch one pitiful little junkie holding two spoons. They wants dealers. They wants to look good Downtown. They wants to bust dealers and cop beaucoup dope so's they can steal it and get rich. Daddy makes a deal with them rats. Says if they drop the charges he'll make me set up Goose. Finger Goose and then stay off Homewood Avenue. Daddy says I'll do that so they let me go.

No way Ima squeal on Goose but I said okay, it's a deal. Soon's I was loose I warned Goose. Pretend like I'm trying to set him up so the cops get off my ass but Goose see me coming know the cops is watching. Helped him, really. Like a lookout. Them dumb motherfuckers got tired playing me. Simon got greedy. Somebody set him up. He got busted for drugs. Still see Garfunkel riding round in his Continental but they took him off the avenue. Too dangerous. Everybody hated them guys.

My lowest day. Didn't know till then I was strung out. That's the first time I was hooked. Started shooting up with Squirrel and Bugs Johnson when Squirrel be coming over to Mom's sometimes. Get up in the morning, go up to the third floor, and shoot up. They was like my teachers. Bugs goes way back. He started with Uncle Carl. Been shooting ever since. Dude's old now. Call him King of the Junkies, he been round so long. Bugs seen it all. You know junkies don't hardly be getting old. Have their day then they gone. Don't see em no more. They in jail or dead. Junkie just don't have no long life. Fast life but your average dopehead ain't round long. Bugs different. He was a pal of Uncle Carl's back in the fifties. Shot up together way back then. Now here he is wit Squirrel and me, still doing this thing. Everybody knows Bugs. He the King.

Let me shoot up wit em but they wouldn't let me go out in the street and hustle wit em. Said I was too young. Too green.

Learning from the King, see. That's how I started the heavy stuff. Me and Squirrel and Bugs first thing in the morning when I got out of bed. Mom was gone to work. They getting themselves ready to hit the street. Make that money. Just like a job. Wasn't no time before I was out there, too. On my own learning to get money for dope. Me and my little mob. We was ready. Didn't take us no time fore we was gangsters. Gon be the next Bugs Johnson. Gon make it to the top.

Don't take long. One day you the King. Next day dope got you and it's the King. You ain't nothing. You lying there naked bout to die and it don't take but a minute. You fall and you gone in a minute. That's the life. That's how it is. And I was out there. I know. Now they got me jammed up in the slammer. That's the way it is. But nobody could tell me nothing then. Hard head. You know. Got to find out for myself. Nobody could tell me nothing. Just out of high school and my life's over and I didn't even know it. Too dumb. Too hardheaded. I was gon do it my way. Youns was square. Youns didn't know nothing. Me, I was gon make mine from the curb. Hammer that rock till I was a supergangster. Be the one dealing the shit. Be the one running the junkies. That's all I knew. Street smarts. Stop being a chump. Forget that nickel-dime hoodlum bag. Be a star. Rise to the top.

You know where that got me. You heard that story. Here I sit today behind that story. Nobody to blame but my ownself. I know that now. But things was fucked up in the streets. You could fall in them streets, Brother. Low. Them streets could snatch you bald-headed and turn you around and wring you inside out. Streets was a bitch. Wake up some mornings and you think you in hell. Think you died and went straight to hell. I know cause I been there. Be days I wished I was dead. Be days worser than that.

. . . .

QUESTIONS FOR A SECOND READING

1. Wideman frequently interrupts this narrative to talk about the problems he is having as a writer. He says, for example, "The hardest habit to break, since it was the habit of a lifetime, would be listening to myself listen to him. That habit would destroy any chance of seeing my brother on his terms; and seeing him in his terms, learning his terms, seemed the whole point of learning his story" (p. 696). What might Wideman mean by this— listening to himself listen? As you reread "Our Time," note the sections in which Wideman speaks to you directly as a writer. What is he saying? Where and how are you surprised by what he says?

   Wideman calls attention to the problems he faces. How does he try to solve them? Are you sympathetic? Do the solutions work, so far as you are concerned?

2. Wideman says that his mother had a remarkable capacity for "[trying] on the other person's point of view." Wideman tries on another point of view himself, speaking to us in the voice of his brother Robby. As you reread this selection, note the passages spoken in Robby's voice and try to infer Robby's point of view from them. If you look at the differences between John and Robby as evidenced by the ways they use language to understand and represent the world, what do you notice?

3. Wideman talks about three ways he could start Robby's story: with Garth's death, with the house in Shadyside, and with the day of Robby's birth. What difference would it make in each case if he chose one and not the others? What's the point of presenting all three?

ASSIGNMENTS FOR WRITING

1. At several points in the essay, Wideman discusses his position as a writer, telling Robby's story, and he describes the problems he faces in writing this piece (or in "reading" the text of his brother's life). You could read this selection, in other words, as an essay about reading and writing.

   Why do you think Wideman talks about these problems here? Why not keep quiet and hope that no one notices? Choose three or four passages in which Wideman refers directly or indirectly to his work as a writer, and write an essay defining the problems Wideman faces and explaining why you think he raises them as he does. Finally, what might this have to do with your work as a writer—or as a student in this writing class?

2. Wideman tells Robby's story in this excerpt, but he also tells the story of his neighborhood, Homewood; of his mother; and of his grandfather John French. Write an essay retelling one of these stories and explaining what it might have to do with Robby and John's.

3. "Our Time" is a family history, but it is also a meditation on the problems of writing family histories—or, more generally, the problems of writing about the "real" world. There are sections in "Our Time" where Wideman speaks directly about the problems he faces as a writer. And the unusual features in the prose stand as examples of how he tried to solve these problems—at certain points Wideman writes as an essayist, at others like a storyteller; at certain points he switches voices; the piece breaks up into sections, it doesn't move from introduction to conclusion. Think of these as part of Wideman's method, as his way of working on the problems of writing as practical problems, where he is trying to figure out how to do justice to his brother and his story.

As you prepare to write this assignment, read back through the selection to think about it as a way of doing one's work, as a project, as a way of writing. What are the selection's key features? What is its shape or design? How does Wideman, the writer, do what he does? And you might ask: What would it take to learn to write like this? How is this writing related to the writing taught in school? Where and how might it serve you as a student?

Once you have developed a sense of Wideman's method, write a Wideman-like piece of your own, one that has the rhythm and the moves, the shape and the design of "Our Time." As far as subject matter is concerned, let Wideman's text stand as an invitation (inviting you to write about family and neighborhood) but don't feel compelled to follow his lead. You can write about anything you want. The key is to follow the essay as an example of a *way* of writing—moving slowly, turning this way and that, combining stories and reflection, working outside of a rigid structure of thesis and proof.

MAKING CONNECTIONS

1. Various selections in this textbook can be said to be "experimental" in their use of nonfiction prose. These are essays that don't do what essays are supposed to do. They break the rules. They surprise. The writers work differently than most writers. They imagine a different project (or they imagine their project differently).

Although any number of the selections in *Ways of Reading* might be read alongside "Our Time," here are some that have seemed interesting to our students: Gloria Anzaldúa, the essays from *Borderlands/La frontera* (pp. 29, 42); Susan Griffin, "Our Secret" (p. 299); and Adrienne Rich, "When We Dead Awaken: Writing as Re-Vision" (p. 520).

Choose one selection to compare with Wideman's and write an essay in which you both explain and explore the projects represented by the two pieces of writing. How do they address a reader's expectations? How do they manipulate the genre? How do they reimagine the features we take for granted in the genre of the essay—sentences and paragraphs; introductions and conclusions; argument, narrative, and exposition? And what is to be gained (or what is at stake) in writing this way? (Would you, for example, argue that these forms of writing should be taught in college?) You should assume that you are writing for someone who is a sophisticated reader but who is not familiar with these particular essays. You will need, that is, to be careful in choosing and presenting examples.

2. Both Harriet Jacobs, in "Incidents in the Life of a Slave Girl" (p. 353), and Wideman speak directly to the reader. They seem to feel that there are problems of understanding in the stories they have to tell and in their relations to their subjects and audiences. Look back over both stories and mark the passages in which the authors address you as a reader. Ask yourself why the authors might do this. What do they reveal about their work as writers at such moments? How would you describe the relationship each writer has with her or his subject matter? As a reader of each of these stories, how would you describe the relationship between the authors and yourself as the "audience"?

   After you have completed this preliminary research, write an essay in which you discuss these two acts of writing *as* acts of writing—that is, as stories in which the writers are self-conscious about their work as writers and make their audience aware of their self-consciousness. What differences or connections exist between you, the authors, and their subject matter? How do these differences or connections influence you as a reader?

3. The "Questions for a Second Reading" that accompany Cornelius Eady's "Brutal Imagination" and Harriet Jacobs's "Incidents in the Life of a Slave Girl" call attention to each as illustrative of the difficulties of narrating or representing the experiences of African Americans—of telling the story, of getting it right, of recovering experience from the representations of others.

   Read one of these alongside "Our Time" and write an essay in which you represent these texts as examples of writers working on a problem that has a particular urgency for black Americans. How might you name this problem? How might you illustrate it? What do you find compelling in these two approaches to the problem? And what might this problem have to do with you—as a writer, a thinker, a citizen?

Assignment
Sequences

Working with Assignment Sequences

EIGHT ASSIGNMENT SEQUENCES follow. Another nine sequences are included in *Resources for Teaching WAYS OF READING*. These assignment sequences are different from the single writing assignments at the end of each essay. The single writing assignments are designed to give you a way back into the works you have read. They define the way you, the reader, can work on an essay by writing about it—testing its assumptions, probing its examples, applying its way of thinking to a new setting or to new material. A single assignment might ask you to read what Paulo Freire has to say about education and then, as a writer, to use Freire's terms and methods to analyze a moment from your own schooling. The single assignments are designed to demonstrate how a student might work on an essay, particularly an essay that is long or complex, and they are designed to show how pieces that might seem daunting are open, manageable, and managed best by writing.

The assignment sequences have a similar function, but with one important difference. Instead of writing one paper, or working on one or two selections from the book, you will be writing several essays and reading several selections. Your work will be sequential as well as cumulative. The work you do on Freire, for example, will give you a way of beginning with Mary Louise Pratt or Adrienne Rich. It will give you an angle of vision. You won't be a newcomer to such discussions. Your previous reading will make the new essay rich with association. Passages or examples will jump out, as if magnetized, and demand your attention. And by reading these essays in context, you will see each writer as a single voice in a larger discussion. Neither Freire, nor Pratt, nor Rich, after all, has had the last word on the subject of education. It is not as though, by working on one of the essays, you have wrapped the subject up, ready to be put on the shelf.

The sequences are designed, then, so that you will be working not only on essays but on a subject, like education (or history, or culture, or the autobiography), a subject that can be examined, probed, and understood through the various frames provided by your reading. Each essay becomes a way of seeing a problem or a subject; it becomes a tool for thinking, an example of how a mind might work, a way of using language to make a subject rich and alive. In the assignment sequences, your reading is not random. Each sequence provides a set of readings that can be pulled together into a single project.

The sequences allow you to participate in an extended academic project, one with several texts and several weeks' worth of writing. You are not just adding one essay to another (Freire + Pratt = ?) but trying out an approach to a subject by revising it, looking at new examples, hearing what someone else has to say, and beginning again to take a position of your own. Projects like these take time. It is not at all uncommon for professional writers to devote weeks or even months to a single essay, and the essay they write marks not the end of their thinking on the subject, but only one stage. Similarly, when readers are working on a project, the pieces they read accumulate on their desks and in their minds and become part of an extended conversation with several speakers, each voice offering a point of view on a subject, a new set of examples, or a new way of talking that resonates with echoes from earlier reading.

A student may read many books, take several courses, write many papers; ideally each experience becomes part of something larger, an education. The work of understanding, in other words, requires time and repeated effort. The power that comes from understanding cannot be acquired quickly—by reading one essay or working for a few hours. A student, finally, is a person who choreographs such experiences, not someone who passes one test only to move on to another. And the assignment sequences are designed to reproduce, although in a condensed period of time, the rhythm and texture of academic life. They invite you to try on its characteristic ways of seeing, thinking, and writing. The work you do in one week will not be lost when it has bearing on the work you do in the next. If an essay by Susan Griffin has value for you, it is not because you proved to a teacher that you read it, but because you have put it to work and made it a part of your vocabulary as a student.

Working with a Sequence

Here is what you can expect as you work with a sequence. You begin by working with a single story or essay. You will need to read each piece twice, the second time with the "Questions for a Second Reading" and the assignment sequence in mind. Before rereading the selection, in other words, you should read through the assignments to get a sense of where you will be headed. And you should read the questions at the end of each selection. (You can use those questions to help frame questions of your own.) The purpose of all these questions, in a sense, is to prepare the text to speak—to bring it to life and insist that it respond to your attention, answer your questions. If you think of the authors as people you can talk to, if you think of their pages as occasions for dialogue (as places where you get to ask questions and insist on responses)—if you prepare your return to those pages in these ways, you are opening up the essays or stories (not closing them down or finishing them off) and creating a scene where you get to step forward as a performer.

While each sequence moves from selection to selection in *Ways of Reading*, the most significant movement in the sequence is defined by the essays you write. Your essays provide the other major texts for the course. In fact, when we teach these sequences, we seldom have any discussion of the assigned readings before our students have had a chance to write. When we talk as a group about Rich's "When We Dead Awaken: Writing as Re-Vision," for example, we begin by reproducing one or two student essays, handing them out to the class, and using them as the basis for discussion. We want to start, in other words, by looking at ways of reading Rich's essay—not at her essay alone.

The essays you write for each assignment in a sequence might be thought of as works-in-progress. Your instructor will tell you the degree to which each essay should be finished—that is, the degree to which it should be revised and copyedited and worked into a finished performance. In our classes, most writing assignments go through at least one revision. After we have had a chance to see a draft (or after a draft has been seen by others in the class), and after we have had some discussion of sample student essays, we ask students to read the assigned essay or story one more time and to rework their essays to bring their work one step further—not necessarily to finish the essays (as though there would be nothing else to say) but to finish up this stage in their work and to feel their achievement in a way a writer simply cannot the first time through. Each assignment, then, really functions as two assignments in the schedule for the course. As a consequence, we don't "cover" as many essays in a semester as students might in another class. But coverage is not our goal. In a sense, we are teaching our students how to read slowly and closely, to return to a text rather than set it aside, to take the time to reread and rewrite and to reflect on what these activities entail. Some of these sequences, then, contain more readings or more writing assignments than you can address in a quarter or semester. Different courses work at different paces. It is important, however, to preserve time for rereading and rewriting. The sequences were written with the assumption that they would be revised to meet the needs of teachers, students, and programs. As you look at your syllabus, you may find, then, that reading or writing assignments have been changed, added, or dropped.

There are alternative selections and assignments at the end of most of these sequences so that the sequences can be customized. Your instructor may wish to replace some of the selections and assignments in the sequence with alternatives.

You will be writing papers that can be thought of as single essays. But you will also be working on a project, something bigger than its individual parts. From the perspective of the project, each piece you write is part of a larger body of work that evolves over the term. You might think of each sequence as a revision exercise, where the revision looks forward to what comes next as well as backward to what you have done. This form of revision asks you to do more than complete a single paper; it invites you to resee a subject or reimagine what you might say about it from a new point of view. You should feel free, then, to draw on your earlier essays when you work on one of the later assignments. There is every reason for you to reuse ideas, phrases, sentences, even paragraphs as your work builds from one week to the next. The advantage of works-in-progress is that you are not starting over completely every time you sit down to write. You've been over this territory before. You've developed some expertise in your subject. There is a body of work behind you.

Most of the sequences bring together several essays from the text and ask you to imagine them as an extended conversation, one with several speakers. The assignments are designed to give you a voice in the conversation as well, to allow you to speak in turn and to take your place in the company of other writers. This is the final purpose of the assignment sequence: after several weeks' work on the essays and on the subject that draws them together, you will begin to establish your own point of view. You will develop a position from which you can speak with authority, drawing strength from the work you have done as well as from your familiarity with the people who surround you.

This book brings together some of the most powerful voices of our culture. They speak in a manner that asks for response. The assignments at the end of each selection and, with a wider range of reference, the assignment sequences here at the end of the book demonstrate that there is no reason for a student, in such company, to remain silent.

The Aims of Education

Paulo Freire

Adrienne Rich

Mary Louise Pratt

Susan Griffin

ALTERNATIVES:

Kwame Anthony Appiah

W. G. Sebald

YOU HAVE BEEN in school for several years, long enough for your experiences in the classroom to seem natural, inevitable. The purpose of this sequence is to invite you to step outside a world you may have begun to take for granted, to look at the ways you have been taught and at the unspoken assumptions behind your education. The eight assignments that follow bring together four essays that discuss how people (and particularly students) become trapped inside habits of thought. These habits of thought (they are sometimes referred to as "structures" of thought; Adrienne Rich calls them the "assumptions in which we are drenched") become invisible (or seem natural) because of the ways our schools work or because of the ways we have traditionally learned to use language when we speak, read, or write.

The essays brought together in this sequence provide powerful critiques of the usual accounts of education. The first two selections (by Paulo Freire and Adrienne Rich) argue that there are, or should be, ways of using language that can enable a person to break free from limited or limiting ways of thinking. The next, by Mary Louise Pratt, examines the classroom as an imagined community and discusses the nature of a student's participation in that community. The last reading in this sequence, the selection from Susan Griffin's *A Chorus of Stones*, is presented as an example of an alternative intellectual or academic project, one driven by a desire to know and understand the past but written outside the usual conventions of history or the social sciences. The writing assignments that accompany the readings provide an opportunity for you to test the arguments in the individual essays by weighing them against scenes and episodes from your own schooling. Some ask you to work within a specific argument (Rich's account of patriarchy, for example), and some ask you to experiment with the conventions of academic prose. (In some classes, students may be asked to work with a selection of these assignments.) The final assignment provides an occasion for you to draw material from all the essays you have written for this sequence into a final and more comprehensive statement on schools and schooling. (Given the number of assignments in this sequence, your instructor may cut one or more to allow time for additional revision. Alternative assignments can also be used.)

•　•　•　•　•　•　•　•　•　•　•　•

ASSIGNMENT **1**

Applying Freire to Your Own Experience as a Student [Freire]

> The teacher talks about reality as if it were motionless, static, compartmentalized, and predictable. Or else he expounds on a topic completely alien to the existential experience of the students. His task is to "fill" the students with the contents of his narration — contents which are detached from reality, disconnected from the totality that engendered them and could give them significance. Words are emptied of their concreteness and become a hollow, alienated, and alienating verbosity. (p. 244)
>
> — PAULO FREIRE
> *The "Banking" Concept of Education*

Surely, anyone who has made it through twelve years of formal education can think of a class, or an occasion outside of class, to serve as a quick example of what Freire calls the "banking" concept of education, where students are turned into "containers" to be "filled" by their teachers. If Freire is to be useful to you, however, he must do more than call up quick examples. He should allow you to say more than that a teacher once treated you like a container (or that a teacher once gave you your freedom).

Write an essay that focuses on a rich and illustrative incident from your own educational experience and read it (that is, interpret it) as Freire would. You will need to provide careful detail: things that were said and done, perhaps the exact wording of an assignment, a textbook, or a teacher's comments. And you will need to turn to the language of Freire's argument, to take key phrases and passages from his argument and see how they might be used to investigate your case.

To do this you will need to read your account as not simply the story of you and your teacher, since Freire is not writing about individual personalities (an innocent student and a mean teacher, a rude teacher, or a thoughtless teacher) but about the roles we are cast in, whether we choose to be or not, by our culture and its institutions. The key question, then, is not who you were or who your teacher was but what roles you played and how those roles can lead you to better understand the larger narrative or drama of Education (an organized attempt to "regulate the way the world 'enters into' the students").

Note: Freire would not want you to work passively or mechanically, as though you were merely following orders. He would want you to make your own mark on the work he has begun. Use your example, in other words, as a way of testing and examining what Freire says, particularly those passages that you find difficult or obscure.

$$\bullet \quad \bullet \quad \bullet \quad \bullet \quad \bullet \quad \bullet \quad \bullet \quad \bullet \quad \bullet \quad \bullet \quad \bullet \quad \bullet$$

A S S I G N M E N T **2**

Studying Rich as a Case in Point
[Freire, Rich]

> The truth is, however, that the oppressed are not "marginals," are not men living "outside" society. They have always been "inside" — inside the structure which made them "beings for others." The solution is not to "integrate" them into the structure of oppression, but to transform that structure so that they can become "beings for themselves." Such transformation, of course, would undermine the oppressors' purposes. . . . (p. 246)
>
> — PAULO FREIRE
> *The "Banking" Concept of Education*

> For a poem to coalesce, for a character or an action to take shape, there has to be an imaginative transformation of reality which is in no way passive. . . . Moreover, if the imagination is to transcend and transform experience it has to question, to challenge,

to conceive of alternatives, perhaps to the very life you are living at that moment. You have to be free to play around with the
notion that day might be night, love might be hate; nothing can
be too sacred for the imagination to turn into its opposite or to
call experimentally by another name. For writing is renaming.
(p. 528)

> — ADRIENNE RICH
> *When We Dead Awaken: Writing as Re-Vision*

Both Freire and Rich talk repeatedly about transformations—about
transforming structures, transforming the world, transforming the way
language is used, transforming the relations between people. In fact, the
changes in Rich's poetry might be seen as evidence of her transforming the
structures from within which she worked. And, when Freire takes a situation we think of as "natural" (teachers talking and students sitting silent)
and names it "banking education," he makes it possible for students and
their teachers to question, challenge, conceive of alternatives, and transform experience. Each, in other words, can be framed as an example in the
language of the other—Freire in Rich's terms, Rich in Freire's. For both,
this act of transformation is something that takes place within and through
the use of language.

Rich's essay could be read as a statement about the aims of education,
particularly if the changes in her work are taken as evidence of something
the poet learned to do. Rich talks about teachers, about people who helped
her to reimagine her situation as a woman and a poet, and about the work
she had to do on her own.

For this assignment, take three of the poems Rich offers as examples of
change in her writing—"Aunt Jennifer's Tigers," the section from "Snapshots of a Daughter-in-Law," and "Planetarium," as well as the additional
poems reprinted in "Sources from Your Native Land, Your Life"—and use
them as a way of talking about revision. What, to your mind, are the key differences between these poems? What might the movement they mark be
said to represent? And what do these poems, as examples, have to do with
the argument about writing, culture, and gender in the rest of the essay?

As you prepare to write, you might also ask some questions in Freire's
name. For example: What problems did Rich pose for herself? How might
this be taken as an example of a problem-posing education? In what ways
might Rich be said to have been having a dialogue with her own work? Who
was the teacher (or the teachers) here and what did the poet learn to do?

You are not alone as you read these poems, in other words. In fact, Rich
provides her own commentary on the three poems, noting what for her are
key changes and what they represent. You will want to acknowledge what
Rich has to say, to be sure, but you should not be bound by it. You, too, are
a person with a point of view on this issue. Rich (with Freire) provides a
powerful language for talking about change, but be sure to carve out space
where you have the opportunity to speak as well.

•   •   •   •   •   •   •   •   •   •   •   •

ASSIGNMENT **3**

Tradition and the Writing
of the Past [Rich]

We need to know the writing of the past, and know it differently than we have ever known it; not to pass on a tradition but to break its hold over us. (p. 522)
— ADRIENNE RICH
When We Dead Awaken: Writing as Re-Vision

"We need to know the writing of the past," Rich says. The "we" of that sentence can be read as an invitation to you. Look back over your own writing (perhaps the drafts and revisions you have written for this course), and think back over comments teachers have made, textbooks you have seen; think about what student writers do and what they are told to do, about the secrets students keep and the secrets teachers keep. You can assume, as Rich does, that there are ways of speaking about writing that are part of the culture of schooling and that they are designed to preserve certain ways of writing and thinking and to discourage others. Write an essay in which you reflect on the writing of the past and its presence in your work as a writer.

One might argue, in other words, that there are ways of writing that are part of schooling. There are traditions here, too. As you look at the evidence of the "past" in your own work, what are its significant features: What might you name this tradition (or these traditions)? What are the official names? What do these names tell us? What do they hide? What difference might it make to name tradition in terms of gender and call it patriarchal?

How would you illustrate the hold this tradition has on your work or the work of students generally? What might you have to do to begin to "know it differently," "to break its hold," or to revise? And, finally, why would someone want (or not want) to make such a break?

•   •   •   •   •   •   •   •   •   •   •   •   •

ASSIGNMENT **4**

The Contact Zone [Pratt]

The idea of the contact zone is intended in part to contrast with
ideas of community that underlie much of the thinking about
language, communication, and culture that gets done in the
academy. (p. 507)

> — MARY LOUISE PRATT
> *Arts of the Contact Zone*

Citing Benedict Anderson and what he calls "imagined communities,"
Pratt argues that our idea of community is "strongly utopian, embodying
values like equality, fraternity, liberty, which the societies often profess but
systematically fail to realize." Against this utopian vision of community,
Pratt argues that we need to develop ways of understanding (even noticing) social and intellectual spaces that are not homogeneous, unified; we
need to develop ways of understanding and valuing difference. And, for
Pratt, the argument extends to schooling. "What is the place," she asks,

> of unsolicited oppositional discourse, parody, resistance, cri-
> tique in the imagined classroom community? Are teachers sup-
> posed to feel that their teaching has been most successful when
> they have eliminated such things and unified the social world,
> probably in their own image? Who wins when we do that? Who
> loses? (p. 509)

Such questions, she says, "may be hypothetical, because in the United
States in the 1990s, many teachers find themselves less and less able to do
that even if they want to."

"In the United States in the 1990s." "The imagined classroom." From
your experience, what scenes might be used to represent schooling in the
1990s and beyond? How are they usually imagined (idealized, represented,
interpreted, valued)? What are the implications of Pratt's argument?

Write an essay in which you use Pratt's terms to examine a representative scene from your own experience with schools and schooling. What examples, stories, or images best represent your experience? How might they
be interpreted as examples of community? as examples of "contact zones"?
As you prepare your essay, you will want to set the scene as carefully as
you can, so that someone who was not there can see it fully. Think about
how someone who has not read Pratt might interpret the scene. And think
through the various ways *you* might interpret your example. And you

should also think about your position in an argum͟
contact zone. What do you (or people like you) stand ͟
you adopt Pratt's point of view?

· · · · · · · · · · · ·

A S S I G N M E N T **5**

The Pedagogical Arts
of the Contact Zone [Pratt]

> Meanwhile, our job in the Americas course remains to figure out
> how to make that crossroads the best site for learning that it can
> be. We are looking for the pedagogical arts of the contact zone.
> These will include, we are sure, exercises in storytelling and in
> identifying with the ideas, interests, histories, and attitudes of
> others; experiments in transculturation and collaborative work
> and in the arts of critique, parody, and comparison (including
> unseemly comparisons between elite and vernacular cultural
> forms); the redemption of the oral; ways for people to engage
> with suppressed aspects of history (including their own histo-
> ries), ways to move *into and out of* rhetorics of authenticity;
> ground rules for communication across lines of difference
> and hierarchy that go beyond politeness but maintain mutual
> respect; a systematic approach to the all-important concept of
> *cultural mediation*. (p. 511)
>
> — MARY LOUISE PRATT
> *Arts of the Contact Zone*

Pratt writes generally about culture and history, but also about reading
and writing and teaching and learning, about the "literate" and "pedagogical" arts of this place she calls the contact zone. Think about the class you
are in — its position in the curriculum, in the institution. Think about its official goals (and its unofficial goals). Think about the positions represented
by the students, the teacher. Think about how to think about the class, in
Pratt's terms, as a contact zone.

And think about the unusual exercises represented by her list: "storytelling," "experiments in transculturation," "critique," "parody," "unseemly
comparisons," moving into and out of "rhetorics of authenticity" — these are
some of them. Take one of these suggested exercises, explain what you take
it to mean, and then go on to discuss how it might be put into practice in a
writing class. What would students do? to what end? How would their work

_valuated? What place would the exercise have in the larger sequence of assignments over the term, quarter, or semester? In your terms, and from your point of view, what might you learn from such an exercise?

Or you could think of the question this way: What comments would a teacher make on one of the papers you have written so far in order that its revision might stand as one of these exercises? How would the revision be different from what you are used to doing?

Write an essay in which you present and discuss an exercise designed to serve the writing class as a contact zone.

• • • • • • • • • • • •

ASSIGNMENT **6**

Writing against the Grain [Griffin]

As you reread "Our Secret," think of Griffin's prose as experimental, as deliberate and crafted. She is trying to do something that she can't do in the "usual" essay form. She wants to make a different kind of argument and engage her reader in a different manner. And so she mixes personal and academic writing. She assembles fragments and juxtaposes seemingly unrelated material in surprising and suggestive relationships. She breaks the "plane" of the page with italicized inter-sections. She organizes her material, that is, but not in the usual mode of thesis-example-conclusion. The arrangement is not nearly so linear. At one point, when she seems to be prepared to argue that German child-rearing practices produced the Holocaust, she quickly says:

> Of course there cannot be one answer to such a monumental riddle, nor does any event in history have a single cause. Rather a field exists, like a field of gravity that is created by the movements of many bodies. Each life is influenced and it in turn becomes an influence. Whatever is a cause is also an effect. Childhood experience is just one element in the determining field.
> (p. 304)

Her prose serves to create a "field," one where many bodies are set in relationship.

It is useful, then, to think about Griffin's prose as the enactment of a method, as a way of doing a certain kind of intellectual work. One way to study this, to feel its effects, is to imitate it, to take it as a model. For this assignment, write a Griffin-like essay, one similar in its methods or organization and argument. You will need to think about the stories you might tell, about the stories and texts you might gather (stories and texts not your own). As you write, you will want to think carefully about arrangement and about commentary (about where, that is, you will speak to your reader *as* the writer of the piece). You should not feel bound to Griffin's subject matter, but you should feel that you are working in her spirit.

• • • • • • • • • • • • •

ASSIGNMENT **7**

The Task of Attention [Griffin]

> I am looking now at the etching called *Poverty*, made in 1897. Near the center, calling my attention, a woman holds her head in her hands. (p. 308)
>
> — SUSAN GRIFFIN
> *Our Secret*

This is one of the many moments where Griffin speaks to us as though in the midst of her work. The point of this assignment is to think about that work—what it is, how she does it, and what it might have to do with schools and schooling. She is, after all, doing much of the traditional work of scholars—going to the archive, studying old materials, traveling and interviewing subjects, learning and writing history.

And yet this is not the kind of prose you would expect to find in a textbook for a history course. Even if the project is not what we usually think of as a research project, Griffin is a careful researcher. Griffin knows what she is doing. Having experimented with a Griffin-like essay, go back now to look again (this time with a writer's eye) at both the features of Griffin's prose and the way she characterizes her work as a scholar, gathering and studying her materials.

Write an essay in which you present an account of *how* Griffin does her work. You should use her words and examples from the text, but you should also feel that it is your job to explain what you present and to comment on it from the point of view of a student. As you reread, look to those sections where Griffin seems to be speaking to her readers about her work—about how she reads and how she writes, about how she gathers her materials and how she studies them. What is she doing? What is at stake in adopting such methods? How might they be taught? Where in the curriculum might (should?) such lessons be featured?

• • • • • • • • • • •

ASSIGNMENT 8

Putting Things Together
[Freire, Rich, Pratt, Griffin]

This is the final assignment of this sequence, and it is the occasion for you to step back and take stock of all that you have done. Perhaps the best way to do this is by making a statement of your own about the role of reading and writing in an undergraduate education. You might, for example, write a document for students who will be entering your school for the first time, telling them what they should expect or what they should know about reading and writing if they want to make the most of their education. Or this might be an essay written for an alumni magazine or a paper for a faculty committee charged with reviewing undergraduate education. Or you might want to think of this essay as primarily autobiographical, as that chapter of your autobiography where you think through your experiences with schooling.

You should feel free to draw as much as you can from the papers you have already written, making your points through examples you have already examined, perhaps using your own work with these assignments as an example of what students might be expected to do.

• • • • • • • • • • •

ALTERNATIVE ASSIGNMENT

Considering Common Pursuits
[Appiah]

When we have taught this essay, "The Ethics of Individuality," our students tended to forget or to ignore or to tune out the final sections: "The Social Scriptorium," "Ethics in Identity," "Individuality and the State," and "The Common Pursuit." It was easier (or more pleasant) to think about the individual; it was harder (or less pleasant) to think about the "State" and "common" pursuits.

If this is the case (even if it is not the case for you), there is reason to reread those sections with particular attention. What is Appiah doing there? What is he getting at? What is the role of education? What does it mean to be educated?

For this assignment, write an essay that addresses these questions and that works closely with the final sections of his essay. Although Appiah makes it clear that he is more interested in exploration than conclusion, that he is not providing "practical advice," you can turn your essay toward an argument or a plan of action if you choose.

* * * * * * * * * * * *

ALTERNATIVE ASSIGNMENT

A Mental Ramble [Sebald]

Let's think for a moment of the two chapters from *The Rings of Saturn* as essays. Each has a distinct way of working. Each presents a character speaking, thinking, and writing. Both are short; they combine the personal with issues and references of general concern. Each moves from the story of a life (travels in the east of England) to the story of a mental or intellectual life. They give special importance to the records (and details) of reading and scholarship—books, authors, paintings. They demonstrate that personal history can include a history of one's thinking and learning. Write a similar essay, one that follows the design and order (if not the style) of Sebald. You can, if you choose, draw on the material you are reading and studying in other courses this semester. You could also include images and illustrations. When you are finished, provide a very brief (one page) preface in which you present your essay as an example of academic writing, as a way of being educated.

SEQUENCE TWO

The Arts of the Contact Zone

Mary Louise Pratt
Gloria Anzaldúa
Harriet Jacobs
Edward Said

ALTERNATIVE:
John Edgar Wideman

THIS SEQUENCE allows you to work closely with the argument of Mary Louise Pratt's "Arts of the Contact Zone," not so much through summary (repeating the argument) as through extension (working under its influence, applying its terms and protocols). In particular, you are asked to try your hand at those ways of reading and writing Pratt defines as part of the "literate arts of the contact zone," ways of reading and writing that have not historically been taught or valued in American schools.

Pratt is one of the country's most influential cultural critics. In "Arts of the Contact Zone," she makes the argument that our usual ways of reading and writing assume identification—that is, we learn to read and write the texts that express our own position and point of view. As a result, texts that reproduce different ways of thinking, texts that allude to different cultural systems, seem flawed, wrong, or inscrutable. As a counterposition, Pratt asks us to imagine scenes of reading, writing, teaching, and learning as "contact zones," places of contact between people who can't or don't or won't necessarily identify with one another.

In the first assignment, you are asked to search for or produce a document to exemplify the arts of the contact zone, working in library archives, searching the streets, surfing the Internet, or writing an "autoethnography." This is a big job, and probably new to most students; it is a project you will want to come back to and revise.

The remaining assignments outline a project where you examine other selections from *Ways of Reading* that exemplify or present moments of cultural contact: Gloria Anzaldúa's *Borderlands/La frontera*, a text that announces itself as the product of a mixed, *mestiza* cultural position; Harriet Jacobs's "Incidents in the Life of a Slave Girl," a classic American slave narrative (and a good example of autoethnography); and Edward Said's "States," an account of Palestinian life written by a Palestinian in exile. The final assignment asks you to think back over both Pratt's argument and the work you have done with that argument in order to fashion a general statement about the arts of the contact zone. An alternative assignment is also included to allow John Edgar Wideman's "Our Time" to be substituted for one of the selections.

· · · · · · · · · · · ·

ASSIGNMENT **1**

The Literate Arts of the Contact Zone [Pratt]

Here, briefly, are two descriptions of the writing one might find or expect in the contact zone:

> Autoethnography, transculturation, critique, collaboration, bilingualism, mediation, parody, denunciation, imaginary dialogue, vernacular expression— these are some of the literate arts of the contact zone. Miscomprehension, incomprehension, dead letters, unread masterpieces, absolute heterogeneity of meaning —these are some of the perils of writing in the contact zone. They all live among us today in the transnationalized metropolis of the United States and are becoming more widely visible, more pressing, and, like Guaman Poma's text, more decipherable to those who once would have ignored them in defense of a stable, centered sense of knowledge and reality. (pp. 506–7)

> We are looking for the pedagogical arts of the contact zone. These will include, we are sure, exercises in storytelling and in identifying with the ideas, interests, histories, and attitudes of others; experiments in transculturation and collaborative work and in the arts of critique, parody, and comparison (including unseemly comparisons between elite and vernacular cultural

forms); the redemption of the oral; ways for people to engage
with suppressed aspects of history (including their own histories), ways to move *into and out of* rhetorics of authenticity;
ground rules for communication across lines of difference and
hierarchy that go beyond politeness but maintain mutual respect; a systematic approach to the all-important concept of *cultural mediation.* (p. 511)

Here are two ways of working on Pratt's idea of the contact zone.
Choose one.

1. One way of working with Pratt's essay, of extending its project, would
    be to conduct your own local inventory of writing from the contact
    zone. You might do this on your own or in teams, with others from
    your class. You will want to gather several similar documents, your
    "archive," before you make a final selection. Think about how to make
    that choice. What makes one document stand out as representative?
    Here are two ways you might organize your search:
    a. You could look for historical documents. A local historical society
        might have documents written by Native Americans ("Indians") to
        the white settlers. There may be documents written by slaves to
        masters or to northern whites explaining their experience. There
        may be documents written by women (suffragettes, for example)
        trying to negotiate for public positions or rights. There may be doc-
        uments from any of a number of racial or ethnic groups—His-
        panic, Jewish, Irish, Italian, Polish, Swedish—trying to explain
        their positions to the mainstream culture. There may, perhaps at
        union halls, be documents written by workers to owners. Your
        own sense of the heritage of your area should direct your search.
    b. Or you could look at contemporary documents in the print that
        is around you, texts that you might otherwise overlook. Pratt refers
        to one of the characteristic genres of the Hispanic community,
        the *"testimonio."* You could look for songs, testimonies, manifestos,
        statements by groups on campus, stories, autobiographies, inter-
        views, letters to the editor, Web pages. You could look at the writ-
        ing of any marginalized group, particularly writing intended, at
        least in part, to represent the experience of outsiders to the domi-
        nant culture (or to be in dialogue with that culture or to respond to
        that culture). These documents, if we follow Pratt's example, would
        encompass the work of young children or students, including col-
        lege students.
        Once you have completed your inventory, choose a document you
        would like to work with and write an essay that presents it carefully
        and in detail (perhaps in even greater detail than Pratt's presentation
        of the *New Chronicle*). You will, in other words, need to set the scene,
        summarize, explain, and work block quotations into your essay. You
        might imagine that you are presenting this to someone who would not

have seen it and would not know how to read it, at le
ample of the literate arts of the contact zone.

2. Another way of extending the project of Pratt's essay w
your autoethnography. It should not be too hard to lc
context in which you are the "other" — the one who s͟p͟ ͟_͟_͟_͟_͟ ͟_͟_͟o͟m͟ ͟o͟u͟t-
side rather than inside the dominant discourse. Pratt says that the position of the outsider is marked not only by differences of language and
ways of thinking and speaking but also by differences in power, authority, status. In a sense, she argues, the only way those in power can
understand you is in *their* terms. These are terms you will need to use
to tell your story, but your goal is to describe your position in ways
that "engage with representations others have made of [you]" without
giving in or giving up or disappearing in their already formed sense of
who you are.

This is an interesting challenge. One of the things that will make
the writing difficult is that the autoethnographic or transcultural text
calls upon skills not usually valued in American classrooms: bilingualism, parody, denunciation, imaginary dialogue, vernacular expression,
storytelling, unseemly comparisons of high and low cultural forms —
these are some of the terms Pratt offers. These do not fit easily with the
traditional genres of the writing class (essay, term paper, summary, report) or its traditional values (unity, consistency, sincerity, clarity, correctness, decorum).

You will probably need to take this essay (or whatever it should be
called) through several drafts. (In fact, you might revise this essay after
you have completed assignments 2 and 3.) It might be best to begin as
Pratt's student, using her description as a preliminary guide. Once you
get a sense of your own project, you may find that you have terms or examples to add to her list of the literate arts of the contact zone.

· · · · · · · · · · · ·

ASSIGNMENT 2

Borderlands [Pratt, Anzaldúa]

In "Arts of the Contact Zone," Pratt talks about the "autoethnographic"
text, "a text in which people undertake to describe themselves in ways
that engage with representations others have made of them," and about
"transculturation," the "processes whereby members of subordinated or
marginal groups select and invent from the materials transmitted by a dominant or metropolitan culture."

Write an essay in which you present a reading of *Borderlands/La frontera* as an example of an autoethnographic and/or transcultural text. You should imagine that you are writing to someone who is not familiar with either Pratt's argument or Anzaldúa's thinking. Part of your work, then, is to present Anzaldúa's text to readers who don't have it in front of them. You have the example of Pratt's reading of Guaman Poma's *New Chronicle and Good Government*. And you have her discussion of the literate arts of the contact zone. Think about how Anzaldúa's text might be similarly read and about how her text does and doesn't fit Pratt's description. Your goal should be to add an example to Pratt's discussion and to qualify it, to alter or reframe what she has said now that you have had a chance to look at an additional example.

. . . .

ASSIGNMENT 3

Autoethnography [Pratt, Jacobs]

Here is Mary Louise Pratt on the autoethnographic text:

> Guaman Poma's *New Chronicle* is an instance of what I have proposed to call an *autoethnographic* text, by which I mean a text in which people undertake to describe themselves in ways that engage with representations others have made of them. Thus if ethnographic texts are those in which European metropolitan subjects represent to themselves their others (usually their conquered others), autoethnographic texts are representations that the so-defined others construct *in response to* or in dialogue with those texts. . . . [T]hey involve a selective collaboration with and appropriation of idioms of the metropolis or the conqueror. These are merged or infiltrated to varying degrees with indigenous idioms to create self-representations intended to intervene in metropolitan modes of understanding. Autoethnographic works are often addressed to both metropolitan audiences and the speaker's own community. Their reception is thus highly indeterminate. Such texts often constitute a marginalized group's point of entry into the dominant circuits of print culture. It is interesting to think, for example, of American slave autobiography in its autoethnographic dimensions, which in some respects distinguish it from Euramerican autobiographical tradition. (pp. 501–2)

Reread Harriet Jacobs's "Incidents in the Life of a Slave Girl" after reading Pratt's essay. Using the example of Pratt's work with the *New Chronicle*, write an essay presenting a reading of Jacobs's text as an autoethnographic and/or transcultural text. You should think about not only how it might be read from this point of view but also how, without this perspective, it might (in Pratt's terms) be misread or unread. Imagine that you are working to put Pratt's ideas to the test but also to see what you can say on your own about "Incidents" as a text, as something written and read.

· · · · · · · · · · · ·

ASSIGNMENT **4**

A Dialectic of Self and Other [Pratt, Said]

In "States," an account of Palestinian life written by a Palestinian in exile, Edward Said says,

> All cultures spin out a dialectic of self and other, the subject "I" who is native, authentic, at home, and the object "it" or "you," who is foreign, perhaps threatening, different, out there. From this dialectic comes the series of heroes and monsters, founding fathers and barbarians, prized masterpieces and despised opponents that express a culture from its deepest sense of national self-identity to its refined patriotism, and finally to its coarse jingoism, xenophobia, and exclusivist bias. (p. 596)

This is as true of the Palestinians as it is of the Israelis—although, he adds, "For Palestinian culture, the odd thing is that its own identity is more frequently than not perceived as 'other.'"

Pratt argues that our idea of community is "strongly utopian, embodying values like equality, fraternity, liberty, which the societies often profess but systematically fail to realize." Against this utopian vision of community, Pratt argues that we need to develop ways of understanding (noticing or creating) social and intellectual spaces that are not homogeneous or unified—contact zones; she argues that we need to develop ways of understanding and valuing difference.

There are similar goals and objects to these projects. Reread Pratt's essay with Said's "States" in mind. As she defines what she refers to as the "literate arts of the contact zone," can you find points of reference in Said's text? Said's thinking always attended to the importance and the conditions of writing, including his own. There are ways that "States" could be imagined as both autoethnographic and transcultural. How might his work allow you to understand the literate arts of the contact zone in practice? How might his work allow you to understand the problems and possibilities of such writing beyond what Pratt has imagined, presented, and predicted?

• • • • • • • • • • •

ASSIGNMENT 5

On Culture
[Pratt, Anzaldúa, Jacobs, Said]

In some ways, the slipperiest of the key words in Pratt's essay "Arts of the Contact Zone" is "culture." At one point Pratt says,

> If one thinks of cultures, or literatures, as discrete, coherently structured, monolingual edifices, Guaman Poma's text, and indeed any autoethnographic work, appears anomalous or chaotic — as it apparently did to the European scholars Pietsch-mann spoke to in 1912. If one does not think of cultures this way, then Guaman Poma's text is simply heterogeneous, as the Andean region was itself and remains today. Such a text is het-erogeneous on the reception end as well as the production end: it will read very differently to people in different positions in the contact zone. (p. 506)

If one thinks of cultures as "coherently structured, monolingual edi-fices," the text appears one way; if one thinks otherwise, the text is "simply heterogeneous." What might it mean to make this shift in the way one thinks of culture? Can you do it—that is, can you read the *New Chronicle* (or its excerpts) from both points of view? Better yet—what about your own culture and its key texts? Can you, for example, think of a group that you participate in as a "community"? Where and how does it represent it-self to others? Where and how does it do this in writing? What are its "liter-ate arts"?

The assignments in this sequence are an exercise in reading texts as het-erogeneous, as contact zones. As a way of reflecting on your work in this se-quence, write an essay in which you explain the work you have been doing to someone not in the course, someone who is interested in reading, writ-ing, and learning, but who has not read Pratt, Anzaldúa, Jacobs, or Said.

* * * * * * * * * * * *

ALTERNATIVE ASSIGNMENT

Counterparts [Wideman]

Here, from "Arts of the Contact Zone," is Mary Louise Pratt on the autoethnographic text:

> Guaman Poma's *New Chronicle* is an instance of what I have proposed to call an *autoethnographic* text, by which I mean a text in which people undertake to describe themselves in ways that engage with representations others have made of them. Thus if ethnographic texts are those in which European metropolitan subjects represent to themselves their others (usually their conquered others), autoethnographic texts are representations that the so-defined others construct *in response to* or in dialogue with those texts. . . . [T]hey involve a selective collaboration with and appropriation of idioms of the metropolis or the conqueror. These are merged or infiltrated to varying degrees with indigenous idioms to create self-representations intended to intervene in metropolitan modes of understanding. . . . Such texts often constitute a marginalized group's point of entry into the dominant circuits of print culture. It is interesting to think, for example, of American slave autobiography in its autoethnographic dimensions, which in some respects distinguish it from Euramerican autobiographical tradition. (pp. 501–2)

John Edgar Wideman's "Our Time" (p. 681) could serve as a twentieth-century counterpart to the *New Chronicle*. Reread it with "Arts of the Contact Zone" in mind. Write an essay that presents "Our Time" as an example of autoethnographic and/or transcultural text. You should imagine that you are working to put Pratt's ideas to the test (*does* it do what she says such texts must do?), but also add what you have to say concerning this text as a literate effort to be present in the context of difference.

Autobiographical Explorations

Richard Rodriguez
Edward Said
W. G. Sebald

ALTERNATIVES:

Kwame Anthony Appiah
Adrienne Rich
John Edgar Wideman
Jane Tompkins
Susan Griffin
Gloria Anzaldúa
Harriet Jacobs

AUTOBIOGRAPHICAL WRITING has been a regular feature of writing courses since the nineteenth century. There are a variety of reasons for the prevalence of autobiography, not the least of which is the pleasure students take in thinking about and writing about their lives and their world. There is also a long tradition of published autobiographical writing, particularly in the United States. The title of this sequence puts a particular spin on that tradition, since it points to a more specialized use of autobiography, phrased here as "exploration." What is suggested by the title is a use of writing (and the example of one's experience, including intellectual experience) to investigate, question, explore, inquire. Often the genre is not used for these purposes at all. Autobiographical writing is often used for purposes of display or self-promotion, or to further (rather than question) an argument (about success, about how to live a good or proper or fulfilling life).

There are two threads to this sequence. The first is to invite you to experiment with the genre of "autobiographical exploration." The second is to foreground the relationship between your work and the work of others, to think about how and why and where you are prepared to write autobiographically (prepared not only by the lessons you've learned in school but by the culture and the way it invites you to tell—and live—the story of your life). And, if you are working inside a conventional field, a predictable way of writing, the sequence asks where and how you might make your mark or assert your position—your identity as a person (a character in a life story) and as a writer (someone working with the conventions of life-writing).

The first three assignments ask you to write from within the example of other writers, writers engaged in "revisionary" projects: Richard Rodriguez, Edward Said, and W. G. Sebald. One of the difficulties, for a student, of an extended project like this is finding a way of writing differently. An autobiographical project *without* the readings (where, in a sense, you were writing on your own) might well produce each week only more of the same, the same story written in the same style. Our goal is to make you aware of the options available to you as a writer as you think about, write, and represent your life. You should think of these assignments as asking not for mere or mechanical imitation, but as invitations to think about areas of your life as these authors have and to imagine the problems and potential of life-writing through the example of their prose, its style and methods.

The last assignment in the sequence is a retrospective assignment. Here you are asked to think back over what you have done and to write a preface to your work, a short essay to prepare other readers to understand what you have been working on and best appreciate the problems and achievements of your work. We will be asking you to think of yourself as an author, to read what you have written and to write about your texts, as, perhaps, you have sometimes been asked to write *about* the works of other authors.

The alternative sequences that follow provide similar assignments but with different readings. They can be substituted for assignments or added to those assignments.

· · · · · · · · · · · ·

ASSIGNMENT 1

Desire, Reading, and the Past [Rodriguez]

In "The Achievement of Desire," Richard Rodriguez tells stories of home but also stories of reading, of moments when things he read allowed him a way of reconsidering or revising ("framing," he calls it) the stories he would tell himself about himself. It is a very particular account of neighborhood, family, ethnicity, and schooling.

At the same time, Rodriguez insists that his story is also everyone's story—that his experience is universal. Take an episode from your life, one that seems in some ways similar to one of the episodes in "The Achievement of Desire," and cast it into a shorter version of Rodriguez's essay. Try to make use of your reading in ways similar to his. Think about what you have read lately in school, perhaps in this anthology.

In general, however, your job in this assignment is to look at your experience in Rodriguez's terms, which means thinking the way he does, noticing what he would notice, interpreting details in a similar fashion, using his key terms, seeing through his point of view; it could mean imitating his style of writing, doing whatever it is you see him doing characteristically when he writes. Imitation, Rodriguez argues, is not necessarily a bad thing; it can, he argues, be one of the powerful ways a person learns. Let this assignment serve as an exercise.

· · · · · · · · · · · ·

ASSIGNMENT 2

A Photographic Essay [Said]

Edward Said, in the introduction to *After the Last Sky*, says of his method in "States":

> Its style and method—the interplay of text and photos, the mixture of genres, modes, styles—do not tell a consecutive story, nor do they constitute a political essay. Since the main features of our present existence are dispossession, dispersion, and yet also a kind of power incommensurate with our stateless exile, I

believe that essentially unconventional, hybrid, and fragmentary forms of expression should be used to represent us. What I have quite consciously designed, then, is an alternative mode of expression to the one usually encountered in the media, in works of social science, in popular fiction. (p. 6)

And later:

The multifaceted vision is essential to any representation of us. Stateless, dispossessed, de-centered, we are frequently unable either to speak the "truth" of our experience or to make it heard. We do not usually control the images that represent us; we have been confined to spaces designed to reduce or stunt us; and we have often been distorted by pressures and powers that have been too much for us. An additional problem is that our language, Arabic, is unfamiliar in the West and belongs to a tradition and civilization usually both misunderstood and maligned. Everything we write about ourselves, therefore, is an interpretive translation—of our language, our experience, our senses of self and others. (p. 6)

Reread "States," paying particular attention to the relationship of text and photograph, and paying attention to form. What *is* the order of the writing in this essay? (We will call it an essay for lack of a better term.) How might you diagram or explain its organization? By what principle(s) is it ordered and arranged? The essay shifts genres—memoir, history, argument. It is, as Said comments, "hybrid." What surprises are there? or disappointments? How might you describe the writer's strategy as he works on his audience, on readers? And, finally, do you find Said's explanation sufficient or useful—does the experience of exile produce its own inevitable style of report and representation?

For this assignment, compose a similar project, a Said-like reading of a set of photos. These can be photos prepared for the occasion (by you or a colleague); they could also be photos already available. Whatever their source, they should represent people and places, a history and/or geography that you know well, that you know to be complex and contradictory, and that you know will not be easily or readily understood by others, both the group for whom you will be writing (most usefully the members of your class) and readers more generally. You must begin with a sense that the photos cannot speak for themselves; you must speak for them.

In preparation, you should reread closely to come to a careful understanding of Said's project. (The first and second "Questions for a Second Reading" should be useful for this.)

•   •   •   •   •   •   •   •   •   •   •   •

ASSIGNMENT 3

Personal Experience as Intellectual Experience
[Sebald]

Let's think for a moment of the two chapters from *The Rings of Saturn* as essays. Each has a distinct way of working. Each presents a character speaking, thinking, and writing. Both are short; they combine the personal with issues and references of general concern. Each moves from the story of a life (travels in the east of England) to the story of a mental or intellectual life. They give special importance to the records (and details) of reading and scholarship—books, authors, paintings. They demonstrate that personal history can include a history of one's thinking and learning. Write a similar essay, one that follows the design and order (if not the style) of Sebald. You can, if you choose, draw on the material you are reading and studying in other courses this semester. You could also include images and illustrations. When you are finished, provide a very brief (one page) preface in which you present to a reader what he or she is about to read.

•   •   •   •   •   •   •   •   •   •   •   •

ASSIGNMENT 4

The "I" of the Personal Essay
[Rodriguez, Said, Sebald]

The assignments in this sequence have been designed to prompt autobiographical writing. They have been invitations for you to tell your story and to think about the ways stories represent a person and a life. They have also, of course, been exercises in imitation, in writing like Rodriguez, Said, and Sebald, in casting your story in their terms. These exercises highlight the ways in which your story is never just your own but also written through our culture's sense of what it means to be a person, to live, grow, change, learn, experience. No writer simply gets to invent childhood. Childhood, like adulthood, is a category already determined by hundreds of thousands of representations of life—in books, in songs, on TV, in paintings, in the stories we tell ourselves about ourselves. As you have written these three personal narratives, you have, of course, been telling the truth, just as you have also, of course, been creating a character, setting scenes, providing certain representations that provide a version of (but that don't begin to sum up) your life.

Read back over the essays you have written (and perhaps revised). As you read, look for examples of where you feel you were doing your best work, where you are proud of the writing and interested in what it allows you to see or to think (where the "investigations" seem most worthwhile).

And think about what is *not* contained in these essays. What experiences are missing? what point of view? what ways of speaking or thinking or writing? If you were to go back to assemble these pieces into a longer essay, what would you keep and what would you add or change? What are the problems facing a writer, like you, trying to write a life, to take experience and represent it in sentences?

With these questions in mind, reread the essays you have written and write a preface, a short piece introducing a reader to what you have written (to your work—and perhaps work you may do on these essays in the future).

· · · · · · · · · · · ·

ALTERNATIVE ASSIGNMENT

Plans of Life [Appiah]

Plans of life. Social choices. Career choices. "We wish to ace our gross anatomy exam, but don't wish to study for it on this sunny afternoon." Sound familiar?

Although Appiah's essay, "The Ethics of Individuality," was written by a philosopher for an adult and academic audience, there is much in it that draws immediately upon the concerns of college students (and their parents) and much that echoes conversations with which you most certainly are familiar. What do you owe your family? What do you owe yourself? What do you owe your race or your gender or your class position or your region or your religious group or your sport or your fraternity or sorority and so on? In Appiah's terms, what "scripts" are offered to you in your project of "self-making"?

For this assignment, write an essay in which you think back and forth between the urgings and the advice—the ways of thinking about plans of life—that are a part of your world, a part of the common thinking for you and your generation (or for people like you) and the concerns and the thought in Appiah's "The Ethics of Individuality." To what uses might this essay be put? What does it have to offer? What, from your point of view, does it miss or just not understand?

· · · · · · · · · · · ·

ALTERNATIVE ASSIGNMENT

Possible Narratives [Appiah]

At one point, Appiah says:

> So we should acknowledge how much our personal histories, the stories we tell of where we have been and where we are going, are constructed, like novels and movies, short stories and folktales, within narrative conventions. Indeed, one of the things that popular narratives (whether filmed or televised, spoken or written) do for us is to provide models for telling our lives. At the same time, part of the function of our collective identities—of the whole repertory of them that a society makes available to its members—is to structure possible narratives of the individual self. (p. 73)

Write an essay in which you present in some detail one or (at most) two of the stories you tell yourself about where you have been and where you are going. And think about these in relation to the models that you are given by our contemporary culture, whether filmed or televised, spoken or written, to use Appiah's language, models drawn from the "whole repertory . . . a society makes available to its members" in order to "structure possible narratives of the individual self." How do you choose? What makes a script possible or powerful? And how, in Appiah's terms, do you understand the ethics of all this?

· · · · · · · · · · ·

ALTERNATIVE ASSIGNMENT

A Moment of Hesitation [Rich]

> I have hesitated to do what I am going to do now, which is to use myself as an illustration. For one thing, it's a lot easier and less dangerous to talk about other[s]. (p. 524)

> Until we can understand the assumptions in which we are drenched we cannot know ourselves. (p. 522)
>
> — ADRIENNE RICH
> *When We Dead Awaken: Writing as Re-Vision*

Write an essay in which you, like Rich (and perhaps with similar hesitation), use your experience as an illustration, as a way of investigating not just your situation but the situations of people like you. Tell a story from your recent past and use it to talk about the ways you might be said to have been shaped or named or positioned by an established and powerful culture. You could imagine that this assignment is a way for you to use (and put to the test) some of Rich's key terms, words like "re-vision," "re-naming," "structure," and "patriarchy."

•　•　•　•　•　•　•　•　•　•　•　•

ALTERNATIVE ASSIGNMENT

Old Habits [Wideman]

Wideman frequently interrupts the narrative in "Our Time" to talk about the problems he is having as a writer. He says, for example, "The hardest habit to break, since it was the habit of a lifetime, would be listening to myself listen to him. That habit would destroy any chance of seeing my brother on his terms; and seeing him in his terms, learning his terms, seemed the whole point of learning his story" (p. 696).

Wideman gives you the sense of a writer who is aware from the inside, while writing, of the problems inherent in the personal narrative. This genre always shades and deflects; it is always partial and biased; in its very attempts to be complete, to understand totally, it reduces its subject in ways that are unacceptable. And so you can see Wideman's efforts to overcome these problems — he writes in Robby's voice; he starts his story three different times, first with Garth, later with the neighborhood, hoping that a variety of perspectives will overcome the limits inherent in each; he stops and speaks to us not as the storyteller but as the writer, thinking about what he is doing and not doing.

Let Wideman's essay provide a kind of writing lesson. It highlights problems; it suggests alternatives. Using Wideman, then, as your writing teacher, write a family history of your own. Yours will most likely be shorter than Wideman's, but let its writing be the occasion for you also to work on a personal narrative as a writing problem, an interesting problem that forces a writer to think about the limits of representation and point of view (about who gets to speak and in whose terms, about who sums things up and what is left out in this accounting).

•   •   •   •   •   •   •   •   •   •   •   •

Personal Experience as Intellectual Experience (II) [Tompkins]

Jane Tompkins's essay "'Indians'" tells the story of a research project, one undertaken as a professor prepares to teach a course, but with reference to its own prehistory, way back to the author's childhood in New York City. Tompkins provides an example of how personal experience is not simply action in the world but also (and often) intellectual experience, a narrative defined by books read, courses taken, changes of mind, new understandings.

Using Tompkins's essay as a model, write a personal essay that tells a similar story, one drawing on your own experiences. You could tell the story of a research project, a paper (most likely a term paper) you prepared for school. This does not have to be a pious or dutiful account. Tompkins, after all, is writing *against* what she takes to be the predictable or expected account of research as the disinterested pursuit of truth—in which a student would go to the library to "find" the truth about the Indians and the settlers. And she writes in a style that is not solemnly academic. Like Tompkins, you can tell what you take to be the untold story of term-paper research, you can reflect on the problem of such research as a story of learning. Or you could tell the story of any important experience you have had as a student or, out of school, as a person who observes, reads, and thinks. Your goal should be to think of your story *as* a story, with characters and scenes (and, perhaps, dialogue), with action, suspense, and surprises.

•   •   •   •   •   •   •   •   •   •   •

The Matrix [Griffin]

At several points in her essay "Our Secret," Susan Griffin argues that we—all of us—are part of a complex web of connections. We live in history and history is determining. At one point she says:

> Who are we? The question is not simple. What we call the self is
> part of a larger matrix of relationship and society. Had we been

> born to a different family, in a different time, to a different world,
> we would not be the same. All the lives that surround us are
> in us. (p. 335)

At another point she asks, "Is there any one of us who can count ourselves outside the circle circumscribed by our common past?" She speaks of a "field"

> like a field of gravity that is created by the movements of many
> bodies. Each life is influenced and it in turn becomes an influ-
> ence. Whatever is a cause is also an effect. Childhood experience
> is just one element in the determining field. (p. 304)

One way of thinking about this concept of the self (and of interrelatedness), at least under Griffin's guidance, is to work on the connections that she implies and asserts. As you reread the selection, look for powerful and surprising juxtapositions, fragments that stand together in interesting and suggestive ways. Think about the arguments represented by the blank spaces on the page or the jumps from section to section. (And look for Griffin's written statements about relatedness.) Look for connections that seem important to the text (and to you) and to be representative of Griffin's thinking (and useful to yours).

Write an essay in which you use these examples to think through the ways Griffin answers the question she raises: Who are we?

• • • • • • • • • • •

A L T E R N A T I V E   A S S I G N M E N T

La conciencia de la mestiza/Toward a New Consciousness [Anzaldúa]

We've included two chapters from Gloria Anzaldúa's *Borderlands/La frontera*. The style of these chapters is unconventional, experimental.

As you reread Anzaldúa, think about her chapters as forming an argument. How does the argument develop? To whom is it directed? What are its key terms and examples? What are the conclusions? To what degree is the style of these chapters part of the argument (or a subtext or a counterpoint)? Write an essay in which you summarize Anzaldúa's argument in these two chapters. Place it in the context of at least one of the texts you have already read in this sequence.

• • • • • • • • • • •

ALTERNATIVE ASSIGNMENT

The Voice of the Unwritten Self [Jacobs]

In the preface to her edition of *Incidents in the Life of a Slave Girl*, Jean Fagin Yellin says the following about Jacobs's narrative:

> Contrasting literary styles express the contradictory thrusts of the story. Presenting herself as a heroic slave mother, Jacobs's narrator includes clear detail, uses straightforward language, and when addressing the reader directly, utilizes standard abolitionist rhetoric to lament the inadequacy of her descriptions and to urge her audience to involve themselves in antislavery efforts. But she treats her sexual experiences obliquely, and when addressing the reader concerning her sexual behavior, pleads for forgiveness in the overwrought style of popular fiction. These melodramatic confessions are, however, subsumed within the text. What finally dominates is a new voice. It is the voice of a woman who, although she cannot discuss her sexual past without expressing deep conflict, nevertheless addresses this painful personal subject in order to politicize it, to insist that the forbidden topic of the sexual abuse of slave women be included in public discussions of the slavery question. By creating a narrator who presents her private sexual history as a subject of public political concern, Jacobs moves her book out of the world of conventional nineteenth-century polite discourse. In and through her creation of Linda Brent, who yokes her success story as a heroic slave mother to her confession as a woman who mourns that she is not a storybook heroine, Jacobs articulates her struggle to assert her womanhood and projects a new kind of female hero.

Yellin's account of the "voice" in Jacobs's text gives us a way to foreground the difference between life and narrative, a person (Harriet Jacobs) and a person rendered on the page ("Linda Brent," the "I" of the narrative), between the experience of slavery and the conventional ways of telling the story of slavery, between experience and the ways in which experience is shaped by a writer, readers, and a culture. It is interesting, in this sense, to read Yellin's account of "Incidents" along with Houston Baker's more general account of the "voice of the Southern slave" (quoted on p. 352). Baker, you may recall, said: "The voice of the unwritten self, once it is subjected to the linguistic codes, literary conventions, and audience expectations of a literate population, is perhaps never again the authentic voice of black American slavery. It is, rather, the voice of a self transformed by an autobiographical act into a sharer in the general public discourse about slavery."

Reread "Incidents in the Life of a Slave Girl," with Yellin's argument and Baker's argument in mind. In the broadest terms, here are the positions they take: Yellin sees "Incidents" as a heroic act of self-assertion. Baker is concerned that the reality of the slave's life becomes lost when it is translated into a conventional romantic narrative. Write an essay in which you provide your account of "Incidents in the Life of a Slave Girl" as an act of self-definition. You might, if it is helpful, write an essay in three parts (or at least three parts), numbered 1, 2, and 3. In the first you might think along with Yellin and in the second you might think along with Baker. In the third, you should take a position of your own. Who is most useful here?

SEQUENCE FOUR

Experts and Expertise

Adrienne Rich

Clifford Geertz

John Edgar Wideman

Walker Percy

ALTERNATIVES:

Kwame Anthony Appiah

Cornelius Eady

Michael McKeon

Linda Nochlin

W. G. Sebald

THE FIRST THREE ASSIGNMENTS in this sequence give you the chance to think about familiar settings or experiences through the work of writers who have had a significant effect on contemporary thought: Adrienne Rich, Clifford Geertz, John Edgar Wideman, and Walker Percy.

In "When We Dead Awaken: Writing as Re-Vision," Adrienne Rich examines the history and possibility of women's writing. Clifford Geertz, in "Deep Play: Notes on the Balinese Cockfight," provides an extended account and interpretation of the cockfight as a feature of Balinese culture. And John Edgar Wideman, in "Our Time," uses a family story to investigate the conditions of life in a black, urban neighborhood.

In each case, you will be given the opportunity to work alongside these thinkers as an apprentice, carrying out work they have begun. The final assignment in the sequence will ask you to look back on what you have done, to take stock, and, with Walker Percy's account of the oppressive nature of expertise in mind, to draw some conclusions about the potential and consequences of this kind of intellectual apprenticeship. There are five alternative assignments following the sequence. Any of these could be used in place of the assignments in the sequence.

. . . .

A S S I G N M E N T **1**

Looking Back [Rich]

> Re-vision—the act of looking back, of seeing with fresh eyes, of entering an old text from a new critical direction—is for women more than a chapter in cultural history: it is an act of survival. Until we can understand the assumptions in which we are drenched we cannot know ourselves. (p. 522)
>
> I have hesitated to do what I am going to do now, which is to use myself as an illustration. For one thing, it's a lot easier and less dangerous to talk about other[s]. (p. 540)
>
> — ADRIENNE RICH
> *When We Dead Awaken: Writing as Re-Vision*

In "When We Dead Awaken," Rich is writing not to tell her story but to tell a collective story, the story of women or women writers, a story in which she figures only as a representative example. In fact, the focus on individual experience might be said to run against the argument she has to make about the shaping forces of culture and history, in whose context knowing oneself means knowing the assumptions in which one is "drenched."

Yet Rich tells her story—offering poems, anecdotes, details from her life. Write an essay in which you too (and perhaps with similar hesitation) use your experience as an illustration, as a way of investigating not just your situation but the situation of people like you. (Think about what materials you might have to offer in place of her poems.) Tell a story of your own and use it to talk about the ways you might be said to have been shaped or named or positioned by an established and powerful culture. You should imagine that this assignment is a way for you to use (and put to the test) some of Rich's key terms, words like "re-vision," "renaming," "structure," and "patriarchy."

•   •   •   •   •   •   •   •   •   •   •   •   •

A S S I G N M E N T   **2**

Seeing Your World through
Geertz's Eyes [Geertz]

> The culture of a people is an ensemble of texts, themselves
> ensembles, which the anthropologist strains to read over the
> shoulders of those to whom they properly belong. (p. 286)
> — CLIFFORD GEERTZ
> *Deep Play: Notes on the Balinese Cockfight*

Geertz talks about "reading" a culture while peering over the shoulders
of those to whom it properly belongs. In "Deep Play," he reads the cockfight over the shoulders of the Balinese. But the cockfight is not a single
event to be described in isolation. It is itself a "text," one that must be understood in context. Or, as Geertz says, the cockfight is a "Balinese reading
of Balinese experience; a story they tell themselves about themselves."

The job of the anthropologist, Geertz says, is "formulating sociological
principles, not . . . promoting or appreciating cockfights." And the question for the anthropologist is this: "What does one learn about such principles from examining culture as an assemblage of texts?" Societies, he says,
"like lives, contain their own interpretations. One has only to learn how to
gain access to them."

Anthropologists are experts at gaining access to cultures and at performing this kind of complex reading. One of the interesting things about being a
student is that you get to (or you have to) act like an expert even though,
properly speaking, you are not. Write an essay in which you prepare a
Geertzian reading of some part of our culture you know well (sorority rush,
window shopping in a shopping mall, slam dancing, studying in the library,
decorating a dorm room, tailgate parties at the football game, whatever).
Ideally, you should go out and observe the behavior you are studying, looking at the players and taking notes with your project in mind. You should
imagine that you are working in Geertz's spirit, imitating his method and
style and carrying out work that he has begun.

•   •   •   •   •   •   •   •   •   •   •   •

ASSIGNMENT 3

Wideman as a Case in Point
[Wideman]

> The hardest habit to break, since it was the habit of a lifetime, would be listening to myself listen to him. That habit would destroy any chance of seeing my brother on his terms; and seeing him in his terms, learning his terms, seemed the whole point of learning his story. However numerous and comforting the similarities, we were different. The world had seized on the difference, allowed me room to thrive, while he'd been forced into a cage. (p. 696)
>
> — JOHN EDGAR WIDEMAN
> *Our Time*

At several points in this selection, Wideman discusses his position as a writer, researching and telling Robby's story, and he describes the problems he faces in writing this piece (and in reading the text of his brother's life). You could read this excerpt, in other words, as an essay on reading and writing.

Why do you think Wideman brings himself and these problems into the text? Why not keep quiet and hope no one notices? Choose three or four passages where Wideman refers directly or indirectly to the work he is doing as he writes this piece, and write an essay describing this work and why you think Wideman refers to it as he does. If he confronts problems, what are they and how does he go about solving them? If Wideman is an expert, how might you describe his expertise? And what might his example say to you as you think about your work as a student? as a writer?

•   •   •   •   •   •   •   •   •   •   •   •

ASSIGNMENT 4

On Experts and Expertise
[Rich, Geertz, Wideman, Percy]

> The whole horizon of being is staked out by "them," the experts. The highest satisfaction of the sightseer (not merely the tourist but any layman seer of sights) is that his sight should be certified

as genuine. The worst of this impoverishment is that there is no sense of impoverishment. (p. 487)

I refer to the general situation in which sovereignty is surrendered to a class of privileged knowers, whether these be theorists or artists. A reader may surrender sovereignty over that which has been written about, just as a consumer may surrender sovereignty over a thing which has been theorized about. The consumer is content to receive an experience just as it has been presented to him by theorists and planners. The reader may also be content to judge life by whether it has or has not been formulated by those who know and write about life. (p. 487)

— WALKER PERCY
The Loss of the Creature

In the last three assignments you were asked to try on other writers' ways of seeing the world. You looked at what you had read or done, and at scenes from your own life, casting your experience in the terms of others.

Percy, in "The Loss of the Creature," offers what might be taken as a critique of such activity. "A reader," he says, "may surrender sovereignty over that which has been written about, just as a consumer may surrender sovereignty over a thing which has been theorized about." Rich, Geertz, and Wideman have all been presented to you as, in a sense, "privileged knowers." You have been asked to model your own work on their examples.

It seems safe to say that, at least so far as Percy is concerned, surrendering sovereignty is not a good thing to do. If Percy were to read over your work in these assignments, how do you think he would describe what you have done? If he were to take your work as an example in his essay, where might he place it? And how would his reading of your work fit with your sense of what you have done? Would Percy's assessment be accurate, or is there something he would be missing, something he would fail to see?

Write an essay in which you describe and comment on your work in this sequence, looking at it both from Percy's point of view and from your own, but viewing that work as an example of an educational practice, a way of reading (and writing) that may or may not have benefits for the reader.

Note: You will need to review carefully those earlier papers and mark sections that you feel might serve as interesting examples in your discussion. You want to base your conclusions on the best evidence you can. When you begin writing, it might be useful to refer to the writer of those earlier papers as a "he" or a "she" who played certain roles and performed his or her work in certain characteristic ways. You can save the first person, the "I," for the person who is writing this assignment and looking back on those texts.

. . . .

A Parallel Project [Appiah]

In the preface to *The Ethics of Identity*, Appiah says that his book is offered "more in the spirit of exploration than of conclusion." (See the first and second "Questions for a Second Reading" following Appiah's selection.) The style and method of "The Ethics of Individuality" provide an enactment of writing in such a spirit. For this assignment, we'd like you to carry out such a project, with Appiah's text as your guide and model. That is, you should begin by talking about Kwame Anthony Appiah and passages from "The Ethics of Individuality," just as Appiah begins by talking about John Stuart Mill and key passages from Mill's work—passages, that is, that are important to the writer. You should turn, then, to some example of an individual life from film or literature or television, just as Appiah turns to the example of Mr. Stevens, the butler in Kazuo Ishiguro's novel, *The Remains of the Day*. You should use subheadings to organize or punctuate your essay; you needn't use as many as Appiah, nor do you need to write an essay quite as long, but you should feel free to use the same terms if and when they can be strategically helpful to you: "Plans of Life," "Invention and Authenticity," "Ethics in Identity." In other words, you are conducting a parallel project, one written from your perspective. You are writing from a similar concern to understand individuality and, to put it more loosely than you need to, what the individual owes the self and others.

. . . .

Writing (and Re-Writing) History [Eady]

This assignment follows from the last of the "Questions for a Second Reading" after "Brutal Imagination." You may wish to work on that question as preparation for this assignment.

> *Brutal Imagination* writes (or rewrites) history. It began, in a sense, as a research project. It is not completely a work of the imagination. There is a Susan Smith. Her children were drowned in a car in a lake. There was an investigation in Union, South

Carolina. There was also a Charles Stuart. The cycle of poems is a way of bringing home the news; in these cases, news from the recent past. And, in fact, both the Smith and the Stuart cases were widely publicized and occupied the nation's attention for an extended time.

As a research project, review some of the articles on the Susan Smith case that were published in major newspapers and magazines. It would be useful to include on your list of possibilities those magazines and newspapers that serve an African American audience—not only *Time* or *Newsweek* but also *Ebony* or *Jet*; not only the *New York Times* or the *Atlanta Constitution* but also the *Chicago Defender* or the *Pittsburgh Courier*. (Note: You can also find the case represented at "crime" Web sites, like *thesmokinggun.com* and *crimelibrary.com*.) All of these provide a *representation* of what happened, one version of who, what, when, where, and why.

With a particular representation of the case as a point of reference, reread "Brutal Imagination," and write an essay on Eady's rewriting of (or intervention in) the popular accounts (the popular history) of Susan Smith. You will need to work closely with your sources. And because you are writing about writing (about two written accounts of the case), you will need to include a substantial block quotation. (Your handbook or your instructor can show you how to work with a block quotation and how to include lines of poetry in a work of prose.)

Note: You can write in a speculative or tentative manner; this is one way of establishing yourself as a careful, thoughtful, and attentive reader. Ideally, you will have the opportunity to come back to this assignment for revision.

· · · · · · · · · · · ·

ALTERNATIVE ASSIGNMENT

Subdividing Interior Spaces [McKeon]

Near the end of the essay McKeon says:

> As the emergence of modern attitudes toward the public and the private is an incremental rather than a rapid historical process, so its contributing elements . . . evince a comparable pattern of change. The most comprehensive abstraction of such patterns that I have used in this study is that of the movement from relations of distinction to relations of separation, and I have stressed the likelihood that in a period of change such as

this one, evidence of what can be abstracted as "before" and "after" will be overlapping and coextensive. (p. 437)

Let's suppose that the organization of public and private space today is different from, but also overlapping and coextensive with, the history McKeon presents.

For this assignment, take up McKeon's project by considering contemporary examples of the "subdivision" of interior spaces. You should work with sites you know well. Most likely you will need to draw your own floor plans. You can certainly find representations in art and advertising. Part of the project will be to work between image and text. As a point of reference, you should present McKeon's basic argument about historical change, about class or social hierarchy, and about relations of distinction and separation. Your primary goal, however, is to extend the discussion to the present, to offer your account of public and private space in the sites of modernity (or postmodernity) that interest you.

•   •   •   •   •   •   •   •   •   •   •

ALTERNATIVE ASSIGNMENT

Practice and Presentation [Nochlin]

Central to Nochlin's essay "Renoir's *Great Bathers*" is the distinction between a *practice* and a *representation*—or, as the subtitle says, between "Bathing as Practice" and "Bathing as Representation." To prepare for this assignment, you should reread the essay to see how Nochlin uses the terms *practice* and *representation* to organize her research project. What is she doing, in other words, when she turns to the history of swimming and swimming pools, and to the "discourses of swimming and bathing" in Paris in the second half of the nineteenth century? What does this allow her to think, to understand, or to say about the paintings?

Once you have a sense of method, gather materials you might use to conduct a similar project—one that considers a set of representations (images and/or texts that matter to you) in relation to the practices to which they allude. Think of your essay as an homage, as carrying out a Nochlin-like project. It would be appropriate to allude to Nochlin's work (and her conclusions) at some point in your essay.

• • • • • • • • • • • •

ALTERNATIVE ASSIGNMENT

A Mental Ramble [Sebald]

Let's think for a moment of the two chapters from *The Rings of Saturn* as essays. Each has a distinct way of working. Each presents a character speaking, thinking, and writing. Both are short; they combine the personal with issues and references of general concern. Each moves from the story of a life (travels in the east of England) to the story of a mental or intellectual life. They give special importance to the records (and details) of reading and scholarship—books, authors, paintings. They demonstrate that personal history can include a history of one's thinking and learning. Write a similar essay, one that follows the design and order (if not the style) of Sebald. You can, if you choose, draw on the material you are reading and studying in other courses this semester. You could include images and illustrations. When you are finished, provide a very brief (one page) preface in which you present to a reader what he or she is about to read.

○—○—○—○—○—○—○—○—○—○—○—○—○—○—○

Reading the Lives of Others

Clifford Geertz

Mary Louise Pratt

Cornelius Eady

John Edgar Wideman

WRITING REMAINS one of the most powerful tools we have for preserving and understanding the past and the present. This is simple to say. What good writing is, and what writing is good for—these questions are constantly debated by writers and academics. There are big philosophical questions here: What is the borderline between fact and fiction, between what is there and what is the product of imagination or point of view? There are practical questions: How do you work on a text? How do you get better at this? And both the philosophical questions and the practical questions have bearing on the work a student performs in the undergraduate curriculum, where students are regularly called upon to read and write textual accounts of human experience. This sequence is designed to give you a chance to do this work firsthand.

The first assignment asks you to prepare a first draft of an ethnography, written in response to the example of Clifford Geertz (an anthropologist). The next assignment takes an additional theoretical step, looking (through Mary Louise Pratt's essay "Arts of the Contact Zone") at problems of representation as they are rooted more generally in culture, history, and ideology (and not just in the work of an individual writer and his or her text). The third assignment asks you to work closely with representation to note how poet Cornelius Eady presents the story of Susan Smith and to situate yourself in relation to Eady's work. The fourth assignment asks you to read

"Our Time," by John Edgar Wideman. Wideman, in professional terms, is neither an anthropologist nor a historian. He is, rather, a fiction writer who has turned his hand to nonfiction, to write about African American culture and his family. You are then asked to consider the work of all the authors in this sequence, to prepare a guide for writers, and, in the final assignment, you are asked to revise your earlier essay.

•   •   •   •   •   •   •   •   •   •   •   •

ASSIGNMENT 1

Close Reading [Geertz]

> As in more familiar exercises in close reading, one can start any-where in a culture's repertoire of forms and end up anywhere else. One can stay, as I have here, within a single, more or less bounded form and circle steadily within it. One can move be-tween forms in search of broader unities or informing contrasts. One can even compare forms from different cultures to define their character in reciprocal relief. But whatever the level at which one operates, and however intricately, the guiding princi-ple is the same: societies, like lives, contain their own interpreta-tions. One has only to learn how to gain access to them. (p. 286)
>
> — CLIFFORD GEERTZ
> *Deep Play: Notes on the Balinese Cockfight*

Geertz says that "the culture of a people is an ensemble of texts, them-selves ensembles, which the anthropologist strains to read over the shoul-ders of those to whom they properly belong." Anthropologists are expert at "reading" in this way; they are trained to do it.

One of the interesting things about being a student is that you get to (or you have to) act like an expert even though you are not officially creden-tialed. Write an essay in which you prepare a Geertzian reading of the activities of some subgroup or some part of our culture you know well. Ideally, you should go out and observe the behavior you are studying ("straining to read over the shoulders" of those to whom this "text" prop-erly belongs), examining it and taking notes with your project in mind. You should imagine that you are working in Geertz's spirit, imitating his method and style and carrying out work that he has begun. (It might be wise, however, to focus more locally than he does. He writes about a na-tional culture—the Balinese cockfight as a key to Bali. You should proba-bly not set out to write about "America" but about something local. And you should write about some group of which you are not already a part, a group which you can imagine as foreign, different, other.)

. . . .

ASSIGNMENT **2**

Reading Others [Pratt]

[handwritten annotations: trading between cultures - lower group using ideas of higher group to reinvent | coordination accusation | King & Book]

Pratt, in "Arts of the Contact Zone," makes the case for the difficulties of reading, as well as writing, the "other":

[handwritten annotations in margin: way non-dominant group describes themselves to dom. group | formal vs informal language]

> Autoethnography, transculturation, critique, collaboration, bilingualism, mediation, parody, denunciation, imaginary dialogue, vernacular expression— these are some of the literate arts of the contact zone. Miscomprehension, incomprehension, dead letters, unread masterpieces, absolute heterogeneity of meaning —these are some of the perils of writing in the contact zone. They all live among us today in the transnationalized metropolis of the United States and are becoming more widely visible, more pressing, and, like Guaman Poma's text, more decipherable to those who once would have ignored them in defense of a stable, centered sense of knowledge and reality. (pp. 506–7)

[handwritten annotation: Salad— all different]

> We are looking for the pedagogical arts of the contact zone. These will include, we are sure, exercises in storytelling and in identifying with the ideas, interests, histories, and attitudes of others; experiments in transculturation, and collaborative work and in the arts of critique, parody, and comparison (including unseemly comparisons between elite and vernacular cultural forms); the redemption of the oral; ways for people to engage with suppressed aspects of history (including their own histories), ways to move *into and out of* rhetorics of authenticity; ground rules for communication across lines of difference and hierarchy that go beyond politeness but maintain mutual respect; a systematic approach to the all-important concept of *cultural mediation.* (p. 511)

One way of working with Pratt's essay, of extending its project, would be to conduct your own local inventory of writing from the contact zone. You might do this on your own or in teams, with others from your class. Here are two ways you might organize your search:

1. You could look for historical documents. A local historical society might have documents written by Native Americans ("Indians") to the white settlers. There may be documents written by slaves to masters or to northern whites. There may be documents written by women to men (written by the suffragettes, for example) negotiating public positions or rights. There may be documents from any of a number of racial or ethnic groups—Hispanic, Jewish, Irish, Italian,

Polish, Swedish —trying to explain their positions to the mainstream culture. There may, perhaps at union halls, be documents written by workers to owners. Your own sense of the heritage of your area should direct your search.

2. Or you could look at contemporary documents in the print that is around you, texts that you might otherwise overlook. Pratt refers to one of the characteristic genres of the Hispanic community, the *"testimonio."* You could look for songs, testimonies, manifestos, statements by groups on campus, stories, autobiographies, interviews, letters to the editor, Web pages. You could look at the writing of any marginalized group, particularly writing intended, at least in part, to represent the experience of outsiders to the dominant culture (or to be in dialogue with that culture or to respond to that culture). These documents, if we follow Pratt's example, would include the work of young children or students, including college students.

Once you have completed your inventory, choose a document you would like to work with and present it carefully and in detail (perhaps in even greater detail than Pratt's presentation of the *New Chronicle*). You might imagine that you are presenting this to someone who would not have seen it and would not know how to read it, at least not as an example of the literate arts of the contact zone.

•   •   •   •   •   •   •   •   •   •   •

ASSIGNMENT 3

Writing (and Re-Writing) History [Eady]

This assignment follows the last of the "Questions for a Second Reading" after "Brutal Imagination." You may wish to turn to it as preparation for this work.

> *Brutal Imagination* writes (or rewrites) history. It began, in a sense, as a research project. It is not completely a work of the imagination. There is a Susan Smith. Her children were drowned in a car in a lake. There was an investigation in Union, South Carolina. There was also a Charles Stuart. The cycle of poems is a way of bringing home the news; in these cases, news from the recent past. And, in fact, both the Smith and the Stuart cases were widely publicized and occupied the nation's attention for an extended time.
>
> As a research project, review some of the articles on the Susan Smith case that were published in major newspapers and maga-

zines. It would be useful to include on your list of possibilities those magazines and newspapers that serve an African American audience—not only *Time* or *Newsweek* but also *Ebony* or *Jet*; not only the *New York Times* or the *Atlanta Constitution* but also the *Chicago Defender* or the *Pittsburgh Courier*. (Note: You can also find the case represented at "crime" websites, such as *thesmokinggun.com* or *crimelibrary.com*.) All of these provide a *representation* of what happened, one version of who, what, when, where, and why.

With a particular representation of the case as a point of reference, reread "Brutal Imagination," and write an essay on Eady's rewriting of (or intervention in) the popular accounts (the popular history) of Susan Smith. You will need to work closely with your sources. And because you are writing about writing (about two written accounts of the case), you will need to include a substantial block quotation. (Your handbook or your instructor can show you how to work with a block quotation and how to include lines of poetry in a work of prose.)

Note: You can write in a speculative or tentative manner; this is one way of establishing yourself as a careful, thoughtful, and attentive reader. Ideally, you will have the opportunity to come back to this assignment for revision.

• • • • • • • • • • • •

ASSIGNMENT 4

A Writer's Guide
[Wideman, Geertz, Pratt, Eady]

While John Edgar Wideman is not writing history in "Our Time," at least not in the strict sense of the term, he is writing about others and about the past—he is trying to recover, represent, and understand the story of his brother Robby, his family, and their neighborhood. He is trying to recover all those factors that might be said to have led to or produced his brother's present situation.

It is interesting to read "Our Time" alongside "Deep Play," "Arts of the Contact Zone," and "Brutal Imagination." All are concerned with the problems of understanding and representation. As you reread these selections, mark passages you might use to illustrate the styles, methods, and/or concerns of each writer. You should reread the essays as a group, as part of a single project investigating the problems of writing about other people and writing about the past. Each essay could be read as both a reflection on writing and a practical guide for those who follow. What do they say about method? What lessons do they offer? what cautions?

Write an essay in which you present your observations in the form of a "Writer's Guide," something that might be of use to students at your college or university.

· · · · · · · · · · · ·

ASSIGNMENT 5

Revision [Geertz]

Revise the first essay you wrote for this sequence. Your goal in revising this paper should be to take it on to its next step, not necessarily to fix it or clean it up or finish it, but to see how you can open up and add to what you have begun. As you prepare, you should consider the guidelines you wrote in assignment 4.

SEQUENCE SIX

On Difficulty

Michel Foucault

Kwame Anthony Appiah

W. G. Sebald

Linda Nochlin

ALTERNATIVES:

Susan Bordo

John Edgar Wideman

THE ASSIGNMENTS in this sequence invite you to consider the nature of difficult texts and how the problems they pose might be said to belong simultaneously to language, to readers, and to writers. The sequence presents four difficult essays (and two alternatives, should you wish to alter the sequence). The assumption the sequence makes is that they are difficult for all readers, not just students, and that the difficulty is necessary, strategic, not a mistake or evidence of a writer's failure.

. . . .

ASSIGNMENT **1**

Foucault's Fabrication [Foucault]

About three-quarters of the way into "Panopticism," Foucault says,

> Our society is one not of spectacle, but of surveillance; under the surface of images, one invests bodies in depth; behind the great abstraction of exchange, there continues the meticulous, concrete training of useful forces; the circuits of communication are the supports of an accumulation and a centralization of knowledge; the play of signs defines the anchorages of power; it is not that the beautiful totality of the individual is amputated, repressed, altered by our social order, it is rather that the individual is carefully fabricated in it, according to a whole technique of forces and bodies. (p. 228)

This prose is eloquent and insists on its importance to our moment and our society; it is also very hard to read or to paraphrase. Who is doing what to whom? How do we think about the individual being carefully fabricated in the social order?

Take this selection as a problem to solve. What is it about? What are its key arguments, its examples and conclusions? Write an essay that summarizes "Panopticism." Imagine that you are writing for readers who have read the chapter (although they won't have the pages in front of them) and who are at sea as to its argument. You will need to take time to present and discuss examples from the text. Your job is to help your readers figure out what it says. You get the chance to take the lead and be the teacher. In addition, you should feel free to acknowledge that you don't understand certain sections even as you write about them.

So how do you write about something you don't completely understand? Here's a suggestion. When you have completed your summary, read it over and treat it as a draft. Ask questions like these: What have I left out? What was I tempted to ignore or finesse? Go back to those sections of the chapter that you ignored and bring them into your essay. Revise by adding discussions of some of the very sections you don't understand. You can write about what you think Foucault might be saying—you can, that is, be cautious and tentative; you can admit that the text is what it is, hard to read. You don't have to master this text. You do, however, need to see what you can make of it.

• • • • • • • • • • • •

ASSIGNMENT 2

Thinking about the State [Appiah]

When we have taught this essay, "The Ethics of Individuality," our students tended to forget or to ignore or to tune out the final sections: "The Social Scriptorium," "Ethics in Identity," "Individuality and the State," and "The Common Pursuit." It was easier (or more pleasant) to think about the individual; it was harder (or less pleasant) to think about the "State" and "common" pursuits.

If this is the case (even if it is not the case for you), there is reason to reread those sections with particular attention. What is Appiah doing there? What is he getting at? Why are these moves (in this essay) important? Why might this section of the essay be said to be hard to read? For this assignment, write an essay that addresses these questions and that works closely with the final sections of his essay.

• • • • • • • • • • • •

ASSIGNMENT 3

Erudition [Sebald]

The speaker (or writer or narrator) in *The Rings of Saturn* has an interest in the early English writer Thomas Browne, "who had practiced as a doctor in Norwich in the seventeenth century and had left a number of writings that defy all comparison" (p. 616). Of Browne's writing, he says

> In common with other English writers of the seventeenth century, Browne wrote out of the fullness of his erudition, deploying a vast repertoire of quotations and the names of authorities who had gone before, creating complex metaphors and analogies, and constructing labyrinthine sentences that sometimes extend over one or two pages, sentences that resemble processions or a funeral cortège in their sheer ceremonial lavishness. It is true that, because of the immense weight of the impediments he is carrying, Browne's writing can be held back by the force of gravitation, but when he does succeed in rising higher and higher through the circles of his spiralling prose, borne aloft like a glider on warm currents of air, even today the reader is overcome by a

sense of levitation. The greater the distance, the clearer the view: one sees the tiniest details with the utmost clarity. It is as if one were looking through a reversed opera glass and through a microscope at the same time. (p. 622)

This is a description of Browne's style—of what the writing *does* rather than what it says in its paraphrasable content. Write an essay in which you provide an account of Sebald's style. ("Questions for a Second Reading" 1 and 5 following Sebald help to prepare for such an essay.) You can begin in the spirit of his description of Browne's writing, but you will need to turn to examples from the text to describe Sebald's writing. If you work with both chapters, think about how they are different and about how chapter 4 could be said to follow chapter 1.

Note: Although it would make your essay a much more ambitious project, it would be interesting to select a passage from Browne's work—from *Urn Burial* (also called *Hydriotaphia*) or *The Garden of Cyrus*—and to present it in relation to a passage from *The Rings of Saturn*. How are they alike? How are they different? What does a seventeenth-century project look like in the late twentieth century? Is Sebald attempting to write in Browne's style? If so, does he succeed?

•   •   •   •   •   •   •   •   •   •   •

ASSIGNMENT 4

Technical Terms [Nochlin]

In Linda Nochlin's essay "Renoir's *Great Bathers*," there are a number of technical terms—key words and phrases that belong to a critical tradition (to the work of other scholars, that is), words and phrases that carry a lot of weight or have a lot of work to do. They make more than "ordinary" sense. Here is a list. You might add others. Sometimes the terms operate in pairs. In the headnote to this selection, we provide a brief gloss of the two French terms listed here. They have a rich and interesting context.

the desiring male gaze, sexual-scopic
representation and practice
natural and artificial
discourse, historically specific discourse, traditional discourse,
    counterdiscourse
l'Informe
rappel à l'ordre

The library, Internet, and dictionaries, particularly a dictionary of critical terms, can help you with these. But you can also work on them in the context of Nochlin's sentences and paragraphs. As you reread, develop a personal glossary, a set of working definitions for these terms. Write an essay in which you provide an extended account of one set of terms, how they serve Nochlin's project, and how they might be applied to a subject close to you. Your goal should be to bring them into your own sentences as you speak and write.

• • • • • • • • • • • •

ASSIGNMENT **5**

A Theory of Difficulty
[Foucault, Wideman, Bordo]

Now that you have worked with these four texts, you are in a good position to review what you have written about each of them in order to say something more general about difficulty—difficulty in writing, difficulty in reading.

Write an essay in which you present a theory of difficulty, a kind of guide, something that might be useful to students who are regularly asked to confront difficult assignments. You will want to work from your previous essays—pulling out sections, revising, reworking examples for this new essay. Don't let your earlier work go unacknowledged. But, at the same time, feel free to move out from these readings to other materials, examples, or situations.

• • • • • • • • • • •

ALTERNATIVE ASSIGNMENT

The Pleasures of the Text [Bordo]

Susan Bordo writes successfully for a broad audience, for readers outside of the academy as well as for those within. It would be wrong to say that her prose is simple or easy, but we think all readers would agree that it is inviting or available in ways that the other selections in the set of readings are not. We've put Bordo into the sequence as a counterexample.

While the prose is not heavygoing, the chapter "Beauty (Re)discovers the Male Body" is long. The writing operates under a set of expectations that does not value efficiency. The writing says, "It is better to take time with this, better to take time rather than hurry, rather than rushing to say what must be said, rather than pushing to be done. Slow down, relax, take your time. This can be fun." While there is attention to a "thesis," the organizing principle of this essay is such that the real work and the real pleasure lie elsewhere. Work and pleasure. As you reread, pay particular attention to how Bordo controls the pace and direction of the essay, where she prolongs the discussion and where and when she shifts direction. Think of this as a way for her (and you) to get work done. And think about it as a way of organizing the pleasure of the text. This is a long essay divided into subsections. The subsections mark stages in the presentation. The subsections allow you to think about form in relation to units larger than the paragraph but smaller than the essay. As you reread, pay attention to these sections. How are they organized internally? How are they arranged? How do they determine the pace or rhythm of your reading, the tonality or phrasing of the text? Which is the slowest, for example? Which is the loudest? And why? And where are they placed? What do they do to the argument?

Take time to reread and to think these questions through. It has become common for scholars and teachers to think about the pleasure, even the "erotics" of the text. This is not, to be sure, the usual language of the composition classroom. Write an essay in which you describe the pleasures (and, if you choose, the problems) of Bordo's writing. Describe how it is organized, and how it organizes your time and attention. Describe how it works (or doesn't) for you as a reader, how it works (or doesn't) for her as a writer and thinker. You can, to be sure, make reference to other things you are reading in (or out of) this sequence or to the writing you are doing (and have done) in school.

. . . .

ALTERNATIVE ASSIGNMENT

A Story of Reading [Wideman]

At several points in "Our Time," Wideman interrupts the narrative to discuss his position as a writer telling Robby's story. He describes the problems he faces in writing this piece (or in reading the text of his brother's life). You could read this selection, in other words, as an essay about reading and writing. It is Wideman's account of his work.

As a narrative, "Our Time" is made up of sections, fragments, different voices. It is left to the reader, in a sense, to put the pieces together and complete the story. There is work for a reader to do, in other words, and one way to account for that work is to call it "practice" or "training." Wideman wants to force a reader's attention by offering a text that makes unusual demands, a text that teaches a reader to read differently. If you think of your experience with the text, of how you negotiated its terrain, what is the story of reading you might tell? In what way do your difficulties parallel Wideman's—at least those he tells us about when he stops to talk about the problems he faces as a writer?

Write an essay in which you tell the story of what it was like to read "Our Time" and compare your experience working with this text with Wideman's account of his own.

A story of reading—this is not a usual school exercise. Usually you are asked what texts mean, not what it was like to read them. As you prepare for this assignment, think back as closely as you can to your experience the first time through. And you will want to reread, looking for how and where Wideman seems to be deliberately working on his reader, defying expectation and directing response. You want to tell a story that is rich in detail, precise in accounting for moments in the text. You want to bring forward the features that can make your story a good story to read—suspense, action, context, drama. Since this is your story, you are one of the characters. You will want to refer to yourself as you were at the moment of reading while also reserving a space for you to speak from your present position, as a person thinking about what it was like to read the text, and as a person thinking about Wideman and about reading. You are telling a story, but you will need to break the narrative (as Wideman breaks his) to account in more general terms for the demands Wideman makes on readers. What habits does he assume a reader will bring to this text? How and why does he want to break them?

SEQUENCE SEVEN

Reading Culture

John Berger

Susan Bordo

Linda Nochlin

Michel Foucault

ALTERNATIVE:

Michael McKeon

IN THIS SEQUENCE, you will be reading and writing about culture. Not Culture, something you get if you go to the museum or a concert on Sunday, but culture—the images, words, and sounds that pervade our lives and organize and represent our common experience. This sequence invites your reflection on the ways culture "works" in and through the lives of individual consumers.

The difficulty of this sequence lies in the way it asks you to imagine that you are not a sovereign individual, making your own choices and charting the course of your life. This is conceptually difficult, but it can also be distasteful, since we learn at an early age to put great stock in imagining our own freedom. Most of the readings that follow ask you to imagine that you are the product of your culture; that your ideas, feelings, and actions, your ways of thinking and being, are constructed for you by a large, organized, pervasive force (sometimes called history, sometimes called culture, sometimes called ideology). You don't feel this to be the case, but that is part of the power of culture, or so the argument goes. These forces hide themselves. They lead you to believe that their constructions are naturally, inevitably there, that things are the way they are because that is just "the way things are." The assignments in this sequence ask you to read against your common sense. You will be expected to try on the role of the critic—to see how and where it might be useful to recognize complex motives in ordinary expressions.

The authors in this sequence all write as though, through great effort, they could step outside culture to see and criticize its workings. The assignments in this sequence will ask you both to reflect on this type of criticism and to participate in it. An alternative assignment, on the work of Michael McKeon, provides an extra option.

· · · · · · · · · · · ·

A S S I G N M E N T **1**

Looking at Pictures [Berger]

> Original paintings are silent and still in a sense that information never is. Even a reproduction hung on the wall is not comparable in this respect for in the original the silence and stillness permeate the actual material, the paint, in which one follows the traces of the painter's immediate gestures. This has the effect of closing the distance in time between the painting of the picture and one's own act of looking at it. . . . What we make of that painted moment when it is before our eyes depends upon what we expect of art, and that in turn depends today upon how we have already experienced the meaning of paintings through reproductions. (p. 116)
>
> —JOHN BERGER
> *Ways of Seeing*

While Berger describes original paintings as silent in this passage, it is clear that these paintings begin to speak if one approaches them properly, if one learns to ask "the right questions of the past." Berger demonstrates one route of approach, for example, in his reading of the Hals paintings, where he asks questions about the people and objects and their relationship to the painter and the viewer. What the paintings might be made to say, however, depends upon the viewer's expectations, his or her sense of the questions that seem appropriate or possible. Berger argues that because of the way art is currently displayed, discussed, and reproduced, the viewer expects only to be mystified.

For this assignment, imagine that you are working against the silence and mystification Berger describes. Go to a museum—or, if that is not possible, to a large-format book of reproductions in the library (or, if that is not possible, to the Internet)—and select a painting that seems silent and still, yet invites conversation. Your job is to figure out what sorts of questions to ask, to interrogate the painting, to get it to speak, to engage with the past in some form of dialogue. Write an essay in which you record this process and what you have learned from it. Somewhere in your essay, perhaps at the end, turn back to Berger's chapter to talk about how this process has or hasn't confirmed what you take to be Berger's expectations.

Note: If possible, include with your essay a reproduction of the painting you select. (Check the postcards at the museum gift shop.) In any event, you want to make sure that you describe the painting in sufficient detail for your readers to follow what you say.

· · · · · · · · · · · ·

ASSIGNMENT 2

Berger and After [Berger, Bordo]

In "Beauty (Re)discovers the Male Body," Bordo refers to John Berger and his work in *Ways of Seeing*, although she refers to a different chapter than the one included here. In general, however, both Berger and Bordo are concerned with how we see and read images; both are concerned to correct the ways images are used and read; both trace the ways images serve the interests of money and power; both are written to teach readers how and why they should pay a different kind of attention to the images around them.

For this assignment, use Bordo's work to reconsider Berger's. Write an essay in which you consider the two chapters as examples of an ongoing project. Berger's essay precedes Bordo's by about a quarter of a century. If you look closely at one or two of their examples, and if you look at the larger concerns of their arguments, are they saying the same things? Doing the same work? If so, how? And why is such work still necessary? If not, how do their projects differ? And how might you explain those differences?

· · · · · · · · · · · ·

ASSIGNMENT 3

Reading the Body [Bordo]

Bordo looks back to the history of advertising (the "cultural genealogy of the ads I've been discussing") and works directly with the ads that prompted and served this chapter in her book. These images are a key part of the writing.

Bordo also speaks directly to you and invites you into her project: "So the next time you see a Dockers or a Haggar ad, think of it not only as an advertisement for khakis but also as an advertisement for a certain notion of what it means to be a man." You don't have to be limited to Dockers, Haggar, or khaki, but as you reread the essay and prepare for this writing assignment, keep your eye out for advertisements that come your way, advertisements that seem perfect for thinking along with Bordo (or advertisements that seem like interesting counterexamples). Clip these or copy them so that you can use them, as she does, as material for writing.

Write an essay in which you take up Bordo's invitation. You should assume an audience that has not read Bordo (or not read her work recently), so you will need to take time to present the terms and direction of her argument. Your goal, however, is to extend her project to your moment in time, where advertising may very well have moved on to different images of men and strategies of presentation. Bordo is quite specific about her age and experience, her point of view. You should be equally specific. You, too, should establish your point of view. You are placed at a different moment in time; your experience is different; your exposure to images has prepared you differently. You write from a different subject position. Your job, then, is not simply to reproduce Bordo's project but to extend it, to refine it, to put it to the test.

●　●　●　●　●　●　●　●　●　●　●

ASSIGNMENT **4**

High and Low [Bordo, Nochlin]

Linda Nochlin's "Renoir's *Great Bathers*" is full of sexually charged images of women; Susan Bordo's "Beauty (Re)discovers the Male Body" is full of sexually charged images of men, the latter in the realm of commerce, the former (or at least most of them) in the realm of "art." Both Nochlin and Bordo are interested in how images of the body circulate, in the work to which these images can be put.

Toward the end of her essay, Nochlin says:

> In concluding, I should like to say once more that in studying a major nineteenth-century theme like bathers, serious attention needs to be paid to alternative points of view, to other modes of visual production rather than the high art studied by conventional art history. Advertising, mass media prints, cartoons, and

so on exist not just as undifferentiated, visually indifferent "sources" for high art but, on the contrary, as alternatives, and, often, as adversaries of it. As alternatives, they have very different work to do and from time to time enter into a positive dialectical relationship with the practices of high art, while at other times, into an equally important relationship of fierce rejection or negation with it. (p. 472)

There are two invitations here. One is to find images of the male body in contemporary "high" art—and there are many that are considered important (and many in Nochlin's book, *Bathers, Bodies, Beauty*)—and to write about them in relation to images from advertising. The purpose would be to read these representations in relation to advertising practice with the goal of making a claim, with Nochlin, for either a "positive dialectical relationship" or a "fierce rejection."

The other invitation is to work more closely between the two essays, as an exercise in close reading. If you follow this lead, as you reread each, look for an extended section of each essay, sections that seem to speak back and forth to each other in interesting or provocative ways. What do both have to say about how images are created and perceived? about how they circulate?

Working closely with these sections, and keeping in mind a reader familiar with neither, write an essay that discusses what you find to be the interesting or important differences between the two writers and their work. Of the two, Nochlin and Bordo, who speaks most powerfully to you (or to your generation) about the body and about images of the body and about how these circulate in contemporary culture? Who makes the most sense—or who seems to you to be doing the kind of work that is most useful or necessary?

• • • • • • • • • • • •

ASSIGNMENT 5

On Agency
[Berger, Bordo, Nochlin, Foucault]

[The Panopticon] is an important mechanism, for it automatizes and disindividualizes power. Power has its principle not so much in a person as in a certain concerted distribution of bodies, surfaces, lights, gazes; in an arrangement whose internal mechanisms produce the relation in which individuals are caught up. The ceremonies, the rituals, the marks by which the sovereign's surplus power was manifested are useless. There is a machinery that assures dissymmetry, disequilibrium, difference.

Consequently, it does not matter who exercises power. Any individual, taken almost at random, can operate the machine: in the absence of the director, his family, his friends, his visitors, even his servants. Similarly, it does not matter what motive animates him: the curiosity of the indiscreet, the malice of a child, the thirst for knowledge of a philosopher who wishes to visit this museum of human nature, or the perversity of those who take pleasure in spying and punishing. The more numerous those anonymous and temporary observers are, the greater the risk for the inmate of being surprised and the greater his anxious awareness of being observed. The Panopticon is a marvelous machine which, whatever use one may wish to put it to, produces homogeneous effects of power. (pp. 216–17)

— MICHEL FOUCAULT
Panopticism

Foucault's work has changed our ways of thinking about "who is doing what to whom." Write an essay in which you explain Foucault's understanding of the Panopticon as a mechanism of power. You will need to paraphrase Foucault's argument, translate his terms, and, where appropriate, cite and deploy his terms. Present Foucault's account as you understand it, and be willing to talk about what you don't understand—or don't quite understand.

As part of your essay, and in order to examine his argument and his terms, use Foucault as a way of thinking about the work of Berger, Bordo, and Nochlin. How might Foucault treat the material they select for their examples? (As you write, it would be strategically useful to limit yourself to one example from each.) How does each of the three writers account for *agency* in their descriptions of the workings of power? What do you make of the differences in their accounts of power and knowledge? What do they imply about how one might live in or understand the world? What might they have to do with the ways you, or people like you, live in and understand the world?

• • • • • • • • • • • •

ASSIGNMENT 6

Reading Culture
[Berger, Bordo, Nochlin, Foucault]

Write an essay in which you revise and bring together the essays you have written for this sequence. You can treat them as individual statements, revising each, ordering them, writing an introduction, conclusion, and necessary transitions. Or you can revise more radically and combine what you have into some other form.

Your goal should be to bring the writers into conversation with each other, to use one selection to weigh, evaluate, and understand another. And your goal should be to find a way, yourself, to enter the conversation — to find a space, a voice, a set of examples and concerns. Where and how do these issues touch you and people like you (some group for whom you feel authorized to speak)? Where do you feel a similar urgency? Where and how would you qualify or challenge the position of these other writers? Where and how would you join them?

· · · · · · · · · · · ·

ALTERNATIVE ASSIGNMENT

The Mechanisms of Power
[Foucault, McKeon]

"Panopticism," the selection from Michel Foucault's *Discipline and Punish*, opens with a scene from the seventeenth century, when measures were being taken to separate the sick and the well. He turns, as well, to the treatment of lepers. He says:

> The constant division between the normal and the abnormal, to which every individual is subjected, brings us back to our own time, by applying the binary branding and exile of the leper to quite different objects; the existence of a whole set of techniques and institutions for measuring, supervising, and correcting the abnormal brings into play the disciplinary mechanisms to which the fear of the plague gave rise. All the mechanisms of power which, even today, are disposed around the abnormal individual, to brand him and alter him, are composed of those two forms from which they distantly derive. (pp. 212–13)

And, at the end, he asks two questions:

> Is it surprising that the cellular prison, with its regular chronologies, forced labor, its authorities of surveillance and registration, its experts in normality, who continue and multiply the functions of the judge, should have become the modern instrument of penalty? Is it surprising that prisons resemble factories, schools, barracks, hospitals, which all resemble prisons? (p. 236)

Although McKeon doesn't write about prisons and schools, and he doesn't use words like *normal* and *abnormal*, he does write about how space is organized in service of power and as the expression of an idea about the relations between individuals and between conceptions of public and private life. Foucault writes:

> Power has its principle not so much in a person as in a certain concerted distribution of bodies, surfaces, lights, gazes; in an arrangement whose internal mechanisms produce the relation in which individuals are caught up. (p. 216)

Read "Panopticism" and then as you reread "Subdividing Inside Spaces," think about why McKeon (unlike many scholars of his generation) does not refer to Foucault in his essay. And, although he is certainly concerned with relations of power, he does not use the word *power* and, if he does, he uses it differently. How is his argument different from Foucault's? As you define that difference, where do you stand? Has McKeon lost something important? Has he made an argument that is more convincing or compelling than Foucault's?

SEQUENCE EIGHT

The Uses of Reading

Richard Rodriguez and Richard Hoggart
Susan Bordo and John Berger
Kwame Anthony Appiah
Alice Walker
David Bartholomae and Anthony Petrosky

ALTERNATIVE:

Cornelius Eady

THIS SEQUENCE focuses attention on authors as readers, on the use of sources, and on the art of reading as a writer. It combines technical lessons with lessons on the practice and rhetoric of citation. The first assignment, for example, calls attention to the block quotations in Richard Rodriguez's essay "The Achievement of Desire." These allow him to work the words of another writer, Richard Hoggart, into his text; they also demonstrate the ways he (Rodriguez) locates himself, his ideas, and his experience in relation to a figure who provides a powerful prior example. At some points he takes Hoggart's words as his own; at others he works to define his position against or beyond what Hoggart has to say. The next two assignments ask you to consider the example of scholars drawing on the work of others, Susan Bordo on John Berger and Kwame Anthony Appiah on John Stuart Mill and Kazuo Ishiguro. This is followed by an assignment asking you to look at Alice Walker's essay "In Search of Our Mothers' Gardens." Walker is in a difficult relationship to her sources. The assignments ask you to think again about how writers use the writing that precedes them in order to move forward, to get work done, to define a position for writing and thinking. The final assignment returns attention to attitudes toward reading and writing in contemporary American education, with *Ways of Reading* offered as an example. An assignment on Cornelius Eady provides an alternative to those included in the sequence.

. . . .

ASSIGNMENT **1**

The Scholarship Boy [Rodriguez, Hoggart]

You could look at the relationship between Richard Rodriguez and Richard Hoggart as a case study of the relation of a reader to a writer or a student to a teacher. Look closely at Rodriguez's references to Hoggart's book, *The Uses of Literacy*, and at the way Rodriguez made use of that book to name and describe his own experience as a student. (An extended selection of *The Uses of Literacy* can be found on pages 180–85 in *Resources for Teaching* WAYS OF READING.) What did he find in the book? How did he use it? How does he use it in his own writing?

Write an essay in which you discuss Rodriguez's use of Hoggart's *The Uses of Literacy*. How, for example, would you compare Rodriguez's version of the "scholarship boy" with Hoggart's? (At one point, Rodriguez says that Hoggart's account is "more accurate than fair." What might he have meant by that?) And what kind of reader is the Rodriguez who is writing "The Achievement of Desire" — is he still a "scholarship boy" or is that description no longer appropriate?

Note: You might begin your research with what may seem to be a purely technical matter, examining how Rodriguez handles quotations and works Hoggart's words into paragraphs of his own. On the basis of Rodriguez's use of quoted passages, how would you describe the relationship between Hoggart's words and Rodriguez's? Who has the greater authority? Who is the expert, and under what conditions? What rules might Rodriguez be said to follow or to break? Do you see any change in the course of the essay in how Rodriguez uses block quotations? in how he comments on them?

•   •   •   •   •   •   •   •   •   •   •   •

ASSIGNMENT 2

Sources (I) [Bordo, Berger]

In "Beauty (Re)discovers the Male Body," Bordo refers to John Berger and his work in *Ways of Seeing,* although she refers to a different chapter than the one included here. In general, however, both Berger and Bordo are concerned with how we see and read images; both are concerned to correct the ways images are used and read; both trace the ways images serve the interests of money and power; both are written to teach readers how and why they should pay a different kind of attention to the images around them.

For this assignment, use Bordo's work to reconsider Berger's. As you reread each essay, mark passages that you might be able to put into interesting conversation with each other. And, when you have completed this work, write an essay in which you consider the two chapters as examples of an ongoing project. Berger's essay precedes Bordo's by about a quarter of a century. If you look closely at one or two of their examples, and if you look at the larger concerns of their arguments, are they saying the same things? doing the same work? If so, how? And why is such work still necessary? If not, how do their projects differ? And how might you explain those differences?

•   •   •   •   •   •   •   •   •   •   •   •

ASSIGNMENT 3

Sources (II) [Appiah]

In the preface to *The Ethics of Identity,* Appiah says that his book is offered "more in the spirit of exploration than of conclusion." (See the first and second "Questions for a Second Reading" following Appiah's selection.) The style and method of "The Ethics of Individuality" provide an enactment of writing in such a spirit. For this assignment, we'd like you to carry out such a project, with Appiah's text as your guide and model. That is, you should begin by talking about Kwame Anthony Appiah and passages from "The Ethics of Individuality," just as Appiah begins by talking about John Stuart Mill and key passages from Mill's work—passages, that is, that are important to the writer. You should turn, then, to some example of an individual life from film or literature or television, just as Appiah turns to the example of Mr. Stevens, the butler in Kazuo Ishiguro's novel, *The Remains of the Day*. You should use subheadings to organize or punctuate your essay; you needn't use as many as Appiah, nor do you need to write an essay quite as long, but you should feel free to use the same terms if and when they can be strategically helpful to you: "Plans of Life," "Invention and Authenticity," "Ethics in Identity." In other words, you are conducting a parallel project, one written from your perspective. You are writing from a similar concern to better understand individuality and, to put it more loosely than you need to, what the individual owes the self and others.

•   •   •   •   •   •   •   •   •   •   •

A S S I G N M E N T **4**

Contrary Instincts [Walker]

In "In Search of Our Mothers' Gardens," Alice Walker uses the term "contrary instincts" when she discusses Phillis Wheatley. The problem for Walker (and others) is that Wheatley would idolize a fair-haired white woman as a goddess of liberty rather than turn to herself as a model or to the black women who struggled mightily for their identities and their liberty.

Walker's essay is filled with allusions to black women artists: Bessie Smith, Roberta Flack, Phillis Wheatley, Zora Neale Hurston; in fact, the essay serves as a kind of book list or reader's guide; it suggests a program of reading. (The references aren't strictly to black women. Jean Toomer was a man and Virginia Woolf was white.)

As you reread this essay, pay attention to the names. (Go to the library and track down some you don't know and take a look at some of their work; skimming is fine.) Write an essay in which you reflect on the use Walker makes of writers and their writing. You might ask yourself how and where her use of the past is similar to or different from what you saw in Rodriguez. Can they provide useful points of reference as you think about (and write about) Alice Walker?

• • • • • • • • • • •

ASSIGNMENT **5**

Ways of Reading
[Bartholomae and Petrosky]

Reread the introduction to *Ways of Reading*. Given the work that you have done in this sequence, you are prepared to read it not as a simple statement of "how things are" but as a position taken in a tradition of concern over the role of reading in the education of Americans. Write an essay in which you consider the introduction in relation to Rodriguez, Hoggart, Bordo, and Eady, and the ways they articulate the proper uses of reading.

And what about you—do you see your own interests and concerns, the values you hold (or those held by people you admire), the abilities you might need or hope to gain—do you see these represented in what you have read?

• • • • • • • • • • •

ALTERNATIVE   ASSIGNMENT

Writing (and Re-Writing) History [Eady]

This assignment follows the last of the "Questions for a Second Reading" following Eady.

> *Brutal Imagination* writes (or rewrites) history. It began, in a sense, as a research project. It is not completely a work of the imagination. There is a Susan Smith. Her children were drowned in a car in a lake. There was an investigation in Union, South Carolina. (There was also a Charles Stuart and Uncle Ben.) The cycle of poems is a way of bringing home the news—in these cases, news from the recent past. And, in fact, both the Smith and the Stuart cases were widely publicized and occupied the nation's attention for an extended period of time.
>
> As a research project, review some of the articles on the Susan Smith case that were published in major newspapers and magazines. It would be useful to include on your list of possibilities those magazines and newspapers that serve an African American audience—not only *Time* or *Newsweek* but also *Ebony* or *Jet*; not only the *New York Times* or the *Atlanta Constitution* but

also *The Chicago Defender* or the *Pittsburgh Courier*. (Note: You can also find the case represented at "crime" Web sites, such as *thesmokinggun.com* and *crimelibrary.com*.) All of these provide a *representation* of what happened, one version of who, what, when, where, and why.

With a particular representation of the case as a point of reference, reread "Brutal Imagination," and write an essay on Eady's rewriting of (or intervention in) the popular accounts (the popular history) of Susan Smith. You will need to work closely with your sources. And because you are writing about writing (about two written accounts of the case), you will need to include substantial block quotations. (Your handbook or your instructor can show you how to work with a block quotation and how to include lines of poetry in a work of prose.)

Note: You can write in a speculative or tentative manner; this is one way of establishing yourself as a careful, thoughtful, and attentive reader. Ideally, you will have the opportunity to come back to this assignment for revision.

right © 1971 by W. W. Norton & Company, Inc., from *Collected Early Poems: 1950–1970* by Adrienne Rich. Parts I, II, III, IV, V, VI, VII, XVIII, XX, XXII, and an excerpt from Part XXIII of "Sources." From *Your Native Land, Your Life: Poems by Adrienne Rich.* Copyright © 1986 by Adrienne Rich. Used by permission of the author and W. W. Norton & Company, Inc.

Richard Rodriguez. "The Achievement of Desire." From *Hunger of Memory: The Education of Richard Rodriguez* by Richard Rodriguez. Copyright © 1982 by Richard Rodriguez. Reprinted by permission of David R. Godine, Publisher, Inc.

Edward Said. "States." From *After the Last Sky* by Edward Said. Copyright © 1999 by Columbia University Press. Reprinted by permission of the publisher.

W. G. Sebald. "Chapter 1" and "Chapter 4." From *The Rings of Saturn* by W. G. Sebald. Translated by Michael Hulse. Copyright © 1995 by Vito von Eichborn Gmbh & Co. Verlag KG. Translation © 1998 by The Harvill Press. Reprinted by permission of New Directions Publishing Corp.

Jane Tompkins. "'Indians': Textualism, Morality, and the Problem of History." First published in *Critical Inquiry*, volume 13, number 1 (Autumn 1986). Reprinted in *Race, Writing, and Difference*, pp. 101–19, Henry Louis Gates, editor. Copyright © 1986 The University of Chicago Press. Reprinted by permission of the publisher. All rights reserved.

Alice Walker. "In Search of Our Mothers' Gardens." From *In Search of Our Mothers' Gardens* by Alice Walker. Copyright © 1974 by Alice Walker. Reprinted by permission of Harcourt, Inc.

John Edgar Wideman. "Our Time." From *Brothers and Keepers* by John Edgar Wideman. Copyright © 1984 by John Edgar Wideman. Reprinted by permission of The Wylie Agency.

Art credits

Gloria Anzaldúa photograph © Jean Weisinger. Cover design from *Borderlands/La Frontera: The New Mestiza*. Copyright © 1987, 1999 by Gloria Anzaldúa. Reproduced by permission of Aunt Lute Books.

Kwame Anthony Appiah photograph courtesy Office of Communications/Princeton University. Cover design from Kwame Anthony Appiah: *The Ethics of Identity* © 2005 Princeton University Press. Reprinted by permission of Princeton University Press.

John Berger photograph © Henri Cartier-Bresson/Magnum Photos. Cover design from *Ways of Seeing* by John Berger, copyright © 1972 by John Berger. Used by permission of Viking Penguin, a division of Penguin Group (USA) Inc. Front cover from *And Our Faces, My Heart, Brief as Photos* by John Berger. Used by permission of Pantheon Books, a division of Random House, Inc. Rene Magritte, "The Key of Dreams" © 2008 C. Herscovici, Brussels/Artists Rights Society (ARS), New York. Frans Hals, "Regents of the Old Men's Alms House" and "Regentesses of the Old Men's Alms House." Reprinted by permission of Frans Halsmuseum. Pablo Picasso, "Still Life with a Wicker Chair" © 2008 Estate of Pablo Picasso/Artists Rights Society (ARS), New York. Leonardo da Vinci, "The Virgin of the Rocks." Reproduced by courtesy of the Trustees, The National Gallery, London. Leonardo da Vinci, "The Madonna of the Rocks, c. 1483," Louvre Museum, Paris. Photo Credit: Scala/Art Resource, NY. Leonardo da Vinci, "The Virgin and Child with St. Anne and St. John the Baptist." Reproduced by courtesy of the Trustees, The National Gallery, London. Sandro Botticelli, "Venus and Mars." Reproduced by courtesy of the Trustees, The National Gallery, London. Pieter Brueghel the Elder, "Jesus Carrying the Cross, or the Way to Calvary, 1564." Photo Credit: Erich Lessing/Art Resource, NY. Details of Pieter Brueghel the Elder, "Jesus Carrying the Cross, or the Way to Calvary, 1564." Photo Credit: Erich Lessing/Art Resource, NY. Vincent van Gogh, "Wheatfield with Crows." Van Gogh Museum Foundation, Amsterdam, The Netherlands, Art Resource, NY. Jan Vermeer, "The Kitchenmaid." Rijkmuseum, Amsterdam, The Netherlands. Art Resource, NY. Rembrandt, "Woman in Bed." National Gallery of Scotland. Michaelangelo Merisi daCaravaggio, "The Calling of St. Matthew." Photo Credit: Scala/Art Resource, NY.

Resource, NY. Auguste Renoir, *The Bathers*. Photo credit: Erich Lessing/Art Resource, NY. Gustave Courbet, *The Two Friends (The Sleepers)*. Photo credit: Erich Lessing/Art Resource, NY.

Walker Percy photograph courtesy of Rhoda K. Faust/Maple Street Book Shop, New Orleans, Louisiana. Jacket design by Janet Halverson from *The Message in the Bottle* by Walker Percy. Jacket design copyright © 1975 by Janet Halverson. Reprinted by permission of Farrar, Straus and Giroux, LLC.

Mary Louise Pratt photograph © Linda A. Cicero/Stanford News Service. Cover design for *Profession 91*. Reprinted by permission of the Modern Language Association of America.

Adrienne Rich photograph © Robert Giard from *The Fact of a Doorframe: Poems, 1950–2001* by Adrienne Rich. Courtesy of W. W. Norton & Company, Inc. Jacket cover from *On Lies, Secrets, and Silence: Selected Prose 1966–1978* by Adrienne Rich. Used by permission of W. W. Norton & Company, Inc. Jacket cover from *Your Native Land, Your Life: Poems* by Adrienne Rich. Used by permission of W. W. Norton & Company, Inc.

Richard Rodriguez photograph © 2001 Christine Alicino. Jacket for *Hunger of Memory* by Richard Rodriguez, reproduced by permission of David R. Godine, Publisher. Copyright 1982 by David R. Godine, Publisher.

Edward Said photograph © Jerry Bauer. Cover image from *After the Last Sky* designed by Benjamin Shin Farber and photographs by Jean Mohr, reprinted by permission of Columbia University Press. Photographs accompanying Edward Said's *After the Last Sky* © Jean Mohr, Geneva.

W. G. Sebald photograph © Jerry Bauer/Courtesy New Directions. Cover from *The Rings of Saturn*. Used by permission of New Directions Publishing Corp. and Eichborn Verlag. Illustrations used by permission of New Directions Publishing Corp. and Eichborn Verlag with exceptions of Rembrandt, *The Anatomy Lesson*. Photo credit: Erich Lessing/Art Resource, NY. "The Burning of the Royals James at the Battle of Solebay, 28 May 1672" by Willem van de Velde, the Younger. National Maritime Museum, Greenwich.

Jane Tompkins photograph courtesy of University of Illinois at Chicago Photo Services. Cover design from *Critical Inquiry*, vol. 13, no. 1 (Autumn 1986) reprinted by permission of University of Chicago Press.

Alice Walker photograph © Jean Weisinger. Book cover from *In Search of Our Mothers' Gardens: Womanist Prose*, copyright 1985 by Alice Walker, reprinted by permission of Harcourt, Inc.

John Edgar Wideman photograph courtesy of the University of Massachusetts, Amherst. Front cover from *Brothers and Keepers*, by John Edgar Wideman. Used by permission of Vintage Books, a division of Random House, Inc.

Need more help with writing and research?
Visit Bedford/St. Martin's *Re:Writing.*

Re:Writing is designed to help with important writing concerns. You'll find advice from experts, models you can rely on, and exercises that will tell you right away how you're doing. And it's all free and available any hour of the day. All of these can be accessed at bedfordstmartins.com/rewriting.

Need help with grammar problems?
> Exercise Central (bedfordstmartins.com/exercisecentral)

Want to see what papers for your other courses look like?
> Model Documents Gallery (bedfordstmartins.com/modeldocs)

Stuck somewhere in the research process? (Maybe at the beginning?)
> The Bedford Research Room (bedfordstmartins.com/researchroom)

Wondering whether a Web site is good enough to use in your paper?
> Tutorial for Evaluating Online Sources
> (bedfordstmartins.com/onlinesourcestutorial)

Having trouble figuring out how to cite a source?
> Research and Documentation Online (bedfordstmartins.com/resdoc)

Confused about plagiarism?
> The St. Martin's Tutorial on Avoiding Plagiarism
> (bedfordstmartins.com/plagiarismtutorial)

Want to get more out of your word processor?
> Using Your Word Processor (bedfordstmartins.com/wordprocessor)

Trying to improve the look of your paper?
> Using Your Word Processor to Design Documents
> (bedfordstmartins.com/docdesigntutorial)

Need to create slides for a presentation?
> Preparing Presentation Slides Tutorial
> (bedfordstmartins.com/presentationslidetutorial)

Interested in creating a Web site?
> Web Design Tutorial (bedfordstmartins.com/webdesigntutorial)